QUEEN'S PARK RANGERS

THE COMPLETE RECORD 1899-2009

QUEEN'S PARK RANGERS

THE COMPLETE RECORD 1899-2009

GORDON MACEY

First published in Great Britain in 2009 by
The Breedon Books Publishing Company Limited
Breedon House, 3 The Parker Centre,
Derby, DE21 4SZ.

This paperback edition published in Great Britain in 2014 by DB Publishing,
an imprint of JMD Media Ltd

ISBN 978-1-78091-409-1

Printed and bound in the UK by Copytech (UK) Ltd Peterborough

Contents

Introduction

When Steve Caron from Breedon Publishing approached me about doing an update to my previous *Complete Record* book I was more than happy to agree to it. It has been 10 years since my Millennium edition was published and in that time there have been many changes at the club, both on and off the pitch. Relegation to the third tier of English football was not one of the better moments, but a Play-off Final appearance followed by automatic promotion the following season were certainly brighter spots.

On more than one occasion financial troubles nearly brought about the end of our club, but following the acquisition by Flavio Briatore and Bernie Ecclestone brighter times are on the horizon. The 're-branding' of the club was not to all die-hard fans' liking, but the results are beginning to bear fruit and the club certainly has a higher profile now, with the potential to move upwards in the football pyramid.

In the book the narrative up to May 1999 has been condensed so that the previously unpublished narrative from the 1999–2000 season onwards can be included in full. All the stats are correct as at the end of the 2008–09 season, with post-season data included as deadlines allowed.

There are a few people that I wish to thank who helped in putting the book contents together. At Breedon Publishing Michelle, Matt and Steve have been a great help, especially with the additional effort required in editing text and data. Another person who helped was Leigh Edwards, who compiled the 100 leading QPR Players and Manager Profiles sections. A special mention must also go to Kenneth Westerberg, who has 'proofed' my line ups and other stats, even though he is based in Finland. Also I would like to record my thanks to Alan Barnes and Joe English for their help detailing the more obscure friendly and youth matches.

At the club I have had assistance from Ian Taylor, Paul Morrissey, Terry Springett and Sheila Marson, who, over many more years than either of us wishes to remember, has been able to help in a number of areas with information.

Although most of the pictures/photographs used are from my collection or held by the club, I would also like to thank Ian Morsman and Tony Williamson for sourcing some of the pictures of players or memorabilia used in the narrative and statistical sections.

Finally, and not least, I would like to thank Gary Waddock for agreeing to provide the Foreword to the book. Gary is greatly respected by fans as a QPR legend, having been a player and manager of the club, so I felt that he was the ideal person to contribute to a publication on the history of the club.

Gordon Macey
QPR Club Historian
June 2009

FOREWORD

I was delighted to be asked to write this foreword for Gordon's new book. I knew him for a number of years at Rangers and I am pleased to have him as a member of my backroom team at Aldershot Town, as this gives me a chance to keep tabs on the latest news. He has a wealth of knowledge on the R's and his detailed records cover all aspects of the club.

Queen's Park Rangers, or 'The Super Hoops', as they are more affectionately known, is a club that I have special affection for. A major part of my life has been connected to the club in one way or another. My association with the club started when I joined the academy/youth set-up in the Under-13 age group, and little did I know that I would continue through many levels, eventually reaching the pinnacle of managing the club.

There have been many highlights of my career at Loftus Road, with the FA Cup Final in 1982 and winning promotion to the (old) Division One being two of the more memorable. I was fortunate to play with a number of Rangers legends, including Stan Bowles, Gerry Francis, Tony Currie and Alan McDonald. The club has always been a 'family friendly' one, and all supporters have a special bond with the club, sometimes going back through two or three generations within their own family. Even when I was forced to retire from playing for the club due to a serious knee injury I always followed the fortunes of the side. When I had the opportunity to re-join the club to work with the youth academy it did not take me long to decide whether or not to return 'home'. Being able to coach and progress some talented youngsters into established first-team players gave me great personal satisfaction because I knew I was helping to build the future of the club.

When circumstances led to me being offered the manager's role it was something that I had no hesitation in accepting. Although things did not work out as well as they could have, I certainly learnt a lot while in the hot seat which has helped me in my later career.

The stability of the club is now assured after the financial difficulties it has been through, with recent doom and gloom replaced by optimism for the future. With the backing of the new investors the sky's the limit, and only time will tell how far the club can go. I will be watching with much interest and hope that it is not long before the club are back at the top of English football in the Premiership.

Gary Waddock
June 2009

The History of QPR

The Queen's Park Rangers story began in 1882 in a newly built residential estate of West London, with the formation of two local youth-club teams, St Jude's Institute and Christchurch Rangers. St Jude's, set up for the boys of Droop Street Board School by Jack McDonald and Fred Weller, supported by the Revd Gordon Young, and the Christchurch boys club team, formed by George Wodehouse (Snr), amalgamated in 1886. George Wodehouse had played in a match between the two sides and was watched by a friend of his who suggested that a merger between the two clubs would be a good idea. Queen's Park Rangers was the name chosen for the new club, and it was suggested by E.D. Robertson because the members were based in the Queen's Park district of West London. The colours adopted were Oxford and Cambridge blue halved shirts, and the earliest details of a Queen's Park Rangers game are from a first-team friendly match against Harlesden United in November 1888 which ended in a 4–1 victory.

Rangers participated in a formal competition for the first time in the **1890–91** season, during which the club were recognised as one of the strongest amateur sides in the West London area. Their first competitive match was on 1 November 1890 in the second round of the London Senior Cup when they met Tottenham Hotspur and drew 1–1 at home. Rangers then lost the replay 2–1 the following week.

Their next competition was the West London Challenge Cup, a small tournament with only eight teams taking part. In the first round St John's Hammersmith were due to be the visitors to Brondesbury, but due to the fact that they could only field a weakened team St John's withdrew from the tie and the match was rearranged as a friendly, which Rangers won 8–0. In the semi-final Rangers' opponents were Hanwell, but they failed to appear at Barn Elms for the game scheduled for 21 February. The organisers of the tournament refused to give Rangers a walkover to the Final and ordered the match to be rearranged, and Rangers won 4–2. For reasons unknown the Final was never played and Rangers were denied the chance to win their first piece of silverware.

The third Cup competition the club entered was the newly instigated West London Observer Challenge Cup. The first-round draw gave Rangers a bye, and so their first match of the competition was against Kensington Rangers in the second round. The tie took nearly a month to decide as initially QPR were not informed of the location of the match, and this was then followed by a successful objection to the condition of the Kensington club's ground. The match was finally settled with a 5–1 victory at the temporary home ground of Barn Elms. In the semi-final, played at the Half Moon ground in Putney, Rangers lost 4–1.

Rangers continued with friendly matches and Cup games until they entered a formal league in the **1892–93** season – the West London League. Before the start of that season they moved home, this time to the Kilburn Cricket Club ground in Harvest Road. At the home match against arch rivals Paddington on 15 October green-and-white shirts were worn for the first time. The club had a moderately successful first season of League football, finishing sixth with 16 points. The highlight of the season was undoubtedly the West London Observer Cup. Rangers received a bye in the first round and were drawn to meet Stanley in the semi-final, which ended in a resounding 4–0 win for Rangers. Rangers' opponents in the Final were the newly crowned League Champions Fulham, and the match was played at the Kensal Rise Athletic ground. Rangers went on to win the match, details of which can be found in the Matches to Remember section of the book. The only downside to the victory was that the members of the winning team did not receive medals as the Association had no money to purchase them.

In the **1893–94** season's West London Observer Cup Rangers received a bye in the first round as holders of the trophy. The semi-final draw gave the club an away fixture at the winners of the tie between West London and Burntwood, and Rangers made it to the Final for the second successive year, but their opponents refused to play. The organisers of the competition asked for the Cup back as it would not be competed for, but Rangers refused, saying that no one had defeated them and therefore they were still the holders. They then added that they would not return it until they had received medals marking their previous year's victory!

OFFICIAL PROGRAMME.

1d. 1d.

QUEEN'S PARK RANGERS

Football and Athletic Club, Ltd.

Office: 89, Lancefield Street, W.

G. H. MOUSELL, Secretary.

Fixtures for October:

5th	Swindon, S.	Home
7th	Southampton, W.	Home
12th	Brentford, S.	Away
12th	Clapton Orient, L.	Home
16th	Southampton, W.	Away
19th	Kettering, S.	Home
19th	Excelsior, L.	Away
21st	Chesham Town, S.E.	Away
26th	Luton, S.	Away
26th	Hitchen, S.E.	Home
28th	Portsmouth, W.	Home

A Queen's Park Rangers programme from the early 1890s.

For the next three seasons Rangers played only friendly matches. Clubs played during this time included Maidenhead, Brentford, Vulcan, Crescent Hampstead and Fulham. The **1894–95** season saw the expansion of the London Senior Cup with more of the 'second' level amateur clubs being invited to enter. For the first time the club also entered the Middlesex Senior Cup and had initial success in their opening match against City Ramblers in the third round. The next round saw Rangers travelling to Harrow Athletic, but Harrow won 2–1.

With an improved team the club entered the English Cup for the first time in the **1895–96** season. Rangers were drawn against their long-time League rivals Old St Stephen's at home. The match, on Saturday 12 October 1895, was played in front of the largest crowd in the club's history. It was estimated that 3,000 people packed into the Harvest Road ground for the game. The match ended in a 1–1 draw, but Rangers lost the replay the following Tuesday. This season also saw the club enter the Amateur Cup competition. Having received a bye in the first qualifying round Rangers were drawn at home to south-west London club Surbiton Hill. The game, attended by 1,000 people, ended as a 2–1 win for Rangers, with both goals scored by Ward. The next round saw a visit of the mighty Casuals side, one of the strongest clubs outside of the professional game in the London area. Not surprisingly Rangers were no match for their respected opponents and lost 5–1.

The services of Jock Campbell, who had previously trained Third Lanark, Woolwich Arsenal and Tottenham, were secured during the **1896–97** season and under his supervision great things were expected of the team. The club joined the London League, playing in the Second Division against long-time adversaries like Fulham, Brentford, Stanley and Harrow Athletic. The crowds grew as a result of these matches; the last home game of the season against Brentford attracted a record gate to the Kensal Rise ground, and the Rangers officials were kept very busy collecting the sixpences of the impatient crowd, some of whom scaled the fences to see the game.

For the **1897–98** season Rangers, together with Bromley and Brentford, were elevated into the First Division of the London League. They won their first League match at the end of November against

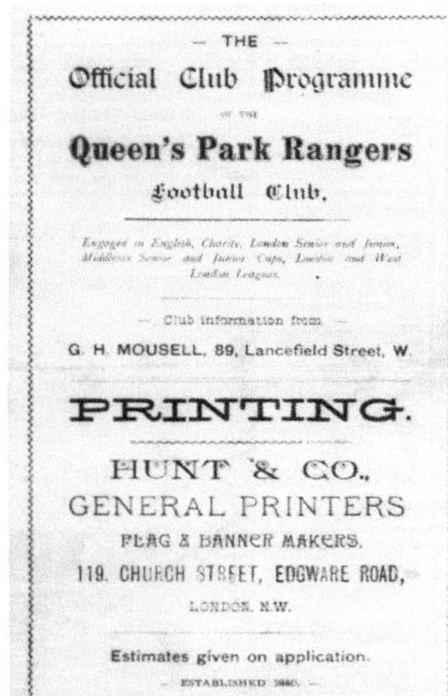

— THE —

Official Club Programme

Queen's Park Rangers

Football Club.

Engaged in English, Charity, London Senior and Junior, Middlesex Senior and Junior Cups, London and West London Leagues.

— Club information from —

G. H. MOUSELL, 89, Lancefield Street, W.

PRINTING.

HUNT & CO.,

GENERAL PRINTERS

FLAG & BANNER MAKERS,

119, CHURCH STREET, EDGWARE ROAD,

LONDON, N.W.

Estimates given on application.

J. T. PARKER, Family Butcher, 630, HARROW ROAD, W.

J. McKENZIE'S BILLIARD SALOON, "ELEPHANT & CASTLE," HARROW ROAD. SPRING HANDICAP. HEATS 200 UP.

TO LET.

Pure Confectionery, &c. CADBURY'S, FRY'S ROWNTREE'S CHOCOLATES, GUMS, &c. C. ANNELL'S 625-626, HARROW ROAD.

Saturday, 12th March, 1898. Kick off 3.30 p.m

QUEEN'S PK. RANGERS CROUCH END VAMPIRES.

G. EDWARDS, Builder & Decorator, 56, WALTERTON ROAD, HARROW ROAD, W.

TO FOOTBALLERS. EXTRACT OF BEEF.

BRAND & CO'S SPECIALTIES FOR INVALIDS

CANTERBURY ARMS, WEST KILBURN. LICENSED FOR MUSIC & DANCING. FINE BILLIARD SALOON.

The cover and inside spread of an early Queen's Park Rangers programme from 1898.

Bromley but then withdrew from the competition, and all their results were expunged from the records. This meant that for the near future the club's only matches were friendly games, with the exception of those coming in the four Cup competitions.

The name of Queen's Park Rangers was now becoming a recognised force in Metropolitan football. In those days visits of provincial Football League sides to the capital were limited to the Cup Finals, and for that reason it was considered to be a rare stroke of business enterprise to get the famous Throstles (West Bromwich Albion) to play Rangers at West Kilburn. The terms agreed were that West Bromwich would receive £40 minimum or half the gate money. As over £140 was taken on the gate, the venture was deemed to be successful. West Bromwich's line up included such names as Basset, Flewitt, McLeod, Reynolds, Williams and Reader. The only downside was the result – Rangers lost 1–4.

Rangers' first appearance in the Charity Cup was in an away tie at Upton when they met Clapton. Aided by stout defending Rangers won a close game with goals from McKenzie and McDonald, with Clapton scoring only once in reply. In the semi-final Rangers were paired with Casuals, who were the current holders of the trophy. Despite the number of internationals in the Casuals side Rangers played above expectations and secured a goalless draw. In the replay at the Queens Club the Casuals' greater experience pulled them through, but only by a single goal.

In the **1898–99** season Queen's Park Rangers moved to the professional level. The change from amateur status was brought about following the English Cup tie against Richmond Association in September. During the game Sammy Brooks was sent off, and the club were fined £4 by the London Football Association and had their ground closed for 14 days. Rangers resented the punishment and initially withdrew from all London FA competitions. This move robbed them of their principal fixtures and caused unrest among the better players, and allied with the fact that the demand for first-class football had become apparent in London, moves were made towards becoming a professional club. A committee was formed and in December 1898 the Queen's Park Rangers Football and Athletic Club became an accomplished fact, with a nominal capital of £5,000 on shares of 10/- (50p) each.

In preparation for the **1899–1900** season Rangers made a successful application to join the Southern League. The reserves applied, also successfully, to become members of the London League.

On the playing front the first team still only participated in the same four Cup competitions as the previous season, with all other games being friendly matches, but with travel becoming more affordable away games at places like King's Lynn, Northampton and Eastbourne were also arranged.

Rangers finished their amateur career on top with the reserves winning the West London League (Division One) title. They were unbeaten in the League and conceded only two goals in the season. Their professional life began in grand style on 2 September 1899 by beating Brighton United 6–0 at home in front of a gate of 6,000, and the victory took them straight to the top of the Southern League. But, unfortunately, as Brighton United, along with Cowes, withdrew from the League before the end of the season the result was expunged from the records. Rangers did not have to wait long for their first recorded professional victory in the Southern League as it came in their second match, 2–0 at home to New Brompton.

They had mixed success in their first professional season, finishing mid-table, winning 12 and losing 14 of their 28 matches. However, the club made a heavy financial loss, despite taking over £1,067 in gate money at two Cup ties. It was only the monetary assistance from the directors that saved the club from extinction.

Rangers had considerable success in the English Cup this season and reached the second-round proper, having had to start their campaign in the preliminary qualifying round. They disposed of London Welsh, Fulham, West Hampstead, Wandsworth and Civil Service in convincing style.

A big crowd turned up for the game at Kensal Rise against Wolverhampton Wanderers and in order to accommodate the numbers the gates were opened three hours prior to the kick-off. The match was played on very heavy ground, which was certainly to Rangers' advantage. The 1–1 tie went to a replay the following Wednesday at Molineux. The First Division side were expected to overcome the 'Southerners' easily on their own immaculate playing surface, but Rangers pulled off a big Cup surprise and beat them 1–0, with Fred Beddingfield scoring the only goal of the game late in the second half.

275 THE GOLDEN PENNY. April 7, 1900.

NOTED FOOTBALL CLUBS.

LXXIII.—QUEEN'S PARK RANGERS (ASSOCIATION).

Early History.

A newspaper article on Queen's Park Rangers from 7 April 1900. The team photograph shows them in their early kit of green and white stripes.

In the next round Rangers were drawn at home against fellow Southern League rivals Millwall Athletic. The 2–0 defeat was a disappointment after the heady success at Wolverhampton, but the preparation for the match was not helped by the fact that some of the players were involved in a brawl the night before the game. Turnbull and Cowie were detained by the police overnight for their part in the disturbance.

There were a large number of changes on the playing staff for the start of the **1900–01** season. Among the departures were Beddingfield, Cowie, Crawford, Hannah, Haywood, Knowles, Smith and White, all of whom had played over 20 games the previous season. The arrivals included James Bellingham, David Christie and William Goldie, all from Scotland. Other arrivals included Jack Cole

(Wales), William Pointing (Southampton), Tom Gray (New Brompton), A. Foxall (Liverpool), Percy Humphreys and William Manning, both from Cambridge.The performances on the field matched those of the previous season, with Rangers finishing eighth again. The season started well with the first home game resulting in a 7–1 victory over Swindon Town, which included the first-ever Rangers League hat-trick, scored by Downing, but away results could hardly have been worse. Off the field, however, the club was in dire straights. At the end of the season the landlord took advantage of a new point decided in the Appeals Court and terminated the club's lease on their ground. The club were in financial straits again so, with the exception of Keech and Newlands, all the players left. Thanks to the efforts of one of the directors, Mr T.R. Eagle, a ground was obtained at the rear of St Quintin's Avenue, near Latimer Road, Notting Hill, in time for the **1901–02** season. The players had to change in the nearby Latimer Arms public house and run down the road to the pitch, much to the delight of the local boys who could not afford the 1d admission to see the games. However, the local residents were never happy having a professional football team in their midst and successfully petitioned the estate owner, who then served notice on Rangers to leave at the end of the season.

Among the incoming players that were signed to replace those that had left at the end of the previous season were Charles Aston (Aston Villa), John Bowman (Stoke City – who later became manager), Harry Collins (Burnley), Ben Freeman (Grays United), Hugh McQueen (Derby County), Harry Millar (Sheffield Wednesday), John Stewart (Hibernian) and Jabez White (Grays United).

The directors faced yet another gloomy season in **1902–03**. They had no ground, scarcely any money and at the end of 1901–02 most of the players had left again. Two of the players who signed

The 1902–03 team.

The 1904–05 team now in the club's traditional hooped shirts.

for the new season were QPR returnees, Alfred Hitch from Nottingham Forest and Harry Skinner from Grimsby. Among the other new arrivals were Harry Abbott (Blackburn Rovers), John Hamilton (Millwall Athletic) and Tom Wilson (London Caledonia).

One of the best players, John Bowman, wanted to return to the amateur game but was persuaded to stay with the club, and he became the new secretary. Bowman was instrumental in the move back to one of the club's former grounds, Kensal Rise. All Saints College, the landlords, charged a rent of £240 per annum for a two-year lease, but thanks to increased gate receipts of £4,500 a profit of £600 resulted at the end of the season.

The **1903–04** season proved to be Rangers' most successful in the Southern League so far with gate receipts rising to £6,000. They finished in fifth place, conceding 37 goals in 34 League games, but only two points behind second-placed Tottenham Hotspur.

Due to the club's increased stability there was not a mass exodus of players at the end of the season. There were some new faces in the team, among them Arthur Archer (New Brompton), William Cross (Third Lanark), George Milward (Chesterfield), Albert Bull (Reading) and Neil Murphy (Sheffield United). In October the ground record was broken for the visit of Southampton, the eventual champions, when 15,000 spectators witnessed the season's only home defeat. If only two of the last five draws had been victories, Rangers would have finished the season as runners-up.

Rangers were on the move again in **1904–05** after a 100 per cent increase in price on the existing ground lease agreement meant that it was beyond their financial capabilities. Rangers offered to increase the rent paid to £300 per annum or to buy the lease for £1,500, but the offers were refused and they ended up moving to the Agricultural Showground in Park Royal.

A crowd of 12,000 came to the first game on the new ground and despite the remoteness the attendances over the season increased. As most fans lived in the Kensal Rise area, public transport and special trains were laid on for home games from Paddington, Westbourne Park, Southall and Hounslow.

MARCH 18, 1905 ILLUSTRATED BUDGET 823

QUEEN'S PARK RANGERS v. LUTON, AT PARK ROYAL: LUTON WON

Queen's Park Rangers: Collins (goal), F. Lyon and Newlands (backs), Bowman, Hitch, and White (half-backs), Murphy, Ronaldson, Bevan, Downing, and Singleton (forwards).
Luton: Lindsay (goal), Turner and McEwen (backs), F. Hawkes, White, and R. Hawkes (half-backs), Eaton, Ross, Lamberton, Moody, and Barnes (forwards)

A Ranger Throw-in

Luton Score their First Goal

A Bold Jump for the Ball

The 1905–06 squad.

In February 1905 Neil Murphy became the first player to gain a full international cap while with Queen's Park Rangers. He was chosen to play for Ireland against England at Middlesbrough and gained two further caps that season against Scotland in Glasgow and Wales in Cliftonville. He also scored one of the goals in the 2–2 draw against the Welsh.

New team members included the Scottish international John Cross (Third Lanark), Fred Bevan (Reading), Harry Singleton (New Brompton) and Arthur Howes (Brighton).

Before the start of the **1905–06** season John Bowman, the club's long-serving player-secretary, moved to Norwich City. His replacement at right-half was William Yenson, who signed from Bolton Wanderers. A number of other players joined Rangers for the new season. They included Matthew Kingsley (West Ham), Sidney Sugden (Nottingham Forest) and James Cowan (Aston Villa).

Despite the poor Southern League performances that season, Rangers did win their first trophy as a professional club, the midweek-based Western League. They finished top with 26 points, one ahead of Southampton, from their 20 matches. The title was not decided until the final match when Plymouth Argyle visited Park Royal on Easter Tuesday, a game for which admission was raised to 3d. If Rangers had lost they would have finished third behind Southampton and Plymouth, but they won the match 1–0 to clinch the Championship.

At the end of a disappointing **1906–07** season, their worst in the Southern League, Rangers learnt that their landlords, The Royal Agricultural Society, were in a financial crisis and had to sell the showground to raise money, thus forcing Rangers into another ground move. They agreed to move to the brand new 60,000-capacity Park Royal stadium built by the Great Western Railway Company. Before the start of the season Rangers appointed their first-team manager, James Cowan, a Scotsman from Aston Villa. While at Villa he had won five League Championship and three English Cup medals.

The newcomers to the team for that season included John McLean (Millwall), Tom Green (Middlesbrough), Dennis O'Donnell (Sunderland), Edward Anderson (Sheffield United) Sid Blake (Newcastle United) and Joseph Fidler (Fulham).

As the Park Royal stadium was not complete for the start of the **1907–08** season Rangers had to play their early home games at the showground. By the end of the season Rangers were favourites for the Championship, but with five matches remaining it was still a two-horse race between Rangers and Plymouth. On Good Friday the two sides met in what was billed as the Championship decider. The match ended in a 1–1 draw, leaving Rangers in pole position. Rangers could have secured the title the following week at home to Northampton but suffered a rare home defeat, but they clinched it two days later on 20 April with a 4–0 home victory over West Ham United. Fred Cannon became the hero of the afternoon by scoring a hat-trick. During the season Evelyn Lintott became the first player to play for the full England team while at the club. (There was a gap of 64 years before Rangers had their second full England cap – Rodney Marsh – in November 1971). Unfortunately Lintott's football career was cut short as he was killed in action during World War One.

Because of their victory in the Southern League Championship Rangers played in the first-ever FA Charity Shield match, facing Football League Champions Manchester United at Stamford Bridge in front of 12,000 fans. It was the biggest occasion in the club's history so far. The United team included many household names of the day, including Billy Meredith, the 'Welsh Wizard'. Rangers took the lead through Fred Cannon and held their advantage until a superb solo goal by Meredith drew United level.

The FA Charity Shield replay, played the following August as a curtain raiser for the new season, was a great opportunity for Rangers to put the upheavals of the summer behind them and get back to playing football. The match was again played at Stamford Bridge and ended in a 4–0 win for the strong United side. After the match both sides went to the Alhambra Theatre in Leicester Square where they watched a bioscope replay of the game. Rangers' share of the gate receipts was £100, which they donated to the following charities: St Mary's Hospital (£50), Willesden College Hospital (£25), Acton College Hospital (£15) and Willesden Children's Aid (£10).

Among the new players signed were Archie Mitchell (Aston Villa), Charlie Shaw (Port Glasgow), Fred Pentland (Brentford), Alfred Gittens (Luton Town), William Barnes (Luton Town), Evelyn Lintott (Plymouth Argyle), John McDonald (Grimsby Town) and Alfred Walker (Nottingham Forest).

Following their success Rangers resigned from the Southern League and applied to join the Football League for the **1908–09** season. Stoke City had resigned from Division Two so a ballot was

proposed for all interested clubs. Much to Rangers' surprise and annoyance, Tottenham Hotspur, who had finished 10 points and seven places below Rangers, were elected. However, after lengthy negotiations the Southern League Management Committee increased the number of teams in the Southern League First Division to 21 so Rangers could be re-admitted. All the upheaval surrounding the failed Football League election bid left the players unsettled and both Fred Pentland and Evelyn Lintott left. The incoming players included J. MacDonald (Lincoln City), Alonzo Drake (Small Heath) and Harry Duff (Manchester City). The biggest coup was made midway through the season when Walter Greer was signed, despite strong competition from Preston North End.

Not surprisingly, Rangers' League performances were nowhere near the previous season's standard, and they finished in 15th place, only three points ahead of the bottom club. The poor performances and the fact that most matches were midweek resulted in lower gates, and a loss of £866 was reported for the season. This loss would have undoubtedly been greater had it not been for the fees received for the sale of Pentland and Lintott and the money raised by supporters in response to the club's appeals.

For the **1909–10** season the fixtures were back to normal and Rangers had a much better season on and off the pitch. New recruits to the team included William Wake (Exeter City), William Steer (Kingston Town), James Travers (Aston Villa) and A. Whyman (New Brompton).

The most exciting part was the Cup run, which took Rangers into the last eight for the first time in their history. In the first round Rangers were drawn away to Norwich City. Rangers had beaten them at home only two weeks earlier and were confident of progressing into the next round, which they did, but only after a replay following a scoreline of 0–0 at The Nest.

Rangers were on the road again for the second round, this time down to coast to face Southend United, with the game ending in another 0–0 draw. Rangers won a closely fought replay 3–0.

For the third successive time Rangers were second out of the bag and had to travel to fellow Southern League side West Ham United, and, also for the third time, the match ended in a draw. After 90 minutes of the replay no goals had been scored so it went to extra time. With just three minutes remaining, William Steer scored his fifth goal in three rounds to send Rangers onwards.

The draw for the fourth round provided Rangers with a long trip to Football League side Barnsley. The match ended in a 1–0 victory for Barnsley, the goal being a fluke according to the Rangers fans!

Such was the fervour of the Rangers fans that by the time the team's train reached Paddington Station several thousand people had assembled to meet it. As the train steamed in, with its engine decked in the club colours of green and white, there was a rush for the team's compartment. But the older hands among the players avoided the crush by getting out of the train on the wrong side and running back to Royal Oak Station.

The following season, **1910–11**, turned out to be a bit of a non-event, but Rangers managed to finish in sixth place, 13 points behind the champions. The season had opened full of optimism as most of the players had decided to stay on at the club. New signings were made to bolster the forwards, these

A London Professional Charity Fund winners' medal from 1910.

The 1911–12 team.

included Horace Brindley (Norwich City), D. McKie (Chorley), Robert Browning and Herbert Butterworth (Oldham Athletic).

Rangers started the **1911–12** season in Championship form, and to bolster the team they signed Arthur Smith (Brierley Athletic), E. Revill (Chesterfield), Gilbert Ovens (Bristol Rovers) and H. Thornton. After 10 matches Rangers were unbeaten and had dropped only two points. By setting such a pace at the top of the League, Rangers had become the team everyone wanted to beat and the first team to do so were Swindon Town, who won 3–1 at Park Royal in front of a crowd of 25,000.

At the turn of the year Rangers were top of the League with 31 points from 21 games, followed by Northampton with 28 points. Plymouth were eight points behind, so the title seemed to be a two-horse race; however, Rangers suffered a minor collapse and only won two of their last seven games. Plymouth won their last six on the trot so Rangers had to avoid defeat in the last match away at Norwich City to clinch the Championship. The match ended in a 1–1 draw so Rangers won it by just one point. As Southern League champions Rangers were invited to play in another Charity Shield match, and the £262 proceeds were sent to the Titanic Disaster appeal.

After the Charity Shield match Rangers travelled overnight to Paris, where they were to play Fulham the next day in an exhibition match. Having left London on Saturday evening, Rangers did not arrive at their hotel until 7 o'clock Sunday morning. The match, at midday, was for the Dubonnet Trophy, and not surprisingly Fulham won quite easily, 4–1. Rangers then played one more game in France before moving on to Germany for another six games. Rangers overcame the opponents of the tour by an aggregate score of 40 to 7. The teams beaten were Paris Red Star 9–2, Saarbrucken 12–1, Kaiserslauten 1–0, Mannheim 3–0, Pforzheim 7–3, Nurenburg 5–1 and Stuttgart 2–0.

Rangers were determined to retain the Southern League title in **1912–13** and signed Jimmy Birch (Aston Villa) and William Thompson (Plymouth Argyle). Birch was to become one of Rangers longest-serving heroes, staying at the club for 14 seasons. Rangers began the defence of their title in fine form by winning six and drawing four of their first 11 matches, but their form deserted them in the New Year and they went nine matches without winning. This period certainly cost them the Championship, but they did have some success in the season when they won the Southern Charity Cup.

Before the start of the **1914–15** season James Cowan resigned as manager and was replaced by James Howie, a former Scottish international. As Howie recognised the good players that Cowan had assembled, he did not make many signings for the new season. The few that he did get the signature of included goalkeeper R. McLeod (Newport County), T. Millington (Bury) and David Donald (Watford).

The outbreak of war meant that crowds were down and Rangers, along with all the other clubs, struggled to keep going. In February 1915 the army commandeered the Park Royal ground and Rangers had to move out. They played the remaining home League fixtures at their old Kensal Rise ground in Harvest Road.

Football continued throughout World War One as best it could. There were no National Leagues, only regional ones. The Football League ran two regional competitions for its clubs in the Midlands and North of England, but as no competition had been organised for the five London clubs it was suggested that they and the Southern League clubs in the London area form their own League. So Rangers, along with their fellow Southern League clubs, joined Football League sides in the newly formed London Combination competition.

The first season of wartime football consisted of two main competitions under the aegis of the London Combination. From September to January was the Primary League and from February to April was the Secondary League. There were no Cup competitions organised to replace the suspended English Cup. Rangers did not fare too well, however, and when the League drew to a close Rangers were in 13th place, one point above bottom-placed Reading.

For the second season of wartime football the London Combination ran only one League with 14 clubs in it. The teams played each other at home and away at least once and then, like the previous season, they played half of the teams again, the difference being that all the results counted in the same League table. Overall Rangers won 10 and lost 20 of their scheduled 40 matches.

For the third season of wartime football the London Combination was reduced to 10 clubs with the teams playing each other at home and away twice. The season started a little better than the previous one, but in the end Rangers only won 14 of their 36 matches. At the end of the season the League gave permission for a War Fund tournament, the only stipulation being that the admission money must be passed on to war charities. Rangers played Crystal Palace and Millwall, winning both home games and losing both away games.

The ceasefire agreements to end the war came too late for the football authorities, so a fourth season of wartime competition was organised for **1918–19.** Due to the economical situation players had only been paid minimal expenses during the war, but when the war was over the Football Association allowed a maximum of 15s (75p) to be paid per week. After the end of hostilities crowds came back to football in an attempt to return to normality, and Rangers had an even start to the season, with two defeats followed by two wins and a draw. An away game at Chelsea over Christmas had a crowd of 15,000, the largest to watch Rangers for over three years, and by the end of the season gates had risen again and 20,000 watched the second away League game at Chelsea. Once Rangers were able to call on a settled side, the results improved and Rangers finished the final war League competition in fifth place, 10 points behind champions Brentford.

During the war several Rangers players were killed in action, among them Lieutenant H. Thornton, J. Butler and J. Pennifer. Another player, D. Higgins, suffered terrible injuries and was never able to play again.

In 1917 the Rangers ground had been turned into allotments to help the war effort, so Rangers moved to the ground of the disbanded Shepherd's Bush Football Club in Ellerslie Road. The ground later became known as Loftus Road, after the street running along its eastern edge. One stand from Park Royal was dismantled and re-erected at the new ground to form the Ellerslie Road Stand.

The **1919–1920** season turned out to be Rangers' last Southern League campaign. After the war Rangers had to re-establish themselves in the League at their new home, and the season started well with no goals conceded in the first four games. In the first 13 games Merrick, the new goalkeeper, had kept 11 clean sheets. The New Year started in fine style with a 7–1 home win over Bristol Rovers, but by the end of the season Rangers had settled in sixth place.

At the end of the season a proposed move to create a regionalised Third Division of the Football League became a reality. Without exception all the First Division clubs left the Southern League to form the new Third Division.

For their new beginning in the Third Division of the Football League Rangers appointed a new manager, Ned Liddell, who had played for Charlton Athletic, Southampton, Clapton Orient and Arsenal. Ned acquired new players for the club over the summer, including G. Grant (Millwall), R. Faulkner (Blackburn Rovers), Herbert Middlemiss (Tottenham Hotspur), E. Grimsdell (Guildford United), goalkeeper Len Hill (Southend United) and future Rangers manager Mick O'Brien, a left-half replacement for Archie Mitchell. Due to the poor financial situation of the club the total outlay on new players was only £25!

Rangers' life in the Football League for season **1920–21** started with two home defeats by Watford and Northampton Town, but despite their shaky start they finished in third position, six points behind the champions Crystal Palace. However, the highlight of the 1920–21 season was undoubtedly the Cup victory over Arsenal. In the first round Rangers were drawn at home to them and were full of confidence as they had not conceded a goal in their previous five matches. The match, played on a mudbath of a pitch in front of a crowd of 20,000, ended in a 2–0 win for Rangers. Unfortunately, in

The 1920–21 team in QPR's first season in the Football League.

the second round Rangers were not so lucky. They put in a gritty performance against Burnley in front of the 41,000 crowd, but lost 4–2 to the eventual First Division champions.

The Football League changed its format for the **1921–22** season. The Northern Clubs formed a further division within the League, resulting in the foundation of the Third Division South and North. The champions of each regional section were to be promoted into the national Second Division and the bottom two had to apply for re-election. Rangers finished that season in fifth place, 12 points behind the leaders Southampton.

Rangers had a busy close season with regard to the signing of players. Among the new recruits were the amateur international Arthur Reed (Tufnell Park), Harold Edgely (Aston Villa), Alex Ramsey (Newcastle United) and J. Bradshaw (Aberdare Athletic).

Action from the 1921–22 season, with Edgeley closing in as Skiller clears.

Money was short during the summer of 1923, and John Gregory, who had been at Rangers for 11 seasons, moved to Yeovil as player-manager and Harold Edgely joined Stockport County. In replacing these experienced players Rangers only spent £150 in acquiring J. Cameron (Heart of Midlothian), James Keen (Newcastle United), G. Benson (Stalybridge Celtic), Richard Oxley (Southport), William Pierce (Bedlington Colliery) and Shirley Abbott (Portsmouth). The other major departure was Arthur Chandler, who was sold to Leicester City for a club record fee of £3,000. The **1923–24** season was another terrible one for Rangers, but fortunately for them all the League teams were re-elected to the Third Division for the forthcoming season.

In the **1925–26** season manager Ned Liddell was replaced by Bob Hewison, the former Northampton Town manager. Along with the departure of Liddell, several of the more experienced players also left. Len Hill, who had been the regular goalkeeper for the past five seasons, signed for Southampton; Ben Marsden, another five seasons man, went to Reading; while Colin Myers, despite topping the goal chart, left after just one season for Exeter City. Hewison did not have much money to spend in replacing the departing players. His signings included goalkeeper George Hebden (Leicester City), John Middleton (Leicester City), Dick Burgess (Aberdare Athletic), Joe Spottiswood (Swansea Town) and Henry Hirst (Preston North End).

The high turnover of playing staff evidently caused problems in the first game when no less than seven of the team were making their debut for the club. The season continued badly and Rangers ended the season bottom of the League, a massive 14 points behind Charlton Athletic, the team above them. So for the second time in three years Rangers had to apply for re-election to the Football League.

The 1926 QPR team, while on a club outing.

Following a successful re-election campaign many changes were made during the summer of 1926. The main non-playing departure was that of the secretary, Mr W.L. Wood. He had been associated with the club since he first saw them play at the Welford Fields in 1887. Later in 1898, when the club turned professional, he became a director and four years later was appointed honorary secretary. When Rangers joined the Football League and the workload increased he became the club's first salaried secretary.

The incoming players signed during the same summer included Howard Hooper (Leicester City), John Young (West Ham United), John Collier (Hull City), Fred Hawley (Brighton), C. Gough (Clapton Orient), Percy Varco (Aston Villa), James Lofthouse (Bristol Rovers) and George Charlesworth (Bristol Rovers). That was not the end of the new players as during the season Rangers made two further significant signings. First was a busman from Redhill by the name of George Goddard, while the mid-season signing was Jimmy Eggleton from Lincoln City.

For all the comings and goings before the new **1926–27** season and the disappointing but improved 14th-place finish, there was an important and long lasting change: the club's colours were changed to blue and white.

The performances continued to improve on the pitch and Rangers had started to develop into a good team, with a 10th-place finish achieved in **1927–28.**

That season only five players left the club: E. Ford (Merthyr Town), George Charlesworth (Crystal Palace), William Young, Jonah Wilcox and George Hebden, all to Gillingham. The players signed as their replacements were J. Stephenson (Watford), W. Turner (Bury), Andy Neil (Brighton), John Duthie (Norwich City), Joseph Cunningham (Newport County) George Rounce (Uxbridge) and J.C. Burns (Crypto).

Rangers finished in sixth place in **1928–29**. Signed to add even more resilience to the centre of the defence were Jock McNab, a Scottish international, and William Cockburn, both signed from Liverpool. The other signings included Ernest Whatmore (Bristol Rovers), Oliver Thompson (Chesterfield) and Stephen Smith (Clapton Orient).

Rangers' placings were improving every season as the club finished in third place in **1929–30**. Among the departures were H. Vallence to Brighton, J. Woodward to Merthyr and Sidney Sweetman to Millwall. The replacements signed included Bernard Harris (Luton Town), H. Moffatt (Walsall), Herbert Young (Newport County), John Yates (Aston Villa) and brothers Harry and George Wiles, amateurs from Sittingbourne.

During the summer of 1931 manager Bob Hewison left the club for Bristol City. He was replaced by John Bowman, who had been player and secretary at the club in the early 1900s. Unfortunately ill health forced him to resign after a couple of months, and he was succeeded by Archie Mitchell. Among the outgoing players that season was Jack Burns, who went to neighbours Brentford. His replacement was the England amateur international player Jim Lewis, who was signed from Walthamstow Avenue. Other signings included Thomas Wyper (Charlton Athletic), Stanley Cribb (West Ham United), William Haley (Fulham) and Ernest Hall (Bedworth Town).

Encouraged by the increase in gates and the success of the club, the board of directors negotiated to play their home games just up the road from the Loftus Road ground at the spacious White City Stadium. The stadium had accommodation for 60,000, including 6,000 under cover. The first game at the White City Stadium on 5 September 1931 attracted a gate of 18,907 who witnessed a 3–0 defeat at the hands of Bournemouth. The **1931–32** season continued badly with only one win, away at Swindon, in the first 13 games, and Rangers finished in 13th place.

In **1932–33** the two goalkeepers used in the previous season were both released; Thomas Pickett went to Bristol Rovers and Joseph Cunningham to Walsall. Ernest Beecham, signed from Fulham, was now the first choice replacement 'keeper. Other new arrivals included Edward Marcroft (Middlesbrough), Albert Brown (Blyth Spartans) and Walter Barrie (West Ham United).

The 1932 QPR squad before meeting Leeds United in the FA Cup.

The QPR players line up for inspection before a friendly against Vienna in 1932.

Despite not attracting bigger gates by moving to the White City, the club remained there for the whole of 1932–33 but by **1933–34** the club's overdraft at the bank had increased to £34,549, so the directors decided to move back to the Loftus Road ground. Most of the debt was owed to the ex-chairman, the late Mr J.H. Fielding. Subsequently his son, Charles, showed great generosity and cancelled the outstanding debt of £20,000. In order to have a fresh start back 'home' the directors appointed the ex-player Mick O'Brien as manager.

O'Brien signed a number of new players for the forthcoming season, including Albert Blake (Watford), George Emmerson (Cardiff City), Frank Eaton (Reading), George Clarke (Crystal Palace), James Allen (Huddersfield Town), Joe Devine (Sunderland), Bill Mason (Fulham) and Alec Farmer (Nottingham Forest).

One of O'Brien's awkward tasks was to bring a youngster named Hurley into line. He was often late for training and was sacked three times by O'Brien. Hurley travelled to the ground on a second-hand motorbike which was not very reliable, so the matter went to the board and they decided to raise Hurley's salary so that he could afford the train fare instead.

After a disappointing 13th place finish in the **1934–35** season the board of directors decided on a change at the helm and appointed William Birrell as manager. Birrell had previously been a player for Middlesbrough and had been manager at Bournemouth for the last four years.

In December 1935 the Queen's Park Rangers Supporters' Club was formed, with the motto 'To Help Not Hinder'. During their first season of operation they handed over a cheque for £100 to help towards the cost of crush barriers on the terracing and to help pay for the trainer's equipment.

That season there was a lot of activity among the playing staff. On the incoming side were William Carr (Derby County), Jonty Rowe (Reading), Ernie Vincent (Manchester United), Harry Lowe (Watford), David Samuel (Reading), Reg Banks (West Bromwich Albion), Jack Fletcher

The 1936–37 team.

(Bournemouth), Frank Lumsden (Huddersfield Town), David Ovenstone (Raith Rovers), Johnny Ballentyne (Patrick Thistle) and Tommy Cheetham.

Signed during the **1936–37** season were Arthur Jefferson (Peterborough United), Wilfred Bott (Newcastle United), Hugh McMahon (Reading) and Arthur Fitzgerald (Reading). After a 13th-place finish more players were signed for the **1937–38** season, including Norman Smith (Charlton Athletic), Jack Cape (Manchester United), John Gilfillan (Portsmouth) and Joe Mallett (Charlton Athletic), resulting in a third place finish.

New players again joined the club during the close season of **1938–39**. One of the new signings was to return to the club in the 1960s and become the most successful Rangers manager – he was, of course, Alec Stock. The other newcomers that season were John Devine (Aberdeen), Arthur Warburton (Fulham) and Harry Pearson (Coventry City). Before the start of the season the supporters' club gave £1,500 to pay for the roof over the new £7,000 terracing at the Loftus Road end of the ground. It was officially opened by the Rt. Hon. Herbert Morrison at the home game against Crystal Palace on 29 October.

At the turn of that year Rangers had 23 points from their 21 games, a record of eight wins, seven draws and six defeats. January's fixtures resulted in two wins and two defeats, and Cheetham scored another hat-trick during the month. In February the club were still £20,000 in debt, and although they had resisted several offers for Cheetham the directors decided to accept the Brentford offer of £5,000 in order to alleviate some of the overdraft. Following Cheetham's departure, however, Rangers lost their way and slid down the table.

Two months after Cheetham's departure William Birrell resigned as manager. He was replaced by Ted Vizzard, who had been manager at Swindon Town for the past six seasons. The reserves had a successful season by finishing as runners-up in the London Combination and winning the London Challenge Cup for the second time. During the season they had a run of one defeat in 28 games.

Before the start of the ill-fated **1939–40** season, Ted Vizzard managed to persuade the old Millwall favourite Dave Mangnall out of retirement to join Rangers. Other new arrivals were Arthur Bonass

(Chesterfield), John Barr (Third Lanark) and John McColgan (Plymouth Argyle). The League lasted for only three games, in which Rangers drew two and lost one, before war was declared and the Football League was suspended. The Football League organised regional competitions for those clubs who wished to continue playing, and Rangers were placed in the South (B) League along with Aldershot, Bournemouth, Brentford, Brighton, Chelsea, Fulham, Portsmouth, Reading and Southampton.

Rangers started their wartime football with a friendly against the army, which Rangers won 10–0. The army side was never made public, the official reason being for security. Rangers' results improved during the season after some poor pre-war results and they finished in second place.

In order to generate more competitiveness in wartime football, the League organised the League War Cup for interested clubs. The first and second rounds were over two legs, with all the other rounds being one game and a replay if necessary. The Final was scheduled to be played at Wembley Stadium. However, a one-leg preliminary round had to be played to reduce the number of entrants. Unfortunately for Rangers, in the preliminary round they were drawn away to Southend United and lost 1–0.

The format of the London Cup, introduced in the **1940–41** season, was two Leagues of six teams, with the teams playing each other at home and away. Following that, the top two sides of each League would go into a knockout to decide the overall winners. Rangers started the London Cup with two defeats by Fulham, 4–1 away and 7–5 at home, but they did manage to win two games in the first half of the competition. The final table saw Rangers in third place with 11 points, just one off a semi-final place. Rangers continued to play in these competitions until the end of wartime football.

Towards the end of the war Dave Mangnall had been offered the role of player-manager, and though at first he had been reluctant to take on the role, he eventually grew into the role and took the club all the way to their first-ever promotion. Mangnall took over from Ted Vizard, who, due to the outbreak of war, had never had the chance to manage Rangers in a competitive game.

Before the start of the final wartime season in **1945–46**, Mangnall gave an interview to a local paper in which he assessed the club's prospects for the next year. In it he expressed his desire to continue with the philosophy of playing the younger players when the regulars were unavailable and only using guest players as a last resort. On the playing side, he said he was looking forward to having Reg Allen and Johnny Barr back at the club following their release from Prisoner of War camps in Germany, where they had both been held for four years. Harry Brown, the current first-choice goalkeeper, was stationed nearby and was available for most matches, but 23 of the club's professionals were still in the forces.

With the expectation of peace on the horizon more teams entered the League competition for the season, causing the South Regional League to be split into South (North) and South (South) Divisions. Rangers were in the South (North) part with 10 other teams. They started off with five successive victories, including a 6–2 win away at Mansfield Town, and after 10 games Rangers were at the top of the League with 18 points and a goal tally of 28 for and only six against. Their first defeat came at Ipswich Town where they lost 2–1, but the setback did not affect them too much as they went on to win the next five games. Their first home defeat was on Boxing Day against Norwich City, but it did not matter as by then Rangers had assured themselves of the title, finishing six points ahead of Norwich City. The mainstays of the side were ever-present Jack Rose and Reg Allen, Harry Daniels, Joe Mallett and Alf Ridyard, all of whom missed only one game. The leading goalscorer for the third successive season was William Heathcote, this time with 22 goals.

For the first season of peacetime football, Rangers relied mostly on players who had joined the club during the war. There were some notable signings made at the beginning of the season, one of whom was a familiar face to the wartime supporters: Cyril Hatton from Notts County, who had guested for the club when he was in London. His transfer fee of £1,000 was the first four-figure sum the club had paid for a player. Dave Mangnall then paid another four-figure fee for the services of Fred Durrant, the Brentford centre-forward. The other newcomers included Don Mills, a miner from Rotherham, Reg Saphin (Ipswich Town) and George Powell from Fulham. On the outgoing side were Harry Brown, the reserve goalkeeper, who went to Notts County as part of the Hatton deal, and Alec Stock, who joined Yeovil Town as manager.

Although Rangers were solvent, it was difficult for them to ignore repeated offers for goalkeeper Reg Allen. One offer was for £10,000, a record for a goalkeeper at that time. Allen was looking to further his career and asked for a move, which the club reluctantly agreed to, but as details of his transfer were being agreed Allen changed his mind and decided to stay.

After a second place finish in **1946–47** Rangers made two costly signings ready for the new season. They paid their record fee of £2,000 for George Smith, the Brentford centre-half, and the same figure to Wolverhampton Wanderers for Fred Ramscar. Ramscar had first appeared for the club as a guest during the latter part of the war.

Rangers started the season as they meant to carry on – with five straight wins, a run in which they scored 13 goals and conceded just one. Not surprisingly Rangers were top of the League and determined to stay there. Rangers' first defeat was 0–2 at home against Swindon Town, which was followed by another, this time 3–1 at Swansea Town. By now the crowds were up to around 25,000, bringing much needed cash into the club.

At the turn of the year Rangers had two five-goal home victories against Watford and Bristol Rovers. Rangers and Bournemouth soon pulled away from the other clubs, and when they met at Dean Court on 14 April it was obvious that Bournemouth had to win to have any chance of catching up. The match attracted a crowd of 25,495, with over 10,000 having to be locked out. Rangers scored 16 minutes from the end to win the game, and as a result they only needed two points from their remaining five games to take the title and the promotion place. They lost 5–2 at Norwich City the following week, but 0–0 against Swansea Town ensured Rangers won promotion for the first time in their history.

Gates had increased dramatically during the promotion-winning season with a total attendance of over a million seeing Rangers through the campaign. The increased revenue enabled the club to make a very important purchase, that of the freehold of the ground together with the 39 houses adjoining in Ellerslie and Loftus Roads. The cost of £26,250 was met by the issue of shares, which due to the club's success were fully taken up.

Action from the 1948 season.

Before the start of the **1948–49** season Rangers became the first British club to make an official trip to Turkey. They played four matches in May, all at the 22,000-capacity Istanbul Stadium. The trip was a success, and the final game against the Turkish Olympic side ended in Rangers' only defeat of the trip, the score being 2–1.

QUEEN'S PARK RANGERS F.C. LTD.
Ellerslie Road, Shepherds Bush, W.12.

No 14890 Admit Bearer to 2/6 Inclnd. Tax

GROUND

SOUTH AFRICA ROAD ENTRANCE

Q.P.R. v. DERBY COUNTY

F.A. CUP—6th Round.

Saturday, 28th February, 1948

Kick-off 3 p.m. G. L. HURLEY, Secretary

A full house in 1948, thought to be the sixth-round FA Cup tie against Derby County.

Before the start of the **1949–50** season George Smith left to join Ipswich Town and was replaced by Horace Woodward of Tottenham Hotspur, who cost a club record fee of £10,500. Other newcomers included Johnny McKay (Irvine) and Stan Gullan (Clyde). On the outgoing side were Johnny Hartburn to Watford and Dougold Campbell to Crewe Alexandra.

The 1949–50 QPR team.

The season turned out to be a very poor one for Rangers, and it was no surprise when a major change in the playing personnel took place during the close season. The main departures were Reg Allen, who joined Manchester United for £11,000, a record fee for a goalkeeper, and Frank Neary, who joined Millwall. On the incoming side were William Waugh (Luton Town), Ernest Shepherd (Hull City), Lewis Clayton (Barnsley), John Poppitt (Derby County), Robert Cameron (Port Glasgow) and Anthony Ingham from Leeds United. Another appointment was that of ex-player Alec Farmer as head trainer, but again the next season was poor.

The **1951–52** season started with a 2–0 home win over West Ham United in front of a crowd of nearly 20,000. The first-ever home League game with Everton provided the most exciting game of the season with the match ending in a 4–4 draw. But the remainder of the first half of the season was a disappointment with just one win in 13 games. At that point Rangers were in 19th place and heading for the relegation zone. In order to boost the team they signed Michael Tompkys from Fulham and Joseph Spence from Portsmouth.

The New Year saw Rangers down in one of the two relegation places with just 17 points from 24 games. The only success in the final weeks of the campaign was the 4–2 home win over Sheffield United. They ended the season with 34 points, level with the other relegated side Coventry City, so after four years in Division Two Rangers were back to their more familiar surroundings of Division Three South.

In an attempt to regain their status Rangers appointed Jack Taylor as manager for the **1952–53** season, replacing Dave Mangnall. Taylor had previously played for Wolverhampton Wanderers, Hull City and Norwich City and had been a successful manager with Dorset side Weymouth. The only signing this season was Gordon Quinn from the local amateur side Eastcote. Nobody left the club pre-season but just after the start William Muir joined Torquay United, and halfway through the season Harry Gilberg signed for Brighton & Hove Albion. Unfortunately, Rangers did not improve much and they finished the season in 21st place.

Before the start of the **1953–54** season a change was made to the kit in an attempt to alter the club's fortunes. The new strip consisted of plain white shirts and blue shorts. Another innovation at Loftus Road was the installation of four floodlight towers, the first in West London, which were officially turned on at a friendly against Arsenal on 5 October.

The 1956–57 squad.

For the start of the season Rangers signed Jim Taylor (Fulham), Bert Hawkins (West Ham United), George Petchey (West Ham United), Derek Barley (Arsenal), Willie Hurrell (Millwall), Peter Fallon (Exeter City) and Peter Angell (Slough Town). The leaving players included Horace Woodward (Walsall), William Waugh (Bournemouth), Oscar Hold (March Town) and Bill Heath (Dover).

The **1955–56** season saw more unusual activity at Loftus Road – the staging of Rugby League matches. Three games were played, with the intention of introducing Londoners to the northern game. One success story of the football season was the reserves winning the London Challenge Cup for the third time.

During the season Rangers signed William McKay (Deal Town), William Nelson (West Ham United), Michael Hellawell (Salts) and George Dawson (Motherwell). Those leaving included Brian Nicholas (Chelsea) and Lewis Clayton (Bournemouth), while Joseph Spence retired on medical advice.

League success in the **1957–58** season was of paramount importance to all clubs in the Third Division North and South regions due to the fact that at the end of the season the top 12 in each region would form a non-regionalised Third Division, with the bottom 12 forming a Fourth Division. In an attempt to secure a top-half place Rangers were busy on the transfer front before the season kicked-off. They signed William Finney (Birmingham City), Edward Smith (Colchester United), Albert Allum (Brentford), Douglas Orr (Hendon) and Bob Fry (Bath City). They released Mike Hellawell, who went to Birmingham as part of the Finney deal, Tom Quigley (Worcester City), Tesi Balogun (Holbeach United) and Albert Pounder (Sittingbourne).

Rangers started the campaign with two 1–0 home wins, over Brentford and Colchester, but then lost several games which left them down in 21st place, a long way from their target position of 12th. But when they were at their lowest position Rangers came into form and won three games on the trot, and by the end of November they had clawed their way back up the table to ninth place. Around Christmas there was a remarkable run of six successive 1–1 draws, three at home and three away.

The New Year saw Rangers just in the wrong half of the table in 13th place with 28 points from their 26 games. So far the away form was causing concern, with seven defeats in the 10 games away from 'The Bush'. Another spell of one win in six was not sufficient to get them up to the halfway mark, but Rangers broke back into the top half with two wins at home at the end of March. They beat Shrewsbury Town at home in April to ensure their Third Division place for the following season, finishing in 10th place.

For the start of the **1958–59** season in the non-regionalised Third Division, Rangers made several signings. They were John Pearson (Brentford) and Clive Clark (Leeds United). Those to leave the club included William Finney (Crewe Alexandra), Edward Smith (Chelmsford), Terence Peacock (Sittingbourne) and Cecil Andrews (Sittingbourne). In addition to those leaving was promising goalkeeper Ron Springett, who went to Sheffield Wednesday in March. His replacement was Ray Drinkwater, signed from Portsmouth.

As there were now four Divisions, the bottom four of the Third would be relegated to the Fourth Division and not re-elected as before. Also, the top two in the Third would be promoted to the Second Division instead of one from the north and south. With the onset of the national League, Rangers were, like many of the other sides in the Division, looking forward to meeting clubs that they had not done before. Rangers ended their first season in the non-regionalised League in 13th place.

Loftus Road was selected for an England v Scotland international match towards the end of the season. It was not a full representative game but one between English and Scottish taxi drivers!

Action from a 1958 game against Halifax.

For the **1959–60** season Jack Taylor left to become manager at Leeds United. He was replaced by the club's ex-player Alec Stock, who, since leaving Rangers just after the war, had taken non-League Yeovil to the fifth round of the FA Cup, in a run which included a famous win over Sunderland. The season started promisingly with three wins, a draw and a defeat, and by the end of the season Rangers were in eighth place with 49 points. The home record had been good with 14 wins and seven draws, but the away form did not match that, with only four wins and 13 defeats.

Stock's signings for the season were Brian Bedford (Bournemouth), Jimmy Andrews (Leyton Orient), Jimmy Golding (Tonbridge), Ken Whitfield (Brighton) and Mike Keen and John Collins. Stock released Tommy Anderson (Torquay), Stuart Richardson (Oldham Athletic), George Whitelaw (Halifax Town), Mike Powell (Yiewsley), Alec Dawson (Sittingbourne) and Robert Cameron (Leeds United).

For the **1960–61** season Rangers reverted back to their more familiar colours of royal blue and white hoops with white shorts, but the change did not bring immediate success. Signed that season were Peter Carey (Leyton Orient), Michael Bottoms (Harrow Town) and David Cockell (Hounslow). Leaving the club were George Petchey and Pat Kerrins, both to Crystal Palace.

After a slow start Rangers had a successful season, and a good spell at the turn of the year saw them reach the top of the table. However, in the end they just missed out on promotion after they dropped some vital points against Chesterfield.

In the **1961–62** season the arrivals included Roy Bentley (Fulham), Jim Towers (Brentford), George Francis (Brentford), Bill Williams (Portsmouth) and John McCelland (Lincoln City). The outgoing players included Arthur Longbottom to Port Vale and Clive Clark to West Bromwich Albion for £17,500. During the season Mark Lazarus was sold to Wolverhampton Wanderers for £26,000 and re-signed five months later for £16,000. This season ended with a fourth-place finish.

Brighton's 'keeper watches the ball go past him in a game in 1961.

The next season, **1962–63**, saw a 13th-place finish, and it was clear that Rangers' form had to improve. The early season transfer activity had seen the signings of Frank Large (Halifax Town), Frank Smith (Tottenham Hotspur), Andy Malcolm (Chelsea) and Jimmy Dugdale (Aston Villa). On the outgoing side were Jim Towers (Millwall), Michael Bottoms (Oxford United) and Rodney Slack (Cambridge United).

The 1962–63 squad.

The players of Queen's Park Rangers training in the snow in the 1960s.

During this season Rangers moved to White City Stadium, after having played there for the 1933–34 season. The move did not last long, however, and after just 10 months Rangers moved back to their old ground at Loftus Road.

Before the start of the **1963–64** season Tony Ingham announced his retirement after a record 555 first-team appearances for the club. Another off-the-field event was the attempt by businessman John Bloom to take control of the club. At the club's AGM in November he lost a vote to unseat Bert Farmer from the board. As it transpired, Rangers were right to reject him as shortly afterwards Bloom's washing machine company, Rolls, went into receivership.

Departures from the squad included Michael Barber (Notts County), Bill Williams (West Bromwich Albion), John McCelland (Portsmouth) and Frank Large (Northampton Town). Stock signed a number of players as replacements, including Dick Whittaker (Peterborough), brothers Ray and Pat Brady, Terry McQuade (Millwall), Derek Gibbs, Malcolm Graham (Leyton Orient) and Peter Springett.

Mr Jim Gregory joined the board in November 1964 after turning down an approach by First Division Fulham, and five months later he was elected chairman of the club, and the rest is, as they say, history. With chairman Gregory's backing Rangers were able to make some significant signings for the **1965–66** season. Arrivals included Les Allen, for a club record fee of £20,000, Ian Watson for £10,000, Keith Sanderson for £5,000, Jim Langley for £2,000, Alan Wilks on a free transfer and Keith Sanderson, who was still an amateur and had a full-time job at NCR in Marylebone Road. After 80 minutes of the away game against Millwall on 2 October that season, Frank Sibley became the first Rangers substitute, when he came on for John Collins.

Post-1966

Interest in football was at its highest level for several years following England's victory in the World Cup Final in July 1966. This, added to their good previous season, meant that Rangers and their fans were looking forward to another successful year. And they were not disappointed.

The League campaign started badly, however, with a home draw and an away defeat. This put Rangers down in 20th place. A 15-game unbeaten run followed, and the 2–1 win at home against Torquay United on 15 November took Rangers to the top of the League. They were not displaced for the rest of the season, a run of 30 games. During February and March 1967 Rangers played 11 games and only conceded a goal in two of them. The biggest victories in that time were 4–0 at home to Bournemouth and Darlington and 5–1 at home to Scunthorpe United. After the Scunthorpe game Rangers needed just two points from their remaining eight matches to clinch the Championship, so hopes were high of a celebratory drink or two on the way back from the game at Walsall. But the champagne had to be kept on ice as Walsall inflicted only the third defeat of the season. However, the next game at Oldham Athletic ended in a 1–0 win and the Championship was Rangers'. The all-important goal was scored by Alan Wilks, who had come in for Rodney Marsh after he was injured in the previous game. By the end of the season Rangers were a record 12 points ahead of second placed Middlesbrough. For the second time in their history Rangers had scored more than 100 goals in a League season, the century coming with Alan Wilks's goal in the 1–1 draw at Swindon Town.

For the season's League Cup competition the Football League decided to replace the two-leg Final with one match at Wembley Stadium to give the Cup more credability among the clubs. Rangers' League Cup campaign started on 23 August with Sir Stanley Rous, President of FIFA, switching on the club's new floodlights. He said that he hoped this was the beginning of a bright new future for the club. Little did he know how prophetic those words would become. The lights must have been to Marsh's liking as he scored four goals in the 5–0 first-round win over Colchester United, the other coming from Mark Lazarus.

The draw for the second round took Rangers to the Recreation Ground to meet Aldershot from the Fourth Division. The match was close, with Aldershot opening the scoring in the first half, while Les Allen equalised before half-time. There was no further scoring in the second half, and the 1–1 draw meant a replay at Loftus Road the following week. In the replay Rangers took the lead through a Jim Langley penalty after 75 minutes and consolidated their position with a second goal from Rodney Marsh in the 81st minute. Following this victory, Rangers reached the third round for the first time, and their next opponents were Swansea Town.

Interest in the Cup was increasing and a crowd of nearly 13,000 came to the game. The Welshmen took the lead in the 32nd minute when Ivor Allchurch went round two defenders before firing the ball past Peter Springett into the net, but Rangers equalised in the 59th minute with a Tony Hazell shot that was deflected past his own 'keeper by the Swansea centre-half Brian Purcell. In the 89th minute Rangers won a corner, and Les Allen sent the ball across for Mike Keen to head the winner.

The draw for the fourth round gave Rangers a home tie against First Division Leicester City. The match attracted a crowd of 20,735, who witnessed an electrifying game. The opening goal was scored by Roger Morgan in the 21st minute, but Derek Dougan equalised within a minute and scored a second after 41 minutes to give Leicester a half-time lead. Rangers came out fighting in the second half and equalised after 56 minutes when Les Allen's chipped shot hit the crossbar, bounced down and went in off Gordon Banks. Rangers regained the lead a minute later when Sanderson released Lazarus down the wing, and Les Allen scored from his cross. Just three minutes later Mark Lazarus scored the fourth, and Rangers held on to win 4–2 to progress to the last eight.

Rangers' next opponents were Carlisle United, who were at the top of the Second Division, and again Rangers got the home draw. The match had another good crowd of 19,146, and Rangers again proved themselves capable in higher company. Rodney Marsh scored twice and Carlisle could only get one goal, so Rangers were through to the last four.

The draw for the two-leg semi-finals paired Rangers with Birmingham City and West Bromwich Albion with West Ham United, giving the possibility of an all-Birmingham or all-London Final. A crowd of 34,295 saw Birmingham take the lead in the first leg after just four minutes through Barry Bridge, but no Rangers fan could have imagined what the second half was to bring. Rangers were not the least bit overawed by their superior opponents. Rodney Marsh scored to bring Rangers back level, and his strike was followed shortly afterwards by another goal, this time from Roger Morgan, before Mark Lazarus added a third to give Rangers a comfortable cushion. But they were not finished as Les Allen scored a fourth to give Rangers an incredible 4–1 win. With a three goal lead Rangers were confident of becoming the first Third Division side to appear in a Wembley Final. The crowd of 24,604 for the second leg was Rangers' biggest home gate of the season. At half-time the match was still goalless, but of course Rangers were still leading the tie by three goals. In the second half Rodney Marsh scored after 53 minutes and then scored another before Birmingham got one back. Mike Keen ended the tie with another goal to give Rangers a 3–1 win and a 7–2 aggregate win overall. In the other semi-final West Bromwich had beaten West Ham United 6–2 on aggregate to get to the Final for the second successive year.

Rodney Marsh scores the equaliser in the League Cup Final against West Bromwich Albion.

The Final attracted a competition record crowd of 97,952 to Wembley Stadium on 4 March 1967. Rangers started very nervously and conceded a goal after just seven minutes, but they fought back and thought that they had scored with a spectacular overhead-kick from Rodney Marsh, but the referee disallowed it stating it was offside. At half-time Rangers went in a little disappointed, as West Bromwich had increased their lead in the 36th minute when Clive Clark beat the Rangers offside trap to fire past a stranded Springett. No one really knows what Alec Stock said to his players during the half-time interval, but it was certainly effective. Albion were still able to control the play, and as the game entered its last half an hour Rangers were still two goals adrift, but after 63 minutes Mark Lazarus was fouled on the right-hand edge of the penalty area. Les Allen took the free-kick and Roger Morgan was able to get a header on target and past 'keeper Shepherd to give Rangers some hope. The crowd urged the Third Division side on, and it must have inspired Marsh as with 75 minutes gone he collected a ball just inside the Albion half and managed to dribble his way through the defence to place a right-footed shot in the far corner of the goal for Rangers' equaliser. It was one of the best goals ever seen at Wembley Stadium and the famous chant of 'Rodnee, Rodnee' boomed around the ground. Tony Brown then had a good chance to give West Bromwich the lead again, but he missed his shot. With just nine minutes remaining Ron Hunt started a run with the ball from just inside his own half. He played a one-two with Mark Lazarus and continued into the Albion penalty area, at which point Shepherd, the West Bromwich 'keeper, came out to smother the ball and collided with Hunt. The ball then ran loose to Mark Lazarus, who kicked it into the unguarded net. All the Albion players were claiming a foul on the 'keeper, but the referee, Walter Crossley, judged that it had been a 50:50 challenge and awarded the goal to Rangers. They held on for those final nail-biting minutes to win the trophy. The unique three-handled Cup was presented to Mike Keen by the Lord Mayor of London, Sir Robert Bellinger. The only disappointment for Rangers was that as they were a Third Division side

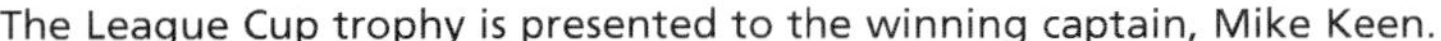

The League Cup trophy is presented to the winning captain, Mike Keen.

they were not allowed to take their place in the following season's Inter-Cities Fairs Cup competition. Instead the place in Europe was given to the losing finalists West Bromwich Albion as only First Division sides were nominated by the League.

Alec Stock relied on practically the same squad of players for the club's return to the Second Division in **1967–68**. The only player movements were the retirement of Jim Langley, who at the age of 38 years and 96 days was the oldest player ever to appear in the first team, and the arrival of Allan Harris from Chelsea as Langley's replacement. Missing at the start of the season was Rodney Marsh, who had broken a bone in his foot during pre-season training.

From the middle of December Rangers had an unbeaten run of nine matches, and at the halfway point Rangers were in second place with 28 points. The unbeaten run took Rangers back to the top of the table. The game at home to Blackpool became crucial as Rangers knew that they could not afford to lose because the Seasiders were only one point behind in third place, but Rangers won 2–0 with goals from Ian Morgan and Clarke. This was the start of a run of four successive victories in which Rangers did not concede a goal. A win and a draw at top-placed Ipswich meant that if Rangers won their last two games they would be promoted, probably on goal average, providing Blackpool did not

The 1967–68 team with the Third Division Championship trophy and the League Cup.

win both their last two games by good margins. The decision eventually went to the last game of the season, when Rangers were ahead of Blackpool by 0.2381 of a goal in the race for the First Division. Rangers were away at Aston Villa and Blackpool were away at Huddersfield Town. Rangers were drawing 1–1 and Blackpool were ahead at Huddersfield. As news came through that Blackpool were now 3–1 ahead, Rangers' travelling fans were getting worried. With eight minutes to go Rangers attacked again and in attempting to clear the ball the Villa full-back Keith Bradley turned the ball past his own goalkeeper to give Rangers the lead. No further scoring took place and Rangers were in the First Division for the first time in their history. The final table saw Ipswich Town on 59 points and Rangers and Blackpool on 58 points – Rangers were promoted by 0.21 of a goal. By winning promotion Rangers became only the second side ever to go from Third Division to First in successive seasons.

In his desire for Rangers to have a stadium worthy of the First Division, the chairman Jim Gregory held discussions with Brentford with a view to merging the two clubs. The new club would use Brentford's Griffin Park ground as it had a capacity of 40,000. The fans of both clubs were against the move and after a few preliminary meetings the idea was dropped. As result of the failed merger Gregory then put all his efforts into turning the Loftus Road ground into a stadium fit for top-level football. Soon after the start of the season a new stand, costing £210,000, was opened on the South Africa Road side of the ground.

Before the first season of First Division football began, Alec Stock resigned from the club and was replaced by Bill Dodgin in a caretaker capacity. So despite having guided Rangers to the First Division Stock never picked a side to play at the top.

The first game of **1968–69** was at home to Leicester City, one of the First Division sides Rangers had beaten on the way to winning the League Cup 18 months before. A crowd of 21,494 were there for the historic occasion, which ended 1–1. At the beginning of November Tommy Docherty was

Division One football for the first time against Leicester City.

appointed manager in place of Bill Dodgin, who had joined Fulham. Docherty lasted only 28 days before being replaced by Les Allen, who became player-manager. By the halfway point of the season Rangers were bottom with only 11 points from their 21 games.

At the beginning of February Rangers sold Roger Morgan to Tottenham Hotspur for £110,000. Morgan's first game for Spurs was against Rangers at Loftus Road, where he lined up against his twin brother Ian for the first time. Rangers then lost the next nine matches to be confirmed as relegated, and they finished the season with just 18 points, an all-time low for the First Division. They had scored just 39 goals and conceded 95 in their 42 League matches.

Terry Venables signs for a club record fee of £70,000 from Tottenham Hotspur.

Following their relegation Rangers went into the transfer market in an attempt to regain their First Division place. They signed Terry Venables for £70,000, a club record, from Tottenham Hotspur, and Clive Clark was re-signed from West Bromwich Albion, as part payment for the transfer of Alan Glover to The Hawthorns, while Bobby Keetch left the club to play for the South African side Durban City and Les Allen gave up playing to concentrate on managing the club. The **1969–70** season started promisingly with four wins and a draw, but Rangers dropped to ninth place at the end of the season, eight points behind promoted Blackpool.

The 1970s

There were many changes on the playing staff for the **1970–71** season. By the early stages of the season the following players had left the club: Barry Bridges (Millwall) for £40,000, Mike Kelly (Birmingham City), Keith Sanderson (Goole Town), Clive Clark (Preston North End), Dave Metchick (Arsenal) and Bobby Turpie (Peterborough United). Their replacements were Frank Saul (Millwall), Phil Parkes (Walsall) and Andy McCulloch (Walton and Hersham). However, despite the changes the season started badly with two defeats. Things improved slightly with a draw and a win away from home, but Rangers were down in 18th place and appeared unlikely to go much higher. After half the season they were in 15th place with only 17 points. The New Year brought a change in the manager's office, with coach Gordon Jago replacing Les Allen, who joined Swindon Town. Subsequently there was a slight improvement in results as the defence had a run of four games without conceding a goal, and Rangers ended the season in 11th place.

Rangers started the **1971–72** season with a fine three-goal victory over Sheffield Wednesday, and the year ended with a run of five wins in six games, enabling Rangers to hold on to third place, just three points behind second placed Millwall. By the end of the season Rangers were in fourth place, just two points behind promoted Birmingham City and three behind champions Norwich City.

In February Rangers arranged a friendly with West Bromwich Albion at short notice as both sides were out of the FA Cup and did not have a match. In order to let people know that the game was on Rangers became the first club to advertise on television. The advert was a still of Rodney Marsh with a voice-over giving details of the game. It must have worked as a larger than expected crowd of 7,087 turned up for the Friday night game.

As Rangers had got so close to promotion, manager Gordon Jago went into the transfer market to buy the extra resources needed to go up. He signed the Eire international Don Givens from Luton Town, while in September Stan Bowles arrived from Carlisle United for a record fee of £110,000. The last signing was Dave Thomas, the Burnley winger. Another new addition to the club was the building of the new Ellerslie Road Stand which replaced the old tin-roofed one. With the development of that side of the ground the club moved the administration offices and dressing rooms to the South Africa Road Stand.

The **1972–73** season started a little disappointingly with just one win in the first five matches. However, by the New Year Rangers were in second place, a position they maintained until the end of the season. January and February saw a run of six unbeaten games in which only one goal was conceded. Despite winning their last four games, Rangers were unable to clinch the title from Burnley, finishing just one point behind them. Rangers' last game of the season was away at Sunderland, who had beaten Leeds United the previous Saturday to win the FA Cup. With promotion assured for Rangers and Sunderland's Cup on display, the 43,265 crowd were expecting to see a friendly game, but the referee had to take both sides off the pitch for 10 minutes to cool down tempers. The tense atmosphere was not helped by Rangers winning 3–0 and Tony Hazell knocking the Cup off its table with a clearance.

For their return to Division One in **1973–74** Jago had a more experienced set of players and was confident of making an impact in the First Division. In fact, he made only one signing, that of Frank McLintock from Arsenal. That season saw a change to the relegation and promotion between Divisions One and Two. Instead of two teams moving each season it would now be three.

Rangers started with four draws and a defeat in the first five games. The crowds were returning to Loftus Road and over 28,000 saw the game against West Ham United. The first half of the season ended with three draws followed by a defeat and a win, and after 21 games Rangers were in sixth place with 23 points.

New Year's Day saw a 3–0 home win over Manchester United in front of a crowd of 32,339 people. On 3 April Phil Parkes and Stan Bowles made their international debuts for England in the 0–0 draw against Portugal in Lisbon. Bowles kept his place for the next England game, against Wales in Cardiff. He scored one of the goals in the 2–0 win and as a result became the first player to score for England while with Rangers. Another ground record was set for the visit of champions Leeds United when 35,353 people watched Rangers lose a close game by one goal to nil. Rangers ended the season with a 1–1 draw at Arsenal to finish eighth with 43 points. It was the highest position ever for the club in the Football League.

During that season's FA Cup Rangers were drawn away to neighbours Chelsea in the third round. The game was typified by the duel between Ron Harris and Stan Bowles. The match ended goalless and meant a replay at Loftus Road, but due to very heavy rain the match was postponed at the last minute and re-arranged for a week later. When the replay was eventually played Chelsea were weakened by injuries and Rangers took full advantage by playing a non-stop attacking game. It was surprising that they only scored once, through Stan Bowles just after the hour. The next round drew Rangers at home to Birmingham City. Mick Leach scored before half-time and when Don Givens scored a second after the break Rangers were on their way to the next round.

In the fifth round Rangers were drawn away at Coventry City. The match was a typical Cup tie with both sides attacking. The only thing the game lacked was a goal. The replay the following Tuesday was just as exciting for the supporters. Cross opened the scoring for Coventry in the first half, but before half-time Givens equalised. The second half followed the same pattern, with Cross giving Coventry the lead again only for Thomas to equalise a couple of minutes later. The game looked certain for extra-time when well into injury time Rangers were awarded a free-kick just outside the area. Stan Bowles ran up to take it and bent the ball round the wall and inside the post for the winning goal. There was not even time to restart the match as Rangers had won with literally the last kick of the match.

Having reached the last eight, Rangers were hoping for a home tie in their quest for their first ever semi-final place. The draw was kind to Rangers as it gave them their longed-for home tie, which would be played against Leicester City. The match attracted a gate of 34,078 to Loftus Road and lived up to expectations, with both sides giving as good as they got. At half-time neither side had managed to score, although Rangers came closest when Bowles headed against the bar. The second half belonged to Waters as he scored twice to kill off any hopes Rangers had of reaching the last four. Rangers had had their chances but they just could not score. So, Leicester progressed to the semi-finals by two goals to nil.

Following their good form the previous season Rangers made only one new signing in the summer. The incoming player was David Webb from Chelsea.

The goals did not exactly rush in at the start of the **1974–75** season, as neither Rangers nor their opponents scored more than once in the first six games. At the beginning of October Gordon Jago resigned as manager in order to join Tampa Bay Rowdies in the United States. His replacement was Dave Sexton, who had led Chelsea to victories in the FA and European Cup-Winners' Cup. After 21 games Rangers were in 17th place with 17 points, and they had won only six of their games and had been beaten 10 times. With two home wins at Easter, Rangers moved up to seventh place, but with only one win in the final seven games they dropped back to 11th place by the end of the season.

Rangers had more representation in the England team that season in the Home international series. The game against Wales saw three Rangers players in the same England side for the first time as Ian Gillard joined Francis and Thomas in the starting line up. In the next game against Scotland Francis scored twice as England beat 'The Auld Enemy' 5–1.

Hopes were high for the **1975–76** season following the establishment of a strong squad of players, the only addition before the start being John Hollins from Chelsea. The optimism increased when during their pre-season games Rangers had beaten the West German champions Borussia Mönchengladbach 4–1 and the Portuguese champions Benfica 4–2. The season could not have got off to a better start as Rangers won their opening game 2–0 against Liverpool in front of a crowd of 27,113. It was the first time that the Merseysiders had lost to Rangers. In the match Gerry Francis scored what turned out to be the BBC Goal of the Season. The first away game was just as spectacular when Rangers won 5–1 against champions Derby, with Bowles getting a hat-trick. In September the England manager Don Revie appointed Gerry Francis as England's captain, a great honour not only for Francis but for the club as well. However, after a great start the year ended badly with three away defeats in four games, the only success being on Boxing

The 1975–76 team.

Day against Norwich City. Another away defeat followed by a home win kept Rangers in fifth place. The next game saw the start of one of the best periods in the club's history, as Rangers gained 23 out of the next 24 points. They won 11 and drew once between 31 January and 10 April 1976.

On 10 April Rangers won 4–2 at home to Middlesbrough, Liverpool drew at Aston Villa and Manchester United lost at Ipswich Town. This meant Rangers were a point clear of Liverpool and had played the same number of games. So if Rangers won their three remaining games they would be League champions, even if Liverpool won all theirs. On Easter Saturday Rangers were at Norwich City and a large number of fans made the trip to East Anglia. The match was a very tense affair. Both sides scored once before half-time, but disaster struck in the second half when Morris scored for Norwich. Boyer then scored a third and Don Givens got one for Rangers, but despite their best efforts they could not equalise. The Rangers players and fans were more disheartened when the news came through from Anfield that Liverpool had beaten Stoke City 5–2. Rangers now had to win their two remaining home games and hope that Liverpool lost one of their two remaining away games. Rangers beat Arsenal on Easter Monday, but Liverpool also won 3–0 at Manchester City. On the last Saturday of the season Rangers were at home to Leeds United, but Liverpool were not playing due to international commitments. Rangers beat Leeds United 2–0 in front of their largest gate of the season, 31,002, and that win meant that Rangers had finished their games and were top of the League. They then had to wait for 10 days until Liverpool played at Wolverhampton Wanderers. As the goal average was so close, a 1–1 or 2–2 draw would also give the title to Liverpool, but a higher scoring draw would keep Rangers on top. Wolves had their own incentive for winning as they needed two points to avoid being relegated if Birmingham City lost their match, which was on the same night. At half-time Wolves led through a John Richards goal. They held on until 13 minutes before the end when Kevin Keegan equalised. When news came through that Birmingham had won so Wolves could not stay up, the fight went out of them and Liverpool scored twice more to win 3–1 and take the title. Rangers were just 13 minutes away from winning the First Division, although they had done enough to reach European competition the following year.

In **1976–77** Sexton was happy with his squad of players and the only transfer activity concerned players who could not command a regular first-team place; John Beck went to Coventry City, Keith Pritchett to Brentford and Richard Teale to Fulham. Just after the season got under way Martyn Busby joined Notts County. The only addition to the squad was Eddie Kelly from Arsenal. There was a change in the League rules concerning the splitting of teams on equal points in the table. It was decided to use goal difference instead of goal average to determine the highest-placed side.

Rangers' performance did not come anywhere near the quality of the end of the previous season and they continued with mixed success. The New Year saw three wins and a draw, but a poor run of just one goal in five games dropped Rangers towards the relegation zone. The next three games produced five points to put Rangers in 15th place but still far too close to the relegation positions for comfort, and four defeats in the next five games put Rangers down to 20th place and in a relegation place. The table was very close, and Rangers' last four games were all against teams in the top half of the League. Luckily for Rangers their form returned and they ended the season in 14th place with 38 points, four away from the three relegation places.

In the League Cup Rangers' second-round opponents were Second Division Cardiff City. Although they were away Rangers soon exerted their superiority with two first-half goals. The scorers were Bowles (32 minutes) and Thomas (37). In the second half Rangers extended their lead in the 63rd minute with a goal from Clement. Cardiff scored a consolation in the 87th minute but it did not prevent Rangers from going through by three goals to one.

The third-round draw paired Rangers with Third Division Bury at Loftus Road. McLintock scored with a header in the first minute from a Masson free-kick, and 17 minutes later another Masson kick was headed in by Givens. Bury fought hard in the second half but did not score until the 89th minute, leaving Rangers to go through by the odd goal in three.

The fourth round took Rangers across London to Upton Park to meet West Ham United. The match did not start well for Rangers as they had lost Dave Thomas, having been fouled by Lampard in the first minute. Rangers did not let the loss affect them too much as they managed to score a goal in each half. The goals came from Bowles after 37 minutes and Clement three minutes before the end. The fifth-round draw gave Rangers another London derby, this time at home to Arsenal. The match turned out to be a very competitive Cup tie, as both sides scored before half-time, Masson for Rangers and Stapleton for Arsenal. In the second half Rangers took the incentive and Webb scored what proved to be the winner.

Rangers had now reached the last four for the second time in their history. The two-legged semi-final draw paired Rangers with Aston Villa, with the first leg to be played at Loftus Road. The match was very even with neither side getting a real opening. It finished goalless, which made Villa favourites to go through to the Final. However, the second leg was one of the games of the season. Again neither side could score in the first half, but after the break Villa took the lead through Deehan. With just eight minutes remaining Rangers were awarded a penalty when Francis was bundled over. Burridge saved Givens's spot-kick and it looked like the end for Rangers. However, two minutes later Francis made up for the miss by scoring the equaliser. The game went to extra-time with both sides looking for the winner. Deehan put Villa back in front only for substitute Eastoe to equalise again. As away goals did not count double in the competition a third game was required. Rangers won the toss for the venue and chose Highbury. The game attracted a crowd of 40,438, which took the total attendance for the semi-final to over 113,000. Rangers looked the more likely to score in the early stages but could not convert their chances, and Aston Villa fought back and Brian Little scored twice before half-time. After the break he completed his hat-trick to kill off Rangers' hopes of reaching a second Final.

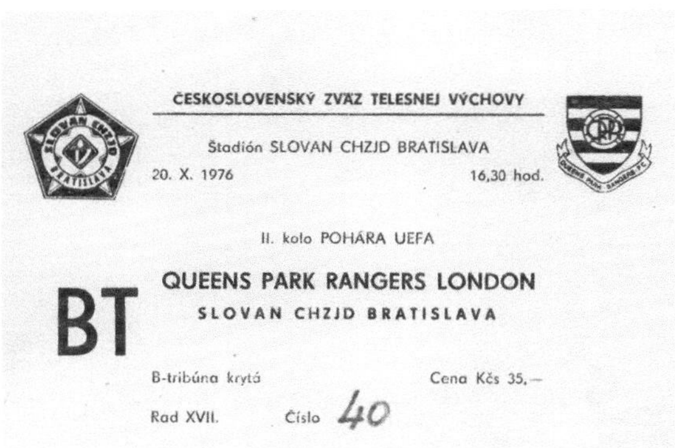

Tickets from Rangers' European games, above versus Slovan Bratislava from the second round and below, against FC Cologne in the third round.

Rangers' first European match was a four-goal victory at home to the Norwegian side Brann Bergen. The match was a good exhibition of European football, with Rangers always looking the better side. The first goal did not come until the 29th minute when Bowles got on the end of a Webb flick-on. Bowles scored again just four minutes later and completed his hat-trick in the 64th minute, while Masson finished the evening off with a fourth after 85 minutes. The second leg was a formality with Rangers scoring another seven goals, including a second European hat-trick for Bowles. The other scorers were Givens, with two, Thomas and Webb.

The second round paired Rangers with Slovan Bratislava of Czechoslovakia. They produced one of the best displays by an English team in Europe, mainly due to the skilful planning of Dave Sexton. Bowles took his European tally to eight with two first-half goals, while Slovan scored once before the break to leave Rangers just in front at the interval. The second half was the reverse of the first, with Bratislava scoring two to Rangers' one, the third Rangers goal being scored by Givens. The entertaining match ended all square at 3–3, which meant that the Czechs had to win the second leg. They came with a very attack-minded side but were no match for Rangers, who managed a three-goal lead by half-time due to Givens's two goals in the 18th and 32nd minutes and a Bowles goal before the break. In the second half Givens completed his hat-trick with a penalty and Clement scored a fifth. Slovan did manage two goals but Rangers went through by an aggregate of eight goals to five.

In the third round Rangers faced the West German side FC Cologne at Loftus Road. Rangers scored twice in the first half through Givens and Webb, and a superb performance was capped with a fine goal from Bowles to ensure they had a three-goal cushion for the return game. The most important thing was that Rangers had not conceded an away goal. The second leg match was played in front of a fanatical 41,000 crowd. Masson scored a very important early goal which meant that the Germans had to score five to go through. They scored three before half-time, and Rangers were not helped by having Dave Clement sent off for punching. Cologne scored again, but Parkes then made three excellent saves to deny the Germans a winning goal. As the tie finished level at 4–4 Rangers went through on the away goals rule.

Rangers had now reached the last eight and had to wait nearly three months for the fourth round to be played. Their opponents were AEK Athens, who had to visit London first. Due to the poor weather Rangers made arrangements to play their home leg at Wembley Stadium on the Thursday, a day later than scheduled. As it was they ended up at Loftus Road as the Greeks insisted on playing on the

Wednesday. The tactics of AEK were soon evident and it was not surprising that Rangers were awarded two penalties before half-time. Francis scored them both and another Bowles goal earned them a three-goal lead to the second leg, just as they had done in the previous round. Rangers went to Athens missing three key players, Thomas and Francis were injured in the previous League game and Clement was suspended. The Greeks attacked right from the start and soon scored three goals. Rangers had to defend strongly to survive, and as they were unable to score a valuable away goal the tie went to extra-time. With neither side managing to score the match had to be decided by penalties, and after the first mandatory five kicks the shoot-out moved into the sudden death phase. The Greeks went first and scored, while Rangers' kicker David Webb missed and sent AEK through to the semi-finals.

Before the **1977–1978** season started manager Dave Sexton resigned and joined Manchester United. He was replaced by ex-Ranger Frank Sibley, who had to try to find cohesion between the experienced players of a couple of seasons' play and the inexperienced youth players. He bought in Dave Needham (Notts County) and Brian Williams (Bury), and gave professional forms to Barry Wallace, Steve Perkins and Paul Goddard, while Martyn Busby rejoined from Notts County. The players to leave included Tony Tagg (Millwall), Eddie Kelly (Leicester City) and Dave Thomas (Everton). His close season changes had an unsettling effect on the side, who had gained only one victory in the first 12 games. By the end of the year they had dropped into the relegation zone with just 15 points from their 24 games. In an attempt to change the club's results Sibley re-entered the transfer market and signed Leighton James (Derby County), Paul McGee (Toronto) and Ernie Howe (Fulham). Before the end of the year other players had

QPR v Liverpool from 1977.

left including David Webb (Leicester City), Don Masson (Derby County) and Dave Needham (Nottingham Forest), after only six months at the club.

January's fixtures produced only the fourth win of the season, but Rangers eventually managed to pull out of the danger zone and into 19th place. With the bottom two clubs, Newcastle United and Leicester City, adrift of the rest of the League there was now just one relegation place to be avoided. Rangers were one point behind West Ham United and Wolverhampton Wanderers but had five games in hand. A 3–0 win at Newcastle lifted Rangers up to 17th place, and so one point then covered the four teams trying to miss the drop. Two goalless draws at home kept Rangers ahead of the others, and although they lost the last game they managed to avoid being relegated by just one point.

Despite their poor League form Rangers put up a good performance in the League Cup. They went out in the third round to a hotly disputed Aston Villa penalty, given in the 40th minute for a tackle by Givens on the Villa centre-half McNaught. Andy Gray scored from the spot and Villa held on to win 1–0.

Following a 4–0 victory over Southern Leaguers Wealdstone, Rangers travelled across London to West Ham United for the fourth round of the FA Cup. The match at Upton Park was a typical Cup tie with both sides going for the win. As it was the match led to a replay at Loftus Road following a 1–1 draw. After four minutes of the replay Robson had put West Ham ahead, but Givens equalised before half-time to set up an eagerly awaited second half. No one could have foreseen what the second 45 minutes would bring. After 49 minutes Shanks hit the post with a header and Hollins netted the rebound, and four minutes later Abbott touched on a Hollins free-kick to Busby, who made it 3–1. Busby then scored again with a header from James's cross. Bowles scored a fifth from the spot after Taylor had handled Gillard's cross, and in the 82nd minute James completed the scoring with a free-kick which bent round the five-man defensive wall. The 6–1 win for Rangers was West Ham's heaviest ever FA Cup defeat.

The fifth-round draw gave Rangers a home tie against Nottingham Forest. Rangers led the game after a 19th-minute goal from a Busby header, and it looked as though they had achieved a victory until O'Neill scored in the last minute to give Forest a replay. The game at the County Ground was just as close as the first one, as a 1–1 draw led them to extra-time. Within the first minute Dave Clement was sent off, which gave the advantage to Forest, but again Rangers showed resoluteness. No more goals were forthcoming and a second replay was required. Rangers lost the toss for the venue and had to return to Nottingham three days later. O'Neill scored early for Forest in the third minute. Again Rangers had to defend strongly, and their efforts paid off in the 64th minute when Bowles equalised after a mistake by Clarke, the Forest full-back. But Forest responded and regained the lead a minute later and sealed the match with a third 10 minutes before the end.

During the summer Frank Sibley resigned as manager, and a permanent appointment was made in August 1978 when Steve Burtenshaw was appointed, replacing temporary manager Alec Stock. Burtenshaw had been at the club previously as coach during Gordon Jago's days. His entry into the transfer market saw the arrival of Glenn Roeder (Orient), Rachid Harkouk (Crystal Palace) and Billy Hamilton (Linfield), while Clive Allen was signed on professional forms. The departures were Don Givens (Birmingham City), Brian Williams (Swindon Town) and Leighton James (Burnley).

The **1978–79** season started disastrously, and at the halfway point of the season Rangers were in 19th place with just 15 points from their 21 games. With New Year results not as good as expected Rangers had several approaches from other clubs regarding the availability of their better players, and in February Phil Parkes was sold to West Ham United for £550,000, a world record for a goalkeeper.

Despite a 5–1 win over Coventry City Rangers could not avoid the drop and chairman Jim Gregory sacked Burtenshaw, with his choice for a replacement being a surprising one – Tommy Docherty. Docherty's previous spell at Rangers was not a success and lasted only 28 days. His arrival did not inspire his new team and they were beaten 4–0 in the final home game against Ipswich Town, signalling relegation.

Rangers' opponents for the second round of the League Cup were Preston North End. With an own-goal and two from Eastoe, Preston were unable to get through the Rangers defence and the match ended 3–1 in Rangers' favour. The third round saw Swansea City visit Loftus Road. Swansea were top of the Third Division so Rangers were expecting a hard game, but Rangers went through as both McGee and Estoe scored twice in the opening four minutes.

The fourth-round draw again saw Rangers at home, this time to Leeds United. The first half was goalless despite referee Clive Thomas awarding a spot-kick to Rangers three minutes before the break when Currie appeared to handle an Eastoe cross. However, following Leeds protests he spoke to a linesman and gave a free-kick a foot outside the box. Nothing came from the free-kick and in the second half Leeds went on to score two goals to leave Rangers rueing their bad luck.

The third-round draw of the FA Cup gave Rangers the short trip across the borough to Craven Cottage to meet Fulham. Rangers' attitude showed their lack of confidence in themselves, while Fulham – fifth in the Second Division – had the more determined approach to the game. It was not surprising when Fulham scored through Margerrison and Davies, killing off any Rangers attempt at a revival, and they went out at the first hurdle for only the second time in seven years.

Due to Docherty's influence there was not an exodus of players from the club following relegation. In fact his presence enabled Rangers to sign three key players for **1979–80**, Chris Woods (Nottingham Forest), Tony Currie (Leeds United) and David McCreery (Manchester United). Also signed were

The QPR team from 1979–80.

apprentices Dean Neal and Gary Waddock along with Peter Davidson (Berwick Rangers), Gary Micklewhite (Manchester United) and Martyn Rogers (Manchester United). The departures saw Gerry Francis leave for Crystal Palace and John Hollins for Arsenal.

Rangers' first game in the Second Division for six seasons ended in a 2–0 home win over Bristol Rovers. The goals came from Goddard and Allen, a partnership that served Rangers well in the coming seasons. The good start did not last and Rangers dropped to 20th place. Docherty re-entered the transfer market and Rangers' form then returned and they went seven games without defeat, moving up to second and eventually top spot. Docherty was not finished with the transfer market, and the greatest surprise was the transfer of fans' favourite Stan Bowles to Brian Clough's Nottingham Forest. The effect on the club of all the 'ins and outs' was felt as Rangers did not win a game in December.

The New Year started in the same way as the old one finished with two more defeats, but form improved and Rangers went back up to fourth place and then down again to sixth place, and with just two games remaining they were four points away from a promotion place. Despite getting those four points with two wins Rangers missed promotion by just one spot.

The League Cup had a change to its second-round format for the **1979–80** season. Instead of a one-leg tie the second round became a two-leg affair, the idea being that as the round was already seeded the lower grade team would be assured of a money-spinning home tie against the better side, making it very difficult for a giant-killing to happen as the giants had a second opportunity in the event of a defeat in the first game. Rangers were drawn at home to Wolverhampton Wanderers in the fourth round, following wins against Bradford City (4–1 on aggregate) and Mansfield Town (3–0). It looked as though Rangers would progress into the next round as they still led after 90 minutes. But Hibbitt scored an injury-time equaliser to take the tie to a replay at Molineux, where Wolves scored after just eight minutes through Carr and managed to hold out, going through to the quarter-final by the only goal. However, their luck did not improve for the FA Cup, as they suffered a 2–1 defeat against long-time rivals Watford in the third round. Rangers also reached the third round of the FA Cup the following season, against Tottenham Hotspur, but bowed out after their 3–1 defeat in the replay.

During the close season Rangers sold top scorer Clive Allen to Arsenal for a club record fee of £1.25 million. Also leaving was Allen's striking partner Paul Goddard, who joined West Ham United. The other players to leave were Karl Elsey (Newport County) and Mick Walsh (FC Porto). Docherty signed Tommy Langley (Chelsea), Andy King (Everton) and Barry Silkman (Brentford) and gave professional forms to apprentices Wayne Fereday, Warren Neill, Mark O'Connor, Andy Pape, Dean Wilkins and Ian Stewart.

The **1980–81** season started badly, and after 14 games Rangers were in the Second Division drop zone. Without the fans' support and with very poor results Docherty's reign as manager ended in November. He was replaced by former player Terry Venables, who went on to win three games in succession, ending the year with two wins and a draw to put Rangers in 12th place after 24 games. At the end of the last home game of the season against Cambridge United on 25 April, fans were invited onto the pitch to take away lumps of grass as souvenirs as the club had announced its intention of laying the first artificial surface in the Football League. The match ended in a resounding 5–0 win, with two goals from debutant Ian Muir. The season ended with an entertaining 3–3 draw at Shrewsbury Town, which left Rangers in eighth place in the table. The change in managership and the different styles of play was evident in the fact that 30 different players appeared during the season.

Rangers' opponents in the second leg of the second round of the League Cup were Derby County. Despite both sides hitting the woodwork neither could score before the 90 minutes or before extra-

The 1982 FA Cup Final squad.

time finished, and the tie went to penalties. Gordon Hill made no mistake for the fifth kick and Rangers became the first side to win a League Cup tie without scoring a goal. The third-round draw gave Rangers another trip to the Midlands, this time to Notts County, who ran out easy winners by four goals to one.

The main factor behind Rangers' decision to install a plastic pitch, at a cost of £350,000, was that the ground could be hired out on non-match days to earn the club extra revenue. The biggest complaint from the players and fans was the high bounce of the ball when hitting the surface. This meant that different skills were required to play on the surface. During the **1981–82** season more sand was put into the pitch which did not reduce the bounce by much, and Rangers had to allow their opponents a day's practice before each League game. Another new innovation for the forthcoming season was the introduction of three points for a League win.

Rangers had difficulty in adapting to a different surface each week as they won various home games and lost away ones, but the season started promisingly with a third-place position achieved by the end of the year. Their form did not improve though, and they finished the season in fifth place, just two points behind promoted Norwich City.

On the transfer front Clive Allen was brought back from Crystal Palace, and John Gregory (Brighton & Hove Albion) and Gary Bannister (Sheffield Wednesday) were also signed. Professional forms were given to apprentices Graham Benstead and Alan McDonald. On the outgoing side were David McCreery and Dean Neal, to North American side Tulsa Roughnecks, Don Shanks (Brighton) and Steve Wicks (Crystal Palace).

Rangers managed to reach the fourth round of the League Cup following an aggregate win of 7–2 against Portsmouth and a 3–0 victory against Bristol City, but a defeat against Watford ended their run. However, the FA Cup was a different story. Rangers' third-round opponents were Middlesbrough. As Rangers were at home they were confident of the game going ahead as scheduled, despite the countrywide freeze at the time. The pitch was in perfect condition and led to an entertaining game. Rangers bought in Hucker for Burridge in goal, a position young Hucker did not give up for the remainder of the historic season. Thompson gave Boro the lead in the first half and try as they might Rangers were not able to score before the break. The second half was all Rangers, with Platt in the Boro goal outstanding. He was finally beaten in the 70th minute by a Stainrod shot after he had weaved his way around the static defence. With no further scoring taking place the tie went to a replay at Ayresome Park. After numerous attempts to play the game it finally took place the Monday before the next round was due to be played. Rangers played some good football and scored twice, both from Stainrod, before the break. After the interval Middlesbrough pulled one back through Otto and equalised two minutes later with a twice-taken Thompson penalty. No more goals came before the 90 minutes were up and extra-time was needed. The match was taking its toll on the older players and Warren Neill came on for Tony Currie after 10 minutes of extra-time. With time running out and no goals forthcoming, it looked as though the tie was heading for a second replay. However, three minutes before the end Neill headed the winning goal to take Rangers to Blackpool the following Saturday.

The match at Bloomfield Road was a hard fought Cup tie with the Fourth Division side giving a good account of themselves and earning a replay with a goalless draw. The replay at Loftus Road was a different matter. Allen scored after only 25 minutes and Stainrod added a second from the spot before half-time. Allen then scored his second early in the second half after a Flanagan shot had rebounded off the bar, and he completed his hat-trick in the 60th minute with an unstoppable header. Entwistle scored for Blackpool but Allen was not finished yet and he scored his fourth and Rangers' fifth five minutes later.

Rangers' fifth-round opponents were Grimsby Town, who had recent experience of the pitch. The scoring was opened by Stainrod in the 27th minute and was followed 10 minutes later by a goal from Allen. After the break Howe extended Rangers' lead in the 65th minute. Although Moore pulled one back for Grimsby in the 72nd minute Rangers went through to the quarter-finals by three goals to one.

Rangers had reached the final eight of the FA Cup for only the fourth time in their history and were hoping for a home draw to help them to gain a semi-final place for the first time. The draw was kind to Rangers, with Crystal Palace coming to Loftus Road. With a lot of tension and nerves on both sides the game was not an entertaining one to watch for the uncommitted. Both sets of supporters had their moments of hope, but with the game heading for a replay both sides seemed content to play out the time. However, in the 88th minute Clive Allen turned in the box and shot past Barron in the Palace goal to put Rangers into the semi-finals for the first time.

A crowd of over 45,000 packed Highbury to see if Rangers could beat West Bromwich Albion to reach their first FA Cup Final. It was ironic that their opponents were the team that they had beaten on their only visit to Wembley Stadium back in March 1967. Terry Venables played a masterstroke and deputed Hazell to follow main threat Cyrille Regis wherever he went. The first half was a dour encounter with neither side creating a clear opportunity. In fact there were no corners at all in the first 45 minutes. But in the 72nd minute when Albion's Ally Robertson tried to clear the ball from his six yard box, Clive Allen stuck out a leg in an attempt to block the clearance and the ball hit his leg and rebounded into the net. Due to Hazell's dominance over Regis, Albion were unable to score in the final 10 minutes and Rangers were on their way to Wembley.

The Final was an all-London affair as Tottenham Hotspur had beaten Leicester City by two goals to nil at Villa Park. Rangers' plans were upset early on with an injury to Clive Allen after just 10

Clive Allen scores the only goal in the FA Cup semi-final against West Bromwich Albion.

minutes. Although he carried on he was not at his most dangerous and was eventually replaced by substitute Gary Micklewhite, who immediately crossed for John Gregory to have a header that was well saved by Clemence. With no real scoring chances and little excitement the match petered out and went into extra-time. After 110 minutes Tottenham took the lead through a Hoddle shot that was deflected past Peter Hucker by Tony Currie. Rangers did not give up, however, and with just five minutes remaining Rangers won a throw-in on the left. Stainrod took a long throw which was headed on by Hazell and Terry Fenwick headed the flick-on in to the net. The game ended in a 1–1 draw which meant a replay the following Thursday, again at Wembley Stadium.

The replay was a much better spectacle for the supporters and the television viewers at home. Rangers had to make a change in defence as captain Glenn Roeder was suspended after being sent off at Luton two weeks earlier. His place was taken by third-round hero Warren Neill. Clive Allen had not recovered from his injury and Gary Micklewhite continued in his place. Roeder's absence meant that Tony Currie was captain for the game. After six minutes Currie tackled Roberts in the penalty area and referee Clive White awarded a penalty, giving Tottenham an early lead. Rangers attacked well and Micklewhite had the ball in the net, but the goal was disallowed due to an offside Stainrod; although whether he was interfering with play was extremely doubtful as he was out on the left wing. In the second half it was all Rangers, with Gregory having a chipped shot headed off the line by Hoddle with Clemence beaten. Fenwick was then fouled in the penalty area and the linesman waved for a penalty but was overruled by the referee. Despite all their valiant efforts Rangers were unable to equalise and the Cup went to North London.

During the summer Rangers faced another attempt by the Football League to get them to replace their artificial playing surface. The League meeting eventually decided to request that any other clubs

The players are introduced before the start of the FA Cup Final against Tottenham Hotspur.

thinking of switching surfaces should get permission from the League first. The concession to Rangers was that they could keep their surface as they had not broken any rules.

Due to the optimism within the club Venables did not feel it necessary to strengthen the squad in his quest for promotion, and as it turned out only 21 players were used during the season. The only players to leave were long-serving Ian Gillard, who joined Aldershot, Ernie Howe (Portsmouth) and John Burridge (Wolverhampton Wanderers).

Rangers' first game of the **1982–83** season was away to Newcastle United, who had just signed Kevin Keegan. His presence attracted a crowd of 36,185 to St James' Park, the largest attendance for a Rangers game all season. Inspired by Keegan, Newcastle won by the only goal of the game. Rangers did not carry on that way though, and they were at second spot by December. It was the lowest they went for the rest of the season.

The 1–0 home win over Leeds United on 23 April assured Rangers of promotion and they now had their sights firmly on the Championship, a title they had not won when gaining promotion before. Rangers finished 10 points ahead of Wolves and a further five ahead of the other promoted side, Leicester City. A lot of critics claimed that Rangers had only won promotion because of the unfair advantage they had with their pitch. What they failed to point out was Rangers' tremendous away record of 10 wins and four draws.

Having been knocked out of the League Cup at the two-leg second-round stage, Rangers were hoping for more success in the FA Cup. Their third-round opponents were West Bromwich Albion, the side that they had beaten in the previous year's semi-final. This time Albion had a home advantage and were looking for revenge on an injury-stricken Rangers. Albion won 3–2, and

Rangers had now lost at the first tie in both Cup competitions. Defeat at the first attempt followed for the next three seasons in the FA Cup.

Towards the end of the previous season chairman Jim Gregory had announced his intention of relinquishing control of the club. He made an offer to manager Terry Venables, but he was unable to raise enough capital to make the deal viable and Gregory decided to stay on at the club.

Before the **1983–84** season started Rangers agreed a deal with the brewery firm Guinness to allow shirt sponsorship for the first time. It was a practise that was already in existence in many European countries and it was felt that the sponsorship would give much-needed income to the clubs.

Venables made his first entry into the transfer market for over year when he signed Mike Fillery from Chelsea. He also signed on professional terms two promising apprentices, David Kerslake and Martin Allen. On the outgoing side were Tony Currie, who joined Vancouver Whitecaps, Dean Wilkins (Brighton) and Ian Muir (Birmingham City).

Rangers' return to the First Division saw them in ninth place at the half-way stage. The New Year started with a flourish including a resounding 6–0 home win over Stoke City, and they soon moved into contention for a European place with an unbeaten run of nine games, including a sequence of six successive wins. Rangers managed to finish fifth in the League and clinch a place in the next season's UEFA Cup competition. Again the consistency of the side meant that only 20 players were used during the season, with nine appearing in 30 or more games.

Rangers' opponents in the second round of the League Cup were Crewe Alexandra. The first leg was drawn to be played at Loftus Road. Crewe played well above their mid-table Fourth Division status and caused Rangers a lot of problems, but they were unable to score more than once. Rangers on the other hand did, and eight times at that! With a seven-goal advantage Rangers relaxed in the

The 1982–83 squad.

The directors of QPR, from left to right: A. Ingham, B.A.V. Henson, A. Framer (vice-president), E. Saunders, Cllr W.C. Smith (vice-president), A. Williamson (deputy chairman), C.J. Armstrong, A. Chandler.

second leg. This allowed Crewe to show what could have been in the first leg as the Cheshire side won by three goals to nil. The third-round draw took Rangers to East Anglia to meet Ipswich Town. The match produced a very entertaining Cup tie. At half-time the match was evenly poised at 1–1, but in the second half the home side took the initiative with two more goals. Gregory managed to pull one back for Rangers, but it was not enough and they went out by the odd goal in five.

Following Venables's departure to Barcelona, Alan Mullery was appointed as his replacement in time for the start of the **1984–85** season. Mullery's only purchase in the transfer market was the signing of Gary Bannister from Sheffield Wednesday, while the only player to leave was Mark O'Connor who joined Bristol Rovers. However, by December things were not harmonious at the club, and following the home win over bottom of the table Stoke City Mullery was sacked as manager. His replacement in a caretaker capacity was Frank Sibley. The New Year bought new hope of a climb away from the foot of the table with two successive away wins. Rangers managed to remain mid-table as they won all their home games but lost all their away games in a run of 12 matches. They finished the season in 19th place, just one point above relegated Norwich City.

Rangers' League Cup trail ended with a fifth-round replay with Ipswich Town. Ipswich led 2–1 by half-time, and the second half was a close affair but the extra man helped Ipswich as they coped with Rangers' attacks. With no goals after the break Ipswich became the first side to beat Rangers in a Cup tie on the artificial pitch.

Having qualified for the UEFA Cup, Rangers were unable to use their home ground due to UEFA not sanctioning their matches to be played on artificial surfaces so Rangers had to play their European home ties at Arsenal's Highbury ground. This was not the first time that Rangers had played at home at Highbury. They had staged a Division Three South game there in March 1930 when the Loftus Road ground was closed following crowd trouble. Rangers' first-round opponents were Icelandic side Reykjavik, with the first leg away. Stainrod scored after 23 minutes and Rangers led the part-timers at half-time. In the 64th minute Stainrod's shot was parried by the 'keeper and Bannister scored from the rebound. Stainrod added a third after 75 minutes to give Rangers a three-goal cushion for the second leg. The match at Highbury was a formality, especially after Bannister, (twice) and Charles had given Rangers a three-goal lead at half-time. Bannister completed his hat-trick in the 60th minute to give Rangers a 7–0 aggregate win. The only disappointing thing about the evening was the low crowd of only 6,196, who looked lost in the spacious Highbury Stadium.

The second round paired Rangers with Partizan Belgrade of Yugoslavia. Rangers were expecting a much harder contest that the previous round as Partizan were experienced European campaigners. The first half was all action with Gregory scoring after 12 minutes only for Klincarski to equalise a minute later. Partizan took the lead in the 24th minute through Mance, but this time Rangers equalised a minute later with a Fereday goal. A minute before the break Stainrod scored to give Rangers the lead again. The second half saw one of the best Rangers performances of recent years when they completely mastered their more experienced opponents. They managed to score three more goals without reply, Neill in the 55th minute and Bannister with two, in the 59th and 83rd minutes. Rangers were confident of progressing as they were taking a four-goal lead into the second leg. The return match in Belgrade was played in front of a very intimidating crowd. Partizan attacked from the start and scored an early goal through Zlvkovic. Rangers nearly held on until half-time but just before the break Wicks fouled Zlvkovic in the area and Kalicanin scored from the spot. Rangers, however, were still two goals ahead over the whole tie. However, disaster struck a minute into the second half when Hucker failed to hold on to a cross and gifted a third goal to Jezic. After 65 minutes the tie was back on level terms when Zlvkovic scored his second and Partizan's fourth. Rangers now had to score to stay in the competition but they were unable to do so. Thus they exited the competition by virtue of the away goals rule. They also made history for all the wrong reasons as this was the first time a British side had gone out of a European competition having held a four-goal lead from the first leg.

During the summer Frank Sibley was replaced as caretaker manager by Jim Smith. Great things were hoped for **1985–86** with the arrival of Smith, who had taken Oxford United into the First Division for the first time in their history, but Rangers finished in a mid-table position of 13th with 50 points.

Rangers' League Cup trail started with a home tie against Second Division Hull City. Smith had made three changes to the previous League side in an effort to improve results. He brought in Barron, Wicks and Kerslake for Hucker, McDonald and Allen, and the changes had the desired effect as Kerslake scored his first goal for Rangers after just 13 minutes. Barron made two good saves to keep the score to 1–0 at half-time, and after the break Rangers scored twice more, through Dawes (52 minutes) and Bannister (63), to take a three-goal advantage to the second leg at Boothferry Park. The match was a very one-sided affair with Rangers winning 5–1 and easily going through to the third round with an aggregate of eight goals to one. The scorers for the Rangers in the second leg were Kerslake and Rosenior, both with two, and Fillery.

The third-round draw paired Rangers with near neighbours Watford, with Rangers having to travel the short distance to Vicarage Road. Again Smith made three changes from the previous week's team. This time he left out Kerslake, James and Rosenior, and brought in Allen, Fillery and Byrne. Watford were awarded a penalty in the 24th minute when Barron pulled down a Watford forward in the area. However, he made amends by saving Jackett's spot-kick. The match remained scoreless at the interval. Rangers battled on in the second half and their efforts were rewarded when Byrne scored after 54 minutes following a good move between Fillery and Fereday. Watford were unable to get back into the game and Rangers recorded their first win at Watford for 16 years.

The fourth-round draw brought Nottingham Forest to Loftus Road. With both sides out on the pitch for their pre-match warm-up the floodlights failed. Despite the efforts of the electricity board and the clubs officials, the referee decided to call the game off after waiting an hour for the power to return. The match was re-scheduled for the following Monday. The evening was very cold and damp and the pitch had to have extra sand put on it to stop the players slipping. Despite the conditions, both sides played their part in an extremely exciting Cup tie. Rangers were awarded a dubious penalty after six minutes, from which Fenwick scored. Forest then set out on attack and were unlucky not to score on several occasions. With no further goals before the interval Rangers were happy with their half-time lead. The second half was much the same as the first. Forest's efforts were rewarded after 80 minutes with a Clough equaliser. With 90 minutes approaching Bannister reacted quickest to a parried save from the 'keeper and scored Rangers' second. Birtles then made a hash of a clearance and Byrne lobbed the ball over Sutton in the Forest goal for Rangers' third.

The fifth-round draw brought Rangers' nearest neighbours Chelsea to Loftus Road. The match attracted a capacity 27,000 crowd who paid club record receipts of £132,572. Rangers took the lead after 12 minutes when Byrne scored after Rougvie failed to cut out a Fereday cross, but Chelsea were back level after 24 minutes when Nevin nipped in after a Murphy corner had been flicked on by Rougvie and Lee. McDonald had an opportunity to give Rangers the lead again in the 27th minute but he just missed with an acrobatic scissors-kick. However, the best chance fell to Bannister just before half-time when he had only the 'keeper to beat, but he missed the target. The second half was just as entertaining with both sides having the chances to score the winner. Chelsea came closest when Dixon's 'goal' was ruled out for offside. The replay at Stamford Bridge was another stirring Cup tie. Again both sides had chances to score but neither could. McDonald was marshalling the Rangers defence well and not letting the Chelsea strikers have much room, while at the other end Niedzwiecki, in the Chelsea goal, was stopping everything shot at him by Byrne and Bannister. After 90 minutes there were still no goals and extra-time was required. Both sides were suffering from tiredness and players were needing constant treatment for cramp. Midway through the first period of extra-time Rangers won a corner which James took. His cross was met firmly by McDonald, who headed into the net to give Rangers the lead. With time running out, Chelsea were trying all sorts of ideas to break through the resolute Rangers defence. A minute from time Niedzwiecki tried to dribble the ball upfield but he lost it to Bannister on the halfway line. He passed it to Robinson, who scored with a 50-yard shot to give Rangers a two-goal victory.

Their reward for beating Chelsea was a two-legged semi-final against Liverpool. The first leg was played at Loftus Road and televised live by ITV. Having already beaten Liverpool in the League at home earlier in the season Rangers were hopeful of a good result to take to the second leg at Anfield. Rangers got off a good start and won early corners while Liverpool were still adapting to the pitch. In the 24th minute Martin Allen crossed from the right and Fenwick scored at the far post. Rangers continued to have the upper hand but despite two good efforts could not add to their tally before half-time. The second half saw Liverpool change their tactics as they tried to squeeze Rangers away from their goal by playing the offside game just inside their own half. This proved to be successful in thwarting Rangers' attacks. Liverpool should have scored after 62 minutes when Rush was unmarked in the area but his shot was weak and Barron saved. With no goals being scored in the second half Rangers took a narrow one-goal lead to the second leg three weeks later at Anfield. Once again the match was televised live by ITV. Liverpool attacked from the start and McMahon scored midway through the first half, and just before half-time the referee adjudged that Dawes had handled a cross in the area and awarded Liverpool a penalty. Robinson, who had joined Rangers from Liverpool, spoke to 'keeper Barron while Molby was waiting to take the kick. The advice must have been good as Molby's spot-kick was saved by Barron by the foot of the right-hand post. With just the one goal before the break, the sides were level on aggregate and an exciting second half was in prospect. In the 58th minute Bannister won the ball from Lawenson and passed to Allen, who crossed hard into the box. In attempting to clear, Beglin hit the ball against Whelan and it ended up behind Grobbelaar in the Liverpool net. Rangers were now back in front on aggregate. However, the lead did not last long as 12 minutes later Johnson scored with a lob from a flick-on by Rush. With extra-time approaching, Rangers attacked again. This time Fereday crossed from the right looking for Robinson in the box, but in trying to beat Robinson in the air Gillespie only managed to head the ball into his own net for Rangers' second goal. Rangers held out for the last five minutes and went through to the Final courtesy of two own-goals.

In the Final Rangers met Jim Smith's old team Oxford United. Following two very entertaining League encounters between the two sides everybody was looking forward to a good contest. A crowd of 90,396 paid £897,646 to see the Final. The game did not live up to expectations, however, and the first half an hour was a fairly dour affair. The Oxford midfield trio of Hebberd, Phillips and Houghton then started to exert their authority on the game and five minutes before half-time Hebberd took a pass from Aldridge and his shot went through Barron. The second half was dominated by Oxford as Rangers seemed to lose their way against a hard-running side. Six minutes after the break Houghton finished off a move that he had begun on the halfway line to score Oxford's second. Rangers replaced Allen with Rosenior, which added a bit of life to the Rangers attack. The first shot on target for Rangers came in the 72nd minute when Dawes had a long-range effort turned over the bar by Judge. Aldridge than missed a couple of good chances before Charles completed the scoring in the 86th minute. This was one of Rangers' worst performances for some time and it had a numbing effect on players and supporters alike.

David Bulstrode, who bought QPR in 1987.

The **1986–87** season did not start too well as Southampton beat Rangers 5–1 at The Dell in the opening game. It did not get much better as halfway through the season Rangers were in 15th place with 24 points, just one point off the relegation places. By the end of the season they dropped one place, finishing 16th after winning only one out of their last 12 matches.

On the transfer front Smith was making a few changes to his line up. In came David Seaman (Birmingham City), Alan Brazil (Coventry City), Sammy Lee (Liverpool) and apprentice Justin Channing, while out went Steve Wicks to Chelsea and Steve Burke to Doncaster Rovers.

During the second half of the season came the news that Jim Gregory had finally found a buyer for his controlling stake in the club. He had sold to Marler Estates, who were run by David Bulstrode and already owned Fulham. As Marler were a property company there was a lot of speculation as to the real reason why they had bought into two football clubs. It was then announced that Rangers and Fulham would merge into one club and would play at Loftus Road. This would enable Marler to develop the Craven Cottage site into a housing estate. The fans' reaction to the proposed 'Fulham Park Rangers' team was severely underestimated and in response the idea was reduced to a ground sharing arrangement. Following a pitch invasion by fans during the home game with Manchester City David Bulstrode changed the plans and personally acquired Rangers from Marler to quash all talk of mergers and ground sharing. Thus both sides were able to keep their identities and grounds.

Rangers reached the third round of the League Cup after victory in the two-leg second round over Blackburn Rovers. The third-round draw took Rangers across London to Selhurst Park to meet Charlton Athletic in stormy conditions. Charlton adapted to the conditions better than Rangers and it was no surprise when Thompson gave them the lead. It looked as though Rangers might get a second chance when the floodlights failed after 69 minutes, but the club's electricians managed to repair the fuse and the game restarted. No further goals were scored in the remaining 20 minutes and so Rangers exited the Cup that they had got to the Final of the year before.

The fourth-round draw of the FA Cup took Rangers to Luton Town, following a 5–2 victory over Leicester City in the third round. As Luton also had an artificial pitch at that time, Rangers were on equal terms with their opponents. Both sides fought hard and had a goal each by the end of the game. The two sides met again at Loftus Road the following Wednesday. Despite Luton's attempts Rangers held on to their 2–1 lead and went through to meet Leeds United at Elland Road, where they were unable to find a second equaliser and so exited the competition.

During the summer there was a large number of changes to the playing personnel as Jim Smith was very active in the transfer market. He bought in Mark Dennis (Southampton), Paul Parker (Fulham), Dean Coney (Fulham), Kevin Brock (Oxford United), David Pizanti (FC Cologne), John O'Neill (Leicester City) and Danny Maddix (Tottenham Hotspur). He also signed on from the apprentices Tony Roberts and Brian Law. He released Mike Fillery (Portsmouth), Robbie James (Leicester City), Sammy Lee (Osasuna), Leroy Rosenior (Fulham), Gary Chivers (Watford) and Clive Walker (Fulham). Also, when Blue Star did not renew their shirt sponsorship deal they were replaced by the Dutch Tourist Board / KLM.

The transfer activity seemed to have paid dividends as Rangers got off to a flying start in the League in **1987–88**, with victories over West Ham United, Chelsea and Portsmouth. At the halfway point of the season Rangers were in sixth place with 33 points. In March Smith made another significant signing when Trevor Francis joined as a free transfer from Glasgow Rangers. The arrival of Francis had an uplifting effect on the club and they won their next five matches. If it was not for the ban on English clubs in European competitions Rangers would have had something to play for in the four remaining matches. As it was they drew two and lost two of those final games to finish in fifth place with 67 points. The home game on 23 April against Sheffield Wednesday was the last match played on the artificial pitch as the club decided to revert back to grass for the new season.

Following a tedious two-leg second-round victory against Millwall, the third-round draw of the League Cup took Rangers to the outskirts of Manchester to meet Third Division Bury. The game was played in heavy rain making the pitch very muddy. Robinson gave Bury the lead after 26 minutes and Rangers nearly scored in the 34th minute but Fereday was cynically tackled from behind when he was just outside the area with only the 'keeper to beat. Rangers increased their tempo after the break and were unlucky when a McDonald header hit the bar. Bury managed to keep their goal intact and pulled off a giant-killing act by one goal to nil.

The Full Members' Cup had been going for two years prior to Rangers entering it. The Cup was for First and Second Division sides and the draw was split into North and South with the two area winners meeting in the Final at Wembley. All ties were to be settled on the night with extra-time and penalties if necessary. There were to be no replays. Rangers were drawn at home against Reading. When the draw was made the gap between the two sides could not have been bigger, Rangers were top of the First Division and Reading were bottom of the Second. Due to an injury to David Seaman, Nicky Johns made his debut in goal for Rangers, who embarassingly lost 3–1. At least Rangers could say that they went out to the eventual winners as Reading won the Final, but incredibly they were relegated to the Third Division and were thus prevented them from defending their first-ever trophy.

Rangers faced Luton Town in the fifth round of the FA Cup after beating Yeovil Town and West Ham United, and as Rangers had home advantage they were looking for the same outcome as in the fourth round the previous season. Rangers had the upper hand in the first half but could not convert their possession into goals and the sides went in level at the break. Rangers took the lead after 59 minutes but they were pulled back level after another seven minutes when Harford's header bounced up higher than expected off the artificial surface. Neither side were able to score again and the tie went to a replay at Kenilworth Road. Again Rangers had more of the play but could not score. After 60 minutes Harford and Neill were chasing a Stein pass when Neill, in attempting to clear the ball for a corner, only succeeded in volleying it past Seaman as it bounced up and hit his shin. Rangers continued to attack without success and went out by the unlucky own-goal.

Activity in the pre-season transfer market saw the arrival of Ossie Ardiles (Tottenham Hotspur), Simon Barker (Blackburn Rovers) and Mark Stein (Luton Town). The players who left were John Byrne (Le Harve), Ian Dawes (Millwall) and Warren Neill (Portsmouth). Smith also signed on professional terms the apprentices Robert Herrera and Bradley Allen.

Rangers' first home match of **1988–89** on the new grass pitch was a friendly against the Egyptian champions Al-Ahly, which ended in a 1–1 draw. Such was the interest in the game that it was televised live to most of North Africa.

After a draw and two losses at the start of the season, the club was hit by the unexpected death of chairman David Bulstrode. Although not popular with the fans on his arrival at the club because of the merger talk, he had won their respect and support following his personal involvement with the club. His replacement was Richard Thompson, who at the age of 24 was the youngest chairman in the League. Rangers had only won four of their first 14 matches and were in 13th place. A 2–1 home win over Coventry was Jim Smith's last as manager, as soon afterwards he resigned to take over as manager of bottom of the table Newcastle United. His replacement in a temporary capacity was his assistant Peter Shreeves. Chairman Thompson told Shreeves that he had a month to prove himself while a permanent appointment was being sought. Two weeks later Trevor Francis was made player-manager and Shreeves left the club. Under Francis's control things did not improve overnight. The year ended with Rangers in 12th place with 23 points, but with the arrival of new players in 1989 results started to improve and Rangers moved up to seventh place. A 2–0 defeat at Liverpool in the final game of the season dropped them back to end the season in ninth place with 53 points.

Following a 2–0 defeat to Arsenal in the first round of the knock-out Centenary Trophy competition, held to mark the Football League's centenary, Rangers managed to reach the quarter-finals of the League Cup against Nottingham Forest. They had beaten Cardiff City, Charlton Athletic

The QPR team at a pre-season cricket match.

and Wimbledon in previous rounds. With Francis, Falco and McDonald missing through injury Rangers met a Forest team in top form. Forest killed the tie off with four goals before half-time, Chapman completing a hat-trick. Stein did get one for Rangers before the break, but having lost Ardiles with a cracked fibula they had no hope of recovery in the second half. After the interval Chapman scored his fourth and Forest's fifth before Kerslake got a late consolation for Rangers.

Rangers were out of the FA Cup at the first hurdle yet again, after a second replay against Manchester United had ended in two draws at Old Trafford. However, Rangers did do well in the Full Members' Cup, which was split into two regional sections as in previous years. Having received a bye in the early rounds, Rangers entered the competition in the third round with an away tie at Sheffield Wednesday. These games did not attract good crowds and only 3,957 people at Hillsborough saw Rangers triumph in extra-time 1–0, the goal coming from Dean Coney. Rangers were now in the quarter-finals and travelled to Watford in their quest for a semi-final place. Rangers had to field three young players, McCarthy, Herrera and Kerslake, due to the non-availability through injury and suspension of first choice players. The reshuffled side did well to hold Watford to a 1–1 draw after extra-time, the Rangers goal coming in the second half of normal time through Coney. The match was decided by penalties, which Rangers won 2–1, following three saves from David Seaman.

The semi-final was against Everton at Goodison Park and was played in heavy rain, which made the pitch slippery. Even with a place at Wembley for the winners only 7,472 people attended. Rangers had several good opportunities to score before Nevin headed the only goal of the game after 68 minutes.

The following three seasons were not too exciting, but Rangers managed 11th, 12th and 11th-place finishes respectively. The main arrival at Loftus Road during the summer before the **1989–90** season began was Don Howe, who joined the coaching staff. Howe had a good reputation as a coach and currently held that position with the England team. In addition to Howe, 1989 also saw the arrival of Kenny Sansom (Newcastle United) and Paul Wright (Aberdeen), and the departure of Wayne Fereday (Newcastle United), Mark Fleming (Brentford), Mark Dennis and Andy Gray (Crystal Palace).

Before the season started Francis reintroduced the Supporters' Club Open Day. This time the afternoon consisted of a cricket match between Rangers and their hosts Shepherd's Bush CC. One or two of the cricketing performances caught the eye, particularly David Seaman's bowling and Alan McDonald's exploits behind the stumps.

Meanwhile in 1989–90 Nigel Spackman, the club's PFA representative, expressed publicly the players' disapproval of Francis's management style and Francis was promptly dropped from the team and was later sacked by chairman Richard Thompson, and coach Don Howe was installed as manager. In order for Howe to concentrate on the footballing side of the job, Clive Berlin was appointed to handle all the financial affairs of the club.

The League Cup was a bit of a non-event that season as Rangers went out of the Cup in the third round following games with Stockport County and Coventry City.

Rangers reached the sixth round of the FA Cup after beating Cardiff, Arsenal and Blackpool in replays. The home match against Liverpool was put back a day so that it could be televised, and what a great match the nation's armchair viewers saw. Rangers had already beaten Liverpool at home in the League and were confident of doing so again to reach the semi-finals for only the second time. Things looked good before Liverpool's Barker grabbed an equaliser two minutes before the end making it 2–2. This meant Rangers had to replay again for the fourth successive time. Rangers were now facing their ninth Cup tie having progressed through just three rounds. As Rangers were unable to turn their extra possession into goals it was Liverpool who progressed in to the semi-finals after scoring a goal.

Rangers sailed through the second and third rounds of the **1990–91** League Cup to face their next opponents, Leeds United, with a home draw. With Leeds in fifth place and Rangers having lost their previous six games their confidence was not very high. It showed early on as Leeds scored after just two minutes through McAllister. Leeds went on to score twice more, denying Rangers' forwards any real scoring opportunities.

For the second time in three years Rangers were drawn away to Manchester United in the third round of the FA Cup. In the second half, with the score at 1–1, the reorganised Rangers defence subdued the lively United attack and it looked as though history would repeat itself and Rangers would get a second chance in the replay. However, McClair scored a goal near the end to shatter Rangers' Cup dreams for another season. The following **1991–92** season's FA Cup campaign ended similarly when Rangers did not get past the third round. They were unable to get into any rhythm and went out by two goals to nil against Southampton.

Rangers entered the Full Members' Cup in the second round having received a bye in the first. The night ended with a fourth Southampton goal courtesy of an own-goal from Law to complete a very miserable and costly evening for Rangers.

During the summer of 1991 chairman Richard Thompson sacked Don Howe, saying that he wanted a younger man to run the club. It was a little unfair on Howe, who had done a good job under extreme difficulties during the previous season. Howe's replacement was Gerry Francis, who had proved his managerial ability with Bristol Rovers, whom he had taken into the Second Division with limited resources. Francis was a popular choice for the fans as they remembered his part in the excellent team of the mid-70s. In his first excursion into the transfer market Francis bought two players who had played under him at Bristol Rovers: Dennis Bailey from Birmingham City and Ian Holloway from Rovers. He also bought Gary Thompson and Tony Witter from Crystal Palace before the season started. The players to leave included Mark Falco to Millwall and Paul Parker, who joined Manchester United for a record free of around £2 million. Yet another new shirt sponsor was signed for the season, following sportswear brand Influence from the previous 1990–91 season. This time it was Brooks, another sportswear manufacturer, who signed a three-year deal. They also redesigned the club's kit and took over the running of the club shop.

Rangers reached the third round of the League Cup to meet Manchester City at Maine Road. Despite their poor League form Rangers gave a good performance and managed to take the tie to a replay at Loftus Road. They got off to the best possible start with a goal after just seven minutes, but Rangers were on their way out of the Cup after City managed three goals by the end of the game. Similarly, Rangers dropped out of the Full Members' Cup in the third round, after losing 3–2 to Crystal Palace.

The **1992–93** season saw one of the biggest changes ever to League football in England. The Football Association formed the Premier League and the Football League was reduced to three divisions. The Premier League was in fact the old First Division. The Second, Third and Fourth Divisions all moved up one to become the First, Second and Third Division respectively. Once again Rangers had a new shirt sponsor. Brooks had not renewed their deal and were replaced by the first national independent radio station Classic FM.

Rangers' Premier League career started in front of the Sky cameras on Monday 17 August at Maine Road. The season continued well, with victories against Coventry City, Tottenham Hotspur, Oldham, Everton and Middlesbrough. In February Rangers had two more additions to their list of current internationals when Les Ferdinand made a scoring debut for England against San Marino at Wembley and Tony Roberts made a well deserved substitute appearance in goal for Wales against the Republic of Ireland in Dublin.

Rangers finished the season in fifth place in the inaugural Premier League and as London's top side. The improved performances increased the average League attendance to over 14,600, the highest figure since the 1985–86 season.

The fourth round of the League Cup saw Rangers visiting Hillsborough to meet Sheffield Wednesday. Despite heavy rain the previous three days the pitch was in perfect condition which suited the play of Wednesday. However, Rangers' performance was so bad that Francis publicly apologised to the travelling fans who saw them lose 4–0.

Rangers' third-round opponents in the FA Cup were Swindon Town, who were near the top of the First Division. They were managed by Glenn Hoddle and the match was billed as a duel between Wilkins and Hoddle. Fortunately Swindon were unable to turn their possession into goals and Rangers went through by three goals to nil. In the next round Manchester City were the visitors to Loftus Road. Rangers had plenty of chances to score, and although they scored in injury time with a goal from Holloway making it 2–1 to City, they went out of the competition having lost their first home FA Cup tie for 13 years. They did not do any better the following season, as Stockport County held on for a justifiable 2–1 victory to go through to the fourth round.

For the start of the second season of the Premier League, **1993–94**, now renamed under sponsorship The Carling Premiership, the only players to leave were Garry Thompson on a free transfer to Cardiff City and Andy Sinton to Sheffield Wednesday. This season also saw the introduction of the innovative squad numbering system which included the players' names on their shirts. This numbering came in for heavy criticism before the end of the season, with some clubs fielding players with shirt numbers in the high 30s and even breaking into the 40s.

Rangers signed a one-year shirt sponsorship deal with Computer Solutions & Finance (CSF) and finished the 1993–94 season in ninth place. The campaign was not very exciting, and the good news that Gerry Francis had been offered and accepted a new contract for another season was matched with disappointment for the fans on the transfer deadline day when Darren Peacock moved to Newcastle United. The fee of £2.75 million broke the record received fee for the second time in the season. The unrest felt by the supporters seemed to get to the players as well with 11 goals being conceded in the next three games. The home game with Leeds United was even disrupted by a pitch invasion by some supporters, who were angry with recent behind-the-scenes happenings at the club. In an attempt to explain the situation Richard Thompson agreed to meet representatives from the supporters so that they could ask questions and hear the club's side of these events.

The highlight of the season from the club's point of view was the success of the Juniors side. They achieved the South East Counties League double by finishing top of the League and beating West Ham United 6–4 on aggregate to lift the League Cup.

Rangers had to fight hard to stop a determined Barnet from leading in the first leg of the League (Coca-Cola) Cup round two. The second leg went more to form with Rangers winning 4–0. They then beat Millwall 3–0 to get to the fourth round against Sheffield Wednesday. This time Rangers were hopeful of a different result as they now had home advantage. However, Rangers were level by half-time, and it looked as though they would have to settle for a replay at Hillsborough when, with just three minutes remaining, Ryan Jones scored to give Wednesday an undeserved 2–1 win. Rangers did not do as well the following season when they exited the Coca-Cola Cup in the third round after losing 4–3 to Manchester City.

Off-the-field news in **1994–95** included the signing of a major three-year shirt sponsorship agreement with Compaq and the stepping-down of Richard Thompson as chairman at the beginning

The 1994–95 QPR team.

of August. Peter Ellis, an existing director, was named as the new chairman and was introduced to the fans at the club's open day.

This season saw the departure of Ray Wilkins to newly promoted Crystal Palace on a free transfer. Other departures before the season began were Stephen Gallen and Darren Findlay to Doncaster Rovers and Dougie Freedman to Barnet, all on free transfers, and Jan Stejskal who returned to his native Czech Republic. The only signing made by Gerry Francis was Sieb Dykstra from Motherwell for £250,000 as a replacement for Stejskal.

Although Rangers had only won one of their first 10 matches of 1994–95, four of the five defeats had been by a single goal. Various behind-the-scenes changes occurred in the first half of the season, and Rangers were quick in appointing a successor following the resignation of Francis, who headed to Tottenham. Former player Ray Wilkins was named as player-manager. Francis was joined at Tottenham by reserve team coach Roger Cross and the youth team coach Des Bulpin. Their replacements were initially Frank Stapleton, who was later replaced by John Hollins following his resignation due to family commitments, and Mark Haverson. However, shortly afterwards Billy Bonds, the former West Ham United manger, became the youth team boss. Wilkins started his managerial career in the best possible manner with a win, at home to Leeds United.

Rangers finished the season in eighth place, with victories over Newcastle United, Chelsea and Arsenal to name a few. They were invited into the Inter-toto Cup, a competition for clubs who just missed out on a UEFA Cup place. Rangers, along with most other invited clubs, declined the chance to play in the summer-based tournament. This was mainly due to the players needing a break and the fact that during the close season the Loftus Road pitch was being dug up to install new drainage and undersoil heating pipes.

When the draw was made for the third round of the FA Cup Rangers were to travel to Diadora League side Aylesbury United. However, as the police would not give the Ducks' side permission to play at home the tie was switched to Loftus Road, with Rangers using the away team's facilities. It never looked as though there would be an upset with Rangers always in control of the game and not allowing Aylesbury's main striker, Cliff Hercules, a chance at goal. Rangers scored three times before half-time, through Maddix (10 minutes), Ferdinand (25) and Gallen (39). Michael Meaker added a fourth in the 78th minute and Rangers were safely through to the next round.

The fourth round drew fellow Premiership side West Ham United as the visitors to Loftus Road. As they had a number of injuries, Rangers had to play some players in unfamiliar positions. It was a well-contested derby Cup tie, with Rangers taking the lead after 20 minutes by means of a strong Andrew Impey shot inside Miklosko's right-hand post. Other good chances were missed by both sides before half-time came with Rangers leading 1–0. The second half saw the Hammers go on the attack once again, but all their efforts were denied by Tony Roberts, who made some excellent saves in the Rangers goal. In the last minute Dichio hit the post and Rangers ended the game as 1–0 winners.

The draw for the fifth round gave Rangers another home tie against Millwall. As Millwall had already beaten two other London Premiership sides, Arsenal and Chelsea, Rangers knew they were in for a very tough game. They were therefore not surprised by the Millwall performance which held Rangers at bay for the whole of the 90 minutes, during which all the goal-bound shots from the Rangers forwards were saved by Keller, the United States international goalkeeper. Millwall were the closest to scoring when Andy Roberts hit the post after 82 minutes, but just as a replay looked the likely outcome the Millwall defender Webber handled the ball inside the area and Rangers had a penalty. The spot-kick, in the second minute of injury time, was coolly converted by Clive Wilson to put Rangers through to the quarter-finals.

The sixth round draw gave Rangers the tie nobody wanted, away to Manchester United. The match was originally switched to Monday evening for Sky Television transmission, but after protests from both clubs and their fans it was re-scheduled for Sunday lunchtime, with a 1pm kick-off. Rangers were supported by a very large contingent of fans, numbering around 7,000, who travelled to Old Trafford. As the players emerged from the tunnel all they could see was a mass of blue-and-white scarves and banners. Ferdinand had an early chance to put Rangers ahead but pulled his shot across the goal. United took the lead after 22 minutes when Bardsley missed a Giggs pass to Sharpe, whose shot went past Roberts into the right-hand corner. Although Rangers had further chances before half-time the United defence was able to clear any danger that arose, and eight minutes into the second half Urwin increased the United lead to 2–0 with a free-kick, following a foul by Maddix on Hughes. Rangers now increased their attacking options by replacing Brevett with Penrice, but, despite efforts by Penrice, Ferdinand and McDonald Rangers were unable to beat Schmeichel in the United goal. Thus, Rangers suffered their second Cup exit at the hands of a Manchester side.

Richard Thompson announced that Les Ferdinand could leave the club for a fee of £6 million. He decided to join Newcastle United at the beginning of June, and his transfer gave an unexpected windfall of £600,000 to his former non-League club Hayes, as they had 10% of any future transfer fee written into the sale agreement to Rangers.

In **1995–96** the record transfer fee paid by the club was broken twice in July. The first time was the signing of Simon Osborn from Reading for the equivalent of £1.1 million, the fee being £600,000 plus Michael Meaker who was valued at £500,000. The second occasion was the signing of Ned Zelic, the Australian international, from Bundesliga champions Borussia Dortmund for £1.25 million. Other arrivals were Gregory Goodridge (Torquay United, £350,0000), Lee Charles (Chertsey Town, £67,500), and Andrew McDermott, who was signed from the Australian Institute of Sport. Players released included Peter Caldwell (Leyton Orient, free), Brian Croft (Torquay United, free), Marvin Bryan (Blackpool, £20,000), Alan McCarthy (Leyton Orient, £25,000) and Dennis Bailey (Gillingham, £50,000).

Along with Wimbledon, Rangers were given a suspended fine and warned by the Football Association following their poor disciplinary record the previous season. QPR had the highest number of cautions in the Premiership, 97 plus four dismissals.

After the New Year a successive run of defeats continued for seven games until the away match at Sheffield Wednesday, which resulted in a fine 3–1 win. Simon Barker scored twice with Gregory Goodridge scoring his first goal for the club direct from a corner, having been booked for time-wasting in taking it. The win left Rangers in 19th place on 21 points, still four points away from, and having played a game more than, the team in the 'safe' position of 17th.

Following eight wins, six draws and 22 losses, Rangers went into their last home game four points away from safety knowing that they had to win both games and then hope that other results went in their favour. The home game against West Ham, attracting the highest home attendance of the season, saw Rangers score three for the third time in succession at home in beating the Hammers. Unfortunately, with Coventry and Southampton both winning Rangers had been relegated. Immediately following relegation to the First Division, Compaq invoked the get-out clause in their contract and withdrew their sponsorship of the club.

The only bright spot in the season was the reserves side, who won the Avon Insurance Combination League. They nearly set a new record for the League in winning the title and scoring in every game.

Rangers' League (Coca-Cola) Cup run reached the fourth round in the 1995–96 season, following wins over Oxford United and York City. The away match against Aston Villa was not very eventful and there were few chances for either side in the first half. After the break the deadlock was settled by a long-range shot from Andy Townsend, who was returning after a lengthy injury.

The League Cup was a bit of a non-event for the next four seasons, as Rangers did not once get past the second round. In fact, in 1997–98 they did not get past the first round, possibly due to a major change in the structure of the competition. Instead of the initial round being for only Second and Third Division sides this time the First Division clubs were included in a non-seeded draw. This resulted in Rangers being drawn against Wolverhampton Wanderers, who had finished third in the League the previous season and therefore were the strongest team in the competition at the time.

In the 54th minute of the third-round FA Cup game against Tranmere Rovers, Quashie played a one-two with Allen and scored with a tremendous shot into the roof of the net. Almost immediately Sinclair hit a post, but he had better success minutes later when he scored the second following a flick-on by Maddix from a Wilkins corner. Despite Tranmere's efforts no more goals were forthcoming and Rangers secured their first FA Cup win away from Loftus Road for eight years.

In the next round neighbours Chelsea were the visitors to Loftus road. After two goals from Chelsea, Rangers had more of the play in the second half and deservedly scored after 67 minutes when Quashie hit a volley from a clearance of a Holloway corner, but with no further scoring, and a missed Rangers penalty, Rangers' interest in the FA Cup ended for another season.

During the close season the club was sold by owner Richard Thompson. He had, as part of Caspian, acquired a stake in Leeds United and therefore under Football League rules had to dispose of his interest in QPR. Chris Wright, owner of Chrysalis Communication, paid a reported £11 million for the club. He also acquired Wasps Rugby Union club for approximately £4 million, with the intention of both clubs using Loftus Road as their home ground. The other financial aspect of the close season was the agreement of Ericsson to be the club sponsors for the next three years.

Prior to the start of the **1996–97** season Rangers were again fined £25,000 by the Football Association due to their poor disciplinary record in the previous season. An additional £50,000 was suspended and would be payable if the record was not improved during the forthcoming season.

There was not much activity on the transfer front prior to the start of the season; Ian Holloway left on a free transfer to become player-manager of Bristol Rovers, and Gregory Goodridge joined Bristol City for £50,000 after Rangers were unable to renew his work permit. Four of the reserve players also left the club: John Cross (Cardiff City), Matthew Lockwood, Grahame Power and Steve Parmenter, all to Bristol Rovers. The only incoming player was Steve Slade, a £350,000 signing from Tottenham Hotspur, who had impressed during the Toulon Under-21 tournament.

In August, after a draw at Wolverhampton Wanderers, where Daniele Dichio scored what was voted the Sky Nationwide Goal of the Season, and a home defeat by fellow relegated team Bolton Wanderers there was a meeting between chairman Chris Wright and manager Ray Wilkins. The result of this meeting was that on 4 September Wilkins announced his resignation, with the reason being given that he wanted to continue playing rather than remaining in managing. Frank Sibley was once again named as caretaker manager until Arsenal's assistant manager Stewart Houston was appointed on 16 September. Four days later he was joined by Bruce Rioch as assistant manager.

At the turn of the year Rangers were in sixth position, the highest they had been since topping the League at the end of August. The first League game in January resulted in an impressive win against Barnsley to give Rangers the double over one of the sides promoted to the Premiership at the end of the season. The next game was memorable as Rangers came back from 4–0 down at half-time to draw 4–4, with three goals in the last eight minutes. However, by March Rangers were losing touch with the teams in the Play-off positions, and despite a late good run which put them back on the edge of the group, Rangers were unable to get into the prized sixth place and finished ninth.

At the end of the season the club gave a free transfer to Alan McDonald, who was soon signed by Swindon Town. Alan had been at the club for over 16 years and had made 483 (476 plus seven sub) appearances, putting him third in the all-time list, just one behind Ian Gillard's 484 (479 plus five sub). In May John Spencer became only the second QPR player to represent Scotland when he played in the friendly international against Wales at Kilmarnock. Another accolade went to Rangers when the BBC voted Trevor Sinclair's goal against Barnsley as their goal of the season. Rangers had got past the third round of the FA Cup to play Barnsley in the fourth round, and Trevor's amazing overhead bicycle-kick after 74 minutes gave Rangers their third goal, and they held on through the seemingly never-ending injury time for a 3–2 victory.

For the fifth-round FA Cup match against Wimbledon, over 15,000 fans attended the away match in support of Rangers. Wimbledon were in the ascendancy in the second half and took the lead to 2–1 after 10 minutes when Earle scored following a run by Leonhardsen. Rangers tried hard for an equaliser but failed. Despite going out of the Cup the Rangers fans gave the team a standing ovation at the end.

During the close season the Loftus Road pitch was relaid and incorporated a new technique which was in use at Huddersfield's McAlpine Stadium. This technique involved the binding of the roots of the grass on the pitch with plastic to make it harder wearing. This meant that with Wasps playing more of their home games at Loftus Road the pitch would stand up to the extra wear and tear. It was also the intention to have the reserve matches return to Loftus road, providing the pitch could take the extra games.

Although Ericsson remained the club sponsor the home kit was redesigned for **1997–98** and manufactured by Le Coq Sportif. The away kit reverted back to the red and black hoops, which seems to be the fans' favourite away strip. Despite not gaining promotion the sales of season tickets increased by 14% to a total of 4,700 at the start of the season.

On 10 November Houston and Rioch were sacked by chairman Chris Wright. At the AGM of Loftus Road plc held the following day Wright was quoted as saying that 'It probably was a mistake to have appointed Houston as he did not have the qualities to manage a First Division club seeking to get into the Premiership. We need a manger that is adept at trading and looking at players from the lower divisions, rather than seeking to buy from Premiership reserve sides.' As there was no immediate replacement in mind John Hollins, currently the reserves' manager, was appointed as caretaker manager until 5 December when it was announced that the new Queen's Park Rangers manager would be Ray Harford, previously at West Bromwich Albion. The announcement had been delayed by a couple of days due to Albion taking out a High Court injunction which tried to stop QPR from 'poaching' Harford.

During the close-season Rangers signed Matthew Rose and Lee Harper from Arsenal for £500,000 and £125,000 (plus £100,000 after a specified number of appearances) respectively and arranged to sell Andrew Impey to West Ham United for £1.2 million. Another incoming player was Mike Sheron, who was signed for a record-equalling transfer fee of £2.35 million from Stoke City.

Rangers did not have a successful season from the start. They went into the New Year in 12th place, the position they had been in for the whole of December. The first four League matches of 1998 resulted in two draws and two defeats, but the most significant factor was that Rangers failed to score in all four. The last defeat, against Stockport County, resulted in a slide down the table to 17th place which was the lowest Rangers had been since their relegation from the Premiership.

In mid-January Rangers signed Antti Heinola, a Finnish international from the Dutch side S.C. Hercules, while at the end of the month those to leave the club included Trevor Sinclair, who joined

West Ham United for a fee valued at around £3.5 million, Jurgeon Summer, who joined Columbus Crew in the United States League for £175,000, and Rufus Brevett who joined up with former manager Ray Wilkins at Fulham for a fee of £375,000. The incoming players were Keith Rowland and Ian Dowie from West Ham United, who joined as part of the Sinclair fee, and Mark Kennedy, who was signed on a month's loan from Liverpool.

The first of the crucial final 10 games of the season resulted in a 1–0 defeat at Birmingham City, managed by ex-Rangers player and manager Trevor Francis. The match was made infamous by the resignation of Francis as manager after the game, due to an incident involving his family in the hospitality areas. He later retracted his resignation and stayed at the club.

Although the match was not of vital importance Rangers lost their last game of the season at home to Bury and avoided the drop to Division Two by one point and one place. Rangers and Portsmouth both finished the season with 49 points, with 51 goals for, 63 goals against. Portsmouth took 20th place ahead of Rangers. This meant that Rangers had finished in their lowest position for 30 years. They had won only 10 games, fewer than any other team in the Division, and had drawn 19 games, more than anybody else.

The highlight for the youth team was reaching the Final of the Southern Junior Floodlight Cup where they were beaten over two legs by Arsenal. The Football Association announced plans for football academies at clubs which would mean that the clubs would have to supply details of their youth policies and those that satisfied the conditions would be awarded accreditation. At the end of May Queen's Park Rangers were one of the very few non-Premiership clubs to be awarded one of these accreditations.

In January Rangers were not looking forward to their FA Cup third-round replay trip against Middlesborough, as they had given what was probably their worst away performance in the League at the Riverside in November. However, this time Rangers played with more spirit and were unlucky to exit both Cup competitions at the first hurdle.

During the summer the players that had been given free transfers were signed by new clubs. Tony Roberts went to Millwall, after a trial at Norwich City; David Bardsley returned to Blackpool, one of his previous clubs, Trevor Challis joined Bristol Rovers; Simon Barker joined Port Vale; while Lee Charles returned to non-League football and signed for Hayes of the Football Conference. The other departure from the club was that of the popular John Hollins, who was appointed manager of Swansea City. The only arrival was Richard Ord, a £675,000 signing from Sunderland.

Rangers did not have much luck the in the FA Cup in the **1998–99** season either. The second half of their third-round game against Huddersfield Town was delayed for 20 minutes due to a freak hailstorm which the referee considered was a danger to the players. Rangers dominated the second half though, and had a number of opportunities to get an equaliser. But in the end time ran out and Huddersfield progressed, winning 1–0.

Behind the scenes before the 1998–99 season began, Stephen Oakley, finance director of Loftus Road plc, left and was replaced by Simon Crane from Coca-Cola in Atlanta, where he was responsible for Coca-Cola's involvement in Euro '96. Various other management changes took place in the first half of the season including the 'sacking' of chief executive Clive Berlin in what was described by the club as a cost-cutting exercise, the resignation of manager Ray Harford, who was replaced, in a caretaker capacity, by reserve team coach Iain Dowie, and the announcement of the return of Gerry Francis to the club, who had been appointed director of football.

Following accreditation as a youth football academy Rangers withdrew from the South East Counties League and entered two sides in the FA Premier Youth League, one in the Under-17s (managed by Gary Waddock) and the other in Under-19s (managed by Warren Neill). The two-year YTS scheme was replaced by a three-year scholarship.

The Annual Report for Loftus Road plc announced an operating loss of £5 million (£3 million before transfers) compared with a loss of £7.1 million for the previous year.

Rangers started the League season with an away match against Sunderland, who had lost the previos season's Play-off Final at Wembley against Charlton Athletic. Despite giving a good account of themselves Rangers lost 1–0 to a Phillips penalty. The penalty was given for handball against Ian Baraclough, who was sent off for the offence. A red card seems to be a frequent occurrence in Rangers' first game of a season.

The first League game of the New Year saw the visit of League leaders Sunderland to Loftus Road. The kick-off was delayed for 15 minutes to allow the near capacity crowd to see the game, which was one of the team's best performances of the season. Rangers were leading 2–1 going in to the last minute, but Quinn equalised to give Rangers only one point instead of the three they looked like getting. The result was the first of four successive draws, which kept the club in 17th place.

By the end of the season, results were not going Rangers' way. The bottom of the table had Bristol City and Oxford United in the last two places with Bury and Rangers on equal points for the remaining relegation place. All teams had one game to play, but in Rangers' favour was the fact that Bury had scored 13 less goals, which meant that Rangers had to get the same or better result than Bury in their final game to stay up. All three teams that could escape the drop, Oxford, Bury and Rangers, were all at home on the final Sunday.

Rangers' opponents were London neighbours Crystal Palace and Bury were facing Port Vale. Oxford would only survive if both Rangers and Bury lost and if they won their game against Stockport by scoring four more goals than Rangers. The game attracted a crowd of 18,498, a record since the stadium was converted to all-seating. It started with Palace having the greater part of the possession in the early minutes. However, it did not last long as Rangers went on to win 6–0 – their biggest victory since the 1985–86 season. With Bury and Oxford both winning Rangers finished in 20th place, as one of four teams on 47 points.

One of the main weaknesses that contributed to the disappointing season was the poor goalscoring record, which was reflected by the leading scorer for the season being Mike Sheron with only nine goals.

Towards the end of the season an approach was made by Ron Noades, the Brentford chairman, to the club concerning a possible ground sharing proposal for Loftus Road. The plan was for Brentford, Rangers and Wasps to all play their matches at the same stadium. Despite the club's well reported poor financial position, the board of Loftus Road plc rejected the offer.

Into the 21st Century

1999–2000

There was limited activity in the transfer market during the summer, mainly due to the lack of available finance at the club. The only new signings were Rob Steiner for £215,000 from Bradford City and Stuart Wardley from Saffron Walden Town for £15,000. Both players had been at the club during the end of the previous season, Steiner on loan and Wardley on trial. Of the players who were out of contract Danny Maddix and Chris Kiwomya were re-signed and Steve Yates was given a free transfer and had a month's trial at Tranmere Rovers. The other players to leave the club were Mark Graham to

Cambridge United, and reserve 'keeper Richard Hurst, who was released and later joined Kingstonian. Despite the previous two disappointing seasons, the sale of season tickets were up 10 per cent in volume and 17 per cent in value, compared to the previous year.

Off the field the Football League made three changes to their rules for the 1999–2000 season. These were the introduction of squad numbers with player's names on shirts, the naming of five substitutes of which three could be used per game and the separating of teams on the same points by goal difference and not goals scored.

The first game of the **1999–2000** season was a home match against Huddersfield Town, who had a new manager, Steve Bruce. At the end of the game Rangers were joint leaders of the Division, having secured a 3–1 win, with goals from Jermaine Darlington (his first for the club), Chris Kiwomya and Gavin Peacock. It was only the second opening day win in 10 years for Rangers. The game also marked Stuart Wardley's debut as he came on as a substitute.

The unbeaten run at the start of the season ended at the first away game played against Bolton Wanderers. Two successive 1–1 draws meant that Rangers were back in a mid-table position, with Gavin Peacock having scored in the first five (League and Cup) games. August ended with a well-deserved 3–2 home win over Port Vale, in which Stuart Wardley, making his full debut, scored twice.

Following an appeal by Loftus Road plc, planning permission was granted for the building of houses on Wasps' rugby ground at Sudbury. This meant that the land could now be sold and the received monies, estimated at approximately £5 million, could be used to pay off some of the club's mounting debts.

Other news at this time was not so good as Antti Heinola, who had injured his cruciate ligaments in the friendly at Luton in July, was likely to be out for at least nine months and therefore expected to miss the whole season. The other long-term injury, Richard Ord, was seeing another specialist to see if the injury he had sustained a year before was liable to heal or whether it would mark the end of his playing career.

Rangers then had an enforced two-week break due to international call-ups for four players and a meningitis scare at the club, which meant the closure of the training ground for five days and the postponement of the home game against Sheffield United. Fortunately, George Kulscar was diagnosed as having the non-fatal viral strain of the disease, and the other players Karl Ready, Matthew Rose and Gavin Peacock who showed symptoms were all cleared. Rangers' next two games both ended in defeat and the club slipped to 18th in the League. The first of these games was away to local rivals Fulham and the game attracted a crowd of 19,623, the Cottagers' largest for nearly 20 years. This game also saw the sending-off of Rob Steiner, for allegedly diving in the penalty area.

Chairman Chris Wright made some funds available to Gerry Francis for the purchase of new players. Francis agreed a transfer fee of £1.2 million with Swindon Town for the sale of their striker George Ndah, but the deal fell through due to Ndah's personal demands. At this time Loftus Road Plc announced a current debt position of £9.5 million, mainly due to player's wages and the loss of all Sky/Premiership monies.

The following two home games saw the start of what was to become Rangers best run for some time. After having failed to score in three successive games, the goals started flowing with a 2–1 win at home over Tranmere and continued on to the next two away games. Both of these games ended in victory, the first being a remarkable 4–1 win at Ipswich (Rangers' first away win in 10 months) followed by a narrow 1–0 victory at the Hawthorns. The only goal was scored by Wardley, his second in successive games. The run was maintained with two home draws and a further away win, the third successive one, at relegated Blackburn Rovers. Rangers were now up to the edge of the Play-off zone in eighth place.

The unbeaten run was extended to eight matches with a 3–3 draw away at Stockport County. This was after Rangers had gone three-nil down early in the second half, with the point being gained by two late goals from substitute Kevin Gallen. The visit of table-topping Manchester City drew a crowd of 19,002 and was Rangers' largest since the introduction of the all-seater stadium. The match ended in a 1–1 draw, thus maintaining the excellent run. With an away game at struggling Crystal Palace to follow, hopes were high on gaining further points in the attempt to reach a top six place.

However, the match at Selhurst Park did not go as expected and ended with a 0–3 defeat and saw Rangers down to nine men at the end, following the dismissals of Chris Kiwomya and Karl Ready. The unbeaten run consisted of four wins and five draws; with more points gained on opponents' grounds than at home. The remaining games in November were evenly spread with one win, one draw and one defeat. A home win over Walsall was achieved, despite the absence of the two key central-defenders of Ready and Maddix, and saw the introduction of Ross Weare, another of Francis's non-League signings. By now Rangers had risen to seventh in the table, their highest position for three seasons.

At the end of November Francis made another venture into the transfer market when he signed Dutchman Samuel Koejoe from Salzburg in Austria for a fee of £250,000. He made his debut immediately when coming on as a substitute at half-time in the away defeat at Huddersfield Town. By now Rangers' long-term injury list was lengthening, with nine players unavailable for selection: Heinola (cruciate ligaments), Maddix (knee operation), Rose (blocked arteries in calf), Ready (back injury), Morrow (ruptured ligaments in shoulder), Breacker (back), Rowland, Peacock (hamstring), and Gallen (hamstring) plus the suspended Slade. With no experienced central-defenders available, Darren Ward, a 21-year-old central-defender, was signed on loan from Watford. He made an impressive debut in the home draw with Charlton Athletic, another match in which Rangers were reduced to 10 men when Chris Kiwomya was sent off. The Christmas/New Year programme ended with two wins and one defeat, lifting Rangers up into seventh place as the new millennium started. Another loan signing, Brian McGovern, a right-sided defender from Arsenal, made his debut in the home win over Crewe Alexandra. The New Year started with the news that McAlpine Homes had purchased the Wasps ground at Sudbury for a reported £8.9 million. Part of the deal was for the Ellerslie Road Stand to be known as the McAlpine Homes Stand for the next season.

On the pitch, Rangers were the only side in the Division with an unbeaten home record, having won six and drawn seven of the matches played. Unfortunately, this record was ended in the very next game when Bolton Wanderers went home with the three points following a 1–0 win. After the game it was announced that Danny Maddix's injury would keep him out of the side for the rest of the season. Following another away defeat, 2–3 at Wolverhampton, Rangers had a run of six successive draws, the first four all being 1–1. The last two matches, at home to Fulham and away at Sheffield United were shown live on Sky Television; having ignored Rangers all season, Sky screened two matches in six days.

During this run of draws both Steiner and McGovern were added to the injured players. As McGovern was on loan he returned to Arsenal and Francis was able to arrange another loan deal, this time the Danish international Mikkel Beck from Derby County. Another player on loan, Ward, had his loan period extended to the end of the season due to some impressive performances, but Watford had included an immediate return clause in case he was needed back at Vicarage Road. Unfortunately for Rangers, Graham Taylor, the Watford manager, had noted Darren Ward's performances and recalled him to assist in Watford's relegation battle. He was replaced as a loan signing by Gareth Taylor, a forward from Manchester City. At the same time Tony Scully joined Walsall on loan, but his stay was brief and he returned within the month to Rangers.

With no wins in their last eight matches Rangers had slipped back down the League to 11th place, and a Play-off place was looking remote. However, the sequence of draws came to an unexpected end with a 3–1 away win at second-placed Manchester City. Two more wins followed, which saw Beck score in three successive games. At the end of March, Le Coq Sportif signed a new three-year kit sponsorship deal, estimated at £500,000.

Rangers' hopes of a Play-off place were temporarily revived with two home games scheduled in four days, but after only getting only one point out of the possible six the Play-offs were once again a distant hope. They were now in a safe place mid-table place, with no possibility of being involved in any relegation situation, but they were too far, points wise, from the fourth Play-off spot.

Mikkel Beck returned to Derby that season, as a further loan deal had been arranged with the club in Beck's home country of Denmark. Taylor also left the club as he became yet another injury victim, returning to Maine Road. The remainder of the season was played out with some entertaining games, and in six of the last seven games clubs either in promotion (automatic or Play-off) or relegation places were involved. The most significant result was the 3–1 defeat of Ipswich Town, which cost them second place in the League and automatic promotion (although they did subsequently win the Play-off at Wembley to gain promotion). Just before the last home game against West Bromwich Albion, a survey was published announcing that the Albion fans were the worst dressed in the League. To show their annoyance at this the travelling fans arrived dressed in eveningwear, which made a spectacular sight behind the School End goal. They were rewarded with a point, thereby keeping them in the Division for the next season.

Rangers ended the season in a creditable 10th place, which with the number of long and short-term injuries suffered was a testament to the coaching and motivation skills of Gerry Francis. The two key success of the season were the performances of Stuart Wardley and Lee Harper. Wardley had been transformed from a central-defender into an attacking central-midfielder and ended the season as joint top goalscorer with 14 goals. Harper had lost his place to Ludek Miklosko the previous season and regained it only when he was injured in September. His return coincided with the up-turn in form of the side and he was able to keep his place for the rest of the season. Both players' contributions were recognised by the supporters, who voted Wardley Player of the Year, with Harper as the runner-up.

The players with the most appearances for the season were Ian Baraclough (49 games), Chris Kiwomya (46 games, plus two sub), Stuart Wardley (44 games, plus two sub) and Richard Langley (41 games, plus five sub). The top goalscorers were Kiwomya with 14 goals (13 League, one Cup), Wardley with 14 (11 League, three Cup) and Gavin Peacock with 10 (8 League and two Cup). The reserves had a successful season under the coaching of Des Bulpin and finished second in the Combination League behind champions Millwall on goal difference. The two Academy sides, Under-17 and Under-19, had positive seasons led by Gary Waddock and Warren Neill. The main disappointment was the short FA Youth Cup run, after being knocked out in their first tie by Watford.

League (Worthington) Cup

Rangers' first-round opponents were Cardiff City, recently promoted from Division Three, with the first leg held at Ninian Park. After an even opening Rangers took the lead in the 32nd minute, with a goal from a Richard Langley overhead-kick. During the break Rangers had had to replace 'keeper Miklosko, who was suffering with a dead-leg. There were not many chances early in the second period, but Rangers increased their lead with a goal from Gavin Peacock in the 65th minute. However, two minutes later Cardiff scored through Bowen to reduce the deficit to one. With no more goals, Rangers took a 2–1 advantage into the home leg.

The home game did not start very promising as ex-Rangers player Matthew Brazier scored just before the interval to put the tie level on aggregate. Despite a number of efforts, Rangers were unable to score before the end of the 90 minutes, thus forcing the game into extra-time. In the 13th minute of extra-time Kiwomya was tripped in the area and Peacock scored from the resulting penalty to put Rangers ahead on aggregate, and the goal gave Peacock a club record of scoring in five successive games from the start of a season. However, five minutes before the end Hughes scored for Cardiff, which meant that penalties would be required. The star of the shoot-out was Hallworth, the Cardiff 'keeper, who saved kicks from Peacock, Baraclough and Kiwomya to give his side a win by three penalties to Rangers' two.

FA Cup

This season the dates of the rounds moved forward in order to accommodate an early finish to the season, in preparation for the start of Euro 2000. As a result the third round was played in the middle of December instead of the traditional first Saturday in January. Missing from the competition were the holders, Manchester United, who withdrew in order to play in the World Club Championship in Brazil during January.

The third-round draw gave Rangers a home tie against Division Three side Torquay United, a team they had not met for over 30 years. Rangers took an early lead in the eighth minute when Stuart Wardley scored from Rob Steiner's cross. It was disappointing for Torquay who had thought that they had scored a minute earlier, only for the goal to be disallowed for offside. The rest of the first half saw Rangers have several chances that were not taken up, either they missed the target or were saved by Neville Southall in goal for Torquay. For the second half Rangers changed 'keepers, with Miklosko making a return to first-team action after a lengthy lay-off due to injury. Torquay had more of the play after the break and it was not really a surprise when they equalised with a free-kick in the 81st minute and with no further scoring, the tie went to a replay at Plainmoor.

The replay was a keenly contested game, despite the severely depleted Rangers team that took to the field. By half-time there had been no goals, but this all changed early after the restart. Bedeau put the Second Division side ahead only for Wardley to equalise six minutes later. After 57 minutes Harper injured his shoulder to be replaced by Miklosko, thereby creating a unique situation where the goalkeeper was substituted due to injury in both the original game and the replay. Rangers should have gone ahead soon after but Neville Southall made an excellent save from a Murray shot. From the resulting corner, Kiwomya scored with a header to give Rangers the lead. The game looked safe when Wardley scored a third, but Thomas gave Torquay hope with their second five minutes before the end. Despite a frantic finish, Torquay were unable to score again and Rangers moved on into the fourth round to an away game at London rivals Charlton Athletic.

The match at The Valley was not very exciting for the crowd of just under 17,000. In the first half there were few opportunities of any note for either side. Rangers lost Kevin Gallen after only 15 minutes and his replacement Iain Dowie caused problems to the Charlton defence, missing a chance when he failed to connect with a cross with only the 'keeper to beat. The second half continued much as the first until the 66th minute when the referee awarded a penalty to Charlton for an apparent shirt pull by Chris Plummer, who was later sent off for a second bookable offence. Wardley took the resultant penalty and put his shot over the bar. However, the respite only lasted two minutes when MacDonald, an 18-year-old making his debut for the first team, connected with a mishit by Newton to score the first goal of the game. With no further chances on either side the match ended in a 1–0 defeat for Rangers and their Cup run was over for another season.

2000–01

At the end of 1999–2000 Rangers released seven players in preparation for the 2000–01 season. Along with first-team player Steve Slade (who joined Cambridge United) were reserve players Michael Mahoney-Johnson (Chesham United) and Wayne Purser (Barnet), together with juniors Matthew Cass, Rik Lopez, John Newall and Brad Piercewright (Scarborough). Soon after the end of the previous season Gerry Francis had made three signings from the lower Football League Divisions, Clarke Carlisle from Blackpool for £250,000, Christer Warren from Bournemouth and Karl Connelly from Wrexham, both on free transfers. Off the pitch another departure from the club was Simon Crane, who resigned to join Jaguar Racing as head of marketing. David Davies, who came from Ogden Entertainment where he had been director of European operations, replaced him as Chief Executive of Loftus Road plc. Ogden have interests in Manchester Storm Ice Hockey club and other sporting areas in the UK and Germany.

After the summer break other players to leave were Kevin Gallen, who was signed on a free 'Bosman' transfer by Huddersfield Town, and Ademole Bankole, who returned to Crewe Alexandra for a £50,000 fee. On the incoming side were Danny Grieves, who had previously played for Maccabi Haifa in Israel, Peter Crouch, a 6ft 6in forward from Tottenham Hotspur who cost £60,000, and Paul Furlong, who joined on a three-month loan deal from Birmingham City. Much to the relief of Francis and the fans, leading scorer Chris Kiwomya, who was out of contract, signed a new one-year deal (it was rumoured that this happened after club secretary Sheila Marson told Kiwomya not to be silly and sign). After the improved performances of the previous season, the sale of season tickets was up 23 per cent (over 5,000) compared to 4,300 at the same stage a year ago.

There were a number of law changes introduced for the new season, the main one being that goalkeepers were now permitted to take any number of steps before releasing the ball, but it must be released within six seconds of controlling the ball with the hands. Another new law stated that if a player encroached at a free-kick he would be cautioned and the ball moved 10 yards nearer to the goal.

Rangers' first game of the **2000–01** season was a home match against Birmingham City, who had narrowly missed out on promotion the season before. Due to the terms of the loan deal, Paul Furlong was not allowed to play against his permanent club. However, Rangers were able to give debuts to new signings Clarke Carlisle and Peter Crouch, but missing were the long-term injury sufferers Danny Maddix, Paul Murray and Rob Steiner. The match ended in a goalless draw and was followed by another draw in the televised match at Selhurst Park against Crystal Palace. The first goal of the season was scored by Clarke Carlisle in the 1–1 draw, which saw debuts for Furlong and Karl Connolly.

Rangers' first win of the new season came in the next game, a 1–0 win against Crewe Alexandra. The winning goal was scored when the Crewe 'keeper kicked a clearance against Furlong and the ball rebounded into the net. However, a high price was paid for the victory as both Karl Ready and Ian Baraclough were carried off with broken bones. This game marked Antti Heinola's first appearance in a game for 16 months after recovering from a number of serious injuries. Another player making his debut in the game was Christer Warren when he came for Ready. The win put Rangers into the top 10 of the League, a height which they never regained during the season.

After the next three games, which yielded just two points from two home draws, Rangers' injury list had grown and was approaching last season's length with three central-defenders missing. In addition to Ready and Baraclough, Maddix, Murray, Steiner, Peacock and Furlong had pulled hamstrings, while Chris Plummer had a broken leg. Due to his injury, Furlong returned to Birmingham after playing just three games of what should have been a three-month loan period.

With another away defeat, this time at Barnsley, Rangers slipped to 17th in the table. The 2–1 win at home against Wimbledon saw Rangers score two goals in a game for the third successive time, but with the weakened defence not many points had been attained. An away draw at Sheffield United in which Sammy Koejoe scored in the 1–1 draw was the last point gained for a month.

The first four games in October all ended in defeat, two away and two at home. The defeat by newly promoted Burnley was the first home loss of the season and was immediately followed by another one against lowly Sheffield Wednesday four days later. Before the Wednesday game Gerry Francis had signed Marlon Broomes as cover for the central defence, on loan from Blackburn Rovers after he had turned down a permanent move. By now Rangers had dropped further down the League to 20th place, just two points away from the relegation places, and had another injury casualty in Jermaine Darlington. This meant that only Clarke Carlisle of the first-choice defence was now available. After the next match Chris Kiwomya was also added to the ever-growing number for the treatment table.

In mid-October the financial results for Loftus Road plc were announced and showed a loss of £4.735 million, compared with £8.379 million for the year before. The main reduction in the loss was due to the sale of the Wasps ground at Sudbury to McAlpine Houses for £3.1 million.

Results on the field did not improve as much as expected, although the run of successive defeats was halted with a 1–1 draw at Tranmere Rovers. Another defeat followed and Francis signed another loan player, Paul Peschisolido from neighbours Fulham, and he made an immediate impact by scoring after just 10 minutes on his debut against Portsmouth. However, his goal was not enough to give Rangers a win and they had to settle for yet another draw. At the beginning of November the news that Rob Steiner would have to retire from the game was not entirely unexpected as he had suffered many setbacks in his recovery period.

Rangers' next three games all ended as draws, which led to Gerry Francis quipping that he should be Manager of the Month as Rangers, despite dropping to 22nd in the table, had been unbeaten in November. By now Rangers had only lost seven times in the League but had drawn over half their games.

Despite Rangers agreeing a transfer fee with Fulham for Peschisolido, they were unable to agree personal terms with the player so he therefore returned to Craven Cottage. He was replaced at the club by another loan signing, Kevin Lisbie from Charlton Athletic, who made his full debut in the goalless draw at Blackburn Rovers. Despite their poor away record, this was the first away game in which Rangers had not scored. However, the result saw Rangers drop to 23rd place and they went bottom of the League during the following week when Huddersfield Town won at Nottingham Forest. Ironically, Forest were Rangers' next opponents and a 1–0 win ensured that Rangers' stay on the bottom was as short as possible. Before the Forest game Francis had made his first permanent signing since the start of the season when Michel Ngonge, a Congo international, joined from Watford in a £60,000 deal. By now Darlington and Baraclough had returned to the side, and with Miklosko replacing Harper in goal Rangers went three games without conceding a goal. Unfortunately, the news on Karl Ready and Paul Murray's injuries was not so good, with both players suffering setbacks which could keep them out for the rest of the season.

Rangers did not prosper over the Christmas/New Year period with only two points from the three games played. The 3–2 defeat on Boxing Day at home to Norwich City saw Rangers return to the bottom of the table and they only moved from last place with a point at home against Crystal Palace on goal difference from Crewe Alexandra. Crewe were due to be Rangers' next opponents, but the game on New Year's Day was postponed due to a frozen pitch at Gresty Road.

Following the introduction of the Bosman ruling players who were out of contract at the end of a season were entitled to speak with other clubs from 1 January. This season marked the end of a large number of contracts, with the players concerned including: Harper, Ready, Rose, Miklosko, Maddix, Kiwomya, Morrow, Graham, Perry, Weare, Ngonge, Bruce, Heinola, Rowland and Scully. In addition to this Iain Dowie's contracts as both player and assistant manager were due for renewal.

Rangers' first League game of the New Year resulted in a 2–0 win over highly placed West Bromwich Albion, the goals coming from Chris Plummer, with his first ever senior goal, and Sammy Koejoe. Despite the win Rangers were still in 23rd place, but now only one point separated the bottom six clubs. This game was followed by a single-goal defeat by Norwich at Carrow Road. At this time Keith Rowland joined Luton Town on a three-month loan deal in order to give him regular first-team action.

The next League game was the re-arranged match against League leaders Fulham. A large crowd saw Rangers outplayed by their neighbours, who won 2–0 and remained 10 points clear at the top of the League. The game had a major impact on the club's attempt at retaining their Division One status for the next season, as both Clarke Carlisle and Richard Langley suffered cruciate knee ligament injuries, which would keep them out for the rest of the season, just the latest in the long line of serious injuries, including six broken legs, keeping key players out for a long period of time.

After the Fulham game Chris Wright announced his intention to resign as chairman of Loftus Road plc and QPR, a club he had supported for over 30 years. When he took on the chairmanship he said that he would remain as long as he felt he had the support and confidence of the fans. His decision was made following incidents in and around the directors' box at the Fulham game, which were the latest in a series of verbal attacks. He said that the loans he had made to the club, totalling £20 million, would remain and he would continue to provide financial support until the club had alternative means of finance.

Three days later Bolton Wanderers, currently in second place in the League, visited Loftus Road. Rangers played some good football, and with the visitors 'keeper being sent off midway through the first half for handling outside of the area, it looked like all three points were for the taking with Michel Ngonge's first goal for the club. Unfortunately, Wanderers scored with four minutes remaining to leave Rangers with just one point. Next followed a disastrous game at Preston, where Rangers conceded five goals in the second half, which,after the midweek games when Rangers did not play, put the club back at the bottom of the League.

On 16 February the club announced that Gerry Francis had decided not to renew his contract when it expired at the end of season, and that he would be relinquishing his first-team duties as soon as a replacement had been appointed. He would, however, be staying at Rangers as director of football until the summer and would be concentrating on the academy and youth aspects of the club. In recognition of what Francis had done for the club, he was invited to join the board of directors, and he said that he would consider the offer at the end of his contract. Ironically, the team were bottom of the League when Francis had joined in October 1998 and were in the same position at the time of his departure. Names bandied about for the role of manager included: Steve Coppell, Laurie Sanchez, Steve Bruce, Graham Rix, Ian Holloway and existing assistant manager Iain Dowie.

What was anticipated as Francis's last home game was against Barnsley, which resulted in 2–0 win, with goals from Kiwomya and Crouch to take Rangers out of the bottom three for the first time in over three months. However, with interviews ongoing and no announcement forthcoming on the appointment of a new manager, Francis continued in the role and saw Rangers gain their first away win of the season at Gillingham, 1–0, with a goal from Kiwomya seven minutes from the end.

Another departure that was announced was that of Des Bulphin, who had been Francis's right-hand man for over 15 years at Bristol Rovers, Tottenham and twice at Rangers. He had been appointed assistant to manager Andy Kilner at Stockport County. Des came to his decision after learning that Gerry would not be continuing the following season.

Francis's last game in charge was the away match at London neighbours Wimbledon and the result was not a pleasant one to end on. For the second time in three weeks Rangers were on the wrong end of a 5–0 thrashing.

The following Monday a press conference was called to announce that ex-player Ian Holloway had been appointed manager, with a contract until the end of the following season. Ian had been at the club from August 1991 until June 1996, making 150 appearances with five goals, when he left to become player-manager at Bristol Rovers. The first piece of good news for Holloway was that both Danny Maddix and Paul Murray had successful run-outs for the reserves during the week. This was Maddix's first match since November 1999 and Murray's first since breaking his ankle for the second time that season.

Holloway's first game in charge, at home to Sheffield United, started well, with Michel Ngonge's goal giving Rangers a half-time lead. However, poor defending allowed the Blades to score three unanswered goals in the second half and Rangers were back in the bottom three, having played more games than the clubs placed above and below them.

A number of off-the-field moves during the week saw assistant manager Iain Dowie leave the club, having had his contract paid up to its expiry at the end of the season. When joining the club Holloway had said that he would be building his own back-room team, but although no appointments had been made, it appeared that there would be no place for Dowie. In the meantime, senior player Tim Breacker would coach the reserves. At this time the club also terminated the contract of Leon Jeanne after a period of notice by the club had run out. The club also lost Antti Heinola, who had decided to retire from football and return to his native Finland to study for an Economics degree.

The next match saw the visit of local rivals Watford for what was a crucial game for both sides. Rangers took the lead with a disputed penalty, as after Peacock's effort had been saved it was ordered to be re-taken, with Ngonge taking responsibility and scoring against his old side. Late in the game, the Hornets equalised to leave Rangers with just one point. The game marked the first-team comeback of Danny Maddix, when he came on as a substitute for the final two minutes.

Before the next match away to League leaders Fulham, Holloway made his first loan signing, Leon Knight, an 18-year-old from Chelsea. The deal was to last until the end of the season but gave Chelsea a 24-hour callback option in case they needed him to return.

The game against Fulham saw another disputed penalty, this time against Rangers, which gave Fulham the lead and they sealed the points with a second in the final minute to send Rangers away with no points.

Ericsson confirmed their decision not to renew the shirt sponsorship deal they had had with Rangers for the past five years. They also ended a similar deal with Wasps, which had been in place for three years. Chris Wright was quoted as saying that he may split Wasps away from QPR as he wished to retain control of the rugby side of Loftus Road plc when he gave up the chairmanship of QPR. Wasps would still play their home matches at Loftus Road, but would use the Centaurs ground in Osterley as a base for training and offices.

In the second week of March Ian Holloway continued to be active in the transfer market and signed Marcus Bignot, for an undisclosed fee from Bristol Rovers, and Alex Higgins, a former Youth international on a free transfer after he had been released by Sheffield Wednesday.

The following Saturday's fixture was a home game against fellow strugglers Grimsby Town, who were just three points ahead of Rangers. A spirited performance from Rangers was not translated into goals due to an inspired performance by Danny Coyne in the visitors' goal. To add to Rangers' problems, Grimsby scored in the final 10 minutes, taking all the points and increasing the gap between the two sides. Rangers were now starting to fall away from the all-important fourth-from-bottom place and were four points away from safety.

Transfer deadline day saw three deals involving the club, with two players joining and one leaving. The in-coming players were Wayne Brown, a centre-half on loan from Ipswich Town until the end of the season, and Andy Thomson, a striker signed on a free transfer from Gillingham. The player leaving was Steve Morrow, who joined Peterborough United on a loan deal to the end of the season. It was also reported that Watford had made a bid of £750,000 for leading goalscorer Peter Crouch, but it had been refused as the club placed a value of double that on him.

Many clubs were not playing the weekend of Rangers' visit to Burnley, due to it being an international fixture weekend. However, for Rangers it was an opportunity to make up some of the lost ground, but it was not to be as the club struggled to a 2–1 defeat. Bignot scored his first goal for the club and Danny Maddix started a game for the first time after his long injury absence. Rangers' plight was not looking good, having gained only one point from Holloway's first five matches. The second away game in a week saw Rangers get a point in a 1–1 draw at Nottingham Forest when Wardley scored a late equaliser. More bad news was the announcement that Paul Murray would not play again this season as he needed another operation on his ankle, this time to repair the pin.

Off the pitch, two events occurred concerning Loftus Road plc. Firstly, on the Friday before the Forest game it was announced that with effect of 7am on Monday 2 April the shares of Loftus Road plc were to be de-listed from the Alternative Investment Market (AIM). At the time the share price was at an all time low of 3.5p. The de-listing and suspension in trading of the shares was caused by the failure of the company to produce interim results for the six months up to end of November 2000.

Secondly, the far more significant event was the decision by the board of directors to put Loftus Road plc and its wholly owned subsidiary of Queen's Park Rangers Football and Athletic Club Ltd into administration. The decision was taken as a result of on-going losses of £570,000 per month for the group. Chairman Chris Wright reaffirmed his intention of honouring his commitments to the group and the club and would provide financial assistant to at least October 2001 if a buyer was not found before. The administrator, Ray Hocking of BDO Stol Hayward, said that he was confident that the club would survive, but he expected it would take some time to find suitable buyers. The component parts of the group were put up for sale individually and buyers were sought for QPR, Wasps, and the Loftus Road and the Twyford Avenue grounds. Hocking revealed that the club owed Chris Wright £9 million and owed £1.5 million to other debtors. Loftus Road plc chief executive David Davies admitted that the calling in of the administrators was the culmination of mistakes made five years ago, which had not been satisfactorily rectified. In order to co-ordinate the views of supporters, the QPR 1st Trust was initiated. At a public meeting, attended by 1,500 people, ideas were aired on how the Trust would be run and what its objectives were.

The Wasps part of the group was sold within three days to London Wasps Holdings Ltd, a company backed by Chris Wright. Although there were at least two firm bids on the table for QPR, Hocking said that the administrators would not be rushed into selling the club or ground, as they wanted to ensure the best deal for the future of the club. One of the bids was reported as being between £6 million and £9 million and was from a consortium led by Andrew Ellis, the son of former chairman Peter Ellis.

Back on the pitch, the situation did not improve as Rangers attempted to avoid relegation. The visit of second-placed Blackburn Rovers started well, with Chris Plummer giving Rangers the lead after 15 minutes. However, by half-time Rovers were 2–1 in front, and with another goal after the break for the visitors, Rangers yet again finished without a point.

The following Tuesday Rangers started a sequence of five games against other teams in the lower third of the Division. In a must-win situation Rangers went into a two-goal lead before half-time against Crewe, with goals from Peter Crouch and recent signing Andy Thomson. Midway through the second half Crouch was sent off, and with four minutes to go Rangers still held their two-goal advantage. After 86 minutes Crewe scored, and with just a minute to go Ready was also dismissed for pulling back Hulse. From the resultant free-kick the home side equalised. The draw meant that Rangers went to the bottom of the League on goal difference, as Tranmere had beaten Birmingham that night. Rangers were eight points from safety with only five games to go.

The first of the two games over Easter saw Rangers journey to the south coast for a match against Portsmouth and they only came away with a point in a 1–1 draw. The point did lift Rangers off the bottom of the League, but they were still seven points adrift of the fourth-from-bottom team, Stockport. With the visit on Easter Monday of Tranmere Rovers, the only team below them, Rangers knew that anything other than a win would mean that they would go bottom and have only a mathematical chance of survival. Tranmere played like a team who knew their fate and Rangers gained their first win under Holloway's management 2–0, with goals from Thomson and Crouch. Rangers were now four points from the drop and had only three games remaining.

The next game was against fellow League strugglers Huddersfield Town, and with the other two sides in the bottom three, Tranmere and Crystal Palace, playing each other, Rangers went into the game knowing that defeat would mean relegation. Huddersfield took the lead in the 33rd minute, with a deflected shot by Gorre, but before half-time Rangers were level through Andy Thomson, with his fourth goal in as many games. After the break, Rangers went on the attack and in the 77th minute Holloway sent on Kiwomya and Richard Pacquette (for his debut) to have a front line of four in an attempt to get the winner. However, it did not produce the longed-for goal, and in the second minute of injury time Delroy Facey scored the fateful goal for Huddersfield after Harper did well to parry a Booth shot. The 2–1 defeat meant that Rangers were relegated to Division Two, as they were seven points behind Portsmouth with only two games to go. The results also meant that Tranmere were relegated, with the third drop-spot undecided. Rangers were returning to the third level of football for the first time since 1967, when they had won the (old) Third Division title.

It was announced on the day prior to the Huddersfield game that Alec Stock, the manager who started the club on the road to success in the early to mid-1960s, had died aged 84 at his home in Devon. He became the most successful manager of the club when he guided them to the Division Three title and a League Cup victory in the first Wembley Final in 1967 and in to the First Division a year later. After leaving Rangers, he went on to manage Fulham and led them to their FA Cup Final appearance in 1975.

The last two matches were of little significance to Rangers. The first of those games saw Stockport County, who were one of the sides attempting to avoid the drop alongside Rangers, visiting a subdued Loftus Road. During the game, which Rangers lost 3–0, first-team debuts were given to three of the successful Under-19 team, Terry McFlynn, Ben Walshe and Justin Cochrane, all as second-half substitutes. Unfortunately, Cochrane's debut did not last long as he was sent off just 17 minutes after coming on.

Before the game the Player of the Season awards were presented. For the first time all six awards went to the same player: Peter Crouch. He was awarded trophies from the Supporters' Club, Players'

Player, Young Player, Junior Rs, Patrons and LSA. The runner-up in most of the categories was Clarke Carlisle, whose season had ended prematurely against Fulham at the end of January.

The season ended at Molineux against mid-table Wolverhampton Wanderers, and Rangers gave two more young players, Alex Higgins and Alvin Bubb, a taste of first-team football in the 1–1 draw.

Before the Wolves games a story had appeared in the Press about a possible merger between Rangers and Wimbledon. The idea was that as Wimbledon did not have a ground of their own and QPR were in financial difficulties the two clubs could get together to solve both of their problems. Apparently, secret talks had taken place at board level between the two clubs and an approach made to the Football League to ascertain their views. The League had reportedly replied that they could not discuss the matter until a formal proposal was put to them, but they would look at it 'favourably'. Not surprisingly both sets of supporters voiced their objection to the possible loss of identity for their clubs. QPR 1st representatives had a meeting with Nick Blackburn and Chris Wright, and during the discussions the idea of a merger seemed to be withdrawn.

With all the injuries and changes of formation and management, 43 different players were used during the season, the highest number ever (excluding the World War Two seasons) in the club's history. Only three players started over 30 games; Peter Crouch in 38, Jermaine Darlington in 33 and Gavin Peacock in 31. The leading scorer was Crouch in his first professional season, with 12 goals (10 League and two Cup), but the only other player in double figures was Chris Kiwomya with 10 (six League and four Cup).

Just prior to the end of the season, Tim Breacker announced his retirement from football due to his long-term ankle injury, and George Kulcsar was released from his contract in May 2001 so that he could take up the chance of playing football during the summer in Singapore.

The reserve side had a good start to the season and were top of the Combination League for the first half of the season, remaining unbeaten until the New Year. With the number of injuries at the club and the use of trialists, 74 different players appeared in the 24 games. The Under-17 Academy side, coached by Gary Waddock, did not have much success and lost the majority of their games. However, the Under-19 side, coached by Warren Neill, had a very successful season and finished 11 points clear at the top of their League and qualified for the semi-finals of the FA Academy Play-offs.

Nikki Bull, QPR's Under-19 goalkeeper.

These two semi-finals saw Rangers' Under-19s at home to Arsenal and Everton playing Nottingham Forest. The match against Arsenal finished as a 1–1 draw and, with no further goals in extra-time (Arsenal did miss a penalty), the tie was decided on penalties. Rangers came out on top 4–3, with Cochrane scoring the decider in sudden death. However, the main reason Rangers went through was the performance of 'keeper Nikki Bull, who made several outstanding saves to keep his side in the match. In the Final Rangers faced Nottingham Forest. The first leg was held at Loftus Road and saw Rangers take a one-goal lead, through Pacquette, into the return at the City Ground. The second leg ended 3–2 to Forest (3–3 on aggregate) at the end of the 90 minutes, Rangers' goals coming from Pacquette and Cochrane. The title looked as though it would be decided on penalties, but two minutes from the end of extra-time Forest scored the decisive goal to win 4–3 overall.

At the Loftus Road plc AGM in December Gerry Francis announced that this would probably be the last season for the academy style set-up, due to conditions imposed by the Football Association that meant they would have to construct an indoor gymnasium for use by the academy players only. Rangers were not only unable to afford to build one, but also unlikely to get planning permission. Following the confirmation, in May 2001, from the FA that Rangers did not meet the required stipulations, the club decided to return to the School of Excellence they had run prior to the creation of the academy scheme.

League (Worthington) Cup

In the first round Rangers were paired with Colchester United, who had been recently promoted to Division Two. The last time these two sides met in the League Cup was at the same stage in the 1966–67 competition, the season Rangers went on to win the trophy at Wembley. The first leg was played at Layer Road and saw Rangers gain an important one-goal lead, with Chris Kiwomya scoring in the 27th minute after a knock-on by Peter Crouch. Colchester had chances during the match, mainly instigated by their 19-year-old Zairian forward Lomana Tresor Lua Lua, who proved to be a handful for Karl Ready. The second leg, a fortnight later, attracted the lowest crowd (4,042) for over 35 years to Loftus Road. Those that stayed away missed one of the most impressive single performances from an opponent seen for a number of years. The star of the evening was the young Lua Lua, who scored a hat-trick to take his side through to the second round. Colchester scored twice, both by Lua Lua, in the first 17 minutes to take a lead in the tie for the first time. Right on half-time Kiwomya scrambled a goal for Rangers to put the tie back level on aggregate, after a previous effort by Breacker had been ruled out for a foul on the 'keeper by Connolly. Shortly after the break Connolly had a chance to put Rangers back in front, but he missed the target. Immediately Lua Lua set up MacGavin, who scored with a powerful shot. With more chances missed by the Rangers forwards the tie was finally settled as Breacker's back pass to Harper was seized on by Lua Lua for his third and Colchester's fourth. With the final aggregate score being 4–2 in the Essex side's favour, Rangers yet again failed to get past the first round.

FA Cup

In the 2000–01 season the third round returned to its traditional first weekend in January, after the previous season's poorly received amendment to the schedule. When the draw was made Rangers were the third-last ball to be drawn which resulted in an away game at the winners of the replayed tie between Darlington and Luton Town. The Hatters were successful, meaning it was just a short journey to Kenilworth Road. With both sides second from bottom in their respective divisions, the Cup tie was a chance to forget their League positions. The initial exchanges were even, with both sides having half-chances, but unfortunately for Rangers the first chance taken was when Fotiadis headed past Miklosko in the 27th minute to put Luton one-up. Only eight minutes later George doubled the Luton lead with a volley, a lead that they held on to until half-time. At the break Francis made two substitutions, bringing on the match fit Peacock and Wardley. Within three minutes Crouch had scored from a Peacock pass and in the 53rd minute Rangers were back on level terms when Crouch scored again, this time from a Connolly pass. Rangers then seemed to have the upper hand but all the effort was wasted in the 76th minute when Douglas scored Luton's third from a long throw-in. With the game going into injury time, it appeared that Rangers' Cup run was over, but from a Langley corner Nogan needlessly handled in the area and Rangers were awarded a penalty. Peacock remained cool and scored to give Rangers a replay back at Loftus Road.

Before the replay the draw was made for the fourth round and for the second time Rangers were drawn in the penultimate tie of the round. This time it would be a home draw against second-placed Premiership side Arsenal, thus giving both Rangers and Luton a big incentive in the replay of their earlier 3–3 stalemate. The game could not have started worse for Rangers as after only 58 seconds Mansell, an 18-year-old YTS trainee, making his first-team debut, scored with a shot that went in off Miklosko's right-hand post. Nine minutes later Luton lost Fraser when he suffered a broken leg when challenging Rose in midfield. With hardly any real chances in the first half-hour Francis made a tactical substitution, bringing on Kiwomya for central-defender Plummer. Just before the break Crouch had an overhead kick that narrowly missed the upright, while two minutes into the second half Kiwomya missed a great chance after a flick-on from Crouch. Another opportunity was lost 10 minutes later and, despite all Rangers' efforts, the equaliser did not look like materialising. Midway through the second half, Luton made some changes and played with Mark Stein, the ex-Rangers player, as a lone striker. Francis countered by bringing on Ngonge for Connolly and played with four forwards. Both sides had chances and when the fourth official signalled that there would be three minutes injury time Rangers were looking like they were exiting the Cup for another season. With less than a minute remaining, however, Langley won a challenge against Mansell and the ball fell to Baraclough, who crossed it into the box for Kiwomya to score. Despite Luton's protests, the game went into extra-time, and Rangers were awarded a penalty after eight minutes when Kiwomya was held down by Ovendale, the Luton 'keeper. With Peacock not playing, Langley took the spot-kick but hit the bar and was unable to convert the follow-up. In the sixth minute of the second period of extra-time Rangers finally took the lead for the first time in the tie when Kiwomya raced on to a Crouch header to beat Ovendale to the ball and score. Rangers survived the inevitable Luton attacks and progressed to the home tie against Arsenal. The game finished at 10:40pm, the latest ever finish for a match at Loftus Road. As the Arsenal tie was to be the next home game the club announced that tickets would be available directly after the game. With thousands of fans queuing for tickets, the box office finally closed at 1.05am the following morning.

With all tickets for the game sold out in two days the game was played in front of a capacity crowd and generated a great atmosphere. Rangers started the match in a positive mood and nearly scored in the first couple of minutes, but Crouch was unable to beat Seaman with his header. Soon afterwards he had another chance, but volleyed into the side netting following a misplaced clearance by Parlour. Miklosko then had to make a save from an Adams header following an Arsenal corner to keep the game goalless. After 31 minutes Rangers thought that they had scored when Crouch's header was cleared off the line, but unfortunately a goal was not signalled and Arsenal broke away to score when Dixon's cross was turned past Miklosko by Plummer for an own-goal. A minute later the lead was doubled when Wiltord's shot was deflected by Baraclough and left Miklosko wrong-footed. At the break Francis brought on two substitutes and re-organised the line up in an attempt to get back into the game. However, within four minutes Rangers went further behind when Cole's cross was sliced into his own net by Rose for the second own-goal of the game. By now Rangers were looking beaten and were not able to create any real chances to worry Seaman. After 56 minutes Wiltord volleyed in from a Parlour corner and two minutes later Pires ran through the centre of the defence to score Arsenal's fifth. The five goals all came in the space of only 27 minutes either side of the interval. The scoring was completed in the 74th minute when Bergkamp finally found the net after missing several previous chances. The defeat was Rangers' biggest ever, home or away, in the FA Cup, doubling the previous worst at home of 0–3 against Luton and Charlton in 1902 and 1930 respectively. It was also one goal worse than the 1–6 reserves away at Hereford in 1957 and Burnley four seasons later.

2001–02

With the club entering the close season still in administration, on 18 May an EGM of Loftus Road plc voted to sell Wasps Rugby Club and the Twyford Avenue facility to London Wasps Holding, a company owned by Chris Wright. A number of consortiums were reported to be negotiating to buy the remaining parts of Loftus Road plc, namely Queen's Park Rangers FC and the Loftus Road ground. One of these interested parties was led by Brian Melzack, a 43-year-old property consultant, who had tabled a bid of £12 million for all of Loftus Road plc prior to the sell-off of Wasps and Twyford Avenue. Another bid was, reportedly, from ex-chairman Richard Thompson who is thought to have made an offer of only £2 million for the club. A third contender was a consortium led by Andrew Ellis, son of former chairman Peter Ellis. Among Ellis's reported intentions was a proposed move to a new ground to the west of London in five years time. Stories circulated which included tales of the club moving to Milton Keynes, Feltham or near to Heathrow. It was a very confusing time for the supporters and the club personnel.

Just before the new season started it was announced that Andrew Ellis had 'shaken hands' on a deal with Chris Wright for the club. However, two days later Ellis withdrew his bid after being discouraged by fans' opposition to a proposed move to a new site near Heathrow within five years. According to the administrators, this still left three bids on the table. A recent offer had come from a consortium led by Maurice Fitzgerald, who stated his intention to leave the club at its present location or move it to a local site. By the time the season started Rangers were still in administration with no short-term resolution evident.

Due to the financial situation at the club a large number of players at the end of their contracts were released. The players concerned were: Ian Baraclough (Notts County), Bertie Brayley (Swindon Town), Alvin Bubb (Bristol Rovers), Richard Graham (Chesham United), Lee Harper (Walsall), Alex Higgins, Chris Kiwomya (AaB, a Danish club), Danny Maddix (Sheffield Wednesday), Terry McFlynn (Woking), Ludek Miklosko (appointed goalkeeping coach by West Ham United), Steve Morrow, Michel Ngonge (Kilmarnock), Karl Ready (Motherwell), Keith Rowland (Chesterfield) and Tony Scully (Cambridge United). Matthew Rose and Paul Bruce were also included in the list of released players but re-signed on new three-month and one-year contracts respectively, prior to the start of the season. Offers were also considered for the players that were still under contract. The players who were transferred for a fee were Peter Crouch, who joined Portsmouth for £1.25 million, and Jermaine Darlington, who went to Wimbledon for £200,000. Other players to leave the club were Ross Weare (Bristol Rovers) and Paul Murray (Southampton). In the week before the season started Gavin Peacock joined Charlton Athletic on a three-month loan deal, with an option to make it a permanent move if Charlton wanted him for longer.

On the incoming side were Leroy Griffiths, who joined from Ryman Premier side Hampton & Richmond Borough for a fee of £40,000, and the free transfer signings of Steve Palmer (Watford), Dave McEwan (Tottenham Hotspur), Terrell Forbes (West Ham United), Hamid Barr (Fisher Athletic), Chris Day (Watford) and Alex Bonnot (Watford). Also joining was Aziz Ben Askar, who was signed on a one-year loan deal from French club Stade Lavallois Mayenne.

Off the field, manager Ian Holloway continued to assemble his backroom staff and appointed Kenny Jackett (ex-Watford) as assistant manager and ex-player Tim Breacker as reserve team manager. Chris Geiler, who was the academy director and had been involved with the youth and schoolboy set-ups for 30 years, left the club. His successor as Centre of Excellence Director was former player Gary Waddock,

The 2001–02 QPR squad.

who had managed the Under-17 side for the past three seasons. Other appointments made included ex-player Tony Roberts (goalkeeper coach), Mel Johnson (chief scout), Prav Mathema (physiotherapist) and Gary Doyle (kit manager). Following the ending by Ericsson of their shirt sponsorship deal a new sponsor was sought and a deal was concluded with J.D. Sports for a one-year contract.

The **2001–02** pre-season saw high profile friendlies against Watford, Chelsea, Birmingham City and a first-ever meeting with Glasgow Celtic. The highlight of these was the 3–1 defeat of a full strength Chelsea squad. During the friendlies a number of trialists were used, with some of them earning contracts. Those who were unsuccessful were Martin Bullock (Barnsley), Gary Holloway, Chris Hutchins, Morello, Jason Price (Swansea), Brkovic, Abdu Tangara, Jason Brissett, Border, Yaldeci De Jesus, Nicky Banger, De Costa and Raphel Nada. Due to the lack of players all the non-first team friendlies were cancelled.

Rangers started the season in Division Two with a 1–0 home victory over Stoke City, the only goal being scored by Andy Thomson. A week later a 2–1 victory at Bury kept Rangers as one of only four clubs with a 100 per cent record after two matches.

Before the Bury game, Holloway was able to sign another player, despite using up the entire budget for players wages allowed by the administrators. The new player was Ebeli M'Bombo (also known as Doudou), a 20-year-old striker born in Zaire, who had made an impression in his two friendly appearances. Supporters Alex and Matthew Winton (owners of Ghost Menswear), who had agreed to sponsor the first year of his wages and accommodation costs, made the deal possible. At the end of

Ebeli M'Bombo.

August Sammy Koejoe had his contract terminated by mutual agreement, as he was frustrated at the lack of first-team opportunities.

In the next home game Rangers lost their 100 per cent record with a 0–0 draw against Reading (Reading had been another side that could boast a 100 per cent record before this game). Rangers then lost their unbeaten record in the next game when they lost to a last-minute goal at Wycombe Wanderers.

At this time Robert Taylor was signed on a one-month loan deal from Wolverhampton Wanderers. He had previously been Andy Thomson's strike partner at Gillingham.

The new ITV sport channel chose to televise Rangers' home game against Bristol City, which ended in another 0–0 draw and saw Ben Asker sent off. After another last-minute defeat, this time at Brighton, Rangers dropped down to 12th in the League. They moved up four places with a 4–1 home win over Port Vale, in which Andy Thomson scored his first hat-trick for the club. September finished with two away games, Leroy Griffiths scored his first goals for the club in the 2–2 draw at Blackpool and a last-minute own-goal by Wigan's Brannan gave Rangers all three points from their first-ever match against Wigan Athletic.

Off the field, the sale of the club was still continuing and on 20 September the consortium led by Brain Melzak were given exclusive rights to talks to buy the club. This meant that they had 21 days to complete the deal with the administrators. At this time a number of other parties were reported as being interested in buying the club, including The Moonies! As the period came to an end the Melzak consortium were given an extra week to finalise details as, according to chief executive David Davies, 'an agreement is so close so it makes sense to extend the period'. At this time Brentford chairman Ron Noades suggested that a new stadium could be built at Feltham and would be ideal for Rangers and Brentford to share.

In order that they could gain some first team experiences, three of last season's successful Under-19 side were loaned out to Ryman League clubs. The players concerned were Danny Murphy, who joined Hampton & Richmond Borough, and Daniel Wright and Adam Rustem, who both joined Chertsey Town. As Nikki Bull was injured, Holloway signed Fraser Digby on a month's loan from Huddersfield as cover for Chris Day.

With two wins and a defeat in the next three games, Rangers were back up into fifth place in the League, just four points off the top. Unfortunately, Rangers then had a run of three successive defeats and dropped to 13th place in the League. The defeats were away at Wrexham, who had just appointed Dennis Smith as their manager, at home to Northampton Town, who, although bottom of the League, had now beaten Rangers twice this season, and at Peterborough United. The game at Peterborough saw Danny Shittu make his debut, having been signed on loan from Charlton Athletic on the morning

QPR score in the away game at Peterborough in the 2001–02 season.

of the game. The game started well when Palmer scored after just four minutes, but by the end Posh had scored four and Shittu had been sent off.

In an attempt to find a goalscoring partnership, Holloway signed another loan player, Dominic Foley from Watford, on a one-month arrangement. He also signed Fernado De Ornelas, a Venezuelan international, on a month's trial, who had been playing for his country in the World Cup qualifying games. After his month's trial De Ornelas was released, as he did not fit into the club's plans.

In the home game against Oldham Athletic Foley made his debut and Doudou scored his first goal for the club. Although the game finished as a 1–1 draw, Rangers had more injury trouble. After 35 minutes Foley pulled a hamstring and was replaced by De Ornelas, but five minutes before the end disaster struck when Chris Day fractured his right leg in two places when attempting to clear a back pass. As Rangers had used all three substitutes, Stuart Wardley went in goal for the final minutes.

Better news followed with a 2–0 away at Notts County, where Fraser Digby, on loan from Huddersfield Town, made his debut and Andy Thomson scored two goals in two minutes. Thomson was now at the head of the Division's leading scorers with 12 League goals. The club was also able to extend Alex Bonnot's contract by three months and Mathew Rose's to the end of the season. Digby's loan from Huddersfield Town was also extended to the end of the season, as Day would not be fit again before the season ended. Another 'keeper, 19-year-old Rhys Evans, was signed on a long-term loan basis from Chelsea. Evans was immediately called-up to the England Under-21 squad, making him unavailable for the weekend's game against Tranmere Rovers. Despite an 88th-minute equaliser by Thomson, Rangers lost 2–1 as Rovers scored a minute later to take the points.

In mid-November the takeover talks again seemed to be having problems. One of the stumbling blocks was reportedly that the club's debts were larger than initially expected. The Melzak consortium were looking for ways of securing the loans required to purchase the club, but had not found a satisfactory solution.

Having missed the first three months of the season recovering from a previous injury, Chris Plummer was ruled out for the remainder of the campaign after breaking his tibia in three places in the Cup tie at Swansea City.

Kevin Gallen made a welcome return to Loftus Road when he signed on a free transfer from Barnsley. He made an immediate impact by creating the first two goals and scoring the third in a 4–0 home victory over Swindon Town. However, more bad news was forthcoming after the game when Oliver Burgess's injury was diagnosed as a ruptured cruciate ligament and he became the third player to be ruled out for the season, and it was not yet the end of November.

At the end of the month it was reported that the Melzak deal had fallen through and that there were no other identified buyers. Again Richard Thompson's name was mentioned but Nick Blackman stated that no offer or communication had been received by the administrator from anyone connected with Thompson. However, a piece of good news on the future of the club was that the administrators had told David Davies that the club has sufficient funds to see it through to the end of the season.

Back on the field two more draws followed, the first of which was a 0–0 at neighbours Brentford in the first League meeting between the two clubs since the 1965–66 season. In the second, a 2–2 home draw against Colchester, Gallen continued his home goalscoring run, claiming both goals. With a blank Saturday due to having been knocked out of the FA Cup and two away Saturdays to follow, the game on 1 December was Rangers' last home game before Christmas; a strange piece of fixture planning.

Gavin Peacock returned from his loan spell at Charlton Athletic, where he had made a number of first-team appearances, while Alex Higgins finally found a club when he signed for Chester City. This left just Steve Morrow as the only player released in the summer who had not been signed by another club. Peacock went straight into the first team and was part of the 3–2 victory away at Chesterfield, which saw Danny Murphy make his first-team debut. After going a goal behind, Rangers scored three times in a period of six minutes. Among the scorers were Rose and Shittu, with his first goal for the club, but unfortunately he also picked up his second red card later in the match. In the following game, a 2–1 win at Bournemouth, Murphy became the second player to be sent off in as many games.

At this time Sunderland transferred Danny Dichio to West Bromwich Albion for £800,000, and, due to a sell-on clause in his transfer from Rangers, the club received £80,000 from the deal. This meant that the club was able to cover Peacock's wages after his return from Charlton and did not go over budget.

Rangers went into the Christmas period in eighth place just two points away from the Play-off places. There was some encouraging news on the long-term injuries as well; Richard Langley had completed 90 minutes of a reserve match, Clarke Carlisle was due to resume contact training, Chris Day was able to put pressure on his leg and walk with the aid of crutches and Oliver Burgess had had a successful operation and was on the road to recovery.

The home game on Boxing Day against Brighton pitted the two leading scorers in the League, Andy Thomson and Bobby Zamora, against each other. However, the match ended in a 0–0 draw, with both defences able to cope with the top marksmen.

The last match of the year was far more eventful, when Wycombe Wanderers made their first-ever trip to Loftus Road. Wanderers had two men sent off following a melee after Rangers had been awarded a penalty, which Thomson subsequently missed. Rangers finally won the game 4–3, with Wycombe scoring from two penalties and an advanced free-kick. The win took the club into a Play-off place in sixth position.

Carl Leaburn joined on a month's loan from Wimbledon and made his debut in the 87th minute in the away defeat at Reading, the first in eight games. Leaburn then decided to return immediately to his own club and is therefore the holder of the record for the shortest QPR career, at just three minutes. Also at this time the club decided to release David McEwan when his six-month contract was not renewed. One player who did stay was Danny Shittu, whose loan deal was made permanent with a £350,000 transfer, which was funded by the Winton brothers.

Two more wins followed, with a 3–0 result at home to Bury and an impressive 1–0 win at Stoke City. The Bury game saw Brian Fitzgerald make his debut as a substitute and Richard Pacquette score his first goal for the club.

In the middle of January Stuart Wardley joined Rushden & Diamonds on a month's loan in order to get some first-team football. The home game against Bournemouth, which ended in 1–1 draw, saw the opposition have at least one man sent off for the third successive home game. A Saturday lunchtime televised defeat at Huddersfield followed and Rangers dropped out of the Play-off places.

At the end of January, Brentford chairman Ron Noades reportedly offered £10 million for the purchase of Loftus Road, or £6 million for 50/50 ownership. The plan was that Brentford would use Loftus Road while a new ground was being developed and then sell Loftus Road back to QPR when the new ground was ready. This offer came at the same time that final negotiations were taking place between QPR and Fulham on a ground-share deal for next season, which if it went ahead would put an end to the Brentford proposal. The ground-sharing deal with Fulham was eventually signed, initially for one season but with the possibility of a second year extension if required. This meant that Wasps would have to find a new home for that period and became involved in discussions with Wycombe Wanderers about using Adams Park. Their 10-year arrangement at Loftus Road, which had six more years to go, would be suspended while Fulham were at Loftus Road. Also at this time Ron Noades successfully applied to the League for a transfer embargo to be placed on the club as they were in administration and as such should not be able to buy players. The club pointed out that both Doudou and Shittu were not purchased using club funds, but by supporters. It also emerged that Noades had been interested in Shittu but had lost out to Rangers. A Football League tribunal refused to lift the transfer embargo and Rangers were only allowed to sign players on loan to cover for injured players. Acting chairman Nick Blackburn led an appeal against the decision, but it was unsuccessful and the embargo remained in place.

Clarke Carlisle played in a reserve game, his first competitive appearance for over a year. However, he lasted only 10 minutes before an unrelated knee injury forced him off and he was out for the remainder of the season .However, he did have some personal success when he won the TV show *Britain's Brainiest Footballer*, with a specialist subject of human biology.

Over 18,000 attended the 0–0 home draw with Cambridge United, the attraction being reduced admission of just £5 for adults and £1 for children, a feature of the League's Family Day initiative.

On the field the next three games resulted in one win, one defeat and one draw. The win was at home against Wrexham and was thanks to Gallen's 89th-minute goal. However, during the game Connolly suffered a knee ligament injury that kept him out for the rest of the season. After the 1–0 defeat at Port Vale, Rangers had dropped to 11th place and a points gap was starting to appear between them and the last Play-off place. In the next game Wigan Athletic made their first League appearance at Loftus Road, and the match ended in a 1–1 draw, with Gallen scoring the equaliser in the third minute of injury time. The match signalled the return of Aziz Ben Askar after his long-term injury, and the debuts of Rhys Evans and Dennis Oli, who came on as a substitute.

Alex Bonnot became another victim of the financial situation at the club when his contract was not renewed at the end of February. He had initially been given a three-month contract in August, which had been renewed on a monthly basis. Ian Holloway stated that the matter was purely financial and not related to the player. Stuart Wardley's loan at Rushden was extended until the end of the season after he had made some impressive appearances in their bid for promotion out of Division Three.

The momentum on the playing side then started to slow down, with just one win in the next four games. The win was against Blackpool and saw Richard Langley score the clinching goal with a superb volley from the edge of the area. Another of the youth players, Wes Daly, made his debut in the away defeat at Colchester.

Talks regarding the purchase of the club were still on-going with various consortia, but on 18 March the Winton brothers announced that they were withdrawing their bid. On 22 March the administrators announced that they were at an advanced stage of negotiations with the current board of directors at the club, regarding a deal to bring the club out of administration. The three main board members involved were David Davies, Nick Blackburn and Ross Jones. No details were given but it was expected that the deal would be centred on obtaining new loans and paying off Chris Wright's loans to the club. However, the announcement did not stop a small group of supporters demonstrating after the home game with Peterborough as they were concerned about the length of time that the club had been in administration.

Transfer deadlines meant that Rangers were involved in three loan deals in March. Arriving were Jerome Thomas from Arsenal and Dominic Foley from Watford, who had been on loan earlier in the season but was unable to complete the loan period due to injury. The other loan deal involved outgoing player reserve 'keeper Nikki Bull, who joined Hayes of the Conference League.

At the end of March the club staged two additional matches, firstly a World Cup warm-up match between Nigeria and Paraguay, and secondly the annual Varsity match between Oxford and Cambridge universities. Danny Shittu made his debut for Nigeria in the match against Paraguay when he came on in the 75th minute as a substitute.

Rangers then managed three wins in a row, which lifted them back up to eighth place, four points behind the sixth-placed team, but there were only two games to go. The first win was a 3–2 victory at Tranmere, in which Jerome Thomas made an impressive debut and Thomson scored the winner in the 90th minute. The next win was also 3–2, this time at home to Notts County after Rangers had been 0–2 down. Ex-Ranger Ian Baraclough scored County's second goal and Foley scored the winner, his first for the club. The third win was a 1–0 victory at Swindon, with Thomas scoring the only goal of the game. In this match Junior Agogo made his debut, after signing as a non-contract player in the week before the game. He had played in America for the San Jose Earthquakes before leaving to join Rangers.

With just two games to go, Rangers' chance of reaching the Play-offs disappeared with a 0–0 home draw against neighbours Brentford. The attendance of 18,346 was the highest for the season and the crowd saw an entertaining game between the two sides. The draw meant that Brentford had to beat Reading in their final game to gain automatic promotion, but a week later that game also ended in a draw so Brentford lost out. Rangers' final game ended in a 1–0 defeat at Oldham Athletic, a performance that led to manager Ian Holloway criticising the players for their lack of commitment. Rangers had finished the season in eighth place, seven points from the elusive Play-off spot.

With the season finishing in mid-April there was still some off-the-field activity going on. Hamid Barr, who had suffered with injury all season, joined Brighton on trial and played against Rangers in the last Combination match. This was a match that saw Tim Breacker's reserve side clinch the

Combination title. With Rushden & Diamonds reaching the Play-offs they wanted to extend Wardley's loan yet again. In the end he was signed on a permanent transfer and he played in the Final at the Millennium Stadium, which Diamonds lost to Cheltenham. Aziz Ben Askar, another player who had suffered from injuries, returned to France for family reasons. Fulham's re-development plans were put on hold for up to a year, due to local residents gaining a High Court injunction calling for a planning inquiry. This meant that Fulham would now ground-share at Loftus Road for two seasons, as their current ground Craven Cottage was not up to Premiership standards. Just prior to the start of the World Cup Nigeria staged another warm-up game at Loftus Road, this time against Jamaica. Although Shittu was once again in the Nigerian squad he did not make an appearance. However, another Rangers player, Richard Langley, came on as a substitute for Jamaica in the second half. Despite being involved in these pre-tournament games, Shittu was not selected for the Nigerian squad that was travelling to the tournament in South Korea and Japan.

Club captain Steve Palmer was the only ever present in the side for the season, while Marcus Bignot and Terrel Forbes only missed a couple of games each. The leading scorer was Andy Thomson with 21 goals, all scored in the League, and the next highest was Kevin Gallen, with seven after his return to the club at the end of November.

The reserve side, coached by Tim Breacker, won the Avon Insurance Combination League, suffering only four defeats all season. This was a great achievement as the beginning of the season had seen a number of trialists used and towards the end of the campaign a number of the junior players had played in the side to give them experience. Regular players were Lyndon Duncan and Danny Murphy, with Richard Pacquette leading the goalscoring list with nine goals in just 10 appearances, plus two more as a substitute.

The juniors, coached by Gary Waddock, played in the Under-19 section of the Football League Youth Alliance for the first time that season, but they did not meet with much success as they were a young side. Their highlight of the season was the FA Youth Cup third-round tie against Manchester United, played at Loftus Road, which they lost 1–3. Next season the club would reintroduce the Under-17 side, which would form part of the School of Excellence and would be coached by Kevin Gallen's brother, Joe.

Just after the end of the season the board of directors announced that the financial deal to take the club out of administration was now in place and all that remained was the legal aspects which would take about two to three weeks to finalise. On 17 May Ray Hocking and Simon James Michael, the joint administrators from BDO Stoy Hayward, announced that the refinancing of Loftus Road plc had been completed and the steps to seek the release from administration for Loftus Road plc and Queen's Park Rangers FC were to be initiated. As a result of the refinancing all unsecured creditors, which included the football, government and trade debts, would be paid in full. This was made possible by Chris Wright agreeing to a 50p in a pound settlement on his loans and by handing back a large portion of his share holding in the company. In recognition of his gesture, the board offered him the position of life vice-president, which he accepted. Roy Hocking said that some of the key features which had enabled the club to return to a solvent position were:

A reduction in playing staff and a more realistic approach to players' wages,
Sale of Peter Crouch and Jermaine Darlington (raising approx. £2.5 million),
The largest creditor, Chris Wright, writing-off some of his debt,
The ground-share agreement with Fulham and co-operation of Wasps Rugby Club,
The support of manager Ian Holloway, playing staff and non-playing staff including the directors,

The support and efforts of Chief Executive David Davies,
The backing of the fans, especially with the number of season tickets sold.

David Davies made a further announcement on behalf of the club in which he added his appreciation of the efforts made by all concerned in making the deal possible. He added some thoughts for those that had lost their jobs through redundancy during the administration period and announced that an application had been made to the high court to have the administration order formally lifted, and this expected to be heard within the next week. The Football League had been informed of the deal and were satisfied with the outcome, thus clearing the way for the club to be included in the following season's fixture list. Davies said that full details of the deal would be given to shareholders at a EGM but he did say that the deal was helped by a £10 million loan from an individual, whose representative, Philip Englefield, had joined the board of directors of Loftus Road plc. Negotiations were also planned with Harold Winton and his sons regarding their involvement with the club and their presence on the board. Finally, Davies sent out a warning that although manager Ian Holloway would have some money to spend, the club would not be spending large sums of money on players. Englefield resigned from the board in mid-July, citing other business commitments as the reason.

The final act in the administration process was completed on 27 May 2002 when the High Court lifted the order on the club. After the hearing, David Davies was quoted as saying, 'This is wonderful news and the conclusion of one of the darkest periods in our history. Having the administration order lifted marks the end of more than a year of tough financial decisions and hard work. This would not have been possible were it not for the commitment of the coaches, players, backroom staff and the hard work of our administrators BDO Stoy Hayward. In addition, none of it would have been possible without the support of the QPR fans. After seeing the club placed into administration, relegated and then lose more than half of our squad, they stuck by us in record numbers and continue to do so. We have faced some tough decisions and learned some hard lessons – these are lessons which many clubs have to learn. But we will come out of this experience in a much stronger position. Gone are the days when players will be paid excessive wages. When we first went into administration QPR was highlighted as being run on the economics of a madhouse. What we have done is brought some sanity to the club – but the hard work is not over. We don't suddenly have a magic wand to wave and make everything better. We are not suddenly flush with cash. With hard work and passion we will improve this club bit by bit and season by season. It won't happen overnight, and it doesn't sound sexy, but that is what we must strain every sinew to achieve. Ian Holloway has restored pride to the team and bought together a hungry and talented bunch of players, we look set once again to post a record number of season tickets holders and with the handcuffs of administration finally removed we can start to build a solid future for QPR. The hard work that has been put into taking QPR out of administration will continue to hopefully ensure that we are not faced with such problems again.'

Paul English, the Loftus Road Financial Controller, said, 'Today is a day to celebrate for all QPR fans. These past 13 months have been a roller-coaster ride for everyone connected with club. Over this period we have discovered a few home truths and we plan to carry forward into the future the lessons we have learned from being in administration.'

Administrator Ray Hocking of BDO Stoy Hayward said that he hoped in a climate of financial uncertainty, QPR's turnaround would give fresh hope to other clubs who were suffering difficulties at the current time. However, he refused to accept that the responsibility of such problems should lie with any one other than the clubs themselves. He said 'Too many clubs are blaming the ITV Digital crisis for their problems, but the fact remains that players are often paid too much money and that is the root cause of the situations they find themselves in.'

After the financial deal was finalised, Nick Blackburn was appointed chairman of Queen's Park Rangers, with Ross Jones becoming chairman of Loftus Road plc. The first action they completed was to negotiate a two-year contract with manager Ian Holloway.

League (Worthington) Cup

In the 2001–02 season a change was made to the format of the League Cup competition that meant that the first and second rounds were now a one-off match and not over two legs as in previous seasons. In round one Rangers were drawn away at fellow Division Two side Northampton Town. The match started well for Rangers and in the 16th minute they took the lead when the Northampton defender Evatt headed the ball into his own net when attempting a clearance. Chris Day then made some good saves from Gabbiadini and Forrester to keep Rangers in front at the interval. In the second half Rangers seemed to do enough to go through, but in the 90th minute Forrester scored for Northampton after Day had saved from Asamoah. Holloway sent on Koejoe and McEwan at the start of extra-time, but Rangers were unable to break down the home defence. In the seventh minute of the second period of extra-time Northampton took the lead when McGregor ran unchallenged to shoot past Day. Despite bringing on another forward, Rangers were unable to find an equaliser and were out of the competition for the third successive season at the first round.

LDV Trophy

Rangers entered this competition, previously known as the Associate Members' Cup, for the first time in 2001–02. The entrants were all Division Two and Three teams with the top six sides from the last season's Nationwide Conference and all matches were one-offs, with the golden goal followed by penalties to decide a tie. In the first (South) round Rangers were drawn away to Yeovil Town, the side with the most famous giant-killing history in the FA Cup.

Although Rangers fielded a full-strength side, Yeovil were on top for the first 30 minutes and only a goalline clearance by Rose kept the game goalless. Almost immediately Yeovil missed another chance, but in the 36th minute they took the lead when Giles headed in a Johnson cross. Before the break the home side could have gone further ahead but failed to take their opportunities. Rangers did not have one shot on target in the first half and had been completely outplayed by their non-League hosts.

Ten minutes after the break Marcus Bignot had Rangers' first shot on target, and, despite all three substitutes being introduced in an attempt to change the game, Rangers continued to struggle. In the 80th minute Grant scored Yeovil's second with a low shot that Day could not get to, and in the final minutes Rangers had Ben Askar sent off for pulling down Johnson, while Giles scored his second in added time to complete a 3–0 win for the Nationwide Conference side. Rangers were out of the competition at the first hurdle, beaten by a side that deserved their win.

FA Cup

Having been relegated to Division Two, Rangers entered the competition at the first round stage for the first time since 1966 and were drawn away to Swansea City, another club suffering from financial problems. This season, the sponsors, AXA Insurance, were awarding prize money to the winners of each game and so, with both clubs needing the £20,000 win bonus, the match was crucial. As the fixture was played on the Sunday evening, both sides already knew that the winners would be away to Macclesfield or Forest Green Rovers in the next round.

Rangers started the game badly and conceded a goal after only six minutes when Williams scored from a Sidibe pass after Digby had saved Sidibe's initial effort. Without Thomson, who was absent to be with his pregnant wife, Rangers lacked the opportunities to make use of their possession. Just before the break Swansea scored their second when Williams headed on a free-kick and Cusack beat Bonnot to the ball and shot past Digby. After five minutes of the second half Holloway made two substitutions in an attempt to break through the Welsh side's organised defence. Rangers did hit the post with a free-kick but they did not look like they were making much progress towards reducing the deficit. By now Rangers were pushing men forward and had used their last substitute in an attempt to get themselves back into the game. However, with 10 minutes remaining Palmer was caught out on the halfway line and Sidibe raced half the length of the pitch to round the advancing 'keeper and push the ball into an empty net to effectively end the game as a contest. Watkins added a fourth in injury time and Rangers went out of the FA Cup in the first round for the first time since the 1955–56 season, a run of 46 years. Despite having the majority of the possession, Rangers only managed seven attempts on goal throughout the game, with only one of them on target. Ian Holloway was reported as saying after the game, 'Character-wise that was appalling. Every man has to have a good look at himself because that was disgusting. If they carry on like that they are no good to QPR'. This completed a distinctly miserable Cup season for Rangers, as they had lost in all three competitions at the first hurdle and to lower-rated sides each time.

2002–03

At the end of the 2001–02 season a number of players who were out of contract were released. These players were: Junior Agogo (who joined Barnet), Hamid Barr (who had a trial at Brighton and St Albans City, before joining Gravesend & Northfleet), Aziz Ben Askar (returned to France), Ricky Browne, Paul Bruce (Dagenham & Redbridge), Nikki Bull (Aldershot Town), Justin Cochrane (Hayes), Mark Perry, Adam Rustem, Christer Warren (trial at Bristol Rovers but later joined Eastleigh) and Daniel Wright. Those players who were also out of contract but who were offered and accepted new terms were: Frazer Digby (six months), Danny Murphy (one year), Mathew Rose (two years), Andy Thomson (two years) and Dennis Oli. Marcus Bignot was offered a new contract but did not accept it and was eventually signed by Rushden & Diamonds at the end of August. Also leaving the club was Gavin Peacock, who, despite still having a year to run on his contract, negotiated a settlement and his contract was terminated by mutual consent.

New players who joined the club on contracts were Gino Padula, a left-back from Argentina, who had previously played for Bristol Rovers, Walsall and Wigan Athletic before returning home to Buenos Aires, Marc Bircham (on a free transfer from Millwall who signed on a two-year contract), and Nick Culkin, a goalkeeper from Manchester United. Having reviewed the players available to him, Ian Holloway decided to make some players available for transfer, even though they had not reached the end of their contracts. The players concerned were Leroy Griffiths (who joined Farnborough Town on a three-month loan), Richard Pacquette, Patrick Gradley, Dave Wattley and Ben Walshe.

Like the previous season a number of high profile pre-season friendlies were played, and once again the first visitors were Scottish champions Celtic, followed by Tottenham Hotspur and former European Cup-winners Steaua Bucharest. During pre-season a number of trialists were played but were not offered contracts. Players trialled included David Sanz Pascal, Sadio Sow, James Panayi (Watford), Mamaby Sidibe (Swansea City), Gregory Goodridge (Torquay United), and Steve Basham (Preston). In order to add to the squad some loan deals were arranged, with Paul Furlong arriving for one month and Tommy Williams for the season, both from Birmingham City. Steve Lovell of Portsmouth was signed on a three-month loan, but he moved to Dundee in a permanent deal before he made an appearance for Rangers.

The first League game of the **2002–03** season was at home to Chesterfield, and after going a goal behind Rangers came back to win 3–1 and head the table on goal difference. The game marked the debuts of Nick Culkin, Tommy Williams and Marc Bircham.

The first week of the season was completed with an away draw and defeat at Stockport and Barnsley respectively. In an attempt to bolster the forwards, D'Jailson Vieira, a Portuguese striker, was signed on a non-contract basis following his international clearance, but following one reserve appearance he was not offered a contract and he left the club. With Culkin injured in the Barnsley game, two other 'keepers under treatment and Chris Day still on the long-term injury list, Rangers had lacked goalkeepers and so signed Simon Royce on a three-month loan from Leicester City. He made his debut in the 2–0 home win over Peterborough United, in which Kevin Gallen scored both goals. The next game was the usual lively affair at Wycombe Wanderers, where Bircham and Marcus Bean, on his debut, were both sent off. Wycombe also had two players dismissed but went on to win the game 4–2.

With the new imposed UEFA transfer window due to 'close' at the end of August, Rangers arranged to loan Jermaine Thomas from Arsenal again for two months, after his successful spell at the club the previous season. This period also saw the end of Vieirs's career at Rangers, as following one reserve appearance he was not offered a contract and subsequently left the club.

At the end of August the club lost one of its greatest servants when Daphne Biggs died. She had been involved with the club for 60 years. A minute's silence was held before the Plymouth game and it was decided to rename the Young Player of the Year trophy in her honour. A memorial service was held at the ground, which was attended by a large number of supporters and ex-players.

In the Plymouth game Rangers recovered from being 0–2 down to draw 2–2, with the equaliser coming in the 90th minute from Pacquette. The side included all four loan players, Royce, Williams, Furlong and Thomas. After the game Paul Furlong was signed on a free transfer from Birmingham and given a permanent contract until the end of the next season.

The next game, at Mansfield Town, signalled the long-awaited return to first-team action for Clarke Carlisle after his 20-month absence. He came on as a substitute for the last six minutes in the 4–0 victory. Soon afterwards, though showing commitment to the club with a number of good performances in the reserves and first team, Richard Pacquette was taken off the transfer list. The next three games all resulted in victories, including an unexpected 3–1 win at high fliers Bristol City, which saw Rangers go top of the League on goal difference. At this time another person with strong connections at the club, Chris Geiler, died. He was a former youth director and had been responsible for the youth and schoolboy squads for over 30 years. He had been instrumental in developing several young players at the club into first-team players.

Rangers maintained their good League form with a fifth successive win, this time 2–0 at home to Colchester United. Simon Royce was recalled by Leicester City due to their goalkeeping situation, but he returned two weeks later on a new deal, missing only the away defeat at Crewe. The Israeli Football Association approached the club concerning the possibility of holding their Euro 2004 qualifying match against Cyprus at Loftus Road. The request was refused after consultation with local resident groups, who expressed concern about the number of games already planned for that week at the ground. The home game with Blackpool was moved to the Monday night to accommodate live transmission by Sky TV. Rangers won the game 2–1, with the winning goal coming from the Blackpool defender Clarke when his goalkeeper completely missed a harmless back pass. Following his period of recuperation Chris Day was given a one-month loan deal at Aylesbury United in order to gain some match experience, while due to limited opportunities in the first team Richard Pacquette went on a three-month loan to Stevenage Borough.

Following a good run of results the next game, away at bottom of the table Cheltenham Town, should have been the opportunity to keep up the pressure on the teams above Rangers in the League. It was not to be, however, and Rangers struggled to a 1–1 draw and Clarke Carlisle was sent off; although the disciplinary committee, following representation from two of the Cheltenham players, later rescinded the red card.

In the next home game, against Oldham Athletic (managed by former player Iain Dowie), Rangers lost their unbeaten home record when they were defeated 1–2. It was the first home defeat since the previous November, a run of 21 games.

After his loan period had expired Jermaine Thomas returned to Arsenal, as the club did not agree to the extension manager Ian Holloway was hoping for.

The next away game at Port Vale included another red card for a Rangers player, this time 'keeper Simon Royce for handling outside of his area. He was the fifth player to be dismissed so far during the season.

Off the field two events occured which would have a financial bearing on the club. Firstly, Lyndon Fuller, the managing director of Fans First Holding Group of companies, was appointed to the board of Queen's Park Rangers FC. Lyndon was the instigator and creator of the successful QPR Financial Services company. Secondly, it was announced by Matt Winton that the 'We Are QPR' (the Supporters' Investment Trust) had not been taken up as hoped for, with less than 100 people subscribing to the offer. He said that plans were being considered for the issuing of a revised proposal with a lower minimum subscription level.

At this time there was a large amount of activity on the loan signings front. Chris Plummer joined Bristol Rovers on a one-month deal in order to continue his attempt to regain full fitness after his serious leg injury sustained a year before. Another player to go out on loan was Leroy Griffiths, who joined Margate after a shortened period at Farnborough Town earlier in the season. Chris Day had his period at Aylesbury extended for another month. Among those joining QPR was Calum Willock, a forward from Fulham, who came in on a one-month arrangement. Finally, Simon Royce had his loan from Leicester extended for another month, although they did not give permission for him to play in the FA Cup. This did not matter initially as he was serving his suspension for being sent off against Port Vale. Richard Langley joined up with the Jamaican international side while serving his suspension for being sent off against Bristol City in the LDV Trophy game. During the two weeks he appeared in three internationals for the 'Reggae Boyz', against Guadeloupe, Grenada and Nigeria.

The poor run of League results continued with another home defeat, this time 1–0 by Northampton Town, with the game also seeing the debut of Calum Willock. Rangers were down to sixth place at that point and were starting to lose touch with the leading group of teams.

Karl Connolly then suffered a foot injury in training and with a number of other forwards injured or not available, Holloway signed Brett Angell on a short two-month contract as cover. Although he had played for Port Vale earlier in the season, Angell had been without a permanent club during the season since being released by Rushden & Diamonds in the summer. His first game was the away match at Luton, which ended in a 0–0 draw despite the home side having two players sent off.

Rangers' goalless run was not ended in the next game as Cardiff inflicted the club's third successive home League defeat with a comprehensive 4–0 victory. The game had been moved to a Friday night on police advice. Despite the recent poor results, Rangers were still sixth and occupying the last Play-off place, but there was a significant gap above them and a group of six clubs within three points below.

Calum Willock's loan period came to an end at this point of the season and he returned to Fulham without having made much of an impact, while Ben Walshe was given a one-month loan deal at Aldershot Town in order to gain some first-team experience. Tommy Williams broke his ankle in a training accident and was expected to be out for eight weeks, while Simon Royce's loan period expired and as Rangers were unable to offer a permanent contract he returned to Leicester.

Another defeat, 0–3 at Notts County, was the fifth successive League game in which Rangers had not scored. Watford winger Lee Cook was yet another player joining on loan when he agreed a one-month deal, and he made his debut in the 1–1 home draw with local rivals Brentford. Marc Bircham scored the goal against Brentford to break the long sequence of 500 minutes without a League goal, however, it was not until the Boxing Day home game against Wycombe Wanderers that Rangers recorded their first win in 13 games. The opening goal was scored by Matthew Rose, playing as a left-back, when he ran over half the length of the pitch before playing a one-two with Gallen to score a rare goal. This marked the halfway point of the season with 23 games having been played. Rangers were in seventh place, level on points with Luton in sixth place but nine points away from the fifth-placed team.

The Christmas period games continued with a 3–0 away defeat at Tranmere Rovers, in which Paul Furlong became yet another player to be sent off for Rangers during the season. Rangers had slipped to 10th place and were only 10 points from the relegation zone. The lower half of the table was bunched up, with just one point covering the clubs between 13th and 20th place.

On 31 December Frazer Digby's contract ended and Ian Holloway decided not to renew it as Chris Day had regained his match fitness and was back in contention for the goalkeeping spot.

The New Year started with a 2–0 win at Peterborough United and a 1–0 win at home to Stockport County. At Peterborough, Langley scored direct from a corner, and in the Stockport game Gallen scored an 88th-minute penalty to earn the points. The good run continued with two more 1–0 victories, at home to Barnsley and away at Plymouth. For the Barnsley game Rangers were missing three players through suspension, Bircham and Shittu (both with five yellows) and Furlong (red card at Tranmere). However, there was an excellent home debut for Gino Padula. At Plymouth, Rangers completed their fourth consecutive shutout, but they did lose Lee Cook when he was sent off in his last game of his loan spell.

Regarding player movement Andy Thomson had talks with Hull City about the possibility of joining Peter Taylor, his former manager at Gillingham. After terms on a two and a half year deal had been agreed, it unfortunately fell through due to Andy's long-term back problems. Lee Cook's loan was extended for another two months, but Watford had a 24-hour recall clause put into the agreement. However, Cook was expected to be suspended for three games after being sent off at Plymouth. Another contract which was renewed was that of Brett Angell, who was given another month, while Craig McAllister, a striker from Ryman League side Basingstoke Town, was given an extended trial after impressing in a reserve game. On the injury front Rose was diagnosed with a medial ligament problem and expected to be out for six weeks, while Langley's injury was similar to what he had suffered with previously. Both Williams and Connolly had suffered setbacks in their recovery and were now going to be out for longer than originally anticipated.

On the pitch Rangers' unbeaten run came to an end with a 1–2 home defeat by Tranmere, the winner being scored in injury time. After the next game, a 4–2 away win at Chesterfield, Kevin Gallen signed an extension to his contact, which tied him to the club until June 2005. Another run of four unbeaten games kept Rangers in sixth place but only three points ahead of ninth-placed Tranmere. The away game at Northampton marked the return of Chris Plummer, when he came on as a substitute, after 15 months out injured. Unfortunately, in training the following week he pulled a hamstring which meant he faced another spell in the treatment room. Thomson had also pulled a hamstring and faced a substantial term on the bench.

Rangers announced a deal with US soccer side Milwaukee Wave United, which involved a partnership for young players to train with the other side. The club also announced a deal with Le Coq Sportif to supply the playing kit and other sportswear for the next four seasons, having had a similar arrangement for the past six years. They detailed the policy for kit changes as follows: in year one and three there would be new home and away kits and in years two and four new away and third kits.

The 4–0 home win over Port Vale saw Padula score his first goal for the club with a hard left-footed shot from the edge of the area, while the 2–2 home draw with Mansfield was eventful with the Stags down to 10 men after 34 minutes and Gallen missing a penalty two minutes after Rangers had gone 2–1 behind. He then salvaged a point when he equalised late into injury time. Angell was given another extension, his third contract, and a testimonial was awarded to Gavin Peacock, who had left the club at the beginning of the season. The opponents for his match in May would be his former club Chelsea. Ian Holloway was named as the Division Two Manager of the Month for February after two wins and two draws in that time.

Rangers then suffered a 3–1 defeat at Swindon, but they recovered to win their next away game four days later at Huddersfield, after their coach broke down on the way to the game. Chris Day returned to the side for that game, after he had been out of first-team action since October 2001. Rangers' next two matches were against teams above them, and by beating fourth-placed Bristol City 1–0 and drawing 0–0 with Oldham Athletic they had closed the gap on the three other teams in the Play-off zone. However, they were still only two points above Tranmere in seventh. With a shortage of fit goalkeepers, Chris Day being the only one match fit, Phil Whitehead (Reading) and Bertrand Bossu (Hayes) were used in reserve matches. The next match was the first ever visit of Cheltenham Town to Loftus Road. Rangers won the game 4–1 with Lee Cook scoring the third goal in his last match before returning to Watford. Williams was carried off after just seven minutes with an injury to the same ankle that had kept him out earlier in the season. Kevin McLeod, a left-sided midfield player, was signed on loan from Everton as cover following William's injury and Cook's departure.

The 2002–03 season saw the announcement by Loftus Road plc of the completion of the sale of the former Wasps training ground at Sudbury, with the final plots being purchased by a company called Sudbury Holdings Ltd. The main shareholders of SHL were named as supporters Matt and Alex Winton, Maurice Fitzgerald, Kevin McGrath and Dawn Adams. They paid £255,000 for the land and said that one-third of any profit from the sale would be paid to Loftus Road plc.

Rangers' Play-off hopes took a knock when top of the table Wigan Athletic beat them 1–0 at home, the match in which McLeod made his debut. On transfer deadline day the only activity Ian Holloway was involved with was the loan signing of Stephen Kelly, a right-sided defensive player from Tottenham Hotspur. The loan was for a month initially but the period could be extended if needed.

Holloway had now used up all of his permitted loan deals. Kelly made his debut in the 3–1 away win at Blackpool, where Richard Langley scored all three for his first hat-trick for the club, and this was followed by a 2–1 win at fellow Play-off contenders Cardiff City, again with Langley scoring, this time an 89th-minute winner. With only five games remaining, just four points covered all four Play-off sides. Rangers were five points ahead of the seventh-placed team and seven points from an automatic promotion spot, having lost only two games in the last 12.

At the supporters' club annual dinner Kevin Gallen was awarded with the Player of the Year trophy, together with the Players' Player trophy and the Goal of the Season award. Danny Shittu was runner-up in the Player of the Year competition and Richard Pacquette won the Young Player of the Year award. At the same time Fulham announced that they would be remaining at Loftus Road for a second year as no planning permission had been received for Craven Cottage and plans to share at Stamford Bridge had been rejected by the council. This period also saw Danny Murphy leaving for Wycombe Wanders on trial and playing in a reserve game for them.

In the first of the final five games Rangers beat Luton 2–0 at home, with both goals coming from McLeod. This was followed by a 2–1 win at neighbours Brentford, with Rangers' winner being scored in the second minute of injury time by Bircham. It was only his second goal for the club, the other being in the home game against Brentford! Rangers were now just three points off third place and five clear of Tranmere in seventh place with a superior goal difference. As Rangers were playing a day earlier than their rivals they moved up to fourth place with a 2–0 home win over Notts County on Easter Monday. Both McLeod and Kelly had their loan periods extended to the end of the season, including the Play-offs.

The last home League match against Crewe ended as a 0–0 draw, despite Rangers having both Carlisle and Kelly sent off for two yellow cards. Rangers were now guaranteed to finish in the Play-off zone and with three sides (including Rangers) on 80 points and one on 81 the final matches would decide who played who in the semi-finals. After the Crewe game chief executive David Davies stated that the referee's report made for 'grim reading' as it mentioned a coin throwing incident, a supporter remonstrating with the referee and a pitch invasion at the end of the game. The final game was held at Colchester United and ended in a 1–0 victory, moving Rangers up to fourth place, level on points with third-placed side Bristol City. The other two sides involved in the Play-offs were Oldham Athletic and Cardiff City, with the pairings for the Play-off semi-finals arranged as Rangers against Oldham, and Bristol City against Cardiff. Rangers had finished the season with a run of seven unbeaten games, in which they conceded only three goals. (See below for details of Rangers' progress in the Play-offs).

At the end of the season Loftus Road plc held their first AGM since entering administration. The AGM had two years of accounts to consider and these were passed on a show of hands. The main decision taken was to change the name of the company from Loftus Road plc to QPR Holdings plc to reflect the change of the constitution of the company following the sale of London Wasps to Chris Wright.

Once again, club captain Steve Palmer was an ever present, playing in 53 games in all competitions. He was followed by Kevin Gallen (44 appearances, plus three substitute), Terrell Forbes and Richard Langley (both 41 apps, plus three subs). The leading goalscorers were Gallen and Paul Furlong, both with 14 goals (13 League and one Cup). The only other player to reach double figures was Langley with 10 (nine League and one other).

The reserves, under Tim Breaker's management, had a mixed season and finished in 14th place in the Avon Insurance Combination League. As in recent years, the side was often comprised of youth players and trialists. The only regular players were Wes Daly (18 appearances, plus two subs), Danny

Murphy (17 appearances, plus two subs) and Marcus Bean (17 appearances); the highest number of goals was just four and was achieved by Angell, Griffiths, Murphy and Pacquette.

The Under-17 side, managed by Joe Gallen, did not meet with much success, winning only three League matches out of the 22 played. As is often said, it is the performance that matters at this level not the result and this was borne out with a number of 'under age' players making up the core of the squad.

The Under-19s, managed by Academy Director Gary Waddock, did not fare much better with just six victories from 27 matches played. Their results did show an improvement towards the end of the season; however, a big disappointment was the FA Youth Cup defeat at non-League Hoddesden Town in the first round.

Division Two Play-off

By finishing fourth Rangers were pitched against fifth-placed Oldham Athletic in the Play-off semi-final, with the first leg held at Boundary Park. Despite three changes in defence from the previous game Rangers started well, with Furlong nearly scoring after three minutes. Oldham then began to exert pressure and scored from a free-kick in the 28th minute, but two minutes after the break Richard Langley equalised from a Tommy Williams cross. The game was littered with niggardly fouls and a number of bookings were made. One of these was Langley, who received a second a minute after his first and was therefore sent off. Rangers had to play the last 10 minutes with reduced numbers, but they managed to hold on to the 1–1 draw.

The second leg at Loftus Road was played in front of a crowd of 17,201, the highest gate of the season so far, home or away. The game started at a frenetic pace, with McLeod having a chance to score in the first minute but was denied by Pogliacomi in the Oldham goal. Rangers had numerous chances and two good penalty appeals turned down before Oldham mounted an attack of their own. Wayne Andrews was causing problems with his pace, but fortunately for Rangers his finishing did not match. Half-time came with no goals and the tie still level at 1–1. Again Rangers began the better team and had numerous chances to take the lead, but they were foiled by good defending and goalkeeping. Low, probably Oldham's best player on the night, had a long range shot which just cleared the bar. Rangers made two substitutions and the changes injected more pace into the attack with Williams providing some good crosses from the left. With 15 minutes remaining, substitute Pacquette thought he had scored but a superb save from the 'keeper denied him. However, with just eight minutes to go, Carlisle cleared a long ball from defence that Furlong got to and he held off challenges from three defenders to score into the bottom left-hand corner of the net. In the final minutes Oldham went all out for the equaliser, but they were unable to break through and Rangers won 1–0 to go through 2–1 on aggregate.

In the Final, played at the Millennium Stadium, Rangers met Cardiff City, who had beaten third-placed Bristol City 1–0 on aggregate. The match was played in front of a crowd of just over 66,000, who saw a scrappy first half with only a couple of chances for Rangers. The first was a Kevin Gallen free-kick which was punched over the bar by Alexander, the Cardiff 'keeper, and the second was when Paul Furlong tried to chip the 'keeper from the left-hand corner of the box. The second half began much better for Rangers, with Gallen having two shots, one saved and one just over. Cardiff did not really threaten and substitute Andy Thompson nearly scored with a header following a poor back pass from a Cardiff defender. With no scoring by the end of 90 minutes, extra-time was needed. In the Play-off matches golden or silver goals do not count so a full 30 minutes had to be played. Clarke Carlisle had a good header from a Gallen cross, but it went just wide, and in the last minute of the first period Chris Day kept Rangers in the game with a reaction save from a Prior header. At the start of the final 15 minutes Tommy Williams ran with the ball from his own penalty area to inside Cardiff's before shooting straight at the 'keeper. However, the decisive moment came just six minutes before the end, when Carlisle misplaced a pass to Kavanagh who played a ball over the top of Shittu for Campbell to run onto. He outpaced Shittu and lobbed the ball over Day into the net for the only goal of the game. With no further chances, Rangers lost the match and were destined for another season in Division Two, despite coming so close to promotion.

League (Worthington) Cup

In the first round Rangers were drawn away to fellow Londoners Leyton Orient, who the season before had finished at the lower end of Division Three. Rangers were unable to field their strongest team due to the non-availability of the short-term loan signings and the suspensions of Bircham and Bean, which meant they had to reorganise defence and midfield. However, the game started well for Rangers, with Thomson going close, but after 33 minutes they fell behind to a Campbell-Ryce goal. Rangers had a chance to equalise before the break but the ball came back off a post. The resulting clearance ended with Orient scoring a second through Thorpe. A re-shuffled side started the second half better and Rangers were awarded a penalty after 70 minutes when Langley was brought down in the box. Thomson scored from the spot to give some hope in retrieving the game. However, Rangers' efforts came to nothing as five minutes later Orient scored a third when Fletcher fired home. Gallen managed to score a second Rangers goal with just two minutes remaining but it was too late. So for the fourth successive season Rangers failed to progress to the second round.

LDV Trophy

This season the competition was expended to include 12 Nationwide Conference clubs, but, despite the extra chance of being paired with a non-League side, for the second successive season Rangers were drawn against Bristol City, one of the strongest sides in the tournament. However, this time Rangers would be at home in a Cup tie, the first time in five ties in all competitions. Home advantage did not count for much, as Rangers went out of yet another Cup competition at the first stage. The match finished goalless after 90 minutes, with few chances for either side, the closest being when Thomson put the ball in the net after 38 minutes but the effort was ruled out for offside. In extra-time Richard Langley was sent off in the 104th minute for an off-the-ball incident. With no goals in the extra 30 minutes the match was decided on penalties. The first was missed by Thomson, but Doudou, Palmer, Williams and Connolly were able to make the score 4–4 after the first five. In sudden death Rose missed his kick and Rosenior scored for City to give them a 5–4 win on penalties.

FA Cup

Once again Rangers came out second in a pairing, this time away to either Hucknall Town or Vauxhall Motors. The two Unibond Premier sides had drawn their fourth qualifying round tie on the Saturday and the replay had ended in a convincing 5–1 win for Vauxhall Motors. As their ground was not considered big enough, the game was switched to Chester's Deva Stadium. Vauxhall were in form, having scored five in each of their last two games, both away. Rangers had a chance early on when Thomson had an effort cleared, but the Motormen responded with two good chances before the break. In the second half, again both sides had chances but with both 'keepers in form neither side could find a way through. In the dying minutes Shittu failed to score when he was just short of connecting with a Burgess cross, and in the last minute Vauxhall's Young saw a header from a corner go just outside of the post. With the game ending in a 0–0 draw a replay 10 days later was arranged.

With Sky announcing that the second-round tie at Macclesfield would be a live televised game, both sides had a large financial incentive in winning the replay. Not only was there the £20,000 round-one winner prize money, but also a half share of the £200,000 television fee at stake. The match started scrappily but it livened up in the 18th minute when Thomson gave Rangers the lead after he received Padula's pass and chipped over the advancing 'keeper. However, the lead only lasted four minutes as Brazier battled through some missed tackles and equalised for the Unibond League team. Both sides had chances before the break, but it remained at 1–1. Vauxhall started the second half full of confidence and created some good moves and chances. Manager Ian Holloway then made tactical substitutions, which seemed to create a fresh approach from Rangers, but they were still unable to break through the opposition's defence to score the all-important goal, and with no further goals the replay went into extra-time. Again Rangers had chances, but with a combination of poor finishing and good keeping the non-League side held out to take the tie to penalties. Furlong missed the first kick, but Palmer, Langley and Thomson all scored theirs. So, reaching the last of the mandatory five, Rangers were lagging 3–4. Connolly had to score to keep the shoot-out going but he scuffed his attempt wide of the right-hand post and Vauxhall Motors were into the next round for the first time in their 15-year history. It was the first occasion Rangers had been beaten by a team three levels below them and it marked their seventh successive Cup tie defeat.

2003–04

At the end of the previous season, 2002–03, the following players were out of contract and not offered a new deal: Brett Angell (who announced his retirement from football), Oliver Burgess (joined Northampton Town), Karl Connolly (Swansea City), Lyndon Duncan, Doudou, Brian Fitzgerald (Northwood), Patrick Gradley (Gravesend & Northfleet), Danny Murphy (Swindon Town) and Chris Plummer (Barnet). Other players to leave were Sam Scully (Aldershot Town), Alistair Heselton (Edgware Town), Mathew Ramsey (Chesham United) and David Wattley (Lincoln City). The following players who were out of contract were offered, and accepted, a renewal: Marcus Bean (two years), Wes Daly (two years), Chris Day (two years), Richard Pacquette (one year), Gino Padula (two years) and Steve Palmer (one year). Although not out of contract Richard Langley and Clarke Carlisle were offered an extension to their existing contracts, but both players rejected the terms and the club announced that they would consider offers for either player. Two players who each had a final year remaining negotiated a termination of their contracts: Leroy Griffiths, who joined Farnborough Town, where he was on loan the previous season, and Andy Thomson, who returned to Scotland and joined Patrick Thistle.

On the incoming side were Eric Sabin (from Swindon Town), Gareth Ainsworth (Cardiff City) and Martin Rowlands (Brentford). All joined on a free transfer under the Bosman ruling. Rowlands was still recovering from a serious leg injury and did not pass his medical until just before the season started.

During the pre-season a number of trialists were given an opportunity to earn a contract. Those involved were Clive Delaney (West Ham United), Tom Newey (Leyton Orient), Marvin Robinson, Killian Brennan, Michael Kathopoulis, Scott Minto (West Ham United), Ben Jones (Merthyr Tydfil), Christopher Kanu (Ajax) and John Bailey (Preston North End).

Off the field it was announced that the new club sponsors would be Binatone Telecom (replacing JD Sports), who had signed a one-year deal worth £150,000. Jim Frayling, who had been marketing manager for the past four years, left the club for a position with Coors Brewers. Bill Power, a life-long supporter from White City, joined the board of QPR Holdings after investing £200,000 in the club. A

The 2003–04 team.

record number of season tickets were sold, with 10 days to go before the first game a total of 7,922 had been purchased, which was 20 per cent up compared to the same stage the previous season. Another income that the club received was from the sell-on clause when Trevor Sinclair left West Ham United to join Manchester City. Rangers also received 10 per cent of the profit on the total £2.4 million (£2.1 million fee plus £300,000 appearance-related extra) the Hammers paid for Sinclair. This gave the club £10,000 but there was a similar clause in the deal with Blackpool when Sinclair moved to Loftus Road, therefore Blackpool gained £2,000, while Rangers kept the other £8,000. However, a big setback to the stability of the club was when an anticipated deal with Australian businessman David Thorne, who had intended to invest £2 million into QPR Holdings, did not materialise. At the end of July he withdrew his offer citing 'significant opposition from a number of quarters, resulting in division and acrimony'. Unconnected to this, Lyndon Fuller resigned from the board for personal and business reasons.

Another far-reaching announcement made was that concerning a restructuring of the youth set-up. David Davies admitted that the overhaul was instigated due to financial constraints on the club. The board had decided to remove four age groups from the Centre of Excellence. The groups being disbanded were the Under-9s, Under-11s, Under-13s and most significantly the Under-19s. This would leave the centre with the Under-10s, Under-12s, Under-14s, Under-15s and Under-17s. Those that would have played for the Under-19s would now be included in the reserve side. Davies was quoted as saying, 'The brutal truth is that the Centre of Excellence structure is not producing the players to justify its cost. Coupled with the uncertainty of funding from Sport England and prospective investments into the club not being realised, we have been faced with the reality of a terribly difficult season. We will save over £100,000 per year with the reduced set-up, and although

I cannot over estimate our sadness at the personal cost to young players, the safeguarding of the club's future is our primary concern. The fact remains that we have brought into the club three excellent players in the close season at no financial cost beyond their wages. Nevertheless, it is important to stress that we have avoided the necessity to disband the set-up altogether and that myself, Ian Holloway and Gary Waddock all believe that the club can look forward to producing outstanding home-grown players in the years to come.' The news was broken to all those concerned at a meeting held at Brunel University. Davies explained that the decision could not have been made sooner as the funding issues were being discussed during the summer months and had only recently come to a head. Manager Ian Holloway admitted that the situation was 'dreadful', but under the current circumstances the board had no choice. Gary Waddock, director of the centre, also stated that he was upset and disappointed, but he stressed his backing of the board and appreciated the thinking behind the course of action.

During the close season Richard Langley joined up with the Jamaican squad for the Gold Cup competition in the Americas and the Caribbean. He played in four games and scored his first full international goal in the pre-tournament game against Cuba in Kingston.

The last pre-season game was a testimonial match against Charlton Athletic for Tony Roberts, who remained at the club as goalkeeping coach.

In the first week of August Ian Holloway tried to arrange some loan deals and was successful in getting Tommy Williams back to the club from Birmingham City, initially on a month arrangement. Another loan deal, that of Mark Yeates from Tottenham Hotspur, fell through due to the player being injured.

The **2003–04** League season opened with a home game against Blackpool. Before the kick-off a minute's silence was held for Ray Harford (manager at QPR from December 1997 until September 1998) who had died that morning, after suffering from cancer for some time.

QPR started the season with a 5–0 win against Blackpool.

The season could not have started any better for one of the debutants, Gareth Ainsworth, who scored after just four minutes. With other goals from Langley, Gallen, Palmer and another from Ainsworth, Rangers won 5–0 to go joint top of the League with Bristol City, who had also had a 5–0 home win. Martin Rowlands and Eric Sabin both made their debuts when coming on as substitutes in the second half.

Before the next League game, which was away against Brighton & Hove Albion and had been moved to Monday night for live transmission by Sky, Richard Langley left the club. He joined Cardiff City for an initial fee of £250,000 with other payments based on Cardiff's progress in the season. Kevin McLeod was signed from Everton for £190,000, initially on loan so that he could play at Brighton. The permanent deal was for a two-year contract. Meanwhile, the game against Brighton & Hove started well as Rangers took the lead from a Padula free-kick. However, Leon Knight, a previous loan player at the club, scored twice to give the home side victory. Another negative for Rangers was the sending off of Terrell Forbes for retaliation after he had been fouled.

Before the next game Tony Thorpe was signed from Luton Town for £50,000 and given a two-year deal. Another player also joining Rangers was Richard Edghill, who had played for Sheffield United the previous season and was without a club. He was signed on a month-long contract as cover for Forbes, who was recovering from his injury and had a three-match suspension to serve. Thorpe made his debut in the 1–0 home win against AFC Bournemouth. Rangers then scored three in each of their next two games, 3–3 draw at Rushden and 3–0 home win over Chesterfield. Edghill made his debut as a substitute in the Chesterfield game and Tony Thorpe opened his goalscoring account with two goals. By the end of August Rangers were up to third in the table. Prior to the Chesterfield game, Clark Carlisle did not appear for training and had a meeting with manager Ian Holloway to explain the reason for his absence. He was suffering from an alcohol-related illness and was to undergo a 28-day recuperation programme at the Sporting Chance clinic.

More loan arrangements were then agreed, with Ben Walshe joining Gravesend & Northfleet for a month and Arthur Gnohere also arriving for a month from Burnley as cover for Carlisle and Matthew Rose, who was suffering from a long-term injury. With the club looking for other means of raising funds, two auctions were held for supporters. One for a place in the squad with a personal number raised £3,500 and the other for the opportunity to travel with the team to the away game at Colchester achieved £500. Gnohere made his debut in the 2–2 draw at Colchester.

Yet more player movements saw Tommy Williams return to Birmingham City, but although he wanted to stay Holloway could not guarantee him first-team football. John Halls of Arsenal and Matt Carragher, previously with Port Vale, were given trials in a reserve game as Holloway sought to bring in more players, while youth-team 'keeper Jake Cole joined Hayes on a 'work experience' programme. Before the Wycombe home game Rangers had a lengthening injury list with five players (Forbes, Carlisle, Rose, Bircham and Daly) definitely out and doubts hanging over Thorpe and Padula. The game against Wycombe ended 0–0, thus ending Rangers' 100 per cent home record, though they were yet to concede a goal at home.

In mid-September the board of QPR Holdings announced that Harold Winton would be taking up the position of honorary life president of QPR FC, and therefore had stepped down as a director of QPR Holdings.

In their next game Rangers recorded their first away win earning a 2–0 victory at Wrexham, with the goals coming from Marcus Bean and Martin Rowlands, their first goals for the club. Another point from a 1–1 draw at Luton Town put Rangers in third place, but only three points away from the club in 13th place.

Further loan deals led to Marien Ifura joining Conference side Farnborough Town and Martyn Williams leaving for Sutton United of the Ryman Premier League, both for a month. Following Dan Shittu's tearing of his anterior cruciate ligament in his knee, which was initially thought to be more serious but was now expected to keep him out of the side for six weeks, Arthur Gnohere's loan from Burnley was extended for another month.

Rangers conceded their first goal at home in the 1–1 draw with Bristol City, although the game was more notable for the fact that this was the first League game that Steve Palmer had not started since he joined the club over two years before.

As a result of incidents which occured in a home game the previous season against Crewe Alexandra, an FA disciplinary meeting imposed the following penalties on the club: the club must publish a notice in the match programme and on the official internet site setting out their responsibilities for ground safety; the FA were to approve the CCTV system at Loftus Road; both goal nets were to be of a finer mesh; and a fine of £25,000, only payable if the club is found guilty of similar offence before the end of 2003–04 season. In addition to the incidents in the Crewe game the injury caused to Tony Butler in the Bristol City match, again from coins thrown, was also taken into account.

Joining the club at this point was Warren Barton, who was signed on a non-contract basis having been released by Derby County at the end of September.

Back on the pitch, Rangers had two successive wins, a 4–0 home win over Barnsley in which they scored three times in a four-minute period in the second half and a 1–0 victory at Grimsby, their first-ever victory at Blundell Park. In the Grimsby game Warren Barton made his debut as a substitute and another substitute, Eric Sabin, scored his first goal for the club in extra-time for the winner. Rangers were now up to second place, just one point behind leaders Brighton.

Rangers' next game, at home to Brentford, had been selected by Sky for live transmission, but due to Brentford having three players called up to international Under-21 squads the game was postponed. The cancellation was a bonus for Marc Bircham as he was called into the Canadian squad for their friendly match against Finland in Tampere. He started the game, adding to the previous 13 caps that he had for his adopted county, the place of his grandfather's birth. Following the LDV game against Kidderminster Harriers, Arthur Gnohere was recalled from his loan period early by Burnley, due to their own injury situation. With two draws and one defeat in the next three games Rangers dropped back to sixth place. In both of the month's away games, at Peterborough and Port Vale, the opposition had a player sent off but Rangers were unable to make any gain from their one-man advantage. More activity on the loan front saw Wes Daly join Gravesend & Northfleet for a month, and Ben Walshe's loan at the same club was extended until the end of the season.

After the 2–1 away win at Stockport County, Rangers' injury list was growing with Barton, Edghill, Padula, Shittu, Rose, Furlong, Bircham and Culkin all undergoing treatment. So, with the FA Cup game up next Rangers needed to recall Wes Daly and Jake Cole from their loans at Gravesend and Hayes respectively. It was to no avail, however, as a weakened Rangers side were knocked out in the first-round tie by Grimsby Town.

After their swift exit from the Cup Rangers bounced back with a 1–0 home win over neighbours Brentford, Tony Thorpe getting the winner that moved them up to second place. On the injury front there was good news regarding Danny Shittu as he made an appearance for the reserves in the game at Crystal Palace.

The next team to visit Loftus Road were top of the table Plymouth Argyle, and Rangers won the match 3–0 in front of 17,049 spectators, the highest gate of the season so far. With two goals from Kevin

Gallen, Rangers replaced the Pilgrims at the top of the table. More good news was that Danny Shittu had agreed a two-year extension to his existing contract, taking him through to the summer of 2006, while Dennis Oli had agreed a loan deal to go to Gravesend & Northfleet for a month. Even better news was that Rangers retained their lead at the top of the table with a 1–1 draw at Swindon Town.

Another season's highest gate (17,313) saw the next home game against Sheffield Wednesday. Rangers won 3–0 to keep themselves one point ahead of Plymouth and four points from third-placed Brighton. Ian Holloway was named as the Nationwide Division Two Manager of the Month for November as Rangers were unbeaten with four wins and a draw, and Clarke Carlisle made it a double celebration as he was awarded the Umbro Isotonic Player of the Month for Division Two. Matthew Rose then made his competitive comeback in a reserve game at Brighton, playing for 60 minutes. However, the match was remembered more for the triple sending off of Paul Furlong, Richard Pacquette and Brighton's centre-half after a brawl. After the match Holloway expressed his annoyance that both players would be serving their three-match suspensions over the busy Christmas/New Year period. Two players who left the club for a period were Wes Daly, who had a trial at Barnet, playing in a Hertfordshire Senior Cup for them, and youth player Lee Barnet, who joined Weston-super-Mare on a work experience scheme.

The next game, after Rangers' enforced break due to the FA Cup second-round fixtures, saw the first-ever visit to Loftus Road of Hartlepool United. The match ended in a comfortable 4–1 win for the home side, with Kevin Gallen scoring two. It was at this time that Chief Executive David Davies issued a warning regarding the club's financial position as at that time no confirmed investor had committed funds to the club. Rangers needed more money to safely complete the season as the first loan repayment of £1 million was due on May 2004. In response to Davies's financial warning, a new fans-based money-raising scheme, called Our QPR, was launched as a joint effort between the LSA, QPR 1st and the official supporters' club.

Rangers next travelled to Boundary Park to meet Oldham Athletic, who the day before the game lost their manager, ex-Ranger Iain Dowie, to Crystal Palace. Rangers lost the game 2–1 and were knocked off the top of the League by Plymouth Argyle, who had beaten Notts County at Home Park.

The festive season started with a 3–3 draw at Notts County, where Rangers had led twice but needed a last-minute equaliser from Gallen to get a point. The next two home games both resulted in wins to send Rangers into the New Year in second place, five points ahead of the third-placed side. The first draw of the In2Win Lottery, which provides funds for the youth academy, took place during half-time of the Rushden & Diamonds game.

Regarding player movement, trials were given to Guy Ipoua and Johan Gudmundsson in a reserve friendly at Wycombe. Ipoua had previously been at Livingston, Gillingham and with Holloway at Bristol Rovers. Wes Daly, having been unsuccessful at Barnet, joined Grays Athletic on a work experience scheme.

With an away win at Blackpool, Rangers closed the gap on leaders Plymouth to just two points. Due to a lack of available experienced midfield players, Dean Marney was signed on a month's loan from Tottenham Hotspur.

A new season's highest gate of 17,839 saw the 2–1 victory over third-placed Brighton & Hove Albion which kept Rangers in an automatic promotion spot. Wes Daly was recalled from Grays due to the non-availability of several players for the game at Bournemouth. Among the injured players were Ainsworth, Bean, Edghill, McLeod and Thorpe, with Carlisle having been suspended. After the surprising 4–0 defeat at Southend in the LDV which followed, Holloway was hoping for an improved performance at Dean Court, and although the team did play better the match ended in a 1–0 defeat. But the biggest blow was the discovery that Dan Shittu, who was injured in the game, had been diagnosed with a ruptured anterior cruciate ligament. It was the same injury that Clark Carlisle had suffered in January 2001 and which kept him out until September 2002. This meant that he would miss the rest of the season and probably at least three months of the next one.

Two more youth players were allowed to join a Ryman Premier Side for vital experience, with Dean Lodge and Jack Perry joining Ford United on loan deals. On the incoming side Jamie Cureton was signed on a free transfer, having been playing for Buscan Icons in Korea since leaving Reading in the summer. Holloway had hoped to sign him before the season started, but Cureton decided at that time to try for a career in the Far East. This did not work out as he had hoped and he returned to the UK at the beginning of the year. His signing was the first deal to be financed by the Our QPR scheme.

Following two successive defeats Rangers were hoping for a better result in the next fixture, but it was not to be as Chesterfield won 4–2. Rangers scored first, through Thorpe, and managed to equalise back to 2–2. Ian Holloway blamed complacency among his team and said he would be addressing the situation during the week prior to the next game.

After Wes Daly had been recalled as cover for the Chesterfield game he rejoined Grays on a work experience arrangement until the end of the season, as he was unable to agree personal terms for a permanent move. Part of the arrangement was that Rangers would not be allowed to recall him again this season. After a successful trial Richard Pacquette joined Mansfield Town on a month's loan.

Rangers continued to maintain their unbeaten home record with a 3–2 win over relegation-threatened Notts County, as Cureton made his debut when he came on a late substitute for McLeod. Rangers remained in second place but were now only two points ahead of Bristol City who had a game in hand. The Ashton Gate side had won their last seven League games to close the gap on the clubs in the automatic promotion places.

In a move to gain valuable first-team experience, Dennis Oli joined Conference side Farnborough Town for a month. Ian Holloway, who was always looking for players to add depth to his squad, gave trials in a reserve game to Paul Warhurst, who had been released by Barnsley and to two youth academy players from Charlton Athletic, Simon Jackson and Darren Beckford.

After a 1–1 draw at Brentford, Rangers held on to second place but only on goal difference. Before Rangers' next game, Plymouth Argyle and Bristol City both played their games in hand, and although Plymouth lost 3–0 at Tranmere, Bristol City won 2–1 to go second and pushed Rangers back into third place. It was the first time since November, a run of 15 games, that Rangers had not been in an automatic promotion place.

More player movements saw Richard Johnson, previously at Watford but recently training with Stoke City, join on a three-month contract, and the return of Arthur Gnohere. Gnohere was signed on a two and a half year deal from Burnley, with the fee being dependent on the number of appearances and whether or not Rangers gained promotion. Dean Marney returned to Tottenham Hotspur, having been restricted to just three appearances due to a hamstring injury suffered midway through his loan period.

Rangers' next home game, against Peterborough United, was chosen for live transmission by Sky and moved to the Friday night. A win would have put Rangers top, but they had to settle for a draw as they nearly lost their unbeaten home record and were only saved by a last-minute equaliser from Gallen. With the game at Tranmere postponed, despite passing an inspection at 11am on the day of the game, Rangers had to watch while their rivals took advantage of their inaction.

The QPR against Oldham game in March 2004.

In the next game, Rangers again scored in the 90th minute, and this time it was the turn of Port Vale to suffer. Vale had scored in the first minute and had thought they had a point after equalising in the 89th, but Jamie Cureton scored his second and Rangers' third to take all three points. Those two goals were Cureton's first for the club, and the other goal, scored by Bircham, was his first which was not scored against Brentford!

More player deals saw Eric Sabin join Boston United on loan for a month, but within two weeks he had signed a permanent deal with Northampton Town. Also leaving was Warren Barton, who signed for Wimbledon before announcing shortly afterwards his retirement from the game. Rangers then had a serious crisis in the goalkeeping area as Culkin joined Day and Cole in the treatment room. Culkin had injured his knee and was expected to be out for six to seven weeks, Day had not resumed training after his injury and young 'keeper Jake Cole had had surgery on his elbow at the beginning of the week. In an attempt to find a replacement, Adriano Basso, a Brazilian 'keeper was given a trial in the reserves at Brentford, but was not taken on. Instead, Lee Camp, an England youth 'keeper, was signed on a month's loan deal from Derby County in time to play in the away game at Hartlepool, which Rangers won 4–1. He nearly kept a clean sheet but 'Pool scored a late consolation goal. Meanwhile, during the home game with Oldham Athletic, which ended in a 1–1 draw, Gino Padula suffered a fractured toe and was expected to be out for six weeks.

Rangers extended their unbeaten run to eight games with a 2–0 win at Wrexham and a 2–2 draw at Wycombe. The game at Wycombe was played in very windy conditions with it being almost impossible to defend into the wind. Rangers played in green and white hoops as both the first and second choice shirts clashed with Wycombe's light and dark blue shirts. Yet more trialists were given opportunities to impress with young Arsenal 'keeper Craig Holloway and Lewis Hamilton, a young Derby County player, appearing in the reserve side.

On 24 March Terrell Forbes was formally charged with the offence of rape and indecent assault on a person under the age of 16. He appeared at Greenwich magistrate's court and was remanded in custody. A remand hearing followed on 26th at the Old Bailey where, along with three others, he was refused bail and remanded back in custody. A preliminary hearing was scheduled for 31 March. David Davies made the following comment: 'This is a terrible situation for all concerned and all we can do at the moment is continue to co-operate with the authorities and offer appropriate support where we can. Naturally, there are internal issues that we, as a club, must confront and we are doing so with regular discussions between the board and the football management. But for the time being, given the highly sensitive nature of this situation, these discussions will remain private.' At the hearing on 31 March Forbes was released on conditional bail and he returned to the club to resume training with the rest of the team.

On transfer deadline day Marcus Bignot was re-signed from Rushden & Diamonds after he had rejected a move to Oldham Athletic to join up with former Diamonds manager Brian Talbot. Bignot's contract was to take him through to the end of next season.

Rangers drew 1–1 at home with Luton and went into the key game with Bristol City with a three-point advantage in second place. The game at Ashton Gate ended Rangers' unbeaten run as they lost 1–0 in front of a crowd of over 19,000. City were now level on points with Rangers, but Rangers' superior goal difference kept them in second place, with a game in hand to play at Tranmere. After this game Rangers announced that Kenny Jackett, Holloway's assistant, had left the club to become manager at Swansea City. David Davies admitted that the club were disappointed to lose Jackett but could not stand in his way. He said, 'Kenny has always been honest with the board and has already stated his ambition to be a manager in his own right. This is an opportunity that he felt he could not pass up and we fully understand and appreciate his desire to take on the role at Swansea. He will be greatly missed by everyone at the club and we wish him the very best of luck for the future'.

Rangers played their game in hand which they drew 0–0 at Tranmere, and Bignot was sent off when he gave away a penalty. Tranmere's Dadi scored from the resultant kick but the referee ordered a retake, which Dadi then missed by hitting the post. Manager Ian Holloway was sent from the dugout for remarks he made to the fourth official during the game.

In recent games players had been picking up a number of cautions or dismissals which led to suspensions. Rowlands had ten yellow cards and would miss the Easter games against Grimsby and Barnsley, while Arthur Gnohere had also received 10 cautions and would miss the Stockport and Plymouth matches. For his red at Tranmere, Bignot was not be available for the Plymouth and Swindon matches.

The Easter fixtures produced a 3–0 home win over Grimsby and a 3–3 draw at Barnsley. Paul Furlong scored twice in each game, including the last-minute equaliser at Oakwell. Lee Camp's loan was extended to the end of the season, including the Play-offs if required. With just four games to go Rangers had a chance to go top if they won their next two games, home to Stockport and away at leaders Plymouth. However, with recent injuries to Padula, Carlisle and Johnson and with Gnohere suspended, Holloway had a selection problem in the centre of defence for the Stockport game and bought in Rose to partner Palmer. With the game ending 1–1, Rangers were unable to take full advantage of the defeats suffered by both Plymouth and Bristol City. Now, with just three games to go, Rangers were still in second place, four points behind leaders Plymouth and just two points in front of third-placed Bristol City.

For the game at Home Park, Rangers had sold out of their allocation of 1,800 tickets and so they arranged for the game to be shown at Harlequin's rugby ground. Padula and Carlisle returned from injury for the match, but it was the home side that won 2–0 and claimed the Division Two

The fans celebrate winning promotion to the Championship.

Championship title. Rangers were now unable to catch Argyle, and with Bristol drawing with Play-off candidates Brighton, they were one point and 13 goals better off than City with two games to go.

On 27 April QPR holdings plc announced that Moorbound Ltd of Leeds had taken a 22 per cent holding of the company's shares, and Gianni Paladini, an Italian football agent, was reported to be the backer of Moorbound and the main decision maker. It was also announced that Azeen Malik had joined the board of QPR Holdings. Chief Executive David Davies confirmed that negotiations were continuing with two parties regarding further investment and commented on the speculation about the arrival of a new rugby club at Loftus Road. There had been stories suggesting that a club based around the local South African community may come into existence and Davies confirmed that discussions had taken place regarding a potential ground-share

Before the final home game the end of season player awards were presented. The winners this season were Martin Rowlands, who won the Supporters' Club and Players' Player of the Year awards, while Kevin Gallen was runner-up in the Supporters' poll and Marcus Bean won the Young Player of the Year award. The Goal of the Season went to Gareth Ainsworth for his first of two in the away game against Rushden & Diamonds.

Although Gnohere was back from suspension for the Swindon game, Bignot still had one game to serve. With Bristol City, Rangers' only challengers for the second automatic promotion place, not playing until the following day, a win was essential to keep the promotion dream alive. Rangers started the game in the best possible way with a goal after just 76 seconds from Rowlands. A long afternoon was endured by the fans as no further goals were scored and Rangers finished their home games with an unbeaten record of 16 wins and seven draws, a goal tally of 47 for and just 12 against. If City lost at Barnsley Rangers would have been promoted, but as it was City won 1–0 and the promotion race had to be settled in the final matches.

For their next game Rangers were away at Sheffield Wednesday as Bristol City faced Blackpool at home. With all their 8,000 allocation sold for the game at Hillsborough Rangers once again arranged for the game to be shown on big screens, this time at Loftus Road, where 10,000 seats were available and only a few remained unsold prior to the game. To be certain of promotion Rangers needed a win, or to at least match the Bristol City result. After 21 minutes City were 2–0 up, leaving Rangers in third place as there had been no goals at Hillsborough. However, after 35 minutes Gallen scored for Rangers and when Furlong added a second three minutes into the second half Rangers were on their way to Division One. Although Shaw pulled one back for the Owls, a Rangers win was confirmed when Carr put one into his own net on 69 minutes to give Rangers a 3–1 winning margin. Bristol City were also pegged back but did win 2–1, which left them in the promotion Play-offs for the second season in succession. Rangers, having finished on 83 points, had gained automatic promotion with champions Plymouth, with Bristol just one point behind. City were joined in the Play-off by Brighton & Hove Albion, Swindon Town and Hartlepool, who edged out Port Vale on goal difference.

The successful season was celebrated with an open-top bus parade to Hammersmith Town Hall for a civic reception with the mayor of Hammersmith and Fulham borough. The route followed Uxbridge Road from the junction with Askew Road, round Shepherd's Bush Green, down Goldhawk Road turning in to Paddenswick Road, down Dalling Road and finally into Kings Street and arriving at the town hall. At the reception the players and coaching staff were presented with the Nationwide Division Two runners-up shield and individual medals.

The leading players for the season were Kevin Gallen with 50 starts and three substitute appearances; he only missed one game throughout the whole of the season. Next were Gino Padula with 42 appearances and Marc Bircham with 41 plus two as a substitute. The top scorers were Kevin Gallen with 17 goals and Paul Furlong with 16. Two other players reached double figures; Martin Rowland with 12 and Tony Thorpe with 11.

The reserves, under the guidance of Tim Breacker, finished in mid-table with an even record of six wins, six defeats and two draws. The side was made up of players that would have played in the Under-19 team, together with a few experienced players who were returning from suspension or injury. As in previous seasons, a number of trialists were given the opportunity to impress the management team, but very few did. The regular players were Richard Pacquette and John Fletcher, with Pacquette the leading scorer with six goals.

Gary Waddock and Joe Gallen's Under-17s had a successful season and finished runners-up in their League. They only lost two out of their 28 League games and ended just one point behind champions Brighton. They had the best attack with 88 goals scored and the best defence with 27 conceded. They went undefeated for the first 19 games and then lost the next two, which effectively lost them the title as the first of these defeats was to Brighton. The regular players were Dean Sylvester, who started all games, 'keeper Patrick Heselton, who only missed one game, and Scott Mulholand with 23 starts and one substitute appearance. The leading scorers were Lee Barnett with 23 goals, Luke Townsend with 19 and Dean Sylvester with 16. The most promising thing from the club's point of view was the numbers from the young squad who were able to progress to the reserve side, while the only disappointment for the youths was the first-round defeat in the FA Youth Cup to non-League side Hayes.

During the post-season internationals Martin Rowlands made his debut for the Republic of Ireland when he came on as a substitute in the 1–0 win against Romania in Dublin. He also featured in the Republic's squad for the Unity Cup Tournament and came off the bench in matches against Nigeria and Jamaica. Marc Bircham added to his caps for Canada when he came on as a substitute in the match against Wales in Wrexham. He was also a member of the squad for the World Cup qualifying games against Belize.

League (Carling) Cup

This season a new name was announced as sponsor for the League Cup, with it now being known as the Carling Cup. The Football League and Coors Brewers, who are owners of the Carling brand name, had signed a three-year agreement. In the first round Rangers were, for the third time in succession, drawn away, this time to fellow Division Two side Cheltenham Town. Since the competition had moved to a single first-round tie, Rangers had not played a tie at home. The game started badly for Rangers when they went behind after just four minutes to a goal from McCann, but Cheltenham's lead only lasted 12 minutes as Gareth Ainsworth equalised after a Furlong shot had been blocked. This came from a free-kick to Rangers which resulted in Furlong being booked for arguing about the distance the wall was from the ball. This has serious consequences as five minutes later Furlong was shown a second yellow for a fouling Duff and was therefore sent off. The home side tried to take advantage of the extra man but failed to turn it into goals. Day made good saves from a number of Cheltenham attempts throughout the second half. Just as it seemed that extra-time, and possibly the dreaded penalties, were going to be required, Gallen rolled a pass into the path of Richard Langley and from a full 25 yards he thumped a shot into the top corner. The remaining four minutes plus the additional time seemed to be endless, but at last the final whistle was blown and Rangers had, after seven failed attempts, finally won a Cup tie.

In the second round Rangers were paired with Sheffield United at Bramall Lane, one of the previous season's losing semi-finalists. As the game was held at Bramall Lane, this meant that once again Rangers had to travel for a League Cup tie. Rangers started the game well against their higher status opponents and had a couple of good chances before they opened the scoring in the 30th minute. The goal came from a move that involved a McLeod run and a Gallen pass to Martin Rowlands, who scored from 10 yards. But Sheffield upped their tempo immediately and caused the Rangers defence some problems. In added on time at the end of the first half another move involving Gallen saw the ball end up with Rowlands to score his and the team's second. At the break United re-organised their formation and in the second half all the pressure came from the home side. They had several chances that were either saved by Day or, in one case, cleared off the line by Padula. However, despite all their efforts, Rangers held on for a well-earned win and a place in the next round.

The third-round draw, which sees those clubs participating in European competitions join in, gave Rangers a long awaited home tie. Their opponents were Premiership side Manchester City, who had two ex-Rangers players, David Seaman and Trevor Sinclair, in their squad. Although still involved in the UEFA Cup City fielded a full strength side. The game began at a frantic pace, with both sides intent on attack. Anelka had a couple of chances for City, before Ainsworth had a shot cleared by the City defence. In the 21st minute City scored a controversial goal on the edge of the area through Wright-Phillips when McLeod, who had been caught by a late challenge, was still getting to his feet by the goalline and was deemed to be playing the entire City front line on side. Before the interval Rowlands and Sinclair both had opportunities for their respective sides. In the second half Rangers continued to take the game to their premiership opponents, with Carlisle, McLeod, Ainsworth and Gallen all having good attempts saved or cleared by the defence, but the best chance came from a free-kick on the edge of the penalty area, which Rowlands put over the bar. City increased their lead in the 76th minute when Wright-Philips scored his second from a quick City counter-attack. Just two minutes later Macken scored a third after a run by Sun from deep in his own half was not halted. Despite further attempts, Rangers were unable to break through a solid City defence and went out of the competition losing 3–0.

LDV Vans Trophy

In the first round of the Southern section Rangers were drawn at home to Division Three side Kidderminster Harriers. This was the first competitive game between the two sides, as Harriers had only been a League team for three seasons following their promotion from the Conference. Rangers made several changes to their normal line up in order to give some players a game. The game started well for the home side, with Oli and Sabin both forcing Brock in the visitors' goal into making good saves, and just before the break a good run and pass from Sabin enabled Pacquette to score from close range. After the interval the game never really got going, with hardly any attacking moves from Kidderminster. The introduction of Gallen and Thorpe lifted the small crowd who had become very quiet. With 10 minutes remaining, a Padula corner was met by Arthur Gnohere, who scored his first goal for the club from just six yards.

The second-round draw again provided Rangers with a home tie, this time against Nationwide Conference side Dagenham & Redbridge. The Essex side contained three ex-Rangers: Tony Roberts, Paul Bruce and Tony Scully. For Roberts, it was an interesting situation as he was at that time the goalkeeping coach at Rangers. As in the previous round, a number of regulars were rested and some reserve players were given a chance in the starting line up. However, after just five minutes Barton had to go off and was replaced by the 'resting' Edghill.

Midway through the first half Eric Sabin had a good run down the right wing, but Roberts easily took his cross. Rangers opened the scoring in the 38th minute from a corner following a fine save from Roberts from a Padula free-kick. Padula took the resultant corner and the ball was adjudged to have crossed the line before being cleared. Dagenham had a couple of chances from their lone forward Braithwaite, but Culkin was equal to them. The game drifted on with neither side showing the enterprise to score. However, with eight minutes remaining McLeod scored with a long-range drive to give Rangers a two-goal cushion. Dagenham responded with an all-out attack and they reduced the deficit three minutes later when Scully scored from a Bentley cross. The real disappointment was the crowd, at just 3,036 it was the lowest post-war attendance for a first-team match.

In the third round Rangers were again at home, the visitors being fellow Division Two side Brighton & Hove Albion. The tie was brought forward and played on the Sunday of the FA Cup second round weekend, as both sides had been knocked out in the first round. The game started brightly with both sides creating chances, and in the 14th minute Brighton midfielder Harding hit the outside of the post with a shot. Four minutes later Rangers took the lead with a strange goal. From a Rowlands corner Steve Palmer headed the ball goalwards only to see his effort wedged against the bar by the Brighton 'keeper, Roberts, who then seemed to fall backwards, releasing the ball, and it was adjudged to have crossed the line before Shittu made sure. In the 23rd minute Ainsworth made a defence-splitting pass to Tony Thorpe, who increased Rangers' lead with a skilful chip over the advancing 'keeper. Before the break both sides continued to attack and Carlisle had a header well saved. At the start of the second half Culkin was again called on to make some telling saves as Brighton went on the offensive. Ex-Rangers loanee Leon Knight did not endear himself to the home fans with his antics and was booked for play acting after going down in the box when a goal-kick had been awarded. Brighton's pressure paid off in the 78th minute when McPhee's shot took a deflection and looped over Nick Culkin, but Rangers managed to hold out for a 2–1 win which saw them progress into the regional semi-final. With two minutes remaining, Matthew Rose received a warm welcome back from the fans when he came on as a substitute for his first competitive action since May's Play-off semi-final.

The Southern section semi-final drew Rangers away to Southend United, with Northampton Town at home to Colchester United in the other tie. Having stated after the Brighton game that 'he was going for the trophy now', Ian Holloway selected a full strength team for the game at Roots Hall. Rangers started well with a couple of chances for Gallen and Furlong; however, after just 12 minutes they were one down following a good turn and shot from Constantine. The rest of the half saw the defences on top and misplaced passes from both midfields, with neither 'keeper really called into action. Rangers started the second half on the attack and had the majority of possession. Chances fell to Shittu and Carlisle from set pieces, but both put their headers wide. It was from a Rangers corner, in the 67th minute, that the game changed. The ball was cleared to Clark, who was well inside his own half when he ran past Forbes and Bircham before scoring past Day with an angled shot. Just two minutes later Rangers went further behind when Broughton fired in a free header from the edge of the six-yard box. The final nail was driven home in the 79th minute when Broughton scored his second and Southend's fourth after Day had parried Cort's goal-bound header. Rangers therefore departed the competition with a performance that was one of the worst seen for sometime, against a team just one place away from a Division Three relegation spot. Ian Holloway said after the game, 'I am humiliated, it is my worse result as a manager'.

FA Cup

The first-round draw gave Rangers an away tie with fellow Division Two side Grimsby Town. It was to be a quick return to Blundell Park, where Rangers had won for the first time just a month earlier. However, due to injuries Rangers started with McLeod at left-back and Sabin and Ainsworth as the wide players. Grimsby began the game with the greater emphasis on scoring and had an early effort that beat Day, only to rebound off the bar. This was followed by another shot, which was well saved by the Rangers 'keeper. The home side continued in the same vein for the rest of the half and Rangers were fortunate to go in to the break level.

Rangers shuffled their formation for the second half but it did not initially make much difference to the pattern of play. They had their first real attack after 50 minutes when Palmer crossed for Ainsworth, who headed just wide. Sabin then had a chance but the home defence blocked it. At the other end Forbes came to Rangers' rescue with a last ditch tackle to thwart another attack. With just 10 minutes to go it looked like the visitors were going to be able to hang on for a replay, but unfortunately for them, Boulding, who had been a threat all through the game, turned on the edge of the box and fired a shot inside Day's right-hand post to give the home side the lead. With no further chances occurring, Rangers went out of the Cup at the first-round stage. In fact, since their relegation they had not progressed through any FA Cup tie.

2004–05

On 28 May 2004 Ian Holloway signed a new one-year rolling contact after agreeing terms with the club. CEO David Davies said: 'We are delighted that Ian has put pen to paper as we firmly believe that he is the man to take this club forward. We are looking forward to the challenge of Division One.' Holloway said: 'I am delighted; it has been a big year for QPR and a big year for Ian Holloway. I felt it was the right job for me, as did the club, and now we can look forward to a new campaign and a new challenge. Again I would like to reiterate this is a business now and we've got a business plan to take us forward. We've got to keep building to get to the promised land of the Premiership but we are a step closer. We have a really good group of lads at the club and now that my contract is settled hopefully we can settle some of theirs. We will sign the players who I think will take us forward'.

Holloway's first activity after signing his new contract was to decide which of the players that were out of contract were to be offered new deals or released. Those he made offers to were Clarke Carlisle, who rejected the terms offered and joined Leeds United on a free transfer; Matthew Rose, who signed a two-year deal; Marc Bircham, who signed a three-year deal; Marien Ifura; Richard Edghill, who signed a one-year contract; Paul Furlong, who accepted a one-year contract; and Richard Johnson, who also signed a one-year contract. After impressing last season, Marcus Bean, who had been at the club since he was 11, signed his first professional contract by agreeing to a one-year extension to his current deal. Although not out of contract, Martin Rowlands was offered and accepted a new three-year deal.

The players released were Terrell Forbes, who was re-engaged on a monthly basis; Steve Palmer, who joined Milton Keynes Dons as player-coach; Richard Pacquette (MK Dons); Dennis Oli (Swansea City); Ben Walshe (St Albans City) and Wes Daly, who had been at Grays Athletic at the end of the previous season. In respect of Steve Palmer, David Davies said: 'The club owes Steve a considerable debt as he came to the club in its darkest hour, and his leadership has enabled the club to move forward, out of shadows. We recognise that Steve still has ambitions to continue playing, and we wish him all the best in his quest to find a new club'.

On the incoming front was Lee Cook, who was signed for a nominal fee decided by the tribunal from Watford; he had had a successful loan period at the club towards the end of the 2002–03 season. Also joining the club was Georges Santos, on a two-year deal, a central-defender released by Ipswich Town, and Lewis Hamilton from Derby County, who had impressed in trials at the end of the previous season and the pre-season friendlies.

At the beginning of June the club announced that 9,789 season tickets had been sold for the **2004–05** season, beating the previous season's record of 9,100. As more were expected to be sold during the summer months the club imposed a limit of 11,300, which would leave approximately 1,500 available on a match-by-match basis. This would enable the club to comply with one of the recommendations of the Football Task Force which was that a number of seats were to be made available to people who cannot afford a season ticket. By the start of the season the number had risen to 10,700, with the 10,000th being sold on 15 June.

Before the start of the season Binatone renewed their sponsorship arrangement for a further two years. This meant that there would be no change to the home shirt for the season. Instead, the club decided on a new second kit of sky blue, which replaced the black design used the season before, and a third kit of green and white hoops that had been used at Wycombe Wanderers.

The board of QPR Holdings announced that there would be no permanent tenants in a ground-share agreement for this season, but that they had agreed terms for one of the 2004 tri-nations rugby league international tournament matches. The match at Loftus Road would be the Australia versus New Zealand game on 23 October 2004, following on from the successful 'home' game for the Australian soccer team played in March 2004.

Before the players returned for their pre-season training, it was announced that, following meetings between the board of QPR Holdings and David Davies regarding the restructuring of the club, it had been mutually agreed that Mr Davies would be leaving the club. He had been at the club for four years and had witnessed QPR's recovery from administration and their resumption of their place in the second level of English football. A week later after another board meeting it was announced that Ross Jones, chairman of the plc, and Nick Blackburn, chairman of the football club, would also both be leaving with immediate effect. Blackburn had been a director since 1996 and chairman for the past three years. He was quoted as saying, 'I have made this decision because I feel that the board has not functioned in a manner that I believe to be correct since April of this year. I also believe that the resignations of David Davies and Ross Jones are not in the best interests of the club'. Ian Holloway also expressed his disappointment at the departures saying, 'I found them to be extremely knowledgeable and very honest. The relationship I had with Nick, David and Ross helped me immensely in achieving our recent successes'. In their places director Bill Power was appointed chairman of the football club and fellow director Kevin McGrath became acting chairman of the plc until the AGM. Returning to the club to take over as chief executive was Mark Devlin, who had held a similar position at Swindon Town for the past two seasons. Mark was previously the commercial and marketing director there and, although a QPR fan, he had left to take up the more senior position with the Wiltshire club. New chairman Bill Power welcomed him back and praised his efforts at Swindon in helping them through their recent financial crisis and hoped his experiences would benefit the club.

Ian Holloway decided that he would not directly replace Kenny Jackett as assistant manager and that there would be no specific reserve-team coach for the new season. Instead, Holloway decided to increase the number of coaching staff and make individual coaches concentrate on specific aspects of training. Tim Breacker would look after the defence, Gary Waddock the midfield, Gary Penrice would take on the strikers full-time and Tony Roberts would continue to coach the goalkeepers. With a first and reserve team squad that was likely to number less than 30, Holloway was keen to foster a unified team spirit between all levels at the club and felt that concentrated coaching from experts in their position would only benefit the players in the long term. Waddock's position as director of the Youth Academy was taken up by Des Bulpin, who returned to club and to the same position he held when Gerry Francis was manager.

Rangers' pre-season included a training camp in Scotland where they played Nairn County and Inverness Caledonian Thistle before returning for a match against Dutch champions Ajax. Other pre-season matches were played against Bristol Rovers and Crystal Palace.

As there were no specific reserve matches the full squad were used in each of the friendlies and during these games a number of trialists were used. These included Lewis Hamilton, on a continuation of his trial from the end of the previous season, Jon Olav Hjelde, a Norwegian international, previously with Nottingham Forest and who had been playing with Buscan Icons in Korea, Serge Branco, released by Vfb Stuttgart, Milos Malenovic, a Swiss Under-19 international, and Ndiwa Lord-Kangana, a Swedish/Congolese player.

The annual report for the accounting year ending May 2003 (the season that ended with a Play-off Final) showed a loss of £3.3 million, compared to a loss of £323,000 the previous year. This was on a turnover £7.3 million (c/f £5.6 million). The most worrying statement was the following under the heading of Going Concern: 'The Directors have reviewed the Group's budget for the coming year and outline projections for the subsequent year including cash flows and forecasts of headroom available against current borrowing facilities, together with other likely sources of cash generation. Following this review the Directors have formed the judgement that the Group does not have sufficient resources to continue operating in the foreseeable future without raising additional working capital.'

The AGM was held on 4 August, with Kevin McGrath acting as chairman for the meeting. The main points to come out of the meeting were:

> As reported, there was a cumulative loss of £4.5 million for the year 2002–03 and there would probably be a loss of approximately the same magnitude for the accounting year of 2003–04. One major reason was an outstanding and as yet unpaid invoice from the Inland Revenue for Tax and VAT of around £2 million.

The proposed resolutions were passed in order to revert the club back to private limited company from plc.

In responses to questions about the ABC loan, Kevin McGrath said that the board were looking very closely at BDO Stoy Hayward's role in arranging the loan that was used to get the club out of administration, as it appears that they were now acting for the ABC Corporation.

A new training ground was being sought by Maurice Fitzgerald to avoid paying rent to London Wasps (Chris Wright).

At end of the meeting Kevin McGrath resigned as chairman of the Ltd Company and was replaced by Bill Power. Power was now chairman of both the plc and the football club.

As an additional fund-raising activity squad number 34 was made available to supporters. The previous season the successful supporter had been the one with the highest bid in an auction, but this season the successful fan would be drawn from a lottery. In order to give everyone the same opportunity the tickets were priced at £10 each. The winner drawn at the home game with Derby was Tony Mulhavil.

The Football League Youth Alliance was formed into two Leagues: Under-16 and Under-18. The rules of the Under-18 League allowed up to a maximum of five over age (Under-19) players to participate, one of whom had to be a goalkeeper. The transitional arrangement was designed to accommodate those clubs who have a number of retained Under-19s on their books who would otherwise have no youth programme to play in. The dispensational arrangement would only remain in place for one season. Rangers had retained only one Under-19, 'keeper Jake Cole. The Under-16s would be coached by Steve Gallen, with brother Joe Gallen continuing to work with the Under-18s.

Rangers kicked-off the newly named Coca-Cola League Championship with a home game against Rotherham United, and just like a year previously Gareth Ainsworth scored after just five minutes. However, there was to be no repeat of an opening day victory as Rotherham equalised and held on for a 1–1 draw. George Santos made his Rangers debut when he came on as a substitute for Bignot after 81 minutes. The next two games were away and a 3–0 defeat at Watford, shown live by Sky, was followed by a 2–2 draw at Sunderland in which Rangers were denied a win when the Wearsiders scored their second equaliser in the second minute of added time at the end of the game. In order to give them some first-team experience, Jack Perry and Wes Daly joined Raith Rovers on a five-month loan deal.

Off the pitch the club's finances were given a boost by the announcement of an investment by New York-based Monte Carlo group Barnaby Holdings. The deal was in excess of £550,000 and saw the group take a 10 per cent stake in the club, with the option for an additional 19.9 per cent. Chairman William Power welcomed Andrea Primicerio, who was to represent the French/Italian investment group on the board. It was later revealed that one of the names behind Barnaby Holdings was Dunga, the Brazilian World Cup-winning captain in 1994.

In the next game Rangers lost their unbeaten home League record which extended back to 22 March 2003, a run of 26 games. The victors at Loftus Road were Derby County, who, with ex-loanee Lee Camp in goal, won 2–0, with both goals coming in the first 15 minutes. Rangers had 'scored' after just 14 seconds but Gallen's effort was disallowed for an infringement against Camp.

In the next competitive game, a Carling Cup game against Swansea City, Danny Shittu made his first appearance after his cruciate ligament injury. It did not go well for him and he lasted only 20 minutes following a robust challenge from a Swansea player.

With a 1–0 win at Gillingham, televised live by Sky, Rangers moved out of the bottom three. The winning goal was controversial as Marcus Bean appeared to knock the ball into the net with the back of his hand.

As a number of players were unavailable for the home game against Sheffield United, Ian Holloway had to shuffle the side around, and, despite a good performance, the visitors went away with all three points following a 1–0 win. This defeat left Rangers in 20th place and just two points away from the bottom. The missing players were Tony Thorpe (ankle), Dan Shittu (knee), Terrell Forbes (thigh), Arthur Gnohere (hamstring), Gareth Ainsworth (leg) and Paul Furlong as his son had been taken to hospital.

With a two-week gap due to international fixtures, there was a large amount of off the pitch activity. Once again the club were forced by the local authority to suspend ticket sales for the next match, against Plymouth. This had happened at every home game since the introduction of a new stewarding company called CES. The authority was not happy with the numbers involved or the level of training that the individuals had received. However, later in the week the restrictions were partially lifted. Chief executive Mark Devlin said it was a situation that must be resolved soon as it was affecting the club financially.

There was also speculation in the media that former Argentine international Ramon Diaz was being lined up as a possible replacement for Ian Holloway. Diaz was a known associate of Barnaby Holdings who held a 10 per cent share in Rangers and had previously been in charge at top Argentinean side River Plate. Rangers issued an immediate denial saying that at no stage had negotiations taken place between the club and Mr Diaz regarding managerial or coaching positions at QPR. At a subsequent press conference which introduced Dunga, the former Brazilian international, and now a figurehead for Barnaby Holdings, Chairman Bill Power announced that the club had plans to extend the stands on three sides of the round to increase capacity to 28,000: a clear indication of the board's desire to stay at Loftus Road.

With the return to fitness of Rose, Gnohere and Shittu, the monthly contract of Terrell Forbes was not renewed and he joined Grimsby Town on a week-to-week basis.

The two-week break seemed to be beneficial as the next three games all ended in victories, a home win over Plymouth and away successes at Crewe and Brighton. The 3–2 win at the Withdean was secured by a Matthew Rose 90th-minute goal and another from Paul Furlong, who had scored in all three games immediately after the break.

Serge Branco was then signed on a short-term contract after being released by Leeds United. Serge had played in two pre-season friendlies for Rangers and he initially signed on a month's deal. He had previously played in Germany for VfB Stuttgart, Eintracht Braunschweig and Eintracht Frankfurt, and was a member of the Cameroon squad that had won the gold medal in the 2000 Olympics in Sydney. Lee Cook's transfer fee was finally set by a League tribunal to be £150,000, with an additional £50,000 payable if Rangers were promoted to the Premiership. As his first-team opportunities were limited at the club, Marian Ifura joined Ryman League side Kingstonian. In a surprise move Des Bulpin was released from his role as academy director. Chief Executive Mark Devlin explained, 'The decision was made on purely financial grounds. His CV is impeccable and he has a history of unearthing players at a number of clubs. Unfortunately, he was appointed as a number of changes took place in the boardroom and we have had to take the very difficult decision to release him due to budgetary constraints.' The running of the Centre of Excellence was now in the hands of Joe Gallen and Gary Waddock, with Waddock also continuing his work with the first team.

The good run of results continued with a 3–2 home win over Leicester City, after being behind 0–2 at half-time. Yet again a 90th-minute winner secured all the points, and this time the scorer of the late goal was Furlong. Leicester had been reduced to 10 men early in the second half when Connolly was sent off for a second yellow after elbowing Santos.

A fifth success in a row was then achieved with a 4–1 home win over Coventry in which Jamie Cureton scored a hat-trick. Furlong scored the other and had now scored seven in the run of five wins. He was the first player to score in five successive matches since Simon Stainrod in September 1983. The run of victories saw Ian Holloway named as Manager of the Month for September. Following Holloway's award, Paul Furlong was named as the *Evening Standard* Player of the Month for September. He was the first QPR player to win the award since Stuart Wardley in November 1999.

Another win, this time at 1–0 at Stoke City, kept the winning run going and helped Rangers move up to third in the table (the winning sequence had come after just one win in the first six games). In a bad-tempered match, Kevin Gallen scored the only goal and Stoke had Taggart sent off for a clash with Bircham.

At the beginning of October another major investor in the club was announced. The latest injection of funds came from Wanlock, a Monaco-based financial and banking institution. They bought shares to the value of £1.1 million, giving them a 20 per cent stake in the club. Announcing the deal, Chairman Bill Power commented on the stewardship of the club under previous regimes. He said, 'Chris Wright still owns 14 per cent of the club, and although he did his best for the club it did not work out. We could pay him around £300,000 for them but that is a month's wages for us and currently not affordable'. Power had already stated his desire to make contact with the mysterious ABC Corporation from whom the club borrowed the £10 million to get out of administration: 'We are paying them £1 million interest per annum and are unable to make any contact with them. This still does not pay off any of the loan, just the interest, so we will have a millstone round our necks for many years to come. The new CEO mark Devlin has had some very unpleasant jobs to do since arriving back at the club and no one likes to see people out of work. But if he hadn't done what he has then the club would not exist'.

Scott Donnelly.

On the field, a club post-war record of seven straight wins was set with a 1–0 home victory over fellow Londoners West Ham United. The only goal of the game was scored by Rose after a series of quick, short passes through the Hammers' defence. The overall club record of eight, set between 7 November and 28 December 1931, was now in sight.

Adam Miller.

Before the next game Holloway agreed a month's loan deal with Frankie Simek, a 20-year-old American defender who was currently on Arsenal's books. He was signed due to the shortage of available central-defenders, as Shittu, Gnohere and Rose were all unavailable through injury.

The away game at Preston was unfortunately the end of the winning sequence when the home side won 2–1, with the help of a disputed penalty for their second goal. It had started well for Rangers when Santos gave them the lead after just eight minutes, but it lasted only a few minutes as Preston quickly equalised. Early in the second half Rangers were lucky when the referee awarded Preston a penalty after the ball ended up in the Rangers net. The spot-kick was missed but the home side were awarded a second penalty a minute later which this time was converted. The game marked the debut of Simek and youth player Scott Donnelly, who came on as a substitute. After giving some impressive performances, Branco had his contract extended for another month. At the same time Richard Johnson was placed on the transfer list, due to his limited first-team opportunities, joining up with former colleagues Steve Palmer and Richard Pacquette when he signed for MK Dons on a month's loan.

A second successive 2–1 away defeat was suffered at Wolverhampton Wanderers in a game played in torrential rain. Furlong missed the game after suffering a groin injury in training the day before. Rangers were now down to fifth in the League, seven points behind leaders Wigan. While Rangers were playing up at Molineux, Loftus Road had played host to a Rugby League Tri Nations match between Australia and New Zealand, which attracted a crowd of 16,750.

At the end of October Tony Thorpe started on the comeback trail in the reserve game at Woking. He scored the opening goal and lasted the full 90 minutes; it was his first game since the beginning of August.

In the next two home games Rangers maintained a Play-off place with a 3–0 win against Burnley and a 1–1 draw with Millwall. Paul Furlong continued his impressive goalscoring run with a goal in each of the games, including the very late equaliser against the Lions.

A boost to the club's financial position came with the announcement that local company Car Giant had secured the sponsorship of the Ellerslie Road Stand. The club also stated that the price of *QPR Live*, the matchday programme, would increase by 50p to £3. It was the first price rise for three years and was due to the increased production and distribution costs incurred by the club and Dunwoody Sport. The price rise would see the number of pages go up by eight to 76 pages per issue.

In the following away game, a 2–1 defeat by West Ham, Gareth Ainsworth returned from injury when he came on as an early substitute for the returning Thorpe. It was later revealed that Thorpe would be out for six weeks with a torn knee ligament. He joined Martin Rowlands on the sidelines, who had been confirmed with a broken metatarsal bone in his right foot.

Another player on the comeback trail was Arthur Gnohere, who played the first half of the reserve game against Aldershot Town. Unfortunately, however, Gnohere was later confirmed as having injured his anterior cruciate ligament in this game and would be out for nine months, thus missing the rest of the season. Following an impressive performance against Rangers reserves, where he scored once and made the other two in a 3–0 win, Aldershot's Adam Miller was signed on a short-term contract until the end of the following season. The fee was made up of an initial £20,000, plus another £10,000 after 10 first-team appearances and the proceeds of two pre-season friendlies with Aldershot.

The next two games saw the inconsistency Rangers had been battling with this season come to the fore. First they inflicted only the second defeat of the season on League leaders Wigan Athletic 1–0 at home, and they followed that up with a 6–1 defeat away at Leeds United. Rangers were 5–1 down at the break, having taken the lead in the second minute. The game marked Matthew Rose's exit from the team with a hamstring injury which would keep him out for around six weeks. With Simek returning to Arsenal after the expiration of his loan spell, Rangers were facing a shortage of experienced defenders. Added to the unavailable list was Padula with a groin strain, also incurred against Leeds, and long-term absentees Rowlands, Thorpe, Edghill and Culkin. With these players unavailable, Serge Branco's month-to-month contract was extended again, this time until the end of December. Rangers had been invited to play in the 2005 Copa de Ibiza summer tournament. It was to be a four team competition and was due to take place between 9 and 16 July at the S.D. Portmany ground. Rangers would be joined by a local select XI and two other Championship sides.

At this time there was speculation linking Ian Holloway to the vacant manager's position at Wolverhampton Wanders, this was initially fuelled by his absence from a training session. It was later revealed that his absence was due to a serious stomach complaint which led him to being kept in hospital for three days observation.

With a hard fought 1–0 home win over Cardiff and a disappointing 1–2 reverse at relegation-threatened Nottingham Forest, Rangers were just hanging on to the final Play-off place. At Forest Adam Miller made an impressive debut and was unlucky to be on the losing side. Rangers' poor run continued with a 4–2 home defeat by high-flying Ipswich Town; their two goals both brilliant long-range efforts from Paul Furlong.

At this time there were movements regarding several players. Luke Townsend, one of the academy players, went on work experience for a month to Conference South side Maidenhead United, while Wes Daly was released early from his three month loan at Raith Rovers as they were unable to afford his wages any longer. Unfortunately, he could not return and play for Rangers until January, as the move was deemed to be an international one and subject to UEFA transfer regulations. Jack Perry had also been at Raith with Daly, but he had returned in October from Scotland and had had his contact terminated by mutual consent. Also on the out-going side was Lewis Hamilton, who, having recovered from his serious knee injury, went on a month's loan to Kingstonian, who were bottom of the Ryman Premier League. He joined up with ex-academy player Giles Coke, who had joined the Surrey side earlier in the season. Incoming was Leon Best, an 18-year-old striker from Southampton, on a month's loan, who had come to the notice of the Rangers management team in the recent FA Youth Cup against the south coast side. Another new recruit was Aaron Brown, who was signed on a non-contract basis having previously played for Bristol City. Another player who was expected to join on a month's loan was Andrew Davies, but Middlesbrough decided against the deal as they needed defensive cover

over the Christmas/New Year period. Completing the player movements was the departure of Richard Johnson, who had his contract terminated by mutual consent so that he could return to his native Australia.

Best made his debut when he came on as a substitute in the televised away game at Reading, but Rangers lost 1–0 and were reduced to 10 men when Jamie Cureton struck out at one of the Reading players, after being conned into leaving a ball by a shout from behind him.

Over the four-game Christmas/New Year period Rangers gained only one point out of the possible 12 and they dropped to 13th place, their lowest League position since the beginning of September. The first match at Plymouth, which ended in 2–1 defeat, saw Santos sent off for two yellow cards in the space of three minutes, and this was followed by a 2–1 defeat at home by Crewe Alexandra, Rangers' fifth successive reverse. In the next game the point-less sequence was ended with a 0–0 home draw against Brighton. In this match Furlong was sent off for striking out at Hinchelwood, and it was Rangers' third red card in four games; although the referee later rescinded the dismissal after evidence from Hinchelwood. The festive period ended with another away defeat, this time 1–0 at Leicester City. Rangers were now nine points away from a Play-off place. An extra game at Loftus Road was the third-round FA Cup tie between Yeading and Newcastle United. As the non-Leaguers' ground was adjudged to not be suitable for the expected 3,000+ crowd it was moved to Loftus Road on safety grounds. A crowd of just over 11,000 saw the Ryman League side give a good performance in their 2–0 defeat by the Premiership side.

In order to boost the defence the club attempted to sign Matt Hill, a central-defender from Bristol City. Rangers had an offer of £100,000 accepted by them, but the bid was matched by Preston North End and the player decided to join the northern club. More player movements saw academy players Lee Barnett and Jake Cole joining Hastings United and AFC Wimbledon respectively on work experience/loan arrangements. Coming in on loan were Simon Royce, from Charlton Athletic, who was previously at the club in the autumn of 2002, and Andrew Davies from Middlesbrough after they had agreed to a new proposal. Two other players to leave the club were Leon Best, returning to Southampton after his loan spell, and Serge Branco whose month-to-month contract was not renewed. Rangers ended their losing run in the next League game with a 1–0 home victory over Stoke City, in front of the Sky TV cameras. The only goal of the game was scored by Lee Cook, and Davies and Royce both made their first appearance of their loan deals.

Away from the pitch Rangers announced the arrival of John O'Brien as youth recruitment officer; he had previously held a similar position at Arsenal and would be responsible for scouring the local area to find some home-grown talent. Another announcement was that a bid had been received by a consortium led by Ron Jones, a former chairman of QPR Holdings. Chief Executive Mark Devlin explained that the current board rejected the deal for a number of reasons. Firstly, there was not enough proposed capital, secondly, it was fronted by a chairman who had been in charge at the time when the club looked like it would have descended into administration and thirdly, there was no consideration of the ABC loan, which continued to be a millstone round the neck of the club. Devlin went on to state that the club had recently placed a bid on a 19-acre site to the west of London to house all training facilities and the QPR Centre of Excellence. He also said that it would appear that Chris Wright's recent offer to sell his shares back to the club had been withdrawn.

Back on the pitch a second successive victory was achieved with a 2–1 win at Coventry City, who had Mickey Adams in charge of his first game for them. The winning goal was scored by Santos in the 90th minute, when the ball was adjudged to have crossed the line by referee Mark Clattenberg, who had recently been involved in the notorious incident at Old Trafford when Tottenham Hotspur were not awarded a goal and the ball was clearly three to four feet over the line after being dropped by Carroll, the United 'keeper.

Off the field, Ian Holloway confirmed that he was having talks regarding a new contract. He was hoping to secure a longer contract to put an end to the speculation regarding his position at the club.

Czech international midfielder Richard Dostalek was training with the club at that time, but, despite interest, he was not signed due to Rangers being asked to pay a fee by his current club, Rubin Kazan of Russia, to take him on loan until the end of the season. These and other conditions prevented Holloway seeing him in a reserve competitive match, so it was decided not to pursue any deal. Two more players were given contracts; firstly, Generoso Rossi, the Italian Under-21 goalkeeper who had previously played for Bari, Palermo, Siena and Lecce in Serie A, was signed until the end of the season. Although the deal was completed at the end of January he was unavailable to play until 15 February as he was serving a ban for his involvement in a betting scandal in Italy. He had come to the notice of the club through Gianni Paladini contacts in Italy. The other signing was a two and a half year professional contract for academy player Pat Kanyuka, who had joined from the Arsenal academy the previous season.

A more important announcement was that chief scout Mel Johnson would be leaving the club in the middle of February to become head scout in the UK for Tottenham Hotspur. During his four years at Rangers Mel was instrumental in the signing of many players, including Palmer, Rowlands, Bircham, Shittu, Cook and Ainsworth.

Rangers' unbeaten run continued with a goalless draw at fellow Londoners Millwall, but it ended with a 2–1 home defeat by Preston in the next game.

Yet more player movement occurred soon afterwards with Wes Daly joining Grays Athletic on non-contract terms after being released from his Rangers contract. Simon Royce's loan was extended by another month until mid-March, although his club, Charlton Athletic, had a 24-hour recall on him. After rejecting a move to Chester City, Kevin McLeod joined Swansea City for a reported fee of £100,000. With him at the Vetch Field was Marcus Bean, who teamed up with his ex-assistant manager Kenny Jackett on a three-month loan until the end of the season. This was in order for him to have some first-team experience as his opportunities at Rangers were limited. In preparation for next season Rangers announced that eight of the second year scholars would be released in the summer. Those being released were John Fletcher, Luke Townsend, Daniel Murphy, Lee Barnet, Andrew Judge, Scott Mulholland, Lee Craig and Sonny Farr, while Ryan Johnson was offered a third year. Other youth players Scott Donnelly and Shabazz Baidoo would begin their second year next season.

However, the biggest news was that Ian Holloway had agreed and signed a new contract for three and half years, taking him up to June 2008. He said that he was delighted with the deal as it gave him, and hopefully the club, the stability required to progress the club further up the football ladder.

After drawing 1–1 at home against Wolverhampton Wanderers, Rangers produced what was probably their best result of the season. They won 2–0 at League leaders Ipswich Town with goals from Furlong and Shittu. The result was recognised as the Performance of the Week by the League Managers' Association.

More loan deals were in the offing with Chris Day going to Preston North End, Lewis Hamilton to AFC Wimbledon and scholar Pat Kanyuka on work experience at Kingstonian; all for a month's duration. In an attempt to bolster the defence, an offer, reportedly for £500,000, for Andrew Davies was made. It was accepted by Middlesbrough, but the club were unable to agree personal terms with the player.

The next two games, both at home, had Rangers moving back up the table with a 0–0 draw with Reading and a 3–1 win over Watford. In the Reading match Les Ferdinand made his last competitive appearance at Loftus Road, but it lasted only 30 minutes as he had to go off injured before the interval. Watford had Gunnarsson sent off after just 20 minutes for deliberate handball, but Gallen missed the resultant penalty. However, he made up for it with two goals in the convincing win.

More players were then signed by Ian Holloway, including Matthew Hislop, an 18-year-old left-back from Arsenal, on a two year contract; former Bristol City winger Aaron Brown, who had spent the season up to that point recovering from a broken leg, on a contract until June 2006; and Simon Royce's existing loan from Charlton was extended for another month, making him available for a further five matches. Leaving the club was Arthur Gnohere, who had been given notice of his contract being terminated due to a series of breaches of club discipline. At the time, he was recovering from a knee injury and the club said that they would continue assisting with his rehabilitation. A player arriving at the club was Andrew Davies, who, having rejected a permanent move, agreed to a loan until the end of the season. He said his reason for not signing earlier was due to him not wanting to move to London and away from his family, but he added that the extended loan would give him an opportunity to try to settle in London.

Two away games followed these changes in the team: firstly a 0–0 draw at Play-off hopefuls Derby County and a 1–0 win over bottom of the table Rotherham United, the goal coming from Rowlands in the 90th minute. Going into the enforced Easter break Rangers were in ninth place, just two points of the Play-off positions.

At Rotherham, Dean Sturridge made his debut when he came off the bench as a substitute. Sturridge's was one of many player deals transacted around transfer deadline day in the middle of March. He was signed from Wolverhampton Wanderers on a free transfer and given an 18-month contract.

Other moves were youth player Ruben Zadkodvitch who, after a successful trial, joined Notts County on a contract until June 2006; Aaron Brown was loaned to Torquay United until the end of the season as part of rebuilding his match fitness; and Tony Thorpe went on a month's loan to Rotherham United. Joining the club was Dominic Shimmin, a 17-year-old centre-half from Arsenal recommended by recently installed youth liaison officer John O'Brien, and Chris Day returned from his spell at Preston. Two welcomed contract deals were those signed by Kevin Gallen and Marcus Bignot, who both extended their stay at the club for another two years. However, there was disappointing news for Gareth Ainsworth who would miss the remainder of the season with a medial ligament strain in his knee, an injury which he suffered in the match at Rotherham. However, he did negotiate and sign a contract extension which would keep him at the club until the summer of 2007.

It was at this time that Rangers fielded what was probably one of their youngest reserves sides ever for the away game at MK Dons. The average age of the out-field players was below 17, with six 16-year-olds, two 17-year-olds and two 18-year-olds, with the odd one out in the starting line up 'keeper Generoso Rossi. At the same time the club announced the signing of some scholars for the following season, including Karl Yelland from Southampton, Andrew Howell from Norwich, Matt O'Connell from QPR Academy and Jon Munday and Ray Jones, who were playing at the club as non-contracts this season.

Rangers' return to action saw them take on League leaders Sunderland at home. After being 1–0 up at half-time, Rangers eventually lost 1–3 in front of a gate of over 18,000. The match saw Adam Miller make his 10th appearance in Rangers' colours, which triggered a further payment to his previous club Aldershot Town.

A home 1–1 draw with Gillingham followed by a 3–2 defeat at Sheffield United virtually ended Rangers' hope of a Play-off place as they slipped to 11th in the League and were 10 points off the all important sixth place, with just five games to go. Against Gillingham, Shabazz Baidoo, at the age of 16 years and 357 days, made his debut as a substitute. At Bramall Lane, Rangers were beaten by a controversial last-minute penalty and were reduced to 10 men in added-on time when Andrew Davies was sent off for a second yellow card, after he was adjudged to have handled the ball on the ground, having been knocked over by a Blades forward. The game also marked the debut of another youngster when Stefan Bailey came on at half-time for Rowlands. Simon Royce returned to Charlton at the end of his loan as they wanted him back for the end of their Premiership campaign.

The club announced the season ticket prices for next season with some prices increasing by over 50 per cent. For example, new prices for the South Africa Road Stand were £514 (c/f £399) for an adult, £262 (c/f £163) for a child and £316 (c/f £200) for a student or OAP. Chief executive Mark Devlin admitted 'that tough decisions had to be made and a considerable price increase was unavoidable.' He stated that this season the tickets were too cheap, as the club had run out of money in January and major shareholders had to stump up the cash to pay the bills. He added, 'what we must do is charge what we believe is needed to fund the club for a whole season. For example, we want to replace the ABC Loan because we are currently paying £1 million a year in interest alone. We have interested parties but they will not do anything with us until they see tangible evidence that the club and business is more financially secure'.

In the 1–1 home draw with Leeds United, Adam Miller became the second player to be sent off in successive games when he was dismissed in the 90th minute for a second caution. In the Supporters' Club annual awards Paul Furlong was voted Player of the Year, with Dan Shittu named as runner-up. After serving his one game suspension Andrew Davies was recalled by Middlesbrough, and as the transfer window was closed a return arrangement was not possible.

For the away game at Burnley, which was lost 0–2, Rangers had 12 players unavailable for selection. There was a serious injury situation at the club with Furlong (hamstring), Rose (hamstring), Bailey (hip), Sturridge (hamstring), Ainsworth (knee) and Rowlands (leg) all receiving treatment, plus long-term absentee Culkin. Santos and Miller were both suspended and new signings Shimmin and Hislop were not yet in full training. Finally, as Thorpe was still in the first month of his loan at Rotherham he could not be recalled. This resulted in starts for debutants Pat Kanyuka and Shabazz Baidoo, and debuts from the bench for Lewis Hamilton, Luke Townsend and Scott Mulholland. The unused subs were Jake Cole and Ryan Johnson, which meant that a total of seven out of the Under-18 squad had made the team selection. In light of the injury situation both Marcus Bean and Aaron Brown were recalled from their loans at Swansea and Torquay respectively.

Two more debuts were also made in the next game at promotion-chasing Wigan Athletic. The game ended as a goalless draw and saw Generoso Rossi start in goal and Aaron Brown appear as a substitute. This meant that eight players had made their debuts in the last five games.

The last home game of the season ended in a 2–1 win over Nottingham Forest, a result which confirmed Forest's relegation to the third level of English League football. Prior to the game Nick Culkin announced his retirement from professional football due to his long-term knee injury, which had kept him out of football for over 18 months.

On a happier note, 36-year-old Paul Furlong signed a new two-year contract keeping him at the club until summer 2007. It was also confirmed by the club that Gnohere's contract had been terminated by mutual consent. His contract, which was due to expire in June 2006, was cancelled in March 2005, but he appealed the decision and an agreement was reached with the assistance of the PFA.

Rangers ended the 2004–05 season with a 0–1 defeat at Cardiff City and finished in 11th place in the League. Despite falling away from the Play-off zone towards the end of the season, it was seen as a satisfactory return to the second level of League football following promotion. At no point in the season were the club looking over their shoulders to see how close to the drop-zone they were.

Captain Kevin Gallen was an ever present, making a total of 49 appearances in the year, and three other players made 40 or more appearances: Marcus Bignot 45 (43 starts, two sub), Lee Cook 45 (40 starts, five sub), Georges Santos 45 (40 starts and five sub) and Paul Furlong 42 (40 starts, two sub). Before his transfer in March Kevin McLeod appeared in 27 out of a possible 32 games, with 21 of them as a substitute. The leading scorer was Paul Furlong with 18 goals (all League), next was Kevin Gallen with 11 (10 League and one Cup) and third in the goalscoring charts were Georges Santos and Jamie Cureton, both with five.

The reserve team, under the leadership of Tim Breacker and Gary Waddock, had a fairly successful season. In this League it is not the result which is the most important factor, it has more to do with how the players played and the overall performance. The Football Combination League sponsored by Pontin's Holidays had a new structure this season and more teams from the Conference joined. The fixtures were arranged strangely with three months between the first two League games, although there was just one Combination Cup game at that time. The best win was the 5–0 away success at Woking, where Luke Townsend scored a fine brace of goals. The heaviest defeat was the loss at home to Aldershot Town, but the 'success' of that match was the signing of the Shots midfielder Adam Miller, who had made two and scored one of the Conference side's three goals. Once again the opportunity was taken to blood some youngsters and to assess some trialists in the games. The most appearances were made by Under-18 players Ryan Johnson (15), Pat Kanyuka (13) and Luke Townsend (11). The leading scorer was Tony Thorpe, who netted five goals from just seven starts.

The Under-18 academy side, led by Joe Gallen, had a successful season and finished second in their League and third in the subsequent Merit Division. They also reached the semi-final of the Football League Youth Alliance League Cup. The only disappointment was a short-lived FA Youth Cup campaign, in which they were beaten by Southampton, the eventual losing finalists. Sean Thomas was an ever present for all 30 games, while Pat Kanyuka, John Fletcher, Danny Murphy and Sonny Farr all made regular appearances. The leading scorer was Shabazz Baidoo with 18 goals from just 16 starts and two substitute appearances. At the end of the season the side was depleted due to the number of players being called-up to the first-team squad, which would probably account for the defeat in the League Cup semi-final. However, with six of the academy players making their first-team debuts during the season, the future of the Academy scheme looked positive.

League (Carling) Cup

In the first round Rangers were drawn at home to Swansea City, which meant a quick return to Loftus Road for Kenny Jackett. Danny Shittu made a surprise return to first-team action following his cruciate ligament injury, but unfortunately he only lasted 20 minutes and had to be replaced as he did not recover from a heavy challenge by one of the Swansea midfielders. Rangers had the better of the game and opened the scoring in the 39th minute when Jamie Cureton connected with a Padula free-kick at the far post. With no changes by either side for the second half, the game continued with Rangers having the upper hand. After 77 minutes Rangers went further ahead when a Gallen effort was deflected onto the post by Cook and Rowlands hit home the rebound. Rangers had a penalty with five minutes remaining when McLeod was brought by Austin, who was sent off, but Gallen missed from the spot as he put his effort over the bar. However, he did score in injury time when he lobbed the 'keeper from the edge of the box, having received a pass from McLeod.

The second-round draw paired Rangers away with Aston Villa, a side they had met before in the competition, most notably in the 1977 semi-final. As before Rangers were away and made the trip up to Villa Park. They started the game well and had a couple of early chances. Cureton had an effort blocked and from the resultant corner Johnson shot over from close in, while Gallen mishit a shot which Sorensen in the Villa goal saved easily. Against the run of play, Villa took the lead when Vassell slotted past Day following a flowing passing move. Immediately McLeod had a chance to restore parity but having successfully lobbed the 'keeper the bouncing ball was cleared by the retreating Villa defence. Just before the break, Villa increased their lead when Angel headed in a Solano free-kick.

At half-time Holloway brought on Furlong and changed the formation to a more effective 4–4–2. His decision seemed to have paid dividends as within two minutes McLeod had scored, following a mix up between Mellberg and Sorensen when the ball rolled towards an empty net. Rangers again had the better of the play and Furlong had two great opportunities to equalise but failed to take advantage on either occasion. Shittu, restored to the side having recovery from his injury, was keeping the Villa attack at bay and limited them to few half chances, but just when it looked as though Rangers would make their possession count, Solano scored with a free-kick which bent round the defensive wall and out of Day's reach to effectively end the game. Overall Rangers had taken the game to their Premiership opponents and were unlucky to lose 3–1.

FA Cup

Following their promotion to the Championship, Rangers entered the competition at the third round stage. The draw was kind to them with a home tie against fellow Championship side Nottingham Forest, who were below Rangers in the table. Rangers went into the game with a much depleted side, as Southampton would not allow Leon Best to play in the FA Cup; Adam Miller was unable to, having played for his old club Aldershot Town in a previous round; Paul Furlong and Georges Santos were suspended and Marcus Bignot and Marc Bircham failed fitness tests on the morning of the game. This meant Serge Branco came in as right-back, Richard Edghill partnered Shittu in the centre of the defence and Kevin McLeod played at left-back. In midfield Martin Rowlands played alongside Marcus Bean in the centre, leaving Kevin Gallen and Jamie Cureton as the two forwards. Another disappointment was the low crowd of just over 11,000, well below the season's average.

Rangers started well and Rowlands had a 25-yard shot saved by Gerrard in the Forest goal. The visitors then had a chance through ex-Ranger Gareth Taylor, but the closest anyone came to scoring in the first quarter was Kevin Gallen's effort which rebounded off the woodwork. Forest took the lead on 22 minutes when Reid scored from a free-kick on the edge of the penalty area, and just three minutes later Rangers were two down when Commons lobbed a shot from 35 yards over Day into the net. Cook and Ainsworth both had good attempts before the break but were unable to find the target.

Rangers started the second half with a succession of corners but again could not get the ball past the last line of the Forest defenders into the net. With 15 minutes remaining, Ian Holloway shuffled the side round and brought on Thorpe and Padula. However, it was Forest who scored again in the 80th minute when Folly's shot from the edge of the area took a deflection to give Day no chance. The game finished 3–0 to the visitors and yet again Rangers exited the FA Cup at the first hurdle.

2005–06

At the end of the 2004–05 season a number of players were released: Chris Day (who joined Oldham Athletic), Jamie Cureton (Swindon Town), Tony Thorpe (Swindon Town), Richard Edghill (Bradford City), Lewis Hamilton (Aldershot Town) and Wes Thomas. These were in addition to the earlier announcement of scholars who were not retained for the coming season. Those concerned were John Fletcher, Luke Townsend, Daniel Murphy, Lee Barnet, Andrew Judge, Scott Mulholland, Lee Craig and Sonny Farr (AFC Wimbledon). Other players to depart were Generoso Rossi, whose short-term contract was not renewed, and Gino Padula, who joined Nottingham Forest. Luke Townsend, who was initially named on the released list, was retained for the new season. Townsend, along with other youth players Stefan Bailey, Patrick Kanyuka, Ryan Johnson, Scott Donnelly and Shabazz Baidoo, was given a first-team squad number.

Chairman Bill Power confirmed that a verbal agreement had been reached with London Wasps, in May 2005, in compensation for the rugby club not returning to Loftus Road. Wasps had decided to stay at their current home of Wycombe Wanderers' ground, which meant that there would be no tenants again sharing the ground with Rangers for the 2005–06 season.

A further off-field financial deal saw Chris Wright sell his shares to chairman Bill Power and donate the entire proceeds from the sale back to the club. The donation was partly in lieu of compensation for the outstanding revenue on the ground-share deal Wasps had for Loftus Road and partly as a goodwill gesture to the club. Bill Power said 'that a substantial amount of money had now come into the club allowing a line to be drawn under the Wasps original ground-share agreement'. He added, 'I believe the club has done very well out of the situation. There are a number of ambiguities in the ground-share deal that could conceivably have seen QPR end up with nothing. Now we have nothing further to do with Wasps, but they were perfect tenants'.

At the end of June the club's funds were further enhanced with the announcement of a £25,000 new commercial partnership with Sellotape, which saw the company's blue and yellow logo placed below the name and number on the back of the home and away shirts until the end of the 2006–07 season. To tie in with the return to red and black hoops for the new season's away kit, another announcement was that of a relationship with D.C. Thompson, publishers of *The Beano*, to have a tie up with their popular Dennis the Menace character. Rangers would be able to market Dennis the Menace items and the comic would feature a story involving the football club.

The annual accounts for the year ending 31 May 2004 were filed with Companies' House. The club made a loss of £4.3 million for the second successive year, with the projected loss for 2004–05 expected to be around £2.5 million. This would be the first accounting year under Bill Power's chairmanship and would show an improvement of £1.8 million on the previous year. The club was planning to break even for the 2005–06 year.

Regarding the ABC loan, Kevin McGrath replied that all repayments had been made on time so far. He added that after five years ABC had the right to increase the interest rate, but that if they wished Rangers had the right to repay or re-finance the loan. Otherwise the loan would run for its original period of 10 years. McGrath mentioned that in the current year (2005–06) there would be an increase in the money received from television rights to over £1 million. In response to a question about the redundancy payment to ex-chief executive David Davies, Bill Power said the club had made the best deal it could in making a payment of £95,000 to Davies.

A welcome boost to the club was the agreement reached with Imperial College London to move the club's training facilities to the Harlington Sports Ground, near Heathrow. The state-of-the-art site

QPR v Aldershot in a pre-season friendly, sponsored by the author, July 2005.

incorporated several full-size pitches, a third-generation floodlight Astroturf pitch and excellent indoor and administrative facilities. Rangers' centre of excellence would also be based there. The site was previously leased by Chelsea until their move to their new facilities at Cobham towards the end of the 2004–05 season.

During the summer break the Professional Footballers' Association (PFA) held their annual golf challenge at St Andrew's, Scotland. This year the event was won by Marc Bircham with a score of 80 points over two rounds. Bircham also won the nearest to the pin competition to round off a successful couple of days.

At the end of the Early Bird Season Ticket renewal scheme the club announced that 8,300 season tickets had been sold. Although compared to last season the numbers were down, the revenue into the club was up by £158,000, due to the price increases involved.

Players moving into the squad included the return of Simon Royce on a free transfer from Charlton Athletic; Ian Evatt, a central-defender, signed in a £150,000 deal from Chesterfield, who agreed the deal in Majorca when Bill Power and Gianni Paladini flew out to meet him on his holiday; Stefan Moore, a forward, signed on a free transfer from Aston Villa; Tommy Doherty, a Northern Ireland international, signed on a three-year contract for a fee of £100,000 from Bristol City; Ugo Ukah, a Nigerian defender, who was signed after impressing on trial in Ibiza and in the Aldershot friendly; Marc Nygaard, a Danish international, signed on a free transfer from Italian club Brescia; and Mauro Milanese, who signed, initially on a month's contract, from Serie A side Perugia. Other good news regarding players was that Dan Shittu agreed a new contract which would keep him at the club for a further three years up to June 2008. Another putting pen to paper was former youth academy 'keeper Jake Cole, who was given a contract up to June 2008.

The pre-season period started with the Ibiza Tournament at the beginning of July in which Rangers were joined by a local Ibizan side, Coventry City and Huddersfield Town. Rangers finished as winners

The 2005 QPR squad.

after overcoming the local side 5–0 in the semi-final and beating Coventry City 3–2 in the Final, with the winner being scored by Kevin Gallen five minutes before the end. Next up was a match at Aldershot Town, which was part of the Adam Miller transfer deal. Other matches were against Iran, as part of their World Cup warm-up preparation, Charlton Athletic and Birmingham City, for Kevin Gallen's testimonial. Not so many trialists were utilised this time as in previous years, with just Ukah, Chambers (West Bromwich), Jamie Vincent (Derby County) and young Aston Villa 'keeper Wayne Henderson being given a chance to impress.

Following the success of the Australia versus New Zealand Rugby League international staged last season, it was announced that this season the Great Britain versus New Zealand Rugby League Tri Nation match would be held at Loftus Road.

The **2005–06** season got underway with an away trip to newly promoted Hull City in their modern KC Stadium. The match, though entertaining, ended in a 0–0 draw and included debuts for Tommy Doherty and substitute Stefan Moore. The game was, unfortunately, remembered more for some of the chants of a small section of the crowd which made reference to the recent bombings in London. Lee Cook, who was injured during the game, was expected to be out for six weeks with a tear to his lateral knee ligament.

Rangers' first home game, the following Tuesday, resulted in a first win of the season when Ipswich Town, who lost in the previous season's Play-offs, were beaten 2–1. Marc Nygaard made his debut when coming on as a sub.

Another 2–1 home win, this time over Sheffield United, saw Rangers go second on goal difference behind early leaders Luton Town. The winner against the Blades was scored in the 90th minute by Stefan Moore, his first for the club. Another player making his debut was substitute Aaron Brown. However, before the game there was allegedly a serious incident involving director Gianni Paladini. He reportedly had a gun held to his head, forcing him to sign a letter of resignation from the board. Police were called and 11 people were arrested. Four of them appeared in court on the following Monday, among them was fellow director David Morris. They were charged with conspiracy to commit blackmail and joint possession of a firearm with intent to commit grievous bodily harm and were remanded in custody until mid-November.

Next up was a trip to Coventry City which was the first match in their new Ricoh Arena stadium. The home side avenged their Ibizan Tournament defeat when they inflicted Rangers' first reverse of the season with a 3–0 win. With injuries to Cook, Santos, Evatt, Rowlands, Doherty, Sturridge and Nygaard, debuts were given to Dominic Shimmin and substitutes Ugo Ukah and Mauro Milanese. There was some good news for Tommy Doherty however, when he was called up to Northern Ireland's squad for the World Cup qualifiers against Azerbaijan and England and would hopefully add to the nine caps he had won before joining the club.

The next two games were both shown live on Sky Sports and saw Rangers gain just one point from a 0–0 home draw with Sheffield Wednesday and a 1–3 away defeat at Wolverhampton Wanderers, as Ian Evatt made his League debut and Gallen scored Rangers' first away goal of the season.

On the evening prior to the Sheffield Wednesday home game the following statement was issued on the club's website: 'The board of QPR Holdings Ltd has decided that Mr Mark Devlin's position as chief executive officer is to be made redundant with immediate effect. Mr Bill Power is no longer chairman of the board but remains as a director. Mr Gualitero Trucco has been appointed interim chairman of the board. Bill Power and director Kevin McGrath do not recognise the validity of these decisions which were taken at yesterday's board meeting in their absence. They are currently seeking legal advice with regards to these decisions.' It appeared that these crucial votes were taken after Bill Power and others had to leave the meeting for personal reasons, and that Dunga (who had not attended any board meeting since his appointment as a director a year ago) was present to add his votes to Paladini's proposal. Dunga was the figurehead of Barnaby, who owned 10 per cent of the club, and Trucco represents Wanlock, who had 19.9 per cent in the club

Gianni Paladini issued a statement in which he said that the recent decisions at board level were made with the club's best interests at heart. He maintained that he was still friends with Bill Power and that they talk each day. He added that it was the supporters who made the club great and he was overwhelmed by their passion and devotion. Paladini went on to say that the investors and directors were ambitious and were going to make steady progress, with the changes being necessary for the long-term stability of the club. He believed that the root of stability lay with the manager and he intended to sit down with Ian Holloway to discuss a new contract.

The following day Bill Power released a statement in which he confirmed his departure as chairman of QPR, after taking advice from his doctor and lengthy discussions with members of his family and the board of directors. He added that he had been considering for a couple of months who should 'take up the baton' from him and said that he was not leaving the club but would be taking a well-earned break. He asked for supporters to give their full support to Gianni, Kevin Gallen and manager Ian Holloway and asked everyone to pull together to get the club through the current situation. At the next regular board meeting Gianni Paladini was appointed chairman of QPR Football Club and QPR Holdings Ltd., replacing interim chairman Gualtiero Trucco.

On the last day of the summer transfer window there was some activity when ex-Ranger Richard Langley from Cardiff City and Steve Lomas from West Ham United were signed, for £50,000 and for free respectively. Marcus Bean re-joined Swansea City on a month's loan and Luke Townsend went on work experience to Northwood. Unfortunately for Luke, his start at Northwood was marred when he broke his wrist just five minutes into his first game, an injury which kept him out for a month.

Rangers' next three games saw them 'break even' with a draw, a win and a defeat. In the draw at Southampton, Rangers took a full away allocation of 3,142 fans who saw Langley and Lomas make their debuts, both of whom came on as a substitute. In the 1–0 home win over Luton Tommy Doherty was sent off for hitting out at an opponent, and in the 0–1 home defeat against Leeds another player was dismissed, this time Healy of Leeds for kicking Bircham.

Another backroom departure from the club was Mark Austin, the commercial and marketing director, who resigned in order to pursue a more normal 'nine to five' job. Three players also left on a temporary basis: Adam Miller on a month's loan to Peterborough United, Aaron Brown to Cheltenham Town also for a month and Ryan Johnson on work experience to Maidenhead United. It was then confirmed that Martin Rowlands would be out for six weeks with a tear to his medial knee ligament, the same injury suffered by Lee Cook earlier in the season.

Rangers gained their first away win with a 2–1 victory at Leicester City, Marc Nygaard marking his first start with his first goal for the club. The winner came from Furlong in the 88th minute, but he was later sent off for a second yellow. Matthew Hislop made his debut in the match, but he did not finish the game due to a serious ankle injury which would keep him out for three to four weeks. In order to cover the lack of available left-sided defenders, Lloyd Dyer was signed on loan from West Bromwich Albion and he immediately made his debut in the 1–1 draw at Millwall. Another televised defeat followed, this time 1–3 to South London rivals Crystal Palace. Rangers went into the enforced two-week break, due to the final round of World Cup qualifiers, in 10th place.

Ian Holloway was fined £1,500 and severely reprimanded by an FA disciplinary panel after admitting a charge of using abusive language and/or insulting words towards a match official. This charge was related to his conduct during the Carling Cup game at Northampton on 23 August.

Marcus Bean's loan at Swansea was extended by another month and youth 'keeper Sean Thomas joined Hendon under the work experience programme. Young player Pat Kanyuka was expected to be out for four months after a double knee operation. He had had surgery to repair damage to his hamstring and lateral knee ligament, which had been damaged in a recent reserve game. As the injury had not responded to treatment the decision was taken to operate, but this meant that due to an extensive rehabilitation programme Pat was not expected to be available again until February.

Back on the field two 1–1 draws followed, away at Preston and home to Plymouth, while in the boardroom Kevin McGrath reportedly resigned from the board of QPR Holdings. This left the board made up entirely of representatives of Moorbound and the two Wanlock and Barnaby consortiums.

An inspired first-half performance against Norwich City gave Rangers a 3–0 win, with all goals coming in the first 45 minutes, their first victory for five games.

After completing his loan time at Peterborough United Adam Miller returned, while Aaron Brown returned from Cheltenham early after being on the bench in recent games and Lloyd Dyer's time at Rangers was extended for another month; mainly due to Matthew Rose having to have an operation which would keep him out for four weeks.

A second successive win saw Rangers come away with all three points from Derby County after a 2–1 success. Rangers were now level on points with the team in the last Play-off place. During the game Paul Furlong was sent off for reportedly kicking out at an opponent and and as a result was out for four games as it was his second red card of the season.

After eight years at the club Phil Harris announced his resignation as communications manager as he had decided to return to his native Norfolk to raise his family and as he added 'to get my weekends back!' His departure led to the restructuring of the communications department, with Jackie Bass assuming overall responsibility for media and public relations, in addition to editing the matchday programme, and with Billy Rice taking over as the club's official webmaster.

Yet more behind the scenes manoeuvrings occurred when, through former Brazilian World Cup star Dunga, Barnaby Holdings increased their shareholding in QPR by purchasing former chairman Bill Power's shares for approximately £1.1 million. They now owned an overall 27.8 per cent stake in the club and when added to the Wanlock shares the two consortia held around 50 per cent of the club equity. Chairman Paladini said that he was delighted and believed it underlined Barnaby's commitment to the club. He added that Barnaby were investing in both the short and long-term future of QPR. He also thanked Bill Power for everything he had done at the club and maintained that although he was no longer financially involved he would always be a big part of the club. In other football-related news, Coors Brewers announced that they had agreed to a three-year extension of their sponsorship of the Carling (League) Cup, therby taking the arrangement through to 2009.

The start of Furlong's suspension period ended in a 1–3 reverse at Watford and was followed by a 1–2 home defeat by high flying Reading. At the start of another two-week break for internationals, Rangers were down in 11th place and just one point from the sides in the Play-off places. At the top Sheffield United and Reading had opened up a gap with nine points between them and third-placed Watford, with Luton a further four points behind. Following them the table was very bunched, with just three points covering the clubs between sixth and 14th spot. At this time Marcus Bean's loan at Swansea was not extended again so he returned to the club.

After the break Rangers did not fare any better and two more defeats followed, a 1–3 defeat at Home Park by Plymouth Argyle and a 0–2 loss at home to Preston. At Plymouth Shabazz Baidoo scored his first goal for the club after coming on as a second-half substitute. The game also marked the return of Martin Rowlands, who had been out for three months with a knee ligament injury.

On the last Thursday in November the loan transfer window closed and for Rangers the only movements were Aaron Brown joining Swindon Town until January and the renewal of Lloyd Dyer's arrangement for another month. The run of four defeats, which coincided with Furlong's suspension, was ended with a 2–2 home draw with Hull City, Ainsworth scoring twice to earn a point after Rangers were 0–2 down just after the break.

The injury list grew longer after the Hull game, with Gallen out for two weeks after suffering a hamstring strain and Santos also out after injuring his left shoulder in the same game. Doherty went for a scan after confirmation that his leg was not broken at Plymouth, and Bircham and Lomas were still two to three weeks away from returning. More welcome news was that Rose and Nygaard had returned to full training and that Shimmin was returning to training within the week.

Mike Pink, the club's commercial and marketing manager, announced that he was leaving to take up the post of head of commercial activity at the new Wembley Stadium. Pink had been at the club for four years in which time he had trebled the turnaround of the club shop and retail operations.

More financial penalties were imposed on the club by the Football League when Rangers were fined £14,000 for failing to control their players in the match at Leicester on 24 September. Leicester were fined £20,000 for their part in the incident that occured in the 20th minute of the match, in which Maybury was sent off for a bad challenge on Furlong. Rangers appealed against the decision.

The next three games saw Rangers break even with an away win 2–1 at Stoke City, a 2–2 draw at Ipswich Town and a 0–1 defeat at home by Coventry. At the end of the Stoke game Simon Royce was assaulted by two Stoke fans as he was retrieving his bag from the net before he left the pitch. At Ipswich the home side equalised in the second minute of injury time to deny Rangers all three points, while in the televised Coventry game Royce was sent off in the 85th minute for bringing down McSheffery. This meant a debut for Jake Cole, whose first action was to face the resulting penalty. With this game moved from the original Saturday date, it meant that from the start of the season to mid-January Rangers had had only five Saturday home games, something that was affecting the gates.

Chairman Gino Paladini announced that Franco Zanotti, a representative of Wanlock, had joined the board. The board now consisted of Paladini, Antonio Caliendo, Carlos Dunga and Paladini's wife Olga. Around this time Rangers avoided an attempt to wind up the company due to an outstanding tax bill for £1.5 million for the period up to July 2005. The current board were unaware of this liability until a letter was received by the club in September. Paladini was able to deal with the matter and the petition was cancelled. Also a preliminary hearing was held at Blackfriars Crown Court relating to the incident at Rangers on 13 August, prior to the Sheffield United match. An application by one defendant to have the charges dismissed was rejected and a trial date was set for the spring of 2006.

Rangers went into the busy Christmas/New Year period of four games in eight days in 14th place, just six points from the Play-off places but also only nine points from the relegation zone. The first game was at lowly Brighton where Rangers lost 0–1 to an early goal, and Jake Cole made his first start as a replacement for the suspended Royce. After the game Lloyd Dyer's loan period expired and following Rose's return to fitness the deal was not renewed and he returned to West Bromwich Albion.

Two days after the Brighton match Rangers recorded a 1–0 home win over Cardiff City. It was a much changed side from the previous game with Rose back from injury, Bircham starting for the first time in two months, Santos and Royce returning after suspension and Nygaard and Cook starting in place of Moore and Ainsworth. The year ended with a 'goal-fest' at Crewe Alexandra where Rangers eventually came out on top winning 4–3, after being 0–1 down, 2–1 up and then 2–3 down, with Langley scoring the winner in the 80th minute.

The New Year started with a 1–1 home draw against Burnley, leaving Rangers in 13th place, five points behind sixth and a healthier 11 points from the drop zone. Off the field, however, there was sad news for all connected with the club with the news that club chaplain David Langdon had died. He had been working with Rangers for 10 years and had been a great source of comfort for players and staff in times of need.

The FA then announced that Rangers were to be charged with 'failing to ensure its players conducted themselves in an orderly fashion and refrained from threatening and/or provocative behaviour'. This related to the incident at the end of the recent game at Stoke City in which Simon Royce was assaulted by a Stoke fan who had run on to the pitch. Rangers' response was that they would appeal against the charge.

More player movements saw Aaron Brown join Swindon Town on a free transfer after a successful loan period at the County Ground, and on the in-coming side were Andy Taylor from Blackburn Rovers on a three-month loan and Marcin Kus from Polonia Warsaw on a six-month loan, with a view to a permanent deal at the end of the season.

The players available for selection for the next game, at home to Southampton, were limited as once again injuries took their toll on the squad. Rowlands had a calf strain sustained during training earlier in the week; Rose had had a scan which showed a significant tear in his oblique muscle; Cole had sprained his ankle ligaments in a reserve game against Wycombe and was likely to be out for six weeks; Gallen was still troubled by a back dysfunction which mimicked a hamstring problem; Bircham was suffering from a neural problem in his right hamstring; Nygaard had resumed light jogging after his calf strain; Shimmin had been for a scan to see how his left groin strain was healing and long-term injury sufferer Doherty had moved into rehab with the fitness coach. Together with the non-availability of Kus, who signed too late the day before, it was to be a thinly stretched squad that took on the Saints. However, Rangers managed to come out on top with a 1–0 victory thanks to a Langley penalty. Late in the second half ex-Ranger Nigel Quashie missed a spot-kick for the visitors, while Andy Taylor made his debut when coming on as a substitute with just over 10 minutes to go.

Chris Pennington, the chief financial officer, announced that he would be leaving the club at the end of February for pastures new. His role was to be taken over by Paolo Mina and the in-house accounts department would be replaced by 'a top London accountancy firm'.

Towards the end of January's transfer window more deals were struck which saw Marcus Bean join Blackpool and Adam Miller join Stevenage Borough, both on free transfers. Ryan Johnson, who was a third year scholar, joined Dagenham & Redbridge on work experience; he had been on a similar arrangement with Maidenhead United since the start of the season. One player to come into the club was Sammy Youssouf, previously with Portuguese side Maritimo, who was given a six month contract.

At this time two financially beneficial announcements were made by the club; firstly that Loftus Road had been chosen to stage a World Cup warm-up match between Trinidad & Tobago and Iceland at the end of February. Secondly, and more significantly, was the announcement that the following season's shirt sponsors would be Car Giant, who currently gave their name to the Ellerslie Road Stand, with the deal being the most lucrative in the club's history, a huge £250,000 per annum.

On the pitch things did not go too well with successive defeats at Luton, 0–2, and at home 2–3 against Leicester City. The most memorable thing about the Leicester game was that four balls disappeared over various stand roofs during the game.

Rangers went back into the loan market and took on two Wolverhampton players, Leon Clarke and Keith Lowe, until the end of the season. One stipulation was that they could not play against their own club in the match later in the season. Luke Townsend joined Woking on a work experience arrangement and was in action for their reserves against Rangers a week later. Then another member of staff announced that they would be leaving the club, this time it was Billy Rice, the recently appointed media manager, who had been at the club for three and a half years.

There were more repercussions to come following the incident at the Stoke away match in December. The Stoke 'fan' who had assaulted Simon Royce was sentenced to a four-month jail term, with another 'fan' given 120 hours of community service for common assault. For his part in the incident, Jake Cole was suspended by the FA for three matches, but as he was out injured he would not actually miss selection for any games. An FA disciplinary hearing fined Rangers £5,000 for 'failing to ensure that their players conducted themselves in an orderly fashion, while at the same FA disciplinary meeting Tim Breacker was warned as to his future conduct for admitting a breach of FA rule E3 of 'foul and abusive language to an official' at the game at Brighton on Boxing Day.

In an attempt to arrest the slide in recent form, Holloway made many changes for the away game at Leeds United. Five players made their debut, including Phil Barnes who was signed from Sheffield United as emergency goalkeeper cover, as Royce was out with an abdomen strain and Cole was another four to six weeks away from recovering from his injury. Other debutants were Marcin Kus, Keith Lowe, Leon Clarke and substitute Sammy Youssouf. With Bignot moving to central midfield, the team had a total of seven changes from the one that lost to Leicester earlier in the week. The game ended in a 0–2 defeat and, with this third defeat in a row, Rangers dropped to 14th in the League.

The day after the Leeds away game the club issued a statement from Paladini, which announced that Ian Holloway had been placed on 'gardening leave', along with coaches Tim Breacker and Gary Penrice. Gary Waddock was appointed caretaker manager and Joe Gallen was named as his one of his assistants. Paladini added: 'QPR has not sacked Ian but we are concerned about recent performances and the effect speculation about Ian joining Leicester City might have on the players. QPR will always be enormously grateful for the contribution he has made over the past five years, in particular gaining promotion in 2004. However, it is critical that the team are focused and able to move forward.' Paladini added that Holloway would not be returning, but that the club would honour the remaining two and a half years of his contract if he did not get another appointment in that time. The following day it was reported that Jim Smith had turned down an offer from Paladini to return to the club as director of football. This appeared to be a change of mind from Smith, who had apparently verbally accepted the role at the end of the previous week. At his first press conference after his appointment Gary Waddock said, 'I am here as a caretaker and just to be given the opportunity to manage this wonderful club is fantastic. I will do it to the best of my ability. My strengths are out on the training ground – training and coaching players. We need another coach and an experience man, which I am working on.' Later in the week ex-Ranger Alan McDonald joined Waddock's team as assistant first-team coach. McDonald was the current Northern Ireland Under-21 coach.

Waddock's first move into transfer dealing was to sign experienced player Paul Jones until the end of the season, as cover for the injured Royce and Cole. Jones had previously been at Southampton, Liverpool and Wolverhampton Wanderers. Waddock also allowed Taylor, Clarke and Lowe to return to their respective clubs before the end of their loan arrangements as he said that he only wanted to work with players contracted to the club. His first game in change was a lively London derby against Millwall, and Rangers came out on top with a 1–0 victory with Paul Jones making his debut. The following Tuesday the new management team had another London derby, this time at Selhurst Park against Crystal Palace, which ended in a narrow 1–2 defeat. In an attempt to stifle the Palace midfield, Waddock and McDonald started with a 4–1–4–1 formation but had to revert to the conventional 4–4–2 when Palace took a two-goal lead. Other bad news was the diagnosis of Rowlands's knee injury as a tear to the medial ligament, which would keep him out for the remainder of the season.

The first away win for the temporary management team came at second-placed Sheffield United, as they took the game to a 3–2 victory, with a key moment being Jones's penalty save.

Two of the club's youth academy players, 17-year-old Scott Donnelly and Stefan Bailey, signed their first professional contracts, both for two years. Other good news was the return to fitness of Kevin Gallen, who made an appearance in the reserves game at Aldershot Town, where he scored twice in a 4–0 win. Paul Jones then became the latest Rangers international player when he played for Wales against Paraguay in the 0–0 draw at Cardiff. Tommy Doherty joined Yeovil Town on a one month emergency loan deal, but his time there was brief as he received a serious ankle injury after just nine minutes of his debut. An MRI scan later showed that he had suffered a syndesomosis sprain of his right ankle, which would keep him out for the rest of the season. In the 0–0 home draw with Wolverhampton Wanderers Stefan Bailey made his full debut, having only appeared as a substitute previously. Simon Royce was back to fitness after missing four weeks and made a return in the reserves game at Crawley Town. Other good news was the return to the squad of Lomas, Bircham and Evatt, in addition to Royce, for the away game at Sheffield Wednesday, which ended in a 1–1 draw.

In mid-March the AGM was held at which the accounts were presented by Chris Pennington, the outgoing chief financial officer. Losses had reduced over the years from £4 million in 2003, £3.4 million in

2004 and £2.5 million in 2005, with projections for 2006 showing a loss of £1.7 million. He added that all (known) outstanding debts, including the tax bills, had been settled. The terms of the ABC loan stated that for five years the interest rate was 10 per cent. After five years there was a break clause, but the clause was not to the club's benefit as ABC could increase the interest rate if the loan was not paid off. A question from the floor was raised on the Gino Padula situation. Paladini admitted that the club had made a mistake in regards to a pre-contact agreement and after Padula's move to Nottingham Forest advisors found a loophole in the agreement which involved the club having to make a settlement payment. A week later on 23 March the club issued a statement stating that all issues relating to a winding up of petitions had been resolved in advance of the hearing. Despite prior resolution of these matters, however, a QPR representative had to appear in court to finalise the paperwork.

On the pitch Rangers continued with two more draws, 1–1 at home to Brighton and 0–0 at Cardiff City, Rangers' fourth successive draw. In the Brighton game Kevin Gallen was sent off for pushing a Brighton player, and the relegation-threatened visitors' equaliser was an own-goal 10 minutes from the end by Bignot. Rangers were still mid-table but the Play-off positions were now out of reach and the clubs below them had closed the gap, making the bottom half of the table very tight; although Rangers were not in too much danger of going into the drop zone as the bottom two clubs, Crewe and Brighton, were a few points adrift of safety. However, with just one point from the following four games Rangers fell to 20th place, but with just two games remaining they were mathematically safe from the drop – but only just. Of these four games three were at home, a 1–2 defeat by Stoke (Ainsworth missed a penalty when 1–0 up), a 1–2 loss to bottom side Crewe and a 1–1 draw with Derby County. The fourth game was a 2–3 defeat at Norwich City, despite having been 2–0 up after an hour. Interestingly, the game marked 30 years to the day since Rangers suffered the same result to effectively lose the (old) Division One title against the same opponents.

Two more of the club's youth players, Sean Thomas and Jon Munday, were signed on professional deals that month. With the season drawing to a close the list of players not available through injury was growing, and for the last home game of the season, against promotion-chasing Watford, Waddock was unable to call on Gallen, Rose, Rowlands, Youssouf, Doherty, Baidoo, Royce and Langley. The match ended in a 1–2 defeat after Nygaard had given Rangers the lead from the penalty spot, and he followed this up by being sent off in the first half for two yellow cards. The visitors' winner was a Santos own-goal.

The final game of the season was at Championship-winners Reading, who needed a win and three goals to round off their season by reaching a record 106 points and scoring 100 League goals. They achieved one of their targets as the game finished in a 2–1 victory for the home side. Rangers had ended the season with a disappointing run of 11 games without a victory.

At the club's annual dinner the Supporters' Player of the Year award went to Danny Shittu, with Gareth Ainsworth named as runner-up. The Players' Player award also went to Shittu and the Young Player of the Year to Shabazz Baidoo. The final award, Goal of the Season, was won by Martin Rowlands for his goal on New Year's Eve against Crewe Alexandra.

With the number of injuries that had occurred throughout the season there had not been much stability to the side. The only two regular players were Danny Shittu, who made 46 appearances, missing just one League game and the Carling Cup tie, and Marcus Bignot, who made 45 appearances, plus one as a substitute. Four other players made over 30 starts: Gareth Ainsworth (33, plus 11 as a substitute), Lee Cook (35 plus six), Paul Furlong (32 plus six) and Simon Royce (32). The leading goalscorers were Gareth Ainsworth and Marc Nygaard, both with nine League goals, while the third highest was Paul Furlong with seven.

The reserve side had a mixed season, but as usual the side was constantly changing and the second half of the season had seen a number of the youth side given first-team games in order to gain valuable experience, with a few of them even gaining full contracts after making good impressions.

The Under-18 side had a successful season finishing second to long-time leaders Brighton in the regional group. A number of the side were playing an age group higher than their age, which was a good sign for the future of the academy. The strength of the squad was shown by the number of the side that made it to the first-team squad towards the end of the season. The highlight for the Under-18s was an impressive performance against Aston Villa in the FA Youth Cup tie, a game they were unfortunate to lose 1–2.

On 18 May there came the news that one of the promising Under-16 players, Kiyan Prince, had been murdered outside of his school, the London Academy in Edgware, when he apparently tried to intervene in a dispute between two other boys. Joe Gallen, the QPR academy manager, stated that Kiyan was a player with a lot of promise and would have had a bright future within the game. A 16-year-old was arrested and charged with his murder.

At the beginning of May the court case began at Blackfriars Crown Court in relation to the alleged incident at Loftus Road prior to the Sheffield United home game in August 2005. The case concerned the alleged threats made to Paladini by fellow director David Morris requesting that he resign from the QPR board, a request reportedly backed with a gun held to Paladini's head by an accomplice. The court heard that Morris and four other defendants (Andy Baker, Barry Powell, Aaron Lacy and John McFarlane) were arrested in one of the club's executive boxes, where £7,000 and the 'letter of resignation' signed by Paladini were found. Another two defendants (Michael Reynolds and David Davenport) were arrested outside of the ground. All seven denied the three charges of conspiracy to blackmail, false imprisonment and possession of a firearm with intent to cause fear or violence. The first week of the trial saw Paladini giving his evidence, followed by former and current members of staff from the club. These testimonies were followed by the case for the defence. On day 16 of the trial Barry Powell was discharged on the instruction of the trial judge due to confusion with evidence of a CCTV tape. After 28 days the jury were sent out to consider their verdicts. On day 30 two defendants, David Morris and John McFarlane, were found not guilty on all three counts by jury. The next day the judge directed the jury to find the remaining defendants not guilty, as the main prosecution case had been built around Morris as the ringleader. Now that he had been acquitted, there was no longer a case to try them with.

League (Carling) Cup

Rangers were seeded for the first-round draw, thus avoiding the other Championship and the top 12 sides from the previous season's Division One. The draw gave Rangers a trip to Division Two side Northampton Town, a return to the ground where they were beaten just four years previously. Due to injuries and the non-availability of suspended Shittu, Holloway only had a thin and inexperienced squad to choose from, especially as the back four had just one first team start between them. Rangers had an early chance when Ukah had a header from a Milanese free-kick, but it was easily dealt with by the home 'keeper. The game continued at a lively pace with Northampton having a couple of good chances, but without really troubling Royce in the Rangers goal. On 29 minutes the home side took the lead when a long through ball hit Ukah on the back as he tried to shepherd it back to Royce and it fell at the feet of Kirk, who lobbed Royce from the edge of the area. Rangers then tried to get back into the game with Gallen and Milanese going close. However, the first half ended disastrously for Rangers when in added-on time Ian Evatt, making his debut, was shown a straight red for bringing down Kirk on the edge of the area. At half-time Holloway shuffled the side around but to no avail. Just after the hour, McGleish increased the home side's lead to 2–0 with an acrobatic overhead-kick. Rangers tried to reduce the arrears and substitute Baidoo and Miller both had efforts saved by the 'keeper. Northampton finished on the up with two more efforts before in added-on time ex-Ranger Sabin was held back by Ukah in the area and he scored from the penalty spot to make the final score 3–0.

FA Cup

The third-round draw gave Rangers a trip to Lancashire to meet in-form Premiership side Blackburn Rovers. Although Rangers started brightly the home side were soon in control and on 17 minutes took the lead when Todd met a cross and headed past Royce from the edge of the six-yard box. Twenty minutes later Rovers increased their lead when Bellamy volleyed home from the edge of the penalty area. Holloway reshuffled the side at the break but Rangers were unable to make any headway against a strong Rovers defence. Furlong nearly took advantage of a poor back header from Todd, but Rovers 'keeper Friedel easily coped with his effort. At the other end Royce was kept very busy with a number of on-target attempts from the home side. Eventually the pressure told and four minutes from the end Bellamy scored his second and Rovers' third when he met Peter's through ball and clipped it over the advancing Royce. Thus, Rangers exited the competition for the fifth successive season at the round they had entered at.

2006–07

On 28 June 2006 Gary Waddock was formally appointed manager of QPR following the announcement by Plymouth Argyle that Ian Holloway had been appointed as their manager. This finally made official the situation regarding the management position at the club since Holloway's 'gardening leave' had commenced in February.

At the end of the 2005–06 season Gary Waddock announced the released and retained list for the new season. The players released were: Georges Santos (who joined Brighton & Hove Albion), Richard Langley (Luton Town), Sammy Youssouf, Marcin Kus, Ryan Johnson (Maidenhead United), Luke Townsend and Dean Sturridge (Kidderminster Harriers). He also placed Stefan Moore, Tommy Doherty, Ian Evatt, Ugo Ukah (Nourese Calcio, an Italian Serie C2 side), Marcus Bignot, Steve Lomas, Matthew Hislop and Marc Bircham on the transfer list. The players retained were Danny Shittu, Lee Cook (who signed a two-year extension taking him to summer 2009), Gareth Ainsworth, Paul Furlong, Kevin Gallen, Martin Rowlands, Matthew Rose, and 'keepers Paul Jones (who signed a new one-year deal), Simon Royce, Jake Cole (who signed an improved contract through to the summer of 2008) and youth 'keeper Sean Thomas; along with youth players Scott Donnelly, Shabazz Baidoo (who signed a two-year deal for his first professional contract), Stefan Bailey, Dominic Shimmin and Pat Kanyuka.

Players joining the club included Jamaican international Damion Stewart, signed from Harbour View on a three-year contract and who had been on season loan to Bradford City; Cameroon international midfielder Armel Tchakounte for £120,000, who signed a one-year deal, with an option of a second year, and who had played the second half of the 2005–06 season at Carshalton Athletic; Australian Nick Ward for £120,000 signed from Perth Glory on a two-year deal (he had won the Australian A-League Rising Star award that year); Adam Czerkas signed on a one-year loan from Polish club side Odra Wodzislaw; and Egutu Oliseh, who signed a two-year contract after he impressed the management team in the friendly against Aldershot Town, having previously played for Belgium League side La Louviere.

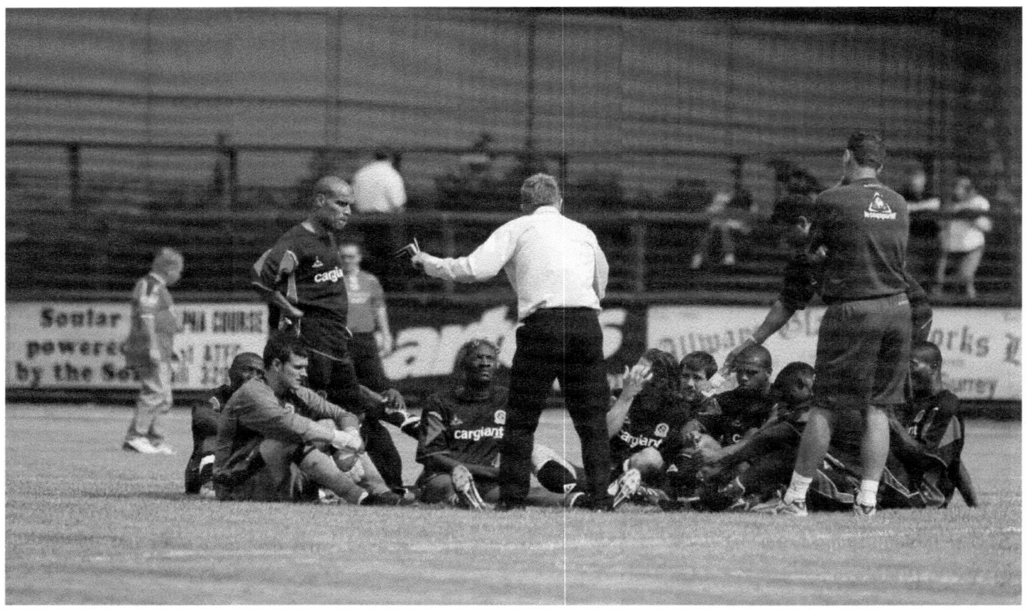

Manager Gary Waddock's half-time team talk at Aldershot, pre-season friendly, July 2006.

Transfers within the backroom staff saw fitness coach Scott Rushton leave after six years at the club and Justin Skinner appointed as reserve team manager after a successful spell as a coach in the academy at Chelsea. Skinner had played alongside Waddock at Bristol Rovers.

On the commercial side Rangers announced that the home shirts for the new season would be based on the red pinstripe design used in the early to mid-1980s with white shorts and socks, while the away kit would be all black with red meshing in the shirts. Both kits would incorporate the Car Giant logo. A new one-year £150,000 sponsorship from G.J. Electrical and Building Ltd and R. Benson Property Maintenance Ltd was also announced. They were to sponsor the home and away shorts for the 2006–07 season, together with the Loft Stand at the ground.

The pre-season preparations started at Aldershot Town, and included games at Stevenage Borough and Gillingham before the first-team squad went on a short break to Sorrento in Italy, with games at Sorrento Calcio and SS Cavese. A few trialists were tried during that period, including Tobi Jinadu against his old club Aldershot Town, but the only one to impress was Oliseh.

The youth side also went overseas and had a pre-season training camp in Edenkoben, Germany, with both the Under-16s and 18s having matches against a South West Germany representative side (SWFV) and Kaiserslauten.

Rangers were for the second time invited to participate in the Masters Tournament and were in the same group as Chelsea, West Ham and Southampton. This year they did much better, finishing runners-up to Chelsea in the Final. The Rangers Masters squad consisted of Tony Roberts, Danny Maddix, Andy Tilson, Steve Palmer, Martin Allen, Maurice Doyle, John Byrne, Karl Connelly and Michael Meaker.

Prior to the start of the **2006–07** League season Carlos Dunga resigned as non-executive director of QPR after his appointment as the new coach of Brazil. He replaced Carlos Alberto Parreira, who had resigned following the defeat by France in the World Cup quarter-finals. Player departures saw

Ian Evatt join Blackpool on a six-month loan, but the biggest loss was that of Danny Shittu, who joined Premiership new boys Watford in a £1.6 million deal, which would rise to £3 million based on appearances and Watford's progress in the season.

The first Championship game was at Burnley and included the debuts of new signings Nick Ward, Damion Stewart and Adam Czerkas. The match finished in a 0–2 defeat and was followed three days later with a 2–2 home draw with Leeds United, with Rangers' equaliser coming in injury time from substitute Baidoo.

After the Leeds game Waddock added three players to his squad: Zesh Rehman from Fulham for £250,000 on a three-year contract as a replacement for Shittu, Dexter Blackstock from Southampton for £500,000 on a three-year contract and youth player Aaron Goode from Walton & Hersham. Rehman and Blackstock both made their debuts in the next home game against newly promoted Southend United, which Rangers won 2–0. One of the goals was scored by Nick Ward, his first for the club. After the first week of the season Rangers were in the mid-table position of 13th with four points.

Gareth Ainsworth signed a one-year extension to his existing contract which would take him through to the end of the 2007–08 season, while in a senior management appointment Graham Mackell was appointed chief operating officer, with a remit to assist the board in improving the off-field activities. At the time of his appointment he was a venue director for UEFA.

In the next week Rangers had a 1–1 draw at Preston North End and progressed through to the second round of the Carling Cup with a 3–2 home win over Northampton Town. The Cup game saw the debuts of youngster Andrew Howell and Egutu Oliseh. In the enforced gap for internationals Rangers had five players called-up at various levels by their countries: Paul Jones (Wales), Damion Stewart (Jamaica), Nick Ward (Australia), Karl Yelland (Wales Under-19) and Ray Jones (England Under-19).

Rangers' return to League action was not a successful one as they suffered a 1–3 home loss to Ipswich Town, in a game that was moved to Friday night for live transmission by Sky Sports. With just one point from the next two games, a 1–1 draw at former manager Ian Holloway's club Plymouth Argyle and a home 0–2 defeat by Birmingham, Rangers had dropped into the bottom three.

More player movements saw Stefan Moore join Port Vale for a month, Tommy Doherty join Wycombe Wanders for three months with a view to a permanent deal when the transfer window reopened at the end of the year, and Pat Kanyuka signing a one-year extension to his current contract, taking him through to the summer of 2008. Following his recent brief appearance for the England Under-19 team, Ray Jones was named in the squad for the Under-19 tournament in Linz, Austria, at the beginning of October.

Two more defeats followed, with a 1–2 reversal at Colchester United and 2–3 loss at Port Vale in the Carling Cup. By now Rangers were holding all the other clubs in the table up, as they were in 24th and last place.

On 20 September Gianni Paladini announced the appointment of former player John Gregory as manager of the club, although Gary Waddock would remain at the club as Gregory's assistant. Gregory admitted it would be a huge challenge, but, he added, 'QPR are very close to my heart and it is a fantastic opportunity.' Waddock said it was the right decision for the club and that he was just thankful that Gianni thought enough of him to keep him as assistant manager. The managerial changes saw the departure from the club of Waddock's assistant, Alan McDonald.

More international recognition for the club's players followed Gregory's appointment with youngster Dean Parrett being named in the England Under-16 squad for the Victory Shield Four Nations tournament involving the four home nations.

The 2006–07 squad.

Gregory's first game in charge resulted in a 2–0 home win over Hull City, which saw Rangers move out of the relegation zone and up to 20th place. Jimmy Smith then joined on loan from Chelsea; Martin Rowlands signed a two-year extension to his existing contract taking him through to the summer of 2009; and Marc Bircham and Marcus were taken off the transfer list. This left three players 'listed', all of whom were at the time out on loan; Doherty at Wycombe Wanderers, Evatt at Blackpool and Moore at Port Vale (extended for another month).

A second successive victory for the new management team followed at Southampton, where Blackstock scored against his old club in the 2–1 win, Jimmy Smith making his debut when coming on as a substitute.

In the two-week gap for internationals, more backroom moves were announced. Leaving the club were reserve-team manager Justin Skinner, head of recruitment John O'Brien, assistant physiotherapist Bobby Baric and team masseur Graham Staddon. Two new appointments were Richard Hill as coach and Joe Dunbar as sports performance coach. Paul Jones made his 50th appearance in goal for Wales in their Euro 2008 qualifier against Slovakia in Cardiff; unfortunately for him, it ended in a 1–5 reverse. Fourteen-year-old Dean Parrett made his international debut for England in the 1–1 draw with Wales at Carmarthen in the Victory Shield Tournament.

Gregory's unbeaten run continued after the international break with a 3–3 home draw with Norwich City, in which Rangers equalised in injury time at the end of the first half and again at the end of the second half; both the goals coming from Rowlands. The good run ended in the next game, however, with a 2–1 defeat at home by Derby County, as another young player, Michael Mancienne from Chelsea, joined the club on a month's loan.

When Gary Waddock left the club after the arrival of Richard Hill, who took over the reserves side, it was announced that this was due to his belief that he did not have the role he initially had anticipated after Gregory's appointment.

The next three games saw Rangers only gain two points, as they lost 3–2 at Sheffield Wednesday, drew 1–1 at home with Leicester and 3–3 away at West Bromwich Albion. Mancienne made his debut at Sheffield, coming on as a substitute. At The Hawthorns Rangers had been 0–2 down and having got back on level terms they found they were now in 20th position in the League. During this time Jimmy Smith's loan from Chelsea was extended for an additional two months which took him through to 27 December, as was Mancienne's.

Rangers were back to their winning ways with a 4–2 home success over Crystal Palace, and the scorers included Lomas with his first for the club. Another three points were earned at Luton with a 3–2 victory; however, the match was remembered more for the comments made by Mike Newell, the Luton manager, regarding female assistant referee Amy Rayner. He later apologised to her but was reprimanded by his club following a board meeting. Stefan Moore returned early from his loan at Port Vale due to an ankle injury, but could return if he regained fitness in the New Year.

The club announced that it had teamed up with Barclays Bank and Deloitte Touche who would provide professional advice on all financial matters relating to the club. This followed the departure of Graham Mackrell, the chief operating officer, after only a few months at QPR Deloitte were to provide an independent review of the business and to address any key business issues requiring attention. After the Australia versus Ghana international friendly, which ended in a 1–1 draw, the Socceroos announced that their next game would also be held at Loftus Road when they would take on Denmark in February.

The next match was at League leaders Cardiff City and was televised live by Sky Sports; it resulted in another win, with Ray Jones scoring the only goal in the 88th minute. Rangers were now up to 14th place and just five points from the Play-off zone. This did not last, however, as all the other sides played the following day and so the gap moved back to seven points. The winning run ended in the next game when Coventry, who had to complete their journey to the ground by underground, due to their coach being stuck in traffic, scored the only goal to beat Rangers. It signalled the start of a poor run as the next four games all ended in defeat as well. First there was a 2–1 home loss to Sunderland, where Furlong made his first appearance of the season as a substitute, followed by away defeats of 3–0 at Crystal Palace and 1–0 at Stoke City, where Rangers were depleted by suspensions for Rehman and Ray Jones and injuries to Cook, Ainsworth, Kanyuka, Shimmin and Lomas. The fifth successive loss then followed with a 1–0 scoreline at home to Wolverhampton Wanderers. Rangers were now down to 20th and just four points from the drop zone.

On the player loan front Smith's deal was extended to the end of the season, but he would be ineligible for the game at Norwich on 30 December as his original loan had to end after 93 days, the maximum allowed under Football League rules, with any new arrangement starting on 1 January when the transfer window re-opened. Doherty returned from Wycombe after his loan period had expired, but he was unavailable for Rangers as he was serving a suspension for his third red card of the season. On the out-going side was Adam Czerkas, whose deal was terminated and he returned to Kolporter Korona SS in Poland.

The busy Christmas/New Year period started with a 1–0 victory over Barnsley, to end the run of successive defeats. However, the next games, both on the road, ended with no points, with a 2–1 loss at Birmingham City on Boxing Day and a 1–0 reverse at Norwich City in the last game of 2006. It was a different story with the first game of the New Year, however, as against Colchester City Rangers started 2007 with a 1–0 home victory, thanks to a Ray Jones goal. With the FA Cup scheduled for the following week, there would not be an immediate opportunity to build on the so far unbeaten League run in 2007.

In the first half of January there were a number of player movements, mostly outbound. The only deal on the incoming side was Sampa Timoska, a Finnish international who joined from My Pa on an 18-month contract. On the outgoing side were Tommy Doherty (Wycombe Wanderers), Sean Thomas (Bristol City) and Kevin Gallen (Plymouth Argyle); all on loan until the end of the season. The club also terminated the contracts of Ian Evatt (who made a permanent move to Blackpool where he had been on loan), Egutu Oliseh, Ugo Ukah (after his return from Nourese Calcio) and Scott Donnelly. Michael Mannicenne's loan from Chelsea was extended to the end of the season and 19-year-old Ray Jones signed a three and a half year contract after reportedly rejecting offers from other clubs. Both Jones and Mancienne were later called into the England Under-19 squad for the match against Poland at Bournemouth. Figures released by the Football League detailing monies committed to agents for the first half of the 2006–07 season showed that Rangers were involved in 35 registrations or transfers. This was made up of 20 new registrations or transfers, 11 updated contracts, one cancelled contract and three loans, and resulted in £187,340 (c/f £131,600 first half 2005–06) being committed to agents.

With their next four away games against the four sides below them in the table, Rangers knew it would be a crucial period in their attempt to pull away from the relegation battle at the foot of the table. The first match was at Hull City in which Timoska made his debut, but it was not the result Rangers wanted as they lost 2–1 and had Lee Cook sent off for two yellow cards.

After the postponement of the FA Cup replay at Luton, Rangers' next game was at home to Southampton. They went into the game with Cook suspended and first choice players like Bignot, Rowlands and Ainsworth out with injuries. The match ended with another defeat, this time 2–0. After the FA Cup exit in a replay at Luton, it was announced that Marc Bircham needed an operation on his lower back which would probably keep him out for the rest of the season.

In mid-January further player movements saw three players leave the club having had their contracts cancelled. These were Mathew Hislop, Jon Munday and Mathew Rose (who joined Yeovil Town). Nick Ward joined Brighton & Hove Albion on loan for the rest of the season and 15-year-old Dean Parret joined Tottenham Hotspur Academy on a student registration as he could not sign as a full-time scholar until July 2008. It was a deal that reportedly could net Rangers £2 million together with a 25 per cent sell-on clause. Joining the club were Adam Bolder from Derby County on a two and a half year contract and Danny Cullip from Nottingham Forest on an 18-month contract. Another player to receive international recognition was Pat Kanyuka, who was called-up by the Democratic Republic of Congo for their match against Gabon, which was played in Stade Jules Deschaseaux in France.

Rangers then lost the crucial away game at Barnsley 2–0, a result which saw them replace their opponents in the relegation zone. The only good news was the return to action for Gareth Ainsworth after being out for two and a half months. However, with a 3–1 home win over Burnley, Rangers moved out of the danger zone up to 19th place.

Before their next League game Rangers played a friendly at the Harlington training ground with the Chinese Olympic team, but the match made the news for all the wrong reasons as it ended in a mass brawl involving players and coaching staff from both sides. A video of the incident was televised in news bulletins all around the world and the most serious injury was revealed to be a broken jaw sustained by one of the Chinese players. Referee Dermot Gallagher had no option but to immediately abandon the game. Afterwards the Chinese sent seven of their players home and their manager made a statement in which he said that he wished to make an official apology and, as team manager, take the responsibility. The Chinese Olympic side were based at Chelsea's Cobham training ground as part of their preparation for the following year's Olympic Games in Beijing. They had previously played a Chelsea XI and were due to finish their three-game schedule with a match against Brentford a week later. Rangers then issued a statement which said: 'Following the incident at the Training Ground on Wednesday 7 February and the subsequent police investigation of the matter, Queen's Park Rangers Football Club have suspended assistant manager Richard Hill from his duties until further notice'. A statement from the Metropolitan Police said that a 43-year-old man had been arrested on suspicion of actual bodily harm and had been bailed to return to a West London police station pending further inquiries. A month later it was announced that Richard Hill would not be facing any criminal changes following his arrest, although following an investigation by the FA the club were charged with misconduct for a breach of FA rule E20(a), for failing to control their staff and players. Rangers admitted the charge and awaited the FA's decision on sanctions. Richard Hill was also charged with misconduct for a breach of FA rule E3, of improper conduct or violent behaviour bringing the game into disrepute.

Back in League action Rangers were next away at bottom side Southend United, a match selected by Sky Sports for live transmission. After the week they had had Rangers could have done without being on the end of a 5–0 defeat, the club's eighth successive away reverse.

In an attempt to bring much-needed stability at the back Lee Camp was signed on loan from Derby County for the remainder of the season, and he had previously been at the club during the 2003–04 season. Camp made his second debut in the 0–0 draw at bottom side Leeds United, a game which saw the home side's biggest gate of the season so far after they had drastically reduced prices in an attempt to attract more people through the turnstiles. The result placed Rangers fourth from bottom and only three points from last place.

Off the pitch Rangers announced an extension to the sponsorship deal with G.J. Electrical and Building Ltd, when they finalised a contract worth £600,000 over four years. They would also sponsor the home and away shorts and would be the main sponsor of the Loft Stand. Youth player Taku Watanabe, who had joined from Crystal Palace in the summer of 2006, had his contract terminated by mutual consent, while there was more movement in the boardroom as the club announced the appointment of three new directors: Nic De Marco, a barrister, and property lawyers Kevin Steele and Jason Kallis. At coaching level Tony Roberts was relieved of his goalkeeper coaching duties at the club.

On the field a 1–1 draw with former manager Ian Holloway's Plymouth left Rangers just on the right side of the 'dotted line'. After a 2–1 defeat at Ipswich Rangers signed Inigo Idiakez on loan from Southampton, initially for a month. He made his debut in the 1–1 home draw with Sheffield Wednesday, which saw the bottom of League get very tight, with only two points separating the bottom side, and Rangers making a drop to fourth from bottom. Despite another draw, this time 1–1 at second-placed Derby County, Rangers dropped into the relegation zone for a day only to move out again on goal difference when Hull City lost 5–2 at Barnsley.

There were some small rays of light at that time, however, as Dan Shittu played his 25th game for Watford triggering another £250,000 instalment of his transfer deal to be paid out, and Rangers managed their first away win for four months when they won 3–1 at Leicester to end a run of seven games without a victory; the goals coming from Idiakez, with his first for the club, and two from Nygaard.

The end of March transfer deadline day saw Rangers only involved with two movements, both loan deals, one in and one out. On the incoming side was Rohan Ricketts from Wolverhampton Wanderers and outgoing was Zesh Rehman to Brighton & Hove Albion. Another arrival was that of former player Warren Neill, who was appointed on a part-time basis to assist John Gregory. The club statement said that he had not been brought in to replace the suspended Richard Hill.

The international break marked the first game to be played at the new Wembley Stadium and Lee Camp played for the England Under-21 side against their Italian counterparts. However, his Wembley career did not start as he would have wished as the Italians scored after just 25 seconds in the 3–3 draw.

On returning to action after the international break Rangers lost 1–2 at home to West Bromwich, a game which included the debut of Rohan Ricketts when he came on as a substitute. A minute after Rangers had equalised they were awarded with a penalty which Furlong missed, and it proved costly as the visitors scored a late winner to keep Rangers just one point and one place out of the relegation places.

In the next eight days Rangers played three games, and it was a run which looked like it would determine the outcome of the season. A 1–0 home win over high-flying Preston was a good start and a successful Easter weekend of a 1–0 away win at Coventry and a 3–2 home win over Luton saw Rangers pick up a valuable nine points in those eight days. In the Luton game Gareth Ainsworth suffered a fractured fibia of his left leg, but Furlong's 90th-minute winner turned out to be a better end to the game. Rangers were up to 18th place and seven points away from the bottom of the table, with just four games to go.

The next game was a trip to League leaders Sunderland, who, not surprisingly, ended up winning 2–1. With teams below them winning, Rangers were back to just four points from safety with three matches remaining. If Rangers won their next match, at home to Cardiff, they could make themselves safe from the drop providing other results that night went their way. Rangers did win, 1–0 thanks to a Blackstock goal, and other results were also favourable – Rangers were now mathematically safe from relegation for the season.

The following week the club announced that John Gregory had agreed a two-year extension to his contract which would keep him at the club until the end of the 2008–09 season. They also announced that Prav Mathema, the club's physiotherapist, would be leaving at the end of the season to take up a similar role at London Wasps Rugby Club. Lee Camp was recalled by Derby County the same week due to them being without a first choice 'keeper after Bywater's three-match suspension, while Inigo Idiakez was recalled by Southampton and Simon Royce joined Gillingham on loan as due to injuries they had a goalkeeping shortage.

The club issued a statement to confirm that following a police investigation and a comprehensive file having been submitted to the Crown Prosecution Service no further action would be taken against the youth-team players involved in an incident at Earls Court tube station the previous November.

With their Championship place secure, Rangers' final two games had little significance and saw them lose 0–2 at Play-off contenders Wolverhampton and end the season with a 1–1 home draw against Stoke. In the Stoke game the referee booked eight QPR players and sent off Timoska for two yellow cards. With the point Rangers finished the season in 18th place.

The end of season presentation of awards saw Lee Cook win both the Supporters' and Players' Player of the Year trophies, while Dexter Blackstock won the Young Player of the Year and Goal of the Season (for his 22-yard strike in the home game against Preston) awards. Aaron Goode won the Kiyan Prince Youth Team Player of the Year, which was voted for by the supporters who attended the youth-team games.

The players who made the most appearances throughout the season were Damion Stewart with 49 appearances, who missed just one game; Lee Cook with 41 games and Dexter Blackstock with 42 games (including two as substitute). The leading goalscorers were Dexter Blackstock with 14 goals (13 League and one Cup) and Martin Rowlands 10 goals (all League); the next highest were Jimmy Smith and Ray Jones with six each.

The reserve side won six out of their 14 League games, but once again the competition was used to give experience to a number of youth players and to give match practice to players returning from injury or those not able to get full games with the first team. The leading appearance makers were Shabazz Baidoo and Aaron Goode, who both featured in 13 games, and the leading goalscorer was Baidoo with five.

The Under-18s won their League and finished unbeaten at home throughout the season, winning 10 out of 11 games. Many off-field factors did not help the consistency of team selection, but manager Joe Gallen and his coaching staff were able to select sides that played to a high level due to their management and coaching skills. Top scorer was Ramone Rose, but towards the end of the season new arrival Angelo Balanta also made a significant contribution. One of the more solid parts of the side was the defence with Aaron Goode and Andrew Howell and 'keeper Goodchild keeping numerous clean sheets. One of the players who made their mark was Dean Parrett, who, after making his England Schoolboys debut, moved mid-season to Tottenham Hotspur in a deal that could be worth £2 million. Regular players were Billy Coyne, who did not miss any of the 22 League games, with Aaron Goode and Matt O'Brien missing just one game each. In the FA Youth Cup Rangers had a quick exit, losing on penalties to Swindon Town in the first round.

The Under-16s again played non-competitive football and won 16 out of 27 games, losing just once at home. Top scorer was Antonio German with 18 goals.

At the end of the season free transfers were given to Marc Bircham, Paul Furlong, Kevin Gallen, Paul Jones, Steve Lomas, Mauro Milanese, Simon Royce and Armel Tchakounte. New contracts were offered to Marcus Bignot and Marc Nygaard, which are in addition to the 12 players with one year and seven players with two years remaining on their existing contracts.

After the season had ended the club issued a statement regarding a loan of £500,000 from Simon Blitz, a director of Oldham Athletic. The club had been in discussion with him concerning the possible re-financing of the ABC loan. After investigation it was found that although the loan was not in breach of the FA or Football League rules, Mr Blitz did not have prior written authorisation from the FA, so the club repaid the loan to him.

The annual report for the 2005–06 season showed a loss before tax and interest of £2.35 million and total loss of £3.34 million. Turnover was up to £9.39 million from £8.75 million in the previous season, playing staff and matchday costs were £6.87 million (c/f £5.78 million) and administration expenses £3.47 million (up £375,000). During the year unsecured convertible loans from directors and other sources amounted to £3.52 million which had kept the club afloat.

On 8 June 2007 the club was served with a winding up order by HM Revenue Services, in respect of unpaid VAT of £700,000 to £800,000, with the High Court hearing scheduled for 4 July. On 15 June, the day of the AGM, it was reported in the press that chairman Gianni Paladini and his fellow directors Antonio Caliendo and Franco Zanotti would be prepared to sell the club for around £4 million, the price they paid for their 62 per cent share of the club's ownership. At the AGM most of the discussion and questions from the floor concerned the financial status of the club. Attempts had been made to refinance the ABC loan at its halfway point, but banks and other financial institutions were reluctant to loan that amount of money to football clubs. The interest on the loan for the remaining five years was to increase from 10 per cent per annum to 11.5 per cent.

At the Football Association disciplinary hearing regarding the incidents at the friendly match with the Chinese Olympic squad the club were fined £40,000 (with £20,000 suspended until 31 May 2008), while Richard Hill was suspended from all football and management activities for three months, until 30 September 2007.

Carling (League) Cup

Once again the draw paired Rangers with Northampton Town, with the game this time at Loftus Road. With an eye on the next League game just three days away, manager Gary Waddock sent out a much changed team, although it was high on experience with players like Gallen, Bircham and Bignot all starting. After a bright opening 15 minutes Lee Cook gave Rangers the lead in the 18th minute with a deflected shot after a long run. Although other chances fell to Gallen, Blackstock and Baidoo, Rangers did not add to their advantage before the break. In the last 15 minutes prior to the interval the visitors wrestled the advantage away from Rangers, who had Jake Cole to thank for keeping their lead intact. Just five minutes after the restart Rangers were awarded a free-kick on the left-hand side of the Northampton penalty area, and Kevin Gallen drilled his shot along the ground with the ball somehow evading all players. Being two down seemed to jolt the visitors into life and they reduced the arrears in the 54th minute with a long-range effort from substitute Watt. On 77 minutes the scores were level when Kirk turned well on the edge of the area and fired in, giving Cole no chance. With just six minutes to go, Waddock made a telling substitution when he brought on youngster Ray Jones, and after three minutes he met a perfect cross from Bignot to head the ball into the corner of the net to give Rangers victory in an entertaining game.

In the second round Rangers were drawn to meet Division One side Port Vale at Vale Park. Four changes from the previous League game seemed to have done the trick as with just nine minutes on the clock Rangers took the lead through Nygaard after he had blocked a clearance from the Vale 'keeper. The visitors continued to apply pressure and were unlucky not to increase their lead when, after a surging run, Cook crossed to Ward, but the 'keeper just got to the ball first. Vale's first attack on 19 minutes ended with Smith hitting a half volley past Cole in the Rangers goal to bring the scores level, while Vale 'keeper Goodlad kept his side in the game with more saves from the Rangers attacks. Just before the half hour Whitaker scored the home side's second after Sodje had hit the post with a header, and after the interval Rangers went back on the attack with Ward having a good chance after a run in from the wing. On 61 minutes Vale had a shot that was deflected round the post and from the resultant corner Walker headed home unchallenged to put Rangers 1–3 behind. With 13 minutes remaining, Stewart shot home from a Cook free-kick to reduce the arrears to one goal. Despite efforts from Bailey and Baidoo in the closing stages, Rangers were unable to produce an equaliser and went out of the competition for another year.

FA Cup

The third-round draw gave Rangers a home tie against fellow Championship side Luton Town. The match started in continuous rain which made the pitch very wet and slippery. Rangers began the brighter, with Smith controlling the midfield and from a Cook cross he had the first meaningful effort on goal. The home side's pressure continued and included the denial of a penalty on 17 minutes when Smith was felled as he went for a rebound off the 'keeper's legs. The visitors then had a chance against the run of play just before the half hour mark but Brkovic's effort went wide. More Rangers pressure resulted in a corner after 32 minutes from which Blackstock headed past Beresford. The lead did not last long, however, as in injury time Vine received a pass from Brkovic and put the ball into the net for an equaliser. Although the rain had eased the second half could not have started worse for Rangers as Luton took the lead when the ball bounced off Feeney in to an empty net in the first minute. Blackstock had a couple of chances to get the home side back on even terms but was unable to finish as he would have liked. Furlong replaced the injured Jones and immediately forced Beresford into a save. With 20 minutes to go, manager Gregory made his last two changes in an attempt to get some fresh legs onto the heavy pitch. Just five minutes later another Rangers corner was headed goal-bound by Stewart, but his effort was cleared off the line and Baidoo followed to score. The Luton defence were up in arms as they claimed, with some justification, that Baidoo had used his hands to get the ball into the net. The remaining 15 minutes saw both sides going all out for a winner, but as neither could score a replay was required.

With the fourth-round draw already made, both sides knew that a victory in the replay at Kenilworth Road would see them at home to Blackburn Rovers in the next round. The first attempt to play the match was postponed just an hour before kick-off due to a waterlogged pitch. The rearranged game a week later saw Cook return from a one-game suspension (which would have kept him out on the original date). The game started poorly, with neither side creating any worthwhile attacks in the first 20 minutes. The first chance fell to Nygaard from a Cook free-kick, but he headed over the bar, and on 30 minutes Smith had a good effort well saved by Brill as Rangers started to take control of the game. Luton did get the ball in the net 10 minutes before the break only to see the linesman's flag raised for offside. Just before the interval Nygaard had another opportunity to open the scoring but he failed to convert Milanese's cross. Rangers had more opportunities after the break with Nygaard, Stewart and Cook all getting close to scoring, but on 72 minutes Rangers were reduced to 10 men when Stefan Bailey was sent off for a two-footed tackle on Brkovic. (After this game, Rangers were charged with not controlling their players and officials following Bailey's sending off. Bailey was also charged with misconduct for his part in the aftermath of his dismissal.) This gave the impetus to the home side for the first time in the match and on 79 minutes Rehman deflected a Morgan volley into his own net to give the home side the lead. Rangers responded by bringing on Ainsworth for his first match since mid-November, but it was to no avail as Rangers were unable to get an equaliser to take the tie into extra-time. So for yet another season Rangers were unable to progress through their first FA Cup tie, which left Luton to face Premier League side Blackburn Rovers live on BBC television the following Saturday.

2007–08

With the renewal of shirt sponsorship by Car Giant for the 2007–08 season, the new home kit was now shirts with a simple hooped design, which carried through on to the sleeves, and a mandarin-style collar, white shorts and white socks with a blue turnover and blue hoop mid-shin with the initials QPR. The away kit returned to the Dennis the Menace-style black and red hoops, with a thin white pinstripe along the edge of the hoops, with the same collar style as the home shirt, red shorts and socks. Alongside the new kit the club agreed a two-year extension with Sellotape for their secondary shirt sponsorship.

Before the start of the season Marcus Bignot was offered and accepted a new contract, while Marc Nygaard signed a one-year extension to his existing deal and Jake Cole signed an extension taking him through to June 2009. New players joining were Chris Barker, signed from Cardiff City on a free transfer; Danny Nardiello from Barnsley on a two-year contract; John Curtis from Nottingham Forest also on a two-year contract; Simon Walton signed from Charlton Athletic on a three-year contract for a fee of £200,000; and Lee Camp, who finally joined the club on a permanent basis from Derby County on a three-year contract for a fee of £300,000. Other players signed were Michael Mancienne of Chelsea, who rejoined on a season-long loan, Ben Sahar, another young player from Chelsea, who joined on loan until January, and Hogan Ephraim from West Ham on a one-month loan. In addition, youth players Andrew Howell, Aaron Goode and Kieron St Aimie all signed their first professional contracts.

The QPR 2007–08 squad.

Players released included Ricky Sappleton, who joined Leicester City, Kevin Gallen to MK Dons, Paul Furlong to Luton Town, Marc Bircham to Yeovil Town, Simon Royce and Steve Lomas to Gillingham.

The main departure was that of Lee Cook, who joined neighbours Fulham in a deal that was initially for £2.5 million, but could rise to £4.5 million depending on appearances. It was later reported that Lee Cook had given 10 per cent of his transfer fee, £250,000, to Rangers. He reportedly stated that as the club had not been paid enough money for him he would give them 10 per cent of the sale. Cook had been a boyhood fan of the club and had acted to help out the club who were struggling financially.

Several backroom staff changes were also made, which saw Joe Gallen, head of youth development, leave the club. In-coming were Mick Harford, who joined as first-team coach, a position he had held at Colchester United the previous season; Paul Parker, appointed commercial and communications director with responsibility for the commercial department and assisting the public relations team; Warren Neill, appointed to the coaching staff on a full-time basis; Paul Hunter, appointed as physio from West Ham, who would work alongside assistant physio Shane Annum and sports performance director Joe Dunbar; while Steve Brown and Keith Ryan joined from Wycombe Wanderers to oversee the Rangers' youth department. Brown was to be youth team manager, while Ryan would be responsible for the full-time scholars' education programme. Also joining was Ed De Goey as a first-team coach and who would be working with the whole squad.

The Football League then released details of payments made by clubs to agents relating to the second half of the 2006–07 season. Rangers were involved with six new registrations, 11 cancelled contracts and eight loans, resulting in £5,000 paid to agents, giving a total of £192,340 for the season.

Rangers had their usual pre-season match schedule against clubs ranging from Harrow Borough and Wycombe Wanderers to the top-flight sides of Celtic and Fulham. Unfortunately, in the Fulham game new signing Simon Walton sustained a traverse fracture of his left tibia which ruled him out of a large part of the season. The same game, which Rangers won 2–1 courtesy of two goals from loanee Ben Sahar, saw the first appearance in a Fulham shirt of Lee Cook.

Just prior to the first League game of **2007–08** Adam Bolder was appointed club captain for the new season. The League campaign started with an away game at Bristol City, which ended in a 2–2 draw. Stewart scored an equaliser in the fourth minute of injury time, after the home side had taken the lead in the 90th minute. The game featured debuts for Curtis, Nardiello and substitute Ephraim. A disappointing exit in the League Cup followed, and, with a 0–2 defeat in their first home game against Cardiff City the following Saturday, Rangers had just one point from their opening two games.

During August a number of developments regarding the current and future financial stability of the club were being reported in the press and referred to by the club. The club were reportedly in talks with three different consortiums about a possible takeover. One group was the consortium led by Renault's Formula One team boss Flavio Briatore, who had made a bid of around £30 million for the club. Other possible consortiums, also of overseas origin, were also meant to be interested and in discussion with the QPR board. It was said that the board had set a deadline of the end of August for any takeover otherwise the club was likely to be placed in administration. The club were £21 million in debt, in addition to the £5 million to £7 million owed to directors for unsecured loans. The Inland Revenue were also owed £1.3 million which was due by the end of August 2007. Confusingly, the club later issued a statement on the official website from Antonio Caliendo saying that the club was not for sale and they were not talking to any interested parties.

On 20 August it was announced that the QPR board of directors had resigned ahead of an expected takeover of the club, reportedly a £22 million deal by Flavio Briatore. Outgoing board members Nick De Marco, James Ferrary and Kevin Steele issued a statement saying, 'We believe the new investment coming into the club will be the most important for years. It will save QPR from the perilous financial position we have found ourselves in and should put the club in an excellent position to move forward.' The statement added that Gianni Paladini and Antonio Caliendo would remain in their current positions. The official website carried a statement from the club saying, 'following recent comments in the press, the board of QPR announces that it is engaged in discussions with a number of parties that may or not may not lead to an offer being made for the entire issued share capital of the company.'

For the second time in 15 months tragedy struck the club when 18-year-old player Ray Jones was killed in a road accident prior to the scheduled away game at Burnley. The accident took place on High Street South, East Ham, and he was pronounced dead at the scene. Police confirmed that Jones was one of three people to have died when a Volkswagen Golf was in collision with a double-decker bus. Two other occupants of the car were taken to hospital, with one seriously injured. The Burnley game was postponed as a mark of respect. Jones had been called-up to the England Under-19 squad the previous season, he had been at the club since he was 15 and had signed a three and a half year contract in January 2007.

Ray Jones.

For the next game, at home to Southampton, all the Rangers players wore shirts with Ray Jones's name on, and the club announced that they would be retiring the number-31 shirt, Jones's squad number, for the 2007–08 season in which he made 34 out of his 36 appearances for the club and scored all of his first-team goals. The match was not the result that Rangers would have hoped for as they lost 0–3. Chris Barker finally made his debut during this game after serving a three-match suspension carried over from last season, while another debutant was Mikele Leigertwood.

Flavio Briatore.

A number of Rangers' players were called-up by their national teams for the round of matches in early September; Michael Mancienne and Dexter Blackstock were chosen for the England Under-21 squad, Daniel Nardiello for the full Wales squad, Daimen Stewart for Jamaica and Sampsa Timoska for the Finnish squad. At the end of the summer transfer window Rangers loaned 'keeper Sean Thomas to Wealdstone for a month and also made a permanent signing when Mikele Leigertwood joined for a £900,000 fee from Sheffield United on a three-year contract.

On 3 September Formula One magnates Flavio Briatore and Bernie Ecclestone unveiled details of a £14 million offer for Queen's Park Rangers Football Club under their company Sarita. Under the deal, the pair would pay £1 million for QPR's shares and take on £13 million of the club's debt. The pair would also loan the club £5 million. The board urged shareholders to accept the deal, saying it represented QPR's best chance of winning promotion to the Premier League 'in time'. Under the terms of the offer Gianni Paladini would remain as chairman but Antonio Caliendo and Franco Zanotti agreed to resign from the board. Mr Briatore said the duo were delighted that their offer had been recommended by the QPR board. 'We are fully aware of the history of QPR and the loyal fan base that it has, and we are therefore totally committed to bringing future success back to the club,' he added, 'Gianni, Bernie and I are all determined to see the club return to the Premiership within the next four years.' (See Appendix for the summary and highlights of the deal.) The club announced that Flavio Briatore, Bruno Michel and Alejandro Agag would be joining the board to replace the departing Caliendo and Zanotti. QPR had been listed on the stock market in 1986, but had hit hard times financially and in 2001 was forced into administration and made in to a private concern.

After the takeover in 2007 Gianni Paladini remained as chairman.

More loan deals involving Rangers were agreed; Aaron Goode joined Kingstonian on a three-month agreement and Ephraim's loan from West Ham was extended for another month until 8 October.

On the pitch, however, things did not improve and the next three games saw just two points gained. A 1–1 draw at Leicester was followed by another home defeat, this time 0–2 by Plymouth Argyle. A better result was the 1–1 home draw with leaders Watford, a match which marked the return to action for Gareth Ainsworth. With the next game, away at West Bromwich, being televised live by Sky Sports, the fans were hoping for a improved performance, especially as their last televised game had been the 5–0 defeat at Southend the previous season. This time Rangers did manage to score but did concede five goals again. The 5–1 reverse put Rangers at the bottom of the League.

The day after the defeat at The Hawthorns John Gregory was sacked and his number two Mick Harford was appointed as caretaker manager. When Gregory had been appointed, just a year earlier, the club were bottom of the League and following the West Bromwich defeat they now found themselves in the same position. Harford immediately moved to bring players to the club, with the loan signings of Jason Jarrett from Preston North End, with a view to a permanent deal in the January transfer window, and Rowan Vine on an initial month deal from Birmingham City. Another 'signing' was made when Dexter Blackstock extended his existing contract by a year taking him through to summer 2010. Ephraim's loan from West Ham was yet again extended by another month and he was joined at the club by another loanee when Martin Cranie of Portsmouth signed a three-month agreement. On the downside, Blackstock had a knee operation that was expected to keep him sidelined for six weeks.

Harford's first game in charge was at Colchester United, the club he left in the summer to join Rangers, but it was not a successful beginning as Rangers lost 4–2. Jarrett and Vine, who scored Rangers' second goal, both made their debuts during the game.

Another televised game, this time at home to Norwich City, saw Rangers gain their first win of the season (in their ninth game). Cranie made his debut in a game in which the only goal came from a Rowland's penalty. The 1–0 win was not enough to take them off the bottom, however, as they needed a two-goal winning margin to overtake Sheffield Wednesday.

Rangers had to wait to extend their 'unbeaten' run as there was another break for international matches. This gave a few players some time to continue their recovery from various injuries. Mancienne had started training after six weeks off with a hamstring/back injury; Barker used the break to have a hernia operation in Germany and planned to be ready for the next game; Blackstock was recovering from his operation to repair a tear in knee cartilage; Nardiello had the same injury as Mancienne but was not yet training; Walton's fracture was healing well, but there was no estimate as to his return to full training; Kanyuka, who had suffered a thigh injury in pre-season, hoped to be training within four weeks; and Nygaard had a calf injury and was expected to be training within two weeks.

It was announced that the result of the offer by Sarita resulted in valid acceptances of 45.76 per cent of the shares by the deadline date; this was in addition to the 19.9 per cent already owned by Sarita. An unconditional offer was made for the remaining shares at the offer price of 1p per share.

Out of the boardroom, yet more loans were arranged which saw Stefan Bailey join Oxford United for a month and Tommy Doherty join Wycombe Wanderers on an emergency loan agreement until January. An international call-up meant that Zesh Rehman joined the Pakistan squad for their two-leg Asian group World Cup qualifier against Iraq.

Once back in action Rangers managed two successive draws, 1–1 at home to Ipswich Town and 0–0 away at Preston North End, where Camp saved a penalty in the first half. These results were not enough to see Rangers off the bottom of the League but they had managed to close the gap on the teams above them.

Rangers were televised once again in the London derby against Charlton Athletic at the Valley, their third appearance on Sky within a month. The game ended in a 1–0 win for the visitors and Rangers were off the bottom, albeit by just one place, and were on a run of four games unbeaten, having conceded just one goal in that time.

Two days later the club announced the appointment of Luigi De Canio as first-team coach, on a contract through to the end of the 2009–10 season. He had previously been in charge at Udinese, Napoli, Reggina, Genoa and most recently Siena in Serie A. Mick Harford decided to leave after being offered a coaching position in the new structure which he did not feel able to accept, while also leaving the club was coach Warren Neill. De Canio appointed fellow Italians Iuri Bartoli as assistant manager, Paolo Pavese as fitness coach, Franco Ceravolo as chief scout and Filippo Orlando as first-team scout, all of whom had worked with him at Siena. The first signing under the new management team was Akos Buzsaky, a Hungarian international on a two-month loan from Plymouth Argyle, who was allocated the vacant number-10 shirt. On the out-going side was Kieran St Aimie, who joined Oxford United on a loan deal.

De Canio's first game in charge was the home match with Hull City which ended in a 2–0 victory for the Hoops and marked the debut of Buzsaky. Coincidentally, John Gregory's first game as manager a year previously had also been a 2–0 home win over Hull City. Another move in the loan market saw Scott Sinclair join on a month's deal from Chelsea.

Three days after the Hull match Rangers faced another home game but this time they lost 1–2 to Coventry City, who scored their winner in added-on time at the end of the game. It was not a good game for Rangers, as, although Sinclair made his debut, loanee Cranie suffered a fractured tibia (and returned to Portsmouth for rehabilitation), Leigertwood received a kick in the face which broke his nose and Nygaard pulled a hamstrin, with all the injuries coming in the first half.

Vine's loan was extended to 1 January, but Ephraim's loan was not renewed and he returned to West Ham United. Going out on loan was Marcus Bignot, who joined Millwall for an initial period of one month. Away from the playing side Paul Parker was sacked from his position as commercial director.

In the second half of November the revolving door for players was still firmly in use. Both Bailey and St Aimie returned from their spells at Oxford United, Bob Malcolm joined from Derby County until the New Year, Dominic Shimmin went to AFC Bournemouth for a month, while Shabazz Baidoo went to Gillingham until the New Year. Also on the outward path was Danny Cullip, whose contract was terminated by mutual agreement and he joined Gillingham in the New Year. In this period Rangers had three games, but only managed two points, with draws at Crystal Palace and at home with Sheffield Wednesday, where Malcolm made his debut. The other match ended in a 1–3 defeat at Stoke, where Blackstock was sent off. This left Rangers in 22nd place, still within the dangerous relegation zone.

Two more defeats followed, 0–1 away at Blackpool and 1–2 by Crystal Palace at home, which left Rangers bottom of the League. In the Palace game Antonio Balanta, one of the youth academy players, made his debut after impressing the management team in recent reserve games. More player activity saw Nick Ward's contract cancelled and he returned to his native Australia to join Melbourne Victory, Matthew Hislop joined Harrow Borough, while Chris Arthur and Reece Crowther, two of the Under-18s, went out on work experience at Hayes & Yeading and Wealdstone respectively. John Curtis was another to have his contract cancelled by mutual agreement, while Aaron Goode returned from his loan at Kingstonian and Dominic Shimmin curtailed his loan at AFC Bournemouth and was reported to be training with Gillingham. Ed de Goey, who had added goalkeeping coaching to his duties, left the club. Back on the pitch, Rangers had two away games and drew 2–2 at Scunthorpe United and won 2–0 at Burnley, a game which marked the debut of Simon Walton after recovering from the broken leg he received in pre-season.

Following the 0–0 home draw with Wolverhampton Wanderers, Sinclair and Sahar both ended their loans at the club and returned to Chelsea, while Franco Cerevolo resigned as chief scout.

Amit Bhatia.

On 20 December it was announced that Lakshmi Mittal, a wealthy Indian steel magnate, had taken a 20 per cent shareholding in QPR Holdings Ltd, making him a significant shareholder along with Flavio Briatore and Bernie Ecclestone. His son-in-law, Amit Bhatia, would have a seat on the board. With Mittal joining the shareholders, the club soon became known as the richest club in the world, due to the combined wealth of its three main backers.

Over the Christmas/New Year period Rangers played four games which resulted in three wins and a defeat. First was a 2–0 home win over Colchester United which, despite having Stewart dismissed for two bookable offences, lifted Rangers out of the danger zone to 24 points. This was followed by a 1–2 defeat at Plymouth, where the home side scored the wining goal in the 94th minute. The referee showed seven yellow cards to Rangers' players during the game and sent off Leigertwood after the match, which resulted in a four-game ban. Next was a 4–2 away win at early season table-toppers Watford, and the festive season ended with a New Year's Day 3–1 home win over Leicester City. Rangers were now up to 18th place and due to the tightness of the League only nine points from a Play-off place.

In the New Year's Honours list ex-QPR player Ivor Powell was awarded an MBE for services to football. Ivor, then aged 91, still helped out with the coaching at Team Bath at Bath University, and was recognised by the *Guinness Book of World Records* as the oldest working football coach in the world.

When the January transfer window opened the player movements, both in and out, went into overdrive. On the incoming side deals were made with Kieron Lee arriving from Manchester United on a six-month loan; Gavin Mahon from Watford for £200,000; Rowan Vine signed a four and half year deal to make his transfer from Birmingham City into a permanent deal for £1 million; Hogan Ephraim returned from West Ham United for £800,000 on a three and a half year contract; Matthew Connolly joined, also on a three and a half year contract, from Arsenal for £1 million; Akos Buzsaky made his move permanent from Plymouth Argyle for a fee of £500,000 with a two and a half year contract; Patrick Agyemang from Preston North End for £350,000 on a four and a half year deal; Fitz Hall from Wigan Athletic also on a four and a half year contract for £700,000; and Damien Delaney from Hull City for an initial £600,000 on a three and a half year contract. After making a good start to his first-team career, Antonio Balanta signed his first professional contract, which ran through to the summer of 2010.

On the outgoing side were Bob Malcolm, who returned to Derby County at the end of his loan spell; Tommy Doherty, who had his contract cancelled and joined Wycombe Wanderers where he had been on loan; and Marcus Bignot, who went to Millwall on a free transfer. The contracts were also cancelled of Shabazz Baidoo, who joined Dagenham & Redbridge; Kieron St Aimie (Barnet); Pat Kanyuka (Swindon Town); Marc Nygaard (returned to Denmark); Stefan Moore (who trialled for Melbourne Victory) and Dominic Shimmin (Crawley Town). Going out on loan were Daniel Nardiello, who went to former club Barnsley until the end of the season, and Simon Walton who went to Hull City, initially for a month, but with the possibility of an extension until the end of the season. Zesh Rehman and Stefan Bailey remained at the club but were placed on the transfer list.

The backroom staff were augmented by Ali Russell, who was appointed deputy managing director. He joined from Heart of Midlothian where he had been commercial director and would take on a similar role at Rangers where he would also be commercial and marketing director, working alongside

David Orman, who had been appointed his deputy. Another new face was John MacDonald, who was appointed stadium director.

Back on the pitch the FA Cup campaign was again short-lived with a 0–1 defeat at neighbours Chelsea, a match that some of the press billed as being between the two richest clubs in the world.

Back in the League, January saw just three games in which Rangers gained only one victory. The first match was a 1–2 loss at Sheffield United, and a week later a home 2–0 win over Barnsley, in which Delaney made his debut, saw Rangers back up to 17th place, and the month ended with a 1–3 defeat at Cardiff City. Rangers were then given permission by the Dutch FA to speak to Stefan Postma regarding a move from ADO Den Haag on an 18-month contract, but the transfer did not materialise due to a failed medical examination.

Even when the transfer window closed, Rangers continued with their player movements. Their search for a new goalkeeper ended when Matt Pickens was signed from Chicago Fire, after an attempt to sign Donovan Ricketts from Bradford City had failed due his work permit not being renewed. Ramone Rose went on work experience at AFC Wimbledon; Liam O'Brien, a youth 'keeper, was released and joined Portsmouth; Sampsa Timoska had his contract cancelled and he returned to Finland in time for their pre-season period; and Adam Bolder went on loan to Sheffield Wednesday, initially for a month. The club then announced that Flavio Briatore was now chairman of QPR Holdings Ltd and Amit Bhatia, who represented Lakshmi Mittal, had been appointed vice-chairman. The club's senior management team also now contained Alejandro Agag as managing director, Ali Russell as deputy managing director and Gavin Taylor as financial controller. A Football League report on agents' fees paid by clubs in the period from July 2007 to December 2007 showed that Rangers paid out £211,000 (c/f £187,000 for the previous year). They were involved with 18 new registrations, six updated contracts, two cancelled contracts and seven loans.

On the pitch, a 3–0 win over Bristol City left Rangers six points above the relegation zone and nine points from a Play-off place. This game was missed by De Canio as he had to return to Italy following the death of his father. Another victory followed, a 3–2 win at Southampton, but the run came to end with a 2–4 home defeat by Burnley in the next game. Rangers had been 2–0 up but were undone by a hat-trick from veteran striker Andrew Cole. Agyemang scored in the game, which stood his record at eight goals in six successive matches, starting with his full debut.

The next four games saw Rangers' progress continue with only one goal conceded. Two draws, 1–1 at home to Sheffield United and 0–0 at Barnsley, were followed by a fine 3–0 home win over Stoke City, with two of goals scored by Leigertwood. Another 0–0 away draw, at Coventry City, helped Rangers move up to 15th in the table. By now Rangers were looking like a mid-table side as they were pulling away from the bottom three but they were not really in with a realistic chance of reaching a Play-off place.

Two of the reserve-team players Andrew Howell and Aaron Goode went out on loan to Wealdstone, while in the backroom David Rouse, a former Manchester United youth coach, joined to concentrate on the coaching of the goalkeepers.

The club's good run came to end at Sheffield Wednesday when the home side won 2–1 and Rangers had Ephraim sent off in the last minute. The setback was soon forgotten, however, as Rangers had a run of scoring three goals in three successive games. First was a 3–2 home win over Blackpool, which was followed by a 3–1 home win over relegation-threatened Scunthorpe United and a 3–3 draw at Wolverhampton Wanderers. It was at this time that Joe Dunbar, the performance manager, left the backroom staff.

At the end of March the club announced that the kit supplier for next season would be Lotto Sport Italia. It was a deal that could be worth £20 million over five seasons, depending on the success of the club. They would supply all home, away and training kits, with new designs due to be unveiled after the end of the current season.

In their next match, Rangers slipped back a couple of places down the table with a 0–0 draw at Ipswich Town. Danny Maguire, another of the younger players, joined AFC Wimbledon for a period of work experience, while, due to a lack of available goalkeepers, David Rouse was forced to don the gloves in the reserve game at Watford. Another backroom appointment saw John Urwin join as youth-team physio, thereby allowing Shane Annun more time with the senior squad.

Prior to the next game, home to Preston North End, Rowan Vine fractured his left leg in training which ruled him out for the remainder of the season. In the Preston game Rangers scored twice in added on time at the end of the game to get a 2–2 draw. It was at this time that Adam Bolder's loan deal at Sheffield Wednesday was extended until the end of the season. Rangers then recorded their fourth successive stalemate with a 1–1 draw at highly placed Hull City. The home side, who were attempting to get an automatic promotion spot, equalised in injury time. The unbeaten run continued with a 1–0 home win over fellow Londoners Charlton Athletic, but was ended in the last away game at Norwich City. Rangers lost 0–3 and were not helped when Stewart was sent off after only five minutes for a foul on the edge of the penalty area.

Before the last game of the season the club launched a new club crest, which retained the traditional blue and white hoops within the design. The stated intention was to give the club a new and refreshed identity. This final match of the season against West Bromwich Albion ended in 0–2 defeat and saw Rowlands sent off towards the end of the first half. Ramone Rose made his debut when he came on as a second-half substitute. West Brom needed the win to confirm themselves as champions – they were already assured of promotion – and the match attracted the highest gate of the season to Loftus Road as a crowd of 18,309 saw the visitors presented with the League trophy. Rangers finished their League campaign in 14th place, six points away from the relegation places.

The end of the season signalled the completion of the sponsorship deals with Car Giant, Sellotape and Le Coq Sportif. The club reported that they would be looking for a more European-based sponsor to raise the profile of the club.

The players released at the end of the season were Sean Thomas, Aaron Goode, Andrew Howell, Stefan Bailey and Matt Pickens, as were second year scholars Lee Brown, Billy Coyne, Aaron Morgan-Cummings, James Folkes and Chris Goodchild. The retained scholars were Danny Maguire, Ramone Rose, Matt O'Brien, Reece Crowther, Josh Ford and Chris Arthur.

Three days after the West Bromwich game it was announced that manager Luigi De Canio had left the club by mutual consent with immediate effect. It was believed that family reasons and his inability to settle in England were the main reasons behind the decision. Leaving with him were his assistants Iuri Bartoli and Paolo Pavese.

The end of season awards saw Martin Rowlands win both the Supporters' and the Players' Player of the Year trophy (named in memory of Ray Jones); Michael Mancienne was named the Young Player of the Year and Goal of the Season went to Akos Buzsaky (for his goal in the home game against Blackpool). Ramone Rose won the Kiyan Prince Youth Team Player of the Year, which was voted for by the supporters who attended the youth-team games. A new award this season was the Community Commitment award which went to Zesh Rehman.

In what was a transitional season, an incredible 38 different players had pulled on the hooped shirt. Those who made the most appearances throughout the season were Lee Camp, who was an ever present with 48 appearances; Martin Rowlands with 46 games (including one as substitute) and Damion Stewart

QPR's Under-18s won the Football League Puma Youth Alliance League for the second year running.

with 41 appearances (including five as substitute). The leading goalscorers were Dexter Blackstock with 10 goals (all League) and Patrick Agyemang nine goals (all League); the next highest were Martin Rowlands and Rowan Vine with seven each.

Once again the reserve league was used mainly to give experience to a number of youth players and to those players returning from injury or those not getting full games with the first team. This season Rangers finished bottom of the Central Division with 14 points from their 18 matches. If they had won their last game against former manager Gary Waddock's Aldershot Town then the wooden spoon would have gone to the Shots, but the visitors won 3–1. The leading appearance makers were Matt O'Brien and Chris Arthur, who featured in 13 and 12 games respectively, and the leading goalscorer was Nardiello with four.

For the second season running, the Under-18s won the Football League Puma Youth Alliance League. They started with an unbeaten run of 13 games and only lost three League games all season. Under the guidance of Steve Brown, the side reached the semi-finals of the Football League Youth Academy Cup, where they lost 0–3 to Colchester United. Unfortunately, their run in the FA Youth Cup was short-lived as they lost 3–5 to Ipswich Town in the third round. In what was a fairly settled side the most appearances were made by Billy Coyne and Matt O'Brien, both with 30, and Josh Ford with 29. The leading goalscorers were Ramone Rose with 14 and Antonio German with 13.

Carling (League) Cup

Rangers were first drawn at home to fellow Londoners Leyton Orient, who had just been promoted to Division One. The match was played in torrential rain with a slippery surface that both sides had difficulty getting to grips with. Rangers started well with Rowlands forcing Orient 'keeper Nelson into an early save. Further efforts from Rowlands and Bailey gave Rangers the upper hand. Boyd had a chance for Orient but Camp was able to watch the effort go just wide of the upright. Just past the half-hour mark Melligan should have scored when he was through on goal but he also shot wide. The half ended with Ward making a solo run which the 'keeper covered to prevent him scoring. On 54 minutes Boyd beat the offside trap and passed to Demetriou, who curled a good shot past the diving Camp to give the visitors the lead. Orient then increased their tempo, calling Camp into action several times. Just past the hour, Cullip brought down Gary in the area and Boyd scored from the resultant penalty to give Orient a two-goal lead. Five minutes later, in the 68th minute, Rowlands was able to scramble the ball in at the far post after St Aimie's cross had eluded Ward. Gregory shuffled the side in an attempt to get an equaliser, but it was to no avail and the game ended in a 2–1 win for the East London side. Rangers' recent poor record in the competition continued as they had now only won one in the last five matches.

FA Cup

Rangers' luck in Cup draws did not change and they were drawn away to the holders, Chelsea, in the third round. After the transfer activity in the week leading up to the game Rangers gave starting debuts to Gavin Mahon, Matthew Connolly and Fitz Hall, and during the game Patrick Agyemang and Kieran Lee made their debuts from the substitutes bench. After an even opening period, Rangers had the first chance when Rowlands had an attempted shot blocked by Sidwell. Chelsea then had a couple of chances and in fortuitous circumstances scored after 29 minutes, when a Pizarro shot rebounded off the post to hit a diving Lee Camp on the back and go into the net. Buzsaky nearly equalised just before the break but his shot went just over the bar.

The second half again saw Rangers match their hosts for effort but they were unable to beat Hilario in the Chelsea goal. The home side were feeling the pressure and brought on some of the big names, like Drogba, Cole and Ballack, but they were unable to add to the score. So, despite their best efforts, Rangers ended the game without forcing an equaliser and once again had failed to get past the third round.

2008–09

On 14 May Iain Dowie was appointed first-team coach to succeed De Canio. Gianni Paladini, named as sporting director, said that 'Iain Dowie has a proven track record in the Championship and we are delighted to have him on board'. Joining Dowie were Tim Flowers as his number two and John Harbin as performance manager; both had been with Dowie previously at Oldham Athletic, Crystal Palace and Coventry City. Gareth Ainsworth was appointed to a player-coach role within the new management team.

In the summer break Zesh Rehman was selected, and appointed captain, for the Pakistan squad for the South Asia Football Federation Tournament in Maldives and Sri Lanka, but unfortunately for him he had to withdraw after failing to recover from a bout of food poisoning he caught during the pre-tournament training camp.

Players joining the club included defender Peter Ramage from Newcastle United on a free transfer, who signed a three-year contract; goalkeeper Radek Cerny from Slavia Prague on a two-year deal, he had been on loan at Tottenham Hotspur the previous season; Matteo Alberti from Serie B side AC Chievo Verona for an undisclosed fee on a four-year contract; Emmanuel Jorge Ledesma on a season-ong loan from Genoa, with a possible permanent move for Euro 3 million at the end of the loan agreement; Samuel Di Carmine from Fiorentina on a season-long loan; Kaspars Gorkss, a Latvian international, from Blackpool on a three-year deal for an undisclosed fee; and Lee Cook rejoined from Fulham on a season-long loan deal.

Signing their first professional contracts with the club were youth players Danny Maguire, Matt O'Brien, Chris Arthur, Ramone Rose, Josh Ford and Lee Browne. Ryan Myers remained on non-contract basis after suffering a knee injury in the first game of the previous season which resulted in him missing the rest of the campaign through injury. Also Reece Crowther and Joe Oastler, who had been released by Portsmouth, were given contracts.

On the outgoing side were Stefan Bailey to Grays Athletic; Jake Cole on a three-month loan to Oxford United; Daniel Nardiello joined Blackpool after his contract was cancelled by mutual agreement; Zesh Rehman went to Blackpool on a six-month loan; Simon Walton to Plymouth Argyle for a fee of £750,000, a record for the Devon club, and Chris Barker also to Plymouth on a three-year contract.

At a press conference held at Somerset House the club launched their new Lotto Sport Italia kit and announced Gulf Air as the shirt sponsor. The arrangement with Gulf Air is for a three-year period and will see the company's logo on all first-team playing and training kit. Reportedly the deal was for £1 million in the first year, rising to another £6 million over the next two years if the club are promoted to the Premiership. A second strip of all red with blue trimmings and a third strip of black and yellow were also launched. Further activity within the commercial side of the club saw a two-year partnership announced with Abbey, who are part of the Santander Group, to become the club's official financial partner. Under the agreement they would explore business and commercial relationships with the football club under a new 'Business in Sport' programme, and would develop a business and community programme to include existing initiatives with schools, charities and local communities. Another company to join forces with the club were Chronotech, who became the club's official timekeeper in a one-year deal worth a six-figure sum. Both Santander and Chronotech were companies who had connections with the Formula 1 racing world.

The club announced that they were imposing a cap on the number of season tickets sold for the coming season. The limit would be 10,000, thus leaving a number of seats available on a match-by-match basis for those who could not afford a season ticket to be able to attend matches. Not long afterwards, the club announced that all 10,000 seasons had been sold.

A major financial announcement was that the £10 million ABC Loan had been repaid. The loan was taken out in 2002 to help get the club out of administration and was due for repayment on or before 31 July 2008, with the ABC Corporation having an option on the Loftus Road ground in the event of non-payment. The payment to ABC had been financed by an advanced loan by Amulya of £10 million over a two-year period at a rate of 8.5 per cent, comparing to 10 per cent from ABC. Amulya Property is a company connected to Briatore and Amit Bhatia.

In the agent's fees reported by Football League, Rangers had been involved in 46 deals during the reported period of January to June 2008, at a cost of £310,000. The breakdown was 14 new registrations of transfers, five updated contracts, 18 cancelled contracts and nine loans. This gave a total of £521,000 for the season of 2007–08.

For the new season Martin Rowlands retained the captain's armband. After the usual round of friendly matches, Rangers finished their pre-season preparations with a home game against AC Chievo Verona, which had been arranged as part of the Alberti deal. Akos Buzsaky was expected to miss the start of the season following surgery on his left ankle after he aggravated the tendon while on international duty with Hungary at the end of March. Also missing for the start of the League campaign, this time due to suspension, were Stewart, who was serving the last match of three-game suspension carried over from last season; Rowlands, who was starting a three-match ban for a red card in last game of last season; and Di Carmine, with a one-game suspension.

The first League game saw Rangers at home to Barnsley and with two goals from Fitz Hall, they won 2–1. He could have had a hat-trick but he missed a second-half penalty. The game saw debuts for Cerny, Ramage, Gorkss, Ledesma, Parejo and Alberti; the last two being as substitutes. Di Carmine made his debut in the following game, the 3–2 win at Swindon Town in the first round of the Carling Cup. The next two League games saw Rangers lose 0–3 at Sheffield United and win 2–0 at home to newly promoted Doncaster Rovers. Following the 4–0 Carling Cup victory over Carlisle United, with

Ledesma scoring a hat-trick, Rangers finished August with a 1–1 draw at Bristol City, in which Ledesma was sent off for two cautionable offences. This left Rangers in ninth place in the League.

Off the pitch Bobby Ross retired from his duties at the club; he had joined in 1978 as coach at the centre of excellence and moved onto schoolboy development officer when the club gained academy status. Recently he had been running the day-to-day side at the Harlington training ground and as assistant to kitman Gary Doyle. He was replaced by Craig Doyle, who joined club as assistant kitman.

There was then a two-week break due to rounds of international matches. Rangers had a number of players called-up for their respective country squads, Agyemang for Ghana v Tanzania, Libya, and Lesotho; Delaney for Republic of Ireland against Norway, Georgia and Montenegro; Gorkss for Latvia against Romania, Moldova and Greece; Balanta for the England Under-19 squad for their match versus Holland; and Parejo for Spanish Under-21 matches against Kazakhstan and Russia. Damiano Tommasi, a former Italian international, was given a contract until the end of the season. He was a free agent having been released by Spanish side Levante at the end of the previous season.

Once back in action Rangers continued with two wins, 4–1 at home to Southampton (a game shown live on Sky) in which Blackstock scored twice against his previous club, the first after just 37 seconds. This was followed by a 1–0 win at Norwich City, which put Rangers up to fourth in the table. The downside was Connolly being sent off for two bookable offences. Rangers then announced a range of match day ticket price increases. Matches would now be categorised A, B or C; with the top price for an A category game would now be platinum £50, gold £40, silver £30 and bronze £20, with category C games £35, £30, £25 and £20 respectively. Derby County, Rangers' next home opponents, objected and appealed to the Football League as their fans were not being charged the admission prices Rangers had given the League at the beginning of the season. The Football League agreed with Derby and ruled that the club has to reduce the prices to the prior announced rate. The club's justification was that it needed more money to make the matches an attraction for the supporters. Later, in an open letter to supporters, Amit Bhatia stated that recently announced price rises were being rescinded and that all remaining home games would be category 'C', with a top price of £35.

On the pitch things did not go as well as the next four games only yielded one point. An away 0–1 defeat at Coventry City was followed by the first home defeat of the season, 0–2 by Derby County (who had not won in any of their previous 25 away matches).The point was gained in the home 1–1 draw with Blackpool in front of a crowd of just 12,500, and the poor run continued with a 0–1 defeat at Birmingham City, another game televised by Sky. Rangers were now down to 11th and a gap was starting to appear to the Play-off places. Another international break followed and Rangers resumed with a 2–1 home win over Nottingham Forest, which saw them move up five places to sixth. The table was now very bunched with 13 teams within three points of Rangers. After the game against Forest, Lee Camp joined them on loan until January 2009.

Next up was a match at newly promoted Swansea City, which ended 0–0 despite the home side playing from the 26th minute with a defender in goal as their 'keeper had to go off injured and they did not have a replacement on the bench. This game was the last one with Iain Dowie as manger, as on the following Friday, 24 October, the club issued a statement announcing that Iain Dowie had been relieved of his duties with immediate effect and that Gareth Ainsworth would be in temporary charge until a permanent appointment was made.

Ainsworth's first game as caretaker was a 0–0 draw at Reading, who had a 100 per cent home record in their previous six games. Next up was a home game against leaders Birmingham City which ended in a 1–0 win with a goal from Di Carmine. The game saw Tommasi make his debut, but also the dismissal of Leigertwood with a straight red card just before half-time. He unsuccessfully appealed against the decision and had his suspension increased to four matches. Ainsworth's unbeaten run came to an end with the next game, a 0–2 defeat at Ipswich Town. Loan deals were then arranged for the following players: Chris Arthur to Kettering for three months; Adam Bolder to Millwall, initially for one month but later extended to January; Angelo Balanta to Wycombe Wanderers initially for two months but later extended for a further two months to mid-February and Ramone Rose to Histon until the end of 2008.

In the 1–0 home victory of Cardiff City the visitors finished with nine men; although the red card for Purse was later rescinded. The Carling Cup tie against Manchester United attracted a crowd of 'only' 62,000; the lowest for the season so far at Old Trafford. Adam Buzsaky suffered an injury to his anterior cruciate ligament and was expected to be out for the rest of the season. Also on the injury front Rowan Vine had further surgery on the leg he fractured in April as the injury had not responded to treatment as well as expected. In what turned out to be the last match under the temporary stewardship of Ainsworth, Rangers lost 0–2 at home to Burnley who had beaten Premiership leaders Chelsea at Stamford Bridge in the Carling Cup on the previous Wednesday.

On 19 November Paulo Sousa was appointed as first-team coach; he had previously been assistant to Luis Felipe Scolari with the Portuguese national side. Sousa brought in Bruno Oliveira as an assistant coach and he retained Gareth Ainsworth, David Rouse and John Harbin in his backroom team. Following Sousa's arrival Tim Flowers left the club as goalkeeping coach, as did first-team scout Filippo Orlando. The first game of Sousa's reign was a 0–3 defeat at Watford in which Hall was sent off late in the game. More loan deals were then arranged; on the incoming side were Heidar Helguson from Bolton Wanderers until the end of 2008 and Gary Borrowdale from Coventry City on an emergency basis.

A more noticeable departure from the club was that of long-serving club secretary Sheila Marson. Sheila had been involved with the secretarial side of the club for over 30 years, first as an assistant to Ron Phillips and then as secretary following his departure in the early 1980s.

The new management team gained their first three points in the home game against Charlton Athletic with a 2–1 win, both goals coming from Blackstock. This was followed by a 0–0 draw at Crystal Palace, a game in which Helguson made his debut from the bench and Rangers failed to score for the seventh successive away League game; a club record. Next up were leaders Wolverhampton Wanderers, and in a game televised by Sky Rangers won 1–0 thanks to a goal from Rowlands. Sousa's unbeaten run ended at Sheffield Wednesday as Rangers lost 0–1 and dropped to ninth in the League. The club recalled Rose early from his loan at Histon as he was not getting the first-team games that the club had hoped he would have. Similarly, Parejo was recalled by Real Madrid, ending his loan period early.

Rangers finally managed to score an away goal as they drew 1–1 at Plymouth when Helguson scored, their first away League goal for nine matches. This was followed by a 3–2 home win over Preston North End in which Helguson scored another two. Rangers went into the Christmas/New Year programme in ninth place, just one point outside of the Play-off zone. In the holiday period Rangers were unbeaten with two draws, 2–2 away at Charlton and 0–0 home to Watford.

When the January transfer window opened Rangers were fairly active. Three loans, Lee Cook, Heidar Helguson and Gary Borrowdale, were made into permanent transfers. Helguson signed until 2011 for a reported fee of £750,000; Borrowdale for £500,000 and Cook for a reported £750,000 fee, both on three and a half year contracts. Also joining was Wayne Routledge from Aston Villa for £300,000, also on a three and a half year deal. Returning to the club after their loans expired were Lee Camp, Zesh Rehman and Adam Bolder. Damiano Tommasi had his contract cancelled and returned to Italy.

Back on the pitch, Rangers were held to another 1–1 draw, this time at home Coventry, and it was their third stalemate in a row, despite the visitors being reduced to 10 men after 37 minutes when Wright was dismissed. Routledge made his debut in the game. Liam Miller was another new recruit when he joined the club on loan from Sunderland until the end of the season. Following the midweek FA Cup defeat, Rangers continued their unbeaten League run with a 2–0 victory over Derby County at Pride Park; the game being the first for the hosts under new manager Nigel Clough. Unfortunately for Rangers, Martin Rowlands incurred an anterior cruciate ligament injury which ruled him out for the rest of the season as he required surgery to repair the tear. With a 3–0 away win over Blackpool, in which Miller made his debut, and a 0–0 home draw with Reading, Rangers kept within touching distance of the Play-off places in seventh place, just two points behind the sixth-placed side.

At the end of January there was more activity on the player moves front with Arthur and Balanta being recalled from their loans at Kettering and Wycombe respectively, and Rehman joining Bradford City on loan until the end of the season. Ledesma's loan was terminated by Genoa and he returned to Italy for a potential permanent transfer to Salernitana Calcio 1919, and Chris Flood and Adam Bolder had their contracts cancelled. Bolder re-joined Millwall, where he had been on loan until the beginning of January.

With heavy snow causing problems across the country the home game with Swansea was postponed as the visitors were unable to travel. Also, the pitch at Loftus Roads was covered by a foot of snow following the previous days' snowfall. Next up was a 2–2 draw at Nottingham Forest; Rangers had now gone nine games without being beaten. In the two-week gap of fixtures caused by postponements and re-arranged FA Cup ties, Rangers signed Jordi Lopez on a three-month contract. He was a free agent after being released by Real Mallorca in December. After their enforced break Rangers' next game was a televised one at home to Ipswich Town, in which after taking the lead they lost 1–3 and dropped down to 11th place in the League.

Steve Brown, the club's youth-team manager, left the club and was replaced by his assistant Keith Ryan. In the following week Rangers drew 0–0 at Cardiff and then were beaten 1–2 at Barnsley, where Lopez made his debut as a substitute. The Football League published their bi-annual agents report covering the period July to December 2008. It showed that the club had been involved in 27 transactions (16 new registrations, one updated contract, four cancelled contracts and six loan deals) resulting in payments of £40,290 to agents, compared with £211,000 for the same period a year earlier. More loans were agreed for players to get match experience – Chris Arthur joined Rushden & Diamonds, Gary Borrowdale joined Brighton & Hove Albion and Jake Cole joined Barnet; all deals were for a month initially.

The poor run continued with no goals being scored in the next four games. The sequence started with a 0–1 home defeat by Norwich City, followed by a 0–0 home draw with Sheffield United. The goalless series continued with two away games, first 0–2 defeat at Doncaster, and secondly another 0–0 this time at Southampton. Rangers had not won for nine games and had dropped to 12th in the League. In an effort to boost the midfield, Adel Taarabt, a young Moroccan international, was signed on loan to the end of the season from Tottenham Hotspur, and he made his debut when coming on as a substitute in the Southampton game. The winless and goalless run came to end when Rangers beat in-form Swansea City 1–0 at home, with Leigertwood scoring the only goal. On the injury front there was good news as Rowan Vine started his comeback, a year after fracturing his leg, when he played for 60 minutes in a reserve game against Charlton Athletic.

Rangers made to it two wins on the trot with a 2–1 victory at home over Bristol City, the goals being the first for the club for Lopez and Taarabt. During the break for international matches Danny Maguire went on loan to Yeovil Town, a deal which was for the remainder of the season; and on loan deadline day Dexter Blackstock joined Nottingham Forest in a similar loan deal. It was a move that later, reportedly, had consequences for manager Sousa. The club made two announcements during the enforced layoff. Firstly Mrs Yuko Yamazaki was appointed as global ambassador, representing the club in the Far East.

She was quoted as saying 'I am looking forward to working on this exciting adventure. QPR is a magical opportunity and I am excited about building the brand in the Far East and maximising the opportunities that I believe are available.' Secondly, and more importantly, the new home kit for the following season was launched. The most noticeable changes were the reversion back to white shorts, a clear Gulf Air logo in white on a blue hoop and the club crest placed centrally on the front of the shirt. It was said that the new kit would be worn in the last home game of the current season against Plymouth.

Back on the pitch, Rangers drew 0–0 with local rivals Crystal Palace. Vine completed his return to first-team action when he came on as a second-half substitute. The match also saw manager Paulo Sousa sent to the stands for complaining to the officials about the number of fouls being committed against his players. Two days after the Palace game the club terminated Bruno Oliveira's contract as assistant first-team coach.

Just three days later, on 9 April, another club statement was issued. It said 'QPR has today [9 April 2009] had to terminate Paulo Sousa's employment with the club with immediate effect. It came to the club's attention that Mr Sousa had without authority divulged highly confidential and sensitive information. The club, with legal advice, responded in this way to protect its position. Player-manager Gareth Ainsworth will take caretaker charge on a temporary basis from now until the end of the season. The club will be making no further comment.' It was reported that Sousa had said that he had not been aware of the Blackstock loan move to Forest, something that the club later refuted.

In a move to appease some of the adverse comments from supporters regarding the previously published details of the following season's season ticket prices and early-bird discount scheme, the club announced a reduction of five per cent in season ticket prices and an extension of a month to the previous published early-bird discount date. After the deadline prices would show a two per cent decrease on the current season to reflect the reduction in the VAT rate. This meant the club would have to send a refund to those that had paid the higher 'discounted' prices.

With just five games remaining Ainsworth started his second spell as caretaker manager with a 0–1 defeat at Play-off chasing Burnley. In the following week the sad news was announced that former club captain Mike Keen had passed away. Keen was skipper of the successful 1966–67 double side that won the League Cup at Wembley and gained promotion from the (old) Division Three. The next game, at home to Sheffield Wednesday, saw Rangers back on the winning track when they came from 0–2 down to win 3–2, with Leigertwood scoring the winner in the 88th minute. With three games to go Rangers were in 10th place, but with no chance of reaching the all important sixth position. Their penultimate away game was at leaders Wolverhampton Wanderers, who won the game 1–0 and sealed their promotion to the Premier League.

One of the successful Under-18 side, 'keeper Elvijs Putnins, received international recognition when he was called-up to the Latvian Under-19 squad for the Baltic Cup tournament at the end of April. Rangers finished their home League campaign with another goalless draw, this time against Plymouth Argyle. The match saw another long-term injury return to action as Patrick Agyemang started the game. At the end-of-season awards function Damion Stewart won both the Supporters' and Players' Player of the Year awards; Young Player of the Year went to Matthew Connolly and Goal of the Season to Martin Rowlands for his goal in the home game against Wolverhampton Wanderers.

In their last game of the season Rangers lost 1–2 at Preston North End, a result that enabled the home side take the last Play-off spot as Cardiff City failed to win their final game. In this game the new away strip for the following season was introduced and it marked a return to the popular 'Dennis the Menace' red and black hoops. The outline design is the same as the new home kit with the club page placed centrally on the shirt.

The new Queen's Park Rangers home shirt for the 2009–10 season.

The season finished with Rangers in mid-table in 11th place, with just 42 goals scored in their 46 games. In fact they were the joint-bottom, with Doncaster Rovers, of the goals scored table. During the campaign 31 different players appeared, with Radek Cerny being the most regular with 47 appearances out of a possible 52 games. The only other players to play in more than 40 games were Mikele Leigertwood, 39 starts and seven subs; Damion Stewart 43 starts; and Damien Delaney 40 starts and two subs. The leading goal scorer was Dexter Blackstock with 12 (11 League plus one Cup), the next highest was Heidar Helguson with just five.

The reserve side once again played in the Central Division of the Football Combination, this season sponsored by Totesport.com. There was also a subsidiary cup competition for Championship sides, but this did not reach a conclusion as a number of the initial group stage games were not played. The coach for the season was Gareth Ainsworth, a role taken over by Steve Gallen towards the end of the season. The side was mainly made up of the more experienced Academy players with first-team squad members using games in the latter stages of their regaining fitness programme. The regular players were Ed Harris and Joe Oastler, both with 16 games; and Ramone Rose with 14 games. The leading scorers were Angelo Balanta and Samuel Di Carmine, both with seven. Di Carmine scored the only hat-trick in the 3–2 win at Aldershot Town. He even went away with the match ball to prove it!

The Under-18s, coached by Steve Brown and latterly by Keith Ryan, had another successful season. Although they were unable to make it three-in-a-row League wins as they did finish runners-up to Southend United. However, they reached the Final of the Football League Youth Alliance Cup after winning the Southern Section. Having only finished third in their group the Under-18s reached the National Final by winning the four knock-out rounds, beating Gillingham in the Southern Final. The Final was played at Loftus Road and the visitors were Northern winners Grimsby Town. Despite taking an early lead through Josh Parker, Rangers did not win the trophy as the Mariners came back to win by two goals to one. The FA Youth Cup saw another remarkable game when in the third round Rangers were 0–3 down at home to Bristol City after 65 minutes, but they managed to go through with a 5–3 win after extra-time; the hero being Josh Parker with a hat-trick.

The success for the Under-18s was mainly due to having a settled regular side available throughout the season, with nine players making 20 or more starts. The most frequent ones being Terry Smith with 30 appearances (29 starts and one sub); Antonio German with 27 appearances and Josh Parker with 26 starts and four subs appearances. The leading scorers were Josh Parker with 17 and Antonio German with 13.

Carling (League) Cup

The draw for the first round gave Rangers a trip to the only other Division Three winners of the League Cup, Swindon Town. This season saw the introduction of seven substitutes in the competition, although only three could be used in a match. Rangers fielded a normal side with just a couple of changes from the previous League game. After being on top for most of the first half-hour, Rangers took the lead on 32 minutes when Balanta scored from close-in following a corner. However, Rangers were unable to hold onto the lead as the home side scored just two minutes later through Cox and again in the 42nd minute when Paynter scored with a diving header, to take a half-time lead. Immediately after the break Rangers were back on level terms when Blackstock headed in a Cook cross. Within 10 minutes Rangers were back in the lead as Delaney scored from 12 yards following another corner that was not cleared properly. Although Swindon had a goal disallowed, Rangers held on for a 3–2 win, their first away victory in the competition for five years.

The second round, which was also seeded this season, drew Rangers at home to Carlisle United. Rangers started well and a Rowlands effort tested the visiting 'keeper early on. Carlisle came back into the game and neat play saw them create some chances, all of which were dealt with by Cerny. At the break neither side had found the net so went in level. The second half started in the best possible way for Rangers when Stewart met a Ledesma in-swinging corner to head into the Carlisle net after 48 minutes. Rangers continued with their pressure with Di Carmine going close, and on 55 minutes Ledesma doubled Rangers' lead when he fired a left-footed shot from the edge of the area in off the post. Just seven minutes later Ledesma had scored again, this time, after a quick interchange with Parejo, he shot across the 'keeper into the far corner. Carlisle now looked a beaten side and did not really trouble Cerny or the Rangers defence. Cook had shot from outside the area which just cleared the bar. On 83 minutes Ledesma completed his hat-trick with the best constructed goal of the evening. Cook ran through from midfield and passed to Balanta, whose quick back-heel was met by Ledesma with a lofted shot over the advancing 'keeper. The game ended in 4–0 win for Rangers, and Ledesma proudly carried off the match ball.

Rangers' reward for reaching the third round for the first time in five seasons was an away tie at Premiership side Aston Villa. Ironically, both sides were in fourth place in their respective Leagues. Rangers made some changes to the side, with Buzsaky making his first appearances after recovering from injury. The home side also made some changes but still fielded a strong first-choice side. Rangers started well with Ledesma and Buzsaky having good chances, while Villa responded with their own opportunities. Although the game was fairly open, neither side could find the net before the break so at half-time Rangers were still level with their higher standard opponents. On 58 minutes Rangers won a corner which Buzsaky took, and the Villa 'keeper could only punch out to Parejo, whose cross was met by Stewart who powered home to give Rangers the lead. This galvanised the home side and for the rest of the match Rangers were under siege and rode their luck to keep the home from scoring. The best chance fell to Gareth Barry on 73 minutes but he got too far under the ball when trying to lob Cerny. Rangers hung on to win a place in the third round for the first time since 1995.

Into the last 16 Rangers were hoping for a home draw, but it was not to be as they were drawn away and had to travel to Old Trafford to meet European Champions League holders Manchester United. In front of a crowd of over 62,500 Rangers faced a 'weakened' United side, which still contained a number of full internationals. The game was played in rain with a strong swirling wind, and United made all the running early on. Cerny was kept busy keeping out the home side's numerous on-target efforts. However, Rangers, despite their lack of possession, went in at the break on level terms at 0–0. Caretaker manager Gareth Ainsworth made a tactical change for the second half with Ledesma coming on for Parejo to bolster the front line. United continued where they had left off in the first half with Rangers hardly getting out of their half. Park hit the post for the home side, before Rangers had one of their very few forays into the United box. But Blackstock could only head tamely at Kuszczak from Ledesma's cross. With a quarter of an hour to go United were awarded a penalty when Welbeck was felled by Ramage on the edge of the box. Tevez scored from the spot by sending Cerny the wrong way. United piled forward for a second but again Cerny and the central-defensive pair of Hall and Stewart kept the onslaught out. Rangers did have the ball in the net just before the end but the effort was ruled out for offside. At the end Rangers had lost 1–0, but with all the efforts United had had, 22 to Rangers' two, the score should have had a wider margin.

FA Cup

In the third-round draw Rangers were paired, at home, with fellow Championship side Burnley, who had reached the semi-final of the Carling Cup by beating Chelsea and Arsenal along the way. Both sides started warily with no real chances at either end in the first 20 minutes. The visitors hit the bar following a corner but the half ended without a clear-cut effort. After the break Gorkss had a volley which went just over the bar. The game continued with neither side having the cutting edge required to make a breakthrough, and not surprisingly the game ended in a 0–0 draw.

For the replay at Turf Moor, manager Sousa made a number of changes to the starting line up in order to 'freshen up' the side. Again both sides started nervously, after which Ledesma had a good chance to score the tie's first goal but was thwarted by a good tackle by Caldwell. The game opened up, with both sides creating chances but without the end product. Burnley started the second half with a series of corners which the Rangers defence were able to deal with. On 54 minutes the deadlock was broken when Di Carmine scored with a right-footed shot following a through ball from Leigertwood. Ledesma had a chance just a minute later to double the lead but this time his shot clipped the topside of the bar. Rangers' lead lasted just six minutes as Thompson was able to take advantage of a poor punch from Cerny and hit home an equaliser following a melee in the Rangers six-yard box. Both sides went for a winner but with no more goals the tie went into extra-time. Both Helguson and Rose had good efforts for Rangers in the extra period, as did MacDonald for the hosts. Just as it looked like penalties would be required, Rodriguez took advantage of some hesitancy in the Rangers defence to prod the ball home passed the on rushing Cerny. There were just 20 seconds on the clock when the goal was scored. So for another season Rangers had gone out of the Cup at their first hurdle. An interesting (but unwanted) fact was the Rangers had never won an FA Cup tie in the eight years of George W. Bush's time as US president!

2009–10

Ahead of the new season there were some activities away from the playing side. Firstly, a significant pitch renovation, costing £60k, was carried out. Special machinery allowed the top layer of organic and dead matter to be removed, before the pitch was redressed with sand allowing the old existing fibres to be brought to the surface, thus keeping the principles of the Desso GrassMaster pitch in tact. Secondly, a new ticketing scheme to be operated by Ticketmaster was announced. Access to the stadium on match days would now be by barcoded season and match day tickets. There would no longer be a season ticket book of vouchers but rather a Season Card instead which had a barcode printed on it. Also, people buying match tickets online would be able to print out their tickets at home, which would also incorporated a bar code.

A five-year, seven-figure catering deal was announced with Azure Catering who were part of the Elior group. The arrangement was for Azure to provide internal and external catering on match days and non-match days; they also had responsibility for selling the stadium catering as part of non-match day usage.

The Football League awards for 2008–09 included one for Radek Cerny who was announced as a joint winner (along with Paddy Kenny of Sheffield United) of the PUMA Golden Gloves award for the Championship, with 19 clean sheets from 47 games.

Players released at the end of the previous season included Zesh Rehman, Liam Miller, Jake Cole and academy players Danny Maguire, Chris Arthur, Michael Wright and Terry Smith.

Second-year scholars Danny Davenport, Josh Parker and Ed Harris all signed one-year professional contracts with the club; along with first-year scholars Max Ehmer and Antonio German, who signed professional contracts. Ramone Rose signed a two-year extension to his existing contract with Joe Oastler and Lee Brown signing one-year extensions. Reece Crowther had his contract terminated by mutual consent.

On 3 June the club announced that Jim Magilton would be the new manager, having agreed a two-year contract. Magilton had previously been manager at fellow Championship side Ipswich Town until April 2009. A week later Magilton appointed John Gorman, his former assistant at Ipswich Town, as his assistant manager at the club.

In the summer Rangers returned to the Screwfix London Masters six-a-side tournament, at Wembley Arena, having not played in the previous two years' tournaments. They won their group with a 3–0 win over Fulham and a 1–1 draw with Chelsea. In the Final they met West Ham United and with the game ending 1–1 after the normal 16 minutes, the trophy was decided on penalties. Rangers eventually succeeding 3–2 on penalties, with Meaker scoring the all-important winner. The victorious squad was Tony Roberts, Danny Maddix (captain), Steve Palmer, Andy Tilson, Andy Sinton, Karl Connolly, Tony Thorpe, Michael Meaker and Bradley Allen. Unfortunately for Palmer, he incurred an Achilles injury in the first game and was unable to continue in the tournament. Tony Roberts was named Player of the Tournament. The success meant Rangers had reached the Masters Final for the first time. The Final was due to be played in the Liverpool Echo Arena in September.

In an attempt to preserve a pristine playing surface for the first team at Loftus Road, the club reached agreement with Aldershot Town to play their Reserve games at The Shots' Recreation Ground.

The club accounts for the year ending May 2008 were published and showed an operating loss of £6.072 million for the year, compared with £4.874 million in the previous year. The report was for the accounting year June 2007 to May 2008, which covered the period when the club was purchased by the Ecclestone/Briatore consortium. Other points of note from the report were:

Turnover up to £9.239 million (c/f £8.224)

Match day revenue fell to an average of £123k per Football League match (down 12 per cent)

Broadcast revenues £1.9 million (c/f £1.0 million)

Retail revenue £700k (c/f £300k, partly due to re-branded merchandise)

Player trading profit £2.1 million (c/f £1.6 million), mainly attributed to the sale of Lee Cook to Fulham.

Expenditure £14.3 million (c/f £9.6 million), a number of factors contributed to this increase: Players wages up 43 per cent, made up of 12 new players plus 11 on loan, but offset by 19 players released from their contracts.

Administration expenses £5.9 million (c/f £3.5 million). Increase consisted of extra non-playing staff and one-off charges relating to the completion of the takeover of the club.

Also reported was, that after the year end, the ABC loan was repaid and financed by a loan from Amulya Property at an interest rate of 8.5 per cent, compared to the ABC loan rate of 11.76 per cent. During the year a total of £1.3 million loans were repaid, along with significant taxation and creditor liabilities. The result was that the Net Debt at 31 May 2008 had increased to £19.9 million (c/f £18 million). A summary comment stated that the board continues to believe that the best long-term policy is to re-invest cash back into the development of the team and key areas of the stadium, and that the business plans and budgets have been prepared with this objective in mind.

In his Chairman's report Flavio Briatore said that the club was saved from certain Administration in November 2007 and that the consortium have the clear aim of achieving promotion from the Championship to the Premier League. He added "We understand the QPR heritage and our role as fans, owners and custodians of the Club. We believe in being courageous in the development of the Club and in taking managed risks. At the same time we remain committed to developing the long-term sustainability of the Club through maintaining a business that pays its own way. An important part of this development was the launch of the new crest, which was designed to combine elements of the past, present and future of the Club. The change is representative of our aim to re-launch the Club into a global brand." He concluded with "The transformation in this club has been immense. The changes have been very important and will allow us to ease our transition to the Premier League. I would like to pay tribute to the shareholders, fans and commercial partners for their continued support and dedication and I look forward to, what I hope will be, a successful season at Loftus Road".

APPENDIX

Details of the Flavio Briatore and Bernie Ecclestone offer to buy the club (September 2007)

(As published in the offer document sent to all shareholders)

The Boards of Sarita Capital and QPR are pleased to announce the terms of a recommended cash offer by Sarita Capital to acquire the entire issued share capital of QPR.

The offer will be one pence in cash for each QPR Share, valuing the existing issued share capital of QPR at approximately £1 million. Together with current total debt of approximately £13 million, this represents an enterprise value of approximately £14 million.

Sarita Capital is a newly formed company, incorporated in the British Virgin Islands, established for the purposes of making the offer. Mr Flavio Briatore is the ultimate beneficial owner of Sarita Capital.

Sarita Capital also announces that it has today purchased a total of 4,900,000 QPR Shares at a price of one pence per QPR Share representing 4.9 per cent of the issued share capital of QPR. Furthermore, Mr Bernie Ecclestone has purchased 15,000,000 QPR Shares at a price of one pence per QPR Share representing, in aggregate, 15 per cent of the issued share capital of QPR. For the purposes of the Takeover Code Sarita Capital and Bernie Ecclestone are deemed to be acting in concert. Both Sarita Capital and Bernie Ecclestone have purchased their shares from Wanlock LLP, which is beneficially owned by Mr Franco Zanotti, a director of QPR.

The Board of QPR are also pleased to announce that Sarita Capital and Bernie Ecclestone have together agreed to invest up to a further £5 million into the Club by way of the Convertible Loan Facilities. Under the Convertible Loan Facilities, Sarita Capital has agreed to loan up to £4.25 million and Bernie Ecclestone has agreed to loan up to £0.75 million to the Company. The Convertible Loan Facilities may be used to meet certain liabilities of the Club and to provide funds for the acquisition of certain additional players. The Loan Facilities are convertible into Ordinary Shares at the price of 1p per share, subject to the passing of a special resolution at the EGM.

Mr Gianni Paladini will remain as chairman of QPR Football Club and a director of the Board of QPR. Mr Flavio Briatore, Mr Bruno Michel and Mr Alejandro Agag will be invited to join the Board and Mr Antonio Caliendo and Mr Franco Zanotti have agreed to resign from the Board.

The Board of QPR intends unanimously to recommend that QPR Shareholders accept the Offer, as the QPR directors have irrevocably undertaken to do in respect of their own beneficial shareholdings of QPR Shares and those certain of their connected persons, which amount, in aggregate, to 42,412,019 QPR Shares, representing approximately 42.4 per cent of the existing issued ordinary share capital of QPR. Mr Zanotti has already sold his holding of 19,900,000 QPR Shares, representing 19.9 per cent of the issued share capital to Sarita Capital and Bernie Ecclestone.

The Board of QPR has taken into account the following considerations in recommending QPR Shareholders accept the Offer:

- The Offer presents an opportunity for QPR Shareholders to realise their entire shareholding in QPR for cash, within a relatively short timescale when the alternative short-term outlook for the Company requires immediate significant further investment;

- No proposals offering better terms for QPR Shareholders have been received, despite the fact that the Board has conducted a process to seek potential offers for the Club given the Club's current financial circumstances;

- The Board of QPR has sought assurances from Sarita Capital in respect of its plans for investment into the Club upon the offer becoming or being declared wholly unconditional. Sarita Capital has provided assurances to the Board of QPR that Sarita Capital and Bernie Ecclestone intend to commit further significant sums to fund the current and continuing working capital requirements of the Club and, in particular, to fund the development of the Club's first team squad, its academy and its scouting system; and

- the Board of QPR believes Sarita Capital's and Bernie Ecclestone's ownership of QPR will help provide the Club with the financial strength necessary to improve its performance in both the Championship and, in time, enable the Club to gain promotion to the FA Premier League.

As at the date of this Announcement, Sarita Capital owns or has received irrevocable undertakings to accept the Offer in respect of 47,312,019 QPR Shares representing approximately 47.3 per cent of QPR's issued ordinary share capital. All of these undertakings will continue to be binding even if a competing offer is made for QPR that exceeds the value of the Offer and even if such higher offer is recommended for acceptance by the Board of QPR.

Sarita Capital and Bernie Ecclestone are deemed to be acting in concert. The Sarita Concert Party therefore owns or has received irrevocable undertakings to accept the Offer in respect of 62,312,019 QPR Shares representing approximately 62.3 per cent of QPR's issued ordinary share capital.

Sarita Capital has also received irrevocable undertakings to vote in favour of the special resolutions at the EGM authorising the conversion of the Convertible Loan Facilities, representing approximately 14.3 per cent of the existing issued ordinary share capital of QPR.

The Offer is conditional, inter alia, on valid acceptances being received relating to QPR Shares carrying in aggregate more than 50 per cent of the voting rights normally exercisable at general meetings of QPR. Given the number of QPR Shares in respect of which irrevocable undertakings have been obtained, the Board of Sarita Capital intend that the Offer once made, will immediately be declared unconditional as to acceptances. The Offer Document and Form of Acceptance will be sent to QPR Shareholders in due course.

Queen's Park Rangers' Grounds

Welford's Dairy
Pre-1887 Rangers played their games here, on a ground located behind the Case is Altered public house, south of Kensal Rise Station.

London Scottish Ground
In 1888 the club moved to the London Scottish Ground at Brondesbury, for an annual rent of £20.

Barn Elms
Early in 1891 Rangers moved temporarily to Barn Elms, due to problems with their London Scottish Ground.

Home Farm
In 1891 the club moved to Home Farm, which was located at Kensal Green.

Kilburn Cricket Club (Harvest Road)
In 1892 the club played their games at the Cricket Club on Harvest Road.

Gun Club
Rangers' next ground from 1893 was the Gun Club situated on Wood Lane at Wormwood Scrubs.

Queen's Park Rangers were formed when the St Jude's team merged with another local side. The St Jude's side had been set up for the boys of Droop Street School.

St Jude's Church.

Kensal Rise Athletic Ground

In 1896 Rangers secured the use of the Kensal Rise Athletic Ground on a 10-year lease, initially £100 per annum rising to £150.

Latimer Road

Rangers' next ground at Latimer Road, which they moved to in 1901, was situated near St Quintin's Avenue. The team would change in the Latimer Arms public house and walk down to the ground in their playing kit. The pitch was not in a very good condition, especially after an open-air celebration for the coronation of King Edward VII had taken place on the ground.

Agricultural Showground, Park Royal

In 1904 the club had to move due to the landlord doubling the rent for the Latimer Road site. The Agricultural Showground was a 100-acre site purchased by the Royal Agricultural Society in 1902 for £26,146. Rangers became tenants of the horse-ring enclosure, which had a large grandstand on the north side and a smaller one on the south side. The capacity of the ground was 40,000.

Park Royal Stadium

In 1907 Rangers moved to the brand new Park Royal Stadium, which was built by the Great Western Railway company just half a mile from the Agricultural Ground. It had a capacity of 60,000, with 9,000 under cover, of which 4,000 were seated.

White City (temporary)

At Easter 1912 Rangers played just two games here due to a rail strike.

An early match being played at Park Royal.

Loftus Road

During World War One the Park Royal Ground was turned into allotments, forcing Rangers to move again. In 1917 they moved to the ground of the disbanded Shepherds Bush Football Club in Ellerslie, an open field on the edge of the White City exhibition area. The only existing structure was a pavilion on the south side, which was replaced by the old stand from Park Royal that was re-erected on the new site and altered to have the dressing rooms and office underneath. After a short while the site became known as Loftus Road, which was the name of the road running along the eastern edge of the ground.

Highbury (temporary)

In March 1930 the Football Association closed Loftus Road for two weeks due to crowd trouble and Rangers had to play a home game at Highbury.

Loftus Road before its upgrading to an all-seater stadium.

The main entrance to the Rangers Stadium.

White City Stadium

In 1931 Rangers moved to this stadium with a 60,000 capacity and Loftus Road was kept for reserve matches. In January 1932 QPR's record crowd of 41,097 witnessed the FA Cup match against Leeds United, while in January 1933 White City held the first public experimental floodlight match.

Loftus Road

In 1933 Rangers moved back to Loftus Road as the club were losing money at White City, partly due to the sparse crowds in the large stadium. At the time of leaving the club had a deficit of £34,549 in the bank.

White City Stadium

In 1962 the club moved back to White City in an attempt to attract larger crowds.

Loftus Road

Rangers moved back after just one season in 1963 as the increase in gates and associated revenue were not forthcoming.

Highbury (temporary)

In 1984 Rangers had to play a UEFA Cup tie at Highbury as European club competitions were not allowed to be played on artificial surfaces.

Matches to Remember

	Date	Opponents	H/A	Result	Reason
1	22 April 1893	Fulham	A	W 3–2	QPR's first piece of silverware
2	2 September 1899	Brighton United	H	W 6–0	First game as a professional club
3	31 January 1900	Wolverhampton W	A	W 1–0	FA Cup giant-killing
4	27 April 1908	Manchester United	A	D 1–1	First-ever Charity Shield match
5	8 January 1921	Arsenal	H	W 2–0	FA Cup shock win
6	26 April 1948	Swansea Town	H	D 0–0	QPR's first-ever promotion
7	3 December 1960	Tranmere Rovers	H	W 9–2	Club's record victory
8	28 April 1965	Tottenham Hotspur	H	D 2–2	SJFC win – basis of the mid-1960s team
9	17 January 1967	Birmingham City	A	W 4–1	Unexpected success in semi-final
10	4 March 1967	West Bromwich Albion	N	W 3–2	League Cup – first Division Three Wembley winners
11	11 May 1968	Aston Villa	A	W 2–1	Promotion to Division One
12	19 March 1969	Manchester United	A	L 1–8	Club's record defeat
13	17 April 1976	Norwich City	A	L 2–3	Championship hopes hit
14	2 March 1977	AEK Athens	H	W 3–0	Stan Bowles' European goalscoring record
15	1 September 1981	Luton Town	H	L 1–2	First match on plastic pitch
16	22 May 1982	Tottenham Hotspur	N	D 1–1	FA Cup Final, played at Wembley
17	22 September 1984	Newcastle United	H	D 5–5	10-goal thriller
18	20 April 1986	Oxford United	N	L 0–3	Milk Cup Final (unforgettable performance!), played at Wembley
19	30 March 1991	Liverpool	A	W 3–1	First-ever win at Anfield
20	1 January 1992	Manchester United	A	W 4–1	First-ever win at Old Trafford – Live on TV
21	9 May 1999	Crystal Palace	H	W 6–0	Relegation avoided
22	26 November 2002	Vauxhall Motors	H	L 1–1	(3–4 pens) Beaten in FA Cup by non-League side
23	25 May 2003	Cardiff City	N	L 0–1 aet	Division Two Play-off Final
24	8 May 2004	Sheffield Wednesday	A	W 3–1	Promoted to Championship

Fulham 2 QPR 3

22 April 1893 – West London Observer Football Challenge Cup Final tie

The two well-known West London teams met at Kensal Rise on a Saturday to contest the Final of the West London Observer Football Challenge Cup. At 4pm Fulham took to the field amid loud and prolonged cheers from their supporters. Queen's Park Rangers soon followed, and the game commenced. Morris started the ball forward for Rangers and King returned it to the Rangers end, where the tussle between Withington and Teagle resulted in a bye.

Fulham should have scored several times, but erratic shooting in front of goal proved to be the means of them losing the game. Teagle and Rushbrook played a sound defensive game and kept the Fulham forwards from Creber, until Withington, after a pretty run, eluded the defence, but his final effort missed by inches. Morris then got away and, passing to Collins, the latter was soon up the field, but Curry stopped him just in time. Returning to midfield, King and Surmon took the ball along the line, and, the latter centring, enabled Fearon to try a shot, which proved ineffectual. Despite trying all they knew Fulham could not score, and the Rangers, although playing against the wind, kept their goal intact.

A fine piece of passing between Withington, Fearon and Pearce ensued, but Harvey upset the combination by forcibly stopping Fearon and passing to Wallington. The latter rushed away and tried a shot, which May easily stopped, and sent the ball on to Fearon, who took it down the line and centred. Teagle cleared, and the Rangers forwards swarmed round the Fulham goal. Shrimpton and Curry were kept busy, and May had to fist out. The game now became fast and exciting and a foul against W. King caused the spectators to groan. Cardwell then stopped Morris, but was deprived by McKenzie.

The wind was now much too high and it upset the calculations of the players to a great extent, but although Fulham tried hard they could not score. Half-time arrived with no score registered on either side. Rangers now had the wind in their favour, and it seemed certain that they would win. Withington started the ball and King was deprived. Morris got on, and, passing out to Collins, the latter broke right away and centred. Rangers kept up a regular fusillade at May, who kept his goal intact in marvellous style, until he was at last beaten by a shot which was difficult to judge due to the wind being so strong. The Rangers supporters were nearly frantic with delight, and encouraged by this success their forwards were soon attacking May again, who had to fist out several hot shots from Morris, Ward and Wallington. Curry relieved the pressure with a big kick but again and again Teagle and Harvey kept the ball well within the Fulham lines. A smart bully in the mouth of the goal resulted in May being beaten again, with the cheers by the Rangers supporters loud and prolonged.

Re-starting Rangers again got away and a bye resulted. Now came an unexpected change over the scene. Withington succeeded in getting his forwards well in line, and some effective passing work between the five Fulham forwards took the ball right up to the Rangers goal. King's shot was stopped by Creber, and the ball was sent to midfield, only to be returned by Cardwell. Withington eluded the defence and sent in a lightening shot, which beat the Rangers goal amid great excitement. There was now only 13 minutes left for play. Some fast and interesting football was now witnessed, each man trying his best to outdo his rival, and a free-kick against the Rangers close to their goal resulted in Fulham making the score two goals each. Both teams strove hard for the winning point but the whistle blew seven minutes before proper time, according to numerous watches held by the spectators, leaving the score Fulham 2 Queen's Park Rangers 2.

The referee ordered an extra half-hour to be played and the ball was again set in motion. The game became fast and furious and spills were frequent. Morris tried a shot at May, which was well fisted out, only to be sent in again, when May had to concede a corner. May was at last beaten by a high shot, which he would have stopped had he not fallen. This had the effect of making matters more lively than ever, and the teams crossed over with the score: Fulham 2 Queen's Park Rangers 3.

The last quarter was entered into with great determination. Fulham, undaunted by their opponents' lead, made great efforts to retrieve their position, but without avail. There was not much play in the final quarter of an hour, owing to the leisurely manner in which Rangers brought the ball back from out of play. The score at the finish was Fulham 2 Queen's Park Rangers 3.

QPR: Henry Creber, Robert J. Rushbrook, Herbert G. Teagle, James McKenzie, Thomas Harvey, Allan Maund, Edward Wallington, William Ward, Charles Davies, Albert Morris, Frank P. Collins.
Fulham: J. May, T.W. Shrimpton, R. Curry, T. Cardross, A. Newport, J. King, G. Pearce, A. Fearon, F. Withington, W. King, A. Sermon, J. Bright, J.G. Shrimpton.
Linesmen: Mr Evan Andrews and Mr W. Coton.
Referee: Mr Gregory (Uxbridge)

A number of gentlemen who took the time of the match state that the first half was seven minutes short of time, a fact which might have had a good deal to do with the result of the game.

QPR 6 Brighton United 0

2 September 1899 – Southern League

For the Southern League fixture against Queen's Park Rangers on Saturday 2 September 1899 the Brighton United Football team made the journey to the ground at Kensal Rise. Up to this point the weather had been bright and sunny, and the match proved a big attraction, with over 5,000 people paying for admission. Winning the toss, the Rangers elected to play with the benefit of the strong gusting wind. Hill kicked-off and the Greenbacks' left-winger got down straight away, crossing over to Mercer, who wound up his effort by shooting over. From the kick-out, Crawford lifted the ball well down the ground, and a miskick by Mills let in the Rangers forwards. They were not slow to make the most of it, putting in shots at close range, but they went the wrong side of the net. Rain now set in heavily but the game continued to be fast and exciting. A good ball by McAvoy and one from Mercer went close. Oakden passed to Mercer, who put in a dashing run by himself but was badly fouled by McConnell close in. The free-kick was cleared by Rangers, who next paid a combined visit to the other end, where Haywood lifted the ball high over the bar. Neatly fed by McAvoy and Parry, the Brighton forwards opened up a very determined attack on the Rangers goal, and Malloch soon forced an opening, but missed the mark by inches. Hero Mercer and Oaken were very conspicuous, putting in several rattling shots. None of them, however, had the desired effect, though once the home goal had a very narrow escape, as, in the nick of time, Clutterbuck dashed out of goal and cleared.

One or two pretty runs by the Rangers forwards were spoiled by defective shooting, but 16 minutes from the start Smith centred to Bedingfield, who scored close in. Scarcely had the ball been restarted when the Rangers front line came down the field again, and a bad mistake by Ashby let in Cowie, who dribbled close in and tapped the leather gently past the Brighton goalkeeper. Thus, before the game was 20 minutes old the Rangers were in the comfortable position of being two goals ahead. In a deluge of rain play was renewed, and soon the players found it very difficult to find their feet. Under the circumstances accurate football was impossible and there was little interest in the play, which for the most part went on in midfield. Malloch put in one or two good centres from the outside-left, but the greasy state of the ball prevented good shooting and spoilt the combination.

The first corner of the game was taken by Rangers, but was not improved upon, and, led by Mercer and Hill, the Greenbacks' front line figured prominently at the Rangers' end. Malloch had hard luck with a long-range shot, while at the other end a corner against Rangers came to nothing. Thirty-five minutes from the start a long dribble and centre by Smith gave Turnbull an opening and he gave Rangers their third goal with a fast grounder. Mercer and Oakden's hard work on the right wing resulted in two corners being conceded by Brighton, but they were both fruitless, and a foul in favour of the Greenbacks shared a similar fate. From this point up to half-time Brighton did most of the pressing but failed to get through. Rangers, on the other hand, were scoring goals all over the place as Cowie scored from a pass by Turnbull. Brighton appealed for offside in vain and half-time arrived with the Rangers leading by four goals to nil.

The rain and wind had both moderated considerably when play was resumed, and after some uninteresting exchanges in midfield Willocks and Malloch got away, the latter finishing up with a long shot which Clutterbuck had plenty of time to get rid of. Perry checked several ugly looking rushes by Smith and Haywood and gave his left wing one more opening, as Willocks and Malloch responded with a smart run, but the latter's centre was headed away by Knowles. McAvoy headed in again but this time Tennant received and the Rangers forwards came away prettily. There was some good work in front of the Brighton posts by Turnbull, Bedingfield and Smith, and on one occasion, after the goalkeeper had saved from Beddingfield, Cowie headed through, only to have his goal disallowed for offside. Fouls were frequent, with Rangers the chief offenders, but they stuck to their work until, with the second half only 20 minutes old, Beddingfield put through a long grounder. Howes slipped up in stopping the ball and before he could get rid of it Cowie put it over the line. This series of misfortunes seemed to thoroughly demoralise the Greenbacks and they were for the most part kept busy defending their own goal.

At length relief came to them in the shape of a short burst up the right wing by Oakden and Mercer, both of whom shot at goal but sent wide. Trying again, the Brighton forwards gave the Rangers defence an anxious time, but the combination in front of the posts left a lot to be desired and the shooting was indifferent. During the last quarter of an hour Brighton tried very hard to place a better complexion on the game but Rangers packed their goal well and frustrated all attempts of the Greenbacks to break through. One good shot by Hill was finely stopped by Clutterbuck, while eight minutes from the end Cowie broke away for the Rangers and wound up with a successful high shot. Willocks came very near to scoring in the last few minutes with a good screw shot, but it hit the wrong side of the net and Brighton were beaten: Queen's Park Rangers 6 Brighton United 0.

Wolverhampton Wanderers 0 QPR 1

31 January 1900 – FA Cup first-round replay

This replayed tie with Wolves took place on Wednesday 31 January at Wolverhampton and proved to be the most sensational match in the whole round. Rangers played exactly the same team as they had on the previous Saturday and Mr Kingscott (Derby) again officiated as referee.

With about 5,000 present, Wolves won the toss and immediately after the kick-off made a sharp attack upon the Rangers goal, which was relieved by Hitch kicking away at a critical moment. Back went White, Bedingfield and Haywood, Bedingfield shooting into Baddeley's hands. A foul was given against the Wolves back for jumping at Bedingfield, but the attack ended by Hitch placing outside the post. Rangers had got into their stride, and the ball travelled from end to end with great rapidity. Miller got down on the left and sent in a splendid shot, while Clutterbuck conceded a corner when trying to save, but it was easily cleared. Baddeley then had another chance to distinguish himself and saved long shots from Bedingfield and Crawford. A foul was then given against Wolves just outside the 12 yards line. Rangers were pressing hard, and with Haywood through and steading to shoot, two heavy backs charged very viciously and poor Adam went down like a log. A penalty was claimed and the referee gave a free-kick. Crawford put it high across the mouth of the goal, but no Rangers head was near and the ball went outside.

Bowen sent in, but this was cleared by Clutterbuck; Miller sent in, and Clutterbuck headed the ball away. A foul against Pheasant allowed Turnbull to get down on the right. He centred and Hannah put it in the net, but the whistle had been blown for offside. From the free-kick Harper got in a fine run. McConnell tackled him but Harper sent it well into the net, just as the referee's whistle blew for a foul against McConnell for the way he had attacked the player. A free-kick was awarded, which was easily cleared. Play became very exciting as half-time drew near, both teams playing for all they were worth.

The Rangers forwards then made a splendid combined run with Bedingfield passing to White, whose shot ended just over the crossbar. McConnell was badly kicked, and the game was delayed a minute or two, but he still struggled gamely on. Immediately afterwards Harper met with an accident and had to leave the field. For the remaining three minutes the Wolves bombarded Clutterbuck's stronghold, and the goal had several narrow shaves.

Half-time came and went with no score. The game was resumed by Wolves kicking-off, with the home team bringing the greatest pressure upon the Rangers defence, but Knowles, McConnell and Clutterbuck withstood stood it. Wolves were kept at bay during the next 10 or 15 minutes, after which their energy expired, and Rangers then had a turn at attacking. Shots were rained upon the Wolves goal, but it remained intact. Rangers pressed severely, but Wolves' sound defence was impregnable. A foul was given against Rangers, Davis took the kick and Clutterbuck brought off another grand save. Bedingfield passed to Turnbull, who failed to take advantage of the opportunity, while White, receiving from Bedingfield, got right through the defence and a goal seemed certain. To the dismay of Rangers, however, he kicked wide.

It was then that at last a penalty was awarded to Wolves. The ball had touched McConnell's arm when he was trying to breast it away, but the referee would not listen to any appeal, and so Pheasant, the deadly penalty shot, took the kick. Clutterbuck came to the six yards line, as Pheasant missed the ball, striking the post and curling outside. A couple of fouls against Wolves carried the play to the other end, and Bedingfield nearly scored, Baddeley saving in fine style. Bedingfield had to leave the field through an injury to his leg, and Rangers were left with 10 men. Another foul fell to Rangers, but the ball was sent into the net without anyone touching it. Immediately afterwards the whistle sounded for the cessation of play, neither side having scored.

Extra-time was ordered by the referee. Both teams had had enough, and begged the referee to allow the game to end, especially as the light was getting bad. The referee coolly said that was his decision and promptly blew his whistle. Most of the team were off the ground and very unwillingly returned. The Rangers captain tossed and won for choice of ends and the game was recommenced. Soon Bedingfield returned to the field and now Rangers went at it hammer and tongs.

Rangers were all round the Wolves stronghold, but they could not find an opening. They then exchanged ends, and again the Rangers forced the pace. After the game had been resumed three minutes Bedingfield got possession and went right through, dashing the ball right into the corner of the net with a wonderful bit of play. This seemed to rouse Rangers to even greater energy and dash, and Turnbull, receiving from White, got right through, but his final shot went outside the net. Wolves were desperate, but the Rangers were playing the usual Cup tie game. Wolves were all round Clutterbuck, but a free-kick was given to the Rangers for offside. The whistle then blew, with Rangers entering the second round as winners of a hard-won fight.

QPR: Clutterbuck, Knowles, McConnell, Crawford, Hitch, Keech, Turnbull, Heywood, Beddingfield, White, Hannah.
Referee: Mr Kingscott (Derby)

MANCHESTER UNITED 1 QPR 1

27 April 1908 – FA Charity Shield

The meeting of the two champion teams of the season, Manchester United, Champions of Division One, and Rangers, Champions of the Southern League, was spoiled as regards the 'gate' by miserable weather, but those who stayed away missed one of the very best games of the season. Rangers added to their reputation, for from start to finish they played a great game, and though they might have been excused some nervousness owing to the reputation of their opponents, this was never in evidence.

Manchester started, but Rangers quickly got going, as Pentland and Cannon initiated a movement that forced the visitors to concede a corner. Nothing came of it, and the First Leaguers got away. Following a foul given against Barnes, Wall put in a beautiful centre which A. Turnbull tried to convert, only for Shaw to save.

From this clearance Rangers went away, and Cannon was getting through when the referee got in the way and Stacey cleared his lines. Back went the ball on the Rangers left, and Barnes placed to Gittins. The latter moved it to Cannon, who raced through and scored with a beautiful shot, yards out of reach of Moger, United's 'keeper. From the restart Rangers were hovering round United's goal and were making straight for Moger, when the ref stopped the game to speak to J. Turnbull. It was hard lines on QPR.

Rangers continued to have the best of the game, Gittins getting in a good drive which Moger just managed to get down to and clear, while Cannon also got very close with a shot. Fidler retired with an injury for a minute or two, and while he was away Cannon spoiled a good chance by getting offside. The Rangers left-back returned to the field of play, and was at once prominent by fouling Roberts within the penalty area. Stacey came to take the kick with a red-hot shot, but Shaw saved in a masterly manner and the whistle went for half-time.

Skilton and Cannon opened the game with a smart attack, which Roberts managed to check in

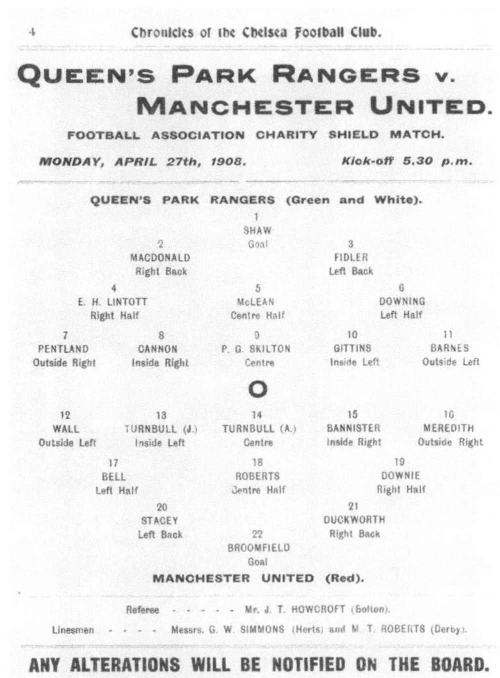
4 Chronicles of the Chelsea Football Club.

QUEEN'S PARK RANGERS v.
MANCHESTER UNITED.

FOOTBALL ASSOCIATION CHARITY SHIELD MATCH.

MONDAY, APRIL 27th, 1908. Kick-off 5.30 p.m.

QUEEN'S PARK RANGERS (Green and White).

1 SHAW Goal

2 MACDONALD Right Back
3 FIDLER Left Back

4 E. H. LINTOTT Right Half
5 McLEAN Centre Half
6 DOWNING Left Half

7 PENTLAND Outside Right
8 CANNON Inside Right
9 P. G. SKILTON Centre
10 GITTINS Inside Left
11 BARNES Outside Left

O

12 WALL Outside Left
13 TURNBULL (J.) Inside Left
14 TURNBULL (A.) Centre
15 BANNISTER Inside Right
16 MEREDITH Outside Right

17 BELL Left Half
18 ROBERTS Centre Half
19 DOWNIE Right Half

20 STACEY Left Back
21 DUCKWORTH Right Back

22 BROOMFIELD Goal

MANCHESTER UNITED (Red).

Referee - - - - - Mr. J. T. HOWCROFT (Bolton).

Linesmen - - - - Messrs. G. W. SIMMONS (Herts) and M. T. ROBERTS (Derby).

ANY ALTERATIONS WILL BE NOTIFIED ON THE BOARD.

Printed and Published for the Proprietors (The Chelsea Football and Athletic Co., Ltd.), by [illegible] & Son, Ltd., London.

The QPR 1907–08 team that faced Manchester United.

the nick of time, and the Manchester lads then had a look in, as twice Shaw saved grandly. United were having just a bit more of the play, and the game had been fought out at a terrific pace, with the going exceedingly heavy. Of the Rangers players, Gittins appeared to feel it most, and he was urged on by the crowd to 'Get at it Gittins', and at this particular moment the visiting players put in an extra dash. Bannister put over to Meredith, the Welsh outside-right, and he got in a long shot which just hit the upright and went across to the other side of the net. United had thus equalised with one of those shots only ever seen once in 100 matches, and one which perhaps no player but Meredith could make. As the ball cannoned off the post, no 'keeper would have been able to anticipate its flight.

For the next quarter of an hour the Rangers defence had a chance to distinguish themselves, and this they did. Rangers made their final rally, as Percy Skilton, after some fine work, was robbed almost under the crossbar, while Cannon sent a wide centre from Pentland. Soon afterwards the whistle went and the game ended in a draw of one goal each.

The match was almost beyond criticism. It was fast and scientific and the teams were well matched. Rangers dominated the first half and United did so for about 20 minutes of the second portion, while Rangers were going strong at the end of the game.

It was a great day for Rangers and it was a pity the elements prohibited many of their supporters being present. About £250 was the total raised for charity.

At the close of the match, Lord Kinnaird, president of the Football Association, complimenting both teams upon their grand display, stated that he hoped that the two teams might meet in early autumn in a replay, when he felt sure everyone present would be delighted to see them opposed to each other again after such an exhibition as they had witnessed that afternoon.

QPR: Shaw, MacDonald, Fidler, Lintott, McLean, Downing, Pentland, Cannon, Skilton, Gittens, Barnes.
Manchester United: Moger, Stacey, Duckworth, Bell, Roberts, Downie, Wall, A. Turnbull, S. Turnbull, Bannister, Meredith.
Referee: Mr J.T. Howcroft

QPR 2 Arsenal 0

8 January 1921 – FA Cup first round

Rangers put in a great performance on 8 January 1921 when they defeated Arsenal 2–0 in the first round of the English Cup. The secret of Rangers' success was their better staying power on a pitch that was no better than a quagmire. Arsenal made three last minute changes, Toney, Baker and Voisey deputising for Dr Patterson, Butler and Graham. With the exception of Grimsdell for Watts, Rangers were as the previous week.

Mitchell won the toss, and Arsenal at once became aggressive, forcing several corners. Rutherford and Toney sent across some splendid centres, but these were all cleared thanks to some brilliant goalkeeping by Hill. After a period of sustained pressure, Rangers began to get a move on and gave Williamson an anxious time, Chandler and Smith sending in shots that were on target. The play for the remainder of the first half was similar to a ding-dong as Arsenal displayed the better combination.

The second half opened sensationally, Chandler scoring in the first five minutes from a weak goal-kick. After this goal the Rangers had one or two lucky escapes. On one occasion Rutherford beat all opposition to pass squarely in front of goal, while Pasnam shot when only two yards from goal, Hill bringing off a save more by luck than judgement. Just after this escape, Hill, in making a save, stumbled and lost the ball, which was promptly returned by an Arsenal player, who only missed sending it into an empty net by inches. Five minutes from time Manning put in a long dropping centre which Williamson caught on the goalline, but before he could clear Smith bundled both goalkeeper and ball into the net. Unfortunately the goalkeeper had to be carried off unconscious. Just after the whistle sounded Rangers were able to celebrate winning by two clear goals.

QPR: Hill, Wingate, Grimsdell, Grant, Mitchell, O'Brien, Manning, Birch, Smith, Chandler, Gregory.

QPR 0 Swansea Town 0

26 April 1948 – Division Three

At 7.40pm on 24 April 1948 a long call on a referee's whistle closed a game which brought reality to the hopes and ambitions of thousands of local football fans: Rangers at long last were in the Second Division.

Manager Dave Mangnall was given a roaring greeting, as, standing in the directors' box, he thanked the crowd for their support. The team were mobbed as they came along the front of the stand from the dressing room, and Captain George Smith said, 'It's been a pleasure to play for you. Thank you very much, and next year we shall do the same into the First Division'.

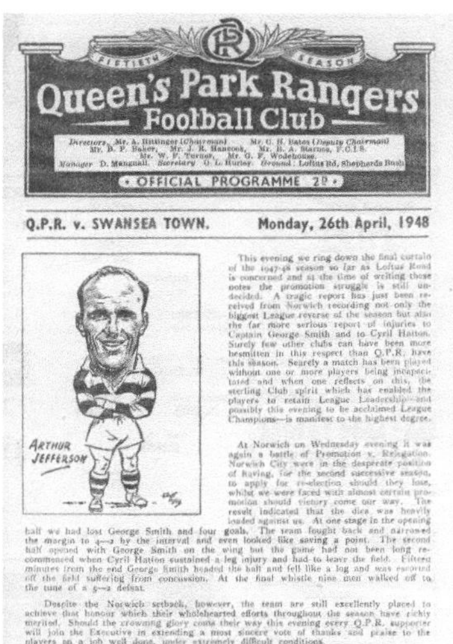

FIFTIETH SEASON

Queen's Park Rangers Football Club

Directors, Mr. A. Hittinger (Chairman) Mr. C. H. Bates (Deputy Chairman) Mr. B. P. Baker, Mr. J. R. Hancock, Mr. B. A. Starnes, F.C.I.S. Mr. W. F. Turner, Mr. G. F. Wodehouse. Manager D. Mangnall. Secretary C. L. Hurley. Ground: Loftus Rd, Shepherds Bush

• OFFICIAL PROGRAMME 2D •

Q.P.R. v. SWANSEA TOWN. Monday, 26th April, 1948

This evening we ring down the final curtain of the 1947-48 season so far as Loftus Road is concerned and at the time of writing these notes the promotion struggle is still undecided. A tragic report has just been received from Norwich recording not only the biggest League reverse of the season but also the far more serious report of injuries to Captain George Smith and to Cyril Hatton. Surely few other clubs can have been more besmitten in this respect than Q.P.R. have this season. Scarcely a match has been played without one or more players being incapacitated and when one reflects on this, the sterling Club spirit which has enabled the players to retain League Leadership—and possibly this evening to be acclaimed League Champions—is manifest to the highest degree.

At Norwich on Wednesday evening it was again a battle of Promotion v. Relegation. Norwich City were in the desperate position of having, for the second successive season, to apply for re-election should they lose, whilst we were faced with almost certain promotion should victory come our way. The result indicated that the dice was heavily loaded against us. At one stage in the opening half we had lost George Smith and four goals. The team fought back and narrowed the margin to 4—2 by the interval and even looked like saving a point. The second half opened with George Smith on the wing but the game had not been long recommenced when Cyril Hatton sustained a leg injury and had to leave the field. Fifteen minutes from the end George Smith headed the ball and fell like a log and was escorted off the field suffering from concussion. At the final whistle nine men walked off to the tune of a 5—2 defeat.

Despite the Norwich setback, however, the team are still excellently placed to achieve that honour which their wholehearted efforts throughout the season have richly merited. Should the crowning glory come their way this evening every Q.P.R. supporter will join the Executive in extending a most sincere vote of thanks and praise to the players on a job well done, under extremely difficult conditions.

To-night our collecting boxes and sheets will be out for a Special Collection to help the widow and family of our late player, Albert Bonass, who was killed in a flying accident whilst on active service during the latter stages of the war. We know all Rangerites will rally to such a deserving cause and on behalf of the recipients we say "Thank you."

Fielding the same team that beat Newport, Rangers almost gave a repeat performance of Saturday's game, when they entertained Swansea on Monday evening. Nothing was seen of the Swansea attack for the first 15 minutes, and although they made some open fine forward raids later on, generally they were well held by a defence which took no chances. Only once in the first half was Allen forced to come out to kick away from Swansea's centre-forward, Powell, and in the second half Rangers' agile goalkeeper made a brilliant one-handed save to block a dangerous cross from left-winger Scrine.

For the rest it was mainly midfield play with long attacks from the Rangers forwards, who found Swansea's goalkeeper

Parry in top form. The home forwards were not as dangerous as on Saturday, mainly because the ball went forward too often in the air and Hatton and the two wing men were crowded out in the centre by the taller and heavier Swansea defenders. The inside men worked hard, but were frequently absent from the line when the attacks reached the scoring stage.

Adams had great difficulty in passing Keane, but may have done better had the passes to his wing been more accurate. Once again it was the Rangers wing-halves, Albert Smith and Ivor Powell, who kept the Swansea defenders on the run with solo efforts, capped with long through passes that were nearly always dangerous.

Hatton got in his first long drive in the 17th minute and Parry could only gather it at the second attempt, and later Stewart just missed the upright with a first-timer following a penalty area scrimmage. The same player later put over a long high cross from near the touchline halfway inside the Swansea half. Parry tipped the ball over the bar and the exertion sent him into the back of the net. The half closed with Hartburn blazing over the bar from close range after he and Hatton had beaten Seeney and Weston.

Five minutes after the interval Hartburn just missed a perfect cross from Adams with his head and landed in the back of the goal. He disentangled himself from the net and came out just in time to have a better go at the return cross from Hatton on the left and flicked a fast header right into Parry's arms.

Rangers' attacks were fewer in the second half and this was mainly due to good work by the Swansea centre-half Weston, who did the work of two men. However, Hatton was unlucky to see a first-time effort fly just wide of the upright with Parry well beaten, and a long ground shot from Hartburn had the goalkeeper vainly chasing it across the goal area, but it just missed the post.

Powell, leading Swansea's attack, had an excellent opportunity to spoil Rangers' promotion hopes in the last few minutes. He beat Jefferson and Ridyard in a run for the ball to put it well over the bar with only Allen to beat.

QPR: Allen, Rose, Jefferson, Powell (L), Ridyard, Smith (A), Adams, Stewart, Hatton, Mills, Hartburn.

QPR 9 Tranmere Rovers 2

3 December 1960 – Division Three

Tranmere Rovers were the victims of a nine-goal blitz inflicted by Rangers at Shepherds Bush on Saturday. Still smarting from their unlucky 2–1 defeat in the Cup the previous week, Rangers were in an angry goal-scoring mood and showed no mercy. Four of their forwards scored twice and Jimmy Andrews returned to the side to add the ninth, but only 4,805 people, the lowest home crowd of the season, braved the wind and rain to see this rare goal-feast. The return of Andrews and the sheer brilliance of the teenaged outside-left Clive Clark sparked off the incredible spree, which had the old faithfuls scratching their heads and wondering if Rangers had ever notched up so many goals.

In fact, according to Club Secretary John Smith, it was the highest home win by Rangers for more than 30 years, but they had scored nine goals at Grimsby after World War Two. Rangers had

also beat Swindon by eight goals before the outbreak of war. It was one occasion where Rangers proved what they were capable of doing. Tranmere showed some good touches and were rewarded with two late goals, but they could not match Rangers' magnificent efforts at shooting.

Super-fit Mark Lazarus played his best game since joining the club, and burly Bernard Evans in the middle chased every ball and showed that he packs plenty of power in his boots, while the goal poaching ability of Brian Bedford made up an all-action attack which gave its most impressive display ever. However, it was not altogether one-sided, as Tranmere's Nigerian leader Onyeall had a goal disallowed. This was followed by Bedford being ruled offside after netting for Rangers.

The spirited runs of Clark and the scheming of Andrews brought about the destruction of Tranmere. It was a dazzling run by Clark which ended in Evans scoring his first goal for the club in the 23rd minute. Bedford was on the spot to head Rangers' second goal from an Andrews left-wing corner after 34 minutes, and the third goal was perhaps the best scored by Rangers during the season. Clark ran into the middle and brilliantly side-footed four defenders before shooting low past the advancing Payne in the 37th minute. Rangers were now in full flight and tearaway Lazarus dashed inside and saw his partially blocked shot trickle in by the near post for the fourth goal three minutes before half-time.

Rangers revelled in the quagmire conditions of the pitch and the inspired Lazarus tricked his way through to add the fifth goal six minutes after the interval. Ten minutes later Lazarus squared the ball across for Clark to hammer home number six.

A clever pass from Mike Keen provided Evans with a chance to put the home team seven ahead after 67 minutes. In a breakaway, Tranmere's inside-right Williams netted and the referee awarded a goal after consulting a linesman, who flagged for an infringement. In the 75th minute, however, Bedford slid home the eighth Rangers goal almost as if to register resentment at Tranmere's audacity in scoring. Tranmere continue to try and play constructive football and were rewarded when Onyeall steered a centre from Eglington past goalkeeper Ray Drinkwater in the 87th minute. It was fitting that Jimmy Andrews claimed the ninth and final Rangers goal during a goalmouth scramble in the last minute. The amazing game ended with the crowd still chanting, 'We want 10!'

QPR: Drinkwater, Woods, Ingham, Keen, Rutter, Angell, Lazarus, Bedford, Evans Andrews, Clark.

Tranmere Rovers: Payne, Millington, Frith, Harrop, Jones, Charlton, Finney, Williams, Onyeall, Neill, Eglington.

QPR 2 Tottenham Hotspur 2

28 April 1965 – Southern Junior Floodlight Cup Final

After 120 minutes of gruelling football the young footballing talents of Rangers and Spurs agreed to become joint winners of the Junior Floodlit Cup and so hold it for six months each. And what a fight these lads had put up. The tension in this action-packed game exploded into near-hysteria nine minutes from time when Spurs snatched their equaliser.

Rangers, who had dominated the game for so long, were leading 2–1 when Spurs earned a free-kick outside the penalty area. Left-back Tony Want took the kick, the ball glided in from the dark areas on the wing, with Steve Pitt's glancing header sending the ball swerving past 'keeper Brooks. Spurs had earned themselves a reprieve, and almost a victory.

The game started off in dismal weather conditions. A darkened sky and a steady downpour had frightened off the anticipated 4,000 fans and only 1,339 trickled through the turnstiles to lose themselves in the vast stadium. The pitch was so waterlogged that the players were almost paddling.

Rangers attacked first. A quick free-kick gave Adams a chance but Spurs' 'keeper Skeet came out fast to save. Then Spurs came away and John Brooks did well to save a low drive from Pearce following a corner-kick. Both teams were a little subdued in the early stages, as Rangers, aided by the first-team experience of the Morgan twins on the wings and half-backs Sibley and Hazell, were the first to overcome the initial attack of nerves and soon settled down to play some good football. Left-half Frank Sibley showed perfect understanding when his low pass was perfectly placed for Roger Morgan to run on to and hit the ball across the Spurs area. Then twin brother Ian Morgan hit a scorching shot from the right wing and seconds later appeared on the left to confuse the Tottenham defence.

It was all Rangers at this stage. Roger Morgan, after some tricky inter-passing with Colin Parker, brought another fine save out of 'keeper Skeet, although his chances of scoring would have improved greatly had he taken the ball closer before shooting. Spurs threatened occasionally with the left-wing pair of Jordan and Mail, and Rangers' goalkeeper Brooks left his goal

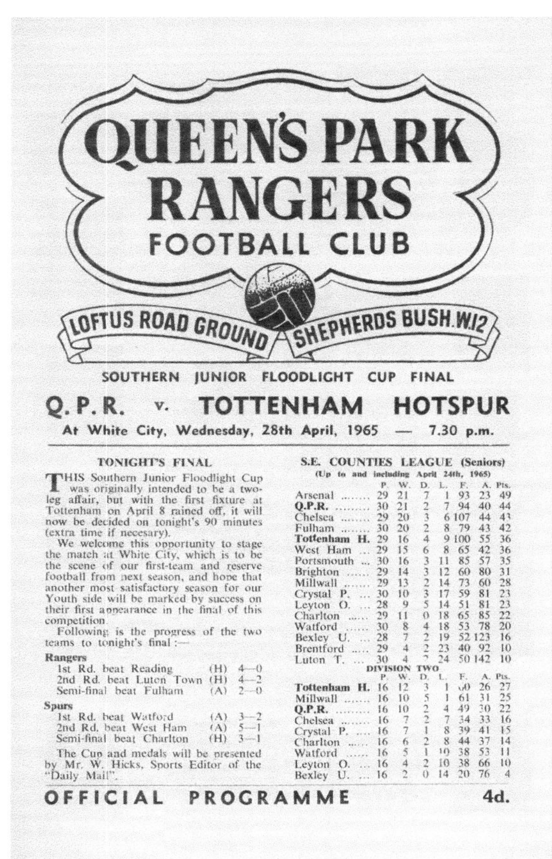

QUEEN'S PARK RANGERS FOOTBALL CLUB

LOFTUS ROAD GROUND SHEPHERDS BUSH W12

SOUTHERN JUNIOR FLOODLIGHT CUP FINAL

Q.P.R. v. TOTTENHAM HOTSPUR

At White City, Wednesday, 28th April, 1965 — 7.30 p.m.

TONIGHT'S FINAL

THIS Southern Junior Floodlight Cup was originally intended to be a two-leg affair, but with the first fixture at Tottenham on April 8 rained off, it will now be decided on tonight's 90 minutes (extra time if necesary).

We welcome this opportunity to stage the match at White City, which is to be the scene of our first-team and reserve football from next season, and hope that another most satisfactory season for our Youth side will be marked by success on their first appearance in the final of this competition.

Following is the progress of the two teams to tonight's final :—

Rangers

1st Rd. beat Reading (H) 4—0
2nd Rd. beat Luton Town (H) 4—2
Semi-final beat Fulham (A) 2—0

Spurs

1st Rd. beat Watford (A) 3—2
2nd Rd. beat West Ham (A) 5—1
Semi-final beat Charlton (H) 3—1

The Cup and medals will be presented by Mr. W. Hicks, Sports Editor of the "Daily Mail".

S.E. COUNTIES LEAGUE (Seniors)
(Up to and including April 24th, 1965)

	P.	W.	D.	L.	F.	A.	Pts.
Arsenal	29	21	7	1	93	23	49
Q.P.R.	30	21	2	7	94	40	44
Chelsea	29	20	3	6	107	44	43
Fulham	30	20	2	8	79	43	42
Tottenham H.	29	16	4	9	100	55	36
West Ham	29	15	6	8	65	42	36
Portsmouth	30	16	3	11	85	57	35
Brighton	29	14	3	12	60	80	31
Millwall	29	13	2	14	73	60	28
Crystal P.	30	10	3	17	59	81	23
Leyton O.	28	9	5	14	51	81	23
Charlton	29	11	0	18	65	85	22
Watford	30	8	4	18	53	78	20
Bexley U.	28	7	2	19	52	123	16
Brentford	29	4	2	23	40	92	10
Luton T.	30	4	2	24	50	142	10

DIVISION TWO

	P.	W.	D.	L.	F.	A.	Pts.
Tottenham H.	16	12	3	1	60	26	27
Millwall	16	10	5	1	61	31	25
Q.P.R.	16	10	2	4	49	30	22
Chelsea	16	7	2	7	34	33	16
Crystal P.	16	7	1	8	39	41	15
Charlton	16	6	2	8	44	37	14
Watford	16	5	1	10	38	53	11
Leyton O.	16	4	2	10	38	66	10
Bexley U.	16	2	0	14	20	76	4

OFFICIAL PROGRAMME 4d.

to make a courageous, diving save following one of Mail's centres. But mainly the first half belonged to Rangers. A goal had to come and minutes before the interval the inevitable happened.

Right-back John Blake took a free-kick and dropped the ball near the far post, as inside-left Adams managed to keep the ball in play and turn it back into the six yard area where Colin Parker pushed it into the net. Rangers led until the interval, but only seconds after the restart Spurs snatched a dramatic equaliser. Inside-right Johnson streaked through on his own and Brooks could only get a hand to the inside-right's shot as it slithered into the net.

It was then that the battle really warmed up. Ian and Roger Morgan tried several long drives that dipped dangerously over the bar and Tony Hazell surged down the right wing and dropped a delicate lob over the goalkeeper's head, only to see it rebound from the crossbar. Rangers took the lead again in the 49th minute. Spurs' 'keeper Skeet dropped a simple ball at the feet of Johnson and then grabbed him by the ankle as the inside-right dribbled past him and prepared to shoot into an open net. It was a blatant, almost comical foul and Tony Hazell lashed the penalty past Skeet so hard that the ball bounced out again from the back of the net. Now Spurs really had their backs to the wall and Skeet was constantly called upon to snatch the ball from the feet of the advancing forwards.

In the 83rd minute the game was thrown wide open again when Spurs grabbed an equaliser. Tony Want dropped a free-kick into the penalty area and outside-right Stephen Pitt rose above the defence to head a brilliant goal. The goal seemed to revitalise Spurs, and as extra-time began Rangers started to fade, and on two occasions only John Brooks's fine positional sense kept his side out of trouble.

Ten minutes after extra-time started an incident occurred that swung the game irrevocably in favour of Tottenham. Rangers' left-half Frank Sibley, who had played a fine game, was spoken to by the referee on the far side of the field. It seemed to be a trifling incident and when Sibley walked off and stood on the touchline little notice was taken of him. However, it turned out that he had been sent off, and it was a decision that marred the whole game. Still, the decision stood, and Rangers were reduced to 10 men with 20 minutes to go.

Tottenham immediately launched themselves against a determined home defence. Right-winger Steve Pitt squirmed past Finch with a dazzling display of footwork and his shot thudded against the bar with Brooks well beaten. Inside-left Jordan was pulled down outside the penalty area as the weary Rangers players struggled to earn the Cup that had seemed to be within their grasp. Rangers dug down into a reserve of courage and energy and somehow survived those last few minutes.

At the end of the game 22 soaking wet and exhausted players were presented with their medals by Mr Bill Hicks, sports editor of the *Daily Mail,* and given a rousing cheer by the crowd.

QPR: John Brooks, John Blake, Bobby Finch, Tony Hazell, Colin Moughton, Frank Sibley, Ian Morgan, Colin Parker, Mick Leach, Lew Adams, Roger Morgan.
Spurs: Stuart Skeet, Joseph Kinnear, Anthony Want, Terrence Reardon, Roger Hoy, John Pratt, Stephen Pitt, Neil Johnson, James Pearce, David Jordan, William Mail.

How they got there
QPR: First round beat Reading (h) 4–0; second round beat Luton (h) 4–2; semi-final beat Fulham (a) 2–0.
Spurs: First round beat Watford (a) 3–2; second round beat West Ham (a) 5–1; semi-final beat Charlton (h) 3–1.

BIRMINGHAM CITY 1 QPR 4

17 January 1967 – League Cup semi-final first leg

It was this game that saw Rodney Marsh head Queen's Park Rangers' 100th goal of the season. It destroyed the lead that Birmingham had held through 50 minutes of their first-leg League Cup semi-final. Marsh was the playmaker and provoked Rangers to a brilliant display that brought three more goals.

Rangers were easily the better side. They were better served in midfield by Sanderson and Sibley, better prompted by Marsh and Allen, and better armed with wingers, in Lazarus and Morgan. This was essentially a great success for an efficient team.

It had taken Birmingham only four minutes to score. Hockey had a fierce shot deflected across goal and Vowden was tackled when about to meet the rebound and from the corner Bullock hit the crossbar. Another corner came and this time Vowden headed on the centre and Bridges sank to his knees to deflect the ball into the roof of the net. Birmingham were always dangerous from corners. Bridges and Thomson both missed good chances when Springett dropped one corner and later Vowden forced the goalkeeper into a brilliant save. The two goalkeepers had a good workout as Springett, from Murray, and Herriott, from Marsh, made incredible one-handed saves.

Ten minutes after half-time came the first of Rangers' goals, as Marsh took his scarlet shirt soaring above a cluster of blue to head the ball high into the net. Having achieved equality, Rangers had to fight to hold it. Bridges streaked through the middle, but as he rounded Springett the goalkeeper's fist edged the ball away. In the 66th minute Rangers shook themselves free from Birmingham's siege and scored a brilliant second goal. Marsh found Lazarus with a casual pass for the winger to move on and centre, as Sanderson edged the ball away from a tackle and Morgan romped in from the left to shoot past Herriot.

Ten minutes later Rangers stole their third. Marsh calmly edged a ball in front of Lazarus and the winger slipped past a tackle to score. Birmingham were clearly beaten but they hardly expected the fourth Rangers goal in the final minutes. That man again, Marsh, slid the ball forward for Allen to edge into the net.

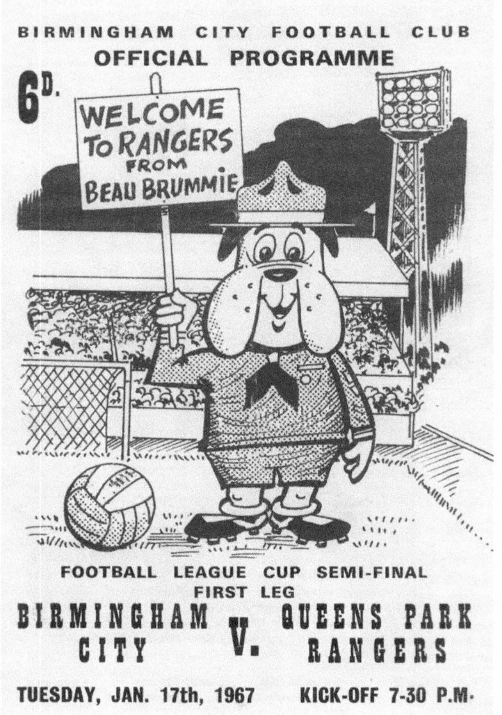

QPR: Springett, Watson, Langley, Keen, Hunt, Sibley, Lazarus, Sanderson, Allen, Marsh, Morgan.
Birmingham City: Herriott, Murray, Green, Thomson, Sharples, Beard, Hockey, Martin, Bullock, Vowden, Bridges.

West Bromwich Albion 2 QPR 3

4 March 1967 – League Cup Final

Out of an almost impossible situation the spirit and dedication of a Third Division team brought glory. Their most ardent supporters were almost ill with disappointment at half-time as their white-shirted heroes trooped off to a scoreline 2–0 down. They went on to win in as thrilling a second half as Wembley had witnessed and in doing so took the League Cup back to Loftus Road.

It was a game dichotomised by the interval, turning from a rout into a startling recovery; a game which produced a goal of genius and a remarkable triumph for the underdogs. The second half belonged almost entirely to Rangers and, long before the end, Albion were staggering on the ropes.

The first half saw Rangers looking slow and deliberate, their build-up so sketchy that Marsh and Allen, the two strikers, perpetually found themselves alone, confronted by a massed defence. Half-time seemed to be a magic watershed, after which they came out transformed, five yards quicker, to pound the Albion goal.

Albion's first goal, after seven minutes, was not only scored by a former Rangers man but also suggested that the greater speed of First Division approach work round the box was more than Rangers could handle. The ball, worked down the left in a rapid shuttle of passes by Brown, Hope and Fraser, was finally slipped through a gap by left-half Clark. Sibley retorted with a shot well taken by Sheppard, but the cries of 'Easy!' appeared to have some basis.

Yet although Albion continued to be so much more co-ordinated, they did not strike hard again until the 25th minute. Clark came away down the left, as Hunt lunged at thin air, and the winger ran on to cross perfectly to Astle. The shot was just as good but Springett turned it brilliantly round the post. Rangers looked set for a spectacular equaliser when Lazarus, on the halfway line in an inside-left position, dummied Collard and had a clear run for goal. However, while in full flight his confidence left him and he squared the ball to a colleague.

Another goal was inevitable and nine minutes from half-time it came. Very smoothly, again, Albion worked the ball across goal right to left to score without hardship. Almost at once, Rangers found themselves presented with a chance, just as they had after the first goal. A left-wing corner dropped over the defence at Keen's feet, but he miskicked past the post.

The second half had barely begun when Rangers produced their first truly incisive move of the afternoon. Quick, clever passes by Morgan and Marsh put Allen through, but he was not quite quick enough to catch the ball. Then a lob from Keen ran off Clarke's back, into a vacant goalmouth from which Kaye cleared. Next Lazarus found Marsh in the area, but Marsh, wheeling effortlessly round two men, shot over the top. Rangers had now set up camp in Albion's half as Sheppard was forced into a marvellous save from Lazarus (though the whistle had gone for a foul) and then to a block from Morgan, by the near post. Flying through the air, he took Keen's powerful long shot, but it was after 63 minutes that Rangers were properly rewarded. Lazarus beat Williams and was callously tripped, allowing Morgan to head one in.

EMPIRE STADIUM
WEMBLEY
THE FOOTBALL LEAGUE
CUP
FINAL
SAT., MARCH 4, 1967
KICK-OFF 3.30 You are advised to take up your position by 3 p.m.
SOUTH STAND
17/6
(SEE PLAN & CONDITIONS ON BACK)
TO BE RETAINED
ENTER AT
A
TURNSTILES
ENTRANCE
29
ROW
17
SEAT
9

A glorious run by Clark followed by a centre across an open goal was almost all West Bromwich provided in the second half. Rangers promptly continued their bombardment and 15 minutes from time they equalised superbly; Marsh got it, with his right foot, off the left-hand post.

It was all white shirts now as Allen took a corner on the right and Lazarus, meeting it first time, hit Sheppard's desperate legs. Then, with eight minutes left, an Albion defender miskicked. Hunt rushed in for the kill, Sheppard saved gallantly at his feet but lost the ball and, as he lay prostrate, Lazarus scored. Three minutes from time he was through again, swerving mazily past two defenders for a shot which chipped the post, but was worth a goal.

WBA: Sheppard, Cram, Williams, Collard, Clarke, Fraser, Brown, Astle, Kaye, Hope, Clark.
Referee: W. Crossley (Lancaster)

Aston Villa 1 QPR 2

11 May 1968 – Division Two

In this game Queen's Park Rangers conceded a goal to a revitalised Aston Villa side at Villa Park and from then on were engaged in a desperate battle to salvage their promotion prospects. Rangers followed their usual technique of allowing their opponents to come at them in the early stages and these tactics almost rebounded against them in the first minute. Villa winger Rudge sent Greenhalgh away and he headed for goal, despite offside protests from Rangers' defenders, but Kelly came out from 10 yards to hold Greenhalgh's drive. That should have been a warning to Rangers to tighten their rearguard, and they were lucky a few minutes later when Greenhalgh netted but was ruled offside.

After 14 minutes Godfrey and Rudge carried out a well-planned move and Mitchinson was unmarked when he drove the ball home from 18 yards. Several Rangers players complained to referee Callaghan about the bustling play of Greenhalgh after he had clashed with Kelly, with the goalkeeper having to receive attention.

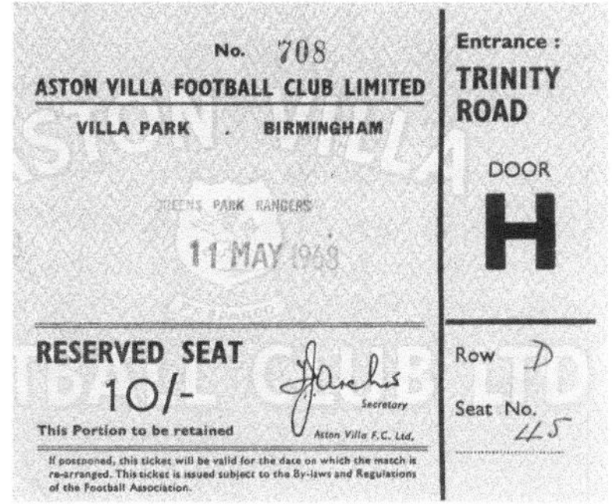

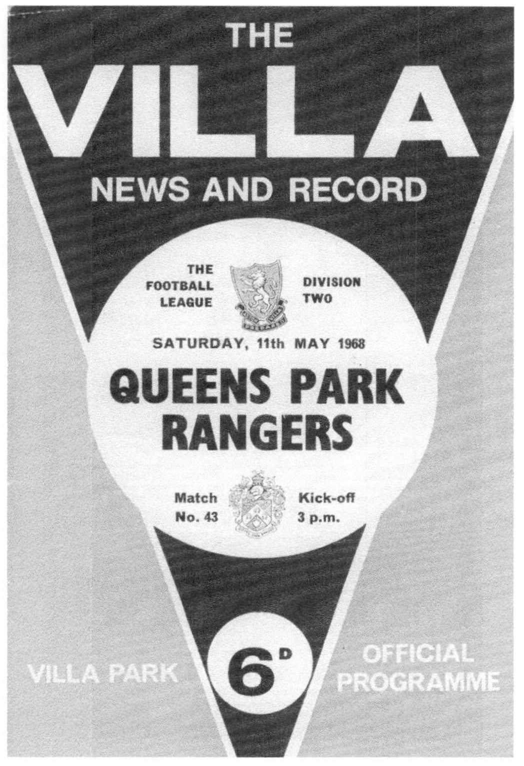

Ian Morgan was Rangers' most dangerous forward and he cleared the Villa crossbar after Clarke had slotted a diagonal pass into the goalmouth. Morgan then spoiled good work when after cleverly rounding two defenders he weakly stabbed the ball straight to a Villa man with Clarke and Marsh both ideally situated for a square pass. In a sudden break Marsh netted during a goalmouth scramble but with his elbow. So enthusiastic were Villa that at times it looked as though they were the side who needed vital points for promotion. Just before the interval Mr Callaghan booked Greenhalgh and Keetch, who had both been engaged in several minor skirmishes.

Within seconds of the resumption Marsh had his legs chopped from under him in a mighty tackle and once more Mr Callaghan's whistle came into use. Morgan passed three defenders to shoot from the penalty spot but Dunn stuck out his left leg to clear off the line. Clarke was the next to try to beat Dunn, who tipped his header over the bar. Rangers now had nine men in the Villa half but could not penetrate a hard-tackling defence firmly guided by skipper Chatterley, who effectively shadowed Clarke. Leach equalised after 70 minutes from a corner which Allen floated into the goalmouth. Immediately afterwards Morgan and Keen had shots blocked, and Rangers went ahead for the first time through an own-goal from Bradley after 82 minutes, going on to win the game 2–1.

QPR: Kelly, Watson, Harris, Keen, Keech, Hazell, I.Morgan, Leach, Clarke, Marsh, Allen.
Referee: Mr Callaghan

Manchester United 8 QPR 1

19 March 1969 – Division One

Desperate defending enabled Rangers to hold out for a short time against a tough United team, and, despite the margin of victory, Spratley, QPR's young goalkeeper, deserved credit for several good saves. United's principal attackers, Law, Kidd and Aston, played notable parts in this success. United's class and dominance was seen to full advantage as they swept four goals past their bewildered opponents in the last seven minutes. Marsh and Glover missed simple chances for Rangers and Stepney made capable saves from Glover, Watson and Ian Morgan, before the Manchester forwards took full command.

Morgan obtained the only goal before the break, a left-footed shot at the far post after Aston had helped on Best's corner on 29 minutes, and he then scored in the 74th and 87th minutes. His second goal came after Best's floated corner had been deflected onto the bar and his third came after Law had won possession in a determined burst.

Best, a constant menace to Rangers with his swift, skilful control and subtle changes of pace and direction, took his two goals in brilliant fashion. He first sent two defenders the wrong way when gathering Kidd's cross to score with a low shot (47 mins) and then left three men trailing with a clever diagonal run from the halfway line before hitting a ferocious cross-shot (66) past the luckless Spratley. Stiles got into the act with a good header (84) and the last two goals arrived in the last two minutes. Kidd, fed by Law, moved to his left to catch Spratley out of position, and Aston rounded off the scoring with a 30-yard shot. There were moments of flair from Marsh (who scored Rangers' only goal) and Glover, but in the end Rangers were outplayed and outclassed.

QPR: Spratley, Watson, Clement, Hazell, Hunt, Sibley, I. Morgan, Leach, Clarke, Marsh, Glover.
Manchester United: Stepney, Fitzpatrick, Dunne, Crerand, James, Stiles, W. Morgan, Kidd, Aston, Law, Best.

Norwich City 3 QPR 2

17 April 1976 – Division One

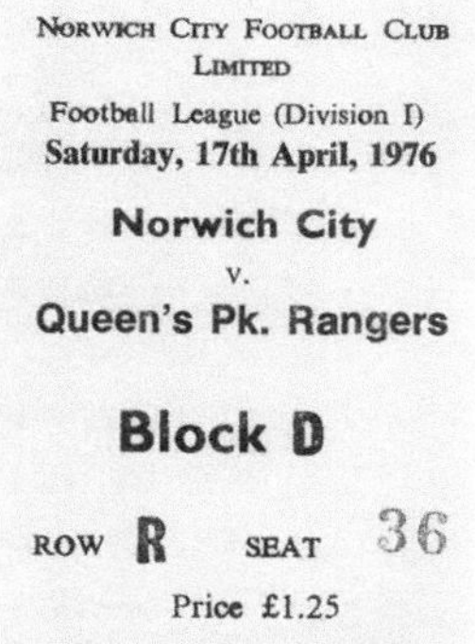

This game saw a defeat by Norwich City that toppled Rangers from the top of the League. In this match, played at Cup tie pace, Norwich were driven with the desire to succeed. They chased everything and their fans kept up a deafening salvo of sound as Rangers plunged to their first defeat in 13 games. Long before the end, scores of policemen were in among the battling fans and there was an astonishing incident on the field when Tony Powell appeared to flatten Stan Bowles with a firm right hook. Referee Keith Styles took no action except for a few brief words with Bowles, who writhed on the pitch clutching his face. Afterwards, Styles cleared up the affair when he said, 'I did not discipline Powell because he did not touch him.'

It was an afternoon of incredible passion, an emotion stoked by Norwich's first goal after 26 minutes when Mick McGuire instigated a sweeping attack. He fed the ball to Colin Suggett and a centre flew into the heart of the Rangers defence. Dave Clement attempted a header that lacked full impact and Ted MacDougall swooped in to tap in his 27th goal of the season. Rangers' response was honest and determined. A minute before half-time Dave Thomas rounded off a series of infuriating misses with a golden pay-off.

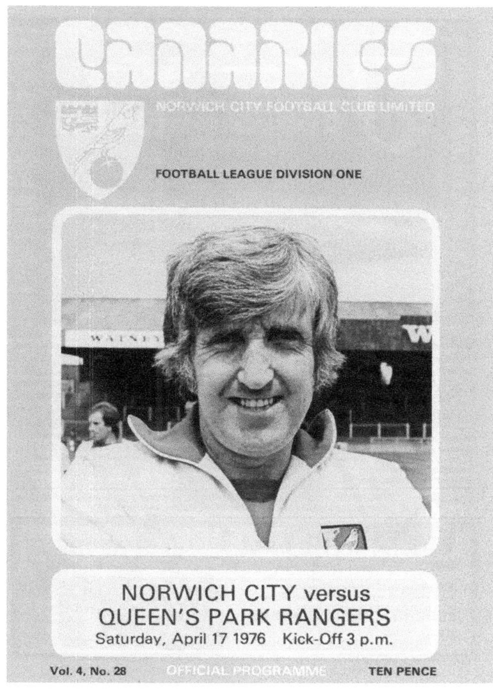

Rangers still seemed likely to win until a sudden intervention by left-back Morris had Norwich's biggest crowd of the season dancing with joy. Suggett's corner was punched out by Phil Parkes, but only as far as Morris, who promptly returned it with unstoppable power from 20 yards. In the 70th minute Norwich sealed it with Morris again in the action. He flung a centre to the far post where Jones headed back into the middle and Phil Boyer merely dipped his shoulders to nod into goal.

Rangers were allowed back into the game when Powell, trying to find his own goalkeeper, lobbed the ball over Keelan's head for an own-goal, but it was too late for Sexton's men to provide a vital equaliser.

After the game Rangers manager Dave Sexton said, 'We can still win the title. We have two home games and the four points we can take should be enough.' Norwich manager John Bond agreed: 'They will win it. I would rather be the manager of them than any of the other contenders.'

Bond's admiration for the efforts of his own men was matched by his glowing tributes to Rangers. He said, 'You have to admire them. They have come a long way. They have built a fine team and a fine stadium. It will be marvellous for them and for the game if they do it.'

QPR: Parkes, Clement, Gillard, Hollins, McLintock, Webb, Thomas, Francis, Masson, Bowles, Givens. Sub: Leach.
Norwich City: Keelan, Jones, Morris, McGuire, Forbes, Powell, Steele, MacDougall, Boyer, Suggett, Peters. Sub: Machin.
Referee: Mr K. Styles

QPR 3 AEK Athens 0

2 March 1977 – UEFA Cup quarter-final first leg

After Gerry Francis had given Queen's Park Rangers a flying start to the first leg of their UEFA Cup quarter-final by converting two penalties in the first few minutes, they were restricted to only one more goal, which was scored by Stan Bowles.

The first gift, in the seventh minute, followed a heavy, unnecessary body check by Tsamis that floored Bowles, who was moving towards a loose ball in the congested penalty box. Ole Amundsen, the Danish referee, immediately pointed to the spot and Francis sent Stergioudes the wrong way by calmly placing his penalty just inside the right post. Four minutes later Givens dribbled round Ravoussis into the box and was tripped by the panicking Nikolaou. This time the goalkeeper charged off his line in a desperate effort to cut off Francis's penalty, which again, flew into the right-hand corner of the net.

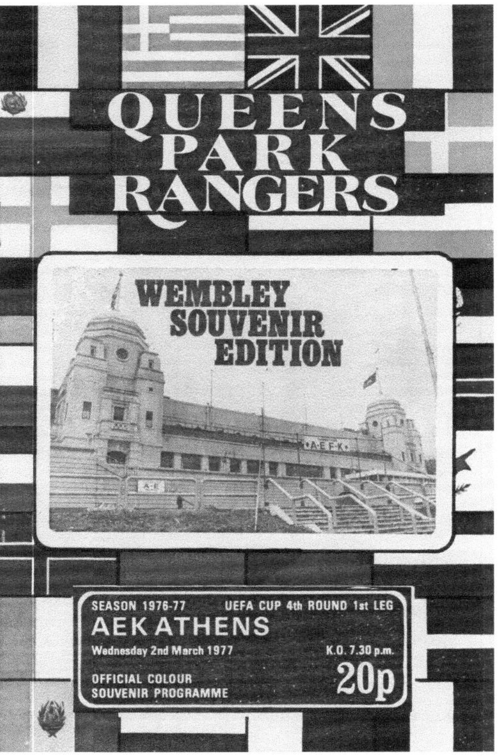

So AEK's task now was to get back into the game as quickly as possible by searching for goals, and indeed QPR were frequently obliged to fall back on defence. The Greeks left themselves open to counter-attacks, and just before half-time, Bowles passed to McLintock, and the ball quickly moved on to Masson, whose final pass was spectacularly driven home by Bowles, thereby breaking the scoring record for a British player in a European competition.

AEK suffered another blow 10 minutes after the interval, when Papadopoulos limped off and was replaced in midfield by Tasos. Despite their misfortunes, AEK kept surging forward, with the gifted Mavros causing all sorts of problems out on the left with his top-speed runs and accurate crosses.

Kelly found himself under such pressure on one occasion that he took the risk of deliberately handling a centre only a few feet outside his own penalty box and was promptly shown the yellow card. Even so, Rangers often looked dangerous and Masson wasted good chances.

QPR: Parkes, Hollins, Gillard, Kelly, McLintock, Webb, Thomas, Francis, Masson, Bowles, Givens.
Referee: Ole Amundsen (Denmark)

QPR 1 Luton Town 2

1 September 1981 – Division Two

In a game marking the first use of the £300,000 weatherproof artificial playing surface Rangers found out the hard way that visitors to Loftus Road were likely to enjoy the experience. David Pleat, the Luton manager, said 'If teams come here wanting to play, there will be some great games on this pitch. We loved the experience'. The synthetic surface, called Omniturf, certainly favoured Rangers in the first half, but Luton clearly learned many lessons from their mistakes and their performance after the interval was brilliant. Once they had mastered the pace it was simply a question of when the speedy

Hill would escape the clutches of Gregory and Waddock, with Horton and Aizlewood masterminding things from the back. Luton took a firm grip of the game – a situation which had seemed unlikely during Rangers' dominance of the first half.

Findlay in the Luton goal was kept busy as Francis and Flanagan kept up a steady stream of passes towards King and Allen, but apart from having to save from Roeder and Allen the goalkeeper was largely able to watch the QPR strikers squander their early chances. Luton were hardly in contention at that stage and it was no real surprise when Rangers went ahead after 35 minutes. Hazell, their big central-defender, chipped an immaculate cross to the far past where King went into the record books by heading the first League goal on a synthetic pitch.

Allen might have made it 2–0 after an hour, but Findlay made a brilliant close range save from his header. From then on it was Luton who showed all the composure, complementing their intricate one-touch play with a series of sweeping counter-attacks. They equalised after 70 minutes with a fine goal, which perhaps might not have been possible on grass. Hill accelerated down the right and hooked a diagonal cross over the Rangers defence to Aizlewood, who was able to take the ball on the half-volley and beat Burridge.

Few would have begrudged Luton their winning goal six minutes from the end. Aizlewood and White pressured the previously composed Francis into losing possession on the edge of the area and there was Hill streaming in behind them to fire an unstoppable drive past Burridge.

QPR: Burridge, Gregory, Fenwick, Waddock, Hazell, Roeder, Flanagan, Francis, Allen, King, Stainrod.
Luton: Findlay, Stephens, Aizlewood, Horton, Saxby, Doughty, Hill, Stein, White, Antic, Ingram.

QPR 1 Tottenham Hotspur 1

22 May 1982 – FA Cup Final

Queen's Park Rangers ended this game level after refusing to be broken by a goal sickeningly deflected into their net in the second half of extra-time and coming back to claim an equaliser that allowed them to contest this FA Cup Final once again a week later. Rangers' 'keeper Peter Hucker had deployed his bulk to such athletic and inspired purpose between the posts that Spurs found themselves in need of deadly finishers on a day when they had none. That combination of Hucker's resistance and the last-stride mistakes of the attackers crowding in on him, particularly the flawed

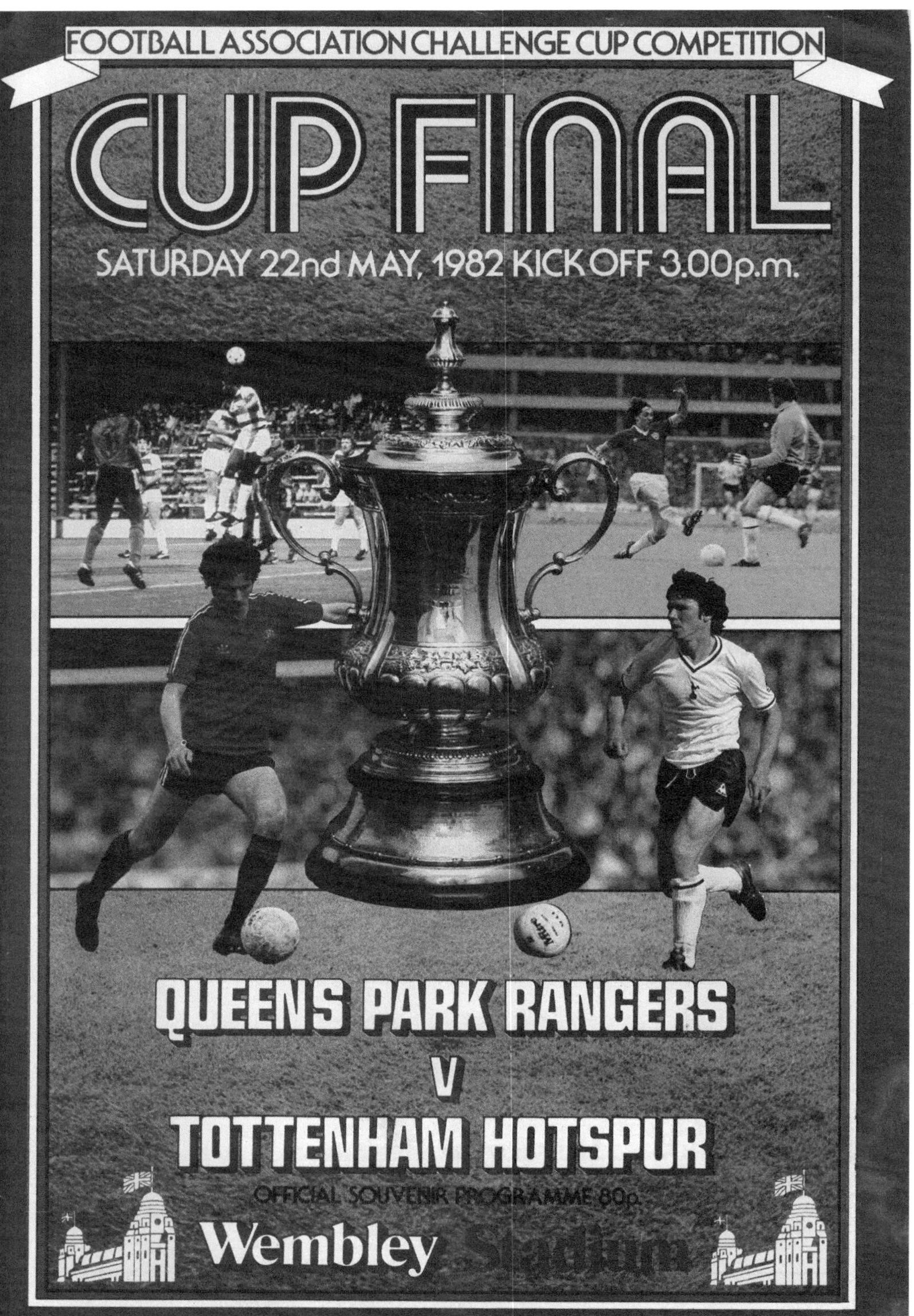
FOOTBALL ASSOCIATION CHALLENGE CUP COMPETITION
CUP FINAL
SATURDAY 22nd MAY, 1982 KICK OFF 3.00p.m.
QUEENS PARK RANGERS
V
TOTTENHAM HOTSPUR
OFFICIAL SOUVENIR PROGRAMME 80p.
Wembley Stadium

shooting of Steve Archibald, kept the teams level for 109 minutes on an afternoon that Tottenham's greater depth of experience and ability might have turned into a parade. When they did score, their goal had so much of the fortuitous about it that it could have shattered Rangers. Not only was the referee an accidental but serious obstacle to Waddock but when Hoddle shot (after exchanging passes with Roberts) the ball spun off the inside of Currie's leg and took a course that ruined Hucker's chances of saving. Yet Rangers, in spite of being aware that they had come near to being killed off in the first FA Cup Final they had ever played, rose above the blow that would have demoralised much bigger battalions.

When Fenwick powerfully headed in the equaliser after a long throw by Stainrod and a back header from Hazell, it was a fine reward for the defiant spirit of Hucker and for the exemplary leadership of Roeder. Micklewhite (who did well as substitute after an injury Allen had received as early as the first minute took that player off in the 52nd) took special honours along with Waddock, but praise was due to all who continued to battle on.

Roberts hustled aggressively in the middle of the field and, although Irishman Waddock was effectively reducing the impact of Hoddle's dramatic talent, that disappointment for Spurs was balanced by Currie's tendency to drop so deep that Hazard was able to thrust forward as an additional menace to Hucker. Rangers were spurred by Micklewhite's arrival in the 52nd minute into producing their best attacks of the match so far. Gregory was right to castigate himself after his header squandered a fine centre from the substitute and both Flanagan and Waddock shot too high after excellent approach play which was initiated by Currie. When Archibald steered the ball to Crooks's feet on the left, the usually efficient finisher could have done much better than hoist it over the crossbar. Crooks sought to compensate by releasing Archibald even more comprehensively but Hucker, sprinting off his line, lunged to his right and pushed the shot wide for a corner. The goalkeeper was equally brilliant soon afterwards when he saved painfully at Perryman's feet after another splendid pass by Hoddle. There was still more outstanding work from Hucker to thwart Hoddle but as the 90 minutes ended it was Stainrod's volley that forced a diving interception from Clemence.

The second half of extra-time had scarcely begun when Brooke announced his presence with a 25-yard drive that Hucker edged over his crossbar. Much worse was to come for the goalkeeper as Waddock's challenge for the ball against Hoddle was impeded by the proximity of the referee and as the Rangers player fell injured Hoddle was able to move on and exchange passes with Roberts. After collecting the return, Hoddle had to reach in a hurry for the shot and was almost on his haunches when he delivered it with his right foot, but a deflection off Currie's leg made the blow deadly and the ball skidded beyond Hucker's right side.

Few teams could have kept up their belief in a good result after that but Queen's Park Rangers, to their credit, certainly did. Within six minutes they were level and Wembley was looking forward to its second Cup Final reply in two years. The goal that took Rangers towards that extra chance started from a long throw near the corner flag on the left. Stainrod's throw was back-headed at the nearpost by Hazell and the ball rose in a high arc across the six yard box and into the path of Fenwick, who headed the ball into the top of the net.

QPR: Hucker, Fenwick, Gillard, Waddock, Hazell, Roeder, Currie, Flanagan, Allen, Stainrod, Gregory. Sub: Micklewhite.
Spurs: Clemence, Hughton, Miller, Price, Hazard, Perryman, Roberts, Archibald, Galvin, Hoddle, Crooks. Sub: Brooke.

QPR 5 Newcastle United 5

22 September 1984 – Division One

Rangers played out of their skin in this game, which saw them look dead and buried after a four-goal first-half hiding. Rangers manager Alan Mullery had admitted that he had told his shattered squad at half-time: 'There is no way you can score four goals.' His players proved him wrong with a second half salvo scripted straight out of the comic books.

Rangers had been appalling in the first half, in which Chris Waddle drummed out a three-goal message to Robson. It looked as if the day would belong exclusively to Waddle as he ripped the heart out of Rangers' ragged rearguard. Single-handedly, he took on Rangers' back four and one by one exposed them to his electrifying pace and stunning skills. He stripped Rangers bare as early as the third minute with a run and cross that gave Neil McDonald the simplest of far-post headers to set the Geordies on their way. Then, in 24 sparkling minutes, Waddle seemed to have killed off Rangers with the first hat-trick of his career. He had slipped his first under 'keeper Peter Hucker in the 17th minute, drilled in a second after Ken Wharton's shot had rebounded from a post in the 25th minute and then curved a 25-yarder beyond the clutching hands of Hucker four minutes from the interval.

Rangers, with Mullery's words of gloom still ringing in their ears, knew they had to score quickly in the second half to stand even the remotest chance. And Gary Bannister did just that within two minutes of the restart, heading home on the rebound after Kevin Carr had parried his first effort. Now it was Newcastle's turn to be put on the rack and in the 56th minute their defensive panic put Rangers right back in the game. Peter Haddock's wild clearance cannoned off Ken Wharton and clipped Simon Stainrod, who gleefully claimed Rangers' second goal. John Gregory's glorious lob from a subtle Micklewhite pass after 74 minutes reduced the gap to just one goal, but that man Waddle interrupted Rangers' celebrations six minutes from time by leaving Steve Wicks sitting on the ground and centring for Wharton to tap in Newcastle's fifth. However, within 60 seconds Wicks had atoned when he headed home a Micklewhite cross.

50p
QPR
DIVISION 1 1984/85
NEWCASTLE UNITED
SATURDAY, 22nd SEPTEMBER 1984 (k.o. 3.00 p.m.)
QPR
GUINNESS

With Rangers' fans on the edges of their seats, it was Micklewhite who conjured up the game's remarkable punchline. Slipping easily onto a pass from substitute Ian Stewart, he rifled a shot into the roof of the net with the scoreboard already indicating that 90 minutes were up.

Afterwards Mullery slumped in a chair as he said: 'I'm sitting down because I am still shaking. I will remember this game for the rest of my life.' He added: 'At half-time we were devastated and to score four times, let alone five, was never on. I told them they had no chance, but to go out and play for their pride. I couldn't believe we had given away goals so easily. No, I can't even remember who scored our goals because, quite honestly, it was something that was never going to happen. A miracle took place and my players made that miracle happen.'

QPR: Hucker, Neill, Dawes, Fereday, Wicks, Fenwick, Micklewhite, Fillery, Bannister, Stainrod, Gregory. Sub: Stewart.
Newcastle United: Carr, Brown, Saunders, Haddock, Anderson, Roeder, McDonald, Wharton, Waddle, Beardsley, McCreery. Sub: Harris.

QPR 0 Oxford United 3

20 April 1986 – Milk Cup Final

This game saw a distinctly subdued performance from Rangers, who were puzzlingly below the superb standards achieved in every other round of the competition. Oxford United achieved the distinction of winning the Milk Cup for the first time with the most decisive victory recorded by any Wembley finalist in this competition of the past 19 years.

Though this was a commendable all-round team performance, the key figure in the resounding triumph for the underdogs was Hebberd. This skilful, former Southampton midfielder took part in three goals that upset the clear odds in favour of a Rangers victory. The crowd had begun to wonder if either team would create a chance, let alone turn it into a goal, in what had been expected to develop into a high scoring final.

Then, after an exceptionally dull half an hour, enlivened only by an unsuccessful penalty appeal from Aldridge, Oxford began to move forward purposefully. With Hebberd, Phillips and Houghton working smoothly in midfield, Rangers' defence came under steady pressure and their confidence was quickly undermined. Five minutes before half-time Oxford took the lead with a simple goal, laid on by Aldridge for

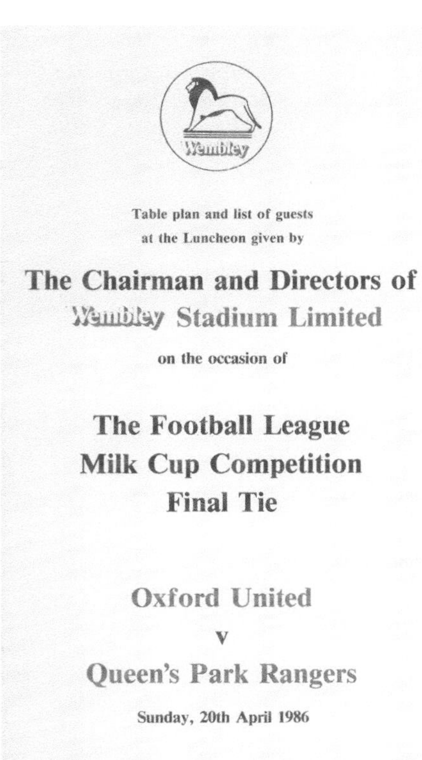
Wembley

Table plan and list of guests
at the Luncheon given by

The Chairman and Directors of
Wembley Stadium Limited

on the occasion of

The Football League
Milk Cup Competition
Final Tie

Oxford United
v
Queen's Park Rangers

Sunday, 20th April 1986

Hebberd, who turned calmly on the left edge of the six yard box to place the ball inside the near post.

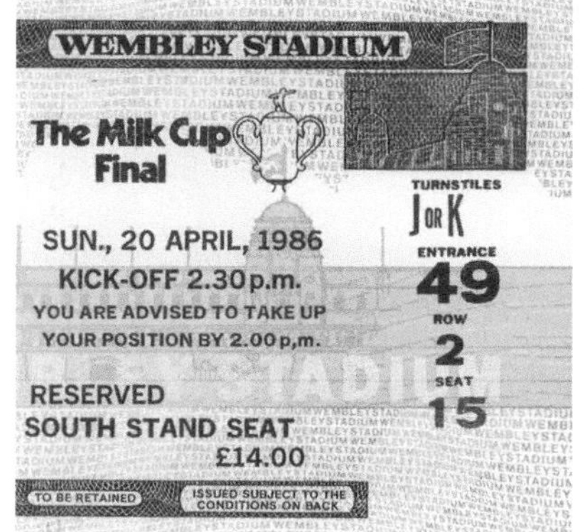

Once they had moved in front, Oxford never looked like they would lose their grip on what ultimately became a one-sided game. Fenwick, James, Robinson and Allen failed to cope defensively with Oxford's free-moving midfield unit and created scarcely an opening in the first hour. Victory slipped still further away from Rangers, with Oxford scoring a goal worthy of the big Wembley occasion. Having checked his stride to counter Rangers' offside trap, Houghton pushed the ball to Hebberd, then ran on to the return and placed the ball firmly beyond Barron's reach.

This had the effect of waking up one or two Rangers players and, with Rosenior replacing Allen, they briefly put Oxford's suspect defence under a little pressure. Yet, though they faced a back four with one of the worst defensive records in the League, Rangers did not fire a shot on target until the 72nd minute and even then Judge tipped a lone one from Dawes over the bar. In contrast, Aldridge, usually a lethal finisher, missed a couple of chances before Oxford put the issue beyond all doubt four minutes from the end. Hebberd's contribution was a perfectly judged pass to Aldridge, whose shot was beaten out by the desperate Barron and promptly planted in the net by Charles.

QPR (13th in Division One): Barron, McDonald, Dawes, Neill, Wicks, Fenwick, Allen, James, Bannister, Byrne, Robinson. Sub: Rosenoir.
Oxford United (20th in Division One): Judge, Langan, Trewick, Phillips, Briggs, Shotton, Houghton, Aldridge, Charles, Hebberd, Brock.

LIVERPOOL 1 QPR 3

30 March 1991 – Division One

This game saw Rangers do London neighbours Arsenal a big favour by clearing the way for the Gunners to return to the top of the First Division. There was no fluke about Rangers' victory, for they were always the slicker, more organised team and it took their unbeaten run to eight games since they had come under the influence of a sports psychologist.

Rangers' confidence grew from the moment goalkeeper Jan Stejskal saved superbly with his right hand from Ian Rush and they soon claimed the lead. Simon Barker centred from the left for Les Ferdinand, who took the ball around David Burrows and fired against an upright. The ball found its way back out to Barker and this time Ferdinand made no mistake as he headed his seventh goal in eight

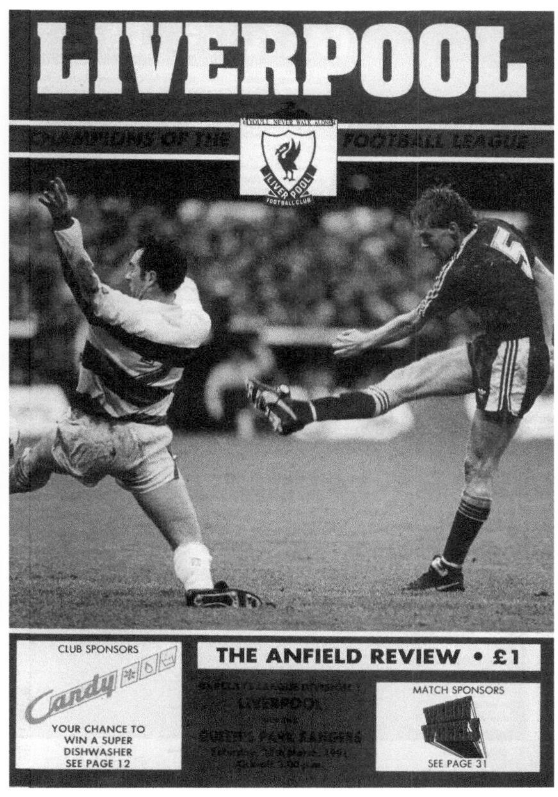

games. Before then Liverpool had been threatened by Rangers, with Roy Wegerle racing from his own half past three defenders to lay on a chance for Andy Sinton which brought a good save out of Mike Hooper. The Liverpool goalkeeper then needed to be agile to tip over the bar a 30-yard shot from the ever-dangerous Ferdinand.

Liverpool lacked accuracy and decisiveness and clearly missed the influence of John Barnes, who was ill with the flu. Perhaps many of their players were feeling the effects of the mid-week international, but whatever the reasons they never looked like table-toppers. Rangers, in contrast, were magnificent, from Stejskal in goal to Sinton in the number-11 shirt, but particularly outstanding was Andy Tillson at the heart of defence and Ray Wilkins, who orchestrated their most dangerous moves from midfield.

With their confidence rising by the minute and Liverpool unable to establish control there were more anxious moments for the champions which culminated in Wegerle putting Rangers two goals ahead just before the break. David Burrows allowed a pass from Steve Staunton to run past him, presumably thinking the ball would safely reach Hooper, but Wegerle pounced to take the ball wide of the goalkeeper and score from an angle.

Liverpool made changes in the second half with Garry Ablett moving from central defence to left-back, as Garry Gillespie switched from right-back to the centre and Steve Nicol dropped into the right-back berth. They thought they had found a way back when Jan Molby tucked away a penalty awarded for handball against Rufus Brevett.

In a thrilling second half, with Liverpool surging forward and gradually turning the screw on the Rangers defence, Peter Beardsley struck the outside of the post and Stejskal somehow pawed away another header from Hysen. Just when it seemed Liverpool's sheer weight of pressure might produce an equaliser, they were stunned by a third Rangers goal. A Ferdinand cross was just too high for the inrushing Wilkins and the ball fell to Nicol in his own six yard box, but as he dithered substitute Clive Wilson stabbed the ball off his toe and into the net with his first touch.

QPR: Stejskal, Bardsley, Brevett, Tillson, Peacock, Maddix, Wilkins, Barker, Ferdinand, Wegerle, Sinton. Subs: Allen, Wilson.

Liverpool: Hooper, Hysen, Burrows, Nicol, Molby, Ablett, Beardsley, Houghton, Rush, Staunton, Gillespie. Sub: Rosenthal.

Referee: M.D. Reid (Birmingham)

MANCHESTER UNITED 1 QPR 4

1 January 1992 – Division One

Manchester United's second and biggest defeat of the season, at the hands of Rangers, knocked them off the top of the First Division as Dennis Bailey scored a hat-trick. Gerry Francis's side, three quarters of the way down the table but hitting peak form, had rocked the Championship favourites with two goals in the first five minutes, and they had then wrapped it up with two more goals in the second half, putting United second and a point behind the leaders.

It was United's worst defeat at Old Trafford since losing 4–0 to Nottingham Forest in December 1978. They were narrowly beaten by Sheffield Wednesday away in October, but otherwise this season they had only lost to Athletico Madrid in the European Cup-Winners' Cup. Ferguson had warned his side not to 'overlook' this comparatively easy looking fixture but United's players had been deaf to the statistics which warned that QPR were on a roll, six games undefeated and only one away defeat in the last 10. 'It was not a lack of planning on my part, it was a lack of determination in clearing the ball and defending properly,' said Ferguson. 'We hadn't started when they were 2–0 up.'

For the first goal Rangers found United's defence fast asleep. Blackmore failed to close down Wegerle on the right, while Bruce failed to intercept his square pass to Barker, and Webb could not close down Andy Sinton whose shot rocketed past Schmeichel. Two minutes later they found the goal wide open again. This time Bailey skipped through the middle, past Blackmore, and although Schmeichel managed to get to the shot, he could not hold it and it rolled past him into the net. United, without Robson and Irwin, and with Giggs 'rested' on the bench, could make only a half-hearted attempt at a comeback even at that stage. Sharpe, making his first start since the European Cup-Winners' Cup Final last May, was back in his familiar role on the left flank. But he was totally shut out of the game by the excellent Manchester-born full-back Bardsley.

The replacement of Phelan, who had taken a knock earlier, by the popular Giggs brought a round of cheering and a ray of hope. He moved into the middle alongside Hughes. However, it was United's defence that needed attention. Bailey decided to test it solo and found the way wide open, calmly chipping the goalkeeper to put QPR three ahead just before the hour. McClair netted twice for a still struggling United

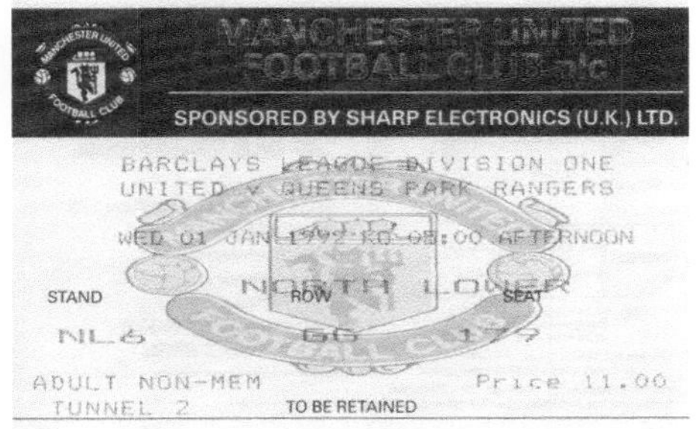

after that. The first time he was ruled offside, and the second time, in the 83rd minute, his strike from a move begun by Giggs wide on the right seemed only a poor consolation rather than the start of a realistic revival. Indeed, it was only a minute later that QPR responded. The magnificent Bardsley again crossed from the right to the far left-hand corner of United's penalty area. Sinton, completely unmarked, had only Schmeichel to beat. Miraculously, the goalkeeper managed to touch the shot onto his far post, and without a red shirt in sight Bailey followed up to complete his hat-trick with only four minutes remaining.

Ferguson, though, refused to moan: 'Perhaps it has come at an appropriate time to remind us that we have got where we are through hard work, and if we desert that route it could end up in embarrassment. Hopefully, this is a one-off and they have got it out of their systems.'

Francis was delighted and was swiftly followed into the dressing room by a tray of six bottles of champagne.

QPR: Stejskal, Bardsley, Wilson, Wilkins, Peacock, McDonald, Holloway, Barker, Bailey, Wegerle, Sinton.
Manchester United: Schmeichel, Parker, Blackmore, Bruce, Webb, Pallister, Phelan, Ince, McClair, Hughes, Sharpe. Sub: Giggs.
Referee: K. Barratt (Coventry)

QPR 6 Crystal Palace 0

9 May 1999 – Division One

Rangers Reprieved
Six of the Best for Francis: I am Ready to Rebuild the Team

The threat of relegation and humiliation was banished in spectacular style in this game, as QPR halted their downward slide just short of the drop into the Second Division. Six years after finishing as London's top club, with a fifth place in the Premiership, they had found themselves fighting in the purgatory of the Nationwide First Division basement. They responded in the nick of time with a six-goal hammering of their London rivals, including a stunning hat-trick from Chris Kiwomya, which had the stadium celebrating as though Rangers had just won the European Cup.

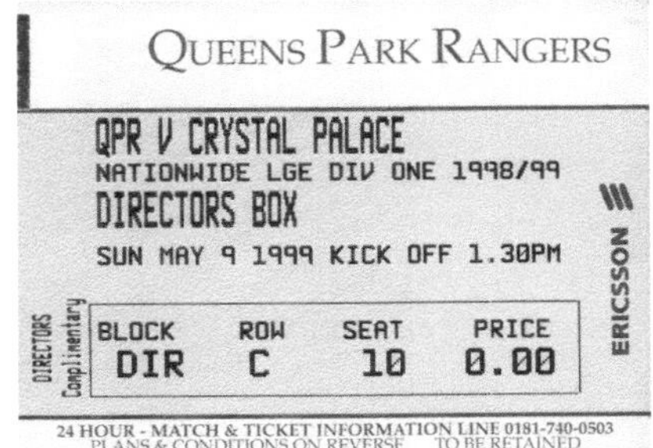

Palace only managed one shot on target in a woeful performance which was always going to end in defeat for the visitors, despite the jitters of the home side following a run of five successive defeats, in which only one goal had been scored. On eight minutes Rangers' nerves were calmed when a clever move involving Kiwomya and Keith Rowland saw the ball cleared to the edge of the Palace area. George Kulscar waited patiently for the ball to come down before thumping a superb volley into the net, with Palace 'keeper Kevin Miller watching in admiration. Two minutes before half-time Miller was at fault as Rangers deservedly took a two-goal lead. A huge clearance by Ludek Miklosko found his opposite number dawdling on his line and Kiwomya took full advantage, getting to the ball before any Palace defender and, after hitting the post, calmly heading in the rebound.

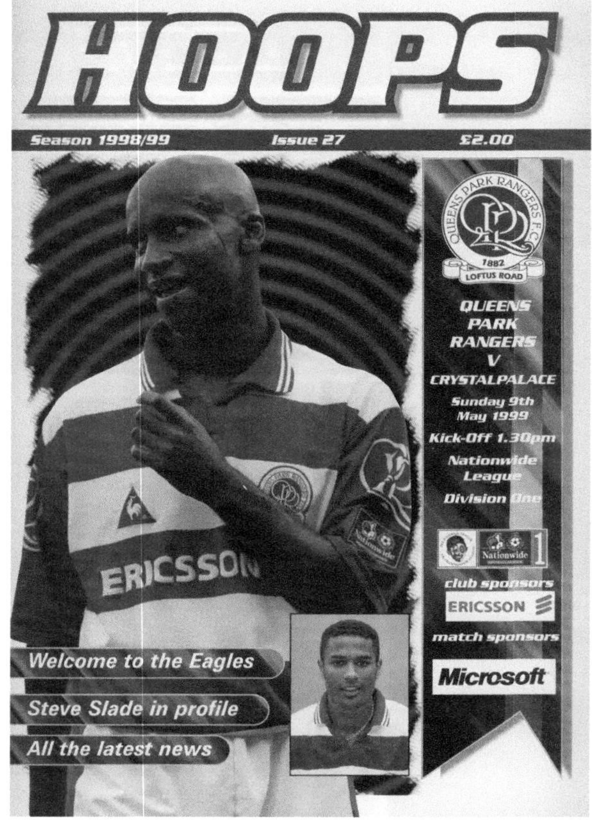

Palace's token resistance all but ended three minutes after the break when they were reduced to 10 men. Palace had won a throw-in and Gavin Peacock, the Rangers midfielder, passed the ball to the referee who juggled with it. As he kicked the ball to the touchline Zhiyi made contact with the referee in an attempt to get the ball back. He was immediately shown the red card, despite appeals from all the Rangers players in the vicinity.

Rangers went for the kill and on 56 minutes they made it 3–0 when Tony Scully's free-kick was knocked on by Steve Slade and forced over the line by Kiwomya in the ensuing scramble. Scully made it four on 76 minutes when he latched on to a Andy Linighan pass to thump in an unstoppable shot from the right-hand corner of the penalty box into the top left-hand corner of the goal. Six minutes later Palace were down to nine men when Woozley was dismissed after pulling down Scully as he was about to shoot into an empty net, following good work by Kiwomya on the wing. Kiwomya was given the opportunity of his hat-tick from the spot, but his effort was blocked by Miller, only for Tim Breacker to follow up and make it 5–0.

Still Rangers were not finished, as three minutes later Scully crossed to Kiwomya, who scored his third goal at the third attempt. Miller saved his first effort, and the subsequent header from the parry, before being beaten at the foot of the post. Kiwomya was then substituted and received a standing ovation from the delighted and extremely relieved Rangers supporters. Before the end came Rowland hit a post and substitute Kevin Gallen had a great effort that went just wide.

The only man who seemed to recognise the hollow nature of the victory against a Palace team, who had ended the match with nine men following the dismissals of Fan Zhiyi and David Woozley, was manager Gerry Francis. Uncomfortable with the thought of revelling in the achievement of simply avoiding a catastrophe, Francis said: 'My job starts tomorrow. It is all very well celebrating today but we should not be celebrating avoiding relegation. We want to be up in the promotion race. It is going to be a slow process because we cannot compete in the transfer market, so we have to bring the kids through and find players from outside of the League who will do a job. I definitely do not want another season like this one.'

QPR: Miklosko, Breacker, Baraclough, Kulscar, Linighan, Maddix, Scully, Peacock, Rowland, Slade, Kiwomya. Subs: Murray, Gallen.
Crystal Palace: Miller, Frampton, Woozley, Austin, Petric, Thompson, Foster, Zhiyi, Martin, Morrison, Mullins. Subs: Tuttle, Burton, Carlisle.
Referee:

QPR 1 VAUXHALL MOTORS 1

26 November 2002 – FA Cup first-round replay (QPR lost 3–4 on penalties)

Tuesday 26 November 2002 will go down in history as one of the most embarrassing nights in the history of Queen's Park Rangers Football Club. Things had seemed to get off to a bright enough start with Rangers having plenty of possession but failing to turn this into genuine chances. That is not to say that Vauxhall Motors were out of their depth, far from it. Left-winger Peter Cumiskey was giving Forbes problems and he had two chances in the opening 15 minutes to give the Motormen the lead.

Rangers opened the scoring through an excellent goal from Andy Thomson. Padula picked him out with a low pass from left-back and Thomson dinked the ball over the advancing Ralph. This should have been the impetus that Rangers needed to go on and win the game comfortably, but instead it galvanised Vauxhall Motors into a devastating 10 minutes of football.

Quick passing and incisive movement cut the Rangers backline open time and time again and they were back on level terms within a few minutes. Tommy Williams was robbed while trying to clear the ball on the edge of his own box and Terry Fearns was played through, and as he attempted to shoot he was felled by Digby. The ball ran loose to former Liverpool trainee Phil Brazier and he fired into an empty net from four yards. The Vauxhall Motors players launched into scenes of wild celebration at their equaliser. The

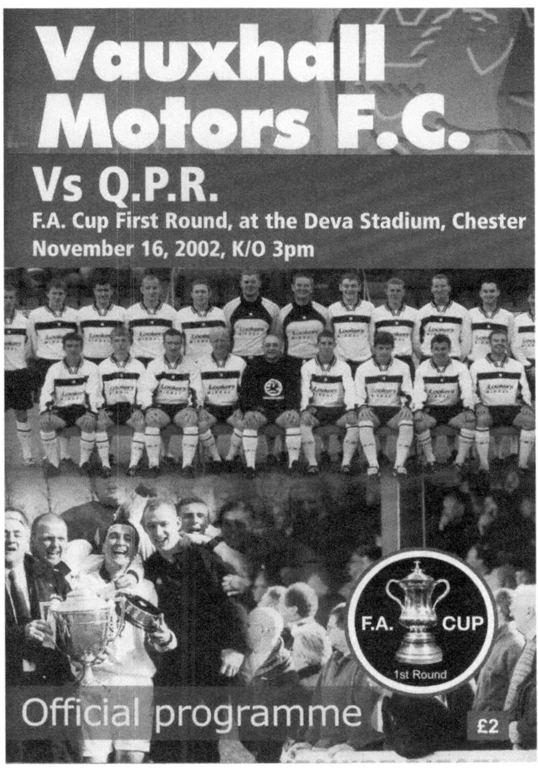

Programme from first match, played at Deva Stadium Chester.

SPOT ON!

Nesbitt a star in QPR drama

VAUXHALL MOTORS FC have been propelled from the relative obscurity of the Unibond League to become FA Cup giantkillers after they held Queens Park Rangers to a draw at Chester, then beat the Second Division side in a thrilling replay.

Carl Nesbitt, above, who works in the Vauxhall plant at Ellesmere Port, scored the third penalty in the shoot-out after extra time at QPR.

The soccer heroes were praised on prime time national television, had their 2nd Round match broadcast live on Sky Sports and generated many columns of newspaper coverage.

Vauxhall Mirror was at each stage of the cup run, even delaying publication of this issue in order to cover both the QPR replay and the second round tie with Macclesfield Town. Our reports and pictures are on pages 15 & 16.

VAUXHALL FA CUP GLORY – PAGES 15 & 16

game continued with wave after wave of Vauxhall attacks and the home crowd became ever more agitated with what they were witnessing.

Rangers had chances, through Thomson, Furlong and Burgess, to regain the lead but they were squandered. Digby then almost gifted Vauxhall a second when he came for a cross only to change his mind as he went to catch it. Young headed goalward but Digby redeemed himself with a fine save.

The start of the second half saw Rangers creating and missing numerous chances, with the crowd getting more restless by the failure to break down a team three divisions below them. Dennis Oli replaced Burgess, and he looked as though he had enough to turn the game in Rangers' favour. Vauxhall soon realised his threat and posted two men on the youngster in an attempt to nullify him. Holloway brought Karl Connolly on for Padula in an attempt to seal the game and in the last couple of minutes of normal time Rangers were still creating chances to win the game. Langley volleyed wide when he probably should have done better and Thomson had a header brilliantly saved by Andy Ralph. The former Tranmere 'keeper had foiled Rangers with numerous saves and seemed to be justifying his Man of the Match award from the first game.

The game went into extra-time and Williams was replaced by Danny Murphy, and again more chances were created and squandered as Ralph denied Rangers time and again. So, with the game finishing 1–1 after extra-time, it was down to penalties. Furlong missed Rangers' first, but Palmer, Thomson and Langley scored theirs. With Vauxhall Motors scoring all four of theirs Connolly had to be successful to keep Rangers alive, but he missed the target and the Vauxhall Motors players were given a rousing ovation by the Loftus Road crowd.

QPR: Digby, Forbes, Palmer, Carlisle, Padula, Burgess, Bircham, Langley, Williams, Thomson, Furlong. Subs: Oli, Connolly, Murphy.

QPR 0 Cardiff City 1 (aet)

25 May 2003 – Division Two Play-off Final

The team for this game virtually picked itself with the only dilemma for manager Ian Holloway being who would partner semi-final hero Paul Furlong in attack. Chris Day started in goal with the usual back four of Kelly, Carlisle, Shittu and Padula in front of him. Gallen was again wide right with Palmer, Bircham and McLeod alongside him, as Richard Pacquette got the nod to partner Furlong in attack.

Cardiff started the quicker of the two sides with Earnshaw firing wildly over the bar, which was followed soon after by Graham Kavanagh smashing a volley wide. This was just about the only look in that Earnshaw got in 90 minutes as Shittu and Carlisle did a superb job on him. Kevin Gallen tested the reflexes of Neil Alexander on the 10-minute mark with a fierce free-kick from the left that the Bluebirds 'keeper tipped over the bar. Richard Pacquette was next to try his luck but rather than opting for the controlled finish he blasted his shot into the massed ranks of the Cardiff fans at the South End of the Millennium Stadium.

The game was so nervy that both teams were struggling to create anything in the way of clear-cut chances. The half chances became more and more important and Furlong should have done better when he shrugged off Gabbidon and chipped both Alexander and his goal. Furlong headed another chance wide before he was the first player entered into Mr Webb's notebook for a wild challenge on Gabbidon. Cardiff's left wing was proving productive for them and Andy Legg was having an excellent game. Kavanagh headed Legg's cross over the bar and minutes later the Irishman was in Webb's book for cleaning out Kelly.

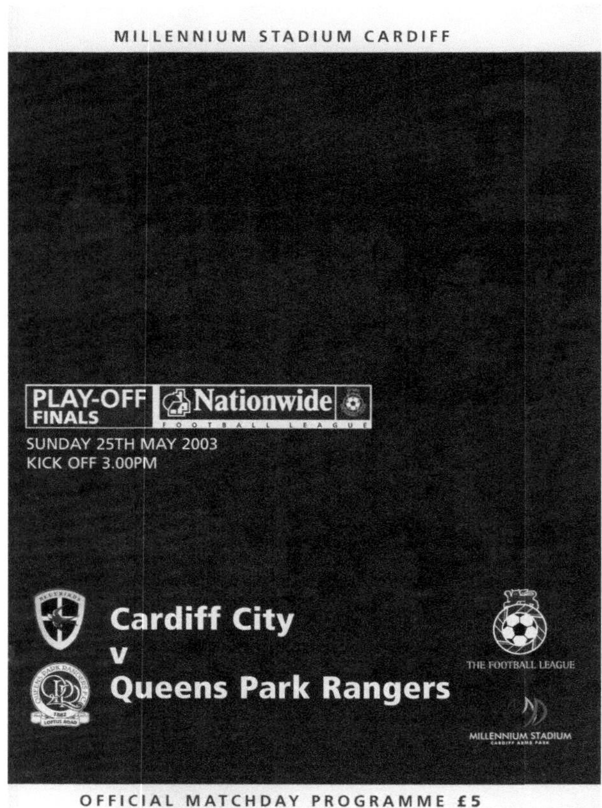

The second period started with Rangers in the ascendancy and both Gallen and Furlong had early chances to snatch the advantage. Firstly Gallen was played in by Furlong but his left-footed shot was straight at Alexander. Furlong then managed to find space in the box but he smashed a wild effort high and wide when he ought to have done better. Pacquette came within millimetres of a goal when McLeod spotted his near post run, but the cross just evaded the striker's boot. Soon after, Thomson replaced Pacquette as Holloway tried to shake things up. Gallen tried his luck again and his volley from just outside the box fizzed over the bar.

Ten minutes from the end, Williams replaced Padula. For Cardiff Andy Campbell replaced Earnshaw, much to the striker's disgust, but this was to prove to be the difference between the two sides.

Thomson fired well wide with five minutes to go and then in the final minute he had the chance to make himself a play-off hero once again. Prior allowed a ball to bounce and Thomson nipped round him to loop a header over Alexander and just wide of the post. With Cardiff enjoying much more possession most of the Rangers players had run themselves to a standstill, yet there was still another 30 minutes to go.

In extra-time Clarke Carlisle produced a magnificent challenge to thwart Campbell and at the other end Furlong was off target with a far post header from a McLeod cross. The chances now started to come in quick succession as tired legs and minds took over. Carlisle surged from the back with the ball and played it into Thomson, who swept it wide to Gallen. The big centre-back had continued his run and Gallen found him with a tremendous cross, for him to plant his header agonisingly wide. At the other end a Graham Kavanagh free-kick found the head of Prior. His header from no more than six yards was accurate, yet somehow Day managed to fling up his arms to turn the ball away.

The second period of extra-time produced yet more chances. Andy Legg cracked a free-kick over the bar and at the other end Tommy Williams set off on a weaving run down the left. He managed to beat two Cardiff players yet with Thomson and Furlong in the box screaming for a cut back he shot right-footed. The shot was weak and failed to trouble Alexander. Then the moment came that condemned Rangers to another season in Division Two and sent the Bluebirds up. Carlisle trapped the ball at the back and tried to knock the ball up-field but his pass was poor and fell straight to Whalley. Campbell was already on his way and the ball to find him was perfect, and Shittu stood for offside but the decision never came. Once he realised this he could not get back to Campbell and the former Boro striker lobbed over the advancing Day to send the Cardiff fans into delirium.

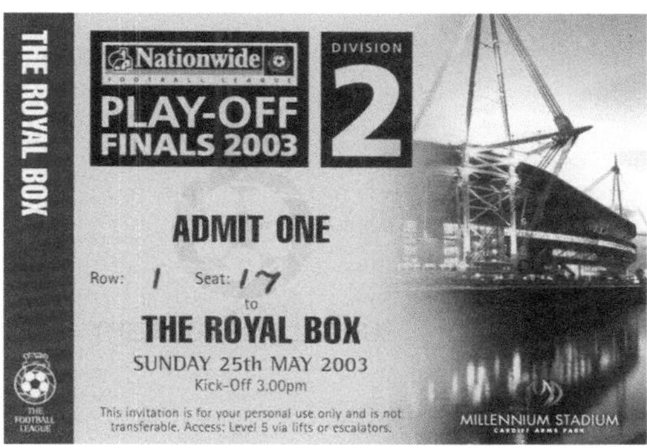

QPR: Day, Kelly, Carlisle, Shittu, Padula, Gallen, Palmer, Bircham, McLeod, Pacquette, Furlong. Subs: Thomson, Williams.
Referee: Mr Webb

Sheffield Wednesday 1 QPR 3

8 May 2004 – Division Two

This game saw Rangers, after enduring a season packed with so many highs and lows, win in style. For the third game in a row manager Ian Holloway named an unchanged line up: Camp was in goal behind Edghill, Carlisle, Rose and Padula. The midfield four were Ainsworth, Johnson, Bircham and Rowlands, with Gallen and Furlong in attack.

Rangers flew out of the traps and could easily have been three or four goals up within the first 10 minutes had they been a bit calmer in front of goal. Bircham, Rowlands and Furlong all saw great chances come and go as Wednesday could not get close to them in a frenetic opening period. The tension began to rise in the Leppings Lane End as a fear that so many missed chances could cost Rangers began to sweep over the fans. Wednesday had started to create some chances of their own now as Carlisle began to look shaky and Matthew Rose was doing all he could to cover for his colleague.

At the other end chances were still coming and Gallen twice tried his luck. First he hit a shot from the edge of the area that flew well over the bar and then he registered Rangers' first shot on target with a low effort that Pressman dived to save. However, his next effort was far more clinical and gave Rangers the lead their pressure had so richly warranted. Gareth Ainsworth careered down the right and sent in a ball that both Rowlands and Furlong had a go at but could not convert. A Wednesday player got half a block on it but could only send the ball into the path of Gallen and he rammed it high into the net to send the Rangers fans into a frenzy. Ainsworth then came within a whisker of making it two only minutes later with a trademark volley. Pressman dived full length across his goal and was grateful to see the ball whistle past the upright rather than inside it. As the half-time whistle approached Rangers suffered a blow when Carlisle went over on his ankle and was forced off the field.

Gnohere replaced him but had little chance to get into the game before the whistle went for half-time.

Rangers made a brilliant start to the second half when Furlong doubled the lead after barely three minutes. Bircham picked him out in the box and in one fluid movement he killed the ball on his chest, rolled defender Chris Carr and slammed the ball right-footed past the helpless Pressman. Rangers' fans were in raptures now and with one foot planted firmly in Division One they roared the team on. Suddenly, though, there was a change in the flow of the game as the Sheffield Wednesday midfield began to overrun the Rangers quartet and create some chances of their own. Time and again Matthew Rose had to step in to quell an attack before it got into a really dangerous area but such was the pressure it only seemed a matter of time before the Rangers defence would be breached. Chris Brunt, an impressive thorn in Rangers' side all afternoon, ran in from the left and managed to evade the attentions of Edghill, Ainsworth and Bircham before feeding Robins on the edge of the box. He in turn picked out Jon Shaw and he drilled a low finish past Lee Camp to jangle the nerves of Rangers. It was time for a response from QPR but Wednesday kept coming. Padula managed to block out another effort from Shaw and Rose made a crucial intervention when Robins managed to break clear on the Rangers left.

Just when it looked as though a Wednesday equaliser might be on the cards Rangers' luck for the season finally turned. The slice of good fortune came courtesy of former Rangers trialist Chris Carr. When Martin Rowlands accelerated down the left and smashed in a wicked cross nobody could have foreseen what would happen next, as Carr stepped forward and took an almighty hack at the ball to send it flying past Pressman to seal the victory that Rangers needed.

There were now 20 minutes to go and Rangers kept coming forward. The introduction of Jamie Cureton for Rowlands with 10 minutes to go put a little fizz into the team. He was bright and energetic and tried to get the ball down and run with it at any opportunity. At last, the referee finally bought the game to an end and Rangers had won by three goals to one.

QPR: Camp, Edghill, Carlisle, Rose, Padula, Ainsworth, Johnson, Bircham, Rowlands, Gallen, Furlong. Subs: Gnohere, Cureton.

100 Leading QPR Players

Total appearance figures do not include those made as a substitute.

Bert Addinall

Born: Paddington, 30 January 1921.

Signed from: RAF.
Debut: 17 March 1945.
Total appearances: 172.
Total goals: 73.

Popular centre-forward Bert Addinall was QPR's top scorer in three successive seasons. Previously with Kilburn United and British Oxygen, he moved to Loftus Road in 1944 and made his League debut in March 1945. He was a member of Dave Mangnall's 1947–48 Third Division South Championship squad, netting 59 goals in 150 League outings for QPR prior to joining Brighton in January 1953. Leading marksman for his new club in the 1953–54 season, he moved to Crystal Palace in July 1954 and then helped Snowdown CW win the Kent League title in 1954–55 and the Kent Senior Cup in 1956. He subsequently became a London black cab driver based in Sunbury and settled in Mytchett in retirement.

Clive Allen

Born: Stepney, 20 May 1961.

Signed from: Apprentice.
Debut: 4 November 1978.
Total appearances: 147.
Total goals: 83.

England international striker Clive Allen was top scorer as QPR finished fifth in the top-flight in 1983–84. A son of former QPR favourite Les Allen, he netted a hat-trick on his full League debut for Rangers against Coventry in November 1978. He was leading marksman in 1979–80 and joined Arsenal for £1.2 million in June 1980. He then followed Terry Venables back to QPR from Crystal Palace in June 1981 and starred as the club were FA Cup finalists in 1982 and Second Division champions in 1982–83. He netted 72 goals in 136 League games overall before joining Spurs for £750,000 in August 1984, scoring in the 1987 FA Cup Final. He later played for Bordeaux, Manchester City, Chelsea, West Ham, Millwall and Carlisle, and he is currently coaching back at Spurs.

Les Allen

Born: Dagenham, 4 September 1937.

Signed from: Tottenham Hotspur.
Debut: 21 August 1965.
Total appearances: 146.
Total goals: 62.

Former England Under-23 centre-forward Les Allen starred alongside Rodney Marsh in QPR's 1966–67 Third Division title and League Cup double triumph. Initially a player with Briggs Sports, he joined Chelsea in September 1954 and moved to Spurs in exchange for Johnny Brooks in December 1959. Ever present in their 1960–61 double success, he joined QPR for a then record £20,000 in July 1965 and was the Third Division's leading goalscorer in 1965–66. He also starred in Rangers' 1967–68 promotion campaign and became player-manager in December 1968. After netting 55 times in 128 League outings he resigned in January 1971, after which he managed Woodford and Swindon. He also worked in the motor industry and currently lives in Hornchurch.

Martin Allen

Born: Reading, 14 August 1965.

Signed from: Apprentice.
Debut: 2 October 1984.
Total appearances: 154.
Total goals: 19.

England Under-21 midfielder Martin Allen played for QPR in the 1986 Milk Cup Final. A cousin of Clive and Bradley Allen, he turned professional at Loftus Road in May 1983 and made his League debut in Rangers' 2–0 defeat at Luton the following year. He missed just two matches in the 1987–88 campaign and netted 16 goals in 136 First Division games for QPR prior to joining West Ham for £550,000 in August 1989. He featured in their 1990–91 and 1992–93 promotion successes and then reunited with Terry Fenwick at Portsmouth in September 1995 and had a spell as their reserve-team boss. 'Mad Dog', as he was known, then became Reading's coach and has since been manager of Barnet, Brentford, MK Dons, Leicester City and currently Cheltenham Town.

Reg Allen

Born: Marylebone, 3 May 1919.

Signed from: Corona.

Debut: 26 November 1938.
Total appearances: 255.
Total goals: 0.

Brilliant goalkeeper Reg Allen was an important figure in QPR's 1947–48 Third Division South title triumph. He was discovered playing for Corona in local football and joined Rangers in May 1938, making his League debut in their 2–0 defeat at Newport County six months later. A wartime commando, he spent four years as a German prisoner of war. He missed just one match for QPR in 1946–47 and helped Rangers take Derby to an FA Cup sixth-round replay in 1947–48, making 183 League appearances before joining Manchester United for a British record for a goalkeeper of £12,000 in June 1950. He featured in their 1951–52 League Championship success before injury ended his career. Settling in Ealing, he died in May 1976.

Peter Angell

Born: Chalvey, 11 January 1932.

Signed from: Slough Town.
Debut: 12 September 1953.
Total appearances: 457.
Total goals: 40.

Long-serving wing-half Peter Angell was ever present in QPR's 1960–61 promotion near-miss. Starting his career with hometown club Slough Town, he moved to Loftus Road in July 1953 and made his League debut in Rangers' 2–0 victory at home to Walsall two months later. He formed a notable half-back line with George Petchey and Keith Rutter, missing just one match in both 1957–58 and 1958–59. He featured in QPR's seven-goal FA Cup wins over Barry Town in 1961–62 and Hinckley Athletic in 1962–63, and he netted 37 goals in 417 League outings before he retired in July 1965. He later became Charlton Athletic's coach and then Orient's trainer in October 1967 and assisted George Petchey, but he tragically died after collapsing during a training session in July 1979.

Gary Bannister

Born: Warrington, 22 July 1960.

Signed from: Sheffield Wednesday.
Debut: 25 August 1984.
Total appearances: 172.
Total goals: 72.

Former England Under-21 striker Gary Bannister was QPR's leading marksman in four successive seasons. Initially a

player with Coventry City, he joined Sheffield Wednesday for £80,000 in August 1981 and was top scorer in their 1983–84 promotion triumph. He moved to Loftus Road for £150,000 in August 1984 and starred as QPR reached the Milk Cup Final in 1986, netting 56 goals in 136 First Division games before he rejoined Coventry for £300,000 in March 1988. Moving to West Brom for £250,000 in March 1990, he later had spells at Nottingham Forest, Stoke City, Hong Kong Rangers, Lincoln City and Darlington, appearing in the 1995–96 Third Division Play-off Final. He now owns holiday accommodation in Porthleven.

David Bardsley

Born: Manchester, 11 September 1964.

Signed from: Oxford United.
Debut: 16 September 1989.
Total appearances: 294.
Total goals: 6.

England international right-back David Bardsley was capped twice while at QPR. Signing professional for Blackpool in November 1982, he moved to Watford for £150,000 in November 1983 and was an influential figure as they were FA Cup finalists in 1984. He joined Oxford United for £250,000 in September 1987 and moved to Loftus Road in a £375,000 deal involving Mark Stein in September 1989. He starred as QPR took Liverpool to an FA Cup sixth-round replay in 1989–90 and made his England debut against Spain in September 1992. He also helped Rangers finish fifth in the Premier League in 1992–93 and was their Player of the Year in 1993–94, netting four goals in 253 League outings prior to rejoining Blackpool in July 1998.

Simon Barker

Born: Farnworth, 4 November 1964.

Signed from: Blackburn Rovers.
Debut: 27 August 1988.
Total appearances: 349.
Total goals: 41.

Former England Under-21 midfielder Simon Barker helped QPR finish fifth in the Premier League in 1992–93. He turned professional with Blackburn Rovers in November 1982 and made his League debut in their 1–0 victory at Swansea in October 1983. He was named Man of the Match in Rovers' 1987 Full Members' Cup Final triumph and

was also ever present and top scorer that season, moving to Loftus Road for £400,000 in July 1988. He scored as QPR took Liverpool to an FA Cup sixth-round replay in 1989–90 and netted 33 goals in 315 League outings for Rangers, and he was given a testimonial match shortly before he joined Port Vale in July 1998. Retiring in May 2000, he subsequently joined the PFA agency that assisted with player contracts.

Billy Barnes

Born: West Ham, 20 May 1879.

Signed from: Luton Town.
Debut: 2 September 1907.
Total appearances: 234.
Total goals: 37.

Tricky winger Billy Barnes was an experienced figure as QPR won the Southern League title in

1907–08 and 1911–12. Initially with Leyton, he joined Sheffield United in July 1898 and scored their winner in the 1902 FA Cup Final replay. In July 1902 he joined West Ham before he moved via Luton Town to Rangers in July 1907. He appeared in both the 1908 and 1912 FA Charity Shield matches for his new club and also represented the Southern League against the Scottish League. Ever present in 1911–12, he netted 36 goals in 216 Southern League outings for QPR and moved to Southend United in July 1913. He later became a trail-blazing coach with Spanish side Bilbao. His brother Alfred became Labour MP for East Ham South, attaining Cabinet rank.

Brian Bedford

Born: Ferndale, 24 December 1933.

Signed from: Bournemouth.
Debut: 22 August 1959.
Total appearances: 284.
Total goals: 180.

Bustling centre-forward Brian Bedford was leading marksman in each of his six seasons at QPR. Signing professional for Reading in April 1954, he moved via Southampton to Bournemouth in August 1956. He starred as they reached the FA Cup sixth round in 1956–57 and joined QPR in July 1959. He featured in successive promotion near-misses under Alec Stock and scored twice in Rangers' record 9–2 victory at home to Tranmere Rovers in December 1960. He netted 161 goals in 258 League games before moving to Scunthorpe United in September 1965. He later played for Brentford, Atlanta Chiefs and Bexley United, before becoming a tennis coach in London and then QPR's clerk of works. He is now living in Cardiff in retirement.

Jimmy Birch

Born: Blackwell, 1888.

Signed from: Aston Villa.
Debut: 5 September 1912.
Total appearances: 363.
Total goals: 144.

Long-serving inside-right Jimmy Birch topped QPR's goalscoring charts on five occasions. He played for Stourbridge prior to joining Aston Villa in May 1906 and gained top-flight experience as understudy to England international Harry Hampton. Moving to QPR in June 1912, he was ever present in 1912–13 and starred as Rangers reached the FA Cup fourth round in 1913–14. His deceptive body swerve and deadly shooting made him a fans' favourite and he soon succeeded Archie Mitchell as captain. Jimmy scored QPR's first-ever Football League goal against Watford in August 1920 and netted 123 times in 328 Southern League/Football League games before joining Brentford in April 1926. He then had a spell on Rangers' coaching staff.

Stan Bowles

Born: Manchester, 24 December 1948.

Signed from: Carlisle United.
Debut: 16 September 1972.
Total appearances: 315.
Total goals: 96.

Skilful England international striker Stan Bowles was a key figure as QPR finished as League Championship runners-up in 1975–76. Initially with Manchester City, he later had spells with Crewe Alexandra and Carlisle United before moving to Loftus Road for £112,000 as Rodney Marsh's replacement in September 1972. 'Stan the Man' starred alongside Don Givens as

QPR won promotion in 1972–73 and were then League Cup semi-finalists and UEFA Cup quarter-finalists in 1976–77. Capped five times, he netted 70 goals in 255 League games prior to joining Nottingham Forest for £250,000 in December 1979, and he then played for Orient and Brentford. He has since helped his sister in the rag trade and been a QPR matchday host.

Barry Bridges

Born: Norwich, 29 April 1941.

Signed from: Birmingham City.
Debut: 24 August 1968.
Total appearances: 82.
Total goals: 35.

Former England international striker Barry Bridges was QPR's leading marksman in two consecutive seasons. One of Ted Drake's 'Ducklings' at Chelsea, he scored on his First Division debut as a 16-year-old and starred in their 1962–63 promotion success. He was leading marksman as they won the League Cup in 1965 and joined Birmingham City for £55,000 in May 1966. He moved to newly-promoted QPR for £50,000 in August 1968 and helped them reach the FA Cup sixth round in 1969–70, and he netted 31 goals in 72 League outings before being sold to Millwall for £40,000 in September 1970. After featuring in their 1971–72 promotion near-miss, he later played for Brighton and Highlands Park, and he then managed several clubs and became a milkman.

Harry Brown

Born: Kingsbury, 9 April 1924.

Signed from: Apprentice.
Debut: 15 November 1941.
Total appearances: 286.
Total goals: 0.

Brave goalkeeper Harry Brown had two spells at QPR. He built a fine reputation with Rangers in wartime football and guested for Arsenal in their famous friendly match against Moscow Dynamo in November 1945. Following the return of Reg Allen, he moved to Notts County in exchange for Cyril Hatton in April 1946 and appeared in their first post-war League match. Harry then joined Derby County as part of the deal for former England international Frank Broome in October 1949 and gained top-flight experience with the Rams before returning to Loftus Road in August 1951. After making 189 League appearances for QPR he moved to Plymouth Argyle in August 1956, then played for Exeter City. He died in Abingdon in June 1982.

John Byrne

Born: Manchester, 1 February 1961.

Signed from: York City.
Debut: 27 October 1984.
Total appearances: 128.
Total goals: 36.

Republic of Ireland international striker John Byrne starred as QPR reached the 1986 Milk Cup Final. Initially with York City, he was leading marksman in their 1983–84 Fourth Division title triumph and moved to Loftus Road for £100,000 in October 1984, shortly after impressing against Rangers in the Milk Cup. He netted 30 goals in 126 First Division games before being sold to French side Le Havre for £175,000 in May 1988. Joining Brighton in September 1990, he moved to Sunderland in October 1991 and was a key figure as they reached the FA Cup Final that season. He joined

Millwall in October 1992, then played for Oxford United, Brighton again and Crawley Town before becoming Shoreham's joint manager.

Bobby Cameron

Born: Greenock, 23 November 1932.

Signed from: Port Glasgow.
Debut: 13 January 1951.
Total appearances: 278.
Total goals: 62.

Former Scotland Schoolboy inside-forward Bobby Cameron formed an exciting partnership with Conway Smith while at QPR. He impressed with Port Glasgow before moving to Loftus Road in June 1950 and made his League debut in Rangers' 3–1 victory at home to Coventry seven months later. Securing a regular first-team slot during the 1952–53 season, he grabbed a hat-trick in QPR's 5–1 win over Newport County in February 1954 and netted 59 goals in 256 League outings before following Jack Taylor to Leeds United in July 1959. He joined Gravesend & Northfleet in July 1962 and helped take Sunderland to an FA Cup fourth-round replay in 1962–63, then played for Southend United and Adamstown before settling in Australia.

Tommy Cheetham

Born: Byker, 11 October 1910.

Signed from: Royal Artillery.
Debut: 12 September 1935.
Total appearances: 135.
Total goals: 93.

Big centre-forward Tommy Cheetham twice topped QPR's goalscoring charts. He played football for the Royal Artillery while serving in India and joined Rangers in July 1935, netting four times on his home debut in the 5–0 hammering of Aldershot two months later. His amazing record of 36 goals in 34 League games in 1935–36 earned him an England trial and he was QPR's leading marksman again in 1938–39. Overall he netted 81 goals in 115 Third Division South outings. He was then sold to top-flight Brentford for £5,000 in March 1939. Also their top scorer that season, he joined Lincoln City in October 1945 and was again leading marksman for his new club in 1946–47. He later worked in the building trade and died in Mansfield in December 1993.

Dave Clement

Born: Battersea, 2 February 1948.

Signed from: Juniors.
Debut: 8 April 1967.
Total appearances: 472.
Total goals: 28.

Long-serving England international right-back Dave Clement was capped five times while at QPR. Signing professional forms at Loftus Road in July 1965, he made his League debut in Rangers' 5–1 victory at home to Scunthorpe United in April 1967 and was ever present in two consecutive seasons, starring as QPR won promotion in 1972–73. He featured prominently alongside Ian Gillard as they were League Championship runners-up in 1975–76 and UEFA Cup quarter-finalists in 1976–77. He scored 22 goals in 405 League games for QPR before moving to Bolton Wanderers for £165,000 in June 1979, and he subsequently played for Fulham and Wimbledon until his tragic death in March 1982. His son Neil currently plays for West Brom.

John Collins

Born: Chiswick, 10 August 1942.

Signed from: Juniors.

Debut: 30 April 1960.
Total appearances: 193.
Total goals: 56.

Inside-forward John Collins scored in QPR's seven-goal FA Cup wins over Barry Town in 1961–62 and Hinckley Athletic in 1962–63. Signing professionally at Loftus Road in August 1959, he made his League debut in Rangers' 1–0 victory at home to Barnsley in April 1960. He secured a regular first-team slot in the 1962–63 season, playing alongside Brian Bedford in QPR's attack and netting 46 goals in 172 Third Division games before joining Oldham Athletic for £10,000 in October 1966. He reunited with Roy Bentley at Reading in August 1967 and linked up again with Alec Stock at Luton Town in August 1969. He then had a spell playing for Cambridge United and later coached at Watford, Fulham and Brighton, and he then worked in the building trade.

Tony Currie

Born: Edgware, 1 January 1950.

Signed from: Leeds United.
Debut: 5 September 1979.

Total appearances: 96.
Total goals: 6.

Former England international midfielder Tony Currie played for QPR in the 1982 FA Cup Final. Rejected by Rangers as a youngster, he impressed with Watford before joining Sheffield United in February 1968. He was ever present as they won promotion in 1970–71 and finished sixth in the top-flight in 1974–75, after which he moved to Leeds United for £240,000 in July 1976. Tommy Docherty paid £400,000 for him in August 1979 but he suffered injury problems and played in only 81 League games (scoring five goals) for Rangers prior to joining Vancouver Whitecaps in May 1983. He later played for Chesham United, Torquay United, Dunstable, Hendon and Goole Town, and since February 1988 he has been Sheffield United's community programme organiser.

Ian Dawes

Born: Croyden, 22 February 1963.

Signed from: Apprentice.
Debut: 22 February 1982.
Total appearances: 270.
Total goals: 4.

Ex-England Schoolboy left-back Ian Dawes was ever present for QPR in four successive seasons. Signing professional at Loftus Road in December 1980, he made his League debut in Rangers' 1–0 defeat at Rotherham in February 1982 and starred alongside Warren Neill as Terry Venables's side won the Second Division title in 1982–83 and finished fifth in the top-flight in 1983–84. He played for QPR in the 1986 Milk Cup Final and netted three goals in 229 League outings before moving to newly-promoted Millwall for £150,000 in August 1988. After helping them qualify for the Second Division Play-offs in 1990–91 he played for Bromley, Dorking and Carshalton, and he then coached at Charlton and Millwall before managing Redhill.

Sam Downing

Born: Willesden, 19 January 1883.

Signed from: West Hampstead.
Debut: 7 November 1903.
Total appearances: 170.
Total goals: 23.

Long-serving wing-half Sam Downing featured prominently

in QPR's 1907–08 Southern League title triumph. Starting with Willesden Green, he also played for Willesden Town, Park Royal and West Hampstead before joining QPR as a forward in April 1903. He netted a hat-trick on his home debut in a 7–1 demolition of Swindon Town and became a constructive wing-half, noted for his powerful long-range shooting. After scoring 22 goals in 179 Southern League games for Rangers he moved to Chelsea in April 1909. He helped them reach the FA Cup semi-finals in 1910–11 and win promotion to the top-flight in 1911–12. He then joined Croydon Common in July 1914 and then became a cricket coach in Maidenhead. Sam died in March 1974.

Ray Drinkwater

Born: Jarrow, 18 May 1931.

Signed from: Portsmouth.
Debut: 15 March 1958.
Total appearances: 216.
Total goals: 0.

Goalkeeper Ray Drinkwater was ever present as QPR narrowly failed to win promotion in 1960–61. He impressed with Guildford City and featured in their 1955–56 Southern League

title campaign before joining Portsmouth for £2,000 in November 1955. After gaining top-flight experience, he moved to Loftus Road in February 1958 as a replacement for Ron Springett. He missed just one match in 1961–62 and made 199 League appearances for Rangers prior to joining Bath City in June 1963, helping them take top-flight Bolton Wanderers to an FA Cup third-round replay in 1963–64. Settling in Guildford, he was a sales rep for Dennis Brothers (fire engine manufacturers) until May 1983, then for Guildford Autos. He died in March 2008.

Terry Fenwick

Born: Seaham, 17 November 1959.

Signed from: Crystal Palace.
Debut: 19 December 1980.

Total appearances: 307.
Total goals: 45.

England international central-defender Terry Fenwick was capped 19 times while at QPR. Signing professional for Crystal Palace in December 1976, he featured in their 1978–79 Second Division title triumph and followed Terry Venables to Loftus Road for £100,000 in December 1980. He scored for QPR in the 1982 FA Cup Final and skippered them to the Second Division title in 1982–83 as well as the 1986 Milk Cup Final. He netted 33 goals in 256 League games for QPR, and then he followed Venables to Spurs for £550,000 in December 1987. He joined Swindon Town in September 1993, also appearing for them in the top-flight, and then he managed Portsmouth, under Terry Venables's chairmanship, before managing Northampton.

Les Ferdinand

Born: Paddington, 18 December 1966.

Signed from: Hayes.
Debut: 20 April 1987.
Total appearances: 169.
Total goals: 90.

England international striker Les Ferdinand gained the first

seven of his 12 caps while at QPR. Initially with Hayes, he moved to Loftus Road in March 1987 and made his League debut for Rangers in the following month's 4–1 defeat at Coventry. During the 1990–91 campaign he returned from loan spells at Brentford and Besiktas to secure a regular first-team slot. 'Sir Les', as he was known, was leading marksman as QPR finished fifth in the Premier League in 1992–93 and netted 80 goals in 163 League games prior to joining Newcastle United for £6 million in June 1995. Reunited with Gerry Francis at Spurs in August 1997, he helped his new club win the Worthington Cup in 1999. He then played for West Ham, Leicester City, Bolton, Reading and Watford.

Wayne Fereday

Born: Warley, 16 June 1963.

Signed from: Apprentice.
Debut: 19 August 1980.
Total appearances: 206.
Total goals: 25.

England Under-21 winger Wayne Fereday helped QPR reach the 1986 Milk Cup Final, but he did not play at Wembley. A former apprentice at Loftus Road, he turned professional in August 1980 and scored twice on his League debut in that month's 4–0 win at home to Bristol Rovers. He secured a regular first-team slot as Rangers qualified for the UEFA Cup in 1983–84, and after netting 21 goals in 196 League games followed Jim Smith to Newcastle United for £300,000 in July 1989. Joining AFC Bournemouth as part of the Gavin Peacock deal in November 1990, he moved to West Brom for £60,000 in December 1991. Later with Cardiff City, Weymouth, Telford United and Christchurch, he became a delivery driver in Bournemouth after his football career ended.

Gerry Francis

Born: Chiswick, 6 December 1951.

Signed from: Apprentice.
Debut: 29 March 1969.
Total appearances: 347.
Total goals: 65.

England international midfielder Gerry Francis was captain of club and country during the mid-1970s. A former apprentice at Loftus Road, he made his League debut against Liverpool three months before turning professional in June 1969. He was ever present in QPR's 1972–73 promotion success and skippered them to League Championship runners'-up spot in 1975–76. Overcoming a series of injuries to join Crystal Palace for £450,000 in July 1979, he followed Terry Venables back to QPR for £150,000 in February 1980 and netted 57 goals in 310

League games overall, moving to Coventry City for £150,000 in February 1982. He later became Exeter City's player-manager and then managed Bristol Rovers (twice), QPR (twice) and Spurs.

Paul Furlong

Born: London, 1 October 1968.

Signed from: Birmingham City.
Debut: 20 August 2000.
Total appearances: 149.
Total goals: 58.

Former England semi-professional striker Paul Furlong starred in QPR's 2003–04 promotion success. He was a prolific scorer for Enfield at the start of his career, netting twice in their 1988 FA Trophy Final replay triumph, before he secured a move to Coventry City for £130,000 in July 1991.

Joining Watford for £250,000 in July 1992, he was twice top scorer and moved to Chelsea for £2.3 million in May 1994. He then joined Birmingham City for £1.5 million in July 1996 and helped them to reach the First Division Play-offs in 1998–99. Moving to QPR in August 2002, after a loan move in 2000, he was twice leading marksman and appeared in the 2002–03 Second Division Play-off Final, netting 56 goals in 168 League games for Rangers before joining Luton Town in August 2007, after which he played for Southend United.

Kevin Gallen

Born: Chiswick, 21 September 1975.

Signed from: Juniors.
Debut: 20 August 1994.
Total appearances: 338.
Total goals: 90.

England Under-21 striker Kevin Gallen was leading marksman in QPR's 2003–04 promotion success. A prolific scorer in youth football, he turned professional at Loftus Road in September 1992 and made his League debut in Rangers' 1–0 defeat at reigning champions Blackburn Rovers in August 1994. He played alongside Les Ferdinand as QPR reached the FA Cup sixth round in 1994–95. He moved to Huddersfield Town in August 2000 and then had a spell at Barnsley before rejoining QPR in November 2001. Starring as they reached the Second Division Play-off Final in 2002–03, he netted 90 goals in 365 League games before joining MK Dons in August 2007. He helped them win the League Two title and Johnstone's Paint Trophy in 2007–08.

Ian Gillard

Born: Hammersmith, 9 October 1950.

Signed from: Apprentice.
Debut: 23 November 1968.
Total appearances: 479.
Total goals: 11.

England international left-back Ian Gillard starred alongside Dave Clement as QPR were League Championship runners-up in 1975–76. A former apprentice at Loftus Road, he turned professional in October 1968 and made his League debut in the following month's 2–1 win at home to Nottingham Forest. He helped QPR reach the FA Cup sixth round in 1969–70 and then regain their top-flight status in 1972–73. Twice ever present, he featured prominently as Rangers were UEFA Cup quarter-finalists in 1976–77. Scoring nine goals in 408 League games for QPR, he made his last appearance for them in the 1982 FA Cup Final and then played for Aldershot, where he became coach. He has since been a contract cleaner in Sandhurst.

Don Givens

Born: Limerick, 9 August 1949.

Signed from: Luton Town.
Debut: 12 August 1972.
Total appearances: 293.
Total goals: 101.

Republic of Ireland international striker Don Givens was capped 26 times while at QPR. A former Manchester United apprentice, he understudied Denis Law before joining Luton Town in April 1970 and moved to Loftus Road for £40,000 in July 1972. He was Rangers' leading marksman on four occasions alongside Stan Bowles, including their 1972–73 promotion success and 1975–76 League Championship near-miss. Scoring 76 goals in 242

League games for QPR, he was sold to Birmingham City for £150,000 in July 1978 and helped them regain their top-flight status at the first attempt in 1979–80. He later played for Sheffield United and leading Swiss side Neuchâtel Xamax, and he has since held various coaching posts.

George Goddard

Born: Gomshall, 20 December 1903.

Signed from: Redhill.
Debut: 11 September 1926.
Total appearances: 260.
Total goals: 186.

Centre-forward George Goddard holds QPR's all-time goalscoring record. He was a prolific scorer with Redhill and represented the Athenian League before turning professional with Rangers in June 1926, netting on his League debut in the 4–2 defeat at local rivals Brentford three months later. Playing alongside Jack Burns and George Rounce in QPR's attack, he netted a club record 37 League goals in 1929–30 and was leading marksman in six successive seasons. He netted 177 goals in 243 League games for Rangers before moving to Brentford in December 1933. He also appeared in the top-flight for Sunderland, before moving to Southend United in July 1935. Later a confectioner/ tobacconist in Molesey, he died in April 1987.

Jack Gregory

Born: Birmingham.

Signed from: Willenhall Swifts.
Debut: 7 December 1912.
Total appearances: 241.
Total goals: 59.

Skilful inside-left Jack Gregory gave QPR fine service during 11 years at the club. He impressed with Willenhall Swifts and joined Rangers in June 1912, securing a regular slot in their Southern League team and helping reach the FA Cup fourth round in 1913–14. His career was disrupted by World War One but he featured in QPR's first Football League match against Watford in August 1920, starred in their 1920–21 FA Cup first-round victory over top-flight Arsenal and missed just two games in 1921–22. He netted 42 goals in 202 Southern League/Football League matches for Rangers before he became Yeovil & Petters' player-manager in May 1923 and took them to the Southern League Western Section title in his first season.

John Gregory

Born: Scunthorpe, 11 May 1954.

Signed from: Brighton.
Debut: 29 August 1981.
Total appearances: 188.
Total goals: 43.

Versatile England international midfielder John Gregory was capped six times while at QPR. Initially with Northampton Town, he starred in their 1975–76 promotion success and joined Aston Villa for £40,000 in June 1977. He was sold to Brighton for £250,000 in July 1979 and moved to Loftus Road for £275,000 in June 1981. He became an influential figure as QPR were FA Cup finalists in 1982 and won the Second Division title in 1982–83. He netted 36 goals in 161 League games prior to joining Derby County for £100,000 in December 1985 and helped them rise from the Third Division to the First. He was later Portsmouth's boss and then coached Leicester and Aston Villa, and he has since managed Wycombe Wanderers, Aston Villa, Derby and QPR.

Allan Harris

Born: Hackney, 28 December 1942.

Signed from: Chelsea.
Debut: 19 August 1967.
Total appearances: 94.
Total goals: 0.

Ex-England Youth left-back Allan Harris was ever present as QPR reached the top-flight for the first time in 1967–68. He turned professional with Chelsea in June 1960 and played alongside his brother Ron in their 1962–63 promotion campaign. After following John Sillett to Coventry City for £35,000 in November 1964, he rejoined Chelsea for £45,000 in May 1966 and was a non-playing substitute in the 1967 FA Cup Final. He moved to Loftus Road for £30,000 in July 1967 and replaced Jim Langley in QPR's defence, making 94 League appearances before being sold to Plymouth Argyle for £9,500 in March 1971. Later with Cambridge United and Hayes as player-manager, he also assisted Terry Venables at Crystal Palace, QPR, Barcelona and Spurs.

Cyril Hatton

Born: Grantham, 14 September 1918.

Signed from: Notts County.
Debut: 14 February 1942.
Total appearances: 206.
Total goals: 93.

Inside-forward Cyril Hatton was leading goalscorer in QPR's 1947–48 Third Division South title triumph. Signing professional for Notts County in July 1936, he was a wartime guest player for QPR and returned to Loftus Road in an exchange deal involving Harry Brown in April 1946. He starred alongside Fred Durrant and Bert Addinall in Rangers' attack and helped the club finish as Third Division South runners-up in 1946–47, and he netted twice in the 1947–48 FA Cup fourth-round win over Stoke City en route to the sixth round. He scored 64 goals in 162 League games before moving to Chesterfield in June 1953, and he later became Grantham's player-manager. He was later a newsagent in Grantham and resided in his native town until his death in July 1987.

Bob Hazell

Born: Kingston, Jamaica, 14 June 1959.

Signed from: Wolverhampton.
Debut: 5 September 1979.
Total appearances: 117.
Total goals: 9.

England Under-21 central-defender Bob Hazell featured prominently as QPR won the Second Division title in 1982–83. Born in West Kingston, Jamaica, he grew up in Edgbaston and turned professional with Wolves in May 1977. His impressive displays in the top-flight tempted Tommy Docherty to pay £240,000 for him in September 1979 and he subsequently played for Rangers in the 1982 FA Cup Final. He scored eight times in 106 League games before he was sold to Leicester City for £100,000 in September 1983. Briefly with Reading, he then joined Port Vale in December 1986 and featured in their 1987–88 FA Cup run and 1988–89 promotion success. A back injury ended his playing career and he has since worked with young offenders in Wolverhampton.

Tony Hazell

Born: High Wycombe, 19 September 1947.

Signed from: Juniors.
Debut: 3 October 1964.
Total appearances: 407.
Total goals: 5.

Long-serving central-defender Tony Hazell was ever present as QPR won promotion to the top-flight in 1967–68. An England Youth international, he turned professional at Loftus Road in October 1964 and immediately secured a regular first-team slot. He also featured prominently in Rangers' 1966–67 Third Division title and League Cup double triumph, the 1969–70 FA Cup run and 1972–73 promotion success. He netted four goals in 369 League games for Rangers before following Gordon Jago to Millwall for £40,000 in December 1974. After helping them win promotion in 1975–76 he reunited with Terry Venables at Crystal Palace, winning promotion again in 1978–79 and then with Charlton in 1980–81. He is currently a telecom engineer in Flackwell Heath.

Ian Holloway

Born: Kingswood, 12 March 1963.

Signed from: Bristol Rovers.
Debut: 17 August 1991.
Total appearances: 150.
Total goals: 5.

Midfielder Ian Holloway helped QPR finish fifth in the Premier League in 1992–93. Signing professional for Bristol Rovers in March 1981, he joined Wimbledon for £35,000 in July 1985 and featured in their 1985–86 promotion campaign. He then played for Brentford before rejoining Bristol Rovers in August 1987, and he was ever present as they won the Third Division title and were Leyland/DAF Cup finalists in 1989–90. He followed Gerry Francis to Loftus Road for £225,000 in August 1991 and 'Olly' featured as Rangers reached the FA Cup sixth round in 1994–95. He netted four goals in 147 League outings before rejoining Bristol Rovers as player-manager in June 1996. He has since managed QPR, Plymouth Argyle and Leicester City.

Peter Hucker

Born: Hampstead, 28 October 1959.

Signed from: Apprentice.
Debut: 2 May 1981.

Total appearances: 188.
Total goals: 0.

England Under-21 goalkeeper Peter Hucker was Man of the Match for QPR in the 1982 FA Cup Final. Signing professional at Loftus Road in July 1977, he made his League debut in Rangers' 3–3 draw at Shrewsbury in May 1981 and displaced John Burridge as first-choice 'keeper midway through the 1981–82 campaign. He was ever present in three successive seasons, including QPR's 1982–83 Second Division title triumph, making 160 League appearances overall before moving to Oxford United for £100,000 in February 1987. He then joined Millwall in November 1989, after which he had spells with Aldershot, Farnborough Town, Enfield and Erith & Belvedere. He later became a classroom welfare support assistant in Putney as well as a goalkeeping coach.

Ron Hunt

Born: Paddington, 19 December 1945.

Signed from: Apprentice.
Debut: 28 December 1964.
Total appearances: 249.
Total goals: 1.

Centre-half Ron Hunt was an important figure in QPR's 1966–67 Third Division title and League Cup double triumph, setting up the Wembley winner. A former QPR apprentice, he turned professional in March 1963 and made his League debut in Rangers' 3–1 victory at home to Bristol Rovers in December 1964. He helped them win promotion to the top-flight for the first time in 1967–68 and his only goal in 219 League games clinched QPR's 1–1 draw at Sheffield United in November 1970. After a knee injury ended his League career in July 1973, he had spells with Molesey, Hillingdon Borough and Walton & Hersham while a professional squash player and coach. He then worked in the petro-chemical industry in Reading.

Andrew Impey

Born: Hammersmith, 13 September 1971.

Signed from: Yeading.
Debut: 9 October 1991.
Total appearances: 199.
Total goals: 18.

England Under-21 winger Andrew Impey was Player of the Year as QPR reached the FA Cup sixth round in 1994–95. Starting

his career with Yeading, he helped them win the FA Vase shortly before moving to Loftus Road in June 1990, and he made his League debut in QPR's 2–2 draw at Coventry in January 1992. He starred as Rangers finished fifth in the Premier League in 1992–93 and netted 13 goals in 187 League outings prior to joining West Ham for £1.2 million in September 1997. Switching to a wing-back role, he was sold to Leicester City for £1.6 million in November 1998 and featured in their 2000 Worthington Cup Final triumph. He helped them regain top-flight status in 2002–03, then played for Nottingham Forest and Coventry City.

Tony Ingham

Born: Harrogate, 18 February 1925.

Signed from: Leeds United.
Debut: 25 November 1950.
Total appearances: 555.
Total goals: 3.

Long-serving left-back Tony Ingham holds QPR's appearance record. Initially with home-town club Harrogate, he joined Leeds United in May 1946 but failed to secure a regular first-team slot and moved to Loftus Road in June 1950. Ever present in five successive seasons, he twice represented the Third Division South and featured in QPR's first-ever League Cup match against Port Vale in 1960–61. He netted three goals in 514 League games before retiring in May 1963. Becoming Rangers' commercial manager, he made a major contribution to that aspect of the development of the club and had a spell as secretary before joining the QPR board in 1981. His outstanding service to the club is marked by the Tony Ingham suite at Loftus Road.

Arthur Jefferson

Born: Goldthorpe, 14 December 1916.

Signed from: Peterborough United.

Debut: 31 August 1936.
Total appearances: 368.
Total goals: 1.

Tough-tackling left-back Arthur Jefferson featured in QPR's 1947–48 Third Division South title triumph. He had spells with Mexborough and Peterborough before joining Rangers in July 1935. He was given his League debut in their 2–0 defeat at Millwall in August 1936, and he overcame a broken leg and missed just two games in 1946–47, starring as QPR took Derby to an FA Cup sixth-round replay in 1947–48. He scored once in 211 League games for Rangers, also making 119 wartime appearances, before joining Aldershot for £1,500 in March 1950. After partnering his younger brother Stan in the Shots' defence, he later owned a fish and chip shop with Bert Smith and was then a newsagent and decorator, residing in Shepherd's Bush until his death in July 1997.

Mike Keen

Born: Wycombe, 19 March 1940.

Signed from: Juniors.
Debut: 7 September 1959.
Total appearances: 440.
Total goals: 45.

Long-serving wing-half Mike Keen skippered QPR to the Third Division title and League Cup double in 1966–67. Discovered with Bucks Boys' Club, he turned professional with Rangers in June 1958 and made his League debut in their 2–1 defeat at York City in September 1959. He was an important figure in QPR's meteoric rise from the Third

Division to the First under Alec Stock. Ever present in five successive seasons, he netted 41 goals in 393 League games before following Stock to Luton Town for £18,500 in January 1969. He captained their 1969–70 promotion success and was then Watford's player-manager and a coach back at QPR. He later managed Northampton, Wycombe Wanderers and Marlow, after which he ran a sports shop in High Wycombe.

Jim Langley

Born: Kilburn, 7 February 1929.

Signed from: Fulham.
Debut: 21 August 1965.
Total appearances: 104.
Total goals: 11.

Former England international left-back Jim Langley was an experienced figure in QPR's

1966–67 Third Division title and League Cup double success. He played for Yiewsley, Hounslow, Uxbridge, Hayes and Guildford City prior to joining Leeds United in June 1952 and moved to Brighton in July 1953. Sold to Fulham for £12,000 in February 1957, he starred in their 1958–59 promotion triumph and joined QPR for £5,000 in July 1965. Ever present in 1965–66, he netted eight goals in 87 League outings before becoming Hillingdon Borough's player-manager in September 1967. He was an FA Trophy finalist in 1971 and had four spells in charge of Hillingdon. He was later a steward at West Drayton British Legion, and he died in December 2007.

Mark Lazarus

Born: Stepney, 5 December 1938.

Signed from: Leyton Orient.
Debut: 17 September 1960.
Total appearances: 233.
Total goals: 84.

Popular winger Mark Lazarus spent three spells at QPR and scored their winner in the 1967 League Cup Final. From a notable boxing family, he exemplified Alec Stock's shrewd

transfer dealings, initially following Stock from Leyton Orient for £3,000 in September 1960. He was sold to Wolves for £26,500 a year later and to Brentford for £8,000 plus George McLeod in January 1964, rejoining QPR each time for a lower fee. He scored 76 goals in 206 League games overall for Rangers before he joined Crystal Palace for £10,000 in November 1967 and starred in their 1968–69 promotion triumph. He featured in four successive promotions as he rejoined Orient to win the Third Division title in 1969–70. He is currently running a haulage firm in Romford.

Mick Leach

Born: Clapton, 16 January 1947.

Signed from: Apprentice.
Debut: 26 February 1965.
Total appearances: 337.
Total goals: 70.

Versatile England Youth international Mick Leach helped QPR win promotion in two consecutive seasons under Alec Stock. A former apprentice at Loftus Road, he turned professional in February 1964 and scored on his League debut

in QPR's 5–0 win at home to Colchester a year later. He was a promotion winner again in 1972–73 and an experienced figure as Rangers were League Championship runners-up in 1975–76. He was given a testimonial match against Red Star Belgrade in February 1976 and netted 61 goals in 313 League games before moving to Detroit Express for £30,000 in March 1978. He joined Cambridge United six months later, then was player-manager of Leatherhead and Dulwich Hamlet. He died of cancer in January 1992.

Evelyn Lintott

Born: Godalming, 2 November 1883.

Signed from: Plymouth Argyle.
Debut: 7 September 1907.
Total appearances: 35.
Total goals: 1.

Influential left-half Evelyn Lintott was QPR's first England international. A schoolteacher by vocation, he gained five England Amateur caps and played for St Luke's College, Woking and Plymouth Argyle prior to joining Rangers as an amateur in September 1907 on his appointment at Oakfield Park School, Willesden. He starred as QPR won the Southern League title for the first time in 1907–08 and turned professional in May 1908. He scored once in 31 Southern League games and gained the first three of his seven caps before joining Bradford City in November 1908. He moved to Leeds City in June 1912 and became chairman of the Players'

Union but was killed in action on the Somme while serving with the 1st Yorkshire Regiment.

Arthur Longbottom

Born: Leeds, 30 January 1933.

Signed from: Methley United.
Debut: 12 March 1955.
Total appearances: 218.
Total goals: 68.

Inside-right Arthur Longbottom was QPR's leading marksman in three successive seasons. Following his RAF service in the Middle East, he had a spell with Methley United before moving to Loftus Road in March 1954. He made his League debut in Rangers' 3–0 defeat at Leyton Orient the following year and netted four times in a 5–1 win at Northampton in November 1957. After scoring 62 goals in

201 League games for QPR he moved to Port Vale in May 1961 and changed his name by deed poll to Langley in December 1962. He joined Millwall in January 1963, then helped Oxford United reach the FA Cup sixth round in 1963–64 before he had a spell playing for Colchester United. Settling in Scarborough, he ran a guest house and was then a window cleaner.

Harry Lowe

Born: Kingskettle, 24 February 1907.

Signed from: Watford.
Debut: 31 August 1935.
Total appearances: 250.
Total goals: 51.

Scottish inside-forward Harry Lowe was ever present for QPR in 1938–39. Initially with St Andrews United, he joined Watford in March 1929 and was ever present for them in 1931–32. He featured in the 1935 Third Division South Cup Final and moved to Loftus Road in exchange for Ted Goodier in June 1935. Netting 40 goals in 161 League games for QPR, he guested for several clubs during the war and then scouted for Chelsea, before he became Guildford City's manager in July 1945. He took charge of Bournemouth in July 1947 and guided them to Third Division South runners'-up spot in 1947–48. He then managed Yeovil Town, scouted for Watford and was Cheshunt's boss. Later director of a lampshade business in Pewsey, he died in October 1988.

Alan McDonald

Born: Belfast, 12 October 1963.

Signed from: Apprentice.
Debut: 24 September 1983.
Total appearances: 476.
Total goals: 18.

Northern Ireland international central-defender Alan McDonald gained a club record 52 caps while at QPR. Signing professional at Loftus Road in September 1981, he made his League debut in QPR's 4–0 win at Wolves two years later and helped them qualify for the UEFA Cup in 1983–84. He was ever present as Rangers were Milk Cup finalists in 1986, then starred as they took Liverpool to an FA Cup sixth-round replay in 1989–90 and finished fifth in the Premier League in 1992–93. Appointed captain of both club and country, he netted 13 goals in 402 League games for QPR before he made the move to Swindon Town in July 1997, where he later joined the coaching staff. He subsequently returned to Rangers as assistant manager.

Frank McLintock

Born: Glasgow, 28 December 1939.

Signed from: Arsenal.
Debut: 22 September 1973.
Total appearances: 162.
Total goals: 6.

Former Scotland international central-defender Frank McLintock was an experienced figure as QPR were League Championship runners-up in 1975–76. Initially with Shawfield Juniors, he joined Leicester City in January 1957 and was an FA Cup finalist in 1961 and 1963, before moving to Arsenal for £80,000 in October 1964. He was twice a League Cup finalist with the Gunners, and he then skippered their 1970 Fairs Cup Final triumph and 1970–71 double success. Moving to QPR for £30,000 in June 1973, he starred as they were League Cup semi-finalists in 1976–77, and he netted five goals in 127 First

Division games before rejoining Leicester as manager in June 1977. He later had a spell as QPR's youth coach before managing Brentford and coaching Millwall.

Danny Maddix

Born: Ashford, 11 October 1967.

Signed from: Tottenham Hotspur.
Debut: 28 November 1987.
Total appearances: 307.
Total goals: 18.

Long-serving Jamaica international central-defender Danny Maddix was an influential figure as QPR took Liverpool to an FA Cup sixth-round replay in 1989–90. A former Spurs apprentice, he turned professional in July 1985 but failed to make an impact and had a loan spell at Southend United before moving to Loftus Road, initially on loan, in July 1987. He helped Rangers finish fifth in the top-flight in 1987–88 and 1992–93, twice returning from long injury layoffs. He netted 13 goals in 292 League outings before he left Rangers to be reunited with Peter Shreeves at Sheffield Wednesday in July 2001. He replaced Des Walker in the heart of their defence, featuring in consecutive relegation battles, then linked up with Martin Allen again at Barnet in July 2003.

Dickie March

Born: Washington, 9 Ocotber 1908.

Signed from: Crawcrook Albion.
Debut: 24 December 1932.
Total appearances: 311.
Total goals: 6.

Hard-working, fearless wing-half Dickie March featured in QPR's record 8–1 FA Cup first-round win at Bristol Rovers in 1937–38. Discovered playing for Crawcrook Albion, he joined Rangers in October 1931 and made his League debut in the 3–1 defeat at Torquay United in December 1932. His excellent timing enabled him to out-jump taller opponents and he soon became a favourite at Loftus Road. He missed just one match during the 1936–37 season and scored twice in 222 Third Division South games for Rangers, then netted a further three goals in 57 wartime matches before he retired in May 1942. He became QPR's catering manager after World War Two and then continued his loyal association as a season-ticket holder.

Rodney Marsh

Born: Hatfield, 11 October 1944.

Signed from: Fulham.
Debut: 12 February 1966.
Total appearances: 242.
Total goals: 134.

England international striker Rodney Marsh was QPR's leading marksman five times, starring in the rise under Alec Stock. Signing professional for Fulham in October 1962, he gained top-flight experience and moved to Loftus Road for £15,000 in March 1966. He scored a club record 44 goals in QPR's 1966–67 Third Division title and League Cup double success. Idolised by Rangers' fans, he was the club's first England international for 63 years and netted 106 times in 211 League games prior to joining Manchester City for £200,000 in March 1972. He was a League Cup finalist in 1974 and later played for Tampa Bay Rowdies and Fulham again, and he then coached in the United States before returning to work in the media with Sky TV.

Billy Mason

Born: Earlsfield, 31 October 1908.

Signed from: Fulham.
Debut: 18 January 1934.

Total appearances: 269.
Total goals: 0.

Long-serving goalkeeper Billy Mason was ever present for QPR in 1936–37. Initially with Wimbledon, he represented Surrey and turned professional with Fulham in November 1928. He made his League debut in that month's 2–0 defeat at Brighton and helped their reserves win the London Challenge Cup in 1932. Following fellow 'keeper Ernie Beecham to Loftus Road in June 1933, he played 154 Third Division South games and a further 91 wartime matches for Rangers. He also guested for Brentford, Fulham, Walsall and Watford during World War Two, then spent 20 years as a police constable in Wimbledon and worked as a security guard until his retirement. He died in Bognor Regis in November 1995.

Don Masson

Born: Banchory, 26 August 1946.

Signed from: Notts County.
Debut: 14 December 1974.
Total appearances: 144.
Total goals: 24.

Scotland international midfielder Don Masson was ever present as QPR were League Championship

runners-up in 1975–76. Signing professional for Middlesbrough in September 1963, he featured in their 1966–67 promotion success and joined Notts County for £12,000 in September 1968, skippering their rise under Jimmy Sirrel. He moved to Loftus Road for £100,000 in December 1974 to replace Terry Venables and starred as QPR reached the League Cup semi-finals in 1976–77. He netted 18 goals in 116 First Division games before joining Derby County in exchange for Leighton James in October 1977, and he returned to Notts County in August 1978 and was then appointed Kettering Town's player-manager. After his football career ended he became a hotelier in Nottingham.

Gary Micklewhite

Born: Southwark, 21 March 1961.

Signed from: Manchester United.
Debut: 5 November 1980.
Total appearances: 115.
Total goals: 17.

Winger Gary Micklewhite scored in QPR's record 8–1 Milk Cup second-round first-leg victory at home to Crewe Alexandra in October 1983. He signed professional forms for

Manchester United in March 1978 but failed to secure a first-team slot, and so he was reunited with Tommy Docherty at Loftus Road in July 1979. He made his League debut in QPR's 2–0 win over Oldham in November 1980 and featured in the 1982 FA Cup Final, and he was then an influential figure in Rangers' 1982–83 Second Division title triumph. He scored 11 times in 106 League games and was sold to Derby County for £75,000 in February 1985, and he was ever present in their rise from the Third Division to the First. He later played for Gillingham and then coached Wycombe Wanderers.

Archie Mitchell

Born: Smethwick, 15 December 1885.

Signed from: Aston Villa.
Debut: 2 September 1907.
Total appearances: 467.
Total goals: 25.

Centre-half Archie Mitchell was an important figure as QPR won the Southern League title in 1907–08 and 1911–12. Initially a player with Oldbury St Johns, he also had a spell with Aston Villa before following James Cowan to QPR in May 1907. He became

captain and represented the Southern League, then helped Rangers consolidate their Football League status in 1920–21. He scored 11 times in 306 Southern League/Football League games for QPR and shared a benefit match with fellow stalwart Jimmy Birch. He then became Brentford's player-manager in August 1921, after which he coached overseas and managed Dartford before rejoining QPR as a coach. He succeeded John Bowman as manager from November 1931 until May 1933, and he died in April 1949.

Ian Morgan

Born: Walthamstow, 14 November 1946.

Signed from: Apprentice.
Debut: 25 September 1964.
Total appearances: 175.
Total goals: 28.

Winger Ian Morgan played on the opposite flank to his identical twin brother Roger during QPR's rise from the Third Division to the First in consecutive seasons. Spotted while playing for Walthamstow Boys, the pair turned professional with QPR in September 1964 and Ian made his League debut in that month's 2–1 win at home to Hull City. A non-playing substitute in the 1967 League Cup Final, he was ever present as Rangers reached the top-flight in 1967–68 and netted 26 goals in 172 League games before reuniting with Mike Keen at Watford for £10,000 in October 1973. He had spells with Barking and Ware, then managed Norwegian sides Ureadd and Storm before joining the London Borough of Hackney Recreation Department.

Roger Morgan

Born: Walthamstow, 14 November 1946.

Signed from: Apprentice.
Debut: 3 October 1964.
Total appearances: 206.
Total goals: 44.

England Youth winger Roger Morgan was a key figure in QPR's 1966–67 Third Division title and League Cup double

success, scoring their first goal in the Wembley Final. Discovered playing for Walthamstow Boys, he and his identical twin brother Ian signed professional at Loftus Road in September 1964 and Roger made his League debut in the following month's 2–2 draw at Gillingham. He helped QPR win promotion in 1967–68 and netted 39 goals in 180 League games before he was sold to Spurs for a then record £110,000 in February 1969. After gaining England Under-23 honours his career was unfortunately ended by a knee injury in April 1973. He was later recreation manager for Haringey Council and has since been West Ham's community officer.

Warren Neill

Born: Acton, 21 November 1962.

Signed from: Apprentice.
Debut: 30 August 1980.
Total appearances: 209.
Total goals: 7.

Ex-England Schoolboy right-back Warren Neill featured prominently in QPR's 1982–83 Second Division title triumph. He played for Ealing Borough in the English Schools Final and was an apprentice at Loftus

Road, making his League debut in Rangers' 1–1 draw at Chelsea a month before turning professional in September 1980. Replacing Glenn Roeder in the 1982 FA Cup Final replay, he formed a notable partnership with Ian Dawes and played in the 1986 Milk Cup Final. He netted three goals in 181 League outings before joining Portsmouth for £110,000 in July 1988, starring in their 1991–92 FA Cup run. After retiring with sciatica in December 1994, he reunited with Roeder at Watford and then rejoined QPR as youth-team coach.

George Newlands

Born: Glasgow, 1882.

Signed from: Parkhead Juniors.
Debut: 29 September 1900.
Total appearances: 186.
Total goals: 1.

Tough-tackling Scottish full-back George Newlands was a key figure in QPR's early Southern League days. Born in Glasgow, he played for various Parkhead sides then Vale of Clyde before joining QPR in September 1900. He was dubbed the 'Little Wonder' and only he and wing-half Billy Keech survived the cost-cutting exercise of 1901. His solitary goal in 174 Southern League games came in Rangers' 3–2 win at home to local rivals Brentford in January 1902. He was given a benefit match against Bristol Rovers before following John Bowman to Norwich City in May 1907. He became their captain and remained a first-team regular for the next three seasons. He later worked as a bricklayer after settling in Dunfermline.

Steve Palmer

Born: Brighton, 31 March 1968.

Signed from: Watford.
Debut: 11 August 2001.
Total appearances: 130.
Total goals: 10.

Ex-England Schoolboy midfielder Steve Palmer skippered QPR's 2003–04 promotion success. A former Cambridge University soccer blue, he captained them in his second Varsity match shortly before joining Ipswich Town in August 1989. He gained Premiership experience while at Portman Road, also appearing in central defence before he moved to Watford for £135,000 in September 1995. He starred as they won the Second Division title in 1997–98 and also featured in their 1998–99 First Division Play-off Final triumph before he joined QPR in July 2001. He was twice ever present for Rangers, appeared in the 2002–03 Second Division Play-off Final and scored nine goals in 127 League games for QPR before becoming MK Dons' player-coach in July 2004.

Paul Parker

Born: West Ham, 4 April 1964.

Signed from: Fulham.
Debut: 15 August 1987.
Total appearances: 156.
Total goals: 1.

England international defender Paul Parker was capped 16 times while at QPR, featuring in the 1990 World Cup semi-final. Signing professional for Fulham in April 1982, he featured in their 1982–83 promotion near-miss and moved to Loftus Road with Dean Coney for £200,000 in June 1987. Ever present in 1987–88, his solitary goal in 125 First Division outings came in the 6–1 win over Luton Town in September 1990. In August 1991 he joined Manchester United for £2 million and helped them win all three major domestic honours before he moved to

Derby County in August 1996, after which he briefly played for Sheffield United, Fulham again and Chelsea before managing Ashford Town and Chelmsford City. He is currently working as a football pundit.

Phil Parkes

Born: Sedgeley, 8 August 1950.

Signed from: Walsall.
Debut: 22 August 1970.
Total appearances: 406.
Total goals: 0.

England international goalkeeper Phil Parkes starred as QPR were League Championship runners-up in 1975–76. Signing professional for Walsall in January 1968, he moved to Loftus Road for £15,000 in June 1970 and was a key figure in QPR's 1972–73 promotion success. He was ever present three times and helped the club reach the League Cup semi-finals in 1976–77. He made 344 League appearances for Rangers prior to joining West Ham for a record £565,000 in February 1979. Starring as the Hammers won the FA Cup in 1980 and were League Cup finalists and Second Division champions in 1980–81, he followed John Lyall to Ipswich Town in August 1990 and has since been a goalkeeping coach as well as running his own building firm.

Darren Peacock

Born: Bristol, 3 February 1968.

Signed from: Hereford United.
Debut: 23 December 1990.
Total appearances: 140.
Total goals: 7.

Tall central-defender Darren Peacock starred as QPR finished fifth in the Premier League in 1992–93. A former Newport County trainee, he made his League debut five months before turning professional in February 1986. He overcame a broken leg prior to joining Hereford United in March 1989 and was Player of the Year as they won the Welsh Cup in 1989–90. Moving to Loftus Road for £350,000 in December 1990, he missed just three matches in 1991–92 and netted six goals in 126 League outings for QPR before being sold to Newcastle United for £2.7 million in March 1994. He featured in successive Premiership title challenges and joined Blackburn Rovers in July 1998, where a serious neck injury ended his playing career.

Gavin Peacock

Born: Eltham, 18 November 1967.

Signed from: Apprentice.
Debut: 29 November 1986.
Total appearances: 206.
Total goals: 42.

England Youth midfielder Gavin Peacock had two spells at QPR. Signing professional at Loftus Road in November 1984, he gained top-flight experience before his father Keith signed him for Gillingham for £40,000 in December 1987. He moved via AFC Bournemouth to Newcastle United in a deal involving Wayne Fereday in November 1990. Top scorer in 1991–92, he starred in their 1992–93 First Division title triumph and joined Chelsea for £1.25 million in August 1993. He was an FA Cup finalist in 1994, and then rejoined QPR in a joint £3.5 million deal with John Spencer in November 1996. Netting 36 goals in 207 League games overall for Rangers, he had a testimonial match in May 2003 and has since worked in the media.

George Petchey

Born: Whitechapel, 24 June 1931.

Signed from: West Ham United.

Debut: 19 August 1953.
Total appearances: 278.
Total goals: 24.

Tough-tackling wing-half George Petchey was ever present for QPR in two consecutive seasons. He turned professional with West Ham in August 1948 but failed to secure a regular first-team slot and moved to Loftus Road in July 1953. He played alongside Peter Angell and Keith Rutter, netting 22 goals in 255 League games for Rangers prior to joining Crystal Palace in June 1960. He helped them win promotion in 1960–61 and 1963–64, after which he joined their coaching staff when his playing career was ended by an eye injury. He became Orient's manager in July 1971 and plotted their 1973–74 promotion near-miss, and he then managed Millwall. Later Brighton's assistant boss, he scouted for several clubs before retiring in Brighton.

Bill Pierce

Born: Ashington, 29 October 1907.

Signed from: Bedlington Colliery.
Debut: 6 October 1923.
Total appearances: 193.
Total goals: 3.

Hard-tackling full-back Bill Pierce gave QPR fine service during eight seasons at Loftus Road. Previously with Bedlington Colliery, he joined Rangers in August 1923 and made his League debut as a 16-year-old in the 2–0 defeat at Swansea two months later. He performed well on either flank and partnered the likes of Sid Sweetman, Jack Young and Bob Pollard in QPR's defence, featuring in consecutive promotion near-misses under Bob Hewison. Helping take Charlton Athletic to an FA Cup third-round replay in 1929–30, he scored twice in 179 Third Division South games prior to joining Carlisle United in June 1931. He was a factory foreman back in his native North East after World War Two and died in September 1976.

George Powell

Born: Fulham, 11 October 1924.

Signed from: Fulham.
Debut: 8 November 1947.
Total appearances: 155.
Total goals: 0.

Locally-born right-back George Powell featured in QPR's 1947–48 Third Division South title triumph. Initially an amateur with Fulham, he

represented the Combined Services during the war and joined Rangers in December 1946. He was given his League debut in QPR's 3–2 defeat at Reading in November 1947 and took over from Reg Dudley for the remainder of that season, helping take Derby County to an FA Cup sixth-round replay when he deputised in goal for the injured Reg Allen. Partnering Arthur Jefferson in Rangers' defence, he made 145 League appearances prior to joining Snowdon Colliery in July 1955, after which he played for Tunbridge Wells. He later managed Addmult and died in Hemel Hempstead in February 1989.

Ivor Powell

Born: Bargoed, 5 July 1916.

Signed from: Bargoed.

Debut: 28 January 1939.
Total appearances: 159.
Total goals: 2.

Welsh international wing-half Ivor Powell was capped four times while at Loftus Road. Initially with Bargoed, he turned professional with QPR in September 1937 and made his League debut at home to Walsall in January 1939. He served in India with Billy McEwan during the war and later starred in Rangers' 1947–48 Third Division South title triumph and FA Cup run. He scored twice in 110 League games before he was sold to Aston Villa for £17,500 in December 1948, and he was ever present for Villa in the top-flight in 1949–50. He later had a spell as Port Vale's player-manager, then held a similar post at Bradford City and was trainer-coach at Leeds United. He managed Carlisle United and Bath City, and was then appointed head football coach at Bath University/Team Bath.

Karl Ready

Born: Neath, 14 August 1972.

Signed from: Trainee.
Debut: 9 October 1991.
Total appearances: 224.
Total goals: 11.

Long-serving Welsh international central-defender Karl Ready was capped five times while at QPR. A former trainee at Loftus Road, he turned professional in August 1990 and made his League debut in Rangers' 1–1 draw at home to Wimbledon in October 1991. He started as a right-back but after suffering an injury he returned in the heart of defence alongside Alan McDonald and secured a regular first-team slot during the 1995–96 relegation battle. Appointed QPR's captain for a spell, he netted 10 goals in 207 League outings prior to joining Motherwell in July 2001. He moved to Aldershot Town in September 2002 and helped win promotion to the Conference that season, and he then had spells with Aylesbury United and Crawley Town.

Glenn Roeder

Born: Woodford, 13 December 1955.

Signed from: Orient.
Debut: 26 August 1978.
Total appearances: 181.
Total goals: 18.

Stylish England B international central-defender Glenn Roeder skippered QPR in the 1982 FA Cup Final. Signing professional forms for Orient in December 1973, he was ever present in their 1977–78 FA Cup run and moved to Loftus Road for a then record £250,000 in August 1978. He missed the 1982 FA Cup Final replay through suspension and lost his place during the 1982–83 Second Division title campaign. He scored 17 goals in 157 League outings for Rangers and then joined Newcastle United for £150,000 in December 1983 and helped them clinch promotion. He later played for Watford, Orient again and Gillingham, and he then rejoined Watford as manager. After holding various coaching posts, he has since managed West Ham, Newcastle and Norwich City.

George Rounce

Born: Grays, 1905.

Signed from: Uxbridge Town.
Debut: 25 February 1928.
Total appearances: 188.
Total goals: 71.

Hard-shooting inside-forward George Rounce formed a lethal partnership with George Goddard while at QPR. He developed as a player with Tilbury and Uxbridge, representing Middlesex Amateurs before joining Rangers in February 1928.

He scored on his League debut in that month's 4–0 victory at Merthyr Town and later grabbed a hat-trick in QPR's 4–0 demolition of Crystal Palace in November 1930, and he also starred in successive promotion challenges under Bob Hewison. He netted 59 goals in 171 Third Division South games for Rangers prior to joining local rivals Fulham in March 1933. Moving to Bristol Rovers in June 1935, he never played for them as he was struck down with tuberculosis shortly after signing and tragically died in October 1936.

Keith Rutter

Born: Leeds, 10 September 1931.

Signed from: Methley United.
Debut: 24 August 1954.
Total appearances: 369.
Total goals: 2.

Commanding centre-half Keith Rutter was ever present for QPR on three occasions. Initially with Yorkshire Amateurs, he moved via Methley United to Loftus Road in July 1954 and later recommended Arthur Longbottom from the same club. He made his League debut in the following month's 2–2 draw at Southend and missed just seven games in six seasons. Scoring once in 339 League

outings for Rangers, he was a key figure in successive promotion challenges under Alec Stock before joining Colchester United for £4,000 in February 1963. He later played for Romford, Ashford Town and was Hastings United's player-manager. After his footballing career he became a builder, a Bournemouth hotelier and a Bridport restaurateur, before settling in Axminster in retirement.

Keith Sanderson

Born: Hull, 9 October 1940.

Signed from: Plymouth Argyle.
Debut: 21 August 1965.
Total appearances: 118.
Total goals: 12.

Inside-forward Keith Sanderson was an influential member of QPR's 1966–67 Third Division title and League Cup double-winning team. A former Cambridge University soccer blue, he played for Harwich & Parkeston before being reunited with Malcolm Allison at Bath City and starring in their 1963–64 FA Cup run. He followed Big Mal to Plymouth Argyle in August 1964 and joined QPR for £4,000 in June 1965. A part-time professional, he combined football with his

job as a strategic systems analyst for IBM in London. He scored 10 goals in 104 League games for Rangers and briefly appeared in the top-flight, before he left for spells with Goole Town and Wimbledon. He later worked for IBM in Portsmouth and has since settled in Hayling Island.

David Seaman

Born: Rotherham, 19 September 1963.

Signed from: Birmingham City.
Debut: 23 August 1986.
Total appearances: 175.
Total goals: 0.

England international goalkeeper David Seaman gained the first three of his 75 caps while at QPR. Initially with Leeds United, he moved via Peterborough United to Birmingham City for £100,000 in October 1984 and helped them regain top-flight status at the first attempt that season. He moved to Loftus Road for £225,000 in August 1986 and missed just one match in the 1986–87 season. Starring in Rangers' 1989–90 FA Cup run, he made 141 First Division appearances before joining Arsenal for £1.3 million in May

1990. He amassed a vast collection of domestic and European honours with the Gunners, including the double in 1997–98 and 2001–02. Moving to Manchester City in July 2003, he retired after suffering a shoulder injury in January 2004.

Don Shanks

Born: Hammersmith, 2 October 1952.

Signed from: Luton Town.
Debut: 7 December 1974.
Total appearances: 201.
Total goals: 11.

Ex-England Youth defender Don Shanks played for QPR in the 1976–77 League Cup semi-final. A former Fulham apprentice, he turned professional with Luton Town in July 1970 and helped win promotion to the top-flight in 1973–74. He moved to Loftus Road for £35,000 in November 1974 and understudied Dave Clement as Rangers were League Championship runners-up in 1975–76. As well as featuring in the 1976–77 UEFA Cup quarter-final second-leg, he was virtually ever present for the next four seasons and netted 10 goals in 180 League games prior to joining Brighton in August 1981. He had spells with various overseas clubs and was a playboy on the London gambling scene, and h e has since worked for a well-known horse racing family.

Ernie Shepherd

Born: Wombwell, 14 August 1919.

Signed from: Hull City.
Debut: 19 August 1950.
Total appearances: 233.
Total goals: 54.

Outside-left Ernie Shepherd missed just one match for QPR in 1950–51. A former Bradford City amateur, he turned professional with Fulham in April 1938 and joined West Brom in exchange for Arthur Rowley in December 1948. He moved to Hull City three months later, helping the club to promotion in 1948–49. Dave Mangnall signed him for Rangers in August 1950 and he netted 51 goals in 219 League outings while at Loftus Road before becoming Hastings United's player-coach in July 1956. He was later trainer at Bradford Park Avenue and Southend United, where he had a spell as manager before he left to assist George Petchey at Orient. Later manager of Al Wasl in Dubai for 10 years, he settled in Southend and died in March 2001.

Danny Shittu

Born: Lagos, Nigeria, 2 September 1980.

Signed from: Charlton Athletic.
Debut: 23 October 2001.
Total appearances: 179.
Total goals: 28.

Nigeria international central-defender Danny Shittu featured in QPR's 2003–04 promotion campaign. Initially with Carshalton Athletic, he joined Charlton Athletic in September 1999 but failed to make an impact and was loaned to Blackpool and QPR before joining Rangers permanently for £250,000 in January 2002 after two fans funded the deal. He was sent-off on his debut in that month's 4–1 defeat at Peterborough but quickly became a popular figure at Loftus Road and starred as QPR reached the Second Division Play-off Final in 2002–03. He netted 17 goals in 169 League outings for Rangers before he joined Watford for £1.6 million in August 2006 and helped them qualify for the Championship Play-offs in 2007–08. He then moved to Bolton Wanderers.

Frank Sibley

Born: Uxbridge, 4 December 1947.

Signed from: Apprentice.
Debut: 4 September 1963.
Total appearances: 165.
Total goals: 5.

Ex-England Youth wing-half Frank Sibley served QPR in various capacities during a 34-year association. Spotted by Derek Healy playing for NW Middlesex Schoolboys, he became an apprentice at Loftus Road and was later QPR's youngest League debutant at 16 years 97 days against Bristol City in March 1964. He was also the club's first substitute in a game against Millwall in October 1965. He later starred in Rangers' 1966–67 Third Division title and League Cup double success. He netted three goals in 143 League games until a knee injury ended his career in May 1971, after which he joined QPR's coaching staff and had two stints as manager in 1977–78 and 1984–85.

Trevor Sinclair

Born: Dulwich, 2 March 1973.

Signed from: Blackpool.
Debut: 18 August 1993.
Total appearances: 185.
Total goals: 21.

Skilful winger Trevor Sinclair was capped 12 times by England after leaving QPR. He turned professional with Blackpool in August 1990 and helped them reach the Fourth Division Play-off Final in 1990–91, then featured in their 1991–92 Play-off Final triumph. Gerry Francis paid £750,000 for him in August 1993, to replace Andy Sinton, and the England Under-21 international featured in QPR's 1994–95 FA Cup run. He missed just one match in Rangers' 1995–96 relegation battle, and he netted 16 goals in 167 League outings while at Loftus Road before joining West Ham in a £2.3 million deal involving Northern Ireland internationals Iain Dowie and Keith Rowland in January 1998. He joined Manchester City for £2.5 million in July 2003.

Andy Sinton

Born: Newcastle, 19 March 1966.

Signed from: Brentford.

Debut: 25 March 1989.
Total appearances: 190.
Total goals: 25.

England international midfielder Andy Sinton was capped 10 times while at QPR. He was Cambridge United's youngest League player at 16 years 228 days against Wolves in November 1982 and moved to Brentford in December 1985. Ever present in two consecutive seasons for Brentford, he joined QPR for £300,000 in March 1989 and was again twice ever present, starring as Rangers finished fifth in the Premier League in 1992–93. He netted 22 goals in 160 League games before reuniting with Trevor Francis at Sheffield Wednesday for £2.7 million in August 1993. Moving to Tottenham Hotspur in January 1996, he helped win the League Cup in 1999, and he then played for Wolves, Burton Albion and Bromsgrove Rovers before managing Fleet Town.

Conway Smith

Born: Huddersfield, 13 July 1926.

Signed from: Huddersfield Town.
Debut: 17 March 1951.
Total appearances: 181.
Total goals: 83.

Inside-forward Conway Smith

topped QPR's goalscoring charts in five successive seasons. The son of former Huddersfield and England star Billy Smith, he turned professional with Huddersfield in May 1945 and gained top-flight experience with his home-town club before moving to Loftus Road in March 1951. Scoring in each of his first three games for QPR, he missed just one match during the 1951–52 relegation battle and netted 81 goals in 174 League outings prior to joining Halifax Town in June 1956. He was twice leading marksman for the Shaymen. Moving to Nelson in June 1962, he later worked in the Rent Office of Huddersfield Corporation Housing Department until he suffered a fatal heart-attack in March 1989.

George Smith

Born: Bromley-by-Bow, 23 April 1915.

Signed from: Brentford.
Debut: 23 August 1947.
Total appearances: 83.
Total goals: 1.

Experienced centre-half George Smith skippered QPR to the Third Division South title in 1947–48. Initially with Bexleyheath & Welling, he moved to Charlton Athletic in May 1938 and helped them win the 1944 Football League South Cup. The England wartime international then joined Brentford in November 1945, moved to Loftus Road in June 1947 and starring as Rangers took Derby to an FA Cup sixth-round replay in 1947–48. Scoring once in 75 League games for QPR, he joined Ipswich Town in September 1949 and then had a spell with Chelmsford City before managing Redhill, Eastbourne United, Sutton United, Crystal Palace and Portsmouth. He was later Pompey's general manager and died in Bodmin in October 1983.

Peter Springett

Born: Fulham, 8 May 1946.

Signed from: Apprentice.
Debut: 18 May 1963.
Total appearances: 161.
Total goals: 0.

Ex-England Youth goalkeeper Peter Springett was ever present in QPR's 1966–67 Third Division title and League Cup double success. Born locally, he turned professional for Rangers in May 1963 and made his League debut in that month's 0–0 draw at home to Peterborough. He played 137 Third Division games for QPR prior to joining Sheffield Wednesday in exchange for his older brother Ron in May 1967. After gaining England Under-23 honours while at Hillsborough, he joined Barnsley in July 1975 and featured in their 1978–79 promotion campaign, and he then played for Scarborough. He later became a constable with South Yorkshire Police, serving at both Sheffield clubs on match days, but he suffered a serious illness and died in September 1997.

Ron Springett

Born: Fulham, 22 July 1935.

Signed from: Victoria United.
Debut: 5 November 1955.
Total appearances: 147.
Total goals: 0.

Former England international goalkeeper Ron Springett helped QPR win promotion to the top-flight for the first time in 1967–68. Born locally, he played for Victoria United before joining QPR in February 1953 and made his League debut in their 3–2 defeat at home to Norwich in November 1955. He was ever present in 1956–57 and moved to Sheffield Wednesday for £15,000 in March 1958. He starred as they were crowned Second Division champions in 1958–59, League Championship runners-up in 1960–61 and FA Cup finalists in 1966, and he rejoined QPR in exchange for his younger brother Peter in May 1967. He made 133 League appearances overall for Rangers, then ran a sports shop and is now a retired decorator in East Sheen.

Simon Stainrod

Born: Sheffield, 1 February 1959.

Signed from: Oldham Athletic.
Debut: 22 November 1980.
Total appearances: 175.
Total goals: 62.

Former England Youth striker Simon Stainrod played for QPR in the 1982 FA Cup Final. Initially with Sheffield United, he joined Oldham Athletic for £60,000 in March 1979 and was leading marksman in 1979–80. He moved to Loftus Road for £270,000 in November 1980 and topped QPR's goalscoring charts in 1981–82. His goals helped the club to win the Second Division title in 1982–83 and finish fifth in the top-flight in 1983–84, and he netted 48 goals in 145 League games for Rangers before joining Sheffield Wednesday for £250,000 in February 1985. He moved to Aston Villa for a similar fee in September 1985, then played for Stoke City, Rouen and Falkirk. Later player-manager of Dundee and Ayr United, he has since become a football agent.

Dave Thomas

Born: Kirkby, 5 October 1950.

Signed from: Burnley.
Debut: 21 October 1972.

Total appearances: 219.
Total goals: 34.

England international winger Dave Thomas gained eight caps while at Loftus Road. He turned professional with Burnley in October 1967 and scored in the 1968–69 League Cup semi-final replay, moving to promotion rivals QPR for £165,000 in October 1972. An influential figure as Rangers regained top-flight status that season and were League Championship runners-up in 1975–76, he netted 28 goals in 182 League games prior to joining Everton for £200,000 in August 1977. Later with Wolves, Vancouver Whitecaps and Middlesbrough, he reunited with Bobby Campbell at Portsmouth in July 1982 and helped them win the Third Division title in 1982–83. He is currently a PE teacher at Bishop Luffa Secondary School in Chichester.

Terry Venables

Born: Bethnall Green, 6 January 1943.

Signed from: Tottenham Hotspur.
Debut: 9 August 1969.
Total appearances: 205.
Total goals: 22.

Ex-England international midfielder Terry Venables was an

influential figure in QPR's 1972–73 promotion success. He turned professional with Chelsea in August 1960, starring as they won promotion in 1962–63 and the League Cup in 1965. Sold to Spurs for £80,000 in May 1966, he was an FA Cup winner in 1967 and joined QPR for £70,000 in June 1969. He skippered Rangers to the FA Cup sixth round in 1969–70, and he netted 19 goals in 177 League outings before joining Crystal Palace in September 1974.

Gary Waddock

Born: Kingsbury, 17 March 1962.

Signed from: Apprentice.
Debut: 28 August 1979.
Total appearances: 227.
Total goals: 10.

Republic of Ireland international midfielder Gary Waddock starred

in QPR's 1982–83 Second Division title triumph. Signing professionally at Loftus Road in July 1979, he made his League debut in Rangers' 2–1 win at Swansea the following month and also played in the 1982 FA Cup Final. He helped QPR qualify for the UEFA Cup in 1983–84, netting eight goals in 203 League outings until a serious injury appeared to end his playing career. But after a spell with Belgian side Charleroi, he joined Millwall in August 1989 and returned to QPR in February 1992. He failed to make any further first-team appearances and joined Bristol Rovers in November 1992, then played for Luton. He was later coach/manager back at QPR before managing Aldershot.

Ian Watson

Born: Hammersmith, 7 January 1944.

Signed from: Chelsea.
Debut: 21 August 1965.
Total appearances: 226.
Total goals: 2.

Versatile full-back Ian Watson was QPR's only ever-present player during their 1968–69 First Division debut campaign. A former Chelsea junior, he turned professional in February 1962 and gained top-flight experience under Tommy Docherty. He moved to Loftus Road for £10,000 in July 1965 and was a valuable member of QPR's 1966–67 Third Division title and League Cup double squad, although he was unlucky not to play at Wembley after a knee injury. Featuring in the vital promotion clincher at Villa Park in May 1968, he helped Rangers regain their top-flight status in 1972–73 and scored once in 202 League games before retiring in May 1974. He has since worked in the building trade, notably with West Park Builders in Copthorne.

David Webb

Born: East Ham, 9 April 1946.

Signed from: Chelsea.
Debut: 16 August 1974.
Total appearances: 146.
Total goals: 11.

Central-defender David Webb was an experienced figure as QPR finished League Championship runners-up in 1975–76. Initially with Leyton Orient, he was swapped for Southampton's George O'Brien in March 1966 and helped clinch promotion that season. He joined Chelsea in exchange for Joe Kirkup in February 1968 and starred as they won the FA Cup in 1970 and European Cup-Winners' Cup in 1971. Reuniting with Dave Sexton at QPR for £120,000 in July 1974, he netted seven goals in 116 First Division games before following Frank McLintock to Leicester City for £50,000 in September 1977. He then had a spell with Derby County before managing AFC

Bournemouth, Torquay United, Southend United, Chelsea, Brentford and Yeovil Town.

Steve Wicks

Born: Reading, 3 October 1956.

Signed from: Derby County.
Debut: 25 September 1979.
Total appearances: 220.
Total goals: 6.

Former England Under-21 central-defender Steve Wicks played for QPR in the 1986 Milk Cup Final. Signing professional for Chelsea in June 1974, he featured prominently as they regained their top-flight status in 1976–77 and joined Derby County for £275,000 in January 1979. He followed Tommy Docherty to Loftus Road for a similar fee in September 1979 and rejoined QPR after nine months with Crystal Palace for

£325,000 in March 1982. Helping Rangers clinch the Second Division title in 1982–83, he netted six goals in 189 League games overall for the club before returning to Chelsea for £400,000 in August 1986. After a back injury ended his playing career he coached at various clubs prior to managing Scarborough and Lincoln City.

Ray Wilkins

Born: Hillingdon, 14 September 1956.

Signed from: Glasgow Rangers.
Debut: 2 December 1989.
Total appearances: 200.
Total goals: 10.

Former England international midfielder Ray Wilkins was ever present for QPR in 1990–91. Initially with Chelsea, he became their youngest captain at the age of 18 in April 1975 and skippered the Blues' 1976–77 promotion success. He reunited with Dave Sexton at Manchester United in August 1979 and scored in their 1983 FA Cup Final triumph. He moved to AC Milan in June 1984 and then played for Paris St Germain and Glasgow Rangers before joining QPR in November 1989. Starring in Rangers' 1989–90 FA Cup run, he had a spell at Crystal Palace prior to rejoining QPR as player-manager in November 1994 and netting seven goals in 175 League games overall. Later with Wycombe, Millwall and Leyton Orient, he has coached at various clubs.

Clive Wilson

Born: Manchester, 13 November 1961.

Signed from: Chelsea.
Debut: 25 August 1990.
Total appearances: 196.
Total goals: 14.

Attacking left-back Clive Wilson featured prominently as QPR finished fifth in the Premier League in 1992–93. He turned professional with Manchester City in December 1979, helping them regain top-flight status in 1984–85 and playing in the 1986 Full Members' Cup Final. Joining Chelsea for £250,000 in May 1987, he featured in their 1988–89 Second Division title triumph and moved to Loftus Road for £450,000 in August 1990. He was QPR's only ever-present player in 1993–94 and was an influential figure as they reached the FA Cup sixth round in 1994–95. The penalty king netted 12 goals in 172 League games before leaving to reunite with Gerry Francis at Spurs in June 1995, after which he then played for Cambridge United and Wingate & Finchley.

Pat Woods

Born: Islington, 29 April 1933.

Signed from: Juniors.
Debut: 3 January 1953.
Total appearances: 333.
Total goals: 16.

Long-serving right-back Pat Woods formed a notable partnership with record appearance holder Tony Ingham while at QPR. A former junior at Loftus Road, he turned professional in June 1950 and made his League debut in Rangers' 2–0 defeat at Coventry City in January 1953. He secured a regular first-team slot during the 1953–54 campaign and was ever present in 1959–60. He featured in QPR's record 9–2 victory over Tranmere Rovers in December 1960 and netted 15 goals in 304 League outings prior to joining Hellenic (Queensland) in May 1961. He also played for Australian rivals South Coast (New South Wales) before moving to Colchester United in August 1963 for a year, after which he then returned to Australia and settled in Nambucca Heads.

QPR Manager Profiles

James Cowan

Former Scotland international centre-half James Cowan managed QPR to the Southern League title in 1907–08 and 1911–12. Initially a player with Vale of Leven, he joined Aston Villa in August 1889 and became the mainstay of their defence, starring as they won the League Championship on five occasions and the FA Cup in 1895 and 1897. He briefly joined their coaching staff, then ran the Grand Turk pub in Aston before becoming QPR's first-ever manager in May 1907. Making several shrewd signings, he managed Rangers in the 1908 and 1912 FA Charity Shield games against Manchester United and Blackburn Rovers, and he remained in charge until illness forced him to resign in 1914. He died in Scotland in December 1915.

Jimmy Howie

Former Scotland international inside-right Jimmy Howie managed QPR to the FA Cup quarter-finals for the first time in 1913–14. Starting his career with Galston Athletic, he joined Kilmarnock in May 1898 and helped them to win the Scottish Second Division title in 1898–99. He then had spells with Kettering Town and Bristol Rovers before he joined Newcastle United in May 1903, featuring prominently in three League Championship triumphs and four FA Cup Finals, including their first-ever success in 1910. He joined Huddersfield Town in December 1910, after which 'Gentleman Jim' managed QPR from November 1913 until March 1920, during which time he oversaw Rangers' first match at Loftus Road. He was then Middlesbrough's secretary-manager for four years. He later became a tobacconist in London and died in January 1963.

Ned Liddell

Ned Liddell guided QPR to the FA Cup quarter-finals in 1922–23. A former centre-half, he played for Whitburn, Southampton, Gainsborough, Clapton Orient, Southend United and Woolwich Arsenal before rejoining Southend as manager in April 1919. He was appointed QPR's boss in April 1920 and managed the side in the club's first season in the Football League. He recruited the likes of Mick O'Brien and Arthur Chandler before he was sacked in June 1925 when the club had to seek re-election. After acting as a scout for Fulham he became their manager for two years in May 1929, and he then scouted for West Ham prior to becoming Luton Town's boss in August 1936. He steered the Hatters to the Third Division South title in 1936–37 and later scouted for Chelsea, Portsmouth, Brentford and Spurs. He died in November 1969.

Bob Hewison

Bob Hewison managed QPR to third place in the Third Division South in 1929–30. Previously a right-half with Newcastle United and Leeds

City, he spent five seasons as Northampton Town's player-manager before taking charge of QPR in July 1925. He managed the first side to play in the new blue and white hoops and signed the club's all-time record goalscorer George Goddard. He suffered a poor first season at Rangers as they finished bottom of the Third Division South and had to apply for re-election. In the 1930–31 season Rangers finishrd in eighth place, and Hewison left the club in March 1931. Appointed Bristol City's manager in April 1932, he plotted their 1934–35 FA Cup run and remained at Ashton Gate for 17 years, for which he gained a Football League long service medal. He later managed Guildford City and Bath City, guiding the latter to the Southern League Championship in 1959–60. He died in Bristol in April 1964.

John Bowman

Influential right-half John Bowman was both a player and manager at QPR. Initially with Sheldon Juniors, he later had spells with Hanley St Judes, Burslem Port Vale and

Stoke, briefly appearing in the top-flight before joining Rangers in June 1901. He scored twice in 103 Southern League games for QPR before becoming Norwich City's first-ever manager in May 1905. He remained in charge of the Canaries until June 1907, and he later spent four years as Croydon Common's boss until the club closed down during World War One, when he returned to QPR as a director. He replaced Bob Hewison as Rangers' manager for eight months until November 1931, when he was forced to step down through ill health, while also running a sports shop in Harlesden during this period. He died in Sudbury in January 1943.

Archie Mitchell

Former captain Archie Mitchell succeeded John Bowman as QPR's manager. A former player for Rangers, after his playing career ended he became Brentford's player-manager in August 1921. He then coached overseas and managed Dartford before rejoining QPR as a coach. Appointed manager in

November 1931 after the sudden retirement of John Bowman, he built a side around George Goddard and oversaw the move to the White City Ground. He remained in charge until May 1933 and died in April 1949.

Mick O'Brien

Irish international centre-half Mick O'Brien was both a player and manager at QPR. At the start of his career he had spells with Walker Celtic and Blyth Spartans before joining Norwich City in August 1919. Moving via South Shields to QPR in May 1920, he netted three goals in 66 League games prior to joining Leicester City in March 1922. He then played for Hull City, Derby County,

Walsall, Norwich again and Watford, returning to QPR as manager from May 1933 until April 1935. He took over with the club in dire circumstances and had to sell star striker George Goddard almost straight away. He did a fine job of lifting the club, however, and they recorded a fourth-place finish in the Southern Section in 1933–34. He left in 1935 after a poor season. After a year as Brentford's assistant boss, he became Ipswich Town's manager in May 1936 and guided them to the Southern League Championship in 1936–37. He left in August 1937 after the death of his wife and resided in Uxbridge until his death in September 1940.

Billy Birrell

Billy Birrell managed QPR to third place in the Third Division South in 1937–38, missing promotion by just three points. Initially a player with Raith Rovers, the inside-right joined Middlesbrough in February 1921 and became a great favourite at Ayresome Park, captaining Boro's 1926–27 Second Division title triumph. He returned to Raith Rovers as player-manager in November 1927, then had five years in charge of Bournemouth. Appointed QPR's manager in April 1935, he remained in charge at Loftus Road until May 1939, when he left to manage top-flight Chelsea. During his time at Rangers he signed Tommy Cheetham, who became the linchpin of the side, and was in charge for Rangers' club record 8–1 FA Cup win over Bristol Rovers. The season before he left, Birrell led the club to third place, just missing out on promotion three points behind Millwall. He guided Chelsea to two wartime Cup Finals, then two FA Cup semi-finals, and he left Stamford Bridge in May 1952. He later worked as a clerk in Kenton and died in November 1968.

Ted Vizard

Former Welsh international outside-left Ted Vizard managed QPR during World War Two. Signing professional for Bolton Wanderers in November 1910, he helped them regain their top-flight status that season and formed a notable partnership with Joe Smith. He was an influential figure as they won the FA Cup in 1923 and 1926, and he became Bolton's A team coach in May 1931. Appointed Swindon Town's boss in April 1933, he took charge at Loftus Road in May 1939 and remained Rangers' manager until April 1944, when he left to replace Major Buckley as Wolves' boss. He led them to third place in the top-flight in 1946–47 and laid the foundations for future success. He was then a licensee in Tattenhall and died in December 1973.

Dave Mangnall

Dave Mangnall managed QPR to the Third Division South title and FA Cup sixth round in 1947–48. He was a centre-forward with Maltby Colliery, Leeds United, Huddersfield, Birmingham and West Ham prior to joining Millwall in July 1936, starring as they reached the FA Cup semi-finals in 1936–37 and claimed the Third Division South Championship in 1937–38. Moving to QPR in May 1939,

he scored 99 goals in 131 wartime games and succeeded Ted Vizard as manager at Loftus Road in April 1944. He guided Rangers to Third Division South runners'-up spot in 1946–47, then to the Second Division for the first time in their history the following season. He was the first manager to spend £5,000 on one player – Fred Durrant – but after four seasons in the Second Division his side began to break up and were eventually relegated in 1952. He retired in June that year and ran a business in Penzance until his death in April 1962.

Jack Taylor

Jack Taylor signed several players from his native Yorkshire during his seven-year reign at Loftus Road. A former full-back, he turned professional with Wolves in January 1934 and played alongside his brother Frank while at Molineux. He featured prominently as Wolves were named League Championship runners-up in 1937–38, before he moved to Norwich City in June 1938 and guested for Barnsley and

Watford during the war. Joining Hull City in July 1947, he helped win the Third Division North title in 1948–49, then had two years as Weymouth's player-manager before taking charge of QPR in June 1952. Taylor did some solid work while at QPR and even uncovered some non-League gems, but success never came on the pitch and attendances dwindled. Crowds also dropped considerably after two humiliating FA Cup defeats to non-League opposition, 4–0 against Walthamstow Avenue and 6–1 against Hereford United. He remained at Loftus Road until May 1959, after which he managed Leeds United for two years and resided in Barnsley until his death in February 1978.

Alec Stock

Alec Stock managed QPR to a Third Division title and League Cup double in 1966–67. He was an inside-forward with Charlton and QPR, then became Yeovil Town's player-manager and plotted their epic 1948–49 FA Cup run. Appointed Leyton Orient's manager in August 1949, he guided them to the Third Division South title in 1955–56 and had brief spells at Arsenal and Roma before taking charge of QPR in August 1959. Stock rebuilt the side and developed a youth set-up, and he also brought in players such as Rodney Marsh. The season in which Rangers

won the Third Division title and League Cup was the greatest season in the club's history to that point. He steered Rangers into the top-flight for the first time in 1967–68 but resigned in August 1968, having never picked a First Division team, and guided Luton Town to promotion in 1969–70, then took Fulham to the 1975 FA Cup Final. Returning to QPR as a director and briefly caretaker manager, he was later AFC Bournemouth's manager. He died in April 2001.

Bill Dodgin Jnr

Former England Under-23 centre-half Bill Dodgin briefly managed QPR at the start of the 1968–69 First Division campaign. The son of the former Fulham manager of the same name, he played for Fulham, Arsenal and Fulham again before coaching Millwall and QPR. He assisted Alec Stock before succeeding him as Rangers' manager for three months as caretaker in August 1968. Rejoining Fulham as boss in December 1968, he led them to promotion in 1970–71, then coached Leicester City before managing Northampton Town to promotion in 1975–76. He took charge of Brentford in September 1976, plotting promotion again in 1977–78, and he then rejoined Northampton as boss in October 1980 before later managing Woking. He died in June 2000.

Tommy Docherty

Colourful manager Tommy Docherty had two spells in charge of QPR. A former Scotland international wing-half, he moved from Celtic to Preston in November 1949 and helped them to win the Second Division title in 1950–51 and reach the FA Cup Final in 1954. He then moved via Arsenal to Chelsea and became their manager in September 1961, guiding them to promotion in 1962–63 and the FA Cup Final in 1967. After a period in charge of Rotherham, he spent 28 days as QPR's manager in November 1968. However, he left due to what he felt was interference coming from chairman John Gregory. 'The Doc' later managed Aston Villa and Scotland, then plotted Manchester United's 1977 FA Cup Final triumph. Later boss of Derby County, then QPR again from May 1979 until October 1980, he also managed Preston, Wolves and Altrincham. When he had joined QPR for the second time in 1979 the club was already doomed to the Second Division, but his name managed to keep many players at Rangers. However, when the team began to struggle in the lower division Docherty left.

Les Allen

Former England Under-23 centre-forward Les Allen managed QPR to the FA Cup sixth round in 1969–70. Initially a player with Briggs Sports, he joined Chelsea in September 1954 and moved to Spurs in exchange for Johnny Brooks in December 1959. Ever present in their 1960–61 double success, he joined QPR for a then record £21,000 fee in July 1965 and starred alongside Rodney Marsh in the 1966–67 Third Division title and League Cup double triumph. He also helped win promotion in 1967–68 and became player-manager in December 1968 after the shock departure of Alex Stock and the stormy, month-long reign of Tommy Docherty. He netted 55 times in 128 League outings before resigning in January 1971. During his time at QPR Allen sgned Terry Venables for a club record fee but could not keep Rangers in the First Division. He later managed Woodford and Swindon, and his sons Clive and Bradley and nephew Martin also played for QPR.

Gordon Jago

Gordon Jago managed QPR back to the top-flight in 1972–73. A former Charlton Athletic centre-half, he coached Eastbourne United, England Youth, Fulham and Baltimore Bays before being appointed QPR's coach in May 1970. He succeeded Les Allen as manager in January 1971 and plotted promotion with shrewd signings including Don Givens, Stan Bowles and

Dave Thomas. He resigned in September 1974, after which he managed Millwall to promotion in 1975–76 and then guided Tampa Bay Rowdies to two consecutive NASL Soccer Bowl triumphs. He also coached California Surf, Dallas Sidekicks and the United States national side. He briefly returned as QPR's general manager in May 1984 and has since settled in the United States.

Dave Sexton

Masterful coach Dave Sexton managed QPR to League Championship runners'-up spot in 1975–76. An early graduate from West Ham's 'Academy', he was also an inside-forward with Luton Town, Leyton Orient, Brighton and Crystal Palace before he became Chelsea's coach in February 1962. He briefly managed Orient, then coached Fulham and Arsenal before rejoining Chelsea as manager in October 1967. He guided the Blues to FA Cup and European Cup-Winners' Cup success, and then he became QPR's boss in October 1974. In his first season Sexton brought Don Masson to the club and led Rangers to 11th place. The following season he led the club to runners'-up spot behind champions Liverpool, thus qualifying for Europe. Sexton led Rangers to the League Cup semi-finals and the UEFA Cup quarter-finals in 1976–77. He left Loftus Road in July 1977 to manage Manchester United, and he later had spells in charge of Coventry City and England Under-21s, while also coaching QPR and Aston Villa.

Frank Sibley

Ex-England Youth wing-half Frank Sibley had two spells as QPR's manager during a 34 year association with the club. After a long playing career with Rangers he joined QPR's coaching staff, and was manager from July 1977 until July 1978, then again as caretaker between December 1984 and June 1985. He was also manager-coach at Walsall, Hounslow and Millwall, and he then assisted Gerry Francis and Ray Wilkins back at Loftus Road.

Steve Burtenshaw

Steve Burtenshaw was unable to prevent QPR's relegation from the top-flight in 1978–79. One of three footballing brothers, he helped Sussex win the FA County Youth Cup shortly before turning professional with Brighton in November 1952. The wing-half helped the Seagulls win the Third Division South title in 1957–58 and joined their coaching staff in July 1964. He later became Arsenal's reserve-team coach, then chief coach before joining QPR in a similar capacity in October 1973. He was appointed Sheffield Wednesday's boss in January 1974, after which he coached Everton before rejoining Rangers as manager from August 1978 until May 1979. While at QPR he signed Glenn Roeder from Orient and Rachid Harkouk from Crystal Palace. The 1978–79 season started badly, however, and with only one win in 20 matches QPR were relegated, with Burtenshaw sacked before the final game of the season. He was later youth-team coach and chief scout back at Arsenal, and he then returned to QPR as chief scout.

Terry Venables

England international midfielder Terry Venables was both a player and manager at QPR during his career. He joined Crystal Palace on leaving Rangers and twice gained promotion, after which he rejoined QPR as boss in October 1980, guiding them to the 1982 FA Cup Final, the Second Division title in 1982–83 and fifth place in the top-flight in 1983–84. In May 1984 he took charge of Barcelona, before he returned to England and managed Spurs and the England national side. He has since assisted Portsmouth, Crystal Palace, Middlesbrough, Leeds United and was also England's assistant boss.

Alan Mullery

Ex-England international midfielder Alan Mullery managed QPR during the 1984–85 season. Initially with Fulham, he helped them win promotion in 1958–59 and joined Spurs in March 1964.

He featured as they won the FA Cup in 1967, League Cup in 1971 and UEFA Cup in 1972. Rejoining Fulham in August 1972, he was Footballer of the Year and an FA Cup finalist in 1975. He became Brighton's manager in July 1976 and led them to promotion in 1976–77, then to the top-flight in 1978–79. Joining Charlton Athletic as boss in July 1981, he later managed Crystal Palace, then succeeded Terry Venables as QPR's manager from June 1984 until December that year. During his brief stay at Rangers, Mullery signed Garry Bannister, John Byrne and Robbie James, and he sold Clive Allen to Spurs. He then had another spell in charge of Brighton before working in the media.

Jim Smith

Jim Smith managed QPR to the 1986 Milk Cup Final. He played for Sheffield United, Aldershot, Halifax Town and Lincoln City before becoming Boston United's player-manager in June 1969. 'Bald Eagle' then joined Colchester United in a similar capacity in

October 1972 and plotted their 1973–74 promotion success, and he then managed Blackburn Rovers. He guided Birmingham City to promotion in 1979–80, then steered Oxford United from the Third Division to the First. Appointed QPR's manager in June 1985, he led them to fifth place in the top-flight in 1987–88, remaining in charge until December 1988. Smith steered the club to the Milk Cup Final, where they lost, ironically, to Oxford United, Smith's former club. He later managed Newcastle United, Portsmouth and Derby County, and he also assisted Harry Redknapp at Portsmouth before rejoining Oxford United.

Trevor Francis

Ex-England international striker Trevor Francis had a spell as QPR's player-manager. He starred as Birmingham City won promotion in 1971–72 and were twice FA Cup semi-finalists, joining Nottingham Forest in the first £1 million transfer in February 1979. Scoring Forest's winner in the 1979

European Cup Final, he later had spells with Manchester City, Sampdoria, Atalanta and Glasgow Rangers, before moving to Loftus Road in March 1988. He became QPR's player-manager in December 1988, replacing caretaker Peter Shreeves. During his spell as player-manager the club suffered an injury crisis, so Francis brought in Andy Sinton and David Bardsley to aid his beleaguered squad. However, his management style was soon facing criticism, particularly in terms of discipline, and, despite securing the services of Ray Wilkins, Francis was forced to leave. He had netted 12 goals in 32 First Division games before he was sacked in November 1989. He later held a similar post at Sheffield Wednesday for four years, taking them to both Cup Finals in 1993, after which he managed Birmingham and Crystal Palace.

Don Howe

Highly respected coach Don Howe managed QPR to the FA Cup sixth round in 1989–90. A former right-back, he turned

professional with West Brom in November 1952 and gained 23 England caps before moving to Arsenal in April 1964. He became their first-team coach and helped to plot their 1970–71 double triumph, before he rejoined West Brom as manager in July 1971. He later returned to Arsenal as chief coach, then manager, and he was Wimbledon's assistant boss when they won the FA Cup in 1988. He then assisted Trevor Francis at QPR before succeeding him as manager from November 1989 until May 1991. His first move after taking over from Francis was to buy Roy Wegerle, who became the first £1 million player in Rangers' history. He briefly managed Coventry City and assisted England in a coaching capacity, after which he was named Arsenal's head youth coach.

Gerry Francis

Ex-England international midfielder Gerry Francis had two spells as QPR's manager. As well as playing for the club, he became QPR's boss in May 1991, and he signed several

players from Bristol Rovers and led Rangers to fifth place in the Premier League in 1992–93. He left for Spurs in November 1994, then managed QPR again between October 1998 and February 2001, before briefly rejoining Bristol Rovers.

Ray Wilkins

Former England international midfielder Ray Wilkins had a spell as QPR's player-manager. He was ever-present for QPR in 1990–91 and had a spell at Crystal Palace before returning to Rangers as player-manager in November 1994. Netting seven goals in 175 League games overall, he remained in charge until September 1996 and has since held various coaching positions. After Wilkins'

resignation, Frank Sibley was once again named as caretaker manager.

Stewart Houston

Former Scotland international defender Stewart Houston managed QPR during the 1996–97 campaign. Initially with Port Glasgow, he joined Chelsea in August 1967 and gained top-flight experience before reuniting with Frank Blunstone at Brentford in March 1972. He helped clinch promotion that season and linked up with Tommy Docherty again at Manchester United in December 1973. Starring in their 1974–75 Second Division title triumph, he was also an FA Cup finalist in 1976 before he joined Sheffield United in July 1980. He featured in the Blades' 1981–82 Fourth Division title triumph, after which he moved to Colchester United. After coaching at various clubs, notably Arsenal, he managed QPR from September 1996 until December 1997. During his time at QPR he signed Gavin Peacock and John Spencer from Chelsea. Houston and his assistant Bruce Rioch were sacked a short while into their second season, with one of the reasons apparently being the manager's transfer policy. John Hollins, the reserve-team manager, was then named as caretaker manager.

Ray Harford

Ray Harford had a disappointing spell as QPR's manager. A central-defender with Charlton, Exeter, Lincoln, Mansfield, Port Vale and Colchester, once his playing career ended he was appointed youth-team coach at Layer Road. He joined Fulham in a similar capacity in June 1981, becoming their manager in April 1984, and then coached Luton before taking charge of the Hatters in June 1987. After plotting their 1988 League Cup Final success, he also led them to that season's Simod Cup Final and then the 1989 League Cup Final. He later managed Wimbledon, then assisted Kenny Dalglish before succeeding him as Blackburn Rovers' boss. After Blackburn he had a spell managing West Brom, and then he moved to QPR and from December 1997 until October 1998, after which he coached Millwall, managed the side. Ray's stay at QPR had started to go downhill at around Christmas time 1997, when the club went into the New Year in 12th place. By mid-January they had slipped to 17th, the lowest they had been since their relegation from the Premiership. Harford readjusted the club's expectations but could not finish any higher than 21st place, the club's lowest finish for 30 years. After he departed the club a management team of Iain Dowie and Gerry Francis was installed. Ray died in August 2003.

Ian Holloway

Ian Holloway led QPR to promotion in 2003–04. Signing professional for Bristol Rovers in March 1981, the midfielder joined Wimbledon in July 1985 and also played for Brentford and helped Bristol Rovers win the Third Division title in 1989–90. He reunited with Gerry Francis at QPR in August 1991, one of several former Bristol Rovers players

who moved to Loftus Road during that period, and netted four goals in 147 League games before returning to Rovers as player-manager in July 1996. Rejoining QPR as manager in February 2001, he led them to the Second Division Play-off Final in 2002–03 and remained in charge until June 2006. He plotted Plymouth Argyle's 2006–07 FA Cup run and then briefly managed Leicester City.

Gary Waddock

Republic of Ireland international midfielder Gary Waddock was both a player and manager at QPR. Initially rejoining Rangers as a coach once his playing career came to a close, he was then appointed manager from June 2006 until he was sacked in September 2006 after a poor run of results left the team bottom of the table. He did, however, remain at Rangers, serving as assistant manager to John Gregory. Now managing Aldershot, he plotted their 2007–08 Blue Square Premier title triumph.

John Gregory

Versatile England international midfielder John Gregory was also both a player and manager at QPR. His first position after his playing days was as Portsmouth's boss, after which he coached Leicester and Aston Villa before managing Wycombe Wanderers, Aston Villa, Derby County and QPR for a year until October 2007. During his time at Rangers it looked as if the club would be relegated, even after a decent start, but a fine run of form late in the season ensured survival. Nevertheless, it was not enough to save Gregory, who was dismisssed a short while into the following season.

Luigi De Canio

Luigi De Canio managed QPR during the 2007–08 season. A former full-back, he began his career with Matera, then played for Chieti, Matera again, Livorno, Galatina Pro Italia and Pisticci, where he became player-manager and plotted promotion at the first attempt in 1988–89. He managed Savoia to promotion

in 1993–94, then had a spell in charge of Siena before leading Carpi to the Play-offs in 1996–97. After managing Lucchese and Pescara, he took charge of Udinese and plotted their 2000 Intertoto Cup Final triumph. He also managed Napoli, Reggina, Genoa and Siena again in Italy before becoming QPR's boss in October 2007, taking over from the recently dismissed John Gregory. During his time at Rangers, De Canio became a popular figure with the fans, despite only managing a 14th-place finish in the League. He remained at Loftus Road until leaving by mutual consent in May 2008, and he is now in charge of Lecce.

Iain Dowie

Former Northern Ireland international striker Iain Dowie was both a player and manager at QPR. He played for St Albans City, Hendon, Luton Town, West Ham, Southampton, Crystal Palace and West Ham again before moving to Loftus Road as part of the Trevor Sinclair deal in January 1998. He scored twice in 30 League outings for

Rangers before joining the coaching staff. Appointed Oldham Athletic's assistant boss in November 2001, he became their manager in May 2002 and guided them to the Second Division Play-offs in 2002–03. He rejoined Crystal Palace as boss in December 2003 and plotted promotion that season, then managed Charlton Athletic, Coventry City and Rangers for five months until he was sacked in October 2008. He had been in charge for only 15 games, and the club were in ninth place in the League.

Paulo Sousa

Portugal-born Sousa was appointed Rangers manager in November 2008; it was his first role as a club manager. His playing career began with Benfica, where he won the League and was twice a national Cup winner. He then moved to Sporting Lisbon and on to Juventus a year later. While with Juve he won the Champions League in 1996 in addition to the Serie A title and Italian Cup. Next he moved to Borussia Dortmund in Germany, where he added a second Champions League title. On the international front he was a member of the FIFA World Youth Championship-winning squad in 1991 and went on to make 51 appearances for the Portuguese senior team.

Sousa had to retire from playing at the age of 32 and moved on to coaching. He started with the Under-15 Portuguese side before joining the coaching staff of the full national side under Carlos Queiroz. His tenure at Rangers lasted just short of six months before he left the club in April 2009. In his 26 games in charge he won seven and lost seven, with the other 11 drawn. In June 2009 Sousa was back in the Championship when he was appointed manager at Swansea City.

Jim Magilton

Magilton joined Rangers as manager in the summer of 2009. Jim was born in Northern Ireland and after failing to make the grade at Liverpool he moved to Oxford United in 1990. His next club was Southampton, where he was a key member of the Saints midfield, being an ever present in the 1994–95 season. He joined Sheffield Wednesday in the summer of 1997 for a fee of £1.6 million, but he soon moved to Ipswich Town, where he made over 300 appearances. Jim also made 52 appearances for his native Northern Ireland and scored five goals. At the end of his playing career he was appointed manager at Portman Road in June 2006, and he led the side to 14th and eighth place (just one point short of the Play-offs) in his first two seasons. In April 2009 he was relieved of his duties as manager following boardroom changes. In June Magilton was appointed manager at Rangers, replacing caretaker manager Gareth Ainsworth.

MANAGERS' RESULTS

Status		First Game	Last Game	SEASON	Total P	W	D	L	F	A	League P	W	D	L	F	A	Cup / Other P	W	D	L	F	A
(Secretary)	G.H. MOUSELL	2 Sep 1899	30 Apr 1902	1899–1900	38	19	4	15	79	66	28	12	2	14	50	58	10	7	2	1	29	8
				1900–01	32	13	5	14	55	53	28	11	4	13	43	48	4	2	1	1	12	5
				1901–02	33	1	6	16	40	57	30	9	6	15	34	55	3	2	0	1	6	2
				TOTAL	103	33	15	45	174	176	86	32	12	42	127	161	17	11	3	3	47	15
				(%)		32.0	14.6	43.7				37.2	14.0	48.8				64.7	17.6	17.6		
(Player / Secretary)	John BOWMAN	3 Sep 1902	29 Apr 1905	1902–03	31	12	6	13	34	45	30	11	6	13	34	42	1	0	0	1	0	3
				1903–04	36	15	12	9	55	41	34	15	11	8	53	37	2	0	1	1	2	4
				1904–05	35	14	8	13	52	48	34	14	8	12	51	46	1	0	0	1	1	2
				TOTAL	102	41	26	35	141	134	98	40	25	33	138	125	4	0	1	3	3	9
				(%)		40.2	25.5	34.3				40.8	25.5	33.7				0.0	25.0	75.0		
(Unknown)	Unknown	2 Sep 1905	27 Apr 1907	1905–06	35	12	7	16	58	45	34	12	7	15	58	44	1	0	0	1	0	1
				1906–07	40	11	11	18	47	56	38	11	10	17	47	55	2	0	1	1	0	1
				TOTAL	75	23	18	34	105	101	72	23	17	32	105	99	3	0	1	2	0	2
				(%)		30.7	24.0	45.3				31.9	23.6	44.4				0.0	33.3	66.7		
	James COWAN	2 Sep 1907	29 Apr 1914	1907–08	41	22	10	9	85	60	38	21	9	8	82	57	3	1	1	1	3	3
				1908–09	43	12	13	18	52	55	40	12	12	16	52	50	3	0	1	2	0	5
				1909–10	49	22	16	11	64	51	42	19	13	10	56	47	7	3	3	1	8	4
				1910–11	39	13	14	12	55	46	38	13	14	11	52	41	1	0	0	1	3	5
				1911–12	41	21	12	8	60	41	38	21	11	6	59	35	3	0	1	2	1	6
				1912–13	40	19	10	11	52	41	38	18	10	10	46	36	2	1	0	1	6	5
				1913–14	43	19	10	14	54	49	38	16	9	13	45	43	5	3	1	1	9	6
				TOTAL	296	128	85	83	422	343	272	120	78	74	392	309	24	8	7	9	30	34
				(%)		43.2	28.7	28.0				44.1	28.7	27.2				33.3	29.2	37.5		
	James HOWIE	1 Sep 1914	30 Apr 1920	1914–15	41	15	12	14	59	59	38	13	12	13	55	56	3	2	0	1	4	3
				1915–16	36	10	8	18	41	78	36	10	8	18	41	78						
				1916–17	39	10	9	20	48	86	39	10	9	20	48	86						
				1917–18	40	16	2	22	56	83	36	14	2	20	48	73	4	2	0	2	8	10
				1918–19	37	16	7	14	69	62	36	16	7	13	69	60	1	0	0	1	0	2
				1919–20	43	18	10	15	63	52	42	18	10	14	62	50	1	0	0	1	1	2
				TOTAL	236	85	48	103	336	420	227	81	48	98	323	403	9	4	0	5	13	17
				(%)		36.0	20.3	43.6				35.7	21.1	43.2				44.4	0.0	55.6		
	Ned LIDDELL	28 Aug 1920	2 May 1925	1920–21	44	23	9	12	65	36	42	22	9	11	61	32	2	1	0	1	4	4
				1921–22	44	18	14	12	54	46	42	18	13	11	53	44	2	0	1	1	1	2
				1922–23	46	19	10	17	62	52	42	16	10	16	54	49	4	3	0	1	8	3
				1923–24	43	11	9	23	38	79	42	11	9	22	37	77	1	0	0	1	1	2
				1924–25	47	16	10	21	52	72	42	14	8	20	42	63	5	2	2	1	10	9
				TOTAL	224	87	52	85	271	285	210	81	49	80	247	265	14	6	3	5	24	20
				(%)		38.8	23.2	37.9				38.6	23.3	38.1				42.9	21.4	35.7		
	Bob HEWISON	29 Aug 1925	2 May 1931	1925–26	46	7	11	28	42	88	42	6	9	27	37	84	4	1	2	1	5	4
				1926–27	42	15	9	18	65	71	42	15	9	18	65	71						
				1927–28	43	17	9	17	73	73	42	17	9	16	72	71	1	0	0	1	1	2
				1928–29	43	19	14	10	84	65	42	19	14	9	82	61	1	0	0	1	2	4
				1929–30	46	23	10	13	86	75	42	21	9	12	80	68	4	2	1	1	6	7
				1930–31	45	22	3	20	92	80	42	20	3	19	82	75	3	2	0	1	10	5
				TOTAL	265	103	56	106	442	452	252	98	53	101	418	430	13	5	3	5	24	22
				(%)		38.9	21.1	40.0				38.9	21.0	40.1				38.5	23.1	38.5		

					Total						League						Cup / Other					
Status		**First Game**	**Last Game**	**SEASON**	**P**	**W**	**D**	**L**	**F**	**A**	**P**	**W**	**D**	**L**	**F**	**A**	**P**	**W**	**D**	**L**	**F**	**A**
	John BOWMAN	29 Aug 1931	31 Oct 1931	1931–32	13	1	6	6	16	26	13	1	6	6	16	26						
				TOTAL	13	1	6	6	16	26	13	1	6	6	16	26						
				(%)		7.7	46.2	46.2				7.7	46.2	46.2								
	Archie MITCHELL	07-Nov-31	6 May 1933	1931–32	33	17	6	10	77	57	29	14	6	9	63	47	4	3	0	1	14	10
				1932–33	47	15	13	19	82	93	42	13	11	18	72	87	5	2	2	1	10	6
				TOTAL	80	32	19	29	159	150	71	27	17	27	135	134	9	5	2	2	24	16
				(%)		40.0	23.8	36.3				38.0	23.9	38.0				55.6	22.2	22.2		
	Mick O'BRIEN	26 Aug 1933	4 May 1935	1933–34	46	26	7	13	81	56	42	24	6	12	70	51	4	2	1	1	11	5
				1934–35	44	17	9	18	66	74	42	16	9	17	63	72	2	1	0	1	3	2
				TOTAL	90	43	16	31	147	130	84	40	15	29	133	123	6	3	1	2	14	7
				(%)		47.8	17.8	34.4				47.6	17.9	34.5				50.0	16.7	33.3		
	William BIRRELL	31 Aug 1935	6 May 1939	1935–36	43	22	9	12	85	56	42	22	9	11	84	53	1	0	0	1	1	3
				1936–37	45	20	9	16	79	54	42	18	9	15	73	52	3	2	0	1	6	2
				1937–38	44	23	9	12	89	50	42	22	9	11	80	47	2	1	0	1	9	3
				1938–39	46	17	15	14	75	52	42	15	14	13	68	49	4	2	1	1	7	3
				TOTAL	178	82	42	54	328	212	168	77	41	50	305	201	10	5	1	4	23	11
				(%)		46.1	23.6	30.3				45.8	24.4	29.8				50.0	10.0	40.0		
	Ted VIZZARD	26 Aug 1939	22 Apr 1944	1939–40	40	22	7	11	91	60	39	22	7	10	91	59	1	0	0	1	0	1
				1940–41	41	19	4	18	91	101	23	8	3	12	47	60	18	11	1	6	44	41
				1941–42	36	13	4	19	60	66	30	11	3	16	52	59	6	2	1	3	8	7
				1942–43	35	22	3	10	81	61	28	18	2	8	64	49	7	4	1	2	17	12
				1943–44	34	19	11	4	90	57	28	14	10	4	65	50	6	5	1	0	25	7
				TOTAL	186	95	29	62	413	345	148	73	25	50	319	277	38	22	4	12	94	68
				(%)		51.1	15.6	33.3				49.3	16.9	33.8				57.9	10.5	31.6		
	Dave MANGNALL	29 Apr 1944	3 May 1952	1943–44	2	0	2	0	4	4	2	0	2	0	4	4						
				1944–45	36	13	12	11	77	69	30	10	10	10	70	61	6	3	2	1	7	8
				1945–46	49	32	11	6	110	37	20	14	4	2	50	15	29	18	7	4	60	22
				1946–47	48	25	14	9	90	50	42	23	11	8	74	40	6	2	3	1	16	10
				1947–48	48	29	11	8	85	46	42	26	9	7	74	37	6	3	2	1	11	9
				1948–49	44	14	12	18	44	67	42	14	11	17	44	62	2	0	1	1	0	5
				1949–50	43	11	12	20	40	59	42	11	12	19	40	57	1	0	0	1	0	2
				1950–51	43	15	10	18	74	86	42	15	10	17	71	82	1	0	0	1	3	4
				1951–52	43	11	12	20	53	84	42	11	12	19	52	81	1	0	0	1	1	3
				TOTAL	356	150	96	110	577	502	304	124	81	99	479	439	52	26	15	11	98	63
				(%)		42.1	27.0	30.9				40.8	26.6	32.6				50.0	28.8	21.2		
	Jack TAYLOR	23 Apr 1952	27 Apr 1959	1952–53	49	12	17	20	66	90	46	12	15	19	61	82	3	0	2	1	5	8
				1953–54	50	18	11	21	65	71	46	16	10	20	60	68	4	2	1	1	5	3
				1954–55	49	15	16	18	73	83	46	15	14	17	69	75	3	0	2	1	4	8
				1955–56	47	14	11	22	64	88	46	14	11	21	64	86	1	0	0	1	0	2
				1956–57	49	20	11	18	67	64	46	18	11	17	61	60	3	2	0	1	6	4
				1957–58	49	19	15	15	69	73	46	18	14	14	64	65	3	1	1	1	5	8
				1958–59	48	20	8	20	75	78	46	19	8	19	74	77	2	1	0	1	1	1
				TOTAL	341	118	89	134	479	547	322	112	83	127	453	513	19	6	6	7	26	34
				(%)		34.6	26.1	39.3				34.8	25.8	39.4				31.6	31.6	36.8		
	Alec STOCK	22 Aug 1959	10 May 1968	1959–60	49	19	14	16	80	61	46	18	13	15	73	54	3	1	1	1	7	7
				1960–61	50	27	11	12	100	69	46	25	10	11	93	60	4	2	1	1	7	9
				1961–62	52	27	12	13	129	84	46	24	11	11	111	73	6	3	1	2	18	11
				1962–63	50	19	11	20	96	84	46	17	11	18	85	76	4	2	0	2	11	8
				1963–64	50	20	9	21	82	84	46	18	9	19	76	78	4	2	0	2	6	6
				1964–65	51	19	13	19	83	91	46	17	12	17	72	80	5	2	1	2	11	11
				1965–66	53	26	12	15	108	73	46	24	9	13	95	65	7	2	3	2	13	8

Status		First Game	Last Game	SEASON	Total						League						Cup / Other					
					P	W	D	L	F	A	P	W	D	L	F	A	P	W	D	L	F	A
				1966–67	58	36	16	6	134	52	46	26	15	5	103	38	12	10	1	1	31	14
				1967–68	46	27	8	11	76	43	42	25	8	9	67	36	4	2	0	2	9	7
				TOTAL	459	220	106	133	888	641	410	194	98	118	775	560	49	26	8	15	113	81
				(%)		47.9	23.1	29.0				47.3	23.9	28.8				53.1	16.3	30.6		
(Caretaker)	Bill DODGIN	10 Aug 1968	2 Nov 1968	1968–69	18	2	5	11	24	44	17	2	5	10	22	40	1	0	0	1	2	4
				TOTAL	18	2	5	11	24	44	17	2	5	10	22	40	1	0	0	1	2	4
				(%)		11.1	27.8	61.1				11.8	29.4	58.8				0.0	0.0	100.0		
	Tommy DOCHERTY	9 Nov 1968	23 Nov 1968	1968–69	3	1	0	2	2	7	3	1	0	2	2	7						
				TOTAL	3	1	0	2	2	7	3	1	0	2	2	7						
				(%)		33.3	0.0	66.7				33.3	0.0	66.7								
	Les ALLEN	7 Dec 1968	2 Jan 1971	1968–69	23	1	5	17	16	50	22	1	5	16	15	48	1	0	0	1	1	2
				1969–70	51	23	12	16	91	70	42	17	11	14	66	57	9	6	1	2	25	13
				1970–71	25	7	6	12	36	40	22	6	6	10	31	36	3	1	0	2	5	4
				TOTAL	99	31	23	45	143	160	86	24	22	40	112	141	13	7	1	5	31	19
				(%)		31.3	23.2	45.5				27.9	25.6	46.5				53.8	7.7	38.5		
	Gordon JAGO	9 Jan 1971	8 Oct 1974	1970–71	20	10	5	5	27	17	20	10	5	5	27	17						
				1971–72	48	22	16	10	66	35	42	20	14	8	57	28	6	2	2	2	9	7
				1972–73	47	26	14	7	89	43	42	24	13	5	81	37	5	2	1	2	8	6
				1973–74	51	18	19	14	71	61	42	13	17	12	56	52	9	5	2	2	15	9
				1974–75	14	3	5	6	13	18	11	2	4	5	9	13	3	1	1	1	4	5
				TOTAL	180	79	59	42	266	174	157	69	53	35	230	147	23	10	6	7	36	27
				(%)		43.9	32.8	23.3				43.9	33.8	22.3				43.5	26.1	30.4		
	Dave SEXTON	12 Oct 1974	23 May 1977	1974–75	35	16	7	12	53	45	31	14	6	11	45	41	4	2	1	1	8	4
				1975–76	48	26	13	9	77	40	42	24	11	7	67	33	6	2	2	2	10	7
				1976–77	59	23	15	21	86	64	42	13	12	17	47	42	17	10	3	4	39	22
				TOTAL	142	65	35	42	216	149	115	51	29	35	159	116	27	14	6	7	57	33
				(%)		45.8	24.6	29.6				44.3	25.2	30.4				51.9	22.2	25.9		
	Frank SIBLEY	20 Aug 1977	2 May 1978	1977–78	50	12	18	20	63	72	42	9	15	18	47	64	8	3	3	2	16	8
				TOTAL	50	12	18	20	63	72	42	9	15	18	47	64	8	3	3	2	16	8
				(%)		24.0	36.0	40.0				21.4	35.7	42.9				37.5	37.5	25.0		
(Temporary)	Alec STOCK				0	0	0	0	0	0												
	Steve BURTENSHAW	19 Aug 1978	28 Apr 1979	1978–79	43	8	13	22	46	67	39	6	13	20	41	62	4	2	0	2	5	5
				TOTAL	43	8	13	22	46	67	39	6	13	20	41	62	4	2	0	2	5	5
				(%)		18.6	30.2	51.2				15.4	33.3	51.3				50.0	0.0	50.0		
(Gap)		4 May 1979	7 May 1979	1978–79	2	0	0	2	4	7	2	0	0	2	4	7						
				TOTAL	2	0	0	2	4	7	2	0	0	2	4	7						
				(%)		0.0	0.0	100.0				0.0	0.0	100.0								
	Tommy DOCHERTY	11 May 1979	1 Nov 1980	1978–79	1	0	0	1	0	4	1	0	0	1	0	4						
				1979–80	48	21	14	13	84	58	42	18	13	11	75	53	6	3	1	2	9	5
				1980–81	18	3	7	8	19	19	15	3	5	7	18	15	3	0	2	1	1	4
				TOTAL	67	24	21	22	103	81	58	21	18	19	93	72	9	3	3	3	10	9
				(%)		35.8	31.3	32.8				36.2	31.0	32.8				33.3	33.3	33.3		
	Terry VENABLES	8 Nov 1980	15 May 1984	1980–81	29	12	9	8	39	34	27	12	8	7	38	31	2	0	1	1	1	3
				1981–82	55	28	10	17	91	56	42	21	6	15	65	43	13	7	4	2	26	13
				1982–83	45	26	8	11	80	41	42	26	7	9	77	36	3	0	1	2	3	5
				1983–84	46	23	7	16	78	46	42	22	7	13	67	37	4	1	0	3	11	9
				TOTAL	175	89	34	52	288	177	153	81	28	44	247	147	22	8	6	8	41	30
				(%)		50.9	19.4	29.7				52.9	18.3	28.8				36.4	27.3	36.4		

					Total						League						Cup / Other					
Status		First Game	Last Game	SEASON	P	W	D	L	F	A	P	W	D	L	F	A	P	W	D	L	F	A
	Alan MULLERY	25 Aug 1984	4 Dec 1984	1984–85	26	11	8	7	46	39	17	5	6	6	23	29	9	6	2	1	23	10
				TOTAL	26	11	8	7	46	39	17	5	6	6	23	29	9	6	2	1	23	10
				(%)		42.3	30.8	26.9				29.4	35.3	35.3				66.7	22.2	11.1		
(Caretaker)	Frank SIBLEY	8 Dec 1984	11 May 1985	1984–85	29	9	6	14	35	46	25	8	5	12	30	43	4	1	1	2	5	3
				TOTAL	29	9	6	14	25	46	25	8	5	12	30	43	4	1	1	2	5	3
				(%)		31.0	20.7	48.3				32.0	20.0	48.0				25.0	25.0	50.0		
	Jim SMITH	17 Aug 1985	3 Dec 88	1985–86	52	21	9	22	71	73	42	15	7	20	53	64	10	6	2	2	18	9
				1986–87	49	16	13	20	61	74	42	13	11	18	48	64	7	3	2	2	13	10
				1987–88	48	22	12	14	58	46	40	19	10	11	48	38	8	3	2	3	10	8
				1988–89	20	8	4	8	25	19	15	5	3	7	16	15	5	3	1	1	9	4
				TOTAL	169	67	38	64	215	212	139	52	31	56	165	181	30	15	7	8	50	31
				(%)		39.6	22.5	37.9				37.4	22.3	40.3				50.0	23.3	26.7		
(Caretaker)	Peter SHREEVES	10 Dec 1988	14 Dec 1988	1988–89	2	1	1	0	2	1	1	0	1	0	1	1	1	1	0	0	1	0
				TOTAL	2	1	1	0	2	1	1	0	1	0	1	1	1	1	0	0	1	0
				(%)		50.0	50.0	0.0				0.0	100.0	0.0				100.0	0.0	0.0		
(Player / Manager)	Trevor FRANCIS	17 Dec 1988	25 Nov 1989	1988–89	29	10	10	9	32	33	22	9	7	6	26	21	7	1	3	3	6	12
				1989–90	18	4	7	7	17	22	15	3	6	6	14	19	3	1	1	1	3	3
				TOTAL	47	14	17	16	49	55	37	12	13	12	40	40	10	2	4	4	9	15
				(%)		29.8	36.2	34.0				32.4	35.1	32.4				20.0	40.0	40.0		
	Don HOWE	2 Dec 1989	11 May 1991	1989–90	32	13	10	9	42	30	23	10	5	8	31	25	9	3	5	1	11	5
				1990–91	44	14	11	19	51	65	38	12	10	16	44	53	6	2	1	3	7	12
				TOTAL	76	27	21	28	93	95	61	22	15	24	75	78	15	5	6	4	18	17
				(%)		35.5	27.6	36.8				36.1	24.6	39.3				33.3	40.0	26.7		
	Gerry FRANCIS	18 Aug 1991	5 Nov 1994	1991–92	49	15	19	15	61	57	42	12	18	12	48	47	7	3	1	3	13	10
				1992–93	48	20	12	16	72	64	42	17	12	13	63	55	6	3	0	3	9	9
				1993–94	47	19	12	16	73	66	42	16	12	14	62	61	5	3	0	2	11	5
				1994–95	17	5	4	8	26	29	14	3	4	7	20	25	3	2	0	1	6	4
				TOTAL	161	59	47	55	232	216	140	48	46	46	193	188	21	11	1	9	39	28
				(%)		36.6	29.2	34.2				34.3	32.9	32.9				52.4	4.8	42.9		
(Player / Manager)	Ray WILKINS	9 Nov 1994	1 Sep 1996	1994–95	32	17	5	10	47	36	28	14	5	9	41	34	4	3	0	1	6	2
				1995–96	44	12	7	25	47	63	38	9	6	23	38	57	6	3	1	2	9	6
				1996–97	4	2	1	1	6	5	4	2	1	1	6	5						
				TOTAL	80	31	13	36	100	104	70	25	12	33	85	96	10	6	1	3	15	8
				(%)		38.8	16.3	45.0				35.7	17.1	47.1				60.0	10.0	30.0		
(Caretaker)	Frank SIBLEY	7 Sep 1996	14 Sep 1996	1996–97	3	1	1	1	4	4	3	1	1	1	4	4						
				TOTAL	3	1	1	1	4	4	3	1	1	1	4	4						
				(%)		33.3	33.3	33.3				33.3	33.3	33.3								
	Stewart HOUSTON	18 Sep 1996	8 Nov 1997	1996–97	45	18	11	16	64	61	39	15	10	14	54	51	6	3	1	2	10	10
				1997–98	18	7	4	7	22	29	16	6	4	6	20	26	2	1	0	1	2	3
				TOTAL	63	25	15	23	86	90	55	21	14	20	74	77	8	4	1	3	12	13
				(%)		39.7	23.8	36.5				38.2	25.5	36.4				50.0	12.5	37.5		
(Caretaker)	John HOLLINS	15 Nov 1997	6 Dec 1997	1997–98	5	1	2	2	6	7	5	1	2	2	6	7						
				TOTAL	5	1	2	2	6	7	5	1	2	2	6	7						
				(%)		20.0	40.0	40.0				20.0	40.0	40.0								

Status		First Game	Last Game	SEASON	Total						League						Cup / Other					
					P	W	D	L	F	A	P	W	D	L	F	A	P	W	D	L	F	A
	Ray HARFORD	12 Dec 1997	26 Sep 1998	1997–98	27	3	14	10	27	34	25	3	13	9	25	30	2	0	1	1	2	4
				1998–99	13	2	4	7	10	19	9	1	3	5	7	15	4	1	1	2	3	4
				TOTAL	40	5	18	17	37	53	34	4	16	14	32	45	6	1	2	3	5	8
				(%)		12.5	45.0	42.5				11.8	47.1	41.2				16.7	33.3	50.0		
(Caretaker)	Iain DOWIE	29 Sep 1998	21 Oct 1998	1998–99	4	1	0	3	3	7	4	1	0	3	3	7						
				TOTAL	4	1	0	3	3	7	4	1	0	3	3	7						
				(%)		25.0	0.0	75.0				25.0	0.0	75.0								
	Gerry FRANCIS	25 Oct 1998	24 Feb 2001	1998–99	34	10	8	16	42	40	33	10	8	15	42	39	1	0	0	1	0	1
				1999–2000	51	18	19	14	69	60	46	16	18	12	62	53	5	2	1	2	7	7
				2000–01	38	8	15	15	40	67	33	6	14	13	33	53	5	2	1	2	7	14
				TOTAL	123	36	42	45	151	167	112	32	40	40	137	145	11	4	2	5	14	22
				(%)		29.3	34.1	36.6				28.6	35.7	35.7				36.4	18.2	45.5		
	Ian HOLLOWAY	3 Mar 2001	5 Feb 2006	2000–01	13	1	5	7	12	22	13	1	5	7	12	22						
				2001–02	49	19	14	16	61	58	46	19	14	13	60	49	3	0	0	3	1	9
				2002–03	53	25	13	15	74	51	46	24	11	11	69	45	7	1	2	4	5	6
				2003–04	54	27	17	10	90	56	46	22	17	7	80	45	8	5	0	3	10	11
				2004–05	49	18	11	20	58	64	46	17	11	18	54	58	3	1	0	2	4	6
				2005–06	34	10	9	15	36	52	32	10	9	13	36	46	2	0	0	2	0	6
				TOTAL	252	100	69	83	331	303	229	93	67	69	311	265	23	7	2	14	20	38
				(%)		39.7	27.4	32.9				40.6	29.3	30.1				30.4	8.7	60.9		
(Caretaker)	Gary WADDOCK	6 Feb 2006	27 Jun 2006	2005–06	14	2	5	7	14	19	14	2	5	7	14	19	0	0	0	0	0	0
		28 Jun 2006	20 Sep 2006	2006–07	10	2	3	5	13	18	8	1	3	4	8	13	2	1	0	1	5	5
				TOTAL	24	4	8	12	27	37	22	3	8	11	22	32	2	1	0	1	5	5
				(%)		16.7	33.3	50.0				13.6	36.4	50.0				50.0	0.0	50.0		
	John GREGORY	20 Sep 2006	01 Oct 2007	2006–07	40	13	9	18	48	58	38	13	8	17	46	55	2	0	1	1	2	3
				2007–08	8	0	3	5	6	18	7	0	3	4	5	16	1	0	0	1	1	2
				TOTAL	48	13	12	23	54	76	45	13	11	21	51	71	3	0	1	2	3	5
				(%)		27.1	25.0	47.9				28.9	24.4	46.7				0.0	33.3	66.7		
(Caretaker)	Mick HARFORD	1 Oct 2007	29 Oct 2007	2007–08	5	2	2	1	5	5	5	2	2	1	5	5						
				TOTAL	5	2	2	1	5	5	5	2	2	1	5	5						
				(%)		40.0	40.0	20.0				40.0	40.0	20.0								
	Luigi DE CANIO	29 Oct 2007	04 May 2008	2007–08	35	12	11	12	50	46	34	12	11	11	50	45	1	0	0	1	0	1
				2008–09																		
				TOTAL	35	12	11	12	50	46	34	12	11	11	50	45	1	0	0	1	0	1
				(%)		34.3	31.4	34.3				35.3	32.4	32.4				0.0	0.0	100.0		
	Iain DOWIE	9 Aug 2008	24 Oct 2008	2008–09	15	8	3	4	21	14	12	5	3	4	13	12	3	3	0	0	8	2
				TOTAL	15	8	3	4	21	14	12	5	3	4	13	12	3	3	0	0	8	2
				(%)		53.3	20.0	26.7				41.7	25.0	33.3				100.0	0.0	0.0		
(Caretaker)	Gareth AINSWORTH	24 Oct 2008	19 Nov 2008	2008–09	6	2	1	3	3	5	5	2	1	2	3	4	1	0	0	1	0	1
				TOTAL	6	2	1	3	3	5	5	2	1	2	3	4		0.0	0.0	100.0		
				(%)		33.3	16.7	50.0				40.0	20.0	40.0								
	Paulo SOUSA	19 Nov 2008	9 Apr 2009	2008–09	26	7	12	7	23	24	24	7	11	6	22	22	2	0	1	1	1	2
				TOTAL	26	7	12	7	23	24	24	7	11	6	22	22		0.0	50.0	50.0		
				(%)		26.9	46.2	26.9				29.2	45.8	25.0								
(Caretaker)	Gareth AINSWORTH	9 Apr 2009	3 May 2009	2008–09	5	1	1	3	4	6	5	1	1	3	4	6						
				TOTAL	5	1	1	3	4	6	5	1	1	3	4	6						
				(%)		20.0	20.0	60.0				20.0	20.0	60.0								
	Jim MAGILTON	8 Aug 2009	(Present)	2009–10																		

1899-1900

Southern League (Div 1)

	P	W	D	L	F	A	Pts
Tottenham Hotspur	28	20	4	4	67	26	44
Portsmouth	28	20	1	7	58	27	41
Southampton	28	17	1	10	70	33	35
Reading	28	15	2	11	41	28	32
Swindon Town	28	15	2	11	50	42	32
Bedminster	28	13	2	13	44	45	28
Millwall Athletic	28	12	3	13	36	37	27
Queen's Park Rangers	28	12	2	14	49	57	26
Bristol City	28	9	7	12	43	47	25
Bristol Rovers	28	11	3	14	46	55	25
New Brompton	28	9	6	13	39	49	24
Gravesend United	28	10	4	14	38	58	24
Chatham	28	10	3	15	38	58	23
Thames Ironworks	28	8	5	15	30	45	21
Sheppey United	28	3	7	18	24	66	13
Brighton United*							
Cowes*							

* Teams resigned from the League.

Match No.	Date		Opponents	Location	Result		Scorers	Atter
	Sep	2	Brighton United	H		6-0	(Resigned from League - Results expunged)	
1		9	Tottenham Hotspur	A	L	0-1		
2		16	New Brompton	H	W	2-0	Turnbull, Bedingfield	
3	Oct	7	Bristol City	A	L	3-5	Tennant, Bedingfield, Evans	
4		11	Gravesend United	A	W	3-1	Bedingfield (2), Haywood	
5		21	Southampton	A	L	1-5	Crawford	
6	Nov	11	Chatham	A	L	3-5	Hitch, Cowie, Turnbull	
7		25	Sheppey United	A	L	1-3	Keech	
8	Dec	2	Reading	H	L	1-2	Cowie	
9		16	Bristol Rovers	H	W	3-0	Haywood (2), White	
10		23	Portsmouth	A	L	1-5	Bedingfield	
11		25	Thames Ironworks	H	W	2-0	Bedingfield (2)	
12		30	Thames Ironworks	A	W	2-1	White, Turnbull	
13	Jan	3	Tottenham Hotspur	H	D	0-0		
		9	Brighton United	A		1-2	(Resigned from League - Results expunged)	
14		12	New Brompton	A	W	3-0	White (3), Evans	
15		19	Gravesend United	H	W	3-1	White, Bedingfield, Smith	
16	Feb	23	Chatham	H	W	5-3	Tennant (2), Bedingfield (2), White	
17	Mar	3	Millwall Athletic	A	W	3-1	Tennant (2), Hannah	
18		5	Bristol City	H	D	1-1	White	
19		10	Sheppey United	H	L	2-3	Bedingfield (2, 1 pen)	
20		24	Reading	A	L	0-2		
21	Apr	7	Portsmouth	H	L	2-4	Bedingfield (pen), Turnbull	
22		14	Bedminster	H	W	2-1	Bedingfield, Turnbull	
23		16	Swindon Town	H	L	3-5	Bedingfield (2), Turnbull	
24		18	Swindon Town	A	L	0-4		
25		21	Bristol Rovers	A	L	0-1		
26		23	Millwall Athletic	H	W	2-0	Evans, Hannah	
27		25	Bedminster	A	L	1-4	Bedingfield	
28		28	Southampton	H	W	1-0	Keech	

Appeara

G

FA Cup

Round	Date		Opponents	Location	Result		Scorers
Pre	Sep	23	London Welsh	H	W	4-2	Bedingfield, Smith, Turnbull (2)
Q1		30	Fulham	H	W	3-0	Haywood, Bedingfield, Turnbull
Q2	Oct	14	West Hampstead	H	W	5-0	Turnbull (3, 1 pen), Smith, Haywood
Q3		28	Wandsworth	A	W	7-1	Keech (3), Evans (2), Hitch, Haywood
Q4	Nov	18	Civil Service	H	W	3-0	Haywood, Hitch, Turnbull
Q5	Dec	9	Luton Town	A	D	1-1	Evans
rep		13	Luton Town	H	W	4-1	Haywood, Bedingfield, White, Smith
R1	Jan	26	Wolverhampton	H	D	1-1	Haywood
rep		30	Wolverhampton	A	W	1-0 aet	Bedingfield
R2	Feb	16	Millwall Athletic	H	L	0-2	

Appeara

G

Total - Appeara

Total - G

Southern District Combination

No.	Date		Opponents	Location	Result		Scorers
1	Sep	13	Southampton	A	L	1-2	Bedingfield
2		25	Millwall Athletic	A	L	0-3	
3	Oct	4	Reading	A	L	0-2	
4		23	Tottenham Hotspur	H	L	1-3	
5	Nov	13	Southampton	H	W	2-0	
6		20	Tottenham Hotspur	A	L	1-3	Haywood
7	Jan	14	Millwall Athletic	H	L	2-3	
8	Feb	4	Chatham	H			
9		20	Portsmouth	H			
10	Mar	7	Chatham	A			
11		12	Portsmouth	A			
12		19	Woolwich Arsenal	A	L	1-5	
13		26	Bristol City	H	D	0-0	
14	Apr	2	Reading	H			
15		4	Bristol City	A	L	1-2	
16		9	Woolwich Arsenal	H	W	3-0	

Clutterbuck	Cowie	Crawford	Evans	Gaylard	Hannah	Haywood	Hitch	Jordan	Keech	Knowles	McConnell	Musslewhite	Skinner	Smith	Tennant	Turnbull	White
1	11	4				8			6	2	3			7	5	10	
1	11	4				8			6		2		3	7	5	10	
1		4	11			8	5	7	6	2	3				9		
1		4				8	5		6	2	3			7	9	11	
1	11	4				8	5		6	2	3			7		10	
1	11	4	10			8	5		6	2	3					7	9
1	11		9		8		5		6	2	3			4		7	10
1	11	4	9			8	5			2	3			6		7	10
1	11	4		2		8	5				3		6	7			10
1		4				8	5			2	3		6	7		10	11
1	11	4				8	5			2	3		6			7	10
1					11	10	5		6	2	3				4	7	8
1	7	4			11	8	5		6	2	3						10
1		4	7		11	8	5		6	2	3						10
1					11	8	5		6	2	3			7	4		10
1		4	11	2			5		6		3			7	9		8
1		4		2	11		5		6		3			7	9		8
1	10	4			11		5		6	2	3			7			8
1		4			11	8	5		6		2		3	7			10
1	11	4		2	7	8	5		6		3					10	9
1					7	11	5		4	2	3		6			8	10
1		7			11				4	2	3	5	6			10	8
1		7			11		5		4	2	3		6			10	8
1		7	8		11		5		4	2	3		6			10	
1		7	8		11				4	2	3		6		5	10	
1		7	8		11				4	2	3		6		5	10	
1		7			11				4	2	3		6		5	10	8
1		7			11				4	2	3		6		5	10	8
28	11	24	9	4	17	17	21	1	24	22	28	1	13	13	12	19	20
	2	1	3		2	3	1		2					1	5	6	7

Clutterbuck	Cowie	Crawford	Evans	Gaylard	Hannah	Haywood	Hitch	Jordan	Keech	Knowles	McConnell	Musslewhite	Skinner	Smith	Tennant	Turnbull	White
1	11	4				8			6	2	3			7	5	10	
1	11	4		2		8			6		3			7	5	10	
1	11	4				8	5		6	2	3			7		10	
1	10	4	11			8	5		9	2	3			7	6		
1	11		9			8	5	7	6	2	3			4		10	
1		4	11	2		8	5				3		6	7			10
1		4	11	2		8	5				3		6	7			10
1		4			11	8	5		6	2	3					7	10
1		4			11	8	5		6	2	3					7	10
1		4			11	8	5		6	2	3			7			10
10	5	9	4	3	3	10	8	1	8	7	10		2	8	3	6	5
			3			6	2		3					3		7	1

Clutterbuck	Cowie	Crawford	Evans	Gaylard	Hannah	Haywood	Hitch	Jordan	Keech	Knowles	McConnell	Musslewhite	Skinner	Smith	Tennant	Turnbull	White
38	16	33	13	7	20	27	29	2	32	29	38	1	15	21	15	25	25
	2	1	6		2	9	3		5					4	5	13	8

1900-01

Southern League (Div 1)

	P	W	D	L	F	A	Pts
Southampton	28	18	5	5	58	26	41
Bristol City	28	17	5	6	54	27	39
Portsmouth	28	17	4	7	56	32	38
Millwall Athletic	28	17	2	9	55	32	36
Tottenham Hotspur	28	16	4	8	55	33	36
West Ham United	28	14	5	9	40	28	33
Bristol Rovers	28	14	4	10	46	35	32
Queen's Park Rangers	28	11	4	13	43	48	26
Reading	28	8	8	12	24	25	24
Luton Town	28	11	2	15	43	49	24
Kettering Town	28	7	9	12	33	46	23
New Brompton	28	7	5	16	34	51	19
Gravesend United	28	6	7	15	32	85	19
Watford	28	6	4	18	24	52	16
Swindon Town	28	3	8	17	19	47	14
W Chatham							

Western League

	P	W	D	L	F	A	Pts
Portsmouth	16	11	2	3	26	22	24
Millwall Athletic	16	9	5	2	33	14	23
Tottenham Hotspur	16	8	5	3	37	19	21
Queen's Park Rangers	16	7	4	5	39	25	18
Bristol City	16	6	4	6	25	26	16
Reading	16	5	5	6	24	29	15
Southampton	16	5	2	9	20	29	12
Bristol Rovers	16	4	1	11	18	32	9
Swindon Town	16	2	2	12	9	35	6

Match No.	Date		Opponents	Location	Result		Scorers	Atten
1	Sep	1	Bristol Rovers	A	L	1-2	Downing	3
2		8	Swindon Town	H	W	7-1	Downing (3), Gray (2), Humphries, Hitch	4
3		15	Reading	A	L	0-3		4
4		22	Watford	H	W	1-0	Goldie	5
5		29	Kettering Town	A	L	1-2	Downing	3
6	Oct	6	Luton Town	H	L	1-3	Humphries	4
7		13	Gravesend United	A	D	2-2	Gray, Downing	3
8		20	Tottenham Hotspur	H	W	2-1	Gray, Humphries	5
9		27	Millwall Athletic	H	L	0-2		5
10	Nov	10	Southampton	H	L	0-1		9
		24	Chatham	H		3-0	(Resigned from League - Results expunged)	
11	Dec	1	New Brompton	A	L	1-2	Ronaldson	2
12		15	Bristol Rovers	H	W	4-3	Hitch (pen), Ronaldson, Humphries, Downing	8
13		22	Swindon Town	A	L	2-4	Humphries, Keech	4
14		29	Reading	H	D	0-0		5
15	Jan	5	Watford	A	W	1-0	Skinner	2
16		12	Luton Town	A	D	2-2	Gray, Humphries	3
17		19	Kettering Town	H	W	2-0	Foxall, Humphries	4
18		26	New Brompton	H	W	2-0	Christie, Humphries	3
19	Feb	9	Bristol City	A	L	0-2		5
20		16	Millwall Athletic	A	W	1-0	Gray	7
21		23	West Ham United	H	L	0-2		6
22	Mar	2	Southampton	A	L	1-5	Gray	4
23		9	Portsmouth	H	W	3-2	Ronaldson (2), Gray	5
24		16	Gravesend United	H	W	4-2	Foxall, Humphries, Hitch, Ronaldson	5
25		23	Bristol City	H	W	2-0	Ronaldson (2)	5
26		30	Tottenham Hotspur	A	L	1-4	Downing	4
27	Apr	5	West Ham United	A	L	1-2	Downing	9
28		27	Portsmouth	A	D	1-1	Ronaldson	3

Appeara
G

FA Cup

Q3	Nov	3	Fulham	H	W	7-0	Goldie (2), Foxall (2), Downing, Gray, Hitch	4
Q4		17	Watford	A	D	1-1	Gray	4
rep		21	Watford	H	W	4-1	Humphries (3), Newbigging	2
Q5	Dec	8	Luton Town	A	L	0-3		5

Appeara
G

Total - Appeara
Total - G

Western League

1	Dec	25	Millwall Athletic	H	W	1-0		6
2	Feb	18	Bristol City	H	L	1-2		1
3	Mar	18	Tottenham Hotspur	H	D	1-1		1
4		27	Southampton	A	L	0-1		
5	Apr	8	Millwall Athletic	A	D	1-1		5
6		9	Bristol City	A	D	2-2		
7		15	Tottenham Hotspur	A	D	2-2		
8		20	Southampton	H	W	6-1		
9			Bristol Rovers	H				
10			Bristol Rovers	A				
11			Portsmouth	H				
12			Portsmouth	A				
13			Reading	H				
14			Reading	A				
15			Swindon Town	H				
16			Swindon Town	A				

Christie	Clutterbuck	Cole	Downing	Foxall	Goldie	Gray	Hitch	Humphries	Keech	Lennox	McConnell	Newbigging	Newlands	Pointing	Ronaldson	Skinner	Turnbull
9	1	2	8	11		7	5		4		3					6	10
	1		8	11	9	7	5	10	4		3					6	
	1		8	11	9	7	5	10	4		3					6	
	1		8	11	9	7	5	10	4					3		6	
9	1		8		11	7	5	10	4				3			6	
	1		8	11		7	5	10	4		3					6	9
	1		8	11		7	5	10	4		3					6	9
	1		8	11		7	5	10	4			9	3			6	
	1		8	11		7	5	10	4			9	3			6	
	1			11	9	7	5	10	4			8	3			6	
	1			11		7	5	10			3	8	4		9	6	
	1		8	11		7	5	10	4		3		2		9	6	
	1		8	11		7	5	10	4		3		2		9	6	
8	1			11		7	5	10		4	3		2		9	6	
	1			11		7	5	10		4	3	8	2		9	6	
	1			11		7	5	10	8	4	3		2		9	6	
8	1			11		7	5	10		4	3		2		9	6	
8	1			11		7	5	10		4	3		2		9	6	
8	1			11		7	5	10		4	3		2		9	6	
8	1			11		7	5	10		4	3		2		9	6	
8	1			11		7	5	10	6	4	3		2		9		
	1		8	11		7	5	10		4	3		2		9	6	
	1		8	11		7	5	10			3		2		9	6	
	1		8	11		7	5	10			3		2		9	6	
	1		8	11		7	5	10			3		2		9	6	
	1		8	11		7	5	10			3		2		9	6	
	1		8	11		7	5	10		4	3		2		9	6	
	1		8	11		7	5	10			3		2		9	6	
8	28	1	18	27	5	28	28	27	14	10	23	5	22	1	18	27	3
1			9	2	1	8	3	9	1						8	1	
	1		8	11	9	7	5	10	4				3			6	
	1			11	9	7	5	10	4		3	8	2			6	
	1			11	9	7	5	10			3	8	4			6	
	1		8	11	9	7	5	10	4		3		2			6	
	4		2	4	4	4	4	4	3		3	2	4			4	
			1	2	2	2	1	3				1					
8	32	1	20	31	9	32	32	31	17	10	26	7	26	1	18	31	3
1	0	0	10	4	3	10	4	12	1	0	0	1	0	0	8	1	0

1901-02

Southern League (Div 1)

	P	W	D	L	F	A	Pts
Portsmouth	30	20	7	3	67	24	47
Tottenham Hotspur	30	18	6	6	61	22	42
Southampton	30	18	6	6	71	28	42
West Ham United	30	17	6	7	45	28	40
Reading	30	16	7	7	57	24	39
Millwall Athletic	30	13	6	11	48	31	32
Luton Town	30	11	10	9	31	35	32
Kettering Town	30	12	5	13	44	39	29
Bristol Rovers	30	12	5	13	43	39	29
New Brompton	30	10	7	13	39	38	27
Northampton Town	30	11	5	14	53	64	27
Queen's Park Rangers	30	8	7	15	34	56	23
Watford	30	9	4	17	36	60	22
Wellingborough	30	9	4	17	34	72	22
Brentford	30	7	6	17	34	61	20
Swindon Town	30	2	3	25	17	93	7

Western League

	P	W	D	L	F	A	Pts
Portsmouth	16	13	1	2	53	16	27
Tottenham Hotspur	16	11	3	2	42	17	25
Reading	16	7	3	6	29	22	17
Millwall Athletic	16	8	1	7	25	29	17
Bristol Rovers	16	8	0	8	25	31	16
Southampton	16	7	1	8	30	28	15
West Ham United	16	6	2	8	30	20	14
Queen's Park Rangers	16	5	1	10	17	43	11
Swindon Town	16	0	2	14	8	53	2

Match No.	Date		Opponents	Location	Result		Scorers	Atte
1	Sep	7	Watford	H	L	0-1		
2		14	Tottenham Hotspur	A	L	0-2		1
3		28	Portsmouth	A	L	0-1		
4	Oct	5	Swindon Town	H	W	4-0	Pryce, Millar, Stewart, McQueen	
5		12	Brentford	A	D	1-1	Millar	
6		19	Kettering Town	H	W	2-1	McQueen, Seeley	
7		26	Luton Town	A	L	0-1		
8	Nov	9	West Ham United	H	W	2-1	McQueen, Pryce	
9		16	Reading	A	L	1-7	Millar	
10		23	Southampton	H	L	0-1		
11	Dec	7	New Brompton	H	D	1-1	McQueen	
12		21	Watford	A	D	1-1	Millar	
13		28	Tottenham Hotspur	H	L	0-3		1
14	Jan	4	Wellingborough	A	L	0-1		
15		11	Portsmouth	H	D	1-1	Stewart	
16		18	Swindon Town	A	W	3-0	Aston (pen), King, Wheldon	
17		25	Brentford	H	W	3-2	Newlands, Wheldon, Stewart	
18	Feb	1	Kettering Town	A	L	0-3		
19		8	Luton Town	H	D	2-2	King, Wheldon	
20		15	Millwall Athletic	H	L	0-2		
21		22	West Ham United	A	L	0-4		
22	Mar	1	Reading	H	W	1-0	McQueen	
23		8	Southampton	A	L	2-4	Wheldon, McQueen (pen)	
24		15	Bristol Rovers	H	D	0-0		
25		22	Northampton Town	A	L	1-4	Millar	
26		27	New Brompton	A	W	1-0	McQueen	
27		29	Northampton Town	H	W	5-1	McQueen (2), Wheldon (2), Millar	
28	Apr	12	Millwall Athletic	A	L	1-6	Millar	
29		19	Wellingborough	H	W	1-0	Seeley	
30		30	Bristol Rovers	A	L	1-4	Edwards	

Appeara
G

FA Cup

Q3	Nov	2	Crouch End Vampires	H	W	2-0	Stewart, Millar
Q4			West Norwood	H		1-0*	(Pryce)
Q4		20	West Norwood	H	W	4-0	Millar (4)
Q5		30	Luton Town	A	L	0-2	

* Match Abandoned after 84 minutes due to Fog

Appeara
G

Total - Appeara
Total - G

Western League

1	Sep	30	Tottenham Hotspur	H	L	1-3
2	Oct	7	Southampton	H	L	2-3
3		16	Southampton	A	L	1-5
4	Dec	9	Tottenham Hotspur	A	L	2-3
5		25	Millwall Athletic	H	L	0-2
6	Mar	3	Millwall Athletic	A	L	0-5
7			Bristol Rovers	H		
8			Bristol Rovers	A		
9			Portsmouth	H		
10			Portsmouth	A		
11			Reading	H		
12			Reading	A		
13			Swindon Town	H		
14			Swindon Town	A		
15			West Ham United	H		
16			West Ham United	A		

London League (Premier Division)

1	Nov	9	West Ham United	A	D	0-0
2	Dec	2	Millwall Athletic	H	L	0-1
3	Feb	3	Woolwich Arsenal	H	D	2-2
4		10	Tottenham Hotspur	H	W	5-1
5		17	Woolwich Arsenal	A	L	0-3
6		22	West Ham United	H	W	3-2
7	Mar	17	Millwall Athletic	A	L	0-3
8	Apr	14	Tottenham Hotspur	A	L	1-2

Southern Professional Charity Cup

No details recorded

Bowman	Christie	Collins	Edwards	Evans	Freeman	Handforth	Jordan	Keech	King	Lennox	McKinlay	McQueen	Millar	Newlands	Pryce	Seeley	Stewart	Wheldon	White
5		1	6		4				7			10	9	2	8	11			
		1			5	11	7	4		6		10	9	2	8				
4	8	1	11					6	7			10	9	2					5
		1			5			4				10	9	2	8	11	7		6
		1			5	11		4				10	9	2	8		7		6
		1			5			4				10	9	2	8	11	7		6
		1			5			4			10	11	9	2	8		7		6
4		1			5			6				10	9	2	8	11	7		
5		1			6				7		4	8	9	3				10	2
4		1			5			6				10	9	2	8	11	7		3
		1			5			6	7				9	4	8	10	11		2
		1			5			6					9	4	8	7	11	10	2
4		1			5						6		9		8	7	11	10	2
4		1			5			6	9			8				7	11	10	2
5		1			6				9			8		4		7	11	10	2
5		1			6				9			8		4		7	11	10	2
5		1			6				9			8		4		7	11	10	2
		1			5			6	9			8		4		7	11	10	2
5		1			6				7			8	9	4			11	10	2
5		1			6		7					8	9	4		11		10	2
		1			5			6				8	9	4		7	11	10	2
		1	6		5			4				8	9	3		7		10	2
5		1			6			4				8	9	3		7	11	10	2
4		1	6	9	5	11		10	7					3	8				2
4		1	6		5				7			10	9	3	8		11		2
4		1	6		5				7			10	9	2	8		11		
4		1	6		5				7			8	9	3			11	10	2
4		1	6		5			10	7			8	9				11		2
5	8	1	6		4							10	9			7	11		2
5		1	6		4						8	10	9			7	11		2
20	2	30	10	1	29	3	2	17	15	1	4	26	24	25	14	19	23	14	26
			1						2			9	7	1	2	2	3	6	

Bowman	Christie	Collins	Edwards	Evans	Freeman	Handforth	Jordan	Keech	King	Lennox	McKinlay	McQueen	Millar	Newlands	Pryce	Seeley	Stewart	Wheldon	White
4		1			5			6				10	9	2	8	11	7		
4		1			5			6				10	9	2	8	11	7		
4		1						6				10	9	2	8	11	7		5
3		3			2			3				3	3	3	3	3	3		1
													5				1		

Bowman	Christie	Collins	Edwards	Evans	Freeman	Handforth	Jordan	Keech	King	Lennox	McKinlay	McQueen	Millar	Newlands	Pryce	Seeley	Stewart	Wheldon	White
23	2	33	10	1	31	3	2	20	15	1	4	29	27	28	17	22	26	14	27
			1						2			9	12	1	2	2	4	6	

1902-03

Southern League (Div 1)

	P	W	D	L	F	A	Pts
Southampton	30	20	8	2	83	20	48
Reading	30	19	7	4	72	30	45
Portsmouth	30	17	7	6	69	32	41
Tottenham Hotspur	30	14	7	9	47	31	35
Bristol Rovers	30	13	8	9	46	34	34
New Brompton	30	11	11	8	37	35	33
Millwall Athletic	30	14	3	13	52	37	31
Northampton Town	30	12	6	12	39	48	30
Queen's Park Rangers	30	11	6	13	34	42	28
West Ham United	30	9	10	11	35	49	28
Luton Town	30	10	7	13	43	44	27
Swindon Town	30	10	7	13	38	46	27
Kettering Town	30	8	11	11	33	40	27
Wellingborough	30	11	3	16	36	56	25
Watford	30	6	4	20	35	87	16
Brentford	30	2	1	27	16	84	5

Western League

	P	W	D	L	F	A	Pts
Portsmouth	16	10	4	2	34	14	24
Bristol Rovers	16	9	2	5	36	22	20
Southampton	16	7	6	3	32	20	20
Tottenham Hotspur	16	6	7	3	20	14	19
Millwall Athletic	16	6	3	7	23	29	15
Reading	16	7	0	9	20	21	14
Queen's Park Rangers	16	6	2	8	18	31	14
Brentford	16	3	4	9	16	34	10
West Ham United	16	2	4	10	15	29	8

Match No.	Date		Opponents	Location	Result		Scorers
1	Sep	3	Wellingborough	H	W	2-0	Busby (2)
2		6	Tottenham Hotspur	A	D	0-0	
3		13	West Ham United	H	D	0-0	
4		20	Portsmouth	A	L	1-2	Hitch
5		27	New Brompton	H	L	1-2	Wilson
6	Oct	4	Swindon Town	A	L	0-2	
7		11	Kettering Town	H	W	4-2	Wilson, Hitch, Busby, Colvin
8		18	Luton Town	A	L	1-4	J.Edwards
9		25	Reading	H	L	1-3	Hamilton
10	Nov	8	Southampton	A	L	0-2	
11		22	Bristol Rovers	A	L	0-4	
12		29	Northampton Town	H	D	0-0	
13	Dec	6	Watford	A	W	2-0	Brown (2)
14		20	Tottenham Hotspur	H	L	0-4	
15		27	West Ham United	A	L	0-2	
16	Jan	3	Portsmouth	H	W	4-3	Blackwood (2), Hitch, Brown
17		10	New Brompton	A	D	0-0	
18		17	Swindon Town	H	W	2-0	Brown (2)
19		24	Kettering Town	A	W	1-0	Brown
20		31	Luton Town	H	W	3-1	Abbott (2), Hamilton
21	Feb	14	Millwall Athletic	H	L	0-1	
22		21	Southampton	H	D	0-0	
23	Mar	4	Brentford	H	W	3-0	Blackwood (2), Freeman
24		7	Bristol Rovers	H	W	2-0	Blackwood, OG (Young)
25		21	Watford	H	W	3-0	Blackwood (2), Brown
26		28	Brentford	A	W	2-0	Blackwood (2)
27		31	Northampton Town	A	D	1-1	Brown
28	Apr	4	Millwall Athletic	A	L	0-6	
29		14	Wellingborough	A	L	1-2	Blackwood
30		18	Reading	A	L	0-1	

Appeara

G

FA Cup

Q3	Nov	1	Luton Town	H	L	0-3	

Appeara

G

Total - Appeara

Total - G

Western League

1	Sep	22	Tottenham Hotspur	H	L	0-2
2	Oct	6	Southampton	H	W	3-2
3	Nov	3	Tottenham Hotspur	A	L	0-3
4		10	Millwall Athletic	A	L	0-4
5	Jan	19	Southampton	A	L	0-6
6	Feb	2	Millwall Athletic	H	W	2-1
7			Brentford	H		
8			Brentford	A		
9			Bristol Rovers	H		
10			Bristol Rovers	A		
11			Portsmouth	H		
12			Portsmouth	A		
13			Reading	H		
14			Reading	A		
15			West Ham United	H		
16			West Ham United	A		

London League (Premier Division)

1	Sep	8	Millwall Athletic	H	D	1-1
2		15	Woolwich Arsenal	H	L	0-2
3		29	Millwall Athletic	A	D	1-1
4	Oct	27	Woolwich Arsenal	A	L	1-3
5	Mar	16	Tottenham Hotspur	H	W	1-0
6		30	Tottenham Hotspur	A	L	0-3
7			Brentford	H	W	3-0
8			Brentford	A	D	2-2
9			West Ham United	H	L	0-2
10			West Ham United	A	L	0-1

Southern Professional Charity Cup

No details recorded

Blackwood	Bowman	Brown	Busby	Clipsham	Collins	Colvin	Edwards A.	Edwards J.	Freeman	Hamilton	Hitch	King	Mayes	Musselwhite	Newlands	Pryce	Skinner	White	Wilson	OG
	4		10		1	7		3		8	5				2		6		11	
	4		10		1	7		3		8	5				2		6		11	
	4		10		1	7		3		8	5	9			2		6		11	
	4		10		1	7		3		8	5				2		6		11	
	4		10		1	7		3		8	5	9			2		6		11	
	4		10		1	7		3		8	5				2		6		11	
	4		11		1	7		3		8	5	9					6	2	10	
			11		1	7		3		8	5				4		6	2	10	
		9	11		1			3	4	8		7		5			6	2	10	
	5	9	11	4	1	7			6	8					3			2		
	4		11	6	1	7		3	5	9		8			2				10	
3		9	11		1	7	6	3	4		5				2				10	
0	4	9			1				6	7	5		8		2			3	11	
0	4	9			1			3	6	7	5							2	11	
0	4				1			3	6	7	5	9						2	11	
0	4	9			1				6	7	5				3			2	11	
	4	9			1			3	6	7	5				2	10			11	
	4	9			1			3	6	7	5				2	10			11	
	4		10		1		6			7	5				3	9		2	11	
0	4	9			1		6			7	5				3			2	11	
	4	9			1			3	6	7	5				2	10			11	
0	4	9			1				6	7	5				3			2	11	
0	4	9			1			3	6	7	5				2				11	
0	4	9			1		6	3	5	7					2				11	
0	4	9			1				6	7	5				3			2	11	
0	4	9			1				6	7	5				3			2	11	
0	4	9			1				6	7	5				3			2	11	
9	4		7		1				6		5				3	10		2	11	
9	4	10			1				6	7	5				3			2	11	
9	4	10			1				6	7	5				3			2	11	
5	27	18	14	2	30	11	4	18	20	28	26	6	1	1	26	5	9	17	29	
0		8	3			1		1	1	2	3								2	1

Blackwood	Bowman	Brown	Busby	Clipsham	Collins	Colvin	Edwards A.	Edwards J.	Freeman	Hamilton	Hitch	King	Mayes	Musselwhite	Newlands	Pryce	Skinner	White	Wilson	OG
	4		11	5	1			3		7		8					6	2	10	
	1		1	1	1			1		1		1					1	1	1	

Blackwood	Bowman	Brown	Busby	Clipsham	Collins	Colvin	Edwards A.	Edwards J.	Freeman	Hamilton	Hitch	King	Mayes	Musselwhite	Newlands	Pryce	Skinner	White	Wilson	OG
5	28	18	15	3	31	11	4	19	20	29	26	7	1	1	26	5	10	18	30	
0		8	3			1		1	1	2	3								2	1

1903-04

Southern League (Div 1)

	P	W	D	L	F	A	Pts
Southampton	34	22	6	6	75	30	50
Tottenham Hotspur	34	16	11	7	54	37	43
Bristol Rovers	34	17	8	9	66	42	42
Portsmouth	34	17	8	9	41	38	42
Queen's Park Rangers	34	15	11	8	53	37	41
Reading	34	14	13	7	48	35	41
Millwall	34	16	8	10	64	42	40
Luton Town	34	14	12	8	38	33	40
Plymouth Argyle	34	13	10	11	44	34	36
Swindon Town	34	10	11	13	30	42	31
Fulham	34	9	12	13	34	35	30
West Ham United	34	10	7	17	39	44	27
Brentford	34	9	9	16	34	48	27
Wellingborough	34	11	5	18	44	63	27
Northampton Town	34	10	7	17	36	60	27
New Brompton	34	6	13	15	26	43	25
Brighton & Hove Albion	34	6	12	16	45	69	24
Kettering Town	34	6	7	21	39	78	19

Western League

	P	W	D	L	F	A	Pts
Tottenham Hotspur	16	11	3	2	33	12	25
Southampton	16	9	3	4	30	18	21
Plymouth Argyle	16	8	4	4	22	18	20
Portsmouth	16	7	2	7	24	22	16
Brentford	16	6	4	6	19	23	16
Queen's Park Rangers	16	5	5	6	15	21	15
Reading	16	4	4	8	16	26	12
Bristol Rovers	16	4	3	9	29	29	11
West Ham United	16	2	4	10	13	31	8

Match No.	Date		Opponents	Location	Result		Scorers	Atter
1	Sep	5	Brentford	H	W	1-0	Brown	1
2		12	West Ham United	A	L	0-1		
3		19	Tottenham Hotspur	H	W	2-0	McGowan, Abbott	
4		26	Luton Town	A	L	0-1		
5	Oct	3	New Brompton	H	W	3-0	McGowan (2), Milward	
6		10	Kettering Town	A	L	1-2	Milward	
7		17	Southampton	H	L	0-3		1
8		24	Fulham	A	D	2-2	Blackwood (2)	1
9	Nov	7	Swindon Town	A	D	1-1	Blackwood	
10		14	Northampton Town	H	W	4-1	Blackwood (3), Milward	
11		21	Reading	H	D	1-1	Blackwood	1
12		28	Wellingborough	A	D	1-1	Murphy	
13	Dec	5	Bristol Rovers	H	W	2-1	Blackwood, Hamilton	
14		12	Brighton	A	W	3-1	Milward (2), Blackwood	
15		19	Portsmouth	H	W	6-1	Blackwood (3),Murphy (2), Hitch	
16		28	Northampton Town	A	L	1-2	Wilson	
17	Jan	2	Brentford	A	W	4-1	Milward (2), Blackwood, Murphy (pen)	
18		9	West Ham United	H	W	2-1	Murphy, Milward	
19		16	Tottenham Hotspur	A	D	2-2	Blackwood (2)	1
20		30	New Brompton	A	L	0-2		
21	Feb	6	Kettering Town	H	W	2-0	Murphy, Blackwood	
22		13	Southampton	A	L	1-2	Blackwood	
23		20	Fulham	H	D	1-1	Cross	1
24		27	Millwall	A	L	0-4		
25	Mar	5	Swindon Town	H	W	1-0	Blackwood	
26		12	Plymouth Argyle	H	W	1-0	Abbott	
27		13	Plymouth Argyle	A	D	1-1	Brown	
28		17	Luton Town	H	W	2-1	Milward, Brown (pen)	
29		19	Reading	A	D	1-1	Blackwood	
30		26	Wellingborough	H	W	3-0	Bowman, Milward, Blackwood	1
31	Apr	2	Bristol Rovers	A	D	1-1	Cross	
32		9	Brighton	H	D	1-1	Milward	
33		16	Portsmouth	A	D	0-0		
34		30	Millwall	H	W	2-1	Murphy, Skilton	

Appeara
G

FA Cup

Q3	Oct	31	Fulham	H	D	1-1	Murphy	1
rep	Nov	4	Fulham	A	L	1-3	Brown	1

Appeara
G

Total - Appeara
Total - G

Western League

1	Oct	5	Tottenham Hotspur	A	L	0-3
2	Nov	2	Southampton	A	L	1-5
3		9	Tottenham Hotspur	H	W	2-0
4		18	Southampton	H	D	0-0
5	Apr	11	West Ham United	H	W	3-1
6	Apr	14	West Ham United	A	L	1-2
7			Brentford	H		
8			Brentford	A		
9			Bristol Rovers	H		
10			Bristol Rovers	A		
11			Plymouth Argyle	H		
12			Plymouth Argyle	A		
13			Portsmouth	H		
14			Portsmouth	A		
15			Reading	H		
16			Reading	A		

London League (Premier Division)

1	Sep	12	West Ham United	H	W	2-1	
2	Dec	25	Millwall	H	L	0-2	10
3	Jan	7	West Ham United	A	D	2-2	
4		11	Woolwich Arsenal	A	L	2-6	
5	Feb	15	Tottenham Hotspur	H	L	0-3	
6	Mar	7	Tottenham Hotspur	A	W	3-1	
7		21	Woolwich Arsenal	H	W	3-1	
8	Apr	4	Millwall	A	L	0-3	
9			Brentford	H			
10			Brentford	A			
11			Fulham	H			
12			Fulham	A			

Southern Professional Charity Cup

No details recorded

Archer	Banner	Blackwood	Bowman	Brown	Bull	Collins	Cross	Downing	Edwards	Freeman	Hamilton	Hitch	Leather	Lyon	McCairns	McGowan	Mayes	Milward	Murphy	Newlands	Skilton	White	Wilson
2		10	4	9		1	7			6		5						8		3			11
2		10	4	9		1				6	7	5						8		3			11
2			4	9	6	1	11				7	5				10				3			
2			4	9	6	1					7	5				10			11	3			
2			4	9	6	1					7	5				10		8		3			11
2			4		6	1	7					5				10		8	9	3			11
2		10	4	9	6	1					7	5								3			11
			4		6	1					7	5		2	8	10			9			3	11
			4			1		6			7	5		2		10		8	9	3			11
2		10	4			1	7	6				5						8	9	3			11
2		10	4			1	11	6			7	5						8	9	3			
2		10	4			1		6	11		7	5						8	9	3			
2		10	4			1		6			7	5						8	9	3			11
2		10	4			1		6			7	5						8	9	3			11
2		10	4			1		6			7	5						8	9	3			11
2	5	10				1	7	4	6									8	9	3			11
2	6	10				1		4			7							8	9	3		5	11
2	4	10				1		6			7	5						8	9	3			11
2		10				1		6			7	5						8	9	3		4	11
2		10	4			1		6			7	5						8	9	3			11
2		10	4			1		6			7	5						8	9	3			11
2		10	4			1		6			7	5						8	9	3			11
2		10	4			1	7	6				5						8	9	3			11
2			4			1	7	6				5					8	10	9	3			11
2		10	4		6	1	7											8	9	3		5	11
2		10	4		6	1	7					5						9		3			11
2			8	9	4	1						5				10		7		3		6	11
2		10	4	9	6	1	7					5						8		3			11
2		10	4	9	6	1	7					5						8		3			11
2		10	5	9	4			6					1				7	8		3			11
2		10	4			1	7	6				5					9	8		3			11
		10		9	4	1		6			7	5						8		3		2	11
2			7	9		1			6			5						8	10	3		4	11
2	7		4			1		6				5						8	10		9	3	11
31	4	24	29	12	13	33	13	20	3	2	19	30	1	2	1	7	3	30	22	32	1	8	30
		20	1	3			2				1	1				3		11	7		1		1

Archer	Banner	Blackwood	Bowman	Brown	Bull	Collins	Cross	Downing	Edwards	Freeman	Hamilton	Hitch	Leather	Lyon	McCairns	McGowan	Mayes	Milward	Murphy	Newlands	Skilton	White	Wilson
			4		6	1					7	5		2	8	10			9	3			11
			4	9	6	1					7	5		2	8	10				3			11
			2	1	2	2					2	2		2	2	2			1	2			2
				1															1				

Archer	Banner	Blackwood	Bowman	Brown	Bull	Collins	Cross	Downing	Edwards	Freeman	Hamilton	Hitch	Leather	Lyon	McCairns	McGowan	Mayes	Milward	Murphy	Newlands	Skilton	White	Wilson
31	4	24	31	13	15	35	13	20	3	2	21	32	1	4	3	9	3	30	23	34	1	8	32
		20	1	4			2				1	1				3		11	8		1		1

1904-05

Southern League (Div 1)

	P	W	D	L	F	A	Pts
Bristol Rovers	34	20	8	6	74	36	48
Reading	34	18	7	9	57	38	43
Southampton	34	18	7	9	54	40	43
Plymouth Argyle	34	18	5	11	57	39	41
Tottenham Hotspur	34	15	8	11	53	34	38
Fulham	34	14	10	10	46	34	38
Queen's Park Rangers	34	14	8	12	51	46	36
Portsmouth	34	16	4	14	61	56	36
New Brompton	34	11	11	12	40	41	33
Watford	34	15	3	16	41	44	33
West Ham United	34	12	8	14	48	42	32
Brighton & Hove Albion	34	13	6	15	44	45	32
Northampton Town	34	12	8	14	43	54	32
Brentford	34	10	9	15	33	38	29
Millwall	34	11	7	16	38	47	29
Swindon Town	34	12	5	17	41	59	29
Luton Town	34	12	3	19	45	54	27
Wellingborough	34	5	3	26	25	104	13

Western League

	P	W	D	L	F	A	Pts
Plymouth Argyle	20	13	4	3	52	18	30
Brentford	20	11	6	3	30	22	28
Southampton	20	11	2	7	45	22	24
Portsmouth	20	10	3	7	29	30	23
West Ham United	20	8	4	8	37	42	20
Fulham	20	7	3	10	29	32	17
Millwall	20	7	3	10	32	40	17
Tottenham Hotspur	20	5	6	9	20	28	16
Reading	20	6	3	11	27	37	15
Bristol Rovers	20	7	1	12	32	44	15
Queen's Park Rangers	20	6	3	11	27	45	15

Match No.	Date		Opponents	Location	Result		Scorers	Atten
1	Sep	3	Plymouth Argyle	H	W	2-1	Blackwood (2)	12
2		10	West Ham United	A	W	3-1	Bevan (2, 1 pen), Hitch	14
3		17	Reading	H	W	4-2	Bevan (2, 1 pen), W.Cross, Hitch	16
4		24	Bristol Rovers	A	D	0-0		6
5	Oct	1	Northampton Town	H	L	1-2	Stewart	9
6		8	Portsmouth	A	L	1-4	Ronaldson	12
7		15	Brentford	H	W	3-2	Ronaldson, W.Cross, Blackwood	12
8		22	Brighton	A	L	0-3		6
9		29	Millwall	A	D	0-0		7
10	Nov	5	Tottenham Hotspur	H	L	1-2	Stewart	16
11		12	Luton Town	A	D	1-1	Ronaldson	6
12		19	Swindon Town	H	W	4-1	Bevan (3), Ronaldson	6
13		26	New Brompton	A	L	0-4		4
14	Dec	3	Wellingborough	H	L	1-2	Hitch	4
15		17	Fulham	H	W	2-0	Bowman, Bevan	14
16		24	Watford	A	L	0-1		6
17		31	Plymouth Argyle	A	L	1-3	Milward	8
18	Jan	7	West Ham United	H	W	1-0	Hitch	7
19		14	Reading	A	L	0-3		8
20		21	Bristol Rovers	H	W	5-0	Milward, Hitch, Skilton, Edwards, Murphy	11
21		28	Northampton Town	A	D	1-1	Ronaldson	4
22	Feb	11	Brentford	A	D	0-0		8
23		18	Brighton	H	L	1-2	Ronaldson	3
24		25	Millwall	H	D	1-1	Bevan	9
25	Mar	4	Tottenham Hotspur	A	L	1-5	Bevan	7
26		11	Luton Town	H	L	1-2	Bevan	4
27		18	Swindon Town	A	D	0-0		4
28		25	New Brompton	H	W	2-0	Ryder (2)	6
29	Apr	1	Wellingborough	A	W	4-0	Bevan (4)	
30		8	Southampton	H	D	1-1	Milward	12
31		15	Fulham	A	W	2-1	Hitch, Bevan	12
32		22	Watford	H	W	4-1	Bevan (3, 1 pen), Hitch	5
33		25	Portsmouth	H	W	2-0	Hitch (pen), Murphy	5
34		29	Southampton	A	W	1-0	Bevan	4

Appearan
G

FA Cup

Q6	Dec	10	Brentford	H	L	1-2	Ryder	10

Appearar
G

Total - Appearan
Total - G

Western League

1	Sep	12	Southampton	H	L	1-4	
2	Nov	7	Southampton	A	L	0-5	
3	Mar	27	Millwall	A	L	1-3	1
4	Apr	3	Millwall	H	W	5-1	2
5			Brentford	H			
6			Brentford	A			
7			Bristol Rovers	H			
8			Bristol Rovers	A			
9			Fulham	H			
10			Fulham	A			
11			Plymouth Argyle	H			
12			Plymouth Argyle	A			
13			Portsmouth	H			
14			Portsmouth	A			
15			Reading	H			
16			Reading	A			
17			Tottenham Hotspur	H			
18			Tottenham Hotspur	A			
19			West Ham United	H			
20			West Ham United	A			

Southern Professional Charity Cup

R1	Oct	26	Millwall	H	D	1-1	4
rep	Nov	21	Millwall	A	D	1-1	3
rep	Dec	12	Millwall	N*	D	1-1	5
rep	Feb	15	Millwall	H	W	2-1	4
R2	No details recorded						

* Played at Tottenham

Bevan	Blackwood	Bowman	Collins	Cross J.	Cross W.	Downing	Edwards	Evans	Hitch	Howes	Leather	Lyon	Milward	Murphy	Newlands	Ronaldson	Ryder	Shufflebottom	Singleton	Skilton	Stewart	White
9	10	4	1	6					5						3	8			11		7	
9	10	4	1	6	7				5						3	8					11	
9		4	1	6	7				5					10	3	8					11	
9		4	1	6	7				5					10	3	8					11	
9		4	1	6	7				5							8	10				11	3
9		4	1	6	7				5							8	10				11	3
9	10	6	1	4	7				5						3	8			11			
9	10		1	4	7	6									3	8			11			5
8	10	5	1	4	7	6									3				11	9		
8	10	4	1	6					5					7	3					9	11	
9		4		6	7				5	1				10	3	8					11	
9		4					6		5	1		3		7		8	10				11	
9		4			7		6		5	1		3				8	10		11			
9	10	4		6	7				5	1		3				8			11			
0		4			7		6		5	1					3	8				9	11	
10		4			7		6		5	1					3	8				9	11	
0		4		6	7				5	1			8	11	3	9						
0			1	4	7	6			5			2	8		3					9	11	
9			1	4		6								7	3	8	10		11			5
		6	1	4	7		11		5			2	8	10	3					9		
		6	1	4	7		11		5			2	8		3	10				9		
9		6	1	4	7		11		5			2	8	10	3							
9		6	1	4					5			2	8		3	10			11		7	
9		4	1			6		7	5			2	8		3	10			11			
0		4				6			5	1		2	8	7	3	9			11			
9		4	1			10			5			2		7	3	8			11			6
9		4	1			7			5				8				10	6	11			3
9		4	1			6			5			2	8	7	3		10		11			
9		4	1			6			5				8	7	3		10		11			
9		4	1		7	6			5			2	8		3		10		11			
9				4		6			5	1		3	8	7			10		11			
9				4		6			5	1		2	8	7	3		10		11			
9				4		6			5	1		2	8	7	3		10		11			
9				4		6			5		1		8	7	3		10		11			2
32	7	27	22	23	19	15	7	1	31	11	1	16	16	17	27	21	13	1	19	7	13	7
20	3	1			2		1		8				3	2		6	2			1	2	
9		4		6	7				5	1		3				8	10				11	
1		1		1	1				1	1		1				1	1				1	
																	1					
33	7	28	22	24	20	15	7	1	32	12	1	17	16	17	27	22	14	1	19	7	14	7
20	3	1			2		1		8				3	2		6	3			1	2	

1905-06

Southern League (Div 1)

	P	W	D	L	F	A	Pts
Fulham	34	19	12	3	44	15	50
Southampton	34	19	7	8	58	39	45
Portsmouth	34	17	9	8	61	35	43
Luton Town	34	17	7	10	64	40	41
Tottenham Hotspur	34	16	7	11	46	29	39
Plymouth Argyle	34	16	7	11	52	33	39
Norwich City	34	13	10	11	46	38	36
Bristol Rovers	34	15	5	14	56	56	35
Brentford	34	14	7	13	43	52	35
Reading	34	12	9	13	53	46	33
West Ham United	34	14	5	15	42	39	33
Millwall	34	11	11	12	38	41	33
Queen's Park Rangers	34	12	7	15	58	44	31
Watford	34	8	10	16	38	57	26
Swindon Town	34	8	9	17	31	52	25
Brighton & Hove Albion	34	9	7	18	30	55	25
New Brompton	34	7	8	19	20	62	22
Northampton Town	34	8	5	21	32	79	21

Western League

	P	W	D	L	F	A	Pts
Queen's Park Rangers	20	11	4	5	33	27	26
Southampton	20	10	5	5	41	35	25
Plymouth Argyle	20	8	8	4	34	23	24
Tottenham Hotspur	20	7	7	6	28	17	21
Bristol Rovers	20	8	3	9	34	34	19
Millwall	20	7	5	8	28	29	19
Portsmouth	20	6	7	7	26	29	19
West Ham United	20	7	5	8	32	35	19
Reading	20	6	6	8	28	35	18
Fulham	20	5	5	10	23	32	15
Brentford	20	6	3	11	25	36	15

Match No.	Date		Opponents	Location	Result		Scorers
1	Sep	2	New Brompton	H	W	4-0	Sugden (3), Bevan
2		9	Portsmouth	A	D	0-0	
3		16	Swindon Town	H	W	3-0	Ryder, Bevan
4		23	Millwall	A	L	0-2	
5		30	Luton Town	H	L	2-3	Sugden, Ryder
6	Oct	7	Tottenham Hotspur	A	L	1-2	Sugden
7		14	Brentford	H	L	1-2	Hitch
8		21	Norwich City	A	L	0-4	
9		28	Plymouth Argyle	H	W	2-0	Yenson, Ryder
10	Nov	4	Southampton	A	L	1-2	Thompson
11		11	Reading	H	W	3-0	Downing (2), Sugden
12		18	Watford	A	W	4-3	Thompson (3), Bevan
13		25	Brighton	H	D	0-0	
14	Dec	2	West Ham United	A	L	0-2	
15		9	Fulham	H	L	1-3	Thompson
16		16	Northampton Town	H	W	6-1	Bevan (3, 1 pen), Ryder, Sugden, Cowan
17		23	Bristol Rovers	A	L	1-2	Ryder
18		30	New Brompton	A	W	2-0	Ryder, Brewis
19	Jan	6	Portsmouth	H	W	2-0	Ryder, Murphy
20		20	Swindon Town	A	W	2-1	Fletcher, Ryder
21		27	Millwall	H	W	2-1	Yenson, Ryder
22	Feb	3	Luton Town	A	L	2-3	Ryder, Murphy
23		10	Tottenham Hotspur	H	D	0-0	
24		17	Brentford	A	D	2-2	Fletcher (2)
25		24	Norwich City	H	D	0-0	
26	Mar	3	Plymouth Argyle	A	D	1-1	Fletcher
27		14	Southampton	H	L	0-3	
28		17	Reading	A	L	0-1	
29		24	Watford	H	W	6-0	Bevan (2), Fletcher, Ryder, Roberts, OG (Brooks)
30		31	Brighton	A	L	2-3	Ryder, Sugden
31	Apr	7	West Ham United	H	L	0-1	
32		14	Fulham	A	L	0-1	
33		21	Northampton Town	A	D	1-1	Yenson
34		28	Bristol Rovers	H	W	7-0	Fletcher (2), Ryder (2), Bevan (2), Thompson

Appeara
G

FA Cup

R1	Jan	13	Fulham	A	L	0-1	

Appeara
G

Total - Appeara
Total - G

Western League

1	Oct	30	Southampton	H	W	5-1
2	Nov	20	Millwall	H	W	2-1
3		27	Southampton	A	W	3-2
4	Feb	26	Millwall	A	D	0-0
5			Brentford	H		
6			Brentford	A		
7			Bristol Rovers	H		
8			Bristol Rovers	A		
9			Fulham	H		
10			Fulham	A		
11			Plymouth Argyle	H		
12			Plymouth Argyle	A		
13			Portsmouth	H		
14			Portsmouth	A		
15			Reading	H		
16			Reading	A		
17			Tottenham Hotspur	H		
18			Tottenham Hotspur	A		
19			West Ham United	H		
20			West Ham United	A		

Southern Professional Charity Cup

R1	Nov	8	Tottenham Hotspur	A	L	0-2

Brewis	Cowan	Downing	Edwards	Fletcher	Fox	Gardner	Guy-Watson	Hitch	Howes	Kingsley	Lyon	McCargill	McLarney	Moger	Murphy	Newlands	Roberts	Ryder	Sugden	Thompson	Wassel	White	Yenson	OG
		5				11		4		1			2		7	3		10	8				6	
		6	11					5		1			2		7	3		10	8				4	
		6				11		5		1			2		7	3		10	8				4	
		6				11		5		1			2		7	3		10	8				4	
		6				11		5		1	2				7	3		10	8				4	
9		6	11					5		1	3		2		7			10	8				4	
		6	11					5		1	3		2		7			10	8				4	
		6						5		1	3		2		7		11	10	8				4	
		6						5		1	2					3	11	10	8	7		4	9	
		6						5		1	2					3	11	10	8	7		4	9	
		6						5		1	2					3	11	10	8	7		4	9	
		6								1	2						11	10	8	7	3	5	4	
		6								1	2						11	10	8	7	3	5	4	
		6								1			2			3	11	10	8	7		5	4	
		6						5		1	2					3	11		8	7		4	9	
	11	6						5		1						3		10	8	7		2	4	
		6		8				5		1					7	3	11	10	9			2	4	
9		6		8				5	1							3	11	10	7			2	4	
		6		8				5	1		11				9	3		10		7		2	4	
		6		8				5	1		11					3		10		7		2	4	
		6		8				5	1						9	3		10		7		2	4	
		6		8				5	1						9	3		10	7			2	4	
		6						5	1							3	9	10	8	7		2	4	
				10				5	1							3	9	6	8	7		2	4	
				10				5		1						3	11	6	8	7		2	4	
				10				5		1						3	11	6	8	7		2	4	
		6		8				5	1							3	11	10	7			2	4	
		6		8				5	1							3	11	10	7			2	4	
		6		8				5	1							3	11	10		7		2	4	
		6		8				5	1							3	11	10	7			2	4	
		6		8				5	1							3	11	10	7			2	4	
				8	3			5		1		6					11	10	7			2	4	
				8		4		5			2	6		1		3	11	10	7				9	
				8			1	5				6					11	10		7	3	2	4	
2	1	28	3	17	1	5	1	31	12	20	13	3	8	1	12	27	22	33	29	17	3	25	34	
1	1	2		7				1							2		1	15	8	6			3	1

Brewis	Cowan	Downing	Edwards	Fletcher	Fox	Gardner	Guy-Watson	Hitch	Howes	Kingsley	Lyon	McCargill	McLarney	Moger	Murphy	Newlands	Roberts	Ryder	Sugden	Thompson	Wassel	White	Yenson	OG
		6		8				5	1		11				9	3		10		7		2	4	
		1		1				1	1		1				1	1		1		1		1	1	

Brewis	Cowan	Downing	Edwards	Fletcher	Fox	Gardner	Guy-Watson	Hitch	Howes	Kingsley	Lyon	McCargill	McLarney	Moger	Murphy	Newlands	Roberts	Ryder	Sugden	Thompson	Wassel	White	Yenson	OG
2	1	29	3	18	1	5	1	32	13	20	14	3	8	1	13	28	22	34	29	18	3	26	35	
1	1	2		7				1							2		1	15	8	6			3	1

1906-07

Southern League (Div 1)

	P	W	D	L	F	A	Pts
Fulham	38	20	13	5	58	32	53
Portsmouth	38	22	7	9	64	36	51
Brighton & Hove Albion	38	18	9	11	53	43	45
Luton Town	38	18	9	11	52	52	45
West Ham United	38	15	14	9	60	41	44
Tottenham Hotspur	38	17	9	12	63	45	43
Millwall	38	18	6	14	71	50	42
Norwich City	38	15	12	11	57	48	42
Watford	38	13	16	9	46	43	42
Brentford	38	17	8	13	57	56	42
Southampton	38	13	9	16	49	56	35
Reading	38	14	6	18	57	47	34
Clapton Orient (Res)	38	11	12	15	38	60	34
Bristol Rovers	38	12	9	17	55	54	33
Plymouth Argyle	38	10	13	15	43	50	33
New Brompton	38	12	9	17	47	59	33
Swindon Town	38	11	11	16	43	54	33
Queen's Park Rangers	38	11	10	17	47	55	32
Crystal Palace	38	8	9	21	46	66	25
Northampton Town	38	5	9	24	29	88	19

Western League

	P	W	D	L	F	A	Pts
Fulham	10	7	1	2	16	9	15
Queen's Park Rangers	10	5	1	4	17	11	11
Brentford	10	5	1	4	19	19	11
Reading	10	4	1	5	12	18	9
Bristol Rovers	10	3	1	6	17	17	7
Chelsea	10	2	3	5	7	14	7

Match No.	Date		Opponents	Location	Result		Scorers
1	Sep	1	Luton Town	A	D	1-1	Anderson
2		8	Crystal Palace	H	W	1-0	Downing
3		15	Brentford	A	L	1-4	Ryder
4		19	Swindon Town	A	D	0-0	
5		22	Millwall	H	W	2-1	O'Donnell, Ryder
6		29	Clapton Orient	A	L	0-3	
7	Oct	6	Portsmouth	H	L	2-3	O'Donnell, Sugden (pen)
8		13	New Brompton	A	L	1-2	Brewis
9		20	Plymouth Argyle	H	D	0-0	
10		27	Brighton	A	L	0-2	
11	Nov	3	Reading	H	L	0-1	
12		10	Watford	A	L	0-1	
13		17	Northampton Town	H	W	5-0	Fletcher (3), Green, Sugden
14		24	Bristol Rovers	H	D	1-1	Green
15	Dec	1	Fulham	A	D	1-1	Thompson
16		8	Southampton	H	L	1-2	Green
17		22	Tottenham Hotspur	H	W	3-1	Ryder, Green, O'Donnell
18		26	Norwich City	H	D	1-1	Fletcher
19		29	Luton Town	H	W	2-0	Green (2)
20	Jan	5	Crystal Palace	A	L	1-5	Fletcher
21		26	Millwall	A	L	0-7	
22	Feb	2	Clapton Orient	H	W	2-0	Sugden (2)
23		9	Portsmouth	A	D	2-2	Sugden, Skilton
24		16	New Brompton	H	W	3-0	Skilton (2), Sugden
25		23	Plymouth Argyle	A	L	1-2	O'Donnell
26		25	West Ham United	A	L	1-2	Anderson
27	Mar	2	Brighton	H	L	0-2	
28		9	Reading	A	D	0-0	
29		11	Brentford	H	D	1-1	Sugden
30		16	Watford	H	D	0-0	
31		23	Northampton Town	A	W	2-1	Yenson (pen), O'Donnell
32		29	Norwich City	A	L	0-1	
33		30	Bristol Rovers	A	L	1-3	Skilton
34	Apr	1	Swindon Town	H	W	6-1	Skilton (2), O'Donnell (2), Sugden (2)
35		6	Fulham	H	L	0-2	
36		13	Southampton	A	W	3-0	Green (2), Anderson
37		20	West Ham United	H	W	2-0	Skilton, Fletcher
38		27	Tottenham Hotspur	A	L	0-2	

Appeara
G

FA Cup

R1	Jan	12	Bristol Rovers	A	D	0-0
rep		14	Bristol Rovers	H	L	0-1

Appearar
G

Total - Appearar
Total - G

Western League

1			Brentford	H			
2			Brentford	A			
3			Bristol Rovers	A			
4			Chelsea	H			
5			Chelsea	A			
6			Fulham	H			
7			Fulham	A			
8			Reading	H			
9			Reading	A			
10	Apr	24	Bristol Rovers	H	W	3-0	(last home game)

Southern Professional Charity Cup

R1	No details recorded					
R2	No details recorded					
SF	Mar	4	Tottenham Hotspur	A	L	0-4

Blake	Brewis	Downing	Fidler	Fletcher	Green	Howes	Lyon	McCargill	McLean	Moger	Newlands	O'Donnell	Ryder	Skilton	Sugden	Taylor	Thompson	Webb	White	Yenson
1		6			7	1			5		3	8	10						2	4
1		6			7	1			5		3	8	10						2	4
1		6			7	1			5		3	8	10						2	4
1		6			7	1			5		3	8	10						2	4
1		6			7	1			5		3	9	10		8				2	4
1		6	3		7	1			5			9	10		8				2	4
1	10				7	1	3		5			9	6		8				2	4
1	9	6			7	1	3		5				10		8				2	4
1	9	6		8	7	1	2				3		10						5	4
1	9	6		8	7	1	2				3		10						5	4
1	9	6		8	7	1	2				3		10						5	4
1		6		8	7	1	2		5		3				10				4	9
		6		8	9	1	2		5		3		11		10		7			4
		6		8	9	1	2		5		3		11		10		7			4
		6		8	9	1	2		5		3		11		10		7			4
		6		8	9	1	2	4	5		3		11		10		7			
		6		8	9	1			5		3	7	11		10				2	4
		6		8	9	1	3		5			7	11		10				2	4
		6		8	9	1	3		5			7	11		10				2	4
		6		8	9	1	2		5		3	7	11						4	
1		6			9		3		5	1			10		8	4	7		2	
		6	3				2		5	1			11	9	10		7			4
		6	3		7	1	2		5				11	9	10					4
		6	3		7	1	2		5				11	9	10					4
		6	3		7	1	2					11		9	10				5	4
		6	3	8	7	1	2					11			10				5	4
		6	3	8	7	1	2		5			11			10					4
		6	3		7	1	2		5			11		9	10					4
		6	3		7		2		5			11		9	10			1		4
		6	3		7		2		5			11		9	10			1		4
		6	3		7		2		5			11		9	10			1		4
		6	3	8	7		2		5			11		9	10			1		4
		6	3	8	7				5			11		9	10			1	2	4
		6	3	8	7				5			11		9	10			1	2	4
		6	3	8	7				5			11		9	10			1	2	4
		6	3	8	7				5			11		9				1	2	4
		6	3	8	7				5			11		9				1	2	4
1		6	3	8	7							10				5		1	2	4
4	5	37	18	21	37	26	25	1	32	2	15	25	23	14	27	2	6	10	25	35
	1	1		6	8							7	3	7	9		1			1
		6		8	9	1			5		3	7	11		10				2	4
		6		8	9	1			5		3	7	11		10				2	4
		2		2	2	2			2		2	2	2		2				2	2
4	5	39	18	23	39	28	25	1	34	2	17	27	25	14	29	2	6	10	27	37
	1	1		6	8							7	3	7	9		1			1

1907-08

Southern League (Div 1)

	P	W	D	L	F	A	Pts
Queen's Park Rangers	38	21	9	8	82	57	51
Plymouth Argyle	38	19	11	8	50	31	49
Millwall	38	19	8	11	49	32	46
Crystal Palace	38	17	10	11	54	51	44
Swindon Town	38	16	10	12	55	40	42
Bristol Rovers	38	16	10	12	59	56	42
Tottenham Hotspur	38	17	7	14	59	48	41
Northampton Town	38	15	11	12	50	41	41
Portsmouth	38	17	6	15	63	52	40
West Ham United	38	15	10	13	47	48	40
Southampton	38	16	6	16	51	60	38
Reading	38	15	6	17	55	50	36
Bradford (Park Avenue)	38	12	12	14	53	54	36
Watford	38	12	10	16	47	59	34
Brentford	38	14	5	19	49	52	33
Norwich City	38	12	9	17	46	49	33
Brighton & Hove Albion	38	12	8	18	46	59	32
Luton Town	38	12	6	20	33	56	30
Clapton Orient (Res)	38	8	11	19	51	73	27
New Brompton	38	9	7	22	44	75	25

Western League

	P	W	D	L	F	A	Pts
Southampton	12	8	1	3	30	12	17
Portsmouth	12	7	1	4	25	13	15
Brighton & Hove Albion	12	6	2	4	19	19	14
Plymouth Argyle	12	5	2	5	14	12	12
Queen's Park Rangers	12	5	1	6	20	23	11
Brentford	12	2	5	5	13	21	9
Leyton	12	2	2	8	11	27	6

Match No.	Date		Opponents	Location	Result		Scorers	Atte
1	Sep	2	Tottenham Hotspur	H	D	3-3	Gittens (2), Hitchcock	
2		7	New Brompton	H	D	2-2	Rogers, Hitchcock	
3		14	Tottenham Hotspur	A	L	2-3	Walker, Barnes	1
4		21	Swindon Town	H	W	2-1	Sugden (2)	
5		28	Crystal Palace	A	W	3-2	Gittens (2), Walker	
6	Oct	5	Luton Town	H	W	3-1	Barnes, Gittens, Pentland	1
7		12	Brighton	A	W	3-2	White, Walker, Gittens	
8		19	Portsmouth	H	W	3-2	Pentland, Skilton, Gittens	1
9		26	Bradford	A	D	2-2	Skilton, Walker	1
10	Nov	2	Millwall	H	L	2-3	Gittens, Walker	1
11		9	Brentford	A	D	1-1	Downing	1
12		16	Bristol Rovers	H	W	5-3	Pentland (2), Barnes, Walker, Skilton	1
13		23	Clapton Orient	A	W	5-2	Walker (2), Gittens (2), Pentland (pen)	
14		30	Reading	H	W	1-0	Pentland (pen)	1
15	Dec	7	Watford	A	W	3-0	Walker, Gittens, Skilton	
16		14	Norwich City	H	W	3-1	Pentland (2), Downing	
17		21	Northampton Town	A	W	2-1	Pentland (2)	
18		25	Plymouth Argyle	H	D	0-0		2
19		26	West Ham United	A	L	0-3		1
20		28	Southampton	H	W	3-0	Walker (2), Sugden	
21	Jan	4	New Brompton	A	W	4-0	Barnes, Sugden, Downing, Gittens	
22		25	Crystal Palace	H	L	1-2	Ainsworth	
23	Feb	8	Brighton	H	W	1-0	Barnes	
24		15	Portsmouth	A	L	0-1		
25		22	Bradford	H	W	2-0	Barnes, Walker	
26		26	Luton Town	A	D	0-0		
27		29	Millwall	A	D	0-0		1
28	Mar	7	Brentford	H	W	1-0	Cannon	1
29		14	Bristol Rovers	A	W	1-0	Downing	1
30		21	Clapton Orient	H	W	5-2	Gittens, Pentland (pen), Skilton, Lintott, Barnes	
31		28	Reading	A	W	3-0	Gittens (2), Cannon	
32	Apr	4	Watford	H	D	3-3	Barnes, Cannon, Pentland	
33		11	Norwich City	A	W	1-0	Gittens	
34		17	Plymouth Argyle	A	D	1-1	Barnes	1
35		18	Northampton Town	H	L	2-3	Pentland, Barnes	1
36		20	West Ham United	H	W	4-0	Cannon (3), Pentland	1
37		25	Southampton	A	L	2-5	Walker, Snelgrove	
38		29	Swindon Town	A	L	3-8	Walker (2), Ainsworth	

Appeara
G

FA Cup

R1	Jan	11	Reading	H	W	1-0	Barnes	2
R2	Feb	1	Swindon Town	A	L	1-2	Walker	

Appeara
G

FA Charity Shield

1	Apr	27	Manchester United	N*		1-1	Cannon	1

* Played at Stamford Bridge

Appeara
G

Total - Appeara
Total - G

Western League

1	Sep	11	Portsmouth	A	W	4-3	Barnes, Pentland, Walker, OG
2		16	Brentford	H	W	3-1	
3		25	Brentford	A	D	1-1	Pentland (pen)
4		30	Portsmouth	H	L	3-5	Gittins, Barnes, Sugden
5	Oct	7	Clapton Orient	A	W	1-0	
6		14	Plymouth Argyle	H	L	0-1	
7		21	Southampton	A	L	0-4	
8		28	Clapton Orient	H	W	2-0	Walker, Downing
9	Nov	4	Southampton	H	L	2-4	Sugden (2)
		11	Brighton	H		0-1*	
10		20	Plymouth Argyle	A	W	2-0	Walker, Barnes
11	Dec	4	Brighton	A	L	0-1	
12		30	Brighton	H	L	2-3	

* (Abanonded after 20 minutes due to fog)

Southern Professional Charity Cup

No details recorded

Anderson	Barnes	Cannon	Corbett	Downing	Fidler	Gittens	Hitchcock	Lowe	Lintott	McDonald	McLean	Mitchell	Morris	Pentland	Rogers	Shaw	Skilton	Snelgrove	Sugden	Walker	White	Yenson
6	11				3	10	9				5	4		7	8	1					2	
	11		2		3	10	9		6		5			7	8	1						4
	11				3	10			6	2	5	4		7	8	1				9		
	11				3	10			6	2	5			7		1			8	9		4
	11				3	10			6	2	5			7	8	1				9		4
	11				3	10			6		5	4		7	8	1				9	2	
	11				3	10			6		5	4		7		1	8			9	2	
	11				3	10			6		5	4		7		1	8			9	2	
	11			6	3	10					5	4				1	8			9	2	7
	11			6	3	10			5			4		7		1	8			9	2	
	11			6	3	10			5			4		7		1	8			9	2	
	11			6	3	10			5			4		7		1	8			9	2	
	11			6	3	10					5	4		7		1	8			9	2	
	11			6	3	10			5					7		1	8			9	2	4
	11			6	3	10					5			7		1	8			9	2	4
	11			6	3	10			5					7		1	8			9	2	4
	11			6	3	10					5			7		1	8			9	2	4
	11			6	3	10			5					7		1	8			9	2	4
	11			6		10			5	3				7		1	8			9	2	4
	11			6		10				3	5			7		1			8	9	2	4
	11			6		10				3	5			7		1			8	9	2	4
				6	3	10			5					7		1			8	9	2	4
	11			6	3	10			4		5			7		1			8		2	9
	11			6	3	10					5	4		7		1	8			9	2	
	11			6	3	10			4		5			7		1			8	9	2	
	11			6	3	10					5			7		1			8	9	2	4
	11	8		6	2	10			4	3	5			7		1				9		
	11	8		6	3	10			4	2	5			7		1				9		
	11	8		6	3	10				2	5			7		1	9					4
	11	8		6	3	10			4	2	5			7		1	9					
	11	8		6	3	10			4	2	5			7		1	9					
	11	8		6	3	10				2	5			7		1	9					4
	11	8		6	3	10			4	2	5			7		1	9					
	11	8		6	3	10				2	5			7		1	9					4
	11			6	3	10					5	4		7		1	9	8			2	
	11	8		6	3	10				2	5			7		1				9		4
	11			6				3					5	7		1		8	10	9	2	4
				6				3					5	7		1		8	10	9	2	4
1	36	9	1	30	33	36	2	2	22	15	28	12	2	37	5	38	21	3	9	28	25	21
	10	6		4		16	2		1					14	1		5	1	4	15	1	
	11			6		10			5	3				7		1			8	9	2	4
	11			6	3	10			4		5			7		1			8	9	2	
	2			2	1	2			2	1	1			2		2			2	2	2	1
	1																			1		
	11	8		6	3	10			4	2	5			7		1	9					
	1	1		1	1	1			1	1	1			1		1	1					
		1																				
1	39	10	1	33	35	39	2	2	25	17	30	12	2	40	5	41	22	3	11	30	27	22
	11	7		4		16	2		1					14	1		5	1	4	16	1	

1908-09

Southern League (Div 1)

	P	W	D	L	F	A	Pts
Northampton Town	40	25	5	10	90	45	55
Swindon Town	40	22	5	13	96	55	49
Southampton	40	19	10	11	67	58	48
Portsmouth	40	18	10	12	68	60	46
Bristol Rovers	40	17	9	14	60	63	43
Exeter City	40	18	6	16	56	65	42
New Brompton	40	17	7	16	48	59	41
Reading	40	11	18	11	60	57	40
Luton Town	40	17	6	17	59	60	40
Plymouth Argyle	40	15	10	15	46	47	40
Millwall	40	16	6	18	59	61	38
Southend United	40	14	10	16	52	54	38
Clapton Orient (Res)	40	15	8	17	52	55	38
Watford	40	14	9	17	51	64	37
Queen's Park Rangers	40	12	12	16	52	50	36
Crystal Palace	40	12	12	16	62	62	36
West Ham United	40	16	4	20	56	60	36
Brighton & Hove Albion	40	14	7	19	60	61	35
Norwich City	40	12	11	17	59	75	35
Coventry City	40	15	4	21	64	91	34
Brentford	40	13	7	20	59	74	33

Western League

	P	W	D	L	F	A	Pts
Brighton & Hove Albion	12	7	2	3	23	13	16
Queen's Park Rangers	12	6	1	5	28	24	13
Crystal Palace	12	5	2	5	23	22	12
Luton Town	12	5	2	5	24	24	12
Croydon Common	12	5	2	5	16	24	12
Reading	12	4	2	6	19	21	10
Leyton	12	4	1	7	16	21	9

Match No.	Date		Opponents	Location	Result		Scorers	Attenc
1	Sep	1	West Ham United	A	L	0-2		7
2		7	Watford	H	W	2-0	McKenzie, Barnes	4
3		10	Northampton Town	A	D	0-0		6
4		14	Portsmouth	H	D	0-0		5
5		16	Watford	A	D	0-0		3
6		19	Plymouth Argyle	H	W	1-0	Cannon	10
7		23	Reading	A	L	0-2		4
8		28	Brentford	A	D	0-0		5
9	Oct	3	Portsmouth	A	L	1-3	Barnes	10
10		12	Coventry City	H	W	4-2	Downing (2), Barnes, Gittens	7
11		17	West Ham United	H	W	3-0	Skilton (2), Rogers	6
12		21	Crystal Palace	A	L	0-3		5
13		26	New Brompton	H	W	2-1	Rogers, Cannon	2
14	Nov	2	Southend United	H	W	2-1	Drake, Barnes	5
15		7	Brentford	H	W	3-0	Drake (2), Barnes	10
16		11	Brighton	A	D	1-1	Barnes	5
17		21	Swindon Town	A	L	1-3	Barnes	5
18		23	Clapton Orient	H	L	0-3		2
19	Dec	5	Millwall	H	D	2-2	Rogers (2)	7
20		25	Norwich City	H	D	2-2	Rogers, Downing	20
21		26	Southampton	A	W	4-1	Skilton, Downing, Rogers, Law	14
22		28	Millwall	A	W	1-0	Greer	5
23	Jan	25	Bristol Rovers	H	W	4-2	Rogers, Drake, Greer, Morris	5
24	Feb	8	Luton Town	A	L	0-1		5
25		20	Exeter City	H	D	1-1	Skilton	7
26		24	Exeter City	A	L	0-1		4
27	Mar	1	Coventry City	A	L	1-2	Drake	5
28		10	New Brompton	A	L	0-1		3
29		15	Luton Town	H	W	4-0	Barnes (2), Downing (pen), Morris	2
30		22	Brighton	H	L	1-2	Downing	3
31		27	Swindon Town	H	W	5-1	Skilton (3), Rogers, Greer	8
32		29	Bristol Rovers	A	D	0-0		2
33	Apr	3	Crystal Palace	H	D	1-1	Greer	6
34		9	Southampton	H	L	1-2	Greer	12
35		10	Plymouth Argyle	A	L	0-2		7
36		12	Norwich City	A	L	2-3	Greer, Rogers	10
37		13	Reading	H	L	2-3	Barnes, Cannon	2
38		19	Northampton Town	H	D	1-1	Skilton	3
39		26	Clapton Orient	A	L	0-1		4
40		28	Southend United	A	D	0-0		2

Appearar
G

FA Cup

R1	Jan	16	West Ham United	H	D	0-0		17
rep		20	West Ham United	A	L	0-1		10

Appearar
G

FA Charity Shield

1	Aug	29	Manchester United	N*	L	0-4		10

* Played at Stamford Bridge

Appearar
G

Total - Appearar
Total - G

Western League

1	Sep	5	Croydon Common	H	W	2-0
2		12	Croydon Common	A	L	1-3
3		30	Luton Town	A	L	1-8
4	Oct	19	Leyton	A	L	1-2
5		30	Reading	H	W	6-1
6	Dec	7	Brighton	H	L	0-1
7		14	Luton Town	H	W	2-0
8		16	Crystal Palace	A	D	2-2
9	Jan	4	Crystal Palace	H	W	5-1
10		20	Brighton	A	W	4-3
11		27	Reading	A	L	1-2
12	Feb	1	Leyton	H	W	3-1

London Challenge Cup

R1	Oct	5	Tottenham Hotspur	A	L	0-1

London Professional Charity Fund

	Mar	1	Fulham	A	L	1-2

Southern Professional Charity Cup

No details recorded

Cannon	Downing	Drake	Duff	Fidler	Gillespie	Gittens	Greer	King	Law	Lintott	MacDonald	McDonald	McEwan	McKenzie	McLean	McNaught	Mitchell	Morris	Rogers	Shaw	Skilton	Snelgrove
8	6	10		3						4	7	2		9	5					1		
8	6	10	4	3						5	7	2		9						1		
8	6	10		3								2		9	5	7	4			1		
8	6	10		3						5		2		9			4		7	1		
8	6	10		3					11			2		9	5		4		7	1		
8	6		4	3		10				5		2		9					7	1		
8	6			3		10						2		9			4	5	7	1		
8	6			3		10						2					4	5	7	1	9	
8	6			3		10				5	7	2					4			1	9	
	6			3		10					7	2		9	5		4		8	1		
	6		4	3		10				5	7	2							8	1	9	
	6	10		3							7	2			5		4		8	1	9	
8	6	10		3						5	9	2					4		7	1		
8	6	10		3							9	2			5		4		7	1		
	6	10		3							7	2			5		4		8	1	9	
8	6	10		3						5	7	2					4			1	9	
		10		3				8		6	7	2			5		4			1	9	
		10		3				8			7	2		6	5		4			1	9	
	6	9	4	3	2				11		7							5	8	1		
	6	10	4	3			9				7	2						5	8	1		
7	6		4						11			2	3					5	8	1	9	
	6		4	3			9		11		7	2					5		8	1		
	6	10	4	3			9				7	2						5	8	1		
	6	10	4	3			9				7	2						5	8	1		
7	6	10	4	3			9					2						5		1	8	
	6	10	4	3								2				7		5	9	1		8
	6	10	4	3								2				7		5	9	1		8
	6		4	3			10				7	2						5	9	1		8
	6		4	3								2				7		5	10	1	9	8
	6		4	3								2				7		5	10	1	9	8
	6		4	3			10					2				7		5		1	9	8
	6			3			10					2				7	4	5		1	9	8
	6			3			10					2				7	4	5		1	9	8
			4	3			10					2				7	6	5	8	1	9	
			4	3			10					2				7	6	5	8	1	9	
9			4	3			10					2			6	7		5	8	1		
9			6	3			10	8				2				7	4	5		1		
				3			10					2			6	7	4	5	8	1	9	
9				3			10					2			6	7	4	5		1	8	
9				3			10					2			6	7	4	5	8	1		
8	31	19	20	39	1	6	16	3	4	9	18	39	1	9	13	15	23	23	27	40	19	8
3	6	5				1	6		1					1				2	9		8	

Cannon	Downing	Drake	Duff	Fidler	Gillespie	Gittens	Greer	King	Law	Lintott	MacDonald	McDonald	McEwan	McKenzie	McLean	McNaught	Mitchell	Morris	Rogers	Shaw	Skilton	Snelgrove
	6	10	4	3			9				7	2						5	8	1		
	6		4	3			9		11		7	2					5		8	1		
	2	1	2	2			2		1		2	2					1	1	2	2		

Cannon	Downing	Drake	Duff	Fidler	Gillespie	Gittens	Greer	King	Law	Lintott	MacDonald	McDonald	McEwan	McKenzie	McLean	McNaught	Mitchell	Morris	Rogers	Shaw	Skilton	Snelgrove
8	6			3		10				4		2			5	7				1	9	
1	1			1		1				1		1			1	1				1	1	

Cannon	Downing	Drake	Duff	Fidler	Gillespie	Gittens	Greer	King	Law	Lintott	MacDonald	McDonald	McEwan	McKenzie	McLean	McNaught	Mitchell	Morris	Rogers	Shaw	Skilton	Snelgrove
9	34	20	22	42	1	7	18	3	5	10	20	42	1	9	14	16	24	24	29	43	20	8
3	6	5				1	6		1					1				2	9		8	

1909-10

Southern League (Div 1)

	P	W	D	L	F	A	Pts
Brighton & Hove Albion	42	23	13	6	69	28	59
Swindon Town	42	22	10	10	92	46	54
Queen's Park Rangers	42	19	13	10	56	47	51
Northampton Town	42	22	4	16	90	44	48
Southampton	42	16	16	10	64	55	48
Portsmouth	42	20	7	15	70	63	47
Crystal Palace	42	20	6	16	69	50	46
Coventry City	42	19	8	15	71	60	46
West Ham United	42	15	15	12	69	56	45
Clapton Orient (Res)	42	16	11	15	60	46	43
Plymouth Argyle	42	16	11	15	61	54	43
New Brompton	42	19	5	18	76	74	43
Bristol Rovers	42	16	10	16	37	48	42
Brentford	42	16	9	17	50	58	41
Luton Town	42	15	11	16	72	92	41
Millwall	42	15	7	20	45	59	37
Norwich City	42	13	9	20	59	78	35
Exeter City	42	14	6	22	60	69	34
Watford	42	10	13	19	51	76	33
Southend United	42	12	9	21	51	90	33
Croydon Common	42	13	5	24	52	96	31
Reading	42	7	10	25	38	73	24

Match No.	Date		Opponents	Location	Result		Scorers	Atte
1	Sep	1	Watford	H	W	4-3	Whyman (2), Hartwell, Travers (pen)	
2		4	Southend United	A	W	1-0	Barnes	
3		8	Watford	A	D	1-1	McNaught	
4		11	Clapton Orient	H	W	2-1	Steer, Whyman	
5		18	Plymouth Argyle	A	W	2-0	Steer, McNaught	
6		25	Southampton	H	D	1-1	Steer	1
7	Oct	2	Croydon Common	A	W	3-0	Travers (2), Steer	
8		4	Reading	H	W	1-0	Steer	
9		9	Millwall	H	L	1-2	McNaught	1
10		16	New Brompton	A	D	1-1	Greer	
11		18	Coventry City	H	W	4-0	Steer (3), Travers	
12		23	Northampton Town	H	W	2-0	Steer, Barnes	1
13		30	Exeter City	H	W	2-0	Barnes, McNaught	1
14	Nov	6	Luton Town	A	D	1-1	Steer	
15		13	Swindon Town	H	L	0-3		1
16		20	Crystal Palace	A	W	1-0	Steer	1
17		27	Brighton	H	W	1-0	Steer	
18	Dec	4	West Ham United	A	W	2-1	Barnes, Hartwell	1
19		11	Portsmouth	H	L	3-5	Whyman, Steer (2)	
20		25	Norwich City	H	W	1-0	Wilson	2
21		28	Coventry City	A	L	0-4		
22	Jan	1	Brentford	A	W	1-0	Steer	1
23		8	Southend United	H	D	2-2	Steer (2)	
24		22	Clapton Orient	A	W	1-0	Steer	
25		29	Plymouth Argyle	H	W	2-1	Whyman, Travers	
26	Feb	12	Croydon Common	H	D	4-4	Barnes (2), Whyman, Travers	
27		26	New Brompton	H	W	1-0	Steer	
28	Mar	12	Exeter City	A	D	0-0		
29		14	Bristol Rovers	A	L	0-2		1
30		19	Luton Town	H	W	4-0	Barnes (2), Steer (2)	
31		25	Brentford	H	D	0-0		2
32		28	Norwich City	A	D	0-0		1
33		30	Reading	A	D	0-0		
34	Apr	2	Crystal Palace	H	L	1-2	Swann	1
35		7	Northampton Town	A	D	0-0		
36		9	Brighton	A	L	0-2		1
37		13	Southampton	A	D	1-1	Steer	
38		16	West Ham United	H	D	3-3	Barnes, Travers, Whyman	
39		18	Millwall	A	L	0-1		
40		23	Portsmouth	A	L	0-4		
41		28	Swindon Town	A	L	0-1		
42		30	Bristol Rovers	H	W	2-1	Whyman, Mitchell (pen)	

Appeara

G

FA Cup

	Date		Opponents	Location	Result		Scorers	
R1	Jan	15	Norwich City	A	D	0-0		1
rep		19	Norwich City	H	W	3-0	Steer, McNaught, Whyman	
R2	Feb	5	Southend United	A	D	0-0		
rep		9	Southend United	H	W	3-2	Steer (2), Travers	1
R3		19	West Ham United	A	D	1-1	Steer	3
rep		24	West Ham United	H	W	1-0 aet	Steer	1
R4	Mar	5	Barnsley	A	L	0-1		2

Appeara

G

Total - Appeara

Total - G

London Challenge Cup

	Date		Opponents	Location	Result		
R1	Sep	16	Clapton	A	W		
R2	Oct	11	Chelsea	A	L	0-1	
SF	Nov	8	Tottenham Hotspur	N*	D	0-0	1
rep		15	Tottenham Hotspur	N**	L	1-4	1

* Played at Stamford Bridge, ** Played at Craven Cottage

London Professional Charity Fund

No details recorded

Southern Professional Charity Cup

	Date		Opponents	Location
	Sep	27	Crystal Palace	H

Dine	Ferguson	Fidler	Greer	Hartwell	Logan	McDonald	McNaught	Mitchell	Morris	Radnage	Shaw	Steer	Swann	Travers	Wake	Wentworth	Whyman	Wilson	Wyatt
		3		5	2		7	4			1	8		9	6		10		
		3		5	2		7	4			1	8		9	6		10		
		3		5		2	7	4			1	8		9	6		10		
		3				2	7			5	1	8		9	6	4	10		
		3				2	7	4	5		1	8		9	6		10		
		3				2	7	4	5		1	8		9	6		10		
		3	10	5		2	7	4			1	8		9	6				
		3	10	5		2	7	4			1	8		9	6				
		3		5		2	7	4			1		8	9	6		10		
		3	11	5		2	7	4			1	8		9	6		10		
		3	11	5		2	7	4			1	8		9	6		10		
		3	10	5		2	7	4			1	8		9	6				
		3		5		2	7	4			1	8		9	6		10		
		3		5		2	7	4			1	8		9	6		10		
		3	10	5		2	7	4			1	8		9			6		
		3	10	5		2	7	4			1	8			6		9		
			10	5	3	2	7	4			1	8			6		9		
			10	5	3	2	7	4			1	8			6		9		
			10	5	3	2	7	4			1	8			6		9		
		3		5		2		4			1	8		7	6		9	10	
		3			5	2	7	4			1	8		9	6		10		
		3		5		2	7	4		6	1	9		8			10		
		3		5		2	7	4			1	9		8	6		10		
		3		5		2	7	4			1	9		8	6		10		
		3	10	5		2	7	4			1	8		9			6		
		3		5	2		7	4			1	9		8	6		10		
		3		5		2	7	4			1	9		8	6		10		
		3		5		2			4		1	9		8	6		10		7
		3		5		2			4		1	9		8	6		10		7
		3		5		2			4		1	9		8	6		10		7
		3		5		2			4		1		8	9	6		10		7
		3		5		2					1	9		8	6	4	10		7
		3		5		2					1	9	7	8	6	4	10		
		3		5		2					1	9	8		6	4	10		7
		3		5		2					1	9		8	6	4	10		7
		3	10	5		2					1			8	6	4	9		7
		3		5		2	7				1	9		8	6	4	10		
4		3	8	5		2	7				1			9	6		10		
		3		5		2	7	4			1	9		8	6		10		
		3	8	5		2		4			1	9			6		10		7
		3	8	5		2	7	4			1	9			6		10		
		3	8	5		2		4			1	9			6		10		7
1		39	16	38	7	39	30	30	6	2	42	38	4	34	39	7	39	1	10
			1	2			4	1				22	1	7			8	1	

Dine	Ferguson	Fidler	Greer	Hartwell	Logan	McDonald	McNaught	Mitchell	Morris	Radnage	Shaw	Steer	Swann	Travers	Wake	Wentworth	Whyman	Wilson	Wyatt
		3		5		2	7	4			1	9		8	6		10		
		3		5		2	7	4			1	9		8	6		10		
		3		5		2	7	4			1	9		8	6		10		
		3		5		2	7	4			1	9		8	6		10		
	7	3		5		2		4			1	9		8	6		10		
	7	3		5		2		4			1	9		8	6		10		
		3		5		2	7	4			1	9		8	6		10		
	2	7		7		7	5	7			7	7		7	7		7		
							1					5		1			1		

Dine	Ferguson	Fidler	Greer	Hartwell	Logan	McDonald	McNaught	Mitchell	Morris	Radnage	Shaw	Steer	Swann	Travers	Wake	Wentworth	Whyman	Wilson	Wyatt
1	2	46	16	45	7	46	35	37	6	2	49	45	4	41	46	7	46	1	10
			1	2			5	1				27	1	8			9	1	

1910-11

Southern League (Div 1)

	P	W	D	L	F	A	Pts
Swindon Town	38	24	5	9	80	31	53
Northampton Town	38	18	12	8	54	27	48
Brighton & Hove Albion	38	20	8	10	58	35	48
Crystal Palace	38	17	13	8	55	48	47
West Ham United	38	17	11	10	63	46	45
Queen's Park Rangers	38	13	14	11	52	42	40
Clapton Orient (Res)	38	16	8	14	57	52	40
Plymouth Argyle	38	15	9	14	54	55	39
Luton Town	38	15	8	15	67	63	38
Norwich City	38	15	8	15	46	48	38
Coventry City	38	16	6	16	65	68	38
Brentford	38	14	9	15	41	42	37
Exeter City	38	14	9	15	51	53	37
Watford	38	13	9	16	49	65	35
Millwall	38	11	9	18	42	54	31
Bristol Rovers	38	10	10	18	42	55	30
Southampton	38	11	8	19	42	67	30
New Brompton	38	11	8	19	34	65	30
Southend United	38	10	9	19	47	64	29
Portsmouth	38	8	11	19	34	53	27

Match No.	Date		Opponents	Location	Result		Scorers	Atter
1	Sep	3	Coventry City	H	W	5-0	Whyman (2), Bradshaw (2), Hartwell	15
2		10	New Brompton	A	L	0-1		10
3		12	West Ham United	H	L	0-2		14
4		17	Millwall	H	W	2-1	Barnes, McKie	15
5		24	Norwich City	A	D	0-0		9
6	Oct	1	West Ham United	A	L	0-3		15
7		8	Luton Town	H	D	3-3	Steer, Browning, McNaught	12
8		15	Portsmouth	A	D	1-1	Browning	9
9		22	Northampton Town	H	D	1-1	Steer	10
10		29	Brighton	A	L	1-2	Steer	12
11	Nov	5	Exeter City	H	W	1-0	Browning	8
12		12	Swindon Town	A	L	1-2	Browning	8
13		19	Bristol Rovers	H	L	1-2	Steer	9
14		26	Crystal Palace	A	L	1-2	Browning	6
15	Dec	3	Brentford	H	W	2-0	Browning, Whyman	15
16		10	Clapton Orient	A	L	1-2	Browning	4
17		17	Watford	H	W	4-1	Browning (3), McKie	4
18		24	Plymouth Argyle	A	D	1-1	Steer	8
19		26	Southampton	A	L	0-1		10
20		27	Southampton	H	W	3-1	McKie (2), Whyman	12
21		31	Coventry City	A	L	2-3	Browning, McKie	6
22	Jan	7	New Brompton	H	W	5-0	Browning (2), Steer (2), Whyman	5
23		21	Millwall	A	D	1-1	Steer	6
24		28	Norwich City	H	D	1-1	Browning	6
25	Feb	11	Luton Town	A	W	1-0	McKie	6
26		18	Portsmouth	H	W	1-0	McKie	7
27		25	Northampton Town	A	D	0-0		5
28	Mar	4	Brighton	H	D	0-0		6
29		11	Exeter City	A	D	2-2	McKie, Steer	8
30		18	Swindon Town	H	W	1-0	Browning	8
31		25	Bristol Rovers	A	D	0-0		6
32	Apr	1	Crystal Palace	H	D	0-0		8
33		8	Brentford	A	D	1-1	Hartwell	8
34		14	Southend United	H	D	1-1	Browning	15
35		15	Clapton Orient	H	W	5-3	McKie (2), Brown (2), Whyman	7
36		17	Southend United	A	W	2-1	Barnes, Browning	6
37		22	Watford	A	L	0-2		6
38		29	Plymouth Argyle	H	W	1-0	Browning	6

Appearar
G

FA Cup

R1	Jan	14	Bradford	A	L	3-5	McKie (2), Steer	25

Appearar
G

Total - Appearar
Total - G

London Challenge Cup

R1	Sep	19	Arsenal	A	L	0-3	1

London Professional Charity Fund

No details recorded

Southern Professional Charity Cup

R1	No details recorded				
R2	No details recorded				
SF	Nov	28	Swindon Town	N*	P-P
SF	Apr	3	Swindon Town	N*	P-P
SF		18	Swindon Town	N**	

* Played at Stamford Bridge, ** Played at Tottenham Hotspur

Bradshaw	Brindley	Brown	Browning	Butterworth	Fidler	Hartwell	Law	Lee	McDonald	McKie	McNaught	Mitchell	Morris	Pullen	Radnage	Shaw	Steer	Wake	Whyman	Wilson
8	7				3	5			2			4				1	9	6	10	
8	7				3	5			2			4				1	9	6	10	
	7				3	5			2	8		4				1	9	6	10	
	7				3	5			2	8		4				1	9	6	10	
					3	5			2		7	4				1	9	6	10	8
					3	5			2	8	7	4				1	9	6	10	
			10		3	5			2		7	4				1	9	6		8
			10		3	5			2		7	4				1	9	6		8
	7		10		3	5			2			4				1	9	6		8
	7		10		3	5			2			4				1	9	6	8	
	7		10		3	5			2			4				1	9	6	8	
			10		3				2		7	4	5			1	9	6	8	
			10		3			2		9	7	4	5		6	1	8			
			10	6	3			2		9	7	4	5			1			8	
			10	6				3	2	9	7	4	5			1			8	
			10	6				3	2	9	7	4	5			1	8			
	11		10	6	3				2	9		4	5			1	8		7	
	11		10	6	3				2	9		4	5			1	8		7	
	11		10	6	3	5			2	9		4				1	8		7	
	11		10	6	3				2	9		4	5			1	8		7	
	11		10	6	3	5			2	9		4				1	8		7	
	11		10	6	3				2	9		4	5			1	8		7	
	7		10	4	3				2	9		5				1	8	6		
	11		10	4	3				2	9		5				1	8	6	7	
	11		10	4	3				2	9		5				1	8	6	7	
	11		10	4	3				2	9		5				1	8	6	7	
			10	4	3				2	9		5				1	8	6	7	
		8	10	4	3				2	9		5				1		6	7	
			10	4	3				2	9		5				1	8	6	7	
			10	4	3				2	9		5				1	8	6	7	
			10	4	3				2	9		5				1	8	6	7	
			10	4	3				2	9		5				1	8	6	7	
		8		4	3	5			2		7					1	9	6		10
		8	10	4	3	5			2	9						1		6	7	
		8	10	4	3	5			2	9						1		6	7	
		8	10	4	3	5			2	9	7					1		6		
		(8)	10	6	3	5			2	9	7	4				1				
		8	10	4	3	5	7			9				2		1		6		
2	17	6	31	25	36	19	1	4	35	28	12	33	9	1	1	38	30	27	28	5
2		2	18			2				10	1						9		6	
	11		10	6	3				2	9		4	5			1	8		7	
	1		1	1	1				1	1		1	1			1	1		1	
										2							1			
2	18	6	32	26	37	19	1	4	36	29	12	34	10	1	1	39	31	27	29	5
2		2	18			2				12	1						10		6	

1911-12

Southern League (Div 1)

	P	W	D	L	F	A	Pts
Queen's Park Rangers	38	21	11	6	59	35	53
Plymouth Argyle	38	23	6	9	63	31	52
Northampton Town	38	22	7	9	82	41	51
Swindon Town	38	21	6	11	82	50	48
Brighton & Hove Albion	38	19	9	10	73	35	47
Coventry City	38	17	8	13	66	54	42
Crystal Palace	38	15	10	13	70	46	40
Millwall	38	15	10	13	60	57	40
Watford	38	13	10	15	56	68	36
Stoke City	38	13	10	15	51	63	36
Reading	38	11	14	13	43	69	36
Norwich City	38	10	14	14	40	60	34
West Ham United	38	13	7	18	64	69	33
Brentford	38	12	9	17	66	65	33
Exeter City	38	11	11	16	48	62	33
Southampton	38	10	11	17	46	63	31
Bristol Rovers	38	9	13	16	41	62	31
New Brompton	38	11	9	18	35	72	31
Luton Town	38	9	10	19	49	61	28
Clapton Orient (Res)	38	7	11	20	29	60	25

Match No.	Date		Opponents	Location	Result		Scorers	Atter
1	Sep	2	Plymouth Argyle	A	W	1-0	Revill	1
2		9	Reading	H	W	3-0	McKie, Revill	1
3		16	Watford	A	W	3-0	McKie, Thornton, Revill	
4		23	New Brompton	H	W	3-0	Revill (2), McKie	1
5		30	Exeter City	A	D	1-1	McKie (pen)	
6	Oct	7	Brentford	H	W	4-0	McKie (2), Revill, Smith	1
7		14	Luton Town	H	W	2-0	Revill, McKie	1
8		21	Millwall	A	D	1-1	Barnes	2
9		28	West Ham United	H	W	4-1	McKie, Smith, Revill, Thornton	2
10	Nov	4	Bristol Rovers	A	W	2-0	McKie, Revill	1
11		11	Swindon Town	H	L	1-3	McKie	2
12		18	Northampton Town	A	L	1-5	McKie	
13		25	Brighton	H	W	2-0	Thornton (pen), Mitchell	
14	Dec	2	Stoke City	A	W	2-0*	Barnes, McKie	
15		9	Coventry City	H	D	0-0		
16		16	Clapton Orient	A	W	1-0	Thornton	
17		23	Norwich City	H	L	1-2	Smith	
18		25	Crystal Palace	H	W	3-2	Thornton (2), Revill	
19		26	Crystal Palace	A	L	0-3		2
20		30	Plymouth Argyle	H	W	2-0	Revill (2)	
21	Jan	6	Reading	A	W	1-0	Ovens	
22		20	Watford	H	D	1-1	Browning	1
23		27	New Brompton	A	W	2-1	Barnes, Thornton	
24	Feb	3	Exeter City	H	D	0-0		
25		10	Brentford	A	W	2-1	Revill, Barnes	
26		17	Luton Town	A	W	3-1	Smith (2), McKie	
27		24	Millwall	H	D	1-1	Mitchell (pen)	
28	Mar	2	West Ham United	A	L	0-3		1
29		9	Bristol Rovers	H	W	4-2	Thornton (2), Revill, McKie	
30		16	Swindon Town	A	D	1-1	Smith	
31		23	Northampton Town	H	W	2-1	Smith, McKie	
32		30	Brighton	A	L	1-3	Revill	
33	Apr	5	Southampton	H**	D	1-1	Tosswill	2
34		6	Stoke City	H**	W	1-0	Whyman	2
35		8	Southampton	A	D	0-0		1
36		13	Coventry City	A	D	0-0		
37		20	Clapton Orient	H	W	1-0	Thornton	
38		27	Norwich City	A	D	1-1	Smith	

* Match Abandoned after 75 minutes, result stood, ** Played at White City

Appeara
G

FA Cup

R1	Jan	13	Bradford City	H	D	0-0		1
rep		18	Bradford City	A	L	0-4		1

Appeara
G

FA Charity Shield

1	May	4	Blackburn Rovers	N +	L	1-2	Revill	

+ Played at White Hart Lane

Appeara
G

Total - Appeara
Total - G

London Challenge Cup

R1	Sep	18	Arsenal	H	L	0-2

London Professional Charity Fund

	Oct	30	Clapton Orient	H	L	0-1

Southern Professional Charity Cup

R1	Oct	11	Crystal Palace	H	W	3-0
R2	Nov	22	Southend United	A	L	4-5

Browing	Butterworth	Fidler	King	McDonald	McKie	Mitchell	Nicholls	Owens	Pullen	Revill	Shaw	Smith	Thornton	Tosswill	Wake	Whyman
0	4	3		2	9	5				8	1	7			6	
	4	3		2	9	5				8	1	7	10		6	
	4	3		2	9	5				8	1	7	10		6	
	4	3		2	9	5				8	1	7	10		6	
	4			2	9	5		3		8	1	7	10		6	
				2	9	5		3		8	1	7	10		6	4
				2	9	5		3		8	1	7	10		6	4
				2	9	5			3	8	1	7	10		6	4
	4			2	9	5			3	8	1	7	10		6	
	4			2	9	5			3	8	1	7	10		6	
	4	3		2	9	5				8	1	7	10		6	
	4	3		2	9	5				8	1	7	10		6	
	4			2	9	5			3	8	1	7	10		6	
	4			2	9	5			3	8	1		10		6	7
	4				9	5		2	3	8	1	7	10		6	
					9	5		2	3	8	1	7	10		6	4
					9	5		2	3	8	1	7	10		6	4
	4	3				5		2		8	1	7	10		6	9
0			8		9	5		2	3		1	7			6	4
0						5		2	3	8	1	7	9		6	4
0				2		5		4	3	8	1	7	9		6	
0				2		5	1	4	3			7	9		6	8
0				2		5		4	3	8	1	7	9		6	
				2	9	5		4	3	8	1	7	10		6	
0				2	9	5		4	3	8	1	7			6	
				2	9	5		4	3	8	1	7	10		6	
0			9	2		5		4	3	8	1	7			6	
				2	9	5		4	3	8	1	7	10		6	
	4			2	9	5			3	8	1	7	10		6	
	4			2	9	5			3	8	1	7	10		6	
				2	9	5		4	3	8	1	7	10		6	
				2	9			4	3	8	1	7	10		6	5
				2	9	5		4	3	7	1		10	8	6	
				2	9	5		4	3	8	1	7	10		6	
			7	2		5		4	3	8	1		10	9	6	
				2	9	5		4	3	8	1	7	10		6	
				2		5		4	3	8	1	7	10	9	6	
				2	9	5		4	3	8	1	7	10		6	
8	15	7	3	32	30	37	1	25	28	36	37	35	34	3	38	11
1					16	2		1		15		8	10	1		1

Browing	Butterworth	Fidler	King	McDonald	McKie	Mitchell	Nicholls	Owens	Pullen	Revill	Shaw	Smith	Thornton	Tosswill	Wake	Whyman
0				2		5		4	3	8	1	7	9		6	
0			9	2		5		4	3	8	1				6	7
2			1	2		2		2	2	2	2	1	1		2	1

Browing	Butterworth	Fidler	King	McDonald	McKie	Mitchell	Nicholls	Owens	Pullen	Revill	Shaw	Smith	Thornton	Tosswill	Wake	Whyman
				2	9	5			3	8	1	7	10		6	4
				1	1	1			1	1	1	1	1		1	1
										1						

Browing	Butterworth	Fidler	King	McDonald	McKie	Mitchell	Nicholls	Owens	Pullen	Revill	Shaw	Smith	Thornton	Tosswill	Wake	Whyman
0	15	7	4	35	31	40	1	27	31	39	40	37	36	3	41	13
1					16	2		1		16		8	10	1		1

1912-13

Southern League (Div 1)

	P	W	D	L	F	A	Pts
Plymouth Argyle	38	22	6	10	77	36	50
Swindon Town	38	20	8	10	66	41	48
West Ham United	38	18	12	8	66	46	48
Queen's Park Rangers	38	18	10	10	46	36	46
Crystal Palace	38	17	11	10	55	36	45
Millwall	38	19	7	12	62	43	45
Exeter City	38	18	8	12	48	44	44
Reading	38	17	8	13	59	55	42
Brighton & Hove Albion	38	13	12	13	48	47	38
Northampton Town	38	12	12	14	61	48	36
Portsmouth	38	14	8	16	41	49	36
Merthyr Town	38	12	12	14	43	60	36
Coventry City	38	13	8	17	53	59	34
Watford	38	12	10	16	43	50	34
Gillingham	38	12	10	16	36	53	34
Bristol Rovers	38	12	9	17	55	64	33
Southampton	38	10	11	17	40	72	31
Norwich City	38	10	9	19	39	50	29
Brentford	38	11	5	22	42	55	27
Stoke City	38	10	4	24	39	75	24

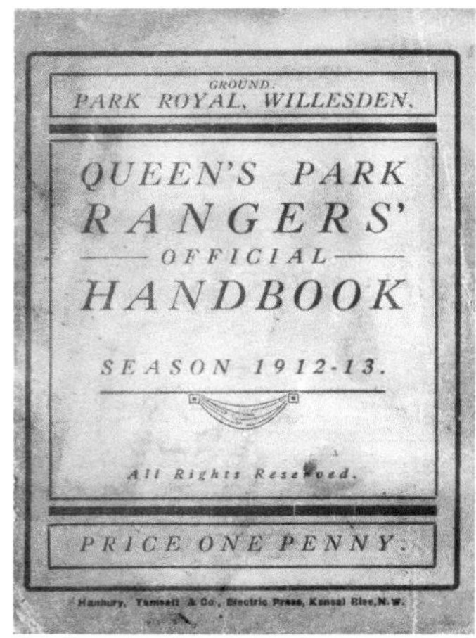

Match No.	Date		Opponents	Location	Result		Scorers	Atten
1	Sep	5	Plymouth Argyle	H	W	2-1	Birch (2)	10
2		7	Norwich City	H	W	1-0	Birch	9
3		14	Gillingham	A	D	0-0		7
4		21	Northampton Town	H	W	3-2	Birch, Anderson, Browning	12
5		28	Stoke City	A	D	0-0		6
6	Oct	5	Brentford	A	W	2-0	Wake, OG (Richards)	13
7		12	Millwall	H	D	1-1	Revill	16
8		19	Bristol Rovers	A	L	0-3		5
9		26	Swindon Town	H	W	2-0	OG (Kay), Ovens	8
10	Nov	2	Portsmouth	A	D	1-1	Birch	12
11		9	Exeter City	H	W	2-1	Mitchell, Revill	8
12		16	West Ham United	A	L	0-1		10
13		23	Brighton	H	D	0-0		11
14	Dec	7	Watford	H	W	2-0	Birch (2)	8
15		14	Merthyr Town	A	D	0-0		3
16		21	Crystal Palace	H	W	2-0	Revill (2)	10
17		25	Southampton	H	W	1-0	Birch	20
18		26	Southampton	A	W	1-0	McKie	3
19		28	Norwich City	A	L	0-2		6
20		30	Coventry City	A	D	1-1	Thompson	5
21	Jan	4	Gillingham	H	W	2-0	Birch, Barnes	7
22		25	Stoke City	H	W	1-0	Whyman	9
23	Feb	8	Brentford	H	W	2-1	Birch, OG (Richards)	16
24		15	Millwall	A	L	1-2	Gaul	14
25		22	Northampton Town	A	D	0-0		6
26	Mar	1	Swindon Town	A	L	1-4	McKie	6
27		8	Portsmouth	H	D	1-1	Birch	8
28		15	Exeter City	A	L	1-3	Birch	6
29		21	Reading	A	L	0-1		15
30		22	West Ham United	H	L	0-1		15
31		24	Reading	H	D	1-1	Gaul	7
32		29	Brighton	A	L	1-4	Birch	5
33	Apr	5	Coventry City	H	W	4-0	Whyman, Gaul, Birch, Revill	6
34		10	Bristol Rovers	H	W	2-0	Gaul (2)	4
35		13	Watford	A	W	2-1	Gaul, Ovens	4
36		19	Merthyr Town	H	W	4-1	Ives (2), Gaul, Revill	7
37		23	Plymouth Argyle	A	L	0-2		4
38		26	Crystal Palace	A	W	2-1	Birch, Gaul	8

Appearar
G

FA Cup

R1	Jan	11	Halifax Town	H	W	4-2	Revill, Birch, Whyman, Ovens	11
R2	Feb	1	Middlesbrough	A	L	2-3	Birch (2)	25

Appearar
G

Total - Appearar
Total - G

London Challenge Cup

R1	Sep	23	London Caledonians	H	W	5-1
R2	Oct	21	West Ham United	A	L	0-2

London Professional Charity Fund

	Oct	7	Clapton Orient	A	W	3-2

Southern Professional Charity Cup

R1	Nov	18	Gillingham	A	W	1-0
R2	Feb	12	Crystal Palace	H	W	7-1
SF	Apr	3	Exeter City	H	W	2-0
F		28	Brighton & Hove Albion	N*	W	4-1

* Played at Millwall

Barnes	Birch	Broster	Browning	Day	Fidler	Gaul	Gregory	Higgins	Ives	Jackman	McDonald	McKie	Mitchell	Nicholls	Owens	Pullen	Revill	Sangster	Shaw	Thompson	Thornton	Wake	Weblin	Whyman	Wingrove	OG
1	9										2		5		4	3	8		1	7		6		10		
1	9										2		5		4	3			1	7	10	6				
1	9		10								2		5		4	3			1	7		6				
1	9		10								2		5		4	3		7	1			6				
1	9		10								2		5		4	3	8		1	7		6				
1	9		10								2		5		4	3	8		1	7		6				
1	9		10								2		5		4	3	8		1	7		6				
1	9		10								2		5		4	3	8		1	7		6				
1	9		10								2		5		4	3	8		1	7		6				
1	9		10								2		5		4	3	8	7	1					6		
1	9		10								2		5		4	3	8		1	7		6				
1	9		10								2		5		4	3	8		1	7		6				
1	9		10		3						2		5				8		1	7		6		4		
1	8						9				2		5		4	3			1	7		6		10		
1	8		10				9						5			3			1	7		6	2	4		
1	8					9							5			3	10		1	7		6	2	4		
1	8				2	9							5			3	10	7	1			6		4		
1	8	6			2							9	5			3	10	7	1					4		
1	8											9	5		4	3	10		1	7		6	2			
1	8											9	5		4	3	10		1	7		6	2			
1	8				2							9	5		4	3	10		1	7		6				
1	8				2								5		4	3	10		1	7		6		9		
1	8					9					2		5		4	3	10		1	7		6				
1	8					9					2	10	5		4	3			1	7		6				
1	8										2	10	5		4	3			1	7		6		9		
1	8										2	10	5		4	3			1	7		6		9		
1	8			9			10				2		5		4	3			1	7		6				
1	8			9							2		5	1	4	3	10			7				6		
	8			9		10		2		11			5		4	3			1	7		6				
1	8										2	9	5			3	10		1	7		4		6		
	8					9		2		11		10	5		4	3			1	7				6		
	8					9				11	2	10	5		4	3			1	7				6		
1	8					9							5		4	3	10		1	7			2	6		
1	8			9									5		4	3	10		1	7			2	6		
1	8					9							5		4	3	10		1	7			2	6		
	8	11				9			7				5		4	3	10		1				2	6		
1	8					9							5		4	3	10		1	7				6	2	
1	8	6				9							5		4	3	10		1	7			2			
4	38	3	12	4	5	12	3	2	1	3	22	10	38	1	32	37	26	4	37	33	1	27	9	20	1	
1	15		1			8			2			2	1		2		6			1		1		2		3
1	8				2								5		4	3	10		1	7		6		9		
1	8				2								5		4	3	10		1	7		6		9		
2	2				2								2		2	2	2		2	2		2		2		
	3														1		1							1		
6	40	3	12	4	7	12	3	2	1	3	22	10	40	1	34	39	28	4	39	35	1	29	9	22	1	
1	18		1			8			2			2	1		3		7			1		1		3		3

1913-14

Southern League (Div 1)

	P	W	D	L	F	A	Pts
Swindon Town	38	21	8	9	81	41	50
Crystal Palace	38	17	16	5	60	32	50
Northampton Town	38	14	19	5	50	37	47
Reading	38	17	10	11	43	36	44
Plymouth Argyle	38	15	13	10	46	42	43
West Ham United	38	15	12	11	61	60	42
Brighton & Hove Albion	38	15	12	11	43	45	42
Queen's Park Rangers	38	16	9	13	45	43	41
Portsmouth	38	14	12	12	57	48	40
Cardiff City	38	13	12	13	46	42	38
Southampton	38	15	7	16	55	54	37
Exeter City	38	10	16	12	39	38	36
Gillingham	38	13	9	16	48	49	35
Norwich City	38	9	17	12	49	51	35
Millwall	38	11	12	15	51	56	34
Southend United	38	10	12	16	41	66	32
Bristol Rovers	38	10	11	17	46	67	31
Watford	38	10	9	19	50	56	29
Merthyr Town	38	9	10	19	38	61	28
Coventry City	38	6	14	18	43	68	26

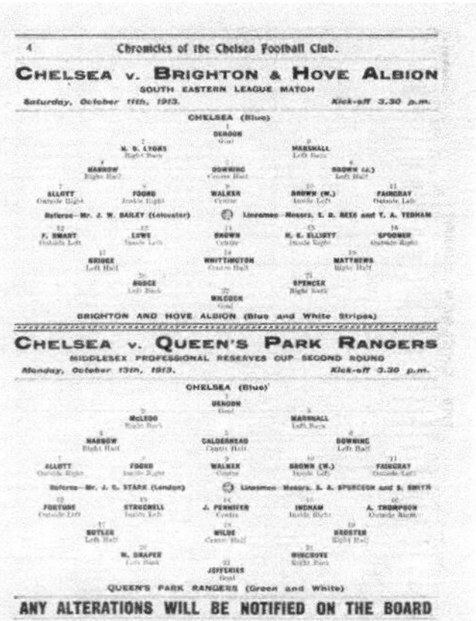
4 Chronicles of the Chelsea Football Club.

CHELSEA v. BRIGHTON & HOVE ALBION
SOUTH EASTERN LEAGUE MATCH
Saturday, October 11th, 1913. Kick-off 3.30 p.m.

CHELSEA (Blue)

BRIGHTON AND HOVE ALBION (Blue and White Stripes)

CHELSEA v. QUEEN'S PARK RANGERS
MIDDLESEX PROFESSIONAL RESERVES CUP SECOND ROUND
Monday, October 13th, 1913. Kick-off 3.30 p.m.

CHELSEA (Blue)

QUEEN'S PARK RANGERS (Green and White)

ANY ALTERATIONS WILL BE NOTIFIED ON THE BOARD

Match No.	Date		Opponents	Location	Result		Scorers
1	Sep	1	Swindon Town	A	L	0-3	
2		6	Gillingham	A	L	0-1	
3		13	Merthyr Town	H	L	0-1	
4		20	Northampton Town	A	D	2-2	Birch, Gaul
5		27	West Ham United	H	D	2-2	Miller, Birch
6	Oct	4	Southend United	A	W	2-1	Gregory, Birch
7		11	Plymouth Argyle	H	D	0-0	
8		18	Brighton	A	L	0-1	
9		25	Southampton	H	W	3-1	Gregory, Ives, Miller
10	Nov	1	Portsmouth	A	D	1-1	Pullen
11		8	Reading	H	W	1-0	Miller
12		15	Millwall	A	L	0-2	
13		22	Crystal Palace	H	W	3-0	Miller (2), Birch
14		29	Exeter City	A	D	0-0	
15	Dec	6	Coventry City	H	W	3-0	Birch (2), Baldock
16		13	Cardiff City	A	L	0-3	
17		20	Watford	H	W	3-2	Birch (2), Mitchell (pen)
18		25	Norwich City	H	D	1-1	Birch
19		26	Norwich City	A	W	3-2	Miller (3)
20		27	Gillingham	H	D	0-0	
21	Jan	3	Merthyr Town	A	W	2-1	Birch, Gregory
22		17	Northampton Town	H	D	0-0	
23		24	West Ham United	A	L	1-4	Miller
24	Feb	7	Southend United	H	D	0-0	
25		14	Plymouth Argyle	A	L	0-2	
26		28	Southampton	A	W	2-0	Birch, Gregory
27	Mar	12	Swindon Town	H	W	4-2	OG (Skiller), Miller (2), Birch
28		21	Millwall	H	W	1-0	Gregory
29		26	Portsmouth	H	W	1-0	Gregory
30		28	Crystal Palace	A	L	1-2	Whyman
31	Apr	4	Exeter City	H	L	2-3	Birch, Miller
32		10	Bristol Rovers	H	W	1-0	Birch
33		11	Coventry City	A	W	1-0	Birch
34		13	Bristol Rovers	A	L	1-2	Thompson
35		18	Cardiff City	H	L	0-2	
36		23	Brighton	H	W	3-0	Miller (2), Birch
37		25	Watford	A	L	0-2	
38		29	Reading	A	W	1-0	Thompson

Appeara

FA Cup

R1	Jan	10	Bristol City	H	D	2-2	Miller, Birch
rep		15	Bristol City	A	W	2-0 aet	Birch, Gregory
R2		31	Swansea Town	A	W	2-1	Birch (2)
R3	Feb	21	Birmingham City	A	W	2-1	Gregory, Miller
R4	Mar	7	Liverpool	A	L	1-2	Mitchell (pen)

Appeara

Total - Appeara

Total -

London Challenge Cup

R1	Sep	22	Arsenal	A	D	1-1
rep		29	Arsenal	H	L	2-3

London Professional Charity Fund

	Oct	2	Fulham	H	L	1-2

Southern Professional Charity Cup

R1	Oct	29	Brentford	A	W	2-1
R2	Feb	19	Norwich City	A	L	0-3

Birch	Blake	Broster	Fortune	Gaul	Gregory	Higgins	Ives	Jefferies	Matthews	Miller	Mitchell	Nicholls	Ovens	Pennifer	Pullen	Strugnell	Thompson	Wake	Weblin	Whyman	Wilde	Wingrove	OG
8							11			9	5	1	4		3	10	7			6		2	
8							11			9	5	1	4		3	10	7			6		2	
8				9			11				5	1	4		3	10	7	6				2	
8				9	10		11				5	1	4		3		7	6				2	
8					10		11	1		9	5				3		7	6		4		2	
				8	10	2	11			9	5	1	4		3		7	6					
8			11		10	2				9		1	4		3		7	6		5			
8					10	2	11			9	5	1	4		3		7	6					
					10	2	11			9	5	1	4		3	8	7	6					
					10	2	11			9	5	1	4		3	8	7	6					
8					10	2	11			9		1	4		3		7	6		5			
					10	2	11			9		1	4		3	8	7	6		5			
8					10	2	11			9	5	1	4		3		7	6					
8					10	2	11			9	5	1	4		3		7	6					
9					10	2	11				5	1	4		3		7	6					
8						2	11				5	1	4	9	3		7	6					
9					10	2	11				5	1			3		7	6		4			
8				9	10		11				5	1	4		3		7	6	2				
8					10	2	11			9	5	1	4		3		7			6			
8			11		10	2				9	5	1	4		3		7	6					
8			11		10	2				9	5	1	4		3		7	6					
8			11		10	2				9	5	1	4		3		7			6			
			11		10					9	5	1	4		3		7	6		8		2	
8			11			2						1	4	9	3	10	7	6		5			
			11		10						5	1		9	3	8	7	6		4		2	
8			11		10					9	5	1	2		3		7	6		4			
8		4			10		11			9	5	1	2		3		7			6			
8		4			10		11			9	5	1	2		3		7			6			
8	9	4			10		11				5	1	2		3		7			6			
8		4			10		11			9	5	1	2		3		7			6			
8					10		11			9	5	1	2		3		7	6		4			
8					10		11			9	5	1	2		3		7	6		4			
8					10		11			9	5	1			3		7	6		4		2	
8	9						11				5	1			3	10	7	6		4		2	
8							11			9	5	1			3	10	7	6		4		2	
8					10		11		1	9	5		2		3		7	6		4			
					10		11			9	5	1	4		3		7	6		8		2	
					10		11		1	9			4		3	8	7		2	6	5		
30	2	4	8	4	31	17	30	1	2	28	33	35	32	3	38	11	38	29	2	25	1	11	
16				1	6		1			14	1				1		2			1			1

Birch	Blake	Broster	Fortune	Gaul	Gregory	Higgins	Ives	Jefferies	Matthews	Miller	Mitchell	Nicholls	Ovens	Pennifer	Pullen	Strugnell	Thompson	Wake	Weblin	Whyman	Wilde	Wingrove	OG
8			11		10	2				9	5	1	4		3		7	6					
8			11		10	2				9	5	1	4		3		7	6					
8			11		10	2				9	5	1	4		3		7	6					
8			11		10	2				9	5	1	4		3		7	6					
8			11		10					9	5	1	4		3		7	6		4			
5			5		5	4				5	5	5	5		5		5	5		1			
4					2					2	1												

Birch	Blake	Broster	Fortune	Gaul	Gregory	Higgins	Ives	Jefferies	Matthews	Miller	Mitchell	Nicholls	Ovens	Pennifer	Pullen	Strugnell	Thompson	Wake	Weblin	Whyman	Wilde	Wingrove	OG
35	2	4	13	4	36	21	30	1	2	33	38	40	37	3	43	11	43	34	2	26	1	11	
20				1	8		1			16	2				1		2			1			1

1914-15

Southern League (Div 1)

	P	W	D	L	F	A	Pts
Watford	38	22	8	8	68	46	52
Reading	38	21	7	10	68	43	49
Cardiff City	38	22	4	12	72	38	48
West Ham United	38	18	9	11	58	47	45
Northampton Town	38	16	11	11	56	51	43
Southampton	38	19	5	14	78	74	43
Portsmouth	38	16	10	12	54	42	42
Millwall	38	16	10	12	50	51	42
Swindon Town	38	15	11	12	77	59	41
Brighton & Hove Albion	38	16	7	15	46	47	39
Exeter City	38	15	8	15	50	41	38
Queen's Park Rangers	38	13	12	13	55	56	38
Norwich City	38	11	14	13	53	56	36
Luton Town	38	13	8	17	61	73	34
Crystal Palace	38	13	8	17	47	61	34
Bristol Rovers	38	14	3	21	53	75	31
Plymouth Argyle	38	8	14	16	51	61	30
Southend United	38	10	8	20	44	64	28
Croydon Common	38	9	9	20	47	63	27
Gillingham	38	6	8	24	43	82	20

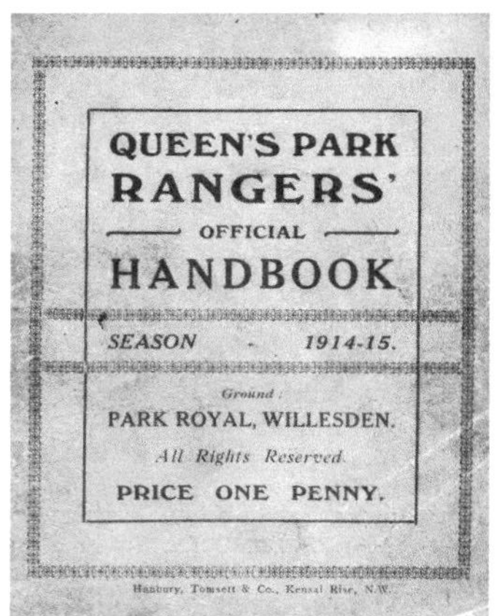

Match No.	Date		Opponents	Location	Result		Scorers	Atten
1	Sep	1	Millwall	A	L	1-3	Miller	6
2		5	Reading	H	L	0-1		4
3		12	Southampton	A	L	0-3		12
4		16	Luton Town	A	W	4-2	Birch (2), Donald, Whyman	4
5		19	Northampton Town	H	D	0-0		5
6		26	Watford	A	D	2-2	Birch, Whyman	5
7	Oct	3	Plymouth Argyle	H	D	1-1	Miller	6
8		10	West Ham United	A	D	2-2	Baldock (2)	7
9		17	Norwich City	H	D	1-1	Baldock	6
10		24	Gillingham	A	W	1-0	Thompson	7
11		31	Brighton	H	L	0-1		5
12	Nov	7	Cardiff City	A	L	0-2		10
13		14	Exeter City	H	L	0-2		10
14		28	Portsmouth	H	L	1-2	Thompson	4
15	Dec	5	Swindon Town	A	W	2-1	Simons, Birch	1
16		12	Southend United	H	W	4-2	Broster, Donald, Miller, Simons	4
17		19	Crystal Palace	A	D	2-2	Simons, Gregory	3
18		25	Bristol Rovers	A	W	3-1	Birch (2), Miller	8
19		26	Bristol Rovers	H	W	2-1	Miller, Simons	3
20		28	Millwall	H	L	0-1		12
21	Jan	2	Reading	A	D	2-2	Birch (2)	5
22		16	Southampton	H	W	4-3	Miller (2), Simons, Birch	4
23		23	Northampton Town	A	D	1-1	Miller	3
24	Feb	6	Plymouth Argyle	A	D	1-1	Birch	3
25		13	West Ham United	H	D	1-1	Birch	5
26		27	Gillingham	H	W	3-0	Miller (2), Mitchell	5
27	Mar	6	Brighton	A	L	0-1		4
28		13	Cardiff City	H	W	3-0	Miller (2), Gregory	4
29		18	Watford	H	L	2-5	Miller, Birch	5
30		20	Exeter City	A	W	1-0	Birch	3
31		24	Norwich City	A	L	1-2	Donald	3
32		27	Luton Town	H	L	0-3		3
33	Apr	2	Croydon Common	H	W	1-0	Baldock	3
34		3	Portsmouth	A	D	1-1	Birch	6
35		5	Croydon Common	A	L	0-1		6
36		10	Swindon Town	H	W	4-2	Birch, Baldock, Thompson, Miller	7
37		17	Southend United	A	D	1-1	Whyman	2
38		24	Crystal Palace	H	W	3-2	Simons (2), Donald	5
								Appearan
								G

FA Cup

R1	Jan	9	Glossop	H	W	2-1	Birch, Miller	7
R2		30	Leeds City	H	W	1-0	Simons	10
R3	Feb	20	Everton	H*	L	1-2	Birch	33

* Played at Stamford Bridge

Appearan
G

Total - Appearan
Total - G

London Challenge Cup

R1	Sep	21	Chelsea	H	W	1-0	
R2	Oct	19	Arsenal	A	L	1-2	4

London Professional Charity Fund

1	Sep	28	Fulham	A	L	0-2

Southern Professional Charity Cup

R1	Oct	8	Brentford	H	W	4-0

irch	Broster	Donald	Gregory	Higgins	Ives	Loney	McKinney	McLeod	Miller	Millington	Mitchell	Ovens	Pullen	Simons	Thompson	Wake	Whyman	Wilde	Wingrove
[illegible]			10		11			1	9	2	5	4	3		7	6			
[illegible]			10		11			1	9	2	5	4	3		7	6			
[illegible]		11	10					1	9	2	5	4	3		7		6		
[illegible]		11	10	2				1	9		5	4	3		7		6		
[illegible]		11	10	2				1	9		5	4	3		7		6		
[illegible]		11	10	2				1	9		5	4	3		7		6		
[illegible]		11	10	2				1	9		5	4	3		7	6			
[illegible]		11		2				1	9		5		3		7	6	4		
[illegible]		11						1	9	2	5	4	3		7	6			
[illegible]	10	11						1	9	2	5	4	3		7	6			
[illegible]	4	11		2				1	9	3					7	6		5	
[illegible]		7	10		11			1		2	5	4	3			6			
[illegible]		11	10					1		2	5	4	3	9	7	6			
[illegible]		11						1		2	5	4	3	9	7		6		
[illegible]	4	11						1	9	2	5		3	10	7	6			
[illegible]	4	11						1	9	2	5		3	10	7	6			
[illegible]	4	11	10					1		2	5		3	9	7		6		
[illegible]	4	11						1	9	2	5		3	10	7		6		
[illegible]	4	11						1	9	2	5		3	10	7		6		
[illegible]	4			2	11			1	9		5		3	10	7	6			
[illegible]	4	7			11			1	9	2	5		3	10			6		
[illegible]	4	11						1	9	2		5	3	10	7		6		
	4	11						1	9	2		5	3	10	7		6		
[illegible]	4	11						1	9	2	5		3	10	7		6		
[illegible]	4	11						1	9	2	5		3	10	7		6		
[illegible]	4	11					7	1	9		5		3	10			6		2
[illegible]	4	11					7	1	9		5		3	10			6		2
[illegible]	4	11	10					1	9				3		7		6	5	2
[illegible]	4	11	10					1	9		5		3		7		6		2
[illegible]	4	11						1	9	2			3	10	7		6	5	
[illegible]	4	11						1	9	2			3	10	7		6	5	
[illegible]	4	11	10					1	9	2			3		7		6	5	
[illegible]	4	11						1	9	2	5		3		7		6		
[illegible]	4	11						1	9	2	5		3		7	6			
[illegible]	4	11						1	9	2	5		3		7	6			
[illegible]	4	11						1	9	2	5		3		7	6			
[illegible]	4	11						1	9	2	5		3	10	7		6		
[illegible]	4	11				2		1		3				9	7		6	5	
7	26	35	13	7	5	1	2	38	33	28	30	14	36	19	34	15	24	6	4
5	1	4	2						14		1			7	3		3		
[illegible]	4	11						1	9	2	5		3	10	7		6		
[illegible]	4	11						1	9	2	5		3	10	7		6		
[illegible]	4	11						1	9	2	5		3	10	7		6		
[illegible]	3	3						3	3	3	3		3	3	3		3		
[illegible]									1					1					
0	29	38	13	7	5	1	2	41	36	31	33	14	39	22	37	15	27	6	4
7	1	4	2						15		1			8	3		3		

1915-16

London Combination (Principal)

Match No.	Date		Opponents	Location	Result		Scorers	Atte
1	Sep	4	Millwall	A	L	1-3	Humphries	
2		11	Croydon Common	H	W	2-1	Fox, Coleman	
3		18	Arsenal	A	L	1-2	Humphries	
4		25	Brentford	H	L	1-2	Humphries	
5	Oct	2	West Ham United	A	L	1-2	Fox	
6		9	Tottenham Hotspur	H	L	0-4		
7		16	Crystal Palace	A	L	0-1		
8		23	Chelsea	H	W	1-0	Coleman	
9		30	Fulham	H	W	2-1	Humphries (2)	
10	Nov	6	Clapton Orient	A	W	2-0	Dale, Simons	
11		13	Millwall	H	L	1-5	Baldock	
12		20	Croydon Common	A	W	1-0	Humphries	
13		27	Arsenal	H	D	1-1	Hicks	
14	Dec	4	Brentford	A	L	0-4		
15		11	West Ham United	H	D	1-1	Dale	
16		18	Tottenham Hotspur	A	L	1-2	Simons	
17		25	Watford	A	L	1-5	Humphries	
18		27	Watford	H	W	3-1	Humphries, Nisbet (2)	
19	Jan	1	Crystal Palace	H	W	5-1	OG, Baldock, Fox, Nisbet, Humphries	
20		8	Chelsea	A	L	1-5	Mitchell (pen)	1
21		15	Fulham	A	W	1-0	Mitchell	
22		22	Clapton Orient	H	D	0-0		

Appeara

London Combination (Subsidiary)

Match No.	Date		Opponents	Location	Result		Scorers	Atte
1	Feb	5	Chelsea	H	L	0-3		
2		12	Watford	A	L	0-6		
3		19	Brentford	H	D	1-1	Simons	
4	Mar	4	Clapton Orient	H	D	1-1	Wagstaffe	
5		11	Tottenham Hotspur	A	D	0-0		
6		18	Watford	H	D	2-2	Birch, Thompson	
7		25	Brentford	A	L	0-4		
8	Apr	1	Reading	H	L	2-6	Mitchell, Hicks	
9		8	Clapton Orient	A	D	1-1	Hicks	
10		15	Tottenham Hotspur	H	L	1-3	Dale	
11		21	Millwall	A	L	2-6	Donald (2)	
12		22	Reading	A	W	2-1	Fox, Simons	
13		24	Millwall	H	W	2-0	Broster, Simons	
14		29	Chelsea	A	L	0-3		1

Appeara

Total - Appeara

Total -

Bellamy (G)	Birch	Blake (G)	Broster	Coleman	Dale	Donald	Draper	Elliott (G)	Fox	Gregory	Hicks	Hooper	Hughes	Humphries	Hunter (G)	Ives	Jackman (G)	Jefferies	Linkson	Loney	McRae (G)	Matthews A.	Matthews F.	Mitchell	Nicholson (G)	Nisbet	Nixon	Poulton (G)	Pullen	Simons	Smith A.	Smith B. (G)	Somerville	Thompson	Wagstaffe (G)	Wake	Walsh (G)	Whyman	Wingrove	Wood	OG
							3		11	6				9						2			1	5		7					4	8									
				8					11	4				9					3	2			1	5		7										6					
				8			3		11	4				9					2				1	5		7										6					
				8			3		11					9						2				5		7	1				4					6					
		9		10			2		7	5				11						3							1			8						4					
				8			2		11	4				9	7					3			1	5						10						6					
							3	7	11									1						5	8					9	4					6				2	
				8					11	10	7			9				1		2				5												6			3	4	
					8				11	4	7			9				1	3	2				5												6					
					8				11		7							1	3	2				5						9						6				4	
					8				11		7			9				1	3	2				5							4									6	
					8				11		7			9				1	3	2				5												6				4	
					10		3		11		8			9				1		2		7		5												6					
					10				11		7							1	3	2				5				8		9						6					
					8				11										3	2				5		7	1			9						6				4	
					8				11										3	2				5		7	1			9						6				4	
2					5				11		8			9				1						3		7				10						6					
					8									9		11		1	3	2				5		7										6		4			
					8				11					9					3	2				5		7	1									6				4	
					8				7					9					2	3				5		11	1									4				6	
					8		3		11					9					2					5		7	1			10								4			
					8		6		11		10			9					3	2				5		7	1														
1		1		6	14		9	1	21	7	9			17	1	1		10	14	18		1	4	21	1	12	8	1		9	4	1				18		2	1	9	
				2	2				3		1			9										2		3				2											1
					6		3		11		8			9					2			7		5		10	1			4											
					4		2		11			3		9			8	1				7											6			5	10				
					8		3		10		7	2		11				1						5						9			4			6					
	8				5	7			11					9					2	4							1		3						10	6					
	5					7			11		8		10						2	4							1		3	9						6					
	8					7	2		11									1			10			5					3				4	9		6					
						7			11		8	4								2			1	5					3	9			10			6					
							2		11		8	7		9				1		5				10					3							6		4			
					8	7			11		10							1		2				5					3					9		6		4			
					8	7			11		10	4						1		2									3	9			5			6					
					8	7	2		11		9							1						5		10			3				4			6					
					8	7	2		11		10							1						5					3	9						6		4			
			4		8	7			11		10							1		2									3	9			5			6					
					8	7			11									1		2				5					3	9						6		4			
	3		1		10	10	7		14		10	5	1	5			1	10	3	8	1	2	1	9		2	3		11	8			7	2	1	13	1	4			
	1		1		1	2			1		2													1						3				1	1						
1	3	1	1	6	24	10	16	1	35	7	19	5	1	22	1	1	1	20	17	26	1	3	5	30	1	14	11	1	11	17	4	1	7	2	1	31	1	6	1	9	
	1		1	2	3	2			4		3			9										3		3				5				1	1						1

uest Player

1916-17

London Combination (Principal)

Match No.	Date		Opponents	Location	Result		Scorers	Atten
1	Sep	2	Luton Town	H	L	1-4	Dale	
2		9	Portsmouth	A	W	3-2	Pennifer, Matthews, OG (Smith)	2
3		16	Millwall	H	L	0-4		4
4		23	Watford	A	L	0-2		1
5		30	Clapton Orient	H	D	0-0		3
6	Oct	7	Fulham	A	L	0-2		5
7		14	Southampton	A	L	1-2	Fox	
8		21	West Ham United	H	L	0-4		3
9		28	Tottenham Hotspur	A	W	5-4	Dale, Salmon (2), Mitchell, OG	4
10	Nov	4	Crystal Palace	H	W	1-0	Lawrence	
11		11	Brentford	A	W	4-1	Lawrence (3), Dale	2
12		18	Chelsea	H	L	1-2	Dale	
13		25	Luton Town	A	L	0-6		3
14	Dec	2	Portsmouth	H	L	1-7	Kinlin	
15		9	Millwall	A	L	1-2	Hassan	5
16		23	Clapton Orient	A	L	1-2	Mitchell	
17		25	Arsenal	H	L	2-3	Dale, Hassan	3
18		26	Arsenal	A	D	0-0		4
19		30	Fulham	H	L	1-7	Lawrence	3
20	Jan	6	Southampton	H	W	4-0	Hassan (2), Lawrence, Baldock	1
21		13	West Ham United	A	L	3-5	Dale, Lawrence, Whyman	5
22		20	Tottenham Hotspur	H	D	1-1	Hassan	1
23		27	Crystal Palace	A	L	0-4		
24	Feb	3	Brentford	H	W	2-0	Whiting, Hassan	1
25		10	Chelsea	A	L	0-3		4
26		17	Watford	H	W	2-1	Lawrence, Hassan	
27		24	Luton Town	A	L	0-2		
28	Mar	3	Fulham	A	D	0-0		3
29		10	Crystal Palace	H	W	3-2	Lawrence, Hassan (2)	
30		17	Millwall	A	L	0-1		5
31		24	Brentford	H	D	2-2	Dale, Barlow	
32		31	Watford	A	W	2-1	Goddard, OG (Grimsdell)	
33	Apr	6	Chelsea	H	D	2-2	Hassan, Baldock	3
34		7	Luton Town	H	D	2-2	Dale (2)	3
35		9	Chelsea	A	L	1-3	Lawrence	7
36		14	Fulham	H	W	2-0	Dale, Baldock	1
37		19	Brentford	A	D	0-0		1
38		21	Crystal Palace	A	L	0-3		
39		28	Millwall	H	D	0-0		6

Appearar
G

Total - Appearar
Total - G

Barrington (G)	Beale (G)	Beckerley (G)	Birch	Birkett (G)	Broster	Brown	Butler	Crossley (G)	Dale	Denoon	Donald	Draper	Drysdale (G)	Durston	Fleming (G)	Fox	Goddard	Green	Grendon	Hassan	Hicks	Hooper	Howie	Hughes	James (G)	Kinlin (G)	Kirk (G)	Langford (G)	Lawrence	Lewis	Loney	Marshall (G)	Matthews	Mitchell	Needham (G)	Nisbet	Pennifer	Richards (G)	Salmon (G)	Saxon (G)	Shutt (G)	Simons	Soffe (G)	Somerville	Strickland (G)	Teabay (G)	Thompson	Thwaites (G)	Toms (G)	Virtue (G)	Wake	Wash (G)	White	Whiting	Whyman	Winyard	Wise (G)	Wren (G)	Wright	OG
			8						4				10	1		11		6													2			5		7	9							3																
									6					1		11		4				3								10	2		8	5		7	9																							
									6			3		1		11														10	2		8	5		7	4			9																				
4									6		11	2		1		7					10	3								8				5			9																							
									10			3		1		11					7	4								8	2			5			9																							
									11			2		1		7														6	3		10	5					8							9														
									10			3				11						2								4				5					8							7	9									1				
									8		7	3				11						6								4	2			5			9										10									1				
									9		7	3				11		4											10		2			5					8																	1				
									9		7	3		1		11		4											10	8	2			5																									6	
									9		7	3		1		11		4											10		2			5																									6	
									9		7	3				11													10		2			5				4																				1	6	
	9			7										1				4				2							10	11				5															3			8							6	
						7								1			11			8						10	2							5							3		9														4		6	
		3																	6	10			8						7					5	9							11								2	4					1				
												3							4	8									10					5	9												7				6				2	1			11	
									9			3					11		4	8		2												5																7	6					1				
							7					3					11		4	8									10					5																					2	1			6	
									9			3					11		4	8		2							10					5																		7				1			6	
												3		1			11			8									10		2			5													7								4				6	
									9	1		3					11		4	8									10		2			5																					6					
										1		3					11		4	8									10					9														5							2				6	
										1		3					7		2	10			6						8			9		5														4												
										1		3							4	8									10		2			5											11									9	6					
									9	1		3					11		4	8									10					5																					2				6	
										1		3					11		4	8									10		2			5																				9					6	
							7		8	1		3					11													10				5															2					9					6	
									11	1		2							6	10									8		3			5																				9	7				4	
									11	1		3			9				4	8									10		2			5																				7					6	
									10	1		3					11		4	8											2			5																				9					6	
							7		10	1		3							2									4						5																				9					6	
									10	1		3					11		4											8	2			5																					6					
								11		1		3							4	8									10	7				5																			2						6	
					6			11	9	1		3							4	8										7	2			5																					10					
							11	7		1		2							6	10									8					5																			3						4	
									10	1		3							4	8					11					7	2			5																									6	
									10	1		11								8								4		7	2			5																			3						6	
									10	1		3								8								4		7	2			5																									6	
									8	1		2							6					10						11				5																			3	9	7				4	
1	1	1	1	1	1	1	4	3	27	19	6	34	1	11	1	12	13	6	21	22	2	8	2	1	1	1	1	3	20	17	22	1	3	39	2	3	6	1	3	1	1	1	1	1	1	2	4	2	2	2	3	2	4	8	11	8	1	1	23	
									10							1	1			10						1			10				1	2			1		2															1	1					3

1	1	1	1	1	1	1	4	3	27	19	6	34	1	11	1	12	13	6	21	22	2	8	2	1	1	1	1	3	20	17	22	1	3	39	2	3	6	1	3	1	1	1	1	1	1	2	4	2	2	2	3	2	4	8	11	8	1	1	23	
									10							1	1			10						1			10				1	2			1		2															1	1					3

est Player

1917-18

London Combination (Principal)

Match No.	Date		Opponents	Location	Result		Scorers	Atte
1	Sep	1	Arsenal	A	L	0-2		
2		8	West Ham United	H	L	0-3		
3		15	Fulham	A	L	1-2	Gregory	
4		22	Crystal Palace	H	W	4-1	Dale, Thurman, Fox (2)	
5		29	Clapton Orient	H	W	2-0	Dale, Thurman	
6	Oct	6	Millwall	A	L	2-4	Mitchell, Dale	
7		13	Tottenham Hotspur	H	L	2-3	Mitchell, Thompson	
8		20	Chelsea	A	W	2-1	Dale (2)	
9		27	Arsenal	H	W	2-0	Mitchell (pen), Brown	
10	Nov	3	West Ham United	A	L	0-4		
11		10	Fulham	H	L	2-3	Dale, Thurman	
12		17	Crystal Palace	A	L	1-4	Dale	
13		24	Clapton Orient	A	W	2-1	Fox, Campbell	
14	Dec	1	Millwall	H	W	1-0	Brown	
15		8	Tottenham Hotspur	A	W	1-0	Smith	
16		15	Chelsea	H	L	0-1		
17		22	Arsenal	A	L	0-3		
18		25	Brentford	A	D	1-1	Walters	
19		26	Brentford	H	L	0-4		
20		29	West Ham United	H	D	1-1	Smith	
21	Jan	5	Fulham	A	L	0-1		
22		12	Crystal Palace	H	W	2-1	Walters, Smith	
23		19	Clapton Orient	H	W	6-1	Brown, Dale, Fox (3), Walters	
24		26	Millwall	A	W	1-0	Mitchell	
25	Feb	2	Tottenham Hotspur	H	L	2-7	Walters, Smith	
26		9	Brentford	A	L	1-6	Jones	
27		16	Arsenal	H	L	0-3		
28		23	West Ham United	A	L	0-4		
29	Mar	2	Fulham	H	L	0-1		
30		9	Crystal Palace	A	W	2-0	MacLinton, Jones	
31		16	Clapton Orient	A	W	1-0	Grendon	
32		23	Millwall	H	W	4-1	MacLinton, Walters (3)	
33		29	Chelsea	A	L	0-1		
34		30	Tottenham Hotspur	A	W	2-1	Fox, Smith	
35	Apr	1	Chelsea	H	L	1-2	Fox	
36		6	Brentford	H	L	2-6	MacLinton (2)	
							Appearances	
							Goals	

War Fund

Match No.	Date		Opponents	Location	Result		Scorers
1	Apr	13	Crystal Palace	H	W	2-1	Britton, Archibald
2		20	Crystal Palace	A	L	1-3	Dale
3		27	Millwall	H	W	4-3	Jefferson, Walters, MacLinton (2)
4	May	4	Millwall	A	L	1-3	Archibald

Appeara
(

Total - Appeara
Total - (

Baldock	Britton (G)	Brown	Campbell (G)	Coleman	Cousins	Crossland (G)	Dale	Denoon	Downing	Draper	Duffield	Edwards (G)	Fox	Green	Gregory	Grendon	Griffen	Hales (G)	Hanford (G)	Hassan	Hawkins (G)	Jefferson	Jones (G)	Kellar (G)	Lewis	Loney	MacLinton	Mitchell	Munson (G)	Over (G)	Read (G)	Sanders (G)	Smith	Steer	Thompson	Thurman	Trindale (G)	Walters	White	Whyman	Wright
							10	1		3			11		9	4												5					8						2	7	6
9							10	1		3			11		8	4									7			5											2		6
							10	1							9	4									7	3		5		8								11	2		6
				8			9	1		3			11			4												5		7						10			2		6
							9	1					11		8	4									7	2		5								10			3		6
							9	1		3			11		8	4									7			5								10			2		6
								1		7			11			4	8									2		5							9	10			3		6
							9	1					11		8	4										2		5							7	10			3		6
8		10					9	1		3			11			4										2		5							7						6
8							9	1		7			11			4										2		5					10						3		6
8							9	1		7			11			4										2		5								10			3		6
7					8		9	1		3		10	11			4	6											5											2		
		8	9					1		3			11			4	7											5								10			2		6
		8	10		7		9	1		6			11			4										3		5											2		
5		8						1		3			11			4						7											9			10			2		6
		8					10	1		3			11			4				9		7						5											2		6
		8					10	1		3			11			4				9		7						5											2		6
		8					10	1					11			4						7				2		5										9	3		6
		8					10	1					11			4						7				2		5										9	3		6
						10	8	1					11			4						7				2		5					9						3		6
							10	1		4			11			6						7				2		5					9					8	3		
		8						1		6			11									7				2		5					9					10	3		4
6		8					9	1		3			11			4						7				2							5					10			
6		8					9	1		3			11			4						7				2		5										10			
1					7		8			3			11			4										2		5					9					10			6
6										3	1		11			4		7	9		2		5	8												10					
		8								3	1		11			4						7						5					9	2				10			6
							10	1		3			11			4												5				8		2		9	7				6
6								1	5	3			11			4				7							8	9						2		10					
3							7	1	5				11			4							9				8							2				10			6
		8					7	1	6	3			11			4											9	5						2				10			
							10	1	6	3			11			4						7					9	5						2				8			
4		10					9	1	3	2			11			6						7						5										8			
4							7	1	6	3			11			5											9	2					8			10					
6							7	1		3			11			5											9	2	8		4							10			
6							7	1	5	3			11			4											8							2		9		10			
	14	2	1	3	1	29	33	7	29	2	1	35		6	35	3	1	1	3	1	13	2	1	4	16	7	31	1	2	1	1	10	7	3	13	1	15	21	1	23	
	3	1				8						8		1	1							2				4	4					5		1	3		7				

Baldock	Britton (G)	Brown	Campbell (G)	Coleman	Cousins	Crossland (G)	Dale	Denoon	Downing	Draper	Duffield	Edwards (G)	Fox	Green	Gregory	Grendon	Griffen	Hales (G)	Hanford (G)	Hassan	Hawkins (G)	Jefferson	Jones (G)	Kellar (G)	Lewis	Loney	MacLinton	Mitchell	Munson (G)	Over (G)	Read (G)	Sanders (G)	Smith	Steer	Thompson	Thurman	Trindale (G)	Walters	White	Whyman	Wright
8	7							1	5	3			11			4											9							2							6
8							9	1	6	3			11			4						7						5						2							
							5			3	1		11	4								7					9							2				8			6
									4	3	1		11									7					9	5						2				8			6
2	1						2	2	3	4	2		4	1		2						3					3	2						4				2			3
	1						1															1					2											1			

Baldock	Britton (G)	Brown	Campbell (G)	Coleman	Cousins	Crossland (G)	Dale	Denoon	Downing	Draper	Duffield	Edwards (G)	Fox	Green	Gregory	Grendon	Griffen	Hales (G)	Hanford (G)	Hassan	Hawkins (G)	Jefferson	Jones (G)	Kellar (G)	Lewis	Loney	MacLinton	Mitchell	Munson (G)	Over (G)	Read (G)	Sanders (G)	Smith	Steer	Thompson	Thurman	Trindale (G)	Walters	White	Whyman	Wright
8	1	14	2	1	3	1	31	35	10	33	4	1	39	1	6	37	3	1	1	3	1	16	2	1	4	16	10	33	1	2	1	1	10	11	3	13	1	17	21	1	26
	1	3	1				9						8		1	1						1	2				6	4					5		1	3		8			

uest Player

1918-19

London Combination (Principal)

Match No.	Date		Opponents	Location	Result		Scorers	Atten
1	Sep	7	Arsenal	H	L	2-3	Smith, Walters	7
2		14	Crystal Palace	A	L	2-4	Jefferson, Walters	3
3		21	Clapton Orient	A	W	5-1	Brown, Dale (4)	
4		28	Millwall	H	W	1-0	Congreve	3
5	Oct	5	Fulham	A	D	3-3	Congreve, Smith (2)	4
6		12	Brentford	H	W	2-1	Fox, Dale	
7		19	West Ham United	A	L	1-4	Dale	6
8		26	Chelsea	H	D	2-2	Dale (2)	7
9	Nov	2	Arsenal	A	L	0-1		6
10		9	Crystal Palace	H	W	3-2	Dale (2), Walters	
11		16	Clapton Orient	H	W	3-1	Fox, Dale, Brown	
12		23	Millwall	A	L	1-4	Downing	5
13		30	Fulham	H	L	0-3		5
14	Dec	7	Brentford	A	L	1-5	Congreve	8
15		14	West Ham United	H	W	1-0	Smith	1
16		21	Chelsea	A	L	0-2		15
17		25	Tottenham Hotspur	H	D	1-1	Mitchell	7
18		26	Tottenham Hotspur	A	D	0-0		6
19		28	Arsenal	H	L	0-2		4
20	Jan	4	Crystal Palace	A	W	2-0	Smith, Congreve	5
21		11	Clapton Orient	A	W	5-1	Mitchell, Smith (2), Gregory, Dale	
22		18	Millwall	H	W	3-0	Gregory, Jefferson, Dale	6
23		25	Fulham	A	L	0-1		12
24	Feb	1	Brentford	H	D	0-0		8
25		8	West Ham United	A	W	4-0	Dale, Gregory, Smith, Jefferson	12
26		15	Tottenham Hotspur	H	W	7-1	Smith, Gregory (3), Mitchell, Dale, Jefferson	9
27		22	Arsenal	A	W	3-1	Gregory, Dale (2)	13
28	Mar	1	Crystal Palace	H	W	3-2	Smith (2), Dale	
29		8	Clapton Orient	H	W	5-2	Smith (3), Gregory, Mitchell	7
30		15	Millwall	A	D	1-1	Gregory	20
31		22	Fulham	H	L	0-1		10
32		29	Brentford	A	D	1-1	Brown	12
33	Apr	5	West Ham United	H	L	1-3	Brown	7
34		12	Tottenham Hotspur	A	W	3-2	Gregory, Smith, OG (Bay)	20
35		18	Chelsea	H	W	3-2	Birch (2), Smith	15
36		21	Chelsea	A	L	0-3		20

Appearan
G

London Victory Cup

Match No.	Date		Opponents	Location	Result		Scorers	Atten
1	Mar	20	Chelsea	A	L	0-2		

Appearar
G

Total - Appearar
Total - G

Birch	Brown	Butler	Congreve	Cope	Dale	Denoon	Dodd	Donald	Downing	Draper	Durston	Fox	Gregory	Grendon	Jefferson	Jenkins	MacLinton	Millington	Mitchell	Page	Pullen	Smith	Steer	Wake	Walters	Whyman	Wingrove	Wright	OG
					8	1				3		11			7				5			9	2		10			4	
	10		6			1	8		3						7		9		5			4	2		11				
	8			7	9	1				3		11		4					5				2		10				
	9		8			1				3		11					7		5				2		10			4	
			8		7	1				3				4	11				5			9	2		10				
	8			7	9	1			6	3		11		4					5				2		10				
	8				9	1				3		11		4			7		5				2		10				
			10		8	1			6	3		11		4			7		5			9	2						
	8					1			5	3		11		4			7		9				2	6	10				
	8				9	1				3		11		4			7		5				2	6	10				
	8			7	9	1			4	3		11				2			5					6					
			8		7	1			5	3		11		4								9	2	6	10				
			8		7	1				3		11		4					5			9	2	6	10				
			10		9	1				3		11		4	7				5			8	2	6					
	8					1				3		11		4	7				5			9		6	10	2			
	8		10							3	1	11		4	7				5			9		6			2		
		7	10		8						1	11		4					5	9			3	6			2		
	8	7	10		9	1						11		4					5					6		3	2		
	8	7	10		9	1						11		4					5					6		3	2		
			10		9	1						11		4	7				5			8				3	2		
					9	1						11	10	4	7				5			8				3	2		
					9	1						11	10	4	7				2			8		5		3			
					9	1						11	10	4	7				5			8				3	2		
					9	1						11	10	4	7				5			8				3	2		
					9	1						11	10	4	7				5			8				3	2		
					9	1						11	10	4	7				5			8				3	2		
					9	1				2		11	10	4	7				5			8				3			
					9	1				2		11	10	4	7				5			8				3			
					9	1						11	10	4	7				5		2	8				3			
					9	1						11	10	4	7				5		2	8				3			
					9	1						11	10	4	7				5		2	8		6		3			
	9					1						11	10	4			7		5		2	8					3		
	9					1						11	10	4	7			2			3	8				5			
					8	1				2		11	10		7						2	9		4		5			
3						1		11					10		7			2	5		3	9						4	
3						1		11				7	10					2	5		3	9				4			
2	14	3	12	3	27	34	1	2	6	18	2	33	16	29	21	1	7	3	33	1	8	26	14	14	12	18	11	3	
2	4		4		18				1			2	10		4				4			16			3				1
					9	1						11	10	4	7				5		2	8				3			
					1	1						1	1	1	1				1		1	1				1			
2	14	3	12	3	28	35	1	2	6	18	2	34	17	30	22	1	7	3	34	1	9	27	14	14	12	19	11	3	
2	4		4		18				1			2	10		4				4			16			3				1

1919-20

Southern League (Div 1)

	P	W	D	L	F	A	Pts
Portsmouth	42	23	12	7	73	27	58
Watford	42	26	6	10	69	42	58
Crystal Palace	42	22	12	8	69	43	56
Cardiff City	42	18	17	7	70	43	53
Plymouth Argyle	42	20	10	12	57	29	50
Queen's Park Rangers	42	18	10	14	62	50	46
Reading	42	16	13	13	51	43	45
Southampton	42	18	8	16	72	63	44
Swansea Town	42	16	11	15	53	45	43
Exeter City	42	17	9	16	57	51	43
Southend United	42	13	17	12	46	48	43
Norwich City	42	15	11	16	64	57	41
Swindon Town	42	17	7	18	65	68	41
Millwall	42	14	12	16	52	55	40
Brentford	42	15	10	17	52	59	40
Brighton & Hove Albion	42	14	8	20	60	72	36
Bristol Rovers	42	11	13	18	61	78	35
Newport County	42	13	7	22	45	70	33
Northampton Town	42	12	9	21	64	103	33
Luton Town	42	10	10	22	51	76	30
Merthyr Town	42	9	11	22	47	78	29
Gillingham	42	10	7	25	34	74	27

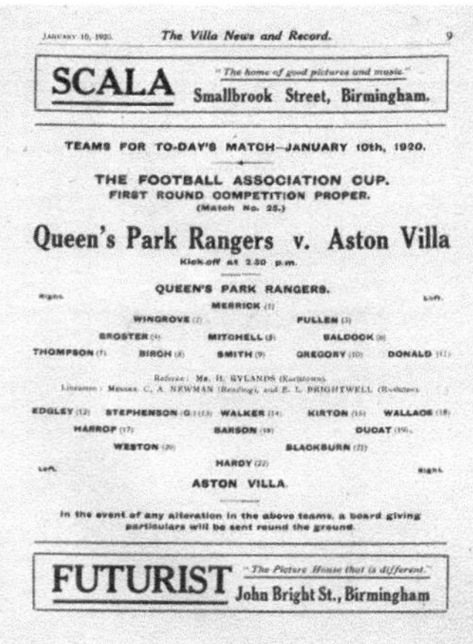

JANUARY 10, 1920. *The Villa News and Record.* 9

TEAMS FOR TO-DAY'S MATCH—JANUARY 10th, 1920.

THE FOOTBALL ASSOCIATION CUP.
FIRST ROUND COMPETITION PROPER.
(Match No. 25.)

Queen's Park Rangers v. Aston Villa

Kick-off at 2.30 p.m.

QUEEN'S PARK RANGERS.

Right. Left.

MERRICK (1)

WINGROVE (2) FULLEN (3)

BROSTER (4) MITCHELL (5) BALDOCK (6)

THOMPSON (7) BIRCH (8) SMITH (9) GREGORY (10) DONALD (11)

Referee: Mr. H. RYLANDS

Linesmen: Messrs. C. A. NEWMAN (Reading), and E. L. BRIGHTWELL

EDGLEY (12) STEPHENSON (C.) (13) WALKER (14) KIRTON (15) WALLACE (16)

HARROP (17) BARSON (18) DUCAT (19)

WESTON (20) BLACKBURN (21)

HARDY (22)

Left. Right.

ASTON VILLA.

In the event of any alteration in the above teams, a board giving particulars will be sent round the ground.

Match No.	Date		Opponents	Location	Result		Scorers
1	Aug	30	Bristol Rovers	A	W	2-0	Donald, Gregory
2	Sep	1	Plymouth Argyle	A	D	0-0	
3		6	Reading	H	D	0-0	
4		8	Plymouth Argyle	H	W	1-0	Mitchell (pen)
5		13	Southampton	A	L	1-2	Donald
6		20	Luton Town	H	W	4-0	Gregory (2), Birch, Smith
7		25	Southend United	H	D	2-2	Birch (2)
8		27	Gillingham	A	W	1-0	Birch
9	Oct	4	Swansea Town	H	W	2-0	Donald, Birch
10		11	Exeter City	A	W	1-0	Gregory
11		16	Newport County	H	W	1-0	Birch
12		18	Cardiff City	H	D	0-0	
13		25	Watford	H	W	3-0	Donald, Whyman, Smith
14	Nov	1	Swindon Town	A	L	2-5	Birch, Gregory
15		8	Millwall	H	L	1-2	Birch
16		15	Brighton	A	W	3-2	Smith (2), Birch
17		29	Portsmouth	A	L	2-4	Baldock, Broster
18	Dec	6	Northampton Town	H	W	5-1	Smith (3), Baldock, Birch
19		13	Crystal Palace	A	L	0-1	
20		25	Brentford	H	W	2-0	Mitchell, Broster
21		26	Brentford	A	L	1-2	Smith
22		27	Norwich City	A	L	1-3	Birch
23	Jan	3	Bristol Rovers	H	W	7-1	Smith (4), Sutch (2), Donald
24		17	Reading	A	W	1-0	Smith
25		24	Southampton	H	W	2-1	Donald, Gregory
26	Feb	14	Swansea Town	A	L	1-3	Smith
27		17	Gillingham	H	D	0-0	
28		21	Exeter City	H	D	0-0	
29		28	Cardiff City	A	L	0-4	
30	Mar	6	Watford	A	L	0-1	
31		13	Swindon Town	H	W	2-1	Birch, Gregory
32		20	Millwall	A	D	0-0	
33		22	Luton Town	A	L	1-2	Birch
34		27	Brighton	H	W	3-1	Gregory (3)
35	Apr	2	Merthyr Town	A	W	4-1	Birch (2), Smith, Ramsey
36		3	Newport County	A	L	0-3	
37		5	Merthyr Town	H	D	0-0	
38		10	Portsmouth	H	D	1-1	Birch
39		17	Northampton Town	A	L	0-2	
40		24	Crystal Palace	H	L	2-3	Gregory (2)
41		26	Southend United	A	D	2-2	Gregory (2)
42		30	Norwich City	H	W	1-0	Gregory

Appeara

FA Cup

R1	Jan	10	Aston Villa	A	L	1-2	Birch

Appeara

Total - Appeara

Total - (

London Challenge Cup

R1	Sep	18	Brentford	H	W	6-0
R2	No details recorded					
SF			Chelsea	N	L	0-1*

* Played at Highbury

London Professional Charity Fund

Oct	23	Brentford	H	W	5-1

Berry	Birch	Blackman	Broster	Cain	Chester	Donald	Fox	Gregory	Haggan	Lowe	Merrick	Miller	Mitchell	Olsen	Pidgeon	Pullen	Ramsey	Smith	Sutch	Thompson	Watts	Whyman	Wilde	Wingrove	Wodehouse
	8	2	4			11		10			1		5			3		9		7					
	8		4			11		10			1		5			3		9		7				2	
	8	2	4			11		10			1		5			3		9		7					
	8	2	4			11		10			1		5			3		9		7					
	8	2	4			11		10			1		5			3		9		7					
	8		4			11		10			1		5			3		9		7		2			
	8		4			11		10			1		5			3		9		7				2	
	8		4			7	11	10			1		5			3		9						2	
	8		4			7	11	10			1		5			3		9						2	
	8		4			7	11	10			1					3		9					5	2	
	8					7	11	10			1		5			3		9					4	2	
	8					7	11	10			1		5			3		9					4	2	
	8		4			11		10			1		5			3		9				7		2	
	8		4			11		10			1		5			3		9				7		2	
	8		4			11				10	1		5			3		9				7		2	
	8	2	4		7		11	10			1		5			3		9							
	8	2	4			7	11	10			1		5			3		9							
	8		4			11		10			1		5			3	7	9						2	
	8		4			11		10			1		5			3	7	9						2	
	8		4			11		10			1		5			3	7	9						2	
	8		4			11		10			1		2				7	9					5	3	
	8					11		10			1		2				7	9				4	5	3	
	8		4			11					1		2					9	10	7			5	3	
	8	3	4			11		10			1		5					9		7				2	
	8	3	4			11		10			1		5					9		7				2	
1	8	3	4			11		10					5					9		7				2	
1	8	3	4			11		10										9		7		5		2	
1	8	3	4			11		10					5					9		7				2	
1	8	3	4			11		10					5					9		7				2	
	8		4			11		10			1		5			3	7	9						2	
	8		4			11		10			1		5			3	7	9						2	
	8		4			11		10			1		5			3	7	9						2	
			4	5		11		10			1	8				3	7	9						2	
	8		4			11		10			1		5			3	7	9						2	
	8		4			11		10			1		5			3	7	9						2	
	8						11	10			1			5		3	7	9						2	4
		2	4	5		11		10			1	8			7			9						3	
	8	2		4		11		10			1		5		7			9						3	
	8	2	4			11		10			1		5		7	3		9							
	8	2	4	5		11		10			1				7			9						3	
	8	2		4		11		10	5		1				7			9						3	
	8	2		4		11		10			1		5		7			9			3				
4	40	18	35	6	1	40	8	40	1	1	38	2	35	1	6	28	12	42	1	14	1	6	6	33	1
	16		2			6		15					2				1	15	2			1			
	8	6	4			11		10			1		5			3		9		7				2	
	1	1	1			1		1			1		1			1		1		1				1	
	1																								
4	41	19	36	6	1	41	8	41	1	1	39	2	36	1	6	29	12	43	1	15	1	6	6	34	1
	17		2			6		15					2				1	15	2			1			

1920-21

Division Three South

	P	W	D	L	F	A	Pts
Crystal Palace	42	24	11	7	70	34	59
Southampton	42	19	16	7	64	28	54
Queen's Park Rangers	42	22	9	11	61	32	53
Swindon Town	42	21	10	11	73	49	52
Swansea Town	42	18	15	9	56	45	51
Watford	42	20	8	14	59	44	48
Millwall	42	18	11	13	42	30	47
Merthyr Town	42	15	15	12	60	49	45
Luton Town	42	16	12	14	61	56	44
Bristol Rovers	42	18	7	17	68	57	43
Plymouth Argyle	42	11	21	10	35	34	43
Portsmouth	42	12	15	15	46	48	39
Grimsby Town	42	15	9	18	49	59	39
Northampton Town	42	15	8	19	59	75	38
Newport County	42	14	9	19	43	64	37
Norwich City	42	10	16	16	44	53	36
Southend United	42	14	8	20	44	61	36
Brighton & Hove Albion	42	14	8	20	42	61	36
Exeter City	42	10	15	17	39	54	35
Reading	42	12	7	23	42	59	31
Brentford	42	9	12	21	42	67	30
Gillingham	42	8	12	22	34	74	28

Attendances

	TOTAL		
	Home	Away	Total
League	297,000	261,000	558,000
Cup/Otherer	20,000	41,007	61,007
TOTAL	317,000	302,007	619,007

	AVERAGE		
	Home	Away	Total
League	14,143	12,429	13,286
Cup/Otherer	20,000	41,007	30,504
TOTAL	14,409	13,728	14,068

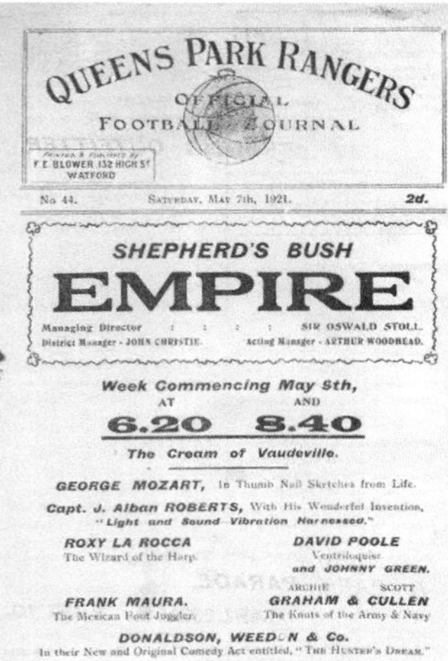

Match No.	Date		Opponents	Location	Result		Scorers	Atten
1	Aug	28	Watford	H	L	1-2	Birch	20
2	Sep	2	Northampton Town	H	L	1-2	Birch	14
3		4	Watford	A	W	2-0	Birch (2)	9
4		6	Northampton Town	A	W	3-0	Gregory, Smith, Middlemiss	6
5		11	Reading	H	W	2-0	Gregory, Smith	15
6		18	Reading	A	D	0-0		9
7		25	Luton Town	H	W	4-1	Birch (2), Gregory (pen), Mitchell	20
8	Oct	2	Luton Town	A	L	1-2	Birch	10
9		9	Southend United	H	W	2-0	Smith, OG (Dorsett)	20
10		16	Southend United	A	L	0-1		8
11		23	Swansea Town	A	W	3-1	Gregory, Birch, Manning	16
12		30	Swansea Town	H	D	1-1	Manning	20
13	Nov	6	Southampton	A	D	2-2	Manning, Gregory	15
14		13	Southampton	H	D	0-0		20
15		20	Grimsby Town	A	L	1-2	Smith	8
16		27	Grimsby Town	H	W	2-0	Smith, Gregory	10
17	Dec	4	Brighton	A	L	1-2	Gregory	9
18		11	Brighton	H	W	4-0	Smith (3), Birch	7
19		18	Crystal Palace	H	W	3-0	Birch (2), Gregory	18
20		25	Brentford	A	W	2-0	Smith (2)	20
21		27	Brentford	H	W	1-0	Birch	25
22	Jan	1	Crystal Palace	A	D	0-0		20
23		15	Merthyr Town	A	L	1-3	Birch	15
24		22	Merthyr Town	H	W	4-2	Gregory, Manning, Birch (pen), Smith	9
25	Feb	5	Norwich City	A	L	0-2		9
26		12	Plymouth Argyle	A	L	0-1		14
27		17	Norwich City	H	W	2-0	Gregory, Birch	4
28		26	Exeter City	A	W	1-0	Smith	10
29	Mar	5	Exeter City	H	W	2-1	Gregory (2)	15
30		12	Millwall	A	D	0-0		25
31		17	Plymouth Argyle	H	W	4-0	Smith (2), Clayton, Gregory	8
32		19	Millwall	H	D	0-0		20
33		25	Bristol Rovers	A	L	0-3		15
34		26	Newport County	H	W	2-0	Mitchell, Smith	10
35		28	Bristol Rovers	H	W	2-1	Mitchell, Smith	15
36	Apr	2	Newport County	A	W	3-1	Smith, Chandler, Manning	15
37		9	Gillingham	H	L	0-1		10
38		16	Gillingham	A	W	2-1	Gregory, Smith	8
39		23	Swindon Town	H	W	1-0	Chandler	12
40		30	Swindon Town	A	W	1-0	Gregory	7
41	May	2	Portsmouth	H	D	0-0		5
42		7	Portsmouth	A	D	0-0		13

Appearances

Goals

FA Cup

R1	Jan	8	Arsenal	H	W	2-0	Chandler, O'Brien	20
R2		29	Burnley	A	L	2-4	Smith, Birch	41

Appearances

Goals

Total - Appearances

Total - Goals

London Challenge Cup

R1	Oct	11	Millwall	H	W	1-0		3
R2	Nov	1	Wimbledon	A	W	2-0		
SF	Feb	21	Crystal Palace	A*	L	2-4	Smith, Chandler	10

* Played at Millwall

London Professional Charity Fund

1	Nov	15	Brentford	A	L	1-3	

Baldock	Birch	Blackman	Chandler	Clayton	Donald	Faulkner	Gould	Grant	Gregory	Grimsdell	Hill	John	McGovern	Manning	Marsden	Middlemiss	Mitchell	O'Brien	Price	Smith	Watts	Wingrove	OG
	8	2				7		5	10				4			11		6	1	9		3	
	8	2				7		5	10				4			11		6	1	9		3	
	8	2				7		4	10	3	1					11	5	6		9			
	8	2				7		4	10	3	1					11	5	6		9			
	8	2				7		4	10	3	1					11	5	6		9			
	8	2				7		4	10	3	1					11	5	6		9			
	8	2				7		4	10	3	1					11	5	6		9			
	8	2				7		4	10	3	1					11	5	6		9			
	8	2				7		4	10	3	1					11	5	6		9			
6	8	2				7		4	10	3	1					11	5			9			
	8	2			11	7		4	6	3	1			10			5			9			
	8	2			11	7		4	6	3	1			10			5			9			
	8	2			11	7		5	6	3		4		10			1			9			
	8	2			11	7		4	6	3	1			10			5			9			
		2			11	7		4	10	3	1			8			5	6		9			
	8	2				7		4	10	3	1					11	5	6		9			
	8	2				7		4	10	3	1					11	5	6		9			
	8	2						4	10	3	1			7		11	5	6		9			
	8							4	10	3	1			7		11	5	6		9		2	
	8							6	10	3	1			7		11	5	4		9		2	
	8							4	10		1			7	2	11	5	6		9		3	
	8		10					4	11		1			7			5	6		9	3	2	
	8		9					4	11	3	1			7			5	6		10		2	
	8		9					5	11		1	4		7				6		10	3	2	
		2	9			7		4	11	3	1			8			5	6		10			
	8	2			11			4	10		1			7				5		9		3	
	8	2			11			4	10		1			7			5	6		9		3	
					11	7		4	10		1			8	2		5			9		3	
					11	7		4	10		1			8	2		5	6		9		3	
					11	7		4	10		1			8	2			5		9		3	
				8	11	7		4	10		1				2			5		9		3	
				8	11	7		4	10		1				2			5		9		3	
					11	7		4	10		1			8	2		5	6		9		3	
			10		11	7	1	4						8	2		5	6		9		3	
				10	11	7	1	4						8	2		5	6		9		3	
			8		11	7		4						10	2		5	6	1	9		3	
			8		11	7		4	10						2		5	6	1	9		3	
			8		11	7		4	10						2		5	6	1	9		3	
		3	8		11	7		4	10						2		5	6	1	9			
			8		11	7		4	10						2		5	6	1	9		3	
			8		11	7		4	10		1				2		5	6		9		3	
			8		11	7		4	10		1				2		5	6		9		3	
1	25	22	12	3	22	33	2	42	39	20	32	2	2	22	16	16	35	36	7	42	2	24	
	15		2	1					15					5		1	3			18			1
	8		10					4	11	3	1			7			5	6		9		2	
	8	2	9					4	11		1			7			5	6		10		3	
	2	1	2					2	2	1	2			2			2	2		2		2	
	1		1															1		1			
1	27	23	14	3	22	33	2	44	41	21	34	2	2	24	16	16	37	38	7	44	2	26	
	16		3	1					15					5		1	3	1		19			1

1921-22

Division Three South

	P	W	D	L	F	A	Pts
Southampton	42	23	15	4	68	21	61
Plymouth Argyle	42	25	11	6	63	24	61
Portsmouth	42	18	17	7	62	39	53
Luton Town	42	22	8	12	64	35	52
Queen's Park Rangers	42	18	13	11	53	44	49
Swindon Town	42	16	13	13	72	60	45
Watford	42	13	18	11	54	48	44
Aberdare Athletic	42	17	10	15	57	51	44
Brentford	42	16	11	15	52	43	43
Swansea Town	42	13	15	14	50	47	41
Merthyr Town	42	17	6	19	45	56	40
Millwall	42	10	18	14	38	42	38
Reading	42	14	10	18	40	47	38
Bristol Rovers	42	14	10	18	52	67	38
Norwich City	42	12	13	17	50	62	37
Charlton Athletic	42	13	11	18	43	56	37
Northampton Town	42	13	11	18	47	71	37
Gillingham	42	14	8	20	47	60	36
Brighton & Hove Albion	42	13	9	20	45	51	35
Newport County	42	11	12	19	44	61	34
Exeter City	42	11	12	19	38	59	34
Southend United	42	8	11	23	34	74	27

Attendances

	TOTAL		
	Home	**Away**	**Total**
League	234,000	243,940	477,940
Cup/Otherer	21,411	31,000	52,411
TOTAL	255,411	274,940	530,351

	AVERAGE		
	Home	**Away**	**Total**
League	11,143	11,616	11,380
Cup/Otherer	21,411	31,000	26,206
TOTAL	11,610	12,497	12,053

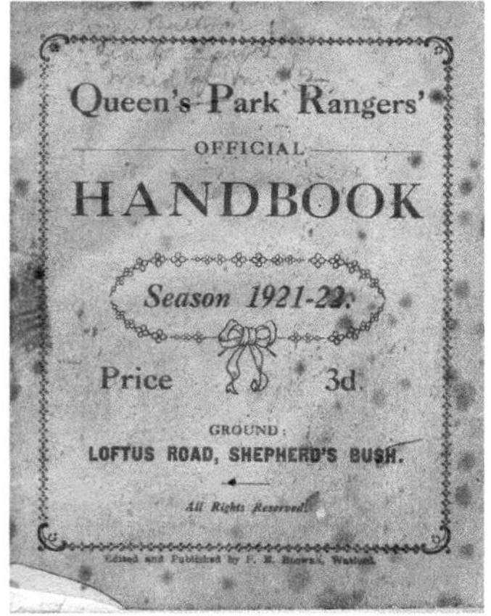

Match No.	Date		Opponents	Location	Result		Scorers	Atter
1	Aug	27	Swindon Town	H	D	0-0		1
2		29	Newport County	A	W	1-0	Birch	1
3	Sep	3	Swindon Town	A	L	0-2		1
4		5	Newport County	H	W	2-1	Birch, Smith	
5		10	Norwich City	A	D	0-0		
6		17	Norwich City	H	W	2-0	Gregory, Smith (pen)	1
7		24	Reading	A	W	1-0	Gregory	1
8	Oct	1	Reading	H	D	1-1	Birch	1
9		8	Bristol Rovers	A	D	1-1	Smith	1
10		15	Bristol Rovers	H	L	1-2	O'Brien	1
11		22	Brentford	A	L	1-5	Birch	1
12		29	Brentford	H	D	1-1	Smith	1
13	Nov	5	Aberdare Athletic	A	L	2-4	Birch, Gregory	1
14		12	Aberdare Athletic	H	W	1-0	Knight	1
15		19	Brighton	A	L	1-2	Faulkner	
16		26	Brighton	H	W	3-0	O'Brien, Birch (2)	1
17	Dec	3	Watford	A	D	2-2	Gregory, Birch	
18		10	Watford	H	D	1-1	Birch	
19		17	Charlton Athletic	A	D	1-1	Chandler	1
20		24	Charlton Athletic	H	W	3-1	O'Brien, Smith, Chandler	1
21		26	Southampton	H	D	2-2	Birch, Chandler	1
22		27	Southampton	A	D	1-1	Birch	2
23		31	Northampton Town	H	W	4-0	Birch (2), Smith (2)	1
24	Jan	14	Northampton Town	A	L	0-1		
25		21	Gillingham	H	W	1-0	Chandler	
26		28	Gillingham	A	W	2-1	Smith (2)	1
27	Feb	4	Millwall	H	W	6-1	Edgley, Smith, Grant, Birch, Chandler (2)	
28		11	Millwall	A	D	0-0		2
29		18	Exeter City	H	W	2-1	Chandler, Gregory	1
30		25	Exeter City	A	W	1-0	Edgley	
31	Mar	4	Swansea Town	H	W	1-0	Birch	
32		11	Swansea Town	A	L	0-1		1
33		18	Southend United	A	W	2-1	Edgley, Birch	
34		25	Southend United	H	W	1-0	Edgley	1
35	Apr	1	Portsmouth	A	L	0-1		
36		8	Portsmouth	H	D	1-1	Chandler	1
37		14	Luton Town	H	W	1-0	Gregory	1
38		15	Merthyr Town	A	L	0-2		
39		17	Luton Town	A	L	1-3	Birch	1
40		22	Merthyr Town	H	D	0-0		
41		29	Plymouth Argyle	A	L	0-4		1
42	May	6	Plymouth Argyle	H	W	2-0	OG (Eastwood), Edgley	1

Appeara

FA Cup

R1	Jan	7	Arsenal	A	D	0-0		3
rep		11	Arsenal	H	L	1-2	Smith	2

Appeara

Total - Appeara

Total -

London Challenge Cup

R1	Oct	17	Custom House	H	W	3-0	Chandler, Gregory, Read
R2		31	Arsenal	A	L	0-2	

London Professional Charity Fund

1	Sep	29	Brentford	H	W	3-0

Bailey	Bain	Birch	Blackman	Bradshaw	Burnham	Chandler	Clayton	Edgley	Faulkner	Grant	Gregory	Hill	John	Knight	Lock	Marsden	O'Brien	Ramsey	Read	Smith	Thompson	Vigrass	OG
		8	3			9		7		4	10	1				2	6	11	5				
		8	3			9		7			10	1	4			2	6	11	5				
		8	3			9		7			10	1	4			2	6	11	5				
		8	3						7		10	1	4			2	6	11	5	9			
			3			8			7		10	1	4			2	6	11	5	9			
			3				10	11	7	4	8	1				2	6		5	9			
			3	7			10	11		4	8	1				2	6		5	9			
		8	3	7				11		4	10	1				2	6		5	9			
		8	3	7				11		4	10	1				2	6		5	9			
		8	3	7				11		4	10	1				2	6		5	9			
		8	3			9	10	11	7	4		1				2	6		5				
		8	3	7				11			10	1	4						5	9	2		
		8	3					11	7	4	10	1				2	5		6	9			
	3	8	2					11	7	4	10			9	1		5		6				
	3	8	2					11	7	4	10			9	1		5		6				
	3	8			6	10			7	4	11				1	2	5			9			
	3	8			6	10			7	4	11				1	2	5			9			
	3	8			6	10			7	4	11				1	2	5			9			
	3	8			6	10			7	4	11				1	2	5			9			
	3	8			6	10		7		4	11	1				2	5			9			
	3	8			6	10		7		4	11	1				2	5			9			
		8	3		6	10		7			11	1				2	5		4	9			
	3	8	2		6	10		7			11	1					5		4	9			
	3	8	2		6	10		7		4		1					5	11		9			
	3	8			6	10		7		4	11	1				2	5			9			
		8	3		6	10		7		4	11	1				2	5			9			
		8	3		6	10		7		4	11	1				2	5			9			
	3	8			6	10		7		4	11	1				2	5			9			
	3	8			6	10		7		4	11	1				2	5			9			
	3	8			6	10		7		4	11	1				2	5			9			
	3	8			6	10		7		4	11	1				2			5	9			
	3	8			6	10		7		4	11	1				2	5			9			
	3	8			6	10		7		4	11	1				2			5	9			
	3	8			6	10		7			11	1	4			2			5	9			
	3	8			6	10		7			11	1	4			2			5	9			
	3	8			5	10		7			11	1	4			2				9			
	3	8			5	9		11	7		10	1	4			2							
	3	8			5			11	7		10	1	4			2				9			
	3	8			5			11	7		10	1	4			2				9			
3		8			5	9		11	7		10	1	4			2						6	
	3				5	9		11	7	4	10	1				2				8		6	
	3	8			5	9		11	7		10	1	4			2						6	
1	25	38	20	5	27	30	3	36	17	27	40	36	13	2	6	37	30	6	21	33	1	3	
		17				8		5	1	1	6			1			3			10			1

Bailey	Bain	Birch	Blackman	Bradshaw	Burnham	Chandler	Clayton	Edgley	Faulkner	Grant	Gregory	Hill	John	Knight	Lock	Marsden	O'Brien	Ramsey	Read	Smith	Thompson	Vigrass	OG
	3	9			6	11		8	7			1	4			2	5			10			
	3	8			6	10		11	7	4		1				2	5			9			
	2	2			2	2		2	2	1		2	1			2	2			2			
																				1			

Bailey	Bain	Birch	Blackman	Bradshaw	Burnham	Chandler	Clayton	Edgley	Faulkner	Grant	Gregory	Hill	John	Knight	Lock	Marsden	O'Brien	Ramsey	Read	Smith	Thompson	Vigrass	OG
1	27	40	20	5	29	32	3	38	19	28	40	38	14	2	6	39	32	6	21	35	1	3	
		17				8		5	1	1	6			1			3			11			1

1922-23

Division Three South

	P	W	D	L	F	A	Pts
Bristol City	42	24	11	7	66	40	59
Plymouth Argyle	42	23	7	12	61	29	53
Swansea Town	42	22	9	11	78	45	53
Brighton & Hove Albion	42	20	11	11	52	34	51
Luton Town	42	21	7	14	68	49	49
Millwall	42	14	18	10	45	40	46
Portsmouth	42	19	8	15	58	52	46
Northampton Town	42	17	11	14	54	44	45
Swindon Town	42	17	11	14	62	56	45
Watford	42	17	10	15	57	54	44
Queen's Park Rangers	42	16	10	16	54	49	42
Charlton Athletic	42	14	14	14	55	51	42
Bristol Rovers	42	13	16	13	35	36	42
Brentford	42	13	12	17	41	51	38
Southend United	42	12	13	17	49	54	37
Gillingham	42	15	7	20	51	59	37
Merthyr Town	42	11	14	17	39	48	36
Norwich City	42	13	10	19	51	71	36
Reading	42	10	14	18	36	55	34
Exeter City	42	13	7	22	47	84	33
Aberdare Athletic	42	9	11	22	42	70	29
Newport County	42	8	11	23	40	70	27

Attendances

	TOTAL		
	Home	Away	Total
League	227,000	225,630	452,630
Cup/Other	53,129	23,454	76,583
TOTAL	280,129	249,084	529,213

	AVERAGE		
	Home	Away	Total
League	10,810	10,744	10,777
Cup/Other	17,710	23,454	19,146
TOTAL	11,672	11,322	11,505

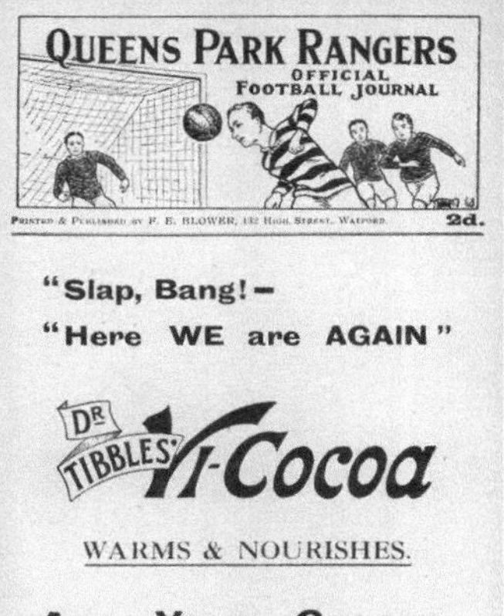

Match No.	Date		Opponents	Location	Result		Scorers	Attend
1	Aug	26	Watford	H	L	1-2	Birch	20
2		28	Norwich City	A	D	1-1	Davis	10
3	Sep	2	Watford	A	W	3-0	Chandler (2), Davis	10
4		4	Norwich City	H	W	2-0	C.Gregory, Birch	8
5		9	Gillingham	H	W	2-1	Birch (2)	9
6		11	Brentford	A	W	3-1	Parker (2, 1 pen), Birch	15
7		16	Gillingham	A	W	1-0	Birch (pen)	8
8		23	Brighton	H	D	0-0		12
9		30	Brighton	A	L	0-2		11
10	Oct	7	Swindon Town	H	L	0-2		12
11		14	Swindon Town	A	L	0-1		8
12		21	Charlton Athletic	H	L	1-2	Birch	11
13		28	Charlton Athletic	A	D	1-1	Birch	10
14	Nov	4	Aberdare Athletic	A	D	0-0		7
15		11	Aberdare Athletic	H	W	4-1	Davis (3), Hart	8
16		18	Newport County	A	L	0-1		8
17		25	Newport County	H	D	1-1	Hart	9
18	Dec	9	Brentford	H	D	1-1	Marsden (pen)	19
19		16	Bristol City	H	L	1-2	Marsden (pen)	12
20		23	Bristol City	A	L	2-3	Davis (2)	15
21		25	Luton Town	H	W	4-0	Parker (2), Birch (2)	16
22		26	Luton Town	A	L	0-1		11
23		30	Portsmouth	H	L	0-1		9
24	Jan	6	Portsmouth	A	D	1-1	Parker	12
25		20	Millwall	H	L	2-3	Parker, Davis	10
26		27	Millwall	A	D	0-0		20
27	Feb	10	Plymouth Argyle	A	L	0-2		11
28		17	Bristol Rovers	H	W	3-1	Parker, Davis, Chandler	9
29	Mar	3	Reading	H	W	1-0	Davis	10
30		15	Plymouth Argyle	H	L	2-3	Birch, Parker	4
31		17	Southend United	A	L	0-2		6
32		21	Reading	A	D	0-0		4
33		24	Southend United	H	W	1-0	Davis	8
34		26	Bristol Rovers	A	W	3-1	Parker, Chandler, Davis	18
35		30	Swansea Town	H	W	2-1	Davis, Chandler	18
36		31	Merthyr Town	A	W	1-0	Parker	5
37	Apr	2	Swansea Town	A	L	0-3		23
38		7	Merthyr Town	H	D	1-1	Vigrass	8
39		14	Exeter City	A	W	2-1	Parker (2)	6
40		26	Exeter City	H	W	2-0	Parker (2)	6
41		28	Northampton Town	A	L	2-4	Parker (2)	7
42	May	6	Northampton Town	H	W	3-2	Chandler, Edgley, OG (Williams)	9

Appearan
G

FA Cup

R1	Jan	13	Crystal Palace	H	W	1-0	J.Gregory	18
R2	Feb	3	Wigan Borough	A	W	4-2	Parker (2), Chandler, Birch	23
R3		24	South Shields	H	W	3-0	Parker (2), Gregory	15
R4	Mar	10	Sheffield United	H	L	0-1		20

Appearan
G

Total - Appearan
Total - G

London Challenge Cup

R1	Oct	16	Charlton Athletic	H	D	2-2	? ?
rep		30	Charlton Athletic	A	L	1-2	Birch

London Professional Charity Fund

1	Oct	9	Brentford	A	L	1-2

Birch	Burnham	Butler	Chandler	Davis	Edgley	Gardner	Gregory C.	Gregory J.	Grimsdell	Hart	Hill	John	Lane	Leach	Marsden	Parker	Rance	Vigrass	Watson	Watts	OG
8	5		10		7		11	4			1			6	2	9					
8			9	10	7		11	6			1	4			2			5			
8			9	10	7		11	6			1	4			2			5			
8			9	10	7		11	6			1	4			2			5			
8			9	10	7		11	6			1	4			2			5			
8			10		7		11	6			1	4			3	9		5	2		
8			10		7		11	6	3		1	4				9		5	2		
8			10		7		11	6			1	4			2	9		5			
8				10	7		11	6			1	4			2	9	5				
8		7	9	10			11	6	2		1	4					5				
8		7		10			11	6			1	4				9	5		2		
8			10		7		11	6			1	4			2	9	5				
8	6		10	9	7		11				1	4			2		5				
8				9	7		11			10	1	4	6		2		5				
8				9	7		11			10	1	4	6		2		5				
8				9	7		11			10	1	4			2		5	6			
8				9	7		11			10	1	4			2		5	6			
8			6	9	7		11			10	1				2			5	4		
		7	10	8			11	6			1	4			2	9		5			
		7	10	8			11	6			1				2	9	5	4			
8		7	10				11				1	4			2	9	5	6			
8		7	10	9	11			6			1		2				5	4			
8		7	10		11			6			1				2	9	5	4			
7			10	8	11			6			1	4			2	9		5			
7			10	8	11			6			1	4			2	9		5			
	6	7	10	8	11			5			1	4				9			2		
7			10	8	11			6			1	4			2	9		5			
7		11	10	8				6			1	4			2	9		5			
7			10	8	11			6			1	4			2	9		5			
7			10	8	11			6			1	4			2	9		5			
7		11	10	8			9	6			1	4	3					5	2		
7		11	10	8				6			1	4			2	9		5			
		7	10	8	11			6			1	4			2	9		5		3	
		7	10	8	11			6			1	4			2	9		5		3	
		7	10	8	11			6			1	4			2	9		5			
		7	10	8			11	6			1	4			2	9		5			
		7	6	8	11		10	3			1	4			2	9		5			
		7	4	8	11	10		6			1				2	9		5			
		7	4	8	11	10		6			1					9		5	2		
10		7	4	8	11			6			1				2	9		5			
8	6	7	4	10	11						1					9		5	2		
8		7	9	10	11						1	4	6		2			5			
32	4	21	36	35	33	2	24	33	2	5	42	33	5	1	34	28	13	33	8	2	
11			6	13	1		1			2					2	16		1			1

Birch	Burnham	Butler	Chandler	Davis	Edgley	Gardner	Gregory C.	Gregory J.	Grimsdell	Hart	Hill	John	Lane	Leach	Marsden	Parker	Rance	Vigrass	Watson	Watts	OG
7			10	8	11			6			1	4			2	9		5			
8			11	10	7			6			1	4			2	9		5			
7			10	8	11			6			1	4			2	9		5			
7			10	8	11			6			1	4			2	9		5			
4			4	4	4			4			4	4			4	4		4			
1			1					2								4					

Birch	Burnham	Butler	Chandler	Davis	Edgley	Gardner	Gregory C.	Gregory J.	Grimsdell	Hart	Hill	John	Lane	Leach	Marsden	Parker	Rance	Vigrass	Watson	Watts	OG
36	4	21	40	39	37	2	24	37	2	5	46	37	5	1	38	32	13	37	8	2	
12			7	13	1		1	2		2					2	20		1			1

1923-24

Division Three South

	P	W	D	L	F	A	Pts
Portsmouth	42	24	11	7	87	30	59
Plymouth Argyle	42	23	9	10	70	34	55
Millwall	42	22	10	10	64	38	54
Swansea Town	42	22	8	12	60	48	52
Brighton & Hove Albion	42	21	9	12	68	37	51
Swindon Town	42	17	13	12	58	44	47
Luton Town	42	16	14	12	50	44	46
Northampton Town	42	17	11	14	64	47	45
Bristol Rovers	42	15	13	14	52	46	43
Newport County	42	17	9	16	56	64	43
Norwich City	42	16	8	18	60	59	40
Aberdare Athletic	42	12	14	16	45	58	38
Merthyr Town	42	11	16	15	45	65	38
Charlton Athletic	42	11	15	16	38	45	37
Gillingham	42	12	13	17	43	58	37
Exeter City	42	15	7	20	37	52	37
Brentford	42	14	8	20	54	71	36
Reading	42	13	9	20	51	57	35
Southend United	42	12	10	20	53	84	34
Watford	42	9	15	18	45	54	33
Bournemouth	42	11	11	20	40	65	33
Queen's Park Rangers	42	11	9	22	37	77	31

Attendances

TOTAL	Home	Away	Total
League	183,000	188,297	371,297
Cup/Other	15,000		15,000
TOTAL	198,000	188,297	386,297

AVERAGE	Home	Away	Total
League	8,714	8,967	8,840
Cup/Other	15,000		15,000
TOTAL	9,000	8,967	8,984

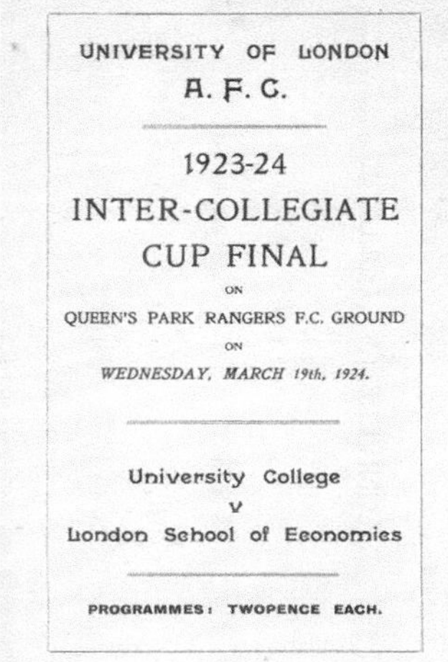

UNIVERSITY OF LONDON
A. F. C.

1923-24
INTER-COLLEGIATE
CUP FINAL
ON
QUEEN'S PARK RANGERS F.C. GROUND
ON
WEDNESDAY, MARCH 19th, 1924.

University College
v
London School of Economies

PROGRAMMES: TWOPENCE EACH.

Match No.	Date		Opponents	Location	Result		Scorers
1	Aug	25	Brentford	H	W	1-0	Parker
2		27	Bristol Rovers	H	L	1-2	Parker
3	Sep	1	Brentford	A	W	1-0	Birch
4		5	Bristol Rovers	A	L	1-2	Davis
5		8	Swindon Town	A	D	0-0	
6		12	Newport County	H	L	0-3	
7		15	Swindon Town	H	D	2-2	Birch, Davis
8		22	Watford	A	W	2-0	Birch, Davis
9		29	Watford	H	W	2-1	Birch, Marsden (pen)
10	Oct	6	Swansea Town	A	L	0-2	
11		13	Swansea Town	H	D	2-2	Davis, Marsden (pen)
12		20	Northampton Town	A	L	0-3	
13		27	Northampton Town	H	W	3-2	Davis (2), Robinson
14	Noc	3	Gillingham	A	D	0-0	
15		10	Gillingham	H	D	1-1	Davis
16	Dec	1	Plymouth Argyle	H	W	3-2	Parker, Birch, Davis
17		8	Plymouth Argyle	A	L	0-2	
18		15	Merthyr Town	H	W	3-0	Parker (2), Marsden (pen)
19		22	Merthyr Town	A	L	0-2	
20		25	Charlton Athletic	H	D	0-0	
21		26	Charlton Athletic	A	L	0-3	
22		29	Portsmouth	H	L	0-2	
23	Jan	1	Newport County	A	L	1-2	Parker
24		5	Portsmouth	A	L	0-7	
25		19	Brighton	H	W	1-0	Parker
26		26	Brighton	A	L	0-3	
27	Feb	2	Luton Town	H	L	0-2	
28		9	Luton Town	A	L	0-2	
29		16	Reading	H	L	1-4	Birch
30		23	Reading	A	L	0-4	
31	Mar	1	Bournemouth	H	L	0-1	
32		8	Bournemouth	A	L	1-3	Johnson
33		15	Millwall	A	L	0-3	
34		22	Millwall	H	D	1-1	Parker
35		29	Aberdare Athletic	A	D	1-1	Birch
36	Apr	5	Aberdare Athletic	H	W	3-0	Parker (2), Johnson
37		12	Southend United	A	L	2-4	Parker, Birch
38		18	Norwich City	H	W	2-1	Parker (pen), Johnson
39		19	Southend United	H	D	0-0	
40		21	Norwich City	A	L	0-5	
41		26	Exeter City	A	L	0-3	
42	May	3	Exeter City	H	W	2-0	Parker (2)

Appeara
G

FA Cup

R1	Jan	12	Notts County	H	L	1-2	Davis

Appeara
G

Total - Appeara
Total - G

London Challenge Cup

R1	Oct	22	Millwall	H	L	0-2

London Professional Charity Fund

1	Oct	1	Brentford	H	L	0-2

Bain	Benson	Birch	Butler	Cameron	Davis	Dobinson	Drabble	Field	Goodman	Hart	Hill	Hurst	John	Johnson	Keen	Knowles	Marsden	Oxley	Parker	Pierce	Robinson	Vigrass	Waller	Waugh	Wood
3	11	8		6	10						1		4		7		2		9			5			
3	11	8		6	10						1		4		7		2		9			5			
3	11	8		6	10						1		4		7		2		9			5			
3	11	8		6	10						1		4		7		2		9			5			
3	11			6	10						1		4		7		2	8	9			5			
3		8	11	6	9						1		4		7		2	10						5	
3		8	11	6	9						1		4		7		2	10						5	
3		8	11	6	9						1		4		7		2	10						5	
3		8	11	6	9						1		4		7		2	10						5	
	11	8		6	10						1		4		7		2	9		3					
3	11			6	10						1		4		7		2	8	9						
3	11	8		6	10	9					1		4		7		2								
		8		6	9					4	1				11		2	7		3	10	5			
		4		6	8						1				11		2	7	9		10	5			
	11	4			8					6	1				7		2		9		10	5			
3	11	4			8						1		6		7		2		9		10	5			
	11	4			7						1		6		8		2		9		10	5			
	11	4			8						1		6		7		2		9	3		5			10
	11	4			8						1		6		7		2		9	3		5			10
	11	4			8						1		6		7		2		9	3		5			10
	11	4			8						1		6		7		2		9	3		5			10
2	11	4			8						1		6		7				9	3				5	10
2	11	4			8						1		6		7				9			5			10
2		8		4	9						1		6		7				11			5			10
2		8	11	6	10			1					4					7	9	3		5			
2		8	11	6	9			1					4					7		3		5			10
2		4	11	6	10			1				8			7				9	3		5			
2			11	6		8					1		4		7				9	3		5			10
2		8	11	6							1		4	10	7				9	3		5			
2		7	11								1		4	10		5			9	3		6			8
3			11	6			1			4				8	7	5			9	2			10		
3		8	7	6			1			4				9		5		11		2			10		
3		8	7								1		4	10		5		11	9			6			
3		8									1		4	10		5		11	9	2		6			7
3		8									1		4	10		5		11	9	2		6			7
3		8									1		4	10		5		11	9	2		6			7
3		8									1		4	10		5		11	9	2		6			7
3		8							11		1		4	10		5			9	2		6			7
		8		6							1		4	10	11	5			9	2					7
		8									1		4	10	11	5			9	2		6			7
		8									1		4	10	11	5			9	2		6			7
3				6							1	8	4	10		5		11	9	2					7
30	17	37	13	24	27	2	2	3	1	4	37	2	36	14	31	13	21	18	33	24	5	30	2	5	19
		8			8									3			3		14		1				
2		8	11	6	10						1		4		7				9	3		5			
1		1	1	1	1						1		1		1				1	1		1			
					1																				
31	17	38	14	25	28	2	2	3	1	4	38	2	37	14	32	13	21	18	34	25	5	31	2	5	19
		8			9									3			3		14		1				

1924-25

Division Three South

	P	W	D	L	F	A	Pts
Swansea Town	42	23	11	8	68	35	57
Plymouth Argyle	42	23	10	9	77	38	56
Bristol City	42	22	9	11	60	41	53
Swindon Town	42	20	11	11	66	38	51
Millwall	42	18	13	11	58	38	49
Newport County	42	20	9	13	62	42	49
Exeter City	42	19	9	14	59	48	47
Brighton & Hove Albion	42	19	8	15	59	45	46
Northampton Town	42	20	6	16	51	44	46
Southend United	42	19	5	18	51	61	43
Watford	42	17	9	16	38	47	43
Norwich City	42	14	13	15	53	51	41
Gillingham	42	13	14	15	35	44	40
Reading	42	14	10	18	37	38	38
Charlton Athletic	42	13	12	17	46	48	38
Luton Town	42	10	17	15	49	57	37
Bristol Rovers	42	12	13	17	42	49	37
Aberdare Athletic	42	14	9	19	54	67	37
Queen's Park Rangers	42	14	8	20	42	63	36
Bournemouth	42	13	8	21	40	58	34
Brentford	42	9	7	26	38	91	25
Merthyr Town	42	8	5	29	35	77	21

Attendances

	TOTAL		
	Home	Away	Total
League	177,000	146,000	323,000
Cup/Other	37,640	9,700	47,340
TOTAL	214,640	155,700	370,340

	AVERAGE		
	Home	Away	Total
League	8,429	6,952	7,690
Cup/Other	12,547	4,850	9,468
TOTAL	8,943	6,770	7,880

Match No.	Date		Opponents	Location	Result		Scorers	Atten
1	Aug	30	Newport County	A	D	0-0		10
2	Sep	3	Watford	H	D	0-0		9
3		6	Bristol Rovers	H	L	1-2	H.Brown	12
4		10	Watford	A	L	0-1		6
5		13	Exeter City	A	W	3-1	H.Brown, Moore, OG (Crompton)	6
6		17	Southend United	A	L	0-1		8
7		20	Swansea Town	H	D	0-0		9
8		24	Plymouth Argyle	A	L	0-1		5
9		27	Reading	A	L	1-2	Hart	1
10	Oct	4	Merthyr Town	H	D	1-1	Birch	7
11		11	Brentford	A	W	1-0	H.Brown	8
12		18	Charlton Athletic	A	L	0-2		5
13		25	Millwall	H	D	0-0		12
14	Nov	1	Luton Town	A	L	0-3		4
15		8	Gillingham	H	D	1-1	Marsden (pen)	9
16		15	Swindon Town	A	L	3-5	Myers (2), Johnson	7
17		22	Brighton	H	W	2-0	Johnson (2)	9
18	Dec	6	Bristol City	H	W	3-0	Moore (2), Johnson	6
19		20	Aberdare Athletic	H	W	4-1	Birch (2), Johnson, Myers	9
20		25	Norwich City	H	L	1-2	Ogley	6
21		26	Norwich City	A	L	0-5		12
22		27	Newport County	H	W	4-3	Ford (2), Johnson, Moore	4
23	Jan	17	Exeter City	H	L	1-4	Moore	10
24		24	Swansea Town	A	L	0-2		6
25		31	Reading	H	W	1-0	Johnson	6
26		7	Merthyr Town	A	W	3-2	Johnson (2), Ford	5
27		14	Brentford	H	W	1-0	C.Brown	10
28		21	Charlton Athletic	H	D	0-0		10
29		28	Millwall	A	L	0-3		16
30	Mar	7	Luton Town	H	W	2-1	Hurst (2)	7
31		14	Gillingham	A	L	0-1		6
32		18	Bristol Rovers	A	L	0-3		5
33		21	Bournemouth	H	L	0-2		7
34		28	Brighton	A	L	0-5		7
35	Apr	4	Plymouth Argyle	H	L	0-1		11
36		11	Bristol City	A	L	0-5		9
37		13	Northampton Town	H	W	2-0	Johnson, Birch	8
38		14	Northampton Town	A	L	0-1		8
39		18	Swindon Town	H	W	1-0	Pierce (pen)	9
40		22	Bournemouth	A	W	2-0	Hurst, John	8
41		25	Aberdare Athletic	A	D	1-1	Birch	4
42	May	2	Southend United	H	W	3-1	Birch, Ogley (pen), Hurst	7

Appearan
G

FA Cup

Q5	Nov	29	Clapton	H	D	4-4	Myers (4)	5
rep	Dec	4	Clapton	A	W	2-0	Birch (2)	4
Q6		13	Charlton Athletic	H	D	1-1	Myers (pen)	13
rep		18	Charlton Athletic	A	W	2-1	Myers, Birch	5
R1	Jan	10	Stockport County	H	L	1-3	Myers	19

Appearan
G

Total - Appearan
Total - G

London Challenge Cup

R1	Oct	27	G.E.R.	A	W	5-2
R2	Nov	10	Brentford	H	W	2-0
SF		24	West Ham United	A	L	0-3

London Professional Charity Fund

No details recorded

Bolam	Brown C.	Brown H.	Dand	Evans	Fenwick	Field	Ford	Harris	Hart	Hill	Hurst	John	Johnson	Knowles	Lillie	Marsden	Moore	Myers	Ogley	Pierce	Pigg	Sweetman	Symes	Thompson	Wicks	Wood	Young	OG
	7	9					11			1		4	10	5	3	2	8		6									
	7	9					11			1		4	10	5	3	2	8		6									
	7	9					11			1		4	10	5	3	2	8		6									
	7	9					11	6		1		4		5		2	10		3									
	7	9					11	6		1		4		5		2	10		3									
	7	9					11	6		1		4		5		2	10		3									
	7	9		2		1	11	6				4		5			10		3									
	7	9		2		1	11	6				4		5			10		3									
	7	9		2		1	11	6	10			4		5					3									
	7	9		2	4		11	6	10	1				5					3									
	7	9			4		11	6		1			10	5		2			3									
	7	9			4		11	6		1			10	5		2			3									
	7	9			4		11	6		1				5		2		10	3									
	7				4		11	6		1				5		2		10	3							9		
	7						11	6				4	9			2	8	10	5				3		1			
	7			3			11	6				4	9	5				10		2					1			
	7						11	6		1		4	9	5				10	3	2								
11	7							6		1		4	9	5			8	10	3	2								
	7				5		11	6				4	9					10	3	2					1			
	7		4		5		11	6					9				10		3	2					1			
	7				4		11	6					9			2	10		5	3					1			
	7				5	1	11						9			2	10		6	3				4				
	7						11	6		1				5			10	9	3	2				4				
	7			3		1	11					4	9	5		2		10	6									
	7					1	11	4					9	5		2	8	10	6				3					
	7			3		1	11	4					9			2		10	6			5						
	7			3		1	11	4					9					10	6	2		5						
	7			3		1	11	4					9					10	6	2		5						
	7			3		1	11	4					9					10	6	2		5						
	7			3		1	11				9		10							2	6	5		4				
	7			3		1	11				9		10							2	6	5		4				
	7			3	6					1	9		10				11			2		5		4				
				3		1	11						9	5		2	10		6					4			8	
	7			3	6	1					9			5		2	11	10						4				
7				3	6	1					9						11	10		2		5		4				
	7			3	5	1							9				11	10	6	2				4				
	7				5	1	11					4	9				10		6	2			3					
	7				5	1	11					4	9				10		6	2			3					
	7				5	1	11					4	9				10		6	2			3					
	7				5	1	11				9	4					10		6	2			3					
	7				5	1	11				9	4					10		6	2			3					
	7				5	1	11				9	4					10		6	2			3					
2	40	13	1	17	19	22	37	24	2	15	8	21	27	22	3	18	26	17	36	22	2	8	8	9	5	1	1	
	1	3					3		1		4	1	10			1	5	3	2	1								1
	7						11	6		1		4	9	5				10	3	2								
	7						11	6		1		4	9	5				10	3	2								
	7						11	6		1		4	9	5				10	3	2								
	7						11	6		1		4	9	5				10	3	2								
	7						11	6		1			9	5				10	3	2				4				
	5						5	5		5		4	5	5				5	5	5				1				
																		7										
2	45	13	1	17	19	22	42	29	2	20	8	25	32	27	3	18	26	22	41	27	2	8	8	10	5	1	1	
	1	3					3		1		4	1	10			1	5	10	2	1								1

1925-26

Division Three South

	P	W	D	L	F	A	Pts
Reading	42	23	11	8	77	52	57
Plymouth Argyle	42	24	8	10	107	67	56
Millwall	42	21	11	10	73	39	53
Bristol City	42	21	9	12	72	51	51
Brighton & Hove Albion	42	19	9	14	84	73	47
Swindon Town	42	20	6	16	69	64	46
Luton Town	42	18	7	17	80	75	43
Bournemouth	42	17	9	16	75	91	43
Aberdare Athletic	42	17	8	17	74	66	42
Gillingham	42	17	8	17	53	49	42
Southend United	42	19	4	19	78	73	42
Northampton Town	42	17	7	18	82	80	41
Crystal Palace	42	19	3	20	75	79	41
Merthyr Town	42	14	11	17	69	75	39
Watford	42	15	9	18	73	89	39
Norwich City	42	15	9	18	58	73	39
Newport County	42	14	10	18	64	74	38
Brentford	42	16	6	20	69	94	38
Bristol Rovers	42	15	6	21	66	69	36
Exeter City	42	15	5	22	72	70	35
Charlton Athletic	42	11	13	18	48	68	35
Queen's Park Rangers	42	6	9	27	37	84	21

Attendances

TOTAL

	Home	Away	Total
League	162,928	162,344	325,272
Cup/Other	17,000	12,411	29,411
TOTAL	179,928	174,755	354,683

AVERAGE

	Home	Away	Total
League	7,758	7,731	7,745
Cup/Other	8,500	6,206	7,353
TOTAL	7,823	7,598	7,711

Match No.	Date		Opponents	Location	Result		Scorers	Atten
1	Aug	29	Gillingham	A	L	0-3		7
2	Sep	3	Reading	H	L	1-2	Campbell	9
3		5	Merthyr Town	H	D	1-1	Spotiswood	8
4		9	Reading	A	L	1-2	Burgess	8
5		12	Newport County	A	L	1-4	Burgess	8
6		19	Luton Town	H	W	1-0	Johnson	5
7		23	Exeter City	A	L	0-3		5
8		26	Brentford	A	W	2-1	Johnson, Birch	9
9	Oct	3	Bristol Rovers	A	L	0-5		7
10		8	Exeter City	H	D	0-0		4
11		10	Swindon Town	H	D	1-1	Middleton	9
12		17	Watford	H	W	2-0	Whitehead, Middleton	10
13		24	Brighton	A	L	1-2	Middleton	8
14		31	Bristol City	H	L	0-2		8
15	Nov	7	Crystal Palace	A	L	0-1		11
16		21	Norwich City	A	D	1-1	Whitehead	6
17	Dec	5	Plymouth Argyle	A	L	1-3	Whitehead	11
18		19	Northampton Town	A	L	2-3	Spotiswood, Burgess	5
19		25	Charlton Athletic	H	D	2-2	Burgess, Brown	8
20		26	Charlton Athletic	A	D	1-1	Burgess	11
21		28	Millwall	H	W	3-0	Cable (2), Whitehead	8
22	Jan	2	Gillingham	H	L	0-1		7
23		16	Merthyr Town	A	L	0-1		4
24		23	Newport County	H	L	0-2		6
25		30	Luton Town	A	L	0-4		6
26	Feb	6	Brentford	H	D	1-1	Burgess	13
27		13	Bristol Rovers	H	W	2-1	Ford (pen), Brown	6
28		20	Swindon Town	A	L	0-2		6
29		25	Aberdare Athletic	H	L	1-3	Burgess	4
30		27	Watford	A	L	1-3	Young	6
31	Mar	4	Southend United	H	D	2-2	Paterson, Young	3
32		6	Brighton	H	L	0-2		8
33		13	Bristol City	A	L	1-3	Paterson	12
34		27	Millwall	A	L	0-3		8
35		30	Crystal Palace	H	L	1-3	Burgess	12
36	Apr	2	Bournemouth	H	D	2-2	Whitehead, Paterson	7
37		3	Norwich City	H	L	0-1		6
38		5	Bournemouth	A	L	1-4	Rowe	5
39		10	Southend United	A	L	1-2	Middleton	6
40		17	Plymouth Argyle	H	L	0-4		9
41		24	Aberdare Athletic	A	L	0-1		3
42	May	1	Northampton Town	H	W	3-2	Birch (2), Middleton	4

Appearar
G

FA Cup

R1	Nov	28	Gravesend & Northfleet	A	D	2-2	Birch (2)	5
rep	Dec	2	Gravesend & Northfleet	H	W	2-0	Birch (2)	6
R2		12	Charlton Athletic	H	D	1-1	Hirst	11
rep		17	Charlton Athletic	A	L	0-1		7

Appearar
G

London Professional Charity Fund

1	Nov	16	Tottenham Hotspur	A	L	0-1		1

Appearar
G

Total - Appearar
Total - G

London Challenge Cup

R1	Sep	14	Clapton Orient	A	L	1-2

Birch	Brown	Burgess	Cable	Campbell	Edwards	Field	Ford	Harris	Hebden	Hirst	John	Johnson	Kerr	Middleton	Murdin	Paterson	Pierce	Pigg	Plunkett	Richmond	Rowe	Smith	Spotiswood	Sweetman	Symes	Thompson	Whitehead	Young
	7	10		9				6	1		4			8			2		3	5			11					
	7	10		9				6	1		4			8			2		3	5			11					
	7			9				6	1	4				10					3	5			11	2				
8	7	9						6	1	4				10					3				11	2				
8	7	9				1		6		4				10					3	5			11	2				
8							7		1	4		9		10			2	6	3	5			11					
10							11		1	4		9		8			2	6	3	5			7					
8	7	10							1	4		9					2	6	3				11			5		
8	7	10							1	4		9					2	6	3				11			5		
8	7								1			10		4			2	6		9			11		3	5		
	7			8			11		1	4		9		10			2	6							3	5		
	7						11		1		4	10		8			2	6							3	5	9	
	7						11		1		4	10		8			2	6							3	5	9	
	7	10					11		1		4			8			2	6							3	5	9	
	7	10					11		1	5	4						2	6							3	8	9	
7		10					11		1	5	4						2	6							3	8	9	
7		10					11		1	5	4						2	6							3	8	9	
	7	10							1	5	4						2	6					11		3	8	9	
	7	10	5					9	1		4						2	6					11		3	8		
	7	10	5			1		9			4						2	6					11		3		8	
	7	10	5			1	11	9			4						2	6							3		8	
	7	10				1	11	9		5	4						2	6							3		8	
		10					11		1	5	4			7		8	2	6							3		9	
	7	10							1	5	4					8	2	6					11		3		9	
	7	10	5						1	6	4	9				8	2		3				11					
7		10					11	6	1	5	4					8	2		3								9	
	7	10					11	6	1	5	4					8	2		3								9	
	7	10					11	6	1	5	4					8	2		3								9	
	7	10					11	6	1	5	4				9	8	2		3									
	7	10					11	6	1					5		9								2	3	4		8
		10	5						1	4				6		9							11	2	3		7	8
		10	5						1	4				6		9	3						11	2			7	8
	7	10	5						1		4			6		9	3						11	2				8
	7	10							1	4			9	6		8	3			5			11	2				
	7	10							1	4			9	6		8	3			5			11	2				
			5		7				1		4			6		10	3						11	2			9	8
			5		7				1		4			6		10	3						11	2			9	8
10			5		7				1		4			6					3		11			2			9	8
7		8	5						1	4				6		10	3				11			2			9	
7		8	5						1	4				6		10	3				11			2			9	
7		8	5								4			6		10					11	1		2	3		9	
7		8					11				4			6		10	3			5		1		2			9	
15	27	32	13	4	3	4	18	14	36	26	26	9	2	26	1	19	35	19	15	10	4	2	22	16	18	13	24	7
3	2	8	2	1			1					2		5		3					1		2				5	2
7		10					11		1	5	4						2	6							3	8	9	
7		10					11		1	5	4						2	6							3	8	9	
7		10					11		1	5	4						2	6							3	8	9	
8	7	10					11		1	5	4						2	6							3		9	
4	1	4					4		4	4	4						4	4							4	3	4	
4										1																		
	7	10		8					1	5	4						2	6					11		3		9	
	1	1		1					1	1	1						1	1					1		1		1	
19	29	37	13	5	3	4	22	14	41	31	31	9	2	26	1	19	40	24	15	10	4	2	23	16	23	16	29	7
7	2	8	2	1			1			1		2		5		3					1		2				5	2

1926-27

Division Three South

	P	W	D	L	F	A	Pts
Bristol City	42	27	8	7	104	54	62
Plymouth Argyle	42	25	10	7	95	61	60
Millwall	42	23	10	9	89	51	56
Brighton & Hove Albion	42	21	11	10	79	50	53
Swindon Town	42	21	9	12	100	85	51
Crystal Palace	42	18	9	15	84	81	45
Bournemouth	42	18	8	16	78	66	44
Luton Town	42	15	14	13	68	66	44
Newport County	42	19	6	17	57	71	44
Bristol Rovers	42	16	9	17	78	80	41
Brentford	42	13	14	15	70	61	40
Exeter City	42	15	10	17	76	73	40
Charlton Athletic	42	16	8	18	60	61	40
Queen's Park Rangers	42	15	9	18	65	71	39
Coventry City	42	15	7	20	71	86	37
Norwich City	42	12	11	19	59	71	35
Merthyr Town	42	13	9	20	63	80	35
Northampton Town	42	15	5	22	59	87	35
Southend United	42	14	6	22	64	77	34
Gillingham	42	11	10	21	54	72	32
Watford	42	12	8	22	57	87	32
Aberdare Athletic	42	9	7	26	62	101	25

Attendances

	TOTAL		
	Home	**Away**	**Total**
League	190,589	183,467	374,056
Cup/Other			
TOTAL	190,589	183,467	374,056

	AVERAGE		
	Home	**Away**	**Total**
League	9,076	8,737	8,906
Cup/Other			
TOTAL	9,076	8,737	8,906

Match No.	Date		Opponents	Location	Result		Scorers	Attend
1	Aug	28	Crystal Palace	A	L	1-2	Varco	18
2	Sep	1	Gillingham	A	D	2-2	Lofthouse, Wilcox	6
3		4	Coventry City	H	D	1-1	Lofthouse	13
4		11	Brentford	A	L	2-4	Paterson, Goddard	17
5		18	Charlton Athletic	A	L	0-2		9
6		20	Aberdare Athletic	A	W	2-0	Goddard (2)	1
7		25	Bristol City	H	L	1-2	Middleton	11
8		30	Aberdare Athletic	H	W	3-0	Goddard, Lofthouse, OG (Brophy)	5
9	Oct	2	Bournemouth	A	L	2-6	Young (pen), Goddard	6
10		9	Plymouth Argyle	H	W	4-2	Lofthouse (2), Middleton, Goddard	12
11		16	Bristol Rovers	H	D	2-2	Burgess, Goddard	11
12		23	Millwall	A	L	1-2	Middleton	14
13		30	Northampton Town	H	W	4-2	Lofthouse (2), Goddard, McAlister	10
14	Nov	6	Brighton	A	L	1-4	Goddard	10
15		13	Norwich City	H	W	4-0	Goddard (2), Lofthouse, Varco	2
16		20	Luton Town	A	L	0-2		5
17	Dec	4	Merthyr Town	A	L	0-4		2
18		11	Plymouth Argyle	A	L	0-2		10
19		18	Swindon Town	A	L	2-6	Goddard (2)	6
20		25	Watford	H	L	2-4	Young, Mustard	11
21		27	Watford	A	W	2-1	Charlesworth, Lofthouse	13
22	Jan	1	Gillingham	H	D	1-1	Goddard	7
23		8	Southend United	H	W	3-2	Charlesworth, Middleton, Goddard	6
24		15	Crystal Palace	H	L	0-2		11
25		22	Coventry City	A	L	0-1		8
26	Feb	5	Charlton Athletic	H	W	2-1	Goddard (2)	8
27		12	Bristol City	A	L	0-1		12
28		19	Bournemouth	H	D	1-1	Lofthouse	6
29		24	Exeter City	H	D	1-1	Lofthouse	2
30	Mar	5	Bristol Rovers	A	L	1-4	Wilcox	4
31		12	Millwall	H	D	1-1	Goddard	14
32		19	Northampton Town	A	L	0-1		5
33		26	Brighton	H	D	2-2	Mustard, Lofthouse	8
34	Apr	2	Norwich City	A	W	1-0	Lofthouse	10
35		9	Luton Town	H	W	1-0	Goddard	4
36		15	Newport County	A	W	2-0	Goddard, Varco	5
37		16	Southend United	A	W	3-0	Charlesworth, Swan, Goddard	7
38		18	Newport County	H	W	2-0	Goddard, Young (pen)	9
39		23	Merthyr Town	H	W	5-1	Young (2, 2 pens), Varco, Paterson, Goddard	8
40		30	Exeter City	A	W	2-0	Lofthouse, Paterson	5
41	May	5	Brentford	H	D	1-1	Hawley	11
42		7	Swindon Town	H	L	0-1		10

Appearar
G

Total - Appearar
Total - G

London Challenge Cup

R1	Sep	27	Barnet	A	W	2-1	
R2	Oct	18	Crystal Palace	H	L	0-1	

London Professional Charity Fund

1	Nov	1	Brentford	H	W	5-3	

Burgess	Cable	Charlesworth	Collier	Cunningham	Drew	Eggleton	Goddard	Gough	Hamilton	Hawley	Hebden	Hooper	Lofthouse	McAlister	Middleton	Mustard	Paterson	Pierce	Salt	Swan	Sweetman	Varco	Waterall	Wilcox	Young	OG
			4					6	7	5	1	2	11				10					8		9	3	
8			4					6	7	5	1	2	11				10							9	3	
8		7	4					6		5	1	2	11				10							9	3	
			4				9	6	7	5	1	2	11				10							8	3	
					7		9	6			1	2	11		4		10						5	8	3	
8		7					9	6			1	2	11		4		10						5		3	
8		7					9	6		5	1	2	11		4		10	3								
8		7					9	6		5	1	2	11		4		10								3	
8		7					9	6			1	2	11		10				5						3	
8							9	6	7	5	1	2	11		10				4						3	
8							9	6	7	5	1	2	11		10				4						3	
	5						9	6	7		1	2	11	8	10				4						3	
10				1			9	6	7	5		2	11	8	4										3	
10	5			1			9		7	4		2	11	8	6			3								
	5			1			9		7			2	11	4	6		10					8			3	
	5			1			9		7			2	11	4	6		10					8			3	
		7		1			9						11	4	6		10	2	5			8			3	
10				1			9			5			11	4	6	7		2				8			3	
10		8		1			9			5			11	4	6	7		2							3	
	5	8					9				1		11	4	6	7		2				10			3	
		7	4			5	9				1		11	8	6	10		2							3	
		7	4			5	9				1		11	8	6	10		2							3	
		7				5	9	6			1		11	4	10	8		2							3	
8		7				5	9	6			1		11	4	10			2							3	
		7				5	9	6			1		11	4	10	8		3			2					
		7				5	9	6			1		11	4	10	8		3			2					
		7				5	9	6			1		11	4		8		3		10	2					
10		7	4			5	9	6			1		11			8		3			2					
		7	4							5	1		11	6	10			3			2	9		8		
			4			5	9				1		11		6	7		3		10	2			8		
		7	4	1		5	9						11		6			3		10	2			8		
		7	4	1		5	9						11		6			3		10	2			8		
			4	1		5	9						11	8	6	7		3		10	2					
			4	1			9			5			11	6		7				10	2	8			3	
		4		1			9			5			11		6	7				10	2	8			3	
		7	4	1			9			5			11	6						10	2	8			3	
		7	4	1			9			5			11	6						10	2	8			3	
		7	4	1			9			5			11	6						10	2	8			3	
			4	1			9			5			11	6			7			10	2	8			3	
			4	1			9			5			11	6			7			10	2	8			3	
			4	1			9			5			11	6			7			10	2	8			3	
			4	1			9			5			11	6			7			10	2	8			3	
4	5	23	20	19	1	12	38	19	10	22	23	16	42	26	28	14	15	19	5	14	18	16	2	9	31	
1		3					23			1			14	1	4	2	3			1		4		2	5	1

Burgess	Cable	Charlesworth	Collier	Cunningham	Drew	Eggleton	Goddard	Gough	Hamilton	Hawley	Hebden	Hooper	Lofthouse	McAlister	Middleton	Mustard	Paterson	Pierce	Salt	Swan	Sweetman	Varco	Waterall	Wilcox	Young	OG
4	5	23	20	19	1	12	38	19	10	22	23	16	42	26	28	14	15	19	5	14	18	16	2	9	31	
1		3					23			1			14	1	4	2	3			1		4		2	5	1

1927-28

Division Three South

	P	W	D	L	F	A	Pts
Millwall	42	30	5	7	127	50	65
Northampton Town	42	23	9	10	102	64	55
Plymouth Argyle	42	23	7	12	85	54	53
Brighton & Hove Albion	42	19	10	13	81	69	48
Crystal Palace	42	18	12	12	79	72	48
Swindon Town	42	19	9	14	90	69	47
Southend United	42	20	6	16	80	64	46
Exeter City	42	17	12	13	70	60	46
Newport County	42	18	9	15	81	84	45
Queen's Park Rangers	42	17	9	16	72	71	43
Charlton Athletic	42	15	13	14	60	70	43
Brentford	42	16	8	18	76	74	40
Luton Town	42	16	7	19	94	87	39
Bournemouth	42	13	12	17	72	79	38
Watford	42	14	10	18	68	78	38
Gillingham	42	13	11	18	62	81	37
Norwich City	42	10	16	16	66	70	36
Walsall	42	12	9	21	75	101	33
Bristol Rovers	42	14	4	24	67	93	32
Coventry City	42	11	9	22	67	96	31
Merthyr Town	42	9	13	20	53	91	31
Torquay United	42	8	14	20	53	103	30

Attendances

TOTAL

	Home	Away	Total
League	218,538	161,790	380,328
Cup/Other	4,000		4,000
TOTAL	222,538	161,790	384,328

AVERAGE

	Home	Away	Total
League	10,407	7,704	9,055
Cup/Other	4,000		4,000
TOTAL	10,115	7,704	8,938

Match No.	Date		Opponents	Location	Result		Scorers
1	Aug	27	Newport County	H	W	4-2	Goddard (2, 1 pen), Lofthouse, Swan
2	Sep	1	Gillingham	H	D	3-3	Goddard (2), Lofthouse
3		3	Swindon Town	A	W	2-0	Swan, Johnson
4		7	Gillingham	A	W	2-1	Johnson, Neil
5		10	Brentford	H	L	2-3	Lofthouse (2)
6		17	Watford	H	W	2-1	Swan, Goddard
7		19	Bournemouth	A	W	2-1	Lofthouse, Goddard
8		24	Charlton Athletic	A	L	0-1	
9	Oct	1	Bristol Rovers	H	W	4-2	Goddard (3), Collier
10		8	Plymouth Argyle	A	L	0-3	
11		15	Merthyr Town	H	D	0-0	
12		22	Crystal Palace	A	D	1-1	Lofthouse
13		29	Millwall	H	L	0-1	
14	Nov	5	Luton Town	A	W	1-0	Goddard
15		12	Exeter City	H	L	0-1	
16		19	Torquay United	A	L	0-1	
17	Dec	3	Northampton Town	A	L	0-1	
18		17	Brighton	A	W	3-1	Goddard (2), Lofthouse
19		24	Bournemouth	H	W	2-0	Goddard, Mustard
20		27	Coventry City	A	D	0-0	
21	Jan	7	Swindon Town	H	L	0-1	
22		14	Southend United	H	W	3-2	Burns, Mustard, Young (pen)
23		21	Brentford	A	W	3-0	Goddard (2), Burns
24		28	Watford	A	D	3-3	Lofthouse (2), Goddard
25	Feb	4	Charlton Athletic	H	D	3-3	Goddard (2), Burns
26		11	Bristol Rovers	A	W	4-0	Goddard (2), Johnson, Lofthouse
27		18	Plymouth Argyle	H	L	0-1	
28		25	Merthyr Town	A	W	4-0	Goddard (3), Rounce
29	Mar	3	Crystal Palace	H	W	2-0	Swan, Goddard
30		10	Millwall	A	L	1-6	Beats
31		17	Luton Town	H	W	3-2	Johnson, Burns, Lofthouse
32		24	Exeter City	A	L	0-4	
33		31	Torquay United	H	L	2-3	Coward, Rounce
34	Apr	6	Newport County	A	W	6-1	Goddard (2), Burns, Young (pen), Coward, Rounce
35		7	Southend United	A	L	0-7	
36		9	Walsall	H	D	1-1	Young (pen)
37		10	Walsall	A	D	2-2	Lofthouse, Rounce
38		14	Northampton Town	H	L	0-4	
39		21	Norwich City	A	L	1-3	Johnson
40		26	Coventry City	H	L	1-5	Rounce
41		28	Brighton	H	W	5-0	Johnson (2), Rounce, Lofthouse, Young (pen)
42	May	3	Norwich City	H	D	0-0	

Appeara

FA Cup

R1	Nov	26	Aldershot	H	Abnd	1-0	
R1		30	Aldershot	H	L	1-2	Johnson

Appeara

Total - Appeara

Total - G

London Challenge Cup

R1	Oct	17	West Ham United	H	W	4-1
R2		31	Charlton Athletic	H	D	2-2
rep	Nov	14	Charlton Athletic	A	L	2-4

London Professional Charity Fund

1	Nov	7	Brentford	H	L	0-1

Burns	Collier	Coward	Crompton	Cunningham	Duthie	Eggleton	Gilhooley	Goddard	Hawley	Johnson	Kellard	Lofthouse	McAllister	Mustard	Neil	Paterson	Pierce	Roberts	Rounce	Stephenson	Swan	Sweetman	Turner	Woodward	Young
	4			1			5	9				11			8					7	10	2	6		3
	4			1			5	9				11			8					7	10	2	6		3
	4			1			5			9		11			8		3			7	10	2	6		
	4			1			5			9		11			8		3			7	10	2	6		
	4			1				9	5			11			8		3			7	10	2	6		
	4			1				9	5			11			8		3			7	10	2	6		
	4			1				9	5			11			8		3			7	10	2	6		
	4			1					5	9		11			8		3			7	10	2	6		
	4			1				9	5			11			8		3			7	10	2	6		
	4			1				9	5			11			8					7	10	2	6		3
	4			1				9	5			11		7	8		3				10	2	6		
	4			1	10	5		9				11		7	8		3					2	6		
	4			1	10	5		9				11		7	8		3					2	6		
	4			1		5		9		10				7		8	3	11				2	6		
	4			1		5		9						7	10	8	3	11				2	6		
	4			1	10	5		9				11			8					7		2	6		3
				1	4	5		9		10		11		7	8		2						6		3
				1	4	5		9				11		8	10		2			7			6		3
				1	4	5		9				11		8	10		2			7			6		3
				1	4	5		9				11		8	10		2			7			6		3
				1	4	5		9				11		8	10		2			7			6		3
8				1		5		9		10		11		7	4		2						6		3
8				1		5		9		10		11		7	4		2						6		3
8				1		5		9		10		11		7	4		2						6		3
8				1		5		9		10		11		7	4		2						6		3
8				1		5		9		10		11		7	4		2						6		3
8				1		5		9		10		11		7	4		2						6		3
				1		5		9				11		7	4		2		8		10		6		3
						5		9				11		7	4		2		8		10		6	1	3
8						5						11		7	4		2				10		6	1	3
8					6	5				9		11			4		2		10	7				1	3
8						5		9				11			4		2		10	7			6	1	3
8		7		1			5	9				11			4		2		10				6		3
8		7		1			5	9				11			4		2		10				6		3
8		7		1			5	9				11			4		2		10				6		3
8		7		1			5	9				11			4		2		10				6		3
8		7		1			5	9				11			4		2		10				6		3
8		7		1		5		9		10					4		2	11					6		3
				1	6	5				9				8	4		2	11	10	7					3
		7		1	6	5				9		11		8	4		2		10						3
8						5				9		11		7	4		2		10				6	1	3
			5			6				9	10	11		7	4		2		8					1	3
6	16	7	1	36	11	26	9	33	7	17	1	38		23	41	2	38	4	13	18	14	16	38	6	30
5	1	2						26		7		13		2	1				6		4				4

Burns	Collier	Coward	Crompton	Cunningham	Duthie	Eggleton	Gilhooley	Goddard	Hawley	Johnson	Kellard	Lofthouse	McAllister	Mustard	Neil	Paterson	Pierce	Roberts	Rounce	Stephenson	Swan	Sweetman	Turner	Woodward	Young
	4			1		5		9		10		11		7	8							2	6		3
	1			1		1		1		1		1		1	1							1	1		1
										1															

Burns	Collier	Coward	Crompton	Cunningham	Duthie	Eggleton	Gilhooley	Goddard	Hawley	Johnson	Kellard	Lofthouse	McAllister	Mustard	Neil	Paterson	Pierce	Roberts	Rounce	Stephenson	Swan	Sweetman	Turner	Woodward	Young
6	17	7	1	37	11	27	9	34	7	18	1	39		24	42	2	38	4	13	18	14	17	39	6	31
5	1	2						26		8		13		2	1				6		4				4

1928-29

Division Three South

	P	W	D	L	F	A	Pts
Charlton Athletic	42	23	8	11	86	60	54
Crystal Palace	42	23	8	11	81	67	54
Northampton Town	42	20	12	10	96	57	52
Plymouth Argyle	42	20	12	10	83	51	52
Fulham	42	21	10	11	101	71	52
Queen's Park Rangers	42	19	14	9	82	61	52
Luton Town	42	19	11	12	89	73	49
Watford	42	19	10	13	79	74	48
Bournemouth	42	19	9	14	84	77	47
Swindon Town	42	15	13	14	75	72	43
Coventry City	42	14	14	14	62	57	42
Southend United	42	15	11	16	80	75	41
Brentford	42	14	10	18	56	60	38
Walsall	42	13	12	17	73	79	38
Brighton & Hove Albion	42	16	6	20	58	76	38
Newport County	42	13	9	20	69	86	35
Norwich City	42	14	6	22	69	81	34
Torquay United	42	14	6	22	66	84	34
Bristol Rovers	42	13	7	22	60	79	33
Merthyr Town	42	11	8	23	55	103	30
Exeter City	42	9	11	22	67	88	29
Gillingham	42	10	9	23	43	83	29

Attendances

TOTAL

	Home	Away	Total
League	283,236	224,586	507,822
Cup/Other		10,000	10,000
TOTAL	283,236	234,586	517,822

AVERAGE

	Home	Away	Total
League	13,487	10,695	12,091
Cup/Other		10,000	10,000
TOTAL	13,487	10,663	12,042

QUEEN'S PARK RANGERS
OFFICIAL PROGRAMME
2d.
Wanted !
Thousands of regular supporters to compete in the Penny-on-the-Ball Competition at every match. Don't miss the opportunity to help yourself and the Club. Buy a
BLUE-&-WHITE TICKET TO-DAY

Match No.	Date		Opponents	Location	Result		Scorers	Atten
1	Aug	25	Torquay United	A	W	4-3	Goddard (3), Burns	7
2		30	Newport County	H	D	0-0		9
3	Sep	1	Gillingham	H	W	1-0	Coward	12
4		6	Newport County	A	D	0-0		5
5		8	Plymouth Argyle	A	W	2-1	Goddard (2)	10
6		15	Fulham	H	W	2-1	Young (pen), Goddard	21
7		22	Brentford	A	D	1-1	Smith	20
8		29	Bristol Rovers	A	D	1-1	Goddard	8
9	Oct	6	Watford	H	W	3-2	Goddard, McNab, Coward	18
10		13	Walsall	A	L	1-3	Rounce	7
11		20	Bournemouth	H	D	0-0		11
12		27	Mertyhr Town	A	W	2-1	Rounce (pen), Goddard	2
13	Nov	3	Southend United	H	W	3-1	Burns, Rounce, Goddard	12
14		10	Exeter City	A	D	1-1	Burns	4
15		17	Brighton	H	W	3-2	Young, Rounce, Goddard	11
16	Dec	1	Charlton Athletic	H	D	2-2	Goddard (2)	10
17		8	Northampton Town	A	L	2-4	Goddard (2)	10
18		15	Coventry City	H	W	3-1	Rogers (2), Goddard	8
19		22	Luton Town	A	L	2-3	Goddard (2)	9
20		25	Swindon Town	H	W	4-2	Rogers, Burns, Goddard, Kellard	14
21		26	Swindon Town	A	L	1-2	OG (Dickenson)	9
22		29	Torquay United	H	W	5-1	Goddard (3), Burns, OG (Oxley)	11
23	Jan	5	Gillingham	A	D	0-0		4
24		19	Plymouth Argyle	H	W	2-0	Burns, McNab	17
25		26	Fulham	A	L	0-5		26
26	Feb	2	Brentford	H	D	2-2	Coward, OG (Herod)	10
27		9	Bristol Rovers	H	L	0-3		10
28		16	Watford	A	L	1-4	Rogers	7
29		23	Walsall	H	D	2-2	Goddard, Young (pen)	8
30	Mar	2	Bournemouth	A	W	3-2	OG (Haywood), Rounce, Goddard	5
31		9	Mertyhr Town	H	W	8-0	Goddard (4), Burns (3), Rounce	11
32		16	Southend United	A	W	3-0	Burns (2), Goddard	6
33		23	Exeter City	H	W	1-0	Goddard	12
34		29	Crystal Palace	A	W	4-1	Goddard (3), Coward	33
35		30	Brighton	A	L	1-2	Pierce	9
36	Apr	1	Crystal Palace	H	D	1-1	Goddard	19
37		6	Norwich City	H	W	3-0	Coward (2), Rounce	12
38		13	Charlton Athletic	A	D	2-2	Coward, Rounce	17
39		20	Northampton Town	H	W	4-1	Rounce, Goddard, Burns, Whatmore	21
40		22	Norwich City	A	L	1-3	Goddard	7
41		27	Coventry City	A	D	0-0		11
42	May	4	Luton Town	H	D	1-1	Goddard	13

Appearar
G

FA Cup

R1	Nov	24	Guildford City	A	L	2-4	Goddard, Burns	10

Appearar
G

Total - Appearar
Total - G

London Challenge Cup

R1	Oct	15	Arsenal	H	W	5-1	Vallence (3), Rounce, Coward	
R2		29	Tottenham Hotspur	H	D	1-1	?	
rep	Nov	5	Tottenham Hotspur	A	L	1-3	Rounce	3

London Professional Charity Fund

1	Nov	12	Brentford	H	L	0-1		

urns	Cockburn	Coward	Cunningham	Eggleton	Foster	Goddard	Johnson	Kellard	McNab	Neil	Nixon	Pierce	Price	Rogers	Rounce	Smith	Sweetman	Thompson	Vallence	Whatmore	Woodward	Young	OG
3	5	7	1			9			4	6			11				2			10		3	
3	5	7	1			9			4	6			11				2			10		3	
3	5	7	1			9			4				11		10		2	6				3	
	5	7	1			9	10		4						8	11	2	6				3	
3	5	7	1			9			4						10	11	2	6				3	
3	5	7	1			9			4						10	11	2	6				3	
3	5	7	1			9			4						10	11	2	6				3	
3	5	7	1			9			4	6					10	11	2					3	
3	5	7	1			9			4	6					10	11	2					3	
3	5	7	1			9			4	6					10	11	2					3	
	5	7	1		8	9			4	6						11	2			10		3	
3	5	7	1			9			4						10	11	2	6				3	
3	5	7	1			9			4	6					10	11	2					3	
3	5	7	1			9						3			10	11	2	6					
3	5	7				9			4	6					10	11	2				1	3	
3	5	7				9			4						10	11	2	6			1	3	
3	5	7	1			9				4					10	11	2	6				3	
3	5	7	1			9				4				10		11	2	6				3	
3	5	7	1			9				4				10		11	2	6				3	
3	5		1			9		7		4				10		11	2			6		3	
3			1	5		9		7		4				10		11	2	6				3	
3		7	1	5		9				4				10		11	2	6				3	
3	5	7	1			9			4					10		11	2	6				3	
3	5	7	1			9			4					10		11	2	6				3	
3	5	7	1			9			4					10		11	2			6		3	
3	5	7	1			9			4					10			2	6		11		3	
	5	7	1			9			4					10	8		2	6		11		3	
		7	1	5		9			4	6				10			2		8	11		3	
3			1	5		9		7		4						11	2	6		10		3	
3	5	7	1			9			4	6		3			10		2			11			
3		7	1			9			4	6	5	3			10		2			11			
3		7	1			9			4	6	5	3			10		2			11			
3		7	1			9			4	6	5	3			10		2			11			
3	5	7	1			9			4	6		3			10		2			11			
3	5	7	1			9			4	6		3			10		2			11			
3	5	7	1			9			4	6	3				10		2			11			
	5	7	1			9		8	4	6	3				10		2			11			
3	5	7				9			4	6		3			10	11	2				1		
3	5	7	1			9			4	6		3			10		2			11			
3	5	7			4	9				6		3			10		2			11	1		
3	5	7	1			9			4	6		3			10		2			11			
3	5	7	1		4	9				6		3			10		2			11			
7	35	39	38	4	3	42	1	4	32	29	5	12	3	11	28	24	42	18	1	21	4	28	
2		7				37		1	2			1		4	9	1				1		3	4
3	5	7				9			4	6					10	11	2				1	3	
1	1	1				1			1	1					1	1	1				1	1	
1						1																	
8	36	40	38	4	3	43	1	4	33	30	5	12	3	11	29	25	43	18	1	21	5	29	
3		7				38		1	2			1		4	9	1				1		3	4

1929-30

Division Three South

	P	W	D	L	F	A	Pts
Plymouth Argyle	42	30	8	4	98	38	68
Brentford	42	28	5	9	94	44	61
Queen's Park Rangers	42	21	9	12	80	68	51
Northampton Town	42	21	8	13	82	58	50
Brighton & Hove Albion	42	21	8	13	87	63	50
Coventry City	42	19	9	14	88	73	47
Fulham	42	18	11	13	87	83	47
Norwich City	42	18	10	14	88	77	46
Crystal Palace	42	17	12	13	81	74	46
Bournemouth	42	15	13	14	72	61	43
Southend United	42	15	13	14	69	59	43
Clapton Orient	42	14	13	15	55	62	41
Luton Town	42	14	12	16	64	78	40
Swindon Town	42	13	12	17	73	83	38
Watford	42	15	8	19	60	73	38
Exeter City	42	12	11	19	67	73	35
Walsall	42	13	8	21	71	78	34
Newport County	42	12	10	20	74	85	34
Torquay United	42	10	11	21	64	94	31
Bristol Rovers	42	11	8	23	67	93	30
Gillingham	42	11	8	23	51	80	30
Merthyr Town	42	6	9	27	60	135	21

Attendances

TOTAL

	Home	Away	Total
League	230,161	205,862	436,023
Cup/Other	35,097	31,300	66,397
TOTAL	265,258	237,162	502,420

AVERAGE

	Home	Away	Total
League	10,960	9,803	10,382
Cup/Other	17,549	15,650	16,599
TOTAL	11,533	10,311	10,922

Match No.	Date		Opponents	Location	Result		Scorers	Atter
1	Aug	31	Crystal Palace	A	D	1-1	H.Wiles	2
2	Sep	5	Walsall	H	D	2-2	Goddard, Moffat	
3		7	Gillingham	H	W	2-1	Goddard, Moffat	1
4		9	Walsall	A	L	0-4		
5		14	Northampton Town	A	L	1-2	Rounce	1
6		16	Fulham	H	D	0-0		1
7		21	Exeter City	H	W	2-0	Young, Rounce	1
8		28	Southend United	A	L	0-1		1
9	Oct	5	Luton Town	H	W	1-0	Goddard	1
10		12	Bournemouth	A	D	0-0		
11		19	Clapton Orient	H	D	1-1	Rounce	1
12		26	Coventry City	A	W	3-2	Howe (2), Goddard	1
13	Nov	2	Watford	H	D	0-0		1
14		9	Newport County	A	W	5-4	H.Wiles (3), Goddard, Rounce	
15		16	Torquay United	H	D	1-1	OG (Fowler)	
16	Dec	7	Swindon Town	A	D	2-2	Coward, Howe	
17		21	Bristol Rovers	A	L	1-4	Goddard	
18		25	Norwich City	A	L	0-3		1
19		26	Norwich City	H	W	3-2	Goddard (3)	1
20		28	Crystal Palace	H	W	4-1	Rounce (2, 1 pen), Burns, Goddard	1
21	Jan	4	Gillingham	A	L	1-3	Goddard	
22		18	Northampton Town	H	L	0-2		1
23		25	Exeter City	A	W	2-0	Moffat, Goddard	
24	Feb	1	Southend United	H	L	2-5	Rounce, Goddard	
25		8	Luton Town	A	L	1-2	Goddard	
26		15	Bournemouth	H	W	3-1	Goddard (2, 1 pen), Coward	
27		22	Clapton Orient	A	W	4-2	Goddard (2), Rounce (2, 1 pen)	1
28	Mar	1	Coventry City	H *	W	3-1	Howe (2), Armstrong	1
29		3	Merthyr Town	A	W	4-1	Goddard (3), H.Wiles	
30		8	Watford	A	D	1-1	OG (Bresford)	1
31		13	Plymouth Argyle	H	L	1-2	Goddard (pen)	
32		15	Newport County	H	W	4-1	Goddard (3), OG (Wheeler)	
33		22	Torquay United	A	W	3-1	Armstrong, Burns, Rounce	
34		27	Brighton	H	W	3-1	Goddard (2), OG (Masrden)	
35		29	Merthyr Town	H	W	2-0	Goddard, Rounce	1
36	Apr	5	Plymouth Argyle	A	L	0-4		1
37		12	Swindon Town	H	W	8-3	Goddard (4), Rounce (3), Coward	
38		18	Brentford	H	W	2-1	Rounce, Goddard (pen)	2
39		19	Brighton	A	W	3-2	Goddard (3)	
40		21	Brentford	A	L	0-3		1
41		26	Bristol Rovers	H	W	2-1	H.Wiles, Armstrong	
42	May	3	Fulham	A	W	2-0	Rounce, Goddard	1

* Played at Highbury

Appeara

G

FA Cup

R1	Nov	30	Luton Town	A	W	3-2	Goddard, Coward, Pierce (pen)	
R2	Dec	12	Lincoln City	H	W	2-1	Burns (2)	1
R3	Jan	11	Charlton Athletic	A	D	1-1	Goddard	2
rep		16	Charlton Athletic	H	L	0-3		2

Appeara

G

London Professional Charity Fund

1	Oct	21	Chelsea	A	W	3-2	Coward (2), Burns	

Appeara

G

Total - Appeara

Total - G

London Challenge Cup

R1	Oct	14	Millwall	A	L	3-4	Goddard (3)

Burns	Cockburn	Coward	Cunningham	Evans	Foster	Goddard	Gretton	Harris	Hebden	Howe	McNab	Moffat	Neil	Nixon	Pickett	Pierce	Pollard	Rogers	Rounce	Whatmore	Wiles G.	Wiles H.	Yates	Young	OG
	5		1			9		3			4	7	6			2			10			8		11	
	5		1			9					4	7	6			2			10		3	8		11	
8			1			9					4	7	6	5		2			10		3			11	
			1		4	9						7		5		2			10		3	8	6	11	
	5		1			9					4	7	6			3	2		8	10				11	
	5		1			9					4	7	6			3	2		8	10				11	
	5		1			9					4	7	6			3	2		8	10				11	
	5		1			9					4	7	6			3	2		8	10				11	
8	5		1			9					4	7	6			3	2		10					11	
8	5		1			9					4	7	6			3	2		10					11	
8	5	7	1			9				11	4		6			3	2		10						
8	5	7	1			9				11	4		6			3	2		10						
8	5	7	1			9				11	4					3	2		10						
	5	7	1			9				11	4					3	2		10	6		8			
8	5	7				9				11	4				1	3	2					10			
8	5	7					1			11	4		6			3	2		10			9			
8	5	7	1			9				11			4			3	2	10		6					
8	5	7	1			9				11	4		6			3	2		10						
8	5	7	1			9				11	4		6			3	2		10						
8	5	7	1			9				11	4		6			2	3		10						
8	5	7	1			9				11	4		6			3	2		10						
8	5		1			9					4	7	6			3	2		10					11	
8	5		1			9					4	7	6			3	2		10					11	
	5			8		9			1		4	7	6			3	2		10					11	
8						9	1	3				7	4	2					10				6	11	
		7				9	1	3		11			4	2					10			8	6		
8		7				9	1	3		11			4	2					10				6		
8		7	1			9		3		11			4	2					10				6		
		7	1			9		3		11			4	2					10			8	6		
8		7	1			9		3		11			4	2					10				6		
8		7	1			9		3		11			4	2					10				6		
8		7	1			9		3		11			4				2		10	6					
8		7	1			9		3		11			4				2		10	6					
8			1			9		3		11		7	4				2		10	6					
8		7	1			9		3		11			4				2		10	6					
8		7	1		4	9		3		11							2		10	6					
8		7	1			9				11						3	2		10		4		6		
8		7	1			9		3		11			4	2					10				6		
8		7	1			9		3		11			4	2					10	6					
8		7	1			9		3		11			4				2		10	6					
8			1			9		3		11			4	2					10	6		7			
8			1			9				11			4	2					10	6	3	7			
31	22	25	36	1	2	41	4	17	1	28	22	15	36	13	1	25	27	1	40	15	5	10	10	14	
2		3				37				5		3							16			6		1	4

Burns	Cockburn	Coward	Cunningham	Evans	Foster	Goddard	Gretton	Harris	Hebden	Howe	McNab	Moffat	Neil	Nixon	Pickett	Pierce	Pollard	Rogers	Rounce	Whatmore	Wiles G.	Wiles H.	Yates	Young	OG
8	5	7				9				11	4		6		1	3	2		10						
8	5	7	1			9				11	4		6			2	3		10						
8	5	7	1			9				11	4		6			3	2		10						
8	5	7	1			9					4		6			3	2		10					11	
4	4	4	3			4				3	4		4		1	4	4		4					1	
2		1				2										1									

Burns	Cockburn	Coward	Cunningham	Evans	Foster	Goddard	Gretton	Harris	Hebden	Howe	McNab	Moffat	Neil	Nixon	Pickett	Pierce	Pollard	Rogers	Rounce	Whatmore	Wiles G.	Wiles H.	Yates	Young	OG
8	5	7	1			9				11	4		6			3	2		10						
1	1	1	1			1				1	1		1			1	1		1						
1		2																							

Burns	Cockburn	Coward	Cunningham	Evans	Foster	Goddard	Gretton	Harris	Hebden	Howe	McNab	Moffat	Neil	Nixon	Pickett	Pierce	Pollard	Rogers	Rounce	Whatmore	Wiles G.	Wiles H.	Yates	Young	OG
36	27	30	40	1	2	46	4	17	1	32	27	15	41	13	2	30	32	1	45	15	5	10	10	15	
5		6				42				5		3				1			19			6		1	4

1930-31

Division Three South

	P	W	D	L	F	A	Pts
Notts County	42	24	11	7	97	46	59
Crystal Palace	42	22	7	13	107	71	51
Brentford	42	22	6	14	90	64	50
Brighton & Hove Albion	42	17	15	10	68	53	49
Southend United	42	22	5	15	76	60	49
Northampton Town	42	18	12	12	77	59	48
Luton Town	42	19	8	15	76	51	46
Queen's Park Rangers	42	20	3	19	82	75	43
Fulham	42	18	7	17	77	75	43
Bournemouth	42	15	13	14	72	73	43
Torquay United	42	17	9	16	80	84	43
Swindon Town	42	18	6	18	89	94	42
Exeter City	42	17	8	17	84	90	42
Coventry City	42	16	9	17	75	65	41
Bristol Rovers	42	16	8	18	75	92	40
Gillingham	42	14	10	18	61	76	38
Walsall	42	14	9	19	78	95	37
Watford	42	14	7	21	72	75	35
Clapton Orient	42	14	7	21	63	91	35
Thames	42	13	8	21	54	93	34
Newport County	42	11	6	25	69	111	28
Norwich City	42	10	8	24	47	76	28

Attendances

	TOTAL		
	Home	Away	Total
League	184,490	160,523	345,013
Cup/Other	17,200	24,000	41,200
TOTAL	201,690	184,523	386,213

	AVERAGE		
	Home	Away	Total
League	8,785	7,644	8,215
Cup/Other	17,200	12,000	13,733
TOTAL	9,168	8,023	8,583

Match No.	Date		Opponents	Location	Result		Scorers	Atten
1	Aug	30	Thames	H	W	3-0	Hoten (2), Goddard	13
2	Sep	3	Bournemouth	A	L	0-2		6
3		6	Norwich City	A	D	1-1	Goddard	12
4		11	Watford	H	L	2-3	Daniels, Goddard	8
5		13	Brighton	H	W	4-1	Rounce (2), Burns, Coward	6
6		17	Watford	A	W	4-0	Rounce, H.Wiles, Daniels, Coward	6
7		20	Walsall	H	W	3-0	Ferguson, H.Wiles, Burns	9
8		27	Coventry City	A	L	0-2		12
9	Oct	4	Fulham	H	L	0-2		14
10		11	Swindon Town	A	L	1-4	Coward	6
11		18	Torquay United	A	L	2-6	Burns, H.Wiles	5
12		23	Northampton Town	H	L	0-2		8
13	Nov	1	Brentford	A	L	3-5	Coward, H.Wiles, Nixon	10
14		8	Crystal Palace	H	W	4-0	Rounce (3, 1 pen), Coward	12
15		15	Southend United	A	L	0-2		5
16		22	Luton Town	H	W	3-1	Burns, Rounce, Sheppard	6
17	Dec	6	Newport County	H	W	7-1	Goddard (3), Burns (2), Armstrong, Rounce	6
18		17	Gillingham	A	D	2-2	Goddard, Howe	2
19		20	Exeter City	H	W	7-2	Goddard (4), Rounce (2), Coward	7
20		25	Notts County	H	W	4-1	Burns (3), Goddard	14
21		26	Notts County	A	L	0-2		13
22		27	Thames	A	L	0-1		3
23	Jan	3	Norwich City	H	W	3-1	Goddard (2), Rounce	6
24		14	Bristol Rovers	A	L	0-3		3
25		17	Brighton	A	D	1-1	Rounce	10
26		24	Walsall	A	W	2-0	OG (John), Hoten	4
27		31	Coventry City	H	W	2-0	Howe, Rounce	7
28	Feb	7	Fulham	A	W	2-0	Coward, Goddard	18
29		14	Swindon Town	H	L	1-2	Daniels	7
30		21	Torquay United	H	L	1-2	Burns	9
31		28	Northampton Town	A	L	0-6		5
32	Mar	7	Brentford	H	W	3-1	Goddard (2), Howe	10
33		14	Crystal Palace	A	L	0-4		14
34		21	Southend United	H	L	0-2		7
35		28	Luton Town	A	L	1-5	Sheppard	6
36	Apr	3	Clapton Orient	H	W	4-2	Goddard (2, 1 pen), Sheppard, Whatmore	7
37		4	Bristol Rovers	H	W	2-0	Rounce, Goddard	8
38		6	Clapton Orient	A	W	3-2	H.Wiles, Rounce, Goddard	5
39		11	Newport County	A	W	3-2	Goddard (2), Sheppard	2
40		18	Gillingham	H	W	1-0	H.Wiles	6
41		25	Exeter City	A	L	0-2		3
42	May	2	Bournemouth	H	W	3-0	Hoten, Lewis, Rounce	6

Appearar
G

FA Cup

R1	Nov	29	Thames	H	W	5-0	Goddard (2, 1 pen), Burns (2), Rounce	9
R2	Dec	13	Crewe Alexandra	A	W	4-2	Goddard (2), Howe, Rounce	8
R3	Jan	10	Bristol Rovers	A	L	1-3	Coward	24

Appearar
G

Total - Appearar
Total - G

London Professional Charity Fund

1	Oct	20	Chelsea	H	W	3-0	H.Wiles (2), Sheppard

Burns	Coward	Cunningham	Daniels	Embleton	Ferguson	Goddard	Harris	Hoten	Howe	Legge	Lewis	Nixon	Pickett	Pierce	Pollard	Rounce	Sales	Sheppard	Smith	Stephenson	Tutt	Vango	Whatmore	Wiles G.	Wiles H.	OG
8		1	11			9	3	10		7		2							4				6			
		1	11			9	3	10		7					2	8			4				6			
8		1	11			9		10		7					2				4				6	3		
8		1	11			9		10		7		2			3				4				6			
6	7	1	11		8							3			2	10			4						9	
6	7	1	11		8							2			3	10			4						9	
6	7	1	11		8							3			2	10			4						9	
6	7	1	11		8	9						2				10			4					3		
6	7	1	11		8							2				10			4					3	9	
	7	1	11					10				2		3		8	4						6		9	
8	7		11									2	1	3		10	4						6		9	
8	7		11									2	1		3		4	10					6		9	
8	7								11			2	1		3	10	4						6		9	
8	7	1					3		11						2	10	4	9					6			
	7	1					3		11						2	10	4	9		8			6			
8	7	1					3		11						2	10	4	9					6			
8	7	1				9	3		11						2	10	4						6			
	7	1			8	9	3		11						2		4	10					6			
8	7	1				9	3		11						2	10	4		5				6			
8	7	1				9	3		11						2	10	4		5				6			
8	7	1			11	9	3								2	10	4		5				6			
8	7	1	11			9	3								2	10	4		5				6			
8		1				9	3	11							2	10	4		5				6		7	
		1				9	3	10		7					2	8	4				11	5	6			
8		1				9	3		11	7					2	10	4		5				6			
8		1			6	9	3	11		7				2		10	4		5							
	7	1			6	9	3		11							8	4		5				10	2		
8	7	1			6	9	3		11							10	4		5					2		
	7	1	11		6	9	3									8	4		5				10	2		
8	7	1				9	3		11							10	4						6	2		
8		1				9	3		11	7					2	10			4				6			
8		1		7	6	9			11						2	10			4					3		
8		1		7	6	9			11						2	10			4					3		
	7	1			6	9	2		11								4	10		8				3		
8	7				6	9							1		2	10	4	11						3		
8	7					9	3						1			10		11	4				6	2		
8	7					9	3						1	2		10		11	4				6			
8						9	3						1		2	10	4	11					6		7	
8						9	3		11				1		2		4	10				5	6		7	
8	7						3						1		2	10	4	11					6		9	
8	7						3			9			1		2	10	4	11					6			
	7						3	9	11		8		1		2	10	4						6			
3	29	31	14	2	15	28	28	9	18	9	1	11	11	4	29	35	28	13	24	2	1	2	31	12	12	
0	7		3		1	23		4	3		1	1				16		4					1		6	1

Burns	Coward	Cunningham	Daniels	Embleton	Ferguson	Goddard	Harris	Hoten	Howe	Legge	Lewis	Nixon	Pickett	Pierce	Pollard	Rounce	Sales	Sheppard	Smith	Stephenson	Tutt	Vango	Whatmore	Wiles G.	Wiles H.	OG
8	7					9	3		11				1		2	10	4						6			
8	7	1				9	3		11						2	10	4						6			
8	7	1				9	3		11						2	10	4		5				6			
3	3	2				3	3		3				1		3	3	3		1				3			
2	1					4			1							2										

Burns	Coward	Cunningham	Daniels	Embleton	Ferguson	Goddard	Harris	Hoten	Howe	Legge	Lewis	Nixon	Pickett	Pierce	Pollard	Rounce	Sales	Sheppard	Smith	Stephenson	Tutt	Vango	Whatmore	Wiles G.	Wiles H.	OG
6	32	33	14	2	15	31	31	9	21	9	1	11	12	4	32	38	31	13	25	2	1	2	34	12	12	
2	8		3		1	27		4	4		1	1				18		5					1		8	1

1931-32

Division Three South

	P	W	D	L	F	A	Pts
Fulham	42	24	9	9	111	62	57
Reading	42	23	9	10	97	67	55
Southend United	42	21	11	10	77	53	53
Crystal Palace	42	20	11	11	74	63	51
Brentford	42	19	10	13	68	52	48
Luton Town	42	20	7	15	95	70	47
Exeter City	42	20	7	15	77	62	47
Brighton & Hove Albion	42	17	12	13	73	58	46
Cardiff City	42	19	8	15	87	73	46
Norwich City	42	17	12	13	76	67	46
Watford	42	19	8	15	81	79	46
Coventry City	42	18	8	16	108	97	44
Queen's Park Rangers	42	15	12	15	79	73	42
Northampton Town	42	16	7	19	69	69	39
Bournemouth	42	13	12	17	70	78	38
Clapton Orient	42	12	11	19	77	90	35
Swindon Town	42	14	6	22	70	84	34
Bristol Rovers	42	13	8	21	65	92	34
Torquay United	42	12	9	21	72	106	33
Mansfield Town	42	11	10	21	75	108	32
Gillingham	42	10	8	24	40	82	28
Thames	42	7	9	26	53	109	23

Attendances

	TOTAL		
	Home	**Away**	**Total**
League	279,368	180,855	460,223
Cup/Other	41,097	46,190	87,287
TOTAL	320,465	227,045	547,510

	AVERAGE		
	Home	**Away**	**Total**
League	13,303	8,612	10,958
Cup/Other	41,097	15,397	21,822
TOTAL	14,567	9,460	11,902

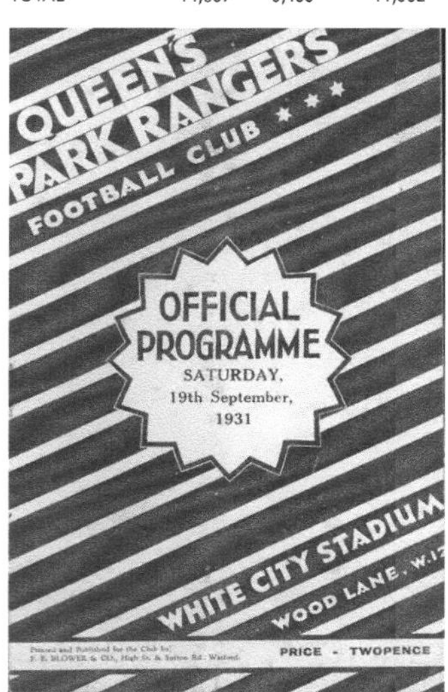

Match No.	Date		Opponents	Location	Result		Scorers	Atte
1	Aug	29	Brentford	A	L	0-1		2
2		31	Bristol Rovers	A	D	1-1	Haley	
3	Sep	5	Bournemouth	H	L	0-3		1
4		10	Swindon Town	H	L	1-2	Lewis	
5		12	Crystal Palace	A	D	1-1	Goddard	1
6		16	Swindon Town	A	W	2-1	Goddard, Cribb	
7		19	Watford	H	D	4-4	Goddard (4)	1
8		26	Mansfield Town	A	D	2-2	OG (England), Lewis	
9	Oct	3	Brighton	H	D	1-1	Goddard	1
10		10	Norwich City	A	L	1-2	Lewis	1
11		17	Exeter City	A	L	2-6	Coward, Lewis	
12		24	Coventry City	H	D	1-1	Wilson	1
13		31	Gillingham	A	L	0-1		
14	Nov	7	Luton Town	H	W	3-1	Cribb (2), Goddard	1
15		14	Cardiff City	A	W	4-0	Cribb (2), Goddard, OG (Roberts)	
16		21	Northampton Town	H	W	3-2	Cribb (2), Coward	1
17	Dec	5	Southend United	H	W	2-1	OG (Robinson), Goddard	1
18		19	Thames	H	W	6-0	Goddard (3), Tutt (2), Wilson (pen)	
19		25	Torquay United	A	W	3-2	Collins (2), Cribb	
20		26	Torquay United	H	W	3-1	Wilson, Cribb, Goddard	2
21		28	Fulham	A	W	3-1	Goddard (2), Cribb	2
22	Jan	2	Brentford	H	L	1-2	Cribb (pen)	3
23		13	Reading	A	L	2-3	Blackman (2)	
24		16	Bournemouth	A	D	2-2	Armstrong, Coward	
25		28	Crystal Palace	H	D	2-2	Blackman, Rounce	
26		30	Watford	A	D	2-2	Howe, Blackman	1
27	Feb	6	Mansfield Town	H	D	1-1	Blackman	1
28		13	Brighton	A	L	0-1		
29		20	Norwich City	H	D	2-2	Blackman, Cribb	
30		27	Exeter City	H	W	1-0	Blackman	1
31	Mar	5	Coventry City	A	L	0-1		1
32		10	Gillingham	H	W	7-0	H.Wiles (4), Haley (2), Coward	
33		19	Luton Town	A	L	1-4	H.Wiles	
34		25	Clapton Orient	A	L	0-3		
35		26	Cardiff City	H	L	2-3	Rounce, Haley	
36		28	Clapton Orient	H	W	3-2	H.Wiles, Coward, Tutt	1
37	Apr	2	Northampton Town	A	L	1-6	H.Wiles	
38		9	Reading	H	W	2-0	H.Wiles (2)	
39		16	Southend United	A	D	0-0		
40		23	Fulham	H	W	3-1	H.Wiles (2), Haley	2
41		30	Thames	A	L	2-3	Rounce (2)	
42	May	7	Bristol Rovers	H	W	2-1	Goddard, Whatmore	

Appeara

G

FA Cup

R1	Nov	28	Barnet	A	W	7-3	Cribb (3), Goddard (2), Coward (2)	
R2	Dec	12	Scunthorpe United	A	W	4-1	Rounce (3), Cribb	
R3	Jan	9	Leeds United	H	W	3-1	Cribb (2), Rounce	4
R4		23	Huddersfield Town	A	L	0-5		3

Appeara

G

Total - Appeara

Total - G

Armstrong	Blackman	Collins	Coward	Cribb	Cunningham	Goddard	Goodier	Haley	Hall	Harris	Howe	Lewis	Nixon	Pickett	Pollard	Rounce	Sales	Smith	Tutt	Vango	Whatmore	Wiles G.	Wiles H.	Wilson	Wyper	OG
5				11		9				3		8		1	2	10	4				6				7	
5				11		9		8		3				1	2	10	4				6				7	
5				11		9				3		8		1	2	10	4				6				7	
5				11		9		10	3			8		1	2	4					6				7	
5				11		9		10	3			8		1	2		4			6					7	
5				11		9		10	3			8		1	2		4			6					7	
5				11		9		8	3					1	2	10	4			6					7	
5				11		9		4	3			8	2	1		10				6					7	
5				11	1	9		4	3			8	2			10				6					7	
5				11	1	9			3			8	2				4			6				10	7	
5			7	11		9		4	3			8	2	1		10				6						
5			7	11		9			3			8		1						6	4	2		10		
5			7	11		9			3	2		8		1		10				6	4					
5		8	7	11		9				3			2	1		10				6	4					
5		8	7	11		9	6			3			2	1		10										
5		8	7	11		9	6			3			2	1		10										
5			7	11		9	6		3	2				1		10								8		
5		10	7			9	6		3	2				1					11					8		
5		10	7	11		9	6		3	2				1										8		
5		10	7	11		9	6		3	2				1										8		
5			7	11		9	6		3	2				1		10								8		
5			7	11		9	6		3	2				1		10								8		
5	9	8	7	11			6		3	2				1		10										
5	9	8	7	11			6		3	2				1		10										
5	9		7	11			6		3					1	2	10								8		
5	9			11			6		3		7			1	2	10								8		
5	9			11			6		3		7			1	2	10								8		
5		8		11			6		3				2	1		10								9	7	
5	9		7	11			6		3				2	1		10								8		
5	9		7				6		3				2	1		10			11					8		
5	9		7				6		3				2	1		10			11					8		
5		11	7				6	8	3				2	1									9	10		
5			7				6	8	3				2	1					11				9	10		
	9		11		1		6		3				2			8		5					7	10		
	9		11				6	8	3				2	1		10		5					7			
5			7				6		3				2	1		10			11				9	8		
5			7				6	8	3				2	1					11				9	10		
5			7		1		6	8	3		11		2			10							9			
5		10	7		1		6	8	3				2								11		9			
5					1	7	6	8	3				2			10					11		9			
5					1	7	6	8	3				2			10					11		9			
5					1	9	6	8	3				2			10					11		7			
40	10	11	26	28	8	25	28	17	36	15	3	11	22	34	10	31	7	2	6	10	11	1	11	20	11	
1	7	2	5	12		17		5			1	4				4			3		1		11	3		3

Armstrong	Blackman	Collins	Coward	Cribb	Cunningham	Goddard	Goodier	Haley	Hall	Harris	Howe	Lewis	Nixon	Pickett	Pollard	Rounce	Sales	Smith	Tutt	Vango	Whatmore	Wiles G.	Wiles H.	Wilson	Wyper	OG
5			7	11		9	6		3	2				1		10								8		
5			7	11		9	6		3	2				1		10								8		
5	9		7	11			6		3	2				1		10								8		
5	9		7	11			6		3	2				1		8					10					
4	2		4	4		2	4		4	4				4		4					1			3		
			2	6		2										4										

Armstrong	Blackman	Collins	Coward	Cribb	Cunningham	Goddard	Goodier	Haley	Hall	Harris	Howe	Lewis	Nixon	Pickett	Pollard	Rounce	Sales	Smith	Tutt	Vango	Whatmore	Wiles G.	Wiles H.	Wilson	Wyper	OG
44	12	11	30	32	8	27	32	17	40	19	3	11	22	38	10	35	7	2	6	10	12	1	11	23	11	
1	7	2	7	18		19		5			1	4				8			3		1		11	3		3

1932-33

Division Three South

	P	W	D	L	F	A	Pts
Brentford	42	26	10	6	90	49	62
Exeter City	42	24	10	8	88	48	58
Norwich City	42	22	13	7	88	55	57
Reading	42	19	13	10	103	71	51
Crystal Palace	42	19	8	15	78	64	46
Coventry City	42	19	6	17	106	77	44
Gillingham	42	18	8	16	72	61	44
Northampton Town	42	18	8	16	76	66	44
Bristol Rovers	42	15	14	13	61	56	44
Torquay United	42	16	12	14	72	67	44
Watford	42	16	12	14	66	63	44
Brighton & Hove Albion	42	17	8	17	66	65	42
Southend United	42	15	11	16	65	82	41
Luton Town	42	13	13	16	78	78	39
Bristol City	42	12	13	17	83	90	37
Queen's Park Rangers	42	13	11	18	72	87	37
Aldershot	42	13	10	19	61	72	36
Bournemouth	42	12	12	18	60	81	36
Cardiff City	42	12	7	23	69	99	31
Clapton Orient	42	8	13	21	59	93	29
Newport County	42	11	7	24	61	105	29
Swindon Town	42	9	11	22	60	105	29

Attendances

TOTAL

	Home	Away	Total
League	161,849	145,938	307,787
Cup/Other	13,000	19,139	32,139
TOTAL	174,849	165,077	339,926

AVERAGE

	Home	Away	Total
League	7,707	6,949	7,328
Cup/Other	6,500	6,380	6,428
TOTAL	7,602	6,878	7,232

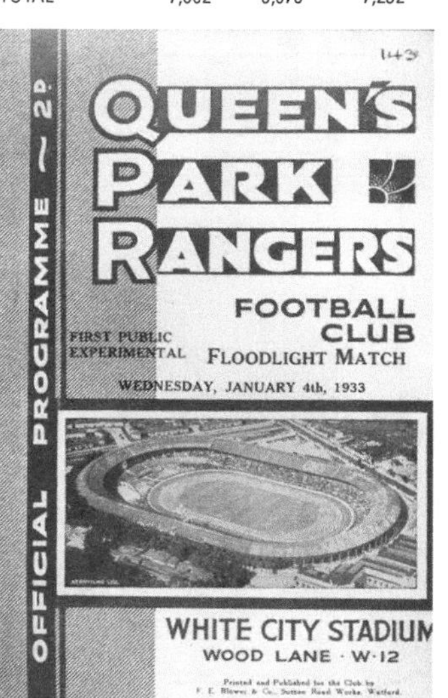

Match No.	Date		Opponents	Location	Result		Scorers	Atter
1	Aug	27	Brentford	H	L	2-3	Goddard, Brown	
2	Sep	1	Aldershot	H	D	2-2	Goddard, Rounce	
3		3	Southend United	A	W	1-0	Rounce	
4		7	Aldershot	A	L	0-2		
5		10	Crystal Palace	H	W	2-1	Wiles, Blackman	
6		17	Gillingham	A	L	1-4	Brown	
7		24	Watford	H	W	2-1	Brown, Marcroft	
8	Oct	1	Cardiff City	A	W	5-2	Marcroft (3), Goodier, Blackman	
9		8	Reading	H	L	0-3		
10		15	Norwich City	A	L	2-3	Marcroft, Goddard	
11		22	Coventry City	H	D	3-3	Gofton, Collins, Brown	
12		29	Bristol City	A	W	3-2	Brown (2), Gofton	
13	Nov	5	Northampton Town	H	D	1-1	Gofton	
14		12	Clapton Orient	A	D	2-2	Howe, Gofton	
15		19	Swindon Town	H	W	4-2	Goddard (2), Gofton (2)	
16	Dec	3	Newport County	H	W	6-1	Brown (2), Gofton (2), Rounce, Marcroft	
17		17	Exeter City	H	L	1-3	Rounce	
18		24	Torquay United	A	L	1-3	Goddard	
19		26	Brighton	H	L	0-1		
20		27	Brighton	A	L	1-4	Brown	
21		31	Brentford	A	L	0-2		
22	Jan	7	Southend United	H	W	6-1	Goddard (2), Brown (2), Blackman, OG (Wilson)	
23		18	Bournemouth	A	L	0-3		
24		21	Crystal Palace	A	W	1-0	Rounce	
25		28	Gillingham	H	D	1-1	Wiles	
26	Feb	4	Watford	A	D	2-2	Howe, Rounce	
27		11	Cardiff City	H	W	5-1	Goddard (2), Rounce (2), Collins	
28		18	Reading	A	L	1-3	Goddard	
29		25	Norwich City	H	D	2-2	Goodier, Howe	
30	Mar	5	Coventry City	A	L	0-7		
31		11	Bristol City	H	D	1-1	Blackman	
32		18	Northampton Town	A	L	1-2	Brown	
33		25	Clapton Orient	H	W	2-1	Howe, Blackman	
34	Apr	1	Swindon Town	A	D	0-0		
35		8	Bournemouth	H	W	3-1	Hill, Blackman, Jones	
36		14	Bristol Rovers	H	D	1-1	Blackman	
37		15	Newport County	A	L	1-5	Marcroft	
38		17	Bristol Rovers	A	L	1-4	Brown	
39		18	Luton Town	A	L	1-3	Blackman	
40		22	Luton Town	H	W	3-1	Blackman (2), Marcroft	
41		29	Exeter City	A	L	0-2		
42	May	6	Torquay United	H	D	1-1	Blackman	

Appearar
G

FA Cup

Round	Date		Opponents	Location	Result		Scorers
R1	Nov	26	Methyr Tydfil	A	D	1-1	Rounce
rep	Dec	1	Methyr Tydfil	H	W	5-1	Goddard (3), Marcroft, Rounce
R2		10	Torquay United	A	D	1-1	Rounce
rep		12	Torquay United	H	W	3-1	Rounce (3)
R3	Jan	14	Darlington	A	L	0-2	

Appearar
G

Total - Appearar
Total - G

Armstrong	Ashman	Barrie	Beecham	Blackman	Brown	Collins	Goddard	Gofton	Goodier	Hall	Hill	Howe	Jobson	Jones	March	Marcroft	Nixon	Rounce	Russell	Wiles	OG
	2		1		11	10	9		6	3			5			7		8			
5	2		1		11		9		6	3	8					7		10			
5	3		1				9		6		8	11				7	2	10			
5	3		1		11		9		6		8					7	2	10			
5	3		1	8	11		9		6					10			2			7	
5	3		1	8	11		9		6					10			2			7	
5		2	1		11		9		6	3				8		7		10			
5		2	1	9	11				6	3				8		7		10			
5		2	1	9	11				6	3				8		7		10			
		2	1	9	10		8		6	3		11	5			7					
5		2	1		10	8		9	6	3		11				7					
5		2	1		10		8	9	6	3		11				7					
5		2	1		10		8	9	6	3		11				7					
5		2	1		10		8	9	6	3		11				7					
5		2	1		11		8	9	6	3						7		10			
5		2	1		11		8	9	6	3						7		10			
5		2	1		11		8	9	6	3						7		10			
	3	2	1	8	11		9		6			7	5		4			10			
5	3	2	1	8	11		9		6			7			4			10			
		2	1	8	11		9		6						4	7	3	10			
5		2	1	7	11		9		6	3	4							10			
5		2	1	7	11		9		6	3	4							10		8	
6		2	1		11	8	9			3	4		5			7		10			
	6	2	1			8	9		5	3	4	11				7		10			
	6	2	1			8			5	3	4	11				7		10		9	
	6	2	1	7		8	9		5		4	11						10	3		
	6	2	1		7	8	9		5	3	4	11						10			
	3	2	1		7	8	9		5		6	11			4			10			
	6	2	1		11	8	9		5			7			4			10	3		
	6	2	1		11	8	9		5			7			4			10	3		
5		2	1	9	11		8		6	3		7			4			10			
5		2	1	9	10		8		6	3		11			4					7	
5		2	1	9					6		8	11		10	4	7			3		
5		2	1	9	11				6		8			10		7			3		
5		2	1	9	11				6		8			10		7			3		
5		2	1	9	11				6		8			10		7			3		
5		2	1	9	11	10	8		6							7			3		
5		2	1	8	10				6	3		11				7				9	
5		2	1	8					6	3		11		10		7				9	
5		2	1	8	11				6	3				10		7				9	
5		2	1	8	11				6	3				10		7				9	
5		2	1	9	11		8		6	3				10		7					
1	15	36	42	23	36	11	30	7	41	26	15	20	4	13	9	29	5	24	8	9	
				11	13	2	11	8	2		1	4		1		8		8		2	1
5		2	1		11		8	9	6	3						7		10			
5		2	1		11		8	9	6	3						7		10			
5		2	1		11		8	9	6	3						7		10			
5		2	1		11		8	9	6	3						7		10			
5		2	1	7	11		9			3	4				6			10		8	
5		5	5	1	5		5	4	4	5	1				1	4		5		1	
							3									1		6			
6	15	41	47	24	41	11	35	11	45	31	16	20	4	13	10	33	5	29	8	10	
				11	13	2	14	8	2		1	4		1		9		14		2	1

1933-34

Division Three South

	P	W	D	L	F	A	Pts
Norwich City	42	25	11	6	88	49	61
Coventry City	42	21	12	9	100	54	54
Reading	42	21	12	9	82	50	54
Queen's Park Rangers	42	24	6	12	70	51	54
Charlton Athletic	42	22	8	12	83	56	52
Luton Town	42	21	10	11	83	61	52
Bristol Rovers	42	20	11	11	77	47	51
Swindon Town	42	17	11	14	64	68	45
Exeter City	42	16	11	15	68	57	43
Brighton & Hove Albion	42	15	13	14	68	60	43
Clapton Orient	42	16	10	16	75	69	42
Crystal Palace	42	16	9	17	71	67	41
Northampton Town	42	14	12	16	71	78	40
Aldershot	42	13	12	17	52	71	38
Watford	42	15	7	20	71	63	37
Southend United	42	12	10	20	51	74	34
Gillingham	42	11	11	20	75	96	33
Newport County	42	8	17	17	49	70	33
Bristol City	42	10	13	19	58	85	33
Torquay United	42	13	7	22	53	93	33
Bournemouth	42	9	9	24	60	102	27
Cardiff City	42	9	6	27	57	105	24

Attendances

TOTAL

	Home	Away	Total
League	210,456	179,608	390,064
Cup/Other	26,000	26,232	52,232
TOTAL	236,456	205,840	442,296

AVERAGE

	Home	Away	Total
League	10,022	8,553	9,287
Cup/Other	13,000	13,116	13,058
TOTAL	10,281	8,950	9,615

Match No.	Date		Opponents	Location	Result		Scorers	Atte
1	Aug	26	Brighton	H	W	2-0	Clarke (2)	1
2		30	Swindon Town	A	L	1-3	Emmerson	
3	Sep	2	Aldershot	A	L	1-3	Devine	
4		7	Swindon Town	H	W	1-0	Eaton	
5		9	Luton Town	H	W	2-1	Emmerson, Clarke	1
6		16	Northampton Town	A	L	1-2	Devine	
7		23	Torquay United	H	W	2-0	Blackman, Emmerson	
8		30	Exeter City	A	D	1-1	Blackman	
9	Oct	7	Newport County	A	W	2-1	OG (Jones), Blackman	
10		14	Norwich City	H	W	5-2	Emmerson (2), Blackman (2), Clarke	
11		21	Cardiff City	H	W	4-0	Blake (2), Emmerson, Blackman	1
12		28	Bournemouth	A	L	2-3	Allen, Clarke	
13	Nov	4	Charlton Athletic	H	W	2-1	Blackman, Clarke	1
14		11	Watford	A	D	0-0		1
15		18	Reading	H	D	0-0		1
16	Dec	2	Southend United	H	W	4-0	Brown, Devine, Emmerson, Blake	
17		16	Crystal Palace	H	W	2-1	Blackman, Blake	1
18		23	Gillingham	A	W	4-1	Blackman (3), Eaton	
19		25	Clapton Orient	H	W	2-0	Blackman, Brown	1
20		26	Clapton Orient	A	D	2-2	Blackman (2)	
21		30	Brighton	A	W	1-0	Blackman	
22	Jan	6	Aldershot	H	L	2-4	Devine, Blake	1
23		18	Coventry City	A	W	1-0	Emmerson	
24		20	Luton Town	A	L	2-4	OG (2 - Kingham (2))	
25		27	Northampton Town	H	W	2-1	Brown (2)	
26	Feb	3	Torquay United	A	D	1-1	Brown	
27		10	Exeter City	H	W	2-0	Emmerson, Blackman	1
28		17	Newport County	H	W	2-1	Devine, Allen	
29		24	Norwich City	A	L	0-1		2
30	Mar	3	Cardiff City	A	L	1-3	Brown	
31		10	Bournemouth	H	W	1-0	Brown	
32		17	Charlton Athletic	A	W	2-1	Emmerson, Blackman	1
33		24	Watford	H	D	0-0		
34		30	Bristol City	H	W	1-0	Blackman	1
35		31	Reading	A	L	0-5		1
36	Apr	2	Bristol City	A	W	2-0	Devine, Blackman	1
37		7	Coventry City	H	L	0-1		
38		14	Southend United	A	W	2-0	Devine, Blackman	
39		18	Bristol Rovers	A	L	1-4	Hammond	
40		21	Bristol Rovers	H	W	1-0	March	
41		28	Crystal Palace	A	L	1-4	Blackman	
42	May	5	Gillingham	H	W	5-0	Blackman (3), Hammond, Devine	

Appeara
G

FA Cup

R1	Nov	25	Kettering Town	H	W	6-0	Blackman (2), Emmerson (2), Allen, Brown	1
R2	Dec	9	New Brighton	H	D	1-1	Blackman	1
rep		11	New Brighton	A	W	4-0	Blackman (4)	
R3	Jan	13	Nottingham Forest	A	L	0-4		2

Appeara
G

Division Three South Cup

R2	Feb	28	Reading	H	W	2-0	Brown (2)	
R3	Mar-	8	Brighton	H	L	1-2	Hammond	

Appeara
G

Total - Appeara
Total - G

Ashman	Barrie	Beecham	Blackman	Blake	Brown	Clarke	Devine	Eaton	Emmerson	Farmer	Goddard	Goodier	Hammond	Jones	Langford	March	Mason	Rivers	Russell	OG
3	2	1		6		11	10	8	7		9	5						4		
3	2	1		6		11	10	8	7		9	5						4		
3	2	1		6		11	10	8	7		9	5				4				
3	2	1		6		11	10	8	7		9	5				4				
3	2	1		6		11		8	7		9	5			10	4				
3	2	1		6		11	10	8	7		9	5				4				
3	2	1	9	6		11	10	8	7			5				4				
3	2	1	9	6		11	10		7			5				4				
3	2	1	9	6		11	10		7			5				4				
3	2	1	9	6		11	10		7			5				4				
3	2	1	9	6		11	10		7			5				4				
3		1	9	6		11	10		7			5				4			2	
3	2	1	9	6		11	10		7			5				4				
3	2	1	9	6		11	10		7			5				4				
3	2	1	9	6		11	10		7			5				4				
3	2	1	9	6	11		10		7			5				4				
3	2	1	9	6	11		10	8	7			5				4				
3	2	1	9	6	11		10	8	7			5				4				
3	2	1	9	6	11		10	8	7			5				4				
3	2	1	9	6	11		10	8	7			5				4				
3	2	1	9	6	11		10	8	7			5				4				
3	2	1	9	6	11		10	8	7			5				4				
3	2		9	6	11			8	7			5			10	4	1			
3	2		9	6	11			8	7			5			10	4	1			
3	2		9	6	11		10		7			5				4	1			
3	2		9	6	11		10		7	5						4	1			
3	2		9		11		10		7	5					6	4	1			
3	2		9		11		10		7	5					6	4	1			
3	2		9		11		10		7			5			6	4	1			
3	2		9	6	11		10		7			5				4	1			
3	2	1	9		11				7			5			10	4		6		
3	2	1	9	6	11		10		7	5						4				
3	2	1	9	6	11		10		7	5						4				
3	2	1	9	6	11		10		7			5				4				
3	2	1	9	6	11		10		7			5				4				
3	2	1	9	6	11		10		7	5						4				
3	2	1	9	6	11		10		7	5						4				
3	2	1	9	6	11		10			5			7			4				
3	2	1	9	6	11		10			5			7			4				
3	2	1	9	6						5			7	11	10	4				
3	2	1	9	6			8			5			7	11	10	4				
3	2	1	9	6			10			5			7	11		4				
42	41	34	36	38	24	15	37	15	37	12	6	30	5	3	9	40	8	3	1	
			24	5	7	6	8	2	10				2			1				3

Ashman	Barrie	Beecham	Blackman	Blake	Brown	Clarke	Devine	Eaton	Emmerson	Farmer	Goddard	Goodier	Hammond	Jones	Langford	March	Mason	Rivers	Russell	OG
3	2	1	9	6	11		10		7			5				4				
3	2	1	9	6	11		10		7			5				4				
3	2	1	9	6	11		10	8	7			5				4				
3	2	1	9	6	11		10	8	7			5				4				
4	4	4	4	4	4		4	2	4			4				4				
			7		1				2											

Ashman	Barrie	Beecham	Blackman	Blake	Brown	Clarke	Devine	Eaton	Emmerson	Farmer	Goddard	Goodier	Hammond	Jones	Langford	March	Mason	Rivers	Russell	OG
	2				11			8	7	5			9		6		1	4	3	
3	2			6		11	10	8	7		5		9			4	1			
1	2			1	1	1	1	2	2	1	1		2		1	1	2	1	1	
					2								1							

Ashman	Barrie	Beecham	Blackman	Blake	Brown	Clarke	Devine	Eaton	Emmerson	Farmer	Goddard	Goodier	Hammond	Jones	Langford	March	Mason	Rivers	Russell	OG
47	47	38	40	43	29	16	42	19	43	13	7	34	7	3	10	45	10	4	2	
			31	5	10	6	8	2	12				3			1				3

1934-35

Division Three South

	P	W	D	L	F	A	Pts
Charlton Athletic	42	27	7	8	103	52	61
Reading	42	21	11	10	89	65	53
Coventry City	42	21	9	12	86	50	51
Luton Town	42	19	12	11	92	60	50
Crystal Palace	42	19	10	13	86	64	48
Watford	42	19	9	14	76	49	47
Northampton Town	42	19	8	15	65	67	46
Bristol Rovers	42	17	10	15	73	77	44
Brighton & Hove Albion	42	17	9	16	69	62	43
Torquay United	42	18	6	18	81	75	42
Exeter City	42	16	9	17	70	75	41
Millwall	42	17	7	18	57	62	41
Queen's Park Rangers	42	16	9	17	63	72	41
Cl apton Orient	42	15	10	17	65	65	40
Bristol City	42	15	9	18	52	68	39
Swindon Town	42	13	12	17	67	78	38
Bournemouth	42	15	7	20	54	71	37
Aldershot	42	13	10	19	50	75	36
Cardiff City	42	13	9	20	62	82	35
Gillingham	42	11	13	18	55	75	35
Southend United	42	11	9	22	65	78	31
Newport County	42	10	5	27	54	112	25

Attendances

TOTAL

	Home	Away	Total
League	154,221	166,761	320,982
Cup/Other	23,000		23,000
TOTAL	177,221	166,761	343,982

AVERAGE

	Home	Away	Total
League	7,344	7,941	7,642
Cup/Other	11,500		11,500
TOTAL	7,705	7,941	7,818

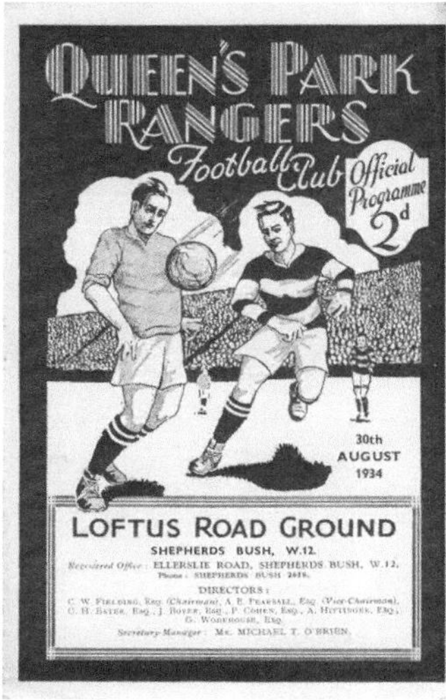

Match No.	Date		Opponents	Location	Result		Scorers	Attend
1	Aug	25	Swindon Town	A	L	1-3	Reed	12,
2		30	Crystal Palace	H	D	3-3	Blake (pen), Crawford, Blackman	9
3	Sep	1	Aldershot	H	W	2-0	Reed (2)	12
4		5	Crystal Palace	A	W	3-2	Hammond, Blackman, Reed	15,
5		8	Cardiff City	A	L	1-2	OG (Farquarson)	12
6		15	Brighton	H	W	2-1	Blackman, Abel	9
7		22	Luton Town	A	D	1-1	Crawford	7,
8		29	Southend United	H	D	1-1	Abel	9
9	Oct	6	Bristol Rovers	A	L	0-2		7
10		13	Charlton Athletic	H	L	0-3		12
11		20	Gillingham	A	D	0-0		5,
12		27	Reading	H	W	2-0	Dutton, Watson	8
13	Nov	3	Millwall	A	L	0-2		12
14		10	Coventry City	H	D	1-1	Crawford	7,
15		17	Watford	A	L	0-2		8
16	Dec	1	Exeter City	A	L	0-3		4
17		15	Northampton Town	A	L	0-1		5
18		22	Bournemouth	H	W	2-1	Crawford, Blackman	4
19		25	Clapton Orient	H	W	6-3	Blackman (2), Emmerson, Crawford, Devine, Allen	9
20		26	Clapton Orient	A	L	1-3	Crawford	11,
21		29	Swindon Town	H	D	1-1	Blake	6,
22	Jan	1	Bristol City	H	W	4-1	Blackman, Crawford, Allen, Emmerson	7
23		5	Aldershot	A	L	0-1		3
24		12	Newport County	H	W	4-1	Blackman (2), Dutton, Emmerson	4,
25		19	Cardiff City	H	D	2-2	Blackman, Dutton	5
26		26	Brighton	A	L	1-5	Allen	5
27	Feb	2	Luton Town	H	W	3-0	Blackman (2), Crawford	6
28		9	Southend United	A	L	0-2		5
29		16	Bristol Rovers	H	W	2-0	Abel, Dutton	2
30		23	Charlton Athletic	A	L	1-3	Allen	17
31	Mar	2	Gillingham	H	W	2-0	Farmer, Blackman	8,
32		9	Reading	A	D	0-0		6
33		16	Millwall	H	W	1-0	Farmer	8
34		23	Coventry City	A	L	1-4	Blackman	8
35		30	Watford	H	W	2-1	Blackman, Blake (pen)	6
36	Apr	6	Newport County	A	L	1-2	Blackman	2
37		13	Exeter City	H	D	1-1	Farmer	5
38		19	Torquay United	H	W	5-1	Blackman (2), Blake, Farmer, Dutton	6
39		20	Bristol City	A	L	1-5	OG (Bridge)	5
40		22	Torquay United	A	L	0-7		3
41		27	Northampton Town	H	W	3-1	Farmer (2), Blackman	3
42	May	4	Bournemouth	A	W	2-0	Farmer, Dutton	4

Appearan
Gc

FA Cup

R1	Nov	24	Walthamstow Avenue	H	W	2-0	Emmerson, Devine	9
R2	Dec	8	Brighton	H	L	1-2	Crawford	14

Appearan
Gc

Division Three South Cup

R2	Oct	18	Luton Town	H	W	2-1	Blackman, Crawford
R3	Feb	13	Watford	A	D	1-1	Blackman
rep		28	Watford	H	D	1-1	Blake
rep	Mar	14	Watford	H	L	0-2 aet	

Appearan
Gc

Total - Appearan
Total - Gc

Allen	Ashman	Barrie	Bartlett	Beecham	Blackman	Blake	Connor	Crawford	Devine	Dutton	Emmerson	Farmer	Goodier	Hammond	Langford	March	Mason	Reed	Ridley	Russell	Trodd	Watson	Wright	OG
8	3	2		1				11	10	6	7		5			4		9						
	3	2		1	8	6		11	10		7	4	5					9						
	3	2		1	8	6		11	10			4	5	7				9						
	3	2		1	8	6		11	10			4	5	7				9						
	3	2		1	8	6		11	10			4	5	7				9						
		2		1	9	6		7	10				5			4				3		11		
		2		1	9	6		7	10				5			4				3		11		
		2		1	9	6		7	10				5			4				3		11		
		2		1	9	6		11	10				5			4				3		7		
8		2		1		6		11	10		7		5			4		9		3				
	3	2			8			7	10	6		4	5				1	9				11		
	3	2			8	4				10		6	5	7			1	9				11		
	3	2	5		7	4			8	10		6					1	9				11		
	3	2				4		11	8	10	7	6	5				1							
	3	2				4		11	8	10	7	6	5				1							
	3	2			9			11	8	10	7	5			6	4	1							
8			5		9			11	10				6	7		4	1		2	3				
8			5		9			11	10		7		6			4	1		2	3				
8		2			9	6		11	10		7		5			4	1			3				
8		2			9	6		11		10	7		5			4	1			3				
8	3	2			9	6		11	10		7		5			4	1							
8	3	2			9	6		11	10		7		5			4	1							
8	3	2			9	6		11			7		5		10	4	1							
8					9	6		11		10	7		5			4	1		2	3				
8		2			9	6				10	7		5			4	1			3		11		
8	3				9	6	11						5	7		4	1		2				10	
8					9	6		11				10	5			4	1		2	3				
8	3				9	6		11				10	5			4	1		2					
8	3				9	6				11		10	5			4	1		2					
8	3				9	6				11		10	5			4	1		2					
					8	6		11				10	5	7		4	1		2	3				
					9	6		11		8		10	5			4	1		2	3				
					9	6	11			8	7	10	5			4	1		2	3				
4					9	6	11			8		10	5				1		2	3				
4					9	6	11			8		10	5				1		2	3				
4					9	6	11			8		10	5				1		2	3				
8					9	6				11		10	5				1		2	3	4			
8					9	6				11		10	5				1		2	3	4			
8					9	6				11		10	5				1		2	3	4			
8	3	2			9	6				11		10	5				1				4			
8	3	2			9	6				11		10	5				1				4			
8	3	2			9	6				11		10	5	7			1				4			
25	21	25	3	10	38	37	5	26	20	23	15	26	40	8	2	24	32	9	17	21	6	8	1	
4					19	4		8	1	6	3	7		1				4				1		2

Allen	Ashman	Barrie	Bartlett	Beecham	Blackman	Blake	Connor	Crawford	Devine	Dutton	Emmerson	Farmer	Goodier	Hammond	Langford	March	Mason	Reed	Ridley	Russell	Trodd	Watson	Wright	OG
	3	2				4		11	8	10	7	5			6		1							
8		4	5		9			11	10				6	7			1		2	3				
1	1	2	1		1	1		2	2	1	1	1	1	1	1		2		1	1				
								1	1		1													

Allen	Ashman	Barrie	Bartlett	Beecham	Blackman	Blake	Connor	Crawford	Devine	Dutton	Emmerson	Farmer	Goodier	Hammond	Langford	March	Mason	Reed	Ridley	Russell	Trodd	Watson	Wright	OG
8	3	2			9			11	10	6	7	5				4	1							
8	3				9	6		11				10	5			4	1		2					
8	3				9	6		11				10	5			4	1		2					
					9		11			8		10	5			4	1		2	3	6			
3	3	1			4	2	1	3	1	2	1	4	3			4	4		3	1	1			
					2	1		1																

Allen	Ashman	Barrie	Bartlett	Beecham	Blackman	Blake	Connor	Crawford	Devine	Dutton	Emmerson	Farmer	Goodier	Hammond	Langford	March	Mason	Reed	Ridley	Russell	Trodd	Watson	Wright	OG
29	25	28	4	10	43	40	6	31	23	26	17	31	44	9	3	28	38	9	21	23	7	8	1	
4					21	5		10	2	6	4	7		1				4				1		2

1935-36

Division Three South

	P	W	D	L	F	A	Pts
Coventry City	42	24	9	9	102	45	57
Luton Town	42	22	12	8	81	45	56
Reading	42	26	2	14	87	62	54
Queen's Park Rangers	42	22	9	11	84	53	53
Watford	42	20	9	13	80	54	49
Crystal Palace	42	22	5	15	96	74	49
Brighton & Hove Albion	42	18	8	16	70	63	44
Bournemouth	42	16	11	15	60	56	43
Notts County	42	15	12	15	60	57	42
Torquay United	42	16	9	17	62	62	41
Aldershot	42	14	12	16	53	61	40
Millwall	42	14	12	16	58	71	40
Bristol City	42	15	10	17	48	59	40
Clapton Orient	42	16	6	20	55	61	38
Northampton Town	42	15	8	19	62	90	38
Gillingham	42	14	9	19	66	77	37
Bristol Rovers	42	14	9	19	69	95	37
Southend United	42	13	10	19	61	62	36
Swindon Town	42	14	8	20	64	73	36
Cardiff City	42	13	10	19	60	73	36
Newport County	42	11	9	22	60	111	31
Exeter City	42	8	11	23	59	93	27

Attendances

TOTAL	Home	Away	Total
League	233,382	192,648	426,030
Cup/Other		7,000	7,000
TOTAL	233,382	199,648	433,030

AVERAGE	Home	Away	Total
League	11,113	9,174	10,144
Cup/Other		7,000	7,000
TOTAL	11,113	9,075	10,070

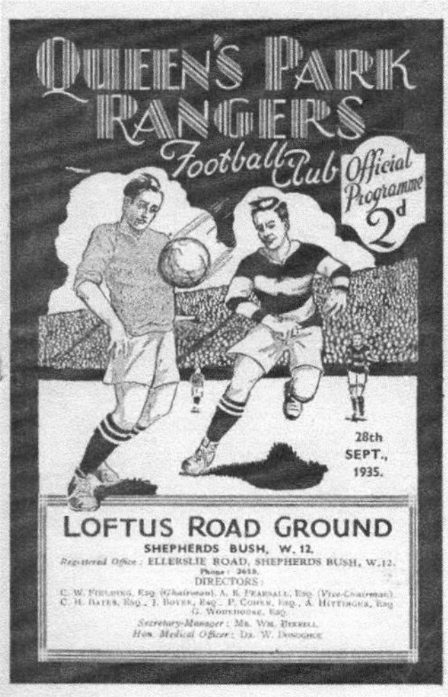

Match No.	Date		Opponents	Location	Result		Scorers	Atten
1	Aug	31	Millwall	H	L	2-3	Blackman, Lowe	13
2	Sep	4	Brighton	A	D	1-1	Hammond	8
3		7	Torquay United	A	L	2-4	Hammond, Samuel	5
4		12	Brighton	H	W	3-2	Cheetham (2), Lowe	6
5		14	Aldershot	H	W	5-0	Cheetham (4), Hammond	9
6		16	Luton Town	A	L	0-2		8
7		21	Swindon Town	A	D	2-2	Crawford, Lowe	11
8		28	Coventry City	H	D	0-0		11
9	Oct	5	Newport County	A	W	4-3	Cheetham (3), Lowe	6
10		12	Exeter City	H	W	3-1	Cheetham (2), Allan	11
11		19	Notts County	A	L	0-3		7
12		26	Bristol Rovers	H	W	4-0	Cheetham (pen), Lumsden (2), Farmer	9
13	Nov	2	Clapton Orient	A	L	0-1		12
14		9	Bournemouth	H	W	2-0	Cheetham, Ovenstone	10
15		16	Northampton Town	A	W	4-1	Ballentyne, Cheetham (2), Ovenstone	6
16		23	Crystal Palace	H	W	3-0	Cheetham (3)	13
17	Dec	7	Cardiff City	H	W	5-1	Lumsden (3), Cheetham (2)	5
18		21	Southend United	H	W	2-1	Ballentyne, Cheetham	8
19		25	Watford	H	W	3-1	Cheetham (2), Ballentyne	14
20		26	Watford	A	L	1-2	Lowe	14
21		28	Millwall	A	L	0-2		14
22	Jan	4	Torquay United	H	W	2-1	Cheetham, Samuel	10
23		15	Reading	A	W	2-1	Cheetham (2)	5
24		18	Aldershot	A	W	3-1	Lowe (2), Abel	3
25		25	Swindon Town	H	W	5-1	Cheetham (2), Lowe (2), Abel	10
26	Feb	1	Coventry City	A	L	1-6	Samuel	20
27		8	Newport County	H	D	1-1	Crawford	10
28		15	Exeter City	A	D	0-0		4
29		22	Notts County	H	D	2-2	Cheetham, Ovenstone	6
30		29	Bournemouth	A	W	1-0	Cheetham	6
31	Mar	7	Gillingham	H	W	5-2	Cheetham (3), Lowe, Crawford	11
32		14	Bristol Rovers	A	W	1-0	Cheetham	7
33		21	Northampton Town	H	L	0-1		13
34		28	Crystal Palace	A	W	2-0	Cheetham, Crawford	22
35	Apr	4	Reading	H	L	0-1		14
36		10	Bristol City	H	W	4-1	Lowe (3), Crawford	15
37		11	Cardiff City	A	L	2-3	Crawford, Lowe	8
38		13	Bristol City	A	D	0-0		10
39		18	Clapton Orient	H	W	4-0	Lowe, Banks, Crawford, Farmer	10
40		22	Gillingham	A	D	2-2	Banks, Cheetham	2
41		25	Southend United	A	W	1-0	Farmer	4
42	May	2	Luton Town	H	D	0-0		17

Appearances
Goals

FA Cup

R1	Nov	30	Margate	A	L	1-3	Cheetham	7

Appearances
Goals

Division Three South Cup

R2	Oct	23	Brighton	A	L	1-2	Crawford	

Appearances
Goals

Total - Appearances
Total - Goals

Allan	Ballentyne	Banks	Barrie	Bartlett	Blackman	Blake	Carr	Cheetham	Clarke	Coggins	Crawford	Farmer	Fletcher	Hammond	Lowe	Lumsden	March	Mason	Molloy	Ovenstone	Rowe	Russell	Samuel	Vincent
		11			9	6	2								8		4	1			3		10	5
						6	2	9			11		8	7	10		4	1			3			5
						6	2				11			7	8		4	1			3		10	5
						6	2	9			11		8	7	10		4	1			3			5
4				5			2	9			11		8	7	10			1	6		3			
4				5			2	9			11		8	7	10			1	6		3			
4				5			2	9			11		8		10	7		1	6		3			
4				5			2	9			11		8		10	7	6	1				3		
4				5			2	9			11		8		10	7	6	1				3		
4				5			2	9			11		8		10	7	6	1				3		
4				5			2	9			11		8		10	7	6	1				3		
4			2	5				9			11	6	8		10	7		1				3		
4		11	2	5		6		9					8		10	7		1				3		
4			2	5				9					8		10	7	6	1		11		3		
4	10		2	5				9							8	7	6	1		11		3		
4	10		2	5				9							8	7	6	1		11		3		
4	10		2	5				9							8	7	6	1		11	3			
	10		2	5		6		9							8	7	4	1		11	3			
4	10		2	5				9							8	7	6	1		11	3			
4			2	5				9					10		8	7	6	1		11	3			
			2	5			3	9		1			10		8	7	6			11				4
			2	5				9		1					8		6			11	3		10	4
4				5				9		1					8		6			11	3	2	10	
4				5				9		1					8		6			11	3	2	10	
4				5				9		1					8		6			11	3	2	10	
4		11	2	5				9		1					8		6				3		10	
4		11	2	5				9			7				8		6	1			3		10	
4			2	5				9							8	7	6	1		11	3		10	
4			2	5				9				10	8			7	6	1		11	3			
4	10		2	5				9					8			7	6	1		11	3			
4	10		2	5				9			11				8	7	6	1			3			
4	10		2	5				9			11		8			7	6	1			3			
4	10		2	5				9			11		8			7	6	1			3			
4	10		2	5				9			11		8			7	6	1			3			
4	10		2	5				9			11		8			7	6	1			3			
4	10		2	5							11	8			9	7	6	1			3			
4	10		2	5							11	8			9	7	6	1			3			
4	10	7	2	5							11	8			9		6	1			3			
4	10	7	2	5							11	8			9		6	1			3			
		11	2	5				9			7	10			8		6	1			3			4
		11		5			2		8		7	10					6	1			3			4
4		11		5			2	9			7	10			8		6	1			3			
33	15	9	26	38	1	6	14	35	1	6	24	9	20	5	35	25	37	36	3	15	32	12	9	8
1	3	2			1			36			7	3		3	15	5				3			3	

Allan	Ballentyne	Banks	Barrie	Bartlett	Blackman	Blake	Carr	Cheetham	Clarke	Coggins	Crawford	Farmer	Fletcher	Hammond	Lowe	Lumsden	March	Mason	Molloy	Ovenstone	Rowe	Russell	Samuel	Vincent
4	10		2	5				9							8	7	6	1		11	3			
1	1		1	1				1							1	1	1	1		1	1			
								1																

Allan	Ballentyne	Banks	Barrie	Bartlett	Blackman	Blake	Carr	Cheetham	Clarke	Coggins	Crawford	Farmer	Fletcher	Hammond	Lowe	Lumsden	March	Mason	Molloy	Ovenstone	Rowe	Russell	Samuel	Vincent
4	10		2	5				9			11	6			8	7		1			3			
1	1		1	1				1			1	1			1	1		1			1			
											1													

Allan	Ballentyne	Banks	Barrie	Bartlett	Blackman	Blake	Carr	Cheetham	Clarke	Coggins	Crawford	Farmer	Fletcher	Hammond	Lowe	Lumsden	March	Mason	Molloy	Ovenstone	Rowe	Russell	Samuel	Vincent
35	17	9	28	40	1	6	14	37	1	6	25	10	20	5	37	27	38	38	3	16	34	12	9	8
1	3	2			1			37			8	3		3	15	5				3			3	

1936-37

Division Three South

	P	W	D	L	F	A	Pts
Luton Town	42	27	4	11	103	53	58
Notts County	42	23	10	9	74	52	56
Brighton & Hove Albion	42	24	5	13	74	43	53
Watford	42	19	11	12	85	60	49
Reading	42	19	11	12	76	60	49
Bournemouth	42	20	9	13	65	59	49
Northampton Town	42	20	6	16	85	68	46
Millwall	42	18	10	14	64	54	46
Queen's Park Rangers	42	18	9	15	73	52	45
Southend United	42	17	11	14	78	67	45
Gillingham	42	18	8	16	52	66	44
Clapton Orient	42	14	15	13	52	52	43
Swindon Town	42	14	11	17	75	73	39
Crystal Palace	42	13	12	17	62	61	38
Bristol Rovers	42	16	4	22	71	80	36
Bristol City	42	15	6	21	58	70	36
Walsall	42	13	10	19	63	85	36
Cardiff City	42	14	7	21	54	87	35
Newport County	42	12	10	20	67	98	34
Torquay United	42	11	10	21	57	80	32
Exeter City	42	10	12	20	59	88	32
Aldershot	42	7	9	26	50	89	23

Attendances

TOTAL

	Home	Away	Total
League	216,153	196,209	412,362
Cup/Other	16,000	19,638	35,638
TOTAL	232,153	215,847	448,000

AVERAGE

	Home	Away	Total
League	10,293	9,343	9,818
Cup/Other	16,000	9,819	11,879
TOTAL	10,552	9,385	9,956

Match No.	Date		Opponents	Location	Result		Scorers	Atten
1	Aug	29	Bristol City	A	L	2-3	Cheetham, Lowe	13
2		31	Millwall	A	L	0-2		16
3	Sep	5	Torquay United	H	W	3-0	Bott (2, 1 pen), Lowe	10
4		12	Notts County	A	W	2-1	Bott (2, 1 pen)	5
5		17	Millwall	H	L	0-1		10
6		19	Clapton Orient	H	W	2-1	Banks, Lowe	15
7		23	Crystal Palace	A	D	0-0		9
8		26	Walsall	A	W	4-2	Cheetham, Allan, Lowe	8
9	Oct	3	Luton Town	H	W	2-1	Bott, Lowe (pen)	20
10		10	Cardiff City	A	L	0-2		21
11		17	Swindon Town	H	D	1-1	Lowe	12
12		24	Aldershot	A	D	0-0		5
13		31	Gillingham	H	L	0-1		5
14	Nov	7	Newport County	A	W	2-1	Lowe (2)	10
15		14	Southend United	H	W	7-2	Fitzgerald (2), Lowe (2), Lumsden, March, Cheetham	11
16		21	Watford	A	L	0-2		12
17	Dec	5	Bournemouth	A	L	1-3	Fitzgerald	7
18		19	Bristol Rovers	A	D	1-1	Cheetham	8
19		25	Exeter City	H	W	4-0	Bott, Fitzgerald, Cheetham, Charlton	12
20		26	Bristol City	H	W	5-0	Cheetham (2), Fitzgerald, Charlton, Bott	9
21		28	Exeter City	A	W	3-0	Bott, Cheetham, Charlton	4
22	Jan	2	Torquay United	A	D	1-1	Fitzgerald	3
23		9	Notts County	H	L	0-2		14
24		21	Brighton	H	L	2-3	Bott, Lowe	4
25		23	Clapton Orient	A	D	0-0		7
26	Feb	4	Walsall	H	W	2-0	Lowe (2)	3
27		6	Luton Town	A	W	1-0	Charlton	13
28		13	Cardiff City	H	W	6-0	Charlton (3), Fitzgerald (3)	11
29		18	Northampton Town	H	W	3-2	Fitzgerald (2), Charlton	3
30		20	Swindon Town	A	D	1-1	Fitzgerald	6
31		27	Aldershot	H	W	3-0	Fitzgerald (2), Lumsden	8
32	Mar	6	Gillingham	A	D	0-0		6
33		13	Newport County	H	W	6-2	Swinden (3), Fitzgerald, Lowe, Lumsden	11
34		20	Southend United	A	L	2-3	Fitzgerald (2)	8
35		26	Reading	H	D	0-0		16
36		27	Watford	H	L	1-2	McMahon	12
37		29	Reading	A	L	0-2		13
38	Apr	3	Brighton	A	L	1-4	Barrie	9
39		10	Bournemouth	H	L	1-2	Cameron	6
40		17	Northampton Town	A	W	1-0	Lowe	4
41		24	Bristol Rovers	H	W	2-1	Lowe (2)	6
42	May	1	Crystal Palace	H	L	1-3	McMahon	6

Appearar
G

FA Cup

R1	Nov	28	Brighton	H	W	5-1	Fitzgerald (3), Cheetham, McMahon	16
R2	Dec	12	South Liverpool	A	W	1-0	Fitzgerald	6
R3	Jan	16	Bury	A	L	0-1		13

Appearar
G

Division Three South Cup

R1	Oct	7	Reading	A	L	1-2	McMahon	

Appearar
G

Total - Appearar
Total - G

Allan	Ballentyne	Banks	Barrie	Bartlett	Bott	Cameron	Carr	Charlton	Cheetham	Clarke	Crawford	Farmer	Fitzgerald	James	Jefferson	Lowe	Lumsden	McMahon	March	Mason	Moralee	Rowe	Swinfen	Vincent
4			2	5	11	10	3		9		7					8			6	1				
4			2	5	11	10			9		7				3	8			6	1				
4	10		2	5	11				9		7				3	8			6	1				
4	10		2	5	11				9						3	8		7	6	1				
4	10		2	5	11				9						3	8		7	6	1				
4		11	2	5					9						3	10		7	6	1			8	
4					11				9						2	8		7	6	1		3	10	5
4	8				11				9						2	10		7	6	1		3		5
4	8				11				9						2	10			6	1		3		5
4	8				11				9						2	10			6	1		3		5
	8			5	11				9						2	10			6	1		3		4
	8				11				9			5			2	10	7		6	1		3		4
	8				11				9					5	2	10	7		6	1		3		4
					11				9				10	5	2	8	7		6	1		3		4
									9				10	5	2	8	7	11	6	1		3		4
									9				10	5	2	8	7	11	6	1		3		4
					7				9				10	5	2	8		11	6	1		3		4
					7			8	9			5	10		2			11	6	1		3		4
					7			8	9			5	10		2	4		11	6	1		3		
					7			8	9			5	10		2	4		11	6	1		3		
					7			8	9			5	10		2	4		11	6	1		3		
	8				7				9			5	10		2	4		11	6	1		3		
					7			8	9			5	10		2	4		11	6	1		3		
					7				9	8		5	10		2	4		11	6	1		3		
4			2		7							5	10		3	8		11		1	6		9	
			2		7			9				5	10		3	8		11	4	1	6			
			2					9				5	10			8	7	11	4	1	6	3		
			2				3	9				5	10			8	7	11	4	1	6			
			2				3	8	9			5	10			4	7	11	6	1				
			2				3	9				5	10			8	7	11	6	1				4
			2				3	9				5	10			8	7	11	6	1				4
			2				3	9				5	10			8	7	11	6	1				4
			2				3					5	10			8	7	11	4	1	6		9	
			2				3	9				5	10			8	7	11	4	1	6			
							3		7			5	10			8		11	4	1	6		9	2
			2				3		7			5	10			8		11	6	1			9	4
			2			8	3	9				5	10			7		11	6	1				4
			2			10	3	9		8		5				7		11	6	1				4
		7	2			8	3					5	10			9		11	4	1	6			
		7	2			8	3					5	10			9		11	4	1	6			
			2			8			9			5	10			7		11	4	1	6			3
			2			8		7				5	10			9		11	4	1	6	3		
1	10	3	23	7	23	8	14	16	28	2	3	26	28	5	25	41	13	33	41	42	11	20	6	20
1		1	1		9	1		8	9				17			17	3	2	1				3	

Allan	Ballentyne	Banks	Barrie	Bartlett	Bott	Cameron	Carr	Charlton	Cheetham	Clarke	Crawford	Farmer	Fitzgerald	James	Jefferson	Lowe	Lumsden	McMahon	March	Mason	Moralee	Rowe	Swinfen	Vincent
					7				9				10	5	2	8		11	6	1		3		4
					7				9			5	10		2	8		11	6	1		3		4
					7			8	9			5	10		2	4		11	6	1		3		
					3			1	3			2	3	1	3	3		3	3	3		3		2
									1				4					1						

Allan	Ballentyne	Banks	Barrie	Bartlett	Bott	Cameron	Carr	Charlton	Cheetham	Clarke	Crawford	Farmer	Fitzgerald	James	Jefferson	Lowe	Lumsden	McMahon	March	Mason	Moralee	Rowe	Swinfen	Vincent
4			3						9						2	10		11	6	1			8	5
1			1						1						1	1		1	1	1			1	1
																	1							

Allan	Ballentyne	Banks	Barrie	Bartlett	Bott	Cameron	Carr	Charlton	Cheetham	Clarke	Crawford	Farmer	Fitzgerald	James	Jefferson	Lowe	Lumsden	McMahon	March	Mason	Moralee	Rowe	Swinfen	Vincent
2	10	3	24	7	26	8	14	17	32	2	3	28	31	6	29	45	13	37	45	46	11	23	7	23
1		1	1		9	1		8	10				21			17	3	4	1				3	

1937-38

Division Three South

	P	W	D	L	F	A	Pts
Millwall	42	23	10	9	83	37	56
Bristol City	42	21	13	8	68	40	55
Queen's Park Rangers	42	22	9	11	80	47	53
Watford	42	21	11	10	73	43	53
Brighton & Hove Albion	42	21	9	12	64	44	51
Reading	42	20	11	11	71	63	51
Crystal Palace	42	18	12	12	67	47	48
Swindon Town	42	17	10	15	49	49	44
Northampton Town	42	17	9	16	51	57	43
Cardiff City	42	15	12	15	67	54	42
Notts County	42	16	9	17	50	50	41
Southend United	42	15	10	17	70	68	40
Bournemouth	42	14	12	16	56	57	40
Mansfield Town	42	15	9	18	62	67	39
Bristol Rovers	42	13	13	16	46	61	39
Newport County	42	11	16	15	43	52	38
Exeter City	42	13	12	17	57	70	38
Aldershot	42	15	5	22	39	59	35
Clapton Orient	42	13	7	22	42	61	33
Torquay United	42	9	12	21	38	73	30
Walsall	42	11	7	24	52	88	29
Gillingham	42	10	6	26	36	77	26

Attendances

TOTAL

	Home	Away	Total
League	289,770	261,619	551,389
Cup/Other		16,000	16,000
TOTAL	289,770	277,619	567,389

AVERAGE

	Home	Away	Total
League	13,799	12,458	13,128
Cup/Other		8,000	8,000
TOTAL	13,799	12,070	12,895

Match No.	Date		Opponents	Location	Result		Scorers	Atter
1	Aug	28	Brighton	H	W	2-1	Cheetham, Fitzgerald	1
2		30	Millwall	A	W	4-1	Lowe, Cape, Cheetham, Fitzgerald	1
3	Sep	4	Bournemouth	A	D	1-1	Cape	
4		9	Millwall	H	L	0-2		
5		11	Cardiff City	H	W	2-1	Cape, Lowe	1
6		15	Torquay United	A	W	2-0	Fitzgerald, Lowe	
7		18	Walsall	A	W	3-0	Prior (2), Bott	
8		25	Northampton Town	H	D	1-1	Cape	1
9	Oct	2	Bristol Rovers	A	D	1-1	Prior	1
10		9	Mansfield Town	H	D	1-1	Bott	1
11		16	Reading	A	L	0-1		1
12		23	Crystal Palace	H	W	1-0	McMahon	1
13		30	Notts County	A	D	2-2	Cape, Cheetham	1
14	Nov	6	Newport County	H	D	0-0		1
15		13	Bristol City	A	L	0-2		1
16		20	Watford	H	W	2-0	Bott (pen), Cheetham	1
17	Dec	4	Exeter City	H	W	4-0	Bott (2), Fitzgerald, Cheetham	1
18		18	Aldershot	H	W	3-0	Fitzgerald, Cheetham, Mallett	
19		25	Southend United	H	W	1-0	Fitzgerald	1
20		27	Southend United	A	L	1-2	Fitzgerald	1
21		28	Swindon Town	A	W	3-1	Cheetham (2), Bott	
22	Jan	1	Brighton	A	L	1-3	Bott	1
23		8	Gillingham	A	W	5-1	Fitzgerald, Mallett, Bott (2), OG (Hartley)	
24		15	Bournemouth	H	L	1-2	Bott	1
25		22	Cardiff City	A	D	2-2	Fitzgerald, Cape	2
26		29	Walsall	H	W	3-1	Charlton, Fitzgerald, OG (Shelton)	1
27	Feb	5	Northampton Town	A	W	2-0	Cape, Fitzgerald	
28		12	Bristol Rovers	H	W	4-0	Bott (2), Mallett, Fitzgerald	1
29		19	Mansfield Town	A	L	2-3	Cape, Charlton	
30		26	Reading	H	W	3-0	Fitzgerald (2), Stock	1
31	Mar	5	Crystal Palace	A	L	0-4		2
32		12	Notts County	H	W	2-1	Fitzgerald, Smith	1
33		19	Newport County	A	D	1-1	Cape	1
34		26	Bristol City	H	L	0-2		2
35	Apr	2	Watford	A	L	1-3	Bott	2
36		9	Gillingham	H	W	2-0	Cheetham, Mallett	1
37		15	Clapton Orient	A	D	1-1	Pattison	1
38		16	Exeter City	A	W	4-0	Cheetham (2), Bott, McCarthy	
39		18	Clapton Orient	H	W	3-2	Bott, Fitzgerald, McCarthy	1
40		23	Swindon Town	H	W	3-0	Bott, Cheetham, McCarthy	1
41		30	Aldershot	A	L	0-1		
42	May	7	Torquay United	H	W	6-3	Cheetham (2), McCarthy (2), Fitzgerald, Bott	

Appeara
G

FA Cup

R1	Nov	27	Bristol Rovers	A	W	8-1	Fitzgerald (3), Cheetham (3), Bott (2)
R2	Dec	11	Swindon Town	A	L	1-2	Cape

Appeara
G

Division Three South Cup

R2	Nov	11	Clapton Orient	H	W	2-0	Lowe, Fitzgerald
R3	Feb	28	Watford	H	L	2-3	Cheetham, McCarthy

Appeara
G

Total - Appeara
Total - G

Barrie	Bott	Cape	Charlton	Cheetham	Clarke	Farmer	Fitzgerald	Gilfillan	Ives	James	Jefferson	Lowe	McCarthy	McMahon	Mallett	March	Mason	Moralee	Pattison	Prior	Reay	Ridyard	Smith	Stock	Swinfen	OG
		7		9		5	10				3	8		11		4	1	6					2			
		7		9		5	10				3	8		11		4	1	6					2			
		7		9		5	10				3	8		11		4	1	6					2			
		7		9		5	10				3	8		11		4	1	6					2			
		7		9			10			5	3	8		11		4	1	6					2			
	11	7					10			5	3	8				4	1	6		9			2			
	11	7					10			5	3	8				4	1	6		9			2			
	11	7				5	10				3	8				4	1	6		9			2			
	11	7			8					5	3	10				4	1	6		9			2			
	11	7			8					5	3	10				4	1	6		9			2			
	11	7			8		10	1		5	3					4		6		9			2			
		7		9			10	1		5	3	4		11	8	6							2			
		7		9				1		5	3	4	10	11	8	6							2			
		7		9				1		5	3	4	10	11	8	6							2			
	11	9					10	1		5	3	7			8	6							2		4	
	11	7		9			10	1		5	3	4			8	6							2			
	11	7		9			10	1		5	3	4			8	6							2			
	11	7		9			10	1		5	3	4			8	6							2			
	11	7		9			10	1		5	3	4			8	6							2			
	11	7		9			10	1		5	3	4			8	6							2			
	11	7		9			10	1		5	3	4			8	6							2			
	11	7		9			10	1		5	3	4			8	6							2			
	11	7		9			10	1		5	3	4			8	6							2			
	11	7		9			10	1		5	3	4			8	6							2			
	11	7		9			10	1		5	3	4			8	6							2			
	11	7	9				10	1		5	3	4			8	6							2			
	11	7	9				10	1		5	3	4			8	6							2			
	11	7	9				10	1		5	3	4			8	6							2			
	11	7	9				10	1		5	3	4			8	6							2			
	11	7					10	1		5	3	4			8	6							2	9		
	11	7		9			10	1		5	3	4			8	6							2			
		7				6	9			5	3	4	10		8		1		11				2			
	11	7					10			5	3	4			8	6	1						2	9		
	11	7					10			5	3	4			8	6	1						2	9		
	11	7					10			5		4			8	6	1				3		2	9		
2		7		9		6						4	10		8		1		11		3	5				
2		7		9								4	10		8	6	1		11		3	5				
2	11			9			10					4	8		7	6	1					5	3			
2	11			9			10					4	8		7	6	1					5	3			
2	11	7		9			10					4	8			6	1					5	3			
2	11	7		9			10					4	8			6	1				3	5				
	11	7		9			6					4	10		8		1				3	5	2			
6	31	40	4	26	3	7	36	21		30	34	41	10	8	29	39	21	11	3	6	5	7	39	4	1	
	17	9	2	14			17					3	5	1	4				1	3			1	1		2

Barrie	Bott	Cape	Charlton	Cheetham	Clarke	Farmer	Fitzgerald	Gilfillan	Ives	James	Jefferson	Lowe	McCarthy	McMahon	Mallett	March	Mason	Moralee	Pattison	Prior	Reay	Ridyard	Smith	Stock	Swinfen	OG
	11	7		9			10	1		5	3	4			8	6							2			
	11	7		9			10	1		5	3	4			8	6							2			
	2	2		2			2	2		2	2	2			2	2							2			
	2	1		3			3																			

Barrie	Bott	Cape	Charlton	Cheetham	Clarke	Farmer	Fitzgerald	Gilfillan	Ives	James	Jefferson	Lowe	McCarthy	McMahon	Mallett	March	Mason	Moralee	Pattison	Prior	Reay	Ridyard	Smith	Stock	Swinfen	OG
	11	7					10			5	3	9			8		1	6							4	
	11			9		2	10	1	7	5	3		8			6									4	
	2	1		1		1	2	1	1	2	2	1	1		1	1	1	1							2	
				1			1					1	1													

Barrie	Bott	Cape	Charlton	Cheetham	Clarke	Farmer	Fitzgerald	Gilfillan	Ives	James	Jefferson	Lowe	McCarthy	McMahon	Mallett	March	Mason	Moralee	Pattison	Prior	Reay	Ridyard	Smith	Stock	Swinfen	OG
6	35	43	4	29	3	8	40	24	1	34	38	44	11	8	32	42	22	12	3	6	5	7	41	4	3	
	19	10	2	18			21					4	6	1	4				1	3			1	1		2

1938-39

Division Three South

	P	W	D	L	F	A	Pts
Newport County	42	22	11	9	58	45	55
Crystal Palace	42	20	12	10	71	52	52
Brighton & Hove Albion	42	19	11	12	68	49	49
Watford	42	17	12	13	62	51	46
Reading	42	16	14	12	69	59	46
Queen's Park Rangers	42	15	14	13	68	49	44
Ipswich Town	42	16	12	14	62	52	44
Bristol City	42	16	12	14	61	63	44
Swindon Town	42	18	8	16	72	77	44
Aldershot	42	16	12	14	53	66	44
Notts County	42	17	9	16	59	54	43
Southend United	42	16	9	17	61	64	41
Cardiff City	42	15	11	16	61	65	41
Exeter City	42	13	14	15	65	82	40
Bournemouth	42	13	13	16	52	58	39
Mansfield Town	42	12	15	15	44	62	39
Northampton Town	42	15	8	19	51	58	38
Port Vale	42	14	9	19	52	58	37
Torquay United	42	14	9	19	54	70	37
Clapton Orient	42	11	13	18	53	55	35
Walsall	42	11	11	20	68	69	33
Bristol Rovers	42	10	13	19	55	61	33

Attendances

TOTAL

	Home	Away	Total
League	224,050	215,257	439,307
Cup/Other	38,408	44,370	82,778
TOTAL	262,458	259,627	522,085

AVERAGE

	Home	Away	Total
League	10,669	10,250	10,460
Cup/Other	38,408	22,185	27,593
TOTAL	11,930	11,288	11,602

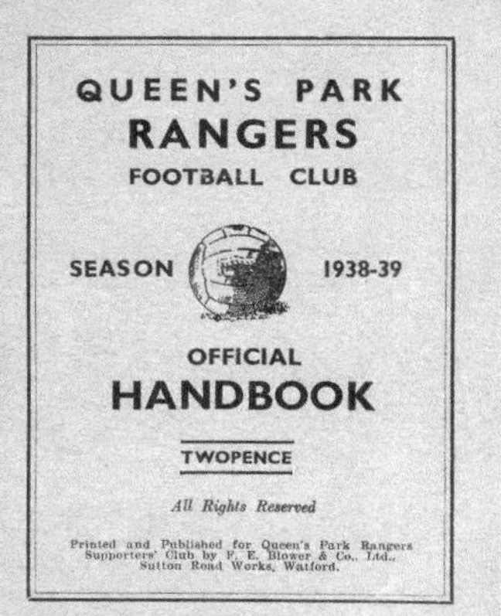

Match No.	Date		Opponents	Location	Result		Scorers	Atten
1	Aug	27	Reading	A	W	4-2	Fitzgerald (2), Bott, OG (Fulwood)	12
2	Sep	1	Exeter City	H	W	5-0	Cheetham (2), Bott (2), Fitzgerald	9
3		3	Bristol Rovers	H	D	1-1	Devine	16
4		7	Southend United	A	L	1-2	McCarthy	6
5		10	Brighton	A	L	1-3	Bott	11
6		17	Bournemouth	H	W	2-0	Cheetham, James	12
7		24	Walsall	A	W	1-0	Cheetham	8
8	Oct	1	Mansfield Town	H	W	3-0	Bott, Cape, Cheetham	12
9		8	Swindon Town	A	D	2-2	Bott, Lowe	12
10		15	Port Vale	H	D	2-2	Cheetham (2)	13
11		22	Torquay United	A	W	3-2	Cheetham (2), Fitzgerald	4
12		29	Crystal Palace	H	L	1-2	Fitzgerald	17
13	Nov	5	Bristol City	A	D	2-2	Cheetham (2)	11
14		12	Aldershot	H	W	7-0	Cheetham (4), McCarthy, March, Swinfen	14
15		19	Notts County	A	D	0-0		13
16	Dec	3	Newport County	A	L	0-2		12
17		17	Watford	A	L	1-4	Pearson	11
18		24	Reading	H	D	2-2	Bott, Devine	4
19		26	Cardiff City	A	L	0-1		26
20		27	Cardiff City	H	W	5-0	Cheetham (2), Devine, McCarthy, Cape	14
21		31	Bristol Rovers	A	D	0-0		9
22	Jan	9	Northampton Town	H	W	3-0	Cheetham (3)	3
23		14	Brighton	H	L	1-2	Cheetham	11
24		21	Bournemouth	A	L	2-4	Cape, Lowe	5
25		28	Walsall	H	W	3-0	Cheetham, Lowe, Fitzgerald	10
26	Feb	4	Mansfield Town	A	D	2-2	OG (Stimpson), Lowe	5
27		11	Swindon Town	H	W	2-1	Bott, Mallett	11
28		18	Port Vale	A	W	2-1	Fitzgerald (2)	7
29		25	Torquay United	H	D	1-1	Lowe	7
30		4	Crystal Palace	A	W	1-0	McEwan	13
31	Mar	11	Bristol City	H	W	3-1	Fitzgerald, McEwan, Stock	9
32		18	Aldershot	A	L	0-2		4
33		25	Notts County	H	L	0-1		9
34	Apr	1	Northampton Town	A	L	0-1		7
35		7	Ipswich Town	H	D	0-0		14
36		8	Newport County	H	D	0-0		14
37		10	Ipswich Town	A	L	0-1		18
38		15	Clapton Orient	A	L	1-2	Smith (pen)	8
39		22	Watford	H	W	1-0	Mallett	7
40		24	Clapton Orient	H	D	1-1	Swinfen	2
41		29	Exeter City	A	D	1-1	Stock	3
42	May	6	Southend United	H	D	1-1	McCarthy	5

Appearar
G

FA Cup

R1	Nov	26	Crystal Palace	A	D	1-1	Cheetham	33
rep		28	Crystal Palace	H	W	3-0	Cheetham (2), Bott (pen)	16
R2	Dec	10	Hartlepools United	A	W	2-0	Cheetham, McCarthy	11
R3	Jan	7	West Ham United	H	L	1-2	Cheetham	22

Appearar
G

Division Three South Cup

R2	Jan	30	Aldershot	H	W	1-0	Bott	
R3	Feb	20	Bournemouth	H	W	3-2	Stock (2), Fitzgerald	
SF	May	4	Port Vale	H	D	0-0		
rep	not played		Port Vale	A				

Appearar
G

League Jubilee

1	Aug	20	Northampton Town	H	D	2-2	Bott, OG (Thayne)	10
2		22	Northampton Town	A	D	0-0		

Appearar
G

Total - Appearar
Total - G

Allen	Black	Bott	Cape	Cheetham	Devine	Farmer	Fitzgerald	Gilmore	James	Jefferson	Lowe	McCarthy	McEwan	Mallett	March	Mason	Pattison	Pearson	Powell	Reay	Ridyard	Smith	Stevens	Stock	Swinfen	Warburton	OG
		11	7	9	8		10		5		4				6	1									2		
		11	7	9	8		10		5		4				6	1									2		
		11	7	9	8		10		5		4				6	1									2		
		11	7	9			10		5		4	8			6	1						2					
		11	7	9					5		4	8			6	1						2				10	
			7	9			10		5		4				6	1	11			3		2				8	
			7	9			10		5		4				6	1	11			3		2				8	
		11	7	9			10		5		4				6	1				3		2				8	
		11		9			10		5		4				6	1		7		3					2	8	
		11		9			10		5		4				6	1		7		3					2	8	
		11		9			10		5		4				6	1		7				3			2	8	
			11	9			10		5		4				6	1		7				3			2	8	
			11	9					5	3	4	10			6	1		7							2	8	
				9					5	3	4	10			6	1	11	7							2	8	
		11		9					5	3	4	10			6	1		7							2	8	
		11		9					5	3	4	10			6			7							2	8	
		11		9					5	3	4	10			6			7							2	8	
		11		9	8		10	6	5	3	4							7							2		
		11	7	9	8		10	6	5	3	4														2		
		11	7	9	8					3	4	10			6						5	2					
	11		7	9	8			6		3	4	10									5	2					
	11		7	9						3	4	10			6						5	2				8	
	11		7	9						3	4	10			6						5	2				8	
	11		7	9			10	6	5	3	4											2				8	
	11		7	9			10		5	3	8				6				4			2					
			7	9			10		5	3	8				6		11		4			2					
		11	7						5	3	4			8	6							2		9		10	
		11	7				10		5	3	4			8	6							2		9			
		11	7				10		5	3	4			8	6							2		9			
							10			3	4		7	8	6		11				5	2		9			
							10		5	3	4		7	8	6		11					2		9			
							10		5	3	4		7	8	6		11					2		9			
							10	6	5	3	4		7	8			11					2		9			
							10		5	3	4		7	8	6		11					2		9			
							6			3	10		7	8			11		4		5	2			9		
							6			3	10		9	8			11		4		5	2		7			
							10		5	3	6		7	8			11		4			2		9			
							10		5	3	6		7	8			11		4			2		9			
		11					10		5	3	4		7	8	6							2			9		
		11					10			3	6		7	8					4		5	2			9		
		10								3	6		7	8				11	4		5	2		9			
							8			3	4	10	7							2	5				9		
7	5	21	21	26	7		30	6	32	30	42	12	13	15	30	15	14	11	8	6	10	29		12	18	17	
		8	3	22	3		9		1		5	4	2	2	1			1				1		2	2		2
		11		9					5	3	4	10			6			7							2	8	
		11		9					5	3	4	10			6			7							2	8	
		11		9					5	3	4	10			6			7							2	8	
		11	7	9				6		3	4	10									5	2				8	
4		4	1	4				1	3	4	4	4			3			3			1	1			3	4	
		1		5								1															
		10		9	8			6	5				7				11		4	3					2		
						5	10	6		3			7	8		1	11		4	2				9			
		10					9	6		3	4			8				7		2	5		11				
2		2		1	1	1	2	3	1	2	1		2	2		1	2	1	2	3	1		1	1	1		
		1					1																	2			
		11	7	9			10		5		4	8			6	1				3					2		1
		1																									1
3	5	27	22	31	8	1	32	10	36	36	47	16	15	17	33	16	16	15	10	9	12	30	1	13	22	21	
		11	3	27	3		10		1		5	5	2	2	1			1				1		4	2		3

1939-40

Division Three South

	P	W	D	L	F	A	Pts
Reading	3	2	1	0	8	2	5
Exeter City	3	2	1	0	5	3	5
Cardiff City	3	2	0	1	5	5	4
Crystal Palace	3	2	0	1	8	9	4
Brighton & Hove Albion	3	1	2	0	5	4	4
Ipswich Town	3	1	2	0	5	3	4
Notts County	2	2	0	0	6	3	4
Southend United	3	1	1	1	3	3	3
Bristol City	3	1	1	1	5	5	3
Clapton Orient	3	0	3	0	3	3	3
Mansfield Town	3	1	1	1	8	8	3
Norwich City	3	1	1	1	4	4	3
Torquay United	3	0	3	0	4	4	3
Bournemouth	3	1	1	1	13	4	3
Walsall	3	1	1	1	3	3	3
Northampton Town	3	1	0	2	2	12	2
Queen's Park Rangers	3	0	2	1	4	5	2
Watford	3	0	2	1	4	5	2
Bristol Rovers	3	0	1	2	2	7	1
Port Vale	2	0	1	1	0	1	1
Aldershot	3	0	1	2	3	4	1
Swindon Town	3	0	1	2	2	4	1

Season abandoned - due to outbreak of war

League South 'B'

	P	W	D	L	F	A	Pts
Queen's Park Rangers	18	12	2	4	49	26	26
Bournemouth	18	11	2	5	52	37	24
Chelsea	18	9	5	4	43	37	23
Reading	18	10	2	6	47	42	22
Brentford	18	8	2	8	42	41	18
Fulham	18	7	4	7	50	51	18
Portsmouth	18	7	2	9	37	42	16
Aldershot	18	5	4	9	38	49	14
Brighton & Hove Albion	18	5	1	12	42	53	11
Southampton	18	4	0	14	41	63	8

League South 'D'

	P	W	D	L	F	A	Pts
Crystal Palace	18	13	1	4	62	32	27
Queen's Park Rangers	18	10	3	5	38	28	23
Watford	18	7	7	4	41	29	21
Southend United	18	8	3	7	41	37	19
Bournemouth	18	8	2	8	40	41	18
Aldershot	18	7	3	8	38	36	17
Clapton Orient	18	7	3	8	33	45	17
Norwich City	18	6	4	8	35	34	16
Reading	18	6	2	10	31	42	14
Brighton & Hove Albion	18	2	4	12	30	65	8

Match No.	Date		Opponents	Location	Result		Scorers
1	Aug	26	Watford	H	D	2-2	Mangnall (2)
2		30	Bournemouth	A	D	2-2	Mangnall, Swinfen
3	Sep	2	Walsall	A	L	0-1	

Appeara
G

Football League Jubilee

1	Aug	19	Northampton Town	H	W	3-2	

League South 'B'

1	Oct	21	Reading	A	L	0-2	
2		28	Fulham	H	D	2-2	Mangnall, McCarthy
3	Nov	4	Portsmouth	A	L	1-2	Mangnall
4		11	Brentford	H	W	1-0	McCarthy
5		18	Aldershot	H	W	4-1	Mangnall (2), Mallett, McEwan
6		25	Bournemouth	A	L	0-3	
7	Dec	2	Chelsea	H	W	3-2	Mallett, Mangnall (2)
8		9	Southampton	A	W	2-1	March, McEwan
9		16	Brighton	H	W	3-2	Mangnall, March, McEwan
10		25	Fulham	A	W	8-3	Mangnall (3), Mallett (3), McCarthy, Bonass
11		26	Portsmouth	H	W	5-2	Mangnall (4), Mallett
12		30	Brentford	A	W	7-0	Mallett, McCarthy, McEwan, Bonass (2), Mangnall, OG
13	Jan	1	Reading	H	W	3-0	Mallett, Mangnall (2)
14		6	Aldershot	A	W	3-1	Mangnall (2), McEwan
15		13	Bournemouth	H	W	2-1	Mangnall, McEwan
16		20	Chelsea	A	D	0-0	
17	Feb	8	Southampton	H	W	4-1	Bonass, McEwan (3)
18	May	4	Brighton	A	L	1-3	OG (Martin)

Appeara
G

League South 'D'

1	Feb	10	Southend United	H	W	3-1	McEwan, March, Bonass
2		24	Crystal Palace	H	L	2-5	McCarthy (2)
3	Mar	2	Reading	A	L	1-4	Mangnall
4		9	Brighton	A	W	2-1	McEwan, Mallett
5		16	Norwich City	H	D	0-0	
6		22	Watford	A	D	1-1	Mangnall
7		23	Aldershot	H	W	3-1	Mangnall (2), McEwan
8		25	Watford	H	W	2-0	McCarthy, McEwan
9		30	Clapton Orient	A	L	3-4	McEwan, Mangnall (2)
10	Apr	3	Bournemouth	A	L	0-1	
11		6	Southend United	A	W	1-0	McEwan
12		10	Aldershot	A	W	1-0	Mangnall
13		20	Brighton	H	W	5-4	Mangnall (3), Mallett, McEwan
14	May	13	Crystal Palace	A	D	2-2	Mangnall (2)
15		18	Clapton Orient	H	W	4-0	McCarthy, Mallett, McEwan, Mangnall
16		23	Reading	H	W	2-1	Mangnall, McEwan
17		25	Norwich City	A	L	1-3	Mangnall
18	Jun	1	Bournemouth	H	W	5-0	Mangnall (2), McCarthy (2), McEwan

Appeara
G

Total - Appeara
Total - G
Total Excludes : League Jubilee, War

War Cup

Pre		13	Southend United	A	L	0-1	

Attendances

	TOTAL		
	Home	Away	Total
League	77,101	59,773	136,874
Cup/Other		4,000	4,000
TOTAL	77,101	63,773	140,874

	AVERAGE		
	Home	Away	Total
League	4,535	3,516	4,026
Cup/Other		4,000	4,000
TOTAL	4,535	3,543	4,025

Allen	Barr	Bonass	Bott	Byrom	Daniels	Devine	Farmer	Fitzgerald	Francis	Jefferson	Kelly	Lowe	Mallett	Mangnall	March	Mason	McCarthy	McColgan	McEwan	Pattison	Powell	Reay	Reid	Ridyard	Stock	Swinfen	OG
1		11						10		3		4	8	9	6				7			2		5			
1		11						10		3		4		9	6							2		5	7	8	
1		11					6	10		3		4		9								2		5	7	8	
3		3					1	3		3		3	1	3	2				1			3		3	2	2	
														3												1	

Allen	Barr	Bonass	Bott	Byrom	Daniels	Devine	Farmer	Fitzgerald	Francis	Jefferson	Kelly	Lowe	Mallett	Mangnall	March	Mason	McCarthy	McColgan	McEwan	Pattison	Powell	Reay	Reid	Ridyard	Stock	Swinfen	OG
	5						6			3		4	8	9		1	10		7	11		2					
													x	x					x								
	5	11					6			3			8	9	4	1	10		7								
	5									3		4	8	9	6	1	10		7	11							
1		11					5			3			8	9	6		10		7		4						
							5			3			8	9	6	1	10		7	11	4						
	5	11					6						8	9	4	1	10	2	7								
	5	11								3			8	9	6	1	10		7		4						
		11					5			3			8	9	6	1	10		7		4						
		11					5	6		3	7		8	9	4	1	10										
		11					5	6		3			8	9	4	1	10		7								
1		11					5			3			8	9	6		10		7		4						
		11					5			3			8	9	6	1	10		7		4						
		11					5			3			8	9	6	1	10		7		4						
2	5	10					11	2		12	1	2	14	14	12	11	13	1	13	3	7	1					
		4											8	20	2		4		9								2

Allen	Barr	Bonass	Bott	Byrom	Daniels	Devine	Farmer	Fitzgerald	Francis	Jefferson	Kelly	Lowe	Mallett	Mangnall	March	Mason	McCarthy	McColgan	McEwan	Pattison	Powell	Reay	Reid	Ridyard	Stock	Swinfen	OG
		11					5			3			8		6	1	10		7		4					9	
		11					5						8	9	6	1	10		7		4	3					
														9	6												
		11					5			3		4	8	9		1	10		7		6	2					
		11				10	5			3		4	8			1			7		6	2					
		11					5			3		4		9		1	10	8	7		6	2					
		11					5			3		4	8	9		1	10		7		6	2					
		11					5			3		4	8	9		1	10		7		6	2					
			11		10					3		4	8	9		1			7		6	2		5			
		11										4	8	9		1			7		6	2	10	5			
		8	1		1	1	7			7		7	8	8	3	9	6	1	9		9	8	1	2		1	
		1											3	17	1		6		10								

Allen	Barr	Bonass	Bott	Byrom	Daniels	Devine	Farmer	Fitzgerald	Francis	Jefferson	Kelly	Lowe	Mallett	Mangnall	March	Mason	McCarthy	McColgan	McEwan	Pattison	Powell	Reay	Reid	Ridyard	Stock	Swinfen	OG
5	8	34	2	1	1	2	28	6	1	30	7	16	33	35	22	34	30	2	35	3	25	18	2	12	2	6	
		5											11	40	3		10		19							1	2

1940-41

League South

	P	W	D	L	F	A	GA
Crystal Palace	27	16	4	7	86	44	1.954
West Ham United	25	14	6	5	70	39	1.794
Coventry City	10	5	3	2	28	16	1.750
Arsenal	19	10	5	4	66	38	1.736
Cardiff City	24	12	5	7	75	50	1.500
Reading	26	14	5	7	73	51	1.431
Norwich City	19	9	2	8	73	55	1.327
Watford	35	15	6	14	96	73	1.315
Portsmouth	31	16	2	13	92	71	1.296
Tottenham Hotspur	23	9	5	9	53	41	1.292
Millwall	31	16	5	10	73	57	1.280
Walsall	32	14	7	11	100	80	1.250
West Bromwich Albion	28	13	5	10	83	69	1.202
Leicester City	33	17	5	11	87	73	1.191
Northampton Town	30	14	3	13	84	71	1.183
Bristol City	20	10	2	8	55	48	1.145
Mansfield Town	29	12	6	11	77	68	1.132
Charlton Athletic	19	7	4	8	37	34	1.088
Aldershot	24	14	2	8	73	68	1.073
Brentford	23	9	3	11	51	51	1.000
Chelsea	23	10	4	9	57	58	0.981
Birmingham City	16	7	1	8	38	43	0.883
Fulham	30	10	7	13	62	73	0.849
Luton Town	35	11	7	17	82	100	0.820
Stoke City	36	9	9	18	76	96	0.791
Queen's Park Rangers	23	8	3	12	47	60	0.783
Brighton & Hove Albion	25	8	7	10	51	75	0.680
Nottingham Forest	25	7	3	15	50	77	0.649
Bournemouth	27	9	3	15	59	92	0.641
Notts County	21	8	3	10	42	66	0.636
Southend United	29	12	4	13	64	101	0.633
Southampton	31	4	4	23	53	111	0.477
Swansea Town	10	2	1	7	12	33	0.363
Clapton Orient	15	1	3	11	19	66	0.287

Attendances

TOTAL	Home	Away	Total
League	16,400	17,667	34,067
Cup/Other	30,964	35,432	66,396
TOTAL	47,364	53,099	100,463

AVERAGE	Home	Away	Total
League	1,491	1,472	1,481
Cup/Other	3,440	4,429	3,906
TOTAL	2,368	2,655	2,512

Match No.	Date		Opponents	Location	Result		Scorers	Atten
1	Aug	31	Fulham	A	L	1-3	Swinfen	3
2	Sep	7	Clapton Orient	H	D	3-3	Bott (2), Ridyard	1
3		21	Charlton Athletic	H	W	2-0	Bott, Swinfen	2
4		28	Arsenal	H	W	3-2	Swinfen (2), Lowe	2
5	Oct	5	Tottenham Hotspur	H	D	1-1	Lowe	1
6		12	Chelsea	H	L	2-3	Daniels, Bott	1
7		19	Chelsea	A	L	1-3	Swinfen	1
8		26	Charlton Athletic	A	L	2-6	Mangnall, OG	
9	Nov	2	Clapton Orient	A	W	3-0	McCarthy (2), Mangnall	
10		16	Fulham	H	L	2-5	Mangnall, Daniels	1
11		23	Millwall	A	L	1-3	Lowe	
12		30	Millwall	H	W	2-1	Mangnall, Lowe	
13	Dec	7	Tottenham Hotspur	A	W	3-2	Mangnall (2), Mallett	1
14		14	Arsenal	A	L	2-3	Bott, Ridyard	1
15		21	Reading	H	W	4-1	Mangnall (2), Lowe, Mallett	
16		25	Brentford	A	L	1-2	Mangnall	1
17		28	Reading	A	L	0-2		2
18	May	10	Aldershot	A	L	1-5	Ling	2
19		17	Watford	H	W	4-2	Ling (2), Mangnall (2)	1
20		24	Watford	A	D	3-3	Ling, Davie, Mangnall	2
21		31	West Ham United	H	L	1-5	Mangnall	2
22	Jun	2	Fulham	H	L	2-3	Bonass, Halford	2
23		7	West Ham United	A	W	3-2	Compton (2), Mills	2

Appearar
G

London Cup

1	Jan	4	Fulham	A	L	1-4	Mangnall	1
2		11	Fulham	H	L	5-7	Lowe. Mallett, Bonass, Bott, Mangnall	2
3		25	Aldershot	H	L	2-3	Mallett (2)	1
4	Feb	1	Chelsea	H	W	5-2	Lowe, Mangnall, McEwan (2), Bott	1
5		8	Aldershot	A	W	4-2	Mangnall, Daniels, Adam, Mallett	2
6	Apr	12	Crystal Palace	A	W	2-1	Mangnall, Fitzgerald	5
7		14	Brentford	A	L	2-4	Mangnall, Daniels	
8		19	Crystal Palace	H	W	2-1	Davie (2)	2
9		26	Brentford	H	D	0-0		6
10	May	3	Chelsea	A	W	3-2	Mangnall (2), Davie	4

Appearan
G

War Cup

R1/1	Feb	15	Crystal Palace	A	W	1-0	Mallett	3
R1/2		22	Crystal Palace	H	W	3-2	OG, Mangnall, Swinfen	3
R2/1	Mar	1	Aldershot	A	L	1-2	Mangnall (pen)	2
R2/2		8	Aldershot	H	W	4-2	Adam, Lowe, Mangnall	2
R3/1		15	Chelsea	H	W	2-0	Mangnall (2)	5
R3/2		22	Chelsea	A	W	4-2	Mangnall (2, 1 pen), Webb, Mallett	7
R4/1		29	Leicester City	H	W	2-1	Mangnall (2)	5
R4/2	Apr	5	Leicester City	A	L	1-6	Mallett	10

Appearar
G

Total - Appearan
Total - G

Adam (G)	Allen	Armstrong	Bacon	Bonass	Bott	Campbell (G)	Compton (G)	Daniels	Davie (G)	Dumsday	Edwards	Farmer	Fitzgerald	Fowler (G)	Griffiths (G)	Halford (G)	Hillard	Jackson (G)	Jefferson	Lievesley (G)	Ling	Lowe	Mahon (G)	Mallett	Mangnall	March	Mason	McCarthy	McEwan	Mills (G)	Mortimer	Pattison	Powell	Reay	Ridyard	Scott (G)	Smith (G)	Swinfen	Webb	Whitfield (G)	Wilson	OG
				11	7														3			4			9	6	1	10							5			8				
				11	9			10											3			4		8		6	1								5			7				
			4	11	9							3										8				6	1	10							5			7				
1								10		2		6									9	7			8	4	1								5							
		7						10	9			5	11									4			8	6	1							2								
				3		5			9					8		11						10			7	4	1													6		
				7					9					8		10						4			5	2	1					11								6		
1		1	1	5	3	1		3	3	1		3	1	2		2			2		1	7		1	5	7	7	2				1		1	4			3		2		
				1	5		2	2	1							1					4	5		2	13			2		1					2			5				1
				11	10							6										8			9	4	1								5			2	7			
				11	10							6										8			9	4	1								5			2	7			
	1			10	9																	4		8		6					3	11			5			2	7			
					11														3			10			9	6	1		8						5			4	7			
1								10				6					7					8			9	4	1								5			2				
											3	6	10			11						8			9	4	1								5				7			
		6									11	3	10									8			9	4	1								5				7			
									9			6	10			11						8				4	1							2	5				7			
1									9			6							3			10			8	4	1							2	5				7			
1									9			6				10			3			7			8	4	1							2	5							
3	1	1		3	4			1	3		2	8	3			3	1		3			10		1	8	10	9		1		1	1		3	10			5	8			
1				1	2			2	3				1									2		4	8				2													
1												4							2			10		8	9	6	1								5			7				
1												4							2			10			9	6	1		8						5			7				
																						4			9	6																
1								10											3			4		8	9	6	1								5				7			
3								1				2							3			4		2	4	4	3		1						3			2	1			
1																						1		3	10													1	1			1
9	1	2	2	19	20	1	1	11	7	1	3	28	4	2	1	6	1	1	16	1	5	39	1	15	32	33	39	11	6	1	1	2	1	4	37	1	1	23	20	4	1	
2				2	7		2	4	4				1			1					4	8		9	31			2	2	1					2			6	1			2

uest Player

1941-42

League South

	P	W	D	L	F	A	Pts
Arsenal	30	23	2	5	108	43	48
Portsmouth	30	20	2	8	105	59	42
West Ham United	30	17	5	8	81	44	39
Aldershot	30	17	5	8	85	56	39
Tottenham Hotspur	30	15	8	7	61	41	38
Crystal Palace	30	14	6	10	70	53	34
Reading	30	13	8	9	76	58	34
Charlton Athletic	30	14	5	11	72	64	33
Brentford	30	14	2	14	80	76	30
Queen's Park Rangers	30	11	3	16	52	59	25
Fulham	30	10	4	16	79	99	24
Brighton & Hove Albion	30	9	4	17	71	108	22
Chelsea	30	8	4	18	56	88	20
Millwall	30	7	5	18	53	82	19
Clapton Orient	30	5	7	18	42	94	17
Watford	30	6	4	20	47	114	16

London Cup - A

	P	W	D	L	F	A	Pts
Brentford	10	4	5	1	25	20	13
Crystal Palace	10	4	4	2	25	18	12
Queen's Park Rangers	10	5	1	4	26	26	11
Aldershot	10	4	2	4	21	24	10
Fulham	10	4	0	6	32	34	8
Chelsea	10	2	2	6	19	26	6

London Cup - 2

	P	W	D	L	F	A	Pts
Brentford	6	4	2	0	17	9	10
Millwall	6	2	3	1	15	12	7
Queen's Park Rangers	6	2	1	3	8	7	5
Aldershot	6	1	0	5	8	20	2

QUEENS PARK RANGERS FOOTBALL CLUB

OFFICIAL TEAM CARD · 1d

Q.P.R. v. FULHAM. Saturday, Sept. 20th, 1941

QUEENS PARK RANGERS — London War League

Right / Left

MASON

ABEL — JEFFERSON

MARCH — RIDYARD — FARMER

MANGNALL — EASTHAM — PATON — MALLETT — HALFORD

CRANFIELD — GALLACHER — ROOKE — MUTTITT — SIBLEY

TOMPKINS — HILES — JONES

TAYLOR — FREEMAN

JOSLIN

Left / Right

FULHAM — Kick-off 3.0

HOME MATCHES :

NEXT SATURDAY : CANADIAN HEADQUARTERS Kick-off 3.0

SAT., OCT. 4th : PORTSMOUTH (League) „

Match No.	Date		Opponents	Location	Result		Scorers
1	Aug	30	Brighton	A	W	5-2	Mahon, Davie (3), Pattison
2	Sep	6	Brentford	H	L	3-4	Mallett, Halford, Mahon
3		13	Crystal Palace	A	L	1-2	Halford
4		20	Fulham	H	L	2-5	Eastham (2)
5		27	Tottenham Hotspur	A	L	1-3	Mangnall
6	Oct	4	Portsmouth	H	L	0-2	
7		11	Chelsea	H	W	2-1	Mahon, Mallett
8		18	Charlton Athletic	H	D	0-0	
9		25	West Ham United	A	L	0-2	
10	Nov	1	Watford	H	L	1-5	Pattison
11		8	Aldershot	A	L	1-4	Pattison
12		15	Millwall	H	W	4-1	Stock (2), Mahon, Pattison
13		22	Arsenal	A	L	1-4	Pattison
14		29	Clapton Orient	A	D	0-0	
15	Dec	6	Reading	A	D	2-2	Armstong, Kirkham
16		13	Brighton	H	W	3-0	Mangnall (2), Armstrong
17		20	Brentford	A	L	3-4	Mangnall (2), Abel
18		25	Crystal Palace	H	L	1-3	Harris
19		27	Fulham	A	W	3-0	Moore, OG, Mangnall
20	Jan	3	Tottenham Hotspur	H	W	1-0	Mallett
21		10	Portsmouth	A	L	1-3	Mangnall
22		17	Chelsea	A	L	1-3	Mangnall
23		24	Charlton Athletic	A	L	1-3	Mangnall
24		31	West Ham United	H	W	2-1	Armstrong, Farmer
25	Feb	14	Aldershot	H	L	0-2	
26		21	Millwall	A	W	2-1	Hatton (2)
27		28	Arsenal	H	L	0-1	
28	Mar	7	Clapton Orient	H	W	2-1	Hatton, Mangnall
29		14	Reading	H	W	4-0	Hatton (2), Mangnall (2)
30	May	2	Watford	A	W	5-0	Heath (2), McEwan (2), Lowe

Appeara
G

London War Cup

Match No.	Date		Opponents	Location	Result		Scorers
1	Mar	21	Millwall	A	D	2-2	Hatton (2)
2		28	Aldershot	A	W	2-0	Kirkham, Hatton
3	Apr	4	Brentford	H	L	1-2	Kirkham
4		6	Aldershot	H	L	1-2	Lowe
5		11	Brentford	A	L	0-1	
6		18	Millwall	H	W	2-0	Hatton (2)

Appeara
G

Total - Appeara
Total - G

Attendances

TOTAL

	Home	Away	Total
League	74,018	55,453	129,471
Cup/Other	7,500	15,310	22,810
TOTAL	81,518	70,763	152,281

AVERAGE

	Home	Away	Total
League	4,935	3,697	4,316
Cup/Other	3,750	5,103	4,562
TOTAL	4,795	3,931	4,351

Armstrong	Blizzard	Bonass	Brown B.	Brown H.	Campbell	Cheetham (G)	Cottam	Dale (G)	Davie (G)	Delaney	Eastham (G)	Edwards E.	Edwards R.	Farmer	Gibbs-Kennett	Gunner	Halford (G)	Harris	Hatton (G)	Heath	Jefferson	Kirkham (G)	Libby	Ling	Lowe	Mahon (G)	Mallett	Mangnall	March	Mason	McEwan	McNickle	Moore	Painter	Paton (G)	Pattison	Reay	Ridyard	Sibley (G)	Smale (G)	Smith	Stock	Swinfen	OG
8									9					6											4	7	10			1						11		5					2	
											8						11								4	7	10	9	6	1								5					2	
10											8			3			11								4	7		9	6	1								5						
											8			6			11				3						10	7	4	1					9			5						
									9												3					11	10	7	4	1				6	8			5						
											10			6			7				3					11		9	4	1					8			5					2	
					4						8			3								9				11	10	7	6	1								5						
					4						8						11				3	9				10		7	6	1								5						
					4						8			3			10					9				11		7	6	1								5						
					4						8											9				7		10	6	1						11		5					2	
	6				4																3				8	7		10		1						11		5				9	2	
	6			1																		8				10	4	7	3							11		5				9		
	6			1																	3	8				10		7	4							11		5				9		
	4											6		3												7		9		1				8		11		5		10				
8	6																				3	10			4					1	7					11		5				9		
8	6			1										4										9		7		10				3				11		5					2	
	6	7									8			3								9					4	10		1						11		5						
8	6	11					7	3						4				9										10		1								5					2	
	6	11												4											7		8	10		1			9	3				5					2	
9	6	7		1										4												11	8	10	3									5						
9	6			1										4							3						8	10								11		5			7			
	6			1																	3					7	4	10								11	2	5			8	9		
9	6			1										4							3						8	10								11	2	5			7			
8				1										6							3	9			7		4	10	11								2	5						
														6					10		3						4	9		1						11	2	5			8		7	
														6					10	9	3						4			1						11	2	5	7		8			
				1										6					10		3	9			2		4	7								11		5			8			
4	6			1										5					10	9					2			8								11			7					
														6					10	11	3	9			4			8		1							2	5	7					
		11		1																9	3			10	7		4				8							5		6			2	
10	14	5		11	5		1	1	2		9	1		20			6	1	5	4	16	11		2	11	15	18	26	13	19	2	1	1	3	3	16	6	29	3	2	6	5	10	
3									3		2			1			2	1	5	2		1			1	4	3	12			2		1			5						2		1

Armstrong	Blizzard	Bonass	Brown B.	Brown H.	Campbell	Cheetham (G)	Cottam	Dale (G)	Davie (G)	Delaney	Eastham (G)	Edwards E.	Edwards R.	Farmer	Gibbs-Kennett	Gunner	Halford (G)	Harris	Hatton (G)	Heath	Jefferson	Kirkham (G)	Libby	Ling	Lowe	Mahon (G)	Mallett	Mangnall	March	Mason	McEwan	McNickle	Moore	Painter	Paton (G)	Pattison	Reay	Ridyard	Sibley (G)	Smale (G)	Smith	Stock	Swinfen	OG
												5		6		4			10	9	3							8		1						11	2		7					
												5		6		4			10		3	9						8		1						11	2		7					
8		11												6		4			10		3	9								1								5	7					
		11	7							3				10	9	4									8				6	1								5						
				1									3	10						9			5				4		6										7		8		2	
		11		1		9													10		3						4				8							5	7		6		2	
1		3	1	2		1				1		2	1	5	1	4			4	2	4	2	1		1		2	2	2	4	1					2	2	3	5		2		2	
																			5			2			1																			

Armstrong	Blizzard	Bonass	Brown B.	Brown H.	Campbell	Cheetham (G)	Cottam	Dale (G)	Davie (G)	Delaney	Eastham (G)	Edwards E.	Edwards R.	Farmer	Gibbs-Kennett	Gunner	Halford (G)	Harris	Hatton (G)	Heath	Jefferson	Kirkham (G)	Libby	Ling	Lowe	Mahon (G)	Mallett	Mangnall	March	Mason	McEwan	McNickle	Moore	Painter	Paton (G)	Pattison	Reay	Ridyard	Sibley (G)	Smale (G)	Smith	Stock	Swinfen	OG
11	14	8	1	13	5	1	1	1	2	1	9	3	1	25	1	4	6	1	9	6	20	13	1	2	12	15	20	28	15	23	3	1	1	3	3	18	8	32	8	2	8	5	12	
3									3		2			1			2	1	10	2		3			2	4	3	12			2		1			5						2		1

uest Player

1942-43

League South

	P	W	D	L	F	A	Pts
Arsenal	28	21	1	6	102	40	43
Tottenham Hotspur	28	16	6	6	68	28	38
Queen's Park Rangers	28	18	2	8	64	49	38
Portsmouth	28	16	3	9	66	52	35
Southampton	28	14	5	9	86	58	33
West Ham United	28	14	5	9	80	66	33
Chelsea	28	14	4	10	52	45	32
Aldershot	28	14	2	12	87	77	30
Brentford	28	12	5	11	64	63	29
Charlton Athletic	28	13	3	12	68	75	29
Clapton Orient	28	11	5	12	54	72	27
Brighton & Hove Albion	28	10	5	13	65	73	25
Reading	28	9	6	13	67	74	24
Fulham	28	10	2	16	69	78	22
Crystal Palace	28	7	5	16	49	75	19
Millwall	28	6	5	17	66	88	17
Watford	28	7	2	19	51	88	16
Luton Town	28	4	6	18	43	100	14

Attendances

	TOTAL		
	Home	Away	Total
League	81,415	83,766	165,181
Cup/Other	22,979	81,028	104,007
TOTAL	104,394	164,794	269,188

	AVERAGE		
	Home	Away	Total
League	5,815	5,983	5,899
Cup/Other	7,660	20,257	14,858
TOTAL	6,141	9,155	7,691

QUEEN'S PARK RANGERS FOOTBALL AND ATHLETIC CLUB, LTD.
Ground - - - Loftus Road, Shepherds Bush, W.12

QUEEN'S PARK RANGERS v. MILLWALL

Saturday, 3rd October, 1942 Kick-off 3.15 p.m.

QUEEN'S PARK RANGERS

RIGHT LEFT

Brown

Reay Abel

Henley Ridyard Smith

Sibley Mangnall Swinfen Hatton Pattison

Referee : L. BROWN

Smith, J. R. Weir Heathcote, W. Davies Grainger

Brolly Cardwell Packard

Smith, E. Calland

Burke

LEFT RIGHT

MILLWALL

Next Home Match - Next Saturday Kick-off 3.15
Q.P.R. JUNIORS v. HAWKER ATHLETIC F.C.

OFFICIAL PROGRAMME—Price 1d.

Match No.	Date		Opponents	Location	Result		Scorers	Attend
1	Aug	29	Chelsea	A	D	1-1	Mallett	6
2	Sep	5	Tottenham Hotspur	H	L	0-1		4
3		12	Clapton Orient	A	W	4-0	Mangnall, Sibley, Stock (2)	1
4		19	Crystal Palace	A	W	1-0	Stock	5
5		26	Brentford	H	W	4-1	Swinfen (3), Mallett	8
6	Oct	3	Millwall	H	W	3-2	Hatton, Swinfen (2)	4
7		10	Reading	A	W	2-1	Hatton, Ridyard	4
8		17	Luton Town	H	D	2-2	Hatton, Burley	4
9		24	Brighton	A	W	3-2	Burley, Swinfen, Sibley	3
10		31	Southampton	H	W	3-1	Swinfen, Hatton, Reay	4
11	Nov	7	West Ham United	H	W	5-2	Hatton, Swinfen (4)	6
12		14	Arsenal	A	L	0-3		14
13		21	Charlton Athletic	A	L	2-3	Hatton, Burley	3
14		28	Chelsea	H	W	4-1	Burley, Swinfen, Sibley, Hatton	8
15	Dec	5	Tottenham Hotspur	A	L	0-6		8
16		12	Clapton Orient	H	W	3-1	Mangnall (3)	4
17		19	Crystal Palace	H	W	3-0	Hatton (2), Burley	3
18		25	Fulham	H	W	2-1	Mangnall, Sibley	4
19		26	Fulham	A	L	2-4	Ridyard, Burley	7
20	Jan	2	Brentford	A	L	0-2		7
21		9	Millwall	A	W	2-1	Mangnall, Smith	4
22		16	Reading	H	W	3-2	Swinfen, Mangnall (2)	4
23		23	Luton Town	A	W	2-1	Burley, Abel	3
24		30	Brighton	H	L	3-4	Sibley, Mangnall (2)	3
25	Feb	6	Southampton	A	L	2-4	Burley, Parkinson	9
26		13	West Ham United	A	W	3-1	Mangnall, Swinfen (2)	6
27		20	Arsenal	H	W	3-2	Heathcote, Burley (2)	13
28		27	Charlton Athletic	H	W	2-0	Pattison, Heathcote	4
								Appearar
								G

League Cup South (Group 2)

1	Mar	6	Brentford	A	W	2-1	McEwan, Burley	10
2		13	Southampton	H	W	2-1	Mallett, McEwan	8
3		20	Clapton Orient	A	D	1-1	Heathcote	3
4		27	Brentford	H	W	2-0	Burley, Heathcote	9
5	Apr	3	Southampton	A	L	1-4	Mallett	13
6		10	Clapton Orient	H	W	8-1	Heathcote (4), Pattison (2), Swinfen, Burley	5
SF		24	Arsenal	N*	L	1-4	Pattison	54
								Appearar
								G

* Played at Stamford Bridge

Total - Appearar
Total - G

Barkas (G)	Beadell	Blizzard	Brown	Burley	Farmer	Fitzgerald	Gadsden	Gunner	Hatton (G)	Heath	Heathcote (G)	Henley (G)	Horsfield (G)	Jefferson	Lowe	Mallett	Mangnall	McEwan	McInnes (G)	Mills (G)	Parkinson	Pattison	Powell	Reay	Ridyard	Rose	Sibley (G)	Smith	Stock	Swinfen
	11		1			6			10	9				3		4								2	5		7	8		
			1	11	5				10				6	3	9	4								2			7	8		
	6		1	11												4	10							2	5		7	8	9	
			1		4											6	10					11		2	5		7	8	9	
			1													6	10	8				11		2	5		7	4		9
			1						10			4					8					11		2	5		7	6		9
			1	11				8	10			4		3										2	5		7	6		
			1	11				4	10					3		6								2	5		7	8		
			1	11				4	10					3		6								2	5		7	8		9
			1	11				4	10					3		6								2	5		7	8		9
			1	11					10					3		6	8							2	5		7	4		9
			1	11					10					3		6	5							2			7	4	8	9
2			1	11					10					3		6	5										7	4	8	9
			1	11					10				2		4	6	8								5		7			9
			1	11					10				2		4	6	8								5		7			9
			1	11					10				2		4		8		6						5		7			9
		6	1	11					10				2			4	9								5		7	8		
		6	1	11			8	4	10					3			9								5		7			
			1	11			8	4						3		6	9								5		7	10		
			1	11	5		8						2			6					10						7	4		9
			1	11				4						3		6	9			10					5		7	8		
			1	11				10						3	4	6	8								5	2	7			9
			1	11				10							4	6	8								5	2	7			9
			1	11											4	6	8				10				5	2	7			9
			1	11											4	6	8				10				5	2	7			9
			1	11	5						9				4	6	8									2		10		7
			1	10							9					6	8					11			5	2		4		7
			1	10							9			3	7	6	8					11			5	2		4		
1	2	2	28	24	4	1	3	9	15	1	3	2	6	14	10	24	21	1	1	1	3	5		12	23	7	25	20	4	17
				9					9		2					2	11				2	1		1	2		5	1	3	15

Barkas (G)	Beadell	Blizzard	Brown	Burley	Farmer	Fitzgerald	Gadsden	Gunner	Hatton (G)	Heath	Heathcote (G)	Henley (G)	Horsfield (G)	Jefferson	Lowe	Mallett	Mangnall	McEwan	McInnes (G)	Mills (G)	Parkinson	Pattison	Powell	Reay	Ridyard	Rose	Sibley (G)	Smith	Stock	Swinfen
			1	10							9					6		8				11			5	2		4		7
			1	11							9					10		8					6		5	2	7	4		
			1	11							9					10	8						6		5	2		4		7
			1	10							9					6	8					11			5	2		4		7
			1	10							9					6	8					11			5	2		4		7
			1	10							9						8					11	6		5	2		4		7
			1	10							9					6		8				11			5	2		4		7
			7	7							7					6	4	3				5	3		7	7	1	7		6
				3							6					2		2				3								1

Barkas (G)	Beadell	Blizzard	Brown	Burley	Farmer	Fitzgerald	Gadsden	Gunner	Hatton (G)	Heath	Heathcote (G)	Henley (G)	Horsfield (G)	Jefferson	Lowe	Mallett	Mangnall	McEwan	McInnes (G)	Mills (G)	Parkinson	Pattison	Powell	Reay	Ridyard	Rose	Sibley (G)	Smith	Stock	Swinfen
1	2	2	35	31	4	1	3	9	15	1	10	2	6	14	10	30	25	4	1	1	3	10	3	12	30	14	26	27	4	23
				12					9		8					4	11	2			2	4		1	2		5	1	3	16

est Player

1943-44

League South

	P	W	D	L	F	A	Pts
Tottenham Hotspur	30	19	8	3	71	36	46
West Ham United	30	17	7	6	74	39	41
Queen's Park Rangers	30	14	12	4	69	54	40
Arsenal	30	14	10	6	72	42	38
Crystal Palace	30	16	5	9	75	53	37
Portsmouth	30	16	5	9	68	59	37
Brentford	30	14	7	9	71	51	35
Chelsea	30	16	2	12	79	55	34
Fulham	30	11	9	10	80	73	31
Millwall	30	13	4	13	70	66	30
Aldershot	30	12	6	12	64	73	30
Reading	30	12	3	15	73	62	27
Southampton	30	10	7	13	67	88	27
Charlton Athletic	30	9	7	14	57	73	25
Watford	30	6	8	16	58	80	20
Brighton & Hove Albion	30	9	2	19	55	82	20
Clapton Orient	30	4	3	23	32	87	11
Luton Town	30	3	5	22	42	104	11

Attendances

TOTAL	Home	Away	Total
League	90,696	123,147	213,843
Cup/Other	28,000	22,367	50,367
TOTAL	118,696	145,514	264,210

AVERAGE	Home	Away	Total
League	6,977	8,210	7,637
Cup/Other	9,333	7,456	8,395
TOTAL	7,419	8,084	7,771

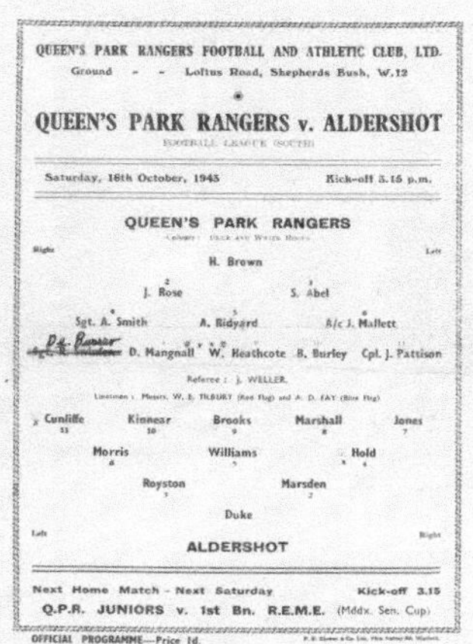
QUEEN'S PARK RANGERS FOOTBALL AND ATHLETIC CLUB, LTD.
Ground - - Loftus Road, Shepherds Bush, W.12

QUEEN'S PARK RANGERS v. ALDERSHOT

FOOTBALL LEAGUE (SOUTH)

Saturday, 16th October, 1943 Kick-off 3.15 p.m.

QUEEN'S PARK RANGERS

H. Brown

J. Rose S. Abel

Sgt. A. Smith A. Ridyard A/c J. Mallett

De Busser D. Mangnall W. Heathcote B. Burley Cpl. J. Pattison

Referee: J. WELLER.

Cunliffe Kinnear Brooks Marshall Jones

Morris Williams Hold

Royston Marsden

Duke

ALDERSHOT

Next Home Match - Next Saturday Kick-off 3.15
Q.P.R. JUNIORS v. 1st Bn. R.E.M.E. (Mddx. Sen. Cup)

OFFICIAL PROGRAMME—Price 1d.

Match No.	Date		Opponents	Location	Result		Scorers
1	Aug	28	Chelsea	A	W	3-1	Heathcote (2), De Busser
2	Sep	4	Tottenham Hotspur	H	W	1-0	Heathcote
3		11	Clapton Orient	A	W	3-2	Heathcote (2), Swinfen
4		18	Watford	H	W	3-1	Heathcote (2), Pattison
5		25	Portsmouth	A	D	1-1	McEwan
6	Oct	2	Reading	A	D	0-0	
7		9	Millwall	H	W	2-0	Mangnall, Burley
8		16	Aldershot	H	D	2-2	Mangnall, Heathcote
9		23	Brighton	A	L	1-3	Heathcote
10		30	Southampton	H	W	7-0	Heathcote (3), McEwan, Pattison (2), Griffths
11	Nov	6	West Ham United	A	D	1-1	Heathcote
12		13	Arsenal	A	L	0-5	
13		20	Charlton Athletic	A	L	0-1	
14		27	Chelsea	H	L	2-11	Swinfen, Pearson
15	Dec	4	Tottenham Hotspur	A	D	2-2	Heathcote (2)
16		11	Clapton Orient	H	W	6-2	Swinfen (2), Burley, Heathcote (2), OG
17		18	Fulham	A	D	2-2	Sibley, Ramscar
18		25	Brentford	A	W	5-2	Somerfield (2), Heathcote (2), Lowes
19		27	Brentford	H	W	3-2	Swinfen, Heathcote, Somerfield
20	Jan	1	Watford	A	D	2-2	Somerfield, Heathcote
21		8	West Ham United	H	W	3-0	Heathcote (2), Little
22		22	Reading	H	W	2-0	Heathcote (2)
23		29	Millwall	A	W	4-3	Lowes, Somerfield, Burley, Heathcote
24	Feb	5	Aldershot	A	W	3-1	Sheen, Burley, Lowes
25		12	Brighton	H	W	1-0	Sheen
26	Apr	1	Southampton	A	D	2-2	De Lisle, Heathcote
27		10	Portsmouth	H	D	1-1	Mangnall
28		22	Fulham	H	D	3-3	Heathcote, Mallett, Jones
29		29	Arsenal	H	D	1-1	Jones
30	May	6	Charlton Athletic	H	D	3-3	Heathcote, Lowes (2)

Appeara
G

League Cup South (Group D)

Match No.	Date		Opponents	Location	Result		Scorers
1	Feb	19	Clapton Orient	A	W	5-2	Swinfen (2), Burley (2), Sibley
2		26	Arsenal	H	D	1-1	Swinfen
3	Mar	4	Luton Town	A	W	4-3	Heathcote (3), Ramscar
4		11	Clapton Orient	H	W	6-0	Dean (2), Swinfen (3), Sheen
5		18	Arsenal	A	W	4-1	Heathcote, Jones, Sheen, Swinfen
6		25	Luton Town	H	W	5-0	Heathcote (3), Swinfen, Jones

Appeara
G

Total - Appeara
Total - G

Alexander	Bacon	Blizzard	Brown	Burley	De Busser	De Lisle	Dean (G)	Dolding	Duke (G)	Evans (G)	Fowler (G)	Gadsden	Gillies (G)	Greenwood (G)	Griffiths	Hardy (G)	Heathcote	Hughes (G)	Hutchinson (G)	Jefferson	Jones (G)	Little (G)	Lowes (G)	Mallett	Mangnall	Martin (G)	Mason	McEwan	McLuckie (G)	Parkinson	Parry (G)	Pattison	Pearson (G)	Ramscar (G)	Ridyard	Rose	Roxburgh (G)	Shaw	Sheen (G)	Sibley (G)	Smith	Somerfield (G)	Swinfen	Webb	Yielleyoye	OG
			1	10	8												9			3				6								11			5						4		7			
			1	10	8												9			3				6								11			5	2					4					
			1	11				10									9							6											5	3					4		7	8		
		7	1														9			3				6						10		11			5	2					4		8			
			1														9			3				6	7			8				11			5	2					4			10		
			1														9			3				6				8				11			5	2					4		7	10		
			1	11													9							6	8										5	2					4		7	10		
			1	10	7												9							6	8							11			5	2					4					
																	9							6	8		1					11			5	2					4		7	10		
			1									10			7		9							6				8				11			5	2					4					
			1	10								8			7		9							6								11			5	2					4					
			1	11													9			2				6				8					10		5						4		7			
			1	11								8			7		9			2				6	5								10								4					
				11						2		4							7					6			1			8			10		5								9			
			1														9			3				6									10	8	5	2					4				11	
				11					1								9			3				6	5									8		2					4		10			
	10		1	11													9							6										8	5	2				7	4	10				
			1	11													9						8	6	5											2				7		10	4			
			1														9			3			8	6	5											2					4	10	7			
			1	11								7					9			2			8	6	5																4	10				
			1	11													9			3		7	8	6											5	2					4	10				
				11								7					9	1					8	6											5	2					4	10				
			1	11													9					7	8	6	5											2					4	10				
			1	11													9					7	8	6											5	2			4			10				
			1	11							8						9					7		6											5	2			10		4					
				11		7											9							5	6											2	1		10		4		8			
5				10								7				11								4	9				8							2	1	6								
			1	11									5				9				7			6	8				10		4					2							3			
			1	11									5				9				7		8	6												2					4	10				
			1	11									5				9				7		8	6												2					4	10				
1	1	1	24	23	3	1		1	1	1	1	7	3		3	1	28	1	1	12	3	4	9	30	13		2	4	2	2	1	9	4	3	19	25	2	1	3	2	25	9	13	5	1	
				4	1	1									1		29				2	1	5	1	3			2				3	1	1					2	1		5	5			1

Alexander	Bacon	Blizzard	Brown	Burley	De Busser	De Lisle	Dean (G)	Dolding	Duke (G)	Evans (G)	Fowler (G)	Gadsden	Gillies (G)	Greenwood (G)	Griffiths	Hardy (G)	Heathcote	Hughes (G)	Hutchinson (G)	Jefferson	Jones (G)	Little (G)	Lowes (G)	Mallett	Mangnall	Martin (G)	Mason	McEwan	McLuckie (G)	Parkinson	Parry (G)	Pattison	Pearson (G)	Ramscar (G)	Ridyard	Rose	Roxburgh (G)	Shaw	Sheen (G)	Sibley (G)	Smith	Somerfield (G)	Swinfen	Webb	Yielleyoye	OG
			1	11													9							6	8										5	2				10	4		7			
			1	11													9							6	5											2			10		4	8	7			
				11										5			9									6								8		2	1		10	7	4					
				11			7						5											6	8											2	1		10		4		9			
				11													9				7			6	5											2	1		10		4		8			
				11									5				9				7			6			1									2			10		4		8			
			2	6			1						2	1			5				2			5	4	1	1							1	1	6	3		5	2	6	1	5			
				2			2										7				2													1					2	1			8			

Alexander	Bacon	Blizzard	Brown	Burley	De Busser	De Lisle	Dean (G)	Dolding	Duke (G)	Evans (G)	Fowler (G)	Gadsden	Gillies (G)	Greenwood (G)	Griffiths	Hardy (G)	Heathcote	Hughes (G)	Hutchinson (G)	Jefferson	Jones (G)	Little (G)	Lowes (G)	Mallett	Mangnall	Martin (G)	Mason	McEwan	McLuckie (G)	Parkinson	Parry (G)	Pattison	Pearson (G)	Ramscar (G)	Ridyard	Rose	Roxburgh (G)	Shaw	Sheen (G)	Sibley (G)	Smith	Somerfield (G)	Swinfen	Webb	Yielleyoye	OG
1	1	1	26	29	3	1	1	1	1	1	1	7	5	1	3	1	33	1	1	12	5	4	9	35	17	1	3	4	2	2	1	9	4	4	20	31	5	1	8	4	31	10	18	5	1	
				6	1	1	2								1		36				4	1	5	1	3			2				3	1	2					4	2		5	13			1

uest Player

1944-45

League South

	P	W	D	L	F	A	Pts
Tottenham Hotspur	30	23	6	1	81	30	52
West Ham United	30	22	3	5	96	47	47
Brentford	30	17	4	9	87	57	38
Chelsea	30	16	5	9	100	55	37
Southampton	30	17	3	10	96	69	37
Crystal Palace	30	15	5	10	74	70	35
Reading	30	14	6	10	78	68	34
Arsenal	30	14	3	13	77	67	31
Queen's Park Rangers	30	10	10	10	70	61	30
Watford	30	11	6	13	66	84	28
Fulham	30	11	4	15	79	83	26
Portsmouth	30	11	4	15	56	61	26
Charlton Athletic	30	12	2	16	72	81	26
Brighton & Hove Albion	30	10	2	18	66	95	22
Luton Town	30	6	7	17	56	104	19
Aldershot	30	7	4	19	44	85	18
Millwall	30	5	7	18	50	84	17
Clapton Orient	30	5	7	18	39	86	17

Attendances

	TOTAL		
	Home	**Away**	**Total**
League	101,944	120,104	222,048
Cup/Other	54,700	44,331	99,031
TOTAL	156,644	164,435	321,079

	AVERAGE		
	Home	**Away**	**Total**
League	6,796	8,007	7,402
Cup/Other	18,233	14,777	16,505
TOTAL	8,702	9,135	8,919

QUEEN'S PARK RANGERS FOOTBALL AND ATHLETIC CLUB, LTD.
Ground - - Loftus Road, Shepherds Bush, W.12

Queen's Park Rangers v. Southampton

FOOTBALL LEAGUE (SOUTH)

Saturday, 2nd September, 1944 — Kick-off 3.15 p.m.

QUEEN'S PARK RANGERS

Duke

Rose — Abel

R. Gunner — Ridyard — Mallett

Jones — Sibley — Heathcote — Fitzgerald — Burley

Referee: A. J. WALTER

Roberts — Walker — Whittingham — Bates — Roper

Stroud — Clements — Dodgin

Roles — Stear

Swindin

SOUTHAMPTON

Here Next Saturday—London War Combination. Kick-off 3.15

FULHAM

OFFICIAL PROGRAMME—Price 1d.

Match No.	Date		Opponents	Location	Result		Scorers	Atten
1	Aug	26	Crystal Palace	A	L	4-7	Heathcote (3), Fitzgerald	7
2	Sep	2	Southampton	H	L	4-5	Sibley, Fitzgerald, Heathcote, Jones	5
3		9	Fulham	A	D	2-2	Fitzgerald (2)	8
4		16	West Ham United	H	L	0-1		8
5		23	Arsenal	A	L	0-2		15
6		30	Reading	A	D	1-1	Mallett	6
7	Oct	7	Millwall	H	W	4-1	Bain, Ridyard, Sibley, Cheetham	6
8		14	Clapton Orient	A	W	3-0	Heathcote, Mallett, Burley	3
9		21	Brentford	A	L	1-3	Jones	16
10		28	Brighton	H	W	4-0	Jones (2), Attwell, E.Smith	6
11	Nov	4	Portsmouth	A	L	1-4	Burley	10
12		11	Aldershot	A	D	1-1	Heathcote	3
13		18	Charlton Athletic	A	W	2-1	Heathcote (2)	6
14		25	Luton Town	H	W	7-1	Abel, Heathcote (3), Mallett, Daniels (2)	5
15	Dec	2	Crystal Palace	H	D	0-0		8
16		9	Southampton	A	W	5-4	Heathcote, Daniels (2), Mallett, Abel	9
17		16	Fulham	H	D	4-4	Heathcote (3), Darragon	10
18		23	Tottenham Hotspur	H	D	0-0		13
19		25	Tottenham Hotspur	A	L	2-4	Abel, Lowes	16
20		30	West Ham United	A	L	2-4	Daniels, Shaw	9
21	Jan	6	Arsenal	H	W	3-2	Heathcote (2), Sibley	10
22		13	Reading	H	W	5-1	Sibley, Somerfield, Daniels, Mallett (2)	6
23		20	Millwall	A	D	3-3	Heathcote (2), Daniels	3
24		27	Clapton Orient	H	D	3-3	Shaw (2), Mallett	2
25	Mar	17	Brentford	H	D	1-1	Darragon	5
26		24	Brighton	A	D	1-1	Shaw	4
27		31	Portsmouth	H	W	1-0	Heathcote	5
28	Apr	14	Aldershot	H	W	3-0	Addinall (2), Gillies	5
29		21	Charlton Athletic	H	L	2-3	Addinall, Shaw	7
30		28	Luton Town	A	L	1-2	Addinall	2

Appearar
G

League Cup South (Group 3)

Match No.	Date		Opponents	Location	Result		Scorers	Atten
1	Feb	3	Tottenham Hotspur	A	D	1-1	Heathcote	20
2		10	Aldershot	H	W	2-1	Daniels, Ridyard	7
3		17	West Ham United	H	D	1-1	Heathcote	17
4		24	Tottenham Hotspur	H	W	1-0	Heathcote	30
5	Mar	3	Aldershot	A	W	2-0	Gillies, OG	4
6		10	West Ham United	A	L	0-5		20

Appearar
G

Total - Appearar
Total - G

Addinall	Alexander	Attwell (G)	Bain (G)	Brook (G)	Brown	Burley	Chalkley (G)	Cheetham (G)	Cruikshank (G)	Daniels	Darragon	Dawes (G)	Dean (G)	Duke (G)	Dukes (G)	Farmer	Farrow	Ferrier (G)	Fitzgerald	Forsyth (G)	Gillies (G)	Gregory (G)	Gunner	Heathcote	Henley (G)	Jefferson	Jones (G)	King	Knight (G)	Laidman (G)	Lowes (G)	Ludford (G)	Mallett	Nevins (G)	Phillips (G)	Ridyard	Robinson (G)	Rose	Shaw	Sibley (G)	Smith A.	Smith E.	Somerfield (G)	Stock	Swinfen	Taylor (G)	Tennant (G)	OG
						11								1					10				4	9									6			5		2		7					8			
						11								1					10					9			7						6			5		2		8	4							
					1	11													10					9			7						6			5		2		8	4							
						11									1				10					9									6			5	8	2		7	4							
			8	10		11						3										1		9									6			5	7	2			4							
			8									3									2	1		9									6			5			10	7	4							
			10			11		9													2	1					7						6			5				8	4							
			10			11						4									2	1		9			7						6			5				8								
			10			11															4	1		9			7						6			5		2		8								
		10				11															4	1		9			7						6			5		2				8						
		10				11						3									4	1		9			7						6			5		2		8								
		10								8		3									4	1		9			7						6			5		2				11						
		10								8		3				5					4	1		9			7						6					2										
										8		3					6				4	1		9									10			5		2		7								
		6								8		3				5					4	1		9								11	10					2		7								
		6								8	7	3									4	1		9									10			5		2										
		6								4	11	3										1		9									10			5		2	8	7								
		6				11				8		3									4	1		9									10			5		2		7								
		6				11				8												1		9							4		10			5		2		7								
		6					2			8	11							4				1		9									10			5			7									
		6								8	11									4		1		9									10			5		2		7								
	5							9		8										4		1											10		6			2		7			11					
		6						11	1	8			7											9						2			10			5				4								
						11				8									6		4	1		9									10			5		2	7									
9								7			11						6				4												8			5		2	10							1		
9								7		6	11										4												8			5		2	10							1		
					1					6	7										4			9									8			5		2	10		11							
9										8	11										4							7					6			5		2	10							1		
9					1					8	11										4							7					6			5		2	10									
9					1					8	11										4												6			5		2	10					7				
5	1	12	5	1	4	13	1	5	1	18	10	11	1	2	1	2	2	1	5	2	19	19	1	23			9	2		1	1	1	30		1	27	2	25	10	17	7	2	1	1	1	3		
4		1	1			2		1		7	2								4		1			20			4				1		7			1			5	4		1	1					
																			8	6	4	1		9		3							10	11		5		2										
					1	10				8									4					9		3							6	11		5		2										
					1	11													7		4			9	6	3							10			5		2									8	
					1	11				8									10		4			9									6			5		2		7								
					1					8	11										4			9		3			10		7		6			5		2										
					1	11				8									10		4			9		3							6			5		2										
					5	4				4	1								5	1	5	1		6	1	5			1		1		6	2		6		6		1							1	
										1											1			3												1												1
5	1	12	5	1	9	17	1	5	1	22	11	11	1	2	1	2	2	1	10	3	24	20	1	29	1	5	9	2	1	1	2	1	36	2	1	33	2	31	10	18	7	2	1	1	1	3	1	
4		1	1			2		1		8	2								4		2			23			4				1		7			2			5	4		1	1					1

uest Player

1945-46

Division Three South (North Region)

	P	W	D	L	F	A	Pts
Queen's Park Rangers	20	14	4	2	50	15	32
Norwich City	20	11	4	5	55	31	26
Port Vale	20	9	6	5	34	25	24
Watford	20	10	2	8	42	47	22
Ipswich Town	20	8	4	8	33	36	20
Notts County	20	8	4	8	39	47	20
Northampton Town	20	8	3	9	37	34	19
Clapton Orient	20	5	6	9	28	43	16
Walsall	20	6	3	11	31	42	15
Southend United	20	5	5	10	33	49	15
Mansfield Town	20	3	5	12	29	42	11

Attendances

TOTAL	Home	Away	Total
League	111,560	113,483	225,043
Cup/Other	186,903	183,508	370,411
TOTAL	298,463	296,991	595,454

AVERAGE	Home	Away	Total
League	11,156	11,348	11,252
Cup/Other	13,350	13,108	13,229
TOTAL	12,436	12,375	12,405

QUEEN'S PARK RANGERS FOOTBALL CLUB

Official Programme - Price 2d

GROUND: LOFTUS ROAD, SHEPHERDS BUSH, W.12

Q.P.R. v. SOUTHEND Utd. Saturday, 1st Sept., 1945

We made a good start at Southend, bringing home two points. Our win was not convincing however, the play at times being very scrappy. Our forwards, with the exception of Freddie Crack, could not get going at all. After getting a nice lead of two goals in the first half-hour, they began to take liberties with the Southend defence and a lot of good spade-work was wasted. I should rank Jefferson as being the best back on the field—he was brilliant. Crack, apart from his two goals, played a nice game; a big fellow with a good turn of speed and a good shot in either foot.

We are all pleased to see Reg. Allen back with us again. The four-and-a-half years he was a prisoner-of-war have not damped his spirits; he played a fine game, with very few mistakes. The Southend goal came from a penalty. Gilberg, a guest player from 'Spurs, took the kick and gave our goalie no chance.

Our Reserves started their campaign in an uncertain fashion, although for the first few minutes of the game our lads were not together and quickly found themselves a goal behind. However, this reverse had the effect of steadying them and very soon they took control. The final score of 6—3 in no way flatters them. Those 2,000 odd spectators who attended this match must have been impressed by the very high standard of play on both sides. As forecast in our programme last week the London Combination will provide keen competition and compares very favourably with the Football Combination of pre-war. The policy of blending seasoned campaigners and youngsters will undoubtedly pay a big dividend in the near future but to enable the Directors to continue this, they need the help of our supporters by regular attendance. Come along and watch the progress of the Rangers of the future!

Looking ahead, whilst promotion at the earliest opportunity must be our first concern, the comfort of spectators is of vital interest to the Directors and Management. A glance at the Loftus Road end of the ground will give tangible evidence of this but the vital need is, as usual, money. Without the loyal and regular attendance of supporters at all matches it will be impossible to attain these objects. Given full support, a programme can be mapped out and brought into being to the advantage of all our supporters. Make it your concern to do this and to encourage all your friends to do the same.

In extending a welcome to Southend United we would remind you of the hard struggle between the teams last week, the result of which might easily have been reversed. This augurs well for to-day's game.

(Continued on Back Page)

Match No.	Date		Opponents	Location	Result		Scorers
1	Aug	25	Southend United	A	W	2-1	Crack (2)
2	Sep	1	Southend United	H	W	4-1	Mallett, Hatton (2), Neary
3		5	Clapton Orient	A	W	2-0	Crack, Heathcote
4		8	Walsall	H	W	4-0	Neary (3), Heathcote
5		12	Mansfield Town	A	W	6-2	Neary (2), Mallett (2), Heathcote, Somerfield
6		15	Walsall	A	D	1-1	Salmon
7		19	Clapton Orient	H	W	3-0	Heathcote (2), Mallett
8		22	Port Vale	A	D	0-0	
9		29	Port Vale	H	W	4-1	Mallett, Heathcote, Neary, Abel
10	Oct	6	Ipswich Town	H	W	2-0	Heathcote, Mallett
11		13	Ipswich Town	A	L	1-2	Mallett
12		20	Northampton Town	A	W	2-0	Neary, Heathcote
13		27	Northampton Town	H	W	4-1	Heathcote (3), Addinall
14	Nov	3	Notts County	H	W	6-0	Neary (2), Heathcote (4)
15		10	Notts County	A	W	1-0	Heathcote
16	Dec	1	Watford	A	W	2-0	Whitehead, Neary
17		25	Norwich City	A	D	1-1	Ridyard
18		26	Norwich City	H	L	1-2	Neary
19		29	Mansfield Town	H	W	3-2	Ridyard, Heathcote (2)
20	Jan	1	Watford	H	D	1-1	Ridyard

Appeara
G

FA Cup

R1/1	Nov	17	Barnet	A	W	6-2	Heatcote, Mallett (2), Neary (3)
R1/2		24	Barnet	H	W	2-1	Swinfen, Neary
R2/1	Dec	8	Ipswich Town	H	W	4-0	Neary, Stock, Addinall (2)
R2/2		15	Ipswich Town	A	W	2-0	Daniels, Addinall
R3/1	Jan	5	Crystal Palace	H	D	0-0	
R3/2		9	Crystal Palace	A	D	0-0*	
rep		16	Crystal Palace	N**	W	1-0	Addinall
R4/1		26	Southampton	A	W	1-0	Addinall
R4/2		30	Southampton	H	W	4-3	Addinall (3), Stock
R5/1	Feb	9	Brentford	H	L	1-3	Pattison
R5/2		14	Brentford	A	D	0-0	

* Abandoned after 117 minutes -result stood, ** Played at Craven Cottage

Appeara
G

Division Three South (North) Cup

Grp	Jan	12	Ipswich Town	H	W	4-1	Stock (2), Heath, Mallett
Grp		19	Ipswich Town	A	L	0-1	
Grp	Feb	2	Bristol City	A	L	0-2	
Grp		16	Southend United	H	W	4-0	Mallett, Stock (2), Heath
Grp		23	Mansfield Town	A	D	0-0	
Grp	Mar	2	Mansfield Town	H	W	3-0	Heath (2), Boxshall
Grp		9	Watford	A	W	3-1	Pattison, Heath (2)
Grp		16	Watford	H	W	2-1	Heath, McEwan
Grp		23	Port Vale	H	W	4-2	Heath (2), McEwan, Neary
Grp		30	Port Vale	A	W	2-0	OG, Neary
Grp	Apr	6	Notts County	H	W	3-1	Mallett, Neary, Chapman
Grp		13	Notts County	A	W	3-0	Pattison (2), McEwan
Grp		17	Southend United	A	D	0-0	
Grp		19	Bristol City	H	W	4-2	Hatton, Pattison, McEwan, Neary
Grp		20	Clapton Orient	A	D	0-0	
Grp		22	Clapton Orient	H	W	6-0	Heathcote, Pattison (2), Neary (2), OG
SF		27	Bournemouth	A	D	1-1	Heathcote
rep	May	1	Bournemouth	H	L	0-1*	

* After 4 periods of extra time. Game ended in 136th minute with 'golden goal'.

Appeara
G

Total - Appeara
Total - G

Addinall	Alexander	Allen	Blizzard	Boxshall	Brown	Chapman	Compton (G)	Crack (G)	Daniels	Darragon	Farrow	Gillies (G)	Hamilton (G)	Hatton	Heath	Heathcote	Hibbs	Jefferson	Johnstone (G)	Jones	Lennon	Mallett	Mangnall	McEwan	Neary	Parkinson	Pattison	Peppitt (G)	Powell	Reay	Ridyard	Rose	Salmon (G)	Shaw	Smith A.	Smith E.	Smith L. (G)	Somerfield (G)	Stock	Swinfen	Webb	Whitehead	Wigglesworth (G)	OG
		1						11	8			4				9		3				6			7						5	2						10						
		1						11	8			4		10		9		3				6			7						5	2												
		1						11	4					10		9						6			7						5	2						8		3				
		1							4	11	6					9						10			7						5	2						8						
		1							4		6					9						10			7						5	2	11					8						
		1							4		6				11	9		3				8									5	2	10					7						
		1							4		6					9						8									5	2	10				7						11	
		1							4		6					9		3				8			7						5	2	10									11		
		1							4		6					9		3				8			7						5	2						10						
		1							4		6					9		3				8			7						5	2						10						
		1							4		6					9		3				8									5	2						10	7					
7	5	1							4		6					9		3				8			10							2										11		
10		1							4		6					9		3				8			7		11				5	2												
10		1							4		6					9		3				8			7		11				5	2												
		1							4		6					9		3				8			7						5	2			10							11		
		1							4		6					9		3				8			10						5	2							7			11		
9					1				4		6										11	8			10						5	2							7					
		1							4		6							3			7	8			9						5	2							10					
		1	11						4				7			9		3				8									5	2							10		6			
		1		7			9										8	3	11									10			5	2		6		4								
4	1	19	1	1	1		1	3	19	1	15	2	1	2	1	17	1	15	1		2	19			15		2	1			19	20	4	1	1	1	1	8	5	1	1	4	1	
1								3						2		18						7			12						3		1					1				1		

Addinall	Alexander	Allen	Blizzard	Boxshall	Brown	Chapman	Compton (G)	Crack (G)	Daniels	Darragon	Farrow	Gillies (G)	Hamilton (G)	Hatton	Heath	Heathcote	Hibbs	Jefferson	Johnstone (G)	Jones	Lennon	Mallett	Mangnall	McEwan	Neary	Parkinson	Pattison	Peppitt (G)	Powell	Reay	Ridyard	Rose	Salmon (G)	Shaw	Smith A.	Smith E.	Smith L. (G)	Somerfield (G)	Stock	Swinfen	Webb	Whitehead	Wigglesworth (G)	OG
		1	10						4		6					9						8			7						5	2								3		11		
		1							4		6					9		3				8			7						5	2								10		11		
9		1							4		6							3				8			7						5	2							10			11		
9		1	7						4		6							3				8									5	2							10			11		
		1							4						6	9		3				8			7		11				5	2							10					
		1							4						6			3				8			9		11				5	2							10			7		
9			7		1				4		6							3				8					11				5	2							10					
9		1							4		6							3				8			7						5	2							10			11		
9		1							4		6							3				8			7		11				5	2							10					
9		1							4		6							3				8					11				5	2							10	7				
9		1							4		6				10			3				8					11			2	5									7				
7		10	3		1				11		9				3	3		10				11			7		6			1	11	10							8	4		6		
8									1							1						2			5		1												2	1				

Addinall	Alexander	Allen	Blizzard	Boxshall	Brown	Chapman	Compton (G)	Crack (G)	Daniels	Darragon	Farrow	Gillies (G)	Hamilton (G)	Hatton	Heath	Heathcote	Hibbs	Jefferson	Johnstone (G)	Jones	Lennon	Mallett	Mangnall	McEwan	Neary	Parkinson	Pattison	Peppitt (G)	Powell	Reay	Ridyard	Rose	Salmon (G)	Shaw	Smith A.	Smith E.	Smith L. (G)	Somerfield (G)	Stock	Swinfen	Webb	Whitehead	Wigglesworth (G)	OG
	3	1	7			5			4		6		8		11							10										2							9					
			7		1				4		6		10					3				8	11								5	2							9					
		1							4		6					9		3				8					11				5	2			10				7					
		1				6			4						10			3				8					11			2	5								9	7				
		1				6			4						10	9		3				8					11			2	5								7					
		1		7					4		6				9			3				8				10	11			2	5													
		1		7					4		6				9			3				8				10	11			2	5													
		1							4		6				9			3				8		7		10	11				5	2												
		1							4		6				9							10		8	7		11			3	5	2												
		1							4		6				9							10		8	7		11			3	5	2												
		1				6			4						9							10		8	7		11			3	5	2												
		1							4					10	3							8		9	7		11		6		5	2												
		1							4		6			10	11					9		8		7							5	2								3				
		1							4					10								8		7	9		11		6		5	2								3				
9		1							4		6				10							8		7			11		3		5	2												
		1				5			4		6					9						10		8	7		11		3			2												
		1				6			4							9						10		8	7		11		3		5	2												
		1				6			4							9						8			7	10	11		3		5	2												
1	1	17	2	2	1	7			18		11		2	3	12	5		7		1		18	1	10	8	4	15		6	7	16	14			1				5	3				
				1		1								1	9	2						3		4	6		6												4					2

Addinall	Alexander	Allen	Blizzard	Boxshall	Brown	Chapman	Compton (G)	Crack (G)	Daniels	Darragon	Farrow	Gillies (G)	Hamilton (G)	Hatton	Heath	Heathcote	Hibbs	Jefferson	Johnstone (G)	Jones	Lennon	Mallett	Mangnall	McEwan	Neary	Parkinson	Pattison	Peppitt (G)	Powell	Reay	Ridyard	Rose	Salmon (G)	Shaw	Smith A.	Smith E.	Smith L. (G)	Somerfield (G)	Stock	Swinfen	Webb	Whitehead	Wigglesworth (G)	OG
12	2	46	6	3	3	7	1	3	48	1	35	2	3	5	16	25	1	32	1	1	2	48	1	10	30	4	23	1	6	8	46	44	4	1	2	1	1	8	18	8	1	10	1	
9				1		1		3	1					3	9	21						12		4	23		7				3		1					1	6	1		1		2

uest Player

1946-47

Division Three South

	P	W	D	L	F	A	Pts
Cardiff City	42	30	6	6	93	30	66
Queen's Park Rangers	42	23	11	8	74	40	57
Bristol City	42	20	11	11	94	56	51
Swindon Town	42	19	11	12	84	73	49
Walsall	42	17	12	13	74	59	46
Ipswich Town	42	16	14	12	61	53	46
Bournemouth	42	18	8	16	72	54	44
Southend United	42	17	10	15	71	60	44
Reading	42	16	11	15	83	74	43
Port Vale	42	17	9	16	68	63	43
Torquay United	42	15	12	15	52	61	42
Notts County	42	15	10	17	63	63	40
Northampton Town	42	15	10	17	72	75	40
Bristol Rovers	42	16	8	18	59	69	40
Exeter City	42	15	9	18	60	69	39
Watford	42	17	5	20	61	76	39
Brighton & Hove Albion	42	13	12	17	54	72	38
Crystal Palace	42	13	11	18	49	62	37
Leyton Orient	42	12	8	22	54	75	32
Aldershot	42	10	12	20	48	78	32
Norwich City	42	10	8	24	64	100	28
Mansfield Town	42	9	10	23	48	96	28

Attendances

TOTAL	Home	Away	Total
League	349,418	368,658	718,076
Cup/Other	53,449	66,577	120,026
TOTAL	402,867	435,235	838,102

AVERAGE	Home	Away	Total
League	16,639	17,555	17,097
Cup/Other	17,816	22,192	20,004
TOTAL	16,786	18,135	17,460

GROUND: LOFTUS ROAD, SHEPHERDS BUSH, W.12

Q.P.R. v. CLAPTON ORIENT. Wednesday, 11th Sept., 1946

BILL WHITEHEAD

OFF TO A GOOD START.

Match No.	Date		Opponents	Location	Result		Scorers	Atten
1	Aug	31	Watford	H	W	2-1	Mallett (2)	2
2	Sep	4	Bournemouth	A	D	1-1	Neary	
3		7	Walsall	A	W	2-0	Neary (2)	1
4		11	Leyton Orient	H	W	2-0	Pattison, Neary	1
5		14	Reading	H	W	2-0	Heath, McEwan	1
6		21	Crystal Palace	A	D	0-0		2
7		25	Bournemouth	H	W	3-0	Pattison (3), Mallett	1
8		28	Torquay United	H	D	0-0		2
9	Oct	5	Mansfield Town	A	W	3-0	Neary, Durrant, Pattison	1
10		12	Bristol Rovers	H	L	0-2		1
11		19	Cardiff City	A	D	2-2	Durrant, Hatton	5
12		26	Norwich City	H	D	1-1	Hatton	1
13	Nov	2	Notts County	A	W	2-1	Neary, Heathcote	2
14		9	Northampton Town	H	W	1-0	McEwan	2
15		16	Aldershot	A	W	2-1	OG (Shepherd), Pattison	
16		23	Brighton	H	W	2-0	Hatton (2)	1
17	Dec	7	Port Vale	H	W	2-0	Harris, Mills	1
18		21	Swindon Town	H	W	7-0	Pattison (2), McEwan (2), Hatton, Mills, Powell	1
19		25	Ipswich Town	H	L	1-3	Hatton	1
20		26	Ipswich Town	A	D	1-1	Hatton	2
21		28	Watford	A	W	2-0	Mallett (2)	1
22	Jan	4	Walsall	H	W	1-0	Boxshall	1
23		18	Reading	A	L	0-1		1
24		25	Crystal Palace	H	L	1-2	Pattison	1
25	Feb	8	Mansfield Town	H	W	3-1	Boxshall, Durrant, Pattison	
26		15	Bristol Rovers	A	L	1-3	Durrant	1
27	Mar	1	Norwich City	A	W	1-0	Mills	1
28		5	Exeter City	A	L	0-3		
29		8	Notts County	H	W	4-1	Pattison, Durrant (2), Chapman	1
30		15	Northampton Town	A	D	4-4	Parkinson (2), Mills, Durrant	1
31		22	Aldershot	H	W	4-1	Hatton (3), Durrant	1
32		29	Brighton	A	W	2-0	McEwan (2)	
33	Apr	4	Southend United	H	W	1-0	Durrant	2
34		5	Exeter City	H	W	2-0	Durrant, Pattison	1
35		7	Southend United	A	W	3-1	Durrant, McEwan, Mills	2
36		12	Port Vale	A	D	2-2	Durrant, Boxshall	1
37		19	Bristol City	H	W	1-0	McEwan	2
38		26	Swindon Town	A	L	2-3	Durrant, Hatton	2
39	May	3	Leyton Orient	A	D	1-1	Hatton	2
40		10	Bristol City	A	D	1-1	Durrant	2
41		17	Torquay United	A	D	0-0		
42		24	Cardiff City	H	L	2-3	OG (Wardle), Pattison	2

Appeara
G

FA Cup

	Date		Opponents	Location	Result		Scorers	Atten
R1	Nov	30	Poole Town	H	D	2-2	Pattison, Hatton	1
rep	Dec	4	Poole Town	A	W	6-0	Mallett (2), Hatton, Harris, Pattison (2)	
R2		14	Norwich City	A	D	4-4	Pattison, McEwan, Mills (2)	2
rep		18	Norwich City	H	W	2-0	Hatton, Mills	1
R3	Jan	11	Middlesbrough	H	D	1-1	Pattison	2
rep		15	Middlesbrough	A	L	1-3	Boxshall	3

Appearan
G

Total - Appearan
Total - G

Allen	Armitage	Barr	Blizzard	Boxshall	Chapman	Daniels	Dudley	Durrant	Harris	Hatton	Heath	Heathcote	Jefferson	McEwan	Mallett	Mills	Neary	Parkinson	Pattison	Powell	Reay	Ridyard	Rose	Saphin	Smith	Swinfen	OG
						4				8		9	3	7	10				11	6		5	2				
						4				10			3	9	8		7		11	6		5	2				
						4							3	7	8		9		11	6		5	2		10		
						4							3	7	8		9		11	6		5	2		10		
	10				5						9		3	7	8				11	6			2		4		
	10				5						9		3	7	8				11	6			2		4		
					5								3	7	8	10			11	6			2		4		
					5			9					3	7	8	10			11	6			2		4		
					5			9					3		8	10	7		11	6			2		4		
					5			9		10					8		7		11	6			2		4	3	
					5			9		10			3		8		7		11	6			2		4		
					5			9		10			3		8		7		11	6	2				4		
		5								10		9	3		8		7		11	6			2		4		
		5								10		9	3	7	8				11	6			2		4		
		5								10		9	3	7	8				11	6			2		4		
		5				4				10	6	9	3		8		7		11				2				
							2		9				3	7	8	10			11	6		5			4		
							2			9			3	7	8	10			11	6		5			4		
							2			9			3	7	8	10			11	6		5			4		
					5		2			9			3	7	8	10			11	6					4		
				7	5		2			10			3	9	8				11	6					4		
				7	5		2			10			3	9	8				11	6					4		
				11	5		2						3	7	8	10				6					4		
				10	5	4	2						3	7	8				11	6							
				10	5		2	9						7	8				11	6	3				4		
				7	6		2	9					3	8	10				11	5					4		
			4		6		2	9					3	7		10		8	11	5							
			4	7	6		2						3	9		10		8	11	5							
			4		6		2	9					3	7		10		8	11	5							
			4		6		2	9					3	7		10		8	11	5							
			4	7	6		2	9		10			3					8	11	5							
					6		2	9		10			3	7				8	11	5				1	4		
					6		2	9		10			3	7				8	11	5					4		
					6		2	9		10			3	7		8			11	5					4		
				11	6		2	9		8			3	7		10				5					4		
				11	6		2	9		10			3	7				8		5					4		
					6		2	9		10			3	7				8	11	5					4		
				11	6		2	9		10			3	7				8		5					4		
				11		6	2	9		8			3	7		10				5					4		
							2	9		8	6		3	7		10			11	5					4		
							2	9		8	6		3	7		10			11	5					4		
							2	9		8	6		3	7		10			11	5					4		
1	2	4	5	12	27	7	26	22	1	26	6	5	40	35	26	18	9	10	37	41	2	7	15	1	33	1	
				3	1			14	1	12	1	1		8	5	5	6	2	12	1							2

Allen	Armitage	Barr	Blizzard	Boxshall	Chapman	Daniels	Dudley	Durrant	Harris	Hatton	Heath	Heathcote	Jefferson	McEwan	Mallett	Mills	Neary	Parkinson	Pattison	Powell	Reay	Ridyard	Rose	Saphin	Smith	Swinfen	OG
						4				10	6		3	7					11	8		5	2				
									9	10			3	7	8				11	6	2	5		1	4		
					5		2			9			3	7	8	10			11	6					4		
							2			9			3	7	8	10			11	6		5			4		
				7	5		2			10			3	9	8				11	6					4		
				7	5		2			10			3	9	8				11	6					4		
5				2	3	1	4		1	6	1		6	6	5	2			6	6	1	3	1	1	5		
				1					1	3				1	2	3			5								

Allen	Armitage	Barr	Blizzard	Boxshall	Chapman	Daniels	Dudley	Durrant	Harris	Hatton	Heath	Heathcote	Jefferson	McEwan	Mallett	Mills	Neary	Parkinson	Pattison	Powell	Reay	Ridyard	Rose	Saphin	Smith	Swinfen	OG
6	2	4	5	14	30	8	30	22	2	32	7	5	46	41	31	20	9	10	43	47	3	10	16	2	38	1	
				4	1			14	2	15	1	1		9	7	8	6	2	17	1							2

1947-48

Division Three South

	P	W	D	L	F	A	Pts
Queen's Park Rangers	42	26	9	7	74	37	61
Bournemouth	42	24	9	9	76	35	57
Walsall	42	21	9	12	70	40	51
Ipswich Town	42	23	3	16	67	61	49
Swansea Town	42	18	12	12	70	52	48
Notts County	42	19	8	15	68	59	46
Bristol City	42	18	7	17	77	65	43
Port Vale	42	16	11	15	63	54	43
Southend United	42	15	13	14	51	58	43
Reading	42	15	11	16	56	58	41
Exeter City	42	15	11	16	55	63	41
Newport County	42	14	13	15	61	73	41
Crystal Palace	42	13	13	16	49	49	39
Northampton Town	42	14	11	17	58	72	39
Watford	42	14	10	18	57	79	38
Swindon Town	42	10	16	16	41	46	36
Leyton Orient	42	13	10	19	51	73	36
Torquay United	42	11	13	18	63	62	35
Aldershot	42	10	15	17	45	67	35
Bristol Rovers	42	13	8	21	71	75	34
Norwich City	42	13	8	21	61	76	34
Brighton & Hove Albion	42	11	12	19	43	73	34

Attendances

TOTAL

	Home	Away	Total
League	459,680	383,572	843,252
Cup/Other	111,022	54,590	165,612
TOTAL	570,702	438,162	1,008,864

AVERAGE

	Home	Away	Total
League	21,890	18,265	20,077
Cup/Other	27,756	27,295	27,602
TOTAL	22,828	19,051	21,018

Q.P.R. v. NOTTS COUNTY. Thursday, 18th Sept., 1947

Match No.	Date		Opponents	Location	Result		Scorers	Atte
1	Aug	23	Norwich City	H	W	3-1	Hatton, McEwan, Pattison	2
2		27	Brighton	A	W	5-0	Hatton (3), Durrant (2)	1
3		30	Bristol Rovers	A	W	1-0	Durrant	1
4	Sep	4	Brighton	H	W	2-0	McEwan, Hatton	1
5		6	Northampton Town	H	W	2-0	McEwan, Pattison	2
6		11	Notts County	A	D	1-1	Durrant	1
7		13	Aldershot	A	W	4-1	Durrant (2), Pattison, Hatton	
8		18	Notts County	H	W	4-1	Pattison (2), Hatton, McEwan	1
9		20	Crystal Palace	H	W	1-0	Chapman	2
10		25	Exeter City	H	W	3-1	Hatton (2), Durrant	1
11		27	Torquay United	A	D	1-1	G.Smith	1
12	Oct	2	Southend United	H	W	3-2	Hatton (2), Pattison	1
13		4	Swindon Town	H	L	0-2		2
14		11	Swansea Town	A	L	1-3	Durrant	2
15		18	Bournemouth	H	W	1-0	Durrant	2
16		25	Ipswich Town	A	L	0-1		2
17	Nov	1	Bristol City	H	W	2-0	Boxshall, Pattison	2
18		8	Reading	A	L	2-3	Durrant, Boxshall	2
19		15	Walsall	H	W	2-1	Hatton, Hartburn	2
20		22	Leyton Orient	A	W	3-1	Durrant, Hatton (2)	1
21	Dec	6	Newport County	A	D	0-0		1
22		26	Watford	A	W	1-0	OG (Jones)	1
23		27	Watford	H	W	5-1	Pattison, Boxshall (2), Hatton, McEwan	1
24	Jan	3	Bristol Rovers	H	W	5-2	McEwan, Hatton, Boxshall (2), Hartburn	2
25		31	Aldershot	H	D	0-0		2
26	Feb	14	Torquay United	H	D	3-3	Ramscar, Boxshall, Hatton	2
27		21	Swindon Town	A	D	0-0		1
28	Mar	13	Ipswich Town	H	W	2-0	Hatton, Boxshall	1
29		15	Crystal Palace	A	W	1-0	Hartburn	2
30		20	Bristol City	A	L	1-2	Hatton	2
31		26	Port Vale	A	W	2-0	Boxshall (2)	1
32		27	Reading	H	W	2-0	Boxshall, Hatton	2
33		29	Port Vale	H	W	2-1	Addinall, A.Smith	2
34	Apr	3	Walsall	A	W	1-0	Addinall	1
35		8	Northampton Town	A	D	1-1	Hartburn	1
36		10	Leyton Orient	H	L	1-2	Stewart	2
37		14	Bournemouth	A	W	1-0	Durrant	2
38		17	Exeter City	A	W	2-1	Hartburn (2)	1
39		21	Norwich City	A	L	2-5	Hatton, A.Smith	3
40		24	Newport County	H	W	1-0	I.Powell	2
41		26	Swansea Town	H	D	0-0		2
42	May	1	Southend United	A	D	0-0		1

Appeara
(

FA Cup

R3	Jan	10	Gillingham	A	D	1-1	Boxshall	2
rep		17	Gillingham	H	W	3-1	Hatton, Hartburn, McEwan	2
R4		24	Stoke City	H	W	3-0	Hatton (2), Ramscar	2
R5	Feb	7	Luton Town	H	W	3-1	Boxshall, Hatton, McEwan	3
R6		28	Derby County	H	D	1-1	Hartburn	2
rep	Mar	6	Derby County	A	L	0-5		3

Appeara
(

Total - Appeara
Total - (

Addinall	Allen	Boxshall	Chapman	Daniels	Dudley	Durrant	Hartburn	Hatton	Heath	Jefferson	McEwan	Mills	Parkinson	Pattison	Powell G.	Powell I.	Ramscar	Reay	Ridyard	Rose	Saphin	Smith A.	Smith G.	Stewart	OG
	1				2	9	7	10	6	3	8			11		4							5		
	1				2	9	7	10	6		8			11		4		3					5		
	1				2	9	7	10	6		8			11		4		3					5		
	1				2	9	7	10	6		8			11		4		3					5		
	1				2	9	7	10	6		8			11		4		3					5		
	1		6		2	9	7	10			8			11		4		3					5		
	1		6		2	9		10			7	8		11		4		3					5		
	1		6		2	9		10			7	8		11		4		3					5		
	1		10		2	9		8			7			11		4		3				6	5		
	1		6		2	9	7	10			8			11		4		3					5		
	1		6		2	9	7	10			8			11		4		3					5		
	1		6		2	9		10			7		8	11		4		3					5		
	1		6		2	9	7	10				8		11		4		3					5		
	1		6		2	9		10			7	8		11		4		3					5		
	1	7	6		2	9		10			8			11				3				4	5		
	1		6		2	9		10			7			11		4	8	3					5		
	1	7	6		2	9				3	8			11		4	10						5		
	1	8	6			9					7			11	2	4	10	3					5		
	1		6			9	11	10		3	7				2	4	8						5		
	1			6		9	11	10		3	7				2	4	8		5						
	1			6		9	11	10		3	7				2	4	8						5		
	1			6		9	11	10		3	7				2	4	8						5		
	1	7		6				10		3	9			11	2	4	8						5		
	1	7		6			11	10		3	9				2	4	8						5		
	1	9		6			11	10		3	7				2	4	8						5		
	1	9		6			11	10		3	7				2	4	8						5		
	1	9					11	10		3	7				2	4	8					6	5		
		7					11	9		3					2	4	10				1	6	5	8	
		7					11	9		3					2	4	10				1	6	5	8	
						9	11	10		3					2	4	8				1	6	5	7	
9		7					11			3		10			2	4					1	6	5	8	
		7					11	9		3		10			2	4					1	6	5	8	
9		7					11			3		10			2	4					1	6	5	8	
9		7					11			3		10			2	4					1	6	5	8	
		7					11		9	3		10			2	4					1	6	5	8	
	1	7					11			3		10			2	4	8					6	5	9	
	1					9	7	8		3		10		11	2	4						6	5		
	1					9	11	8		3		10			2	4						6	5	7	
	1					9	11	8		3		10			2	4						6	5	7	
	1						11	9		3		10				4			5	2		6		8	
	1						11	9		3		10				4			5	2		6		8	
	1	7				9		10		3		11			2	4			5			6		8	
3	34	17	14	7	17	27	31	35	6	26	26	16	1	20	23	41	16	16	4	2	8	18	38	14	
2		11	1			12	6	21			6			8		1	1					2	1	1	1

Addinall	Allen	Boxshall	Chapman	Daniels	Dudley	Durrant	Hartburn	Hatton	Heath	Jefferson	McEwan	Mills	Parkinson	Pattison	Powell G.	Powell I.	Ramscar	Reay	Ridyard	Rose	Saphin	Smith A.	Smith G.	Stewart	OG
	1	9		6				10		3	7			11	2	4	8						5		
	1	9		6			11	10		3	7				2	4	8						5		
	1	9		6			11	10		3	7				2	4	8						5		
	1	7		6			11	10		3	9				2	4	8						5		
	1	7					11	10	9	3					2	4	8					6	5		
	1	9					11	10		3	7				2	4	8					6	5		
	6	6		4			5	6	1	6	5			1	6	6	6					2	6		
		2					2	4			2						1								

Addinall	Allen	Boxshall	Chapman	Daniels	Dudley	Durrant	Hartburn	Hatton	Heath	Jefferson	McEwan	Mills	Parkinson	Pattison	Powell G.	Powell I.	Ramscar	Reay	Ridyard	Rose	Saphin	Smith A.	Smith G.	Stewart	OG
3	40	23	14	11	17	27	36	41	7	32	31	16	1	21	29	47	22	16	4	2	8	20	44	14	
2		13	1			12	8	25			8			8		1	2					2	1	1	1

1948-49

Division Two

	P	W	D	L	F	A	Pts
Fulham	42	24	9	9	77	37	57
West Bromwich Albion	42	24	8	10	69	39	56
Southampton	42	23	9	10	69	36	55
Cardiff City	42	19	13	10	62	47	51
Tottenham Hotspur	42	17	16	9	72	44	50
Chesterfield	42	15	17	10	51	45	47
West Ham United	42	18	10	14	56	58	46
Sheffield Wednesday	42	15	13	14	63	56	43
Barnsley	42	14	12	16	62	61	40
Luton Town	42	14	12	16	55	57	40
Grimsby Town	42	15	10	17	72	76	40
Bury	42	17	6	19	67	76	40
Queen's Park Rangers	42	14	11	17	44	62	39
Blackburn Rovers	42	15	8	19	53	63	38
Leeds United	42	12	13	17	55	63	37
Coventry City	42	15	7	20	55	64	37
Bradford Park Avenue	42	13	11	18	65	78	37
Brentford	42	11	14	17	42	53	36
Leicester City	42	10	16	16	62	79	36
Plymouth Argyle	42	12	12	18	49	64	36
Nottingham Forest	42	14	7	21	50	54	35
Lincoln City	42	8	12	22	53	91	28

Attendances

	TOTAL		
	Home	**Away**	**Total**
League	458,966	564,027	1,022,993
Cup/Other	26,000	31,075	57,075
TOTAL	484,966	595,102	1,080,068

	AVERAGE		
	Home	**Away**	**Total**
League	21,856	26,858	24,357
Cup/Other	26,000	31,075	28,538
TOTAL	22,044	27,050	24,547

Match No.	Date		Opponents	Location	Result		Scorers	Atten
1	Aug	21	Luton Town	A	D	0-0		22
2		26	Leicester City	H	W	4-1	Addinall (3), Hartburn	24
3		28	Bradford	H	W	1-0	Addinall	26
4		30	Leicester City	A	W	3-2	Hatton (2), Mills	36
5	Sep	4	Southampton	A	L	0-3		27
6		9	Cardiff City	H	D	0-0		20
7		11	Barnsley	H	D	2-2	Addinall (2)	21
8		13	Cardiff City	A	L	0-3		40
9		18	Grimsby Town	A	L	1-4	Pattison	15
10		25	Nottingham Forest	H	W	2-1	Hartburn, Pattison	19
11	Oct	2	Fulham	A	L	0-5		30
12		9	Brentford	H	W	2-0	Hartburn, Hudson	25
13		16	Tottenham Hotspur	A	L	0-1		69
14		23	West Ham United	H	W	2-1	Hatton, Hudson	27
15		30	Bury	A	D	0-0		19
16	Nov	6	West Bromwich	H	L	0-2		24
17		13	Chesterfield	A	L	1-2	Hartburn	12
18		20	Lincoln City	H	W	2-0	Hatton, Gibbons	19
19		27	Sheffield Wednesday	A	L	0-2		34
20	Dec	4	Coventry City	H	L	0-3		16
21		11	Leeds United	A	W	2-1	Gibbons, Pattison	26
22		18	Luton Town	H	L	0-3		16
23		25	Blackburn Rovers	A	L	0-2		31
24		27	Blackburn Rovers	H	W	4-2	Parkinson (2), Hatton, Hartburn	17
25	Jan	1	Bradford	A	D	0-0		15
26		22	Barnsley	A	L	0-4		20
27		29	Southampton	H	L	1-3	Pointon	20
28	Feb	5	Grimsby Town	H	L	1-2	Hudson	19
29		12	Nottingham Forest	A	D	0-0		26
30		26	Fulham	H	W	1-0	Ramscar	28
31	Mar	5	Brentford	A	W	3-0	Hudson, Pointon, Duggan	29
32		12	Tottenham Hotspur	H	D	0-0		25
33		19	West Ham United	A	L	0-2		26
34		26	Bury	H	W	3-1	Duggan, Jefferson, Ramscar	20
35	Apr	2	West Bromwich	A	D	1-1	Pointon	35
36		9	Chesterfield	H	D	1-1	Hill	25
37		15	Plymouth Argyle	H	W	2-1	Stewart, Pointon	22
38		16	Lincoln City	A	D	0-0		11
39		18	Plymouth Argyle	A	L	1-3	Addinall	20
40		23	Sheffield Wednesday	H	L	1-3	Heath	25
41		30	Coventry City	A	D	1-1	Stewart	14
42	May	7	Leeds United	H	W	2-0	Addinall (2)	16

Appearar
G

FA Cup

R3	Jan	8	Huddersfield Town	H	D	0-0 aet	26
rep		15	Huddersfield Town	A	L	0-5	31

Appearar
G

Total - Appearar
Total - G

Addinall	Allen	Bennett	Campbell	Dudley	Duggan	Durrant	Farrow	Gibbons	Hartburn	Hatton	Heath	Hill	Hudson	Jefferson	Lennon	McEwan	Millbank	Mills	Muir	Nicholas	Parkinson	Pattison	Pointon	Powell G.	Powell I.	Ramscar	Reay	Smith A.	Smith G.	Stewart	Wardle
9	1								11	10				3		7		8						2	4			6	5		
9	1								11	10				3		7		8						2	4			6	5		
9	1								11	10				3		7		8						2	4			6	5		
9	1								11	10				3		7		8						2	4			6	5		
9	1								11	10				3		7		8						2	4			6	5		
9	1								11	10				3		7		8						2	4			6	5		
9	1								11	10				3		7	4	8						2				6	5		
9	1									10						7		6	3			11		2	5	8		4			
9	1			2					7									10				11		3	4	8		6	5		
9	1			3					7	10												11		2	4	8		6	5		
9	1								7	10				3								11		2	4	8		6	5		
9	1						6		7	10			11	3										2	4	8			5		
9	1						6		7	10	5		11	3										2	4	8					
	1						6	9	7	10	5		11	3										2	4	8					
	1						6	9		10	5			3		7								2	4	8					
	1						6		11					3		9								2	4	8			5	10	
	1						6	9	11	10				3		7								2	4	8			5		
	1						6	9	11	10				3		7								2	4	8			5		
	1						10	9	11		6			3		7								2	4	8			5		
	1						6	9	11	10				3	8	7								2	4				5		
	1						6	9	7	10				3							4	11		2					5	8	
	1						6	9	7	10				3							4	11		2					5	8	
	1								7		6			3				10			4	11		2	9				5	8	
	1					9	6		7	10				3							4	11		2					5	8	
	1					9	6		7	10				3							4	11		2					5	8	
	1						6	7						3				10			4	11	9	2		8			5		
	1						6				5		11	3							4	10	9	2						8	7
0	1				8						6		11	3							4		9	2					5		7
0	1				8		6						11	3							4		9	2					5		7
	1				8		6						11	3							4		9	2		10			5		7
0	1				7						6		11	3							4		9	2		8			5		
0	1				7						6		11	3							4		9	2		8			5		
		1			10						6		11	3							4		9	2		8			5		7
	1				10				11		6			3							4		9	2		8			5		7
	1				7						6	10		3							4		9	2		8			5		11
	1				7						6	10		3							4		9	2		8			5		11
	1				7				11		6	10		3							4		9	2					5	8	
0	1				7				11		6			3							4		9	2					5	8	
0	1				7						6			3							4		9	2					5	8	11
0		1			7						6			3							4		9				2		5	8	11
0	1				7						6			3							4		9				2		5	8	11
0	1				7							6		3						4			9			8	2		5		11
2	40	2		2	15	2	17	9	26	21	18	4	10	39	1	14	1	11	1	1	21	11	17	39	20	21	3	11	37	12	12
9					2			2	5	5	1	1	4	1				1			2	3	4			2				2	

Addinall	Allen	Bennett	Campbell	Dudley	Duggan	Durrant	Farrow	Gibbons	Hartburn	Hatton	Heath	Hill	Hudson	Jefferson	Lennon	McEwan	Millbank	Mills	Muir	Nicholas	Parkinson	Pattison	Pointon	Powell G.	Powell I.	Ramscar	Reay	Smith A.	Smith G.	Stewart	Wardle
	1					9	6		7	10				3							4	11		2					5	8	
	1		7			9	6							3				10			4	11		2					5	8	
	2		1			2	2		1	1				2				1			2	2		2					2	2	

Addinall	Allen	Bennett	Campbell	Dudley	Duggan	Durrant	Farrow	Gibbons	Hartburn	Hatton	Heath	Hill	Hudson	Jefferson	Lennon	McEwan	Millbank	Mills	Muir	Nicholas	Parkinson	Pattison	Pointon	Powell G.	Powell I.	Ramscar	Reay	Smith A.	Smith G.	Stewart	Wardle
2	42	2	1	2	15	4	19	9	27	22	18	4	10	41	1	14	1	12	1	1	23	13	17	41	20	21	3	11	39	14	12
9					2			2	5	5	1	1	4	1				1			2	3	4			2				2	

1949-50

Division Two

	P	W	D	L	F	A	Pts
Tottenham Hotspur	42	27	7	8	81	35	61
Sheffield Wednesday	42	18	16	8	67	48	52
Sheffield United	42	19	14	9	68	49	52
Southampton	42	19	14	9	64	48	52
Leeds United	42	17	13	12	54	45	47
Preston North End	42	18	9	15	60	49	45
Hull City	42	17	11	14	64	72	45
Swansea Town	42	17	9	16	53	49	43
Brentford	42	15	13	14	44	49	43
Cardiff City	42	16	10	16	41	44	42
Grimsby Town	42	16	8	18	74	73	40
Coventry City	42	13	13	16	55	55	39
Barnsley	42	13	13	16	64	67	39
Chesterfield	42	15	9	18	43	47	39
Leicester City	42	12	15	15	55	65	39
Blackburn Rovers	42	14	10	18	55	60	38
Luton Town	42	10	18	14	41	51	38
Bury	42	14	9	19	60	65	37
West Ham United	42	12	12	18	53	61	36
Queen's Park Rangers	42	11	12	19	40	57	34
Plymouth Argyle	42	8	16	18	44	65	32
Bradford Park Avenue	42	10	11	21	51	77	31

Attendances

TOTAL

	Home	Away	Total
League	405,188	516,000	921,188
Cup/Other	22,433		22,433
TOTAL	427,621	516,000	943,621

AVERAGE

	Home	Away	Total
League	19,295	24,571	21,933
Cup/Other	22,433		22,433
TOTAL	19,437	24,571	21,945

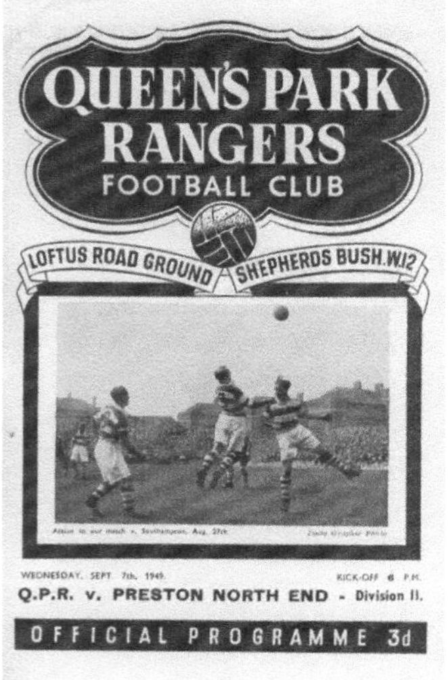

Match No.	Date		Opponents	Location	Result		Scorers	Atte
1	Aug	20	Leeds United	A	D	1-1	Pointon	3
2		24	Brentford	H	D	3-3	Pattison (2, 2 pens), Pointon	2
3		27	Southampton	H	W	1-0	Hudson	2
4		31	Brentford	A	W	2-0	Hatton, Hudson	2
5	Sep	3	Coventry City	A	D	0-0		2
6		7	Preston North End	H	D	0-0		2
7		10	Luton Town	H	W	3-0	Addinall, Duggan, Hatton	2
8		14	Preston North End	A	L	2-3	Addinall, OG (Robertson)	2
9		17	Barnsley	A	L	1-3	Addinall	1
10		24	West Ham United	H	L	0-1		2
11	Oct	1	Sheffield United	A	D	1-1	Ramscar	3
12		8	Hull City	H	L	1-4	Duggan	2
13		15	Sheffield Wednesday	A	L	0-1		3
14		22	Plymouth Argyle	H	L	0-2		1
15		29	Chesterfield	A	L	1-2	Neary	1
16	Nov	5	Bradford	H	L	0-1		
17		12	Leicester City	A	L	2-3	Addinall, Parkinson	2
18		19	Bury	H	W	1-0	Neary	1
19		26	Tottenham Hotspur	A	L	0-3		6
20	Dec	3	Cardiff City	H	L	0-1		1
21		10	Blackburn Rovers	A	D	0-0		1
22		17	Leeds United	H	D	1-1	Best	1
23		24	Southampton	A	W	2-1	Neary (2)	2
24		26	Grimsby Town	A	D	1-1	Hudson	2
25		27	Grimsby Town	H	L	1-2	Addinall	2
26		31	Coventry City	H	W	2-0	McEwan, Best	1
27	Jan	14	Luton Town	A	W	2-1	Neary, Mills	1
28		21	Barnsley	H	L	0-5		1
29	Feb	4	West Ham United	A	L	0-1		2
30		18	Sheffield United	H	L	1-3	McKay	2
31		25	Hull City	A	D	1-1	Mills	2
32	Mar	4	Sheffield Wednesday	H	D	0-0		2
33		11	Plymouth Argyle	A	W	2-0	Addinall, Best	2
34		18	Chesterfield	H	W	3-2	Addinall (2), Wardle	1
35		25	Bradford	A	L	0-1		1
36	Apr	1	Tottenham Hotspur	H	L	0-2		2
37		7	Swansea Town	H	D	0-0		2
38		8	Cardiff City	A	L	0-4		1
39		10	Swansea Town	A	W	1-0	Hudson	2
40		15	Leicester City	H	W	2-0	Addinall (2)	1
41		22	Bury	A	D	0-0		1
42		29	Blackburn Rovers	H	L	2-3	Addinall, Hatton	1

Appeara
G

FA Cup

R3	Jan	7	Everton	H	L	0-2		2

Appeara
G

Total - Appeara
Total - G

Addinall	Allen	Best	Chapman	Dudley	Duggan	Farrow	Hatton	Heath	Hill	Hudson	Jefferson	McEwan	McKay	Mills	Neary	Nelson	Parkinson	Pattison	Pointon	Powell	Ramscar	Reay	Saphin	Wardle	Woodward	OG
	1				7		10		6		3						4	11	9		8	2			5	
	1				7		10		6		3						4	11	9		8	2			5	
	1			2	7		10		6	11	3						4		9		8				5	
	1			2	7		10		6	11	3						4		9		8				5	
9	1			2	7		10	3	6	11							4				8				5	
9	1			2	7		10		6	11	3						4				8				5	
9	1			2	7		10		6	11	3						4				8				5	
9	1			2	7		10		6	11	3						4				8				5	
9	1			2	7		10		6	11	3						4				8				5	
9	1			2	7		10		6		3						4	11			8				5	
9	1		5	2	7		10		6		3						4		11		8					
9	1			3	10		4		6										11	2	8			7	5	
9	1			2	7	6	10	3									4				8			11	5	
	1			2	7	6	10				3						4		9		8			11	5	
10	1				7	6	8				3				9		4	11		2					5	
10	1					6	8				3				9		4	11		2					5	
7	1					10		5	6		3				9		8	11		2					4	
8	1		5			10			6		3		11		9					2				7	4	
	1		5			6	8		10		3		11		9					2				7	4	
	1		5			6	10				3				7		4		9	2				11	8	
10	1	8	5			6	4	3				7			9					2				11		
10	1	8	5			6	4	3				7			9					2				11		
10	1	8	5			6	4	3				7			9					2				11		
10	1		5			6	4	3		11		8			9					2				7		
10	1		5			6	4	3		11		7			9					2				8		
	1	10	5			6	4	3				8			9			11		2				7		
	1	9	5			6	4	3				8		10	7					2				11		
		9	5			6	4	3				8			7				10	2			1	11		
	1		5		10		4	3	6			8	11		9					2				7		
	1				8		6	3					11	10	9	4				2				7	5	
	1				8		6	3					11	10	9	4				2				7	5	
	1				8		6	3					11	10	9	4				2				7	5	
8	1	9					6	3					11	10		4				2				7	5	
8	1	9					6	3					11	10		4				2				7	5	
8	1	9			10	6		3					11			4				2				7	5	
8	1	9				6		3					11	10		4				2				7	5	
8	1	9					6	3					11	10		4				2				7	5	
8	1	9		2		6		3					11	10		4								7	5	
8	1	9					6	3		11				10		4				2				7	5	
9	1					6	8	3		11				10		4				2				7	5	
9	1					6	8	3		11				10		4				2				7	5	
9	1					6	8	3		11				10		4				2				7	5	
28	41	13	13	13	20	22	37	25	16	13	17	9	12	13	18	13	17	7	9	28	14	2	1	28	32	
11		3			2		3			4		1	1	2	5		1	2	2		1			1		1
	1	10	5			6	4	3		11		8			9					2				7		
	1	1	1			1	1	1		1		1			1					1				1		
28	42	14	14	13	20	23	38	26	16	14	17	10	12	13	19	13	17	7	9	29	14	2	1	29	32	
11		3			2		3			4		1	1	2	5		1	2	2		1			1		1

1950-51

Division Two

	P	W	D	L	F	A	Pts
Preston North End	42	26	5	11	91	49	57
Manchester City	42	19	14	9	89	61	52
Cardiff City	42	17	16	9	53	45	50
Birmingham City	42	20	9	13	64	53	49
Leeds United	42	20	8	14	63	55	48
Blackburn Rovers	42	19	8	15	65	66	46
Coventry City	42	19	7	16	75	59	45
Sheffield United	42	16	12	14	72	62	44
Brentford	42	18	8	16	75	74	44
Hull City	42	16	11	15	74	70	43
Doncaster Rovers	42	15	13	14	64	68	43
Southampton	42	15	13	14	66	73	43
West Ham United	42	16	10	16	68	69	42
Leicester City	42	15	11	16	68	58	41
Barnsley	42	15	10	17	74	68	40
Queen's Park Rangers	42	15	10	17	71	82	40
Notts County	42	13	13	16	61	60	39
Swansea Town	42	16	4	22	54	77	36
Luton Town	42	9	14	19	57	70	32
Bury	42	12	8	22	60	86	32
Chesterfield	42	9	12	21	44	69	30
Grimsby Town	42	8	12	22	61	95	28

Attendances

TOTAL

	Home	Away	Total
League	358,894	439,612	798,506
Cup/Other	25,777		25,777
TOTAL	384,671	439,612	824,283

AVERAGE

	Home	Away	Total
League	17,090	20,934	19,012
Cup/Other	25,777		25,777
TOTAL	17,485	20,934	19,169

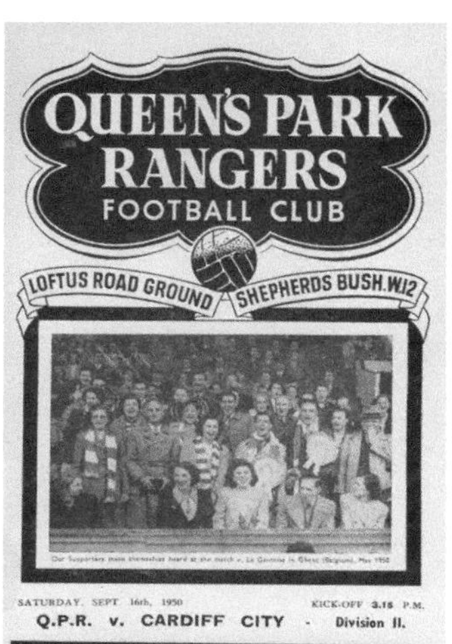

Match No.	Date		Opponents	Location	Result		Scorers	Atter
1	Aug	19	Chesterfield	H	D	1-1	Hatton	25
2		24	Notts County	H	W	1-0	Hatton	16
3		26	Leicester City	A	L	2-6	Addinall, Shepherd	28
4		31	Notts County	A	D	3-3	Addinall (2), Wardle	33
5	Sep	2	Manchester City	H	L	1-2	Hatton	21
6		6	Bury	A	W	1-0	Addinall	8
7		9	Coventry City	A	L	0-3		22
8		16	Cardiff City	H	W	3-2	Hatton (pen), Heath, Wardle	19
9		23	Birmingham City	A	D	1-1	Addinall	27
10		30	Grimsby Town	H	W	7-1	Shepherd (3), Addinall (2), Hatton (2)	16
11	Oct	7	West Ham United	A	L	1-4	Addinall	26
12		14	Swansea Town	H	D	1-1	Addinall	19
13		21	Luton Town	A	L	0-2		15
14		28	Leeds United	H	W	3-0	Shepherd, Hatton (pen), Mills	15
15	Nov	4	Barnsley	A	L	0-7		20
16		11	Sheffield United	H	W	2-1	Hatton, Wardle	16
17		18	Hull City	A	L	1-5	Hatton	33
18		25	Doncaster Rovers	H	L	1-2	Hatton	16
19	Dec	2	Brentford	A	L	1-2	Addinall	23
20		9	Blackburn Rovers	H	W	3-1	Addinall (2), Hatton (pen)	13
21		16	Chesterfield	A	L	1-3	Addinall	[illegible]
22		23	Leicester City	H	W	3-0	Addinall, Hatton, Shepherd	11
23		25	Preston North End	H	L	1-4	Waugh	16
24		26	Preston North End	A	L	0-1		36
25	Jan	13	Coventry City	H	W	3-1	Addinall, Hatton (pen), Shepherd	17
26		20	Cardiff City	A	L	2-4	Shepherd (2)	20
27		27	Brentford	H	D	1-1	Davies	26
28	Feb	3	Birmingham City	H	W	2-0	Farrow (pen), Shepherd	12
29		17	Grimsby Town	A	D	2-2	Farrow, Shepherd	14
30		24	West Ham United	H	D	3-3	Clayton, Farrow, Duggan	21
31	Mar	3	Swansea Town	A	L	0-1		20
32		10	Luton Town	H	D	1-1	Shepherd	13
33		17	Leeds United	A	D	2-2	Shepherd, Smith	18
34		23	Southampton	H	W	2-0	Farrow, Smith	19
35		24	Barnsley	H	W	2-1	Waugh, Smith	15
36		26	Southampton	A	D	2-2	Addinall (2)	20
37		31	Sheffield United	A	L	0-2		16
38	Apr	4	Manchester City	A	L	2-5	Hatton, Smith	21
39		7	Hull City	H	W	3-1	Farrow (2), Smith	14
40		14	Doncaster Rovers	A	W	2-0	Clayton, Smith	17
41		25	Blackburn Rovers	A	L	1-2	Hatton	9
42	May	5	Bury	H	W	3-2	Hatton, Shepherd, Smith	11
								Appeara
								G

FA Cup

R3	Jan	6	Millwall	H	L	3-4	Parkinson (2), Addinall	25
								Appeara
								G

Total - Appeara
Total - G

Cameron	Chapman	Clayton	Davies	Duggan	Farrow	Gullan	Hatton	Heath	Ingham	McKay	Mills	Muir	Nelson	Nicholas	Parkinson	Poppitt	Powell	Saphin	Shepherd	Smith	Stewart	Wardle	Waugh	Woodward
							8	3			10		4		6		2	1	11				7	5
							10	3			8		4		6		2	1	11				7	5
					6		10	3			8		4		5		2	1	11			7		
	5				6		10	3			8			4			2	1	11			7		
	5				6		10	3			8			4			2	1	11			7		
	5				6	1	10	3			8			4			2				11	7		
	5	4		10	6	1		3			8						2		11			7		
	5				6	1	10	3			8		4				2		11			7		
	5				6	1	10	3			8		4			2			11			7		
	5				6	1	10	3			8		4			2			11			7		
	5				6	1	10	3			8		4			2			11			7		
	5			7	6	1	10	3			8		4			2			11					
	5			7	6	1		3		8	10		4			2			11					
	5				6	1	10	3			8		4			2			11			7		
	5				6	1	10	3			8		4			2			11			7		
	5				6	1	10	3			8		4			2			11			7		
	5				6	1	10	3			8		4			2			11			7		
	5				6	1	10	3	2		8		4			7			11					
	5				6	1	10	3	2				4		8				11			7		
					6	1	10		3				4		8	2			11				7	5
					6	1	10		3				4		8	2			11				7	5
					6	1	10		3				4		8	2			11				7	5
					6	1	10		3					4	8	2			11				7	5
				10	6			3						4	8	2		1	11				7	5
				8	6		10		3						4	2		1	11				7	5
8				10	6				3						4	2		1	11				7	5
		6	9	8					3						4	2		1	11				7	5
		6			10				3			8			4	2		1	11				7	5
		6		8	10				3						4	2		1	11				7	5
		6		8	10				3						4	2		1	11				7	5
		6		8	10				3						4	2		1	11				7	5
		6		8	10				3						4	2		1	11				7	5
		6			10				3						4	2		1	11	8			7	5
		6			10				3						4	2		1	11	8			7	5
		6			10				3						4	2		1	11	8			7	5
		6		8	10				3						4	2		1	11				7	5
		6			10				3						4	2		1	11	8			7	5
					6		10	3							4	2		1	11	8			7	5
		6			10	1	9		3						4	2			11	8			7	5
		6			10	1	9		3						4	2			11	8			7	5
		6			10	1	9		3						4	2			11	8			7	5
		6			10	1	9		3						4	2			11	8			7	5
1	16	16	1	12	39	22	27	21	23	1	18	1	18	5	27	33	8	20	41	9	1	14	25	25
		2	1	1	6		16	1			1								14	7		3	2	
				10			4	3						6	8	2		1	11				7	5
				1			1	1						1	1	1		1	1				1	1
															2									
1	16	16	1	13	39	22	28	22	23	1	18	1	18	6	28	34	8	21	42	9	1	14	26	26
		2	1	1	6		16	1			1				2				14	7		3	2	

1951-52

Division Two

	P	W	D	L	F	A	Pts
Sheffield Wednesday	42	21	11	10	100	66	53
Cardiff City	42	20	11	11	72	54	51
Birmingham City	42	21	9	12	67	56	51
Nottingham Forest	42	18	13	11	77	62	49
Leicester City	42	19	9	14	78	64	47
Leeds United	42	18	11	13	59	57	47
Everton	42	17	10	15	64	58	44
Luton Town	42	16	12	14	77	78	44
Rotherham United	42	17	8	17	73	71	42
Brentford	42	15	12	15	54	55	42
Sheffield United	42	18	5	19	90	76	41
West Ham United	42	15	11	16	67	77	41
Southampton	42	15	11	16	61	73	41
Blackburn Rovers	42	17	6	19	54	63	40
Notts County	42	16	7	19	71	68	39
Doncaster Rovers	42	13	12	17	55	60	38
Bury	42	15	7	20	67	69	37
Hull City	42	13	11	18	60	70	37
Swansea Town	42	12	12	18	72	76	36
Barnsley	42	11	14	17	59	72	36
Coventry City	42	14	6	22	59	82	34
Queen's Park Rangers	42	11	12	19	52	81	34

Attendances

TOTAL	Home	Away	Total
League	346,589	454,213	800,802
Cup/Other		35,000	35,000
TOTAL	346,589	489,213	835,802

AVERAGE	Home	Away	Total
League	16,504	21,629	19,067
Cup/Other		35,000	35,000
TOTAL	16,504	22,237	19,437

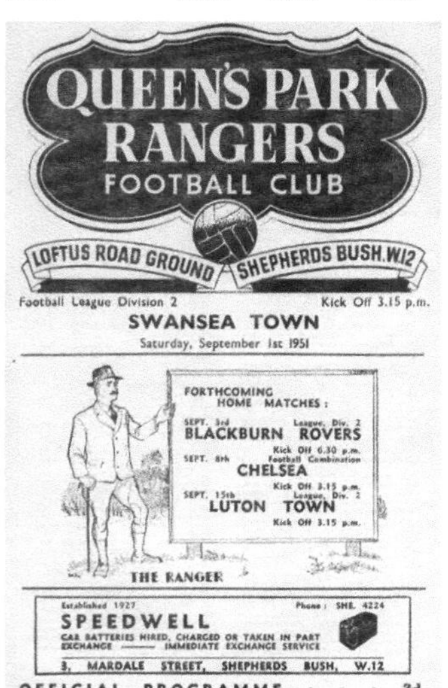

Match No.	Date		Opponents	Location	Result		Scorers	Atte
1	Aug	18	West Ham United	H	W	2-0	Addinall, Shepherd	1
2		20	Hull City	H	D	1-1	Smith	1
3		25	Coventry City	A	D	0-0		2
4		30	Hull City	A	L	1-4	Smith	1
5	Sep	1	Swansea Town	H	D	1-1	Smith	1
6		3	Blackburn Rovers	H	W	2-1	Addinall (2)	1
7		8	Bury	A	L	1-3	Clayton	1
8		15	Luton Town	H	D	0-0		1
9		22	Notts County	A	D	0-0		2
10		29	Brentford	H	W	3-1	Gilberg, Shepherd, Smith	2
11	Oct	6	Doncaster Rovers	A	L	0-4		2
12		13	Everton	H	D	4-4	Shepherd (2), Waugh, Gilberg	1
13		20	Southampton	A	D	1-1	Smith	1
14		27	Sheffield Wednesday	H	D	2-2	Addinall, Smith	1
15	Nov	3	Leeds United	A	L	0-3		2
16		10	Rotherham United	H	L	2-3	Gilberg, Smith	1
17		17	Cardiff City	A	L	1-3	Gilberg	2
18		24	Birmingham City	H	L	0-2		1
19	Dec	1	Leicester City	A	L	0-4		2
20		8	Nottingham Forest	H	W	4-3	Smith, Hatton (pen), Shepherd, Gilberg	1
21		15	West Ham United	A	L	2-4	Gilberg, Hatton (pen)	1
22		22	Coventry City	H	L	1-4	Smith	1
23		25	Barnsley	A	L	1-3	Hatton	1
24		26	Barnsley	H	D	1-1	Smith	1
25		29	Swansea Town	A	W	3-2	Gilberg, Hill, Addinall	1
26	Jan	1	Blackburn Rovers	A	L	2-4	Nicholas, Addinall	2
27		5	Bury	H	W	3-2	Addinall, Gilberg, Smith	1
28		19	Luton Town	A	W	1-0	Addinall	1
29		26	Notts County	H	L	1-4	Gilberg	1
30	Feb	9	Brentford	A	D	0-0		2
31		16	Doncaster Rovers	H	L	0-2		1
32	Mar	1	Everton	A	L	0-3		3
33		8	Southampton	H	W	2-1	Addinall, Hold	1
34		15	Sheffield Wednesday	A	L	1-2	Muir	4
35		22	Leeds United	H	D	0-0		1
36		29	Rotherham United	A	L	0-1		
37	Apr	5	Cardiff City	H	D	1-1	Smith (pen)	1
38		12	Birmingham City	A	L	0-1		2
39		14	Sheffield United	H	W	4-2	Addinall (2), Farrow, Muir	1
40		19	Leicester City	H	W	1-0	Addinall	1
41		26	Nottingham Forest	A	L	1-3	Muir	1
42	May	3	Sheffield United	A	W	2-1	Stewart, Smith	

Appeara
G

FA Cup

R3	Jan	12	Brentford	A	L	1-3	Shepherd	3

Appeara
G

Total - Appeara
Total - G

Brown	Cameron	Chapman	Clayton	Farrow	Gilberg	Gullan	Hatton	Heath	Hill	Hold	Ingham	McKay	Muir	Nicholas	Poppitt	Powell	Richardson	Shepherd	Smith	Spence	Stewart	Tomkys	Underwood	Waugh
1		5	4		6		10	3							2			11	8					7
1		5	4		6			3					7		2			11	8		10			
1		5	4		6			3				11	7		2				8		10			
1		5	4		6			3					7		2			11	8		10			
1		5	4		6			3					7		2			11	8		10			
1	10		4		6			5							2	3		11	8					7
1	10	5	4		6			3								2		11	8					7
1	10	5		6	4			3							2			11	8					7
		5	4	6	10	1									2	3		11	8					7
1	8	5	4	6	10										2	3		11	9					7
1	8	5	4	6	10										2	3		11	9					7
1		5	4	6	10										2	3		11	8					7
1		5	4	6	10										2	3		11	8					7
1		5	4	6	10										2	3		11	8					7
1		5	4	6	10										2	3		11	8					7
1			4	6	10			5							2	3		11	8					7
1				6	4			5							2	3		11	8		10			7
1				6	4			5			3					2		11	8		10	7		
1				6	4			5	8		3					2		11			10			7
1				6	10		4	5							2	3		11	8					7
1				6	10		4	5							2	3		11	8					7
1		5		6	8		10							4	2	3		11	9					7
1				6	8		10		7					4	2	3			9	5				11
1				6	8		10		7					4	2	3			9	5				11
1					8			6	7		3			4		2			10	5				11
1					8			6	7		3			4		2			10	5				11
1					8			6	7		3			4		2			10	5				11
				6	4	1			10							3	2	11	8	5				7
				6	4				10							3	2	11	8	5			1	7
				6	4				10		3					2		11	8	5			1	7
				6	8	1		4	7		3					2			9	5	10			11
				6	8	1		4			3	11				2			10	5				7
1				6	4					8	3		7			2			10	5				11
1				6	4					8	3		7			2			10	5				11
1				6	4					8	3		7			2			10	5				11
1			4	6	10						3					2		11	8	5				7
1			4	6	10						3					2		11	8	5				7
1			4	6	10						3					2		11	8	5				7
1			4	6	10								7		3	2			8	5				11
1			4	6							3		8		2			11	10	5				7
1			4	6	8						3		7		2			11	10	5				
1			4	6							3				2			11	8	5	10			7
36	5	15	22	32	40	4	6	19	10	3	17	2	10	6	25	33	2	30	41	20	9	1	2	36
			1	1	9		3		1	1			3	1				5	13		1			1

Brown	Cameron	Chapman	Clayton	Farrow	Gilberg	Gullan	Hatton	Heath	Hill	Hold	Ingham	McKay	Muir	Nicholas	Poppitt	Powell	Richardson	Shepherd	Smith	Spence	Stewart	Tomkys	Underwood	Waugh
1					4			6	10		3					2		11	8	5				7
1					1			1	1		1					1		1	1	1				1
																		1						

Brown	Cameron	Chapman	Clayton	Farrow	Gilberg	Gullan	Hatton	Heath	Hill	Hold	Ingham	McKay	Muir	Nicholas	Poppitt	Powell	Richardson	Shepherd	Smith	Spence	Stewart	Tomkys	Underwood	Waugh
37	5	15	22	32	41	4	6	20	11	3	18	2	10	6	25	34	2	31	42	21	9	1	2	37
			1	1	9		3		1	1			3	1				6	13		1			1

1952-53

Division Three South

	P	W	D	L	F	A	Pts
Bristol Rovers	46	26	12	8	92	46	64
Millwall	46	24	14	8	82	44	62
Northampton Town	46	26	10	10	109	70	62
Norwich City	46	25	10	11	99	55	60
Bristol City	46	22	15	9	95	61	59
Coventry City	46	19	12	15	77	62	50
Brighton & Hove Albion	46	19	12	15	81	75	50
Southend United	46	18	13	15	69	74	49
Bournemouth	46	19	9	18	74	69	47
Watford	46	15	17	14	62	63	47
Reading	46	19	8	19	69	64	46
Torquay United	46	18	9	19	87	88	45
Crystal Palace	46	15	13	18	66	82	43
Leyton Orient	46	16	10	20	68	73	42
Newport County	46	16	10	20	70	82	42
Ipswich Town	46	13	15	18	60	69	41
Exeter City	46	13	14	19	61	71	40
Swindon Town	46	14	12	20	64	79	40
Aldershot	46	12	15	19	61	77	39
Queen's Park Rangers	46	12	15	19	61	82	39
Gillingham	46	12	15	19	55	74	39
Colchester United	46	12	14	20	59	76	38
Shrewsbury Town	46	12	12	22	68	91	36
Walsall	46	7	10	29	56	118	24

Attendances

	TOTAL		
	Home	**Away**	**Total**
League	277,624	310,414	588,038
Cup/Other	11,475	8,799	20,274
TOTAL	289,099	319,213	608,312

	AVERAGE		
	Home	**Away**	**Total**
League	12,071	13,496	12,783
Cup/Other	11,475	4,400	6,758
TOTAL	12,046	12,769	12,415

Match No.	Date		Opponents	Location	Result		Scorers	Attend
1	Aug	23	Exeter City	A	D	2-2	Smith (2)	15,
2		25	Watford	H	D	2-2	Stewart, Smith	23
3		30	Coventry City	H	L	0-4		14,
4	Sep	4	Watford	A	D	1-1	Shepherd	22,
5		6	Norwich City	A	L	0-2		26,
6		8	Walsall	H	W	4-2	Tomkys (2), Gilberg, Smith	9,
7		13	Colchester United	H	W	1-0	Muir	13,
8		18	Walsall	A	D	1-1	Cameron	7,
9		20	Aldershot	A	L	1-4	Shepherd	8,
10		25	Leyton Orient	A	L	0-5		8,
11		27	Swindon Town	H	D	1-1	Addinall	10,
12	Oct	2	Shrewsbury Town	A	W	3-0	Shepherd (2), Smith	5,
13		4	Southend United	H	W	3-2	Smith (2), Addinall	14,
14		11	Brighton	A	L	0-2		18,
15		18	Newport County	H	W	4-2	Quinn, Shepherd (2), Addinall	14
16		25	Crystal Palace	A	L	2-4	Addinall, Ingham	19,
17	Nov	1	Bristol City	H	W	2-1	Mountford, Addinall	14,
18		8	Torquay United	A	D	1-1	Parsons	6,
19		15	Northampton Town	H	D	2-2	Shepherd, Gilberg	14
20		29	Ipswich Town	H	D	2-2	Addinall (2)	8,
21	Dec	13	Bournemouth	H	W	2-1	Nicholas (pen), Cameron	7,
22		20	Exeter City	H	D	1-1	Clayton	6,
23		26	Bristol Rovers	H	L	0-1		13,
24		27	Bristol Rovers	A	L	1-2	Gilberg	30,
25	Jan	3	Coventry City	A	L	0-2		15,
26		10	Gillingham	A	L	0-3		11,
27		17	Norwich City	H	W	3-1	Tomkys, Waugh (2)	12,
28		24	Colchester United	A	D	1-1	OG (Harrison)	7,
29		31	Gillingham	H	D	1-1	Tomkys	10
30	Feb	7	Aldershot	H	D	2-2	Smith, Waugh	10
31		14	Swindon Town	A	W	3-1	Hatton (2), Smith	6,
32		21	Southend United	A	L	0-2		12,
33		28	Brighton	H	D	3-3	Higgins, Hatton, OG (Jennings)	15,
34	Mar	7	Newport County	A	L	0-2		8,
35		14	Crystal Palace	H	D	1-1	Cameron	12,
36		21	Bristol City	A	D	4-4	Mountford, Cameron, Smith (2)	19
37		28	Torquay United	H	L	0-1		8,
38	Apr	3	Millwall	A	L	1-2	Smith	23,
39		4	Northampton Town	A	L	2-4	Tomkys, Cameron	12,
40		6	Millwall	H	L	1-3	Shepherd	12,
41		11	Leyton Orient	H	L	0-1		10,
42		18	Ipswich Town	A	W	1-0	Hatton	8,
43		20	Shrewsbury Town	H	W	1-0	Shepherd	7,
44		25	Reading	H	W	1-0	Harrison	10,
45		29	Reading	A	L	0-2		8,
46	May	2	Bournemouth	A	L	0-1		8,

Appearan

Gc

FA Cup

R1	Nov	22	Shrewsbury Town	H	D	2-2	Cameron (2)	11,
rep		27	Shrewsbury Town	A	D	2-2 aet	Addinall, Smith	5,
rep	Dec	2	Shrewsbury Town	N*	L	1-4	Smith	3,

* Played at Villa Park

Appearan

Gc

Total - Appearan

Total - Gc

Brown	Cameron	Chapman	Clayton	Crickson	Farrow	Gilberg	Gullan	Harrison	Hatton	Heath	Higgins	Hold	Ingham	Mountford	Muir	Nicholas	Parsons	Poppitt	Powell G.	Powell M.	Quinn	Shepherd	Smith	Spence	Stewart	Tomkys	Waugh	Woods	OG
1			4			6							3					2				11	8	5	10		7		
1			4			6							3					2				11	8	5	10		7		
1			4			6						10	3					2				11	8	5			7		
1	10					8							3			4		2		5		11	7	6		9			
1	10					8										4		2	3	5		11	7	6		9			
1	10					8										4		2	3	5		11	7	6		9			
1	10					8							3		7	4		2		5		11		6		9			
1	10				6	8							3		7	4		2		5		11				9			
1	10				6	8							3		7	4		2		5		11				9			
1	10				6	8				5			3		11	4		2								7			
1	10				6	11							3		7	4		2		5			8						
1	10		4		6	7							3					2				11	8	5					
1	10		4		6	7							3					2				11	8	5					
1	10		4		6	7							3					2				11	8	5					
1			4		6	7							3					2			10	11	8	5					
1			4			6							3	7				2			10	11	8	5					
1						6							3	7		4		2			10	11	8	5					
1	10					8							3	7		4	6	2				11		5					
1	10					8							3	7		4	6	2				11		5					
1	10					6							3	7		4		2				11	8	5					
1	10		6			8							3	7		4		2				11		5					
1	10		6			8							3	7		4		2				11		5					
1	10		6			8							3	7		4		2				11		5					
1	10		6			8							3	7		4		2		5		11				9			
1	8					10		6					3	7		4				5		11						2	
1	8					10		6					3			4			2			11		5			7		
1	10	5											3	8		4			2			11		6		9	7		
	10	5					1						3	8		4			2			11		6		9	7		
	10	5					1						3	8		4			2			11		6		9	7		
		5					1		10				3			4			2			11	8	6		9	7		
1		5	6						10				3			4			2			11	8			9	7		
1		5	6						10				3			4			2			11	8			9	7		
1		5							10		9		3	8		4			2			11		6			7		
1		5									9		3	8		4			2			11	10	6			7		
1	10	5											3	7		4			2			11	8	6		9			
1	10	5	6										3	7		4		2				11	8			9			
1	10	5	6										3	7		4		2				11	8			9			
1	10		6								9		3			4		2		5		11	8				7		
1	10	6											3	7		4			2	5		11	8			9			
1	8		6	4					10				3					2		5		11				9	7		
1	10		6	4									3	7				2		5			8			9	11		
1	8		4					9	10				3	7				2		5		11		6					
1	8		4					9	10				3	7				2		5		11		6					
1	8		4					9	10				3	7				2		5		11		6					
1	8		4					9	10				3	7				2		5		11		6					
1	10		6						9					7		4		3	2	5		11	8						
43	35	12	24	2	8	26	3	6	10	1	3	1	43	25	5	32	2	34	14	18	3	43	25	31	2	20	15	1	
	5		1			3		1	4		1		1	2	1	1	1				1	9	12		1	5	3		2
1	10					8							3	7		4	6	2				11		5					
1	10					8							3	7		4		2				11	6	5					
1	10		4			8							3	7				2				11	6	5					
3	3		1			3							3	3		2	1	3				3	2	3					
	2																						2						
46	38	12	25	2	8	29	3	6	10	1	3	1	46	28	5	34	3	37	14	18	3	46	27	34	2	20	15	1	
	7		1			3		1	4		1		1	2	1	1	1				1	9	14		1	5	3		2

1953-54

Division Three South

	P	W	D	L	F	A	Pts
Ipswich Town	46	27	10	9	82	51	64
Brighton & Hove Albion	46	26	9	11	86	61	61
Bristol City	46	25	6	15	88	66	56
Watford	46	21	10	15	85	69	52
Northampton Town	46	20	11	15	82	55	51
Southampton	46	22	7	17	76	63	51
Norwich City	46	20	11	15	73	66	51
Reading	46	20	9	17	86	73	49
Exeter City	46	20	8	18	68	58	48
Gillingham	46	19	10	17	61	66	48
Leyton Orient	46	18	11	17	79	73	47
Millwall	46	19	9	18	74	77	47
Torquay United	46	17	12	17	81	88	46
Coventry City	46	18	9	19	61	56	45
Newport County	46	19	6	21	61	81	44
Southend United	46	18	7	21	69	71	43
Aldershot	46	17	9	20	74	86	43
Queen's Park Rangers	46	16	10	20	60	68	42
Bournemouth	46	16	8	22	67	70	40
Swindon Town	46	15	10	21	67	70	40
Shrewsbury Town	46	14	12	20	65	76	40
Crystal Palace	46	14	12	20	60	86	40
Colchester United	46	10	10	26	50	78	30
Walsall	46	9	8	29	40	87	26

Attendances

TOTAL	Home	Away	Total
League	251,272	251,156	502,428
Cup/Other	48,866	13,083	61,949
TOTAL	300,138	264,239	564,377

AVERAGE	Home	Away	Total
League	10,925	10,920	10,922
Cup/Other	16,289	13,083	15,487
TOTAL	11,544	11,010	11,288

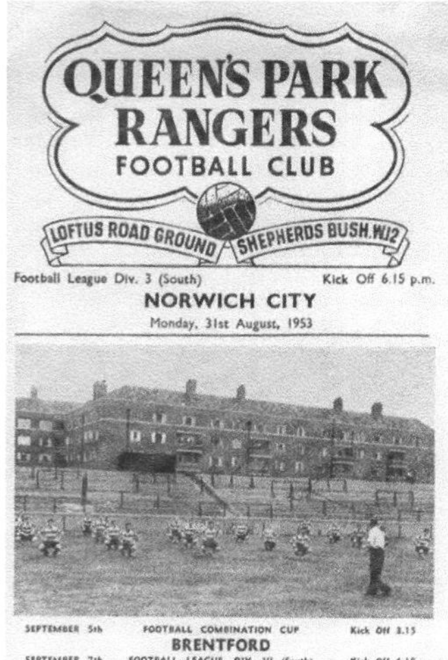

Match No.	Date		Opponents	Location	Result		Scorers	Atten
1	Aug	19	Brighton	H	L	1-2	Shepherd	16
2		22	Bristol City	A	W	2-1	Petchey, Cameron	20
3		26	Norwich City	A	D	2-2	Clayton, Hawkins	23
4		29	Aldershot	H	L	0-2		12
5		31	Norwich City	H	L	0-2		11
6	Sep	5	Swindon Town	A	W	1-0	Cameron	15
7		7	Southampton	H	L	0-1		11
8		12	Walsall	H	W	2-0	Petchey, Hawkins	12
9		16	Southampton	A	L	1-3	Hawkins	16
10		19	Shrewsbury Town	A	D	1-1	Smith	11
11		21	Crystal Palace	H	D	1-1	Shepherd	7
12		26	Exeter City	H	D	0-0		12
13		30	Crystal Palace	A	W	3-0	Smith (2), Shepherd	9
14	Oct	3	Newport County	A	L	1-2	Hurrell	6
15		10	Northampton Town	H	D	1-1	Shepherd	13
16		17	Torquay United	A	D	2-2	Smith (2)	8
17		24	Watford	H	L	0-4		15
18	Nov	7	Southend United	H	W	1-0	Tomkys	9
19		14	Reading	A	L	1-3	Shepherd	14
20		28	Millwall	A	L	0-4		17
21	Dec	5	Ipswich Town	H	W	3-1	Petchey, Woods, Shepherd	13
22		19	Bristol City	H	L	0-1		8
23		25	Colchester United	A	L	0-5		6
24		26	Colchester United	H	D	0-0		10
25	Jan	2	Aldershot	A	W	4-1	Petchey (3), Cameron	5
26		16	Swindon Town	H	L	0-2		9
27		23	Walsall	A	L	0-2		8
28		30	Coventry City	H	L	0-3		5
29	Feb	6	Shrewsbury Town	H	D	0-0		7
30		13	Exeter City	A	D	0-0		8
31		20	Newport County	H	W	5-1	Cameron (3), Kerrins, Smith	10
32		27	Northampton Town	A	L	1-2	Clark	8
33	Mar	6	Torquay United	H	W	5-1	Clark, Smith (2, 1 pen), Kerrins, Cameron	11
34		18	Leyton Orient	A	D	2-2	Clark, Angell	4
35		20	Millwall	H	W	4-0	Kerrins, Clark, Pounder, Smith	13
36		27	Southend United	A	L	1-4	Angell	10
37	Apr	3	Reading	H	W	2-0	Smith, Tomkys	9
38		7	Bournemouth	A	W	1-0	Clark	5
39		10	Ipswich Town	A	L	1-2	Cameron	15
40		12	Coventry City	A	L	1-3	Clark	4
41		16	Gillingham	A	L	0-1		10
42		17	Bournemouth	H	W	2-1	Shepherd, Smith	10
43		19	Gillingham	H	W	3-1	Smith, Kerrins, OG (Lewin)	9
44		24	Watford	A	W	2-0	Angell, Cameron	10
45		26	Leyton Orient	H	W	2-1	Cameron, OG (Aldous)	9
46		30	Brighton	A	L	1-3	Pounder	10
								Appearan
								G

FA Cup

R1	Nov	21	Shrewsbury Town	H	W	2-0	Hurrell (2)	13
R2	Dec	12	Nuneaton Borough	H	D	1-1	Tomkys	18
rep		17	Nuneaton Borough	A	W	2-1	Petchey, Shepherd	13
R3	Jan	9	Port Vale	H	L	0-1		17
								Appearar
								G

Total - Appearar

Total - G

Angell	Barley	Brown	Cameron	Clark	Clayton	Fallon	Gullan	Hawkins	Hurrell	Ingham	Kerrins	Mountford	Nicholas	Petchey	Poppitt	Pounder	Powell	Quinn	Shepherd	Smith	Spence	Taylor G.	Taylor J.	Tomkys	Woods	OG
		1			6			9	10	3		7			2				11	8	4		5			
		1	8		6			9		3		7		10	2				11		4		5			
		1	8		6			9		3		7		10	2				11		4		5			
	9	1	8		6					3		7		10	2				11		4		5			
	9	1	8		6					3		7	4		2				11	10			5			
	9	1	8		6					3		7	4	10	2				11				5			
	9	1	8		6					3		7	4	10	2				11				5			
11		1	8		6			9		3		7	4	10									5		2	
		1	8					9		3		7	4	10					11		6		5		2	
		1	8		4	6		9		3		7							11	10			5		2	
		1	8		6			9		3			4						11	10			5	7	2	
					6		1	9		3			4					8	11	10			5	7	2	
6					9		1			3			4					8	11	10			5	7	2	
6					9		1		10	3			4						11	8			5	7	2	
6					9		1			3			4				5	8	11	10				7	2	
9					6		1			3			4				5	8	11	10				7	2	
9		1	8		6					3			4						11	10			5	7	2	
		1	8		6					3			4	9					11	10			5	7	2	
6		1	8						10	3			4	9					11				5	7	2	
6		1	8						10	3			4	9					11				5	7	2	
6		1	10						8				4	9	3				11				5	7	2	
6		1	8						10	3			4	9					11				5	7	2	
6		1	8							3			4	9	2				11	10		7	5			
6		1	10							3			4	9	2			8	11				5	7		
6		1	10							3			4	9	2			8				11	5	7		
6		1	10							3			4	9	2			8	11				5	7		
6		1	10										4	8	3		9		11				5	7	2	
6		1	10		4									9	3			8	11				5	7	2	
6		1	10	9						3			4				5		11	8			2	7		
6		1	8	9						3	11		4			7	5			10			2			
6		1	10	9						3	11		4			7	5			8			2			
6		1	8	9						3	11		4			7	5			10			2			
6		1	8	9						3	11		4			7	5			10			2			
6			8	9			1			3	11		4			7	5			10			2			
6		1	8	9						3	11		4			7	5			10			2			
6		1	8	9						3	11		4			7	5			10			2			
6			8	9	4		1			3	11						5			10			2	7		
6			8	9	4		1			3							5		11	10			2			
6			8	9	4		1			3						7	5		11	10			2			
6		1	8	9	4					3				10		7	5		11				2			
		1	8	9	4					3							5		11	10			2	7	6	
		1		9	4						7			6			5	8	11	10			2		3	
				9	4		1				7			6			5	8	11	10			2		3	
6			8	9	4		1			3	7						5		11	10					2	
6			8	9	4		1			3	11					7	5			10					2	
6			8	9	4		1			3	11					7	5			10					2	
31	4	33	38	18	28	1	13	8	6	41	13	10	30	21	14	11	21	10	34	29	5	2	41	20	23	
3			10	6	1			3	1		4			6		2			7	12				2	1	2

Angell	Barley	Brown	Cameron	Clark	Clayton	Fallon	Gullan	Hawkins	Hurrell	Ingham	Kerrins	Mountford	Nicholas	Petchey	Poppitt	Pounder	Powell	Quinn	Shepherd	Smith	Spence	Taylor G.	Taylor J.	Tomkys	Woods	OG
6		1	8						10	3			4	9					11				5	7	2	
6		1	8		5				10	3			4	9					11					7	2	
6		1	8						10	3			4	9					11				5	7	2	
6		1	10							3			4	9	2			8	11				5	7		
4		4	4		1				3	4			4	4	1			1	4				3	4	3	
									2					1					1					1		

Angell	Barley	Brown	Cameron	Clark	Clayton	Fallon	Gullan	Hawkins	Hurrell	Ingham	Kerrins	Mountford	Nicholas	Petchey	Poppitt	Pounder	Powell	Quinn	Shepherd	Smith	Spence	Taylor G.	Taylor J.	Tomkys	Woods	OG
35	4	37	42	18	29	1	13	8	9	45	13	10	34	25	15	11	21	11	38	29	5	2	44	24	26	
3			10	6	1			3	3		4			7		2			8	12				3	1	2

1954-55

Division Three South

	P	W	D	L	F	A	Pts
Bristol City	46	30	10	6	101	47	70
Leyton Orient	46	26	9	11	89	47	61
Southampton	46	24	11	11	75	51	59
Gillingham	46	20	15	11	77	66	55
Millwall	46	20	11	15	72	68	51
Brighton & Hove Albion	46	20	10	16	76	63	50
Watford	46	18	14	14	71	62	50
Torquay United	46	18	12	16	82	82	48
Coventry City	46	18	11	17	67	59	47
Southend United	46	17	12	17	83	80	46
Brentford	46	16	14	16	82	82	46
Norwich City	46	18	10	18	60	60	46
Northampton Town	46	19	8	19	73	81	46
Aldershot	46	16	13	17	75	71	45
Queen's Park Rangers	46	15	14	17	69	75	44
Shrewsbury Town	46	16	10	20	70	78	42
Bournemouth	46	12	18	16	57	65	42
Reading	46	13	15	18	65	73	41
Newport County	46	11	16	19	60	73	38
Crystal Palace	46	11	16	19	52	80	38
Swindon Town	46	11	15	20	46	64	37
Exeter City	46	11	15	20	47	73	37
Walsall	46	10	14	22	75	86	34
Colchester United	46	9	13	24	53	91	31

Attendances

TOTAL

	Home	Away	Total
League	257,936	257,421	515,357
Cup/Other	16,299	22,439	38,738
TOTAL	274,235	279,860	554,095

AVERAGE

	Home	Away	Total
League	11,215	11,192	11,203
Cup/Other	16,299	11,220	12,913
TOTAL	11,426	11,194	11,308

Match No.	Date		Opponents	Location	Result		Scorers	Atten
1	Aug	21	Watford	H	W	2-1	Cameron, Clark	19
2		24	Southend United	A	D	2-2	Cameron, Smith	8
3		28	Bournemouth	A	D	2-2	Smith (2)	13
4		30	Southend United	H	D	1-1	Shepherd	11
5	Sep	4	Brentford	A	D	1-1	Smith	9
6		7	Aldershot	H	W	5-0	Smith (2, 2 pens), Fidler (2), Petchey	10
7		11	Newport County	H	W	2-0	Shepherd, Rutter	13
8		15	Aldershot	A	L	0-2		5
9		18	Exeter City	A	L	1-2	Cameron	8
10		22	Swindon Town	A	L	0-2		6
11		25	Colchester United	H	W	4-1	Pounder, Clark, Cameron, OG (Elder)	11
12		27	Swindon Town	H	W	3-1	Smith (2, 1 pen), Pounder	8
13	Oct	2	Norwich City	A	D	1-1	Smith	20
14		9	Southampton	H	D	2-2	Smith, OG (Wilkins)	16
15		16	Millwall	A	W	1-0	Clark	21
16		23	Leyton Orient	H	W	2-0	Smith, Clark	22
17		30	Brighton	A	L	1-4	Shepherd	14
18	Nov	6	Reading	H	L	2-3	Shepherd, Smith	13
19		13	Shrewsbury Town	A	L	0-1		7
20		27	Bristol City	A	D	1-1	Tomkys	17
21	Dec	4	Torquay United	H	W	4-2	Smith (2, 1 pen), Cameron (2)	8
22		18	Watford	A	D	1-1	Cameron	11
23		25	Northampton Town	H	W	1-0	Clark	8
24		27	Northampton Town	A	W	3-1	Clark (2), Angell	12
25	Jan	1	Bournemouth	H	D	1-1	Angell	8
26		15	Brentford	H	D	1-1	Clark	9
27		22	Newport County	A	L	0-4		5
28		29	Coventry City	H	W	3-2	Smith (pen), Cameron, Kerrins	12
29	Feb	5	Exeter City	H	L	1-2	Smith	9
30		12	Colchester United	A	L	0-1		4
31		19	Norwich City	H	W	2-1	Angell, Cameron	6
32		26	Southampton	A	D	2-2	Clark, Shepherd	12
33	Mar	5	Millwall	H	L	1-2	Shepherd	11
34		12	Leyton Orient	A	L	0-3		17
35		19	Brighton	H	W	3-2	Clark (2), Shepherd	9
36		26	Reading	A	L	1-3	Kerrins	6
37	Apr	2	Shrewsbury Town	H	W	2-0	Clark, Cameron	8
38		8	Crystal Palace	A	L	1-2	Clark	17
39		9	Walsall	A	L	1-4	Smith	13
40		11	Crystal Palace	H	W	1-0	Clark	8
41		16	Bristol City	H	D	1-1	Shepherd (pen)	12
42		20	Gillingham	A	L	1-3	Pounder	9
43		23	Torquay United	A	L	2-3	Longbottom, Cameron	6
44		25	Walsall	H	D	1-1	Cameron	6
45		30	Gillingham	H	D	1-1	Cameron	9
46	May	2	Coventry City	A	L	1-5	Clark	7

Appearar
G

FA Cup

R1	Nov	20	Walthamstow Avenue	H	D	2-2	Fidler, Smith	16
rep		23	Walthamstow Avenue	A	D	2-2 aet	Fidler, Tomkys	10
rep		29	Walthamstow Avenue	N*	L	0-4		11

* Played at Highbury

Appearar
G

Total - Appearar
Total - G

Brown	Cameron	Clark	Fidler	Gullan	Ingham	Kerrins	Longbottom	Nicholas	Patchey	Pounder	Powell	Rutter	Shepherd	Silver	Smith	Tomkys	Woods	OG
	8	9			3			4		7	5		11		10		2	
	8		9					4		7	5	3	11		10		2	
	8		9					4		7	5	3	11		10		2	
	8		9	1				4		7	5	3	11		10		2	
	8		9	1				4	6	7	5	3	11		10		2	
	8		9	1				4	6	7	5	3	11		10		2	
	8	9		1				4	6	7	5	3	11		10		2	
	8	9		1				4	6	7	5	3	11		10		2	
	8	9		1	3			4	6	7	5	2	11		10			
	8	9			3	7		4	10		5	2	11					
	8	9			3			4	10	7	5	2	11					
	8	9			3			4		7	5	2	11		10			
	8	9			3				4	7	5	2	11		10			
		9			3			4	8	7	5	2	11		10			
	8	9			3				4	7	5	2	11		10			
	8	9			3				4	7	5	2	11		10			
	8	9			3				4	7	5	2	11		10			
	8	9			3				4	7	5	2	11		10			
	8		9		3			4	6		5				10	7	2	
	8		9		3	11		4			5				10	7	2	
	8	9	7		3	11		1	4			5			10		2	
	8	9	7		3			4				5	11		10		2	
	8	9	7		3			4				5	11		10		2	
	8	9	7		3			4			5	2	11		10			
	8	9			3			4			5	2	11		10	7		
	8	9				11		4			5	3			10	7	2	
		9			3	11		4	8		5	2			10	7		
	8	9			3	7		4			5		11		10		2	
	8	9			3	7		4			5		11		10		2	
	10	9	7		3			4			5		11		8		2	
	10	9			3	7		4			5		11		8		2	
	10	9			3	7		4			5		11		8		2	
	10	9			3	7		4			5		11		8		2	
	10	9			3		8	4			5		11			7	2	
	10	9			3	7	8	4			5		11				2	
	10	9			3	7	8	4			5	2	11					
	10	9			3	7	8	4			5		11				2	
	10	9			3			4		7	5		11		8		2	
	10	9			3	11		4		7	5				8		2	
	10	9			3	7	8	4				5	11				2	
	10	9			3		8	4		7		5	11				2	
	10	9			3		8	4		7		5	11				2	
	10	9			3		8		4	7		5	11				2	
	10	9			3		8	4		7		5	11				2	
	10	9			3		8	4				5	11			7	2	
	10	9			3		8	4				5	11			7	2	
9	44	39	12	6	38	15	11	40	17	23	36	32	40		33	8	32	
	13	15	2			2	1		1	3		1	8		17	1		2

Brown	Cameron	Clark	Fidler	Gullan	Ingham	Kerrins	Longbottom	Nicholas	Patchey	Pounder	Powell	Rutter	Shepherd	Silver	Smith	Tomkys	Woods	OG
	8		9		3				4	7	5		11		10		2	
	8		9		3				4		5		11		10	7	2	
	8	9			3	11		4			5			1	10	7	2	
2	3	1	2		3	1		1	2	1	3		2	1	3	2	3	
			2												1	1		

Brown	Cameron	Clark	Fidler	Gullan	Ingham	Kerrins	Longbottom	Nicholas	Patchey	Pounder	Powell	Rutter	Shepherd	Silver	Smith	Tomkys	Woods	OG
1	47	40	14	6	41	16	11	41	19	24	39	32	42	1	36	10	35	
	13	15	4			2	1		1	3		1	8		18	2		2

1955-56

Division Three South

	P	W	D	L	F	A	Pts
Leyton Orient	46	29	8	9	106	49	66
Brighton & Hove Albion	46	29	7	10	112	50	65
Ipswich Town	46	25	14	7	106	60	64
Southend United	46	21	11	14	88	80	53
Torquay United	46	20	12	14	86	63	52
Brentford	46	19	14	13	69	66	52
Norwich City	46	19	13	14	86	82	51
Coventry City	46	20	9	17	73	60	49
Bournemouth	46	19	10	17	63	51	48
Gillingham	46	19	10	17	69	71	48
Northampton Town	46	20	7	19	67	71	47
Colchester United	46	18	11	17	76	81	47
Shrewsbury Town	46	17	12	17	69	66	46
Southampton	46	18	8	20	91	81	44
Aldershot	46	12	16	18	70	90	40
Exeter City	46	15	10	21	58	77	40
Reading	46	15	9	22	70	79	39
Queen's Park Rangers	46	14	11	21	64	86	39
Newport County	46	15	9	22	58	79	39
Walsall	46	15	8	23	68	84	38
Watford	46	13	11	22	52	85	37
Millwall	46	15	6	25	83	100	36
Crystal Palace	46	12	10	24	54	83	34
Swindon Town	46	8	14	24	34	78	30

Attendances

TOTAL

	Home	Away	Total
League	199,994	212,763	412,757
Cup/Other		15,000	15,000
TOTAL	199,994	227,763	427,757

AVERAGE

	Home	Away	Total
League	8,695	9,251	8,973
Cup/Other		15,000	15,000
TOTAL	8,695	9,490	9,101

Match No.	Date		Opponents	Location	Result		Scorers	Atte
1	Aug	20	Brighton	A	D	1-1	Clark	1
2		22	Brentford	H	D	1-1	Cameron	1
3		27	Southampton	H	W	4-0	Shepherd (2), Smith, Angell	1
4		30	Brentford	A	L	0-2		1
5	Sep	3	Shrewsbury Town	A	D	1-1	Shepherd	1
6		5	Crystal Palace	H	L	0-3		
7		10	Ipswich Town	H	D	1-1	Clark	1
8		14	Crystal Palace	A	D	1-1	Shepherd	1
9		17	Walsall	A	D	2-2	Smith, Clark	1
10		19	Northampton Town	A	L	2-5	Smith (2)	
11		24	Torquay United	H	W	3-1	Cameron (2), Smith	1
12		26	Swindon Town	H	W	1-0	Cameron	
13	Oct	1	Newport County	A	L	1-2	Smith	
14		8	Southend United	H	L	1-2	Shepherd	1
15		15	Exeter City	A	L	0-2		
16		22	Leyton Orient	H	L	0-1		1
17		29	Colchester United	A	L	1-4	Clark	
18	Nov	5	Norwich City	H	L	2-3	Petchey, Smith	1
19		12	Bournemouth	A	L	0-1		
20		26	Millwall	A	L	0-2		
21	Dec	3	Reading	H	D	3-3	Smith (2), Angell	
22		17	Brighton	H	W	2-1	Cameron, Clark	
23		24	Southampton	A	L	0-4		
24		26	Aldershot	A	W	2-1	Smith (2)	
25		27	Aldershot	H	D	2-2	Cameron (2)	
26		31	Shrewsbury Town	H	D	1-1	Smith	
27	Jan	7	Gillingham	H	D	2-2	Smith (2)	
28		14	Ipswich Town	A	L	1-4	Clark	1
29		21	Walsall	H	W	3-2	Petchey (2), Pounder	
30		28	Watford	A	W	1-0	Angell	
31	Feb	4	Torquay United	A	L	0-2		
32		11	Newport County	H	D	0-0		
33		18	Southend United	A	L	1-5	Smith	
34		25	Exeter City	H	W	1-0	Cameron	
35	Mar	3	Leyton Orient	A	L	1-7	Shepherd	1
36		10	Colchester United	H	W	6-2	Shepherd (2), Kerrins, Cameron, Smith, Petchey	
37		17	Norwich City	A	L	0-1		1
38		24	Bournemouth	H	L	0-1		
39		30	Coventry City	H	L	1-2	Cameron	1
40		31	Gillingham	A	W	2-0	Clark, Cameron	
41	Apr	3	Coventry City	A	L	1-4	Clark	1
42		7	Millwall	H	W	4-0	Clark, Shepherd, Ingham, Smith (pen)	1
43		14	Reading	A	L	1-3	Cameron	
44		21	Watford	H	W	3-2	Kerrins, Cameron, Angell	
45		25	Swindon Town	A	W	1-0	Smith	
46		28	Northampton Town	H	W	3-2	Clark (2), Smith	

Appeara

FA Cup

R1	Nov	19	Southend United	A	L	0-2		1

Appeara

Southern Floodlight Cup

R1	Oct	31	Leyton Orient	H	L	0-1		

Appeara

Total - Appeara

Total -

Brown	Cameron	Clark	Crickson	Dawson	Dean	Hellawell	Ingham	Kerrins	Longbottom	McKay	Nelson	Petchey	Pounder	Powell	Quinn	Rhodes	Rutter	Shepherd	Smith	Springett	Temby	Tomkys	Woods
1	10	9					3	7	8			4		5				11					2
1	10	9	4				3	7	8					5				11					2
1	10	9					3	7				4		5				11	8				2
1	10				9		3			7		4		5				11	8				2
1	10	9					3	7				4		5	8			11					2
1	10	9					3	7				4		5	8			11					2
1	8	9					3	7				4		5	10			11					2
1	10	9					3			7		4		5				11	8				2
1	10	9					3			7		4		5				11	8				2
1	10	9					3					4	7	5				11	8				2
1	10	9					3			7	2	4		5				11	8				
1	10	9					3	7				4		5				11	8				2
1	10	9					3	7				6		5				11	8				2
1	10	9					3			7		4		5				11	8				2
1	10	9					3		7			4					5	11	8				2
1	10	9					3	11	8			4	7				5						2
1	10	9									3	4					5	11	8			7	2
	10						3					9					5	11	8	1	4	7	2
	10						3		7			9					5	11	8	1	4		2
1	10		4		8		3					9	7	5				11					2
1	4						3				2	9	7	5	10			11	8				
1	10	9					3				2	4	7				5	11	8				
1	10	9					3				2	4	7				5	11	8				
1	10						3					4	7				5	11	8			9	2
	10	9					3	11				4	7				5		8	1			2
	10	9					3					4	7				5	11	8	1			2
1	10	9			6		3					4	7				5		8				2
1	10	9			6		3					4	7				5		8				2
1	8	9					3					4	7				5	11	10				2
1		9							8		3	4	7				5		10			11	2
1		9							8		3	4	7				5		10			11	2
1		9							8		3	4	7				5		10			11	2
1		9							8		3	4	7				5		10			11	2
1	9					11	3		8			4	7				5		10				2
1	9						3		8			4	7				5	11	10				2
1	10	9		6			3	7				4		5				11	8				2
1	10	9					3	7				4		5				11	8				2
1	10	9	4				3	7						5				11	8				2
1	10	9			4		3	11	8	7				5									2
1	10	9			4		3	11	8				7	5									2
1	10	9			4		3							5				11	8			7	2
	10	9			6		3	7				4		5				11	8	1			2
	10	9			6		3	7				4		5		2		11	8	1			
	10	9			6		3	7				4		5		2			8	1			
	10	9			6		3	7				4				2	5		8	1			
	10	9			6		3	7				4				2	5		8	1			
37	42	38	3	1	12	1	41	20	13	6	9	41	19	25	4	4	21	32	37	9	2	8	38
	13	11					1	2				4	1					9	19				
1	10		4		8		3					9	7				5	11					2
1	1		1		1		1					1	1				1	1					1
1	10	9					3					4					5	11	8			7	2
1	1	1					1					1					1	1	1			1	1
39	44	39	4	1	13	1	43	20	13	6	9	43	20	25	4	4	23	34	38	9	2	9	40
	13	11					1	2				4	1					9	19				

1956-57

Division Three South

	P	W	D	L	F	A	Pts
Ipswich Town	46	25	9	12	101	54	59
Torquay United	46	24	11	11	89	64	59
Colchester United	46	22	14	10	84	56	58
Southampton	46	22	10	14	76	52	54
Bournemouth	46	19	14	13	88	62	52
Brighton & Hove Albion	46	19	14	13	86	65	52
Southend United	46	18	12	16	73	65	48
Brentford	46	16	16	14	78	76	48
Shrewsbury Town	46	15	18	13	72	79	48
Queen's Park Rangers	46	18	11	17	61	60	47
Watford	46	18	10	18	72	75	46
Newport County	46	16	13	17	65	62	45
Reading	46	18	9	19	80	81	45
Northampton Town	46	18	9	19	66	73	45
Walsall	46	16	12	18	80	74	44
Coventry City	46	16	12	18	74	84	44
Millwall	46	16	12	18	64	84	44
Plymouth Argyle	46	16	11	19	68	73	43
Aldershot	46	15	12	19	79	92	42
Crystal Palace	46	11	18	17	62	75	40
Exeter City	46	12	13	21	61	79	37
Gillingham	46	12	13	21	54	85	37
Swindon Town	46	15	6	25	66	96	36
Norwich City	46	8	15	23	61	94	31

Attendances

TOTAL	Home	Away	Total
League	212,466	231,536	444,002
Cup/Other	9,764	42,027	51,791
TOTAL	222,230	273,563	495,793

AVERAGE	Home	Away	Total
League	9,238	10,067	9,652
Cup/Other	9,764	21,014	17,264
TOTAL	9,260	10,943	10,118

Match No.	Date		Opponents	Location	Result		Scorers	Atten
1	Aug	18	Reading	A	L	0-1		11
2		20	Plymouth Argyle	A	W	2-1	Angell, Longbottom	15
3		25	Newport County	H	D	1-1	Hellawell	7
4		27	Plymouth Argyle	H	W	3-0	Quigley (2), Hellawell	8
5	Sep	1	Colchester United	A	D	1-1	Quigley	8
6		6	Northampton Town	A	L	0-3		7
7		8	Norwich City	H	W	3-1	Angell, Locke, Quigley	12
8		10	Northampton Town	H	W	1-0	Longbottom	10
9		15	Coventry City	A	L	1-5	Quigley	18
10		19	Swindon Town	A	L	0-1		8
11		22	Southampton	H	L	1-2	Hellawell	12
12		24	Swindon Town	H	W	3-0	Quigley (2), Temby	9
13		29	Exeter City	A	D	0-0		7
14	Oct	6	Aldershot	A	L	2-4	Cameron, Hellawell	5
15		13	Watford	H	W	3-1	Hellawell, Balogun, OG (Brown)	14
16		20	Shrewsbury Town	A	D	0-0		8
17		27	Walsall	H	W	1-0	Kerrins	9
18	Nov	3	Ipswich Town	A	L	0-4		12
19		10	Bournemouth	H	W	2-1	Petchey, Locke	8
20		24	Millwall	H	D	0-0		10
21	Dec	1	Brighton	A	L	0-1		9
22		15	Reading	H	D	1-1	Peacock	5
23		22	Newport County	A	D	1-1	Peacock	7
24		25	Crystal Palace	A	L	1-2	Peacock	9
25		26	Crystal Palace	H	W	4-2	Cameron (2), Kerrins (2)	5
26		29	Colchester United	H	D	1-1	Kerrins	8
27	Jan	12	Norwich City	A	W	2-1	Longbottom, OG (Pointer)	11
28		19	Coventry City	H	D	1-1	Petchey	7
29	Feb	2	Southampton	A	W	2-1	Hellawell, Longbottom	17
30		9	Exeter City	H	W	5-3	Longbottom (3), Kerrins, Andrews	8
31		16	Aldershot	H	L	0-1		10
32		23	Watford	A	W	4-2	Temby, Cameron, Balogun, OG (Shipwright)	4
33	Mar	2	Shrewsbury Town	H	W	2-1	Balogun, Temby	9
34		9	Gillingham	A	W	1-0	Kerrins	7
35		16	Ipswich Town	H	L	0-2		12
36		23	Bournemouth	A	L	0-1		12
37		25	Southend United	H	W	3-0	Peacock, Longbottom, Hellawell	6
38		30	Torquay United	H	L	0-1		9
39	Apr	6	Millwall	A	L	0-2		10
40		13	Brighton	H	D	0-0		6
41		15	Southend United	A	L	0-3		6
42		19	Brentford	A	L	0-2		13
43		20	Walsall	A	W	2-0	Longbottom (2)	7
44		22	Brentford	H	D	2-2	Longbottom, OG (Dargie)	9
45		27	Torquay United	A	L	0-3		8
46		29	Gillingham	H	W	5-0	Longbottom (3), Kerrins, Cameron	6
								Appearan
								G

FA Cup

R1	Nov	17	Dorchester	H	W	4-0	Hellawell, Balogun, Locke, Cameron	9
R2	Dec	8	Tooting & Mitcham	A	W	2-0	Balogun, Longbottom	11
R3	Jan	5	Sunderland	A	L	0-4		30
								Appearan
								G

Southern Floodlight Cup

R1	Oct	8	Millwall	H	W	5-2	Balogun (2), Locke (2), Woods (pen)	5
R2	Nov	26	Reading	H	L	1-2	OG (McLaren)	3
								Appearan
								G

Total - Appearan
Total - G

ngell	Balogun	Cameron	Dawson	Dean	Hellawell	Ingham	Kerrins	Lay	Locke	Longbottom	Peacock	Petchey	Powell	Quigley	Quinn	Rhodes	Rutter	Springett	Temby	Woods	OG
1		10			7	3						4	5	9	8			1		2	
1					7	3				8		4		9	10		5	1		2	
1					7	3				8		4		9	10		5	1		2	
1					7	3			10	8		4		9			5	1		2	
1					7	3			10	8		4		9			5	1		2	
1					7	3			10	8		4		9			5	1		2	
1					7	3			10	8		4		9			5	1		2	
1					7	3			10	8		4		9			5	1		2	
1					7	3			10	8		4		9			5	1		2	
					7	3	11			8		4		9	10		5	1		2	
					7	3	11		10	8		4		9			5	1		2	
					7	3	11		10			4		9			5	1	8	2	
1					7	3			10			4		9			5	1	8	2	
1		8			7	3			10			4		9			5	1		2	
	9	8			7	3	11		10			4					5	1		2	
	9	8			7	3	11		10			4					5	1		2	
	9	8			7	3	11		10			4					5	1		2	
	9	8			7	3	11		10			4					5	1		2	
	9	8			7	3	11		10			4					5	1		2	
1	9				7	3			10	8		4					5	1		2	
1					7	3			10	8		4		9			5	1		2	
		10			7	3	11			8	9	4					5	1		2	
		10			7	3	11			8	9	4					5	1		2	
		10			7	3	11			8	9	4					5	1		2	
		9			7	3	11	5	10	8		4						1		2	
		9			7	3	11		10	8		4					5	1		2	
		10			7	3	11			8	9	4					5	1		2	
		10			7	3	11			8	9	4					5	1		2	
		10			7	3	11			8	9	4					5	1		2	
		10			7	3	11			8	9	4					5	1		2	
		10			7	3	11			8	9	4					5	1		2	
	9	10			7	3	11					4					5	1	8	2	
	9	10			7	3	11					4					5	1	8	2	
	9	10			7	3	11			8		4					5	1		2	
	9	10			7	3	11			8		4					5	1		2	
	9	10			7	3	11			8		4					5	1		2	
		10		4	7	3	11			8	9						5	1		2	
		10		4	7	3	11			8	9						5	1		2	
		10		4	7	3	11			8				9			5	1		2	
	9	10	7			3	11			8		4					5	1		2	
	9	10			7	3	11			8		4				2	5	1			
		9		10	7	3	11			8		4					5	1		2	
1		10				3	7			8	9	4					5	1		2	
1					7	3			10	8	9	4					5	1		2	
1		10			7	3				8	9	4					5	1		2	
		10			7	3	11			8	9	4					5	1		2	
6	13	31	1	4	44	46	31	1	20	35	14	43	1	16	4	1	44	46	4	45	
2	3	5			7		7		2	14	4	2		7					3		4
	9	8			7	3	11		10			4					5	1		2	
	9	10			7	3	11			8		4					5	1		2	
		10			7	3	11			8	9	4					5	1		2	
	2	3			3	3	3		1	2	1	3					3	3		3	
	2	1			1				1	1											
1	9	8			7	3			10			4					5	1		2	
1					7	3			10	8		4		9			5	1		2	
2	1	1			2	2			2	1		2		1			2	2		2	
	2								2											1	1
8	16	35	1	4	49	51	34	1	23	38	15	48	1	17	4	1	49	51	4	50	
2	7	6			8		7		5	15	4	2		7					3	1	5

1957-58

Division Three South

	P	W	D	L	F	A	Pts
Brighton & Hove Albion	46	24	12	10	88	64	60
Brentford	46	24	10	12	82	56	58
Plymouth Argyle	46	25	8	13	67	48	58
Swindon Town	46	21	15	10	79	50	57
Reading	46	21	13	12	79	51	55
Southampton	46	22	10	14	112	72	54
Southend United	46	21	12	13	90	58	54
Norwich City	46	19	15	12	75	70	53
Bournemouth	46	21	9	16	81	74	51
Queen's Park Rangers	46	18	14	14	64	65	50
Newport County	46	17	14	15	73	67	48
Colchester United	46	17	13	16	77	79	47
Northampton Town	46	19	6	21	87	79	44
Crystal Palace	46	15	13	18	70	72	43
Port Vale	46	16	10	20	67	58	42
Watford	46	13	16	17	59	77	42
Shrewsbury Town	46	15	10	21	49	71	40
Aldershot	46	12	16	18	59	89	40
Coventry City	46	13	13	20	61	81	39
Walsall	46	14	9	23	61	75	37
Torquay United	46	11	13	22	49	74	35
Gillingham	46	13	9	24	52	81	35
Millwall	46	11	9	26	63	91	31
Exeter City	46	11	9	26	57	99	31

Attendances

TOTAL	Home	Away	Total
League	215,875	251,072	466,947
Cup/Other	12,786	22,000	34,786
TOTAL	228,661	273,072	501,733

AVERAGE	Home	Away	Total
League	9,386	10,916	10,151
Cup/Other	12,786	11,000	11,595
TOTAL	9,528	10,923	10,239

Match No.	Date		Opponents	Location	Result		Scorers
1	Aug	24	Brentford	H	W	1-0	Petchey
2		26	Colchester United	H	W	1-0	Cameron
3		31	Southend United	A	L	0-6	
4	Sep	2	Colchester United	A	L	1-2	Finney
5		7	Brighton	H	L	0-1	
6		11	Swindon Town	A	D	1-1	Angell
7		14	Southampton	A	L	0-5	
8		16	Swindon Town	H	W	2-1	Locke (2)
9		21	Newport County	H	D	1-1	Woods
10		23	Millwall	H	W	3-0	Locke (3)
11		28	Port Vale	A	L	1-2	Locke
12		30	Millwall	A	L	0-5	
13	Oct	5	Plymouth Argyle	H	W	1-0	Locke
14		12	Norwich City	A	L	0-2	
15		19	Bournemouth	H	W	3-0	Angell, Woods, OG (Woollard)
16		26	Walsall	A	W	2-1	Longbottom (2)
17	Nov	2	Coventry City	H	W	3-0	Kerrins (2), Locke
18		9	Shrewsbury Town	A	L	1-2	Longbottom
19		23	Northampton Town	A	W	5-1	Longbottom (4), Smith
20		30	Watford	H	W	3-0	Ingham, Longbottom, Petchey
21	Dec	14	Torquay United	H	D	1-1	Woods
22		21	Brentford	A	D	1-1	Cameron
23		25	Gillingham	A	D	1-1	Standley
24		26	Gillingham	H	D	1-1	Woods
25		28	Southend United	H	D	1-1	Standley
26	Jan	11	Brighton	A	D	1-1	Longbottom
27		18	Southampton	H	W	3-2	Longbottom (2), Woods (pen)
28		25	Reading	A	L	0-3	
29	Feb	1	Newport County	A	L	2-4	Dawson, Longbottom
30		8	Port Vale	H	W	2-1	Cameron, Longbottom
31		15	Plymouth Argyle	A	L	1-3	Cameron
32		22	Norwich City	H	D	1-1	Cameron
33	Mar	1	Bournemouth	A	L	1-4	Dawson
34		3	Aldershot	H	L	0-1	
35		8	Walsall	H	W	1-0	Cameron
36		15	Coventry City	A	D	1-1	Locke
37		17	Reading	H	W	3-0	Woods, Longbottom, Petchey
38		22	Northampton Town	H	W	1-0	Longbottom
39		29	Torquay United	A	L	1-3	Locke
40	Apr	4	Exeter City	H	D	1-1	Cameron
41		7	Exeter City	A	D	0-0	
42		12	Watford	A	D	0-0	
43		16	Crystal Palace	A	W	3-2	Longbottom, Kerrins, Locke
44		19	Crystal Palace	H	W	4-2	Kerrins, Longbottom, Cameron, Locke
45		24	Aldershot	A	D	1-1	Kerrins
46		28	Shrewsbury Town	H	W	3-0	Kerrins (2), Locke

Appeara
G

FA Cup

R1	Nov	16	Clapton	A	D	1-1	Dawson
rep		18	Clapton	H	W	3-1	Longbottom, Locke, OG (Walsh)
R2	Dec	7	Hereford United	A	L	1-6	Smith

Appeara
G

Southern Floodlight Cup

R1	Oct	4	Reading	H	D	0-0	
rep	Nov	6	Reading	A	L	2-5	Kerrins, Locke

Appeara
G

Total - Appeara
Total - G

Andrews	Angell	Cameron	Colgan	Dawson	Drinkwater	Finney	Fry	Ingham	Kerrins	Locke	Longbottom	Orr	Peacock	Petchey	Powell	Rutter	Smith	Springett	Standley	Tomkys	Woods	OG
6	11	8				9		3			7			4		5	10	1			2	
6	11	8				9		3			7			4		5	10	1			2	
6	11	8				9		3			7			4		5	10	1			2	
6	11					9		3			8			4		5	10	1			2	
6	11					9		3	7		8			4		5	10	1			2	
6	11					10		3	7		8		9	4		5		1			2	
6	11					10		3	7		8		9	4		5		1			2	
	6	9				8		3	7	10		11		4		5		1			2	
	6	8				9		3	7	10		11		4		5		1			2	
6	11	8						3		10	7			4		5	9	1			2	
6	11	8						3		10	7			4		5	9	1			2	
6	11	8						3		10	7			4		5	9	1			2	
	6	8		7				3	11	10				4		5	9	1			2	
	6	8		7				3	11	10				4		5	9	1			2	
	6	8		7				3	11	10				4		5	9	1			2	
	6			7				3	11	10	8			4		5	9	1			2	
	6			7				3	11	10	8			4		5	9	1			2	
	6			7				3	11	10	8			4		5	9	1			2	
	6	9		7				3	11		8			4		5	10	1			2	
	6	9		7				3	11		8			4		5	10	1			2	
	6	9		7			1	3	11		8			4		5	10				2	
	6	10		7				3	11		8			4		5		1	9		2	
	6	10		7				3	11		8			4		5		1	9		2	
6		10		7				3	11		8			4		5		1	9		2	
	6	10	2	7				3	11		8			4		5		1	9			
	6	9		7				3	11		8			4		5	10	1			2	
	6	10		7				3	11		8			4		5		1	9		2	
	6	10		7				3	11		8			4		5		1	9		2	
	6	10		7				3	11		8			4		5		1	9		2	
	6	10		7				3	11		8			4		5		1	9		2	
	6	10		7				3	11		8			4		5		1	9		2	
	6	10		7		8		3	11					4		5		1	9		2	
	6	10	2	7				3	11		8			4		5		1	9			
	6	10		7				3	11		8			4		5		1	9		2	
	6	9		7				3		10	8			4		5		1		11	2	
11	6			7	1			3		10	8			4		5				9	2	
	6			7	1			3		10	8			4	9	5				11	2	
	6	9		7	1			3		10	8			4		5				11	2	
	6	9		7	1			3		10	8			4		5				11	2	
	6	9		7	1			3		10	8	11		4		5					2	
	6	10			1			3		11	8	7		4		5			9		2	
	6	10		7	1			3		11	8			4		5			9		2	
	6	10		7	1			3	9	11	8			4		5					2	
	6	10		7	1			3	9	11	8			4		5					2	
	6	10		7	1			3	9		8	11		4		5					2	
	6	10		7	1			3	9	11	8			4		5					2	
12	45	37	2	33	11	10	1	46	31	22	40	5	2	46	1	46	18	34	14	5	44	
	2	8		2		1		1	7	13	17			3			1		2		6	1

Andrews	Angell	Cameron	Colgan	Dawson	Drinkwater	Finney	Fry	Ingham	Kerrins	Locke	Longbottom	Orr	Peacock	Petchey	Powell	Rutter	Smith	Springett	Standley	Tomkys	Woods	OG
	6	9		7				3	11	10	8			4		5		1			2	
	6	9		7				3	11	10	8			4		5		1			2	
6		9		7				3	11		8			4		5	10	1			2	
1	2	3		3				3	3	2	3			3		3	1	3			3	
				1						1	1						1					1

Andrews	Angell	Cameron	Colgan	Dawson	Drinkwater	Finney	Fry	Ingham	Kerrins	Locke	Longbottom	Orr	Peacock	Petchey	Powell	Rutter	Smith	Springett	Standley	Tomkys	Woods	OG
9	6	8		7				3	11					4		5	10	1			2	
	6			7			1	3	11	10	8			4		5	9				2	
1	2	1		2			1	2	2	1	1			2		2	2	1			2	
									1	1												

Andrews	Angell	Cameron	Colgan	Dawson	Drinkwater	Finney	Fry	Ingham	Kerrins	Locke	Longbottom	Orr	Peacock	Petchey	Powell	Rutter	Smith	Springett	Standley	Tomkys	Woods	OG
14	49	41	2	38	11	10	2	51	36	25	44	5	2	51	1	51	21	38	14	5	49	
	2	8		3		1		1	8	15	18			3			2		2		6	2

1958-59

Division Three

	P	W	D	L	F	A	Pts
Plymouth Argyle	46	23	16	7	89	59	62
Hull City	46	26	9	11	90	55	61
Brentford	46	21	15	10	76	49	57
Norwich City	46	22	13	11	89	62	57
Colchester United	46	21	10	15	71	67	52
Reading	46	21	8	17	78	63	50
Tranmere Rovers	46	21	8	17	82	67	50
Southend United	46	21	8	17	85	80	50
Halifax Town	46	21	8	17	80	77	50
Bury	46	17	14	15	69	58	48
Bradford City	46	18	11	17	84	76	47
Bournemouth	46	17	12	17	69	69	46
Queen's Park Rangers	46	19	8	19	74	77	46
Southampton	46	17	11	18	88	80	45
Swindon Town	46	16	13	17	59	57	45
Chesterfield	46	17	10	19	67	64	44
Newport County	46	17	9	20	69	68	43
Wrexham	46	14	14	18	63	77	42
Accrington Stanley	46	15	12	19	71	87	42
Mansfield Town	46	14	13	19	73	98	41
Stockport County	46	13	10	23	65	78	36
Doncaster Rovers	46	14	5	27	50	90	33
Notts County	46	8	13	25	55	96	29
Rochdale	46	8	12	26	37	79	28

Attendances

TOTAL

	Home	Away	Total
League	210,462	244,292	454,754
Cup/Other	13,166	15,123	28,289
TOTAL	223,628	259,415	483,043

AVERAGE

	Home	Away	Total
League	9,151	10,621	9,886
Cup/Other	13,166	15,123	14,145
TOTAL	9,318	10,809	10,063

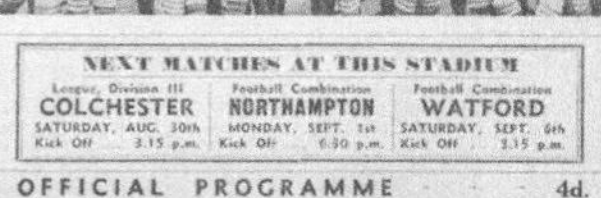

Match No.	Date		Opponents	Location	Result		Scorers	Atten
1	Aug	23	Reading	A	D	2-2	Longbottom (2)	16
2		25	Tranmere Rovers	H	D	1-1	Cameron	12
3		30	Colchester United	H	W	4-2	Kerrins (2), Longbottom, Locke	9
4	Sep	1	Tranmere Rovers	A	L	0-2		13
5		6	Bournemouth	A	L	0-2		11
6		9	Doncaster Rovers	A	L	0-2		10
7		13	Norwich City	H	W	2-1	Longbottom, Kerrins	10
8		15	Doncaster Rovers	H	W	3-1	Longbottom, Cameron, Kerrins	10
9		20	Southend United	A	L	0-4		13
10		22	Stockport County	A	W	3-2	Longbottom (3)	7
11		27	Bury	H	W	2-1	Tomkys (2)	9
12		29	Stockport County	H	D	0-0		7
13	Oct	4	Mansfield Town	A	W	4-3	Longbottom, Dawson, Cameron, Angell	10
14		7	Rochdale	A	D	2-2	Cameron, Tomkys	4
15		11	Chesterfield	H	D	2-2	Kerrins, Tomkys	9
16		20	Newport County	A	L	1-3	Cameron	8
17		25	Halifax Town	H	W	3-1	Longbottom (3)	9
18	Nov	1	Accrington Stanley	A	W	4-2	Dawson (2), Tomkys, Longbottom	6
19		8	Southampton	H	D	2-2	Longbottom, Petchey	11
20		22	Brentford	H	L	1-2	Kerrins	13
21		29	Hull City	A	L	0-1		11
22	Dec	13	Swindon Town	A	L	0-2		8
23		20	Reading	H	W	2-0	Kerrins, Pearson	6
24		26	Plymouth Argyle	A	L	2-3	Angell, Tomkys	30
25		27	Plymouth Argyle	H	W	2-1	Pearson, Longbottom	15
26	Jan	3	Colchester United	A	L	0-3		8
27		17	Bournemouth	H	L	0-4		6
28		31	Norwich City	A	L	1-5	Longbottom	16
29	Feb	7	Southend United	H	L	1-3	Petchey	6
30		14	Bury	A	L	1-3	Clark	5
31		21	Mansfield Town	H	D	1-1	Locke	5
32		28	Chesterfield	A	W	3-2	Locke (2), Tomkys	8
33	Mar	7	Newport County	H	W	4-2	Longbottom (2), Locke, Angell	5
34		14	Halifax Town	A	L	1-2	Locke	5
35		16	Bradford City	H	W	3-0	Pearson (2), Whitelaw	7
36		21	Accrington Stanley	H	W	3-1	Anderson, Pearson, OG (Tighe)	8
37		27	Notts County	H	W	2-1	Whitelaw, Pearson	12
38		28	Southampton	A	L	0-1		9
39		30	Notts County	A	W	1-0	Angell (pen)	6
40	Apr	4	Wrexham	H	W	5-0	Anderson (2), Whitelaw, Angell (pen), Longbottom	8
41		8	Wrexham	A	L	0-1		5
42		11	Brentford	A	L	0-1		15
43		18	Hull City	H	D	1-1	Whitelaw	9
44		20	Rochdale	H	W	3-0	Angell, Longbottom, Whitelaw	7
45		25	Bradford City	A	L	0-1		6
46		27	Swindon Town	H	W	2-1	Angell, Tomkys	7

Appearan
G

FA Cup

R1	Nov	15	Walsall	A	W	1-0	Dawson	15
R2	Dec	6	Southampton	H	L	0-1		13

Appearar
G

Southern Floodlight Cup

R1	Oct	13	Fulham	H	L	0-4		8

Appearar
G

Total - Appearar
Total - G

Angell	Cameron	Clark	Colgan	Dawson	Drinkwater	Ingham	Kelly	Kerrins	Locke	Longbottom	Pearson	Petchey	Powell	Richardson	Rutter	Tomkys	Welton	Whitelaw	Woods	OG
6	10			7	1	3		9	11	8		4			5				2	
6	10			7	1	3		9	11	8		4			5				2	
6	10			7	1	3		9	11	8		4			5				2	
6	10			7	1	3		9		8	11	4			5				2	
6	10	11		7	1	3		9		8		4			5				2	
6	10			7	1	3		9	11	8		4			5				2	
6	10				1	3		9	11	8		4			5	7			2	
6	10			7	1	3		9	11	8		4			5				2	
6	10			7	1	3		9	11	8		4			5				2	
6	10			7	1	3		9		8		4			5	11			2	
6				7	1	3		9	10	8		4			5	11			2	
6	10			7	1	3		9	11	8		4			5				2	
6	10			7	1	3		9	11	8		4			5				2	
6	10			7	1	3		9		8		4			5	11			2	
6	10			7	1	3		9		8		4			5	11			2	
6	10			7	1	3		9		8		4			5	11			2	
6	10			7	1	3		9		8		4			5	11			2	
6	10			7	1	3		9		8		4			5	11			2	
6	10			7	1	3		9		8		4			5	11			2	
6	10			7	1	3		9		8		4			5	11			2	
6	10				1	3		9		8		4			5	11			2	
6	10				1	3	9	11		8		4			5	7			2	
6					1	3	9	11		8	10	4			5	7			2	
6					1	3	9	11		8	10	4			5	7			2	
6					1	3	9	11		8	10	4			5	7			2	
					1	3	9	11		8	10	4		6	5	7			2	
6					1	3	9	11		8	10	4	5		2	7				
6	9	11			1	3		7	10	8		4			5				2	
6		11		7		3		9		8	10	4			5		1		2	
6		11		7		3			10		8	4	5			9	1		2	
6		11		7		3			10	8		4	5			9	1		2	
6		11		7	1	3			10	8		4			5	9			2	
6		11		7	1	3			10	8		4			5	9			2	
6		11		7	1	3			10	8		4			5	9			2	
6		11			1	3			10		8	4			5			9	2	
6		11			1	3			10		8	4			5			9	2	
6		11			1	3			10		8	4			5			9	2	
6		11			1	3			10		8	4			5	7		9	2	
6			2		1	3			11	8	10	4			5			9		
6		11			1	3				8	10	4			5			9	2	
6		11			1	3				8	10	4			5			9	2	
6		11			1	3				8	10	4			5			9	2	
6		11			1	3			10	8		4			5			9	2	
6		11			1	3			10	8		4			5			9	2	
6		11			1	3			10	8		4	9		5	7			2	
6		11			1	3			10	8		4			5	7		9	2	
5	22	19	1	25	43	46	6	29	25	41	16	46	4	1	44	25	3	11	44	
7	5	1		3				7	6	20	6	2				8		5		1

Angell	Cameron	Clark	Colgan	Dawson	Drinkwater	Ingham	Kelly	Kerrins	Locke	Longbottom	Pearson	Petchey	Powell	Richardson	Rutter	Tomkys	Welton	Whitelaw	Woods	OG
6	10			7	1	3		9		8		4			5	11			2	
6	10			7	1	3		11		8		4			5	9			2	
2	2			2	2	2		2		2		2			2	2			2	
				1																

Angell	Cameron	Clark	Colgan	Dawson	Drinkwater	Ingham	Kelly	Kerrins	Locke	Longbottom	Pearson	Petchey	Powell	Richardson	Rutter	Tomkys	Welton	Whitelaw	Woods	OG
6	10			7	1	3		9		8		4			5	11			2	
1	1			1	1	1		1		1		1			1	1			1	

Angell	Cameron	Clark	Colgan	Dawson	Drinkwater	Ingham	Kelly	Kerrins	Locke	Longbottom	Pearson	Petchey	Powell	Richardson	Rutter	Tomkys	Welton	Whitelaw	Woods	OG
8	25	19	1	28	46	49	6	32	25	44	16	49	4	1	47	28	3	11	47	
7	5	1		4				7	6	20	6	2				8		5		1

1959-60

Division Three

	P	W	D	L	F	A	Pts
Southampton	46	26	9	11	106	75	61
Norwich City	46	24	11	11	82	54	59
Shrewsbury Town	46	18	16	12	97	75	52
Grimsby Town	46	18	16	12	87	70	52
Coventry City	46	21	10	15	78	63	52
Brentford	46	21	9	16	78	61	51
Bury	46	21	9	16	64	51	51
Queen's Park Rangers	46	18	13	15	73	54	49
Colchester United	46	18	11	17	83	74	47
Bournemouth	46	17	13	16	72	72	47
Reading	46	18	10	18	84	77	46
Southend United	46	19	8	19	76	74	46
Newport County	46	20	6	20	80	79	46
Port Vale	46	19	8	19	80	79	46
Halifax Town	46	18	10	18	70	72	46
Swindon Town	46	19	8	19	69	78	46
Barnsley	46	15	14	17	65	66	44
Chesterfield	46	18	7	21	71	84	43
Bradford City	46	15	12	19	66	74	42
Tranmere Rovers	46	14	13	19	72	75	41
York City	46	13	12	21	57	73	38
Mansfield Town	46	15	6	25	81	112	36
Wrexham	46	14	8	24	68	101	36
Accrington Stanley	46	11	5	30	57	123	27

Attendances

	TOTAL		
	Home	**Away**	**Total**
League	242,957	215,608	458,565
Cup/Other	11,143	18,379	29,522
TOTAL	254,100	233,987	488,087

	AVERAGE		
	Home	**Away**	**Total**
League	10,563	9,374	9,969
Cup/Other	11,143	9,190	9,841
TOTAL	10,588	9,359	9,961

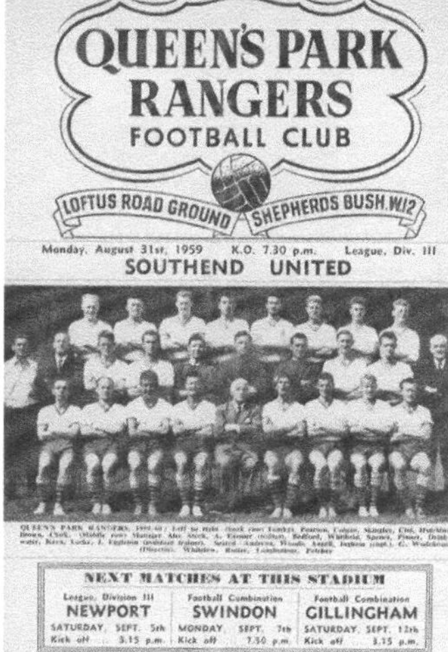

Match No.	Date		Opponents	Location	Result		Scorers	Atte
1	Aug	22	Swindon Town	H	W	2-0	Longbottom, Whitelaw	1
2		24	Southend United	A	L	2-3	Whitelaw (2)	1
3		29	Chesterfield	A	W	4-0	Pearson (2), Bedford, Whitelaw	
4		31	Southend United	H	D	0-0		1
5	Sep	5	Newport County	H	W	3-0	Bedford (2), Longbottom	1
6		7	York City	A	L	1-2	Pearson	1
7		12	Accrington Stanley	A	W	2-1	Andrews, Longbottom	
8		14	York City	H	D	0-0		1
9		19	Bournemouth	H	W	3-0	Bedford, Golding, OG (Nelson)	1
10		21	Coventry City	A	D	0-0		1
11		26	Tranmere Rovers	A	W	3-0	Golding (2), Bedford	1
12		28	Coventry City	H	W	2-1	Golding (2)	1
13	Oct	3	Wrexham	H	W	2-1	Angell (2)	1
14		5	Grimsby Town	H	D	0-0		1
15		10	Mansfield Town	A	L	3-4	Locke (2), Petchey	
16		13	Grimsby Town	A	L	1-3	Angell	
17		17	Halifax Town	H	W	3-0	Longbottom, Whitelaw, Petchey	1
18		24	Bury	A	L	0-2		1
19		31	Brentford	H	L	2-4	Bedford (2)	1
20	Nov	7	Southampton	A	L	1-2	Bedford	1
21		21	Shrewsbury Town	A	D	1-1	Bedford	1
22		28	Port Vale	H	D	2-2	Bedford (2)	
23	Dec	12	Barnsley	A	L	1-2	Bedford	
24		19	Swindon Town	A	L	1-2	Andrews	
25		26	Colchester United	H	W	3-1	Bedford (2), Angell	
26		28	Colchester United	A	L	0-2		
27	Jan	16	Newport County	A	W	3-2	Bedford (3)	
28		23	Accrington Stanley	H	W	5-1	Andrews (2), Kerrins, Locke, Bedford	
29		30	Norwich City	A	L	0-1		1
30	Feb	6	Bournemouth	A	D	1-1	Bedford	
31		13	Tranmere Rovers	H	W	2-1	Andrews, Keen	
32		27	Mansfield Town	H	W	2-0	Woods (pen), Longbottom	
33	Mar	5	Halifax Town	A	L	1-3	Wooods (pen)	
34		7	Reading	H	W	2-0	Andrews, Bedford	
35		12	Bury	H	W	2-0	Cini, Andrews	
36		19	Port Vale	A	D	0-0		
37		26	Southampton	H	L	0-1		1
38		28	Chesterfield	H	D	3-3	Bedford (2), Petchey	1
39	Apr	2	Reading	A	L	0-2		
40		9	Shrewsbury Town	H	D	1-1	Bedford	
41		15	Bradford City	H	W	5-0	Bedford (2), Longbottom, Petchey, Andrews	
42		16	Brentford	A	D	1-1	Golding	1
43		18	Bradford City	A	L	1-3	Andrews	
44		23	Norwich City	H	D	0-0		1
45		30	Barnsley	H	W	1-0	Andrews	
46	May	4	Wrexham	A	D	1-1	Woods	

Appeara
G

FA Cup

R1	Nov	14	Colchester United	A	W	3-2	Petchey, Bedford, Angell	
R2	Dec	5	Port Vale	H	D	3-3	Longbottom (2), Bedford	1
rep		7	Port Vale	A	L	1-2	Andrews	

Appeara
G

Southern Floodlight Cup

R1	Oct	26	Leyton Orient	H	L	1-2	Longbottom	

Appeara
G

Total - Appeara
Total - G

Angell	Bedford	Cini	Clark	Collins	Drinkwater	Golding	Hasty	Ingham	Keen	Kerrins	Locke	Longbottom	Pearson	Petchey	Pinner	Rutter	Whitelaw	Whitfield	Woods	OG
6	10	7						3				8		4	1	5	9		2	
6	10	7						3				8		4	1	5	9		2	
6	8							3				7	10	4	1	5	9		2	
6	8		11					3				7		4	1	5	9		2	
6	8							3				7	10	4	1	5	9		2	
	8							3	6			7	10	4	1	5	9		2	
6	8							3				7	10	4	1	5	9		2	
6	8					7		3					10	4	1	5	9		2	
6	10					7		3				8		4	1	5	9		2	
6	10					7		3				8		4	1	5	9		2	
6	9				1	7		3				8		4		5		10	2	
6	9					7		3				8		4	1	5		10	2	
6	9					7		3				8		4	1	5		10	2	
6						7		3	10			8		4	1	5	9		2	
6					1	7		3	10		9	8		4		5			2	
6	10							3			7	8		4	1	5	9		2	
6	10					7		3				8		4	1	5	9		2	
6	10					7		3				8		4	1	5	9		2	
6	10					7		3				8		4	1	5	9		2	
6	10				1	7		3	9			8		4		5			2	
6	10				1	7		3	4					9		5		8	2	
6	10		7					3	4					9	1	5		8	2	
6	10		7		1			3	4			8		9		5			2	
	9		7		1			3	6			8		4		5		10	2	
6	10	7			1		9	3				8		4		5			2	
6	9	7			1			3			11	8		4		5			2	
	9				1			3	4	7	11	8		6		5			2	
	9				1			3	4	7	11	8		6		5			2	
	9				1			3	4	7	11	8				5		6	2	
	9				1			3	4	7	11	8		6		5			2	
	9		11		1			3	4	7		8		6		5			2	
6	9		11		1			3	4	7		8				5			2	
10	9				1	7		3	4			8		6		5			2	
6	9	8	11		1			3	4			7				5			2	
6	9	8	11		1			3	4			7				5			2	
6	8	7	11		1			3	4					9		5			2	
6	9		11		1			3	4	7	8					5			2	
6	8		11		1			3	4		7			9		5			2	
6	9		11		1	7		3	4					8		5			2	
6	9		11		1	7		3				8		4		5			2	
	9		11		1	7		3	4			8		6		5			2	
	9		11		1	7		3	4			8		6		5			2	
	9		11		1	7		3	4			8		6		5			2	
	9		11		1	7		3	4			8		6		5			2	
	9		11	8	1	7		3	4					6		5			2	
	9		11	8	1	7		3	4					6		5			2	
33	44	7	18	2	27	22	1	46	27	7	10	37	5	41	19	46	15	7	46	
4	25	1				6			1	1	3	6	3	4			5		3	1

Angell	Bedford	Cini	Clark	Collins	Drinkwater	Golding	Hasty	Ingham	Keen	Kerrins	Locke	Longbottom	Pearson	Petchey	Pinner	Rutter	Whitelaw	Whitfield	Woods	OG
6	10					7		3	4			8		9	1	5			2	
6	9		7					3	4			8			1	5		10	2	
6	9		7		1			3	4			8				5		10	2	
3	3		2		1	1		3	3			3		1	2	3		2	3	
1	2											2		1						

Angell	Bedford	Cini	Clark	Collins	Drinkwater	Golding	Hasty	Ingham	Keen	Kerrins	Locke	Longbottom	Pearson	Petchey	Pinner	Rutter	Whitelaw	Whitfield	Woods	OG
6	10					7		3				8		4	1	5	9		2	
1	1					1		1				1		1	1	1	1		1	
												1								

Angell	Bedford	Cini	Clark	Collins	Drinkwater	Golding	Hasty	Ingham	Keen	Kerrins	Locke	Longbottom	Pearson	Petchey	Pinner	Rutter	Whitelaw	Whitfield	Woods	OG
37	48	7	21	2	29	24	1	50	30	7	9	41	5	43	21	50	16	9	50	
5	27	1				6			1	1	3	9	3	5			5		3	1

1960-61

Division Three

	P	W	D	L	F	A	Pts
Bury	46	30	8	8	108	45	68
Walsall	46	28	6	12	98	60	62
Queen's Park Rangers	46	25	10	11	93	60	60
Watford	46	20	12	14	85	72	52
Notts County	46	21	9	16	82	77	51
Grimsby Town	46	20	10	16	77	69	50
Port Vale	46	17	15	14	96	79	49
Barnsley	46	21	7	18	83	80	49
Halifax Town	46	16	17	13	71	78	49
Shrewsbury Town	46	15	16	15	83	75	46
Hull City	46	17	12	17	73	73	46
Torquay United	46	14	17	15	75	83	45
Newport County	46	17	11	18	81	90	45
Bristol City	46	17	10	19	70	68	44
Coventry City	46	16	12	18	80	83	44
Swindon Town	46	14	15	17	62	55	43
Brentford	46	13	17	16	56	70	43
Reading	46	14	12	20	72	83	40
Bournemouth	46	15	10	21	58	76	40
Southend United	46	14	11	21	60	76	39
Tranmere Rovers	46	15	8	23	79	115	38
Bradford City	46	11	14	21	65	87	36
Colchester United	46	11	11	24	68	101	33
Chesterfield	46	10	12	24	67	87	32

Attendances

TOTAL

	Home	Away	Total
League	229,099	234,247	463,346
Cup/Other	20,900	6,800	27,700
TOTAL	249,999	241,047	491,046

AVERAGE

	Home	Away	Total
League	9,961	10,185	10,073
Cup/Other	6,967	6,800	6,925
TOTAL	9,615	10,044	9,821

Match No.	Date		Opponents	Location	Result		Scorers	Atten
1	Aug	20	Bournemouth	A	L	0-1		12
2		25	Notts County	A	L	1-2	Andrews	15
3		27	Bradford City	H	W	1-0	Bedford	7
4		29	Notts County	H	W	2-0	Clark (2)	8
5	Sep	3	Barnsley	A	D	3-3	Whitfield (2), Bedford	6
6		5	Coventry City	A	D	4-4	Bedford (2), Andrews, Clark	15
7		10	Newport County	H	W	2-0	Whitfield, Barber	7
8		12	Coventry City	H	W	2-1	Bedford, Woods	9
9		17	Colchester United	A	W	1-0	Lazarus	5
10		19	Brentford	H	D	0-0		12
11		24	Grimsby Town	H	W	2-0	Andrews, Longbottom	10
12		27	Brentford	A	L	0-2		15
13	Oct	1	Hull City	A	L	1-3	Bedford	9
14		3	Reading	H	W	5-2	Bedford (2), Lazarus (2), Barber	8
15		8	Torquay United	H	D	3-3	Lazarus (2), Bedford	7
16		15	Port Vale	A	W	1-0	Bedford	8
17		22	Southend United	H	W	2-1	Woods (pen), Bedford	6
18		29	Chesterfield	A	W	1-0	Carey	4
19	Nov	12	Walsall	A	L	3-4	Bedford (2), Lazarus	10
20		19	Shrewsbury Town	H	D	1-1	Bedford	7
21	Dec	3	Tranmere Rovers	H	W	9-2	Bedford (2), Clark (2), Lazarus (2), Evans (2), Andrews	4
22		10	Watford	A	W	3-0	Lazarus, Woods (pen), Clark	15
23		17	Bournemouth	H	W	3-1	Bedford (2), Evans	6
24		26	Bristol City	A	D	1-1	Bedford	10
25		27	Bristol City	H	D	1-1	Woods (pen)	15
26		31	Bradford City	A	D	1-1	Evans	8
27	Jan	14	Barnsley	H	W	4-2	Bedford, Andrews, Evans, Keen	8
28		23	Newport County	A	W	3-1	Evans (2), Bedford	6
29		28	Bury	H	W	3-1	Bedford (3)	14
30	Feb	4	Colchester United	H	W	3-2	Evans, Bedford, Lazarus	10
31		11	Grimsby Town	A	L	1-3	Bedford	10
32		18	Hull City	H	W	2-1	Keen, Bedford	12
33		25	Tranmere Rovers	A	W	2-1	Evans, Woods (pen)	9
34	Mar	4	Port Vale	H	W	1-0	Evans	12
35		11	Southend United	A	D	0-0		10
36		18	Chesterfield	H	L	1-2	Bedford	8
37		25	Bury	A	L	0-1		14
38		31	Swindon Town	H	W	3-1	Angell, Barber, Evans	14
39	Apr	1	Walsall	H	W	1-0	Longbottom	14
40		3	Swindon Town	A	L	0-1		11
41		8	Shrewsbury Town	A	L	1-4	Evans	8
42		15	Halifax Town	H	W	5-1	Bedford (4), Lazarus	9
43		17	Halifax Town	A	D	1-1	Andrews	4
44		22	Torquay United	A	W	6-1	Evans (3), Lazarus, Bedford, OG (Bettany)	5
45		26	Reading	A	L	1-3	Longbottom	15
46		29	Watford	H	W	2-1	Evans, Longbottom	10

Appearar

G

FA Cup

R1	Nov	5	Walthamstow Avenue	H	W	3-2	Bedford (3)	5
R2		26	Coventry City	H	W	1-2	Longbottom	8

Appearar

G

League Cup

R1	Oct	17	Port Vale	H	D	2-2	Lazarus, Rutter	6
rep		19	Port Vale	A	L	1-3	Bedford	6

Appearar

G

Total - Appearar

Total - G

Angell	Baker	Barber	Bedford	Bottoms	Carey	Clark	Cockell	Drinkwater	Evans	Golding	Ingham	Keen	Lazarus	Longbottom	Pinner	Rutter	Whitaker	Whitfield	Woods	OG
6			9		2	11		1		7	3	4		8		5				
6			9		2	11		1		7	3	4		8		5				
6			10		4	11		1		7	3			8		5		9	2	
6			9		4	11		1		7	3			8		5			2	
6			8		4	11		1		7	3					5		9	2	
6		7	8		4	11		1			3					5		9	2	
6		7	8		4	11		1			3					5		9	2	
6		7	8		4	11		1			3					5		9	2	
6			8		4	11		1			3		7			5		9	2	
6			8		4			1			3		7	10		5		9	2	
6					4	11		1			3		7	8		5		9	2	
6					4	11		1			3		7	8		5		9	2	
6			8		4	11		1		7	3					5		9	2	
6		7	9			11		1			3	4	8			5			2	
6		7	9			11		1			3	4	8			5			2	
6		7	9	10		11		1			3	4	8			5			2	
6		7	9			11		1			3	4	8	10		5			2	
6		11	10		8			1			3	4	7			5		9	2	
6			10		8			1			3	4	7	11		5		9	2	
6			10				4	1	9		3	8	7	11		5			2	
6			8			11		1	9		3	4	7			5			2	
6			8			11		1	9		3	4	7			5			2	
6			8			11		1	9		3	4	7			5			2	
6			8					1	9		3	4	7	11		5			2	
6			8			11		1	9		3	4	7			5			2	
6			8			11	4	1	9		3		7			5			2	
6			8				4	1	9		3	10	7			5			2	
6			8				4	1	9		3	10	7			5			2	
6			8				4	1	9		3	10		7		5			2	
6			8				4	1	9		3	10	7			5			2	
6		7	8	10				1	9		3	4		11		5			2	
6			8					1	9		3	4	7	10		5	11		2	
6			8					1	9	7	3	4		10		5	11		2	
6	2		8					1	9	7	3	4		10		5	11			
6	2		8					1	9		3	4	7	10		5	11			
6	2		8					1	9		3	4	7			5	11			
6	2		8				4	1	9		3	10		7		5				
1	2	7	8				6	1	9		3	4				5				
6	2		8					1	9		3	4		7		5	11			
6	2		8					1	9		3	4		7		5	11			
6	2		8					1	9		3	4	7	11		5	10			
6	2		10					1	9		3	4	7	8		5				
6	2		10					1	9		3	4	7	8		5				
6	2		10					1	9		3	4	7	8		5				
6	2	11	10					1	9		3	4	7	8		5				
6	2	11	10					1	9		3	4	7	8		5				
6	13	12	44	2	15	21	8	46	27	8	46	34	29	26		46	8	12	31	
		3	33		1	6			16			2	12	4				3	5	1

Angell	Baker	Barber	Bedford	Bottoms	Carey	Clark	Cockell	Drinkwater	Evans	Golding	Ingham	Keen	Lazarus	Longbottom	Pinner	Rutter	Whitaker	Whitfield	Woods	OG
6			10		8			1			3	4	7			5		9	2	
			10			11	6	1			3	4	7	8		5		9	2	
			2		1	1	1	2			2	2	2	1		2		2	2	
			3											1						

Angell	Baker	Barber	Bedford	Bottoms	Carey	Clark	Cockell	Drinkwater	Evans	Golding	Ingham	Keen	Lazarus	Longbottom	Pinner	Rutter	Whitaker	Whitfield	Woods	OG
		7	9	10	4	11	6				3		8		1	5			2	
6		7	9			11		1			3	4	8			5			2	
		2	2	1	1	2	1	1			2	1	2		1	2			2	
			1										1			1				

Angell	Baker	Barber	Bedford	Bottoms	Carey	Clark	Cockell	Drinkwater	Evans	Golding	Ingham	Keen	Lazarus	Longbottom	Pinner	Rutter	Whitaker	Whitfield	Woods	OG
8	13	14	48	3	17	24	10	49	27	8	50	37	33	27	1	50	8	14	35	
		3	37		1	6			16			2	13	5		1		3	5	1

1961-62

Division Three

	P	W	D	L	F	A	Pts
Portsmouth	46	27	11	8	87	47	65
Grimsby Town	46	28	6	12	80	56	62
Bournemouth	46	21	17	8	69	45	59
Queen's Park Rangers	46	24	11	11	111	73	59
Peterborough United	46	26	6	14	107	82	58
Bristol City	46	23	8	15	94	72	54
Reading	46	22	9	15	77	66	53
Northampton Town	46	20	11	15	85	57	51
Swindon Town	46	17	15	14	78	71	49
Hull City	46	20	8	18	67	54	48
Bradford Park Avenue	46	20	7	19	80	78	47
Port Vale	46	17	11	18	65	58	45
Notts County	46	17	9	20	67	74	43
Coventry City	46	16	11	19	64	71	43
Crystal Palace	46	14	14	18	83	80	42
Southend United	46	13	16	17	57	69	42
Watford	46	14	13	19	63	74	41
Halifax Town	46	15	10	21	62	84	40
Shrewsbury Town	46	13	12	21	73	84	38
Barnsley	46	13	12	21	71	95	38
Torquay United	46	15	6	25	76	100	36
Lincoln City	46	9	17	20	57	87	35
Brentford	46	13	8	25	53	93	34
Newport County	46	7	8	31	46	102	22

Attendances

TOTAL

	Home	Away	Total
League	252,683	230,878	483,561
Cup/Other	33,091	38,852	71,943
TOTAL	285,774	269,730	555,504

AVERAGE

	Home	Away	Total
League	10,986	10,038	10,512
Cup/Other	11,030	12,951	11,991
TOTAL	10,991	10,374	10,683

Match No.	Date		Opponents	Location	Result		Scorers	Atter
1	Aug	19	Brentford	H	W	3-0	Towers, Bedford, Evans	1
2		21	Reading	H	L	3-6	Lazarus (2), Angell	1
3		28	Barnsley	A	W	4-2	Bedford, Angell (pen), Towers, Evans	
4		30	Reading	A	W	2-0	Towers (2)	1
5	Sep	2	Portsmouth	H	L	0-1		1
6		4	Swindon Town	H	W	6-1	Lazarus (2), Towers (2), Barber, Evans	1
7		9	Crystal Palace	A	D	2-2	Lazarus (2)	2
8		16	Bournemouth	H	D	1-1	Lazarus	1
9		23	Watford	A	L	2-3	Towers, McClelland	1
10		25	Halifax Town	H	W	6-2	Bedford (3), Evans (2), McClelland	1
11		30	Hull City	H	D	1-1	Francis	
12	Oct	7	Newport County	A	W	4-2	McClelland, Bedford, Barber, Evans	
13		9	Lincoln City	H	L	1-3	Evans	
14		14	Southend United	H	W	5-3	Bedford (4), Angell	1
15		17	Swindon Town	A	D	0-0		1
16		21	Grimsby Town	A	D	1-1	Collins	
17		28	Coventry City	H	W	4-1	Barber (2), Bedford, Evans	
18	Nov	11	Port Vale	H	W	2-1	Bedford, Angell (pen)	
19		18	Bristol City	A	L	0-2		1
20	Dec	2	Notts County	A	D	0-0		
21		9	Shrewsbury Town	H	W	3-1	Bedford (3)	
22		16	Brentford	A	W	4-1	Bedford (2), McClelland, OG (Reeves)	1
23		26	Torquay United	A	D	2-2	McClelland, Keen	
24		30	Torquay United	H	W	6-0	Evans (3), Towers (2), Collins	
25	Jan	13	Portsmouth	A	L	1-4	Towers	1
26		20	Crystal Palace	H	W	1-0	Evans	1
27	Feb	3	Bournemouth	A	L	1-3	Towers	1
28		10	Watford	H	L	1-2	McClelland	1
29		16	Hull City	A	L	1-3	Bedford	
30		19	Peterborough United	A	L	1-5	Collins	1
31		24	Newport County	H	W	4-0	Bedford, McClelland, Lazarus (2)	
32	Mar	3	Southend United	A	W	3-2	Bedford, Collins, OG (Shields)	
33		10	Grimsby Town	H	W	3-2	Bedford (2), Angell	
34		14	Coventry City	A	W	3-2	Bedford (3)	
35		19	Barnsley	H	W	3-0	Keen, Bedford, Evans	1
36		24	Peterborough United	H	D	3-3	Evans, McClelland, Bedford	1
37		31	Port Vale	A	W	3-2	Collins, Bedford, Angell	
38	Apr	7	Bristol City	H	W	4-1	Evans (2), Bedford (2)	1
39		11	Bradford	H	L	1-2	Lazarus	1
40		14	Bradford	A	D	3-3	Bedford (3)	
41		21	Notts County	H	W	2-0	Bedford, McClelland	
42		23	Northampton Town	H	W	2-0	Evans, Towers	1
43		24	Northampton Town	A	D	1-1	McClelland	1
44		28	Shrewsbury Town	A	W	2-1	Towers, McClelland	
45		30	Lincoln City	A	W	5-0	Lazarus (2), Towers (2), Collins	
46	May	3	Halifax Town	A	D	1-1	Evans	

Appeara

G

FA Cup

R1	Nov	4	Barry Town	A	D	1-1	OG (McLellan)	
rep		6	Barry Town	H	W	7-0	Bedford (3), Collins (2), Evans (2)	1
R2		25	Ashford Town	A	W	3-0	Collins, McClelland, Evans	
R3	Jan	6	Burnley	A	L	1-6	Evans	2

Appeara

G

League Cup

R1	Sep	13	Crystal Palace	H	W	5-2	Bedford (2), Francis (2), Angell	1
R2	Oct	11	Nottingham Forest	H	L	1-2	Towers	1

Appeara

G

Total - Appeara

Total - G

Andrews	Angell	Baker	Barber	Bedford	Bentley	Cockell	Collins	Drinkwater	Evans	Francis	Ingham	Keen	Lazarus	McClelland	Rutter	Slack	Towers	Williams	OG
	6	2	11	8	5			1	9		3	4	7				10		
11	6	2		8	5			1	9		3	4	7				10		
11	6			8	2			1	9		3	4	7		5		10		
11	6			8	2			1	9		3	4	7		5		10		
11	6			8	2			1	9		3	4	7		5		10		
	6		11	8	2			1	9		3	4	7		5		10		
	6		11	8	2			1	9		3	4	7		5		10		
	6	2	11	8				1		9		4	7		5		10	3	
	6	2	11	8				1	9		3	4		7	5		10		
	6	2	11	8				1	9		3	4		7	5		10		
	6	2	11	8				1		9	3	4		7	5		10		
	6	2	11	8				1	9		3	4		7	5		10		
	6	2	11	8				1	9		3	4		7	5		10		
	6		11	8	2		10		9		3	4		7	5	1			
	6		11	8	2		10	1	9			4		7	5			3	
	6		11	8	2		10	1	9			4		7	5			3	
	6		11	8	2		10	1	9			4		7	5			3	
	6			8	2		10	1	9			4		7	5		11	3	
	6		11	8	2		10	1	9			4		7	5			3	
	6		11	8	2		10	1	9		3	4		7	5				
	6		11	8	2			1	9		3	4		7	5		10		
	6		11	8	2			1	9		3	4		7	5		10		
	6		11	8	2			1	9		3	4		7	5		10		
	6		11		2		8	1	9		3	4		7	5		10		
	6		11	8	2			1	9		3	4		7	5		10		
				8	2		11	1	9		3	4		7	5		10		
			11		2		10	1	9		3	4		7	5		8		
			11		2		10	1	9		3	4		7	5		8		
			11	8			10	1	9		3	4		7	5			2	
			11	8		6	10	1	9		3	4		7	5			2	
	6			8			10	1	9		3	4	11	7	5			2	
	6			8			10	1	9		3	4	11	7	5			2	
	6			8			10	1	9		3	4	11	7	5			2	
	6			8			10	1	9		3	4	11	7	5			2	
	6			8			10	1	9		3	4	11	7	5			2	
	6			8			10	1	9		3	4	11	7	5			2	
	6			8			10	1	9		3	4	11	7	5			2	
	6			8			10	1	9		3	4	11	7	5			2	
	6			8			10	1	9		3	4	11	7	5			2	
	6			8	2			1	9		3	4	11	7	5		10		
	6			8	2			1	9		3	4	11	7	5		10		
	6			8	2			1	9		3	4	11	7	5		10		
				8	2		10	1	9		3	4	11	7	5			6	
				8	2			1	9		3	4	11	7	5		10	6	
	6			8	2		10	1			3	4	11	7			9	5	
	6			8	2		10	1	9		3	4	11	7	5				
4	39	8	23	43	29	1	24	45	43	2	40	46	24	38	43	1	27	20	
	6		4	34			6		18	1		2	12	11			15		2

Andrews	Angell	Baker	Barber	Bedford	Bentley	Cockell	Collins	Drinkwater	Evans	Francis	Ingham	Keen	Lazarus	McClelland	Rutter	Slack	Towers	Williams	OG
	6			8	2		10	1	9			4		7	5		11	3	
	6		11	8	2		10	1	9			4		7	5			3	
	6			8	2		10	1	9		3	4		7	5		11		
	6			8	2		11	1	9		3	4		7	5		10		
	4		1	4	4		4	4	4		2	4		4	4		3	2	
				3			3		4					1					1

Andrews	Angell	Baker	Barber	Bedford	Bentley	Cockell	Collins	Drinkwater	Evans	Francis	Ingham	Keen	Lazarus	McClelland	Rutter	Slack	Towers	Williams	OG
	6	2	11	8				1		9	3	4	7		5		10		
	6		11	8	2		7	1	9		3	4			5		10		
	2	1	2	2	1		1	2	1	1	2	2	1		2		2		
	1			2						2							1		

Andrews	Angell	Baker	Barber	Bedford	Bentley	Cockell	Collins	Drinkwater	Evans	Francis	Ingham	Keen	Lazarus	McClelland	Rutter	Slack	Towers	Williams	OG
4	45	9	26	49	34	1	29	51	48	3	44	52	25	42	49	1	32	22	
	7		4	39			9		22	3		2	12	12			16		3

1962-63

Division Three

	P	W	D	L	F	A	Pts
Northampton Town	46	26	10	10	109	60	62
Swindon Town	46	22	14	10	87	56	58
Port Vale	46	23	8	15	72	58	54
Coventry City	46	18	17	11	83	69	53
Bournemouth	46	18	16	12	63	46	52
Peterborough United	46	20	11	15	93	75	51
Notts County	46	19	13	14	73	74	51
Southend United	46	19	12	15	75	77	50
Wrexham	46	20	9	17	84	83	49
Hull City	46	19	10	17	74	69	48
Crystal Palace	46	17	13	16	68	58	47
Colchester United	46	18	11	17	73	93	47
Queen's Park Rangers	46	17	11	18	85	76	45
Bristol City	46	16	13	17	100	92	45
Shrewsbury Town	46	16	12	18	83	81	44
Millwall	46	15	13	18	82	87	43
Watford	46	17	8	21	82	85	42
Barnsley	46	15	11	20	63	74	41
Bristol Rovers	46	15	11	20	70	88	41
Reading	46	16	8	22	74	78	40
Bradford Park Avenue	46	14	12	20	79	97	40
Brighton & Hove Albion	46	12	12	22	58	84	36
Carlisle United	46	13	9	24	61	89	35
Halifax Town	46	9	12	25	64	106	30

Attendances

TOTAL	Home	Away	Total
League	229,509	242,193	471,702
Cup/Other	36,265	12,500	48,765
TOTAL	265,774	254,693	520,467

AVERAGE	Home	Away	Total
League	9,979	10,530	10,254
Cup/Other	12,088	12,500	12,191
TOTAL	10,222	10,612	10,409

Match No.	Date		Opponents	Location	Result		Scorers	Attend
1	Aug	18	Brighton	H	D	2-2	Lazarus, Bedford	11
2		20	Halifax Town	H	W	5-0	Bedford (2), McClelland, Keen, Lazarus	10
3		24	Carlisle United	A	W	5-2	Lazarus (2, 1 pen), Bedford (2), Evans	8
4		27	Halifax Town	A	W	4-1	McClelland, Angell (pen), Bedford, Lazarus	7
5	Sep	1	Swindon Town	H	D	2-2	McClelland, Large	12
6		3	Crystal Palace	H	W	4-1	Bedford (2), Angell (pen), Large	16
7		8	Peterborough United	A	W	2-1	McClelland, Bedford	14
8		12	Crystal Palace	A	L	0-1		21
9		15	Barnsley	H	W	2-1	Large (2)	11
10		17	Wrexham	H	L	1-2	Lazarus	13
11		22	Northampton Town	A	L	0-1		15
12		29	Southend United	A	W	3-1	Barber, Lazarus, McClelland	12
13	Oct	6	Notts County	H	L	0-1		15
14		10	Wrexham	A	L	1-3	Lazarus	15
15		13	Bournemouth	A	L	1-2	Bedford	11
16		22	Hull City	H	W	4-1	Bedford (3), Lazarus	18
17		27	Bradford	A	W	3-0	McClelland (3)	8
18	Nov	10	Bristol City	A	W	4-2	Bedford (2), Barber, McClelland	13
19		17	Reading	H	W	3-2	Large, Collins, Malcolm	10
20	Dec	1	Shrewsbury Town	H	D	0-0		10
21		8	Millwall	A	D	0-0		13
22		15	Brighton	A	D	2-2	Bedford, Lazarus	11
23		22	Carlisle United	H	D	2-2	Lazarus (2)	9
24	Jan	12	Swindon Town	A	L	0-5		7
25	Feb	9	Northampton Town	H	L	1-3	Bedford	14
26		23	Notts County	A	L	2-3	Lazarus, Bedford	8
27	Mar	2	Bournemouth	H	W	1-0	Bedford	8
28		9	Coventry City	A	L	1-4	Leary	15
29		16	Bradford	H	L	1-2	Malcolm	7
30		23	Watford	A	W	5-2	Bedford (2), Lazarus (2), Malcolm	10
31		30	Bristol City	H	W	3-1	Collins, Leary, Barber	5
32	Apr	1	Colchester United	H	L	1-2	Malcolm	7
33		5	Reading	A	D	1-1	Bedford	7
34		8	Southend United	H	W	1-0	Lazarus	7
35		12	Bristol Rovers	H	L	3-5	Bedford, Leary, Lazarus	10
36		13	Port Vale	H	W	3-1	Leary (2), Collins	5
37		15	Bristol Rovers	A	D	0-0		12
38		20	Shrewsbury Town	A	W	3-0	Lazarus, Malcolm, Leary	3
39		22	Colchester United	A	L	1-2	McClelland	6
40		25	Hull City	A	L	1-4	Leary	5
41		27	Millwall	H	L	2-3	Leary, McClelland	8
42		29	Port Vale	A	L	2-3	Leary, OG (Sporson)	5
43	May	10	Barnsley	A	D	0-0		4
44		13	Watford	H	D	2-2	Barber, Collins	5
45		18	Peterborough United	H	D	0-0		5
46		22	Coventry City	H	L	1-3	Collins	3

Appearan
G

FA Cup

R1	Nov	3	Newport County	H	W	3-2	Barber (2), Large	12
R2		24	Hinkley Athletic	H	W	7-2	Bedford (3), McClelland, Collins, Lazarus, Large	13
R3	Jan	26	Swansea Town	A	L	0-2		12

Appearan
G

League Cup

R1	Sep	24	Preston North End	H	L	1-2	Collins	11

Appearan
G

Total - Appearan
Total - G

Baker	Barber	Bedford	Bentley	Collins	Drinkwater	Dugdale	Evans	Ingham	Keen	Large	Lazarus	Leary	Malcolm	McClelland	Rutter	Smith	Springett	Taylor	Williams	OG
		8	2		1		9	3	4	10	11			7	5					
		8	2	10	1		9	3	4	6	11			7	5					
		8	2	10	1		9	3	4	6	11			7	5					
		8	2	10	1			3	4	9	11			7	5					
		8	2	10	1			3	4	9	11			7	5					
		8	2	10	1			3	4	9	11			7	5					
		8	2	10	1			3	4	9	11			7	5					
		8	2	10	1			3	4	9	11			7	5					
		8	2	10	1				4	9	11			7	5				3	
		8	2	10	1				4	9	11			7	5				3	
	11	8			1		9		4	6	10			7	5				2	
	11		2	10	1				4	9	8			7	5				3	
	11		2	10	1				4	9	8			7	5				3	
	11	10			1		9	3	4		8			7	5				2	
	11	10		8	1		9	3	4		7				5				2	
		8	2		1	5	9	3	10		11		4	7						
		8	2	10	1	5	9	3			11		4	7						
	11	8	2	10	1	5		3		9			4	7						
		8	2	10	1	5		3		9	11		4	7						
2		8			1	5		3	10	9	11		4	7						
2		8		10	1	5		3		9	11		4	7						
2		8			1	5		3	10		11	9	4	7						
2		8			1	5		3	10		11	9	4	7						
	10	8			1			3	5	6	11	9	4	7						
		8		10	1			3	6		11	9	4	7	5					
	11	10			1			3	6		8	9	4	7	5					
	11	10			1	5		3	6		8	9	4	7						
	11	10				5		3			8	9	4	7		1			2	
	11	8						3	6		10	9	4	7		1			5	
	11	8						3	4		10	9	6	7		1		2	5	
	11	8		7				3	4		10	9	6			1		2	5	
	11	8		7				3	4		10	9	6			1		2	5	
	11	8		7				3	4		10	9	6			1		2	5	
	11	8		10				3	6		7	9	4			1		2	5	
	11	6		10				3	5		8	9	4	7		1		2		
	11	8		10				3	6		7	9	4			1		2	5	
	11	8		10				3	6		7	9	4			1		2	5	
	11	8		10				3	6		7	9	4			1		2	5	
	11	8		10				3	6			9	4	7		1		2	5	
	11	8		10				3	6			9	4	7		1		2	5	
	11	8		10				3	6			9	4	7		1		2	5	
	11	8		10				3	6		7	9	4			1			5	
2	11	8		10				3	6		7	9	4			1			5	
2	11	8		10				3	6		7	9	4			1			5	
	11			10				3	4		7	9	8				1	6	5	
	11	9		10				3	8		7		4				1	6	5	
6	28	43	16	33	27	10	8	41	41	18	42	24	31	33	17	17	2	14	25	
	4	23		5			1		1	5	18	9	5	11						1

Baker	Barber	Bedford	Bentley	Collins	Drinkwater	Dugdale	Evans	Ingham	Keen	Large	Lazarus	Leary	Malcolm	McClelland	Rutter	Smith	Springett	Taylor	Williams	OG
	11		2	10	1	5		3		9	7		4	8						
		8	2	10	1	5		3		9	11		4	7						
		10			1	5		3	8	6	11	9	4	7						
	1	2	2	2	3	3		3	1	3	3	1	3	3						
	2	3		1						2	1			1						

Baker	Barber	Bedford	Bentley	Collins	Drinkwater	Dugdale	Evans	Ingham	Keen	Large	Lazarus	Leary	Malcolm	McClelland	Rutter	Smith	Springett	Taylor	Williams	OG
		8		10			9		4	6	11			7	5	1			2	
		1		1			1		1	1	1			1	1	1			1	
				1																

Baker	Barber	Bedford	Bentley	Collins	Drinkwater	Dugdale	Evans	Ingham	Keen	Large	Lazarus	Leary	Malcolm	McClelland	Rutter	Smith	Springett	Taylor	Williams	OG
6	29	46	18	36	30	13	9	44	43	22	46	25	34	37	18	18	2	14	26	
	6	26		7			1		1	7	19	9	5	12						1

1963-64

Division Three

	P	W	D	L	F	A	Pts
Coventry City	46	22	16	8	98	61	60
Crystal Palace	46	23	14	9	73	51	60
Watford	46	23	12	11	79	59	58
Bournemouth	46	24	8	14	79	58	56
Bristol City	46	20	15	11	84	64	55
Reading	46	21	10	15	79	62	52
Mansfield Town	46	20	11	15	76	62	51
Hull City	46	16	17	13	73	68	49
Oldham Athletic	46	20	8	18	73	70	48
Peterborough United	46	18	11	17	75	70	47
Shrewsbury Town	46	18	11	17	73	80	47
Bristol Rovers	46	19	8	19	91	79	46
Port Vale	46	16	14	16	53	49	46
Southend United	46	15	15	16	77	78	45
Queen's Park Rangers	46	18	9	19	76	78	45
Brentford	46	15	14	17	87	80	44
Colchester United	46	12	19	15	70	68	43
Luton Town	46	16	10	20	64	80	42
Walsall	46	13	14	19	59	76	40
Barnsley	46	12	15	19	68	94	39
Millwall	46	14	10	22	53	67	38
Crewe Alexandra	46	11	12	23	50	77	34
Wrexham	46	13	6	27	75	107	32
Notts County	46	9	9	28	45	92	27

Attendances

TOTAL

	Home	Away	Total
League	179,667	223,727	403,394
Cup/Other	12,141	29,000	41,141
TOTAL	191,808	252,727	444,535

AVERAGE

	Home	Away	Total
League	7,812	9,727	8,769
Cup/Other	12,141	9,667	10,285
TOTAL	7,992	9,720	8,891

Match No.	Date		Opponents	Location	Result		Scorers	Atten
1	Aug	24	Oldham Athletic	A	L	1-2	Graham	
2		26	Shrewsbury Town	A	W	2-1	Bedford (2)	
3		31	Peterborough United	H	W	3-0	Leary (2), Angell	
4	Sep	7	Southend United	A	W	3-1	Lazarus (2), Leary	
5		9	Shrewsbury Town	H	L	3-4	Graham (2), Bedford	
6		14	Watford	H	W	1-0	Bedford	
7		17	Bristol Rovers	A	D	0-0		
8		21	Colchester United	A	L	0-2		
9		28	Millwall	H	W	2-0	Bedford, McQuade	
10		30	Bristol Rovers	H	W	1-0	Lazarus	
11	Oct	4	Barnsley	A	L	1-3	Bedford	
12		7	Bournemouth	H	W	1-0	Angell	
13		12	Mansfield Town	A	L	0-1		
14		16	Bournemouth	A	L	2-4	Collins, Vafiadis	
15		19	Notts County	H	W	3-2	Collins, Lazarus, OG (Birkinshaw)	
16		21	Hull City	H	L	0-2		
17		26	Crewe Alexandra	A	L	0-2		
18		30	Hull City	A	L	0-3		
19	Nov	2	Crystal Palace	H	L	3-4	Collins (2), Bedford	
20		9	Walsall	A	W	2-0	Lazarus, Graham	
21		23	Luton Town	A	D	4-4	Leary (2), Graham, McQuade	
22		30	Coventry City	H	L	3-6	Bedford (2), Keen	
23	Dec	14	Oldham Athletic	H	W	3-2	Bedford (2), Leary	
24		21	Peterborough United	A	L	1-2	Angell	
25		28	Bristol City	H	L	0-2		
26	Jan	11	Southend United	H	L	4-5	Leary (2), Vafiadis, Bedford	
27		18	Watford	A	L	1-3	Graham	
28	Feb	1	Colchester United	H	D	0-0		
29		8	Millwall	A	D	2-2	McLeod, Leary	
30		22	Mansfield Town	H	W	2-0	OG (Humble), Bedford	
31		29	Brentford	A	D	2-2	Bedford (2)	
32	Mar	7	Crewe Alexandra	H	W	2-0	Graham, OG (Riggs)	
33		10	Bristol City	A	L	1-2	McLeod	
34		14	Crystal Palace	A	L	0-1		
35		20	Brentford	H	D	2-2	Bedford (2)	
36		27	Wrexham	H	W	1-0	Collins	
37		28	Reading	A	W	2-1	McLeod (2)	
38		30	Wrexham	A	W	1-0	Collins	
39	Apr	6	Port Vale	A	L	0-2		
40		11	Coventry City	A	L	2-4	Collins (2)	
41		14	Reading	H	W	4-2	Bedford, Keen, Vafiadis, Leary	
42		18	Port Vale	H	W	3-0	Bedford (2), Leary	
43		25	Notts County	A	D	2-2	Vafiadis, Leary	
44		27	Barnsley	H	D	2-2	Bedford (2)	
45		29	Luton Town	H	D	1-1	Bedford	
46	May	1	Walsall	H	W	3-0	Keen (2), Collins	

Appeara
G

FA Cup

R1	Nov	16	Gillingham	H	W	4-1	Bedford, Leary, Malcolm, Graham	
R2	Dec	7	Colchester United	A	W	1-0	Leary	
R3	Jan	4	Carlisle United	A	L	0-2		

Appeara
G

League Cup

R1	Sep	4	Aldershot	A	L	1-3	Bedford	

Appeara
G

Total - Appeara
Total - G

Bedford	Brady P.	Brady R.	Collins	Gibbs	Graham	Keen	Lazarus	Leary	McLeod	McQuade	Malcolm	Sibley	Smith	Springett	Taylor	Vafiadis	Whittaker	OG
8		5	11	6	10	4	7	9						1			2	
8		5	11	6	10	4	7	9						1			2	
8		5	10	4	11	6	7	9						1			2	
8		5	10	4	11	6	7	9						1			2	
8		5	10	4	11	6	7	9						1			2	
8		5	10	4	11	6	7	9						1			2	
8		5	10			6	7	9		11	4			1			2	
8		5	10			6	7	9		11	4			1			2	
8		5	10	6		4		9		11				1		7	2	
8		5	10	6		4	7	9						1		11	2	
8		5	10	6		4	7	9		11				1			2	
8		5	10	6		4	7	9						1		11	2	
8			10	4	11	6		9						1	5	7	2	
8		5	10	6		4	7	9						1		11	2	
8		5	10	6		4	7	9						1		11	2	
		5	10	8		6	7	9		11	4			1			2	
8		5	11		10	4	7	9			6			1			2	
8	2	5	10	9		4	7				6		1			11		
10	2	5	11	6		8	7	9			4			1				
8	2	5			10	6	7	9		11	4			1				
9	2	5		4	10	6	7	8		11				1				
9	2	5	10			6	7	8		11	4			1				
10	3	5		9		6	7	8		11	4			1				
8	3	5		9		6	7	10		11	4			1				
8	3	5		9		6	7	10		11	4			1				
8	3	5			10	6		9	11		4			1	2	7		
8	3	5			10	6		9	11		4			1	2	7		
	3	5	8	9	10	6			11	7	4		1		2			
8	2	5	7		10	6		9	11		4		1					
8	2	5			10	6		9	11	7	4		1					
8	2	5			10	6		9	11	7	4		1					
8	2	5		6	10	4		9	11	7			1					
8	2			6	10	5		9	11		4	7	1					
8	2	5	7		10	6		9	11		4		1					
8	2	5	11		10	6		9		7	4		1					
8	2	5	10			6		9	11	7	4		1					
8	3	5	10			6		9	11		4	7	1		2			
8	3	5	10			6		9	11		4	7	1		2			
8	3	5	10			6		9	11	7	4		1		2			
8	3	5	7	6		10		9	11		4		1					
8	2	5	10			6		9	11		4		1			7		
8	2	5	10			6		9	11		4		1			7		
8	2	5	10			6		9	11		4		1			7		
8	2	5	11		10	6		9			4		1			7		
8	2		10			6		9		11	4		1		5	7		
8	3	5	10	6		9				11	4		1		2	7		
44	29	43	35	25	21	46	23	43	17	20	31	3	20	26	9	15	17	
23			9		7	4	5	12	4	2						4		3

Bedford	Brady P.	Brady R.	Collins	Gibbs	Graham	Keen	Lazarus	Leary	McLeod	McQuade	Malcolm	Sibley	Smith	Springett	Taylor	Vafiadis	Whittaker	OG
9	2	5			10	6	7	8		11	4			1				
8	3	5		9		6	7	10		11	4			1				
	3	5	10	9		6	7	8		11	4			1				
2	3	3	1	2	1	3	3	3		3	3			3				
1					1			2			1							

Bedford	Brady P.	Brady R.	Collins	Gibbs	Graham	Keen	Lazarus	Leary	McLeod	McQuade	Malcolm	Sibley	Smith	Springett	Taylor	Vafiadis	Whittaker	OG
8	3	5			10	6		9		11	4	7		1			2	
1	1	1			1	1		1		1	1	1		1			1	
1																		

Bedford	Brady P.	Brady R.	Collins	Gibbs	Graham	Keen	Lazarus	Leary	McLeod	McQuade	Malcolm	Sibley	Smith	Springett	Taylor	Vafiadis	Whittaker	OG
47	33	47	36	27	23	50	26	47	17	24	35	4	20	30	9	15	18	
25			9		8	4	5	14	4	2	1					4		3

1964-65

Division Three

	P	W	D	L	F	A	Pts
Carlisle United	46	25	10	11	76	53	60
Bristol City	46	24	11	11	92	55	59
Mansfield Town	46	24	11	11	95	61	59
Hull City	46	23	12	11	91	57	58
Brentford	46	24	9	13	83	55	57
Bristol Rovers	46	20	15	11	82	58	55
Gillingham	46	23	9	14	70	50	55
Peterborough United	46	22	7	17	85	74	51
Watford	46	17	16	13	71	64	50
Grimsby Town	46	16	17	13	68	67	49
Bournemouth	46	18	11	17	72	63	47
Southend United	46	19	8	19	78	71	46
Reading	46	16	14	16	70	70	46
Queen's Park Rangers	46	17	12	17	72	80	46
Workington	46	17	12	17	58	69	46
Shrewsbury Town	46	15	12	19	76	84	42
Exeter City	46	12	17	17	51	52	41
Scunthorpe United	46	14	12	20	65	72	40
Walsall	46	15	7	24	55	80	37
Oldham Athletic	46	13	10	23	61	83	36
Luton Town	46	11	11	24	51	94	33
Port Vale	46	9	14	23	41	76	32
Colchester United	46	10	10	26	50	89	30
Barnsley	46	9	11	26	54	90	29

Attendances

TOTAL

	Home	Away	Total
League	131,395	194,848	326,243
Cup/Other	17,428	22,271	39,699
TOTAL	148,823	217,119	365,942

AVERAGE

	Home	Away	Total
League	5,713	8,472	7,092
Cup/Other	5,809	11,136	7,940
TOTAL	5,724	8,685	7,175

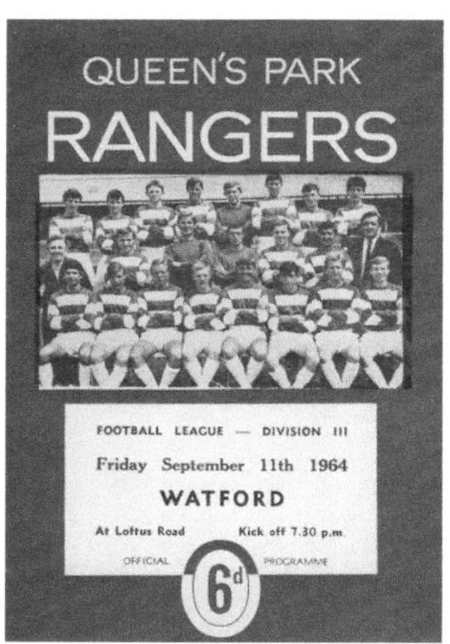

Match No.	Date		Opponents	Location	Result		Scorers	Atten
1	Aug	22	Barnsley	A	D	0-0		5
2		24	Southend United	H	W	2-0	Bedford, Leary	6
3		28	Scunthorpe United	H	W	2-1	Keen (2)	7
4		31	Southend United	A	D	0-0		10
5	Sep	5	Walsall	A	L	1-4	Collins	4
6		7	Reading	H	L	0-1		7
7		11	Watford	H	D	2-2	Bedford, Leary	8
8		16	Reading	A	L	3-5	Keen (2), Bedford	10
9		18	Workington	A	D	0-0		7
10		25	Hull City	H	W	2-1	Keen, McAdams	6
11	Oct	3	Gillingham	A	D	2-2	Keen, Bedford	12
12		5	Shrewsbury Town	H	W	2-1	Bedford, R.Morgan	5
13		9	Brentford	H	L	1-3	Keen	11
14		13	Bristol City	A	L	0-2		11
15		17	Colchester United	A	W	2-1	Collins, OG (Jones)	3
16		19	Bristol City	H	W	1-0	Bedford	5
17		23	Port Vale	H	W	3-1	Bedford, I.Morgan, R.Morgan	4
18		30	Carlisle United	A	L	0-2		9
19	Nov	6	Luton Town	H	W	7-1	Bedford (3), Keen (3, 2 pens), R.Morgan	5
20		21	Grimsby Town	H	D	1-1	R.Morgan	6
21		28	Peterborough United	A	L	1-6	Collins	8
22	Dec	11	Barnsley	H	W	3-2	Bedford (3)	3
23		18	Scunthorpe United	A	L	1-2	McAdams	5
24		26	Bristol Rovers	A	L	1-3	R.Morgan	17
25		28	Bristol Rovers	H	W	3-1	Bedford (2), Keen	5
26	Jan	1	Walsall	H	W	1-0	Bedford	4
27		16	Watford	A	W	2-0	Leary, I.Morgan	7
28		29	Bournemouth	H	D	1-1	Bedford	3
29	Feb	6	Hull City	A	L	1-3	McAdams	23
30		13	Gillingham	H	W	3-1	Bedford, Collins, McAdams	6
31		20	Brentford	A	L	2-5	I.Morgan, Keen	12
32		26	Colchester United	H	W	5-0	McAdams (3), Bedford, Leach	4
33	Mar	6	Bournemouth	A	L	0-2		6
34		12	Carlisle United	H	L	1-2	Bedford	5
35		15	Mansfield Town	A	L	1-8	Bedford	9
36		20	Luton Town	A	L	0-2		3
37		26	Mansfield Town	H	W	2-0	Bedford, Collins	5
38		31	Exeter City	A	D	2-2	Leary (2)	5
39	Apr	3	Grimsby Town	A	D	0-0		3
40		5	Workington	H	W	2-1	Hazell, Leary	4
41		10	Peterborough United	H	W	3-2	Bedford, Leary, Collins	4
42		12	Shrewsbury Town	A	L	2-3	McAdams, I.Morgan	3
43		16	Oldham Athletic	A	L	3-5	Collins (2), Keen	7
44		17	Port Vale	A	D	0-0		4
45		19	Oldham Athletic	H	D	1-1	Leary	3
46		23	Exeter City	H	D	0-0		4

Appearar
G

FA Cup

R1	Nov	14	Bath City	H	W	2-0	Collins, Leary	7
R2	Dec	5	Peterborough United	H	D	3-3	R.Brady, Keen (pen), Bedford	6
rep		9	Peterborough United	A	L	1-2	McAdams	15

Appearar
G

League Cup

R1	Sep	2	Aldershot	H	W	5-2	Bedford (2), Collins (2), Angell	3
R2		23	Reading	A	L	0-4		7

Appearar
G

Total - Appearar
Total - G

Bedford	Brady P.	Brady R.	Collins	Gibbs	Hazell	Hunt	Jacks	Keen	Leach	Leary	McAdams	McLeod	McQuade	Malcolm	Morgan I.	Morgan R.	Nash	Sibley	Smith	Springett	Taylor	OG
3	2	5	7					10		9		11		4					1		3	
3	2	5	7					10		9		11		4					1		3	
3	2	5	7					10		9		11		4					1		3	
3	2	5	7					10		9		11		4					1		3	
3	2	5	7					10		9		11		4					1		3	
3	2	5	7	4				10		9		11							1		3	
3	2	5	7					10		9		11		4					1		3	
3	2	5	7	4				10		9		11							1		3	
3	2	5	10					4		9		11						7		1	3	
0	2	5	8					6			9	11		4	7		3			1		
0	2	5	8		4			6			9				7	11	3			1		
0	2	5	8		4			6			9				7	11	3			1		
0	2	5	8					6			9			4	7	11	3			1		
0	2	5	8		4			6			9				7	11	3			1		
0	2	5	8		4			6			9				7	11	3			1		
0	2	5	8		4			6		9					7	11	3			1		
0	2	5	8		4			6		9					7	11	3			1		
0	2	5	8		4			6		9					7	11	3			1		
0	2	5	8		4			6		9					7	11	3			1		
0		5	8		4			6		9					7	11	3		1		2	
0		5	8		4			6		9		7				11	3		1		2	
0	2	5			6			8			9	11		4	7		3		1			
0	2	5	8		3			6			9	11		4	7				1			
0	2	5	8		3			6			9			4	7	11			1			
0		3	8		2	5		6			9			4	7	11			1			
0		3	8		2	5		6			9			4	7	11			1			
		3	10		2	5		6		8	9			4	7	11			1			
3		3	10		2	5		6			9			4	7	11			1			
0		3			2	5		6		8	9	11		4	7				1			
0		3	8		2	5		6			9			4	7	11			1			
0		3	8		2	5		6			9			4	7	11			1			
0		6			2	5		4	8		9				7	11	3		1			
			8		2	5		6	10		9	11		4	7		3		1			
3			10		2	5		6			9			4	7	11	3		1			
3		5	10		2			6			9			4	7	11			1		3	
3	2	5	10		4			6			9				7	11				1	3	
3	2	5	10		4			6		9		11				7			1		3	
	2	5						6	10	9	8	11				7		4		1	3	
	2	5			4			6	10	9	8	11				7				1	3	
0	2	5			4			6	8	9		11				7				1	3	
3	2	5	10		4			6		9		11				7				1	3	
	2	5	8					6		10	9	11			7			4		1	3	
	2	5	8					6		9	10	11			7			4		1	3	
3	2	5	7					6		9	10	11						4		1	3	
0	2	5	8					6		9		11			7		3	4		1		
3	2	5	7				10	6			9			4	11				1		3	
0	33	44	40	2	29	10	1	46	5	26	27	24		22	30	27	17	6	26	20	22	
3			8		1			13	1	8	8				4	5						1
0	2	5	8		4			6		9					7	11	3		1			
9		5	8		2			6		10				4	7	11			1			
0	2	5	7		3			6		9	8			4		11			1			
3	2	3	3		3			3		3	1			2	2	3	1		3			
1		1	1					1		1	1											
3	2	5	7					10		9			11	4					1		3	
0	2	5	7					4		8		11						9		1	3	
2	2	2	2					2		2		1	1	1				1	1	1	2	
2			2																			
5	37	49	45	2	32	10	1	51	5	31	28	25	1	25	32	30	18	7	30	21	24	
6		1	11		1			14	1	9	9				4	5						1

1965-66

Division Three

	P	W	D	L	F	A	Pts
Hull City	46	31	7	8	109	62	69
Millwall	46	27	11	8	76	43	65
Queen's Park Rangers	46	24	9	13	95	65	57
Scunthorpe United	46	21	11	14	80	67	53
Workington	46	19	14	13	67	57	52
Gillingham	46	22	8	16	62	54	52
Swindon Town	46	19	13	14	74	48	51
Reading	46	19	13	14	70	63	51
Walsall	46	20	10	16	77	64	50
Shrewsbury Town	46	19	11	16	73	64	49
Grimsby Town	46	17	13	16	68	62	47
Watford	46	17	13	16	55	51	47
Peterborough United	46	17	12	17	80	66	46
Oxford United	46	19	8	19	70	74	46
Brighton & Hove Albion	46	16	11	19	67	65	43
Bristol Rovers	46	14	14	18	64	64	42
Swansea Town	46	15	11	20	81	96	41
Bournemouth	46	13	12	21	38	56	38
Mansfield Town	46	15	8	23	59	89	38
Oldham Athletic	46	12	13	21	55	81	37
Southend United	46	16	4	26	54	83	36
Exeter City	46	12	11	23	53	79	35
Brentford	46	10	12	24	48	69	32
York City	46	9	9	28	53	106	27

Attendances

TOTAL	Home	Away	Total
League	190,046	200,892	390,938
Cup/Other	33,776	33,708	67,484
TOTAL	223,822	234,600	458,422

AVERAGE	Home	Away	Total
League	8,263	8,734	8,499
Cup/Other	8,444	11,236	9,641
TOTAL	8,290	9,023	8,649

Match No.	Date		Opponents	Location	Result		Scorers	Atte
1	Aug	21	Brentford	A	L	1-6	R.Morgan	1
2		23	Brighton	H	W	4-1	Keen (pen), Collins, Allen, McAdams	1
3		28	Mansfield Town	H	L	1-2	McAdams	
4	Sep	4	Hull City	A	W	3-1	Allen (2), R.Morgan	2
5		11	Reading	H	L	0-2		
6		14	Scunthorpe United	A	W	2-1	Allen, Collins	
7		18	Exeter City	A	D	0-0		
8		25	Peterborough United	H	W	2-1	Collins, Langley (pen)	
9	Oct	2	Millwall	A	L	1-2	Leach	1
10		4	Scunthorpe United	H	W	1-0	Keen	
11		9	York City	A	D	2-2	Allen, I.Morgan	
12		16	Oxford United	H	L	2-3	Sanderson, Allen	
13		23	Swansea Town	A	L	2-4	Collins, Allen	
14		30	Walsall	H	W	2-1	Sibley, Langley (pen)	
15	Nov	5	Workington	A	D	1-1	McAdams	
16		20	Southend United	A	W	3-1	Allen (2), Lazarus	
17		23	Brighton	A	W	2-0	Allen (2)	1
18		27	Swindon Town	H	W	3-2	Allen (3)	
19	Dec	11	Grimsby Town	H	W	3-0	Collins, R.Morgan, OG (Thompson)	
20		18	Oxford United	A	W	3-1	Allen (2), R.Morgan	
21	Jan	1	York City	H	W	7-2	Allen (3), Collins (2), Lazarus, R.Morgan	
22		8	Bournemouth	A	D	1-1	R.Morgan	
23		15	Swansea Town	H	W	6-2	R.Morgan (3), Collins (2), Lazarus	
24		29	Brentford	H	W	1-0	R.Morgan	1
25	Feb	5	Mansfield Town	A	L	1-2	Collins	
26		15	Watford	H	D	1-1	Langley (pen)	
27		19	Hull City	H	D	3-3	Collins (3)	1
28	Mar	5	Watford	A	W	2-1	Keen, R.Morgan	1
29		12	Exeter City	H	W	1-0	Allen	
30		19	Peterborough United	A	D	1-1	Collins	
31		26	Millwall	H	W	6-1	Marsh (2), Collins, Allen, Lazarus, R.Morgan	1
32	Apr	2	Workington	H	W	4-1	Marsh, Allen (2), Lazarus	
33		8	Bristol Rovers	H	W	4-1	Allen, Collins, Marsh, Lazarus	1
34		9	Shrewsbury Town	A	D	0-0		
35		12	Bristol Rovers	A	L	0-1		
36		16	Southend United	H	W	2-1	Lazarus (2)	
37		23	Swindon Town	A	L	1-2	Keen	1
38		25	Gillingham	H	L	1-3	Marsh	
39		30	Shrewsbury Town	H	W	2-1	Allen, Marsh	
40	May	2	Oldham Athletic	H	D	1-1	Allen	
41		7	Grimsby Town	A	L	2-4	R.Morgan, Marsh	
42		13	Reading	A	L	1-2	Collins	
43		18	Gillingham	A	L	1-3	Collins	
44		21	Bournemouth	H	W	5-0	Lazarus (3), Allen (2)	
45		25	Oldham Athletic	A	W	2-0	Allen, Marsh	
46		28	Walsall	A	W	1-0	Allen	

Appeara
Sub appeara

FA Cup

R1	Nov	13	Colchester United	A	D	3-3	Collins, Allen, Sanderson	
rep		17	Colchester United	H	W	4-0	Allen (2), R.Morgan, Sanderson	
R2	Dec	4	Guildford City	H	W	3-0	OG (Hunt), Sibley, Lazarus	
R3	Jan	22	Shrewsbury Town	H	D	0-0		1
rep		26	Shrewsbury Town	A	L	0-1		1

Appeara

League Cup

R1	Sep	1	Walsall	H	D	1-1	OG (Sissons)	
rep		7	Walsall	A	L	2-3	R.Morgan, Collins	1

Appeara

Total - Appeara
Total - Sub appeara
Total -

Bedford	Brady	Collins	Hazell	Hunt	Keen	Langley	Lazarus	Leach	Leary	McAdams	Marsh	Morgan I.	Morgan R.	Mortimore	Moughton	Sanderson	Sibley	Smith	Springett	Taylor	Watson	OG
	5	7	4		6	3				9			11			10		1			2	
		7	6	5	4	3				9			11			10			1		2	
		7	4	5	6	3				9			11			10			1		2	
		7	6	5	4	3				9			11			10			1		2	
		7	6		4	3				9			11	5		10			1		2	
		7	6		4	3		9					11	5		10			1		2	
		7	6		4	3		9					11	5		10			1		2	
		7	4		6	3			9				11	5		10			1		2	
		7[a]	4		6	3		9				11		5		10	12		1		2	
			4		6	3		9				7	11	5		10	12		1		2[a]	
			4		6	3		9				7	11	5		10			1	2		
			4		6	3		9				7	11	5		10			1		2	
		7[a]	6		10	3		9					11	5		12	4	1		2		
		7	12		4	3		9					11	5[a]		10	6		1	2		
		11		5	4	3	7			9						10	6		1		2	
		8		5	4	3	7						11			10	6		1		2	
		8		5	4	3	7						11			10	6		1		2	
		8		5	4	3	7						11			10	6		1		2	
		8		5	4	3	7						11			10	6		1		2	
		8		5	4	3	7						11			10	6		1		2	
		8		5	4	3	7						11			10	6		1		2	
		8		5	4	3	7						11			10	6		1		2	
		8		5	4	3	7						11			10	6		1		2	
		8		5	4	3	7						11			10	6		1		2	
		8		5	4	3	7	9					11			10	6		1		2	
		8		5	4	3	7						11			10	6		1		2	
		8	12	5	4	3	7						11			10	6		1		2	
		8		5	4	3	7						11			10	6		1		2	
		8		5	4	3	7	10					11				6		1		2	
		8		5	4	3	7				10		11				6		1		2	
		8[a]		5	4	3	7				10		11			12	6		1		2	
				5	4	3	7				10		11			8	6		1		2	
		8		5	4	3	7				10		11				6		1		2	
				5	4	3	7				10		11			8	6		1		2	
		10		5	4	3	7				9[a]		11			8	6		1		2	
		7		5	4	3	9				10		11			8	6		1		2	
				5	4	3	7				10		11			8	6		1		2	
		8	6	5	4	3	7[a]				10		11			12			1		2	
		7		5	4	3					10		11			8	6		1		2	
		8		5	4	3					10	7	11			6			1		2	
			2	5	4	3	7				10		11			8	6		1			
		8	6	5	4	3						7	11			10			1	2		
		8		5[a]	4	3	12				10	7	11			6			1		2	
					5	3	7				10	8	11		6	4			1		2	
					5	3	7				10	8	11		6				1	4	2	
			2		5	3	7				10	11	8		6	4			1			
	1	36	17	32	46	46	28	10	1	6	16	10	44	10	3	39	27	2	44	5	40	
			2				1									3	2					
		18			4	3	11	1		3	8	1	13			1	1					1

Bedford	Brady	Collins	Hazell	Hunt	Keen	Langley	Lazarus	Leach	Leary	McAdams	Marsh	Morgan I.	Morgan R.	Mortimore	Moughton	Sanderson	Sibley	Smith	Springett	Taylor	Watson	OG
		7		5	4	3				9			11			10	6		1		2	
		7		5	4	3				9			11			10	6		1		2	
		8		5	4	3	7						11			10	6		1		2	
		8		5	4	3	7						11			10	6		1		2	
		8		5	4	3	7						11			10	6		1		2	
		5		5	5	5	3			2			5			5	5		5		5	
		1					1						1			2	1					1

Bedford	Brady	Collins	Hazell	Hunt	Keen	Langley	Lazarus	Leach	Leary	McAdams	Marsh	Morgan I.	Morgan R.	Mortimore	Moughton	Sanderson	Sibley	Smith	Springett	Taylor	Watson	OG
10		11	6	5	4	3				9						7			1		2	
		7	6	5	4	3				9			11			10			1		2	
1		2	2	2	2	2				2			1			2			2		2	
		1											1									1

Bedford	Brady	Collins	Hazell	Hunt	Keen	Langley	Lazarus	Leach	Leary	McAdams	Marsh	Morgan I.	Morgan R.	Mortimore	Moughton	Sanderson	Sibley	Smith	Springett	Taylor	Watson	OG
1	1	43	19	39	53	53	31	10	1	10	16	10	50	10	3	46	32	2	51	5	47	
			2				1									3	2					
		20			4	3	12	1		3	8	1	15			3	2					3

stitutions are listed as:
replaced by player 12

1966-67

Division Three

	P	W	D	L	F	A	Pts
Queen's Park Rangers	46	26	15	5	103	38	67
Middlesbrough	46	23	9	14	87	64	55
Watford	46	20	14	12	61	46	54
Reading	46	22	9	15	76	57	53
Bristol Rovers	46	20	13	13	76	67	53
Shrewsbury Town	46	20	12	14	77	62	52
Torquay United	46	21	9	16	73	54	51
Swindon Town	46	20	10	16	81	59	50
Mansfield Town	46	20	9	17	84	79	49
Oldham Athletic	46	19	10	17	80	63	48
Gillingham	46	15	16	15	58	62	46
Walsall	46	18	10	18	65	72	46
Colchester United	46	17	10	19	76	73	44
Orient	46	13	18	15	58	68	44
Peterborough United	46	14	15	17	66	71	43
Oxford United	46	15	13	18	61	66	43
Grimsby Town	46	17	9	20	61	68	43
Scunthorpe United	46	17	8	21	58	73	42
Brighton & Hove Albion	46	13	15	18	61	71	41
Bournemouth	46	12	17	17	39	57	41
Swansea Town	46	12	15	19	85	89	39
Darlington	46	13	11	22	47	81	37
Doncaster Rovers	46	12	8	26	58	117	32
Workington	46	12	7	27	55	89	31

Attendances

TOTAL

	Home	Away	Total
League	302,707	251,783	554,490
Cup/Other	112,454	177,634	290,088
TOTAL	415,161	429,417	844,578

AVERAGE

	Home	Away	Total
League	13,161	10,947	12,054
Cup/Other	14,057	44,409	24,174
TOTAL	13,392	15,904	14,562

Match No.	Date		Opponents	Location	Result		Scorers	Atten
1	Aug	20	Shrewsbury Town	H	D	2-2	Allen, Marsh	[illegible]
2		27	Watford	A	L	0-1		[illegible]
3	Sep	3	Swindon Town	H	W	3-1	Lazarus (2), R.Morgan	[illegible]
4		6	Middlesbrough	H	W	4-0	Marsh (3), Allen	[illegible]
5		10	Reading	A	D	2-2	Langley (pen), I.Morgan	[illegible]
6		17	Doncaster Rovers	H	W	6-0	R.Morgan (2), Keen (2), Sanderson, Marsh	[illegible]
7		24	Mansfield Town	A	W	7-1	Marsh (3), Allen (2), Langley (pen), Sanderson	[illegible]
8		26	Middlesbrough	A	D	2-2	Marsh, Lazarus	1
9	Oct	1	Grimsby Town	H	W	5-1	Allen (2), Marsh, Lazarus, R.Morgan	[illegible]
10		8	Swansea Town	H	W	4-2	Allen (2), Sanderson, Marsh	1
11		15	Bournemouth	A	W	3-1	R.Morgan (2), Marsh	1
12		19	Torquay United	A	D	1-1	Langley (pen)	[illegible]
13		22	Leyton Orient	H	W	4-1	Allen (2), Lazarus, Marsh	1
14		29	Gillingham	A	D	2-2	Keen, Marsh	1
15	Nov	5	Workington	H	W	4-1	Marsh (2), Langley (pen), Allen	[illegible]
16		12	Scunthorpe United	A	W	2-0	Marsh (2)	[illegible]
17		15	Torquay United	H	W	2-1	R.Morgan, Allen	1
18		19	Oldham Athletic	H	L	0-1		1
19	Dec	3	Bristol Rovers	H	W	3-0	Allen, Sanderson, Lazarus	1
20		10	Colchester United	A	W	3-1	R.Morgan (2), Marsh	[illegible]
21		17	Shrewsbury Town	A	D	0-0		[illegible]
22		26	Brighton	H	W	3-0	Sanderson, Lazarus, Marsh	1
23		27	Brighton	A	D	2-2	R.Morgan, Wilks	2
24		31	Watford	H	W	4-1	Marsh (2), Sibley, Lazarus	1
25	Jan	14	Reading	H	W	2-1	Marsh, R.Morgan	1
26		21	Doncaster Rovers	A	D	1-1	Keen	1
27	Feb	4	Mansfield Town	H	D	0-0		1
28		11	Grimsby Town	A	D	1-1	I.Morgan	[illegible]
29		20	Peterborough Ubited	A	W	2-0	OG (Crawford), Lazarus	[illegible]
30		25	Swansea Town	A	W	3-1	Lazarus (3)	1
31	Mar	7	Bournemouth	H	W	4-0	Marsh (2), Allen, Keen	2
32		11	Peterborough United	H	D	0-0		1
33		18	Leyton Orient	A	D	0-0		1
34		24	Darlington	H	W	4-0	Marsh, Langley (pen), Lazarus, Allen	1
35		25	Gillingham	H	W	2-0	I.Morgan, Marsh	1
36		27	Darlington	A	D	0-0		[illegible]
37	Apr	1	Workington	A	W	2-0	I.Morgan, Langley (pen)	[illegible]
38		8	Scunthorpe United	H	W	5-1	Marsh (2), Lazarus (2), Keen	1
39		11	Walsall	A	L	0-2		1
40		15	Oldham Athletic	A	W	1-0	Wilks	1
41		22	Oxford United	H	W	3-1	Wilks (2), Lazarus	1
42		25	Walsall	H	D	0-0		1
43		29	Bristol Rovers	A	L	1-2	Leach	1
44	May	2	Swindon Town	A	D	1-1	Wilks	2
45		6	Colchester United	H	W	2-1	Sanderson, Allen	1
46		13	Oxford United	A	L	1-2	Marsh	1

Appearan
Sub appeara
G

FA Cup

R1	Nov	26	Poole Town	H	W	3-2	Marsh (3)	[illegible]
R2	Jan	7	Bournemouth	H	W	2-0	Langley (pen), Lazarus	1
R3		28	Sheffield Wednesday	A	L	0-3		4

Appearan
Sub appeara
G

League Cup

R1	Aug	23	Colchester United	H	W	5-0	Marsh (4), Lazarus	[illegible]
R2	Sep	14	Aldershot	A	D	1-1	Allen	5
rep		20	Aldershot	H	W	2-0	Langley (pen), Marsh	7
R3	Oct	12	Swansea Town	H	W	2-1	Hazell, Keen	1
R4		25	Leicester City	H	W	4-2	R.Morgan, Allen (2), Lazarus	2
R5	Dec	7	Carlisle United	H	W	2-1	Marsh (2)	1
SF1	Jan	17	Birmingham City	A	W	4-1	Marsh, R.Morgan, Lazarus, Allen	3
SF2	Feb	7	Birmingham City	H	W	3-1	Marsh (2), Keen	2
F	Mar	4	West Bromwich	W	W	3-2	R.Morgan, Marsh, Lazarus	97

Appearan
Sub appearan
G

Total - Appearan
Total - Sub appearan
Total - G

Clement	Collins	Hazell	Hunt	Keen	Keetch	Kelly	Langley	Lazarus	Leach	Marsh	Morgan I.	Morgan R.	Moughton	Sanderson	Sibley	Springett	Watson	Wilks	OG
	8	3	5	4				7		10		11			6	1	2		
		2	5	4			3	7		10		11		8	6	1			
		3	5	4				7		10		11		8	6	1	2		
		3	5	4				7		10		11		8	6	1	2		
		3		5			12	7		10	8	11		4	6	1	2[a]		
		2	5	4			3	7		10		11		8	6	1			
		2	5	4			3			10	7	11		8	6	1			
		2	5	4			3	7		10	8	11			6	1			
		2	5	4			3	7		10		11		8	6	1			
		2	5	4			3	7		10		11		8	6	1			
		2	5	4			3	7		10		11		8	6	1			
			5	4			3	7	9	10		11		8	6	1	2		
		2	5	4			3	7		10		11		8	6	1			
		2	5	4			3	7		10		11		8	6	1			
		2	5	4			3	7		10		11		8	6	1			
		2	5	4			3	7		10		11		8	6	1			
		2	5	4			3	7		10		11		8	6	1			
		2	5	4			3	7		10		11		8	6	1			
			5	4			3	7		10		11		8	6	1	2		
			5	4			3	7		10		11		8	6	1	2		
			5	4			3	7		10	12	11		8	6	1	2		
			5	4			3	7		10		11		8	6	1	2		
			5	4			3	7		10		11		8	6	1	2	9	
			5	4			3	7		10		11		8	6	1	2		
			5	4			3	7		10		11		8	6	1	2		
			5	4			3	7		10		11		8	6	1	2		
		2	5	4			3	7		10		11		8	6	1			
		2	5	4			3	7		10	8	11			6	1			
		2	5	4			3	7		10		11		8	6	1			
		2	5	4			3	7		10[a]	12	11		8	6	1		9	
		2	5	4			3	7		10	12	11		8[a]	6	1			
		2	5	4	3			7		10	8	11			6	1			
		2	5	4			3	7		10		11		8	6	1			
		2	5	4			3	7		10	11			8	6	1			
		2	5	4			3	7		10	11			8	6	1			
		2	5	4			3	7		10		11		8	6	1			
		2	5	4			3	7[a]		10	12	11	6	8		1			
5		2		4			3	7		10		11	6	8		1			
		2	5	4	12		3	7		10[a]		11		8	6	1			
		2	5	4			3				7	11		8	6	1	12	10[a]	
		2	5	4			3	7				11		8	6	1		10	
		2	5	4			3	7				11		8	6	1		10	
		3	5	4				7	9		8	11	6			1	2	10	
		6	5	4			3	7			8	11				1	2	10	
		2	5	4			3	7		10		11		8	6	1			
		2	5	4			3	7		10		11		8	6	1			
	1	37	44	46	1		40	44	2	41	10	44	3	40	42	46	15	7	
					1		1				4						1		
				6			6	16	1	30	4	11		6	1			5	1

Clement	Collins	Hazell	Hunt	Keen	Keetch	Kelly	Langley	Lazarus	Leach	Marsh	Morgan I.	Morgan R.	Moughton	Sanderson	Sibley	Springett	Watson	Wilks	OG
		2[a]	5	4		1	3	7		10	12	11		8	6				
			5	4			3	7		10		11		8	6	1	2		
			5	4			3	7		10	12	11		8	6	1	2[a]		
		1	3	3		1	3	3		3		3		3	3	2	2		
											2								
							1	1		3									

Clement	Collins	Hazell	Hunt	Keen	Keetch	Kelly	Langley	Lazarus	Leach	Marsh	Morgan I.	Morgan R.	Moughton	Sanderson	Sibley	Springett	Watson	Wilks	OG
			5	4			3	7		10		11		8	6	1	2		
		2	5	4			3	7		10	8	11		6		1			
		2	5	4			3	7		10		11		8	6	1			
		3	5	4				7		10		11		8	6	1	2		
		2	5	4			3	7		10		11		8	6	1			
			5	4			3	7		10		11		8	6	1	2		
			5	4			3	7		10		11		8	6	1	2		
		2	5	4			3	7		10		11		8	6	1			
		2	5	4			3	7		10		11		8	6	1			
		6	9	9			8	9		9	1	9		9	8	9	4		
		1		2			1	4		11		3							

Clement	Collins	Hazell	Hunt	Keen	Keetch	Kelly	Langley	Lazarus	Leach	Marsh	Morgan I.	Morgan R.	Moughton	Sanderson	Sibley	Springett	Watson	Wilks	OG
	1	44	56	58	1	1	51	56	2	53	11	56	3	52	53	57	21	7	
					1		1				6						1		
		1		8			8	21	1	44	4	14		6	1			5	1

1967-68

Division Two

	P	W	D	L	F	A	Pts
Ipswich Town	42	22	15	5	79	44	59
Queen's Park Rangers	42	25	8	9	67	36	58
Blackpool	42	24	10	8	71	43	58
Birmingham City	42	19	14	9	83	51	52
Portsmouth	42	18	13	11	68	55	49
Middlesbrough	42	17	12	13	60	54	46
Millwall	42	14	17	11	62	50	45
Blackburn Rovers	42	16	11	15	56	49	43
Norwich City	42	16	11	15	60	65	43
Carlisle United	42	14	13	15	58	52	41
Crystal Palace	42	14	11	17	56	56	39
Bolton Wanderers	42	13	13	16	60	63	39
Cardiff City	42	13	12	17	60	66	38
Huddersfield Town	42	13	12	17	46	61	38
Charlton Athletic	42	12	13	17	63	68	37
Aston Villa	42	15	7	20	54	64	37
Hull City	42	12	13	17	58	73	37
Derby County	42	13	10	19	71	78	36
Bristol City	42	13	10	19	48	62	36
Preston North End	42	12	11	19	43	65	35
Rotherham United	42	10	11	21	42	76	31
Plymouth Argyle	42	9	9	24	38	72	27

Attendances

	TOTAL		
	Home	**Away**	**Total**
League	387,704	437,660	825,364
Cup/Other	76,236		76,236
TOTAL	463,940	437,660	901,600

	AVERAGE		
	Home	**Away**	**Total**
League	18,462	20,841	19,652
Cup/Other	19,059		19,059
TOTAL	18,558	20,841	19,600

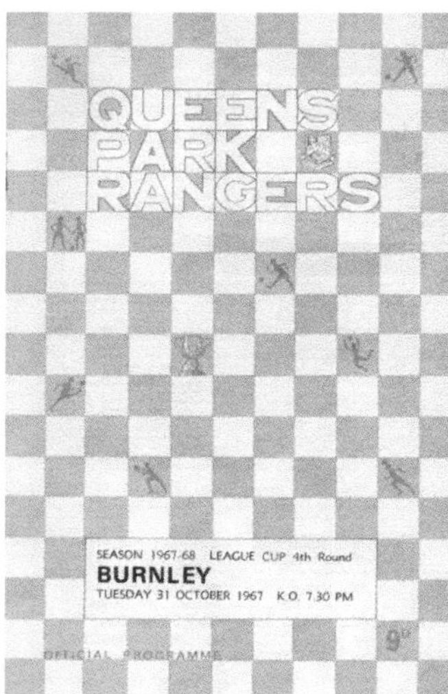

Match No.	Date		Opponents	Location	Result		Scorers	Atte
1	Aug	19	Portsmouth	A	D	1-1	R.Morgan	2
2		22	Bristol City	A	W	2-0	Leach (2)	2
3		26	Norwich City	H	W	2-0	Keen, I.Morgan	1
4		29	Bristol City	H	W	3-1	I.Morgan, Allen, R.Morgan	1
5	Sep	2	Rotherham United	A	W	3-1	Leach, Allen, Lazarus	
6		5	Aston Villa	H	W	3-0	Sanderson (2), Lazarus	2
7		9	Derby County	H	L	0-1		1
8		16	Preston North End	A	W	2-0	R.Morgan, Leach	1
9		23	Charlton Athletic	H	W	2-1	I.Morgan, Allen	1
10		30	Crystal Palace	A	L	0-1		3
11	Oct	7	Bolton Wanderers	H	W	1-0	Wilks	1
12		14	Hull City	A	L	0-2		1
13		21	Millwall	H	W	3-1	R.Morgan, Keen, Allen	2
14		28	Blackpool	A	W	1-0	Allen	2
15	Nov	11	Carlisle United	A	L	1-3	Sibley	1
16		18	Middlesbrough	H	D	1-1	Marsh	1
17		25	Huddersfield Town	A	L	0-1		1
18	Dec	2	Ipswich Town	H	W	1-0	Marsh	1
19		9	Birmingham City	A	L	0-2		2
20		12	Blackburn Rovers	H	W	3-1	Marsh, Wilks, Sanderson	1
21		16	Portsmouth	H	W	2-0	I.Morgan, Keen	2
22		23	Norwich City	A	D	0-0		2
23		26	Plymouth Argyle	A	W	1-0	Keen (pen)	2
24		30	Plymouth Argyle	H	W	4-1	Marsh (2), Keen (2)	1
25	Jan	6	Rotherham United	H	W	6-0	I.Morgan (2), Leach (2), R.Morgan, Marsh	1
26		20	Preston North End	H	W	2-0	Marsh (2)	1
27	Feb	3	Charlton Athletic	A	D	3-3	R.Morgan (2), Marsh	2
28		10	Crystal Palace	H	W	2-1	I.Morgan, Wilks	1
29		17	Derby County	A	L	0-4		2
30		24	Bolton Wanderers	A	D	1-1	R.Morgan	1
31	Mar	9	Hull City	H	D	1-1	Marsh (pen)	1
32		16	Millwall	A	D	1-1	Marsh	2
33		23	Blackpool	H	W	2-0	I.Morgan, Clarke	1
34		30	Blackburn Rovers	A	W	1-0	Clarke	1
35	Apr	6	Carlisle United	H	W	1-0	Clarke	1
36		12	Cardiff City	H	W	1-0	I.Morgan	2
37		13	Middlesbrough	A	L	1-3	Allen	2
38		16	Cardiff City	A	L	0-1		2
39		20	Huddersfield Town	H	W	3-0	Marsh (2), OG (Legg)	1
40		27	Ipswich Town	A	D	2-2	Marsh (pen), Leach	2
41	May	4	Birmingham City	H	W	2-0	Leach, I.Morgan	2
42		11	Aston Villa	A	W	2-1	Leach, OG (Bradley)	3

Appeara
Sub appeara
G

FA Cup

R3	Jan	27	Preston North End	H	L	1-3	Keen	1

Appeara
Sub appeara
G

League Cup

R2	Sep	12	Hull City	H	W	2-1	Leach, Keen	1
R3	Oct	10	Oxford United	H	W	5-1	Wilks (5)	1
R4		31	Burnley	H	L	1-2	Sibley	2

Appeara
Sub appeara
G

Total - Appeara
Total - Sub appeara
Total - G

Clarke	Clement	Finch	Harris	Hazell	Hunt	Keen	Keetch	Kelly	Lazarus	Leach	McGovern	Marsh	Morgan I.	Morgan R.	Sanderson	Sibley	Springett	Watson	Wilks	OG
	2		3	6		4	5		7	10			8	11			1			
	2		3	6		4	5		7	10			8	11			1			
	2[a]		3	6	5	4			7	10			8	11			1	12		
	2[a]		3	6	5	4		1	7	10			8	11				12		
			3	6	5	4			7	10			8	11	12		1	2		
	2		3	6	5	4			7	10			8	11	9		1			
	2		3	6	5	4			7	9			8[a]	11	10		1			
	2		3	6	5	4			12	10			7[a]	11	8		1			
	2		3	6	5	4			7	10			8	11			1			
	2[a]		3	6	5	4	12		7	10			8	11			1			
	2		3	6	12	4	5			9			7	11	8[a]		1		10	
	2		3	6		4	5			9			7	11			1		10	
			3	2		4	5		7				8	11		6	1		10	
	2		3	6		4	5		7	12			8	11		10	1			
	2		3	6		4	5		7				8	11		10	1			
			3	2		4	5		7			10	8	11		6	1			
			3	2		4	5		7[a]			10	8	11	12	6	1			
	2		3	6		4	5					10	8	11			1		7	
	2		3	6		4	5					10	7	11	8		1		12	
	2		3	6		4	5					10	7	11	8		1		9	
	2		3	6		4	5					10	7	11	8		1		9	
	2		3	6		4	5					10	7	11	8		1	12	9[a]	
	2		3	6		4	5				9	10	7	11	8		1			
	2		3	6		4	5					10	7	11	8		1		9	
	2		3	6		4	5			9		10	7	11	8		1			
	2		3	6		4	5			9		10	7	11	8		1			
	2		3	6		4	5			9		10	7	11	8		1			
	2		3	6		4	5					10	7	11	8		1		9	
	2		3	6		4	5			9		10	7	11	8		1			
9	2		3	6		4	5					10	7	11	8		1			
9			3	6		4	5					10	8	11			1	2	7	
9	2		3	6		4	5					10	7	11			1			
9	2		3	6		4	5					10	7	11			1			
9	2		3	6		4	5					10	7	11			1			
9	2[a]		3	6		4	5					10	7	11			1	12		
9			3	6		4	5						7	11			1	2	10	
9			3	6	5	4				12			7	11[a]			1	2	10	
9		2	3	6	5	4		1		8		10	7	11						
9		2	3	6		4	5	1		8		10	7	11						
9		2	3	6		4	5	1		8		10	7	11[a]						
9[a]			3	6		4	5	1		8		10	7					2	12	
9			3	6		4	5	1		8		10	7					2		
3	30	3	42	42	10	42	32	6	14	21	1	25	42	40	16	5	36	6	12	
					1		1		1	2					2			4	2	
3						6			2	9		14	10	8	3	1			3	

Clarke	Clement	Finch	Harris	Hazell	Hunt	Keen	Keetch	Kelly	Lazarus	Leach	McGovern	Marsh	Morgan I.	Morgan R.	Sanderson	Sibley	Springett	Watson	Wilks	OG
	2[a]		3	6		4	5			9		10	7	11	8		1		12	
	1		1	1		1	1			1		1	1	1	1		1			
																			1	
						1														

Clarke	Clement	Finch	Harris	Hazell	Hunt	Keen	Keetch	Kelly	Lazarus	Leach	McGovern	Marsh	Morgan I.	Morgan R.	Sanderson	Sibley	Springett	Watson	Wilks	OG
	2		3	6	5	4			7	10			8	11			1			
	2		3		5	4	6			9			7	11			1		10	
	2		3	6		4	5		7				8	11		10	1			
	3		3	2	2	3	2		2	2			3	3		1	3		1	
						1				1						1			5	

Clarke	Clement	Finch	Harris	Hazell	Hunt	Keen	Keetch	Kelly	Lazarus	Leach	McGovern	Marsh	Morgan I.	Morgan R.	Sanderson	Sibley	Springett	Watson	Wilks	OG
3	34	3	46	45	12	46	35	6	16	24	1	26	46	44	17	6	40	6	13	
					1		1		1	2					2			4	3	
3						8			2	10		14	10	8	3	2			8	2

1968-69

Division One

	P	W	D	L	F	A	Pts
Leeds United	42	27	13	2	66	26	67
Liverpool	42	25	11	6	63	24	61
Everton	42	21	15	6	77	36	57
Arsenal	42	22	12	8	56	27	56
Chelsea	42	20	10	12	73	53	50
Tottenham Hotspur	42	14	17	11	61	51	45
Southampton	42	16	13	13	57	48	45
West Ham United	42	13	18	11	66	50	44
Newcastle United	42	15	14	13	61	55	44
West Bromwich Albion	42	16	11	15	64	67	43
Manchester United	42	15	12	15	57	53	42
Ipswich Town	42	15	11	16	59	60	41
Manchester City	42	15	10	17	64	55	40
Burnley	42	15	9	18	55	82	39
Sheffield Wednesday	42	10	16	16	41	54	36
Wolverhampton W	42	10	15	17	41	58	35
Sunderland	42	11	12	19	43	67	34
Nottingham Forest	42	10	13	19	45	57	33
Stoke City	42	9	15	18	40	63	33
Coventry City	42	10	11	21	46	64	31
Leicester City	42	9	12	21	39	68	30
Queen's Park Rangers	42	4	10	28	39	95	18

Attendances

TOTAL

	Home	Away	Total
League	453,005	623,081	1,076,086
Cup/Other		51,262	51,262
TOTAL	453,005	674,343	1,127,348

AVERAGE

	Home	Away	Total
League	21,572	29,671	25,621
Cup/Other		25,631	25,631
TOTAL	21,572	29,319	25,622

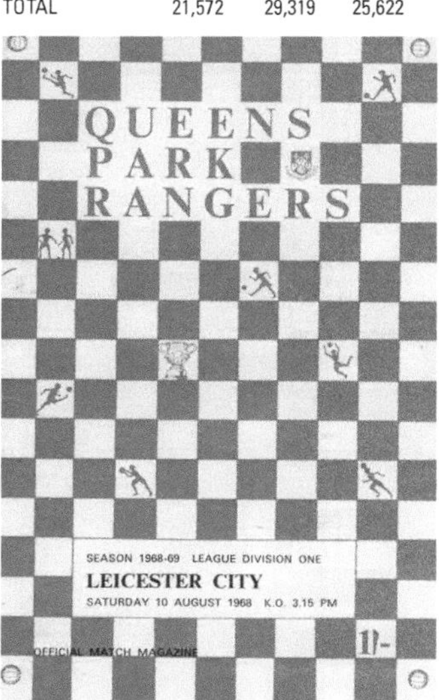

Match No.	Date		Opponents	Location	Result		Scorers	Atten
1	Aug	10	Leicester City	H	D	1-1	Allen	21
2		14	Leeds United	A	L	1-4	Wilks	31
3		17	Wolverhampton	A	L	1-3	I.Morgan	30
4		20	Sunderland	H	D	2-2	Allen, Clarke	20
5		24	Manchester City	H	D	1-1	Bridges	19
6		27	Ipswich Town	A	L	0-3		24
7		31	Arsenal	A	L	1-2	Wilks	44
8	Sep	7	Liverpool	A	L	0-2		46
9		14	Chelsea	H	L	0-4		26
10		21	Stoke City	A	D	1-1	R.Morgan	15
11		28	Southampton	H	D	1-1	Allen	20
12	Oct	5	West Bromwich	A	L	1-3	Clarke	23
13		8	Ipswich Town	H	W	2-1	Bridges, R.Morgan	17
14		12	Sheffield Wednesday	H	W	3-2	Wilks, Bridges, Leach	19
15		19	Newcastle United	A	L	2-3	Wilks, OG (Moncur)	34
16		26	Manchester United	H	L	2-3	Leach, Wilks	31
17	Nov	2	West Ham United	A	L	3-4	Leach (2), Bridges	36
18		9	Burnley	H	L	0-2		22
19		16	Everton	A	L	0-4		42
20		23	Nottingham Forest	H	W	2-1	Marsh, Hazell	18
21	Dec	7	Coventry City	H	L	0-1		17
22		14	Sheffield Wednesday	A	L	0-4		22
23		21	Newcastle United	H	D	1-1	Bridges	16
24		26	West Bromwich	H	L	0-4		18
25	Jan	11	West Ham United	H	D	1-1	Clarke	28
26		18	Burnley	A	D	2-2	Marsh, Leach	12
27		24	Leeds United	H	L	0-1		26
28		29	Tottenham Hotspur	A	L	2-3	Clement, Clarke (pen)	38
29	Feb	1	Everton	H	L	0-1		26
30		15	Tottenham Hotspur	H	D	1-1	Clarke	30
31		22	Coventry City	A	L	0-5		26
32	Mar	4	Nottingham Forest	A	L	0-1		21
33		8	Wolverhampton	H	L	0-1		17
34		12	Leicester City	A	L	0-2		24
35		15	Manchester City	A	L	1-3	Leach	28
36		19	Manchester United	A	L	1-8	Marsh	37
37		22	Arsenal	H	L	0-1		23
38		29	Liverpool	H	L	1-2	Bridges	16
39	Apr	5	Southampton	A	L	2-3	Marsh, Bridges	22
40		7	Sunderland	A	D	0-0		18
41		12	Stoke City	H	W	2-1	Leach (2)	12
42		19	Chelsea	A	L	1-2	Bridges	41

Appearar
Sub appearar
G

FA Cup

R3	Jan	4	Aston Villa	A	L	1-2	I.Morgan	39

Appearar
Sub appearar
G

League Cup

R2	Sep	3	Peterborough United	A	L	2-4	Keen, Clarke	11

Appearar
Sub appearar
G

Total - Appearar
Total - Sub appearar
Total - G

Bridges	Clarke	Clement	Finch	Francis	Gillard	Glover	Harris	Hazell	Hunt	Keen	Keetch	Kelly	Leach	McGovern	Marsh	Metchick	Morgan I.	Morgan R.	Sanderson	Sibley	Spratley	Springett	Watson	Wilks	OG
	9[a]		2				3	6		4							7	11		8		1	5	10	
			2				3	6		4							7	11		8		1	5	10	
							3	6		4	5	1	9				7	11		8			2	10	
	9						3	2		4		1	10[a]				7	11	12	6			5		
9							3	2		4		1					7	11	10	6			5		
9	10						3	2		4		1	8				7			6			5	11	
9		2					3	8		4		1	10[a]				7			6			5	12	
1	9[a]						3	8	12	4	5						7		10	6		1	2		
9							3	8	12	4	5		11[a]				7		10	6		1	2		
9							3	4			5	1	8[a]				7	11		6			2	12	
9							3	4	5			1	8				7	11		6			2		
0	9						3	4	5			1	8			12	7[a]	11		6			2		
7							3	6		4	5	1	8					11					2	10	
7							3	6	5	4		1	8[a]			12		11					2	10	
7							3	6	5	4		1	8					11					2	10	
7							3	6	5	4		1	8					11					2	10	
7							3	6	5	4			8					11				1	2	10	
7							3	6	5	4[a]		1	8				12	11					2	10	
7		3						6	8	5		1			10			11		4			2		
9		2			3			6				1		8	10		7	11		4			5		
		2					3	6					9		10		7	11		4		1	2	8	
7							3	6	5	4			9		10		8	11				1	2		
7	9						3	6	5	8	4				10			11				1	2		
[a]	9						3	6	5	8	4				10			11				1	2		
	9	3				12			5		6		8		10[a]		7	11		4	1		2		
	9	3			12				5		6		8		10		7	11		4	1[a]		2		
	9	3			12				5		6	1	8[a]		10		7	11		4			2		
	9	3						12	5		6[a]	1			10		7	11		4			2	8	
	9	3	12					4	5			1			10		7	11		6			2	8[a]	
1	9	3						4	5			1			10		7			6			2		
1	9	3					6	4	5			1	8		10		7						2		
	9	12			3			4	5		6		8[a]		10		7				1		2	11	
	9	12			3	8		4	5		6				10		7				1		2	11[a]	
	9					11	3	4	5		6		8		10		7				1		2		
	9				3	11		4	5		6		8		10		7				1		2		
	9[a]	3				11		4	5		12		8		10		7			6	1		2		
3		3				11		4	5				9		10		7			6	1		2		
1	9			12			3	4	5[a]		6		8		10						1		2	7	
1	9	2					3	6	5				8		10		7				1		4		
1		2					3	6	5				9				7			8	1		4	10	
1	9	2					3	6	5				10				7			8[a]	1		4	12	
1	9	2					3	6	5				8		10		7				1		4		
7	23	17	2		4	5	29	38	29	19	16	20	30	1	22		32	25	3	25	13	9	42	17	
		2	1	1	2	1		1	2		1					2	1		1					3	
3	5	1						1					8		4		1	2						5	1
	9	3				10			5		4		8				7	11		6	1		2		
	1	1				1			1		1		1				1	1		1	1		1		
																	1								
9	12	2	3					8		4		1					7[a]			6			5	10	
1		1	1					1		1		1					1			1			1	1	
	1																								
	1									1															
8	24	19	3		4	6	29	39	30	20	17	21	31	1	22		34	26	3	27	14	9	44	18	
	1	2	1	1	2	1		1	2		1					2	1		1					3	
3	6	1						1		1			8		4		2	2						5	1

1969-70

Division Two

	P	W	D	L	F	A	Pts
Huddersfield Town	42	24	12	6	68	37	60
Blackpool	42	20	13	9	56	45	53
Leicester City	42	19	13	10	64	50	51
Middlesbrough	42	20	10	12	55	45	50
Swindon Town	42	17	16	9	57	47	50
Sheffield United	42	22	5	15	73	38	49
Cardiff City	42	18	13	11	61	41	49
Blackburn Rovers	42	20	7	15	54	50	47
Queen's Park Rangers	42	17	11	14	66	57	45
Millwall	42	15	14	13	56	56	44
Norwich City	42	16	11	15	49	46	43
Carlisle United	42	14	13	15	58	56	41
Hull City	42	15	11	16	72	70	41
Bristol City	42	13	13	16	54	50	39
Oxford United	42	12	15	15	35	42	39
Bolton Wanderers	42	12	12	18	54	61	36
Portsmouth	42	13	9	20	66	80	35
Birmingham City	42	11	11	20	51	78	33
Watford	42	9	13	20	44	57	31
Charlton Athletic	42	7	17	18	35	76	31
Aston Villa	42	8	13	21	36	62	29
Preston North End	42	8	12	22	43	63	28

Attendances

TOTAL

	Home	Away	Total
League	368,025	413,382	781,407
Cup/Other	142,831	82,079	224,910
TOTAL	510,856	495,461	1,006,317

AVERAGE

	Home	Away	Total
League	17,525	19,685	18,605
Cup/Other	23,805	27,360	24,990
TOTAL	18,921	20,644	19,732

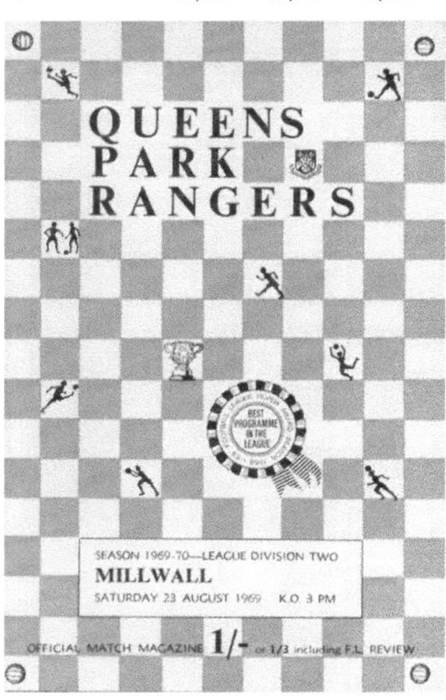

Match No.	Date		Opponents	Location	Result		Scorers	Atte
1	Aug	9	Hull City	H	W	3-0	Clark, Clarke, Leach	1
2		16	Preston North End	A	D	0-0		1
3		20	Watford	A	W	1-0	Bridges	2
4		23	Millwall	H	W	3-2	Bridges (2), Clement	1
5		26	Blackpool	H	W	6-1	Marsh (3), Bridges (2), Venables (pen)	1
6		30	Birmingham City	A	L	0-3		3
7	Sep	6	Huddersfield Town	H	W	4-2	Marsh, Morgan, Bridges, Venables (pen)	1
8		13	Portsmouth	A	W	3-1	Clement, Francis, Bridges	2
9		17	Blackburn Rovers	A	W	1-0	Leach	1
10		20	Swindon Town	H	W	2-0	Wilks, Clarke (pen)	2
11		27	Cardiff City	A	L	2-4	Venables (pen), Bridges	3
12	Oct	4	Middlesbrough	H	W	4-0	Bridges (2), Clarke, Clement	2
13		7	Preston North End	H	D	0-0		2
14		11	Norwich City	A	L	0-1		2
15		18	Carlisle United	A	L	2-3	Clement, Clarke	1
16		25	Charlton Athletic	H	D	1-1	Metchick	2
17	Nov	1	Aston Villa	A	D	1-1	Marsh	3
18		8	Sheffield United	H	W	2-1	Bridges, Clarke	1
19		11	Watford	H	W	2-1	Clarke, Hazell	1
20		15	Bristol City	A	L	0-2		1
21		22	Leicester City	H	D	1-1	Bridges	2
22		29	Bolton Wanderers	A	L	4-6	Leach, Bridges, Clement, Marsh	
23	Dec	6	Oxford United	H	L	1-2	Bridges	1
24		13	Portsmouth	H	W	2-0	Clarke, Bridges	1
25		26	Millwall	A	L	0-2		1
26		27	Birmingham City	H	W	2-1	Bridges (2)	1
27	Jan	10	Swindon Town	A	D	0-0		1
28		17	Cardiff City	H	W	2-1	Gillard, Marsh	2
29		20	Huddersfield Town	A	L	0-2		2
30		31	Middlesbrough	A	L	0-1		2
31	Feb	14	Hull City	A	W	2-1	Marsh, Clarke	1
32		17	Norwich City	H	W	4-0	Venables (pen), Clarke, Bridges, Marsh	1
33		24	Sheffield United	A	L	0-2		2
34		28	Aston Villa	H	W	4-2	Bridges (2), Marsh (2)	1
35	Mar	14	Bolton Wanderers	H	L	0-4		1
36		21	Oxford United	A	D	0-0		1
37		27	Carlisle United	H	D	0-0		1
38		28	Bristol City	H	D	2-2	Bridges, Francis	1
39		31	Charlton Athletic	A	D	1-1	Watson	1
40	Apr	4	Blackpool	A	D	1-1	Leach	1
41		14	Blackburn Rovers	H	L	2-3	Venables (pen), Hazell	1
42		18	Leicester City	A	L	1-2	Marsh (pen)	2

Appeara
Sub appeara
G

FA Cup

R3	Jan	3	South Shields	H	W	4-1	Marsh (2), Clarke, Ferguson	1
R4		24	Charlton Athletic	A	W	3-2	Marsh (2), Clarke	3
R5	Feb	7	Derby County	H	W	1-0	OG (Mackay)	2
R6		21	Chelsea	H	L	2-4	Venables (pen), Bridges	3

Appeara
Sub appeara
G

League Cup

R2	Sep	3	Mansfield Town	A	D	2-2	Bridges, Watson	
rep		9	Mansfield Town	H	W	4-0	Venables (pen), Clement, Marsh, Clarke	1
R3		23	Tranmere Rovers	H	W	6-0	Marsh (4), Leach, Clarke	1
R4	Oct	15	Wolverhampton	H	W	3-1	Clarke (2), Bridges	2
R5		29	Manchester City	A	L	0-3		4

Appeara
Sub appeara
G

Total - Appeara
Total - Sub appeara
Total - G

Busby	Clark	Clarke	Clement	Ferguson	Francis	Gillard	Harris	Hazell	Hunt	Kelly	Leach	McGovern	Marsh	Metchick	Mobley	Morgan	Sibley	Spratley	Turpie	Venables	Watson	Wilks	OG
	11	9	3					6	5	1	12		10			8				4[a]	2		
	11	9	3					6	5	1			10			8				4	2		
		9	3				12	6	5	1	11		10				8[a]			4	2		
		9[a]	3				12	6	5	1	11		10				8			4	2		
	11		3					6	5	1	9		10				8			4	2		
	11		3					6	5	1	9		10				8			4	2		
			3					6	5	1	9		10			11	8			4	2		
		9	3		11			6	5	1[a]			10				4		12		2	8	
		9	2					6	5		7		10			11	4	1	3			8	
		9	3					6	5		7		10			11	4	1			2	8	
		9	3					6	5		8		10			11		1		4	2		
		9	3					6			8		10		5	11				4	2		
		9	2			3		6		1	8		10		5	11[a]	12			4			
		9	3					6	12	1	11		10		5		8[a]			4	2		
		9	3					6	8	1	11		10		5					4	2		
	11[a]	9	3					6		1	8		10	12	5					4	2		
		9				12	3	6	8	1	11[a]		10		5					4	2		
	12	9					3	6	8	1	11		10		5					4[a]	2		
	11	9					3	6	4	1	8		10		5						2		
	11	9	12				3	6	4	1	8		10		5[a]						2		
		9	2	8	7		3	6	5		4		10					1					
		9	2	8			3	6	5		7		10					1		4			
		9	2	10	11		3	6	5		8							1		4			
		9	2	11		3		6		1	10						4			8	5		
		9	2	10		3		6		1	11				5					8	4		
		9	2	10	11	3		6	4	1										8	5		
		9	2	11		3		6		1			10				4			8	5		
		9	2	11		3		6					10				4	1		8	5		
		9	2	11		3		6		1			10		12		4[a]			8	5		
		9	2	11[a]		3		6		1	12		10		5					8	4	7	
		9	2	11		3		6		1			10		5					8	4		
		9[a]	2	11		3		6		1	12		10		5					8	4		
			2	11		3		6		1	9		10		5[a]	12				8	4		
		9	2	11		3		6		1			10			8				4	5		
		9	2	11		3[a]	12	6	5	1			10			8				4			
							3	6			9	4	10		5			1		8	2	11	
					12		3	6			9	4	10		5			1		8[a]	2	11	
				11	8		3	6			9	4	10		5			1			2		
				11	8		3	6			9		10		5			1		4	2		
				11	8		3	6			9		10		5			1		4	2		
				11	8		3	6			9		10		5	12		1		4	2		
4			2	11	8	3		6			9		10		5	7		1					
1	7	31	32	20	9	14	13	42	21	28	30	3	38		21	11	13	14	1	34	35	6	
	1		1		1	1	3		1		3			1	1	2	1		1				
	1	9	5		2	1		2			4		12	1		1				5	1	1	

Busby	Clark	Clarke	Clement	Ferguson	Francis	Gillard	Harris	Hazell	Hunt	Kelly	Leach	McGovern	Marsh	Metchick	Mobley	Morgan	Sibley	Spratley	Turpie	Venables	Watson	Wilks	OG
		9	2	8	11	3		6		1			10							4	5		
		9	2	11		3		6		1			10		5					8	4		
		9	2	11		3		6		1			10		5					8	4		
			2	11		3		6		1	9		10		5					8	4		
		3	4	4	1	4		4		4	1		4		3					4	4		
		2		1									4							1			1

Busby	Clark	Clarke	Clement	Ferguson	Francis	Gillard	Harris	Hazell	Hunt	Kelly	Leach	McGovern	Marsh	Metchick	Mobley	Morgan	Sibley	Spratley	Turpie	Venables	Watson	Wilks	OG
	11		3					6	5	1	9		10				8			4	2		
		12	3					6	5	1	9[a]		10			11	8			4	2		
		9	4			3		6	5		7		10			11		1			2	8	
	11	9	3					6		1	8		10		5					4	2		
		9	3					6		1	8		10	11	5					4	2		
	2	3	5			1		5	3	4	5		5	1	2	2	2	1		4	5	1	
		1																					
		4	1								1		5							1	1		

Busby	Clark	Clarke	Clement	Ferguson	Francis	Gillard	Harris	Hazell	Hunt	Kelly	Leach	McGovern	Marsh	Metchick	Mobley	Morgan	Sibley	Spratley	Turpie	Venables	Watson	Wilks	OG
1	9	37	41	24	10	19	13	51	24	36	36	3	47	1	26	13	15	15	1	42	44	7	
	1	1	1		1	1	3		1		3			1	1	2	1		1				
	1	15	6	1	2	1		2			5		21	1		1				7	2	1	1

1970-71

Division Two

	P	W	D	L	F	A	Pts
Leicester City	42	23	13	6	57	30	59
Sheffield United	42	21	14	7	73	39	56
Cardiff City	42	20	13	9	64	41	53
Carlisle United	42	20	13	9	65	43	53
Hull City	42	19	13	10	54	41	51
Luton Town	42	18	13	11	62	43	49
Middlesbrough	42	17	14	11	60	43	48
Millwall	42	19	9	14	59	42	47
Birmingham City	42	17	12	13	58	48	46
Norwich City	42	15	14	13	54	52	44
Queen's Park Rangers	42	16	11	15	58	53	43
Swindon Town	42	15	12	15	61	51	42
Sunderland	42	15	12	15	52	54	42
Oxford United	42	14	14	14	41	48	42
Sheffield Wednesday	42	12	12	18	51	69	36
Portsmouth	42	10	14	18	46	61	34
Orient	42	9	16	17	29	51	34
Watford	42	10	13	19	38	60	33
Bristol City	42	10	11	21	46	64	31
Charlton Athletic	42	8	14	20	41	65	30
Blackburn Rovers	42	6	15	21	37	69	27
Bolton Wanderers	42	7	10	25	35	74	24

Attendances

TOTAL

	Home	Away	Total
League	270,098	341,419	611,517
Cup/Other	29,865	31,729	61,594
TOTAL	299,963	373,148	673,111

AVERAGE

	Home	Away	Total
League	12,862	16,258	14,560
Cup/Other	14,933	31,729	20,531
TOTAL	13,042	16,961	14,958

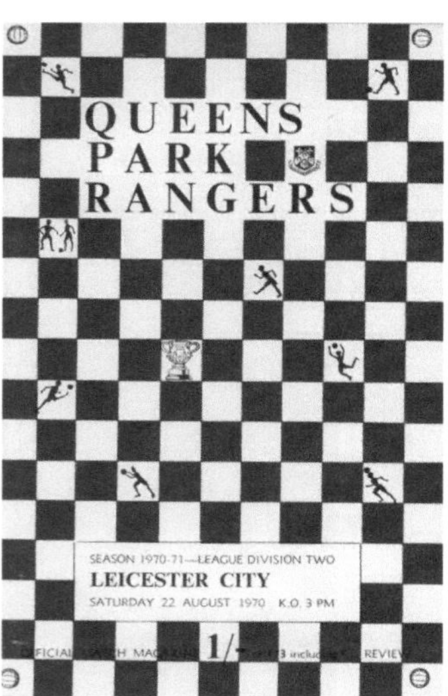

Match No.	Date		Opponents	Location	Result		Scorers	Atten
1	Aug	15	Birmingham City	A	L	1-2	Bridges	30
2		22	Leicester City	H	L	1-3	Venables (pen)	17
3		29	Bolton Wanderers	A	D	2-2	Venables (2, 1 pen)	10
4	Sep	2	Blackburn Rovers	A	W	2-0	Leach, Saul	7
5		5	Watford	H	D	1-1	Venables (pen)	18
6		12	Sheffield Wednesday	A	L	0-1		14
7		19	Bristol City	H	W	2-1	Marsh, Bridges	13
8		26	Middlesbrough	A	L	2-6	Clement, Marsh	16
9		29	Luton Town	H	L	0-1		19
10	Oct	3	Orient	H	W	5-1	Marsh (2), Morgan (2), Venables (pen)	14
11		10	Swindon Town	A	L	0-1		17
12		17	Birmingham City	H	W	5-2	Marsh (3), Venables, McCulloch	13
13		21	Oxford United	A	W	3-1	Venables, Ferguson, Francis	15
14		24	Portsmouth	H	W	2-0	Clement, Morgan	14
15		31	Millwall	A	L	0-3		15
16	Nov	7	Cardiff City	H	L	0-1		11
17		14	Sheffield United	A	D	1-1	Hunt	19
18		21	Hull City	A	D	1-1	Leach	15
19		28	Charlton Athletic	H	L	1-4	Leach	14
20	Dec	5	Sunderland	A	L	1-3	Leach	14
21		12	Carlisle United	H	D	1-1	Marsh	8
22		19	Leicester City	A	D	0-0		23
23	Jan	9	Luton Town	A	D	0-0		22
24		16	Oxford United	H	W	2-0	Francis, Marsh	10
25	Feb	6	Sunderland	H	W	2-0	Venables, Leach	11
26		13	Carlisle United	A	L	0-3		9
27		20	Hull City	H	D	1-1	Marsh	13
28		27	Millwall	H	W	2-0	Francis, Marsh	15
29	Mar	6	Portsmouth	A	L	0-2		10
30		13	Sheffield United	H	D	2-2	Marsh (2)	12
31		20	Cardiff City	A	L	0-1		23
32		23	Norwich City	H	L	0-1		9
33		27	Watford	A	W	2-1	Marsh (2)	16
34	Apr	3	Bolton Wanderers	H	W	4-0	Marsh (3), Leach	8
35		6	Sheffield Wednesday	H	W	1-0	Marsh	11
36		10	Norwich City	A	L	0-3		15
37		12	Orient	A	W	1-0	McCulloch	11
38		17	Swindon Town	H	W	4-2	Clement, Venables (2), McCulloch	11
39		20	Charlton Athletic	A	W	3-0	McCulloch (2), Marsh	16
40		24	Bristol City	A	D	0-0		12
41		27	Blackburn Rovers	H	W	2-0	Marsh, Francis	9
42	May	1	Middlesbrough	H	D	1-1	Francis	10

Appearar
Sub appearar
G

FA Cup

R3	Jan	2	Swindon Town	H	L	1-2	Marsh (pen)	14

Appearar
Sub appearar
G

League Cup

R2	Sep	8	Cardiff City	H	W	4-0	Bridges, Saul, Marsh, Venables (pen)	15
R3	Oct	6	Fulham	A	L	0-2		31

Appearar
Sub appearar
G

Total - Appearar
Total - Sub appearar
Total - G

usby	Clement	Evans	Ferguson	Francis	Gillard	Harris	Hazell	Hunt	Leach	McCulloch	McGovern	Marsh	Mobley	Morgan	Parkes	Salvage	Saul	Sibley	Spratley	Venables	Watson	Wilks
	2			11	3		6	5	10								9	8	1	4		
	2			12	3		6	5	11			10			1		9	8		4		
	3		8				2	5	11			10			1		9	6		4		
	3		11	12			2	5	8[a]			10			1		9	6		4		
	3		11	8			2	5				10			1		9	6		4		
2	3		11[a]	8			2	5				10			1		9	6		4		
	3		11	8			2	5				10			1		9	6		4		
	3[a]		11	8			2	5				10		7	1		9	6		4	12	
4	3			7								10	5	11	1		9	6		8	2	
9	3		7				6	4				10	5	11	1					8	2	
	2		7		3		6	4				10		11	1		9			8	5	
	2		11		3		6	4		9		10		7	1					8	5	
a	2		11	12	3		6	5				10		7	1					8	4	
	2		11	9	3[a]		6	4		12		10	5	7	1					8		
	4			8	3	12	6	5		9		10		7	1		11				2[a]	
6	4			11		3	2	5	7			10			1		9			8		
6	4		11	7		3	2	5	9			10			1					8		
6	4		11	7		3	2	5	9	12		10[a]			1					8		
4	2		11	7		3	6	5	9	8					1					10		
6	2		11	7		3	4	5	10						1		9			8		
6	2		11	7		3	4	5	9			10		12	1					8[a]		
4	3			11				5	9		7	10			1		8	6			2	
	3		11	8				5	9[a]	12		10		7	1			6		4	2	
	3		11	8			6	5	9			10		7	1					4	2	
	3		11	8				5	9			10		7[a]	1			6		4	2	12
	3		11	8[a]			12	5	9			10		7	1			6		4	2	
	3		11	8				5	9	12		10		7[a]	1			6		4	2	
	3		11	8				5	9		12	10			1			6		4[a]	2	7
	3		11	8				5	9		4	10			1			6			2	7
	3		11	8			2	5	9		7	10			1			6		4		
2	3			8			2	5	9		11[a]	10		7	1			6		4		
	3		11	8			2	5	9			10		7	1			6		4		
	2			8	3		6	5	7[a]		4	10		12	1	11	9					
	2		7	8	3		6	5	9			10			1	11				4		
	2	5	7	8	3		6		9	12		10			1	11[a]				4		
	2	5	11	8	3		6		7			10			1		9			4		
a	2	5	7	8	3		6			9		10			1		11			12		
a	2	5		8	3		6			9		10		12	1		11			7		
	2	5		7	3		6	4		9[a]		10		12	1		11			8		
	9	5		7	3		6	4				10			1		11			8	2	
	2	5	7[a]	8	3		12	4		9		10			1		11			4		
	2	5		7	3		6	4		9		10			1		11			8		
2	42	8	30	35	17	6	33	37	25	8	5	39	3	15	41	3	22	19	1	37	15	2
2				3		1	2			5	1			4						1	1	1
	3		1	5				1	6	5		21		3			1			10		

usby	Clement	Evans	Ferguson	Francis	Gillard	Harris	Hazell	Hunt	Leach	McCulloch	McGovern	Marsh	Mobley	Morgan	Parkes	Salvage	Saul	Sibley	Spratley	Venables	Watson	Wilks
4	3			11				5	9		7	10			1			6		8	2	
	1			1				1	1		1	1			1			1		1	1	
												1										

usby	Clement	Evans	Ferguson	Francis	Gillard	Harris	Hazell	Hunt	Leach	McCulloch	McGovern	Marsh	Mobley	Morgan	Parkes	Salvage	Saul	Sibley	Spratley	Venables	Watson	Wilks
2	3[a]		11	8			2	5				10			1		9	6		4		
9	3		7				6	4				10	5	11	1					8	2	
	2		2	1			2	2				2	1	1	2		1	1		2	1	
												1					1			1		

usby	Clement	Evans	Ferguson	Francis	Gillard	Harris	Hazell	Hunt	Leach	McCulloch	McGovern	Marsh	Mobley	Morgan	Parkes	Salvage	Saul	Sibley	Spratley	Venables	Watson	Wilks
4	45	8	32	37	17	6	35	40	26	8	6	42	4	16	44	3	23	21	1	40	17	2
3				3		1	2			5	1			4						1	1	1
	3		1	5				1	6	5		23		3			2			11		

1971-72

Division Two

	P	W	D	L	F	A	Pts
Norwich City	42	21	15	6	60	36	57
Birmingham City	42	19	18	5	60	31	56
Millwall	42	19	17	6	64	46	55
Queen's Park Rangers	42	20	14	8	57	28	54
Sunderland	42	17	16	9	67	57	50
Blackpool	42	20	7	15	70	50	47
Burnley	42	20	6	16	70	55	46
Bristol City	42	18	10	14	61	49	46
Middlesbrough	42	19	8	15	50	48	46
Carlisle United	42	17	9	16	61	57	43
Swindon Town	42	15	12	15	47	47	42
Hull City	42	14	10	18	49	53	38
Luton Town	42	10	18	14	43	48	38
Sheffield Wednesday	42	13	12	17	51	58	38
Oxford United	42	12	14	16	43	55	38
Portsmouth	42	12	13	17	59	68	37
Orient	42	14	9	19	50	61	37
Preston North End	42	12	12	18	52	58	36
Cardiff City	42	10	14	18	56	69	34
Fulham	42	12	10	20	45	68	34
Charlton Athletic	42	12	9	21	55	77	33
Watford	42	5	9	28	24	75	19

Attendances

TOTAL	Home	Away	Total
League	305,680	357,035	662,715
Cup/Other	68,507	48,554	117,061
TOTAL	374,187	405,589	779,776

AVERAGE	Home	Away	Total
League	14,556	17,002	15,779
Cup/Other	17,127	24,277	19,510
TOTAL	14,967	17,634	16,245

Match No.	Date		Opponents	Location	Result		Scorers	Atte
1	Aug	14	Sheffield Wednesday	H	W	3-0	Marsh (2, 1 pen), Francis	1
2		21	Middlesbrough	A	L	2-3	McCulloch, Marsh	2
3		28	Millwall	H	D	1-1	Marsh	1
4		31	Fulham	A	W	3-0	Saul, OG (Matthewson), McCulloch	2
5	Sep	4	Swindon Town	A	D	0-0		1
6		11	Preston North End	H	W	2-1	McCulloch, Saul	1
7		18	Burnley	A	L	0-1		1
8		25	Watford	H	W	3-0	Marsh (2), McCulloch	1
9		29	Oxford United	A	L	1-3	Busby	1
10	Oct	2	Norwich City	A	D	0-0		2
11		9	Birmingham City	H	W	1-0	Marsh	1
12		16	Sheffield Wednesday	A	D	0-0		1
13		19	Luton Town	H	W	1-0	Leach	1
14		23	Blackpool	A	D	1-1	Marsh	1
15		30	Portsmouth	H	D	1-1	Morgan	1
16	Nov	6	Cardiff City	A	D	0-0		1
17		13	Bristol City	H	W	3-0	O'Rourke, OG (Merrick), Marsh	1
18		20	Hull City	H	W	2-1	O'Rourke, Morgan	1
19		27	Charlton Athletic	A	L	1-2	Clement	1
20	Dec	4	Sunderland	H	W	2-1	Marsh, O'Rourke	1
21		11	Carlisle United	A	W	4-1	Leach, O'Rourke, Marsh (2)	
22		18	Swindon Town	H	W	3-0	Marsh (2), Venables	1
23		27	Orient	A	L	0-2		1
24	Jan	1	Burnley	H	W	3-1	Leach (2), Marsh	1
25		8	Millwall	A	D	0-0		2
26		22	Oxford United	H	W	4-2	Marsh (2), Saul, Leach	1
27		29	Luton Town	A	D	1-1	Francis	1
28	Feb	12	Blackpool	H	L	0-1		1
29		19	Portsmouth	A	L	0-1		1
30	Mar	4	Bristol City	A	L	0-2		1
31		11	Birmingham City	A	D	0-0		3
32		18	Middlesbrough	H	W	1-0	Clement	1
33		25	Preston North End	A	D	1-1	O'Rourke	1
34		31	Watford	A	W	2-0	Evans, Salvage	1
35	Apr	1	Orient	H	W	1-0	O'Rourke	1
36		3	Norwich City	H	D	0-0		2
37		8	Hull City	A	D	1-1	O'Rourke	1
38		15	Charlton Athletic	H	W	2-0	Francis, Leach	1
39		22	Sunderland	A	W	1-0	Busby	1
40		25	Fulham	H	D	0-0		2
41		29	Carlisle United	H	W	3-0	Clement, Leach, O'Rourke	1
42	May	2	Cardiff City	H	W	3-0	Ferguson, O'Rourke, Leach	

Appeara
Sub appeara
G

FA Cup

R3	Jan	15	Fulham	H	D	1-1	Mancini	2
rep		18	Fulham	A	L	1-2	Clement	2

Appeara
Sub appeara
G

League Cup

R2	Sep	7	Birmingham City	H	W	2-0	Francis, Marsh	1
R3	Oct	5	Lincoln City	H	W	4-2	Morgan, McCulloch, Marsh, Saul	1
R4		26	Bristol Rovers	H	D	1-1	Marsh	1
rep	Nov	2	Bristol Rovers	A	L	0-1		2

Appeara
Sub appeara
G

Total - Appeara
Total - Sub appeara
Total - G

Clement	Evans	Ferguson	Francis	Gillard	Hazell	Hunt	Leach	McCulloch	McGovern	Mancini	Marsh	Morgan	O'Rourke	Parkes	Salvage	Saul	Seary	Venables	Watson	OG
2			8	3	6	5	11	9			10			1				4		
2			8	3	6	5	11	9			10			1	12			4		
2			8	3	6	5	11	9			10			1				4		
2			8	3	6	5		9			10			1		11		4		
2				3	6	5[a]		9			10			1	8	11	12	4		
2			8	3	6	5[a]		9	12		10			1		11		4		
2			8	3	6	5		9			10			1		11		4		
2			8	3	6	5		9			10			1		11		4		
2			8	3	6	5		9			10			1		11		4		
2			8	3	6	5		9			10	7		1		11		4		
2			8[a]	3	6	5		9			10			1	12	11		4		
2				3	4	5	12	9[a]		6	10			1		11		8		
2				3	6	12	8			5	10		9[a]	1		11		4		
3					2	5	8	9		6	10			1		11		4		
3			8		2	5				6	10	12	9	1		11		4		
2			8[a]		3	6		11		5	10	7	9	1		12		4		
2			8		3	6	9			5	10	7	11	1		4				
2			8		3	6[a]	9			5	10	7	11	1		12		4		
2			8[a]		3	5	9			6	10	7	11	1		12		4		
2			8		3	5	9			6	10	7	11	1				4		
2			8		3	5	9	12		6	10	7	11	1				4[a]		
2			8		3	5	9			6	10	7	11	1				4		
2			8		3	5	9	12		6	10	7[a]	11	1				4		
2			8		3	5	9			6	10		11	1		7		4		
2			8		3	5	9			6	10		11	1		7		4		
2		11	8		3	5	9			6	10			1		7		4		
2		11	8		3	5	9			6	10			1		7		4		
2		11	8[a]		3	5	9			6	10			1		7		4		
2		11	8		3	5	9			6	10		7	1						
2			7	3	5	4	12	9		6	10[a]		11	1						
2	5	10	7	3	6		12	8					9[a]	1	11					
2	5	10	8	3	6			9					7	1	11					
2	5	10	8	3	6		9	12					7	1	11					
2	5	10	8	3	6		9						7	1	11					
2	5	10	8	3	6		9						7	1	11					
2	5	10	8	3	6		9						7	1	11					
2	5	10	8	3	6		9	12					7	1	11[a]					
2	5[a]	10	8	3	6		9	12					7	1	11					
2		10	8	3	6		9			5			7	1	11					
2		10	8	3	6		9	12		5			7	1	11[a]					
2		10	8		6		9			5			7	1	11				3	
2		10	8		6		9			5			7	1	11				3	
42	8	16	38	24	42	29	28	17		23	30	9	26	42	13	18		27	2	
						1	3	6	1			1			2	3	1			
3	1	1	3				8	4			17	2	9		1	3		1		2

Clement	Evans	Ferguson	Francis	Gillard	Hazell	Hunt	Leach	McCulloch	McGovern	Mancini	Marsh	Morgan	O'Rourke	Parkes	Salvage	Saul	Seary	Venables	Watson	OG
2			8		3	5	9	12		6	10		11	1		7[a]		4		
2			8		3	5	9			6	10		11	1		7		4		
2			2		2	2	2			2	2		2	2		2		2		
								1												
1										1										

Clement	Evans	Ferguson	Francis	Gillard	Hazell	Hunt	Leach	McCulloch	McGovern	Mancini	Marsh	Morgan	O'Rourke	Parkes	Salvage	Saul	Seary	Venables	Watson	OG
2			8	3	6	5		9			10			1		11		4		
2			8	3	6	5		9			10	7		1		11		4		
3	6		8		2	5		9[a]			10	12		1		11		4		
2	5	11	8		3	6					10	7		1	12	9[a]		4		
4	2	1	4	2	4	4		3			4	2		4		4		4		
												1			1					
			1					1			3	1				1				

Clement	Evans	Ferguson	Francis	Gillard	Hazell	Hunt	Leach	McCulloch	McGovern	Mancini	Marsh	Morgan	O'Rourke	Parkes	Salvage	Saul	Seary	Venables	Watson	OG
48	10	17	44	26	48	35	30	20		25	36	11	28	48	13	24		33	2	
						1	3	7	1			2			3	3	1			
4	1	1	4				8	5		1	20	3	9		1	4		1		2

1972-73

Division Two

	P	W	D	L	F	A	Pts
Burnley	42	24	14	4	72	35	62
Queen's Park Rangers	42	24	13	5	81	37	61
Aston Villa	42	18	14	10	51	47	50
Middlesbrough	42	17	13	12	46	43	47
Bristol City	42	17	12	13	63	51	46
Sunderland	42	17	12	13	59	49	46
Blackpool	42	18	10	14	56	51	46
Oxford United	42	19	7	16	52	43	45
Fulham	42	16	12	14	58	49	44
Sheffield Wednesday	42	17	10	15	59	55	44
Millwall	42	16	10	16	55	47	42
Luton Town	42	15	11	16	44	53	41
Hull City	42	14	12	16	64	59	40
Nottingham Forest	42	14	12	16	47	52	40
Orient	42	12	12	18	49	53	36
Swindon Town	42	10	16	16	46	60	36
Portsmouth	42	12	11	19	42	59	35
Carlisle United	42	11	12	19	50	52	34
Preston North End	42	11	12	19	37	64	34
Cardiff City	42	11	11	20	43	58	33
Huddersfield Town	42	8	17	17	36	56	33
Brighton & Hove Albion	42	8	13	21	46	83	29

Attendances

TOTAL	Home	Away	Total
League	309,002	307,216	616,218
Cup/Other	13,626	73,358	86,984
TOTAL	322,628	380,574	703,202

AVERAGE	Home	Away	Total
League	14,714	14,629	14,672
Cup/Other	13,626	18,340	17,397
TOTAL	14,665	15,223	14,962

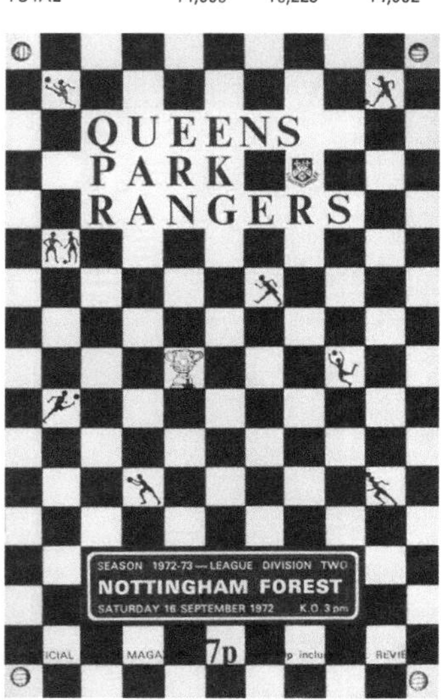

Match No.	Date		Opponents	Location	Result		Scorers	Attenc
1	Aug	12	Swindon Town	A	D	2-2	Busby, Leach	14
2		19	Sheffield Wednesday	H	W	4-2	Francis, O'Rourke, Givens, Leach	12
3		26	Preston North End	A	D	1-1	O'Rourke	9
4	Sep	2	Middlesbrough	H	D	2-2	Givens, O'Rourke	10
5		9	Burnley	A	D	1-1	Busby	10
6		16	Nottingham Forest	H	W	3-0	Givens, Bowles, McCulloch	12
7		19	Bristol City	H	D	1-1	Francis	11
8		23	Orient	A	D	2-2	Leach, Bowles	9
9		26	Hull City	A	L	1-4	Givens	8
10		30	Cardiff City	H	W	3-0	Givens (2), Bowles	11
11	Oct	7	Carlisle United	H	W	4-0	Leach, Busby, Evans, Francis	11
12		14	Aston Villa	A	W	1-0	Francis	34
13		17	Fulham	A	W	2-0	Bowles, Givens	17
14		21	Sunderland	H	W	3-2	Bowles (2), Givens	17
15		28	Blackpool	A	L	0-2		14
16	Nov	4	Hull City	H	D	1-1	Bowles	13
17		11	Bristol City	A	W	2-1	Givens (2)	12
18		18	Millwall	H	L	1-3	Bowles	15
19		25	Portsmouth	A	W	1-0	Givens	8
20	Dec	2	Oxford United	H	D	0-0		9
21		9	Luton Town	A	D	2-2	Givens, Clement	13
22		23	Brighton	A	W	2-1	Givens (2)	13
23		26	Orient	H	W	3-1	Leach, Givens, Thomas	15
24		30	Sheffield Wednesday	A	L	1-3	Leach	20
25	Jan	6	Preston North End	H	W	3-0	Givens (2), Francis	10
26		20	Middlesbrough	A	D	0-0		8
27		27	Burnley	H	W	2-0	Leach, Givens	22
28	Feb	6	Huddersfield Town	H	W	3-1	Givens (2), Thomas	13
29		10	Nottingham Forest	A	D	0-0		11
30		17	Swindon Town	H	W	5-0	Bowles (3), Francis, Givens	13
31	Mar	3	Carlisle United	A	W	3-1	Thomas, Bowles, Clement	8
32		6	Huddersfield Town	A	D	2-2	Francis, Leach	8
33		10	Aston Villa	H	W	1-0	Leach	21
34		24	Blackpool	H	W	4-0	Bowles, Francis, Thomas, OG (Hatton)	15
35		31	Portsmouth	H	W	5-0	Thomas, OG (Lewis), Venables, Leach, Mancini	14
36	Apr	7	Oxford United	A	L	0-2		12
37		14	Luton Town	H	W	2-0	Mancini, Givens	16
38		18	Cardiff City	A	D	0-0		11
39		21	Millwall	A	W	1-0	Givens	16
40		24	Brighton	H	W	2-0	Francis, Bowles	16
41		28	Fulham	H	W	2-0	Clement, Bowles	22
42	May	9	Sunderland	A	W	3-0	Bowles (2), Thomas	43

Appearan
Sub appearan
Go

FA Cup

R3	Jan	13	Barnet	H	D	0-0		13
rep		16	Barnet	A	W	3-0	Leach, Bowles, Mancini	10
R4	Feb	3	Oxford United	A	W	2-0	Clement, Givens	16
R5		24	Derby County	A	L	2-4	Leach, Givens	38

Appearan
Sub appearan
Go

League Cup

R2	Sep	6	West Bromwich	A	L	1-2	Givens	8

Appearan
Sub appearan
Go

Total - Appearan
Total - Sub appearan
Total - Go

Bowles	Busby	Clement	Delve	Evans	Ferguson	Francis	Gillard	Givens	Hazell	Hunt	Leach	McCulloch	Mancini	Morgan	O'Rourke	Parkes	Salvage	Spratley	Thomas	Venables	Watson	OG
	7	2		5		8		11	6		10				9	1				4	3	
	7	2		5		8		11	6		10				9	1				4	3	
	7	2		5		8		11	6		10				9	1				4	3	
	7	2		5		8		11	6		10				9	1				4	3	
	7	2		5		8		11	6			9			10[a]	1	12			4	3	
10	7	2		5		8		11[a]	6			9				1	12			4	3	
10	7	2		5		8		11	6			9				1				4	3	
10	7	2		5		8			6		11	9				1				4	3	
10	7	2		5		8		11	6			9				1				4	3	
10	7	2		5	12	8	3[a]	11	6		9					1				4		
10	7	2		5		8		11	6		9					1				4	3	
10	7	2		5		8		11	6		9					1				4	3	
10	7[a]	2		5		8		11	6		9	12				1				4	3	
10		2		5		8		11	6		9					1			7	4	3	
10		2		5		8		11	6		9					1			7	4	3	
10		2		5		8		11	6		9					1			7	4	3	
10		2		5		8		11	6		9					1			7	4	3	
10		2		5[a]		8	3	11	6		9				12	1			7	4		
10		2				8	3	11	6		12		5	7	9[a]	1				4		
10		2				8	3	11	6				5	7	9	1			4			
10		2	9			8	3	11	6				5			1			7	4		
10		2				8	3	11	6		9		5			1			7	4		
10		2[a]				8	3	11	6		9		5			1			7	4		
10			12			8	3	11	6		9		5			1			7	4[a]	2	
10					7	8		11	2	6	4[a]		5			1	12		9		3	
10[a]		3	12			8		11	6		4		5			1			9	7	2	
10		2	4			8		11	6		9		5					1	7		3	
10		2	4			8		11		6	9		5			1			7		3	
10		2	4			8		11	6		9		5			1			7		3	
10		2				8		11	6		9		5			1			7	4	3	
10		2				8		11	6		9		5			1			7	4	3	
		2	10			8		11	6		9		5			1			7	4	3	
		2	10			8		11	6		9		5			1			7	4	3	
10		2				8		11	6		9		5			1			7	4	3	
10		2				8		11	6		9		5			1			7	4	3	
10		2				8		11	6		9		5			1			7	4	3	
10		2[a]	12			8		11	6		9		5			1			7	4	3	
10		2				8		11	6		9		5			1			7	4	3	
10		2				8		11	6		9		5			1			7	4	3	
10		2				8		11	6		9		5			1			7	4	3	
10		2				8		11	6		9		5			1			7	4	3	
10		2				8		11	6		9		5			1			7	4	3	
35	13	40	6	18	1	42	8	41	41	2	35	5	24	2	7	41		1	28	37	35	
			3		1						1	1			1		3					
17	3	3		1		9		23			10	1	2		3				6	1		2
10		3			7			11	2	6	4		5			1	8		9			
10		3			7	8		11	4		6		5			1			9		2	
10		2	4			8		11	6[a]	12	9		5					1	7		3	
10		2				8		11	6		9		5			1			7	4	3	
4		4	1		2	3		4	4	1	4		4			3	1	1	4	1	3	
										1												
1		1						2			2		1									
	7	2		5		8		11	6		10	12			9[a]	1				4	3	
	1	1		1		1		1	1		1				1	1				1	1	
												1										
								1														
39	14	45	7	19	3	46	8	46	46	3	40	5	28	2	8	45	1	2	32	39	39	
			3		1					1	1	2			1		3					
18	3	4		1		9		26			12	1	3		3				6	1		2

1973-74

Division One

	P	W	D	L	F	A	Pts
Leeds United	42	24	14	4	66	31	62
Liverpool	42	22	13	7	52	31	57
Derby County	42	17	14	11	52	42	48
Ipswich Town	42	18	11	13	67	58	47
Stoke City	42	15	16	11	54	42	46
Burnley	42	16	14	12	56	53	46
Everton	42	16	12	14	50	48	44
Queen's Park Rangers	42	13	17	12	56	52	43
Leicester City	42	13	16	13	51	41	42
Arsenal	42	14	14	14	49	51	42
Tottenham Hotspur	42	14	14	14	45	50	42
Wolverhampton W	42	13	15	14	49	49	41
Sheffield United	42	14	12	16	44	49	40
Manchester City	42	14	12	16	39	46	40
Newcastle United	42	13	12	17	49	48	38
Coventry City	42	14	10	18	43	54	38
Chelsea	42	12	13	17	56	60	37
West Ham United	42	11	15	16	55	60	37
Birmingham City	42	12	13	17	52	64	37
Southampton	42	11	14	17	47	68	36
Manchester United	42	10	12	20	38	48	32
Norwich City	42	7	15	20	37	62	29

Attendances

TOTAL

	Home	Away	Total
League	480,104	603,617	1,083,721
Cup/Other	172,496	61,621	234,117
TOTAL	652,600	665,238	1,317,838

AVERAGE

	Home	Away	Total
League	22,862	28,744	25,803
Cup/Other	24,642	30,811	26,013
TOTAL	23,307	28,923	25,840

Match No.	Date		Opponents	Location	Result		Scorers	Atter
1	Aug	25	Southampton	H	D	1-1	Givens	18
2		29	Norwich City	A	D	0-0		24
3	Sep	1	Manchester United	A	L	1-2	Francis	44
4		4	West Ham United	H	D	0-0		28
5		8	Stoke City	H	D	3-3	Leach, Venables (pen), Mancini	18
6		10	West Ham United	A	W	3-2	Givens (2), Abbott	26
7		15	Everton	A	L	0-1		30
8		22	Birmingham City	H	D	2-2	OG (Hynd), Bowles	18
9		29	Newcastle United	A	W	3-2	Thomas, Francis, Leach	26
10	Oct	6	Chelsea	H	D	1-1	Bowles	31
11		13	Burnley	A	L	1-2	Thomas	18
12		20	Wolverhampton	A	W	4-2	Bowles (2), Leach, Francis (pen)	19
13		27	Arsenal	H	W	2-0	Givens, Bowles	29
14	Nov	3	Derby County	A	W	2-1	Francis, Bowles	30
15		10	Coventry City	H	W	3-0	Bowles, Francis, Venables	20
16		17	Manchester City	A	L	0-1		30
17		24	Liverpool	H	D	2-2	Bowles, McLintock	26
18	Dec	1	Leeds United	A	D	2-2	Thomas, Bowles	32
19		8	Sheffield United	H	D	0-0		15
20		15	Leicester City	A	L	0-2		17
21		22	Newcastle United	H	W	3-2	Clement, Givens, Bowles	15
22		26	Tottenham Hotspur	A	D	0-0		30
23		29	Stoke City	A	L	1-4	Leach	18
24	Jan	1	Manchester United	H	W	3-0	Bowles (2), Givens	32
25		12	Everton	H	W	1-0	Givens	19
26		19	Southampton	A	D	2-2	Thomas, Francis (pen)	22
27	Feb	2	Leicester City	H	D	0-0		22
28		5	Norwich City	H	L	1-2	Bowles	12
29		23	Chelsea	A	D	3-3	Bowles (2), Givens	34
30		27	Burnley	H	W	2-1	Thomas, Bowles (pen)	21
31	Mar	2	Tottenham Hotspur	H	W	3-1	Givens, Bowles, Francis	25
32		16	Wolverhampton	H	D	0-0		21
33		23	Coventry City	A	W	1-0	Francis	18
34		30	Derby County	H	D	0-0		19
35	Apr	6	Liverpool	A	L	1-2	Thomas	54
36		9	Manchester City	H	W	3-0	Leach (2), Bowles	20
37		12	Ipswich Town	H	L	0-1		27
38		15	Ipswich Town	A	L	0-1		26
39		20	Sheffield United	A	D	1-1	Givens	17
40		23	Birmingham City	A	L	0-4		39
41		27	Leeds United	H	L	0-1		35
42		30	Arsenal	A	D	1-1	Bowles	40

Appeara
Sub appeara
G

FA Cup

R3	Jan	5	Chelsea	A	D	0-0		31
rep		15	Chelsea	H	W	1-0	Bowles	28
R4		26	Birmingham City	H	W	2-0	Leach, Givens	23
R5	Feb	16	Coventry City	A	D	0-0		30
rep		19	Coventry City	H	W	3-2	Givens, Thomas, Bowles	28
R6	Mar	9	Leicester City	H	L	0-2		34

Appeara
Sub appearar
G

League Cup

R2	Oct	8	Tottenham Hotspur	H	W	1-0	Givens	23
R3	Nov	6	Sheffield Wednesday	H	W	8-2	OG (Cameron), OG (Mullen), Francis, Bowles, Givens (2), Leach (2)	16
R4		20	Plymouth Argyle	H	L	0-3		19

Appeara
Sub appearar
G

Total - Appearar
Total - Sub appeara
Total - G

Beck	Bowles	Busby	Clement	Delve	Evans	Francis	Gillard	Givens	Hazell	Leach	McLintock	Mancini	Parkes	Thomas	Venables	Watson	OG
	10		2	8				11	6	9		5	1	7	4	3	
	10		2	8				11	6	9		5	1	7	4	3	
	10		2			8		11	6	9		5	1	7	4	3	
	10		2			8		11	6	9		5	1	7	4	3	
	10		2			8		11	6	9		5	1	7	4	3	
	10		2			8		11	6	9		5	1		4	3	
	10				6	8	3	11	2	9		5	1	7	4		
	10		2			8		11	3	9[a]	6	5	1	7	4		
	10		2			8		11	3	9	6	5	1	7	4		
	10		2			8		11	3	9	6	5	1	7	4		
	10		2		5	8		11	3	9	6		1	7	4		
	10		2	12		8		11[a]	3	9	6	5	1	7	4		
	10		2			8		11	3	9	6	5	1	7	4		
	10		2			8		11	3	9	6	5	1	7	4		
	10		2	12		8		11	3	9[a]	6	5	1	7	4		
	10	9[a]	2	12		8		11	3		6	5	1	7	4		
	10		2			8		11	3	9	6	5	1	7	4		
	10		2			8		11	3	9	6	5	1	7	4		
12	10		2	4[a]		8		11	3	9	6	5	1	7			
	10		2			8		11	3	9	6	5	1	7	4		
	10		2			8	3	11		9	6	5	1	7	4		
	10		2			8	3	11		9	6	5	1	7	4		
12	10		2		5	8	3	11		9	6		1	7	4[a]		
	10		2			8	3	11		9	6	5	1	7	4		
	10		2			8	3	11		9	6	5	1	7	4		
	10		2			8	3	11	6	9		5	1	7	4		
	10		2			8	3	11		9	6	5	1	7	4		
	10		2			8	3	11		9	6	5	1	7	4		
	10		2			8	3	11		9	6	5	1	7[a]	4		
	10		2			8	3	11		9	6	5	1	7			
	10		2			8	3	11	12	9	6	5	1	7			
	10		2			8	3	11	12	9	6	5	1	7	4[a]		
	10	4	2			8	3	11[a]		9	6	5	1	7			
	10	12	2			8	3	11		9	6	5	1	7	4[a]		
	10		2			8	3	11	6	9		5	1	7	4		
4	10		2			8	3	11	6	9		5	1	7			
4	10		2			8	3	11	6	9		5	1	7			
	10		2[a]			8	3	11	6	9		5	1	7	4		
	10	9[a]			6	8	3	11	2	12		5	1	7	4		
	10	9			6	8	3	11	2			5	1	7	4		
	10	2				8	3	11	6	9		5	1	7	4		
12	10		2[a]			8	3	11	6	9		5	1	7	4		
2	42	5	38	3	5	40	23	42	29	39	26	40	42	41	36	6	
3		1		3					2	1							
	19		1			8		10		6	1	1		6	2		1

Beck	Bowles	Busby	Clement	Delve	Evans	Francis	Gillard	Givens	Hazell	Leach	McLintock	Mancini	Parkes	Thomas	Venables	Watson	OG
	10		2			8	3	11		9	6	5	1	7	4		
	10[a]		2			8	3	11	12	9	6	5	1	7	4		
	10		2			8	3	11		9	6	5	1	7	4		
	10					8	3	11	2	9	6	5	1	7	4		
	10					8	3	11	2	9	6	5	1	7	4		
	10		2			8	3	11		9	6	5	1	7	4		
	6		4			6	6	6	2	6	6	6	6	6	6		
									1								
	2							2		1				1			

Beck	Bowles	Busby	Clement	Delve	Evans	Francis	Gillard	Givens	Hazell	Leach	McLintock	Mancini	Parkes	Thomas	Venables	Watson	OG
	10[a]	12	2			8		11	3	9	6	5	1	7	4		
	10	12	2			8		11	3	9	6[a]	5	1	7	4		
	10	9[a]	2	12		8		11	3		6	5	1	7	4		
	3	1	3			3		3	3	2	3	3	3	3	3		
		2		1													
	1					1		3		2							2

Beck	Bowles	Busby	Clement	Delve	Evans	Francis	Gillard	Givens	Hazell	Leach	McLintock	Mancini	Parkes	Thomas	Venables	Watson	OG
2	51	6	45	3	5	49	29	51	34	47	35	49	51	50	45	6	
3		3		4					3	1							
	22		1			9		15		9	1	1		7	2		3

1974-75

Division One

	P	W	D	L	F	A	Pts
Derby County	42	21	11	10	67	49	53
Liverpool	42	20	11	11	60	39	51
Ipswich Town	42	23	5	14	66	44	51
Everton	42	16	18	8	56	42	50
Stoke City	42	17	15	10	64	48	49
Sheffield United	42	18	13	11	58	51	49
Middlesbrough	42	18	12	12	54	40	48
Manchester City	42	18	10	14	54	54	46
Leeds United	42	16	13	13	57	49	45
Burnley	42	17	11	14	68	67	45
Queen's Park Rangers	42	16	10	16	54	54	42
Wolverhampton W	42	14	11	17	57	54	39
West Ham United	42	13	13	16	58	59	39
Coventry City	42	12	15	15	51	62	39
Newcastle United	42	15	9	18	59	72	39
Arsenal	42	13	11	18	47	49	37
Birmingham City	42	14	9	19	53	61	37
Leicester City	42	12	12	18	46	60	36
Tottenham Hotspur	42	13	8	21	52	63	34
Luton Town	42	11	11	20	47	65	33
Chelsea	42	9	15	18	42	72	33
Carlisle United	42	12	5	25	43	59	29

Attendances

	TOTAL		
	Home	Away	Total
League	428,085	546,380	974,465
Cup/Other	75,031	69,043	144,074
TOTAL	503,116	615,423	1,118,539

	AVERAGE		
	Home	Away	Total
League	20,385	26,018	23,202
Cup/Other	18,758	23,014	20,582
TOTAL	20,125	25,643	22,827

Match No.	Date		Opponents	Location	Result		Scorers	Atten
1	Aug	16	Sheffield United	A	D	1-1	Francis	16
2		21	Leeds United	A	W	1-0	Francis	31
3		24	Stoke City	H	L	0-1		21
4		27	Leeds United	H	D	1-1	Givens	24
5		31	Luton Town	A	D	1-1	Bowles (pen)	18
6	Sep	7	Birmingham City	H	L	0-1		16
7		14	Leicester City	A	L	1-3	Francis	19
8		21	Newcastle United	H	L	1-2	OG (Keeley)	18
9		24	Everton	H	D	2-2	Givens, Busby	16
10		28	Manchester City	A	L	0-1		30
11	Oct	5	Ipswich Town	H	W	1-0	Francis	19
12		12	Arsenal	A	D	2-2	Bowles (2 pens)	26
13		19	Liverpool	H	L	0-1		27
14		26	Wolverhampton	A	W	2-1	Givens (2)	20
15	Nov	2	Coventry City	H	W	2-0	Bowles, Givens	17
16		9	Derby County	A	L	2-5	Leach, Bowles	23
17		16	Carlisle United	H	W	2-1	Thomas, Bowles	15
18		23	Middlesbrough	A	W	3-1	Bowles, Givens, Rogers	27
19		27	Stoke City	A	L	0-1		22
20		30	West Ham United	H	L	0-2		28
21	Dec	7	Burnley	A	L	0-3		16
22		14	Sheffield United	H	W	1-0	Rogers	13
23		21	Tottenham Hotspur	A	W	2-1	Bowles (2, 1 pen)	21
24		26	Leicester City	H	W	4-2	Beck, Thomas, Givens, Westwood	17
25		28	Chelsea	A	W	3-0	Givens (2), Francis	38
26	Jan	11	Burnley	H	L	0-1		19
27		18	West Ham United	A	D	2-2	Masson, Bowles (pen)	28
28	Feb	1	Derby County	H	W	4-1	Givens (3), Thomas	20
29		8	Coventry City	A	D	1-1	Leach	18
30		22	Carlisle United	A	W	2-1	Givens (2)	13
31		25	Middlesbrough	H	D	0-0		18
32	Mar	1	Luton Town	H	W	2-1	Givens, Rogers	19
33		8	Everton	A	L	1-2	Givens	39
34		15	Manchester City	H	W	2-0	Rogers (2)	22
35		18	Chelsea	H	W	1-0	Thomas	25
36		22	Birmingham City	A	L	1-4	Thomas	32
37		29	Tottenham Hotspur	H	L	0-1		25
38		31	Newcastle United	A	D	2-2	Francis (pen), Gillard	28
39	Apr	5	Wolverhampton	H	W	2-0	Givens, Thomas	16
40		12	Ipswich Town	A	L	1-2	Gillard	28
41		19	Arsenal	H	D	0-0		24
42		26	Liverpool	A	L	1-3	Francis (pen)	42

Appearar
Sub appearar
G

FA Cup

R3	Jan	4	Southend United	A	D	2-2	Gillard, Francis	18
rep		7	Southend United	H	W	2-0	Givens (2)	21
R4		24	Notts County	H	W	3-0	Thomas, Bowles (pen), Givens	23
R5	Feb	15	West Ham United	A	L	1-2	Clement	39

Appearar
Sub appearar
G

League Cup

R2	Sep	10	Orient	H	D	1-1	Francis	14
rep		17	Orient	A	W	3-0	Francis, Givens, Bowles	11
R3	Oct	8	Newcastle United	H	L	0-4		15

Appearar
Sub appearar
G

Total - Appearar
Total - Sub appearar
Total - G

eck	Bowles	Busby	Clement	Francis	Gillard	Givens	Hazell	Leach	McLintock	Mancini	Masson	Parkes	Pritchett	Rogers	Shanks	Teale	Thomas	Venables	Webb	Westwood	OG
0			2	8	3	11				5		1					7	4	6		
0		12	2	8	3	11				5[a]		1					7	4	6		
9	10[a]	4	2	8	3	11		12		5		1					7		6		
9	10	12	2[a]	8	3	11				5		1					7	4	6		
9	10	2		8	3	11				5		1					7	4	6		
9	10	2		8[a]	3	11		12		5						1	7	4	6		
	10	9	2	8	3	11	6	4				1					7		5		
	10	9	2	8	3	11	6	4				1					7		5		
		9	2	8	3	11	6	4				1		12			7		5		
4		9	2	8	3	11[a]	6					1		12			7		5		
4	10		2	8	3	11	6	9[a]		5		1		12			7				
	10		2	8	3	11		4	5			1		9			7		6		
4	10		2	8	3	11			5			1		9			7		6		
	10		2	8	3	11	4		5			1		9			7		6		
	10		2		3	11	4	9	5			1		8			7		6		
2	10		2	8	3	11	4	9[a]	5			1					7		6		
	10		6	8	3	11	2	4	5			1		9			7				
	10		2	8	3	11	6	4	5			1		9			7				
	10		2	8	3	11	6	4	5			1		9			7				
	10		2	8	3	11	4		5			1		9			7		6		
	10		2	8	3	11		9	5			1			4		7		6		
0			2	8	3	11		9	5		4	1		7					6		
3	10		2		3	11		9	5		4	1					7		6		
3			6		3	11		9[a]	5		4	1			2		7		10	12	
9	10		2	8	3	11			5		4	1					7		6		
9	10		2	8	3	11			5		4	1					7		6		
9	10		2	8	3	11			5		4	1					7		6		
9	10		2	8	3	11			5		4	1					7		6		
9	10		2	8[a]	3	11		12	5		4	1					7		6		
9	10	12	6		3	11			5		4[a]	1		8	2		7				
9	10		2	8	3	11			5		4	1					7		6		
9	10	8	2		3	11			5		4	1		12			7[a]		6		
9	10	8	2		3	11			5		4	1					7		6		
	10	9		8	3				5		4	1		11	2		7		6		
2	10	9		8	3				5		4	1		11	2		7		6[a]		
	10[a]	9		8	3	11			5		4	1		12	2		7		6		
9				8	3	11			5		4	1		10	2		7		6		
9				8	6	11[a]		10	5		4	1	3		2		7				
9	10			8	6	11			5[a]		4	1	3		2		7				
9	10			8	6	11			5[a]		4	1	3		2		7				
9	10				6	11		8			4	1	3		2		7				
9				8	3	11		12	5[a]		4	1			2		7		6		
7	33	12	31	35	42	40	12	16	30	7	21	41	4	13	12	1	41	5	33		
2		3						4						5						1	
	10	1		7	2	17		2			1			5			6			1	1

eck	Bowles	Busby	Clement	Francis	Gillard	Givens	Hazell	Leach	McLintock	Mancini	Masson	Parkes	Pritchett	Rogers	Shanks	Teale	Thomas	Venables	Webb	Westwood	OG
	10		2	8	3	11		9	5		4	1							6		
9	10		2	8	3	11			5		4	1					7		6		
9	10		2	8	3	11			5		4	1					7		6		
9	10[a]		2		3	11		8	5		4	1		12			7		6		
4	4		4	3	4	4		2	4		4	4					3		4		
														1							
	1		1	1	1	3											1				

eck	Bowles	Busby	Clement	Francis	Gillard	Givens	Hazell	Leach	McLintock	Mancini	Masson	Parkes	Pritchett	Rogers	Shanks	Teale	Thomas	Venables	Webb	Westwood	OG
	10	9	2	8	3	11				5						1	7	4	6		
2	10	6		8	3	11	4	9				1					7		5		
4	10		2	8	3	11	6			5		1					7		12	9[a]	
2	3	2	2	3	3	3	2	1		2		2				1	3	1	2	1	
																			1		
	1			2		1															

eck	Bowles	Busby	Clement	Francis	Gillard	Givens	Hazell	Leach	McLintock	Mancini	Masson	Parkes	Pritchett	Rogers	Shanks	Teale	Thomas	Venables	Webb	Westwood	OG
3	40	14	37	41	49	47	14	19	34	9	25	47	4	13	12	2	47	6	39	1	
2		3						4						6					1	1	
	12	1	1	10	3	21		2			1			5			7			1	1

1975-76

Division One

	P	W	D	L	F	A	Pts
Liverpool	42	23	14	5	66	31	60
Queen's Park Rangers	42	24	11	7	67	33	59
Manchester United	42	23	10	9	68	42	56
Derby County	42	21	11	10	75	58	53
Leeds United	42	21	9	12	65	46	51
Ipswich Town	42	16	14	12	54	48	46
Leicester City	42	13	19	10	48	51	45
Manchester City	42	16	11	15	64	46	43
Tottenham Hotspur	42	14	15	13	63	63	43
Norwich City	42	16	10	16	58	58	42
Everton	42	15	12	15	60	66	42
Stoke City	42	15	11	16	48	50	41
Middlesbrough	42	15	10	17	46	45	40
Coventry City	42	13	14	15	47	57	40
Newcastle United	42	15	9	18	71	62	39
Aston Villa	42	11	17	14	51	59	39
Arsenal	42	13	10	19	47	53	36
West Ham United	42	13	10	19	48	71	36
Birmingham City	42	13	7	22	57	75	33
Wolverhampton W	42	10	10	22	51	68	30
Burnley	42	9	10	23	43	66	28
Sheffield United	42	6	10	26	33	82	22

Attendances

TOTAL

	Home	Away	Total
League	500,436	609,254	1,109,690
Cup/Other	61,698	80,058	141,756
TOTAL	562,134	689,312	1,251,446

AVERAGE

	Home	Away	Total
League	23,830	29,012	26,421
Cup/Other	20,566	26,686	23,626
TOTAL	23,422	28,721	26,072

Match No.	Date		Opponents	Location	Result		Scorers
1	Aug	16	Liverpool	H	W	2-0	Francis, Leach
2		19	Aston Villa	H	D	1-1	Francis
3		23	Derby County	A	W	5-1	Bowles (3, 1 pen), Thomas, Clement
4		26	Wolverhampton	A	D	2-2	Givens (2)
5		30	West Ham United	H	D	1-1	Givens
6	Sep	6	Birmingham City	A	D	1-1	Thomas
7		13	Manchester United	H	W	1-0	Webb
8		20	Middlesbrough	A	D	0-0	
9		23	Leicester City	H	W	1-0	Leach
10		27	Newcastle United	H	W	1-0	Leach
11	Oct	4	Leeds United	A	L	1-2	Bowles (pen)
12		11	Everton	H	W	5-0	Francis (2), Givens, Masson, Thomas
13		18	Burnley	A	L	0-1	
14		25	Sheffield United	H	W	1-0	Givens
15	Nov	1	Coventry City	A	D	1-1	Givens
16		8	Tottenham Hotspur	H	D	0-0	
17		15	Ipswich Town	A	D	1-1	Givens
18		22	Burnley	H	W	1-0	Bowles
19		29	Stoke City	H	W	3-2	Masson, Clement, Webb
20	Dec	6	Manchester City	A	D	0-0	
21		13	Derby County	H	D	1-1	Nutt
22		20	Liverpool	A	L	0-2	
23		26	Norwich City	H	W	2-0	Masson, Bowles
24		27	Arsenal	A	L	0-2	
25	Jan	10	Manchester United	A	L	1-2	Givens
26		17	Birmingham City	H	W	2-1	Masson (2)
27		24	West Ham United	A	L	0-1	
28		31	Aston Villa	A	W	2-0	Hollins, Francis
29	Feb	7	Wolverhampton	H	W	4-2	Givens (2), Thomas, Francis (pen)
30		14	Tottenham Hotspur	A	W	3-0	Francis (2), Givens
31		21	Ipswich Town	H	W	3-1	OG (Wark), Webb, Thomas
32		25	Leicester City	A	W	1-0	Thomas
33		28	Sheffield United	A	D	0-0	
34	Mar	6	Coventry City	H	W	4-1	Thomas, Francis, Givens, Masson
35		13	Everton	A	W	2-0	Bowles, Leach
36		20	Stoke City	A	W	1-0	Webb
37		27	Manchester City	H	W	1-0	Webb
38	Apr	3	Newcastle United	A	W	2-1	McLintock, Bowles
39		10	Middlesbrough	H	W	4-2	Francis (2, 1 pen), Givens, Bowles
40		17	Norwich City	A	L	2-3	Thomas, OG (Powell)
41		19	Arsenal	H	W	2-1	McLintock, Francis (pen)
42		24	Leeds United	H	W	2-0	Thomas, Bowles

Appeara
Sub appeara

FA Cup

R3	Jan	3	Newcastle United	H	D	0-0	
rep		7	Newcastle United	A	L	1-2	Masson

Appeara
Sub appeara

League Cup

R2	Sep	9	Shrewsbury Town	A	W	4-1	Webb, Masson, Thomas, Leach
R3	Oct	7	Charlton Athletic	H	D	1-1	Bowles
rep		14	Charlton Athletic	A	W	3-0	Thomas, Masson, Bowles
R4	Nov	11	Newcastle United	H	L	1-3	Leach

Appeara
Sub appeara

Total - Appeara
Total - Sub appeara
Total -

Beck	Bowles	Busby	Clement	Francis	Gillard	Givens	Hollins	Leach	McLintock	Masson	Nutt	Parkes	Shanks	Tagg	Thomas	Webb	OG
	10		2	8	3	11	4[a]	12	5	9		1			7	6	
2	10		2	8	3	11		4	5[a]	9		1			7		
2	10		2	8	3	11		4		9		1		6	7[a]		
	10		2	8	3	11		4		9		1		6	7		
	10		2	8[a]	3	11	12	4		9		1		6	7		
	10		2			11	8	4		9		1		6	7	3	
	10		2	8	3	11		4	5	9		1			7	6	
	10		2	8	3	11[a]	12	4	5	9		1			7	6	
	10		2	8	3	11		4	5	9		1			7	6	
	10		2	8	3	11		4	5	9		1			7	6	
	10		2	8	3	11	4		5	9		1			7	6	
	10		2	8	3	11		4	5	9		1			7	6	
	10		2	8	3	11	5	4		9		1			7	6	
	10		2	8	3	11		4	5	9		1			7	6	
	10		2	8	3	11		4	5	9		1			7	6	
	10		2	8	3	11		4	5	9		1			7	6	
			2	8	3	11	10	4	5	9		1			7	6	
	10		2	8	3	11		4	5	9		1			7	6	
8	10		2		3		4	11[a]	5	9	12	1			7	6	
			2	8	3	11	4	10	5	9		1			7	6	
			2	8	3	11	4	10	5	9[a]	12	1			7	6	
	10		2	8	3	11	4		5	9		1			7	6	
	10		2	8	3	11		4	5	9		1			7	6	
	10		2	8	3	11	4		5	9		1			7	6	
	10[a]		2	8	3	11	4	7	5	9		1				6	
8	10		2		3	11	4		5	9		1			7	6	
8			2		3	11	4	10	5[a]	9	12	1			7	6	
			2	8	3	11	4	10	5	9		1			7	6	
	10		2	8	3	11	5	4		9		1			7	6	
	10		2	8	3	11	5	4		9		1			7	6	
	10		2	8	3	11	5	4[a]	12	9		1			7	6	
	10		2	8	3	11	4		5	9		1			7	6	
	10		2		3	11	4	8	5	9		1			7	6	
	10		2	8	3	11	4		5	9		1			7	6	
	10		2	8[a]	3	11	4	12	5	9		1			7	6	
	10		2		3	11	4	8	5	9		1			7	6	
	10			8	3	11	4	12	5[a]	9		1	2		7	6	
	10			8	3	11	4		5	9		1	2		7	6	
	10		2	8	3	11	4		5	9		1			7	6	
	10		2	8	3	11	4		5	9		1			7	6	
	10		2	8	3	11	4		5	9		1			7	6	
	10		2	8	3	11	4		5	9		1			7	6	
3	37		40	36	41	41	28	28	34	42		42	2	4	41	38	
2							2	3	1		3						
	10		2	12		13	1	4	2	6	1				9	5	2

Beck	Bowles	Busby	Clement	Francis	Gillard	Givens	Hollins	Leach	McLintock	Masson	Nutt	Parkes	Shanks	Tagg	Thomas	Webb	OG
	10		2	8	3	11[a]	12	4	5	9		1			7	6	
	10[a]	12	2	8	3	11	4	7	5	9		1				6	
	2		2	2	2	2	1	2	2	2		2			1	2	
		1					1										
										1							

Beck	Bowles	Busby	Clement	Francis	Gillard	Givens	Hollins	Leach	McLintock	Masson	Nutt	Parkes	Shanks	Tagg	Thomas	Webb	OG
	10		2	8		11		4	5	9		1			7	3	
	10		2	8	3	11		4	5	9		1			7	6	
	10		2	8	3	11	12	4	5[a]	9		1			7	6	
	10[a]		2	8	3	11	12	4	5	9		1			7	6	
	4		4	4	3	4		4	4	4		4			4	4	
							2										
	2							2		2					2	1	

Beck	Bowles	Busby	Clement	Francis	Gillard	Givens	Hollins	Leach	McLintock	Masson	Nutt	Parkes	Shanks	Tagg	Thomas	Webb	OG
3	43		46	42	46	47	29	34	40	48		48	2	4	46	44	
2		1					5	3	1		3						
	12		2	12		13	1	6	2	9	1				11	6	2

1976-77

Division One

	P	W	D	L	F	A	Pts
Liverpool	42	23	11	8	62	33	57
Manchester City	42	21	14	7	60	34	56
Ipswich Town	42	22	8	12	66	39	52
Aston Villa	42	22	7	13	76	50	51
Newcastle United	42	18	13	11	64	49	49
Manchester United	42	18	11	13	71	62	47
West Bromwich Albion	42	16	13	13	62	56	45
Arsenal	42	16	11	15	64	59	43
Everton	42	14	14	14	62	64	42
Leeds United	42	15	12	15	48	51	42
Leicester City	42	12	18	12	47	60	42
Middlesbrough	42	14	13	15	40	45	41
Birmingham City	42	13	12	17	63	61	38
Queen's Park Rangers	42	13	12	17	47	52	38
Derby County	42	9	19	14	50	55	37
Norwich City	42	14	9	19	47	64	37
West Ham United	42	11	14	17	46	65	36
Bristol City	42	11	13	18	38	48	35
Coventry City	42	10	15	17	48	59	35
Sunderland	42	11	12	19	46	54	34
Stoke City	42	10	14	18	28	51	34
Tottenham Hotspur	42	12	9	21	48	72	33

Attendances

TOTAL	Home	Away	Total
League	442,776	586,508	1,029,284
Cup/Other	168,565	330,482	499,047
TOTAL	611,341	916,990	1,528,331

AVERAGE	Home	Away	Total
League	21,085	27,929	24,507
Cup/Other	21,071	36,720	29,356
TOTAL	21,081	30,566	25,904

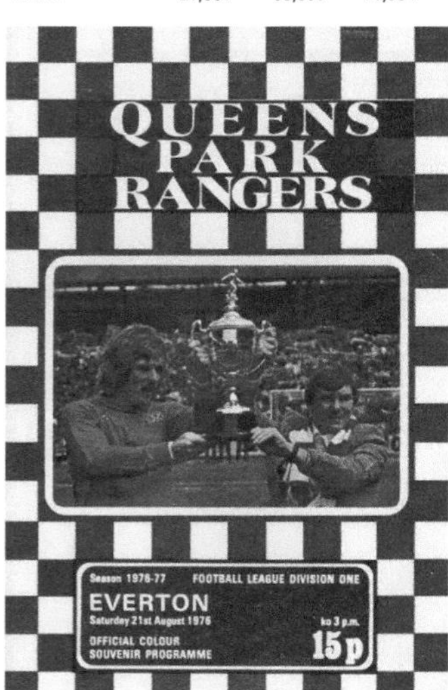

Match No.	Date		Opponents	Location	Result		Scorers	Atten
1	Aug	21	Everton	H	L	0-4		24
2		23	West Ham United	A	L	0-1		31
3		28	Ipswich Town	A	D	2-2	Givens, Masson	24
4	Sep	4	West Bromwich	H	W	1-0	Gillard	18
5		11	Aston Villa	H	W	2-1	Masson, Clement	23
6		18	Leicester City	A	D	2-2	Givens, Hollins	18
7		25	Stoke City	H	W	2-0	Bowles, Givens	21
8	Oct	2	Arsenal	A	L	2-3	Thomas, McLintock	39
9		5	Norwich City	H	L	2-3	Masson (pen), Webb	16
10		16	Manchester City	A	D	0-0		40
11		23	Sunderland	H	W	2-0	McLintock, Bowles	22
12		30	Birmingham City	A	L	1-2	Eastoe	31
13	Nov	6	Derby County	H	D	1-1	Givens	22
14		9	Coventry City	A	L	0-2		16
15		20	Middlesbrough	H	W	3-0	Givens (pen), Masson, Bowles	16
16		27	Newcastle United	A	L	0-2		39
17	Dec	11	Liverpool	A	L	1-3	Eastoe	37
18		27	Norwich City	A	L	0-2		27
19	Jan	11	Tottenham Hotspur	H	W	2-1	Bowles, Clement	24
20		22	Everton	A	W	3-1	Leach, Masson, Bowles	26
21	Feb	12	West Bromwich	A	D	1-1	Francis	18
22		26	Leicester City	H	W	3-2	Givens, Hollins, Francis (pen)	20
23	Mar	5	Stoke City	A	L	0-1		15
24		8	Leeds United	H	D	0-0		20
25		12	Arsenal	H	W	2-1	Francis, Hollins	26
26		19	Bristol City	A	L	0-1		22
27		22	Manchester City	H	D	0-0		17
28	Apr	2	Sunderland	A	L	0-1		27
29		4	West Ham United	H	D	1-1	Eastoe	24
30		9	Tottenham Hotspur	A	L	0-3		32
31		14	Coventry City	H	D	1-1	Masson (pen)	15
32		16	Middlesbrough	A	W	2-0	Abbott, Masson	14
33		19	Manchester United	H	W	4-0	Eastoe (2), Givens, Kelly	28
34		23	Newcastle United	H	L	1-2	Givens	20
35		26	Bristol City	H	L	0-1		14
36		30	Manchester United	A	L	0-1		50
37	May	7	Liverpool	H	D	1-1	Givens	29
38		11	Derby County	A	L	0-2		21
39		14	Leeds United	A	W	1-0	Eastoe	22
40		16	Ipswich Town	H	W	1-0	Givens	19
41		20	Aston Villa	A	D	1-1	Abbott	28
42		23	Birmingham City	H	D	2-2	Masson, Webb	14

Appearar
Sub appearar
G

FA Cup

R3	Jan	8	Shrewsbury Town	H	W	2-1	Bowles, Givens	18
R4		29	Manchester United	A	L	0-1		57

Appearar
Sub appearar
G

League Cup

R2	Sep	1	Cardiff City	A	W	3-1	Bowles, Thomas, Clement	23
R3		21	Bury	H	W	2-1	McLintock, Givens	13
R4	Oct	27	West Ham United	A	W	2-0	Bowles, Clement	24
R5	Dec	1	Arsenal	H	W	2-1	Masson, Webb	27
SF1	Feb	1	Aston Villa	H	D	0-0		28
SF2		16	Aston Villa	A	D	2-2 aet	Francis, Eastoe	48
rep		22	Aston Villa	N*	L	0-3		40

* Played at Highbury

Appearar
Sub appearar
G

UEFA Cup

R1/1	Sep	15	Brann Bergan	H	W	4-0	Bowles (3), Masson	14
R1/2		29	Brann Bergan	A	W	7-0	Bowles (3), Givens (2), Thomas, Webb	11
R2/1	Oct	20	Slovan Bratislava	A	D	3-3	Bowles (2), Givens	40
R2/2	Nov	3	Slovan Bratislava	H	W	5-2	Givens (3, 1 pen), Bowles, Clement	22
R3/1		24	FC Cologne	H	W	3-0	Givens, Webb, Bowles	21
R3/2	Dec	7	FC Cologne	A	L	1-4*	Masson	50
QF/1	Mar	2	AEK Athens	H	W	3-0	Francis (2 pens), Bowles	23
QF/2		16	AEK Athens	A	L	0-3**		35

* Won on Away Goals Rule, b, After extra-time, Lost on penalties

Appearar
Sub appearar
G

Total - Appearar
Total - Sub appearar
Total - G

Bowles	Busby	Clement	Cunningham	Eastoe	Francis	Gillard	Givens	Hollins	Kelly	Leach	McLintock	Masson	Nutt	Parkes	Richardson	Shanks	Thomas	Webb
0	8[a]	2				3	11	4		6	5	9		1		12	7	
0		2				3	11	4		8	5	9		1			7	
0		2				3	11	4		8	5	9		1			7	
0		2				3	11	4		8	5	9		1			7	6
0		2				3	11	4	8[a]	12	5	9		1			7	6
0		2				3	11	4	8[a]	12	5	9		1			7	6
0		2				3	11	4	8		5	9		1			7	6
0		2	8			3	11	4			5	9	12	1[a]			7	6
0		2				3	11	4	8		5	9		1			7	6
0		2		12		3	11[a]	4	8		5	9		1			7	6
0		2				3	11	4	8		5	9		1			7	6
0		2		7		3	11	4		8	5	9		1				6
0		2				3	11	4	8		5	9		1			7	6
0		2				3	11	4		8	5	9		1			7	6
0							11	3	8	4	5	9		1		2	7	6
		2		10		3	11	4	8		5	9		1			7	6
0		2		7		3	11	5	4	8		9		1				6
0		2		12		3	11	5	4	8		9		1			7	6[a]
0		2		7		3	11	4		8	5	9		1				6
0		2[a]	12	7		3	11	4		8	5	9		1				6
0		2			8	3	11	4			5	9		1			7	6
		2		9	8	3	11	4	10	12	5[a]			1			7	6
0		12			8	3	11[a]	3	4		5	9		1			7	6
		2		11	8	3		4	10		5	9			1		7	6
		2		12	8	3	11	4	10		5	9			1		7[a]	6
0[a]		2	8	7		3	11	4			5	9		1		12		6
		2		8		3	11	4	10			9		1		12	7[a]	6
			10	7		3	11	4		8		9		1		2		6
				7		3	11	4		8	5	9		1		2		10
				10		3	11		4	8		9		1		2	7	6
			12	10		3	11		4	8		9		1		2	7[a]	6
		2		7		3	11	4	8		5	9		1				6
		2[a]		7	8	3	11	4	10		5	9		1				6
				7		3	11	4	8		5	9		1		2		6
		2		7	8	3	11	4	10		5	9[a]		1			12	6
		2		7	8	3	11	4	10		5	9		1				6
		2		10	8	3	11	4			5	9		1			7	6
		2[a]		10		3	11	4	8		5	9		1		12	7	6
				10	8	3	11	2	4		5	9		1			7	6
				10	8[a]	3	11	2	4	12	5	9		1			7	6
		2		10		3	11	4	8		5	9		1			7	
				10		3	11	2	4[a]	8	5	9		1			7	6
2	1	32	3	24	11	41	41	40	28	16	36	41		40	2	6	30	38
		1	2	3						4			1			4	1	
		2		6	3	1	10	3	1	1	2	8					1	2

Bowles	Busby	Clement	Cunningham	Eastoe	Francis	Gillard	Givens	Hollins	Kelly	Leach	McLintock	Masson	Nutt	Parkes	Richardson	Shanks	Thomas	Webb
0		2		7		3	11	4		8	5	9		1				6
0				7		3	11	4		8	5	9		1		2		6
2		1		2		2	2	2		2	2	2		2		1		2
							1											

Bowles	Busby	Clement	Cunningham	Eastoe	Francis	Gillard	Givens	Hollins	Kelly	Leach	McLintock	Masson	Nutt	Parkes	Richardson	Shanks	Thomas	Webb
0		2				3	11[a]	4		8	5	9		1		12	7	6
0		2				3	11	4	8		5	9		1			7	6
0		2				3	11	4	8	12	5	9		1			7[a]	6
0		2				3	11	4	8	12	5[a]	9		1			7	6
0				9		3	12	4[a]		8	5	9		1		2	7	6
0		2		12	8	3	11	4[a]			5	9		1			7	6
0		2		9	8	3	11				5	9		1			7	6
7		6		2	2	7	6	6	3	2	7	7		7		1	7	7
				1			1			2						1		
2		2		1	1		1				1	1					1	1

Bowles	Busby	Clement	Cunningham	Eastoe	Francis	Gillard	Givens	Hollins	Kelly	Leach	McLintock	Masson	Nutt	Parkes	Richardson	Shanks	Thomas	Webb
0		2				3	11	4		8	5	9		1			7	6
0	14	2				3	11	4		8b	5	9		1			7	6
0		2				3	11	4		8	5	9		1			7	6
0		2				3	11	4		8	5	9		1			7	6
0		2				3	11	4		8	5	9		1			7	6
0		2		14		3	11	4		8b	5	9		1			7	6
0					8	3	11	2	4		5	9		1			7	6
0				7		3	11	4	8		5	9		1		2		6
8		6		1	1	8	8	8	2	6	8	8		8		1	7	8
	1			1														
1		1			2		7					2					1	2

Bowles	Busby	Clement	Cunningham	Eastoe	Francis	Gillard	Givens	Hollins	Kelly	Leach	McLintock	Masson	Nutt	Parkes	Richardson	Shanks	Thomas	Webb
9	1	45	3	29	14	58	57	56	33	26	53	58		57	2	9	44	55
	1	1	2	5			1			6			1			5	1	
9		5		7	6	1	19	3	1	1	3	11					3	5

1977-78

Division One

	P	W	D	L	F	A	Pts
Nottingham Forest	42	25	14	3	69	24	64
Liverpool	42	24	9	9	65	34	57
Everton	42	22	11	9	76	45	55
Manchester City	42	20	12	10	74	51	52
Arsenal	42	21	10	11	60	37	52
West Bromwich Albion	42	18	14	10	62	53	50
Coventry City	42	18	12	12	75	62	48
Aston Villa	42	18	10	14	57	42	46
Leeds United	42	18	10	14	63	53	46
Manchester United	42	16	10	16	67	63	42
Birmingham City	42	16	9	17	55	60	41
Derby County	42	14	13	15	54	59	41
Norwich City	42	11	18	13	52	66	40
Middlesbrough	42	12	15	15	42	54	39
Wolverhampton W	42	12	12	18	51	64	36
Chelsea	42	11	14	17	46	69	36
Bristol City	42	11	13	18	49	53	35
Ipswich Town	42	11	13	18	47	61	35
Queen's Park Rangers	42	9	15	18	47	64	33
West Ham United	42	12	8	22	52	69	32
Newcastle United	42	6	10	26	42	78	22
Leicester City	42	5	12	25	26	70	22

Attendances

TOTAL

	Home	Away	Total
League	417,899	544,571	962,470
Cup/Other	77,024	142,134	219,158
TOTAL	494,923	686,705	1,181,628

AVERAGE

	Home	Away	Total
League	19,900	25,932	22,916
Cup/Other	19,256	35,534	27,395
TOTAL	19,797	27,468	23,633

Match No.	Date		Opponents	Location	Result		Scorers	Atte
1	Aug	20	Aston Villa	H	L	1-2	Eastoe	2
2		23	Wolverhampton	A	L	0-1		2
3		27	Norwich City	A	D	1-1	Needham	1
4	Sep	3	Leicester City	H	W	3-0	Givens, Francis, Needham	1
5		10	West Ham United	A	D	2-2	Eastoe, OG (Lock)	2
6		17	Manchester City	H	D	1-1	Francis	2
7		24	Chelsea	H	D	1-1	Masson	2
8	Oct	1	Bristol City	A	D	2-2	Masson, Eastoe	2
9		4	Birmingham City	A	L	1-2	Masson	2
10		8	Everton	H	L	1-5	Eastoe	2
11		15	Arsenal	A	L	0-1		3
12		22	Nottingham Forest	H	L	0-2		2
13		29	West Bromwich	H	W	2-1	Eastoe, Bowles	1
14	Nov	5	Middlesbrough	A	D	1-1	Busby	1
15		12	Liverpool	H	W	2-0	James, Bowles	2
16		19	Coventry City	A	L	1-4	Givens	2
17		26	Manchester United	H	D	2-2	Needham, Givens	2
18	Dec	3	Leeds United	A	L	0-3		2
19		10	Newcastle United	H	L	0-1		1
20		17	Liverpool	A	L	0-1		3
21		26	Derby County	H	D	0-0		1
22		27	Ipswich Town	A	L	2-3	Bowles (pen), McGee	2
23		31	Wolverhampton	H	L	1-3	Shanks	1
24	Jan	2	Aston Villa	A	D	1-1	OG (Smith)	3
25		14	Norwich City	H	W	2-1	Eastoe, Cunningham	1
26		21	Leicester City	A	D	0-0		1
27	Feb	11	Manchester City	A	L	1-2	Abbott	3
28		25	Bristol City	H	D	2-2	Bowles (pen), Busby	1
29	Mar	4	Everton	A	D	3-3	Shanks, Hollins, Howe	3
30		14	West Ham United	H	W	1-0	Cunningham	2
31		22	West Bromwich	A	L	0-2		2
32		25	Ipswich Town	H	D	3-3	McGee (2), James	1
33		27	Derby County	A	L	0-2		2
34	Apr	1	Middlesbrough	H	W	1-0	Busby	1
35		8	Manchester United	A	L	1-3	Bowles (pen)	4
36		11	Arsenal	H	W	2-1	Shanks, Bowles	2
37		15	Coventry City	H	W	2-1	Goddard, James	1
38		18	Nottingham Forest	A	L	0-1		3
39		22	Newcastle United	A	W	3-0	Givens, McGee, Hollins	1
40		25	Birmingham City	H	D	0-0		1
41		29	Leeds United	H	D	0-0		2
42	May	2	Chelsea	A	L	1-3	James	2

Appeara
Sub appeara
G

FA Cup

R3	Jan	7	Wealdstone	H	W	4-0	Givens, James, Bowles (pen), Howe	1
R4		28	West Ham United	A	D	1-1	Howe	3
rep		31	West Ham United	H	W	6-1	Givens, Hollins, Busby (2), Bowles (pen), James	2
R5	Feb	18	Nottingham Forest	H	D	1-1	Busby	2
rep		27	Nottingham Forest	A	D	1-1 aet	Shanks	4
rep	Mar	2	Nottingham Forest	A	L	1-3	Bowles	3

Appeara
Sub appeara
G

League Cup

R2	Aug	31	Bournemouth	H	W	2-0	Givens, Eastoe	1
R3	Oct	26	Aston Villa	A	L	0-1		3

Appeara
Sub appeara
G

Total - Appeara
Total - Sub appeara
Total - G

Bowles	Busby	Clement	Cunningham	Eastoe	Francis	Gillard	Givens	Goddard	Hollins	Howe	James	Leach	McGee	Masson	Needham	Parkes	Perkins	Richardson	Shanks	Wallace	Webb	Williams	OG
10		2		7	8[a]	3	11		4					9	5	1					6	12	
10		2		7		3	11		4			12		9	5	1					6		
10		2		7		3	11[a]		4			8		9	5	1					6	12	
10		2		7	8		11		4					9	5	1			3		6		
10		2		7	8		11[a]		4					9	5	1			3		6	12	
10		2		7[a]	8	3	11							9	5	1					6	4	
10		2		7	8[a]	3	11		4					9	5	1					6	12	
10	8	2		7		3[a]	11		4					9	5	1						12	
10	8	2		7[a]			11					4		9	5	1			3			12	
10	8	2		7			11		12			4[a]		9	5	1			3				
10	8	2		7		3	11		4					9	5	1			6				
10	8	2		7		3	11[a]		4					9	5	1			6			12	
10		2[a]		7		3	9		4		8					1			6	12		11	
10	7					3	9		4		8				5			1	2	12		11[a]	
10	6		12	7[a]		3	9		4		8				5			1	2			11	
10	6					3	9		4		8		7[a]		5			1	2			11	
10			6			3	9		4		8	7			5			1	2	11			
10			6			3	9		4		8	7			5			1	2	11			
10			6		8	3	9		4		7				5			1	2	11			
	12		6		8	3	9		4	5		10						1	2	11[a]		7	
10			6	11	8	3	9		4	5	7							1	2				
10			6	11[a]	8	3	9		4	5	7		12					1	2				
10			6	9[a]	8	3	11		4	5	7		12					1	2				
10	12		6	9[a]	8	3	11		4	5	7					1			2				
10			6	7	8	3	11		4	5	9[a]					1			2	12			
10			6		8[a]	3	11		4	5	9					1			2	7		12	
10	8	2				3	11		4	5	9					1			7				
10	8	2				3	11		4	5	9					1			7				
10	8[a]	2	6			3	11		4	5			9			1			7	12			
10	8	2	6			3	11		4	5	9[a]		12			1			7				
	8	2	6			3	11		4	5	9		10			1			7				
10	8	2	6			3	11[a]		4	5	9		12			1			7				
10	8	2	6			3			4	5	9		11[a]			1			7	12			
10	8	2				3			4	5			11			1	6		7	9			
10	8	2				3			4	5	12		11[a]			1	6		7	9			
10	8	2				3	11[a]	12	4	5	9		7			1			6				
10	8[a]	2				3		11	4	5	9		7			1			6			12	
10		2				3		11	4	5	9		7			1			6			8	
10		2				3	11	12	4	5	9		7[a]			1			6			8	
10		2				3	11	12	4	5	9		8			1			6			7[a]	
10		2				3	11	12	4	5	9		7			1			6	8[a]			
10		2				3	11	7	4	5	9		8[a]					1	6			12	
40	19	29	15	19	13	38	37	3	39	23	26	6	13	12	18	31	2	11	36	8	7	9	
	2		1					4	1		1	1	4							5		10	
6	3		2	6	2		4	1	2	1	4		4	3	3				3				2

Bowles	Busby	Clement	Cunningham	Eastoe	Francis	Gillard	Givens	Goddard	Hollins	Howe	James	Leach	McGee	Masson	Needham	Parkes	Perkins	Richardson	Shanks	Wallace	Webb	Williams	OG
10			6			3	11		4	5	9	7[a]				1			2	8		12	
10	8	2				3	11		4	5	9					1			7				
10	8	2				3	11		4	5	9					1			7				
10	8	2				3	11		4	5	9					1			7				
10	8	2				3	11		4	5	9[a]		12			1			7				
10	8		8			3	11[a]		4	5			7			1			2			12	
6	5	4	2			6	6		6	6	5	1	1			6			6	1			
													1									2	
3	3						2		1	2	2								1				

Bowles	Busby	Clement	Cunningham	Eastoe	Francis	Gillard	Givens	Goddard	Hollins	Howe	James	Leach	McGee	Masson	Needham	Parkes	Perkins	Richardson	Shanks	Wallace	Webb	Williams	OG
10		2		7	8	3[a]	11		4					9	5	1					6	12	
10		2		7		3	9		4						5[a]	1			6	11		8	
2		2		2	1	2	2		2					1	2	2			1	1	1	1	
																						1	
				1			1																

Bowles	Busby	Clement	Cunningham	Eastoe	Francis	Gillard	Givens	Goddard	Hollins	Howe	James	Leach	McGee	Masson	Needham	Parkes	Perkins	Richardson	Shanks	Wallace	Webb	Williams	OG
48	24	35	17	21	14	46	45	3	47	29	31	7	14	13	20	39	2	11	43	10	8	10	
	2		1					4	1		1	1	5							5		13	
9	6		2	7	2		7	1	3	3	6		4	3	3				4				2

1978-79

Division One

	P	W	D	L	F	A	Pts
Liverpool	42	30	8	4	85	16	68
Nottingham Forest	42	21	18	3	61	26	60
West Bromwich Albion	42	24	11	7	72	35	59
Everton	42	17	17	8	52	40	51
Leeds United	42	18	14	10	70	52	50
Ipswich Town	42	20	9	13	63	49	49
Arsenal	42	17	14	11	61	48	48
Aston Villa	42	15	16	11	59	49	46
Manchester United	42	15	15	12	60	63	45
Coventry City	42	14	16	12	58	68	44
Tottenham Hotspur	42	13	15	14	48	61	41
Middlesbrough	42	15	10	17	57	50	40
Bristol City	42	15	10	17	47	51	40
Southampton	42	12	16	14	47	53	40
Manchester City	42	13	13	16	58	56	39
Norwich City	42	7	23	12	51	57	37
Bolton Wanderers	42	12	11	19	54	75	35
Wolverhampton W	42	13	8	21	44	68	34
Derby County	42	10	11	21	44	71	31
Queen's Park Rangers	42	6	13	23	45	73	25
Birmingham City	42	6	10	26	37	64	22
Chelsea	42	5	10	27	44	92	20

Attendances

TOTAL

	Home	Away	Total
League	342,021	499,105	841,126
Cup/Other	41,282	36,032	77,314
TOTAL	383,303	535,137	918,440

AVERAGE

	Home	Away	Total
League	16,287	23,767	20,027
Cup/Other	20,641	18,016	19,329
TOTAL	16,665	23,267	19,966

Match No.	Date		Opponents	Location	Result		Scorers	Atten
1	Aug	19	Liverpool	A	L	1-2	McGee	50
2		22	West Bromwich	H	L	0-1		15
3		26	Nottingham Forest	H	D	0-0		17
4	Sep	2	Arsenal	A	L	1-5	McGee	33
5		9	Manchester United	H	D	1-1	Gillard	23
6		16	Middlesbrough	A	W	2-0	Harkouk, Eastoe	12
7		23	Aston Villa	H	W	1-0	Harkouk	16
8		30	Wolverhampton	A	L	0-1		14
9	Oct	7	Bristol City	H	W	1-0	Busby	15
10		14	Southampton	A	D	1-1	Goddard	22
11		21	Everton	H	D	1-1	Gillard	21
12		28	Ipswich Town	A	L	1-2	Francis	20
13	Nov	4	Chelsea	H	D	0-0		22
14		11	Liverpool	H	L	1-3	Eastoe	26
15		18	Nottingham Forest	A	D	0-0		28
16		25	Derby County	A	L	1-2	Howe	19
17	Dec	2	Bolton Wanderers	H	L	1-3	Harkouk	11
18		9	Coventry City	A	L	0-1		18
19		16	Manchester City	H	W	2-1	Hamilton (2)	12
20		26	Tottenham Hotspur	H	D	2-2	Bowles (pen), Shanks	24
21		30	Leeds United	H	L	1-4	Eastoe	17
22	Jan	20	Middlesbrough	H	D	1-1	Goddard	9
23		31	Norwich City	A	D	1-1	Francis	14
24	Feb	10	Wolverhampton	H	D	3-3	Roeder, Busby, Gillard	11
25		13	Arsenal	H	L	1-2	Shanks	21
26		24	Southampton	H	L	0-1		13
27		28	Manchester United	A	L	0-2		36
28	Mar	3	Everton	A	L	1-2	Goddard	24
29		6	Birmingham City	A	L	1-3	Busby	12
30		17	Chelsea	A	W	3-1	Goddard, Roeder, Busby	25
31		20	Aston Villa	A	L	1-3	Allen	24
32		24	West Bromwich	A	L	1-2	McGee	23
33		31	Derby County	H	D	2-2	Goddard, Walsh	13
34	Apr	3	Bristol City	A	L	0-2		15
35		7	Bolton Wanderers	A	L	1-2	Goddard	21
36		13	Norwich City	H	D	0-0		14
37		14	Tottenham Hotspur	A	D	1-1	Clement	28
38		21	Manchester City	A	L	1-3	Busby	30
39		28	Coventry City	H	W	5-1	Allen (3), Shanks, Walsh (pen)	10
40	May	4	Leeds United	A	L	3-4	Walsh, Roeder, Busby	20
41		7	Birmingham City	H	L	1-3	Roeder	9
42		11	Ipswich Town	H	L	0-4		9

Appearan
Sub appearar
G

FA Cup

R3	Jan	9	Fulham	A	L	0-2		21

Appearar
Sub appearar
G

League Cup

R2	Aug	29	Preston North End	A	W	3-1	OG (Baxter), Eastoe (2)	14
R3	Oct	3	Swansea City	H	W	2-0	McGee, Eastoe	18
R4	Nov	11	Leeds United	H	L	0-2		22

Appearar
Sub appearar
G

Total - Appearar
Total - Sub appearar
Total - G

Allen	Bowles	Busby	Clement	Cunningham	Eastoe	Elsey	Francis	Gillard	Goddard	Hamilton	Harkouk	Hollins	Howe	James	McGee	Parkes	Richardson	Roeder	Shanks	Wallace	Walsh	OG
	10	7	2		9		8	3				4	5		11	1			6			
	10	9[a]	2		7		8	3				4	5	11	12	1			6			
	10	9			7		8	3			12	4[a]	5		11	1		2	6			
	10	9			7		8	3				4	5		11	1		6	2			
	10	6			7		8	3	12		9[a]	4	5		11	1			2			
	10	9		6	7			3			8	4	5		11[a]	1			2			
	10	9		6	7			3			8	4	5		11	1			2			
	10			6[a]	7		8	3			9	4	5		11		1		2			
	10	12		6	7		8	3			9[a]	4	5		11	1			2			
	10	6		7	9			3[a]	12		11	4	5		8	1			2			
	10	6			7		8	3			9	4	5		11	1			2			
	10	6		11	7		8[a]	3			9	4	5		12	1			2			
2	10	6		11	7[a]			3			9	4	5		8	1			2			
	10	8	2		7			3			9	4	5		11	1			6			
	10	9	2	11	7		8	3				4	5			1			6			
		9	2	11	7		8	3				4	5		12	1			6	10[a]		
		9	2		7		8	3		12	11	4	5		10[a]	1			6			
		10	2		7			3[a]	12	9	11	4	5			1		8	6			
	10		2		9		8[a]	3		12	11	4	5			1		6	7			
	10		2		8			3		9	11[a]	4	5		12	1		6	7			
2	10		2		8			3	11	9		6	5[a]			1		4	7			
	10		2				8	3	11	9		6	5			1		4	7			
	10	12	2				8	3	11	9		4	5			1		6	7[a]			
	10	12	2				8	3	11	9		4	5[a]			1		6	7			
	10	6	2				8	3	11	9		4				1		5	7			
2	10	6	2				8	3	11	9[a]		4					1	5	7			
	10	6	2		9		8	3	11			4					1	5	7			
	10		2		9[a]		8	3	11	12		4	5				1	6	7			
	10	12	2[a]		9		8	3	11			4	5				1	6	7			
	10	12	2		9		8	3	11[a]			4	5				1	6	7			
2	10	11	2		9[a]		8	3				4	5				1	6	7			
		9	2			11	8	3				4	5		10		1	6	7			
	10	12	2				8	3[a]	11			4	5				1	6	7		9	
2		8	2						11			4	5		10		1	6	3[a]	7	9	
		10	2				8		11			4	5		7		1	6		3	9	
2		10	2						11			4	5		7		1	6	8	3[a]	9	
	10	7	2				8		11			4	5				1	6	3		9	
		4	2				8	3	11				5		10		1	6	7		9	
1		7	2					3	10			4	5				1	6	8		9	
1		7				12	8	3	10[a]			4	5				1	6	2		9	
1						7[a]	8	3	10			4	5				1	6	2	12	9	
1		7	2				8	3	10			4					1	5	6		9	
4	30	29	29	9	26	2	31	38	20	8	14	41	38	1	18	24	18	27	41	4	10	
5		6				1			3	3	1				4					1		
4	1	6	1		3		2	3	6	2	3		1		3			4	3		3	
	10	11[a]	2	4	8			3		9	12	6	5			1			7			
	1	1	1	1	1			1		1		1	1			1			1			
											1											
	10	9			7		8	3				4	5		11	1		6	2			
	10[a]			6	7		8	3			9	4	5		11		1		2			
	10	8	2	12	7			3			9[a]	4	5		11	1			6			
	3	2	1	1	3		2	3			2	3	3		3	2	1	1	3			
				1																		
					3										1							1
4	34	32	31	11	30	2	33	42	20	9	16	45	42	1	21	27	19	28	45	4	10	
5		6		1		1			3	3	2				4					1		
4	1	6	1		6		2	3	6	2	3		1		4			4	3		3	1

1979-80

Division Two

	P	W	D	L	F	A	Pts
Leicester City	42	21	13	8	58	38	55
Sunderland	42	21	12	9	69	42	54
Birmingham City	42	21	11	10	58	38	53
Chelsea	42	23	7	12	66	52	53
Queen's Park Rangers	42	18	13	11	75	53	49
Luton Town	42	16	17	9	66	45	49
West Ham United	42	20	7	15	54	43	47
Cambridge United	42	14	16	12	61	53	44
Newcastle United	42	15	14	13	53	49	44
Preston North End	42	12	19	11	56	52	43
Oldham Athletic	42	16	11	15	49	53	43
Swansea City	42	17	9	16	48	53	43
Shrewsbury Town	42	18	5	19	60	53	41
Orient	42	12	17	13	48	54	41
Cardiff City	42	16	8	18	41	48	40
Wrexham	42	16	6	20	40	49	38
Notts County	42	11	15	16	51	52	37
Watford	42	12	13	17	39	46	37
Bristol Rovers	42	11	13	18	50	64	35
Fulham	42	11	7	24	42	74	29
Burnley	42	6	15	21	39	73	27
Charlton Athletic	42	6	10	26	39	78	22

Attendances

TOTAL	Home	Away	Total
League	295,810	321,626	617,436
Cup/Other	48,942	46,871	95,813
TOTAL	344,752	368,497	713,249

AVERAGE	Home	Away	Total
League	14,086	15,316	14,701
Cup/Other	16,314	15,624	15,969
TOTAL	14,365	15,354	14,859

Match No.	Date		Opponents	Location	Result		Scorers	Atte
1	Aug	18	Bristol Rovers	H	W	2-0	Allen, Goddard	1
2		22	Cardiff City	A	L	0-1		1
3		25	Leicester City	H	L	1-4	Allen (pen)	1
4	Sep	1	Notts County	A	L	0-1		
5		8	Fulham	H	W	3-0	Goddard, Allen, Currie	1
6		15	Swansea City	A	W	2-1	Burke, OG (Stephenson)	1
7		22	West Ham United	H	W	3-0	Allen (2), Goddard	2
8		29	Oldham Athletic	A	D	0-0		
9	Oct	6	Watford	A	W	2-1	Allen, Roeder	2
10		9	Cardiff City	H	W	3-0	Allen (2), Roeder	1
11		13	Preston North End	H	D	1-1	Goddard	1
12		20	Sunderland	A	L	0-3		2
13		27	Burnley	H	W	7-0	Goddard (2), Allen (2), Roeder, Shanks, McCreery	1
14	Nov	3	Bristol Rovers	A	W	3-1	OG (Thomas), Roeder, Allen	
15		10	Luton Town	A	D	1-1	Allen	1
16		17	Shrewsbury Town	H	W	2-1	McCreery, Roeder	1
17		24	Charlton Athletic	H	W	4-0	Allen (2, 1 pen), Roeder, Bowles	1
18	Dec	1	Cambridge United	A	L	1-2	Bowles	
19		8	Wrexham	H	D	2-2	Goddard (2)	1
20		15	Newcastle United	A	L	2-4	Goddard, Roeder	2
21		18	Chelsea	H	D	2-2	Allen (2)	2
22		27	Leicester City	A	L	0-2		2
23	Jan	1	Birmingham City	A	L	1-2	Allen	2
24		12	Notts County	H	L	1-3	Allen	
25		19	Fulham	A	W	2-0	Waddock, Burke	1
26	Feb	2	Swansea City	H	W	3-2	Allen (pen), Goddard (2)	1
27		9	West Ham United	A	L	1-2	Goddard	2
28		12	Orient	H	D	0-0		1
29		16	Oldham Athletic	H	W	4-3	Allen (2, 1 pen), McCreery, Goddard	
30		23	Preston North End	A	W	3-0	Allen, Roeder, Goddard	1
31	Mar	1	Sunderland	H	D	0-0		1
32		8	Burnley	A	W	3-0	Gillard, Allen, Shanks	
33		14	Watford	H	D	1-1	Currie	1
34		22	Luton Town	H	D	2-2	Goddard (2)	1
35		29	Shrewsbury Town	A	L	0-3		
36	Apr	2	Chelsea	A	W	2-0	Busby, Burke	3
37		5	Birmingham City	H	D	1-1	Burke	1
38		8	Orient	A	D	1-1	Allen	1
39		12	Cambridge United	H	D	2-2	Allen, Busby	1
40		19	Charlton Athletic	A	D	2-2	Allen (2)	
41		26	Newcastle United	H	W	2-1	Roeder, McCreery	1
42	May	3	Wrexham	A	W	3-1	Currie, Hazell, Allen	

Appeara
Sub appeara
G

FA Cup

R3	Jan	5	Watford	H	L	1-2	Hazell	1

Appeara
Sub appeara
G

League Cup

R2	Aug	28	Bradford City	H	W	2-1	McCreery, Neal	
rep	Sep	5	Bradford City	A	W	2-0	Gillard, Roeder	1
R3		25	Mansfield Town	A	W	3-0	Bowles, Allen, Currie	
R4	Oct	30	Wolverhampton	H	D	1-1	Allen	2
rep	Nov	6	Wolverhampton	A	L	0-1		2

Appeara
Sub appeara
G

Total - Appeara
Total - Sub appeara
Total - G

Bowles	Burke	Busby	Currie	Davidson	Elsey	Gillard	Goddard	Hamilton	Harkouk	Hazell	Hill	Howe	McCreery	Neal	Pape	Roeder	Rogers	Shanks	Waddock	Wallace	Walsh	Wicks	Woods	OG
					2	3	11	10				5	4	7		6		8					1	
		4			2	3	7					5	8	11		6		10					1	
		11		12	2[a]	3	10					5	4	7		6		8					1	
11					2	3	10		12			5[a]	4	7		6		8					1	
7	11		10			3	8		12	5[a]			4			6		2					1	
7	11					3	8		10[a]	5			4			6		2	12				1	
7	11		8			3	10			5			4			6		2					1	
7			8[a]			3	10		12	5			4			6		2				11	1	
7	11					3	10			5			4			8		2				6	1	
7	11					3	10[a]			5			4			8		2			12	6	1	
7	11[a]					3	10			5			4			8		2			12	6	1	
7	11					3	10			5			4			8		2			12	6	1	
7	11[a]					3	10						4			5		2		8	12	6	1	
7			10			3	11			5[a]			4			8		2			12	6	1	
7	12		10[a]			3	11			5			4			8		2				6	1	
7			10			3[a]	11			5			4			8		2	12			6	1	
7	12						11[a]			5			4			8		2	10	3		6	1	
7							10			5	11[a]		4			8		2	12	3		6	1	
7			12			3	10			5	11		4			8[a]		2				6	1	
		12	10[a]			3	7			5	11		4			8		2				6	1	
	11[a]	12				3	7			5			4			8		2	10			6	1	
			10			3	7[a]			5	11		4			8		2	12			6	1	
	12	6	8[a]								11		4					2	10	3	7	5	1	
	11						8						4	12		6		2	10	3	7[a]	5	1	
	11		10			3[a]	7						4			6		2	8	12		5	1	
	11		10			3[a]	7						4			6		2	8	12		5	1	
	11[a]		10			3	7			8			4			6		2	12			5	1	
	11		8			3	10			6			4					2	7			5	1	
	11		8[a]			3	10			5			4			7		2	12			6	1	
	11		10			3	7			5			4			8		2				6	1	
	11		10			3	7			5			4			8		2				6	1	
	11		10[a]			3	7			5	12		4			8		2				6	1	
	11[a]		10			3	7			5	12		4			8		2				6	1	
	11		10			3	7		12	5			4			8[a]		2				6	1	
	11		10			3	7			5			4	9[a]		8		2	12			6	1	
	11	9	10			3	7						4			6		2	8			5	1	
	11	8	10			3	7						4			6		2				5	1	
	11	8	10			3	7						4			6		2				5	1	
	11	8	10			3[a]	7			12			4			6		2				5	1	
	11	7[a]	10			3	8						4		1	6		2	12			5		
	11		10			3	7[a]			12	8		4			6	2	4				5	1	
	11		10			3				7	8		4			6	2					5	1	
16	28	8	27		4	38	40	1	1	27	7	4	42	5	1	40	2	41	8	5	2	35	41	
	3	2	1	1					4	2	2			1					8	2	5			
2	4	2	3			1	16			1			4			9		2	1					2

	12		10							6	11		4					2	8	3	7[a]	5	1	
			1							1	1		1					1	1	1	1	1	1	
	1																							
										1														

11		4				3	10[a]					5	8	7		6		2	12				1	
7			10			3	8		11	5			4			6		2					1	
7	11[a]		8			3	10			5			4			6		2				12	1	
7			10[a]			3	12			5			4			8		2			11	6	1	
7[a]	12		10			3	11			5			4			8		2				6	1	
5	1	1	4			5	4		1	4		1	5	1		5		5			1	2	5	
	1						1												1			1		
1			1			1							1	1		1								
21	29	9	32		4	43	44	1	2	32	8	5	48	6	1	45	2	47	9	6	4	38	47	
	5	2	1	1			1		4	2	2			1					9	2	5	1		
3	4	2	4			2	16			2			5	1		10		2	1					2

1980-81

Division Two

	P	W	D	L	F	A	Pts
West Ham United	42	28	10	4	79	29	66
Notts County	42	18	17	7	49	38	53
Swansea City	42	18	14	10	64	44	50
Blackburn Rovers	42	16	18	8	42	29	50
Luton Town	42	18	12	12	61	46	48
Derby County	42	15	15	12	57	52	45
Grimsby Town	42	15	15	12	44	42	45
Queen's Park Rangers	42	15	13	14	56	46	43
Watford	42	16	11	15	50	45	43
Sheffield Wednesday	42	17	8	17	53	51	42
Newcastle United	42	14	14	14	30	45	42
Chelsea	42	14	12	16	46	41	40
Cambridge United	42	17	6	19	53	65	40
Shrewsbury Town	42	11	17	14	46	47	39
Oldham Athletic	42	12	15	15	39	48	39
Wrexham	42	12	14	16	43	45	38
Orient	42	13	12	17	52	56	38
Bolton Wanderers	42	14	10	18	61	66	38
Cardiff City	42	12	12	18	44	60	36
Preston North End	42	11	14	17	41	62	36
Bristol City	42	7	16	19	29	51	30
Bristol Rovers	42	5	13	24	34	65	23

Attendances

TOTAL	Home	Away	Total
League	229,643	243,413	473,056
Cup/Other	40,073	59,666	99,739
TOTAL	269,716	303,079	572,795

AVERAGE	Home	Away	Total
League	10,935	11,591	11,263
Cup/Other	20,037	19,889	19,948
TOTAL	11,727	12,628	12,187

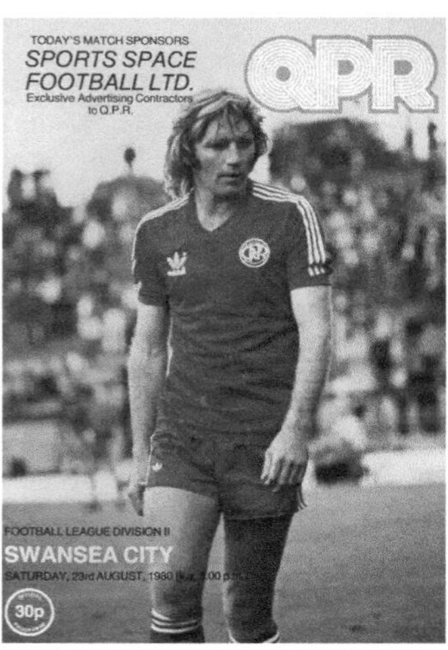

Match No.	Date		Opponents	Location	Result		Scorers	Atten
1	Aug	16	Oldham Athletic	A	L	0-1		6
2		19	Bristol Rovers	H	W	4-0	Fereday (2), Hazell, Shanks	9
3		23	Swansea City	H	D	0-0		10
4		30	Chelsea	A	D	1-1	Langley	23
5	Sep	6	Notts County	A	L	1-2	Hill (pen)	7
6		13	Newcastle United	H	L	1-2	Hazell	10
7		20	Sheffield Wednesday	A	L	0-1		15
8		27	Bristol City	H	W	4-0	Neal (2), Langley, Shanks	8
9	Oct	4	Blackburn Rovers	A	L	1-2	Neal	12
10		7	Orient	H	D	0-0		9
11		11	Bolton Wanderers	H	W	3-1	Langley, Burke (pen), Neal	8
12		18	Derby County	A	D	3-3	King (2), Langley	16
13		22	Cardiff City	A	L	0-1		4
14		25	Wrexham	H	L	0-1		9
15	Nov	1	Grimsby Town	A	D	0-0		10
16		8	Luton Town	H	W	3-2	Neal (2), King	10
17		11	Bristol Rovers	A	W	2-1	King, Langley	6
18		15	Oldham Athletic	H	W	2-0	Silkman (pen), Neal	8
19		22	Preston North End	A	L	2-3	Roeder, Neal	6
20		29	Shrewsbury Town	H	D	0-0		7
21	Dec	6	Cambridge United	A	L	0-1		6
22		19	Bolton Wanderers	A	W	2-1	Stainrod, Flanagan	6
23		26	West Ham United	H	W	3-0	Silkman, Currie, Stainrod	23
24		27	Watford	A	D	1-1	King	22
25	Jan	10	Preston North End	H	D	1-1	Stainrod	8
26		17	Chelsea	H	W	1-0	Langley	22
27		31	Swansea City	A	W	2-1	Langley, King	12
28	Feb	3	Cardiff City	H	W	2-0	Fenwick, Langley	9
29		7	Newcastle United	A	L	0-1		20
30		14	Notts County	H	D	1-1	Howe	11
31		21	Bristol City	A	W	1-0	Waddock	10
32		28	Sheffield Wednesday	H	L	1-2	Stainrod	15
33	Mar	7	Blackburn Rovers	H	D	1-1	Francis	9
34		21	Derby County	H	W	3-1	Francis (2), Flanagan	8
35		28	Wrexham	A	D	1-1	Waddock	5
36		31	Orient	A	L	0-4		6
37	Apr	4	Grimsby Town	H	W	1-0	Francis (pen)	8
38		11	Luton Town	A	L	0-3		12
39		18	Watford	H	D	0-0		10
40		21	West Ham United	A	L	0-3		24
41		25	Cambridge United	H	W	5-0	Sealy (2), Muir (2), Roeder	6
42	May	2	Shrewsbury Town	A	D	3-3	Fenwick, Waddock, Flanagan	5

Appearances
Sub appearances
Goals

FA Cup

R3	Jan	3	Tottenham Hotspur	H	D	0-0		28
rep		7	Tottenham Hotspur	A	L	1-3	Stainrod	36

Appearances
Sub appearances
Goals

League Cup

R2/1	Aug	26	Derby County	H	D	0-0		11
R2/2	Sep	3	Derby County	A	D	0-0*		16
R3		23	Notts County	A	L	1-4	Langley	6

* Won 5-3 on penalties

Appearances
Sub appearances
Goals

Total - Appearances
Total - Sub appearances
Total - Goals

Burridge	Currie	Fenwick	Fereday	Flanagan	Francis	Gillard	Hazell	Howe	Hill	Hucker	King	Langley	McCreery	Micklewhite	Muir	Neal	Neill	Roeder	Sealy	Shanks	Silkman	Stainrod	Stewart	Waddock	Walsh	Wicks	Wilkins	Woods
	10					3			7				2			12		6		8				4	9[a]	5		1
	10		7			3	9[a]		12				2					6		8				4		5		1
	10		7[a]			3	12					9	2					6		8				4		5		1
	10		7			3						9	2				12	6		8				4		5		1
			7[a]			3	12		11			9	2				10	6		8				4		5		1
	10		7[a]			3	5		12			9	2					6		8				4				1
	10					3[a]			11		8	9	7					6		2				4		5		1
	10					3						9	2			7		6		8				4		5		1
	10					3					7	9[a]	2			11		6		8			12	4		5		1
	10					3					7	8	11			9		6		2				4		5		1
	10					3	6				7	8[a]	4			9				2				12		5		1
						3					8	10	7			9		6		2				4		5		1
						3	12				8	10	7			9		6		2				4		5		1
			12			3					8	10	7			9		6		2				4		5		1
						3		7			8	10				9		6[a]		2	11			4		5	12	1
						3		6			8	10	12			9[a]		7		2	11			4		5		1
						3		6			8	10				9		7		2	11			4		5		1
						3		6			8	10		12		9		7		2[a]	11			4		5		1
						3		6			8					9		7		2	11	10		4		5		1
						3					8	6				9		7		2	11	10		4		5		1
	6					3					8					9		7		2	11	10		4		5		1
	10	4		7		3					8							6		2	11	9				5		1
	10[a]	4		7		3					8							6		2	11	9		12		5		
		4		7		3					8							6		2	11	9		10		5		
	10	4				3					8					7		6		2	11	9				5		
	10	4				3					8	7						6		2	11	9				5		
	10	4				3					8	7						6		2	11[a]	9		12		5		
	10	4				3					8	7						6		2	11	9				5		
	10	4				3					8	7						6		2	11	9				5		
	10	4				3	5	6			8	7								2	11	9						
	10	4				3	6[a]				8	7								2	11	9		12		5		
	10	4		12	8	3						7						6		2	11[a]	9				5		
	10[a]	4		7	8	3						12						6		2	11	9				5		
	10	4		7	8	3					12							6	9	2	11[a]					5		
	10	4		9	8	3					12							6	7	2				11[a]		5		
	10	4		7	8	3[a]												6	9	2	12			11		5		
	10			7	8	3												6	9	2	4			11		5		
	10			7	8	3[a]												6	9	2	4			11		5		
	10	4		9	8	3											2	6						7		5		
	10	4		9	8	3											2	6	11					7		5[a]		
	10	2		9	8	3		5							11			6	7					4				
	10	2		9		3		5		1					11			6	8					7			4	
9	31	19	5	13	10	42	5	8	3	1	24	24	14		2	15	3	39	8	38	22	15		29	1	38	1	22
			1	1			3		2		2	1	1	1		1	1				1		1	4			1	
	1	2	2	3	4		2	1	1		6	8			2	8		2	2	2	2	4		3				

Burridge	Currie	Fenwick	Fereday	Flanagan	Francis	Gillard	Hazell	Howe	Hill	Hucker	King	Langley	McCreery	Micklewhite	Muir	Neal	Neill	Roeder	Sealy	Shanks	Silkman	Stainrod	Stewart	Waddock	Walsh	Wicks	Wilkins	Woods
		4		7		3					8							6		2	11	9		10		5		
	10	4		7[a]		3					8		12					6		2	11	9				5		
2	1	2		2		2					2							2		2	2	2		1		2		
													1															
																						1						

Burridge	Currie	Fenwick	Fereday	Flanagan	Francis	Gillard	Hazell	Howe	Hill	Hucker	King	Langley	McCreery	Micklewhite	Muir	Neal	Neill	Roeder	Sealy	Shanks	Silkman	Stainrod	Stewart	Waddock	Walsh	Wicks	Wilkins	Woods
	10					3	7					9	2					6		8				4		5		1
	10[a]		7			3			11			9	2				12	6		8				4		5		1
	10[a]						12				7	9	2			11		6		8				4		5		1
	3		1			2	1		1		1	3	3			1		3		3				3		3		3
							1										1											
												1																

Burridge	Currie	Fenwick	Fereday	Flanagan	Francis	Gillard	Hazell	Howe	Hill	Hucker	King	Langley	McCreery	Micklewhite	Muir	Neal	Neill	Roeder	Sealy	Shanks	Silkman	Stainrod	Stewart	Waddock	Walsh	Wicks	Wilkins	Woods
1	35	21	6	15	10	46	6	8	4	1	27	27	17		2	16	3	44	8	43	24	17		33	1	43	1	25
			1	1			4		2		2	1	2	1		1	2				1		1	4			1	
	1	2	2	3	4		2	1	1		6	9			2	8		2	2	2	2	5		3				

1981-82

Division Two

	P	W	D	L	F	A	Pts
Luton Town	42	25	13	4	86	46	88
Watford	42	23	11	8	76	42	80
Norwich City	42	22	5	15	64	50	71
Sheffield Wednesday	42	20	10	12	55	51	70
Queen's Park Rangers	42	21	6	15	65	43	69
Barnsley	42	19	10	13	59	41	67
Rotherham United	42	20	7	15	66	54	67
Leicester City	42	18	12	12	56	48	66
Newcastle United	42	18	8	16	52	50	62
Blackburn Rovers	42	16	11	15	47	43	59
Oldham Athletic	42	15	14	13	50	51	59
Chelsea	42	15	12	15	60	60	57
Charlton Athletic	42	13	12	17	50	65	51
Cambridge United	42	13	9	20	48	53	48
Crystal Palace	42	13	9	20	34	45	48
Derby County	42	12	12	18	53	68	48
Grimsby Town	42	11	13	18	53	65	46
Shrewsbury Town	42	11	13	18	37	57	46
Bolton Wanderers	42	13	7	22	39	61	46
Cardiff City	42	12	8	22	45	61	44
Wrexham	42	11	11	20	40	56	44
Orient	42	10	9	23	36	61	39

Attendances

TOTAL	Home	Away	Total
League	264,103	229,206	493,309
Cup/Other	84,514	288,014	372,528
TOTAL	348,617	517,220	865,837

AVERAGE	Home	Away	Total
League	12,576	10,915	11,745
Cup/Other	14,086	41,145	28,656
TOTAL	12,912	18,472	15,742

Match No.	Date		Opponents	Location	Result		Scorers
1	Aug	29	Wrexham	A	W	3-1	King, Allen (2)
2	Sep	1	Luton Town	H	L	1-2	King
3		5	Newcastle United	H	W	3-0	King, Roeder, Stainrod
4		12	Grimsby Town	A	L	1-2	Gregory
5		19	Crystal Palace	H	W	1-0	Stainrod
6		22	Oldham Athletic	A	L	0-2	
7		26	Derby County	A	L	1-3	Gregory
8	Oct	3	Blackburn Rovers	H	W	2-0	Gregory, Allen
9		10	Norwich City	H	W	2-0	Gregory, Stainrod
10		18	Orient	A	D	1-1	Gillard
11		24	Leicester City	H	W	2-0	Stainrod, Gregory
12		31	Charlton Athletic	A	W	2-1	Stainrod, Allen
13	Nov	7	Rotherham United	H	D	1-1	Flanagan
14		14	Sheffield Wednesday	A	W	3-1	Stainrod (3)
15		21	Shrewsbury Town	A	L	1-2	Flanagan
16		24	Oldham Athletic	H	D	0-0	
17		28	Cardiff City	H	W	2-0	Stainrod (2)
18	Dec	5	Bolton Wanderers	A	L	0-1	
19		12	Barnsley	H	W	1-0	Flanagan
20		26	Chelsea	H	L	0-2	
21	Jan	16	Wrexham	H	D	1-1	Stainrod
22		30	Crystal Palace	A	D	0-0	
23	Feb	6	Grimsby Town	H	W	1-0	Gregory
24		9	Cambridge United	A	L	0-1	
25		16	Blackburn Rovers	A	L	1-2	Allen
26		20	Derby County	H	W	3-0	Hazell, Fenwick, Flanagan
27		27	Norwich City	A	W	1-0	Roeder
28	Mar	9	Watford	A	L	0-4	
29		13	Leicester City	A	L	2-3	Currie, Stainrod
30		20	Charlton Athletic	H	W	4-0	Allen (3), Fenwick
31		27	Rotherham United	A	L	0-1	
32		29	Sheffield Wednesday	H	W	2-0	Flanagan, Stainrod
33	Apr	6	Orient	H	W	3-0	Hazell, Flanagan, Stainrod
34		10	Chelsea	A	L	1-2	Gregory
35		12	Watford	H	D	0-0	
36		17	Shrewsbury Town	H	W	2-1	Flanagan, Allen
37		24	Cardiff City	A	W	2-1	Allen, Micklewhite
38	May	1	Bolton Wanderers	H	W	7-1	Gregory, Micklewhite, Flanagan (2), Fenwick (pen), Allen, Stainrod
39		5	Newcastle United	A	W	4-0	Gregory, Allen, Flanagan, Stainrod
40		8	Barnsley	A	L	0-3	
41		11	Luton Town	A	L	2-3	Fenwick, Stainrod
42		15	Cambridge United	H	W	2-1	Allen, Fenwick (pen)

Appeara
Sub appeara

FA Cup

R3	Jan	2	Middlesbrough	H	D	1-1	Stainrod
rep		18	Middlesbrough	A	W	3-2 aet	Stainrod (2), Neill
R4		23	Blackpool	A	D	0-0	
rep		26	Blackpool	H	W	5-1	Allen (4), Stainrod (pen)
R5	Feb	13	Grimsby Town	H	W	3-1	Stainrod, Allen, Howe
R6	Mar	6	Crystal Palace	H	W	1-0	Allen
SF	Apr	3	West Bromwich	N*	W	1-0	Allen
F	May	22	Tottenham Hotspur	W**	D	1-1	Fenwick
rep		27	Tottenham Hotspur	W**	L	0-1	

* Played at Highbury
** Played at Wembley

Appeara
Sub appeara

League Cup

R2/1	Oct	6	Portsmouth	H	W	5-0	OG (Ellis), Gregory (2), Micklewhite (2)
R2/2		27	Portsmouth	A	D	2-2	Flanagan, Micklewhite
R3	Nov	10	Bristol City	H	W	3-0	Flanagan, Stainrod, Allen
R4	Dec	1	Watford	A	L	1-4	Stainrod (pen)

Appeara
Sub appeara

Total - Appeara
Total - Sub appeara
Total -

Burke	Burridge	Currie	Dawes	Fenwick	Fereday	Flanagan	Francis	Gillard	Gregory	Hazell	Howe	Hucker	King	Micklewhite	Neill	O'Connor	Roeder	Sealy	Stainrod	Stewart	Waddock	Wicks	Wilkins	OG
	1			3		7	8		2	5			10				6		11		4			
	1			3		7	8		2	5			10				6		11		4			
	1	4		3		7	8	12	2	5			10				6		11					
	1	4		3		7	8	12	2		5		10[a]				6		11					
	1	10		3		7		11	2	5							6		8		4			
	1	10		3		7		11	2	5							6		8		4			
	1	10		3		7[a]		11	2	5							6	12	8		4			
	1	10		3				11	2	5				7			6		8		4			
12	1	10		3				11	2	5				7[a]			6		8		4			
12	1			3		8		11	2	5				7			6		10		4			
12	1			3		8	7[a]	11	2	5							6		10		4			
	1			3		8	7	11	2	5							6		10		4			
9	1			3		8	7[a]	11	2	5							6	12	10		4			
	1			3		8		11	2	12	5			7			6		10		4			
	1			3		8		11	2		5			7			6		10		4			
	1			3		8		11	2		5			7			6	12	10		4			
	1			3		8		11	2		5			7			6	9	10		4			
12	1			3[a]		8		11	2		5			7			6	9	10		4			
	1			3	12	8		11	2		5			7			6	9[a]		10	4			
	1			3		8		11			5			7		2	6	9[a]		10	4			
		9		3		12		11	8		5	1			2[a]		6		10		4			
		8		2				3	11		5	1		9			6		10		4			
		8		2	9			3	11		5	1					6		10		4			
		8[a]		2	9			3	11		5	1		12			6		10		4			
				2		8		3	11		5	1		7	4		6		10					
				2		8		3	11[a]	5		1		7	4		6		10				12	
		7				8		3	11	5	2	1			4		6		10					
		7				8		3	11	5	9	1			2		6		10		4			
12		7				8		3	11[a]	5	2	1					6		10		4			
12		7		4		8		3[a]		5		1		11	2		6		10					
12			11	3		8				5		1[a]		7	2				10		4	6		
		7	3			8			11			1		4	2		6		10			5		
		7		2		8		3		5		1		11			6		10[a]	12	4			
		7				8		3	11	5		1			2		6		10		4			
			3			8				5		1		11	2		7		10		4	6		
10		7[a]	3	2	12	8						1		11			6				4	5		
				2		8		3	11			1		7			6		10		4	5		
12				2[a]		8		3	11			1		7			6		10		4	5		
12				2		7		3	11			1		8[a]			6		10		4	5		
12				2		8		3		5		1		7			11		10[a]		4	6		
			3	11		8						1		7	2		6		10		4	5		
		7		2		8		3	11	5		1		12			6		10		4[a]			
2	20	20	5	36	2	36	7	33	34	23	16	22	4	24	11	1	41	4	39	2	35	9		
10					2	1		2		1				2				3		1			1	
		1		5		10		1	9	2			3	2			2		17					

Burke	Burridge	Currie	Dawes	Fenwick	Fereday	Flanagan	Francis	Gillard	Gregory	Hazell	Howe	Hucker	King	Micklewhite	Neill	O'Connor	Roeder	Sealy	Stainrod	Stewart	Waddock	Wicks	Wilkins	OG
				3		8		11			5	1		7	2		6		10	9	4			
		8[a]		2		9		3	11		5	1			12		6		10		4			
		8		2		9		3	11		5	1					6		10		4			
		8		2		9[a]		3	11		5	1					6		10	12	4			
				2	12	8		3	11		5	1		7			6		10		4[a]			
		7				8		3	11	5		1			2		6		10		4			
		7		2		8		3		5		1		11			6		10		4			
		7		2		8		3	11	5		1		12			6		10		4			
12		7		2		8		3	11	5		1		9[a]	6				10		4			
		7		8		9		9	7	4	5	9		4	3		8		9	1	9			
1					1									1	1					1				
				1							1				1				5					

Burke	Burridge	Currie	Dawes	Fenwick	Fereday	Flanagan	Francis	Gillard	Gregory	Hazell	Howe	Hucker	King	Micklewhite	Neill	O'Connor	Roeder	Sealy	Stainrod	Stewart	Waddock	Wicks	Wilkins	OG
12	1	10[a]		3				11	2	5				7			6		8		4			
9	1			3		8		11	2	5[a]				7			6		10	12	4			
	1			3		8[a]		11	2	5				7			6		10	12			4	
	1			3		8		11	2	7[a]	5			12			6	9	10		4			
1	4	1		4		3		4	4	4	1			3			4	1	4		3		1	
1														1						2				
						2			2					3					2					1

Burke	Burridge	Currie	Dawes	Fenwick	Fereday	Flanagan	Francis	Gillard	Gregory	Hazell	Howe	Hucker	King	Micklewhite	Neill	O'Connor	Roeder	Sealy	Stainrod	Stewart	Waddock	Wicks	Wilkins	OG
3	24	28	5	48	2	48	7	46	45	31	22	31	4	31	14	1	53	5	52	3	47	9	1	
12					3	1		2		1				4	1			3		4			1	
		1		6		12		1	11	2	1		3	5	1		2		24					1

1982-83

Division Two

	P	W	D	L	F	A	Pts
Queen's Park Rangers	42	26	7	9	77	36	85
Wolverhampton W	42	20	15	7	68	44	75
Leicester City	42	20	10	12	72	44	70
Fulham	42	20	9	13	64	47	69
Newcastle United	42	18	13	11	75	53	67
Sheffield Wednesday	42	16	15	11	60	47	63
Oldham Athletic	42	14	19	9	64	47	61
Leeds United	42	13	21	8	51	46	60
Shrewsbury Town	42	15	14	13	48	48	59
Barnsley	42	14	15	13	57	55	57
Blackburn Rovers	42	15	12	15	58	58	57
Cambridge United	42	13	12	17	42	60	51
Derby County	42	10	19	13	49	58	49
Carlisle United	42	12	12	18	68	70	48
Crystal Palace	42	12	12	18	43	52	48
Middlesbrough	42	11	15	16	46	67	48
Charlton Athletic	42	13	9	20	63	86	48
Chelsea	42	11	14	17	51	61	47
Grimsby Town	42	12	11	19	45	70	47
Rotherham United	42	10	15	17	45	68	45
Burnley	42	12	8	22	56	66	44
Bolton Wanderers	42	11	11	20	42	61	44

Attendances

TOTAL

	Home	Away	Total
League	268,933	240,351	509,284
Cup/Other	9,653	22,131	31,784
TOTAL	278,586	262,482	541,068

AVERAGE

	Home	Away	Total
League	12,806	11,445	12,126
Cup/Other	9,653	11,066	10,595
TOTAL	12,663	11,412	12,024

Match No.	Date		Opponents	Location	Result		Scorers	Attenc
1	Aug	28	Newcastle United	A	L	0-1		36
2		31	Cambridge United	H	W	2-1	Sealy (2)	9
3	Sep	4	Derby County	H	W	4-1	Gregory, Fenwick (pen), Stainrod (2)	10
4		7	Fulham	A	D	1-1	Stainrod	15
5		11	Oldham Athletic	A	W	1-0	Gregory	4
6		18	Sheffield Wednesday	H	L	0-2		13
7		25	Leicester City	A	W	1-0	OG (O'Neill)	10
8		28	Crystal Palace	H	D	0-0		12
9	Oct	2	Burnley	H	W	3-2	Neill, Allen, Micklewhite	9
10		9	Barnsley	A	W	1-0	Allen	13
11		16	Shrewsbury Town	H	W	4-0	Allen, Flanagan, Micklewhite, Gregory	9
12		23	Middlesbrough	A	L	1-2	Allen	7
13		30	Bolton Wanderers	H	W	1-0	Stainrod	9
14	Nov	6	Rotherham United	A	D	0-0		7
15		13	Blackburn Rovers	H	D	2-2	Allen, Fenwick (pen)	9
16		20	Cambridge United	A	W	4-1	Wicks, Sealy, Allen (2)	5
17		27	Carlisle United	H	W	1-0	Fenwick	9
18	Dec	4	Leeds United	A	W	1-0	Allen	11
19		11	Grimsby Town	H	W	4-0	Neill, Sealy, Gregory, Micklewhite	9
20		18	Wolverhampton	A	L	0-4		15
21		27	Chelsea	H	L	1-2	Sealy	23
22		29	Charlton Athletic	A	W	3-1	Micklewhite (2), Sealy	13
23	Jan	3	Derby County	A	L	0-2		14
24		15	Newcastle United	H	W	2-0	Gregory (2)	13
25		22	Crystal Palace	A	W	3-0	Allen (2), Hazell	14
26	Feb	5	Oldham Athletic	H	W	1-0	Sealy	8
27		19	Barnsley	H	W	3-0	Gregory, Sealy, Flanagan	10
28		26	Shrewsbury Town	A	D	0-0		4
29	Mar	5	Middlesbrough	H	W	6-1	Allen (3), Micklewhite, Flanagan, Gregory	9
30		12	Bolton Wanderers	A	L	2-3	Gregory (pen), Sealy	6
31		19	Rotherham United	H	W	4-0	Sealy, Flanagan, Gregory (2)	9
32		22	Charlton Athletic	H	W	5-1	Sealy (2), Hazell, Gregory, Stainrod	10
33		26	Blackburn Rovers	A	W	3-1	Stainrod (2), Flanagan	5
34	Apr	4	Chelsea	A	W	2-0	Gregory, Sealy	20
35		9	Leicester City	H	D	2-2	Gregory, Sealy	16
36		19	Sheffield Wednesday	A	W	1-0	Flanagan	11
37		23	Leeds United	H	W	1-0	OG (Hart)	19
38		30	Carlisle United	A	L	0-1		5
39	May	2	Fulham	H	W	3-1	Gregory, Sealy, Stainrod	24
40		7	Wolverhampton	H	W	2-1	Flanagan, Hazell	19
41		10	Burnley	A	L	1-2	Sealy	7
42		14	Grimsby Town	A	D	1-1	Stainrod	9

Appearar
Sub appearan
G

FA Cup

R3	Jan	8	West Bromwich	A	L	2-3	Fenwick (pen), Micklewhite	16

Appearan
Sub appearan
G

League Cup

R2/1	Oct	5	Rotherham United	A	L	1-2	Gregory	5
R2/2		26	Rotherham United	H	D	0-0		9

Appearar
Sub appearan
G

Total - Appearan
Total - Sub appearan
Total - G

Benstead	Burke	Currie	Dawes	Duffield	Fenwick	Fereday	Flanagan	Grregory	Hazell	Hucker	Micklewhite	Neill	O'Connor	Roeder	Sealy	Stainrod	Steewart	Waddock	Wicks	Wilkins	OG
	12		3		6			11	5	1	7[a]	2			9	10	8	4			
			3		6			11	5	1	7	2			9	10	8	4			
			3		6			11	5	1	7	2			9	10	8[a]	4		12	
			3		6			11	5	1	7	2			9	10	8	4			
			3		6			11	5	1	7	2			9	10	8[a]	4		12	
	12		3		6			11	5	1	7[a]	2			9	10	8	4			
			3		6	12		11	5	1	7	2			9	10	8[a]	4			
			3		6	12		11	5	1	7[a]	2			9	10	8	4			
			3		6			11	5	1	7	2			9		8	4			
			3		6			11	5	1	7	2				10	8	4		12	
			3		6	12	8[a]	11	5	1	7	2			10			4			
			3		6	12		11	5	1	7	2			10		8[a]	4			
		12	3		6			11	5	1	7	2				10	8[a]	4			
			3		6			11	5	1	7	2			12	10	8[a]	4			
		10	3		6			11	5	1	7[a]	2	12		4		8				
			3		6			11	5	1	7	2			8	10	12		4[a]		
			3		6			11	5	1	7	2		4	8	10					
			3		6			11	5	1	7	2		4	8	10					
			3		6		12	11	5	1	7	2		4	8	10[a]					
			3		6			11	5	1	7	2		4	8	10	12				
	12		3		6			11	5	1	7[a]		2	4	8		10				
			3		6		10[a]	11	5	1	7	2		4	8		12				
			3		6		8	11[a]	5	1	7	2		4	10		12				
			3		6		10	11	5	1	7	2			8			4			
			3		6		10	11	5	1	7	2			8			4			
			3		6		10	11		1	7	2			8			4	5		
			3		6		10	11		1	7	2			8	12		4	5		
			3		6		10	11		1	7	2			8	12		4	5		
			3				10	11	5	1	7			2	8			4	6		
			3[a]			12	10	11	5	1				2	8	7		4	6		
			3		6		10	11	5	1	7	2			8	9		4			
			3		6		10	11	5	1	7[a]	2			8	9		4			
			3		6		10	11	5	1	7	2			8	9		4			
			3		6		10	11	5	1		2			8[a]	9		4	7		
			3		6		10	11	5	1	7	2			8	9		4			
			3		6		10	11	5	1		2			8	9		4	7		
			3		6		10	11	5	1		2			8	9		4	7		
	12		3		6		10[a]	11	5	1		2			8	9		4	7		
			3		6		10	11	5	1		2			8	9		4	7		
			3		6		10[a]	11	5	1	12	2			8	9		4	7		
			3		6			11	5	1		2			8	9		4	7		
	6		3	12			10[a]	11	5	1		2			8	9		4	7		
	1	1	42		39		21	42	39	42	33	39	1	9	39	29	15	33	14		
	4	1		1		5	1				1		1		1	2	4			3	
					3		7	15	3		6	2			16	9			1		2

Benstead	Burke	Currie	Dawes	Duffield	Fenwick	Fereday	Flanagan	Grregory	Hazell	Hucker	Micklewhite	Neill	O'Connor	Roeder	Sealy	Stainrod	Steewart	Waddock	Wicks	Wilkins	OG
1	12		3		4		9		5[a]		7	2		6	11			8			
1			1		1		1		1		1	1		1	1			1			
	1																				
					1						1										

Benstead	Burke	Currie	Dawes	Duffield	Fenwick	Fereday	Flanagan	Grregory	Hazell	Hucker	Micklewhite	Neill	O'Connor	Roeder	Sealy	Stainrod	Steewart	Waddock	Wicks	Wilkins	OG
			3		6			11	5	1	7	2			9	10		4			
			3		6			11	5	1	7	2			8[a]	10	12	4			
			2		2			2	2	2	2	2			2	2		2			
																	1				
								1													

Benstead	Burke	Currie	Dawes	Duffield	Fenwick	Fereday	Flanagan	Grregory	Hazell	Hucker	Micklewhite	Neill	O'Connor	Roeder	Sealy	Stainrod	Steewart	Waddock	Wicks	Wilkins	OG
1	1	1	45		42		22	44	42	44	36	42	1	10	42	31	15	36	14		
	5	1		1		5	1				1		1		1	2	5			3	
					4		7	16	3		7	2			16	9			1		2

1983-84

Division One

	P	W	D	L	F	A	Pts
Liverpool	42	22	14	6	73	32	80
Southampton	42	22	11	9	66	38	77
Nottingham Forest	42	22	8	12	76	45	74
Manchester United	42	20	14	8	71	41	74
Queen's Park Rangers	42	22	7	13	67	37	73
Arsenal	42	18	9	15	74	60	63
Everton	42	16	14	12	44	42	62
Tottenham Hotspur	42	17	10	15	64	65	61
West Ham United	42	17	9	16	60	55	60
Aston Villa	42	17	9	16	59	61	60
Watford	42	16	9	17	68	77	57
Ipswich Town	42	15	8	19	55	57	53
Sunderland	42	13	13	16	42	53	52
Norwich City	42	12	15	15	48	49	51
Leicester City	42	13	12	17	65	68	51
Luton Town	42	14	9	19	53	66	51
West Bromwich Albion	42	14	9	19	48	62	51
Stoke City	42	13	11	18	44	63	50
Coventry City	42	13	11	18	57	77	50
Birmingham City	42	12	12	18	39	50	48
Notts County	42	10	11	21	50	72	41
Wolverhampton W	42	6	11	25	27	80	29

Attendances

TOTAL

	Home	Away	Total
League	326,753	410,954	737,707
Cup/Other	8,911	27,927	36,838
TOTAL	335,664	438,881	774,545

AVERAGE

	Home	Away	Total
League	15,560	19,569	17,564
Cup/Other	8,911	9,309	9,210
TOTAL	15,257	18,287	16,838

Match No.	Date		Opponents	Location	Result		Scorers	Atte
1	Aug	27	Manchester United	A	L	1-3	Allen	4
2		29	Southampton	A	D	0-0		1
3	Sep	3	Aston Villa	H	W	2-1	Stainrod, OG (Withe)	1
4		6	Watford	H	D	1-1	Stainrod	1
5		10	Nottingham Forest	A	L	2-3	Dawes, Stainrod	1
6		17	Sunderland	H	W	3-0	Fenwick (pen), Stainrod, Allen	1
7		24	Wolverhampton	A	W	4-0	Allen (2), Gregory, Stainrod	1
8	Oct	1	Arsenal	H	W	2-0	Gregory, Neill	2
9		15	Ipswich Town	A	W	2-0	Stainrod, Gregory	1
10		22	Liverpool	H	L	0-1		2
11		29	Norwich City	A	W	3-0	Fenwick (2, 1 pen), Stainrod	1
12	Nov	5	Luton Town	H	L	0-1		1
13		12	Coventry City	A	L	0-1		1
14		19	Birmingham City	H	W	2-1	Stainrod, Fenwick	1
15		26	Tottenham Hotspur	A	L	2-3	Stainrod, Fenwick (pen)	3
16	Dec	3	Notts County	H	W	1-0	Waddock	1
17		10	West Bromwich	A	W	2-1	Fenwick, Stainrod	1
18		17	Everton	H	W	2-0	Charles (2)	1
19		24	Leicester City	A	L	1-2	Fenwick (pen)	1
20		31	Aston Villa	A	L	1-2	Charles	
21	Jan	2	Wolverhampton	H	W	2-1	Wicks, Gregory	1
22		13	Manchester United	H	D	1-1	Fenwick	1
23		17	Stoke City	H	W	6-0	Charles (2), Stainrod, Gregory, Stewart, Fillery	
24	Feb	4	Arsenal	A	W	2-0	Stewart, Fenwick	3
25		7	West Ham United	H	D	1-1	Stainrod	2
26		11	Nottingham Forest	H	L	0-1		1
27		14	Norwich City	H	W	2-0	Dawes, Waddock	1
28		25	Liverpool	A	L	0-2		3
29	Mar	3	Luton Town	A	D	0-0		1
30		7	Sunderland	A	L	0-1		1
31		10	Coventry City	H	W	2-1	Stainrod, Allen	
32		17	Watford	A	L	0-1		1
33		24	Southampton	H	W	4-0	Wicks, Micklewhite, Allen, Waddock	1
34		31	West Ham United	A	D	2-2	Allen (2)	2
35	Apr	7	Ipswich Town	H	W	1-0	Allen	1
36		14	Birmingham City	A	W	2-0	Gregory, Fenwick	
37		21	Leicester City	H	W	2-0	Allen, Fereday	1
38		23	Stoke City	A	W	2-1	Allen, Fereday	
39		28	Tottenham Hotspur	H	W	2-1	Fereday, Gregory	2
40	May	5	Notts County	A	W	3-0	Allen (3)	
41		7	West Bromwich	H	D	1-1	Fereday	1
42		12	Everton	A	L	1-3	Micklewhite	2

Appeara
Sub appeara

FA Cup

R3	Jan	7	Huddersfield Town	A	L	1-2	Gregory	1

Appeara
Sub appeara

League Cup

R2/1	Oct	4	Crewe Alexandra	H	W	8-1	Stainrod (3), Waddock, Allen, Stewart, Micklewhite, McDonald	
R2/2		25	Crewe Alexandra	A	L	0-3		
R3	Nov	9	Ipswich Town	A	L	2-3	Stewart, Gregory	1

Appeara
Sub appeara

Total - Appeara
Total - Sub appeara
Total - (

	Burke	Charles	Dawes	Fenwick	Fereday	Fillery	Flanagan	Gregory	Hazell	Hucker	McDonald	Micklewhite	Neill	Roeder	Sealy	Stainrod	Stewart	Wadock	Wicks	OG
			3			12	8[a]	11	5	1		7	2	6		10		4		
			3	6		8[a]	12	11	5	1		7	2			10		4		
			3	6		8		11[a]	5	1		7	2			10	12	4		
			3	6			12	11	5	1		7	2			10	8[a]	4		
			3	6				11	5	1		7	2		9	10	8	4		
			3	6				11	5[a]	1		7	2		12	10	8	4		
			3	6				11[a]		1	5	7	2		12	10	8	4		
			3	6				11		1	5	7	2			10	8	4		
			3	6	12			11		1	5	7	2[a]			10	8	4		
			3	6	2			11		1	5	7				10	8	4		
			3	6	12			11		1		7	2			10	8	4	5	
			3	6				11		1		7	2			10	8	4	5	
			3	6			12	11		1	5	7	2		9	10	8	4[a]		
			3	6		11				1		7	2		9	10	8	4	5	
			3	6		11	12			1		7	2		9	10[a]	8	4	5	
			3	6		7		11		1			2		9	10	8	4	5	
		12	3	6		7		11		1			2		9[a]	10	8	4	5	
		9	3	6		7		11		1			2			10	8	4	5	
		9	3	6		7		11		1			2			10	8	4	5	
		9	3	6		7		11		1			2			10	8	4	5	
		9	3	6	12	7		11		1			2			10	8	4[a]	5	
		9	3	6		7		11		1			2			10	8	4	5	
		9[a]	3	6		7		11		1		12	2			10	8	4	5	
		9[a]	3	6	12	7		11		1			2			10	8	4	5	
			3	6	9	7[a]		11		1		12	2			10	8	4	5	
		9[a]	3	6	12	7		11		1			2			10	8	4	5	
	9		3	6		7		11		1			2			10	8	4	5	
	12	9	3	6		7[a]		11		1			2			10	8	4	5	
		9[a]	3	6		7		11		1			2			10	8	4	5	
			3	6		7[a]		11		1		12	2			10	8	4	5	
			3	6				11		1		7	2			10	8	4	5	
			3	6				11		1		7	2			10	8	4	5	
			3	6	11	8				1		7	2			10		4	5	
	12		3	6	11[a]	8				1		7	2			10		4	5	
			3	6	11	8				1		7	2			10		4	5	
			3	6	12	8		11		1		7	2			10		4[a]	5	
	12		3	6	4	8		11[a]		1		7	2			10			5	
			3	6	4	8		11		1		7	2			10			5	
	12		3	6	4	8[a]		11		1		7	2			10			5	
			3	6	4	8		11		1		7	2			10			5	
			3	6	4	8		11		1		7	2			10			5	
		12	3	6	4	8		11[a]		1		7	2				10		5	
	1	10	42	41	11	29	1	37	6	42	5	27	41	1	6	41	30	36	31	
	4	2			6	1	4					3			2		1			
		5	2	10	4	1		7				2	1			13	2	3	2	1

	Burke	Charles	Dawes	Fenwick	Fereday	Fillery	Flanagan	Gregory	Hazell	Hucker	McDonald	Micklewhite	Neill	Roeder	Sealy	Stainrod	Stewart	Wadock	Wicks	OG
		9	3	6	12	7		11		1			2			10	8[a]	4	5	
		1	1	1		1		1		1			1			1	1	1	1	
					1															
								1												

	Burke	Charles	Dawes	Fenwick	Fereday	Fillery	Flanagan	Gregory	Hazell	Hucker	McDonald	Micklewhite	Neill	Roeder	Sealy	Stainrod	Stewart	Wadock	Wicks	OG
			3	6	12			11		1	5	7[a]	2			10	8	4		
			3	6	2	11				1	5	7[a]			12	10	8	4		
			3	6		12		11		1	5	7	2			10	8	4		
			3	3	1	1		2		3	3	3	2			3	3	3		
					1	1									1					
								1			1	1				3	2	1		

	Burke	Charles	Dawes	Fenwick	Fereday	Fillery	Flanagan	Gregory	Hazell	Hucker	McDonald	Micklewhite	Neill	Roeder	Sealy	Stainrod	Stewart	Wadock	Wicks	OG
	1	11	46	45	12	31	1	40	6	46	8	30	44	1	6	45	34	40	32	
	4	2			8	2	4					3			3		1			
		5	2	10	4	1		9			1	3	1			16	4	4	2	1

1984-85

Division One

	P	W	D	L	F	A	Pts
Everton	42	28	6	8	88	43	90
Liverpool	42	22	11	9	68	35	77
Tottenham Hotspur	42	23	8	11	78	51	77
Manchester United	42	22	10	10	77	47	76
Southampton	42	19	11	12	56	47	68
Chelsea	42	18	12	12	63	48	66
Arsenal	42	19	9	14	61	49	66
Sheffield Wednesday	42	17	14	11	58	45	65
Nottingham Forest	42	19	7	16	56	48	64
Aston Villa	42	15	11	16	60	60	56
Watford	42	14	13	15	81	71	55
West Bromwich Albion	42	16	7	19	58	62	55
Luton Town	42	15	9	18	57	61	54
Newcastle United	42	13	13	16	55	70	52
Leicester City	42	15	6	21	65	73	51
West Ham United	42	13	12	17	51	68	51
Ipswich Town	42	13	11	18	46	57	50
Coventry City	42	15	5	22	47	64	50
Queen's Park Rangers	42	13	11	18	53	72	50
Norwich City	42	13	10	19	46	64	49
Sunderland	42	10	10	22	40	62	40
Stoke City	42	3	8	31	24	91	17

Attendances

TOTAL

	Home	Away	Total
League	297,321	433,118	730,439
Cup/Other	75,259	98,168	173,427
TOTAL	372,580	531,286	903,866

AVERAGE

	Home	Away	Total
League	14,158	20,625	17,391
Cup/Other	10,751	16,361	13,341
TOTAL	13,306	19,677	16,434

Match No.	Date		Opponents	Location	Result		Scorers	Atten
1	Aug	25	West Bromwich	H	W	3-1	Stainrod (2), Fenwick	12
2		28	Watford	A	D	1-1	Bannister	23
3	Sep	1	Liverpool	A	D	1-1	Fereday	33
4		8	Nottingham Forest	H	W	3-0	Fereday (2), Bannister	13
5		15	Tottenham Hotspur	A	L	0-5		31
6		22	Newcastle United	H	D	5-5	Bannister, Stainrod, Gregory, Wicks, Micklewhite	14
7		29	Southampton	A	D	1-1	Fereday	18
8	Oct	6	Luton Town	H	L	2-3	Fillery, Bannister	12
9		13	Ipswich Town	A	D	1-1	Gregory	15
10		20	Coventry City	H	W	2-1	Stainrod (2)	10
11		27	Norwich City	A	L	0-2		14
12	Nov	3	Sunderland	A	L	0-3		16
13		10	Sheffield Wednesday	H	D	0-0		13
14		17	Arsenal	A	L	0-1		34
15		24	Aston Villa	H	W	2-0	Gregory, Bannister	11
16	Dec	1	Leicester City	A	L	0-4		10
17		4	Stoke City	H	W	2-0	Bannister, Gregory	8
18		8	Everton	H	D	0-0		14
19		15	Manchester United	A	L	0-3		36
20		21	Liverpool	H	L	0-2		11
21		26	Chelsea	H	D	2-2	Bannister, McDonald	26
22		29	Stoke City	A	W	2-0	James, Fillery	10
23	Jan	1	West Ham United	A	W	3-1	Byrne, Bannister, Waddock	20
24		12	Tottenham Hotspur	H	D	2-2	Bannister (2)	27
25		26	West Bromwich	A	D	0-0		9
26	Feb	2	Southampton	H	L	0-4		10
27		9	Nottingham Forest	A	L	0-2		12
28		23	Sunderland	H	W	1-0	Byrne	10
29	Mar	2	Norwich City	H	D	2-2	Fereday, Wicks	12
30		9	Coventry City	A	L	0-3		8
31		16	Ipswich Town	H	W	3-0	Fereday (2), Bannister	9
32		23	Luton Town	A	L	0-2		9
33		30	Watford	H	W	2-0	Fillery (2)	12
34	Apr	6	Chelsea	A	L	0-1		20
35		8	Wst Ham United	H	W	4-2	Byrne, Bannister (2), Fenwick (pen)	16
36		13	Newcastle United	A	L	0-1		20
37		20	Arsenal	H	W	1-0	James	20
38		23	Sheffield Wednesday	A	L	1-3	Fillery	22
39		27	Aston Villa	A	L	2-5	Bannister (2)	12
40	May	4	Leicester City	H	W	4-3	Fillery, Gregory, Bannister, Robinson	9
41		6	Everton	A	L	0-2		50
42		11	Manchester United	H	L	1-3	Bannister	20

Appearar
Sub appearar
G

FA Cup

R3	Jan	5	Doncaster Rovers	A	L	0-1		10

Appearar
Sub appearar
G

League Cup

R2/1	Sep	25	York City	A	W	4-2	Bannister (2), Fenwick (pen), Fereday	10
R2/2	Oct	9	York City	H	W	4-1	Bannister (2), Fereday, Micklewhite	7
R3		30	Aston Villa	H	W	1-0	Gregory	12
R4	Nov	20	Southampton	A	D	1-1	Fenwick (pen)	14
rep		27	Southampton	H	D	0-0		13
rep	Dec	12	Southampton	H	W	4-0	Waddock, Neill, Fenwick (2, 1 pen)	12
R5	Jan	23	Ipswich Town	A	D	0-0		16
rep		28	Ipswich Town	H	L	1-2	Bannister	14

Appearan
Sub appearan
G

UEFA Cup

R1/1	Sep	18	FC Reykjavik	A	W	3-0	Stainrod (2), Bannister	1
R1/2	Oct	2	FC Reykjavik	H*	W	4-0	Bannister (3), Charles	6
R2/1		24	Partizan Belgrade	H*	W	6-2	Gregory, Fereday, Neill, Stainrod, Bannister (2)	7
R2/2	Nov	7	Partizan Belgrade	A	L	0-4		45

* Home matches played at Highbury

Appearan
Sub appearan
G

Total - Appearan
Total - Sub appearan
Total - G

Bannister	Burke	Byrne	Charles	Chivers	Cooper	Dawes	Fenwick	Fereday	Fillery	Gregory	Hucker	James	Kerslake	McDonald	Micklewhite	Neill	Robinson	Stainrod	Stewart	Wadock	Wicks
9[a]						3	6	12	8	11	1				7	2		10	4		5
9						3	6	12	8	11	1				7	2		10	4[a]		5
9						3	6	4	8	11	1				7	2		10			5
9						3	6	4	8	11	1				7	2		10			5
9						3	6	4	8	11	1				7	2		10			5
9						3	6	4	8[a]	11	1				7	2		10	12		5
9						3	6	4	8	11	1				7	2		10[a]	12		5
9						3	6	4	8	11	1				7	2		10			5
9						3	6	4	8	11	1			5	7	2		10			
9						3	6	4	8	11	1				7[a]	2		10	12		5
9		12				3	6	4	8	11	1				7[a]	2		10			5
9		12				3	6		8[a]	11	1				7	2		10		4	5
9		10[a]		2		3	6	7		11	1				12				8	4	5
9		8		2		3	6	7[a]		11	1	12						10		4	5
9						3	6	7		11	1					2		10	8	4	5
9						3	6	7		11	1					2		10	8	4	5
9		7[a]				3	6			11	1	8				2		10	12	4	5
9						3	6			11	1	12		7		2[a]		10	8	4	5
9						3	6			11	1			7		2		10	8	4	5
9		12		5		3	6			11	1			7		2[a]		10	8	4	
9		10		5		3	6		8	11	1	2		7						4	
9		10[a]		5		3	6		8	11	1	2		7			12			4	
9		10		5		3	6		8	11	1	2[a]		7			12			4	
9		10		5		3	6		8	11	1	2		7						4	
9		10[a]		5		3	6		8		1	2			11		12			4	7
9		10		5		3	6		8	11	1	2								4	7
9		10		5		3	6		8	11	1	2[a]			12					4	7
9		10				3	6	2	8	11	1						7			4	5
9		10			8[a]	3	6	2		11	1	12					7			4	5
9		10		12		3	6	2	8	11	1						7[a]			4	5
9		12		2		3	6	10	8	11	1						7[a]			4	5
9		7[a]		2		3		10	8	11	1	6		5						4	
9		10		2		3	6	11[a]	8		1			7					12	4	5
9		10		2		3	6	11	8		1			7						4	5
9		10		2		3	6	11[a]	8		1	12		7						4	5
9		10		2		3	6		8		1	7	12							4	5
9		10[a]		2		3	6		8	12	1	5		7						4	
9				2		3	6	12	8	10[a]	1	5		7						4	
9				2		3	6		8	12	1	10		7[a]			11			4	5
9				2		3	6	12	8[a]	11	1	10					7			4	5
9				2		3	6		8	11[a]	1	10		12			7			4	5
9				2		3	6	12		11	1	10					7			4	5
2		19		22	1	42	41	21	32	35	42	16		15	13	18	8	19	8	31	33
		4		1				5		2		4	1	1	2		3		5		
7		3					2	7	6	5		2		1	1		1	5		1	2

Bannister	Burke	Byrne	Charles	Chivers	Cooper	Dawes	Fenwick	Fereday	Fillery	Gregory	Hucker	James	Kerslake	McDonald	Micklewhite	Neill	Robinson	Stainrod	Stewart	Wadock	Wicks
9		10[a]		5		3	6	12	8	11	1			7			2			4	
1		1		1		1	1		1	1	1			1			1			1	
								1													

Bannister	Burke	Byrne	Charles	Chivers	Cooper	Dawes	Fenwick	Fereday	Fillery	Gregory	Hucker	James	Kerslake	McDonald	Micklewhite	Neill	Robinson	Stainrod	Stewart	Wadock	Wicks
9						3	6	4	8	11	1				7	2		10			5
9					12	3	6	4	8[a]	11	1				7	2		10			5
9			12		7[a]	3	6	4		11	1					2		10		8	5
9						3	6	7		11	1					2		10	8	4	5
9						3	6	7[a]		11	1					2		10	8	4	5
9						3	6	12		11	1			7		2		10	8[a]	4	5
9				5		3	6		8		1				11	2		10		4	7
9				5		3	6	12	8[a]	11	1				2			10		4	7
8				2	1	8	8	5	4	7	8			1	4	7		8	3	6	8
			1		1			2													
5							4	2		1					1	1				1	

Bannister	Burke	Byrne	Charles	Chivers	Cooper	Dawes	Fenwick	Fereday	Fillery	Gregory	Hucker	James	Kerslake	McDonald	Micklewhite	Neill	Robinson	Stainrod	Stewart	Wadock	Wicks
9[c]			15			3	6	4[d]	8	11	1				7	2		10	16		5
9			10		14	3	6	4	8[b]	11	1					2d			7		5
9	16					3	6	4	8	11	1					2		10	7[d]		5
9				2		3	6	4	8	11	1				14			10		7[b]	5
4			1	1		4	4	4	4	4	4				1	3		3	2	1	4
	1		1		1										1				1		
6			1					1		1						1		3			

Bannister	Burke	Byrne	Charles	Chivers	Cooper	Dawes	Fenwick	Fereday	Fillery	Gregory	Hucker	James	Kerslake	McDonald	Micklewhite	Neill	Robinson	Stainrod	Stewart	Wadock	Wicks
5		20	1	26	2	55	54	30	41	47	55	16		17	18	28	9	30	13	39	45
	1	4	2	1	2			8		2		4	1	1	3		3		6		
8		3	1				6	10	6	7		2		1	2	2	1	8		2	2

e UEFA Cup substitutions are listed as:
replaced by player 12
replaced by player 14
replaced by player 15
replaced by player 16

1985-86

Division One

	P	W	D	L	F	A	Pts
Liverpool	42	26	10	6	89	37	88
Everton	42	26	8	8	87	41	86
West Ham United	42	26	6	10	74	40	84
Manchester United	42	22	10	10	70	36	76
Sheffield Wednesday	42	21	10	11	63	54	73
Chelsea	42	20	11	11	57	56	71
Arsenal	42	20	9	13	49	47	69
Nottingham Forest	42	19	11	12	69	53	68
Luton Town	42	18	12	12	61	44	66
Tottenham Hotspur	42	19	8	15	74	52	65
Newcastle United	42	17	12	13	67	72	63
Watford	42	16	11	15	69	62	59
Queen's Park Rangers	42	15	7	20	53	64	52
Southampton	42	12	10	20	51	62	46
Manchester City	42	11	12	19	43	57	45
Aston Villa	42	10	14	18	51	67	44
Coventry City	42	11	10	21	48	71	43
Oxford United	42	10	12	20	62	80	42
Leicester City	42	10	12	20	54	76	42
Ipswich Town	42	11	8	23	32	55	41
Birmingham City	42	8	5	29	30	73	29
West Bromwich Albion	42	4	12	26	35	89	24

Attendances

TOTAL

	Home	Away	Total
League	320,062	365,409	685,471
Cup/Other	62,124	168,389	230,513
TOTAL	382,186	533,798	915,984

AVERAGE

	Home	Away	Total
League	15,241	17,400	16,321
Cup/Other	15,531	28,065	23,051
TOTAL	15,287	19,770	17,615

Match No.	Date		Opponents	Location	Result		Scorers	Atte
1	Aug	17	Ipswich Town	H	W	1-0	Byrne	1
2		20	West Ham United	A	L	1-3	Byrne	1
3		24	Aston Villa	A	W	2-1	Bannister (2)	1
4		27	Nottingham Forest	H	W	2-1	Bannister, Fenwick (pen)	1
5		31	Newcastle United	A	L	1-3	Fenwick	2
6	Sep	3	Arsenal	H	L	0-1		1
7		7	Everton	H	W	3-0	Bannister (2), Byrne	1
8		14	Watford	A	L	0-2		1
9		21	Luton Town	A	L	0-2		
10		28	Birmingham City	H	W	3-1	Rosenior, Bannister, Dawes	1
11	Oct	5	Liverpool	H	W	2-1	Fenwick, Bannister	2
12		12	Manchester United	A	L	0-2		4
13		19	Manchester City	H	D	0-0		1
14		26	Southampton	A	L	0-3		1
15	Nov	2	Sheffield Wednesday	H	D	1-1	James	1
16		9	West Bromwich	A	W	1-0	Robinson	
17		16	Leicester City	H	W	2-0	Wicks, Fereday	1
18		23	Tottenham Hotspur	A	D	1-1	Byrne	2
19		30	Coventry City	H	L	0-2		1
20	Dec	7	West Ham United	H	L	0-1		2
21		14	Ipswich Town	A	L	0-1		1
22		17	Aston Villa	H	L	0-1		1
23		28	Arsenal	A	L	1-3	Bannister	2
24	Jan	1	Oxford United	H	W	3-1	Allen, Fereday, Byrne	1
25		11	Everton	A	L	3-4	Bannister (2), Byrne	2
26		18	Newcastle United	H	W	3-1	Fenwick (2, 1 pen), Robinson	1
27	Feb	1	Nottingham Forest	A	L	0-4		1
28		8	Manchester City	A	L	0-2		2
29		22	Luton Town	H	D	1-1	Byrne	1
30	Mar	1	Birmingham City	A	L	0-2		
31		8	Liverpool	A	L	1-4	Rosenior	2
32		11	Southampton	H	L	0-2		1
33		15	Manchester United	H	W	1-0	Byrne	2
34		19	Chelsea	A	D	1-1	Kerslake	1
35		22	Watford	H	W	2-1	Fenwick (pen), Robinson	1
36		29	Oxford United	A	D	3-3	Walker, Allen, Fenwick (pen)	1
37		31	Chelsea	H	W	6-0	Bannister (3), Byrne (2), Rosenior	1
38	Apr	8	Sheffield Wednesday	A	D	0-0		1
39		12	West Bromwich	H	W	1-0	Bannister	1
40		14	Leicester City	A	W	4-1	Allen, Bannister, Robinson, Byrne	
41		26	Tottenham Hotspur	H	L	2-5	Rosenior, Bannister	1
42	May	3	Coventry City	A	L	1-2	Byrne	1

Appeara
Sub appeara
G

FA Cup

R3	Jan	13	Carlisle United	A	L	0-1		

Appeara
Sub appeara
G

League Cup

R2/1	Sep	24	Hull City	H	W	3-0	Kerslake, Dawes, Bannister	
R2/2	Oct	8	Hull City	A	W	5-1	Kerslake (2), Rosenior (2), Fillery	
R3		29	Watford	A	W	1-0	Byrne	1
R4	Nov	25	Nottingham Forest	H	W	3-1	Fenwick (pen), Bannister, Byrne	1
R5	Jan	22	Chelsea	H	D	1-1	Byrne	2
rep		29	Chelsea	A	W	2-0	McDonald, Robinson	2
SF 1	Feb	12	Liverpool	H	W	1-0	Fenwick	1
SF 2	Mar	5	Liverpool	A	D	2-2	OG (Whelan), OG (Gillespie)	2
F	Apr	20	Oxford United	W	L	0-3		9

Appeara
Sub appeara
G

Total - Appeara
Total - Sub appeara
Total - G

Bakholt	Bannister	Barron	Byrne	Chivers	Dawes	Fenwick	Fereday	Fillery	Gregory	Hucker	James	Kerslake	McDonald	Neill	Robinson	Rosenior	Waddock	Walker	Wicks	OG
	9		12	2	3	6	10		11	1	7[a]		5		8		4			
	9		7	2	3	6	10		11	1	12		5		8[a]		4			
	9		10[a]	2	3	6	12		11	1	8		5				4			
	9		10	2	3	6			11	1	8		5				4			
	9		10[a]	2	3	6	12		11	1	8		5				4			
	9		10	2[a]	3	6	8		11	1			5			12	4			
	9		10	2	3	6	8		11	1			5				4			
	9		10	2	3	6	8		11	1			5			12	4[a]			
	9		10	2	3	6	8		11	1			5				4			
	9	1			3	6	8		11			7	2			10	4		5	
	9	1			3	6	8	11				7	2			10	4		5	
	9	1			3	6	8	11				7[a]	2			10	4		5	
	9	1	12		3	6		8[a]	11			7	2			10	4		5	
	9	1	12		3	6	11				8	7[a]	2			10	4		5	
	9	1	10		3		11	8			12		2		6		4[a]		5	
	9	1	10[a]		3	6	11	8			7		2		4				5	
	9	1	10		3	6	11	8			7[a]		2		4				5	
	9	1	10		3	6	11[a]	8			7		2		4				5	
	9	1	10		3	6		8			7	12	2		4				5	
	9[a]	1	10		3	6	11	8					2		4	12			5	
		1	10	6	3		11	8			7		2		4				5	
		1	10	2	3		11	8			9		6		4			7	5	
	9	1	10		3	6	12	8					4	2	7			11[a]	5	
	9	1	10		3	6	11						2	4	7				5	
	9	1	10		3	6	11				12		2	4	7[a]				5	
	9	1	10		3	6	11				8		2	4	7				5	
	9	1	10		3		11	6			8		2	4	7[a]				5	
12	9		10		3	6				1	7		2	4		8		11[a]		
	9	1	10		3	6	11	7					2	4					5	
		1	10[a]		3	6	11	7				12	2	4		9			5	
		1			3	6		11			8	12	2	4	7	9			5	
		1	12		3	6					8	10	2	4	7	9[a]		11	5	
	9	1	10		3	6					8	11[a]	2	4	12				5	
	9[a]	1			3	6		10			8	12	2	4	11				5	
	9	1			3	6	10[a]				8	12	2	4	11				5	
	9	1	12		3	5					6		2[a]	4	7	11		10		
	9	1	10		3	6[a]	4				8		2		11	12			5	
	9	1	10		3	6	4				8		2		11				5	
	9	1	10		3	6	4				8		2		11	12			5	
	9	1	12	5	3	6	4[a]						2	8	11	10				
	9	1	10	5	3		4				8	6	2		11[a]	12				
			10	12	3	6[a]	11			1	8	7	2	4		9			5	
	36	31	30	13	42	37	30	17	11	11	25	9	42	16	25	12	15	5	29	
1			6	1			3				3	5			1	6				
	16		12		1	7	2				1	1			4	4		1	1	
	9	1	10		3	6					7		2	4[a]	11	12			5	
	1	1	1		1	1					1		1	1	1				1	
																1				
	9	1	10	2[a]	3	6	8		11			7				12	4		5	
	9	1	12		3	6		11[a]				7	2			10	4		5	
	9	1	10		3	6[a]	11	8					2		12		4		5	
	9	1	10		3	6		8			7	11[a]	2		4				5	
	9	1	10		3	6	11				8		2	4	7				5	
	9	1	10[a]		3		11	6			8		2	4	7				5	
	9	1	10		3	6	11				8		2	4					5	
	9[a]	1			3	6	12	11			8		2	4	7				5	
	9	1	10		3	6					8		2	4	11	12			5	
	9	9	7	1	9	8	5	5	1		6	3	8	5	5	1	3		9	
			1				1								1	2				
	2		3		1	2		1				3	1		1	2				2
	46	41	38	14	52	46	35	22	12	11	32	12	51	22	31	13	18	5	39	
1			7	1			4				3	5			2	9				
	18		15		2	9	2	1			1	4	1		5	6		1	1	2

1986-87

Division One

	P	W	D	L	F	A	Pts
Everton	42	26	8	8	76	31	86
Liverpool	42	23	8	11	72	42	77
Tottenham Hotspur	42	21	8	13	68	43	71
Arsenal	42	20	10	12	58	35	70
Norwich City	42	17	17	8	53	51	68
Wimbledon	42	19	9	14	57	50	66
Luton Town	42	18	12	12	47	45	66
Nottingham Forest	42	18	11	13	64	51	65
Watford	42	18	9	15	67	54	63
Coventry City	42	17	12	13	50	45	63
Manchester United	42	14	14	14	52	45	56
Southampton	42	14	10	18	69	68	52
Sheffield Wednesday	42	13	13	16	58	59	52
Chelsea	42	13	13	16	53	64	52
West Ham United	42	14	10	18	52	67	52
Queen's Park Rangers	42	13	11	18	48	64	50
Newcastle United	42	12	11	19	47	65	47
Oxford United	42	11	13	18	44	69	46
Charlton Athletic	42	11	11	20	45	55	44
Leicester City	42	11	9	22	54	76	42
Manchester City	42	8	15	19	36	57	39
Aston Villa	42	8	12	22	45	79	36

Attendances

TOTAL

	Home	Away	Total
League	293,733	390,047	683,780
Cup/Other	32,042	56,057	88,099
TOTAL	325,775	446,104	771,879

AVERAGE

	Home	Away	Total
League	13,987	18,574	16,280
Cup/Other	10,681	14,014	12,586
TOTAL	13,574	17,844	15,753

Match No.	Date		Opponents	Location	Result		Scorers	Atten
1	Aug	23	Southampton	A	L	1-5	Allen	14
2		26	Watford	H	W	3-2	Allen, Fereday, Bannister	14
3		30	Aston Villa	H	W	1-0	Bannister	13
4	Sep	3	Newcastle United	A	W	2-0	Byrne, Bannister (pen)	23
5		6	Everton	A	D	0-0		30
6		13	West Ham United	H	L	2-3	James, Byrne	19
7		20	Manchester City	A	D	0-0		17
8		27	Leicester City	H	L	0-1		10
9	Oct	4	Norwich City	A	L	0-1		15
10		11	Wimbledon	H	W	2-1	Bannister, McDonald	14
11		18	Nottingham Forest	A	L	0-1		17
12		25	Tottenham Hotspur	H	W	2-0	Allen, Byrne	21
13	Nov	1	Luton Town	A	L	0-1		9
14		8	Liverpool	H	L	1-3	Bannister	24
15		15	Oxford United	H	D	1-1	Byrne	12
16		22	Manchester United	A	L	0-1		42
17		29	Sheffield Wednesday	H	D	2-2	Bannister, McDonald	10
18	Dec	6	Arsenal	A	L	1-3	Bannister	34
19		13	Charlton Athletic	H	D	0-0		10
20		20	West Ham United	A	D	1-1	Fenwick (pen)	17
21		27	Coventry City	H	W	3-1	Byrne, Bannister, Allen	10
22		28	Oxford United	A	W	1-0	James	11
23	Jan	1	Chelsea	A	L	1-3	Byrne	20
24		3	Everton	H	L	0-1		19
25		24	Southampton	H	W	2-1	Byrne, Bannister	10
26	Feb	7	Aston Villa	A	W	1-0	OG (Keown)	13
27		14	Newcastle United	H	W	2-1	Byrne, Fillery	10
28		28	Manchester City	H	W	1-0	Allen	12
29	Mar	7	Tottenham Hotspur	A	L	0-1		21
30		14	Nottingham Forest	H	W	3-1	Bannister, Fereday, McDonald	11
31		18	Liverpool	A	L	1-2	Fillery	28
32		21	Wimbledon	A	D	1-1	Rosenior	6
33		25	Leicester City	A	L	1-4	Rosenior	7
34		28	Norwich City	H	D	1-1	Rosenior	9
35	Apr	6	Watford	A	W	3-0	Bannister (3)	13
36		11	Luton Town	H	D	2-2	Byrne (2)	11
37		18	Chelsea	H	D	1-1	Bannister	18
38		20	Coventry City	A	L	1-4	Bannister	20
39		25	Manchester United	H	D	1-1	Byrne	17
40	May	2	Sheffield Wednesday	A	L	1-7	Peacock	16
41		4	Arsenal	H	L	1-4	McDonald	13
42		9	Charlton Athletic	A	L	1-2	Rosenior	7

Appearar
Sub appearar
G

FA Cup

R3	Jan	10	Leicester City	H	W	5-2	Fenwick (2, 1 pen), Lee, James, Byrne	9
R4		31	Luton Town	A	D	1-1	Fenwick (pen)	12
rep	Feb	4	Luton Town	H	W	2-1	Fenwick, Byrne	15
R5		21	Leeds United	A	L	1-2	OG (Rennie)	31

Appearar
Sub appearar
G

League Cup

R2/1	Sep	23	Blackburn Rovers	H	W	2-1	Byrne, Brazil	6
R2/2	Oct	7	Blackburn Rovers	A	D	2-2	Bannister, Walker	5
R3		28	Charlton Athletic	A	L	0-1		6

Appearar
Sub appearar
G

Total - Appearar
Total - Sub appearar
Total - G

Bannister	Barron	Brazil	Byrne	Channing	Chivers	Dawes	Fenwick	Ferdinand	Fereday	Fillery	James	Kerslake	Lee	Maguire	McDonald	Neill	Peacock	Robinson	Rosenior	Seaman	Waddock	Walker	OG
a		12	10		6	3			11		4				5	2		7		1			
9			12		6	3			11		8	7[a]			5	2			10	1			
9			10		6	3			11		8		7		5	2				1			
9			10		6	3			11		8		7		5	2				1			
			10		6	3			11		8		7		5	2			9	1			
			10		6	3			11[a]		8		7		5	2		12	9	1			
9		12	10[a]		6	3			11		8		7		5			2		1			
9		12	10		6	3	5[a]		2		8		7							1		11	
9		10[a]			6	3			2		8				5			12		1	7	11	
9			10		6	3			2		8		7		5			12		1		11	
9			10		6	3			2		8		7		5					1	11[a]	12	
9			10		6	3			2		8				5					1	7	11	
a			10	11	6	3	5		2		8					7				1		12	
9			10		6	3	7		2		8				5				12	1		11	
9			10		6	3	7		2[a]		8				5			11		1		12	
9			10		6	3	7		2[a]		12		8		5				11	1			
9			10		6	3	7						8		5	2	11[a]		12	1			
9			10		6	3	7		11				8[a]		5	2	12			1			
9			10		6[a]	3	8		11		12		7		5	2				1			
9			10[a]				6			12	3		7		5	2	11	8		1			
9			10			3	6				2		7		5		11[a]	8	12	1			
9			12		6	3					2		7	11	5			8	10[a]	1			
			10		6	3			9		2		7	11[a]	5			8		1		12	
			10		6		9		12		3		7		5	2		8		1		11[a]	
9			10				6		11	8[a]	3		7		5	2			12	1		4	
			10				6		11	8	3			2	5				9	1		4	
9			10				6		11	8	3				5	2				1		4	
9			10				6		11	8	3			5		2	12			1		4[a]	
9			10				6		11	8	3		12	4[a]	5	2				1			
9			10				6		11	8	3		4		5	2				1			
9			10				6		11	8	3		4		5	2				1			
9			10				6			8	3		4		5	2			12	1		11[a]	
9			10[a]				6		11	8	3		4	12	5	2			7	1			
9			10				6		11	8	3		4		5	2			7	1			
9			12						11	8	3		4	6	5	2	10[a]		7	1			
9			10						11	8	3		4	6	5	2			7	1			
9			10						11	8	3		4	6	5	2	12		7[a]	1			
9				3				12	11	8[a]			4	6	5	2	10		7	1			
9			10						11	8[a]	3		4	6	5	2	12			1			
	1		9			3[a]		12	11	8	6			4	5	2	7		10				
			10						11	8	3	7[a]		6	5	2	12		9	1	4		
			10		4				11		3	12	7	6	5	2	8[a]		9	1			
4	1	1	37	2	23	23	21		36	17	37	2	29	13	39	29	7	8	15	41	4	11	
		3	3					2	1	1	2	1	1	1			5	3	5			4	
5			11				1		2	2	2				4		1		4				1
b			10				6		11[a]	8	3		7		5	2	12		14	1		4	
9			10				6		11		3		7		5	2			12	1		4[a]	
a			10				6		11	8	3			2	5				12	1		4	
9			10		5		6		11	8[b]	3		12	14		2				1		4[a]	
4			4		1		4		4	3	4		2	1	3	3				4		4	
													1	1			1		3				
			2				4				1		1										1
b		12	10		6	3			11[a]		8		7					2	5	1		14	
9		10[a]			6	3			2		8		7		5			12		1		11	
9			10		6	3	12		2		8				5				14	1	7[a]	11[b]	
3		1	2		3	3			3		3		2		2			1	1	3	1	2	
		1					1											1	1			1	
		1	1																			1	
1	1	2	43	2	27	26	25		43	20	44	2	33	14	44	32	7	9	16	48	5	17	
		4	3				1	2	1	1	2	1	2	2			6	4	9			5	
6		1	14				5		2	2	3		1		4		1		4			1	2

1987-88

Division One

	P	W	D	L	F	A	Pts
Liverpool	40	26	12	2	87	24	90
Manchester United	40	23	12	5	71	38	81
Nottingham Forest	40	20	13	7	67	39	73
Everton	40	19	13	8	53	27	70
Queen's Park Rangers	40	19	10	11	48	38	67
Arsenal	40	18	12	10	58	39	66
Wimbledon	40	14	15	11	58	47	57
Newcastle United	40	14	14	12	55	53	56
Luton Town	40	14	11	15	57	58	53
Coventry City	40	13	14	13	46	53	53
Sheffield Wednesday	40	15	8	17	52	66	53
Southampton	40	12	14	14	49	53	50
Tottenham Hotspur	40	12	11	17	38	48	47
Norwich City	40	12	9	19	40	52	45
Derby County	40	10	13	17	35	45	43
West Ham United	40	9	15	16	40	52	42
Charlton Athletic	40	9	15	16	38	52	42
Chelsea	40	9	15	16	50	68	42
Portsmouth	40	7	14	19	36	66	35
Watford	40	7	11	22	27	51	32
Oxford United	40	6	13	21	44	80	31

Attendances

TOTAL	Home	Away	Total
League	262,706	379,237	641,943
Cup/Other	54,876	37,180	92,056
TOTAL	317,582	416,417	733,999

AVERAGE	Home	Away	Total
League	13,135	18,962	16,049
Cup/Other	13,719	9,295	11,507
TOTAL	13,233	17,351	15,292

Match No.	Date		Opponents	Location	Result		Scorers
1	Aug	15	West Ham United	A	W	3-0	OG (Stewart), Bannister, Brock
2		19	Derby County	H	D	1-1	Bannister
3		22	Arsenal	H	W	2-0	Byrne, McDonald
4		29	Southampton	A	W	1-0	Brock
5	Sep	2	Everton	H	W	1-0	Allen
6		5	Charlton Athletic	A	W	1-0	Coney
7		12	Chelsea	H	W	3-1	Bannister (3)
8		19	Oxford United	A	L	0-2	
9		26	Luton Town	H	W	2-0	Coney, Fenwick (pen)
10	Oct	3	Wimbledon	A	W	2-1	Bannister, Fenwick (pen)
11		17	Liverpool	A	L	0-4	
12		24	Portsmouth	H	W	2-1	Byrne, Fenwick
13		31	Norwich City	A	D	1-1	Allen
14	Nov	7	Watford	H	D	0-0	
15		14	Tottenham Hotspur	A	D	1-1	Coney
16		21	Newcastle United	H	D	1-1	OG (Wharton)
17		28	Sheffield Wednesday	A	L	1-3	Bannister
18	Dec	5	Manchester United	H	L	0-2	
19		13	Nottingham Forest	A	L	0-4	
20		18	Coventry City	H	L	1-2	Falco
21		26	Chelsea	A	D	1-1	Kerslake
22		28	Oxford United	H	W	3-2	Falco (2), Allen
23	Jan	1	Southampton	H	W	3-0	Bannister, Falco, Fereday
24		2	Arsenal	A	D	0-0	
25		16	West Ham United	H	L	0-1	
26	Feb	6	Charlton Athletic	H	W	2-0	Falco, Byrne
27		13	Everton	A	L	0-2	
28		27	Wimbledon	H	W	1-0	Byrne
29	Mar	5	Liverpool	H	L	0-1	
30		16	Nottingham Forest	H	W	2-1	Coney, Fereday
31		19	Norwich City	H	W	3-0	Channing, Coney, Fereday
32		26	Portsmouth	A	W	1-0	Coney
33	Apr	1	Watford	A	W	1-0	McDonald
34		4	Tottenham Hotspur	H	W	2-0	Kerslake (2)
35		9	Newcastle United	A	D	1-1	Kerslake (pen)
36		13	Derby County	A	W	2-0	Allen, Fereday
37		19	Luton Town	A	L	1-2	Kerslake (pen)
38		23	Sheffield Wednesday	H	D	1-1	Coney
39		30	Manchester United	A	L	1-2	McDonald
40	May	7	Coventry City	A	D	0-0	

Appeara
Sub appeara

FA Cup

R3	Jan	9	Yeovil Town	A	W	3-0	Falco (2), Brock
R4		30	West Ham United	H	W	3-1	Pizanti, Bannister, Allen
R5	Feb	20	Luton Town	H	D	1-1	Neill
rep		24	Lution Town	A	L	0-1	

Appeara
Sub appeara

League Cup

R2/1	Aug	23	Millwall	H	W	2-1	Bannister, McDonald
R2/2	Oct	6	Millwall	A	D	0-0	
R3		27	Bury	A	L	0-1	

Appeara
Sub appeara

Simod Cup

R1	Dec	21	Reading	H	L	1-3	Allen

Appeara
Sub appeara

Total - Appeara
Total - Sub appeara
Total -

Bannister	Brock	Byrne	Channing	Coney	Dawes	Dennis	Falco	Fenwick	Ferdinand	Fereday	Fleming	Francis	Johns	Kerslake	Law	Maddix	Maguire	McDonald	Neill	O'Neill	Parker	Peacock	Pizanti	Roberts	Seaman	OG
9	11	10		8		3		6		2								5			4				1	
9	11	10		8		3		6		2								5			4				1	
9	11	10[b]		8		3		6		2								5			4	14			1	
9	11	10		8	3			6		2								5			4				1	
9	11	10		8	3			6		2								5			4				1	
9	11	10[b]		8	3			6		2								5			4	14			1	
9	11	10		8	3			6		2								5			4				1	
9	11	10[b]		8	3[a]			6		2								5	12		4	14			1	
9	11	10		8	3			6		2[a]								5	12		4				1	
9	11	10		8	3			6										5	2		4				1	
9	11	10		8[a]	3			6									14	5	2[b]		4		12		1	
9	11	10[b]		8	3			6		14							12	5	2[a]		4				1	
		10[b]	11	8	3			6		9									2	5	4		14		1	
	11	10	9[a]	8	3			6		14							12	5	2[b]		4				1	
	11	10[b]	9	8		3		6		2								5			4	14			1	
9	11	10[b]	12	8		3		6		2								5[a]			4	14			1	
9	11[a]	14	10	8	3			6		2[b]						12				5	4				1	
9	11	10		14	3		8[b]	6		2							5				4				1	
9	11[a]	10		8[b]		3	14	6		2							12	5			4				1	
9[b]	11	10		14		3	8	6		2								5			4			1		
9	11				3		8	6					1	10[b]			14	5	2		4					
9[b]	11				3		8	6		14			1	10				5	2		4					
9	11			12	2	3	8[a]			14			1	10[b]			6	5			4					
9	11[a]		12		2	3	8			10			1				6	5			4					
9	11[a]	14			2	3	8			10[b]			1	12			6	5			4					
9	11[a]	14			2		8			10			1	12			6	5			4		3[b]			
9	11	14			2[a]				8	10			1				6	5	12		4		3[b]			
		9			2		8			10	14			11		5	6		3		4				1	
		9[a]		12	2		8			10	14			11		7[b]	6	5	3		4				1	
		8[a]	12	9	2					10				7		11	6	5	3		4				1	
		14	11	9[b]	3	12				10				8		6		5	2		4				1	
			11[b]	9	3		14			10		12		8[a]		6		5	2		4				1	
			14	9	3					10		11		8[b]			6	5	2		4				1	
			14	12	3		9			10		11[a]		8			6	5	2		4				1	
				12	3		9			10		11[b]		8[a]		14	6	5	2		4				1	
					3		9			10		11		8[b]		14	6	5	2		4				1	
			6	12	3		9			10		11[b]		8[a]				5	2		4		14		1	
				9	3		12			10		11[b]		8	14	6[a]		5	2		4				1	
			12	9	3		6			10[a]		11		8				5	2		4				1	
			12	9	3		14			10		11		8				5	2[b]		4		6[a]		1	
4	26	22	7	25	33	10	15	22	1	33		8	7	16		6	13	36	20	2	40		3	1	32	
		5	7	7		1	4			4	2	1		2	1	3	5		3			5	3			
3	2	4	1	7			5	3		4				5				3								2

Bannister	Brock	Byrne	Channing	Coney	Dawes	Dennis	Falco	Fenwick	Ferdinand	Fereday	Fleming	Francis	Johns	Kerslake	Law	Maddix	Maguire	McDonald	Neill	O'Neill	Parker	Peacock	Pizanti	Roberts	Seaman	OG
9[a]	11			12	2	3	8			10[b]			1	14			6	5			4					
9	11	14			2		8			10[b]			1				6	5			4		3			
9[b]	11	14			2		8			10			1				6	5	3		4					
	11	9		12	2		8[a]			10				14			6	5	3[b]		4				1	
3	4	1			4	1	4			4			3				4	4	2		4		1		1	
		2		2										2												
1	1						2												1				1			

Bannister	Brock	Byrne	Channing	Coney	Dawes	Dennis	Falco	Fenwick	Ferdinand	Fereday	Fleming	Francis	Johns	Kerslake	Law	Maddix	Maguire	McDonald	Neill	O'Neill	Parker	Peacock	Pizanti	Roberts	Seaman	OG
9	11	10		8	3			6		2								5			4				1	
9	11	10		8	3			6										5	2		4				1	
9[a]		10	12		3			6	14	8[b]								5	2		4		11		1	
3	2	3		2	3			3		2								3	2		3		1		3	
			1						1																	
1																		1								

Bannister	Brock	Byrne	Channing	Coney	Dawes	Dennis	Falco	Fenwick	Ferdinand	Fereday	Fleming	Francis	Johns	Kerslake	Law	Maddix	Maguire	McDonald	Neill	O'Neill	Parker	Peacock	Pizanti	Roberts	Seaman	OG
	11	10[a]	2		8	3	9	6					1	12				5			4					
	1	1	1		1	1	1	1					1					1			1					
														1												

Bannister	Brock	Byrne	Channing	Coney	Dawes	Dennis	Falco	Fenwick	Ferdinand	Fereday	Fleming	Francis	Johns	Kerslake	Law	Maddix	Maguire	McDonald	Neill	O'Neill	Parker	Peacock	Pizanti	Roberts	Seaman	OG
40	33	27	8	27	41	12	20	26	1	39		8	11	16		6	17	44	24	2	48		5	1	36	
		7	8	9		1	4		1	4	2	1		5	1	3	5		3			5	3			
0	3	4	1	7			7	3		4				5				4	1				1			2

1988-89

Division One

	P	W	D	L	F	A	Pts
Arsenal	38	22	10	6	73	36	76
Liverpool	38	22	10	6	65	28	76
Nottingham Forest	38	17	13	8	64	43	64
Norwich City	38	17	11	10	48	45	62
Derby County	38	17	7	14	40	38	58
Tottenham Hotspur	38	15	12	11	60	46	57
Coventry City	38	14	13	11	47	42	55
Everton	38	14	12	12	50	45	54
Queen's Park Rangers	38	14	11	13	43	37	53
Millwall	38	14	11	13	47	52	53
Manchester United	38	13	12	13	45	35	51
Wimbledon	38	14	9	15	50	46	51
Southampton	38	10	15	13	52	66	45
Charlton Athletic	38	10	12	16	44	58	42
Sheffield Wednesday	38	10	12	16	34	51	42
Luton Town	38	10	11	17	42	52	41
Aston Villa	38	9	13	16	45	56	40
Middlesbrough	38	9	12	17	44	61	39
West Ham United	38	10	8	20	37	62	38
Newcastle United	38	7	10	21	32	63	31

Attendances

TOTAL

	Home	Away	Total
League	233,433	378,039	611,472
Cup/Other	57,538	136,353	193,891
TOTAL	290,971	514,392	805,363

AVERAGE

	Home	Away	Total
League	12,286	19,897	16,091
Cup/Other	11,508	17,044	14,915
TOTAL	12,124	19,052	15,791

Welcome to Al-Ahly FC

Sunday 21st August 1988
Kick-off: 3.00 pm
at Rangers Stadium

Official Programme 50p

Match No.	Date		Opponents	Location	Result		Scorers	Atten
1	Aug	27	Manchester United	A	D	0-0		46
2	Sep	3	Southampton	H	L	0-1		9
3		10	Norwich City	A	L	0-1		11
4		17	Sheffield Wednesday	H	W	2-0	Francis (2, 1 pen)	8
5		24	Derby County	A	W	1-0	Stein	14
6	Oct	1	Millwall	A	L	2-3	Allen, Francis	14
7		8	Nottingham Forest	H	L	1-2	Stein	11
8		15	West Ham United	H	W	2-1	Maddix, Stein	14
9		22	Arsenal	A	L	1-2	Falco	33
10		29	Luton Town	A	D	0-0		8
11	Nov	5	Newcastle United	H	W	3-0	Maddix, Allen, Falco	11
12		12	Middlesbrough	A	L	0-1		20
13		19	Liverpool	H	L	0-1		20
14		26	Tottenham Hotspur	A	D	2-2	Falco, Francis	26
15	Dec	3	Coventry City	H	W	2-1	Francis, Falco	9
16		10	Charlton Athletic	A	D	1-1	Francis	6
17		17	Everton	H	D	0-0		10
18		26	Aston Villa	A	L	1-2	Francis	25
19		31	Southampton	A	W	4-1	Allen, Barker, Falco (2)	15
20	Jan	2	Norwich City	H	D	1-1	Falco	12
21		14	Wimbledon	A	L	0-1		7
22		21	Derby County	H	L	0-1		9
23	Feb	4	Millwall	H	L	1-2	Falco (pen)	10
24		11	Nottingham Forest	A	D	0-0		19
25		18	Arsenal	H	D	0-0		20
26		25	West Ham United	A	D	0-0		17
27	Mar	11	Newcastle United	A	W	2-1	Stein, Clarke	21
28		21	Luton Town	H	D	1-1	Clarke	9
29		25	Sheffield Wednesday	A	W	2-0	Falco, Allen	18
30		27	Aston Villa	H	W	1-0	Sinton	11
31	Apr	1	Everton	A	L	1-4	Falco (pen)	23
32		8	Wimbledon	H	W	4-3	Clarke, Spackman, Falco, Reid	9
33		15	Middlesbrough	H	D	0-0		10
34		22	Coventry City	A	W	3-0	Clarke (2), Channing	11
35		29	Charlton Athletic	H	W	1-0	Sinton	13
36	May	8	Manchester United	H	W	3-2	Sinton, Gray (2)	10
37		13	Tottenham Hotspur	H	W	1-0	Falco	21
38		16	Liverpool	A	L	0-2		38

Appearar
Sub appearar
G

FA Cup

R3	Jan	7	Manchester United	A	D	0-0		36
rep		11	Manchester United	H	D	2-2 aet	Stein, McDonald	22
rep		23	Manchester United	A	L	0-3		47

Appearar
Sub appearar
G

League Cup

R2/1	Sep	28	Cardiff City	H	W	3-0	Francis, Fereday, Allen	6
R2/2	Oct	12	Cardiff City	A	W	4-1	Falco (2), Maddix, Stein	2
R3	Nov	2	Charlton Athletic	H	W	2-1	Francis (2)	8
R4		30	Wimbledon	H	D	0-0		10
rep	Dec	14	Wimbledon	A	W	1-0	Falco	6
R5	Jan	18	Nottingham Forest	A	L	2-5	Stein, Kerslake	24

Appearar
Sub appearar
G

Simod Cup

R3	Feb	1	Sheffield Wednesday	A	W	1-0	Coney	3
R4		14	Watford	A	D	1-1 [a]	Coney	8
SF		27	Everton	A	L	0-1		7

a Won on penalties

Appearar
Sub appearar
G

Mercantile Centenary Credit Trophy

R1	Aug	31	Arsenal	H	L	0-2		10

Appearar
Sub appearar
G

Total - Appearar
Total - Sub appearar
Total - G

Allen M.	Ardiles	Barker	Brock	Channing	Clarke	Coney	Dennis	Falco	Fereday	Fleming	Francis	Gray	Herrera	Johns	Kerslake	Law	Maddix	Maguire	McCarthy	McDonald	Parker	Pizanti	Reid	Seaman	Sinton	Spackman	Stein
7	6	11	8				3	9	2		10[a]									5	4			1			12
7	6	11	8[a]				3	9	2		10[b]						12			5	4			1			14
7	12	8[a]	11[b]			9	3	14	2								6			5	4			1			10
7			11				3		9		8					2	6			5	4			1			10
7		11				12	3		9		8				2		6			5	4			1			10[a]
7		12	11[a]				3[b]	14	9		8			1	2			6		5	4						10
7			11			10	3[a]		9		8			1			2	6		5	4						12
3		2	11[b]			12		7	9		8			1	14		6			5	4						10[a]
3		2	11					7	9		8[b]				14		6			5	4			1			10
3		2[a]	11			12		7	9		8[b]				14		6			5	4			1			10
3		2[a]	12					7	9		8				14		6	11		5	4			1			10[b]
3	14	2	12					7	9		8						6	11[a]		5	4			1			10[b]
3	12	2[b]	11					7	9		8[a]				14		6			5	4	10		1			
3	5[b]	2[a]	11					7	9		8				12		6	14			4	10		1			
3			11			2	14	7	9		8						6	5			4[b]	10		1			
3								7	9		8				11		6	5		2	4	10		1			
		11[a]				10	3[b]	7	9		8				12		6			2	4	5		1			14
		11				10		7	9[b]		8				6		12	3[a]		2	4	5		1			14
1	14	12				10		7			8					3	6			2	4	5[a]		1			9[b]
1		10						7			8				12	5	6			2	4	3		1			9[a]
	2	8				10			9				14		11[a]	5	6				4	3b[b]		1			7
		8				10			9[a]	2			12		11	5	6				4	3		1			7
		12				10		9	11[a]			8				3[b]	2			5	4	14		1		6	7
		9		2		10						8[a]			12		5				4	3	11	1		6	7
		7[b]		2		10	3[a]	9				8			14		5					11	4	1		6	12
		7		2		14	3[a]	9[b]				8					10			5		12	4	1		6	11
					9	14	3		2			7[a]					12			5	4	11[b]	10	1		6	8
1		12			9				3			7[a]					2			5	4		10	1		6	8
1					9[b]		3	12	2								14			5	4		10	1	7	6	8[a]
b					9		3	8[a]	2								14			5	4		10	1	11	6	12
a					9		3	8	2											5	4		10	1	11	6	12
7				2[b]	9		3	8[a]	14											5	4		10	1	11	6	12
7				2	9		3	8[a]	14											5[b]	4		10	1	11	6	12
2				2	9				3			7[a]			8		5				4		10	1	11	6	
2				2	9				3			7[a]			8		5				4		10[b]	1	11	6	14
				2	9				3[b]			7			8		5			14	4		10[a]	1	11	6	12
3		10		2[b]	9			14				7			8[a]		5			12	4			1	11	6	
3		2			9			14				7[b]			8		5			12	4		10[a]	1	11	6	
6	4	21	12	9	12	11	16	22	29	1	19	11		3	11	6	28	7		27	36	13	14	35	10	16	19
2	4	4	2			5	1	5	2				2		10		5	1		3		2					12
4		1		1	5			12			7	2					2						1		3	1	4

Allen M.	Ardiles	Barker	Brock	Channing	Clarke	Coney	Dennis	Falco	Fereday	Fleming	Francis	Gray	Herrera	Johns	Kerslake	Law	Maddix	Maguire	McCarthy	McDonald	Parker	Pizanti	Reid	Seaman	Sinton	Spackman	Stein
1		12				10		7[b]	9		8[a]					5	6			2	4	3		1			14
	14	8				10	12		9						11	5[a]	6			2	4	3[b]		1			7
		8		11		10				12					9[a]	5	6[b]			2	4	3		1			7
		2		1		3		1	2		1				2	3	3			3	3	3		3			2
	1	1					1			1																	1
																				1							1

Allen M.	Ardiles	Barker	Brock	Channing	Clarke	Coney	Dennis	Falco	Fereday	Fleming	Francis	Gray	Herrera	Johns	Kerslake	Law	Maddix	Maguire	McCarthy	McDonald	Parker	Pizanti	Reid	Seaman	Sinton	Spackman	Stein
7		12	11				3		9[b]		8			1	2		6	14		5	4						10[a]
		2	11[b]			12		7	9		8[a]			1	14		6	3		5	4						10
3		2	11					7[b]	9		8				14		6			5	4			1			10
3	5[b]		11			2		7	9		8						6	14			4	10		1			
3						10	5	7	9		8				11[b]		6			2	4	14		1			
	2[a]	8				10			9				14		11	5[b]	6				4	3		1			7
4	2	3	4			3	2	4	6		5			2	3	1	6	1		4	6	2		4			4
		1				1							1		2			2				1					
								3	1		3				1		1										2

Allen M.	Ardiles	Barker	Brock	Channing	Clarke	Coney	Dennis	Falco	Fereday	Fleming	Francis	Gray	Herrera	Johns	Kerslake	Law	Maddix	Maguire	McCarthy	McDonald	Parker	Pizanti	Reid	Seaman	Sinton	Spackman	Stein
		8		2		10	11[b]	9[a]	6						12		14			5	4	3		1			7
		9		2		10				12			11		8		5		4[a]			3		1		6	7
		7		2[a]		10	3						14		8		12			5	4	11[b]		1		6	9
		3		3		3	2	1	1				1		2		1		1	2	2	3		3		2	3
										1			1		1		2										
						2																					

Allen M.	Ardiles	Barker	Brock	Channing	Clarke	Coney	Dennis	Falco	Fereday	Fleming	Francis	Gray	Herrera	Johns	Kerslake	Law	Maddix	Maguire	McCarthy	McDonald	Parker	Pizanti	Reid	Seaman	Sinton	Spackman	Stein
7	6[b]	11[a]	8				3	9	2		10						12			5	4			1			14
	1	1	1				1	1	1		1									1	1			1			
																	1										1

Allen M.	Ardiles	Barker	Brock	Channing	Clarke	Coney	Dennis	Falco	Fereday	Fleming	Francis	Gray	Herrera	Johns	Kerslake	Law	Maddix	Maguire	McCarthy	McDonald	Parker	Pizanti	Reid	Seaman	Sinton	Spackman	Stein
2	7	30	17	13	12	20	21	29	39	1	26	11	1	5	18	10	38	8	1	37	48	21	14	46	10	18	28
2	5	6	2			6	2	5	2	2			4		13		8	3		3		3					14
5		1		1	5	2		15	1		10	2			1		3			1			1		3	1	7

1989-90

Division One

	P	W	D	L	F	A	Pts
Liverpool	38	23	10	5	78	37	79
Aston Villa	38	21	7	10	57	38	70
Tottenham Hotspur	38	19	6	13	59	47	63
Arsenal	38	18	8	12	54	38	62
Chelsea	38	16	12	10	58	50	60
Everton	38	17	8	13	57	46	59
Southampton	38	15	10	13	71	63	55
Wimbledon	38	13	16	9	47	40	55
Nottingham Forest	38	15	9	14	55	47	54
Norwich City	38	13	14	11	44	42	53
Queen's Park Rangers	38	13	11	14	45	44	50
Coventry City	38	14	7	17	39	59	49
Manchester United	38	13	9	16	46	47	48
Manchester City	38	12	12	14	43	52	48
Crystal Palace	38	13	9	16	42	66	48
Derby County	38	13	7	18	43	40	46
Luton Town	38	10	13	15	43	57	43
Sheffield Wednesday	38	11	10	17	35	51	43
Charlton Athletic	38	7	9	22	31	57	30
Millwall	38	5	11	22	39	65	26

Attendances

TOTAL

	Home	Away	Total
League	251,285	342,375	593,660
Cup/Other	98,950	103,045	201,995
TOTAL	350,235	445,420	795,655

AVERAGE

	Home	Away	Total
League	13,226	18,020	15,623
Cup/Other	14,136	20,609	16,833
TOTAL	13,471	18,559	15,913

Match No.	Date		Opponents	Location	Result		Scorers	Atte
1	Aug	19	Crystal Palace	H	W	2-0	Wright (2, 1 pen)	1
2		22	Chelsea	A	D	1-1	Clarke	2
3		26	Norwich City	A	D	0-0		1
4		30	Luton Town	H	D	0-0		1
5	Sep	9	Manchester City	A	L	0-1		2
6		16	Derby County	H	L	0-1		1
7		23	Aston Villa	A	W	3-1	Francis (3)	1
8		30	Tottenham Hotspur	A	L	2-3	Bardsley, Francis	2
9	Oct	14	Southampton	H	L	1-4	Francis	1
10		21	Charlton Athletic	H	L	0-1		1
11		28	Nottingham Forest	A	D	2-2	Sinton, Wright	
12	Nov	4	Wimbledon	A	D	0-0		
13		11	Liverpool	H	W	3-2	Wright (2, 1 pen), Falco	1
14		18	Arsenal	A	L	0-3		3
15		25	Millwall	H	D	0-0		
16	Dec	2	Crystal Palace	A	W	3-0	Maddix, Sinton (2)	1
17		9	Chelsea	H	W	4-2	Ferdinand (2), Falco, Clarke	1
18		16	Sheffield Wednesday	A	L	0-2		1
19		26	Coventry City	H	D	1-1	Falco	
20		30	Everton	H	W	1-0	Sinton	1
21	Jan	1	Manchester United	A	D	0-0		3
22		13	Norwich City	H	W	2-1	Falco, Clarke	1
23		20	Luton Town	A	D	1-1	Falco	
24	Feb	10	Derby County	A	L	0-2		1
25		24	Millwall	A	W	2-1	Barker, Wegerle	1
26	Mar	3	Arsenal	H	W	2-0	Wilkins, Wegerle	1
27		17	Tottenham Hotspur	H	W	3-1	Clarke, Sinton, Barker	1
28		20	Aston Villa	H	D	1-1	Clarke	1
29		24	Nottingham Forest	H	W	2-0	Sinton, Barker	1
30		31	Charlton Athletic	A	L	0-1		
31	Apr	3	Southampton	A	W	2-0	Maddix, Wegerle	1
32		7	Everton	A	L	0-1		1
33		11	Manchester City	H	L	1-3	Wegerle	
34		14	Manchester United	H	L	1-2	Channing	1
35		16	Coventry City	A	D	1-1	Maddix	1
36		21	Sheffield Wednesday	H	W	1-0	Clarke	1
37		28	Liverpool	A	L	1-2	Wegerle	3
38	May	5	Wimbledon	H	L	2-3	Wegerle, Channing	

Appeara
Sub appeara
(

FA Cup

R3	Jan	6	Cardiff City	A	D	0-0		1
rep		10	Cardiff City	H	W	2-0	Wilkins, Wegerle	1
R4		27	Arsenal	A	D	0-0		4
rep		31	Arsenal	H	W	2-0	Sansom, Sinton	2
R5	Feb	18	Blackpool	A	D	2-2	Clarke (2)	
rep		21	Blackpool	H	D	0-0 aet		1
rep		26	Blackpool	H	W	3-0	Sinton, Sansom, Barker	1
R6	Mar	11	Liverpool	H	D	2-2	Wilkins, Barker	2
rep		14	Liverpool	A	L	0-1		3

Appeara
Sub appeara
(

League Cup

R2/1	Sep	20	Stockport County	H	W	2-1	Spackman, Clarke	
R2/2	Oct	2	Stockport County	A	D	0-0		
R3		25	Coventry City	H	L	1-2	Wright (pen)	

Appeara
Sub appeara
(

Total - Appeara
Total - Sub appeara
Total - (

Bardsley	Barker	Channing	Clarke	Falco	Ferdinand	Francis	Herrera	Iorfa	Kereslake	Law	Maddix	McDonald	Parker	Reid	Roberts	Rutherford	Sansom	Seaman	Sinton	Spackman	Stein	Wegerle	Wilkins	Wright
		2	9a	12							14	5	4	8b			3	1	11	6				10
		2	9	12							14	5	4	8			3	1	11b	6				10a
	7	2	9b	12					14			5	4	8			3	1	11	6				10a
	14	2	9	12								5	4	8b			3	1	11	6	7a			10
	7a	2	9								14	5	4	8			3	1	11	6	12			10b
7	14	2	9			12						5	4	8b			3	1	11	6				10a
7		2	9			10b					12	5	4	8a			3	1	11	6				14
7	8	2	9	12		10a						5	4				3	1	11	6				
7	14	2	9			10					3	5	4a	8b				1	11	6				12
7	8	2	9								4	5				14	3	1	11	6b				10
7	6	2	9									5	4	8		10b	3	1	11					14
7		2	9		14						10	5	4	8			3	1	11b	6				
	7	2	14	9							6	5	4	8			3	1	11					10b
	7	2b	12	9a						6		5	4	8	1		3		11	14				10
2	7		9		10a						6	5	4	8b	1		3		11	14				12
2			14	9	10b						6	5	4	8	1		3		11				7	
2	12		14	9	10b						6	5	4	8a	1		3		11				7	
2a	8	12		9	10b						6	5	4		1		3		11			14	7	
2	8			9							6	5	4				3	1	11			10	7	
2	8			9						4	6	5					3	1	11			10	7	
2	8			9						4	6	5					3	1	11			10b	7	14
2	8		14	9b							6	5	4				3	1	11			10	7	
2	8		14	9b							6	5	4				3	1	11			10	7	
2	8	12	9								6a	5	4				3	1	11			10b	7	14
2	8		9							4	6	5					3	1	11			10	7	
2	8		9								6	5	4				3	1	11			10	7	
2	8		9a	12							6	5	4				3	1	11			10	7	
2	8		9b	14							6	5	4				3	1	11			10	7	
2	8		9b	14							6	5	4				3	1	11			10	7	
2	8		9	14						5	6		4				3	1	11			10b	7	
2	8		9							5	6		4				3	1	11			10	7	
2	8	12	9							5a	6		4				3	1	11			10	7	
2	8a	12	9							5	6		4				3	1	11			10	7	
2		8	14	9b	10						6	5	4				3	1	11				7	
2		8	9	14	10						6	5	4				3b	1	11				7	
2		8	9								6	5	4				3	1	11			10	7	
2		8	9		14		3			4	6b	5						1	11			10	7	
2		8	9a		12			14		4	6	5					3	1	11			10b	7	
31	24	19	27	11	6	3	1			10	28	34	32	15	5	1	36	33	38	11	1	18	23	9
	4	4	7	10	3	1		1	1		4					1				2	1	1		6
1	3	2	6	5	2	5					3								6			6	1	5

Bardsley	Barker	Channing	Clarke	Falco	Ferdinand	Francis	Herrera	Iorfa	Kereslake	Law	Maddix	McDonald	Parker	Reid	Roberts	Rutherford	Sansom	Seaman	Sinton	Spackman	Stein	Wegerle	Wilkins	Wright
2	8			9							6	5	4				3	1	11			10	7	
2	8			9							6	5	4				3	1	11			10	7	
2	8		9								6	5	4				3	1	11			10b	7	14
2	8		9								6	5	4				3	1	11			10	7	
2	8		9								6	5	4				3	1	11			10	7	
2	8		9								6	5	4				3	1	11			10b	7	14
2	8		9								6	5	4				3	1	11			10	7	
2	8		9	14							6	5	4				3	1	11			10b	7	
2	8		9	14							6	5	4				3	1	11			10b	7	
9	9		7	2							9	9	9				9	9	9			9	9	
				2																				2
	2		2														2		2			1	2	

Bardsley	Barker	Channing	Clarke	Falco	Ferdinand	Francis	Herrera	Iorfa	Kereslake	Law	Maddix	McDonald	Parker	Reid	Roberts	Rutherford	Sansom	Seaman	Sinton	Spackman	Stein	Wegerle	Wilkins	Wright
	8	2	9a	12		7b						5	4	14			3	1	11	6				10
	7	2	9			10						5	4	8			3	1	11	6				
	6	2	9			10b					4	5		7		14	3	1	11					8
	3	3	3			3					1	3	2	2			3	3	3	2				2
				1										1		1								
			1																	1				1

Bardsley	Barker	Channing	Clarke	Falco	Ferdinand	Francis	Herrera	Iorfa	Kereslake	Law	Maddix	McDonald	Parker	Reid	Roberts	Rutherford	Sansom	Seaman	Sinton	Spackman	Stein	Wegerle	Wilkins	Wright
40	36	22	37	13	6	6	1			10	38	46	43	17	5	1	48	45	50	13	1	27	32	11
	4	4	7	13	3	1		1	1			4		1		2				2	1	1		8
1	5	2	9	5	2	5						3					2		8	1		7	3	6

stitutions are listed as:
replaced by player 12
replaced by player 14

1990-91

Division One

	P	W	D	L	F	A	Pts
Arsenal	38	24	13	1	74	18	83
Liverpool	38	23	7	8	77	40	76
Crystal Palace	38	20	9	9	50	41	69
Leeds United	38	19	7	12	65	47	64
Manchester City	38	17	11	10	64	53	62
Manchester United	38	16	12	10	58	45	59
Wimbledon	38	14	14	10	53	46	56
Nottingham Forest	38	14	12	12	65	50	54
Everton	38	13	12	13	50	46	51
Tottenham Hotspur	38	11	16	11	51	50	49
Chelsea	38	13	10	15	58	69	49
Queen's Park Rangers	38	12	10	16	44	53	46
Sheffield United	38	13	7	18	36	55	46
Southampton	38	12	9	17	58	69	45
Norwich City	38	13	6	19	41	64	45
Coventry City	38	11	11	16	42	49	44
Aston Villa	38	9	14	15	46	58	41
Luton Town	38	10	7	21	42	61	37
Sunderland	38	8	10	20	38	60	34
Derby County	38	5	9	24	37	75	24

Attendances

	TOTAL		
	Home	Away	Total
League	256,963	417,298	674,261
Cup/Other	32,944	47,681	80,625
TOTAL	289,907	464,979	754,886

	AVERAGE		
	Home	Away	Total
League	13,524	21,963	17,744
Cup/Other	10,981	15,894	13,438
TOTAL	13,178	21,135	17,157

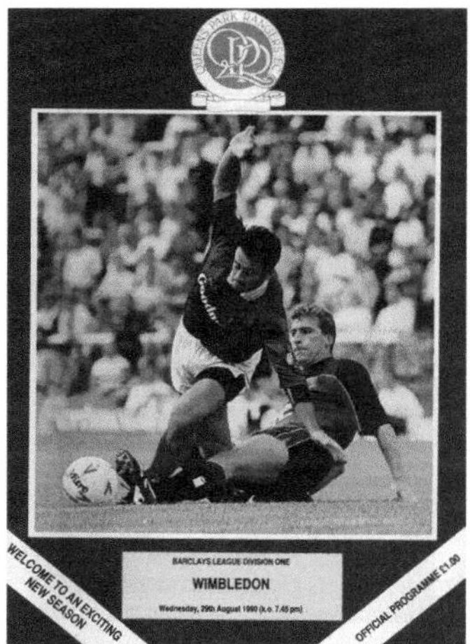

Match No.	Date		Opponents	Location	Result		Scorers	Atten
1	Aug	25	Nottingham Forest	A	D	1-1	Wegerle	21
2		29	Wimbledon	H	L	0-1		9
3	Sep	1	Chelsea	H	W	1-0	Wegerle (pen)	19
4		8	Manchester United	A	L	1-3	Wegerle (pen)	43
5		15	Luton Town	H	W	6-1	Wegerle (2), Sinton, Wilkins, Falco, Parker	10
6		22	Aston Villa	A	D	2-2	Wegerle (pen), Sinton	23
7		29	Coventry City	A	L	1-3	Ferdinand	9
8	Oct	6	Tottenham Hotspur	H	D	0-0		21
9		20	Leeds United	A	W	3-2	Wegerle (2), Wilkins	27
10		27	Norwich City	H	L	1-3	Wegerle (pen)	11
11	Nov	3	Everton	A	L	0-3		22
12		10	Southampton	A	L	1-3	Falco	15
13		17	Crystal Palace	H	L	1-2	Wegerle	14
14		24	Arsenal	H	L	1-3	Wegerle (pen)	18
15	Dec	1	Manchester City	A	L	1-2	Sinton	25
16		8	Wimbledon	A	L	0-3		5
17		15	Nottingham Forest	H	L	1-2	Wegerle (pen)	10
18		23	Derby County	A	D	1-1	Wegerle	16
19		26	Liverpool	H	D	1-1	Falco	17
20		29	Sunderland	H	W	3-2	Maddix, Wegerle (pen), Falco	11
21	Jan	1	Sheffield United	A	L	0-1		21
22		12	Chelsea	A	L	0-2		19
23		19	Manchester United	H	D	1-1	Falco	18
24	Feb	2	Luton Town	A	W	2-1	Ferdinand (2)	8
25		16	Crystal Palace	A	D	0-0		15
26		23	Southampton	H	W	2-1	Ferdinand (2)	11
27	Mar	2	Manchester City	H	W	1-0	Ferdinand	12
28		16	Coventry City	H	W	1-0	Ferdinand	9
29		23	Tottenham Hotspur	A	D	0-0		30
30		30	Liverpool	A	W	3-1	Ferdinand, Wegerle, Wilson	37
31	Apr	1	Derby County	H	D	1-1	Wegerle (pen)	12
32		6	Sunderland	A	W	1-0	Tilson	17
33		10	Aston Villa	H	W	2-1	Allen, Tilson	11
34		13	Sheffield United	H	L	1-2	Allen	13
35		17	Leeds United	H	W	2-0	Wegerle, Barker	10
36		23	Arsenal	A	L	0-2		42
37	May	4	Norwich City	A	L	0-1		13
38		11	Everton	H	D	1-1	Wegerle	12

Appearar
Sub appearar
G

FA Cup

R3	Jan	7	Manchester United	A	L	1-2	Maddix	35

Appearar
Sub appearar
G

League Cup

R2/1	Sep	26	Peterborough United	H	W	3-1	Ferdinand, Maddix, Wegerle	8
R2/2	Oct	9	Peterborough United	A	D	1-1	Ferdinand	7
R3		31	Blackburn Rovers	H	W	2-1	Falco, Barker	8
R4	Nov	27	Leeds United	H	L	0-3		15

Appearar
Sub appearar
G

Zenith Data Systems Cup

R2	Nov	20	Southampton	A	L	0-4		5

Appearar
Sub appearar
G

Total - Appearar
Total - Sub appearar
Total - G

…ardsley	Barker	Brevett	Caeser	Channing	Falco	Ferdinand	Herrera	Iorfa	Law	Maddix	McCarthy	McDonald	Meaker	Parker	Peacock	Roberts	Sansom	Sinton	Stejskal	Tilson	Wegerle	Wilkins	Wilson
2	12			4	9[b]	14				6		5				1	3	11			10	7[a]	8
2	12			4[a]	9	14				6		5				1	3	11			10[b]	7	8
2				6	9							5		4		1	3	11			10	7	8
2	12				9					6[a]		5		4		1	3	11			10	7	8
2					9[b]	14				6		5		4		1	3	11			10	7	8
2						9				6		5		4		1	3	11			10	7	8
[a]	14			12		9				6		5		4		1	3[b]	11			10	7	8
2	8				14	9[b]				6		5		4		1	3	11			10	7	
2	8				14	9[b]				6		5		4			3	11	1		10	7	
2	8			12	14	9[b]				6		5[a]		4			3	11	1		10	7	
2	8				9					6[b]		5		4			3	11	1		10	7	14
[b]	8				9					6		5		4			3	11	1		10	7	
2	8				9				6			5		4		1	3	11			10	7	
2	8						4	14	6		5					1	3	11			10	7	9[b]
2	8		5				4	9[a]	6				12			1	3	11			10	7	
2	8		5		9		4[a]				12					1	3	11			10	7	6
[b]	8		5		9					6			14				3	11	1		10	7	4
2	8				9					6					5		3	11	1	4	10	7	
2	8		5		9					6							3	11	1	4	10	7	
2	8		5		9					6			14				3	11	1	4	10[b]	7	
2	8				9					6			14		5		3	11[b]	1	4	10	7	
2	8				9					6			14		5		3	11	1	12	10[b]	7	4[a]
2	8				9	10[b]				6			14		5		3	11	1	4		7	
2	8					10				6			14		5		3	11[b]	1	4		7	
2	8				9[a]	10				6					5		3	11	1	4		7	
2	8					9				6					5		3	11	1	4	10	7	
2	8					9		14		6					5		3	11	1	4	10[b]	7	
2	8					9[b]		14		6					5		3	11	1	4	10	7	
2	8	3				9				6					5			11	1	4	10	7	
2	8	3				9				6					5			11[b]	1	4	10[a]	7	14
[a]	8	3						14		6				12	5			11	1	4	10	7	
2	8	3				9				6					5			11	1	4	10	7	
2	8[a]	3				9[b]				6				12	5			11	1	4	10	7	
[a]	8	3								6			14	12	5			11	1	4	10[b]	7	
2	8	3								6		9			5			11	1	4	10	7	
2	8	3								6[b]		9		12	5			11	1	4	10	7	
2	8	3						12				6[a]		4	5			11	1		10	7	
2	8	3								6[b]		9		4	5			11	1		10	7	
8	31	10	5	3	17	15	3	1	3	32	1	17		13	19	12	28	38	26	18	35	38	11
	4			2	3	3		5			1		8	4						1			2
	1				5	8				1				1				3		2	18	2	1
2	8			5[a]	9	14				6	12						3[b]	11	1		10	7	4
	1			1	1					1							1	1	1		1	1	1
						1					1												
										1													
2	12					9				6		5		4		1	3	11			10	7	8[a]
2	8					9				6		5		4		1	3	11			10	7	
2	8				9				12	6		5[a]		4			3	11	1		10	7	
2	8						4	9	6							1	3	11			10	7	5
4	3				1	2	1	1	1	3		3		3		3	4	4	1		4	4	2
	1								1														
	1				1	2				1											1		
2	8								5		6		14	4		1	3	11[a]			10[b]	7	12
	1								1		1			1		1	1	1			1	1	
													1										1
4	36	10	5	4	19	17	4	2	5	36	2	20		17	19	16	34	44	28	18	41	44	14
	5			2	3	4		5	1		2		9	4						1			3
	2				6	10				3				1				3		2	19	2	1

1991-92

Division One

	P	W	D	L	F	A	Pts
Leeds United	42	22	16	4	74	37	82
Manchester United	42	21	15	6	63	33	78
Sheffield Wednesday	42	21	12	9	62	49	75
Arsenal	42	19	15	8	81	46	72
Manchester City	42	20	10	12	61	48	70
Liverpool	42	16	16	10	47	40	64
Aston Villa	42	17	9	16	48	44	60
Nottingham Forest	42	16	11	15	60	58	59
Sheffield United	42	16	9	17	65	63	57
Crystal Palace	42	14	15	13	53	61	57
Queen's Park Rangers	42	12	18	12	48	47	54
Everton	42	13	14	15	52	51	53
Wimbledon	42	13	14	15	53	53	53
Chelsea	42	13	14	15	50	60	53
Tottenham Hotspur	42	15	7	20	58	63	52
Southampton	42	14	10	18	39	55	52
Oldham Athletic	42	14	9	19	63	67	51
Norwich City	42	11	12	19	47	63	45
Coventry City	42	11	11	20	35	44	44
Luton Town	42	10	12	20	38	71	42
Notts County	42	10	10	22	40	62	40
West Ham United	42	9	11	22	37	59	38

Attendances

	TOTAL		
	Home	Away	Total
League	285,683	419,959	705,642
Cup/Other	20,776	38,637	59,413
TOTAL	306,459	458,596	765,055

	AVERAGE		
	Home	Away	Total
League	13,604	19,998	16,801
Cup/Other	6,925	9,659	8,488
TOTAL	12,769	18,344	15,613

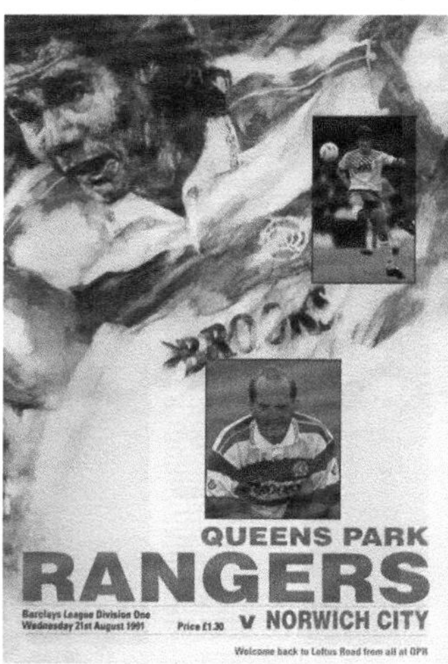

Match No.	Date		Opponents	Location	Result		Scorers	Atte
1	Aug	17	Arsenal	A	D	1-1	Bailey	3
2		21	Norwich City	H	L	0-2		1
3		24	Coventry City	H	D	1-1	Wegerle	
4		28	Liverpool	A	L	0-1		3
5		31	Sheffield Wednesday	A	L	1-4	Bailey	2
6	Sep	4	West Ham United	H	D	0-0		1
7		7	Southampton	H	D	2-2	Barker, Thompson	
8		14	Tottenham Hotspur	A	L	0-2		3
9		17	Luton Town	A	W	1-0	Barker	
10		21	Chelsea	H	D	2-2	Wilson,. Peacock	1
11		28	Crystal Palace	A	D	2-2	Barker, Wegerle	1
12	Oct	5	Nottingham Forest	H	L	0-2		1
13		19	Wimbledon	A	W	1-0	Bailey	
14		26	Everton	H	W	3-1	Bailey, Barker (2)	1
15	Nov	2	Aston Villa	H	L	0-1		1
16		16	Leeds United	A	L	0-2		2
17		23	Oldham Athletic	H	L	1-3	Ferdinand	
18		30	Notts County	A	W	1-0	Ferdinand	
19	Dec	7	Sheffield United	H	W	1-0	Wegerle	1
20		14	Manchester City	A	D	2-2	Wegerle, Bailey	2
21		21	Norwich City	A	W	1-0	Bailey	1
22		26	Liverpool	H	D	0-0		2
23		28	Sheffield Wednesday	H	D	1-1	Wilkins	1
24	Jan	1	Manchester United	A	W	4-1	Sinton, Bailey (3)	3
25		11	Coventry City	A	D	2-2	Penrice (2)	1
26		18	Arsenal	H	D	0-0		2
27	Feb	1	Wimbledon	H	D	1-1	Penrice	
28		8	Everton	A	D	0-0		1
29		15	Oldham Athletic	A	L	1-2	Wegerle	1
30		22	Notts County	H	D	1-1	Ferdinand	
31		29	Sheffield United	A	D	0-0		1
32	Mar	7	Manchester City	H	W	4-0	Ferdinand (2), Wilson (pen), Barker	1
33		11	Leeds United	H	W	4-1	Ferdinand, Allen, Sinton, Wilson (pen)	1
34		14	Aston Villa	A	W	1-0	Ferdinand	1
35		21	West Ham United	A	D	2-2	Allen (2)	2
36		28	Manchester United	H	D	0-0		2
37	Apr	4	Southampton	A	L	1-2	Ferdinand	1
38		11	Totttenham Hotspur	H	L	1-2	Sinton	2
39		18	Chelsea	A	L	1-2	Allen	1
40		20	Luton Town	H	W	2-1	Ferdinand (2)	1
41		25	Nottingham Forest	A	D	1-1	Allen	2
42	May	2	Crystal Palace	H	W	1-0	OG (Humphrey)	1

Appeara
Sub appeara
G

FA Cup

R3	Jan	4	Southampton	A	L	0-2		1

Appeara
Sub appeara
G

League Cup

R2/1	Sep	24	Hull City	A	W	3-0	Thompson, Barker (2)	
R2/2	Oct	9	Hull City	H	W	5-1	Bardsley, Thompson (2), Bailey (2)	
R3		29	Manchester City	A	D	0-0		1
rep	Nov	20	Manchester City	H	L	1-3	Penrice	1

Appeara
Sub appeara
G

Zenith Data Systems Cup

R2	Oct	23	Norwich City	A	W	2-1	Sinton, Impey	
QF	Nov	26	Crystal Palace	H	L	2-3	Bardsley, Wilkins	

Appeara
Sub appeara
G

Total - Appeara
Total - Sub appeara
Total - G

Bailey	Bardsley	Barker	Brevett	Channing	Ferdinand	Herrera	Holloway	Impey	Iorfa	McCarthy	McDonald	Maddix	Meaker	Peacock	Penrice	Ready	Roberts	Sinton	Stejskal	Thompson	Tilson	Walsh	Wegerle	Wilkins	Wilson	OG
7	2	8	3		9		12					6		5				11	1				10	4[a]		
7[b]	2	8	3		9		4					6		5				11	1	14			10			
7	2	8	12		9[b]		4					6		5				11	1	14			10		3[a]	
7	2	8			9[b]		4					6		5				11	1	14			10		3	
7	2	8			9		4					6		5					1	14			10		3	
7	2	8	3		14		4[b]					6		5					1	9			10		11	
7	2	8	3								12	6[a]		5				4	1	9			10		11	
	2[a]	8	3				12		14		5	6					1	11		9	4		10[b]		7	
14	2	8	3[a]				12				5	6						11	1	10	4	9[b]			7	
	2	8					4				5	6		3				11	1	9		10			7	
14	2	8					4				5	6		3				11	1	9			10[b]		7	
12	2	8			9		7					6		5[a]				11	1		4		10		3	
10	2	8					7					6		5				11	1	9	4				3	
10	2	8					7					6		5				11	1	9	4				3	
10	2	8					7					6		5	12			11	1	9	4[a]				3	
	2	8			12		7					6		5	10			11	1	9[a]	4[b]			14	3	
7[b]	2	8			9		14					6		5	10			11	1					4	3	
	2	8			9					7	6			5	10			11	1					4	3	
	2	8					12			7	6			5	9[a]			11	1				10	4	3	
14	2	8					12			7[b]	6			5	9			11	1				10	4	3[a]	
9	2	8					7				6			5				11	1				10	4	3	
9	2	8					7				6			5				11	1				10	4	3	
9[a]	2	8					7				6			5				11	1	12			10	4	3	
9	2	8					7				6			5				11	1				10	4	3	
9	2	8					7	11			6			5	12				1				10[a]	4	3	
9[a]	2	8					7				6			5	10			11	1				12	4	3	
9		8[b]					7							5	10	2		11	1		6		14	4	3	
9[a]	2[b]	8					7				6			5	10			11	1		14		12	4	3	
	2	8[a]					7				6		12	5	9			11	1				10	4	3	
	2				9		8	7			6			5	10			11	1					4	3	
	2				9		8				6			5	10			11	1		4			7	3	
	2	14			9		8	4			6			5	10[b]			11	1					7	3	
	2	14			9		8	4			6			5				11[b]	1					7	3	
	2				9		8	4			6			5				11	1					7	3	
	2	14			9		8	4			6			5				11	1					7	3	
	2				9		8	4			6			5				11	1					7	3	
	2	7			9		8	4			6	5			14			11[b]	1						3	
	2				9[b]		8	4			6			5	14			11	1					7	3	
	2				9		8	4[a]			6			5	10			11	1					7	3	
	2				9		8	4			6			5	12			11	1					7	3	
	2				9[b]		8	4				6		5	14			11	1					7	3	
14	2	11			9[b]		8	4			6			5					1					7	3	
19	41	31	6		21		34	13		3	27	19		39	13	1	1	38	41	10	9	2	18	26	40	
5		3	1		2		6		1		1		1		6					5	1		3	1		
9		6			10									1	3			3		1			5	1	3	1

Bailey	Bardsley	Barker	Brevett	Channing	Ferdinand	Herrera	Holloway	Impey	Iorfa	McCarthy	McDonald	Maddix	Meaker	Peacock	Penrice	Ready	Roberts	Sinton	Stejskal	Thompson	Tilson	Walsh	Wegerle	Wilkins	Wilson	OG
9	2	8					7				6[a]			5	12			11	1				10	4	3	
1	1	1					1				1			1				1	1				1	1	1	
															1											

Bailey	Bardsley	Barker	Brevett	Channing	Ferdinand	Herrera	Holloway	Impey	Iorfa	McCarthy	McDonald	Maddix	Meaker	Peacock	Penrice	Ready	Roberts	Sinton	Stejskal	Thompson	Tilson	Walsh	Wegerle	Wilkins	Wilson	OG
	2	8			12	14	4				5	6		3				11[b]	1	9			10[a]		7	
10	2	8					7	14				6[a]		5		12		11[b]	1	9	4				3	
10	2	8					7					6		5				11	1	9	4				3	
7	2	8	3		9							6		5	10				1					4	11	
3	4	4	1		1		3				1	4		4	1			3	4	3	2		1	1	4	
					1	1		1								1										
2	1	2													1					3						

Bailey	Bardsley	Barker	Brevett	Channing	Ferdinand	Herrera	Holloway	Impey	Iorfa	McCarthy	McDonald	Maddix	Meaker	Peacock	Penrice	Ready	Roberts	Sinton	Stejskal	Thompson	Tilson	Walsh	Wegerle	Wilkins	Wilson	OG
10	2	8					7	12				6		5				11[a]	1	9	4				3	
	2	8[a]		7[b]	9		12	14			6			5	10		1	11						4	3	
1	2	2		1	1		1				1	1		2	1		1	2	1	1	1			1	2	
							1	2																		
	1							1										1						1		

Bailey	Bardsley	Barker	Brevett	Channing	Ferdinand	Herrera	Holloway	Impey	Iorfa	McCarthy	McDonald	Maddix	Meaker	Peacock	Penrice	Ready	Roberts	Sinton	Stejskal	Thompson	Tilson	Walsh	Wegerle	Wilkins	Wilson	OG
24	48	38	7	1	23		39	13		3	30	24		46	15	1	2	44	47	14	12	2	20	29	47	
5		3	1		3	1	7	3	1		1		1		7	1				5	1		3	1		
11	2	8			10			1						1	4			4		4			5	2	3	1

1992-93

Premier League

	P	W	D	L	F	A	Pts
Manchester United	42	24	12	6	67	31	84
Aston Villa	42	21	11	10	57	40	74
Norwich City	42	21	9	12	61	65	72
Blackburn Rovers	42	20	11	11	68	46	71
Queen's Park Rangers	42	17	12	13	63	55	63
Liverpool	42	16	11	15	62	55	59
Sheffield Wednesday	42	15	14	13	55	51	59
Tottenham Hotspur	42	16	11	15	60	66	59
Manchester City	42	15	12	15	56	51	57
Arsenal	42	15	11	16	40	38	56
Chelsea	42	14	14	14	51	54	56
Wimbledon	42	14	12	16	56	55	54
Everton	42	15	8	19	53	55	53
Sheffield United	42	14	10	18	54	53	52
Coventry City	42	13	13	16	52	57	52
Ipswich Town	42	12	16	14	50	55	52
Leeds United	42	12	15	15	57	62	51
Southampton	42	13	11	18	54	61	50
Oldham Athletic	42	13	10	19	63	74	49
Crystal Palace	42	11	16	15	48	61	49
Middlesbrough	42	11	11	20	54	75	44
Nottingham Forest	42	10	10	22	41	62	40

Attendances

TOTAL	Home	Away	Total
League	314,339	419,706	734,045
Cup/Other	38,033	30,284	68,317
TOTAL	352,372	449,990	802,362

AVERAGE	Home	Away	Total
League	14,969	19,986	17,477
Cup/Other	12,678	10,095	11,386
TOTAL	14,682	18,750	16,716

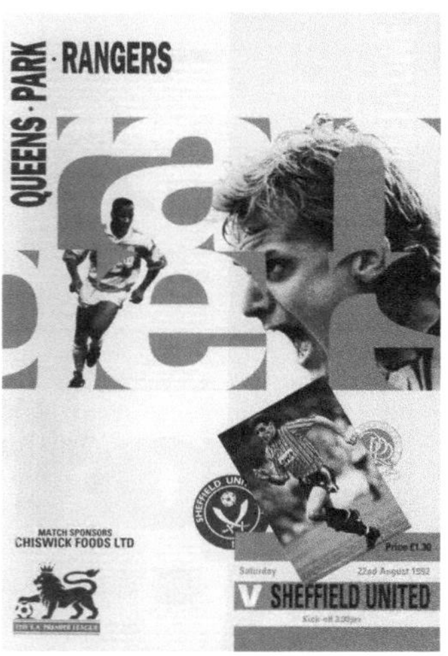

Match No.	Date		Opponents	Location	Result		Scorers	Atten
1	Aug	17	Manchester City	A	D	1-1	Sinton	24
2		19	Southampton	H	W	3-1	Ferdinand (2), Bardsley	10
3		22	Sheffield United	H	W	3-2	Barker, Ferdinand, Bailey	10
4		26	Coventry City	A	W	1-0	Impey	13
5		29	Chelsea	A	L	0-1		22
6	Sep	2	Arsenal	H	D	0-0		20
7		5	Ipswich Town	H	D	0-0		12
8		12	Southampton	A	W	2-1	Sinton, Channing	14
9		19	Middlesbrough	H	D	3-3	Ferdinand, Penrice, Sinton (pen)	12
10		26	Manchester United	A	D	0-0		33
11	Oct	3	Tottenham Hotspur	H	W	4-1	Holloway, Wilkins, Penrice (2)	19
12		17	Norwich City	A	L	1-2	Allen	16
13		24	Leeds United	H	W	2-1	Bardsley, Ferdinand	19
14	Nov	1	Aston Villa	A	L	0-2		20
15		7	Wimbledon	A	W	2-0	Wilkins, Allen	6
16		23	Liverpool	H	L	0-1		21
17		28	Blackburn Rovers	A	L	0-1		15
18	Dec	5	Oldham Athletic	H	W	3-2	Ferdinand (2), Penrice	11
19		12	Crystal Palace	H	L	1-3	Penrice	14
20		19	Sheffield Wednesday	A	L	0-1		23
21		28	Everton	H	W	4-2	Sinton (3), Penrice	14
22	Jan	9	Middlesbrough	A	W	1-0	Ferdinand	15
23		18	Manchester United	H	L	1-3	Allen	20
24		27	Chelsea	H	D	1-1	Allen	15
25		30	Sheffield United	A	W	2-1	Allen, Holloway	16
26	Feb	6	Manchester City	H	D	1-1	Wilson (pen)	13
27		9	Ipswich Town	A	D	1-1	White	17
28		20	Coventry City	H	W	2-0	Peacock, OG (Pearce)	12
29		24	Nottingham Forest	A	L	0-1		22
30		27	Tottenham Hotspur	A	L	2-3	Peacock, White	32
31	Mar	6	Norwich Citty	H	W	3-1	Ferdinand (2), Wilson	13
32		10	Liverpool	A	L	0-1		30
33		13	Wimbledon	H	L	1-2	Ferdinand	12
34		20	Oldham Athletic	A	D	2-2	Allen, Sinton	10
35		24	Blackburn Rovers	H	L	0-3		10
36	Apr	3	Crystal Palace	A	D	1-1	Allen	14
37		10	Nottingham Forest	H	W	4-3	Ferdinand (3), Wilson (pen)	15
38		12	Everton	A	W	5-3	Impey, Ferdinand (3), Bardsley	19
39	May	1	Leeds United	A	D	1-1	Ferdinand	31
40		4	Arsenal	A	D	0-0		18
41		9	Aston Villa	H	W	2-1	Ferdinand, Allen	18
42		11	Sheffield Wednesday	H	W	3-1	Allen (2), Ferdinand	12

Appearar
Sub appearar
G

FA Cup

R3	Jan	4	Swindon Town	H	W	3-0	Ferdinand (2), Penrice	12
R4		23	Manchester City	H	L	1-2	Holloway	18

Appearar
Sub appearar
G

League Cup

R2/1	Sep	23	Grimsby Town	H	W	2-1	Ferdinand (2)	7
R2/2	Oct	6	Grimsby Town	A	L	1-2*	Bailey	8
R3		27	Bury	A	W	2-0	Allen, Peacock	4
R4	Dec	2	Sheffield Wednesday	A	L	0-4		17

* Won 6-5 on penalties

Appearar
Sub appearar
G

Total - Appearar
Total - Sub appearar
Total - G

Bailey	Bardsley	Barker	Brevett	Channing	Doyle	Ferdinand	Holloway	Impey	Maddix	McDonald	Meaker	Peacock	Penrice	Ready	Roberts	Sinton	Stejskal	Thompson	White	Wilkins	Wilson	OG
0	2					9[a]	8	7		6		5				11	1	12		4	3	
0	2					9[a]	8	7		6		5			1	11		12		4	3	
0	2	7				9	8[a]			6		5				11	1	12		4	3	
0	2	8				9[a]		7		6		5	12			11	1			4	3	
0[a]	2	8				9		7		6		5	12			11	1			4	3	
0[a]	2	8				9		7		6		5	12		1	11				4	3	
0[a]	2	8				9		7		6		5	12			11	1			4	3	
		8		2[a]		9		7	12	6		5	10			11	1			4	3	
		8		2		9	14	7	12	6		5[b]	10			11	1			4	3[a]	
	2	12	3			9[a]	8	7	6			5	10			11	1			4		
9	2						8	7		6		5	10			11	1			4	3	
9	2						8	7	14	6		5	10[a]			11[b]	1			4	3	
	2	12				9	8	7		6		5				11	1			4	3	
2	2	11				9	8	7[a]		6		5			1					4	3	
	2					9	8	7		6		5			1	11				4	3	
	2					9	8	7		6		5			1	11				4	3	
0[a]	2					9	8	7		6		5	12			11	1			4	3	
	2					9[b]	8	7	14	6		5	10			11[a]	1			4	3	
	2					9	8	7		6		5	10			11	1			4	3	
	2	12				9	8	7[a]		6		5	10		1	11				4	3	
	2	7				9	8			6		5	10		1	11				4	3	
	2	8	3			9		7	14	6		5	10[a]		1	11[b]					4	
9	2	4					8	7		6		5[a]			1	11		12			3	
	2	4	3			9	8	11	5	6					1				14		7[b]	
	2	4	3			9	8	7[a]	5	6		12			1						11	
	2	4	3			9		8	5	6					1	11					7	
	2		3		4[b]	9		8[a]	5	6		12			1	11			14		7	
	2	4	3			9		8				5		6	1	11					7	
2	2	4	3			9		8	6			5			1	11					7	
	2	4[b]	3			9		14	8	6		5			1	11			10		7	
	2		3		4	9		7	5	6	11				1				10[a]		8	
	2		3		4	9		7	5[b]	6	11	14			1				10		8	
	2		3		4	9[a]		7		6	11	5			1[c]		13		12		8	
	2				4	9	8	7		6		5		14	1	11[b]					3	
9	2		3				8	7		6				5	1	11					4	
9	2		3				8	7		6		5			1	11[b]			14		4	
	2					9	8	7		6		5			1	11				4	3	
	2	12				9	8	7		6		5			1	11[a]				4	3	
	2	8				9		7		6		5			1	11				4	3	
	2	8[b]	14			9		7		6		5			1	11				4	3	
	2	8				9		7		6		5			1	11				4	3	
	2	8				9		7		6		5			1	11				4	3	
3	40	21	14	2	5	37	23	39	9	39	3	35	10	2	28	36	14		3	27	41	
2		4	1				1	1	5			3	5	1			1	4	4			
1	3	1		1		20	2	2				2	6			7			2	2	3	1
	2	7				9	8	12		6		5	10[a]		1	11				4	3	
4	2	4	3			9	8		5	6					1	11[b]					7	
	2	2	1			2	2		1	2		1	1		2	2				1	2	
1								1														
						2	1						1									
0[a]			3	2		9	8	7	6			5	12		1	11				4		
9	2						8	7		6		5	10[a]			11	1	12		4	3	
	2	7				9	8			6		5			1	11		12		4	3	
	2					9	8	7[a]		6		5	10			11	1			4	3	
2	3	1	1	1		3	4	3	1	3		4	2		2	4	2			4	3	
													1					2				
1						2						1										
5	45	24	16	3	5	42	29	42	11	44	3	40	13	2	32	42	16		3	32	46	
3		4	1				1	2	5			3	6	1			1	6	4			
2	3	1		1		24	3	2				3	7			7			2	2	3	1

stitutions are listed as:
replaced by player 12
replaced by player 14
replaced by player 13

1993-94

Premier League

	P	W	D	L	F	A	Pts
Manchester United	42	27	11	4	80	38	92
Blackburn Rovers	42	25	9	8	63	36	84
Newcastle United	42	23	8	11	82	41	77
Arsenal	42	18	17	7	53	28	71
Leeds United	42	18	16	8	65	39	70
Wimbledon	42	18	11	13	56	53	65
Sheffield Wednesday	42	16	16	10	76	54	64
Liverpool	42	17	9	16	59	55	60
Queen's Park Rangers	42	16	12	14	62	61	60
Aston Villa	42	15	12	15	46	50	57
Coventry City	42	14	14	14	43	45	56
Norwich City	42	12	17	13	65	61	53
West Ham United	42	13	13	16	47	58	52
Chelsea	42	13	12	17	49	53	51
Tottenham Hotspur	42	11	12	19	54	59	45
Manchester City	42	9	18	15	38	49	45
Everton	42	12	8	22	42	63	44
Southampton	42	12	7	23	49	66	43
Ipswich Town	42	9	16	17	35	58	43
Sheffield United	42	8	18	16	42	60	42
Oldham Athletic	42	9	13	20	42	68	40
Swindon Town	42	5	15	22	47	100	30

Attendances

	TOTAL		
	Home	Away	Total
League	298,792	462,731	761,523
Cup/Other	33,757	11,138	44,895
TOTAL	332,549	473,869	806,418

	AVERAGE		
	Home	Away	Total
League	14,228	22,035	18,132
Cup/Other	11,252	5,569	8,979
TOTAL	13,856	20,603	17,158

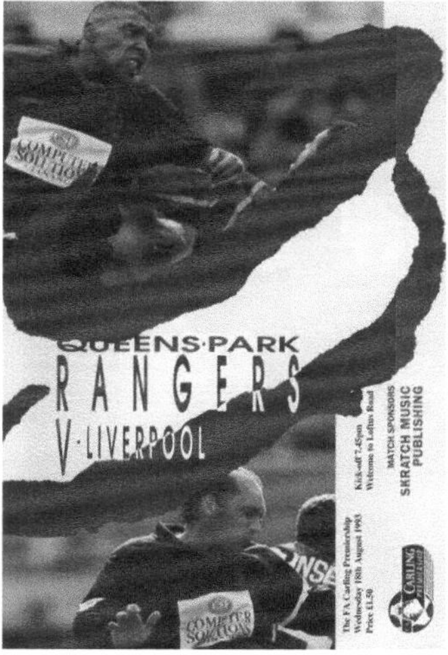

Match No.	Date		Opponents	Location	Result		Scorers	Atter
1	Aug	14	Aston Villa	A	L	1-4	Ferdinand	3
2		18	Liverpool	H	L	1-3	Wilkins	1
3		21	Southampton	H	W	2-1	Penrice, Wilson (pen)	1
4		25	Chelsea	A	L	0-2		2
5		28	West Ham United	A	W	4-0	Ferdinand (2), Peacock, Penrice	1
6	Sep	1	Sheffield United	H	W	2-1	Sinclair, Wilson (pen)	1
7		11	Manchester City	A	L	0-3		2
8		18	Norwich City	H	D	2-2	Sinclair, Ferdinand	1
9		27	Wimbledon	A	D	1-1	McDonald	
10	Oct	2	Ipswich Town	H	W	3-0	White (2), Barker	1
11		16	Newcastle United	A	W	2-1	Ferdinand, Allen	3
12		23	Coventry City	H	W	5-1	Ferdinand, Allen (2), Impey, Barker	1
13		30	Manchester United	A	L	1-2	Allen	4
14	Nov	6	Blackburn Rovers	H	W	1-0	OG	1
15		20	Everton	A	W	3-0	Allen (3)	1
16		24	Swindon Town	A	L	0-1		1
17		27	Tottenham Hotspur	H	D	1-1	Ferdinand	1
18	Dec	4	Aston Villa	H	D	2-2	Penrice, OG	1
19		8	Liverpool	A	L	2-3	Barker, Ferdinand	2
20		11	Southampton	A	W	1-0	Ferdinand	1
21		27	Oldham Athleetic	H	W	2-0	White, Penrice	1
22		29	Leeds United	A	D	1-1	Meaker	3
23	Jan	1	Sheffield Wednesday	H	L	1-2	Ferdinand	1
24		3	Arsenal	A	D	0-0		3
25		16	Newcastle United	H	L	1-2	Penrice	1
26		22	Coventry City	A	W	1-0	White	1
27	Feb	5	Manchester United	H	L	2-3	Wilson (pen), Ferdinand	2
28	Mar	5	Manchester City	H	D	1-1	Penrice	1
29		12	Norwich City	A	W	4-3	Barker, Peacock, White, Penrice	1
30		16	Sheffield United	A	D	1-1	Barker	1
31		19	Wimbledon	H	W	1-0	Peacock	1
32		26	Ipswich Town	A	W	3-1	Impey (2), Ferdinand	1
33	Apr	2	Oldham Athletic	A	L	1-4	Ferdinand	1
34		4	Leeds United	H	L	0-4		1
35		9	Sheffield Wednesday	A	L	1-3	White	2
36		13	Chelsea	H	D	1-1	Ferdinand	1
37		16	Everton	H	W	2-1	White, Ferdinand	1
38		24	Blackburn Rovers	A	D	1-1	Ready	1
39		27	Arsenal	H	D	1-1	Penrice	1
40		30	Swindon Town	H	L	1-3	Ferdinand	
41	May	3	West Ham United	H	D	0-0		1
42		7	Tottenham Hotspur	A	W	2-1	Sinclair (2)	2

Appeara
Sub appeara
G

FA Cup

R3	Jan	8	Stockport County	A	L	1-2	Barker	

Appeara
Sub appeara
G

League Cup

R2/1	Sep	21	Barnet	A	W	2-1	Ferdinand, Barker	
R2/2	Oct	6	Barnet	H	W	4-0	Allen (3), Impey	
R3		27	Millwall	H	W	3-0	Sinclair, Barker, Ferdinand	1
R4	Dec	1	Sheffield Wednesday	H	L	1-2	Meaker	1

Appeara
Sub appeara
G

Total - Appeara
Total - Sub appeara
Total - G

Bardsley (2)	Barker (14)	Brevett (15)	Doyle (20)	Ferdinand (9)	Holloway (8)	Impey (7)	McCarthy (25)	McDonald (6)	Meaker (22)	Peacock (5)	Pennice (12)	Ready (18)	Roberts (1)	Sinclair (11)	Stejskal (13)	White (19)	Wilkins (4)	Wilson (3)	Witter (21)	Yates (24)	OG
	11			9	8[a]	7				5		2	1			A	4	3	6		
	8			9		7				5	10	2	1	11[a]		A	4	3		6	
	8	A		9		7				5	10[b]	2	1	11[a]		B	4	3		6	
	8	3[a]		9		7				5	10	2	1	A			4	11		6	
2	8			9		7		6		5	10[b]	A	1	11			4[a]	3			
2	8			9		7		6		5	10	A	1	11[a]			4	3			
2			8	9		7		6		5	10		1	11[a]			4	3			
2	8			9		7		6		5	10			11	1		4	3			
2	8			9[b]		7		6		5	10[a]	B		11	1	A	4	3			
2	8	A				7		6		5				11[a]	1	9	4	3			
2	8			9		7		6		5				11[a]	1		4	3		A	
2	8			9	A	7[a]		6		5				11	1		4	3			
2	8			9	A	7		6		5				11	1		4[a]	3			
2	8			9	A	7		6		5				11	1		4[a]	3			
2	8			9		7				5				11	1		4	3		6	
2	8			9	4	7				5				11	1			3		6	
2	8			9	4	7		6	11	5					1			3			
2	8				A	7		6[a]	11		9	5			1		4	3			
2	8			9		7			11[a]	5	A	6			1		4	3			
2	8			9	A	7				5		6		11	1		4[a]	3		B	
2		A			8				7	5	9			11	1	10	4[a]	3		6	
2				9	8	A			7	5	10			11[a]	1		4	3		6	
2		8		9					7	5	10			11	1		4	3		6	
2	8			9					7	5	10			11	1		4	3		6	
2	8			9		7[a]			A	5	10		1	11			4	3		6	
2	8				7				A	5	10			11	1	9	4[a]	3		6	
2	8			9	7				A	5	10			11[a]	1		4	3		6	
2	8			9		7				5	10			11	1		4	3		6	
2	8				A				7[a]	5	10			11	1	9	4	3		6	
2	8			A					7	5	10[a]			11	1	9	4	3		6	
				9	8				7	5		2		11	1	10	4	3		6	
	11			9	8[a]	7	5				B	2			1	10[b]	4	3		6	
	11[a]			9	8	7	5				A	2			1	10	4	3		6	
2	11			9	8[a]	7					10	5			1		4	3		6	
2	4			9	8	7			11[a]			5	1			A		3		6	
2	11[a]			9	8	7						5	1	A		10	4	3		6	
2	A			9	8	7						5	1	11		10	4[a]	3		6	
2	A			9[a]	8	7						5	1	11		10	4	3		6	
2	11				8	7					9	5	1			10[a]	4	3		6	
	11			9	8	7[a]	2				10	5	1				4	3		6	
	11	A		9	8[a]		2				10[b]	5	1	7			4	3		6	
	11	2		9[b]	8	B						5	1	7		A	4	3		6	
32	35	3	1	34	35	31	4	12	11	30	23	19	16	30	26	12	39	42	1	27	
	2	4		1	6	2			3		3	3		2		6				2	
	5			16		3		1	1	3	8	1		4		7	1	3			2
2	8			9		B			7	5	10		A	11[b]	1[a]		4	3		6	
1	1			1					1	1	1			1	1		1	1		1	
						1							1								
	1																				
2	8			9		7		6		5	10			11	1		4	3			
2	8	A				7[a]		6		5				11	1	9	4	3			
2	8			9	A	7		6		5				11	1		4[a]	3			
2	8			9		7[a]		6	11	5					1	A	4	3			
4	4			3		4		4	1	4	1			3	4	1	4	4			
		1			1											1					
	2			2		1			1					1							
37	40	3	1	39	19	35	4	16	13	35	25	19	16	34	31	13	44	47	1	28	
	2	5		1	7	3			3		3	3	1	2		7				2	
	8			18		4		1	2	3	8	1		5		7	1	3			2

stitutions are now listed as:

replaced by player A

replaced by player B

replaced by player C

1994-95

Premier League

	P	W	D	L	F	A	Pts
Blackburn Rovers	42	27	8	7	80	39	89
Manchester United	42	26	10	6	77	28	88
Nottingham Forest	42	22	11	9	72	43	77
Liverpool	42	21	11	10	65	37	74
Leeds United	42	20	13	9	59	38	73
Newcastle United	42	20	12	10	67	47	72
Tottenham Hotspur	42	16	14	12	66	58	62
Queen's Park Rangers	42	17	9	16	61	59	60
Wimbledon	42	15	11	16	48	65	56
Southampton	42	12	18	12	61	63	54
Chelsea	42	13	15	14	50	55	54
Arsenal	42	13	12	17	52	49	51
Sheffield Wednesday	42	13	12	17	49	57	51
West Ham United	42	13	11	18	44	48	50
Everton	42	11	17	14	44	51	50
Coventry City	42	12	14	16	44	62	50
Manchester City	42	12	13	17	53	64	49
Aston Villa	42	11	15	16	51	56	48
Crystal Palace	42	11	12	19	34	49	45
Norwich City	42	10	13	19	37	54	43
Leicester City	42	6	11	25	45	80	29
Ipswich Town	42	7	6	29	36	93	27

Attendances

	TOTAL		
	Home	**Away**	**Total**
League	306,596	498,708	805,304
Cup/Other	52,413	67,817	120,230
TOTAL	359,009	566,525	925,534

	AVERAGE		
	Home	**Away**	**Total**
League	14,600	23,748	19,174
Cup/Other	13,103	22,606	17,176
TOTAL	14,360	23,605	18,888

Match No.	Date		Opponents	Location	Result		Scorers	Atten
1	Aug	20	Manchester United	A	L	0-2		4
2		24	Sheffield Wednesday	H	W	3-2	Ferdinand, Sinclair, Gallen	1
3		27	Ipswich Town	H	L	1-2	Ferdinand	1
4		31	Leicester City	A	D	1-1	OG	1
5	Sep	10	Coventry City	H	D	2-2	Penrice (2)	1
6		17	Everton	A	D	2-2	Ferdinand (2)	2
7		24	Wimbledon	H	L	0-1		1
8	Oct	2	Nottingham Forest	A	L	2-3	Ferdinand, Allen	2
9		8	Tottenham Hotspur	A	D	1-1	Impey	2
10		15	Manchester City	H	L	1-2	Wilson	1
11		22	Norwich City	A	L	2-4	Barker, Gallen	1
12		29	Aston Villa	H	W	2-0	Dichio, Penrice	1
13		31	Liverpool	H	W	2-1	Sinclair, Ferdinand	1
14	Nov	5	Newcastle United	A	L	1-2	Dichio	3
15		19	Leeds United	H	W	3-2	Ferdinand (2), Gallen	1
16		26	Blackburn Rovers	A	L	0-4		2
17	Dec	4	West Ham United	H	W	2-1	Ferdinand, Sinclair	1
18		10	Manchester United	H	L	2-3	Ferdinand (2)	1
19		17	Sheffield Wednesday	A	W	2-0	Ferdinand, Maddix	2
20		26	Crystal Palace	A	D	0-0		1
21		28	Southampton	H	D	2-2	Barker, Gallen	1
22		31	Arsenal	A	W	3-1	Gallen, Allen, Impey	3
23	Jan	14	Aston Villa	A	L	1-2	Yates	2
24		24	Leeds United	A	L	0-4		2
25	Feb	4	Newcastle United	H	W	3-0	Ferdinand (2), Barker	1
26		11	Liverpool	A	D	1-1	Gallen	3
27		26	Nottingham Forest	H	D	1-1	Barker	1
28	Mar	4	Wimbledon	A	W	3-1	Ferdinand (2), Holloway	
29		8	Leicester City	H	W	2-0	McDonald, Wilson	1
30		15	Norwich City	H	W	2-0	Ferdinand, Gallen	1
31		18	Everton	H	L	2-3	Ferdinand, Gallen	1
32		22	Chelsea	H	W	1-0	Gallen	1
33	Apr	1	Coventry City	A	W	1-0	Sinclair	1
34		4	Blackburnm Rovers	H	L	0-1		1
35		8	Arsenal	H	W	3-1	Impey, Gallen, Ready	1
36		11	Ipswich Town	A	W	1-0	Ferdinand	1
37		15	Southampton	A	L	1-2	Ferdinand	1
38		17	Crystal Palace	H	L	0-1		1
39		29	Chelsea	A	L	0-1		2
40	May	3	West Ham United	A	D	0-0		2
41		6	Tottenham Hotspur	H	W	2-1	Ferdinand (2)	1
42		14	Manchester City	A	W	3-2	Ferdinand (2), Dichio	2

Appeara
Sub appeara
G

FA Cup

R3	Jan	7	Aylesbury	A*	W	4-0	Maddix, Ferdinand, Gallen, Meaker	1
R4		28	West Ham United	H	W	1-0	Impey	1
R5	Feb	18	Millwall	H	W	1-0	Wilson (pen)	1
R6	Mar	12	Manchester United	A	L	0-2		4

* Played at Home

Appearar
Sub appearar
G

League Cup

R2/1	Sep	20	Carlisle United	A	W	1-0	Ferdinand	
R2/2	Oct	5	Carlisle United	H	W	2-0	Allen, Wilson (pen)	
R3		25	Manchester City	H	L	3-4	Gallen, Sinclair, Penrice	1

Appeara
Sub appearar
G

Total - Appearar
Total - Sub appearar
Total - G

ardsley (2)	Barker (14)	Brevett (15)	Dichio (24)	Dykstra (13)	Ferdinand (9)	Gallen (20)	Hodge (25)	Holloway (8)	Impey (7)	Maddix (16)	McCarthy (18)	McDonald (6)	Meaker (22)	Penrice (12)	Ready (5)	Roberts (1)	Sinclair (11)	White (19)	Wilkins (26)	Wilson (3)	Yates (4)	OG
2	4				9a	10b		8	7	B		5		A		1	11			3	6	
2	4				9	10a		8	7	A		5				1	11			3	6	
2	4				9	10		8	7a			5		A		1	11			3	6	
2	4				9	A		8	7			5		10a		1	11			3	6	
2	4	3			9	A		8	7			5		10a		1	11				6	
2	4	3			9a			8	7			5		10	A	1				11	6	
2	4	3			9	A			7			5	11	10		1				8a	6	
2	4	3			9			8	7	10		5a				1	11				6	
2	4a				9			8	7	A		5				1	11			3	6	
2	4				9	A		8	7			5				1	11			3	6a	
2	4			1		10		8				5	7a				11	9		3	6	
2	4		9	1		10b	7	8a		A		5		B			11			3	6	
2	4			1	9	10	8		7			5					11			3	6	
2	4		A	1	9	10	8a		7			5					11			3	6	
	4			1	9	10	8a	A	7			5			2		11			3	6	
	4			1	9	10	8		7			5			2		11			3	6	
	4a			1	9	10	8	A	7	6		5					11			3	2	
2	4			1	9	10	8		7	6		5					11			3		
2	4			1	9	10	8	A	7	6		5					11a			3		
	4			1	9	10	8		7	6		5	A				11a			3	2	
	4	A		1	9	10	8		7a	6		5	11							3	2	
2	4				9a	10	8		7	6		5	11			1				3		
2					9	10	8	4	7	6	A		11			1				3a	5	
2		3			9	10b	8a	4	7	6	B		11			1	A				5	
2	4	3	A		9a	10		8	7	6		5				1	11					
2	4	11			9	10		8	7	6		5				1				3		
	4				9	10		8	7	6		5	11b	A	B	1				3	2a	
	4	11			9a	10		8	7	6		5		A	2	1				3		
	4		9			10a		8	7	6		5		A	2	1	11			3		
2	4				9	10		8	7	6		5				1	11			3		
2	4a				9	10		8	7	6		5		A		1	11			3		
2	4		9			10		8	7			5			6	1	11			3		
	4	3	9			10		8	7			5			6	1	11			2		
	4	3	A		9	10a		8	7			5			6	1	11			2		
	4	3			9	10a		8	7			5		A	6	1	11			2		
	4b	3			9	10a		8	7	B		5		A	6	1	11			2		
2		3			9	10a	8		7b	5				A	6	1	11		B	4		
2		3b	B		9			8	7	A		5		10	6a	1	11			4		
2		3			9	A	11		7	6		5		10		1			8a	4		
2	4	A			9	B		8	7	6		5		10b		1	11			3a		
2	4	3			9			8	7	6		5		10		1	11					
2	4	3	B		9	10b			7	6		5		8		1	11a				A	
0	37	17	4	11	37	31	15	28	40	21		39	7	9	11	31	32	1	1	36	22	
		2	5			6		3		6	2		1	10	2		1		1		1	
	4		3		24	10		1	3	1		1		3	1		4			2	1	1
2	4b				9	10a	8	B	7	6		5	11			1				3		
2	4		9			10		8	7	6		5				1	11				3	
2	4				9	10		8	7	6		5	11			1				3		
2	4	11a			9	10		8	7	6		5		A		1				3		
4	4	1	1		3	4	1	3	4	4		4	2			4	1			3	1	
								1						1								
					1	1			1	1			1							1		
2	4				9			8	7			5		10	A	1	11a			3	6	
2	4				9a	A		8	7			5				1	11			3	6	
2	4a		9	1		10		8				5	7	A			11			3	6	
3	3		1	1	2	1		3	2			3	1	1		2	3			3	3	
						1								1	1							
					1	1								1			1			1		
7	44	18	6	12	42	36	16	34	46	25		46	10	10	11	37	36	1	1	42	26	
		2	5			7		4		6	2		1	12	3		1		1		1	
	4		3		26	12		1	4	2		1	1	4	1		5			4	1	1

1995-96

Premiership

	P	W	D	L	F	A	Pts
Manchester United	38	25	7	6	73	35	82
Newcastle United	38	24	6	8	66	37	78
Liverpool	38	20	11	7	70	34	71
Aston Villa	38	18	9	11	52	35	63
Arsenal	38	17	12	9	49	32	63
Everton	38	17	10	11	64	44	61
Blackburn Rovers	38	18	7	13	61	47	61
Tottenham Hotspur	38	16	13	9	50	38	61
Nottingham Forest	38	15	13	10	50	54	58
West Ham United	38	14	9	15	43	52	51
Chelsea	38	12	14	12	46	44	50
Middlesbrough	38	11	10	17	35	50	43
Leeds United	38	12	7	19	40	57	43
Wimbledon	38	10	11	17	55	70	41
Sheffield Wednesday	38	10	10	18	48	61	40
Coventry City	38	8	14	16	42	60	38
Southampton	38	9	11	18	34	52	38
Manchester City	38	9	11	18	33	58	38
Queen's Park Rangers	38	9	6	23	38	57	33
Bolton Wanderers	38	8	5	25	39	71	29

Attendances

TOTAL	Home	Away	Total
League	297,775	509,575	807,350
Cup/Other	40,721	42,658	83,379
TOTAL	338,496	552,233	890,729

AVERAGE	Home	Away	Total
League	15,672	26,820	21,246
Cup/Other	13,574	14,219	13,897
TOTAL	15,386	25,102	20,244

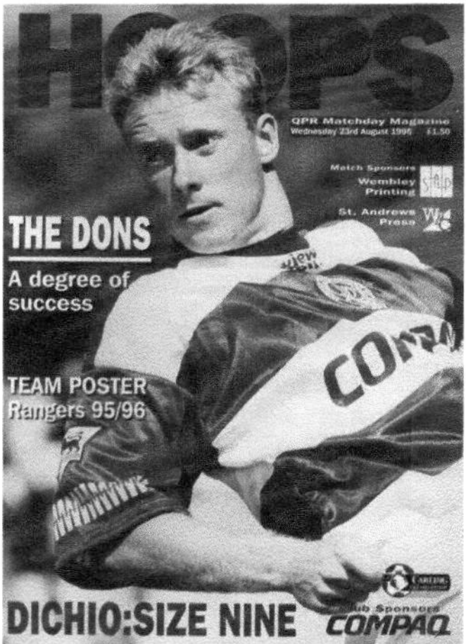

Match No.	Date		Opponents	Location	Result		Scorers	Atter
1	Aug	19	Blackburn Rovers	A	L	0-1		2
2		23	Wimbledon	H	L	0-3		1
3		26	Manchester City	H	W	1-0	Barker	1
4		30	Liverpool	A	L	0-1		3
5	Sep	9	Sheffield Wednesday	H	L	0-3		1
6		16	Leeds United	A	W	3-1	Dichio (2), Sinclair	3
7		25	Tottenham Hotspur	H	L	2-3	Dichio, Impey	1
8		30	Bolton Wanderers	A	W	1-0	Dichio	1
9	Oct	14	Newcastle United	H	L	2-3	Dichio (2)	1
10		21	Middlesbrough	A	L	0-1		2
11		28	Nottingham Forest	H	D	1-1	Sinclair	1
12	Nov	4	Southampton	A	L	0-2		1
13		19	Coventry City	H	D	1-1	Barker	1
14		22	Everton	A	L	0-2		3
15		25	West Ham United	A	L	0-1		2
16	Dec	2	Middlesbrough	H	D	1-1	McDonald	1
17		9	Tottenham Hotspur	A	L	0-1		2
18		16	Bolton Wanderers	H	W	2-1	Osborn, Impey	1
19		23	Aston Villa	H	W	1-0	Gallen	1
20		26	Arsenal	A	L	0-3		3
21		30	Manchester United	A	L	1-2	Dichio	4
22	Jan	2	Chelsea	H	L	1-2	Allen	1
23		13	Blackburn Rovers	H	L	0-1		1
24		20	Wimbledon	A	L	1-2	Hateley	
25	Feb	3	Manchester City	A	L	0-2		2
26		11	Liverpool	H	L	1-2	Dichio	1
27		17	Sheffield Wednesday	A	W	3-1	Barker (2), Goodridge	2
28	Mar	2	Arsenal	H	D	1-1	Gallen	1
29		6	Leeds United	H	L	1-2	Gallen	1
30		9	Aston Villa	A	L	2-4	Gallen, Dichio	2
31		16	Manchester United	H	D	1-1	OG (Irwin)	1
32		23	Chelsea	A	D	1-1	Barker	2
33		30	Southampton	H	W	3-0	Brevett, Dichio, Gallen	1
34	Apr	6	Newcastle United	A	L	1-2	Holloway	3
35		8	Everton	H	W	3-1	Impey, Hateley, Gallen	1
36		13	Coventry City	A	L	0-1		2
37		27	West Ham United	H	W	3-0	Ready, Gallen (2)	1
38	May	5	Nottingham Forest	A	L	0-3		2

Appeara
Sub appeara
G

FA Cup

R3	Jan	6	Tranmere Rovers	A	W	2-0	Sinclair, Quashie	1
R4		29	Chelsea	H	L	1-2	Quashie	1

Appeara
Sub appeara
G

League Cup

R2/1	Sep	19	Oxford United	A	D	1-1	Dichio	
R2/2	Oct	3	Oxford United	H	W	2-1 aet	Ready, Gallen	
R3		25	York City	H	W	3-1	Sinclair, Impey, Dichio	1
R4	Nov	29	Aston Villa	A	L	0-1		2

Appeara
Sub appeara
G

Total - Appeara
Total - Sub appeara
Total - G

Bardsley (2)	Barker (4)	Brazier (27)	Brevett (3)	Challis (24)	Charles (22)	Dichio (9)	Gallen (10)	Goodridge (18)	Hateley (26)	Holloway (8)	Impey (7)	Maddix (6)	McDonald (5)	Murray (30)	Osborn (15)	Penrice (12)	Plummer (29)	Quashie (19)	Ready (14)	Roberts (1)	Sinclair (11)	Sommer (25)	Wilkins (20)	Yates (21)	Zelic (16)	OG
2a	7		5			11	10			8	6	4	3		A					1	9					
2	7b		5			11	10			8	6	4	3a							1	9		B		A	
2	7		5			11	10a			8	6	4	3			A				1	9					
2	7		5			11	10				6	4	3			A				1	9		8a			
2	7		5a			11	10			8	6	4	3			A				1	9					
2	7		5			10				8		6	3		11				4		9	1				
	7		5			10				8	2	6	3		11a				4		9	1				
	7		5			10				8a	2	6	3		11				4		9	1	A			
	7		5			10		A		8	2	6			11a				4		9	1		3		
2	7		5a			10	A			8	11	6							4		9	1		3		
2	7c	A	5				10	B			11a	6			C				4b		9	1	8	3		
2	7		5			10	A					6							4a		9	1	8	3	11	
	7		5a	A		10	11				2	6							4		9b	1	B	3	8	
	7	9		5b		A	11				6	4	B						2		10a	1		3	8	
	7	6			A	10	9			8	2a	B	3						4			1	11b	5		
	7			2		A	10a		11	6	8		3						4		9	1		5		
2	7b			4	B		10a		11	6	8		3		A						9	1		5		
2	7			4b			A		11	6	8		3		10a				B		9	1		5		
2	7	A	5				10b		11c		8		3						C		9	1	6a	4		
2	7		5			A	10b		11	B	8		3								9	1	6a	4		
2b		6	5			A				7	8	3						11	B		9	1		4		
A		6		3		B				7	8	2						11b	4a		9	1		5		
2		6a		4				B	A		8b	C	3					11			9	1	7c	5		
2	7	6		4b		A		B	11				3					8			9	1		5		
	7	C		4		B	A		11b	6		2	3					8c			9	1		5		
2	7		3			11	10			6		4						8			9	1		5		
2	7		3				10b	A		6	11a	4						8			9	1		5		
2	7			3		A	10			6	11a							8	4		9	1		5		
2	7a	A		3		11	10b	B		6								8	4		9	1		5		
2	7		3			11	10	A		6								8a	4		9	1		5		
2	7		3			11b	10c		B	6	A		4					8a	C		9	1		5		
2	7	C	3			11	10b		B		8	6a	4						A		9	1		5c		
2	7		3			11	10			6	8		4								9	1		5		
2			3			11a	10		A	6	8		4								9	1	7	5		
2			3				10		11	6	8		4								9	1	7	5		
2	7		3				10		11a	6	8		4								9	1	A	5		
	6		3		A	11	10		7a				4						2		9	1	8	5		
2c	6		3		B	11	10						4a	7			A		C		9	1	8b	5		
28	33	6	27	10		22	26		10	26	28	20	25	1	5			11	16	5	37	33	11	30	3	
1		5		1	4	8	4	7	4	1	1	2	1		3	3	1		6				4		1	
	5		1			10	8	1	2	1	3		1		1				1		2					1

Bardsley (2)	Barker (4)	Brazier (27)	Brevett (3)	Challis (24)	Charles (22)	Dichio (9)	Gallen (10)	Goodridge (18)	Hateley (26)	Holloway (8)	Impey (7)	Maddix (6)	McDonald (5)	Murray (30)	Osborn (15)	Penrice (12)	Plummer (29)	Quashie (19)	Ready (14)	Roberts (1)	Sinclair (11)	Sommer (25)	Wilkins (20)	Yates (21)	Zelic (16)	OG
		6		2		C		B			8	A	3					11	4b		9	1	7	5a		
2a				4					11	6	8	A	3					7			9	1		5		
1		1		2					1	1	2		2					2	1		2	2	1	2		
						1		1				2														
																		2			1					

Bardsley (2)	Barker (4)	Brazier (27)	Brevett (3)	Challis (24)	Charles (22)	Dichio (9)	Gallen (10)	Goodridge (18)	Hateley (26)	Holloway (8)	Impey (7)	Maddix (6)	McDonald (5)	Murray (30)	Osborn (15)	Penrice (12)	Plummer (29)	Quashie (19)	Ready (14)	Roberts (1)	Sinclair (11)	Sommer (25)	Wilkins (20)	Yates (21)	Zelic (16)	OG
	7		5			10				8	2	6	3		11				4	1	9					
	7c	A	5			10	9	B		8	2	6	3b		11a				4	1			C			
2	7		5			10					11	6							4	1	9		8	3		
2	7	6					10a		A		8		3						4	1	9		11	5		
2	4	1	3			3	2			2	4	3	3		2				4	4	3		2	2		
		1						1	1														1			
						2	1				1								1		1					

Bardsley (2)	Barker (4)	Brazier (27)	Brevett (3)	Challis (24)	Charles (22)	Dichio (9)	Gallen (10)	Goodridge (18)	Hateley (26)	Holloway (8)	Impey (7)	Maddix (6)	McDonald (5)	Murray (30)	Osborn (15)	Penrice (12)	Plummer (29)	Quashie (19)	Ready (14)	Roberts (1)	Sinclair (11)	Sommer (25)	Wilkins (20)	Yates (21)	Zelic (16)	OG
31	37	8	30	12		25	28		11	29	34	23	30	1	7			13	21	9	42	35	14	34	3	
1		6		1	4	9	4	9	5	1	1	4	1		3	3	1		6				5		1	
	5		1			12	9	1	2	1	4		1		1			2	2		4					1

1996-97

Division One

	P	W	D	L	F	A	Pts
Bolton Wanderers	46	28	14	4	100	53	98
Barnsley	46	22	14	10	76	55	80
Wolverhampton W	46	22	10	14	68	51	76
Ipswich Town	46	20	14	12	68	50	74
Sheffield United	46	20	13	13	75	52	73
Crystal Palace	46	19	14	13	78	48	71
Portsmouth	46	20	8	18	59	53	68
Port Vale	46	17	16	13	58	55	67
Queen's Park Rangers	46	18	12	16	64	60	66
Birmingham City	46	17	15	14	52	48	66
Tranmere Rovers	46	17	14	15	63	56	65
Stoke City	46	18	10	18	51	57	64
Norwich City	46	17	12	17	63	68	63
Manchester City	46	17	10	19	59	60	61
Charlton Athletic	46	16	11	19	52	66	59
West Bromwich Albion	46	14	15	17	68	72	57
Oxford United	46	16	9	21	64	68	57
Reading	46	15	12	19	58	67	57
Swindon Town	46	15	9	22	52	71	54
Huddersfield Town	46	13	15	18	48	61	54
Bradford City	46	12	12	22	47	72	48
Grimsby Town	46	11	13	22	60	81	46
Oldham Athletic	46	10	13	23	51	66	43
Southend United	46	8	15	23	42	86	39

Attendances

TOTAL	Home	Away	Total
League	288,741	300,727	589,468
Cup/Other	33,069	42,052	75,121
TOTAL	321,810	342,779	664,589

AVERAGE	Home	Away	Total
League	12,554	13,075	12,815
Cup/Other	11,023	14,017	12,520
TOTAL	12,377	13,184	12,781

Match No.	Date		Opponents	Location	Result		Scorers	Atte
1	Aug	17	Oxford United	H	W	2-1	Gallen, Dichio	1
2		23	Portsmouth	A	W	2-1	Gallen (2)	
3		28	Wolverhampton	A	D	1-1	Dichio	2
4	Sep	1	Bolton Wanderers	H	L	1-2	McDonald	1
5		7	West Bromwich Albion	H	L	0-2		1
6		11	Norwich City	A	D	1-1	Impey	1
7		14	Barnsley	A	W	3-1	Dichio, Perry, Barker	1
8		21	Swindon Town	H	D	1-1	Murray	1
9		28	Birmingham City	A	D	0-0		1
10	Oct	2	Port Vale	H	L	1-2	Barker	
11		5	Grimsby Town	A	L	0-2		
12		12	Manchester City	H	D	2-2	Sinclair, Murray	1
13		16	Bradford City	H	W	1-0	Brazier	
14		20	Tranmere Rovers	A	W	3-2	Slade, McDonald, Charles	
15		26	Sheffield United	A	D	1-1	Slade	1
16		30	Ipswich Town	H	L	0-1		1
17	Nov	2	Stoke City	H	D	1-1	Sinclair	1
18		10	Crystal Palace	A	L	0-3		1
19		16	Charlton Athletic	H	L	1-2	Sinclair	1
20		23	Reading	A	L	1-2	Spencer	1
21		30	Sheffield United	H	W	1-0	Barker (pen)	1
22	Dec	7	Oldham Athletic	A	W	2-0	Spencer, Peacock	
23		14	Southend United	H	W	4-0	Barker (pen), OG (Harris), Spencer, Peacock	1
24		21	Huddersfield Town	A	W	2-1	Dichio, Brazier	1
25		26	Norwich City	H	W	3-2	Peacock, Dichio, McDermott	1
26		28	West Bromwich Albion	A	L	1-4	Spencer	1
27	Jan	11	Barnsley	H	W	3-1	Spencer (3)	1
28		19	Port Vale	A	D	4-4	OG (Holwyn), Impey, Murray, Spencer	
29		29	Birmingham City	H	D	1-1	Spencer	1
30	Feb	1	Crystal Palace	H	L	0-1		1
31		5	Swindon Town	A	D	1-1	Hateley	1
32		8	Ipswich Town	A	L	0-2		1
33		22	Stoke City	A	D	0-0		1
34	Mar	1	Oldham Athletic	H	L	0-1		1
35		4	Charlton Athletic	A	L	1-2	Dichio	1
36		8	Huddersfield Town	H	W	2-0	McDermott, Spencer	
37		12	Reading	H	L	0-2		1
38		15	Southend United	A	W	1-0	OG (Roget)	
39		22	Portsmouth	H	W	2-1	Murray, Spencer	1
40		29	Oxford United	A	W	3-2	Yates, Spencer, Peacock	
41		31	Wolverhampton	H	D	2-2	Spencer, Peacock	1
42	Apr	5	Bolton Wanderers	A	L	1-2	Morrow	1
43		12	Grimsby Town	H	W	3-0	Spencer, Murray, Slade	1
44		19	Manchester City	A	W	3-0	Spencer (2), Slade	2
45		26	Tranmere Rovers	H	W	2-0	Dichio, Spencer	1
46	May	4	Bradford City	A	L	0-3		1

Appeara
Sub appeara
G

FA Cup

R3	Jan	4	Huddersfield Town	H	D	1-1	Hateley	1
R3 rep		14	Huddersfield Town	A	W	2-1	Peacock, McDonald	1
R4		25	Barnsley	H	W	3-2	Spencer, Peacock, Sinclair	1
R5	Feb	15	Wimbledon	A	L	1-2	Hateley	2

Appeara
Sub appeara
G

League Cup

R2/1	Sep	18	Swindon Town	A	W	2-1	Dichio, Impey	7
R2/2		25	Swindon Town	H	L	1-3 aet	Brazier	6

Appeara
Sub appeara
G

Total - Appeara
Total - Sub appeara
Total - G

razier	Brevett	Challis	Charles	Dichio	Gallen	Graham M.	Hateley	Impey	Jackson	Maddix	Mahoney-Johnson	McDermott	McDonald	Morrow	Murray	Peacock	Perry	Plummer	Quashie	Ready	Roberts	Sinclair	Slade	Sommer	Spencer	Wilkins	Yates	OG
	3			12	10		9[a]						5							2		11		1		8	6	
	3			9	10[c]			7[a]	2	14			5		12							11		1		8	6	
	3			9				7	2				5		12							11	10	1		8[a]	6	
1	3			9					2				5		7				4			10	12	1		8[a]	6	
	3	7	12	9					2	14			5[c]		4[a]				8			11	10	1			6	
	3	7[b]		9				10	2				5		13				8			11		1			6	
3	3			9				10	2	14[b]			5		7		8					11		1			6[c]	
	3			9		12		10	2				5		8			6[a]				11		1				
	3			9		2							5		8			6	10			11		1				
	3			9		2					12		5				8[a]	6	10			11		1				
	3			9		8		10[a]		14	12		5					6[c]		2		11		1				
3	3		14			8		10					5		6				7[b]	2		11	9[c]	1				
	3		9			2							5		8					6		11	10	1				
	3		12	9[a]		2							5		8				14	6		11	10[c]	1				
	3			9[c]		2	14						5		8			12		6		11	10[a]	1				
	3					2	9	12					5		8					6		11	10[a]	1				
a	3			9		2		12					5		8					6		11	10	1				
	3		13	9		2		7					5		8					6		11	10[b]	1				
4	3		13	9[b]		2		7					5		8					6		11	10	1				
	3		9[a]	12				10		2			5			8				6	1	11			7			
	3		9[a]	12		2		10					5		13	8				6	1	11			7			
0	3		9[c]	14		2							5			8				6	1	11			7			
0	3			9			14					2	5			8				6	1	11			7[c]			
0	3			9								2	5			8				6	1	11			7			
0[b]	3			9				13		14		2	5[c]			8				6	1	11			7			
0	3			9				13		5		2				8				6	1	11[b]			7			
0	3			12		2	9[a]	14		13			5		4[b]	8				6	1	11[c]			7			
0[c]	3			12		2[b]	9[a]	14		13			5		4	8				6	1	11			7			
0	3			9				2		6			5		4	8						11		1	7			
0	3			9[a]			12	2		6			5		4	8						11		1				
	3						9	2		4			5			8				6		11		1	7			
4	3[c]					2	9						5			8				6		11		1	7		4	
	3		12	10[a]			9						5		7	8				6		11		1			2	
4	3						9			2			5		10	8				6		11		1	7			
	3[c]			9[a]			12	10		2			5		14	8				6		11		1	7			
			9					10		5		2				8				6		11		1	7			
b			9[a]				12	10		5		2	13			8				6		11		1	7			
	3			9				10		2			5			8				6		11		1	7			
	3			9				10		2			5		14	8				6		11[c]		1	7			
	3			9				10		2			5		11	8								1	7		6	
	3			9[c]				10		2			5		11	8			13				14	1	7		6	
	3			9[c]				10		2				6	11	8			13				14	1	7		5	
	3			9[b]		14		10		2				6	11	8[a]			13		1		12		7		5	
	3			9[c]				10		2				6	11	8			4		1		14		7		5	
	3			9[c]				10		2				6	11	8			4		1		14		7		5	
	3							10		2				6	11	8			4	12	1		9		7		5[a]	
2	44	2	6	31	2	16	8	26	7	18		6	38	5	26	27	2	4	9	28	13	39	11	33	25	4	16	
			6	6		2	5	6		7	2		1		6			1	4	1			6					
			1	7	3		1	2				2	2	1	5	5	1					3	4		17		1	3
0[c]	3			9[a]		2	12	14		5						8				6	1	11			7			
0	3			12		2	9						5		4	8				6	1	11			7[a]			
	3			9			12	10		2			5		4	8				6	1	11			7[a]			
	3[c]			14			9						5		10	8				6		11		1	7		2	
	4			2		2	2	1		2			3		3	4				4	3	4		1	4		1	
				2			2	1																				
							2						1			2						1			1			
	3			9		7		10					5		8			6				11		1				
	3		12	9		2		10[a]					5		8[c]			6	14			11		1				
	2			2		2		2					2		2			2				2		2				
			1																1									
				1				1																				
	50	2	6	35	2	20	10	29	7	20		6	43	5	31	31	2	6	9	32	16	45	11	36	29	4	17	
			7	8		2	7	7		7	2		1		6			1	5	1			6					
			1	8	3		3	3				2	3	1	5	7	1					4	4		18		1	3

1997-98

Division One

	P	W	D	L	F	A	Pts
Nottingham Forest	46	28	10	8	82	42	94
Middlesbrough	46	27	10	9	77	41	91
Sunderland	46	26	12	8	86	50	90
Charlton Athletic	46	26	10	10	80	49	88
Ipswich Town	46	23	14	9	77	43	83
Sheffield United	46	19	17	10	69	54	74
Birmingham City	46	19	17	10	60	35	74
Stockport County	46	19	8	19	71	69	65
Wolverhampton W	46	18	11	17	57	53	65
West Bromwich Albion	46	16	13	17	50	56	61
Crewe Alexandra	46	18	5	23	58	65	59
Oxford United	46	16	10	20	60	64	58
Bradford City	46	14	15	17	46	59	57
Tranmere Rovers	46	14	14	18	54	57	56
Norwich City	46	14	13	19	52	69	55
Huddersfield Town	46	14	11	21	50	72	53
Bury	46	11	19	16	42	58	52
Swindon Town	46	14	10	22	42	73	52
Port Vale	46	13	10	23	56	66	49
Portsmouth	46	13	10	23	51	63	49
Queen's Park Rangers	46	10	19	17	51	63	49
Manchester City	46	12	12	22	56	57	48
Stoke City	46	11	13	22	44	74	46
Reading	46	11	9	26	39	78	42

Attendances

	TOTAL		
	Home	Away	Total
League	300,908	352,462	653,370
Cup/Other	21,734	40,215	61,949
TOTAL	322,642	392,677	715,319

	AVERAGE		
	Home	Away	Total
League	13,083	15,324	14,204
Cup/Other	10,867	20,108	15,487
TOTAL	12,906	15,707	14,306

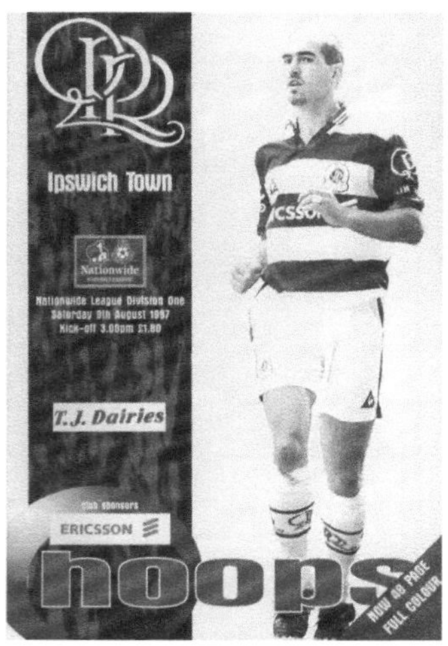

Match No.	Date		Opponents	Location	Result		Scorers	Atte
1	Aug	9	Ipswich Town	H	D	0-0		1
2		15	Tranmere Rovers	A	L	1-2	Peacock	
3		23	Stockport County	H	W	2-1	Sinclair (2)	1
4		30	Nottingham Forest	A	L	0-4		1
5	Sep	2	Reading	A	W	2-1	Spencer, OG (Swayne)	1
6		13	West Bromwich Albion	H	W	2-0	Sheron, Peacock	1
7		20	Crewe Alexandra	A	W	3-2	Spencer, Maddix, Sinclair	
8		24	Portsmouth	H	W	1-0	Spencer	1
9		27	Port Vale	A	L	0-2		
10	Oct	4	Charlton Athletic	H	L	2-4	Sheron (2)	1
11		18	Sheffield United	A	D	2-2	Murray, Morrow	1
12		21	Bury	A	D	1-1	Spencer	
13		26	Manchester City	H	W	2-0	Ready, Peacock (pen)	1
14		1	Birmingham City	H	D	1-1	Barker	1
15	Nov	5	Swindon Town	A	L	1-3	Peacock	1
16		8	Middlesbrough	A	L	0-3		3
17		15	Stoke City	H	D	1-1	Barker (pen)	1
18		22	Huddersfield Town	H	W	2-1	Quashie (2)	1
19		29	Wolverhampton Wanderers	A	L	2-3	Sheron, Peacock	2
20	Dec	3	Norwich City	H	D	1-1	Peacock	1
21		6	Sunderland	H	L	0-1		1
22		12	Oxford United	A	L	1-3	Peacock	
23		21	Bradford City	H	W	1-0	Peacock (pen)	
24		26	Portsmouth	A	L	1-3	Sheron	1
25		28	Reading	H	D	1-1	Spencer	1
26	Jan	10	Ipswich Town	A	D	0-0		1
27		17	Tranmere Rovers	H	D	0-0		1
28		24	Nottingham Forest	H	L	0-1		1
29		31	Stockport County	A	L	0-2		
30	Feb	7	Crewe Alexandra	H	W	3-2	Kennedy (2), Ready	1
31		14	West Bromwich Albion	A	D	1-1	Dowie	1
32		17	Charlton Athletic	A	D	1-1	Peacock (pen)	1
33		21	Port Vale	H	L	0-1		1
34		25	Sheffield United	H	D	2-2	Sheron, Ready	
35		28	Norwich City	A	D	0-0		1
36	Mar	4	Middlesbrough	H	W	5-0	OG (Vickers), Bruce, Gallen, Sheron (2)	1
37		7	Birmingham City	A	L	0-1		1
38		14	Swindon Town	H	L	1-2	Quashie	1
39		21	Stoke City	A	L	1-2	Barker (pen)	1
40		28	Huddersfield Town	A	D	1-1	Jones	1
41	Apr	1	Wolverhampton Wanderers	H	D	0-0		1
42		10	Sunderland	A	D	2-2	Sheron (2)	4
43		14	Oxford United	H	D	1-1	Gallen	1
44		19	Bradford City	A	D	1-1	Gallen	1
45		25	Manchester City	A	D	2-2	Sheron, OG (Pollock)	3
46	May	3	Bury	H	L	0-1		1

Appeara
Sub appeara
(

FA Cup

R3	Jan	3	Middlesbrough	H	D	2-2	Spencer, Gallen	1
rep		13	Middlesbrough	A	L	0-2		2

Appeara
Sub appeara
(

League Cup

R1/1	Aug	12	Wolverhampton Wanderers	H	L	0-2		
R1/2		27	Wolverhampton Wanderers	A	W	2-1	Peacock, Murray	1

Appeara
Sub appeara
(

Total - Appeara
Total - Sub appeara
Total - (

Bardsley	Barker	Brazier	Brevett	Bruce	Dowie	Gallen	Graham M.	Harper	Heinola	Jones	Kennedy	Kulcsar	Maddix	Mahoney-Johnson	Morrow	Murray	Peacock	Perry	Quashie	Ready	Roberts	Rose	Rowland	Ruddock	Scully	Sheron	Sinclair	Slade	Spencer	Yates	OG
	4	9[a]	3			10[c]		1					5[b]		6	11	8	13				2					12	14	7		
	4	12	3			10[c]		1							6	9	8	2				5					11[a]	14	7		
	4		3			9[a]		1					5		6	10[b]	8		13			2					11	12	7[c]	14	
	4[a]		3			14		1					5		6	9	8	7				2					11	10[c]		12	
			3					1					5		6	9	8		4			2				10	11		7		
			3					1					5		6	9	8		4	12		2[a]				10	11		7		
			3					1					5		6	9	8		4	2						10[a]	11	12	7		
			3					1					5		6[b]	9	8		4	2		13				10	11		7		
	14		3					1					5			9[c]	8		4[b]	6		2				10	11	13	7		
	14		3					1					5		6	9	8		4[c]			2				10	11	13	7[b]		
	11[a]		3					1					5		6	9	8			4		2[c]				10[b]	12	13	7	14	
	2		3					1					5		6	9	8			4						10	11		7		
	12		3					1					5		6	9[a]	8			4		2[c]				10[b]	11	13	7	14	
	9		3			13		1					5		6		8			4[a]		2				10	11		7[b]	12	
	7[c]	3				9[a]		1					5		6		8		14	4		2				10	11	12[b]		13	
	7[a]	3						1					5		6		8		9	4		2				10	11	12			
	4	3														9[c]	8	2	14	5	1					10	11		7	6	
	4	3[c]	14													9	8	2	7	5	1					10	11			6	
	4	3	14												6	9	8		7	5	1					10	11			2[c]	
	4[c]	3	14										2		6	9	8		7	5	1					10	11				
	4	14												13	3	2[c]	8		9	5	1					10[b]	11		7	6	
		13	3[b]										14			4	8	2[c]	9	5	1					10	11		7	6	
			3			14						4[a]	6			12	8		9	5	1					10[c]	11		7	2	
		3				14							6			9	8		4	5	1					10[c]	11		7	2	
			3										6			9	8		4	5	1					10	11		7	2	
			3			14							6			9	8		4	5	1					10	11		7[c]	2	
	11[c]		3	14		9		1							6	7	8		4	5						10[a]		12		2	
	11[a]		3			10[b]		1	13						6	9	8		4	5								12	7	2	
					9			1			11				6	10[a]	8		4	5			3			12			7	2	
					9	10[a]		1			11	14			6	7[c]	8		4	5			3			12				2	
					9	10[a]		1			11	4			6	7	8			5			3			12				2	
	4[b]				9	12		1	13		11				6	7	8			5			3			10[a]				2	
	4[a]			13	9	10[b]		1			11				6	7	8	14		5			3			12				2[c]	
2					9[a]	12		1			11	4			6[b]	7	8			5			3			10				13	
2					9			1	14		11	4			6	7[c]	8			5			3[b]			10				13	
2				14		10[a]		1	13		11	4			3			7[c]	8[b]	5						9		12		6	
2				11[a]		10		1	14			4	13		3[b]		8		7	5						9		12		6[c]	
2[c]				13[a]	9	10		1	14			4	6				8[b]		7	5						11		12		3	
	8				9[b]	13		1	14			4[a]	6		3					5					11	10		12		2[c]	
2	7				14	10[c]		1		4									8	5				6	11	9					
2					14	10		1		4					3[c]				8	5				6	11	9					
2						10[b]		1		4[a]		7							8	5		13		6	11	9		12			
2						10		1	13	4		7[a]							8[b]	5				6	11	9		12			
2						10		1		4		7[a]							8	5				6	11	9		12			
2						10		1	13	4			5				14		8			12		6[b]		9[a]		11[c]		7	
2						10		1	13	4[b]							8		9	5				6[a]	11			7		12	
12	20	8	20	1	9	19		36		7	8	11	23		31	31	38	6	30	38	10	13	7	7	7	36	24	3	22	21	
	3	3	3	4	2	8			10			1	2	1		1	1	2	3	1		3				4	2	19		9	
	3			1	1	3				1	2		1		1	1	9		3	3						11	3		5		3

Bardsley	Barker	Brazier	Brevett	Bruce	Dowie	Gallen	Graham M.	Harper	Heinola	Jones	Kennedy	Kulcsar	Maddix	Mahoney-Johnson	Morrow	Murray	Peacock	Perry	Quashie	Ready	Roberts	Rose	Rowland	Ruddock	Scully	Sheron	Sinclair	Slade	Spencer	Yates	OG
			3			15							5			9	8		4	6	1					10e	11	16	7d	2	
			3[c]	14		15		1							5	9	8		4	6						10e	11	16	7d	2	
			2					1					1		1	2	2		2	2	1					2	2		2	2	
				1		2																						2			
						1																							1		

Bardsley	Barker	Brazier	Brevett	Bruce	Dowie	Gallen	Graham M.	Harper	Heinola	Jones	Kennedy	Kulcsar	Maddix	Mahoney-Johnson	Morrow	Murray	Peacock	Perry	Quashie	Ready	Roberts	Rose	Rowland	Ruddock	Scully	Sheron	Sinclair	Slade	Spencer	Yates	OG
	4	12	3[a]			10[c]	13	1							6	9	8	2[b]				5					11	14	7		
	4		3			14		1					5		6	9	8	7				2					11	10[c]			
	2		2			1		2					1		2	2	2	2				2					2	1	1		
		1				1	1																					1			
																1	1														

Bardsley	Barker	Brazier	Brevett	Bruce	Dowie	Gallen	Graham M.	Harper	Heinola	Jones	Kennedy	Kulcsar	Maddix	Mahoney-Johnson	Morrow	Murray	Peacock	Perry	Quashie	Ready	Roberts	Rose	Rowland	Ruddock	Scully	Sheron	Sinclair	Slade	Spencer	Yates	OG
12	22	8	24	1	9	20		39		7	8	11	25		34	35	42	8	32	40	11	15	7	7	7	38	28	4	25	23	
	3	4	3	5	2	11	1		10			1	2	1		1	1	2	3	1		3				4	2	22		9	
	3			1	1	4				1	2		1		1	2	10		3	3						11	3		6		3

1998-99

Division One

	P	W	D	L	F	A	Pts
Sunderland	46	31	12	3	91	28	105
Bradford City	46	26	9	11	82	47	87
Ipswich Town	46	26	8	12	69	32	86
Birmingham City	46	23	12	11	66	37	81
Watford	46	21	14	11	65	56	77
Bolton Wanderers	46	20	16	10	78	59	76
Wolverhampton W	46	19	16	11	64	43	73
Sheffield United	46	18	13	15	71	66	67
Norwich City	46	15	17	14	62	61	62
Huddersfield Town	46	15	16	15	62	71	61
Grimsby Town	46	17	10	19	40	52	61
West Bromwich Albion	46	16	11	19	69	76	59
Barnsley	46	14	17	15	59	56	59
Crystal Palace	46	14	16	16	58	71	58
Tranmere Rovers	46	12	20	14	63	61	56
Stockport County	46	12	17	17	49	60	53
Swindon Town	46	13	11	22	59	81	50
Crewe Alexandra	46	12	12	22	54	78	48
Portsmouth	46	11	14	21	57	73	47
Queen's Park Rangers	46	12	11	23	52	61	47
Port Vale	46	13	8	25	45	75	47
Bury	46	10	17	19	35	60	47
Oxford United	46	10	14	22	48	71	44
Bristol City	46	9	15	22	57	80	42

Attendances

	TOTAL		
	Home	Away	Total
League	272,488	319,958	592,446
Cup/Other	23,234	15,417	38,651
TOTAL	295,722	335,375	631,097

	AVERAGE		
	Home	Away	Total
League	11,847	13,911	12,879
Cup/Other	7,745	7,709	7,730
TOTAL	11,374	13,415	12,374

Match No.	Date		Opponents	Location	Result		Scorers	Atten
1	Aug	8	Sunderland	A	L	0-1		41
2		15	Bristol City	H	D	1-1	Ready	13
3		22	Norwich City	A	L	2-4	Peacock (pen), Sheron	16
4		29	Bury	H	D	0-0		8
5		31	Portsmouth	A	L	0-3		12
6	Sep	8	Tranmere Rovers	H	D	0-0		8
7		12	Watford	A	L	1-2	Slade	14
8		19	Stockport County	H	W	2-0	Gallen (2)	8
9		26	Oxford United	A	L	1-4	Scully	7
10		29	Wolverhampton W.	A	W	2-1	Sheron (2)	20
11	Oct	3	Grimsby Town	H	L	1-2	Maddix	10
12		17	Huddersfield Town	A	L	0-2		14
13		21	West Bromwich Albion	A	L	0-2		11
14		25	Birmingham City	H	L	0-1		10
15		31	Swindon Town	A	L	1-3	Sheron	8
16	Nov	4	Barnsley	H	W	2-1	Langley, Gallen	8
17		7	Bolton Wanderers	H	W	2-0	Gallen, Sheron	11
18		14	Crewe Alexandra	A	W	2-0	Peacock, Sheron	5
19		21	Sheffield United	H	L	1-2	Peacock (pen)	12
20		28	Bradford City	A	W	3-0	Peacock, Gallen, Sheron	15
21	Dec	2	Ipswich Town	H	D	1-1	Gallen	12
22		5	Port Vale	H	W	3-2	Maddix, OG (Talbot), Sheron	10
23		12	Crewe Alexandra	H	L	0-1		11
24		19	Crystal Palace	A	D	1-1	Steiner	17
25		26	Norwich City	H	W	2-0	Murray, Peacock	15
26		28	Barnsley	A	L	0-1		14
27	Jan	9	Sunderland	H	D	2-2	Maddix, Gallen	17
28		16	Bury	A	D	1-1	Dowie	4
29		30	Portsmouth	H	D	1-1	Peacock	12
30	Feb	5	Bristol City	A	D	0-0		13
31		13	Tranmere Rovers	A	L	2-3	Maddix, Rowland	5
32		20	Watford	H	L	1-2	Peacock	14
33		27	Stockport County	A	D	0-0		7
34	Mar	3	Oxford United	H	W	1-0	Steiner	9
35		6	Wolverhampton W.	H	L	0-1		13
36		13	Bolton Wanderers	A	L	1-2	Rowland (pen)	17
37		20	Swindon Town	H	W	4-0	Steiner, Kiwomya (2), Rowland	11
38	Apr	3	Huddersfield Town	H	D	1-1	Baraclough	11
39		5	Ipswich Town	A	L	1-3	Kiwomya	22
40		10	West Bromwich Albion	H	W	2-1	Ready, Peacock	11
41		13	Grimsby Town	A	L	0-1		4
42		17	Sheffield United	A	L	0-2		14
43		20	Birmingham City	A	L	0-1		20
44		24	Bradford City	H	L	1-3	Gallen	11
45	May	1	Port Vale	A	L	0-2		9
46		9	Crystal Palace	H	W	6-0	Kulscar, Kiwomya (3), Scully, Breacker	18

Appearar
Sub appearar
G

FA Cup

R3	Jan	2	Huddersfield Town	H	L	0-1		11

Appearar
Sub appearar
G

League Cup

R1/1	Aug	11	Walsall	A	D	0-0		3
R1/2		26	Walsall	H	W	3-1 aet	Sheron, Slade, Maddix	5
R2/1	Sep	16	Charlton Athletic	H	L	0-2		6
R2/2		22	Charlton Athletic	A	L	0-1		11

Appearar
Sub appearar
G

Total - Appearar
Total - Sub appearar
Total - G

Breaker	Darlington	Dowie	Gallen	Graham R.	Harper	Heinola	Jeanne	Jones	Kiwomya	Kulscar	Langley	Linighan	Maddix	Miklosko	Morrow	Murray	Peacock	Perry	Plummer	Ready	Rose	Rowland	Scully	Sheron	Slade	Steiner	Yates	OG
			10		1	2							6			7	8			5		9	11		12		4[a]	
			10[c]		1	2							6			7	8			5		14	11	9	12		4[a]	
			10		1	2[b]							6			7	8			5	13	3	11	9	12		4[a]	
			10[c]		1				14				6			4	8			5	2		11	9	7			
			10		1				14				6			4	8			5[b]	2	13	11	9[c]	7			
		13	10		1	2		12					6			4	8			5			11[a]	9[b]	7			
			10		1	2		4					6			7	8			5			11	9[a]	12			
			10		1	2				9[c]			6			11	8			5			14		7		4	
			10		1	2[a]				9[b]			6			11[c]	8			5	13		12	14	7		4	
			10	13	1								6		7	2[b]	8			5	11			9	12		4[a]	
4			10	13									6	1	7	2[c]	8			5	11		14	9				
[a]			10										6	1	7	2[b]	8			5	11[c]	12	13	9	14			
			10		1								6		4		8			5	2	11[c]	7	9	14			
		14	10										6[b]	1	4	11	8			5	2	13[c]	7	12	9[a]			
			10[a]		1	2					13				6	8		7[b]		5	4	11	12	9				
		14	10			2					7[c]			1	6	8[a]	12			5	4[b]	11	13	9				
			10[c]			2				4	7			1	6		8			5		11		9		14		
			10			2				4	7			1	6		8				5	11		9				
			10			2[b]					7			1	6		8			5	4	11[c]	13	9		14		
			10			2					7		6	1	4		8			5	11[a]	12		9				
			10			2					7[b]		6	1	4	11	8[a]			5		12	13	9[c]		14		
			10			2							6	1	4[a]	8				5	7	11		9		12		
			10			2				3[b]			6	1	4	8				5	7[a]	11	13	9		12		
			10			2							6[c]	1	4	11[a]	8			5	7	14		9		12		
			10			2							6	1	4	11	8			5	7			9[a]		12		
		14	10			2							6	1	4	11[b]	8			5	7		13			9[c]		
		9	10			2			11				6	1	4		8			5	7							
		9	10			2[b]			11				6	1	4	13	8		5		7							
		9	10										6[a]	1	4	7	8		2	5	11[b]	12	13					
		9	10			2[c]			11[b]				6	1	4	14	8		7	5			13					
[c]		9	10										6	1	4	11[b]	8		7	5		12	13		14			
2		9	10				13						6	1	4[a]	11	8		12	5	7	3[b]						
2		9	10				11			7				1			8		6	5	4							
2			10				11[b]			7			6[a]	1		13	8		12	5	4					9		
2		12	10[c]				11		14	7[b]				1		13	8		6	5	4					9[a]		
2		13	9				10[c]		14		11			1		7			6[a]	5	4	12				8[b]		
2		13	12						11	5			6	1		7[a]	8				4	10				9[b]		
2		14	10[c]				13		11	4			6	1		7	8			12	5[a]	9[b]						
2		12					10		11	9		14	6	1	4[a]	7	8			5[c]								
2	4[a]		10[b]						11	9		3	6	1		7[c]	8			5		14			12			
2	9[c]		10						11	4[b]		3[a]	6	1		7	8			5		14			12			
2	4[a]	14	10[b]		1				11	9		12	6			7[c]	8			5		13						
2		14			1	4[b]	9[c]		11				6			13	8			5		7			10			
2		12	10		1		9[c]			4[a]		14	6			13	8			5		7[b]			11			
[b]	3		14				13		11	7[a]		6		1		9[c]	8		5			12			10			
2			12						11[a]	4		5	6	1		14	8					9[c]	7		10			
8	4	7	41		15	23	7	1	12	17	7	4	37	31	24	32	41	1	8	40	27	16	10	21	10	5	6	
		12	3	2			3	1	4		1	3				7			2	1	2	14	13	2	10	7		
		1	8						6	1	1		4			1	8			2		3	2	8	1	3		1
		12	10			2			15					1	4	11[a]	8			5	7	6			9d			
			1			1								1	1	1	1			1	1	1			1			
		1							1																			
			10[a]		1	2							6			7	8			5			11	9	12		4	
			10		1					15			6			7	8			5	2		11d	9	12		4[a]	
			10		1	2				16			6			4	8			5		11[a]	9e	12	7			
		14	10		1	2			15				6			9d	8			5			11[a]	12	7e		4	
			4		4	3							4			4	4			4	1	1	4	2	2		3	
		1							1	2														2	2			
													1											1	1			
8	4	7	46		19	27	7	1	12	17	7	4	41	32	25	37	46	1	8	45	29	18	14	23	13	5	9	
		14	3	2			3	1	6	2	1	3				7			2	1	2	14	13	4	12	7		
		1	8						6	1	1		5			1	8			2		3	2	9	2	3		1

1999-2000

Division One

	P	W	D	L	F	A	Pts
Charlton Athletic	46	27	10	9	79	45	91
Manchester City	46	26	11	9	78	40	89
Ipswich Town	46	25	12	9	71	42	87
Barnsley	46	24	10	12	88	67	82
Birmingham City	46	22	11	13	65	44	77
Bolton Wanderers	46	21	13	12	69	50	76
Wolverhampton W	46	21	11	14	64	48	74
Huddersfield Town	46	21	11	14	62	49	74
Fulham	46	17	16	13	49	41	67
Queen's Park Rangers	46	16	18	12	62	53	66
Blackburn Rovers	46	15	17	14	55	51	62
Norwich City	46	14	15	17	45	50	57
Tranmere Rovers	46	15	12	19	57	68	57
Nottingham Forest	46	14	14	18	53	55	56
Crystal Palace	46	13	15	18	57	67	54
Sheffield United	46	13	15	18	59	71	54
Stockport County	46	13	15	18	55	67	54
Portsmouth	46	13	12	21	55	66	51
Crewe Alexandra	46	14	9	23	46	67	51
Grimsby Town	46	13	12	21	41	67	51
West Bromwich Albion	46	10	19	17	43	60	49
Walsall	46	11	13	22	52	77	46
Port Vale	46	7	15	24	48	69	36
Swindon Town	46	8	12	26	38	77	36

Attendances

TOTAL

	Home	Away	Total
League	289,536	318,171	607,707
Cup/Other	15,028	27,732	42,760
TOTAL	304,564	345,903	650,467

AVERAGE

	Home	Away	Total
League	12,589	13,834	13,211
Cup/Other	7,514	9,244	8,552
TOTAL	12,183	13,304	12,754

Match No.	Date		Opponents	Location	Result		Scorers
1	Aug	7	Huddersfield Town	H	W	3-1	Darlington, Kiwomya, Peacock
2		14	Bolton Wanderers	A	L	1-2	Peacock (pen)
3		21	Wolverhampton W.	H	D	1-1	Peacock
4		28	Nottingham Forest	A	D	1-1	Ready
5		31	Port Vale	H	W	3-2	Wardley (2), Kiwomya
6	Sep	18	Fulham	A	L	0-1	
7		25	Birmingham City	A	L	0-2	
8	Oct	2	Blackburn Rovers	H	D	0-0	
9		9	Tranmere Rovers	H	W	2-1	Steiner, Peacock
10		16	Ipswich Town	A	W	4-1	Peacock, Wardley, Steiner (2)
11		19	West Bromwich Albion	A	W	1-0	Wardley
12		23	Portsmouth	H	D	0-0	
13		27	Birmingham City	H	D	2-2	Kiwomya, Steiner
14		30	Blackburn Rovers	A	W	2-0	Wardley, Gallen
15	Nov	2	Stockport County	A	D	3-3	Maddix, Gallen (2)
16		6	Manchester City	H	D	1-1	Kiwomya
17		14	Crystal Palace	A	L	0-3	
18		20	Walsall	H	W	2-1	Wardley, Kiwomya
19		23	Grimsby Town	A	L	1-2	Kiwomya
20		27	Barnsley	H	D	2-2	Darlington, Steiner
21		30	Sheffield United	H	W	3-1	Steiner, Wardley, Breacker
22	Dec	4	Huddersfield Town	A	L	0-1	
23		18	Charlton Athletic	H	D	0-0	
24		26	Norwich City	A	L	1-2	Wardley
25		28	Crewe Alexandra	H	W	1-0	Wardley
26	Jan	3	Swindon Town	A	W	1-0	Langley
27		15	Bolton Wanderers	H	L	0-1	
28		22	Wolverhampton W.	A	L	2-3	Peacock, Slade
29		29	Nottingham Forest	H	D	1-1	Kiwomya
30	FEb	5	Port Vale	A	D	1-1	Wardley
31		12	Stockport County	H	D	1-1	Kiwomya
32		19	Barnsley	A	D	1-1	Rose
33		28	Fulham	H	D	0-0	
34	Mar	5	Sheffield United	A	D	1-1	Beck
35		8	Manchester City	A	W	3-1	Kiwomya, OG (Wiekens), Beck (pen)
36		11	Grimsby Town	H	W	1-0	Beck (pen)
37		18	Walsall	A	W	3-2	OG (Larusson), Wardley, Kiwomya
38		22	Crystal Palace	H	L	0-1	
39		25	Norwich City	H	D	2-2	Kiwomya (2)
40		31	Charlton Athletic	A	L	1-2	Taylor
41	Apr	8	Swindon Town	H	W	2-1	Ready, Beck (pen)
42		15	Crewe Alexandra	A	L	1-2	Langley
43		22	Ipswich Town	H	W	3-1	Peacock, Koejoe, Kiwomya
44		24	Tranmere Rovers	A	D	1-1	Peacock (pen)
45		29	West Bromwich Albion	H	D	0-0	
46	May	7	Portsmouth	A	W	3-1	Langley, Gallen, OG (Myers)

Appeara
Sub appeara
G

FA Cup

R3	Dec	11	Torquay United	H	D	1-1	Wardley
rep		21	Torquay United	A	W	3-2	Wardley (2), Kiwomya
R4	Jan	8	Charlton Athletic	A	L	0-1	

Appeara
Sub appeara
G

League Cup

R1/1	Aug	10	Cardiff City	A	W	2-1	Langley, Peacock
R1/2		25	Cardiff City	H	L	1-2*	Peacock (pen)

* (Lost 2-3 on penalties)

Appeara
Sub appeara
G

Total - Appeara
Total - Sub appeara
Total - G

Baraclough (3)	Beck (36)	Breacker (2)	Bruce (30)	Darlington (22)	Dowie (25)	Gallen (10)	Harper (13)	Jeanne (23)	Kiwomya (11)	Koejoe (31)	Kulscar (15)	Langley (21)	Maddix (6)	McGovern (35)	Miklosko (1)	Morrow (4)	Murray (7)	Peacock (8)	Perry (24)	Plummer (17)	Ready (5)	Rose (12)	Rowland (16)	Scully (20)	Slade (18)	Steiner (9)	Taylor (37)	Ward (32)	Wardley (27)	Weare (29)	OG
3		2		11[a]		B			10[b]			7[c]	6		1	4		8				5	C			9			A		
3		2[b]		11		A			10			7[a]	6		1	4		8				5		B		9					
3		2[b]				9			10			7	6		1	4[a]		8			5	11		A	B						
3				11		9			10[a]			7[b]	6		1			8			5	2	B	A					4		
3				11		10[a]			A			7[b]	6		1	B		8			5	2				9			4		
3						A			10[a]			7	6		1			8			5	2		11		9			4		
3				11[a]		C	B		10			7[c]	6		1[b]			8			5	2		A		9			4		
3				11		9[a]	1	B	10			7[b]	6					8			5	2			A				4		
3				11[c]		C	1[a]		10			7[b]	6					8			5	2	B			9			4		
3		2		11[b]		B	1		10			7	6[c]				C	8[a]			5		A			9			4		
3		2		11[b]		B	1		10			7	6				A	8[a]			5					9			4		
3		2		11			1		10			7	6								5	8				9			4		
3		2		11			1		10			7[a]	6				A				5	8				9			4		
3				11		A	1		10			B	6				7				5	8	2[b]			9[a]			4		
3				11		A	1		10			B	6				7				5	8[a]	2[b]			9			4		
3				11		A	1		10			B	6				7				5	2[a]	8[b]			9			4		
3		C		11		A[c]	1		10				6				7[b]	B			5	2[a]	8			9			4		
3		5		11			1		10[b]			7[a]				6		8				2	A			9			4	B	
3		5		11			1		10							6		8		2			7[a]			9			4	A	
3		5		11			1		10		8	C				6[a]	7[c]			A		2				9			4[b]	B	
3		5		11		10	1				8						7[b]			6		2[c]	B	C		9[a]			4	A	
3		5		11		10[c]	1		C	B	8[a]	A					7			6		2				9[b]			4		
		5	2	11			1		10		A	8[a]					7			6						9		3	4		
3		5		11		A			10			8			1		7[a]			6						9		2	4		
3		5[b]		11[a]		B	1		10[c]		C	8		A			7			6						9		2	4		
3			11			10	1					8		5			7			6						9		2	4		
3			5[b]	11			1		10	A	8[a]			B			7			6						9		2	4		
3			5[a]	11			1		10	9[c]		6		8			7[b]	A					C		B			2	4		
3			C				1		10	B		7[c]		5[a]				8			A	6		11[b]	9			2	4		
3				11			1		10	B		7[a]						8			5	6	A		9[b]			2	4		
3	A			11		C	1		10			7[b]						8			5	6	B		9[c]			2[a]	4		
3	9[b]			11			1		10[a]		7						A	8			5	6			B			2	4		
3	9			11			1		10[b]		C	7[c]					A	8			5	6[a]			B			2	4		
3	9[b]			11[a]		B	1		10[c]			7					4	8		6	5		A		C			2			
3	9			11			1		10			7[b]					4	8[a]		6	5	B						2	A		
3	9			11		A	1		10			7[a]					8[b]			6	5	B						2	4		
3	9[c]			11[b]			1		10		B	7					8		A	6[a]	5	2					C		4		
3	9					C	1		10		A	7[c]					8[b]		11	6[a]	5	2					B		4		
3	9[c]					C	1	6[b]	10			7					8	B	11		5	2[a]					A		4		
3	9[a]		2	11[c]		C	1		10			7					8[b]	B	6		5						A		4		
3	9		2[a]				1		10	B	C	7					A	8	11		5						6[b]		4[c]		
3			2[b]			B	1		10	A		7[c]					9	8	11		5			C			6[a]		4		
3			2[b]			A	1		10	9[a]	B	7						8	11	6	5								4		
3			2[b]			A			10	9[a]		7			1		B	8	11	6	5								4		
3			2[b]			A	1		10	9[a]		7					B	8	11	6	5								4		
3			2[b]			C	1		10[c]	9	B	7					A	8	11	6	5								4		
45	10	15	11	34		7	37	1	42	5	5	36	17	3	9	6	21	26	9	17	32	27	5	2	3	24	2	14	41		
	1	1	1			24	1	1	2	6	8	5		2		1	9	4	1	1	1	2	10	6	6		4		2	4	
	4	1		2		4			13	1		3	1					8			2	1			1	6	1		11		3

Baraclough (3)	Beck (36)	Breacker (2)	Bruce (30)	Darlington (22)	Dowie (25)	Gallen (10)	Harper (13)	Jeanne (23)	Kiwomya (11)	Koejoe (31)	Kulscar (15)	Langley (21)	Maddix (6)	McGovern (35)	Miklosko (1)	Morrow (4)	Murray (7)	Peacock (8)	Perry (24)	Plummer (17)	Ready (5)	Rose (12)	Rowland (16)	Scully (20)	Slade (18)	Steiner (9)	Taylor (37)	Ward (32)	Wardley (27)	Weare (29)	OG
3		5	2	11			1[a]		10[b]	B		8			A		7			6						9			4		
		5	2	11			1[a]		10	9[b]	3	8			A		7			6									4	B	
3			5	11[c]	A	10[a]	1					8					7[b]			6			C	B		9		2	4		
2		2	3	3		1	3		2	1	1	3					3			3						2		1	3		
					1					1					2								1	1						1	
									1																				3		

Baraclough (3)	Beck (36)	Breacker (2)	Bruce (30)	Darlington (22)	Dowie (25)	Gallen (10)	Harper (13)	Jeanne (23)	Kiwomya (11)	Koejoe (31)	Kulscar (15)	Langley (21)	Maddix (6)	McGovern (35)	Miklosko (1)	Morrow (4)	Murray (7)	Peacock (8)	Perry (24)	Plummer (17)	Ready (5)	Rose (12)	Rowland (16)	Scully (20)	Slade (18)	Steiner (9)	Taylor (37)	Ward (32)	Wardley (27)	Weare (29)	OG
3		2		11		B	A		10[b]			7	6		1[a]	4		8				5				9					
3		2[a]				9[b]			10			7	6		1	4[c]		8			5	11	C	A	B						
2		2		1		1			2			2	2		2	2		2			1	2				1					
						1	1																1	1	1						
												1						2													

Baraclough (3)	Beck (36)	Breacker (2)	Bruce (30)	Darlington (22)	Dowie (25)	Gallen (10)	Harper (13)	Jeanne (23)	Kiwomya (11)	Koejoe (31)	Kulscar (15)	Langley (21)	Maddix (6)	McGovern (35)	Miklosko (1)	Morrow (4)	Murray (7)	Peacock (8)	Perry (24)	Plummer (17)	Ready (5)	Rose (12)	Rowland (16)	Scully (20)	Slade (18)	Steiner (9)	Taylor (37)	Ward (32)	Wardley (27)	Weare (29)	OG
49	10	19	14	38		9	40	1	46	6	6	41	19	3	11	8	24	28	9	20	33	29	5	2	3	27	2	15	44		
	1	1	1		1	25	2	1	2	7	8	5		2	2	1	9	4	1	1	1	2	12	8	7		4		2	5	
	4	1		2		4			14	1		4	1					10			2	1			1	6	1		14		3

2000-01

Division One

	P	W	D	L	F	A	Pts
Fulham	46	30	11	5	90	32	101
Blackburn Rovers	46	26	13	7	76	39	91
Bolton Wanderers	46	24	15	7	76	45	87
Preston North End	46	23	9	14	64	52	78
Birmingham City	46	23	9	14	59	48	78
West Bromwich Albion	46	21	11	14	60	52	74
Burnley	46	21	9	16	50	54	72
Wimbledon	46	17	18	11	71	50	69
Watford	46	20	9	17	76	67	69
Sheffield United	46	19	11	16	52	49	68
Nottingham Forest	46	20	8	18	55	53	68
Wolverhampton W	46	14	13	19	45	48	55
Gillingham	46	13	16	17	61	66	55
Crewe Alexandra	46	15	10	21	47	62	55
Norwich City	46	14	12	20	46	58	54
Barnsley	46	15	9	22	49	62	54
Sheffield Wednesday	46	15	8	23	52	71	53
Grimsby Town	46	14	10	22	43	62	52
Stockport County	46	11	18	17	58	65	51
Portsmouth	46	10	19	17	47	59	49
Crystal Palace	46	12	13	21	57	70	49
Huddersfield Town	46	11	15	20	48	57	48
Queen's Park Rangers	46	7	19	20	45	75	40
Tranmere Rovers	46	9	11	26	46	77	38

Attendances

TOTAL	Home	Away	Total
League	276,279	322,204	598,483
Cup/Other	37,440	12,577	50,017
TOTAL	313,719	334,781	648,500

AVERAGE	Home	Away	Total
League	12,012	14,009	13,011
Cup/Other	12,480	6,289	10,003
TOTAL	12,066	13,391	12,716

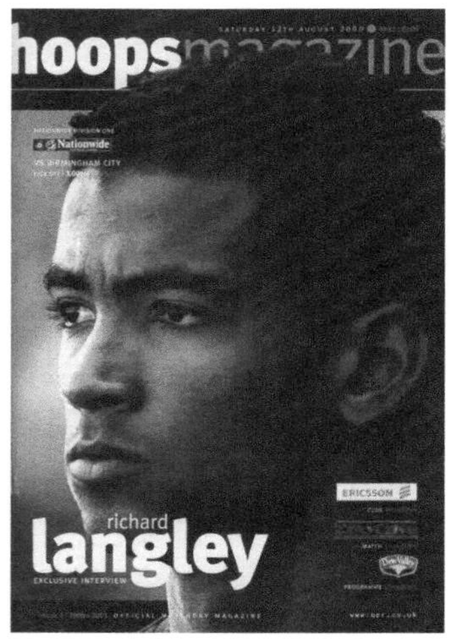

Match No.	Date		Opponents	Location	Result		Scorers	Attend
1	Aug	12	Birmingham City	H	D	0-0		13,
2		20	Crystal Palace	A	D	1-1	Carlisle	19
3		26	Crewe Alexandra	H	W	1-0	Furlong	9
4		28	West Bromwich Albion	A	L	1-2	Kiwomya	14
5	Sep	9	Preston North End	H	D	0-0		11
6		13	Gillingham	H	D	2-2	Crouch, Kiwomya	10
7		16	Barnsley	A	L	2-4	Kiwomya (2)	12,
8		23	Wimbledon	H	W	2-1	Wardley, Crouch	11
9		30	Sheffield United	A	D	1-1	Koejoe	13
10	Oct	14	Watford	A	L	1-3	Connolly	17,
11		17	Grimsby Town	A	L	1-3	Connolly	4,
12		21	Burnley	H	L	0-1		11
13		25	Sheffield Wednesday	H	L	1-2	Peacock (pen)	10
14		28	Tranmere Rovers	A	D	1-1	Connolly	7
15		31	Bolton Wanderers	A	L	1-3	Crouch	10,
16	Nov	4	Portsmouth	H	D	1-1	Peschisolido	12
17		11	Stockport County	A	D	2-2	Carlisle, Langley	6
18		18	Huddersfield Town	H	D	1-1	Connolly	11
19		25	Wolverhampton W.	H	D	2-2	Peacock (2)	11
20	Dec	2	Sheffield Wednesday	A	L	2-5	Crouch (2)	21
21		9	Blackburn Rovers	A	D	0-0		16
22		16	Nottingham Forest	H	W	1-0	Crouch	14,
23		23	Birmingham City	A	D	0-0		24
24		26	Norwich City	H	L	2-3	Carlisle, Wardley	12
25		30	Crystal Palace	H	D	1-1	Crouch	14,
26	Jan	13	West Bromwich Albion	H	W	2-0	Plummer, Koejoe	11
27		20	Norwich City	A	L	0-1		16
28		31	Fulham	H	L	0-2		16
29	Feb	3	Bolton Wanderers	H	D	1-1	Ngonge	10
30		10	Preston North End	A	L	0-5		14
31		17	Barnsley	H	W	2-0	Kiwomya, Crouch	9
32		20	Gillingham	A	W	1-0	Kiwomya	10,
33		24	Wimbledon	A	L	0-5		9
34	Mar	3	Sheffield United	H	L	1-3	Ngonge	11
35		7	Watford	H	D	1-1	Ngonge (pen)	12,
36		10	Fulham	A	L	0-2		16
37		17	Grimsby Town	H	L	0-1		17
38		24	Burnley	A	L	1-2	Bignot	14
39		31	Nottingham Forest	A	D	1-1	Wardley	22
40	Apr	7	Blackburn Rovers	H	L	1-3	Plummer	12
41		10	Crewe Alexandra	A	D	2-2	Crouch, Thomson	6
42		14	Portsmouth	A	D	1-1	Thomson	13
43		16	Tranmere Rovers	H	W	2-0	Thomson, Crouch	9
44		21	Huddersfield Town	A	L	1-2	Thomson	12
45		28	Stockport County	H	L	0-3		10
46	May	6	Wolverhampton W.	A	D	1-1	Bruce	17,

Appearan
Sub appearan
G

FA Cup

R3	Jan	6	Luton Town	A	D	3-3	Crouch (2), Peacock (pen)	8
rep		17	Luton Town	H	W	2-1 aet	Kiwomya (2)	14
R4		27	Arsenal	H	L	0-6		19

Appearan
Sub appearan
G

League Cup

R1/1	Aug	23	Colchester United	A	W	1-0	Kiwomya	3
R1/2	Sep	6	Colchester United	H	L	1-4	Kiwomya	4

Appearan
Sub appearan
G

Total - Appearan
Total - Sub appearan
Total - G

Bignot (23)	Breacker (2)	Broomes (36)	Brown (33)	Bruce (30)	Bubb (nn)	Burgess (37)	Carlisle (18)	Cochrane (40)	Connolly (10)	Crouch (28)	Darlington (22)	Dowie (25)	Furlong (33)	Harper (13)	Heinola (14)	Higgins (25)	Kiwomya (11)	Knight (14)	Koejoe (31)	Kulcsar (15)	Langley (21)	Lisbie (38)	Maddix (6)	McFlynn (35)	Miklosko (1)	Morrow (4)	Murray (7)	Ngonge (9)	Pacquette (38)	Peacock (8)	Perry (24)	Peschisolido (37)	Plummer (17)	Ready (5)	Rose (12)	Rowland (16)	Scully (20)	Thomson (36)	Walshe (39)	Wardley (27)	Warren (19)
							3			10	2			1			11				7					4				9	A			5						8	
							3		A	B			10[b]	1			11[a]				7					4				9	2			5						8	
							3						10	1	B		11				7					4				9	2			5[a]						8	A
	B						3		C	A	6[b]		10[a]	1			11				7					4					2[c]		5							8	9
							3			B	6			1			11		10[b]		7					A					2		5[a]		4	9				8	
							3			A	2			1			11		10		7					5[a]									4	9				8	6
	A						3			10	2			1			11		B		7					5[a]									4[b]	9				8	6
	5						3			10[c]	6			1			11		A	C	7					4					2[b]					9[a]				8	B
	5[a]						3			10	2			1			11		9	7						4					A									8	6
							3		A	10	2			1					11	7[a]	8					4				B	6[b]									9	5
							3		11	10	2			1					9		8					4				7	5[a]									A	6
							3		11	10	2			1					B		9[b]						A			8	5[a]				4					7	6
		5					3		9	10	2[a]			1			11		B		7									8	A[b]				4						6
		5					3		9	10				1			11		B		7[c]									8	2[b]			A	4					C	6[a]
	2	5					3		11	10				1					A		9[b]					7[a]				8					4					B	6
	2	5					3		9[a]	10				1							8									7		11			4					A	6
	2	5[c]					3		9[a]	10				1					B		8					A				7		11		C	4						6[b]
	2								9	10											8				1	5				7		11		3	4						A
	2						3		9	10									A		8				1					7		11[b]		5[a]	4					B	6
	2						3[b]		9[a]	10									A			B			1	8				7		11		5	4						6[c]
							3		A		2								10		8	11[a]			1					7			5		4					9	
							3		9[b]	10	2								A		8				1	B		11[a]					5		4					7	
							3			10	2								B	9[c]	8				1	4		11[b]			A		5[a]							7	C
							3		B	10	2						A				8				1	7[b]		11[a]					5		4					9	
							3		9	10	2								11		8				1						A		5		4					7[a]	
							3		9[a]	10	6						B		11[b]		7				1	A				8	2		5								
							3			10	6						11		A		7				1	8[a]		B			2[b]		5							9	
				A			3[a]		9	10[c]							11			B	7[b]				1			C		8	2		5		4						
									9	10[a]	2	A								7					1	4		11		8					3					6	
									9[b]		2						11			7					1	4[a]		10		8				A	3		B			6	
									9[b]	10	5						11			7					1					8	2		B	4	3[a]					6	
										10	6						11[b]			8					1	B				9	2[a]		5	4	3					7	
										10	6						11			8					1			A		9	2[a]		5	4	3					7	
									C	10										9[a]					1	A	B	11		8	2		5[c]	3	4					7[b]	6
										10	9[b]			1			A						C				8	11[a]		7	2		3[c]	4			6				B
										10	9			1			A	11[b]		C							7[a]			8	2		5	3	4[c]						B
A										10	9			1			11	6									7[a]			8	2		3	4							
8			3							10[b]	9			1			11[a]	6		C			4				7[c]	B			2							A			
7			4[b]	A						10	9			1			11	6												8[c]	2[a]		3	B						C	
2				6		A				10[b]				1				B	C											9			5[c]	3	8			11		7	
2				6[c]						10				1			A	7[b]		C								B		9			5	3	8			11[a]			
2				6						10	B			1				7												9			5	3	8[a]			11		A	
7				9						10	2			1				6										A		8			4	3				11[a]			
7										10	9			1			A	6[a]											B	8	2[b]		4	3				11		C	
7[a]								C			9			1				6						A					10		2		3					11	B	8[c]	5[b]
				9	C					10	2			1		B		6[a]						7							A		4	3				11[c]		8	
8	8	5	2	5			27		17	38	32		3	29			20	10	8	9	26	1	1	1	17	18	4	7	1	31	23	5	24	19	27	4	1	7		26	16
1	2			2	1	1		1	6	4	1	1			1	1	6	1	13	5		1	1	1		6	2	6	1	1	6		1	4			1	1	1	8	6
1				1			3		4	10			1				6		2		1							3		3		1	2					4		3	

Bignot (23)	Breacker (2)	Broomes (36)	Brown (33)	Bruce (30)	Bubb (nn)	Burgess (37)	Carlisle (18)	Cochrane (40)	Connolly (10)	Crouch (28)	Darlington (22)	Dowie (25)	Furlong (33)	Harper (13)	Heinola (14)	Higgins (25)	Kiwomya (11)	Knight (14)	Koejoe (31)	Kulcsar (15)	Langley (21)	Lisbie (38)	Maddix (6)	McFlynn (35)	Miklosko (1)	Morrow (4)	Murray (7)	Ngonge (9)	Pacquette (38)	Peacock (8)	Perry (24)	Peschisolido (37)	Plummer (17)	Ready (5)	Rose (12)	Rowland (16)	Scully (20)	Thomson (36)	Walshe (39)	Wardley (27)	Warren (19)
							3		9	10	2								11	8[b]	7				1	4[a]				B			5							A	
							3		9[b]	10	6						A		11[c]		7				1			B			2		5[a]		8					C	
							3		A	10	2						11		B[c]		7				1			C		8	9[a]		5[b]		4						
							3		2	3	3						1		2	1	3				3	1				1	2		3		2						
									1								1		1									2		1										2	
										2							2													1											

Bignot (23)	Breacker (2)	Broomes (36)	Brown (33)	Bruce (30)	Bubb (nn)	Burgess (37)	Carlisle (18)	Cochrane (40)	Connolly (10)	Crouch (28)	Darlington (22)	Dowie (25)	Furlong (33)	Harper (13)	Heinola (14)	Higgins (25)	Kiwomya (11)	Knight (14)	Koejoe (31)	Kulcsar (15)	Langley (21)	Lisbie (38)	Maddix (6)	McFlynn (35)	Miklosko (1)	Morrow (4)	Murray (7)	Ngonge (9)	Pacquette (38)	Peacock (8)	Perry (24)	Peschisolido (37)	Plummer (17)	Ready (5)	Rose (12)	Rowland (16)	Scully (20)	Thomson (36)	Walshe (39)	Wardley (27)	Warren (19)
							3			10[a]				1	B		11		A		7					4				9[b]	2			5						8	
	2			B			3		9	A	6			1			11		10[b]		8					4[a]					7				5						
	1						2		1	1	1			2			2		1		2					2				1	2			1	1					1	
				1						1					1				1																						
																	2																								

Bignot (23)	Breacker (2)	Broomes (36)	Brown (33)	Bruce (30)	Bubb (nn)	Burgess (37)	Carlisle (18)	Cochrane (40)	Connolly (10)	Crouch (28)	Darlington (22)	Dowie (25)	Furlong (33)	Harper (13)	Heinola (14)	Higgins (25)	Kiwomya (11)	Knight (14)	Koejoe (31)	Kulcsar (15)	Langley (21)	Lisbie (38)	Maddix (6)	McFlynn (35)	Miklosko (1)	Morrow (4)	Murray (7)	Ngonge (9)	Pacquette (38)	Peacock (8)	Perry (24)	Peschisolido (37)	Plummer (17)	Ready (5)	Rose (12)	Rowland (16)	Scully (20)	Thomson (36)	Walshe (39)	Wardley (27)	Warren (19)
8	9	5	2	5			32		20	42	36		3	31			23	10	11	10	31	1	1	1	20	21	4	7	1	33	27	5	27	20	30	4	1	7		27	16
1	2			3	1	1		1	7	5	1	1			2	1	7	1	15	5		1	1	1		6	2	8	1	2	6		1	4			1	1	1	10	6
1				1			3		4	12			1				10		2		1							3		4		1	2					4		3	

2001-02

Division Two

	P	W	D	L	F	A	Pts
Brighton & Hove Albion	46	25	15	6	66	42	90
Reading	46	23	15	8	70	43	84
Brentford	46	24	11	11	77	43	83
Cardiff City	46	23	14	9	75	50	83
Stoke City	46	23	11	12	67	40	80
Huddersfield Town	46	21	15	10	65	47	78
Bristol City	46	21	10	15	68	53	73
Queen's Park Rangers	46	19	14	13	60	49	71
Oldham Athletic	46	18	16	12	77	65	70
Wigan Athletic	46	16	16	14	66	51	64
Wycombe Wanderers	46	17	13	16	58	64	64
Tranmere Rovers	46	16	15	15	63	60	63
Swindon Town	46	15	14	17	46	56	59
Port Vale	46	16	10	20	51	62	58
Colchester United	46	15	12	19	65	76	57
Blackpool	46	14	14	18	66	69	56
Peterborough United	46	15	10	21	64	59	55
Chesterfield	46	13	13	20	53	65	52
Notts County	46	13	11	22	59	71	50
Northampton Town	46	14	7	25	54	79	49
Bournemouth	46	10	14	22	56	71	44
Bury	46	11	11	24	43	75	44
Wrexham	46	11	10	25	56	89	43
Cambridge United	46	7	13	26	47	93	34

Attendances

TOTAL	Home	Away	Total
League	270,016	189,486	459,502
Cup/Other		12,298	12,298
TOTAL	270,016	201,784	471,800

AVERAGE	Home	Away	Total
League	11,740	8,239	9,989
Cup/Other		4,099	4,099
TOTAL	11,740	7,761	9,629

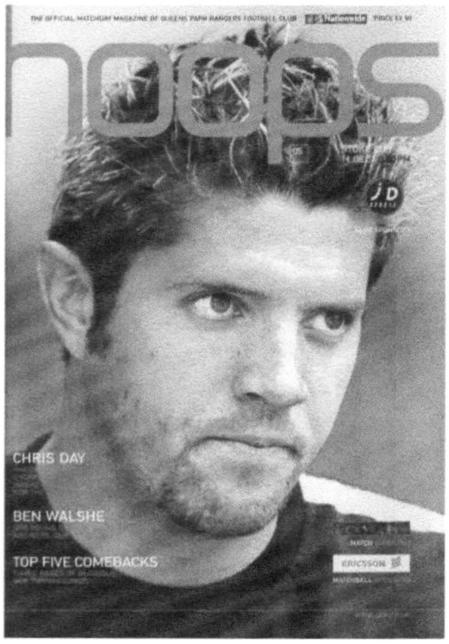

Match No.	Date		Opponents	Location	Result		Scorers	Atte
1	Aug	11	Stoke City	H	W	1-0	Thomson	
2		18	Bury	A	W	2-1	Thomson (pen), Bruce	
3		25	Reading	H	D	0-0		
4		27	Wycombe Wanderers	A	L	0-1		
5		30	Bristol City	H	D	0-0		
6	Sep	8	Brighton & Hove Albion	A	L	1-2	Thomson	
7		15	Port Vale	H	W	4-1	Palmer, Thomson (3, 1 pen)	
8		18	Blackpool	A	D	2-2	Griffiths (2)	
9		22	Wigan Athletic	A	W	2-1	Thomson, OG (Brannan)	
10		25	Cardiff City	H	W	2-1	Thomson (2, 1 pen)	
11		29	Cambridge United	A	L	1-2	Connolly	
12	Oct	7	Huddersfield Town	H	W	3-2	Thomson, Rose, Palmer	
13		13	Wrexham	A	L	0-1		
14		20	Northampton Town	H	L	0-1		
15		23	Peterborough United	A	L	1-4	Palmer	
16		27	Oldham Athletic	H	D	1-1	Doudou	
17	Nov	3	Notts County	A	W	2-0	Thomson (2)	
18		10	Tranmere Rovers	H	L	1-2	Thomson	
19		21	Swindon Town	H	W	4-0	Doudou, Burgess, Gallen, Thomson	
20		24	Brentford	A	D	0-0		
21	Dec	1	Colchester United	H	D	2-2	Gallen (2)	
22		15	Chesterfield	A	W	3-2	Thomson (pen), Shittu, Rose	
23		22	Bournemouth	A	W	2-1	Thomson (2, 1 pen)	
24		26	Brighton & Hove Albion	H	D	0-0		
25		29	Wycombe Wanderers	H	W	4-3	Thomson, Gallen, Connolly, Peacock	
26	Jan	5	Reading	A	L	0-1		
27		12	Bury	H	W	3-0	Griffiths, Pacquette, Bignot	
28		19	Stoke City	A	W	1-0	Peacock	
29		22	Bournemouth	H	D	1-1	Palmer	
30		26	Huddersfield Town	A	L	0-1		
31	Feb	2	Cambridge United	H	D	0-0		
32		5	Bristol City	A	L	0-2		
33		9	Northampton Town	A	D	2-2	Connolly (2,1 pen)	
34		16	Wrexham	H	W	2-1	Langley, Gallen	
35		23	Port Vale	A	L	0-1		
36		26	Wigan Athletic	H	D	1-1	Gallen	
37	Mar	2	Blackpool	H	W	2-0	Gallen, Langley	
38		5	Cardiff City	A	D	1-1	Pacquette	
39		9	Chesterfield	H	D	0-0		
40		16	Colchester United	A	L	1-3	Doudou	
41		23	Peterborough United	H	W	1-0	Thomson (pen)	
42		30	Tranmere Rovers	A	W	3-2	Thomson (2), Langley	
43	Apr	1	Notts County	H	W	3-2	Shittu, Rose, Foley	
44		6	Swindon Town	A	W	1-0	Thomas	
45		13	Brentford	H	D	0-0		
46		20	Oldham Athletic	A	L	0-1		

Appeara
Sub appeara
G

FA Cup

R1	Nov	18	Swansea City	A	L	0-4	

Appeara
Sub appeara
G

League Cup

R1	Aug	21	Northampton Town	A	L	1-2 aet	OG (Evatt)

Appeara
Sub appeara
G

LDV Trophy

S1	Oct	16	Yeovil Town	A	L	0-3	

Appeara
Sub appeara
G

Total - Appeara
Total - Sub appeara
Total - G

Barr (16)	Ben Askar (28)	Bignot (11)	Bonnot (26)	Bruce (3)	Burgess (24)	Connolly (10)	Daly	Day (1)	De Ornelas (32)	Digby (30)	Doudou (29)	Evans (33)	Fitzgerald (35)	Foley (18/34)	Forbes (17)	Gallen (18)	Griffiths (14)	Koejoe (18)	Langley (9)	Leaburn (34)	McEwan (19)	Murphy (23)	Oli (36)	Pacquette (22)	Palmer (4)	Peacock (8)	Perry (2)	Plummer (6)	Rose (12)	Shittu (31)	Taylor (18)	Thomas (26)	Thomson (27)	Wardley (7)	Warren (15)	OG
	3	7	8	5		9[c]		1							2		A[b]	B							4		6						10	11[a]	C	
	3	7	8[c]	5		9[a]		1							2			B							4		6		C				10	11[b]	A	
	3	7	8			9		1			A				2						B			C	4		6[a]		5				10[c]	11[b]		
	3	5	8			9[b]		1			6				2						11[a]			A	4		7						10		B	
	3	8	C	5		9[c]		1			6				2		A				B				4		7				11[b]		10[a]			
	3	7		5		8[c]		1			A				2		9				10[a]				4		6		C		11[b]		B			
		6	8	4		5		1			A				2		9								3				7		11[a]		10			
		7		4		5[a]		1			6				2		9								3				8		B		10[b]	11	A	
	3	7				9		1			A				2		11								4		6		8				10[a]		5	
	3	8				9[a]		1			A				2		11								4		6		7				10	B	5[b]	
	3	C	8[c]			B		1			9[a]				2		11[b]							A	4		6		7				10		5	
	3	6	8			9[a]		1							2		11[b]								4		B		7				10	A	5	
	3	6[b]	8	5		9[c]		1			A				2		11[a]								4		B		7				10	C		
		7	8	9	6	A		1			B						11[c]							C	4		2[b]		3				10		5[a]	
		7	8	5	6	10		1			9[a]						B							11[b]	4				2	3			A			
		7	8	5	6[c]	9		1	C		10			11[a]	2						A[b]				4				3					B		
		8		5		9			7[a]	1	11[b]				2		B								4		6		3				10	A		
		8		5		9				1	11				2		A								4		6[a]	3					10	7		
		A	8		6[a]	9				1	11[b]				2	10									7				4	3			B		5	
		6	8			9				1	11[a]				2	10									7				4	3			A		5	
		6	8			9				1	A				2	11									7				4	3			10		5[a]	
	3	B	C			9[a]				1	A[c]				2	11						6[b]			4	7			8	5			10			
		6	A			B				1	9[b]				2	11						5			4	7			8	3			10[a]			
		6[a]				A				1	9				2	11						5			4	7			8	3			10			
	3	A				9[a]				1	6				2	11						5			4	7			8				10			
	3	6	A	5[b]		9[c]				1					2	11			B	C					4	7			8[a]				10			
		6	8							1	10		B		2		9					5[a]		11[b]	4	7	A			3						
		6				B				1	10[b]				2		9					5		11[a]	4	7			8	3			A			
		6				A				1	11[b]				2		9		B			5[a]			4	7			8	3			10			
		6				B				1	A				2	11	9[b]					5[a]		C	4	7			8	3			10[c]			
		5				B				1	6				2[c]	11[a]	9		C					A	4	7			8	3			10[b]			
						C				1	6[c]				2	10	9		8			5[a]		11[b]	4				7	3			B		A	
		5				11				1	A				2	10	9[a]		6						4	7			8	3						
		5	C			11[c]				1	A				2[a]	10	9[b]		6					B	4	7			8	3						
		5	7							1	11					10	9[a]		6			B		A	4		2[b]		8	3						
	4	5	8								A	1			2	10	9[b]		6				B	11[a]	7					3						
	4	5									A	1			2	10	9		6					11[a]	7				8	3						
	4	5										1			2	10[a]	9		6					11	7				8	3			A			
	4	5									A	1			2[c]	10	9[a]		6					11[b]	7	C			8	3			B			
		5					8[b]				A	1			2	11			6			9[a]			4	7				3			10		B	
		5									6[a]	1			2	11	A		9				B		4	7			8	3			10[b]			
		5										1			2	11	A		6						4	7			8	3		9[a]	10			
		5										1		A	2	11			6						4	7			8	3		9	10[a]			
		5										1		10[a]	2	11			6						4	7			8	3		9				
		5										1		10[a]	2	11			6						4	7			8	3		9	A			
		5[c]										1		B	2	11[b]	9[a]		6			C			4	7			8	3			10			
	18	41	17	13	4	24	1	16	1	19	20	11		3	43	25	23		15		2	10		8	46	19	13	1	37	27	3	4	29	5	8	
		4	5			9			1		16		1	2			7	2	3	1	3	2	2	8		1	3		2		1		9	5	6	
		1		1	1	4					3			1		7	3		3					2	4	2			3	2		1	21			1

Barr (16)	Ben Askar (28)	Bignot (11)	Bonnot (26)	Bruce (3)	Burgess (24)	Connolly (10)	Daly	Day (1)	De Ornelas (32)	Digby (30)	Doudou (29)	Evans (33)	Fitzgerald (35)	Foley (18/34)	Forbes (17)	Gallen (18)	Griffiths (14)	Koejoe (18)	Langley (9)	Leaburn (34)	McEwan (19)	Murphy (23)	Oli (36)	Pacquette (22)	Palmer (4)	Peacock (8)	Perry (2)	Plummer (6)	Rose (12)	Shittu (31)	Taylor (18)	Thomas (26)	Thomson (27)	Wardley (7)	Warren (15)	OG
		7	8	A	B	9				1	11				2		10[c]							C	4		6[b]	3							5[a]	
		1	1			1				1	1				1		1								1		1	1							1	
				1	1																			1												

Barr (16)	Ben Askar (28)	Bignot (11)	Bonnot (26)	Bruce (3)	Burgess (24)	Connolly (10)	Daly	Day (1)	De Ornelas (32)	Digby (30)	Doudou (29)	Evans (33)	Fitzgerald (35)	Foley (18/34)	Forbes (17)	Gallen (18)	Griffiths (14)	Koejoe (18)	Langley (9)	Leaburn (34)	McEwan (19)	Murphy (23)	Oli (36)	Pacquette (22)	Palmer (4)	Peacock (8)	Perry (2)	Plummer (6)	Rose (12)	Shittu (31)	Taylor (18)	Thomas (26)	Thomson (27)	Wardley (7)	Warren (15)	OG
	3	7[c]	8	5				1			10[a]				2			B			A			C	4		6							11[b]	9	
	1	1	1	1				1			1				1										1		1							1	1	
																		1			1			1												
											1																									

Barr (16)	Ben Askar (28)	Bignot (11)	Bonnot (26)	Bruce (3)	Burgess (24)	Connolly (10)	Daly	Day (1)	De Ornelas (32)	Digby (30)	Doudou (29)	Evans (33)	Fitzgerald (35)	Foley (18/34)	Forbes (17)	Gallen (18)	Griffiths (14)	Koejoe (18)	Langley (9)	Leaburn (34)	McEwan (19)	Murphy (23)	Oli (36)	Pacquette (22)	Palmer (4)	Peacock (8)	Perry (2)	Plummer (6)	Rose (12)	Shittu (31)	Taylor (18)	Thomas (26)	Thomson (27)	Wardley (7)	Warren (15)	OG
C	3	2[b]	7[c]	5		9		1			B													A	4		6		8				10	11[a]		
	1	1	1	1		1		1																	1		1		1				1	1		
1											1													1												

Barr (16)	Ben Askar (28)	Bignot (11)	Bonnot (26)	Bruce (3)	Burgess (24)	Connolly (10)	Daly	Day (1)	De Ornelas (32)	Digby (30)	Doudou (29)	Evans (33)	Fitzgerald (35)	Foley (18/34)	Forbes (17)	Gallen (18)	Griffiths (14)	Koejoe (18)	Langley (9)	Leaburn (34)	McEwan (19)	Murphy (23)	Oli (36)	Pacquette (22)	Palmer (4)	Peacock (8)	Perry (2)	Plummer (6)	Rose (12)	Shittu (31)	Taylor (18)	Thomas (26)	Thomson (27)	Wardley (7)	Warren (15)	OG
	20	44	20	15	4	26	1	18	1	20	22	11		3	45	25	24		15		2	10		8	49	19	16	2	38	27	3	4	30	7	10	
1		4	5	1	1	9			1		17		1	2			7	3	3	1	4	2	2	11		1	3		2		1		9	5	6	
		1		1	1	4					3			1		7	3		3					2	4	2			3	2		1	21			2

2002-03

Division Two

	P	W	D	L	F	A	Pts
Wigan Athletic	46	29	13	4	68	25	100
Crewe Alexandra	46	25	11	10	76	40	86
Bristol City	46	24	11	11	79	48	83
Queen's Park Rangers	46	24	11	11	69	45	83
Oldham Athletic	46	22	16	8	68	38	82
Cardiff City	46	23	12	11	68	43	81
Tranmere Rovers	46	23	11	12	66	57	80
Plymouth Argyle	46	17	14	15	63	52	65
Luton Town	46	17	14	15	67	62	65
Swindon Town	46	16	12	18	59	63	60
Peterborough United	46	14	16	16	51	54	58
Colchester United	46	14	16	16	52	56	58
Blackpool	46	15	13	18	56	64	58
Stockport County	46	15	10	21	65	70	55
Notts County	46	13	16	17	62	70	55
Brentford	46	14	12	20	47	56	54
Port Vale	46	14	11	21	54	70	53
Wycombe Wanderers	46	13	13	20	59	66	52
Barnsley	46	13	13	20	51	64	52
Chesterfield	46	14	8	24	43	73	50
Cheltenham Town	46	10	18	18	53	68	48
Huddersfield Town	46	11	12	23	39	61	45
Mansfield Town	46	12	8	26	66	97	44
Northampton Town	46	10	9	27	40	79	39

Attendances

	TOTAL		
	Home	Away	Total
League	303,784	176,564	480,348
Cup/Other	27,289	86,736	114,025
TOTAL	331,073	263,300	594,373

	AVERAGE		
	Home	Away	Total
League	13,208	7,677	10,442
Cup/Other	9,096	21,684	16,289
TOTAL	12,734	9,752	11,215

Match No.	Date		Opponents	Location	Result		Scorers	Atten
1	Aug	10	Chesterfield	H	W	3-1	Furlong, Langley, Gallen	12
2		13	Stockport County	A	D	1-1	Connolly (pen)	5
3		17	Barnsley	A	L	0-1		9
4		24	Peterborough United	H	W	2-0	Gallen (2)	11
5		26	Wycombe Wanderers	A	L	1-4	Furlong	8
6		31	Plymouth Argyle	H	D	2-2	Thomas, Pacquette	14
7	Sep	7	Mansfield Town	A	W	4-0	Furlong, Shittu, Gallen, Thomson	4
8		14	Swindon Town	H	W	2-0	Gallen, Langley	11
9		17	Huddersfield Town	H	W	3-0	Shittu, Williams, Carlisle	11
10		21	Bristol City	A	W	3-1	Connolly (2), Gallen	12
11		28	Colchester United	H	W	2-0	Connolly, Gallen	12
12	Oct	5	Crewe Alexandra	A	L	0-2		7
13		14	Blackpool	H	W	2-1	Langley, OG (Clarke)	11
14		19	Cheltenham Town	A	D	1-1	Thomas	6
15		26	Oldham Athletic	H	L	1-2	Rose	15
16		29	Wigan Athletic	A	D	1-1	Thomson	6
17	Nov	2	Port Vale	A	D	0-0		4
18		9	Northampton Town	H	L	0-1		11
19		23	Luton Town	A	D	0-0		9
20		29	Cardiff City	H	L	0-4		14
21	Dec	14	Notts County	A	L	0-3		5
22		21	Brentford	H	D	1-1	Bircham	15
23		26	Wycombe Wanderers	H	W	2-1	Rose, Gallen	14
24		28	Tranmere Rovers	A	L	0-3		8
25	Jan	1	Peterborough United	A	W	2-0	Carlisle, Langley	6
26		4	Stockport County	H	W	1-0	Gallen (pen)	10
27		11	Barnsley	H	W	1-0	Pacquette	11
28		18	Plymouth Argyle	A	W	1-0	Pacquette	10
29		25	Tranmere Rovers	H	L	1-2	Palmer	12
30	Feb	2	Chesterfield	A	W	4-2	Pacquette, Shittu, Furlong, Thomson	4
31		8	Northampton Town	A	D	1-1	Furlong	5
32		15	Port Vale	H	W	4-0	Shittu, Furlong, Padula, Gallen	13
33		22	Mansfield Town	H	D	2-2	Furlong, Gallen	11
34	Mar	1	Swindon Town	A	L	1-3	Shittu	7
35		4	Huddersfield Town	A	W	3-0	Furlong (2), Shittu	8
36		8	Bristol City	H	W	1-0	Gallen (pen)	14
37		15	Oldham Athletic	A	D	0-0		7
38		18	Cheltenham Town	H	W	4-1	Gallen, OG (M.Duff), Cook, Furlong	11
39		22	Wigan Athletic	H	L	0-1		14
40		29	Blackpool	A	W	3-1	Langley (3)	8
41	Apr	5	Cardiff City	A	W	2-1	Furlong, Langley	15
42		12	Luton Town	H	W	2-0	McLeod (2)	15
43		19	Brentford	A	W	2-1	Shittu, Bircham	9
44		21	Notts County	H	W	2-0	Furlong, Langley	13
45		26	Crewe Alexandra	H	D	0-0		16
46	May	3	Colchester United	A	W	1-0	Furlong	5

Appearar
Sub appearar
G

Play-off

SF1	May	10	Oldham Athletic	A	D	1-1	Langley	12
SF2		14	Oldham Athletic	H	W	1-0	Furlong	17
F		25	Cardiff City	N	L	0-1 aet		66

Appearar
Sub appearar
G

FA Cup

R1	Nov	16	Vauxhall Motors	A	D	0-0		3
R1 rep		26	Vauxhall Motors	H	L	1-1*	Thomson	5

* Lost 3-4 on pens

Appearar
Sub appearar
G

League Cup

R1/1	Sep	10	Leyton Orient	A	L	2-3	Thomson (pen), Gallen	4

Appearar
Sub appearar
G

LDV Trophy

R1-S	Oct	22	Bristol City	H	L	0-0*		4

* Lost 5-4 on pens

Appearar
Sub appearar
G

Total - Appearar
Total - Sub appearar
Total - G

ean (22)	Bircham (8)	Burgess (18)	Carlisle (5)	Connolly (11)	Cook (15)	Culkin (13)	Daly (21)	Day (1)	Digby (30)	Doudou (12)	Forbes (2)	Furlong (29)	Gallen (10)	Griffiths (23)	Kelly (32)	Langley (9)	McLeod (15)	Murphy (16)	Oli (20)	Pacquette (24)	Padula (3)	Palmer (4)	Plummer (14)	Rose (7)	Royce (15)	Shittu (6)	Thomas (32)	Thomson (27)	Walshe (26)	Williams (33)	Willock (32)	OG
	7			9		1	6[b]				2	A	11			B		5[c]				4		8		3		10[a]		C		
	7			9[a]		1				A	2	10	11			6						4		8		3				5		
	7			9		1				B	2	10[a]	11			6					A	4		8		3				5[b]		
	7									9	2	10[a]	11			6				A		4		8	1	3				5		
	7			9[a]						B	2	10	11			6[b]						4		8	1	3				5		
	7			C						6[a]	2	10[b]	11							A		4		8	1	3	9[c]	B		5		
	7		B	A							2	10	11[c]			6						4			1	3	9[a]	C		5		
			4	9							2		11			7			10[a]			8		6	1	3		A		5		
			4	9							2		11			7		B	10[a]	A		8		6[b]	1	3				5		
	A		4	9[c]							2		11			7[b]		B	10[a]			8		6	1	3		C		5		
			4	9							2	A	11			7			10[a]			8		6	1	3				5		
	A		4[a]	9[b]					1		2[c]	10	11			7			B			8		6		3		C		5		
			4	A							2	10[c]	11			8			C			5		7[b]	1	3	9[a]	B		6		
			4	10[b]							2		11[a]			8			B			5		7	1	3	9	A		6		
			4	10					B		2					7			A		C	8		6	1[b]	3[a]	9	11		5[c]		
			4	9[a]							2					7			10			8		6	1	3	A	11		5		
			4						A	C	2			B		7			10[b]		9[a]	8		6	1	3		11[c]		5		
	7	B	4	A						9[a]	2[c]								C			8[b]		6	1	3		11		5	10	
	7	6	4								2	A	B[c]						C			8			1	3		11[a]		5	9	
	6		4								2	A	10			7			B			8			1	3				5	9[b]	
	7		4			1	A				2	B	10			6		5	9[a]			3		8[c]				C				
	7		4		9[a]	1					2	11	10			6		5				3		8				A				
	6[a]		4		9[b]	1	A				2	11[c]	10			7						8		5		3		B				
			4		9[c]	1	6[a]			C	2	11	10			7		B	A			8		5		3[b]						
	6		4[a]		9	1					2		10			7		A				8		5		3						
	6[b]	B	4		9[c]	1					2		10			7		C		A		8		5		3						
		C	4		9	1	A				2		10			7[c]			6[b]	11	5	8		3[a]								
	8		4		9	1					2		6					A	B	11[b]	5[a]	7				3						
	8		4		9[b]	1					2		6	B				5		11[a]		7				3		A				
	8	6[b]				1					2	C	7							11	5	4				3		A	9[a]			
	8					1	7[a]			C	2	10	11	9[c]							5	4	B			3		6[b]				
	7					1				A	2	10	11	9		8					5	4				3						
	7		C			1					2	10	11	9		8		B	A		5[b]	4				3[c]						
	7		2		9[a]	1						10[c]	11			8				B	5[b]	4				3				A		
	6		4		9[a]			1			2	10	11			7					5	8				3				A		
	7		4		9[a]			1			2	10	11	A		6						8				3				5		
	7		4		9[a]			1			2	10	11			6					A	8				3				5[b]		
	7		4		9			1			2	10[c]	11[b]			6					A	8				3		B		5[a]		
	7		4					1			2	10	11			6[a]	9				5	8				3		A				
	7		4					1				10[a]	11		2	6	9				5	8		A		3						
	7		4					1				10	11		2	6	9[a]				5	8		A		3						
	7		4					1				10	11		2	6	9				5	8				3						
	7		4					1				10	11		2	6	9				5	8				3						
	7		4					1				10	11		2	6	9				5	8				3						
	7		4					1				10[c]	11		2	6[a]	9[b]			C	5	8		A		3				B		
	7							1				10	11		2[b]	6[a]	9			A	5	8	B	4		3						
	34	2	34	12	13	17	3	12	1	3	38	27	41	3	7	38	8	4	8	4	17	46		25	16	43	5	7	1	22	3	
	2	3	2	4			3		2	7		6	1	3		1		7	10	7	4		2	3			1	14		4		
	2		2	4	1							13	13			9	2			4	1	1		2		7	2	3		1		2

ean (22)	Bircham (8)	Burgess (18)	Carlisle (5)	Connolly (11)	Cook (15)	Culkin (13)	Daly (21)	Day (1)	Digby (30)	Doudou (12)	Forbes (2)	Furlong (29)	Gallen (10)	Griffiths (23)	Kelly (32)	Langley (9)	McLeod (15)	Murphy (16)	Oli (20)	Pacquette (24)	Padula (3)	Palmer (4)	Plummer (14)	Rose (7)	Royce (15)	Shittu (6)	Thomas (32)	Thomson (27)	Walshe (26)	Williams (33)	Willock (32)	OG
	7							1			2	10	11			6	9			A		8		4[a]		3				5		
	7		4					1				10	6		2		9			A	5[b]	8				3		11[a]		B		
	7		4					1				10	6		2		9			11[a]	5[b]	8				3		A		B		
	3		2					3			1	3	3		2	1	3			1	2	3		1		3		1		1		
																				2								1		2		
												1				1																

ean (22)	Bircham (8)	Burgess (18)	Carlisle (5)	Connolly (11)	Cook (15)	Culkin (13)	Daly (21)	Day (1)	Digby (30)	Doudou (12)	Forbes (2)	Furlong (29)	Gallen (10)	Griffiths (23)	Kelly (32)	Langley (9)	McLeod (15)	Murphy (16)	Oli (20)	Pacquette (24)	Padula (3)	Palmer (4)	Plummer (14)	Rose (7)	Royce (15)	Shittu (6)	Thomas (32)	Thomson (27)	Walshe (26)	Williams (33)	Willock (32)	OG
	8	6	4	9[c]					1		A		B						10[b]		C	2		7[a]		3		11		5		
	7	6[a]	4	B					1		2	11				8		C	A		5[b]	3						10		9[c]		
	2	2	2	1					2		1	1				1			1		1	2		1		1		2		2		
				1							1		1					1	1		1											
			1																													

ean (22)	Bircham (8)	Burgess (18)	Carlisle (5)	Connolly (11)	Cook (15)	Culkin (13)	Daly (21)	Day (1)	Digby (30)	Doudou (12)	Forbes (2)	Furlong (29)	Gallen (10)	Griffiths (23)	Kelly (32)	Langley (9)	McLeod (15)	Murphy (16)	Oli (20)	Pacquette (24)	Padula (3)	Palmer (4)	Plummer (14)	Rose (7)	Royce (15)	Shittu (6)	Thomas (32)	Thomson (27)	Walshe (26)	Williams (33)	Willock (32)	OG
			4[a]	9[c]					1	A	2		B			7			C	11[b]		8		6		3		10		5		
			1	1					1		1					1				1		1		1		1		1		1		
										1			1						1													
													1															1				

ean (22)	Bircham (8)	Burgess (18)	Carlisle (5)	Connolly (11)	Cook (15)	Culkin (13)	Daly (21)	Day (1)	Digby (30)	Doudou (12)	Forbes (2)	Furlong (29)	Gallen (10)	Griffiths (23)	Kelly (32)	Langley (9)	McLeod (15)	Murphy (16)	Oli (20)	Pacquette (24)	Padula (3)	Palmer (4)	Plummer (14)	Rose (7)	Royce (15)	Shittu (6)	Thomas (32)	Thomson (27)	Walshe (26)	Williams (33)	Willock (32)	OG
		6[b]		9			7[c]			A	2					8			11[a]		B	4		3	1			10		5		
		1		1			1				1					1			1			1		1	1			1		1		
										1											1											

ean (22)	Bircham (8)	Burgess (18)	Carlisle (5)	Connolly (11)	Cook (15)	Culkin (13)	Daly (21)	Day (1)	Digby (30)	Doudou (12)	Forbes (2)	Furlong (29)	Gallen (10)	Griffiths (23)	Kelly (32)	Langley (9)	McLeod (15)	Murphy (16)	Oli (20)	Pacquette (24)	Padula (3)	Palmer (4)	Plummer (14)	Rose (7)	Royce (15)	Shittu (6)	Thomas (32)	Thomson (27)	Walshe (26)	Williams (33)	Willock (32)	OG
	39	5	39	15	13	17	4	15	4	3	42	31	44	3	9	42	11	4	10	6	20	53		29	17	48	5	12	1	27	3	
	2	3	2	5			3		2	9	1	6	3	3		1		8	12	9	6		2	3			1	15		6		
	2		2	4	1							14	14			10	2			4	1	1		2		7	2	5		1		2

2003-04

Division Two

	P	W	D	L	F	A	Pts
Plymouth Argyle	46	26	12	8	85	41	90
Queen's Park Rangers	46	22	17	7	80	45	83
Bristol City	46	23	13	10	58	37	82
Brighton & Hove Albion	46	22	11	13	64	43	77
Swindon Town	46	20	13	13	76	58	73
Hartlepool United	46	20	13	13	76	61	73
Port Vale	46	21	10	15	73	63	73
Tranmere Rovers	46	17	16	13	59	56	67
Bournemouth	46	17	15	14	56	51	66
Luton Town	46	17	15	14	69	66	66
Colchester United	46	17	13	16	52	56	64
Barnsley	46	15	17	14	54	58	62
Wrexham	46	17	9	20	50	60	60
Blackpool	46	16	11	19	58	65	59
Oldham Athletic	46	12	21	13	66	60	57
Sheffield Wednesday	46	13	14	19	48	64	53
Brentford	46	14	11	21	52	69	53
Peterborough United	46	12	16	18	58	58	52
Stockport County	46	11	19	16	62	70	52
Chesterfield	46	12	15	19	49	71	51
Grimsby Town	46	13	11	22	55	81	50
Rushden & Diamonds	46	13	9	24	60	74	48
Notts County	46	10	12	24	50	78	42
Wycombe Wanderers	46	6	19	21	50	75	37

Attendances

	TOTAL		
	Home	**Away**	**Total**
League	340,657	205,236	545,893
Cup/Other	31,016	23,243	54,259
TOTAL	371,673	228,479	600,152

	AVERAGE		
	Home	**Away**	**Total**
League	14,811	8,923	11,867
Cup/Other	7,754	5,811	6,782
TOTAL	13,766	8,462	11,114

Match No.	Date		Opponents	Location	Result		Scorers	Atte
1	Aug	9	Blackpool	H	W	5-0	Ainsworth (2), Langley, Gallen, Palmer	1
2		18	Brighton & Hove Albion	A	L	1-2	Padula	
3		23	AFC Bournemouth	H	W	1-0	Furlong	1
4		25	Rushden & Diamonds	A	D	3-3	Ainsworth (2), Furlong	
5		30	Chesterfield	H	W	3-0	Thorpe (2), Furlong	1
6	Sep	6	Colchester United	A	D	2-2	Furlong (2)	
7		13	Wycombe Wanderers	H	D	0-0		1
8		16	Wrexham	A	W	2-0	Bean, Rowlands	
9		20	Luton Town	A	D	1-1	Furlong	
10		27	Bristol City	H	D	1-1	Padula	1
11		30	Barnsley	H	W	4-0	Gallen, Rowlands, Ainsworth, Thorpe	1
12	Oct	4	Grimsby Town	A	W	1-0	Sabin	
13		18	Peterborough United	A	D	0-0		
14		21	Port Vale	A	L	0-2		
15		25	Tranmere Rovers	H	D	1-1	Gallen	1
16	Nov	1	Stockport County	A	W	2-1	Gallen, Rowlands	
17		11	Brentford	H	W	1-0	Thorpe	1
18		15	Plymouth Argyle	H	W	3-0	Gallen (2), Thorpe	1
19		22	Swindon Town	A	D	1-1	Rowlands	1
20		29	Sheffield Wednesday	H	W	3-0	Palmer, Thorpe, McLeod	1
21	Dec	13	Hartlepool United	H	W	4-1	Gallen (2), Padula, Ainsworth	1
22		20	Oldham Athletic	A	L	1-2	Thorpe	
23		26	Notts County	A	D	3-3	Palmer, OG (Richardson), Gallen	
24		28	Colchester United	H	W	2-0	Gallen, Thorpe	1
25	Jan	3	Rushden & Diamonds	H	W	1-0	Gallen	1
26		10	Blackpool	A	W	1-0	Rowlands	
27		17	Brighton & Hove Albion	H	W	2-1	Rowlands, Gallen	1
28		24	AFC Bournemouth	A	L	0-1		
29		31	Chesterfield	A	L	2-4	Thorpe, Palmer	
30	Feb	7	Notts County	H	W	3-2	McLeod, Thorpe, Furlong	1
31		14	Brentford	A	D	1-1	Furlong	
32		20	Peterborough United	H	D	1-1	Gallen	1
33	Mar	2	Port Vale	H	W	3-2	Bircham, Cureton (2)	1
34		6	Oldham Athletic	H	D	1-1	Gallen (pen)	1
35		13	Hartlepool United	A	W	4-1	Furlong (2), Gallen, Rowlands	
36		16	Wrexham	H	W	2-0	Carlisle, McLeod	1
37		20	Wycombe Wanderers	A	D	2-2	Gallen, Rowlands	
38		27	Luton Town	H	D	1-1	Furlong	1
39	Apr	3	Bristol City	A	L	0-1		1
40		6	Tranmere Rovers	A	D	0-0		
41		10	Grimsby Town	H	W	3-0	Furlong (2), Bircham	1
42		12	Barnsley	A	D	3-3	OG (Kay), Furlong (2)	1
43		17	Stockport County	H	D	1-1	Rowlands	1
44		24	Plymouth Argyle	A	L	0-2		1
45	Mar	1	Swindon Town	H	W	1-0	Rowlands	1
46		8	Sheffield Wednesday	A	W	3-1	Gallen, Furlong, OG (Carr)	2

Appeara
Sub appeara
G

FA Cup

R1	Nov	8	Grimsby Town	A	L	0-1	

Appeara
Sub appeara
G

League Cup

R1	Aug	12	Cheltenham Town	A	W	2-1	Ainsworth, Langley
R2	Sep	23	Sheffield United	A	W	2-0	Rowlands (2)
R3	Oct	28	Manchester City	H	L	0-3	

Appeara
Sub appeara
G

LDV Trophy

R1-S	Oct	14	Kidderminster Harriers	H	W	2-0	Pacquette, Gnohere
R2-S	Nov	4	Dagenham & Redbridge	H	W	2-1	Padula, McLeod
QF-S	Dec	7	Brighton & Hove Albion	H	W	2-1	Palmer, Thorpe
SF-S	Jan	20	Southend United	A	L	0-4	

Appeara
Sub appeara
G

Total - Appeara
Total - Sub appeara
Total - G

Barton (20)	Bean (17)	Bignot (12)	Bircham (8)	Camp (31)	Carlisle (5)	Culkin (13)	Cureton (28)	Daly (16)	Day (1)	Edghill (23)	Forbes (2)	Furlong (29)	Gallen (10)	Gnohere (24)/(20)	Johnson (30)	Langley (9)	Marney (27)	McLeod (22)	Oli (18)	Pacquette (15)	Padula (3)	Palmer (4)	Rose (7)	Rowlands (14)	Sabin (12)	Shittu (6)	Thorpe (9)	Walshe (19)	Williams (33)	OG
			7		3				1		2	11[a]	10[c]			9					5	8		B	A	4			C	
	B		7		3				1		2	11						A	C		5	8		6[b]	10[a]	4			9[c]	
	B		7[b]		3				1			11	A					9			5	8		2		4	10[a]			
	A		7[a]		3				1			11[b]	10								5	8		2		4	B		9	
	A								1	B		11[a]	7					9			5	3		2		4	10		8[b]	
	A								1	B		11	7	4				9	C			8		2		3	10[a]		5[c]	
	7								1			11	10	4				9			5	8		2		3				
	7								1	A		11[a]	10	4				9			5	8		2	B	3				
	7		C						1	2		11	10	4				9[b]			5	8[c]		6[a]		3	B			
	7[c]		8						1	2[a]	3	11	10	4				9[b]	C		5	B		6						
	7		8[a]					A	1		2		10	4							5	3		9			11			
A	7		8						1		3	11	9								5	4		2	B		10[a]			
2	7		8						1		3	11[a]	10					9[c]			5	4		6[b]	C		A			
2[a]	7[c]		8		A				1		3		10					9		C	5	4		6			11[b]			
			8		4				1	2	3		10					9		B	5			7	A		11[a]			
			8[a]		4				1	2	3		10					9			5	A		7			11			
	7		8		4				1	2[b]	3		10					9			5	B		6[a]			11			
	7		8		4				1	2[a]	3		10					9			5			6		A	11			
	7[c]		8		4				1	2[a]	3		10								5	C		9	6[b]	A	11			
	7[b]				3				1	C	2	A	10					B			5[c]	8		9		4	11			
	7				3	1					2	B	10[b]					A			5[c]	8	C	9		4	11[a]			
	7		A						1		2		10					9			5	8[a]	3			4	11			
			7		3				1		2		10					9[a]			5	8[b]		6	B	4	11			
	7		8[a]		3				1		2		10					9			5	B	A	6		4[b]	11			
	7		8		3				1		2	11	10					9[a]			5			6		4				
	7		8		3				1		2	11	10					9[a]			5		A	6		4				
	7[a]		6		3				1		2	11	10				B				5	A	8[b]	9		4				
			7						1		2	11	10				6[a]				5	3	8	9		4	A			
			7		4			C	1		3	11[a]	9					A			5	8	2[b]	6[c]	B		10			
			7		4	1	B				2	A	10					9[b]			5	8	3	6			11[a]			
			7		4		A		1		2	11	10								5	8	3	9	6[a]					
			7		3	1	B				2	11[a]	10	4	C			9			5	8[c]	6[b]				A			
			7		3	1	B				2	A	10	4	8			9[b]			5			6			11[a]			
			7		3	1	B				2	A	10	4	8			9[a]			5			6			11[b]			
	A		7[b]	1	3						2	11	10	4	8[a]			9				B	5	6						
			7	1	3						2	11	10	4	8			9					5[a]	6			A			
	C		7[c]	1	3		B			A	2[a]	11	9	4	8			5[b]						6			10			
	7[b]	2		1	3		B			5		11	9	4	8			A						6			10[a]			
	7[a]	2		1	3		A					11	10	4	8[b]			9[c]				B	5	6			C			
	7	2	8[a]	1	3					5		11	10	4								A	B	9[b]						
	7[b]	2	8	1	3[a]		10			5		11	9	4				C				B	A							
	B[c]	2	7	1			10[b]			5		11	9	4				A				8	3				C			
	7	2	8	1			B			5		11	10					A[c]				3	4	9[a]			C			
			7[a]	1	3		C			2		11	10		8			B			5[c]	A	4	9						
			7	1	3					2		11	10		8						5		4	9						
			7	1	3[a]		B			2		11	10	A	8						5		4	9[b]						
2	23	6	36	12	32	5	2		29	15	30	31	44	17	10	1	1	26			36	24	15	41	3	18	22		4	
1	8		2		1		11	2		5		5	1	1	1		1	9	3	2		11	5	1	7	2	9		1	
	1		2		1		2					16	17			1		3			3	4		10	1		10			3

Barton (20)	Bean (17)	Bignot (12)	Bircham (8)	Camp (31)	Carlisle (5)	Culkin (13)	Cureton (28)	Daly (16)	Day (1)	Edghill (23)	Forbes (2)	Furlong (29)	Gallen (10)	Gnohere (24)/(20)	Johnson (30)	Langley (9)	Marney (27)	McLeod (22)	Oli (18)	Pacquette (15)	Padula (3)	Palmer (4)	Rose (7)	Rowlands (14)	Sabin (12)	Shittu (6)	Thorpe (9)	Walshe (19)	Williams (33)	OG
	7				4			A	1		3		10					5	B			8		2[a]	9		11			
	1				1				1		1		1					1				1		1	1		1			
								1											1											

Barton (20)	Bean (17)	Bignot (12)	Bircham (8)	Camp (31)	Carlisle (5)	Culkin (13)	Cureton (28)	Daly (16)	Day (1)	Edghill (23)	Forbes (2)	Furlong (29)	Gallen (10)	Gnohere (24)/(20)	Johnson (30)	Langley (9)	Marney (27)	McLeod (22)	Oli (18)	Pacquette (15)	Padula (3)	Palmer (4)	Rose (7)	Rowlands (14)	Sabin (12)	Shittu (6)	Thorpe (9)	Walshe (19)	Williams (33)	OG
			7		3				1		2	11	10[a]			9					5	8			A	4				
	7		8						1	2	3	11	10					9			5			6[a]		4				
			8		4				1	2	3		10					9		11[a]	5			7	A					
	1		3		2				3	2	3	2	3			1		2		1	3	1		2		2				
2																														
																1								2						

Barton (20)	Bean (17)	Bignot (12)	Bircham (8)	Camp (31)	Carlisle (5)	Culkin (13)	Cureton (28)	Daly (16)	Day (1)	Edghill (23)	Forbes (2)	Furlong (29)	Gallen (10)	Gnohere (24)/(20)	Johnson (30)	Langley (9)	Marney (27)	McLeod (22)	Oli (18)	Pacquette (15)	Padula (3)	Palmer (4)	Rose (7)	Rowlands (14)	Sabin (12)	Shittu (6)	Thorpe (9)	Walshe (19)	Williams (33)	OG
2	7		8[c]			1					3		B	4					11[b]	10[a]	5	C		9	6		A			
2[a]	7[b]				4	1				A	3		B					9		11[c]	5	8			6		C			
	7				3	1				5[b]	2	A	10									8	B	9		4	11			
			7[b]		3				1		2	11	10[c]				6[a]		C		5	B	8	9	A	4				
2	3		2		3	3			1	1	4	1	2	1			1	1	1	2	3	2	1	3	2	2	1			
										1		1	2						1			2	1		1		2			
														1				1		1	1	1					1			

Barton (20)	Bean (17)	Bignot (12)	Bircham (8)	Camp (31)	Carlisle (5)	Culkin (13)	Cureton (28)	Daly (16)	Day (1)	Edghill (23)	Forbes (2)	Furlong (29)	Gallen (10)	Gnohere (24)/(20)	Johnson (30)	Langley (9)	Marney (27)	McLeod (22)	Oli (18)	Pacquette (15)	Padula (3)	Palmer (4)	Rose (7)	Rowlands (14)	Sabin (12)	Shittu (6)	Thorpe (9)	Walshe (19)	Williams (33)	OG
4	28	6	41	12	38	8	2		34	18	38	34	50	18	10	2	2	30	1	3	42	28	16	47	6	22	24		4	
1	8		2		1		11	3		6		6	3	1	1		1	9	5	2		13	6	1	10	2	11		1	
	1		2		1		2					16	17	1		2		4		1	4	5		12	1		11			3

2004-05

Championship

	P	W	D	L	F	A	Pts
Sunderland	46	29	7	10	76	41	94
Wigan Athletic	46	25	12	9	79	35	87
Ipswich Town	46	24	13	9	85	56	85
Derby County	46	22	10	14	71	60	76
Preston North End	46	21	12	13	67	58	75
West Ham United	46	21	10	15	66	56	73
Reading	46	19	13	14	51	44	70
Sheffield United	46	18	13	15	57	56	67
Wolverhampton W	46	15	21	10	72	59	66
Millwall	46	18	12	16	51	45	66
Queen's Park Rangers	46	17	11	18	54	58	62
Stoke City	46	17	10	19	36	38	61
Burnley	46	15	15	16	38	39	60
Leeds United	46	14	18	14	49	52	60
Leicester City	46	12	21	13	49	46	57
Cardiff City	46	13	15	18	48	51	54
Plymouth Argyle	46	14	11	21	52	64	53
Watford	46	12	16	18	52	59	52
Coventry City	46	13	13	20	61	73	52
Brighton & Hove Albion	46	13	12	21	40	65	51
Crewe Alexandra	46	12	14	20	66	86	50
Gillingham	46	12	14	20	45	66	50
Nottingham Forest	46	9	17	20	42	66	44
Rotherham United	46	5	14	27	35	69	29

Attendances

TOTAL	Home	Away	Total
League	369,283	415,374	784,657
Cup/Other	16,022	26,975	42,997
TOTAL	385,305	442,349	827,654

AVERAGE	Home	Away	Total
League	16,056	18,060	17,058
Cup/Other	8,011	26,975	14,332
TOTAL	15,412	18,431	16,891

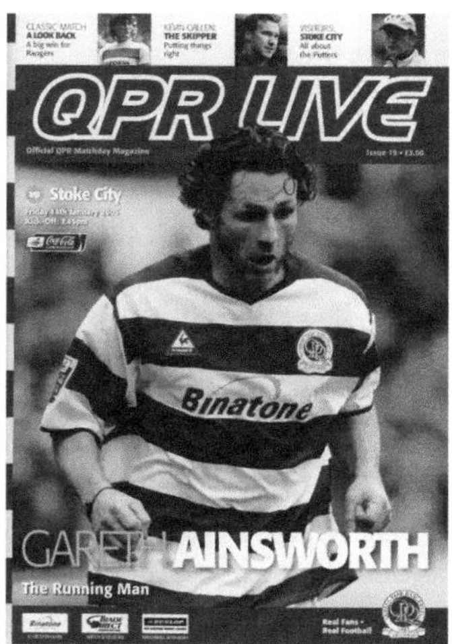

Match No.	Date		Opponents	Location	Result		Scorers	Atten
1	Aug	7	Rotherham United	H	D	1-1	Ainsworth	14
2		9	Watford	A	L	0-3		14
3		14	Sunderland	A	D	2-2	Furlong, Rowlands	26
4		21	Derby County	H	L	0-2		15
5		27	Gillingham	A	W	1-0	Bean	7
6		31	Sheffield United	H	L	0-1		13
7	Sep	11	Plymouth Argyle	H	W	3-2	Furlong (2), Gallen	15
8		14	Crewe Alexandra	A	W	2-0	Furlong, Santos	5
9		18	Brighton & Hove Albion	A	W	3-2	Gallen, Furlong, Rose	6
10		25	Leicester City	H	W	3-2	Cook, Furlong (2)	15
11		28	Coventry City	H	W	4-1	Cureton (3), Furlong	14
12	Oct	2	Stoke City	A	W	1-0	Gallen	16
13		16	West Ham United	H	W	1-0	Rose	18
14		19	Preston North End	A	L	1-2	Santos	10
15		23	Wolverhampton Wand.	A	L	1-2	Gallen	27
16		30	Burnley	H	W	3-0	Gallen (pen), Santos, Furlong	15
17	Nov	2	Millwall	H	D	1-1	Furlong	16
18		6	West Ham United	A	L	1-2	McLeod	31
19		13	Wigan Athletic	H	W	1-0	Furlong	15
20		20	Leeds United	A	L	1-6	Ainsworth	29
21		27	Cardiff City	H	W	1-0	Shittu	15
22	Dec	4	Nottingham Forest	A	L	1-2	Santos	26
23		11	Ipswich Town	H	L	2-4	Furlong (2)	18
24		18	Reading	A	L	0-1		20
25		26	Plymouth Argyle	A	L	1-2	Furlong	19
26		28	Crewe Alexandra	H	L	1-2	Shittu	15
27	Jan	1	Brighton & Hove Albion	H	D	0-0		15
28		3	Leicester City	A	L	0-1		23
29		14	Stoke City	H	W	1-0	Cook	13
30		22	Coventry City	A	W	2-1	Cureton, Santos	16
31	Feb	5	Millwall	A	D	0-0		15
32		12	Preston North End	H	L	1-2	Furlong	15
33		22	Wolverhampton Wand.	H	D	1-1	Gallen	15
34		26	Ipswich Town	A	W	2-0	Furlong, Shittu	29
35	Mar	5	Reading	H	D	0-0		16
36		12	Watford	H	W	3-1	Furlong, Gallen (2)	16
37		16	Derby County	A	D	0-0		24
38		19	Rotherham United	A	W	1-0	Rowlands	5
39	Apr	2	Sunderland	H	L	1-3	Shittu	18
40		5	Gillingham	H	D	1-1	Furlong	16
41		9	Sheffield United	A	L	2-3	Rowlands, Gallen	20
42		16	Leeds United	H	D	1-1	Gallen	18
43		19	Burnley	A	L	0-2		10
44		23	Wigan Athletic	A	D	0-0		12
45		30	Nottingham Forest	H	W	2-1	OG (Curtis), Bircham	17
46	May	8	Cardiff City	A	L	0-1		15

Appearar
Sub appearar
G

FA Cup

R3	Jan	8	Nottingham Forest	H	L	0-3		11

Appearar
Sub appearar
G

League Cup

R1	Aug	24	Swansea City	H	W	3-0	Cureton, Rowlands, Gallen	4
R2	Sep	22	Aston Villa	A	L	1-3	McLeod	26

Appearar
Sub appearar
G

Total - Appearar
Total - Sub appearar
Total - G

Baidoo (34)	Bailey (18)	Bean (16)	Best (28)	Bignot (2)	Bircham (8)	Branco (19)	Brown (27)	Cole (13)	Cook (17)	Culkin (12)	Cureton (15)	Daly (20)	Davies (6)	Day (1)	Donnelly (25)	Edghill (4)	Forbes (19)	Furlong (29)	Gallen (10)	Gnohere (22)	Hamilton (24)	Johnson (6)	Kanyuka (35)	McLeod (18)	Miller (21)	Mulholland (30)	Padula (3)	Rossi (19)	Rose (7)	Rowlands (14)	Royce (32)	Santos (23)	Shittu (5)	Simek (28)	Sturridge (20)	Thorpe (9)	Townsend (31)	OG
		7[c]		2[a]										1				11	10	4		8		B			5		3[b]	9		A				C		
		A		2					C					1				B	10	4		8		9[b]			5		7	6[c]		3[a]				11		
		7		2[b]					A					1			B	11	10	4		8[c]					5		3	9		C						
		7		2[b]					9[c]		C			1			3	11	10			8		B			5		4[a]	6		A						
		7		2	B				9[c]		C			1		A	3[a]	11	10			8[b]					5			6		4						
		7[c]		2	B				9		11			1		4[a]			10			8[b]		C			5		A	6		3						
		7		2	8				9[a]		B			1				11	10					A			5		3	6[b]		4						
		7		2	8				9					1				11	10								5		3	6		4						
				2	8				9[c]		7			1		A		11	10					B			5[a]		3	6[b]		4	C					
				2	7	B			9[b]		10			1				11	8					A					5	6[a]		4	3					
				2	7	A			9[a]		10[c]			1		5		11	8					C					B	6		4[b]	3					
		A		2	7[b]	C			9[c]		10			1				11	8					B					5	6[a]		4	3					
				2	7[b]	B			9		10[a]			1				11	8					A			C		5	6		4	3[c]					
				2	7				9					1	A			10	8					11			5[a]			6		4		3				
		7[a]		2	8	6			9					1	A				11					B					5	10		4		3[b]				
		A		2	8	7[b]			9					1				11	10					B			C		5[c]	6[a]		4		3				
				6	8	7[a]			9					1				11	10					B			5[b]		4			3		2		A		
					7				9[b]		10			1				11	8					B			C		5			4	3	2[c]		6[a]		
		7		2					9[b]		10			1				11	8					A			B		5			4	3					
		C		2	7				B		10[c]			1				11	8					9[b]			A		5[a]			4	3					
		B		2	7				9[a]		10[b]			1				11	8					A			5					4	3					
		7		2					10[a]		B			1				11	9					A	8		5					4	3					
		7[a]		2	8[c]						B			1				11	10					C	9		5			A		4	3					
			A	2	7				B		10			1				11	8						9[c]		5[a]			6[b]		4	3					
			A	2	8				9[c]					1		B		11	10						7[a]		5[b]			6		4	3					
			10	2	7[c]				9[b]					1		4		11	8					A	C		5[a]			6			3					
		7	10[a]	2										1		5		11	8					A						9		3	4					
			B	2	7						A			1		5		11	10[b]					9	8[a]					6		3	4					
		B							9[c]		10[b]		4[a]			2		11	7					C			5		A		1	8	3					
				C					9		10[a]		4			2		11	7								5[c]			B	1	8	3			A		
									9		10[a]		4			2		11	7								5		C	B	1	8	3			A[c]		
				C	A				9[b]		10[a]		4			2[c]		11	7								5			B	1	8	3					
				2	7[a]				9[b]							5		11	10						A				4	6	1	8	3					
				2	7				9[b]							5		11	10						A				4[a]	6	1	8	3					
				2	7[b]				9[c]		B					5[a]		11	10										4	6	1	8	3			C		
				2	7				9[c]							A		11[b]	10						B				5[a]	8	1	4	3			C		
				2	7[a]				9				4			B		11	10										5[b]	6	1	8	3					
				2	7[c]				9[b]		A		4					11	10										5	8	1	C	3		B			
				2	7[c]				9		B		4					11	10						C		5			6[a]	1	8	3		A[b]			
B				2	7				9		A		4					11[a]	10						6[b]				5		1	8	3					
	A			2	7				9		B		4						10						8		5[b]			6[a]	1	11	3					
C	8[c]			2	7				6		A			1		B		11[a]	10						9		5		3[b]				4					
1[a]				2	7[c]				9		6			1		8			10		A[b]		3			C	5						4				B	
1[a]		8		2			B		9[b]		6					C			7						10[c]		5	1				3	4				A	
		A		2	7[a]				9									11	8								5	1		6		3	4			10		
				2	7				9		11								8								5	1		6		3	4			10		
2	1	13	2	41	32	3			38		18		9	30		13	2	39	46	3		6	1	4	9		28	3	24	31	13	39	33	5		4		
2	1	7	3	2	3	4	1		4		12				2	7	1	1			1			20	5	1	5		4	4		4	1		2	6	2	
		1			1				2		4							18	10					1					2	3		5	4					1
		7				2[b]			9[a]		11			1		4			10					5			A			8			3			B		
		1				1			1		1			1		1			1					1						1			1					
		1									1																											
		A		2	B				9		10[b]			1			3	11[c]	8					C			5			6		7	4[a]					
				2		8			C		11			1		5		A	10	4[b]		7[a]		9						6[c]		B	3					
				2		1			1		2			2		1	1	1	2	1		1		1			1			2		1	2					
		1			1				1									1						1								1						
											1								1					1						1								
2	1	14	2	43	32	5			40		21		9	33		15	3	40	49	4		7	1	6	9		29	3	24	34	13	40	36	5		4		
2	1	8	3	2	4	4	1		5		12				2	7	1	2			1			21	5	1	6		4	4		5	1		2	7	2	
		1			1				2		5							18	11					2					2	4		5	4					1

2005-06

Championship

	P	W	D	L	F	A	Pts
Reading	46	31	13	2	99	32	106
Sheffield United	46	26	12	8	76	46	90
Watford	46	22	15	9	77	53	81
Preston North End	46	20	20	6	59	30	80
Leeds United	46	21	15	10	57	38	78
Crystal Palace	46	21	12	13	67	48	75
Wolverhampton W	46	16	19	11	50	42	67
Coventry City	46	16	15	15	62	65	63
Norwich City	46	18	8	20	56	65	62
Luton Town	46	17	10	19	66	67	61
Cardiff City	46	16	12	18	58	59	60
Southampton	46	13	19	14	49	50	58
Stoke City	46	17	7	22	54	63	58
Plymouth Argyle	46	13	17	16	39	46	56
Ipswich Town	46	14	14	18	53	66	56
Leicester City	46	13	15	18	51	59	54
Burnley	46	14	12	20	46	54	54
Hull City	46	12	16	18	49	55	52
Sheffield Wednesday	46	13	13	20	39	52	52
Derby County	46	10	20	16	53	67	50
Queen's Park Rangers	46	12	14	20	50	65	50
Crewe Alexandra	46	9	15	22	57	86	42
Millwall	46	8	16	22	35	62	40
Brighton & Hove Albion	46	7	17	22	39	71	38

Attendances

	TOTAL		
	Home	Away	Total
League	309,133	414,922	724,055
Cup/Other		17,242	17,242
TOTAL	309,133	432,164	741,297

	AVERAGE		
	Home	Away	Total
League	13,441	18,040	15,740
Cup/Other		8,621	8,621
TOTAL	13,441	17,287	15,444

Match No.	Date		Opponents	Location	Result		Scorers	Atten
1	Aug	6	Hull City	A	D	0-0		2
2		9	Ipswich Town	H	W	2-1	Gallen, Rowlands	1
3		13	Sheffield United	H	W	2-1	Bircham, Moore	1
4		20	Coventry City	A	L	0-3		2
5		26	Sheffield Wednesday	H	D	0-0		1
6		30	Wolverhampton Wanderers	A	L	1-3	Gallen	2
7	Sep	10	Southampton	A	D	1-1	Shittu	2
8		13	Luton Town	H	W	1-0	Cook	1
9		17	Leeds United	H	L	0-1		1
10		24	Leicester City	A	W	2-1	Nygaard, Furlong	2
11		27	Millwall	A	D	1-1	Nygaard	1
12	Oct	3	Crystal Palace	H	L	1-3	Ainsworth	1
13		15	Preston North End	A	D	1-1	Shittu	1
14		18	Plymouth Argyle	H	D	1-1	Gallen (pen)	1
15		22	Norwich City	H	W	3-0	Nygaard, Furlong, Santos	1
16		29	Derby County	A	W	2-1	Ainsworth, Gallen	2
17	Nov	1	Watford	A	L	1-3	Shittu	1
18		5	Reading	H	L	1-2	Cook	1
19		19	Plymouth Argyle	A	L	1-3	Baidoo	1
20		22	Preston North End	H	L	0-2		1
21		26	Hull City	H	D	2-2	Ainsworth (2)	1
22	Dec	3	Stoke City	A	W	2-1	Furlong, Langley (pen)	1
23		10	Ipswich Town	A	D	2-2	Moore, Furlong	2
24		19	Coventry City	H	L	0-1		1
25		26	Brighton & Hove Albion	A	L	0-1		
26		28	Cardiff City	H	W	1-0	Nygaard	1
27		31	Crewe Alexandra	A	W	4-3	Cook, Baidoo, Rowlands, Langley	
28	Jan	2	Burnley	H	D	1-1	Ainsworth	1
29		14	Southampton	H	W	1-0	Langley (pen)	1
30		21	Luton Town	A	L	0-2		
31		31	Leicester City	H	L	2-3	Ainsworth, Shittu	1
32	Feb	4	Leeds United	A	L	0-2		2
33		11	Millwall	H	W	1-0	Nygaard	1
34		14	Crystal Palace	A	L	1-2	Furlong	1
35		25	Sheffield United	A	W	3-2	Nygaard, OG (Morgan), Furlong	2
36	Mar	4	Wolverhampton Wanderers	H	D	0-0		1
37		11	Sheffield Wednesday	A	D	1-1	Bircham	2
38		18	Brighton & Hove Albion	H	D	1-1	Ainsworth	1
39		25	Cardiff City	A	D	0-0		1
40		29	Stoke City	H	L	1-2	Nygaard	1
41	Apr	1	Crewe Alexandra	H	L	1-2	Ainsworth	1
42		8	Burnley	A	L	0-1		1
43		15	Derby County	H	D	1-1	Nygaard	1
44		17	Norwich City	A	L	2-3	Ainsworth, Cook	2
45		22	Watford	H	L	1-2	Nygaard (pen)	1
46		30	Reading	A	L	1-2	Furlong	2

Appeara
Sub appeara
G

FA Cup

R3	Jan	7	Blackburn Rovers	A	L	0-3		1

Appeara
Sub appeara
G

League Cup

R1	Aug	23	Northampton Town	A	L	0-3		

Appeara
Sub appeara
G

Total - Appeara
Total - Sub appeara
Total - G

Baidoo (28)	Bailey (23)	Barnes (21)	Bean (16)	Bignot (2)	Bircham (8)	Brown (19)	Clarke (36)	Cole (12)	Cook (17)	Doherty (6)	Donnelly (27)	Dyer (33)	Evatt (4)	Furlong (29)	Gallen (10)	Hislop (22)	Johnson (26)	Jones P. (21)	Jones R. (36)	Kanyuka (24)	Kus (19)	Langley (40)	Lomas (31)	Lowe (37)	Milanese (3)	Miller (21)	Moore (18)	Nygaard (30)	Rose (7)	Rowlands (14)	Royce (1)	Santos (15)	Shimmin (20)	Shittu (5)	Sturridge (9)	Taylor (33)	Townsend (25)	Ukah (32)	Youssouf (16)	OG
				2	7				9	8[b]				11	10												C		5	6[a]	1	4		3	A[c]					
				2	7					8				11[b]	10												A	B	5	9	1	4		3						
			C	2	7	B				8[a]				11	10												A		5	9[c]	1	4		3						
			C	2[b]	8[c]	9[a]								11	7										A		10		5		1		4	3				B		
				2	7					8				11	10										5	9[a]	A		4		1			3						
			A	6	7[b]					8[a]			2	11	10										5		9				1	4		3						
				2	7				9	8[b]				11[c]								C	B		5		6	A			1	4		3	10[a]					
				2	7				9	8				11[b]								A	C		5		10[c]	B			1	4		3						
				2	7				9				A	11									8		5[a]		A			B	1	4		3	10[a]					
				2	7				9[c]				C	11		5[a]						6[b]	8					10			1	4	A	3						
				2	7				9			5										6[a]	8				B	10			1	4		3	11[b]					
B				2[c]	7				9	8[a]		5	C	11								A					10[b]				1	4		3						
				2					9[b]	A		5	3	11	7								6[a]					10			1	8		4						
				2	7				9[c]	8[a]		5	3	11[b]	6													10			1	C		4	B					
				2	7[b]				9[c]	8		5	3	11	6													10[a]			1	B		4	A					
				2						7[b]		5	3	11	9							B			C		A				1	8		4	10[a]					
				2					A	7		5	3		9							C					11[c]	B			1	8[b]		4	10					
				2					9	7		5	3		8							6									1	10		4	11[a]					
B			C	2					9	8[a]		5	3		10							7[b]								A	1	11[c]		4						
1[b]			C	2					9[a]			5	3		10							8					A			7	1	B		4						
				2					A			9	3	11	10[b]							7			5		B			8	1	4[a]								
C			8	2					B			5[a]	A	11								7			4		10[c]			9	1			3						
			8	2					C			5[a]	B	11								7[b]			4		10			9[c]	1	A		3						
			8[a]	2	B			C	A			5	3									9					11			7	1	10[b]		4						
			8[b]	2	C			1	B			5	3	11								9					10[a]	A		7				4						
A				2	7[c]				9[b]					11								8			C			10[a]	5	6	1	4		3						
1				2	7[a]				9					C								8			B			10[c]	5	6	1	4[b]		3						
1				2					9		C			A								8[c]			5			10[a]	3[b]	7	1	B		4						
0[b]				2					9		C			11								8	7				B		5		1	4[a]		3		A				
0[a]				2[c]					9					11								8	7				B	A	5		1	4		3		C				
A				2					9		C			11[b]								8	7				B	10[a]	5		1	4		3						
		1		8			10		9[b]												2[c]	C	7	4			11	A						3		5			B	
A				2	7[b]				9				3	11				1				B	8		5			10[a]						4						
B				2[a]					10		7[b]		3	A				1				8	9		5			11	6					4						
				2	7				9				3	11				1				6	8[b]					10[a]	5			B		4					A	
	8			2					9					11	10[a]			1				7			5				4					3					A	
B				2	7				9[a]				C	11[b]	10			1				A	8		5				4[c]					3						
B				2	8				9[b]				4		10			1					7		5			11[a]						3					A	
				2	8				9				4	A				1				B	7		5			11[b]						3					10[a]	
				2	8[b]				9				4	C				1				B	7		5		A	11						3					10[a]	
				2[a]	8				9				4	11[b]				1				A	7		5		B	10						3						
1					8[b]				9		B		4					1			2[a]	7	A		5			10						3						
	8								9		10[a]		4	A				1			2	7			5			11						3						
	7			2					9					11				1					8		5			10				4		3						
	7			2[a]					9		A			11				1	B				8[b]		5			10				4		3						
	7[b]			2				A	9		10			11				1[a]	B			8			5							4		3						
6	5	1	4	44	24	1	1	1	34	14	3	15	21	31	18	1		14			3	22	18	1	22	1	11	20	15	12	30	25	1	45	6	1			2	
9			5		2	1		2	6	1	5		6	6					2			11	3		4		14	7		2		6	1		3	2		1	4	
2					2				4					7	4							3					2	9		2		1		4						1
0				2					9[b]		B			11[c]								8			5		C		4	6	1	7[a]		3						
1				1					1					1								1			1				1	1	1	1		1						
											1																1													
B			7	A	8[b]	9							3		10										5	6	11[a]				1		4					2		
			1		1	1							1		1										1	1	1				1		1					1		
1				1																																				
7	5	1	5	45	25	2	1	1	35	14	3	15	22	32	19	1		14			3	23	18	1	24	2	12	20	16	13	32	26	2	46	6	1		1	2	
0			5	1	2	1		2	6	1	6		6	6					2			11	3		4		15	7		2		6	1		3	2		1	4	
2					2				4					7	4							3					2	9		2		1		4						1

2006-07

Championship

	P	W	D	L	F	A	Pts
Sunderland	46	27	7	12	76	47	88
Birmingham City	46	26	8	12	67	42	86
Derby County	46	25	9	12	62	46	84
West Bromwich Albion	46	22	10	14	81	55	76
Wolverhampton W	46	22	10	14	59	56	76
Southampton	46	21	12	13	77	53	75
Preston North End	46	22	8	16	64	53	74
Stoke City	46	19	16	11	62	41	73
Sheffield Wednesday	46	20	11	15	70	66	71
Colchester United	46	20	9	17	70	56	69
Plymouth Argyle	46	17	16	13	63	62	67
Crystal Palace	46	18	11	17	59	51	65
Cardiff City	46	17	13	16	57	53	64
Ipswich Town	46	18	8	20	64	59	62
Burnley	46	15	12	19	52	49	57
Norwich City	46	16	9	21	56	71	57
Coventry City	46	16	8	22	47	62	56
Queen's Park Rangers	46	14	11	21	54	68	53
Leicester City	46	13	14	19	49	64	53
Barnsley	46	15	5	26	53	85	50
Hull City	46	13	10	23	51	67	49
Southend United	46	10	12	24	47	80	42
Luton Town	46	10	10	26	53	81	40
Leeds United	46	13	7	26	46	72	36

Attendances

	TOTAL		
	Home	**Away**	**Total**
League	297,537	448,188	745,725
Cup/Other	14,633	11,044	25,677
TOTAL	312,170	459,232	771,402

	AVERAGE		
	Home	**Away**	**Total**
League	12,936	19,486	16,211
Cup/Other	7,317	5,522	6,419
TOTAL	12,487	18,369	15,428

Match No.	Date		Opponents	Location	Result		Scorers	Atten
1	Aug	5	Burnley	A	L	0-2		12
2		8	Leeds United	H	D	2-2	Rowlands (pen), Baidoo	13
3		12	Southend United	H	W	2-0	Rowlands, Ward	12
4		19	Preston North End	A	D	1-1	Ainsworth	11
5		25	Ipswich Town	H	L	1-3	Gallen	10
6	Sep	9	Plymouth Argyle	A	D	1-1	Blackstock	12
7		12	Birmingham City	H	L	0-2		10
8		16	Colchester United	A	L	1-2	OG (Brown)	5
9		23	Hull City	H	W	2-0	R.Jones, Blackstock	11
10		30	Southampton	A	W	2-1	Blackstock, R.Jones	25
11	Oct	14	Norwich City	H	D	3-3	Smith, Rowlands (2)	14
12		17	Derby County	H	L	1-2	Smith	10
13		21	Sheffield Wednesday	A	L	2-3	Blackstock (2)	23
14		28	Leicester City	H	D	1-1	Rowlands (pen)	12
15		31	West Bromwich Albion	A	D	3-3	Stewart, Gallen, Nygaard	17
16	Nov	4	Crystal Palace	H	W	4-2	Smith (2), Lomas, Gallen (pen)	13
17		11	Luton Town	A	W	3-2	Smith, OG (Heikkinen), Blackstock	9
18		17	Cardiff City	A	W	1-0	R.Jones	13
19		25	Coventry City	H	L	0-1		12
20		28	Sunderland	H	L	1-2	R.Jones	13
21	Dec	2	Crystal Palace	A	L	0-3		17
22		9	Stoke City	A	L	0-1		16
23		16	Wolverhampton Wanderers	H	L	0-1		12
24		23	Barnsley	H	W	1-0	Rowlands	11
25		26	Birmingham City	A	L	1-2	Cook	29
26		30	Norwich City	A	L	0-1		25
27	Jan	1	Colchester United	H	W	1-0	R.Jones	11
28		13	Hull City	A	L	1-2	Blackstock	19
29		20	Southampton	H	L	0-2		14
30		30	Barnsley	A	L	0-2		9
31	Feb	3	Burnley	H	W	3-1	Cook, Blackstock, Lomas	10
32		9	Southend United	A	L	0-5		10
33		20	Leeds United	A	D	0-0		29
34		24	Plymouth Argyle	H	D	1-1	Cook	13
35	Mar	3	Ipswich Town	A	L	1-2	Furlong	21
36		10	Sheffield Wednesday	H	D	1-1	Rowlands (pen)	15
37		13	Derby County	A	D	1-1	Rowlands	27
38		17	Leicester City	A	W	3-1	Idiakez, Nygaard (2, 1 pen)	24
39		31	West Bromwich Albion	H	L	1-2	Blackstock	14
40	Apr	3	Preston North End	H	W	1-0	Blackstock	11
41		7	Coventry City	A	W	1-0	Smith	22
42		9	Luton Town	H	W	3-2	Blackstock (2, 1 pen), Furlong	14
43		14	Sunderland	A	L	1-2	Rowlands (pen)	39
44		21	Cardiff City	H	W	1-0	Blackstock	12
45		28	Wolverhampton Wanderers	A	L	0-2		24
46	May	6	Stoke City	H	D	1-1	Rowlands	16

Appearar

Sub appearar

G

FA Cup

R3	Jan	6	Luton Town	H	D	2-2	Blackstock, Baidoo	10
R3 rep		23	Luton Town	A	L	0-1		7

Appearar

Sub appearar

G

League Cup

R1	Aug	22	Northampton Town	H	W	3-2	Cook, Gallen, R.Jones	4
R2	Sep	19	Port Vale	A	L	2-3	Nygaard, Stewart	3

Appearar

Sub appearar

G

Total - Appearar

Total - Sub appearar

Total - G

Baidoo (22)	Bailey (23)	Bignot (2)	Bircham (8)	Blackstock	Bolder (7)	Camp (20)	Cole (12)	Cook (17)	Cullip (4)	Czerkas (27)	Donnelly (20)	Furlong (29)	Gallen (10)	Howell A. (33)	Idiakez (28)	Jones P. (21)	Jones R. (31)	Kanyuka (24)	Lomas (16)	Mancienne (38)	Milanese (3)	Moore (18)	Nygaard (30)	Oliseh (28)	Rehmann (5)	Ricketts (34)	Rose M. (7)	Rowlands (14)	Royce (1)	Shimmin (15)	Smith (37)	Stewart (25)	Timoska (27)	Ward (9)	OG
		2	B					9		11[b]	C					1	A		8[a]		5						4	7[c]				3		10	
3		2[b]	C					9		11[a]						1	A		8		5						4	7[c]				3		10	
				11				9					B			1	10[b]		A		5				4		2	7[a]				3		8	
C				11				9					B			1	10[b]		A		5				4		2	7[a]				3		8	
3			A	11				9					6			1	10		7[a]		5[b]				4		2					3		8	
			8[a]	11[b]				9					C			1	B		A		5		10[c]	6	4		2					3		7	
3			8	11[a]				9								1	A				5		10	6	4[b]		2					3		7	
[b]			8				1	9		A	B						11[a]				5		10		4		2					3		7	
	8[b]	2	7[c]	11				9								1	10	A	B						3		5[a]	6				4		C	
	8[c]	2	7[b]	11				9								1	10	A	B						3		5[a]	6			C	4			
		5	7	11				9					A			1	10[a]		2[b]						3		B	6			8	4			
		5	7	11				9			B		A			1	10[a]		2[b]						3			6			8	4			
		5[c]	7[a]	11				9					C			1	10		2	A					3			6[b]			8	4		B	
		5		11				9					B					4[a]	7	A			10[b]		2			6[c]	1		8	3			
		5		11[a]				9					10						7	2			A		3				1		8	4			
		5		11				9					10[a]						7	2			A		3				1		8[b]	4		B	
	7	5		11[a]				9					A[b]							2			10		3				1		8	4		B	
	7	5		11[b]				9									B			2			10		3				1		8	4		A	
	7[c]	5		11[a]				9					B				A			2			10[b]		3			C	1		8	4		6	
		5		11[b]				9[a]				B	10				A			2					3			8	1		7	4		6	
		5		11[b]								B	8				9			2			10[a]		3			6	1		7	4		A	
C	6	2		11[a]								A	9							3	5		10[c]					7[b]	1		8	4		B	
		2	7[a]	11								A	9				10			3	5				4			6	1		8				
		2	B	11				9				C					10[c]		7	4	5[a]				A			6	1		8[b]	3			
	A	6	7[a]	11[c]				9				10					C			4	5[b]				2			B	1		8	3			
		2		B				9				10	6[b]				11		8	4	5							7[a]	1			3		A	
A		5		11				9				B	8				10[b]	2	7	4									1			3		6[a]	
3		5[a]	6[b]	11[c]				9				C					10	2	7	4									1		8	3	A		
5	A		8[a]	11													10[b]		7	4			B		2				1		9	3	5		
				11	6			9				10[a]					A		7[b]	4			C		2[c]				1		8	3	5		
				10	6			11	3										7	2								9	1			4	8		
				10	6			11	3[b]								B		7	2					A			8	1			4	9[a]		
				10	8	1		11	3										7	2								9				4	5		
				10	8	1		11	3			A							7	2								9[a]				4	5		
					8	1		11	3			A					10		7[b]	2								9			B	4	5		
		5		11[a]	8	1		9	3			10			7[b]					2			A					6				4			
		5						9	3			10[b]			8		B		7[c]	2			11					6[a]	1		C	4			
		5			7	1		9	3			10[b]			8[a]		B		A	2			11								C	4			
		5		B	7	1		9	3			10			8[a]				A	2			11[b]			C						4			
		5		11	8	1		9[b]	3									A	7	2[a]			10			B[c]					C	4			
		A		11	8[c]	1			3			10[b]						2	C			9	B								7	4	5[a]		
		5		11	8	1			3			C						2[b]	7			9	10[c]								A	4	B		
		2		11	8	1			3[a]			B			C			A	7[c]			10[b]						9			6	4	5		
		2		11[b]	8	1		9				B						3	7				10					6[a]			A	4	5		
	C	2			8[c]		1					10[b]					B	3[a]	7		5		11					6			9	4	A		
	8	5	B	11[a]	7[b]		1					A					C						10[c]					6		4	9	3	2		
2	7	32	12	37	16	11	3	37	13	2		9	9		4	12	17	7	26	26	14	3	17	2	23		10	27	20	1	22	45	11	11	
7	3	1	5	2						1	3	13	9		1		14	4	8	2			6		2	2	1	2			7		3	8	
				13				3				2	3		1		5		2				3					10			6	1		1	2
C		5	B	11				9				A					10[a]	2	7[b]	4									1		8	3		6[c]	
	8			11				9									A		7	4	5		10[a]		2				1		6[b]	3			
	1	1		2				2									1	1	2	2	1		1		1				2		2	2		1	
			1									1					1																		
				1																															
6	7	2	8[b]	11			1	9					10[a]	5			B	C						A	4							3[c]			
C	8	2	7				1	9		10							A	4			5[b]		11[a]				B					3		6[c]	
	2	2	2	1			2	2		1			1	1				1			1		1		1							2		1	
																	2	1						1			1								
								1					1				1						1									1			
3	10	35	14	40	16	11	5	41	13	3		9	10	1	4	12	18	9	28	28	16	3	19	2	25	0	10	27	22	1	24	49	11	13	
9	3	1	6	2						1	3	14	9		1		17	5	8	2			6	1	2	2	2	2			7		3	8	
2				14				4				2	4		1		6		2				4					10			6	2		1	2

2007-08

Championship

	P	W	D	L	F	A	Pts
West Bromwich Albion	46	23	12	11	88	55	81
Stoke City	46	21	16	9	69	55	79
Hull City	46	21	12	13	65	47	75
Bristol City	46	20	14	12	54	53	74
Crystal Palace	46	18	17	11	58	42	71
Watford	46	18	16	12	62	56	70
Wolverhampton W	46	18	16	12	53	48	70
Ipswich Town	46	18	15	13	65	56	69
Sheffield United	46	17	15	14	56	51	66
Plymouth Argyle	46	17	13	16	60	50	64
Charlton Athletic	46	17	13	16	63	58	64
Cardiff City	46	16	16	14	59	55	64
Burnley	46	16	14	16	60	67	62
Queen's Park Rangers	46	14	16	16	60	66	58
Preston North End	46	15	11	20	50	56	56
Sheffield Wednesday	46	14	13	19	54	55	55
Norwich City	46	15	10	21	49	59	55
Barnsley	46	14	13	19	52	65	55
Blackpool	46	12	18	16	59	64	54
Southampton	46	13	15	18	56	72	54
Coventry City	46	14	11	21	52	64	53
Leicester City	46	12	16	18	42	45	52
Scunthorpe United	46	11	13	22	46	69	46
Colchester United	46	7	17	22	62	86	38

Attendances

TOTAL

	Home	Away	Total
League	321,049	397,960	719,009
Cup/Other	5,260	41,289	46,549
TOTAL	326,309	439,249	765,558

AVERAGE

	Home	Away	Total
League	13,959	17,303	15,631
Cup/Other	5,260	41,289	23,275
TOTAL	13,596	18,302	15,949

Match No.	Date		Opponents	Location	Result		Scorers	Atte
1	Aug	11	Bristol City	A	D	2-2	Blackstock, Stewart	1
2		18	Cardiff City	H	L	0-2		1
3	Sep	1	Southampton	H	L	0-3		1
4		15	Leicester City	A	D	1-1	Leigertwood	2
5		18	Plymouth Argyle	H	L	0-2		1
6		22	Watford	H	D	1-1	Moore	1
7		30	West Bromwich Albion	A	L	1-5	Ainsworth	2
8	Oct	3	Colchester United	A	L	2-4	Ephraim, Vine	
9		8	Norwich City	H	W	1-0	Rowlands (pen)	1
10		20	Ipswich Town	H	D	1-1	Nygaard	1
11		23	Preston North End	A	D	0-0		1
12		27	Charlton Athletic	A	W	1-0	Bolder	2
13	Nov	3	Hull City	H	W	2-0	Ephraim, Leigertwood	1
14		6	Coventry City	H	L	1-2	Buzsaky	1
15		10	Crystal Palace	A	D	1-1	Sinclair	1
16		24	Sheffield Wednesday	H	D	0-0		1
17		27	Stoke City	A	L	1-3	Vine	1
18	Dec	1	Blackpool	A	L	0-1		
19		4	Crystal Palace	H	L	1-2	Stewart	1
20		8	Scunthorpe United	A	D	2-2	Buzsaky (2)	
21		11	Burnley	A	W	2-0	Stewart, Vine	1
22		15	Wolverhampton Wanderers	H	D	0-0		1
23		22	Colchester United	H	W	2-1	Buzsaky (2)	1
24		26	Plymouth Argyle	A	L	1-2	Vine	1
25		29	Watford	A	W	4-2	Rowlands (2, 1 pen), Stewart, Buzsaky	1
26	Jan	1	Leicester City	H	W	3-1	Stewart, Bolder, Blackstock	1
27		12	Sheffield United	A	L	1-2	Agyemang	2
28		19	Barnsley	H	W	2-0	Agyemang, Vine	1
29		29	Cardiff City	A	L	1-3	Agyemang	1
30	Feb	2	Bristol City	H	W	3-0	Agyemang (2), Buzsaky	1
31		9	Southampton	A	W	3-2	Rowlands, Agyemang (2)	2
32		12	Burnley	H	L	2-4	Mahon, Agyemang	1
33		23	Sheffield United	H	D	1-1	Balanta	1
34		26	Barnsley	A	D	0-0		
35	Mar	2	Stoke City	H	W	3-0	Leigertwood (2), Buzsaky	1
36		6	Coventry City	A	D	0-0		1
37		8	Sheffield Wednesday	A	L	1-2	Delaney	1
38		11	Blackpool	H	W	3-2	Buzsaky, Vine, Rowlands	1
39		15	Scunthorpe United	H	W	3-1	Rowlands (pen), Agyemang, Vine	1
40		22	Wolverhampton Wanderers	A	D	3-3	Buzsaky, Blackstock (pen), Leigertwood	2
41		29	Ipswich Town	A	D	0-0		2
42	Apr	5	Preston North End	H	D	2-2	Blackstock, Ainsworth	1
43		12	Hull City	A	D	1-1	Blackstock	2
44		19	Charlton Athletic	H	W	1-0	Blackstock	1
45		26	Norwich City	A	L	0-3		2
46	May	4	West Bromwich Albion	H	L	0-2		1

Appeara
Sub appeara
(

FA Cup

R3	Jan	5	Chelsea	A	L	0-1		4

Appeara
Sub appeara
(

League Cup

R1	Aug	14	Leyton Orient	H	L	1-2	Rowlands	

Appeara
Sub appeara
(

Total - Appeara
Total - Sub appeara
Total - (

Ainsworth (11)	Bailey (23)	Balanta (36)	Barker (3)	Bignot (2)	Blackstock (9)	Bolder (7)	Buzsaky (10)	Camp (1)	Cole (12)	Connolly (16)	Cranie (33)	Cullip (4)	Curtis (21)	Delaney (2)	Ephraim (25)	Hall (29)	Jarrett (16)	Lee (21)	Leigertwood (32)	Mahon (4)	Malcolm (25)	Mancienne (6)	Moore (18)	Nardiello (8)	Nygaard (30)	Rehman (28)	Rose (37)	Rowlands (14)	Sahar (17)	Sinclair (34)	St. Aimie (20)	Stewart (5)	Timoska (27)	Vine (26)	Walton (19)	Ward (29)
	8				11[b]	7		1					5		A							4	6	10[a]	B	2		9				3				
					11	7		1					5		8							4	6[a]	10[b]	B	2		9				3				A
			5		11[a]	8		1				C	2		9				7			4[c]		B	A			6	10[b]			3				
			5		11	8[b]		1				2			B				7				9	A		4		6	10[a]			3				
			5	B	11	8		1				2			A				7				9[a]	10[c]		4[b]		6	C			3				
6[b]			5		11	8		1				4			A				7				B	10[a]				9				3	2			
6			5[c]	C	11	7		1				3	A		B								9			2[a]		8	10[b]			4				
6[b]			5		10	7		1				4			9		8[a]		3				B					2	A					11		
6[b]			5			8		1			4				9[c]		B		7				A					2	10[a]			3	C	11		
6[b]			5			7		1			4				10				8			2[a]	B		A			9				3		11		
6[a]			5			7		1			4				10				8			2			A			9				3		11		
			5			7		1			4				9				8			2			10			6				3		11		
B			5			A	8[b]	1			4				9				7			2		C	10[a]			6				3		11[c]		
			5			B	8	1			4[a]								7[b]			2		C	10[c]			6		9		3	A	11		
A			5			8[b]	10	1											7			4				B		6[a]	C	9		3	2	11[c]		
			5		10[b]		8	1											7		4[a]	2			B			6		9		3	A	11		
			5		10	C	8	1											7		A	4[a]			B			6[c]		9		3	2	11[b]		
B			5			8	7[c]	1											4		2		C		A			6	10[a]	9		3		11[b]		
		B	5			C	8[c]	1											7		2				A	4		6[a]	10[b]	9		3		11		
C			5			8	6[c]	1											9		2				B	4[a]		7		10[b]		3	A	11		
6[c]			5		A	7		1											8		2		C		10[b]	4				9[a]		3		11	B	
6			5		10[a]		8	1											7		2				11	4		9		A		3				
6			5		10[a]	8	9	1											7[b]		2				A	4						3		11	B	
6			5		B	8	10[b]	1											7		2				A	4		9[a]						11	3	
6[a]		8[b]	5		10	7	B	1													2				11[c]	4		9				3		A	C	
6[a]			5		10[c]	7[b]	8	1												A	2				B	4		9				3		11	C	
			5[a]		A		10	1		2						3		6		7								8				4		9		
					10[c]		9	1		2				5	C	3[a]		B	8			A						7				4[b]		6		
					B		9[c]	1		2[b]				5	C	3[a]			8	7		A						6				4		10		
							6	1		B				5	9[a]			A	C	7		2				4[b]		8				3		10[c]		
					B		A	1		3				5	9[c]			6[a]	C	7		2				4		8						10		
					B		6	1		2[c]				5	9[b]				A	7		C				4		8[a]				3		10		
		9[b]			B			1		4[a]				5	6	3			8			2						7				A		10		
		9[a]			10[b]		6[c]	1		4				5	A	3			8			2						7				C		B		
C					A		6	1		4				5	9	3[b]			8			2						7[c]				B		10[a]		
B					A		6	1		4				5	9	3			8			2						7[b]						10		
		C			10		6[c]	1		4				5	A				7[b]	B		2						8				3		9[a]		
					10		6[b]	1		4				5		3		B	7	A		2				C		8[c]						9		
					10		6[a]	1		4				5		3		C	7	A		2						8[b]				B		9		
C					10		6[c]	1		4[b]				5		3			7	A		2				B		8[a]						9		
		C			10			1		5					9[c]	4		B	7[a]	8		2						A				3		6[b]		
B		A			10			1		5					9[a]	4			6	7[b]		2						8				3				
6[c]		B			10[a]			1		C				5	9	4			A	7		2						8				3				
6[b]		11			10		B	1		2				5	9[c]	4[a]			C	7		A						8				3				
6[a]		11			10			1		4				5	9[b]				A	7		2				B		8				3				
6		11[a]			10			1		4				5	9[b]				A	7		2				3	B	8								
16	1	6	25		26	20	24	46		18	6	5	3	17	20	14	1	2	33	11	10	26	5	4	6	17		43	6	8		35	3	31	1	
8		5		2	9	4	3			2		1	1		9		1	5	7	5	1	4	6	4	13	4	1	1	3	1		4	4	2	4	1
2		1			6	2	10							1	2				5	1			1		1			6		1		5		7		
6[a]		C	5		11		10[b]	1		2					9[c]	3		B		8								7				4				
1			1		1		1	1		1					1	1				1								1				1				
		1																1																		
	8			5[c]		7		1				3	C									4	10[a]		11	2[b]		9			A	B				6
	1			1		1		1				1										1	1		1	1		1								1
													1																		1	1				
			1																																	
17	2	6	26	1	27	21	25	48		19	6	6	3	17	21	15	1	2	33	12	10	27	6	4	7	18		45	6	8		36	3	31	1	1
8		6		2	9	4	3			2		1	2		9		1	6	7	5	1	4	6	4	13	4	1	1	3	1	1	5	4	2	4	1
2		1			6	2	10							1	2				5	1			1		1			7		1		5		7		0

2008-09

Championship

	P	W	D	L	F	A	Pts
Wolverhampton W	46	27	9	10	80	52	90
Birmingham City	46	23	14	9	54	37	83
Sheffield United	46	22	14	10	64	39	80
Reading	46	21	14	11	72	40	77
Burnley	46	21	13	12	72	60	76
Preston North End	46	21	11	14	66	54	74
Cardiff City	46	19	17	10	65	53	74
Swansea	46	16	20	10	63	50	68
Ipswich Town	46	17	15	14	62	53	66
Bristol City	46	15	16	15	54	54	61
Queen's Park Rangers	46	15	16	15	42	44	61
Sheffield Wednesday	46	16	13	17	51	58	61
Watford	46	16	10	20	68	72	58
Doncaster Rovers	46	17	7	22	42	53	58
Crystal Palace	46	15	12	19	52	55	57
Blackpool	46	13	17	16	47	58	56
Coventry City	46	13	15	18	47	58	54
Derby County	46	14	12	20	55	67	54
Nottingham Forest	46	13	14	19	50	65	53
Barnsley	46	13	13	20	45	58	52
Plymouth Argyle	46	13	12	21	44	57	51
Norwich City	46	12	10	24	57	70	46
Southampton	46	10	15	21	46	69	45
Charlton Athletic	46	8	15	23	52	74	39

Attendances

TOTAL	Home	Away	Total
League	324,078	416,329	740,407
Cup/Other	16,917	95,070	111,987
TOTAL	340,995	511,399	852,394

AVERAGE	Home	Away	Total
League	14,090	18,101	16,096
Cup/Other	8,459	23,768	18,665
TOTAL	13,640	18,941	16,392

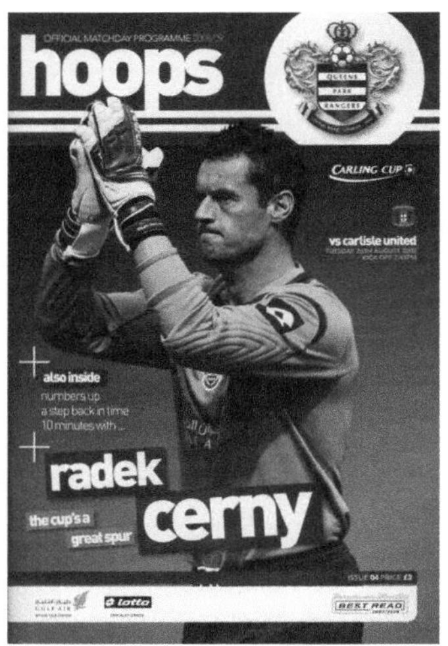

Match No.	Date		Opponents	Location	Result		Scorers	Atten
1	Aug	9	Barnsley	H	W	2-1	Hall (2)	14
2		16	Sheffield United	A	L	0-3		25
3		23	Doncaster Rovers	H	W	2-0	Blackstock, Ledesma	15
4		30	Bristol City	A	D	1-1	Blackstock	17
5	Sep	13	Southampton	H	W	4-1	Blackstock (2), Stewart, Agyemang	13
6		17	Norwich City	A	W	1-0	Rowlands	24
7		20	Coventry City	A	L	0-1		16
8		27	Derby County	H	L	0-2		14
9		30	Blackpool	H	D	1-1	Blackstock	12
10	Oct	4	Birmingham City	A	L	0-1		18
11		18	Nottingham Forest	H	W	2-1	Balanta, Buzsaky	15
12		21	Swansea City	A	D	0-0		13
13		25	Reading	A	D	0-0		20
14		28	Birmingham City	H	W	1-0	Di Carmine	13
15	Nov	1	Ipswich Town	A	L	0-2		20
16		8	Cardiff City	H	W	1-0	Mahon	13
17		15	Burnley	H	L	1-2	Blackstock	13
18		22	Watford	A	L	0-3		16
19		25	Charlton Athletic	H	W	2-1	Blackstock (2)	12
20		29	Crystal Palace	A	D	0-0		16
21	Dec	6	Wolverhampton Wanderers	H	W	1-0	Rowlands	13
22		9	Sheffield Wednesday	A	L	0-1		14
23		13	Plymouth Argyle	A	D	1-1	Helguson	10
24		20	Preston North End	H	W	3-2	Helguson (2), Blackstock	14
25		26	Charlton Athletic	A	D	2-2	Cook, Blackstock	21
26		28	Watford	H	D	0-0		16
27	Jan	10	Coventry City	H	D	1-1	Blackstock	13
28		17	Derby County	A	W	2-0	Routledge, Leigertwood	28
29		27	Blackpool	A	W	3-0	Helguson (2, 1 pen), Ephrain	6
30		31	Reading	H	D	0-0		17
31	Feb	7	Nottingham Forest	A	D	2-2	Alberti (2)	25
32		21	Ipswich Town	H	L	1-3	Di Carmine	13
33		25	Cardiff City	A	D	0-0		17
34		28	Barnsley	A	L	1-2	Delaney	11
35	Mar	3	Norwich City	H	L	0-1		13
36		7	Sheffield United	H	D	0-0		13
37		10	Doncaster Rovers	A	L	0-2		10
38		14	Southampton	A	D	0-0		18
39		17	Swansea City	H	W	1-0	Leigertwood	12
40		21	Bristol City	H	W	2-1	Lopez, Taarabt	14
41	Apr	4	Crystal Palace	H	D	0-0		15
42		11	Burnley	A	L	0-1		15
43		13	Sheffield Wednesday	H	W	3-2	Vine, Mahon, Stewart	13
44		18	Wolverhampton Wanderers	A	L	0-1		27
45		25	Plymouth Argyle	H	D	0-0		14
46	May	3	Preston North End	A	L	1-2	Agyemang	18

Appeara
Sub appeara
G

FA Cup

R3	Jan	3	Burnley	H	D	0-0		8
R3 rep		13	Burnley	A	L	1-2 aet	Di Carmine	3

Appeara
Sub appeara
G

League Cup

R1	Aug	12	Swindon Town	A	W	3-2	Balanta, Blackstock, Delaney	7
R2		26	Carlisle United	H	W	4-0	Stewart, Ledesma (3)	8
R3	Sep	24	Aston Villa	A	W	1-0	Stewart	21
R4	Nov	11	Manchester United	A	L	0-1		62

Appeara
Sub appeara
G

Total - Appeara
Total - Sub appeara
Total - G

Alberti (21)	Balanta (19)	Blackstock (9)	Bolder (12)	Buzsaky (10)	Camp (1)	Cerny (24)	Cole (23)	Connolly (16)	Cook (17)	Delaney (2)	Di Carmine (22)	Ephraim (25)	German (32)	Gorkss (13)	Hall (5)	Helguson (27)	Ledesma (20)	Leigertwood (6)	Lopez (20)	Mahon (4)	Miller (18)	Parejo (7)	Ramage (15)	Rehman (18)	Rose (30)	Routledge (7)	Rowlands (14)	Stewart (3)	Taarabt (39)	Tommasi (18)	Vine (8)
B		11				1			9	5				4	3		8[b]	7		6		A	2								
B	10[a]	11				1		5	9[b]	2	A			4	3		6	7				8									
	B	11				1		A	9[b]	5					3[a]		10	7		6		8[c]	2				C	4			
		11				1		3	9[a]	5							6	7		8		10[b]	2				A	4			
		11				1		3	9	5		6[a]						7		8		10[b]	2				B	4			
		11[b]		C		1		3	9[a]	5				A			10[c]	7		8			2				6	4			
		11[c]		A		1			9	5				3			10[a]	7		8		B	2[b]				6	4			
		11		10[a]		1		2	A	5					3		6[c]	B		7[b]		9					8	4			
		11		C		1			9	5					3		10[b]	A		7[c]		6[a]	2				8	4			
		11		A		1		C	9	5					3		B	7		8[a]			2[c]				6[b]	4			
	10[b]	11		7[c]		1		A	9	5	B				3[a]			8		C			2				6	4			
		11		10		1		C	9[b]	5					3		B	7		8		A	2[c]				6[a]	4			
	B	A		6		1		5	9		10[a]				3			2		7		11[b]					8	4			
		11[b]		B		1		5	9[a]		10[c]	C			3		6	2		A							7	4		8	
		A		10[b]		1		2	9	5	11[a]				3		B					6					7	4		8	
		10		A		1		5	9		11[c]				3		6[a]			B			2				7	4		8[b]	
		10				1		5[a]	9	A	11	6[c]			3					B			2				7	4		8[b]	
		10[c]				1				5	C	9			3		6[b]	7		8[a]		B	2					4		A	
		10				1				5	11[a]	6		4			C	7		B		9[c]	2					3		8[b]	
		11[b]				1				5	C	10		4		A		7		8		9[a]	2				B	3			
		11[a]				1			A[c]	5	C	6		4		10[b]				7			2				8	3		B	
						1			A	5[c]	B	6[a]		4	C	10		9		7[b]			2				8	3			
		B				1			9[a]	5		A		4	C	10		8		7			2[c]				6	3			
		C				1			9	5[b]		6		4	B	10		A		7[a]			2[c]				8	3			
6[a]		11				1		5	9[b]		10[c]	A		4	3	C	B	7					2				8				
		A				1			9[a]	5		6			3	10		B		7[b]			2				8	4			
		11				1		2		5[a]	B	6[c]		4	C	10	A	7[b]								9	8	3			
C						1		2	10[c]	5	B	A		4		11[b]		8		7						6	9[a]	3			
		B			1			2[c]	10	5		A		4	C	11[b]		8		7	9[a]					6		3			
		B			1			2	10[c]	5	C	A		4		11[b]		8		7[a]	9					6		3			
10[c]	C	A			1			2		5	11[a]	B		4				8		7	9[b]					6		3			
	C	B			1			2	10	5[b]	11[a]			4	3	A		8		7	9[c]					6					
A		B				1		2	10	5	C			4		11[c]		8		7[b]	9[a]					6		3			
7[b]		10				1		2		5	C			4		11[c]		8	B		9[a]				A	6		3			
		10				1		2		5	B	A		4[c]	C	11[b]		8	9		7[a]					6		3			
A	B	10				1		2		5	11[b]	C		4				8[c]	9		7[a]					6		3			
9[b]		10				1		5			11			4[a]				8[c]	A	7	C		2		B	6		3			
		11				1		5				6[b]	A	4				8[c]	9	C	7[a]		2			10		3	B		
10						1		5		B	11[a]	6		4	3[b]	A		8	9[c]		C		2						7		
10[a]						1		3[b]	C	5	11[c]	6		4		B		8	9				2			A			7		
	C					1		3	A	5	11[c]	9		4				8			7[a]		2			6			10[b]		B
C						1		3	A	5	10[a]	9[b]		4				7	B				2			6			8		11c
						1		5	10			B		4		11		C	7[b]	8[c]			2			6		3	9[a]		A
						1		5	9[a]			A		4		11		C	7[c]	8			2			6		3	B		10b
	A					1		5	9[a]				C	4		11		2		8	7[b]		B			6		3			
	B					1		3		5		9	A	4				7		8[b]			2			6					11
6	2	26		5	4	42		31	28	35	15	16		30	18	15	11	36	7	29	11	10	30			18	20	37	5	5	3
5	8	10		6				4	6	2	12	11	3	1	6	5	6	6	3	6	2	4	1		2	1	4		2	2	2
2	1	11		1					1	1	2	1			2	5	1	2	1	2						1	2	2	1		1
		11				1			9[a]	5	10[c]	B		4			A	6		7[b]			2				8	3			
6						1				5	11[c]	A		4	2	C	10[a]	7		8[b]					B		9	3			
1		1				2			1	2	2			2	1		1	2		2			1				2	2			
												2				1	1								1						
											1																				
B	11	10[a]			1			2	9	5	A			3			6[b]	7				8						4			
	C		A			1		3	9	5[b]	11[c]			B			6			8[a]		10	2				7	4			
	C			10[b]		1		2		5	A				3		6[c]	B		7		9					8	4			
		11		8[a]		1		5	9						3		B			6		10[b]	2				7	4			
	1	2		2	1	3		4	3	3	1			1	2		3	1		3		4	2				3	4			
1	2		1								2			1			1	1													
	1	1								1							3											2			
7	3	29		7	5	47		35	32	40	18	16		33	21	15	15	39	7	34	11	14	33			18	25	43	5	5	3
6	10	10	1	6				4	6	2	14	13	3	2	6	6	8	7	3	6	2	4	1		3	1	4		2	2	2
2	2	12		1					1	2	3	1			2	5	4	2	1	2						1	2	4	1		1

Club Honours

TEAM	COMPETITION	RESULT	SEASON
FIRST	Division One	Runners-up	1975–76
	Division Two	Champions	1982–83
	Division Two	Runners-up	1967–68, 1972–73, 2003–04
	Division Two	Play-off Finalists	2002–03
	Division Three	Champions	1966–67
	Division Three South	Champions	1947–48
	Division Three South	Runners-up	1946–47
	Division Three (Regional)	Champions	1945–46
	Southern League	Champions	1907–08, 1911–12
	Western League	Champions	1905–06
	FA Cup	Finalists	1981–82
	League Cup	Winners	1966–67
	League Cup	Finalists	1985–86
	FA Charity Shield	Runners-up	1908–09, 1911–12
	Southern Charity Cup	Winners	1912–13
	West London Challenge Cup	Finalists	1890–91
	West London Observer Cup	Winners	1892–93
	West London Observer Cup	Finalists	1893–94
RESERVES	Football Combination	Champions	1944–45, 1981–82, 1982–83, 1995–96, 2001–02
	Football Combination	Runners-up	1920–21, 1938–39
	London Mid-Week League	Runners-up	1966–67
	London League	Runners-up	1901–02, 1902–03
	South Eastern League	Runners-up	1901–02, 1902–03, 1913–14
	West London League	Champions	1898–99
	West London League	Runners-up	1897–98
	London Challenge Cup	Winners	1932–33, 1938–39, 1955–56, 1965–66
YOUTH	South East Counties League	Champions	1963–64, 1965–66, 1967–68, 1977–78 1981–82, 1993–94
	South East Counties League	Runners-up	1962–63, 1964–65, 1979–80
	London Mid-Week League	Champions	1949–50, 1953–54
	FA Youth Cup	Semi-finalists	1963–64, 1965–66
	FA Academy Under-19	Finalists	2000–01
	FL Youth Alliance (South East)	Winners	2006–07, 2007–08
	FL Youth Alliance (South East)	Runners-up	2008–09
	FL Youth Alliance League Cup	Runners-up	2008–09
	Southern Junior Floodlight Cup	Winners	1964–65, 1976–77, 1982–83, 1987–88
	Southern Junior Floodlight Cup	Runners-up	1979–80, 1997–98
	South East Counties League Cup	Winners	1976–77, 1993–94,
	South East Counties League Cup	Runners-up	1967–68
	South East Anglian League Cup	Runners-up	1960–61
	London Youth Cup	Winners	1964–65
	London Youth Cup	Runners-up	1958–59
5-a-side	London Championship	Winners	1971, 1972, 1974, 1980, 1985
	London Championship	Runners-up	1976, 1978
	World Sportacular	Winners	1971

Club Records

Attendance	League	(Home)	35,353 v Leeds United 27 April 1974, Division One
		(Away)	69,718 v Tottenham Hotspur 16 October 1948, Division Two
	FA Cup	(Home)	41,097 v Leeds United 9 January 1932, round three
		(Away)	100,000 v Tottenham Hotspur 22 May 1982, Final
	League Cup	(Home)	28,739 v Aston Villa 1 February 1977, semi-final
		(Away)	97,952 v West Bromwich Albion 4 March 1967, Final
	European	(Home)	23,009 v AEK Athens 16 March 1977, round four
		(Away)	50,000 v FC Köln 7 December 1976, round three
Victory	League	(Home)	9–2, Tranmere Rovers 3 December 1960, Division Three
		(Away)	7–1, Mansfield Town 24 September 1966, Division Three
	FA Cup	(Home)	7–0, Barry Town 6 November 1961, round one
		(Away)	8–1, Bristol Rovers 27 November 1937, round one
	League Cup	(Home)	8–1, Crewe Alexandra 4 October 1983, round two
		(Away)	5–1, Hull City 8 October 1985, round two
	European	(Home)	6–2, Partizan Belgrade 24 October 1984, UEFA round two
		(Away)	7–0, Brann Bergen 29 September 1976, UEFA round one
Defeat	League	(Home)	0–5, Burnley 21 January 1950, Division Two
		(Away)	1–8, Mansfield Town 15 March 1963, Division Three
			1–8, Manchester United 19 March 1969, Division One
	FA Cup	(Home)	0–6, Arsenal 27 January 2001, round four
		(Away)	1–6, Burnley 6 January 1962, round three
			1–6, Hereford United 7 December 1957, round two
	League Cup	(Home)	0–4, Newcastle United 8 October 1974, round three
		(Away)	0–4, Reading 23 September 1964, round two
			0–4, Sheffield Wednesday 2 December 1992, round four
	European	(Home)	none
		(Away)	0–4, Partizan Belgrade 7 November 1984, UEFA round two

Most Points	(2 for a win)	67, Division Three 1966–67
	(3 for a win)	85, Division Two 1982–83
Least Points	(2 for a win)	18, Division One 1968–69
	(3 for a win)	33, Premier 1995–96
Most League Goals in Season		111, Division Three 1961–62
Least League Goals in Season		37, Division Three South 1923–24
		37, Division Three South 1925–26
Most Appearances	(Career)	555, Tony Ingham (514 League, 30 FA Cup, 4 League Cup, 7 Others)
Most Goals	(Career)	186, George Goddard (174 League, 12 FA Cup)
	(Season)	44, Rodney Marsh 1966–67 (30 League, 3 FA Cup, 11 League Cup)

Oldest Player	(Last Game)	39 years 352 days, Ray Wilkins 1 September 1996
Youngest Player	(Debut)	15 years 275 days, Frank Sibley, 4 September 1963 15 years 342 days, William Pierce, 6 October 1923 16 years 17 days, Brian Nicholas, 7 May 1949 16 years 299 days, Scott Donnelly, 19 October 2004 16 years 314 days, Mick McGovern, 26 December 1967 16 years 329 days, Martyn Busby, 18 April 1970 16 years 357 days, Shabazz Baidoo, 5 April 2005
Shortest Career		3 minutes, Carl Leaburn, 5 January 2002 9 minutes, Alex Higgins, 6 May 2001 9 minutes, Alvin Bubb, 6 May 2001
Transfer Fee	(Received)	£6 million, Les Ferdinand to Newcastle United, June 1995
	(Paid)	£2.35 million, John Spencer from Chelsea, November 1996 £2.35 million, Mike Sheron from Stoke City, July 1997
Most Capped Player	(while at club)	52, Alan McDonald (Northern Ireland)

Hat-tricks for QPR

Season	Date	Player	Goals	Opponents	Competition
1899–1900	4 October 1899	Peter Turnbull	3	West Hampstead	FA Cup
1899–1900	28 October 1899	William Keech	3	Wandsworth	FA Cup
1900–01	8 September 1900	Samuel Downing	3	Swindon Town	Southern League
1900–01	21 November 1900	Percy Humphries	3	Watford	FA Cup
1901–02	20 November 1901	Harry Millar	4	West Norwood	FA Cup
1903–04	14 November 1903	John Blackwood	3	Northampton Town	Southern League
1903–04	19 December 1903	John Blackwood	3	Portsmouth	Southern League
1904–05	19 November 1904	Fred Bevan	3	Swindon Town	Southern League
1904–05	1 April 1905	Fred Bevan	4	Wellingborough	Southern League
1904–05	22 April 1905	Fred Bevan	3	Watford	Southern League
1905–06	2 September 1905	Sidney Sugden	3	New Brompton	Southern League
1905–06	18 November 1905	A. Thompson	3	Watford	Southern League
1905–06	16 December 1905	Fred Bevan	3	Northampton Town	Southern League
1906–07	17 November 1906	Jack Fletcher	3	Northampton Town	Southern League
1907–08	20 April 1908	Fred Cannon	3	West Ham United	Southern League
1908–09	27 March 1909	Percy Skilton	3	Swindon Town	Southern League
1909–10	18 October 1909	William Steer	3	Coventry City	Southern League
1910–11	17 December 1910	Robert Browning	3	Watford	Southern League
1913–14	26 December 1913	J. Miller	3	Norwich City	Southern League
1916–17	11 November 1916	Walter Lawrence	3	Brentford	London Combination
1917–18	19 January 1918	G. Fox	3	Clapton Orient	London Combination
1917–18	23 March 1918	Walters	3	Millwall	London Combination
1918–19	21 September 1918	George Dale	4	Clapton Orient	London Combination
1918–19	8 March 1919	Jack Smith	3	Clapton Orient	London Combination
1919–20	6 December 1919	Jack Smith	3	Northampton Town	Southern League

Season	Date	Player	Goals	Opponents	Competition
1918–19	15 December 1919	John Gregory	3	Tottenham Hotspur	London Combination
1919–20	3 January 1920	Jack Smith	4	Bristol Rovers	Southern League
1919–20	27 March 1920	John Gregory	3	Brighton & Hove Albion	Southern League
1920–21	11 December 1920	Jack Smith	3	Brighton & Hove Albion	Division 3
1922–23	11 November 1922	Arthur Davis	3	Aberdare Athletic	Division Three South
1924–25	29 December 1924	Colin Myers	4	Clapton	FA Cup
1927–28	1 October 1927	George Goddard	3	Bristol Rovers	Division Three South
1927–28	25 February 1928	George Goddard	3	Merthyr Tydfil	Division Three South
1928–29	25 August 1928	George Goddard	3	Torquay United	Division Three South
1928–29	29 December 1928	George Goddard	3	Torquay United	Division Three South
1928–29	9 March 1929	Jack Burns	3	Merthyr Tydfil	Division Three South
1928–29	9 March 1929	George Goddard	4	Merthyr Tydfil	Division Three South
1928–29	29 March 1929	George Goddard	3	Crystal Palace	Division Three South
1929–30	9 November 1929	Harry Wiles	3	Newport County	Division Three South
1929–30	26 December 1929	George Goddard	3	Norwich City	Division Three South
1929–30	3 March 1930	George Goddard	3	Merthyr Tydfil	Division Three South
1929–30	15 March 1930	George Goddard	3	Newport County	Division Three South
1929–30	12 April 1930	George Goddard	4	Swindon Town	Division Three South
1929–30	12 April 1930	George Rounce	3	Swindon Town	Division Three South
1929–30	19 April 1930	George Goddard	3	Brighton & Hove Albion	Division Three South
1930–31	8 November 1930	George Rounce	3	Crystal Palace	Division Three South
1930–31	6 December 1930	George Goddard	3	Newport County	Division Three South
1930–31	20 December 1930	George Goddard	4	Exeter City	Division Three South
1930–31	25 December 1930	Jack Burns	3	Notts County	Division Three South
1931–32	19 September 1931	George Goddard	4	Watford	Division Three South
1931–32	28 November 1931	Stanley Cribb	3	Barnet	FA Cup
1931–32	12 December 1931	George Rounce	3	Scunthorpe United	FA Cup
1931–32	19 December 1931	George Goddard	3	Thames	Division Three South
1931–32	10 March 1932	Harry Wiles	4	Gillingham	Division Three South
1932–33	1 October 1932	Edward Marcroft	3	Cardiff City	Division Three South
1932–33	28 November 1932	George Goddard	3	Merthyr Tydfil	FA Cup
1932–33	12 December 1932	George Rounce	3	Torquay United	FA Cup
1933–34	11 December 1933	Jack Blackman	4	New Brighton	FA Cup
1933–34	23 December 1933	Jack Blackman	3	Gillingham	Division Three South
1933–34	5 May 1934	Jack Blackman	3	Gillingham	Division Three South
1935–36	14 September 1935	Tommy Cheetham	4	Aldershot	Division Three South
1935–36	5 October 1935	Tommy Cheetham	3	Newport County	Division Three South
1935–36	23 November 1935	Tommy Cheetham	3	Crystal Palace	Division Three South
1935–36	7 December 1935	Frank Lumsden	3	Cardiff City	Division Three South
1935–36	7 March 1936	Tommy Cheetham	3	Gillingham	Division Three South
1935–36	10 April 1936	Harry Lowe	3	Bristol City	Division Three South
1936–37	28 November 1936	Alfred Fitzgerald	3	Brighton & Hove Albion	FA Cup
1936–37	13 February 1937	William Charlton	3	Cardiff City	Division Three South
1936–37	13 February 1937	Alfred Fitzgerald	3	Cardiff City	Division Three South
1936–37	13 March 1937	Reg Swinfen	3	Newport County	Division Three South
1937–38	27 November 1937	Tommy Cheetham	3	Bristol Rovers	FA Cup
1937–38	27 November 1937	Alfred Fitzgerald	3	Bristol Rovers	FA Cup
1938–39	12 November 1938	Tommy Cheetham	4	Aldershot	Division Three South
1938–39	9 January 1939	Tommy Cheetham	3	Northampton Town	Division Three South

Season	Date	Player	Goals	Opponents	Competition
1939–40	25 December 1939	Joe Mallet	3	Fulham	League South
1939–40	25 December 1939	Dave Mangnall	3	Fulham	League South
1939–40	26 December 1939	Dave Mangnall	4	Portsmouth	League South
1939–40	8 February 1940	Billy McEwan	3	Southampton	League South
1939–40	20 April 1940	Dave Mangnall	3	Brighton & Hove Albion	League South
1941–42	30 August 1941	John Davie	3	Brighton & Hove Albion	London League
1942–43	26 September 1942	Reg Swinfen	3	Brentford	League South
1942–43	7 November 1942	Reg Swinfen	4	West Ham United	League South
1942–43	12 December 1942	Dave Mangnall	3	Clapton Orient	League South
1942–43	10 April 1943	William Heathcote	4	Clapton Orient	League Cup
1943–44	30 October 1943	William Heathcote	3	Southampton	League South
1943–44	4 March 1944	William Heathcote	3	Luton Town	League Cup
1943–44	11 March 1944	Reg Swinfen	3	Clapton Orient	League Cup
1943–44	25 March 1944	William Heathcote	3	Luton Town	League Cup
1944–45	26 August 1944	William Heathcote	3	Crystal Palace	League South
1944–45	25 November 1944	William Heathcote	3	Luton Town	League South
1944–45	16 December 1944	William Heathcote	3	Fulham	League South
1945–46	8 September 1945	Frank Neary	3	Walsall	League South (North)
1945–46	27 October 1945	William Heathcote	3	Northampton Town	League South (North)
1945–46	3 November 1945	William Heathcote	4	Notts County	League South (North)
1945–46	17 November 1945	Frank Neary	3	Barnet	FA Cup
1945–46	30 January 1946	Bert Addinall	3	Southampton	FA Cup
1946–47	22 March 1947	Cyril Hatton	3	Aldershot	Division Three South
1947–48	22 August 1947	Cyril Hatton	3	Brighton & Hove Albion	Division Three South
1948–49	26 August 1948	Bert Addinall	3	Leicester City	Division Two
1950–51	30 September 1950	Ernest Shepherd	3	Grimsby Town	Division Two
1953–54	2 January 1954	George Petchey	3	Aldershot	Division Three South
1953–54	20 February 1954	Robert Cameron	3	Newport County	Division Three South
1956–57	9 February 1957	Arthur Longbottom	3	Exeter City	Division Three South
1956–57	29 April 1957	Arthur Longbottom	3	Gillingham	Division Three South
1957–58	23 September 1957	Leslie Locke	3	Millwall	Division Three South
1957–58	23 November 1957	Arthur Longbottom	4	Northampton Town	Division Three South
1958–59	22 September 1958	Arthur Longbottom	3	Stockport County	Division Three
1958–59	25 October 1958	Arthur Longbottom	3	Halifax Town	Division Three
1959–60	16 January 1960	Brian Bedford	3	Newport County	Division Three
1960–61	5 November 1960	Brian Bedford	3	Walthamstow Avenue	FA Cup
1960–61	28 January 1961	Brian Bedford	3	Bury	Division Three
1960–61	15 April 1961	Brian Bedford	4	Halifax Town	Division Three
1960–61	22 April 1961	Bernard Evans	3	Torquay United	Division Three
1961–62	25 September 1961	Brian Bedford	3	Halifax Town	Division Three
1961–62	14 October 1961	Brian Bedford	4	Southend United	Division Three
1961–62	6 November 1961	Brian Bedford	3	Barry Town	FA Cup
1961–62	9 December 1961	Brian Bedford	3	Shrewsbury Town	Division Three
1961–62	30 December 1961	Bernard Evans	3	Torquay United	Division Three
1961–62	14 March 1962	Brian Bedford	3	Coventry City	Division Three
1961–62	14 April 1962	Brian Bedford	3	Bradford (Park Avenue)	Division Three
1962–63	22 October 1962	Brian Bedford	3	Hull City	Division Three
1962–63	27 October 1962	John McCelland	3	Bradford (Park Avenue)	Division Three
1962–63	24 November 1962	Brian Bedford	3	Hinkley Athletic	FA Cup

Season	Date	Player	Goals	Opponents	Competition
1964–65	6 November 1964	Brian Bedford	3	Luton Town	Division Three
1964–65	6 November 1964	Mike Keen	3	Luton Town	Division Three
1964–65	11 December 1964	Brian Bedford	3	Barnsley	Division Three
1964–65	26 February 1965	Billy McAdams	3	Colchester United	Division Three
1965–66	27 November 1965	Les Allen	3	Swindon Town	Division Three
1965–66	1 January 1966	Les Allen	3	York City	Division Three
1965–66	15 January 1966	Roger Morgan	3	Swansea Town	Division Three
1965–66	19 February 1966	John Collins	3	Hull City	Division Three
1965–66	21 May 1966	Mark Lazarus	3	Bournemouth	Division Three
1966–67	23 August 1966	Rodney Marsh	4	Colchester United	League Cup
1966–67	6 September 1966	Rodney Marsh	3	Middlesbrough	Division Three
1966–67	24 September 1966	Rodney Marsh	3	Mansfield Town	Division Three
1966–67	26 November 1966	Rodney Marsh	3	Poole Town	FA Cup
1966–67	25 February 1967	Mark Lazarus	3	Swansea Town	Division Three
1967–68	10 October 1967	Allan Wilks	5	Oxford United	League Cup
1969–70	26 August 1969	Rodney Marsh	3	Blackpool	Division Two
1969–70	23 September 1969	Rodney Marsh	4	Tranmere Rovers	League Cup
1970–71	17 October 1970	Rodney Marsh	3	Birmingham City	Division Two
1970–71	3 April 1971	Rodney Marsh	3	Bolton Wanderers	Division Two
1972–73	17 February 1973	Stan Bowles	3	Swindon Town	Division Two
1974–75	1 February 1975	Don Givens	3	Derby County	Division One
1975–76	23 August 1975	Stan Bowles	3	Derby County	Division One
1976–77	15 September 1976	Stan Bowles	3	Brann Bergen	UEFA Cup
1976–77	29 September 1976	Stan Bowles	3	Brann Bergen	UEFA Cup
1976–77	3 November 1976	Don Givens	3	Slovan Bratislava	UEFA Cup
1978–79	28 April 1979	Clive Allen	3	Coventry City	Division One
1981–82	14 November 1981	Simon Stainrod	3	Sheffield Wednesday	Division Two
1981–82	26 January 1982	Clive Allen	4	Blackpool	FA Cup
1981–82	20 March 1982	Clive Allen	3	Charlton Athletic	Division Two
1982–83	5 March 1983	Clive Allen	3	Middlesbrough	Division Two
1983–84	4 October 1983	Simon Stainrod	3	Crewe Alexandra	League Cup
1983–84	5 May 1984	Clive Allen	3	Notts County	Division One
1984–85	2 October 1984	Gary Bannister	3	Reykjavik	UEFA Cup
1985–86	31 March 1986	Gary Bannister	3	Chelsea	Division One
1986–87	6 April 1987	Gary Bannister	3	Watford	Division One
1987–88	12 September 1987	Gary Bannister	3	Chelsea	Division One
1989–90	23 September 1989	Trevor Francis	3	Aston Villa	Division One
1991–92	1 January 1992	Dennis Bailey	3	Manchester United	Division One
1992–93	28 December 1992	Andy Sinton	3	Everton	Premier
1992–93	10 April 1993	Les Ferdinand	3	Nottingham Forest	Premier
1992–93	12 April 1993	Les Ferdinand	3	Everton	Premier
1993–94	6 October 1993	Clive Allen	3	Barnet	League Cup
1993–94	20 November 1993	Clive Allen	3	Everton	Premier
1996–97	11 January 1997	John Spencer	3	Barnsley	Division One
1998–99	9 May 1999	Chris Kiwomya	3	Crystal Palace	Division One
2001–02	15 September 2001	Andy Thomson	3	Port Vale	Division Two
2002–03	29 March 2003	Richard Langley	3	Blackpool	Division Two
2004–05	28 September 2004	Jamie Cureton	3	Coventry City	Championship
2008–09	26 August 2008	Emmanuel Ledesma	3	Carlisle United	Carling Cup

Against other Clubs

Opponents	Type	Total P	Total W	Total D	Total L	Total F	Total A	Home W	Home D	Home L	Home F	Home A	Away W	Away D	Away L	Away F	Away A
ABERDARE	3RD	12	6	3	3	22	12	5	0	1	16	5	1	3	2	6	7
	TOTAL	**12**	**6**	**3**	**3**	**22**	**12**	**5**	**0**	**1**	**16**	**5**	**1**	**3**	**2**	**6**	**7**
ACCRINGTON STANLEY	3RD	4	4	0	0	14	5	2	0	0	8	2	2	0	0	6	3
	TOTAL	**4**	**4**	**0**	**0**	**14**	**5**	**2**	**0**	**0**	**8**	**2**	**2**	**0**	**0**	**6**	**3**
AEK ATHENS	O-EU	2	1	0	1	3	3	1	0	0	3	0	0	0	1	0	3
	TOTAL	**2**	**1**	**0**	**1**	**3**	**3**	**1**	**0**	**0**	**3**	**0**	**0**	**0**	**1**	**0**	**3**
ALDERSHOT	3RD	30	12	6	12	57	40	7	4	4	37	15	5	2	8	20	25
	FAC	1	0	0	1	1	2	0	0	1	1	2					
	LC	4	2	1	1	9	6	2	0	0	7	2	0	1	1	2	4
	D3CUP	1	1	0	0	1	0	1	0	0	1	0					
	WW2-L	11	6	2	3	22	18	3	1	1	12	6	3	1	2	10	12
	WW2-C	8	5	0	3	18	12	2	0	2	9	8	3	0	1	9	4
	TOTAL	**55**	**26**	**9**	**20**	**108**	**78**	**15**	**5**	**8**	**67**	**33**	**11**	**4**	**12**	**41**	**45**
ARSENAL	1ST	40	11	12	17	39	52	9	6	5	23	17	2	6	12	16	35
	FAC	6	2	2	2	5	8	2	0	2	5	8	0	2	0	0	0
	LC	1	1	0	0	2	1	1	0	0	2	1					
	MC	1	0	0	1	0	2	0	0	1	0	2					
	WW1-L	12	2	2	8	11	21	1	1	4	7	12	1	1	4	4	9
	WW2-L	10	3	1	6	13	25	3	1	1	10	8	0	0	5	3	17
	WW2-C	3	1	1	1	6	6	0	1	0	1	1	1	0	1	5	5
	TOTAL	**73**	**20**	**18**	**35**	**76**	**115**	**16**	**9**	**13**	**48**	**49**	**4**	**9**	**22**	**28**	**66**
ASHFORD TOWN	FAC	1	1	0	0	3	0						1	0	0	3	0
	TOTAL	**1**	**1**	**0**	**0**	**3**	**0**						**1**	**0**	**0**	**3**	**0**
ASTON VILLA	1ST	32	15	6	11	43	42	10	3	3	21	12	5	3	8	22	30
	2ND	6	5	1	0	12	4	3	0	0	8	2	2	1	0	4	2
	FAC	2	0	0	2	2	4						0	0	2	2	4
	LC	8	2	2	4	5	10	1	1	0	1	0	1	1	4	4	10
	TOTAL	**48**	**22**	**9**	**17**	**62**	**60**	**14**	**4**	**3**	**30**	**14**	**8**	**5**	**14**	**32**	**46**
AYLESBURY	FAC	1	1	0	0	4	0						1	0	0	4	0
	TOTAL	**1**	**1**	**0**	**0**	**4**	**0**						**1**	**0**	**0**	**4**	**0**

Opponents	Type	Total P	Total W	Total D	Total L	Total F	Total A	Home W	Home D	Home L	Home F	Home A	Away W	Away D	Away L	Away F	Away A
BARNET	FAC	5	4	1	0	18	6	1	1	0	2	1	3	0	0	16	5
	LC	2	2	0	0	6	1	1	0	0	4	0	1	0	0	2	1
	TOTAL	**7**	**6**	**1**	**0**	**24**	**7**	**2**	**1**	**0**	**6**	**1**	**4**	**0**	**0**	**18**	**6**
BARNSLEY	2ND	26	11	5	10	33	45	9	3	1	23	14	2	2	9	10	31
	3RD	16	8	5	3	32	21	7	1	0	20	7	1	4	3	12	14
	FAC	2	1	0	1	3	3	1	0	0	3	2	0	0	1	0	1
	TOTAL	**44**	**20**	**10**	**14**	**68**	**69**	**17**	**4**	**1**	**46**	**23**	**3**	**6**	**13**	**22**	**46**
BARRY TOWN	FAC	2	1	1	0	8	1	1	0	0	7	0	0	1	0	1	1
	TOTAL	**2**	**1**	**1**	**0**	**8**	**1**	**1**	**0**	**0**	**7**	**0**	**0**	**1**	**0**	**1**	**1**
BATH CITY	FAC	1	1	0	0	2	0						1	0	0	2	0
	TOTAL	**1**	**1**	**0**	**0**	**2**	**0**						**1**	**0**	**0**	**2**	**0**
BEDMINSTER	SL	2	1	0	1	3	5	1	0	0	2	1	0	0	1	1	4
	TOTAL	**2**	**1**	**0**	**1**	**3**	**5**	**1**	**0**	**0**	**2**	**1**	**0**	**0**	**1**	**1**	**4**
BIRMINGHAM CITY	1ST	16	4	4	8	19	29	3	3	2	12	11	1	1	6	7	18
	2ND	28	6	9	13	22	31	6	5	3	18	13	0	4	10	4	18
	FAC	2	2	0	0	4	1	1	0	0	2	0	1	0	0	2	1
	LC	3	3	0	0	9	2	2	0	0	5	1	1	0	0	4	1
	TOTAL	**49**	**15**	**13**	**21**	**54**	**63**	**12**	**8**	**5**	**37**	**25**	**3**	**5**	**16**	**17**	**38**
BLACKBURN ROVERS	1ST	8	1	1	6	2	12	1	0	3	1	5	0	1	3	1	7
	2ND	24	11	5	8	38	30	6	3	3	24	17	5	2	5	14	13
	FAC	1	0	0	1	0	3						0	0	1	0	3
	LC	3	2	1	0	6	4	2	0	0	4	2	0	1	0	2	2
	CS	1	0	0	1	1	2						0	0	1	1	2
	TOTAL	**37**	**14**	**7**	**16**	**47**	**51**	**9**	**3**	**6**	**29**	**24**	**5**	**4**	**10**	**18**	**27**
BLACKPOOL	2ND	12	6	3	3	22	10	4	1	1	16	5	2	2	2	6	5
	3RD	6	5	1	0	15	4	3	0	0	9	1	2	1	0	6	3
	FAC	5	2	3	0	10	3	2	1	0	8	1	0	2	0	2	2
	TOTAL	**23**	**13**	**7**	**3**	**47**	**17**	**9**	**2**	**1**	**33**	**7**	**4**	**5**	**2**	**14**	**10**
BOLTON WANDERERS	1ST	4	2	0	2	5	6	1	0	1	3	4	1	0	1	2	2
	2ND	20	7	3	10	35	33	6	1	3	20	10	1	2	7	15	23
	TOTAL	**24**	**9**	**3**	**12**	**40**	**39**	**7**	**1**	**4**	**23**	**14**	**2**	**2**	**8**	**17**	**25**

Opponents	Type	Total						Home					Away				
		P	W	D	L	F	A	W	D	L	F	A	W	D	L	F	A
BOURNEMOUTH	3RD	70	30	14	26	97	92	21	7	7	58	29	9	7	19	39	63
	FAC	1	1	0	0	2	0	1	0	0	2	0					
	LC	1	1	0	0	2	0	1	0	0	2	0					
	WW2-L	4	2	0	2	7	5	2	0	0	7	1	0	0	2	0	4
	WW2-C	2	0	1	1	1	2	0	0	1	0	1	0	1	0	1	1
	D3CUP	1	1	0	0	3	2	1	0	0	3	2					
	ABND	1	0	1	0	2	2						0	1	0	2	2
	TOTAL	**80**	**35**	**16**	**29**	**114**	**103**	**26**	**7**	**8**	**72**	**33**	**9**	**9**	**21**	**42**	**70**
BRADFORD (PA)	2ND	4	1	1	2	1	2	1	0	1	1	1	0	1	1	0	1
	3RD	4	1	1	2	8	7	0	0	2	2	4	1	1	0	6	3
	FAC	1	0	0	1	3	5						0	0	1	3	5
	SL	2	1	1	0	4	2	1	0	0	2	0	0	1	0	2	2
	TOTAL	**11**	**3**	**3**	**5**	**16**	**16**	**2**	**0**	**3**	**5**	**5**	**1**	**3**	**2**	**11**	**11**
BRADFORD CITY	2ND	6	3	1	2	7	7	2	0	1	3	3	1	1	1	4	4
	3RD	6	3	1	2	11	5	3	0	0	9	0	0	1	2	2	5
	FAC	2	0	1	1	0	4	0	1	0	0	0	0	0	1	0	4
	LC	2	2	0	0	4	1	1	0	0	2	1	1	0	0	2	0
	TOTAL	**16**	**8**	**3**	**5**	**22**	**17**	**6**	**1**	**1**	**14**	**4**	**2**	**2**	**4**	**8**	**13**
BRENTFORD	2ND	8	4	3	1	15	7	2	2	0	9	5	2	1	1	6	2
	3RD	54	17	19	18	70	81	9	12	6	36	32	8	7	12	34	49
	FAC	4	0	1	3	3	8	0	0	2	2	5	0	1	1	1	3
	SL	26	15	8	3	44	21	10	2	1	26	8	5	6	2	18	13
	WW1-L	16	3	6	7	18	38	2	3	3	10	16	1	3	4	8	22
	WW2-L	11	5	1	5	29	21	3	1	1	12	8	2	0	4	17	13
	WW2-C	6	2	1	3	7	8	1	1	1	3	2	1	0	2	4	6
	TOTAL	**125**	**46**	**39**	**40**	**186**	**184**	**27**	**21**	**14**	**98**	**76**	**19**	**18**	**26**	**88**	**108**
BRIGHTON & HOVE ALBION	2ND	6	3	2	1	8	5	1	2	0	3	1	2	0	1	5	4
	3RD	64	25	13	26	102	99	19	7	6	64	32	6	6	20	38	67
	FAC	2	1	0	1	6	3	1	0	1	6	3					
	AM	1	1	0	0	2	1	1	0	0	2	1					
	D3CUP	2	0	0	2	2	4	0	0	1	1	2	0	0	1	1	2
	SL	26	8	5	13	28	36	5	4	4	13	9	3	1	9	15	27
	WW2-L	12	8	1	3	32	22	5	0	1	19	10	3	1	2	13	12
	TOTAL	**113**	**46**	**21**	**46**	**180**	**170**	**32**	**13**	**13**	**108**	**58**	**14**	**8**	**33**	**72**	**112**

Opponents	Type	Total P	Total W	Total D	Total L	Total F	Total A	Home W	Home D	Home L	Home F	Home A	Away W	Away D	Away L	Away F	Away A
BRISTOL CITY	1ST	6	1	2	3	5	8	1	1	1	3	3	0	1	2	2	5
	2ND	18	9	7	2	29	15	6	3	0	21	7	3	4	2	8	8
	3RD	48	18	11	19	71	69	13	5	6	40	21	5	6	13	31	48
	FAC	2	1	1	0	4	2	0	1	0	2	2	1	0	0	2	0
	LC	1	1	0	0	3	0	1	0	0	3	0					
	AM	1	0	0	1	0	0	0	0	1	0	0					
	SL	4	1	1	2	5	7	1	1	0	2	0	0	0	2	3	7
	WW2-C	2	1	0	1	4	4	1	0	0	4	2	0	0	1	0	2
	TOTAL	**82**	**32**	**22**	**28**	**121**	**105**	**23**	**11**	**8**	**75**	**35**	**9**	**11**	**20**	**46**	**70**
BRISTOL ROVERS	2ND	4	4	0	0	11	2	2	0	0	6	0	2	0	0	5	2
	3RD	54	21	11	22	79	84	17	3	7	56	33	4	8	15	23	51
	FAC	4	1	1	2	9	5	0	0	1	0	1	1	1	1	9	4
	LC	2	0	1	1	1	2	0	1	0	1	1	0	0	1	0	1
	SL	34	18	6	10	66	42	14	2	1	52	17	4	4	9	14	25
	TOTAL	**98**	**44**	**19**	**35**	**166**	**135**	**33**	**6**	**9**	**115**	**52**	**11**	**13**	**26**	**51**	**83**
BURNLEY	1ST	8	2	1	5	6	12	2	0	2	3	4	0	1	3	3	8
	2ND	20	8	2	10	33	24	6	1	3	25	12	2	1	7	8	12
	FAC	4	0	1	3	4	12	0	1	0	0	0	0	0	3	4	12
	LC	1	0	0	1	1	2	0	0	1	1	2					
	TOTAL	**33**	**10**	**4**	**19**	**44**	**50**	**8**	**2**	**6**	**29**	**18**	**2**	**2**	**13**	**15**	**32**
BURY	2ND	12	5	5	2	14	11	4	1	1	10	6	1	4	1	4	5
	3RD	8	5	0	3	13	9	4	0	0	10	2	1	0	3	3	7
	FAC	1	0	0	1	0	1						0	0	1	0	1
	LC	3	2	0	1	4	2	1	0	0	2	1	1	0	1	2	1
	TOTAL	**24**	**12**	**5**	**7**	**31**	**23**	**9**	**1**	**1**	**22**	**9**	**3**	**4**	**6**	**9**	**14**
CAMBRIDGE UNITED	2ND	8	4	1	3	16	9	3	1	0	11	4	1	0	3	5	5
	3RD	2	0	1	1	1	2	0	1	0	0	0	0	0	1	1	2
	TOTAL	**10**	**4**	**2**	**4**	**17**	**11**	**3**	**2**	**0**	**11**	**4**	**1**	**0**	**4**	**6**	**7**
CARDIFF CITY	2ND	34	14	6	14	33	35	12	2	3	24	8	2	4	11	9	27
	3RD	22	10	4	8	55	35	7	1	3	35	16	3	3	5	20	19
	FAC	2	1	1	0	2	0	1	0	0	2	0	0	1	0	0	0
	LC	6	5	0	1	17	5	2	0	1	8	2	3	0	0	9	3
	PO	1	0	0	1	0	1						0	0	1	0	1
	SL	6	1	1	4	3	11	1	1	1	3	2	0	0	3	0	9
	TOTAL	**71**	**31**	**12**	**28**	**110**	**87**	**23**	**4**	**8**	**72**	**28**	**8**	**8**	**20**	**38**	**59**

Opponents	Type	Total P	Total W	Total D	Total L	Total F	Total A	Home W	Home D	Home L	Home F	Home A	Away W	Away D	Away L	Away F	Away A
CARLISLE UNITED	1ST	2	2	0	0	4	2	1	0	0	2	1	1	0	0	2	1
	2ND	12	6	2	4	20	13	4	2	0	10	1	2	0	4	10	12
	3RD	4	1	1	2	8	8	0	1	1	3	4	1	0	1	5	4
	FAC	2	0	0	2	0	3						0	0	2	0	3
	LC	4	4	0	0	9	1	3	0	0	8	1	1	0	0	1	0
	TOTAL	**24**	**13**	**3**	**8**	**41**	**27**	**8**	**3**	**1**	**23**	**7**	**5**	**0**	**7**	**18**	**20**
CHARLTON ATHLETIC	1ST	8	3	2	3	6	5	2	1	1	3	1	1	1	2	3	4
	2ND	24	11	7	6	46	31	7	2	3	25	14	4	5	3	21	17
	3RD	20	4	9	7	23	32	3	5	2	15	15	1	4	5	8	17
	FAC	8	2	3	3	8	11	0	2	1	2	5	2	1	2	6	6
	LC	6	2	1	3	6	6	1	1	1	3	4	1	0	2	3	2
	WW2-L	10	3	2	5	16	20	2	2	1	9	6	1	0	4	7	14
	TOTAL	**76**	**25**	**24**	**27**	**105**	**105**	**15**	**13**	**9**	**57**	**45**	**10**	**11**	**18**	**48**	**60**
CHATHAM	SL	2	1	0	1	8	8	1	0	0	5	3	0	0	1	3	5
	TOTAL	**2**	**1**	**0**	**1**	**8**	**8**	**1**	**0**	**0**	**5**	**3**	**0**	**0**	**1**	**3**	**5**
CHELSEA	1ST	32	8	13	11	43	43	6	8	2	26	18	2	5	9	17	25
	2ND	8	3	2	3	10	9	1	1	2	4	6	2	1	1	6	3
	FAC	5	1	1	3	4	7	1	0	2	4	6	0	1	1	0	1
	LC	2	1	1	0	3	1	0	1	0	1	1	1	0	0	2	0
	WW1-L	16	3	2	11	14	35	2	2	4	10	14	1	0	7	4	21
	WW1-C	1	0	0	1	0	2						0	0	1	0	2
	WW2-L	10	4	2	4	19	26	3	0	2	13	18	1	2	2	6	8
	WW2-C	4	4	0	0	14	6	2	0	0	7	2	2	0	0	7	4
	TOTAL	**78**	**24**	**21**	**33**	**107**	**129**	**15**	**12**	**12**	**65**	**65**	**9**	**9**	**21**	**42**	**64**
CHELTENHAM TOWN	3RD	2	1	1	0	5	2	1	0	0	4	1	0	1	0	1	1
	LC	1	1	0	0	2	1						1	0	0	2	1
	TOTAL	**3**	**2**	**1**	**0**	**7**	**3**	**1**	**0**	**0**	**4**	**1**	**1**	**1**	**0**	**3**	**2**
CHESHAM GENERALS	FAC	1	1	0	0	4	0	1	0	0	4	0					
	TOTAL	**1**	**1**	**0**	**0**	**4**	**0**	**1**	**0**	**0**	**4**	**0**					
CHESTERFIELD	2ND	6	1	2	3	8	11	1	2	0	5	4	0	0	3	3	7
	3RD	12	7	3	2	29	18	2	3	1	12	8	5	0	1	17	10
	TOTAL	**18**	**8**	**5**	**5**	**37**	**29**	**3**	**5**	**1**	**17**	**12**	**5**	**0**	**4**	**20**	**17**
CIVIL SERVICE	FAC	1	1	0	0	3	0	1	0	0	3	0					
	TOTAL	**1**	**1**	**0**	**0**	**3**	**0**	**1**	**0**	**0**	**3**	**0**					

Opponents	Type	Total P	Total W	Total D	Total L	Total F	Total A	Home W	Home D	Home L	Home F	Home A	Away W	Away D	Away L	Away F	Away A
CLAPTON	FAC	5	2	2	1	10	7	1	1	0	7	5	1	1	1	3	2
	TOTAL	**5**	**2**	**2**	**1**	**10**	**7**	**1**	**1**	**0**	**7**	**5**	**1**	**1**	**1**	**3**	**2**
COLCHESTER UNITED	2ND	4	2	0	2	6	7	2	0	0	3	1	0	0	2	3	6
	3RD	32	15	7	10	52	44	11	4	1	37	14	4	3	9	15	30
	FAC	4	3	1	0	11	5	1	0	0	4	0	2	1	0	7	5
	LC	3	2	0	1	7	4	1	0	1	6	4	1	0	0	1	0
	TOTAL	**43**	**22**	**8**	**13**	**76**	**60**	**15**	**4**	**2**	**50**	**19**	**7**	**4**	**11**	**26**	**41**
COVENTRY CITY	1ST	40	17	10	13	56	50	12	5	3	40	19	5	5	10	16	31
	2ND	18	5	5	8	16	23	3	1	5	12	14	2	4	3	4	9
	3RD	42	11	11	20	56	95	8	6	7	35	38	3	5	13	21	57
	FAC	3	1	1	1	4	4	1	0	1	4	4	0	1	0	0	0
	LC	1	0	0	1	1	2	0	0	1	1	2					
	SL	12	6	3	3	25	12	5	1	0	20	2	1	2	3	5	10
	TOTAL	**116**	**40**	**30**	**46**	**158**	**186**	**29**	**13**	**17**	**112**	**79**	**11**	**17**	**29**	**46**	**107**
CREWE ALEXANDRA	2ND	12	7	1	4	21	16	3	0	3	7	7	4	1	1	14	9
	3RD	4	1	1	2	2	4	1	1	0	2	0	0	0	2	0	4
	FAC	1	1	0	0	4	2						1	0	0	4	2
	LC	2	1	0	1	8	4	1	0	0	8	1	0	0	1	0	3
	TOTAL	**19**	**10**	**2**	**7**	**35**	**26**	**5**	**1**	**3**	**17**	**8**	**5**	**1**	**4**	**18**	**18**
CROUCH END	FAC	1	1	0	0	2	0	1	0	0	2	0					
	TOTAL	**1**	**1**	**0**	**0**	**2**	**0**	**1**	**0**	**0**	**2**	**0**					
CROYDON COMMON	SL	4	2	1	1	8	5	1	1	0	5	4	1	0	1	3	1
	WW1-L	2	2	0	0	3	1	1	0	0	2	1	1	0	0	1	0
	TOTAL	**6**	**4**	**1**	**1**	**11**	**6**	**2**	**1**	**0**	**7**	**5**	**2**	**0**	**1**	**4**	**1**
CRYSTAL PALACE	1ST	10	3	4	3	11	9	2	0	3	5	6	1	4	0	6	3
	2ND	22	5	8	9	23	26	4	3	4	16	11	1	5	5	7	15
	3RD	52	22	13	17	81	71	14	5	7	51	35	8	8	10	30	36
	FAC	7	4	3	0	7	1	3	1	0	5	0	1	2	0	2	1
	LC	1	1	0	0	5	2	1	0	0	5	2					
	FM	1	0	0	1	2	3	0	0	1	2	3					
	SL	20	8	3	9	28	33	5	2	3	17	12	3	1	6	11	21
	WW1-L	14	9	0	5	28	25	7	0	0	21	9	2	0	5	7	16
	WW1-C	2	1	0	1	3	4	1	0	0	2	1	0	0	1	1	3
	WW2-L	8	2	2	4	14	19	1	1	2	6	8	1	1	2	8	11
	WW2-C	4	4	0	0	8	4	2	0	0	5	3	2	0	0	3	1
	TOTAL	**141**	**59**	**33**	**49**	**210**	**197**	**40**	**12**	**20**	**135**	**90**	**19**	**21**	**29**	**75**	**107**

		Total						Home					Away				
Opponents	**Type**	**P**	**W**	**D**	**L**	**F**	**A**	**W**	**D**	**L**	**F**	**A**	**W**	**D**	**L**	**F**	**A**
DAGENHAM & REDBRIDGE	0-AM	1	1	0	0	2	1	1	0	0	2	1					
	TOTAL	**1**	**1**	**0**	**0**	**2**	**1**	**1**	**0**	**0**	**2**	**1**					
DARLINGTON	3RD	2	1	1	0	4	0	1	0	0	4	0	0	1	0	0	0
	FAC	1	0	0	1	0	2						0	0	1	0	2
	TOTAL	**3**	**1**	**1**	**1**	**4**	**2**	**1**	**0**	**0**	**4**	**0**	**0**	**1**	**1**	**0**	**2**
DERBY COUNTY	1ST	20	5	8	7	24	25	1	7	2	10	9	4	1	5	14	16
	2ND	16	5	4	7	21	24	3	1	4	12	10	2	3	3	9	14
	FAC	4	1	1	2	4	10	1	1	0	2	1	0	0	2	2	9
	LC	2	0	2	0	0	0	0	1	0	0	0	0	1	0	0	0
	TOTAL	**42**	**11**	**15**	**16**	**49**	**59**	**5**	**10**	**6**	**24**	**20**	**6**	**5**	**10**	**25**	**39**
DONCASTER ROVERS	2ND	6	2	0	4	5	10	1	0	2	3	4	1	0	2	2	6
	3RD	4	2	1	1	10	4	2	0	0	9	1	0	1	1	1	3
	FAC	1	0	0	1	0	1						0	0	1	0	1
	TOTAL	**11**	**4**	**1**	**6**	**15**	**15**	**3**	**0**	**2**	**12**	**5**	**1**	**1**	**4**	**3**	**10**
DORCHESTER TOWN	FAC	1	1	0	0	4	0	1	0	0	4	0					
	TOTAL	**1**	**1**	**0**	**0**	**4**	**0**	**1**	**0**	**0**	**4**	**0**					
EVERTON	1ST	40	14	9	17	57	62	10	5	5	32	23	4	4	12	25	39
	2ND	2	0	1	1	4	7	0	1	0	4	4	0	0	1	0	3
	FAC	2	0	0	2	1	4	0	0	2	1	4					
	FM	1	0	0	1	0	1						0	0	1	0	1
	TOTAL	**45**	**14**	**10**	**21**	**62**	**74**	**10**	**6**	**7**	**37**	**31**	**4**	**4**	**14**	**25**	**43**
EXETER CITY	3RD	58	27	17	14	86	63	18	7	4	56	23	9	10	10	30	40
	SL	16	5	7	4	14	14	3	3	2	8	7	2	4	2	6	7
	TOTAL	**74**	**32**	**24**	**18**	**100**	**77**	**21**	**10**	**6**	**64**	**30**	**11**	**14**	**12**	**36**	**47**
FC COLOGNE	EU	2	1	0	1	4	4	1	0	0	3	0	0	0	1	1	4
	TOTAL	**2**	**1**	**0**	**1**	**4**	**4**	**1**	**0**	**0**	**3**	**0**	**0**	**0**	**1**	**1**	**4**

Opponents	Type	Total P	Total W	Total D	Total L	Total F	Total A	Home W	Home D	Home L	Home F	Home A	Away W	Away D	Away L	Away F	Away A
FULHAM	2ND	14	7	3	4	17	12	4	2	1	9	3	3	1	3	8	9
	3RD	8	5	1	2	12	10	2	1	1	5	4	3	0	1	7	6
	FAC	8	2	2	4	14	10	2	2	0	12	2	0	0	4	2	8
	LC	1	0	0	1	0	2						0	0	1	0	2
	SPFC	1	0	0	1	0	4	0	0	1	0	4					
	SL	8	2	3	3	9	11	1	1	2	4	6	1	2	1	5	5
	WW1-L	14	3	2	9	12	25	2	0	5	7	16	1	2	4	5	9
	WW2-L	13	3	5	5	35	37	1	3	3	17	23	2	2	2	18	14
	WW2-C	2	0	0	2	6	11	0	0	1	5	7	0	0	1	1	4
	TOTAL	**69**	**22**	**16**	**31**	**105**	**122**	**12**	**9**	**14**	**59**	**65**	**10**	**7**	**17**	**46**	**57**
GILLINGHAM	2ND	4	2	2	0	5	3	0	2	0	3	3	2	0	0	2	0
	3RD	54	22	19	13	88	62	14	9	4	54	24	8	10	9	34	38
	FAC	3	2	1	0	8	3	2	0	0	7	2	0	1	0	1	1
	SL	34	19	7	8	53	21	12	4	1	36	6	7	3	7	17	15
	TOTAL	**95**	**45**	**29**	**21**	**154**	**89**	**28**	**15**	**5**	**100**	**35**	**17**	**14**	**16**	**54**	**54**
GLOSSOP	FAC	1	1	0	0	2	1	1	0	0	2	1					
	TOTAL	**1**	**1**	**0**	**0**	**2**	**1**	**1**	**0**	**0**	**2**	**1**					
GRAVESEND & NORTHFLEET	FAC	2	1	1	0	4	2	1	0	0	2	0	0	1	0	2	2
	TOTAL	**2**	**1**	**1**	**0**	**4**	**2**	**1**	**0**	**0**	**2**	**0**	**0**	**1**	**0**	**2**	**2**
GRAVESEND UNITED	SL	4	3	1	0	12	6	2	0	0	7	3	1	1	0	5	3
	TOTAL	**4**	**3**	**1**	**0**	**12**	**6**	**2**	**0**	**0**	**7**	**3**	**1**	**1**	**0**	**5**	**3**
GRIMSBY TOWN	2ND	20	6	4	10	28	26	6	0	4	20	8	0	4	6	8	18
	3RD	16	7	5	4	27	18	6	2	0	19	4	1	3	4	8	14
	FAC	2	1	0	1	3	2	1	0	0	3	1	0	0	1	0	1
	LC	2	1	0	1	3	3	1	0	0	2	1	0	0	1	1	2
	TOTAL	**40**	**15**	**9**	**16**	**61**	**49**	**14**	**2**	**4**	**44**	**14**	**1**	**7**	**12**	**17**	**35**
GUILDFORD CITY	FAC	2	1	0	1	5	4	1	0	0	3	0	0	0	1	2	4
	TOTAL	**2**	**1**	**0**	**1**	**5**	**4**	**1**	**0**	**0**	**3**	**0**	**0**	**0**	**1**	**2**	**4**
HALIFAX TOWN	3RD	10	6	2	2	30	12	5	0	0	22	4	1	2	2	8	8
	FAC	1	1	0	0	4	2	1	0	0	4	2					
	TOTAL	**11**	**7**	**2**	**2**	**34**	**14**	**6**	**0**	**0**	**26**	**6**	**1**	**2**	**2**	**8**	**8**

Opponents	Type	Total P	Total W	Total D	Total L	Total F	Total A	Home W	Home D	Home L	Home F	Home A	Away W	Away D	Away L	Away F	Away A
HARTLEPOOL	3RD	2	2	0	0	8	2	1	0	0	4	1	1	0	0	4	1
	FAC	1	1	0	0	2	0						1	0	0	2	0
	TOTAL	**3**	**3**	**0**	**0**	**10**	**2**	**1**	**0**	**0**	**4**	**1**	**2**	**0**	**0**	**6**	**1**
HEREFORD UNITED	FAC	1	0	0	1	1	6						0	0	1	1	6
	TOTAL	**1**	**0**	**0**	**1**	**1**	**6**						**0**	**0**	**1**	**1**	**6**
HINCKLEY ATHLETIC	FAC	1	1	0	0	7	2	1	0	0	7	2					
	TOTAL	**1**	**1**	**0**	**0**	**7**	**2**	**1**	**0**	**0**	**7**	**2**					
HUDDERSFIELD TOWN	2ND	16	7	4	5	25	19	6	2	0	19	7	1	2	5	6	12
	3RD	4	3	0	1	9	3	2	0	0	6	2	1	0	1	3	1
	FAC	7	1	2	4	4	15	0	2	1	1	2	1	0	3	3	13
	TOTAL	**27**	**11**	**6**	**10**	**38**	**37**	**8**	**4**	**1**	**26**	**11**	**3**	**2**	**9**	**12**	**26**
HULL CITY	2ND	22	6	10	6	29	34	5	5	1	19	12	1	5	5	10	22
	3RD	14	4	3	7	20	28	3	3	1	13	10	1	0	6	7	18
	LC	5	5	0	0	18	3	3	0	0	10	2	2	0	0	8	1
	TOTAL	**41**	**15**	**13**	**13**	**67**	**65**	**11**	**8**	**2**	**42**	**24**	**4**	**5**	**11**	**25**	**41**
IPSWICH TOWN	1ST	26	11	6	9	34	30	8	2	3	19	12	3	4	6	15	18
	2ND	20	5	7	8	24	29	3	3	4	12	15	2	4	4	12	14
	3RD	14	3	4	7	13	22	2	3	2	9	9	1	1	5	4	13
	FAC	2	2	0	0	6	0	1	0	0	4	0	1	0	0	2	0
	LC	3	0	1	2	3	5	0	0	1	1	2	0	1	1	2	3
	WW2-L	2	1	0	1	3	2	1	0	0	2	0	0	0	1	1	2
	WW2-C	2	1	0	1	4	2	1	0	0	4	1	0	0	1	0	1
	TOTAL	**69**	**23**	**18**	**28**	**87**	**90**	**16**	**8**	**10**	**51**	**39**	**7**	**10**	**18**	**36**	**51**
KETTERING	FAC	1	1	0	0	6	0	1	0	0	6	0					
	SL	8	5	0	3	13	10	4	0	0	10	3	1	0	3	3	7
	TOTAL	**9**	**6**	**0**	**3**	**19**	**10**	**5**	**0**	**0**	**16**	**3**	**1**	**0**	**3**	**3**	**7**
KIDDERMINSTER HARRIERS	AM	1	1	0	0	2	0	1	0	0	2	0					
	TOTAL	**1**	**1**	**0**	**0**	**2**	**0**	**1**	**0**	**0**	**2**	**0**					
KR REJKJAVIK	EU	2	2	0	0	7	0	1	0	0	4	0	1	0	0	3	0
	TOTAL	**2**	**2**	**0**	**0**	**7**	**0**	**1**	**0**	**0**	**4**	**0**	**1**	**0**	**0**	**3**	**0**
LEEDS CITY	FAC	1	1	0	0	1	0	1	0	0	1	0					
	TOTAL	**1**	**1**	**0**	**0**	**1**	**0**	**1**	**0**	**0**	**1**	**0**					

Opponents	Type	Total						Home					Away				
		P	W	D	L	F	A	W	D	L	F	A	W	D	L	F	A
LEEDS UNITED	1ST	26	9	6	11	33	43	5	3	5	16	17	4	3	6	17	26
	2ND	16	5	7	4	17	20	3	4	1	10	5	2	3	3	7	15
	FAC	2	1	0	1	4	3	1	0	0	3	1	0	0	1	1	2
	LC	2	0	0	2	0	5	0	0	2	0	5					
	TOTAL	**46**	**15**	**13**	**18**	**54**	**71**	**9**	**7**	**8**	**29**	**28**	**6**	**6**	**10**	**25**	**43**
LEICESTER CITY	1ST	22	10	5	7	33	30	8	2	1	22	9	2	3	6	11	21
	2ND	26	11	5	10	43	44	7	3	3	26	18	4	2	7	17	26
	FAC	2	1	0	1	5	4	1	0	1	5	4					
	LC	1	1	0	0	4	2	1	0	0	4	2					
	WW2-C	2	1	0	1	3	7	1	0	0	2	1	0	0	1	1	6
	TOTAL	**53**	**24**	**10**	**19**	**88**	**87**	**18**	**5**	**5**	**59**	**34**	**6**	**5**	**14**	**29**	**53**
LEYTON ORIENT	2ND	12	5	5	2	17	12	4	2	0	12	2	1	3	2	5	10
	3RD	34	15	9	10	60	56	12	2	3	39	19	3	7	7	21	37
	LC	4	1	1	2	7	6	0	1	1	2	3	1	0	1	5	3
	D3CUP	1	1	0	0	2	0	1	0	0	2	0					
	SPFC	2	0	0	2	1	3	0	0	2	1	3					
	SL	12	8	0	4	23	17	5	0	1	15	9	3	0	3	8	8
	WW1-L	14	9	4	1	34	11	4	3	0	17	5	5	1	1	17	6
	WW2-L	14	10	3	1	42	16	5	2	0	24	10	5	1	1	18	6
	WW2-C	6	4	2	0	26	4	3	0	0	20	1	1	2	0	6	3
	TOTAL	**99**	**53**	**24**	**22**	**212**	**125**	**34**	**10**	**7**	**132**	**52**	**19**	**14**	**15**	**80**	**73**
LINCOLN CITY	2ND	2	1	1	0	2	0	1	0	0	2	0	0	1	0	0	0
	3RD	2	1	0	1	6	3	0	0	1	1	3	1	0	0	5	0
	FAC	1	1	0	0	2	1	1	0	0	2	1					
	LC	1	1	0	0	4	2	1	0	0	4	2					
	TOTAL	**6**	**4**	**1**	**1**	**14**	**6**	**3**	**0**	**1**	**9**	**6**	**1**	**1**	**0**	**5**	**0**
LIVERPOOL	1ST	40	6	6	28	34	68	5	4	11	20	28	1	2	17	14	40
	FAC	3	0	1	2	3	5	0	1	0	2	2	0	0	2	1	3
	LC	2	1	1	0	3	2	1	0	0	1	0	0	1	0	2	2
	TOTAL	**45**	**7**	**8**	**30**	**40**	**75**	**6**	**5**	**11**	**23**	**30**	**1**	**3**	**19**	**17**	**45**
LONDON WELSH	FAC	1	1	0	0	4	2	1	0	0	4	2					
	TOTAL	**1**	**1**	**0**	**0**	**4**	**2**	**1**	**0**	**0**	**4**	**2**					

		Total						Home					Away				
Opponents	**Type**	**P**	**W**	**D**	**L**	**F**	**A**	**W**	**D**	**L**	**F**	**A**	**W**	**D**	**L**	**F**	**A**
LUTON TOWN	1ST	20	6	8	6	24	21	4	4	2	18	11	2	4	4	6	10
	2ND	24	9	8	7	29	30	6	3	3	17	13	3	5	4	12	17
	3RD	42	18	8	16	63	63	16	4	1	45	15	2	4	15	18	48
	FAC	15	5	5	5	22	24	4	2	1	14	10	1	3	4	8	14
	D3CUP	1	1	0	0	2	1	1	0	0	2	1					
	SL	28	11	7	10	50	39	8	2	4	33	19	3	5	6	17	20
	WW1-L	4	0	1	3	3	14	0	1	1	3	6	0	0	2	0	8
	WW2-L	4	2	1	1	12	6	1	1	0	9	3	1	0	1	3	3
	WW2-C	2	2	0	0	9	3	1	0	0	5	0	1	0	0	4	3
	TOTAL	**140**	**54**	**38**	**48**	**214**	**201**	**41**	**17**	**12**	**146**	**78**	**13**	**21**	**36**	**68**	**123**
MANCHESTER CITY	1ST	32	9	11	12	31	35	8	6	2	21	10	1	5	10	10	25
	2ND	8	3	3	2	16	13	1	2	1	6	5	2	1	1	10	8
	FAC	1	0	0	1	1	2	0	0	1	1	2					
	LC	5	0	1	4	4	13	0	0	3	4	10	0	1	1	0	3
	TOTAL	**46**	**12**	**15**	**19**	**52**	**63**	**9**	**8**	**7**	**32**	**27**	**3**	**7**	**12**	**20**	**36**
MANCHESTER UNITED	1ST	38	6	10	22	41	67	5	7	7	28	28	1	3	15	13	39
	FAC	6	0	2	4	3	10	0	1	0	2	2	0	1	4	1	8
	LC	1	0	0	1	0	1						0	0	1	0	1
	CS	2	0	1	1	1	5						0	1	1	1	5
	TOTAL	**47**	**6**	**13**	**28**	**45**	**83**	**5**	**8**	**7**	**30**	**30**	**1**	**5**	**21**	**15**	**53**
MANSFIELD TOWN	3RD	22	9	7	6	47	34	5	5	1	18	8	4	2	5	29	26
	LC	3	2	1	0	9	2	1	0	0	4	0	1	1	0	5	2
	WW2-L	2	2	0	0	9	4	1	0	0	3	2	1	0	0	6	2
	WW2-C	2	1	1	0	3	0	1	0	0	3	0	0	1	0	0	0
	TOTAL	**29**	**14**	**9**	**6**	**68**	**40**	**8**	**5**	**1**	**28**	**10**	**6**	**4**	**5**	**40**	**30**
MARGATE	FAC	1	0	0	1	1	3						0	0	1	1	3
	TOTAL	**1**	**0**	**0**	**1**	**1**	**3**						**0**	**0**	**1**	**1**	**3**
MARLOW	FAC	1	0	0	1	1	3	0	0	1	1	3					
	TOTAL	**1**	**0**	**0**	**1**	**1**	**3**	**0**	**0**	**1**	**1**	**3**					
MERTHYR TOWN	3RD	20	10	5	5	40	22	5	5	0	25	6	5	0	5	15	16
	FAC	2	1	1	0	6	2	1	0	0	5	1	0	1	0	1	1
	SL	6	3	2	1	10	4	1	1	1	4	2	2	1	0	6	2
	TOTAL	**28**	**14**	**8**	**6**	**56**	**28**	**7**	**6**	**1**	**34**	**9**	**7**	**2**	**5**	**22**	**19**

Opponents	Type	Total P	W	D	L	F	A	Home W	D	L	F	A	Away W	D	L	F	A
MIDDLESBROUGH	1ST	16	7	7	2	22	11	3	5	0	13	7	4	2	2	9	4
	2ND	14	4	4	6	26	23	4	3	0	20	5	0	1	6	6	18
	3RD	2	1	1	0	6	2	1	0	0	4	0	0	1	0	2	2
	FAC	7	1	3	3	10	14	0	3	0	4	4	1	0	3	6	10
	TOTAL	**39**	**13**	**15**	**11**	**64**	**50**	**8**	**11**	**0**	**41**	**16**	**5**	**4**	**11**	**23**	**34**
MILLWALL	1ST	4	1	1	2	5	6	0	1	1	1	2	1	0	1	4	4
	2ND	14	5	6	3	15	15	4	2	1	12	8	1	4	2	3	7
	3RD	42	10	10	22	50	65	8	5	8	39	22	2	5	14	11	43
	FAC	3	1	0	2	4	6	1	0	2	4	6					
	LC	3	2	1	0	5	1	2	0	0	5	1	0	1	0	0	0
	SPFC	1	1	0	0	5	2	1	0	0	5	2					
	SL	34	9	9	16	30	58	6	4	7	20	22	3	5	9	10	36
	WW1-L	16	6	2	8	21	31	5	1	2	12	10	1	1	6	9	21
	WW1-C	2	1	0	1	5	6	1	0	0	4	3	0	0	1	1	3
	WW2-L	10	8	1	1	27	16	5	0	0	15	5	3	1	1	12	11
	WW2-C	2	1	1	0	4	2	1	0	0	2	0	0	1	0	2	2
	TOTAL	**131**	**45**	**31**	**55**	**171**	**208**	**34**	**13**	**21**	**119**	**81**	**11**	**18**	**34**	**52**	**127**
NEW BRIGHTON	FAC	2	1	1	0	5	1	0	1	0	1	1	1	0	0	4	0
	TOTAL	**2**	**1**	**1**	**0**	**5**	**1**	**0**	**1**	**0**	**1**	**1**	**1**	**0**	**0**	**4**	**0**
NEWCASTLE UNITED	1ST	28	12	5	11	49	42	6	3	5	27	21	6	2	6	22	21
	2ND	8	4	0	4	14	9	3	0	1	8	3	1	0	3	6	6
	FAC	2	0	1	1	1	2	0	1	0	0	0	0	0	1	1	2
	LC	2	0	0	2	1	7	0	0	2	1	7					
	TOTAL	**40**	**16**	**6**	**18**	**65**	**60**	**9**	**4**	**8**	**36**	**31**	**7**	**2**	**10**	**29**	**29**
NEWPORT CITY	3RD	58	31	13	14	121	80	19	8	2	72	27	12	5	12	49	53
	FAC	1	1	0	0	3	2	1	0	0	3	2					
	SL	2	1	0	1	1	3	1	0	0	1	0	0	0	1	0	3
	TOTAL	**61**	**33**	**13**	**15**	**125**	**85**	**21**	**8**	**2**	**76**	**29**	**12**	**5**	**13**	**49**	**56**
NORTHAMPTON TOWN	3RD	62	25	9	28	97	103	19	4	8	55	38	6	5	20	42	65
	LC	3	1	0	2	4	7	1	0	0	3	2	0	0	2	1	5
	JUB	3	1	2	0	5	4	1	1	0	5	4	0	1	0	0	0
	SL	30	10	14	6	50	35	8	5	2	37	14	2	9	4	13	21
	WW2-L	2	2	0	0	6	1	1	0	0	4	1	1	0	0	2	0
	TOTAL	**100**	**39**	**25**	**36**	**162**	**150**	**30**	**10**	**10**	**104**	**59**	**9**	**15**	**26**	**58**	**91**

Opponents	Type	Total						Home					Away				
		P	W	D	L	F	A	W	D	L	F	A	W	D	L	F	A
NORWICH CITY	1ST	32	10	10	12	42	41	7	5	4	26	19	3	5	8	16	22
	2ND	28	9	8	11	33	32	7	4	3	25	13	2	4	8	8	19
	3RD	48	17	12	19	66	75	14	6	4	48	25	3	6	15	18	50
	FAC	4	2	2	0	9	4	2	0	0	5	0	0	2	0	4	4
	FM	1	1	0	0	2	1						1	0	0	2	1
	SL	22	6	9	7	22	27	4	6	1	13	9	2	3	6	9	18
	WW2-L	4	0	2	2	3	6	0	1	1	1	2	0	1	1	2	4
	TOTAL	**139**	**45**	**43**	**51**	**177**	**186**	**34**	**22**	**13**	**118**	**68**	**11**	**21**	**38**	**59**	**118**
NOTTS COUNTY	1ST	4	3	1	0	6	1	1	1	0	2	1	2	0	0	4	0
	2ND	8	1	3	4	8	14	1	1	2	4	8	0	2	2	4	6
	3RD	30	15	7	8	51	40	11	1	3	33	17	4	6	5	18	23
	FAC	2	1	0	1	4	2	1	0	1	4	2					
	LC	1	0	0	1	1	4						0	0	1	1	4
	WW2-L	2	2	0	0	7	0	1	0	0	6	0	1	0	0	1	0
	WW2-C	2	2	0	0	6	1	1	0	0	3	1	1	0	0	3	0
	TOTAL	**49**	**24**	**11**	**14**	**83**	**62**	**16**	**3**	**6**	**52**	**29**	**8**	**8**	**8**	**31**	**33**
NOTTINGHAM FOREST	1ST	30	7	8	15	30	45	7	3	5	22	18	0	5	10	8	27
	2ND	16	6	6	4	21	21	6	1	1	15	8	0	5	3	6	13
	FAC	5	0	2	3	3	12	0	1	1	1	4	0	1	2	2	8
	LC	3	1	0	2	6	8	1	0	1	4	3	0	0	1	2	5
	TOTAL	**54**	**14**	**16**	**24**	**60**	**86**	**14**	**5**	**8**	**42**	**33**	**0**	**11**	**16**	**18**	**53**
NUNEATON BOROUGH	FAC	2	1	1	0	3	2	0	1	0	1	1	1	0	0	2	1
	TOTAL	**2**	**1**	**1**	**0**	**3**	**2**	**0**	**1**	**0**	**1**	**1**	**1**	**0**	**0**	**2**	**1**
OLD ST STEPHEN'S	FAC	2	0	1	1	1	2	0	1	0	1	1	0	0	1	0	1
	TOTAL	**2**	**0**	**1**	**1**	**1**	**2**	**0**	**1**	**0**	**1**	**1**	**0**	**0**	**1**	**0**	**1**
OLDHAM ATHLETIC	1ST	6	2	1	3	10	13	2	0	1	6	5	0	1	2	4	8
	2ND	10	5	2	3	10	7	3	1	1	7	4	2	1	2	3	3
	3RD	14	3	5	6	16	19	1	4	2	8	9	2	1	4	8	10
	PO	2	1	1	0	2	1	1	0	0	1	0	0	1	0	1	1
	TOTAL	**32**	**11**	**9**	**12**	**38**	**40**	**7**	**5**	**4**	**22**	**18**	**4**	**4**	**8**	**16**	**22**
OXFORD UNITED	1ST	6	3	2	1	11	9	2	1	0	7	4	1	1	1	4	5
	2ND	14	6	3	5	20	21	4	2	1	11	6	2	1	4	9	15
	3RD	4	2	0	2	9	7	1	0	1	5	4	1	0	1	4	3
	FAC	1	1	0	0	2	0						1	0	0	2	0
	LC	4	2	1	1	8	5	2	0	0	7	1	0	1	1	1	4
	TOTAL	**29**	**14**	**6**	**9**	**50**	**42**	**9**	**3**	**2**	**30**	**15**	**5**	**3**	**7**	**20**	**27**

		Total						Home					Away				
Opponents	**Type**	**P**	**W**	**D**	**L**	**F**	**A**	**W**	**D**	**L**	**F**	**A**	**W**	**D**	**L**	**F**	**A**
PARTISAN BELGRADE	EU	2	1	0	1	6	6	1	0	0	6	2	0	0	1	0	4
	TOTAL	**2**	**1**	**0**	**1**	**6**	**6**	**1**	**0**	**0**	**6**	**2**	**0**	**0**	**1**	**0**	**4**
PETERBOROUGH UNITED	3RD	18	8	6	4	26	26	5	4	0	15	7	3	2	4	11	19
	FAC	2	0	1	1	4	5	0	1	0	3	3	0	0	1	1	2
	LC	3	1	1	1	6	6	1	0	0	3	1	0	1	1	3	5
	TOTAL	**23**	**9**	**8**	**6**	**36**	**37**	**6**	**5**	**0**	**21**	**11**	**3**	**3**	**6**	**15**	**26**
PLYMOUTH ARGYLE	2ND	16	5	5	6	20	22	3	3	2	11	10	2	2	4	9	12
	3RD	30	12	1	17	38	50	9	1	5	29	18	3	0	12	9	32
	LC	1	0	0	1	0	3	0	0	1	0	3					
	SL	26	11	10	5	25	20	9	4	0	15	4	2	6	5	10	16
	TOTAL	**73**	**28**	**16**	**29**	**83**	**95**	**21**	**8**	**8**	**55**	**35**	**7**	**8**	**21**	**28**	**60**
POOLE TOWN	FAC	3	2	1	0	11	4	1	1	0	5	4	1	0	0	6	0
	TOTAL	**3**	**2**	**1**	**0**	**11**	**4**	**1**	**1**	**0**	**5**	**4**	**1**	**0**	**0**	**6**	**0**
PORT VALE	2ND	8	2	2	4	12	16	2	0	2	7	7	0	2	2	5	9
	3RD	26	15	6	5	46	27	11	2	0	33	12	4	4	5	13	15
	FAC	3	0	1	2	4	6	0	1	1	3	4	0	0	1	1	2
	LC	3	0	1	2	5	8	0	1	0	2	2	0	0	2	3	6
	D3CUP	1	0	1	0	0	0	0	1	0	0	0					
	WW2-L	2	1	1	0	4	1	1	0	0	4	1	0	1	0	0	0
	WW2-C	2	2	0	0	6	2	1	0	0	4	2	1	0	0	2	0
	TOTAL	**45**	**20**	**12**	**13**	**77**	**60**	**15**	**5**	**3**	**53**	**28**	**5**	**7**	**10**	**24**	**32**
PORTSMOUTH	1ST	2	2	0	0	3	1	1	0	0	2	1	1	0	0	1	0
	2ND	20	10	6	4	29	18	6	4	0	17	4	4	2	4	12	14
	3RD	10	0	4	6	3	18	0	2	3	1	5	0	2	3	2	13
	LC	2	1	1	0	7	2	1	0	0	5	0	0	1	0	2	2
	SL	32	8	12	12	46	56	8	4	4	33	25	0	8	8	13	31
	WW1-L	2	1	0	1	4	9	0	0	1	1	7	1	0	0	3	2
	WW2-L	8	2	2	4	11	15	2	1	1	7	5	0	1	3	4	10
	TOTAL	**76**	**24**	**25**	**27**	**103**	**119**	**18**	**11**	**9**	**66**	**47**	**6**	**14**	**18**	**37**	**72**
PRESTON NORTH END	2ND	28	7	12	9	32	35	5	6	3	17	15	2	6	6	15	20
	FAC	1	0	0	1	1	3	0	0	1	1	3					
	LC	2	1	0	1	4	3	0	0	1	1	2	1	0	0	3	1
	TOTAL	**31**	**8**	**12**	**11**	**37**	**41**	**5**	**6**	**5**	**19**	**20**	**3**	**6**	**6**	**18**	**21**

Opponents	Type	Total P	Total W	Total D	Total L	Total F	Total A	Home W	Home D	Home L	Home F	Home A	Away W	Away D	Away L	Away F	Away A
READING	2ND	10	1	4	5	6	11	0	3	2	2	5	1	1	3	4	6
	3RD	64	22	13	29	84	99	17	7	8	53	36	5	6	21	31	63
	FAC	1	1	0	0	1	0	1	0	0	1	0					
	LC	1	0	0	1	0	4						0	0	1	0	4
	D3CUP	2	1	0	1	3	2	1	0	0	2	0	0	0	1	1	2
	FM	1	0	0	1	1	3	0	0	1	1	3					
	SPFC	3	0	1	2	3	7	0	1	1	1	2	0	0	1	2	5
	SL	32	11	8	13	30	37	7	4	5	20	14	4	4	8	10	23
	WW1-L	2	1	0	1	4	7	0	0	1	2	6	1	0	0	2	1
	WW2-L	14	8	3	3	29	17	7	0	0	23	5	1	3	3	6	12
	TOTAL	**130**	**45**	**29**	**56**	**161**	**187**	**33**	**15**	**18**	**105**	**71**	**12**	**14**	**38**	**56**	**116**
RICHMOND ASSOCIATION	FAC	1	0	0	1	0	3						0	0	1	0	3
	TOTAL	**1**	**0**	**0**	**1**	**0**	**3**						**0**	**0**	**1**	**0**	**3**
ROCHDALE	3RD	2	1	1	0	5	2	1	0	0	3	0	0	1	0	2	2
	TOTAL	**2**	**1**	**1**	**0**	**5**	**2**	**1**	**0**	**0**	**3**	**0**	**0**	**1**	**0**	**2**	**2**
ROTHERHAM UNITED	2ND	10	4	3	3	18	8	2	2	1	14	5	2	1	2	4	3
	LC	2	0	1	1	1	2	0	1	0	0	0	0	0	1	1	2
	TOTAL	**12**	**4**	**4**	**4**	**19**	**10**	**2**	**3**	**1**	**14**	**5**	**2**	**1**	**3**	**5**	**5**
RUSHDEN & DIAMONDS	3RD	2	1	1	0	4	3	1	0	0	1	0	0	1	0	3	3
	TOTAL	**2**	**1**	**1**	**0**	**4**	**3**	**1**	**0**	**0**	**1**	**0**	**0**	**1**	**0**	**3**	**3**
SCUNTHORPE UNITED	2ND	2	1	1	0	5	3	1	0	0	3	1	0	1	0	2	2
	3RD	6	5	0	1	13	5	3	0	0	8	2	2	0	1	5	3
	FAC	1	1	0	0	4	1						1	0	0	4	1
	TOTAL	**9**	**7**	**1**	**1**	**22**	**9**	**4**	**0**	**0**	**11**	**3**	**3**	**1**	**1**	**11**	**6**
SHEFFIELD UNITED	1ST	14	6	6	2	14	10	5	1	1	9	5	1	5	1	5	5
	2ND	28	8	10	10	37	44	6	4	4	22	20	2	6	6	15	24
	FAC	1	0	0	1	0	1	0	0	1	0	1					
	LC	1	1	0	0	2	0						1	0	0	2	0
	TOTAL	**44**	**15**	**16**	**13**	**53**	**55**	**11**	**5**	**6**	**31**	**26**	**4**	**11**	**7**	**22**	**29**

Opponents	Type	Total P	Total W	Total D	Total L	Total F	Total A	Home W	Home D	Home L	Home F	Home A	Away W	Away D	Away L	Away F	Away A
SHEFFIELD WEDNESDAY	1ST	24	8	6	10	30	43	5	5	2	18	15	3	1	8	12	28
	2ND	28	7	7	14	31	39	5	5	4	19	16	2	2	10	12	23
	3RD	2	2	0	0	6	1	1	0	0	3	0	1	0	0	3	1
	FAC	1	0	0	1	0	3						0	0	1	0	3
	LC	3	1	0	2	9	8	1	0	1	9	4	0	0	1	0	4
	FM	1	1	0	0	1	0						1	0	0	1	0
	TOTAL	**59**	**19**	**13**	**27**	**77**	**94**	**12**	**10**	**7**	**49**	**35**	**7**	**3**	**20**	**28**	**59**
SHEPPEY UNITED	SL	2	0	0	2	3	6	0	0	1	2	3	0	0	1	1	3
	TOTAL	**2**	**0**	**0**	**2**	**3**	**6**	**0**	**0**	**1**	**2**	**3**	**0**	**0**	**1**	**1**	**3**
SHREWSBURY TOWN	2ND	8	3	3	2	12	10	3	1	0	8	2	0	2	2	4	8
	3RD	28	11	12	5	40	28	7	6	1	23	13	4	6	4	17	15
	FAC	7	1	3	3	9	10	1	2	1	6	3	0	1	2	3	7
	LC	1	1	0	0	4	1						1	0	0	4	1
	TOTAL	**44**	**16**	**18**	**10**	**65**	**49**	**11**	**9**	**2**	**37**	**18**	**5**	**9**	**8**	**28**	**31**
SK BRANN	EU	2	2	0	0	11	0	1	0	0	4	0	1	0	0	7	0
	TOTAL	**2**	**2**	**0**	**0**	**11**	**0**	**1**	**0**	**0**	**4**	**0**	**1**	**0**	**0**	**7**	**0**
SLOVAN BRATISLAVA	EU	2	1	1	0	8	5	1	0	0	5	2	0	1	0	3	3
	TOTAL	**2**	**1**	**1**	**0**	**8**	**5**	**1**	**0**	**0**	**5**	**2**	**0**	**1**	**0**	**3**	**3**
SOUTH LIVERPOOL	FAC	1	1	0	0	1	0						1	0	0	1	0
	TOTAL	**1**	**1**	**0**	**0**	**1**	**0**						**1**	**0**	**0**	**1**	**0**
SOUTH SHIELDS	FAC	2	2	0	0	7	1	2	0	0	7	1					
	TOTAL	**2**	**2**	**0**	**0**	**7**	**1**	**2**	**0**	**0**	**7**	**1**					
SOUTHAMPTON	1ST	32	12	8	12	46	48	7	4	5	26	22	5	4	7	20	26
	2ND	16	8	4	4	22	21	5	0	3	11	10	3	4	1	11	11
	3RD	18	3	7	8	23	33	2	4	3	14	12	1	3	5	9	21
	FAC	4	2	0	2	5	6	1	0	1	4	4	1	0	1	1	2
	LC	3	1	2	0	5	1	1	1	0	4	0	0	1	0	1	1
	FM	1	0	0	1	0	4						0	0	1	0	4
	SL	34	12	6	16	43	54	7	4	6	22	21	5	2	10	21	33
	WW1-L	2	1	0	1	5	2	1	0	0	4	0	0	0	1	1	2
	WW2-L	8	5	1	2	29	18	3	0	1	18	7	2	1	1	11	11
	WW2-C	2	1	0	1	3	5	1	0	0	2	1	0	0	1	1	4
	TOTAL	**120**	**45**	**28**	**47**	**181**	**192**	**28**	**13**	**19**	**105**	**77**	**17**	**15**	**28**	**76**	**115**

Opponents	Type	Total P	Total W	Total D	Total L	Total F	Total A	Home W	Home D	Home L	Home F	Home A	Away W	Away D	Away L	Away F	Away A
SOUTHEND UNITED	2ND	4	3	0	1	7	5	2	0	0	6	0	1	0	1	1	5
	3RD	70	34	12	24	115	108	23	7	5	75	43	11	5	19	40	65
	FAC	5	2	2	1	7	6	2	0	0	5	2	0	2	1	2	4
	AM	1	0	0	1	0	4						0	0	1	0	4
	SL	12	5	7	0	19	13	2	4	0	11	8	3	3	0	8	5
	WW2-L	4	4	0	0	10	3	2	0	0	7	2	2	0	0	3	1
	WW2-C	3	1	1	1	4	1	1	0	0	4	0	0	1	1	0	1
	TOTAL	**99**	**49**	**22**	**28**	**162**	**140**	**32**	**11**	**5**	**108**	**55**	**17**	**11**	**23**	**54**	**85**
STOCKPORT CITY	2ND	8	2	4	2	10	12	2	1	1	5	5	0	3	1	5	7
	3RD	6	3	3	0	8	5	1	2	0	2	1	2	1	0	6	4
	FAC	2	0	0	2	2	5	0	0	1	1	3	0	0	1	1	2
	LC	2	1	1	0	2	1	1	0	0	2	1	0	1	0	0	0
	TOTAL	**18**	**6**	**8**	**4**	**22**	**23**	**4**	**3**	**2**	**10**	**10**	**2**	**5**	**2**	**12**	**13**
STOKE CITY	1ST	14	8	2	4	25	15	5	1	1	18	7	3	1	3	7	8
	2ND	12	4	4	4	13	12	2	3	1	8	5	2	1	3	5	7
	3RD	2	2	0	0	2	0	1	0	0	1	0	1	0	0	1	0
	FAC	1	1	0	0	3	0	1	0	0	3	0					
	SL	4	3	1	0	4	0	2	0	0	2	0	1	1	0	2	0
	TOTAL	**33**	**18**	**7**	**8**	**47**	**27**	**11**	**4**	**2**	**32**	**12**	**7**	**3**	**6**	**15**	**15**
SUNDERLAND	1ST	10	5	2	3	12	9	4	1	0	11	4	1	1	3	1	5
	2ND	16	5	4	7	21	24	3	2	3	11	11	2	2	4	10	13
	FAC	1	0	0	1	0	4						0	0	1	0	4
	TOTAL	**27**	**10**	**6**	**11**	**33**	**37**	**7**	**3**	**3**	**22**	**15**	**3**	**3**	**8**	**11**	**22**
SWANSEA CITY	2ND	12	6	5	1	14	9	2	4	0	6	4	4	1	1	8	5
	3RD	16	6	4	6	25	25	4	4	0	16	8	2	0	6	9	17
	FAC	3	1	0	2	2	7						1	0	2	2	7
	LC	3	3	0	0	7	1	3	0	0	7	1					
	SL	2	1	0	1	3	3	1	0	0	2	0	0	0	1	1	3
	TOTAL	**36**	**17**	**9**	**10**	**51**	**45**	**10**	**8**	**0**	**31**	**13**	**7**	**1**	**10**	**20**	**32**
SWINDON TOWN	1ST	2	0	0	2	1	4	0	0	1	1	3	0	0	1	0	1
	2ND	3	2	0	1	6	6	0	0	1	1	3	2	0	0	5	3
	3RD	74	31	18	25	119	99	23	7	7	81	37	8	11	18	38	62
	FAC	4	1	0	3	6	6	1	0	1	4	2	0	0	2	2	4
	LC	2	1	0	1	3	4	0	0	1	1	3	1	0	0	2	1
	SL	34	17	4	13	70	61	14	0	3	51	21	3	4	10	19	40
	TOTAL	**133**	**58**	**27**	**48**	**230**	**192**	**44**	**8**	**14**	**160**	**72**	**14**	**19**	**34**	**70**	**120**

Opponents	Type	Total P	Total W	Total D	Total L	Total F	Total A	Home W	Home D	Home L	Home F	Home A	Away W	Away D	Away L	Away F	Away A
THAMES	3RD	4	2	0	2	11	4	2	0	0	9	0	0	0	2	2	4
	FAC	1	1	0	0	5	0	1	0	0	5	0					
	TOTAL	**5**	**3**	**0**	**2**	**16**	**4**	**3**	**0**	**0**	**14**	**0**	**0**	**0**	**2**	**2**	**4**
TOOTING & MITCHAM	FAC	1	1	0	0	2	0						1	0	0	2	0
	TOTAL	**1**	**1**	**0**	**0**	**2**	**0**						**1**	**0**	**0**	**2**	**0**
TORQUAY UNITED	3RD	46	18	15	13	97	79	12	7	4	59	29	6	8	9	38	50
	FAC	4	2	2	0	8	5	1	1	0	4	2	1	1	0	4	3
	TOTAL	**50**	**20**	**17**	**13**	**105**	**84**	**13**	**8**	**4**	**63**	**31**	**7**	**9**	**9**	**42**	**53**
TOTTENHAM HOTSPUR	1ST	38	12	13	13	53	55	9	6	4	32	23	3	7	9	21	32
	2ND	4	0	1	3	0	6	0	1	1	0	2	0	0	2	0	4
	FAC	4	0	2	2	2	5	0	1	0	0	0	0	1	2	2	5
	LC	1	1	0	0	1	0	1	0	0	1	0					
	SL	18	3	5	10	18	35	3	3	3	11	14	0	2	7	7	21
	WW1-L	14	5	4	5	26	29	1	2	4	14	20	4	2	1	12	9
	WW2-L	10	3	3	4	11	19	2	2	1	3	2	1	1	3	8	17
	WW2-C	2	1	1	0	2	1	1	0	0	1	0	0	1	0	1	1
	TOTAL	**91**	**25**	**29**	**37**	**113**	**150**	**17**	**15**	**13**	**62**	**61**	**8**	**14**	**24**	**51**	**89**
TRANMERE ROVERS	2ND	10	4	4	2	14	10	3	2	0	6	1	1	2	2	8	9
	3RD	12	5	3	4	23	17	2	2	2	15	9	3	1	2	8	8
	FAC	1	1	0	0	2	0						1	0	0	2	0
	LC	1	1	0	0	6	0	1	0	0	6	0					
	TOTAL	**24**	**11**	**7**	**6**	**45**	**27**	**6**	**4**	**2**	**27**	**10**	**5**	**3**	**4**	**18**	**17**
VAUXHALL MOTORS	FAC	2	0	1	1	1	1	0	0	1	1	1	0	1	0	0	0
	TOTAL	**2**	**0**	**1**	**1**	**1**	**1**	**0**	**0**	**1**	**1**	**1**	**0**	**1**	**0**	**0**	**0**
WALSALL	2ND	2	2	0	0	5	3	1	0	0	2	1	1	0	0	3	2
	3RD	40	25	8	7	69	44	15	5	0	38	13	10	3	7	31	31
	FAC	1	1	0	0	1	0						1	0	0	1	0
	LC	4	1	2	1	6	5	1	1	0	4	2	0	1	1	2	3
	WW2-L	2	1	1	0	5	1	1	0	0	4	0	0	1	0	1	1
	ABND	1	0	0	1	0	1						0	0	1	0	1
	TOTAL	**50**	**30**	**11**	**9**	**86**	**54**	**18**	**6**	**0**	**48**	**16**	**12**	**5**	**9**	**38**	**38**
WALTHAMSTOW AVENUE	FAC	5	2	2	1	9	10	2	1	0	7	4	0	1	1	2	6
	TOTAL	**5**	**2**	**2**	**1**	**9**	**10**	**2**	**1**	**0**	**7**	**4**	**0**	**1**	**1**	**2**	**6**

Opponents	Type	Total P	Total W	Total D	Total L	Total F	Total A	Home W	Home D	Home L	Home F	Home A	Away W	Away D	Away L	Away F	Away A
WANDSWORTH	FAC	1	1	0	0	7	1						1	0	0	7	1
	TOTAL	**1**	**1**	**0**	**0**	**7**	**1**						**1**	**0**	**0**	**7**	**1**
WATFORD	1ST	10	5	3	2	13	8	3	2	0	8	4	2	1	2	5	4
	2ND	24	8	8	8	29	33	3	7	2	14	10	5	1	6	15	23
	3RD	68	32	18	18	119	92	18	9	7	64	46	14	9	11	55	46
	FAC	3	1	1	1	6	4	1	0	1	5	3	0	1	0	1	1
	LC	2	1	0	1	2	4						1	0	1	2	4
	D3CUP	4	0	2	2	4	7	0	1	2	3	6	0	1	0	1	1
	FM	1	0	1	0	1	1						0	1	0	1	1
	SL	30	16	7	7	57	32	10	3	2	38	17	6	4	5	19	15
	WW1-L	7	3	1	3	10	18	2	1	0	7	4	1	0	3	3	14
	WW2-L	10	5	4	1	24	15	3	1	1	11	9	2	3	0	13	6
	WW2-C	2	2	0	0	5	2	1	0	0	2	1	1	0	0	3	1
	ABND	4	0	1	0	2	2	0	1	0	2	2					
	TOTAL	**165**	**73**	**46**	**43**	**272**	**218**	**41**	**25**	**15**	**154**	**102**	**32**	**21**	**28**	**118**	**116**
WEALDSTONE	FAC	1	1	0	0	4	0	1	0	0	4	0					
	TOTAL	**1**	**1**	**0**	**0**	**4**	**0**	**1**	**0**	**0**	**4**	**0**					
WELLINGBOROUGH	SL	8	4	1	3	13	6	3	0	1	7	2	1	1	2	6	4
	TOTAL	**8**	**4**	**1**	**3**	**13**	**6**	**3**	**0**	**1**	**7**	**2**	**1**	**1**	**2**	**6**	**4**
WEST BROMWICH ALBION	1ST	14	6	3	5	14	17	4	1	2	8	8	2	2	3	6	9
	2ND	16	4	4	8	16	27	3	1	4	7	9	1	3	4	9	18
	FAC	2	1	0	1	3	3						1	0	1	3	3
	LC	2	1	0	1	4	4						1	0	1	4	4
	TOTAL	**34**	**12**	**7**	**15**	**37**	**51**	**7**	**2**	**6**	**15**	**17**	**5**	**5**	**9**	**22**	**34**
WEST HAM UNITED	1ST	32	9	14	9	44	37	5	7	4	18	15	4	7	5	26	22
	2ND	14	5	1	8	19	23	5	1	1	14	5	0	0	7	5	18
	FAC	10	4	3	3	15	9	4	1	1	12	4	0	2	2	3	5
	LC	1	1	0	0	2	0						1	0	0	2	0
	SL	32	10	6	16	37	49	7	5	4	25	15	3	1	12	12	34
	WW1-L	12	2	2	8	13	31	1	2	3	4	12	1	0	5	9	19
	WW2-L	10	5	1	4	20	19	3	0	2	11	9	2	1	2	9	10
	WW2-C	2	0	1	1	1	6	0	1	0	1	1	0	0	1	0	5
	TOTAL	**113**	**36**	**28**	**49**	**151**	**174**	**25**	**17**	**15**	**85**	**61**	**11**	**11**	**34**	**66**	**113**
WEST HAMPSTEAD	FAC	1	1	0	0	5	0	1	0	0	5	0					
	TOTAL	**1**	**1**	**0**	**0**	**5**	**0**	**1**	**0**	**0**	**5**	**0**					

Opponents	Type	Total P	Total W	Total D	Total L	Total F	Total A	Home W	Home D	Home L	Home F	Home A	Away W	Away D	Away L	Away F	Away A
WEST NORWOOD	FAC	1	1	0	0	4	0	1	0	0	4	0					
	TOTAL	**1**	**1**	**0**	**0**	**4**	**0**	**1**	**0**	**0**	**4**	**0**					
WIGAN ATHLETIC	2ND	2	1	1	0	1	0	1	0	0	1	0	0	1	0	0	0
	3RD	4	1	2	1	4	4	0	1	1	1	2	1	1	0	3	2
	TOTAL	**6**	**2**	**3**	**1**	**5**	**4**	**1**	**1**	**1**	**2**	**2**	**1**	**2**	**0**	**3**	**2**
WIGAN BOROUGH	FAC	1	1	0	0	4	2						1	0	0	4	2
	TOTAL	**1**	**1**	**0**	**0**	**4**	**2**						**1**	**0**	**0**	**4**	**2**
WIMBLEDON	1ST	20	8	4	8	23	25	4	1	5	12	15	4	3	3	11	10
	2ND	2	1	0	1	2	6	1	0	0	2	1	0	0	1	0	5
	FAC	1	0	0	1	1	2						0	0	1	1	2
	LC	2	1	1	0	1	0	0	1	0	0	0	1	0	0	1	0
	TOTAL	**25**	**10**	**5**	**10**	**27**	**33**	**5**	**2**	**5**	**14**	**16**	**5**	**3**	**5**	**13**	**17**
WINDSOR & ETON	FAC	1	1	0	0	3	0	1	0	0	3	0					
	TOTAL	**1**	**1**	**0**	**0**	**3**	**0**	**1**	**0**	**0**	**3**	**0**					
WOLVERHAMPTON W.	1ST	14	6	3	5	25	20	3	2	2	12	10	3	1	3	13	10
	2ND	22	3	10	9	22	33	2	7	2	9	9	1	3	7	13	24
	FAC	2	1	1	0	2	1	0	1	0	1	1	1	0	0	1	0
	LC	5	2	1	2	6	6	1	1	1	4	4	1	0	1	2	2
	TOTAL	**43**	**12**	**15**	**16**	**55**	**60**	**6**	**11**	**5**	**26**	**24**	**6**	**4**	**11**	**29**	**36**
WOLVERTON	FAC	1	1	0	0	2	1						1	0	0	2	1
	TOTAL	**1**	**1**	**0**	**0**	**2**	**1**						**1**	**0**	**0**	**2**	**1**
WORKINGTON	3RD	6	4	2	0	13	4	3	0	0	10	3	1	2	0	3	1
	TOTAL	**6**	**4**	**2**	**0**	**13**	**4**	**3**	**0**	**0**	**10**	**3**	**1**	**2**	**0**	**3**	**1**
WREXHAM	2ND	6	2	3	1	10	7	0	2	1	3	4	2	1	0	7	3
	3RD	12	7	1	4	18	10	5	0	1	13	4	2	1	3	5	6
	TOTAL	**18**	**9**	**4**	**5**	**28**	**17**	**5**	**2**	**2**	**16**	**8**	**4**	**2**	**3**	**12**	**9**
WYCOMBE WANDERERS	3RD	6	2	2	2	9	11	2	1	0	6	4	0	1	2	3	7
	TOTAL	**6**	**2**	**2**	**2**	**9**	**11**	**2**	**1**	**0**	**6**	**4**	**0**	**1**	**2**	**3**	**7**
YEOVIL TOWN	FAC	1	1	0	0	3	0						1	0	0	3	0
	AM	1	0	0	1	0	3						0	0	1	0	3
	TOTAL	**2**	**1**	**0**	**1**	**3**	**3**						**1**	**0**	**1**	**3**	**3**

		Total						Home					Away				
Opponents	**Type**	**P**	**W**	**D**	**L**	**F**	**A**	**W**	**D**	**L**	**F**	**A**	**W**	**D**	**L**	**F**	**A**
YORK CITY	3RD	4	1	2	1	10	6	1	1	0	7	2	0	1	1	3	4
	LC	3	3	0	0	11	4	2	0	0	7	2	1	0	0	4	2
	TOTAL	**7**	**4**	**2**	**1**	**21**	**10**	**3**	**1**	**0**	**14**	**4**	**1**	**1**	**1**	**7**	**6**

COMPETITIONS	**Type**	**P**	**W**	**D**	**L**	**F**	**A**	**W**	**D**	**L**	**F**	**A**	**W**	**D**	**L**	**F**	**A**
(Div.1 / Premiership)	1ST	822	277	223	322	1028	1111	187	117	107	607	457	90	106	215	421	654
(Div.2 / Div.1 / Championship)	2ND	1006	368	288	350	1343	1284	254	140	109	827	498	114	148	241	516	786
(Div.3 South / Div.3 / Div.2 / Div.1)	3RD	1710	719	416	575	2772	2432	494	207	154	1732	895	225	209	421	1040	1537
(Div.4 / Div.3 / Div.2)	4TH	0	0	0	0	0	0	0	0	0	0	0	0	0	0	0	0
FA Cup	FAC	287	112	71	104	479	396	73	36	32	293	156	39	35	72	186	240
League Cup	LC	156	78	27	51	287	204	50	12	20	182	94	28	15	31	105	110
Associate Members' Cup	AM	6	3	0	3	6	9	3	0	1	6	2	0	0	2	0	7
Charity Shield	CS	3	0	1	2	2	7						0	1	2	2	7
Division 3 (S) Cup	D3CUP	13	5	3	5	17	16	5	2	3	14	11	0	1	2	3	5
UEFA Cup	EU	12	8	1	3	39	18	6	0	0	25	4	2	1	3	14	14
Full Members' Cup	FM	7	2	1	4	7	13	0	0	2	3	6	2	1	2	4	7
League Jubilee	JUB	3	1	2	0	5	4	1	1	0	5	4	0	1	0	0	0
Centenary Trophy	MC	1	0	0	1	0	2	0	0	1	0	2					
Play-Off	PO	3	1	1	1	2	2	1	0	0	1	0	0	1	1	1	2
South. Prof. Floodlight Cup	SPFC	7	1	1	5	9	16	1	1	4	7	11	0	0	1	2	5
Southern League	SL	608	245	155	208	877	799	173	71	60	574	302	72	84	148	303	497
1st World War (League)	WW1-L	147	50	26	71	206	297	29	16	28	121	138	21	10	43	85	159
1st World War (Cups)	WW1-C	5	2	0	3	8	12	2	0	0	6	4	0	0	3	2	8
2nd World War (League)	WW2-L	197	97	39	61	439	352	62	17	19	257	151	35	22	42	182	201
2nd World War (Cups)	WW2-C	62	36	10	16	140	89	22	3	5	87	35	14	7	11	53	54
Abandoned Seasons	ABND	3	0	2	1	4	5	0	1	0	2	2	0	1	1	2	3
	TOTAL	**5058**	**2005**	**1267**	**1786**	**7670**	**7068**	**1363**	**624**	**545**	**4749**	**2772**	**642**	**643**	**1241**	**2921**	**4296**

OTHER FIRST-TEAM MATCHES

Season	Date	Opponents	H/A	Result	Score	Goalscorers	Gate
1899–1900	4 November 1899	Rushden	H				
1899–1900	6 September 1899	Richmond Association	H	W	4–1	Turnbull, ?, ?, ?	
1899–1900	6 December 1899	Richmond Association	A				
1900–01	26 September 1900	Bristol City	A	D	0–0		500
1900–01	10 October 1900	Southampton	H	W	1–0		
1900–01	24 October 1900	Tottenham Hotspur	A	L	0–7		
1900–01	31 October 1900	Bristol City	H	L	1–2		
1910–11	27 March 1911	Chelsea	H	W	1–0		
1910–11	26 April 2011	Brentford	A	L	0–4		
1911–12	4 September 1911	Pontypridd	A	L	1–2		
1911–12	8 November 1911	Brentford	H	W	4–1		
1911–12	17 April 1912	Maidstone United	A	W	8–1		
1911–12	5 May 1912	Fulham	A	L	1–4	McKie	
1911–12	7 May 1912	Paris Red Star	A	W	9–2	Tosswill (3), McKie (3), Birch (3)	
1911–12	11 May 1912	Saarbrucken	A	W	12–0	Revill (6), Birch (3), Whyman, Sangster, Tosswill	
1911–12	12 May 1912	Kaiserslauten	A	W	1–0	Browning	
1911–12	15 May 1912	Mannheim	A	W	3–0	Wake, Tosswill, McKie	
1911–12	17 May 1912	Pforzheim	A	W	7–3	Browning (4), Radnage, Revill, McKie	
1911–12	18 May 1912	Nuremberg	A	W	5–1	Browning (2), McKie, Marchant, Tosswill	
1911–12	19 May 1912	Stuttgart	A	W	2–1	Wake, Revill	
1912–13	3 September 1912	Llanelly	A	W	1–0		
1912–13	12 September 1912	Newport	A				
1912–13	30 September 1912	West Ham United	H	W	3–2		
1912–13	14 October 1912	West Ham United	A	L	2–3		
1912–13	30 October 1912	Brentford	A	L	0–2		
1912–13	18 January 1913	Boscombe	A	W	6–0		
1913–14	11 September 1913	Woolwich Arsenal	H	L	0–2		
1913–14	27 April 1914	Brentford	H	W	2–1		
1919–20	22 January 1919	Reading	H	W	4–2		
1920–21	19 February 1921	Coventry City	A	W	2–1		
1920–21	9 March 1921	Watford	A				
1920–21	4 April 1921	Caerphilly	A	W	2–0		
1920–21	18 April 1921	Chelsea	H	W	1–0		
1922–23	2 December 1922	Watford	A	D	1–1	Hart	
1923–24	17 November 1923	Corinthians	H	L	1–3		
1923–24	May 1924	Holland National XI	A	D	1–1	Opp og	5,000
1925–26	7 January 1926	Fulham	A				
1925–26	9 January 1926	Watford	H	L	2–3		
1926–27	27 November 1926	Plymouth Argyle	H	L	1–6		
1927–28	12 September 1927	Huddersfield Town	H	L	0–5		
1927–28	10 December 1927	Corinthians	H	L	3–4		
1930–31	15 April 1931	Wycombe Wanderers	A				
1931–32	12 November 1931	London University	H	W	6–1		
1932–33	30 January 1933	First Vienna	H	L	0–3		
1933–34	27 January 1934	RAF	H	W	5–2		
1934–35	12 September 1934	Sutton United	A	L	2–4	Blackman, Palmer	
1934–35	23 January 1935	Dutch XI	A				
1935–36	11 January 1936	Corinthians	H	W	4–2		

Season	Date	Opponents	H/A	Result	Score	Goalscorers	Gate
1935–36	30 April 1936	Ex-Rangers	H	D	2–2	Abel, Farmer / Chandler, Rivers	
1936–37	30 January 1937	Hamilton Academicals	H	W	4–1	Fitzgerald, Swinfen (3)	
1936–37	22 April 1937	Brentford	H	W	5–2		
1936–37	29 April 1937	Fulham	A				
1937–38	5 May 1938	Anglo Scots	H	W	8–3		
1937–38	9 May 1938	Ipswich Town	A	L	3–4	Bott (2, 1 pen), McCarthy	
1938–39	1 May 1939	Reserves	H		P–P		
1939–40	9 September 1939	The Army	H	W	10–2		
1939–40	16 September 1939	Aldershot	A	W	1–0		
1939–40	23 September 1939	Swindon Town	A	L	0–1		
1939–40	30 September 1939	Southend United	A	L	2–3		
1939–40	14 October 1939	Luton Town	A	W	2–1		
1939–40	14 December 1939	Chelsea	H				
1939–40	27 April 1940	Northampton Town	H	W	2–0		
1939–40	8 June 1940	Walthamstow Avenue	A	L	4–5	McEwan (2), Swinfen, Mangnall	
1940–41	14 September 1940	Norwich City	A		n–p		
1941–42	25 April 1942	Fulham	H	D	0–0		2,500
1942–43	17 April 1943	Tottenham Hotspur	H	D	1–1		
1942–43	24 April 1943	Watford	A				
1942–43	26 April 1943	Watford	H	W	3–2		
1943–44	8 April 1944	Brentford	A	L	1–2		
1943–44	15 April 1944	Staines	A	W	3–1		
1944–45	5 May 1945	Millwall	A	L	2–3		
1944–45	19 May 1945	Fulham	A	W	3–0	Heathcote (2), Mallett	
1945–46	22 December 1945	Bristol City	H	L	1–2	Addinall	
1945–46	24 April 1946	BAOR	A	L	0–5		
1946–47	8 May 1947	Willesden	A	W	5–2		10,000
1946–47	4 June 1947	Rejkjavik	A	W	9–0	Pattison (3), Hatton (3), Hartburn, Durrant (2)	7,000
1946–47	6 June 1947	Fram	A	W	6–1	Pattison (2), Hatton, Durrant (2), ?	
1946–47	9 June 1947	Rejkjavik	A	W	5–0	McEwan (2), Hatton, Pattison, Durrant	
1946–47	11 June 1947	Rejkjavik	A	W	6–1	Hatton, Pattison (2), Durrant (3)	
1947–48	29 November 1947	Rotherham United	A	L	0–1		
1947–48	13 December 1947	Rotherham United	H	W	2–1	Hartburn (2)	
1947–48	29 April 1948	Willesden	A	D	2–2	Mills, E. Worthington	4,000
1947–48	3 May 1948	Brentford	A	W	1–0	Hatton (pen)	
1947–48	22 May 1948	Fenerbache	A	D	1–1	Durrant	
1947–48	29 May 1948	Besiktas	A	W	5–2	Stewart (2), Hatton (2), Hartburn	
1947–48	30 May 1948	Turkey Olympic	A	L	1–2	Hatton	
1947–48	May 1948	Galatasaray	A	D	1–1	Hatton (pen)	
1948–49	2 May 1949	Leyton Orient	A				
1948–49	5 May 1949	Willesden	A				
1948–49	25 May 1949	Demirspor	A	L	1–2		
1948–49	26 May 1949	Gencler Birligi	A	W	3–2		
1948–49	28 May 1949	KSK	A	W	5–1		
1948–49	29 May 1949	Altinordu / Althay	A	W	3–1		
1948–49	2 June 1949	Fenerbache	A	D	1–1		
1948–49	5 June 1949	Besiktas	A	L	0–4		
1948–49	9 June 1949	Galatasaray	A	W	4–2		
1949–50	28 January 1950	Preston North End	A	W	3–1	Neary, Wardle, McKay	
1949–50	11 February 1950	Millwall	A	L	1–2	Neary	
1949–50	13 March 1950	St Just	A				
1949–50	6 May 1950	Charlton Athletic	H	W	3–0	Hatton (3), Hudson	

Season	Date	Opponents	H/A	Result	Score	Goalscorers	Gate
1949–50	May 1950	La Gantoise	A				
1950–51	14 September 1950	Galatasaray	H	W	4–1	Wardle, Addinall (2), Shepherd	
1950–51	10 February 1951	British Army	N	W	1–0	Addinall	
1950–51	16 April 1951	Clyde	H	W	1–0	Hatton	
1950–51	21 April 1951	Brentford	H	D	1–1	Hatton	
1950–51	7 May 1951	S.V.V. Schiedam	H	D	1–1 a	Hatton	
1950–51	10 May 1951	La Gantoise	H	D	4–4		
1951–52	11 April 1952	Arbroath	A	W	5–1		
1951–52	12 April 1952	Ayr United	A	W	2–1		
1951–52	28 April 1952	Alec Stock XI	H	W	2–1	Shepherd, ?	
1951–52	5 May 1952	Kilmarnock	A	L	0–2		
1951–52	9 May 1952	Arbroath	A				
1951–52	12 May 1952	St Johnstone	A				
1951–52		Uxbridge	A	W	3–2	Hill, Tomkys, Opp og	
1951–52		Ipswich Town	A	L	1–3	Parsons	
1952–53	2 February 1953	Gloucester	A	D	2–2	Smith (pen), Allen	
1952–53	9 February 1953	Headington United	A	L	0–1		
1952–53	13 April 1953	Ernie Adams XI	H				
1952–53	27 April 1953	La Gantoise	H	W	5–0	Tomkys (3), Smith, Quinn	
1952–53		Weymouth	A	D	6–6	Cameron (4), Smith, Shepherd	
1953–54	5 October 1953	Arsenal	H	L	1–3	Quinn	16,028
1953–54	14 October 1953	Fenerbache	H	D	2–2	Angell, Smith	
1953–54	19 October 1953	Brentford	H	W	1–0	Tomkys	8,000
1953–54	31 October 1953	Brighton	A	L	1–2	Van Geersdaele	3,500
1953–54	2 November 1953	West Ham United	H	L	2–4	Hawkins, Hurrell	5,000
1953–54	20 January 1954	Gravesend & Northfleet	A	W	3–2	Shepherd, Powell, Tomkys	
1953–54	1 March 1954	Hereford United	A	L	0–1		
1953–54	8 March 1954	Chelsea	H	L	2–5	Pounder (2)	
1953–54	15 March 1954	Amsterdam	H	W	5–2	Nicholas, Angell, Cameron, Clark (2)	
1953–54	22 March 1954	Charlton Athletic	H	D	2–2	Shepherd (2)	
1953–54	29 March 1954	Manchester United	H	L	1–4	Bent og	15,529
1953–54	5 April 1954	Middlesex Wanderers	H	W	3–2	Cameron, Kerrins, Clark	4,319
1954–55	11 October 1954	Tottenham Hotspur	H	W	2–1	Shepherd (2)	9,737
1954–55	18 October 1954	Stoke City	H	W	3–1	Angell (2), Powell	8,631
1954–55	25 October 1954	Hull City	H	L	0–2		7,319
1954–55	8 January 1955	Headington United	A	L	1–2	Smith	
1954–55	3 February 1955	Lask Linz	H	W	3–0	Clark (2), Smith	6,944
1954–55	16 February 1955	1st Simmering Sport	H	W	3–1	Dean, Cameron, Longbottom	1,847
1954–55	2 March 1955	Columbia, Vienna	H	W	4–0	Cameron, Shepherd, Kerrins, Clark	2,965
1954–55	14 March 1955	Middlesex Wanderers	H	D	2–2	Tomkys, Shepherd	
1954–55	21 March 1955	Brentford	A	D	2–2		
1954–55	28 March 1955	Fulham	H		P–P		
1954–55	4 April 1955	All Stars XI	H	D	1–1	Smith	
1954–55	5 May 1955	Weymouth	A	W	4–0		
1955–56	10 October 1955	England Olympic XI	H	W	2–1	Clark, Shepherd	
1955–56	17 October 1955	Portsmouth	H	L	1–3	Cameron	3,000
1955–56	10 December 1955	Oldham Athletic	A	W	3–0	Smith (2), Pounder	
1955–56	5 March 1956	All Star Manager XI	H	L	0–2		
1955–56	12 March 1956	Fulham	H	L	0–2		4,225
1955–56	19 March 1956	England Amateur XI	H	L	2–4	Clark, Cameron	
1955–56	9 April 1956	Middlesex Wanderers	H	W	3–1		
1955–56	18 April 1956	Rampla Juniors	H	D	0–0		
1955–56	30 April 1956	Dover	A	D	0–0		2,000

Season	Date	Opponents	H/A	Result	Score	Goalscorers	Gate
1956–57	5 November 1956	All Star Managers XI	H	D	1–1	Locke	
1956–57	January 1957	Headington United	A	L	1–2		
1956–57	26 January 1957	Brentford	A	W	3–2	Peacock (2), Longbottom	
1956–57	18 March 1957	Middlesex Wanderers	H	L	1–2		
1956–57	2 April 1957	Headington United	A	W	3–2		
1956–57	May 1957	Chalvey	A	W	4–3		
1957–58	4 January 1958	Pegasus	H	D	1–1		
1957–58	24 March 1958	Showbiz XI	H	W	5–3	Cameron (3), Kerrins, Locke	
1957–58	26 April 1958	Reading	A	D	1–1		
1958–59	27 October 1958	All Stars XI	H	L	1–6	Locke	
1958–59	24 January 1959	Leyton Orient	A	L	1–9	Cameron	
1958–59	2 May 1959	Crystal Palace	A	L	1–2		
1959–60	9 January 1960	Southend United	H	D	2–2	Longbottom, Angell	
1959–60	14 March 1960	Middlesex Wanderers	H	L	1–2	Petchey	
1959–60	22 March 1960	Cambridge City	A	L	1–2		
1960–61	6 August 1960	GB Olympic XI	A	L	2–4	Barber, Bedford	
1960–61	8 October 1960	Margate	A	L	1–4	Golding	759
1961–62	9 August 1961	Aldershot	A	W	6–3	Bedford (4), Towers, Francis	3,200
1961–62	12 August 1961	Brighton	H	W	3–2	Evans (2), Bedford	
1961–62	15 August 1961	Brighton	A	L	1–3	Bedford	
1961–62	27 January 1962	Chelsea	H	D	1–1	Keen	
1962–63	8 August 1962	Brentford	A	W	2–1	McCelland, Towers	5,580
1962–63	10 August 1962	Aldershot	A	W	3–2	Towers (pen), Bedford, Lazarus	3,272
1962–63	13 August 1962	Brentford	H	L	0–1		6,000
1963–64	13 August 1963	Brentford	A	L	1–4	McQuade	
1963–64	19 August 1963	Brentford	H	W	3–0	Lazarus, Leary, Collins	
1963–64	25 September 1963	Romford	A	W	5–1	Bedford (2), Keen, McQuade, Collins	
1963–64	15 February 1964	Hibernian	H	W	5–1	Bedford (2), Graham (2), McQuade	
1964–65	8 August 1964	Bath City	A	D	1–1	Leach	
1964–65	11 August 1964	Brentford	A	L	1–2	Bedford	6,000
1964–65	17 August 1964	Brentford	H	D	0–0		2,716
1964–65	19 August 1964	Wembley	A	W	6–2	Bedford (3), Angell (2, 2 pen), McQuade	
1964–65	22 October 1964	Sutton United	A	W	1–0	Leach	
1965–66	7 August 1965	Arsenal	H	W	5–1	Collins (2), Watson, Keen, Opp og	
1965–66	10 August 1965	Charlton Athletic	H	W	4–2	Collins, Keen, McAdams, R. Morgan	
1965–66	12 August 1965	Wimbledon	A	W	1–0		
1965–66	14 August 1965	Portsmouth	A	L	2–5	R.Morgan, Keen	
1965–66	16 August 1965	Bedford	A	L	0–5		2,279
1965–66	23 February 1966	Hastings United	A	W	2–1		
1965–66	18 April 1966	England Amateur XI	H	W	2–1		5,985
1966–67	6 August 1966	Aldershot	A	W	1–0	Keen (pen)	1,950
1966–67	9 August 1966	Norwich City	H	W	1–0	Marsh	2,300
1966–67	11 August 1966	Wimbledon	A	W	5–2		
1966–67	13 August 1966	Norwich City	A	W	2–0	Allen, R.Morgan	3,567
1966–67	15 August 1966	Maidenhead	A	D	2–2	De'ath, Wilks	
1966–67	17 August 1966	Dover	A	L	1–2		
1966–67	27 October 1966	Southall	A				
1966–67	3 May 1967	International XI	H		4–6	R.Morgan (2), I. Morgan, Allen	
1966–67	11 May 1967	Yeovil Town	A				
1966–67	15 May 1967	Bletchley	A				
1966–67	9 June 1967	Jaen	A	L	0–1		
1966–67	10 June 1967	Malaga	A	L	1–5	Hazell	
1967–68	5 August 1967	Italian Olympic XI	H	W	5–1	I. Morgan, R. Morgan, Keen (Pen), Lazarus, Leach	

Season	Date	Opponents	H/A	Result	Score	Goalscorers	Gate
1967–68	8 August 1967	Southend United	A	W	3–2	Lazarus, Allen, Wilks	
1967–68	12 August 1967	Oldham Athletic	A	L	1–2	Allen	
1967–68	15 August 1967	Brentford	H	W	2–0	I. Morgan, Leach	
1967–68	4 March 1968	Inter Bratislava	H	W	4–3	Clarke, Marsh (2, 1 pen), Wilks	8,306
1967–68	6 May 1968	Chelsea	A	L	3–6	Marsh, Glover, Watson	20,969
1967–68	13 May 1968	Chelsea	H	L	1–2	Allen	14,298
1967–68	14 May 1968	Wycombe Wanderers	A	L	0–1		
1967–68	15 May 1968	Bath City	A				
1967–68	23 May 1968	Athletico Bilbao	A				
1967–68	26 May 1968	Real Santander	A				
1968–69	27 July 1968	Aldershot	A	W	3–2	Clarke (2), Leach	4,146
1968–69	1 August 1968	Raith Rovers	A	W	3–1		
1968–69	3 August 1968	Dundee	A	W	2–0	I. Morgan (2)	
1968–69	1 March 1969	Arbroath	H	W	6–3	Marsh (3), Clarke (2), Leach	4,010
1968–69	24 April 1969	Brentford	A	L	1–2	Clarke	6,630
1969–70	28 July 1969	Colchester United	A	W	3–1	Marsh (2), Venables (pen)	
1969–70	2 August 1969	Glasgow Rangers	H	D	3–3	Venables (pen), Bridges, I. Morgan	16,725
1969–70	7 May 1970	Calella	A	W	5–3	Venables (2), Bridges (2), Marsh	
1969–70	10 May 1970	Español	A	W	2–0	Venables, Marsh	
1970–71	3 August 1970	Torquay United	A	D	0–0		
1970–71	5 August 1970	Bournemouth	A	D	1–1	Marsh	
1970–71	8 August 1970	Southampton	A	L	0–3		
1970–71	23 February 1971	Brighton	A	W	1–0	Marsh	
1970–71	3 May 1971	London XI	H	D	4–4	Marsh (2), Venables, R. Morgan	7,750
1970–71	May 1971	Español	A	L	1–3	Marsh	
1970–71	May 1971	Badalona	A	W	1–0	Abbott	
1970–71	May 1971	Sabadell	A	W	2–1	Abbott (2)	
1971–72	31 July 1971	Swansea City	A	W	2–1	Marsh, McCulloch	3,000
1971–72	3 August 1971	Leicester City	H		P–P		
1971–72	3 August 1971	Enfield	A	W	5–0	Marsh (2), Evans, McGovern, Hazell	
1971–72	6 August 1971	West Ham United	H	W	2–0	Leach, Marsh	7,030
1971–72	9 November 1971	Guernsey Island XI	A	W	6–2	O'Rourke (2), ?, ?, ?, ?	
1971–72	4 February 1972	West Bromwich	H	L	1–2	Marsh	7,082
1972–73	17 July 1972	Viking FC	A	W	4–1	Venables, Evans, Leach, Givens	
1972–73	19 July 1972	Alesund	A	W	1–0	O'Rourke	
1972–73	22 July 1972	Clausengen	A	W	2–1	McCulloch (2)	
1972–73	24 July 1972	Rosenburg	A	D	1–1	Leach	
1972–73	29 July 1972	Brighton	A	W	2–1	O'Rourke, Givens	
1972–73	7 August 1972	Vale Recreation	A	W	6–1	Evans, O'Rourke (2), Leach, Givens (2)	
1972–73	12 December 1972	Manchester City	H	L	0–1		
1972–73	30 April 1973	Charlton Athletic	A	W	2–1		2,420
1973–74	30 July 1973	Karlstad	A	D	2–2	Abbott, Mayes	
1973–74	1 August 1973	Amal	A	W	3–1	Givens (3)	
1973–74	3 August 1973	Frederikstad	A	W	5–0	Francis (3), Clement, Bowles	
1973–74	6 August 1973	Kungshan	A	W	2–0	Mancini, Abbott	
1973–74	15 August 1973	Orient	A	L	0–1		4,177
1973–74	18 August 1973	Millwall	A	L	0–2		6,056
1973–74	3 May 1974	Crystal Palace	H	W	2–1	Bowles (2)	4,383
1973–74	14 May 1974	Santos	A	W	2–0	Leach, Abbott	
1973–74	17 May 1974	Boystown	A	W	2–0	Givens (2)	
1973–74	19 May 1974	Jamaica All Stars	A	D	0–0		
1974–75	1 August 1974	Elinkwijk (Utrecht)	A	W	4–0	Bowles (2), Busby, Westwood	
1974–75	3 August 1974	AZ 67	A	D	2–2	Givens (2)	

Season	Date	Opponents	H/A	Result	Score	Goalscorers	Gate
1974–75	6 August 1974	Royal Liege	A	L	1–2	Clement	
1974–75	8 August 1974	Telstar	A	W	1–0	Thomas	
1974–75	3 September 1974	Crystal Palace	A	D	1–1	Westwood	12,000
1974–75	3 March 1975	Brighton	A	L	1–2		
1974–75	14 May 1975	Vard	A	W	9–4	Westwood (4), Bowles (2), Abbott, Masson, Rogers	
1974–75	16 May 1975	Brann Bergen	A	L	0–1		
1974–75	21 May 1975	France A	A	L	0–3		
1975–76	20 July 1975	Borussia Mönchengladbach	A	W	4–1	Webb (2), Bowles (2)	
1975–76	25 July 1975	Wuppertal	A	W	2–1	Clement, Givens	
1975–76	27 July 1975	Paderborn	A	W	6–2	Bowles, Beck, Francis, Givens, Leach, Opp og	
1975–76	8 August 1975	Benfica	A	W	4–2	Bowles, Clement, Webb, Hollins	
1975–76	9 August 1975	Bilbao	A	L	0–3		
1975–76	1 October 1975	Reading	A	W	3–2		7,480
1975–76	9 December 1975	Willesden	A	W	2–1	Rogers (2)	
1975–76	2 February 1976	Red Star Belgrade	H	W	4–0	Thomas, Francis (2, 1 pen), Masson	8,806
1975–76	2 March 1976	Moscow Dynamo	H	W	1–0	McLintock	8,710
1975–76	10 March 1976	Watford	A	W	6–0	Leach, Shanks (2), Bowles (pen), Nutt, Givens	
1975–76	3 May 1976	Southampton	A	D	2–2	McLintock, Eastoe	29,508
1976–77	27 July 1976	Rot-Weiss Essen	A	W	2–0	Bowles, Clement	
1976–77	29 July 1976	Preussen Münster	A	W	3–0	Givens, Busby, Eastoe	
1976–77	1 August 1976	Kaiserslauten	A	L	1–2	Givens	
1976–77	3 August 1976	Red Star Belgrade	A	L	0–1		
1977–78	23 July 1977	Borussia Dortmund	A	W	2–0	Abbott, Thomas	
1977–78	24 July 1977	DJK Wanheimerort	A	W	7–0	Bowles, Eastoe, Francis, Leach, Webb (2), Opp og	
1977–78	26 July 1977	FC Kaiserslauten	A	D	0–0		
1977–78	30 July 1977	Go Ahead Eagles	A	W	3–1	Eastoe, Givens, Thomas	
1977–78	10 August 1977	Wimbledon	A	W	3–1	Bowles, Eastoe, Webb	2,984
1977–78	13 August 1977	Wycombe Wanderers	A	W	1–0	Givens	2,500
1977–78	2 April 1978	Hungerford Town	A	W	2–1	Howe, R. Francis	
1977–78	5 May 1978	Manchester United	H	W	4–2	Goddard (2), McGee, Givens	6,700
1977–78	8 May 1978	Charlton Athletic	A	W	3–1	Goddard, Givens (2)	2,545
1977–78	18 May 1978	Omonoia	A	D	1–1	Busby	
1977–78	21 May 1978	AEK Athens	A	L	0–2		
1977–78	22 May 1978	Aris Salonika	A	D	2–2	Allen, Cunningham (pen)	
1978–79	21 July 1978	FC Homburg	A	D	0–0		500
1978–79	22 July 1978	FC Trier	A	L	1–2	Busby	5,500
1978–79	24 July 1978	FC Würztburg 04	A	W	2–0	Buckley, Busby	3,300
1978–79	2 August 1978	NAC Breda	A	D	1–1	Harkouk	3,600
1978–79	5 August 1978	Bad Honnef	A	W	3–1	Goddard (2), Busby	2,000
1978–79	6 August 1978	FC Viktoria	A	W	6–0	Viljoen, Harkouk, Busby, McGee (3)	2,000
1978–79	12 August 1978	Brighton	A	L	1–2	Hollins	11,359
1978–79	27 November 1978	Chelsea	A	D	2–2		3,981
1978–79	24 April 1979	Tottenham Hotspur	H	L	1–3	Elsey	3,937
1978–79	29 April 1979	Burnham	A				
1978–79	2 June 1979	IICC	A	D	1–1	Harkouk	
1978–79	4 June 1979	Raccah	A	D	1–1	McGee	
1978–79	9 June 1979	Nigeria XI	A	W	2–0	Walsh (2)	
1979–80	29 July 1979	Frederikshavn	A	W	1–0	Goddard	
1979–80	31 July 1979	Ikant	A	W	2–0	Goddard, Elsey	

Season	Date	Opponents	H/A	Result	Score	Goalscorers	Gate
1979–80	2 August 1979	Randers Freja	A	W	2–1	Goddard, Howe	
1979–80	12 August 1979	Drogheda	A	W	1–0	Allen (pen)	
1979–80	5 May 1980	Sunderland	A	L	2–3	Hazell, Hill	
1980–81	14 July 1980	Sochaux Auxerre	A	L	0–1		
1980–81	16 July 1980	Racing Strasbourg	A	D	3–3	Neal (2), Walsh	
1980–81	20 July 1980	Olympiakos Athens	A	L	2–3	Goddard, Neal	
1980–81	29 July 1980	Uleaborg	A	W	6–0	Goddard (2), Hill (2), Hazell, Wilkins	
1980–81	31 July 1980	Helsinki	A	W	2–0	Goddard, Hazell	
1980–81	1 August 1980	Jaro	A	W	8–0	Hill (4), Roeder, Goddard, Hazell, Neal	
1980–81	3 August 1980	IF Kamraterna	A	W	6–0	Goddard (3), Hill (3)	
1980–81	4 August 1980	Rauma Pallo	A	W	8–1	Hill (3), Goddard, McCreey (2), Wilkins, Waddock	
1980–81	24 January 1981	Newport County	A	L	0–2		
1981–82	25 July 1981	Stugens BK	A	W	6–0	Stainrod (2), King (2), Burridge, Sealy	
1981–82	27 July 1981	Skargarden	A	W	8–1	Stainrod, Micklewhite (2), Waddock, Sealy (2), Flanagan, Muir	
1981–82	29 July 1981	Spanga IS	A	W	1–0	Micklewhite	
1981–82	31 July 1981	Enkopings	A	W	9–1	Flanagan (3), Stainrod (2), Allen (2), Muir, Micklewhite	
1981–82	2 August 1981	Ludvika / Grangesberg	A	W	4–1	Stainrod (2), Flanagan, Gregory	
1981–82	8 August 1981	Wimbledon	A	W	4–1	Flanagan (2), Allen (2)	
1981–82	12 August 1981	Maidstone United	A	D	3–3	Stewart (2), Fereday	772
1981–82	16 August 1981	Athlone Town	A	W	4–3	Stainrod (3), Flanagan	
1981–82	18 August 1981	Bohemians	A	W	3–0	Stainrod (2), Allen	
1981–82	22 August 1981	Cambridge United	A	D	0–0		14,418
1981–82	8 September 1981	Birmingham City	A	W	2–1		
1981–82	19 December 1981	Notts County	H	W	3–0	Fenwick (pen), Stewart, Flanagan	6,000
1981–82	17 May 1982	Dave Clement XI	H	W	6–2	Flanagan, Allen, Dawes, Stainrod (2), Stewart	6,486
1981–82	26 May 1982	Tulsa Roughnecks	A	W	3–1	Gregory (2), Flanagan	
1981–82	31 May 1982	San Jose Earthquakes	A	D	3–3	Flanagan, Roeder, Neill	
1982–83	25 July 1982	IS Halmia	A	W	3–2	Stainrod, Fenwick, Wicks	
1982–83	27 July 1982	Myresjö IF	A	W	1–0	C. Allen	
1982–83	28 July 1982	Kalmar FF	A	L	0–2		
1982–83	31 July 1982	Veberoed AIR	A	W	5–0	C. Allen (2), Sealy (2), Neill	
1982–83	2 August 1982	Hjaernarp GIF	A	W	8–0	Flanagan (3), Hazell (2), Sealy, Dawes, Stewart	
1982–83	11 August 1982	Finn Harps	A	W	4–0	Stainrod (2), Neill (2)	
1982–83	13 August 1982	St Patricks	A	L	0–1		
1982–83	15 August 1982	Drogheda United	A	W	6–0	Stainrod (3), Burke, Stewart, Wilkins	
1982–83	18 August 1982	Brighton	A	D	2–2	Gregory (2)	
1982–83	21 August 1982	Gillingham	A	W	2–0	Stainrod, Currie	1,741
1982–83	23 August 1982	Wimbledon	A	W	2–0	Stewart, Gregory	
1982–83	31 January 1983	Southampton	H	L	2–5	Flanagan, Sealy	1,584
1982–83	14 April 1983	Aston Villa	A	L	0–1		
1982–83	4 May 1983	Wimbledon	A	W	2–1	Allen, O'Connor	1,113
1982–83	18 May 1983	Western Australia	A	W	6–1	Neill, Fereday, Sealy, Micklewhite, Stainrod, OG	10,000
1982–83	22 May 1983	Canterbury	A	W	1–0	C. Allen	
1982–83	24 May 1983	Wellington	A	W	2–0	Stainrod, Fenwick (pen)	
1982–83	29 May 1983	Auckland	A	D	2–2	Roeder, Fereday	
1982–83	1 June 1983	New Caledonia	A	L	2–3	C. Allen (2)	
1982–83	3 June 1983	District Assoc. XI	A	W	2–1	Burke, Stainrod	

Season	Date	Opponents	H/A	Result	Score	Goalscorers	Gate
1983–84	6 August 1983	Hibernian	A	W	2–1	C. Allen, Waddock	1,000
1983–84	8 August 1983	Motherwell	A	D	1–1	Micklewhite	
1983–84	10 August 1983	Dundee United	A	D	1–1	Stainrod	
1983–84	13 August 1983	St Mirren	A	L	2–3	C. Allen, Stainrod	2,289
1983–84	16 August 1983	Crystal Palace	A	W	2–1	Hazell, Stainrod	2,000
1983–84	20 August 1983	Chelsea	A	L	1–2	Micklewhite	4,461
1983–84	22 August 1983	AEK Athens	A	L	0–2		
1983–84	18 October 1983	Hayes	A	W	4–1	Sealy (3), Flanagan	
1983–84	15 November 1983	Brentford	A	L	2–3	Flanagan, Comfort	1,414
1983–84	27 January 1984	Fulham	A	W	3–0	Stainrod (3)	
1983–84	19 February 1984	Oman	A	W	3–1	Neill, Allen, Fenwick	
1983–84	21 February 1984	Oman	A	D	2–2	Waddock, Allen	
1983–84	30 April 1984	Crystal Palace	A	L	1–4		1,000
1983–84	22 May 1984	Indonesia FA	A	W	3–2	Kerslake, Stainrod, Fenwick	
1983–84	25 May 1984	Feyenoord	A	L	1–3	Allen	
1984–85	27 July 1984	Waterford	A	W	3–1	Fereday (2), Stainrod	
1984–85	29 July 1984	Drogheda United	A	W	3–0	Gregory, Bannister, Chivers	
1984–85	30 July 1984	Longford Town	A	W	3–0	Fenwick, Allen (pen), Cooper (pen)	
1984–85	4 August 1984	Falkirk	A	D	1–1	Allen	
1984–85	7 August 1984	Heart of Midlothian	A	L	2–3	Micklewhite, Gregory	5,068
1984–85	18 August 1984	Barking	A	W	2–0	Bannister, Gregory	
1984–85	20 August 1984	Portsmouth	A	W	2–0	Bannister, Fenwick (pen)	6,099
1984–85	16 February 1985	Gibraltar XI	A	W	2–0	Bannister (2)	2,000
1984–85	23 May 1985	Hamburg	A	L	3–7		
1985–86	1 August 1985	Cottingham	A	W	5–0	Bannister (3), James, Fenwick	700
1985–86	10 August 1985	Millwall	A	W	3–1	McDonald, Bannister, Fillery	2,320
1985–86	16 September 1985	Maidstone United	A	L	2–3	Byrne (2)	546
1985–86	24 February 1986	Weymouth	A	L	1–2	Walker	
1985–86	26 February 1986	Ottery St Mary	A	W	7–0	Loram, Rosenior, Bannister, Byrne, Walker (2), Chivers	1,364
1985–86	10 March 1986	Ruislip Town	A	W	3–1	Beggs, Walker, Chivers	1,459
1985–86	5 July 1986	Tampa Bay	A				
1985–86	May 1986	Oxford United	A	D	2–2	Allen, Byrne	
1986–87	26 July 1986	Alingsas IF	A	D	1–1	Bannister	750
1986–87	29 July 1986	Falkenbergs FF	A	W	3–2	Allen, Byrne, Fereday	2,025
1986–87	31 July 1986	Osterlenlaget	A	W	6–2	Loram, McDonald, Allen, Rosenior (2), Channing	800
1986–87	2 August 1986	Hoganas BK	A	W	6–0	Hebbard, Channing, Bannister, Robinson, Sage, ?	
1986–87	4 August 1986	Ljungby	A	W	5–0	Allen, Bannister, Byrne (2), Loram	1,330
1986–87	8 August 1986	Enfield	A	L	0–6		
1986–87	9 August 1986	Gillingham	A	D	0–0		1,156
1986–87	13 August 1986	Brentford	A	W	1–0	Fereday	2,254
1986–87	16 August 1986	Portsmouth	A	D	0–0		
1986–87	18 August 1986	Cambridge United	A	L	0–3		
1986–87	25 November 1986	Merthyr Tydfil	A	D	1–1	Robinson	2,300
1986–87	9 February 1987	Dawlish Town	A	W	4–0	Walker (2), Bannister, Loram	1,400
1986–87	15 May 1987	Brentford	A	D	3–3	Byrne (2), Opp og	7,049
1987–88	19 July 1987	Hounslow	A	W	7–0	Walker (2), Coney, Ferdinand, Byrne, Fenwick (pen), Maddix	600
1987–88	10 October 1987	HAC (Le Harve)	A	D	1–1	Coney	
1987–88	9 November 1987	Leicester United	A	W	8–2	Kerslake (3), Peacock (2), Pizanti (2), Brock	1,500

Season	Date	Opponents	H/A	Result	Score	Goalscorers	Gate
1987–88	25 January 1988	Truro	A	W	8–0	Falco (4), Bannister (2), Kerslake, Byrne	2,000
1987–88	8 February 1988	Le Harve	H	W	2–0	Allen, Fereday	849
1987–88	15 February 1988	Charleroi	H	D	1–1	Byrne	4,473
1987–88	9 May 1988	Colchester United	A	W	2–0	Falco, Pizanti	
1988–89	25 July 1988	Nassjo FF	A	W	1–0	Opp og	1,735
1988–89	27 July 1988	Falkenbergs FF	A	D	1–1	Francis	7,798
1988–89	28 July 1988	Orgryte	A	L	0–2		
1988–89	31 July 1988	Rydobruk FF	A	W	9–0	Allen (3), Falco, Francis (2), Barker (2), Channing	
1988–89	2 August 1988	Aarhus	A	W	2–1	Allen, Coney	
1988–89	10 August 1988	Weymouth	A	W	1–0	Barker	
1988–89	13 August 1988	Bournemouth	A	D	0–0		
1988–89	16 August 1988	Yeovil Town	A	D	1–1	Francis (pen)	
1988–89	19 August 1988	Aldershot	A	W	3–0	Brock, Falco, Francis	1,387
1988–89	21 August 1988	Al Ahly	H	D	1–1	McDonald	3,471
1988–89	3 May 1989	Trinidad	A	D	2–2	Stein, Gray	
1988–89	5 May 1989	Trinidad	A	D	0–0		
1989–90	24 July 1989	Bodmin Town	A	W	2–1	Gray, Wright	2,119
1989–90	26 July 1989	Cardiff City	A	W	1–0	Clarke	1,473
1989–90	28 July 1989	Plymouth Argyle	A	L	2–3	Gray, Clarke	4,072
1989–90	31 July 1989	St Mirren	A	D	2–2	Spackman, Wright	1,600
1989–90	2 August 1989	Falkirk	A	W	2–0	Clarke, Gray (pen)	3,500
1989–90	5 August 1989	Dundee	A	D	2–2	Ferdinad, Gray	2,967
1989–90	9 August 1989	Brentford	A	L	0–1		4,667
1989–90	12 August 1989	Wolverhampton	A	D	1–1	Spackman	3,000
1989–90	11 May 1990	Chelsea	H	L	2–4	Sinton, McDonald (pen)	3,652
1990–91	3 August 1990	Taby	A	W	6–1	Falco (3), Wilson, Iorfa, McDonald	
1990–91	6 August 1990	Västeras SK	A	W	3–0	Wegerle (2), Channing	929
1990–91	8 August 1990	Sodertalje FF	A	D	1–1	Sinton	
1990–91	9 August 1990	Uppland SK	A	D	3–3	Ferdinand, Iorfa (2)	2,568
1990–91	14 August 1990	Kingstonian	A	W	4–1	Wegerle (2), Falco (2)	
1990–91	18 August 1990	Portsmouth	A	L	1–2	Wilson	
1990–91	21 August 1990	Wycombe Wanderers	A	W	4–1	Wegerle, Sinton, Barker, Ferdinand	2,575
1991–92	22 July 1991	Gloucester City	A	W	1–0		
1991–92	28 July 1991	Edsbro IF	A	W	5–0	Wegerle, Sinton, Ferdinand, Allen (2)	
1991–92	29 July 1991	IK Viljan	A	W	4–0	Ferdinand, Sinton, Parker, Iorfa	500
1991–92	31 July 1991	IFK Kumla	A	W	7–1	Ferdinand, Barker, Falco, Iorfa, Wilson, Allen, Maddix	1,012
1991–92	3 August 1991	Krylbo IF	A	W	11–0	Sinton (3), Bailey (2), Falco (2), Wegerle (2), Peacock, Ferdinand	1,709
1991–92	7 August 1991	Aldershot	A	W	4–0	Bailey (2), Tilson, Holloway	1,630
1991–92	9 August 1991	Watford	A	W	4–1	Webster, Falco, Ferdinand (2)	2,969
1991–92	10 August 1991	Millwall	A	W	3–0	Falco, Bailey, Bardsley	2,784
1991–92	15 January 1992	Cambridge United	A	D	1–1		
1991–92	22 April 1992	Q.P.R. Select XI	H	W	3–1	Allen, Channing, Sinton	
1992–93	21 July 1992	Sarpsborg FK	A	W	4–1	Ferdinand, Allen, Wilson (pen), Bailey	1,066
1992–93	23 July 1992	Pressens Lag	A	W	2–1	Bailey, Wilson	860
1992–93	24 July 1992	SKI	A	W	3–1	Barker, Ferdinand (2)	572
1992–93	26 July 1992	Baerum SK	A	W	4–0	Ferdinand, Bailey, Wilkins, Maddix	500
1992–93	28 July 1992	Kongsvinger IL	A	W	2–0	Sinton, Ferdinand	900
1992–93	29 July 1992	Raufor	A	W	2–0	Meaker, Impey	
1992–93	1 August 1992	Brentford	A	W	2–1	Ferdinand (2)	4,441
1992–93	8 August 1992	Fulham	A	W	2–1	Holloway, Bailey	2,421

Season	Date	Opponents	H/A	Result	Score	Goalscorers	Gate
1992–93	10 August 1992	Luton Town	A	D	0–0		2,519
1993–94	21 July 1993	GAIS	A	W	3–1	Impey, Meaker, Ferdinand	
1993–94	23 July 1993	Myresjö IF	A	W	7–2	Meaker, Ferdinand, Witter, Impey, Bailey, Allen, Barker	
1993–94	25 July 1993	Hvidovre	A	W	2–0	Ferdinand, Impey	
1993–94	26 July 1993	IF Leiken	A	W	6–1	White (3), Penrice, Sinton, Brevett	
1993–94	28 July 1993	IFK Gothenburg	A	W	2–1	McDonald, Sinton	
1993–94	31 July 1993	Bournemouth	A	W	2–0	Ferdinand, Barker	2,629
1993–94	4 August 1993	Watford	A	D	1–1	Peacock	5,078
1993–94	7 August 1993	Oxford United	A	W	2–0	White, Sinton	
1994–95	25 July 1994	Vänersborg	A	W	5–1	Ferdinand, Penrice, Sinclair, Allen, White	
1994–95	26 July 1994	Asa	A	W	3–0	Allen (2), Holloway	
1994–95	26 July 1994	Gais	A	W	1–0	Ferdinand	
1994–95	28 July 1994	Jonsereds	A	L	1–2	White	
1994–95	30 July 1994	Fargelanda	A	W	13–1	Holloway, Ferdinand (2), Gallen (2), Penrice, Meaker (2), Allen (2), White (3)	
1994–95	31 July 1994	Skövde AIK	A	W	3–2	Allen (3)	
1994–95	3 August 1994	Brentford	A	D	0–0		4,614
1994–95	6 August 1994	Bristol Rovers	A	W	2–1	Gallen (2)	3,022
1994–95	9 August 1994	Derby County	A	L	1–2	Penrice	3,453
1994–95	May 1995	Barbados	A	W	2–0	Ferdinand, Sinclair	
1994–95	May 1995	Trinidad & Tobago	A	W	2–0		
1995–96	22 July 1995	Aylesbury	A	W	8–0	Dichio (2), Gallen (2), Allen (2), Osborn, Opp og	1,913
1995–96	25 July 1995	Leyton Orient	A	W	1–0	Dichio	2,537
1995–96	29 July 1995	Charlton Athletic	A	W	2–1	Maddix, Dichio	3,703
1995–96	2 August 1995	Brighton	A	D	1–1	Gallen	4,424
1995–96	5 August 1995	Crystal Palace	A	W	3–1	Gallen, Sinclair, Dichio	2,048
1995–96	7 August 1995	Millwall	A	W	2–1	Barker, Charles	5,699
1995–96	12 August 1995	Hibernian	A	L	1–2	Dichio	6,005
1996–97	26 July 1996	Wycombe Wanderers	A	W	3–1	Sinclair, Murray, Hateley	
1996–97	31 July 1996	Barnet	A	W	2–0	Slade, Hateley	
1996–97	2 August 1996	Brentford	A	L	1–2	Gallen	
1996–97	3 August 1996	Leyton Orient	A	W	1–0	Slade	
1996–97	6 August 1996	Fulham	A	W	1–0	Gallen	
1996–97	10 August 1996	Wimbledon	H	L	0–1		3,024
1997–98	11 July 1997	St Albans	A	W	5–2	Gallen (2), Spencer (2), Mahoney-Johnson	1,200
1997–98	16 July 1997	Exeter City	A	L	1–2		2,443
1997–98	18 July 1997	Plymouth Argyle	A	W	2–0	Gallen (2)	
1997–98	22 July 1997	Gillingham	A	L	0–1		
1997–98	25 July 1997	Wycombe Wanderers	A	L	2–3	Spencer (2)	3,628
1997–98	29 July 1997	Bournemouth	A	W	2–1	Gallen, Peacock	2,600
1997–98	2 August 1997	West Ham United	A	L	0–2		12,658
1997–98	22 March 1998	Jamaica	H	L	1–2	Slade	16,978
1998–99	18 July 1998	Glentoran	A	W	2–1	Sheron, Heinola	1,400
1998–99	21 July 1998	Portadown	A	W	5–0	Dowie, Bruce, Sheron (2), Rowland	750
1998–99	24 July 1998	Millwall	A	L	0–1		2,879
1998–99	28 July 1998	Brentford	A	D	0–0		4,706
1998–99	1 August 1998	Tottenham Hotspur	H	D	0–0		9,700
1999–2000	13 July 1999	Bournemouth	A	W	1–0	Murray	2,000
1999–2000	14 July 1999	Weymouth	A	D	1–1	R. Graham	720

Season	Date	Opponents	H/A	Result	Score	Goalscorers	Gate
1999–2000	17 July 1999	Basingstoke	A	W	4–2	Langley (2), Yates, Scully	1,743
1999–2000	20 July 1999	Sheffield Wednesday	H	L	1–2	Gallen	3,685
1999–2000	24 July 1999	Brentford	A		P–P	(Ground not ready)	
1999–2000	26 July 1999	Bristol Rovers	A	L	0–3		2,106
1999–2000	28 July 1999	Tottenham Hotspur	H	D	2–2	Peacock (pen), Steiner	10,515
1999–2000	31 July 1999	Luton Town	A	L	1–3	Rowland	2,296
2000–01	18 July 2000	Tiverton Town	A	W	5–0	Koejoe, Crouch, Wardley, Dowie, Jeanne	
2000–01	19 July 2000	Exeter City	A	W	4–1	Peacock (pen), Koejoe, Burrows og, Wardley	
2000–01	22 July 2000	Brentford	A	W	2–0	Wardley, Langley	
2000–01	25 July 2000	Wycombe Wanderers	A	D	2–2	Dowie, Wardley	2,362
2000–01	29 July 2000	Aldershot	A	W	2–0	Crouch, Langley	1,902
2000–01	5 August 2000	Tottenham Hotspur	H	L	0–2		12,042
2001–02	14 July 2001	Glasgow Celtic	H	L	0–2		17,337
2001–02	21 July 2001	Watford	H	D	0–0		4,411
2001–02	28 July 2001	Chelsea	H	W	3–1	Griffiths, Connolly, Peacock	11,988
2001–02	4 August 2001	Birmingham City	H	W	1–0	Thomson	2,360
2001–02	6 August 2001	Hampton & Richmond	A	W	5–0	M'Bombo, Pacquette, Perry, Wardley, Connolly	1,220
2002–03	13 July 2002	Glasgow Celtic	H	L	3–7	Gallen, Burgess, Sidibe	15,556
2002–03	20 July 2002	Aylesbury	A	W	2–1	Shittu, Carlisle	1,265
2002–03	28 July 2002	Tottenham Hotspur	H	W	3–2	Carlisle, Thomson, Rose	7,335
2002–03	3 August 2002	Steaua Bucharest	H	W	2–1	Thomson, Connolly	2,707
2003–04	12 July 2003	Farnborough Town	A	D	0–0		1,000
2003–04	14 July 2003	Aylesbury United	A	W	2–0	Ainsworth, Sabin	
2003–04	19 July 2003	Kettering Town	A	W	2–1	Ainsworth, Furling	1,216
2003–04	26 July 2003	Watford	H	L	1–2	Langley (pen)	3,000
2003–04	2 August 2003	Dagenham & Redbridge	A	W	3–0	Pacquette (2), Furlong	1,105
2003–04	4 August 2003	Charlton Athletic	H	L	1–3	Gallen	
2004–05	14 July 2004	Nairn County	A	W	3–0	Rowlands, Gallen, Thorpe	
2004–05	17 July 2004	Inverness Caledonian T.	A	D	1–1	Cureton	850
2004–05	21 July 2004	Ajax	H	L	0–1		9,582
2004–05	27 July 2004	Bristol Rovers	A	W	2–0	Furlong, Thorpe	5,924
2004–05	31 July 2004	Crystal Palace	H	W	3–0	Thorpe, Furlong, Gallen	5,070
2005–06	17 July 2005	Aldershot Town	A	W	3–0	Brown (2), Moore	1,620
2005–06	23 July 2005	Iran	H	W	3–0	Furlong, Ainsworth, Santos	5,843
2005–06	26 July 2005	Charlton Athletic	H	L	0–3		3,256
2005–06	30 July 2005	Birmingham City	H	W	2–1	Gallen, Furlong	5,801
2006–07	8 July 2006	Aldershot Town	A	D	1–1	Doherty	1,340
2006–07	19 July 2006	Stevenage Borough	A	W	4–1	Ainsworth, Donnelly, Gallen (2)	
2006–07	22 July 2006	Gillingham	A	W	1–0	R. Jones	1,472
2006–07	24 July 2006	Sorrento Calcio	A	L	1–5	Czerkas	
2006–07	28 July 2006	San Antonio Abate	A	W	4–0	Ward, Nygaard, Baidoo, R. Jones	
2007–08	15 July 2007	Celtic	H	L	1–5	St Aimie	
2007–08	28 July 2007	Wycombe Wanderers	A	W	1–0	Rowlands	3,045
2007–08	31 July 2007	Harrow Borough	A	W	3–0	Nygaard, Bolder, Baidoo	
2007–08	3 August 2007	Fulham	H	W	2–1	Sahar (2)	
2008–09	23 July 2008	Northampton Town	A	W	1–0	Blackstock	2,562
2008–09	26 July 2008	Falkirk	A	L	0–2		
2008–09	29 July 2008	Kilmarnock	A	L	0–1		
2008–09	2 August 2008	AC Chievo Verona	H	L	1–2	Blackstock	

International Appearances

Name	Country	Caps	Level	Date	Against	Venue	W/D/L	Score	Goals	Sub	Capt
Sam ABEL	Met. Police	1		20/05/1942	Royal Navy	Ipswich	W	7–5			
Bert ADDINALL	FA	1		01/11/1950	Diables Rouges						
Bradley ALLEN	England	1	Youth	20/09/1988	Eire	Rio De Janeiro	W	2–0		Sub	
	England	2	Youth	26/10/1988	Greece	Birkenhead	W	5–0		Sub	
	England	3	Youth	15/11/1988	France	Bradford	D	1–1		Sub	
	England	4	Youth	15/06/1990	Spain	Faro	L	0–1			
	England	5	Youth	18/06/1990	Syria	Faro	D	3–3			
	England	6	Youth	20/06/1990	Uruguay	Faro	D	0–0			
	England	7	Youth	24/06/1990	Belgium	Nyiregyhaza	D	1–1	1	Sub	
	England	8	Youth	26/07/1990	USSR	Debrecen	L	1–3			
	England	1	U21	12/05/1992	Hungary	Vac	D	2–2	1		
	England	2	U21	24/05/1992	Mexico	Toulon	D	1–1	1		
	England	3	U21	26/05/1992	Czechoslavakia	La Sage	L	1–2			
	England	4	U21	28/05/1992	France	Aubagne	D	0–0			
	England	5	U21	12/10/1992	Norway	Peterborough	L	0–2		Sub	
	England	6	U21	17/11/1992	Turkey	Leyton	L	0–1			
	England	7	U21	06/06/1993	Portugal	Miramas	W	2–0			
	England	8	U21	09/06/1993	RCS	Saint-Cyr	D	1–1		Sub	
Clive ALLEN	England	1	Youth	05/05/1978	Turkey	Wodzislaw	D	1–1		Sub	
	England	2	Youth	07/05/1978	Spain	Bukowas	W	1–0	1	Sub	
	England	3	Youth	09/05/1978	Poland	Chorzow	L	0–2			
	England	4	Youth	08/10/1978	Las Palmas	Las Palmas	W	4–2	3		
	England	5	Youth	10/10/1978	USSR	Las Palmas	W	1–0			
	England	6	Youth	12/10/1978	Las Palmas	Las Palmas	W	3–0	1		
	England	7	Youth	13/11/1978	Portugal	Monte Carlo	W	2–0	1		
	England	8	Youth	15/11/1978	Yugoslavia	Monte Carlo	D	1–1			
	England	9	Youth	17/11/1978	Spain	Monte Carlo	D	1–1			
	England	10	Youth	17/01/1979	Belgium	Brussels	W	4–0			
	England	11	Youth	28/02/1979	Italy	Rome	W	1–0			
	England	12	Youth	26/05/1979	Malta	Salzburg	W	3–0	1		
	England	13	Youth	28/05/1979	West Germany	Salzburg	W	2–0		Sub	
	England	14	Youth	31/05/1979	Bulgaria	Vienna	L	0–1			
	England	15	Youth	02/06/1979	France	Vienna	D	0–0		Sub	
	England	1	U21	23/04/1980	East Germany	Jena	L	0–1		Sub	
	England	2	U21	09/09/1980	Norway	Southampton	W	3–0			
	England	3	U21	14/10/1980	Romania	Ploiesti	L	0–4			
	England	1	Full	10/06/1984	Brazil	Rio De Janeiro	W	2–0		Sub	
	England	2	Full	13/06/1984	Uruguay	Montevideo	L	0–2			
	England	3	Full	17/06/1984	Chile	Santiago	D	0–0			
Martin ALLEN	England	1	Youth	03/06/1985	USSR	Toulon	L	0–2			
	England	2	Youth	05/06/1985	Mexico	Toulon	W	2–0		Sub	
	England	3	Youth	07/06/1985	France	Toulon	L	1–3			
	England	1	U21	09/09/1986	Sweden	Ostersund	D	1–1		Sub	
	England	2	U21	10/11/1987	Yugoslavia	Zemun	W	5–1		Sub	
Reg ALLEN	British Army	1		11/02/1940	French Army	Paris	D	1–1			
	British Army	2		15/02/1940	French Army	Lille	W	1–0			
	Army in England	3		30/11/1940	Army in Scotland	Ibrox	W	4–1			
	FA	1		03/11/1948	Army	Ipswich	L	0–2			
Kurt BAKHOLT	Denmark	1	U21	26/03/1986	England	Maine Road	D	1–1			
BALL	FA XI	1		30/03/1940	RAF	Dulwich	L	2–3			
David BARDSLEY	England	1	Full	09/09/1992	Spain	Santander	L	0–1		Sub	

Stan Bowles

John Byrne

Name	Country	Caps	Level	Date	Against	Venue	W/D/L	Score	Goals	Sub	Capt
	England	2	Full	19/05/1993	Poland	Katowice	D	1–1			
William BARNES	Southern League	1		24/10/1910	Scottish League	Millwall	W	1–0			
Graham BENSTEAD	England	1	Youth	03/09/1981	Austria	Umag	W	3–0		Sub	
Marc BIRCHAM	Canada	1	Full	11/10/2003	Finland	Tampere	L	2–3			
	Canada	2	Full	18/11/2003	Republic of Ireland	Dublin	L	0–3			
	Canada	3	Full	30/05/2004	Wales	Wrexham	L	0–1		Sub	
	Canada	4	Full	16/06/2004	Belize	Kingston	W	4–0			
Dexter BLACKSTOCK	England	1	U21	07/09/2007	Montenegro	Podgorica	W	3–0		Sub	
	England	2	U21	10/05/2008	Wales	Wrexham	W	2–0		Sub	
Albert BONASS	Met. Police	1		26/03/1942	Welsh Guards	Staines					
	Met. Police	2		02/01/1943	Army	Aldershot	D	5–5			
Tommy BONNER	Scotland	1	U16	14/10/2003	Switzerland	Switzerland	W	3–0			
	Scotland	2	U16	16/10/2003	Belgium	Switzerland	W	1–0		Sub	
Stan BOWLES	Football League	1		27/03/1974	Scottish League	Manchester	W	5–0	1		
	England	1	Full	03/04/1974	Portugal	Lisbon	D	0–0			
	England	2	Full	11/05/1975	Wales	Cardiff	W	2–0	1		
	England	3	Full	15/05/1975	Northern Ireland	Wembley	W	1–0			
	England	4	Full	17/11/1976	Italy	Rome	L	0–2			
	England	5	Full	09/02/1977	Holland	Wembley	L	0–2			
Ray BRADY	Eire	1	Full	25/09/1963	Austria	Vienna	D	0–0			
	Eire	2	Full	13/10/1963	Austria	Dublin	W	3–2			
	Eire	3	Full	11/03/1964	Spain	Seville	L	1–5			
	Eire	4	Full	08/04/1964	Spain	Dublin	L	0–2			
	Eire	5	Full	10/05/1964	Poland	Krakow	L	1–3			
	Eire	6	Full	13/05/1964	Norway	Oslo	W	4–1			
Kevin BROCK	England	1	B	14/10/1987	Malta	Ta'Qali	W	2–0			
Harry BROWN	FA XI	1		27/11/1943	Civil Defence	Luton	W	5–4			
	FA XI	2		22/01/1944	RAF	Bristol	L	2–4			
	London	1		21/11/1951	Berlin	Berlin	D	1–1			
Paul BRUCE	England	1	U16	1994	Tour to Oman						
	England	2	U16	1994	Tour to Oman						
	England	3	U16	/06/1994	France	Wembley					
Martyn BUSBY	England	1	Youth	31/03/1971	Spain	Pamplona	L	2–3			
	England	2	Youth	22/05/1971	Yugoslavia	Bardejov	W	1–0			
	England	3	Youth	24/05/1971	Sweden	Poprad	W	1–0			
	England	4	Youth	26/05/1971	Poland	Presov	D	0–0			
	England	5	Youth	28/05/1971	USSR	Prague	D	1–1			
	England	6	Youth	30/05/1971	Portugal	Prague	W	3–0			
Akos BUZSAKY	Hungary	1	Full	17/11/2007	Moldova	Chisinau	L	0–3		Sub	
	Hungary	2	Full	21/11/2007	Greece	Budapest	L	1–2	1		
	Hungary	3	Full	06/02/2008	Slovakia	Budapest	D	1–1			
	Hungary	4	Full	11/10/2008	Albania	Budapest	W	2–0		Sub	
	Hungary	5	Full	15/11/2008	Malta	Valletta	L	0–1		Sub	
John BYRNE	Eire	1	Full	05/02/1985	Italy	Dublin	L	1–2			
	Eire	2	Full	26/05/1985	England	Wembley	L	1–2		Sub	
	Eire	3	Full	26/05/1985	Spain	Cork	D	0–0		Sub	
	Eire	4	Full	18/02/1987	Scotland	Glasgow	L	0–1		Sub	
	Eire	5	Full	29/04/1987	Belgium	Dublin	D	0–0		Sub	
	Eire	6	Full	23/05/1987	Brazil	Dublin	W	1–0			
	Eire	7	Full	28/05/1987	Luxembourg	Luxembourg	W	2–0		Sub	
	Eire	8	Full	09/09/1987	Luxembourg	Dublin	W	2–1			
	Eire	9	Full	14/10/1987	Bulgaria	Dublin	W	2–0		Sub	
	Eire	10	Full	10/11/1987	Israel	Dublin	W	5–0	1		
	Eire	11	Full	23/03/1988	Romania	Dublin	W	2–0			
	Eire	12	Full	27/04/1988	Yugoslavia	Dublin	W	2–0		Sub	

Name	Country	Caps	Level	Date	Against	Venue	W/D/L	Score	Goals	Sub	Capt
	Eire	13	Full	22/05/1988	Poland	Dublin	W	3–0		Sub	
Peter CALDWELL	England	1	U15	/03/1987	France	Sheffield	L	0–1			
Robert CAMERON	Army	1		07/11/1951	FA	Highbury	L	2–4			
	London	1		04/05/1956	Basle	Tottenham	W	1–0			
Clarke CARLISLE	England	1	U21	31/08/2000	Georgia	Middlesbrough	W	6–1		Sub	
	England	2	U21	06/10/2000	Germany	Derby	D	1–1		Sub	
	England	3	U21	10/10/2000	Finland	Valkeakoski	D	2–2		Sub	
Trevor CHALLIS	England	1	U18	07/09/1993	Romania	Port Vale	D	1–1		Sub	
	England	2	U18	13/10/1993	Romania	Bucharest	D	1–1		Sub	
	England	1	U21	28/05/1996	Angola	Cuers	L	0–2			
	England	2	U21	30/05/1996	Portugal	Arles	L	1–3			
Justin CHANNING	England	1	Youth	20/03/1986	Hungary	Cannes	W	2–0			
	England	2	Youth	29/03/1986	Brazil	Cannes	D	0–0		Sub	
Jeremy CHARLES	Wales	1	Full	14/12/1983	Yugoslavia	Cardiff	D	1–1		Sub	
	Wales	2	Full	28/02/1984	Scotland	Glasgow	L	1–2			
Colin CLARKE	Northern Ireland	1	Full	26/04/1989	Malta	Valetta	W	2–0	1		
	Northern Ireland	2	Full	26/05/1989	Chile	Belfast	L	0–1			
	Northern Ireland	3	Full	06/09/1989	Hungary	Belfast	L	1–2			
	Northern Ireland	4	Full	11/10/1989	Eire	Dublin	L	0–3			
	Northern Ireland	5	Full	27/03/1990	Norway	Belfast	L	2–3			
Dave CLEMENT	England	1	Youth	23/05/1966	France	Rijeka	L	1–2			
	England	2	Youth	25/05/1966	Italy	Rijeka	D	1–1			
	England	1	Full	24/03/1976	Wales	Wrexham	W	2–1		Sub	
	England	2	Full	08/05/1976	Wales	Cardiff	W	1–0			
	England	3	Full	28/05/1976	Italy	New York	W	3–2			
	England	4	Full	17/11/1976	Italy	Rome	L	0–2			
	England	5	Full	09/02/1977	Holland	Wembley	L	0–2			
Alan COMFORT	England	1	Youth	07/04/1982	Portugal	Cannes	W	3–0			
	England	2	Youth	09/04/1982	Holland	Cannes	W	1–0			
	England	3	Youth	11/04/1982	Czechoslavakia	Cannes	L	0–1			
	England	4	Youth	12/04/1982	France	Cannes	L	0–1			
	England	5	Youth	13/07/1982	Norway	Levanger	L	1–4			
Dean CONEY	England	1	U21	13/10/1987	Turkey	Sheffield	D	1–1			
Barry CONLON	Eire	1	U18		France	Opporto	D	1–1	1		
	Eire	2	U18		Russia	Opporto	D	1–1	1		
	Eire	3	U18		Portugal	Opporto	L	0–2			
Gary COOPER	England	1	Youth	04/04/1983	Qatar	Cannes	D	1–1			
	England	1	U17	12/07/1983	Poland	Slagelse	W	1–0			
	England	2	U17	14/07/1983	Norway	Slagelse	W	1–0			
	England	3	U17	16/07/1983	Denmark	Slagelse	L	0–1			
	England	2	Youth	01/09/1983	Switzerland	Porec	W	4–2	1		
	England	3	Youth	03/09/1983	Hungary	Umag	W	3–2			
	England	4	Youth	08/09/1983	Yugoslavia	Pula	D	2–2			
	England	5	Youth	01/11/1983	Iceland	Selhurst Park	W	3–0			
	England	6	Youth	25/05/1984	East Germany	Moscow	D	1–1			
	England	7	Youth	27/05/1984	USSR	Moscow	D	1–1			
	England	8	Youth	29/05/1984	Luxembourg	Moscow	W	2–0			
	England	9	Youth	03/06/1985	USSR	Toulon	L	0–2			
	England	10	Youth	07/06/1985	France	Toulon	L	1–3			
Damian DELANEY	Eire	1	Full	24/05/2008	Serbia	Dublin	W	1–0			
	Eire	2	Full	29/05/2008	Colombia	Fulham	W	1–0			
Daniele DICHIO	England	1	U21	10/10/1995	Norway	Stavanger	D	2–2		Sub	
David DONALD	London Combination	1		07/04/1921	London League	West Ham	L	1–2			
Scott DONNELLY	England	1	U17	29/07/2003	Iceland	Hamar	W	3–0	1		
	England	2	U17	30/07/2003	Denmark	Hamar	L	0–3		Sub	

Colin Clarke

Iain Dowie

Name	Country	Caps	Level	Date	Against	Venue	W/D/L	Score	Goals	Sub	Capt
	England	3	U17	01/08/2003	Norway	Norway	D	1–1		Sub	
	England	4	U17	03/08/2003	Sweden	Norway	L	1–3			
Iain DOWIE	Northern Ireland	1	Full	25/03/1998	Slovakia	Belfast	W	1–0			
	Northern Ireland	2	Full	22/04/1998	Switzerland	Belfast	W	1–0			
	Northern Ireland	3	Full	03/06/1998	Spain	Santander	L	1–4			
	Northern Ireland	4	Full	05/09/1998	Turkey	Istanbul	L	0–3			Capt
	Northern Ireland	5	Full	10/10/1998	Finland	Belfast	W	1–0			
	Northern Ireland	6	Full	18/11/1998	Moldova	Belfast	D	2–2	1		
	Northern Ireland	7	Full	27/03/1999	Germany	Belfast	L	0–3			
	Northern Ireland	8	Full	31/03/1999	Moldova	Chisinau	D	0–0			
	Northern Ireland	9	Full	27/04/1999	Canada	Belfast	D	1–1			
	Northern Ireland	10	Full	29/05/1999	Republic of Ireland	Dublin	W	1–0			Capt
	Northern Ireland	11	Full	18/08/1999	France	Belfast	L	0–1			
	Northern Ireland	12	Full	04/09/1999	Turkey	Belfast	L	0–3			
	Northern Ireland	13	Full	08/09/1999	Germany	Dortmund	L	0–4			
Martin DUFFIELD	England	1	Youth	23/03/1982	Scotland	Coventry	D	2–2			
Lyndon DUNCAN	England	1	U17	05/09/2000	Czech Republic	(neutral)	D	2–2		Sub	
	England	2	U17	08/09/2000	Poland	(neutral)	L	1–2			
	England	3	U17	14/06/2001	Italy	Tivoli	L	1–4		Sub	
	England	1	U19	01/10/2001	Iceland	York	W	2–0			
	England	2	U19	04/10/2001	Russia	Barnsley	L	0–1		Sub	
	England	1	U20	11/06/2003	Portugal	Nimes	L	0–3			
	England	2	U20	13/06/2003	Argentina	Toulon	L	0–8			
	England	3	U20	15/06/2003	Turkey	Toulon	L	0–1			
Ian EVANS	Wales	1	U23	29/11/1972	England	Swansea	L	0–3			
	Wales	2	U23	27/02/1974	Scotland	Aberdeen	L	0–3			
Des FARROW	FA	1		25/10/1950	RAF	Fulham	W	6–1			
Terry FENWICK	England	1	U21	09/09/1980	Norway	Southampton	W	3–0			
	England	2	U21	14/10/1980	Romania	Ploiesti	L	0–4			
	England	3	U21	18/11/1980	Switzerland	Ipswich	W	5–0			Capt
	England	4	U21	25/02/1981	Eire	Liverpool	W	1–0			
	England	5	U21	28/04/1981	Romania	Swindon	W	3–0			
	England	6	U21	08/09/1981	Norway	Dramen	D	0–0			
	England	7	U21	17/11/1981	Hungary	Nottingham	W	2–0			
	England	8	U21	19/04/1982	Scotland	Glasgow	W	1–0			
	England	9	U21	28/04/1982	Scotland	Manchester	D	1–1			
	England	10	U21	21/09/1982	West Germany	Sheffield	W	3–1			
	England	11	U21	12/10/1982	West Germany	Bremen	L	2–3			
	England	1	Full	02/05/1984	Wales	Wrexham	L	0–1		Sub	
	England	2	Full	26/05/1984	Scotland	Glasgow	D	1–1			
	England	3	Full	02/06/1984	USSR	Wembley	L	0–2			
	England	4	Full	10/06/1984	Brazil	Rio De Janeiro	W	2–0			
	England	5	Full	13/06/1984	Uruguay	Montevideo	L	0–2			
	England	6	Full	17/06/1984	Chile	Santiago	D	0–0			
	England	7	Full	22/05/1985	Finland	Helsinki	D	1–1			
	England	8	Full	25/05/1985	Scotland	Glasgow	L	0–1			
	England	9	Full	09/06/1985	Mexico	Mexico City	L	0–1			
	England	10	Full	16/06/1985	USA	Los Angeles	W	5–0			
	England	11	Full	11/09/1985	Romania	Wembley	D	1–1			
	England	12	Full	16/10/1985	Turkey	Wembley	W	5–0			
	England	13	Full	13/11/1985	Northern Ireland	Wembley	D	0–0			
	England	14	Full	29/01/1986	Egypt	Cairo	W	4–0			
	England	15	Full	17/05/1986	Mexico	Los Angeles	W	3–0			
	England	16	Full	03/06/1986	Portugal	Monterrey	L	0–1			
	England	17	Full	06/06/1986	Morocco	Monterrey	D	0–0			

Terry Fenwick

Name	Country	Caps	Level	Date	Against	Venue	W/D/L	Score	Goals	Sub	Capt
	England	18	Full	11/06/1986	Poland	Monterrey	W	3–0			
	England	19	Full	22/06/1986	Argentina	Mexico City	L	1–2			
Les FERDINAND	England	1	Full	17/02/1993	San Marino	Wembley	W	6–0	1		
	England	2	Full	28/04/1993	Holland	Wembley	D	2–2			
	England	3	Full	02/06/1993	Norway	Oslo	L	0–2			
	England	4	Full	09/06/1993	USA	Boston	L	0–2			
	England	5	Full	08/09/1993	Poland	Wembley	W	3–0	1		
	England	6	Full	17/11/1993	San Marino	Bologna	W	7–1	1		
	England	7	Full	07/09/1994	USA	Wembley	W	2–0		Sub	
Wayne FEREDAY	England	1	U21	13/11/1984	Turkey	Bursa	D	0–0			
	England	2	U21	25/03/1985	Eire	Portsmouth	W	3–2		Sub	
	England	3	U21	21/05/1985	Finland	Mikkeli	L	1–3			
	England	4	U21	15/10/1985	Turkey	Bristol	W	3–0		Sub	
	England	5	U21	23/04/1986	Italy	Swindon	D	1–1			
Joseph FIDLER	London	1		25/10/1909	Birmingham	Fulham	L	1–3			
	Southern League	1		02/10/1911	Scottish League	Glasgow	L	2–3			
Brian FITZGERALD	Eire	1	U18	20/09/2000	Switzerland	Dublin					
Gerry FRANCIS	England	1	U23	13/11/1973	Denmark	Portsmouth	D	1–1			
	England	2	U23	13/03/1974	Scotland	Newcastle	W	2–0			
	England	3	U23	11/05/1974	Turkey	Ankara	D	0–0			
	England	4	U23	15/05/1974	Yugoslavia	Zrenjanin	L	0–1		Sub	
	England	5	U23	19/05/1974	France	Valence	D	2–2			
	England	1	Full	30/10/1974	Czechoslavakia	Wembley	W	3–0			
	England	2	Full	20/11/1974	Portugal	Wembley	D	0–0			
	England	3	Full	21/05/1975	Wales	Wembley	D	2–2			
	England	4	Full	24/05/1975	Scotland	Wembley	W	5–1	2		
	England	5	Full	03/09/1975	Switzerland	Basle	W	2–1			Capt
	England	6	Full	30/10/1975	Czechoslavakia	Bratislava	L	1–2			Capt
	England	7	Full	19/11/1975	Portugal	Lisbon	D	1–1			Capt
	England	6	U23	10/03/1976	Hungary	Budapest	L	0–3			Capt
	England	8	Full	08/05/1976	Wales	Cardiff	W	1–0			Capt
	England	9	Full	11/05/1976	Northern Ireland	Wembley	W	4–0	1		Capt
	England	10	Full	15/05/1976	Scotland	Glasgow	L	1–2			Capt
	England	11	Full	23/05/1976	Brazil	Los Angeles	L	0–1			Capt
	England	1	Other	31/05/1976	Team America	Philadelphia	W	3–1	1		Capt
	England	12	Full	13/06/1976	Finland	Helsinki	W	4–1			Capt
Kevin GALLEN	England	1	U18	30/03/1993	Denmark	Stoke	W	4–2	1	Sub	
	England	2	U18	18/07/1993	France	Stoke	W	2–0	1	Sub	
	England	3	U18	20/07/1993	Holland	Walsall	W	4–1	1		
	England	4	U18	22/07/1993	Spain	Walsall	W	5–1			
	England	5	U18	25/07/1993	Turkey	Nottingham	W	1–0			
	England	6	U18	24/08/1993	Eire	Port Vale	D	2–2			
	England	7	U18	07/09/1993	Romania	Port Vale	D	1–1			
	England	8	U18	13/10/1993	Romania	Bucharest	D	1–1	1		
	England	9	U18	27/10/1993	France	(Away)	L	0–2			
	England	10	U18	16/11/1993	France	Yeovil	D	3–3	2		
	England	1	U21	27/03/1995	Eire	Dublin	W	2–0			
	England	2	U21	25/04/1995	Latvia	Riga	W	1–0			
	England	3	U21	07/06/1995	Latvia	Burnley	W	4–0			
	England	4	U21	23/04/1996	Croatia	Sunderland	L	0–1			
Stephen GALLEN	Eire	1	U21	09/03/1993	Germany	Dublin	L	0–1			
	Eire	2	U21	12/10/1993	Spain	Drogheda	L	0–2		Sub	
	Eire	3	U21	/06/1993	Albania	(Away)	D	1–1			
Ian GILLARD	England	1	U23	13/03/1974	Scotland	Newcastle	W	2–0			
	England	2	U23	11/05/1974	Turkey	Ankara	D	0–0			

Les Ferdinand

Name	Country	Caps	Level	Date	Against	Venue	W/D/L	Score	Goals	Sub	Capt
	England	3	U23	15/05/1974	Yugoslavia	Zrenjanin	L	0–1			
	England	4	U23	19/05/1974	France	Valence	D	2–2	1		
	England	5	U23	18/12/1974	Scotland	Aberdeen	W	3–0			
	England	1	Full	12/03/1975	West Germany	Wembley	W	2–0			
	England	2	Full	21/05/1975	Wales	Wembley	D	2–2			
	England	3	Full	30/10/1975	Czechoslavakia	Bratislava	L	1–2			
Don GIVENS	Eire	1	Full	15/11/1972	France	Dublin	W	2–1	1		
	Eire	2	Full	13/05/1973	USSR	Moscow	L	0–1			
	Eire	3	Full	16/05/1973	Poland	Warsaw	L	0–2			
	Eire	4	Full	19/05/1973	France	Paris	D	1–1			
	Eire	5	Full	06/06/1973	Norway	Oslo	D	1–1			
	All Ireland	1		03/07/1973	Brazil	Dublin	L	3–4			
	Eire	6	Full	21/10/1973	Poland	Dublin	W	1–0			
	Eire	7	Full	05/05/1974	Brazil	Rio De Janeiro	L	1–2			
	Eire	8	Full	08/05/1974	Uruguay	Montevideo	L	0–2			
	Eire	9	Full	12/05/1974	Chile	Santiago	W	2–1			
	Eire	10	Full	30/10/1974	USSR	Dublin	W	3–0	3		
	Eire	11	Full	20/11/1974	Turkey	Izmir	D	1–1	1		
	Eire	12	Full	11/03/1975	West Germany	Dublin	W	1–0			
	Eire	13	Full	11/05/1975	Switzerland	Dublin	W	2–1			
	Eire	14	Full	18/05/1975	USSR	Moscow	L	1–2			
	Eire	15	Full	21/05/1975	Switzerland	Basle	L	0–1			
	Eire	16	Full	29/10/1975	Turkey	Dublin	W	4–0	4		
	Eire	17	Full	24/03/1976	Norway	Dublin	W	3–0			
	Eire	18	Full	26/05/1976	Poland	Warsaw	W	2–0	2		
	Eire	19	Full	08/09/1976	England	Wembley	D	1–1			
	Eire	20	Full	13/10/1976	Turkey	Ankara	D	3–3	1		
	Eire	21	Full	17/11/1976	France	Paris	L	0–2			
	Eire	22	Full	09/02/1977	Spain	Dublin	L	0–1			
	Eire	23	Full	30/03/1977	France	Dublin	W	1–0			
	Eire	24	Full	01/06/1977	Bulgaria	Sofia	L	1–2	1		
	Eire	25	Full	12/10/1977	Bulgaria	Dublin	D	0–0			
	Eire	26	Full	21/05/1978	Norway	Oslo	D	0–0			
	Eire	27	Full	24/05/1978	Denmark	Copenhagen	D	3–3			
Gregory GOODRIDGE	Barbados	1	Full	19/05/1996	Dominica	Bridgetown	W	1–0	1		
Kaspars GORKSS	Latvia	1	Full	20/08/2008	Romania	Urziceni	L	0–1			
	Latvia	2	Full	06/09/2008	Moldova	Tiraspol	W	2–1			
	Latvia	3	Full	10/09/2008	Greece	Riga	L	0–2			
	Latvia	4	Full	11/10/2008	Switzerland	St Gallen	L	1–2			
	Latvia	5	Full	15/10/2008	Israel	Riga	D	1–1			
	Latvia	6	Full	11/02/2009	Armenia	Kipra	D	0–0			
	Latvia	7	Full	28/03/2009	Luxembourg	Luxembourg	W	4–0			
	Latvia	8	Full	01/04/2009	Luxembourg	Riga	W	2–0			
Mark GRAHAM	Northern Ireland	1	B	21/02/1995	Scotland	Hibernian	L	0–3		Sub	
	Northern Ireland	2	B	11/02/1998	Eire	Tolka Park	W	1–0		Sub	
	Northern Ireland	3	B	10/10/1995	Norway	Coleraine	W	3–0		Sub	
	Northern Ireland	4	B	28/03/1997	Portugal	Lurgan	W	2–0		Sub	
Richard GRAHAM	Northern Ireland	1	U16	/08/96	Zambia	Coleraine					
	Northern Ireland	2	U16	/08/96	Turkey	Coleraine					
	Northern Ireland	3	U16	/08/96	Wales	Coleraine					
	Northern Ireland	1	U18	/10/96	Finland	York					
	Northern Ireland	2	U18	/10/96	England	York	L	0–4			
	Northern Ireland	3	U18	/11/97	Croatia	Belfast	L	1–2			
	Northern Ireland	4	U18	/11/97	Andorra	Belfast	W	5–0	1		
	Northern Ireland	1	U21	09/10/1998	Finland	Belfast	W	2–0		Sub	

Paul Goddard

Name	Country	Caps	Level	Date	Against	Venue	W/D/L	Score	Goals	Sub	Capt
	Northern Ireland	2	U21		Moldova						
	Northern Ireland	3	U21		Republic of Ireland					Sub	
	Northern Ireland	4	U21	17/08/1999	France	Belfast	W	3–1		Sub	
	Northern Ireland	5	U21	03/09/1999	Turkey	Belfast	L	1–2		Sub	
	Northern Ireland	6	U21	07/09/1999	Germany	Augsburg	L	0–1		Sub	
	Northern Ireland	7	U21	08/10/1999	Finland	(away)	L	1–2		Sub	
	Northern Ireland	8	U21	28/03/2000	Malta	(away)	W	2–1			
	Northern Ireland	9	U21	29/05/2000	Scotland	(neutral)	D	1–1			
	Northern Ireland	10	U21	02/06/2000	Wales	(neutral)	D	2–2			
	Northern Ireland	11	U21	01/09/2001	Malta	(home)	D	1–1			
	Northern Ireland	12	U21	06/10/2000	Denmark	Belfast	L	0–3			
	Northern Ireland	13	U21	23/03/2001	Czech Republic	Ballymena	L	0–2		Sub	
	Northern Ireland	14	U21	01/06/2001	Bulgaria	Belfast	D	1–1		Sub	
	Northern Ireland	15	U21	05/06/2001	Czech Republic	Prague	L	0–4		Sub	
Walter GREER	Ireland	1	Full	13/02/1909	England	Bradford	L	0–4			
	Ireland	2	Full	15/03/1909	Scotland	Glasgow	L	0–5			
	Ireland	3	Full	20/03/1909	Wales	Belfast	L	2–3			
John GREGORY	England	1	Full	12/06/1983	Australia	Sydney	D	0–0			
	England	2	Full	15/06/1983	Australia	Brisbane	W	1–0			
	England	3	Full	19/06/1983	Australia	Melbourne	D	1–1			
	England	4	Full	21/09/1983	Denmark	Wembley	L	0–1			
	England	5	Full	12/10/1983	Hungary	Budapest	W	3–0			
	England	6	Full	02/05/1984	Wales	Wrexham	L	0–1			
Ernest GRIMSDELL	FA XI	1		18/11/1920	Canbridge University	Cambridge	L	0–1			
Billy HAMILTON	Northern Ireland	1	Full	13/05/1978	Scotland	Glasgow	D	1–1		Sub	
Ambrose HARTWELL	Southern League	1		11/04/1910	Football League	Chelsea	D	2–2			
	Southern League	2		14/11/1910	Football League	Tottenham	W	3–2			
Cyril HATTON	FA	1		03/11/1948	Army	Ipswich	L	0–2			
	FA	2		08/11/1950	Army	Highbury	W	3–2	1		
Tony HAZELL	England	1	Youth	17/04/1964	Spain	Heilbronn	D	0–0			
	England	2	Youth	30/03/1966	Spain	Swindon	W	3–0			
	England	3	Youth	21/05/1966	Czechoslavakia	Rijeka	L	2–3			
	England	4	Youth	23/05/1966	France	Rijeka	L	1–2			
	England	5	Youth	25/05/1966	Italy	Rijeka	D	1–1			
William HEATHCOTE	London District	1		11/03/1944	Eastern Command		W	5–0			
	London District	2		10/04/1944	Eastern Command	Ipswich	W	4–1			
	Army	1		09/08/1944	Moray Services	Elgin	W	8–3			
	Army	2		10/08/1944	North Scotland Services	Fort George	W	6–3			
	Army	3		12/08/1944	Combined Services	Inverness	W	7–1			
	London District	3		13/01/1945	Eastern Command	Brentford	W	7–6	4		
	London District	4		17/03/1945	Western Command	Stoke	L	0–5			
	Combined Services	1		09/05/1945	Police & Civil Defence	Wembley	W	3–1	1		
Chris HERRON	Northern Ireland	1	U21	28/03/2003	Armenia	Abovyan	L	0–2			
	Northern Ireland	2	U21	01/04/2003	Greece	Glentoran	L	2–6			
D HIGGINS	The South	1		24/01/1914	The North	Oxford	L	2–3			
Leonard HILL	Football League	1		10/11/1921	The Army	Leyton	W	4–1			
John HOLLINS	England	1	B	30/05/1978	Malaysia	Kuala Lumpur	D	1–1			
	England	2	B	07/06/1978	New Zealand	Christchurch	W	4–0	1		
	England	3	B	11/06/1978	New Zealand	Wellington	W	3–1			
	England	4	B	14/06/1978	New Zealand	Auckland	W	4–0			
	England	5	B	18/06/1978	Singapore	Singapore	W	8–0			
Peter HUCKER	England	1	U21	18/04/1984	Italy	Manchester	W	3–1			
	England	2	U21	17/05/1984	Spain	Seville	W	1–0			
Andrew IMPEY	England	1	U21	17/11/1992	Turkey	Leyton	L	0–1			
Leighton JAMES	Wales	1	Full	14/12/1977	West Germany	Dortmund	D	1–1			

John Gregory

Name	Country	Caps	Level	Date	Against	Venue	W/D/L	Score	Goals	Sub	Capt
Robbie JAMES	Wales	1	Full	26/02/1985	Norway	Wrexham	D	1–1			
	Wales	2	Full	27/03/1985	Scotland	Glasgow	W	1–0			
	Wales	3	Full	30/04/1985	Spain	Wrexham	W	3–0			
	Wales	4	Full	05/06/1985	Norway	Bergen	L	2–4			
	Wales	5	Full	10/09/1985	Scotland	Cardiff	D	1–1			
	Wales	6	Full	25/02/1986	Saudi Arabia	Dhahran	W	2–1			
	Wales	7	Full	26/03/1986	Eire	Dublin	W	1–0			
	Wales	8	Full	21/04/1986	Uruguay	Cardiff	D	0–0			
	Wales	9	Full	10/05/1986	Canada	Toronto	L	0–2			
	Wales	10	Full	20/06/1986	Canada	Vancouver	W	3–0			
	Wales	11	Full	10/09/1986	Finland	Helsinki	D	1–1			
	Wales	12	Full	18/02/1987	USSR	Swansea	D	0–0			
	Wales	13	Full	01/04/1987	Finland	Wrexham	W	4–0			
	Wales	14	Full	29/04/1987	Czechoslavakia	Wrexham	D	1–1			
Leon JEANNE	Wales	1	U16	24/03/1997	Northern Ireland	Flint					
	Wales	1	U18								
	Wales	2	U18	/09/1998	Northern Ireland						
	Wales	3	U18	/09/1998	Moldova				1		
	Wales	1	U21	18/11/1998	Portugal	(A)	L	0–3		Sub	
	Wales	2	U21	30/03/1999	Switzerland	(A)	L	0–1			
	Wales	3	U21	05/06/1999	Italy	Ferrara	L	2–6	1		
	Wales	4	U21		Belarus						
	Wales	5	U21	08/10/1999	Switzerland	Newtown	L	0–0			
	Wales	6	U21	31/05/2000	Scotland	(neutral)	L	0–1			
	Wales	7	U21	02/06/2000	Northern Ireland	(neutral)	D	2–2	1		
	Wales	8	U21	01/09/2000	Belarus	(away)	L	1–4			
Arthur JEFFERSON	Western Command	1		20/10/1944	Northern Command	Newcastle	L	1–6			
	Western Command	2		11/11/1944	A.A. Command	Bolton	D	3–3			
	Western Command	3		01/01/1945	Scottish Command	Ayr	W	2–0			
	Western Command	4		24/02/1945	Northern Command	Molineux	W	2–0			
	Western Command	5		17/03/1945	London District	Stoke	W	5–0			
Ivean JONES	Wales	1	Youth	23/01/1980	Northern Ireland	Wrexham	D	0–0			
	Wales	2	Youth	13/02/1980	Northern Ireland	Bangor	W	0–2			
Paul JONES	Wales	1	Full	01/03/2006	Paraguay	Cardiff	D	0–0			
	Wales	2	Full	15/08/2006	Bulgaria	Swansea	D	0–0			
	Wales	3	Full	02/09/2006	Czech Republic	Teplice	L	1–2			
	Wales	4	Full	08/09/2006	Brazil	Tottenham	L	0–2			
	Wales	5	Full	07/10/2006	Slovakia	Cardiff	L	1–5			
Ray JONES	England	1	U19	05/09/2006	Holland	Walsall	D	0–0		Sub	
William KEECH	Southern League	1		25/02/1900	Amateurs of the South	Queens Club	W	7–2			
David KERSLAKE	England	1	Youth	07/04/1982	Portugal	Cannes	W	3–0	1		
	England	2	Youth	09/04/1982	Holland	Cannes	W	1–0			
	England	3	Youth	11/04/1982	Czechoslavakia	Cannes	L	0–1			
	England	4	Youth	12/04/1982	France	Cannes	L	0–1			
	England	5	Youth	13/07/1982	Norway	Levanger	L	1–4			
	England	6	Youth	15/07/1982	Denmark	Stjordal	W	5–2			
	England	7	Youth	17/07/1982	Poland	Steinkjer	W	3–2	1		
	England	8	Youth	02/09/1982	R.I. Istra	Istra	W	3–1			
	England	9	Youth	04/09/1982	USSR	Umag	W	1–0			
	England	10	Youth	06/09/1982	Switzerland	Porec	W	2–0	1		
	England	11	Youth	09/09/1982	Yugoslavia	Pala	W	1–0			
	England	12	Youth	21/02/1983	Israel U21	Tel Aviv	W	4–0			
	England	13	Youth	23/02/1983	Israel Olympic	Tel Aviv	W	4–2	2		
	England	14	Youth	13/04/1983	Belgium	Birmingham	D	1–1			
	England	15	Youth	13/05/1983	Spain	Stoke	W	1–0			

Name	Country	Caps	Level	Date	Against	Venue	W/D/L	Score	Goals	Sub	Capt
	England	16	Youth	15/05/1983	Scotland	Birmingham	W	3–0			
	England	17	Youth	17/05/1983	USSR	Villa Park	L	0–2			
	England	18	Youth	20/05/1983	Czechoslavakia	Highbury	D	1–1			
	England	19	Youth	22/05/1983	Italy	Watford	D	1–1			
	England	1	U17	12/07/1983	Poland	Slagelse	W	1–0			
	England	2	U17	14/07/1983	Norway	Slagelse	W	1–0	1		
	England	3	U17	16/07/1983	Denmark	Slagelse	L	0–1			
	England	20	Youth	01/09/1983	Switzerland	Porec	W	4–2			
	England	21	Youth	03/09/1983	West Germany	Umag	W	3–2			
	England	22	Youth	05/09/1983	Hungary	Pazin	W	2–0	1		
	England	23	Youth	08/09/1983	Yugoslavia	Pula	D	2–2			
	England	24	Youth	12/10/1983	Iceland	Reykjavik	W	3–0			
	England	25	Youth	01/11/1983	Iceland	Selhurst Park	W	3–0			
	England	26	Youth	01/06/1985	Cameroon	Toulon	W	1–0			
	England	27	Youth	03/06/1985	USSR	Toulon	L	0–2			
	England	28	Youth	05/06/1985	Mexico	Toulon	W	2–0	1		
	England	29	Youth	07/06/1985	France	Toulon	L	1–3			
	England	1	U21	15/10/1985	Turkey	Bristol	W	3–0			
KYLE	A.A. Command	1		08/01/1944	Southern Command	Bristol	D	1–1			
Richard LANGLEY	Jamaica	1	Full	18/05/2002	Nigeria	Loftus Road	L	0–1		Sub	
	Jamaica	2	Full	11/11/2002	Guadaloupe	Grenada	W	2–0			
	Jamaica	3	Full	13/11/2002	Grenada	Grenada	W	4–1			
	Jamaica	4	Full	20/11/2002	Nigeria	Lagos	D	0–0			
	Jamaica	5	Full	06/07/2003	Cuba	Kingston	L	1–2	1		
	Jamaica	6	Full	09/07/2003	Paraguay	Kingston	W	2–0	1		
	Jamaica	7	Full	13/07/2003	Colombia	Miami	L	0–1			
	Jamaica	8	Full	20/07/2003	Mexico	Mexico City	L	0–5			
	England		U16								
Brian LAW	Wales	1	Full	25/04/1990	Sweden	Stockholm	L	2–4			
	Wales	1	U21	19/05/1990	Poland	(Home)	W	2–0			
	Wales	2	U21	15/12/1990	England	Tranmere	D	0–0			
Mick LEACH	England	1	Youth	11/05/1963	Northern Ireland	Oldham	D	1–1			
	England	2	Youth	18/05/1963	Scotland	Dumfries	W	3–1	1		
	England	3	Youth	17/04/1964	Spain	Heilbronn	D	0–0			
Evelyn LINTOTT	England	1	Amateur	07/12/1907	Ireland	Tottenham	W	6–1			
	England	2	Amateur	21/12/1907	Holland	Darlington	W	12–2			
	England	1	Full	15/02/1908	Ireland	Cliftonville	W	3–1			
	England	2	Full	16/03/1908	Wales	Wrexham	W	7–1			
	England	3	Amateur	23/03/1908	France	Park Royal	W	12–0			
	England	3	Full	04/04/1908	Scotland	Glasgow	D	1–1			
	England	4	Amateur	18/04/1908	Belgium	Brussels	W	8–2			
	England	5	Amateur	20/04/1908	Germany	Berlin	W	5–1			
Harry LOWE	Met. Police	1		20/05/1942	Royal Navy	Ipswich	W	7–5	2		
	Civil Defence	1		14/11/1942	Army	Millwall	L	2–8			
Alan McCARTHY	England	1	Youth	20/09/1988	Eire	Dublin	W	2–0			
	Wales	1	U21	07/09/1993	RCS	Ebbw Vale	L	0–4			
	Wales	2	U21	13/10/1993	Cyprus	Cwmbran	W	6–2			
	Wales	3	U21	16/11/1993	Romania	Ebbw Vale	L	1–2			
	Wales	1	B	02/02/1994	Scotland	Wrexham	W	2–1			
Doug McCLURE	England	1	Youth	07/04/1982	Portugal	Cannes	W	3–0			
	England	2	Youth	09/04/1982	Holland	Cannes	W	1–0			
	England	3	Youth	11/04/1982	Czechoslavakia	Cannes	L	0–1			
	England	4	Youth	12/04/1982	France	Cannes	L	0–1			
	England	5	Youth	13/07/1982	Norway	Levanger	L	1–4			
	England	6	Youth	15/07/1982	Denmark	Stjordal	W	5–2			

Evelyn Lintott

Name	Country	Caps	Level	Date	Against	Venue	W/D/L	Score	Goals	Sub	Capt
	England	7	Youth	17/07/1982	Poland	Steinkjer	W	3–2			
	England	8	Youth	02/09/1982	R.I. Istra	Istra	W	3–1			
	England	9	Youth	04/09/1982	USSR	Umag	W	1–0			
	England	10	Youth	06/09/1982	Switzerland	Porec	W	2–0			
	England	11	Youth	09/09/1982	Yugoslavia	Pala	W	1–0			
David McCREEY	Northern Ireland	1	Full	17/10/1979	England	Belfast	L	1–5			
	Northern Ireland	2	Full	21/11/1979	Eire	Belfast	W	1–0			
	Northern Ireland	3	Full	16/05/1980	Scotland	Belfast	W	1–0		Sub	
	Northern Ireland	4	Full	20/05/1980	England	Wembley	D	1–1		Sub	
	Northern Ireland	5	Full	23/05/1980	Wales	Cardiff	W	1–0		Sub	
	Northern Ireland	6	Full	11/06/1980	Australia	Sydney	W	2–1		Sub	
	Northern Ireland	7	Full	15/06/1980	Australia	Melbourne	D	1–1			
	Northern Ireland	8	Full	15/10/1980	Sweden	Belfast	W	3–0		Sub	
	Northern Ireland	9	Full	19/11/1980	Portugal	Lisbon	L	0–1		Sub	
Alan McDONALD	Northern Ireland	1	Schools	1977	England	Carlisle	D	0–0			
	Northern Ireland	2	Schools	1977	Scotland	(Away)					
	Northern Ireland	3	Schools	1977	Wales	Ballymena	W	4–0			
	Northern Ireland	4	Schools	1978	Eire	Dublin	W	3–1	1		
	Northern Ireland	5	Schools	1978	West Germany	Stoke	W	4–3			
	Northern Ireland	6	Schools	1978	Eire	Merseyside	W	4–1	1		
	Northern Ireland	7	Schools	1978	Scotland	Crewe	W	1–0			
	Northern Ireland	8	Schools	1978	Wales	Manchester	W	2–1			
	Northern Ireland	1	Full	16/10/1985	Romania	Bucharest	W	1–0			
	Northern Ireland	2	Full	13/11/1985	England	Wembley	D	0–0			
	Northern Ireland	3	Full	26/02/1986	France	Paris	D	0–0			
	Northern Ireland	4	Full	26/03/1986	Denmark	Belfast	D	1–1	1		
	Northern Ireland	5	Full	23/04/1986	Morocco	Belfast	W	2–1			
	Northern Ireland	6	Full	03/06/1986	Algeria	Guadalajara	D	1–1			
	Northern Ireland	7	Full	07/06/1986	Spain	Guadalajara	L	1–2			
	Northern Ireland	8	Full	12/06/1986	Brazil	Guadalajara	L	0–3			
	Northern Ireland	9	Full	15/10/1986	England	Wembley	L	0–3			
	Northern Ireland	10	Full	12/11/1986	Turkey	Izmir	D	0–0			
	Northern Ireland	11	Full	18/02/1987	Israel	Tel Aviv	D	1–1			
	Northern Ireland	12	Full	01/04/1987	England	Belfast	L	0–2			
	Northern Ireland	13	Full	23/04/1987	Yugoslavia	Belfast	L	1–2			
	Northern Ireland	14	Full	14/10/1987	Yugoslavia	Sarajevo	L	0–3			
	Northern Ireland	15	Full	11/11/1987	Turkey	Belfast	W	1–0			
	Northern Ireland	16	Full	23/03/1988	Poland	Belfast	D	1–1			
	Northern Ireland	17	Full	27/04/1988	France	Belfast	D	0–0			
	Northern Ireland	18	Full	21/05/1988	Malta	Belfast	W	3–0			
	Northern Ireland	19	Full	14/09/1988	Eire	Belfast	D	0–0			
	Northern Ireland	20	Full	19/10/1988	Hungary	Budapest	L	0–1			
	Northern Ireland	21	Full	21/12/1988	Spain	Seville	L	0–4			
	Northern Ireland	22	Full	26/05/1989	Chile	Belfast	L	0–1			Capt
	Northern Ireland	23	Full	06/09/1989	Hungary	Belfast	L	1–2			
	Northern Ireland	24	Full	11/10/1989	Eire	Dublin	L	0–3			
	Northern Ireland	25	Full	18/05/1990	Uruguay	Belfast	W	1–0			Capt
	Northern Ireland	26	Full	12/09/1990	Yugoslavia	Belfast	L	0–2			Capt
	Northern Ireland	27	Full	17/10/1990	Denmark	Belfast	D	1–1			Capt
	Northern Ireland	28	Full	14/11/1990	Austria	Vienna	D	0–0			Capt
	Northern Ireland	29	Full	01/05/1991	Faroe Islands	Belfast	D	1–1			Capt
	Northern Ireland	30	Full	11/09/1991	Faroe Islands	Landskrona	W	5–0	1		Capt
	Northern Ireland	31	Full	19/02/1992	Scotland	Glasgow	L	0–1			Capt
	Northern Ireland	32	Full	28/04/1992	Lithuania	Belfast	D	2–2			Capt
	Northern Ireland	33	Full	02/06/1992	Germany	Bremen	D	1–1			Capt

Alan McDonald

Name	Country	Caps	Level	Date	Against	Venue	W/D/L	Score	Goals	Sub	Capt
	Northern Ireland	34	Full	09/09/1992	Albania	Belfast	W	3–0			Capt
	Northern Ireland	35	Full	14/10/1992	Spain	Belfast	D	0–0			Capt
	Northern Ireland	36	Full	18/11/1992	Denmark	Belfast	L	0–1			Capt
	Northern Ireland	37	Full	17/02/1993	Albania	Tirane	W	2–1	1		Capt
	Northern Ireland	38	Full	31/03/1993	Eire	Dublin	L	0–3			Capt
	Northern Ireland	39	Full	28/04/1993	Spain	Seville	L	1–3			Capt
	Northern Ireland	40	Full	25/05/1993	Lithuania	Vilnius	W	1–0			Capt
	Northern Ireland	41	Full	02/06/1993	Latvia	Riga	W	2–1			Capt
	Northern Ireland	42	Full	13/10/1993	Denmark	Copenhagen	L	0–1			Capt
	Northern Ireland	43	Full	17/11/1993	Eire	Belfast	D	1–1			Capt
	Northern Ireland	44	Full	07/09/1994	Portugal	Belfast	L	1–2			Capt
	Northern Ireland	45	Full	12/10/1994	Austria	Vienna	W	2–1			Capt
	Northern Ireland	46	Full	29/03/1995	Eire	Dublin	D	1–1			Capt
	Northern Ireland	47	Full	26/04/1995	Latvia	Riga	W	1–0			Capt
	Northern Ireland	48	Full	22/05/1995	Canada	Edmonton	L	0–2			Capt
	Northern Ireland	49	Full	25/05/1995	Chile	Edmonton	L	1–2			Capt
	Northern Ireland	50	Full	07/06/1995	Latvia	Belfast	L	1–2			Capt
	Northern Ireland	51	Full	15/11/1995	Austria	Belfast	W	5–3		Sub	
	Northern Ireland	52	Full	27/03/1996	Norway	Belfast	L	0–2			Capt
Terry McFLYNN	Northern Ireland	1	U16	23/02/1998	Belgium						
	Northern Ireland	2	U16	27/02/1998	Eire						
	Northern Ireland	1	U21	28/03/2000	Malta	(away)	W	2–1		Sub	
	Northern Ireland	2	U21	02/06/2000	Wales	(neutral)	D	2–2		Sub	
	Northern Ireland	3	U21	01/09/2000	Malta	(home)	D	1–1		Sub	
	Northern Ireland	4	U21	23/03/2001	Czech Republic	Ballymena	L	0–2		Sub	
	Northern Ireland	5	U21	27/03/2001	Bulgaria	Vrasta	L	0–2		Sub	
	Northern Ireland	6	U21	01/06/2001	Bulgaria	Belfast	D	1–1		Sub	
	Northern Ireland	7	U21	05/06/2001	Czech Republic	Prague	L	0–4			
	Northern Ireland	1	U18	/09/1999	Sweden				2		
	Northern Ireland	2	U18	/09/1999	Luxembourg				2		
	Northern Ireland	3	U18	/09/1999	Estonia				1		
Paul McGEE	Eire	1	Full	05/04/1978	Turkey	Dublin	W	4–2	1		
	Eire	2	Full	21/05/1978	Norway	Oldham	D	0–0		Sub	
	Eire	3	Full	24/05/1978	Denmark	Copenhagen	D	3–3		Sub	
	Eire	4	Full	20/09/1978	Northern Ireland	Dublin	D	0–0			
	Eire	5	Full	25/10/1978	England	Dublin	D	1–1			
	Eire	6	Full	02/05/1979	Denmark	Dublin	W	2–0		Sub	
	Eire	7	Full	19/05/1979	Bulgaria	Sofia	L	0–1		Sub	
	Eire	8	Full	29/05/1979	Argentina	Dublin	D	0–0		Sub	
	Eire	9	Full	17/10/1979	Bulgaria	Dublin	W	3–0			
Danny MADDIX	Jamaica	1	Full	20/04/1998	Macedonia	Tehran	L	1–2			
	Jamaica	2	Full	22/04/1998	Iran	Tehran	L	0–1			
Michael MAHONEY-JOHNSON	England	1	U17	13/03/1994	Combined Services	(Away)	W	5–1	1		
	England	2	U17	06/04/1994	ESFA	(Away)	W	5–1			
Joe MALLETT	RAF	1		08/03/1941	Army	Aldershot	D	2–2			
	RAF	2		03/04/1941	Police Pros	New Cross	D	0–0			
Terry MANCINI	Eire	1	Full	21/10/1973	Poland	Dublin	W	1–0			
	Eire	2	Full	05/05/1974	Brazil	Rio De Janeiro	L	1–2	1		
	Eire	3	Full	09/05/1974	Uruguay	Montevideo	L	0–2			
	Eire	4	Full	12/05/1974	Chile	Santiago	W	2–1			
Dave MANGNALL	London Pros	1		10/02/1940	London Amateurs	Selhurst	W	4–2			
	FA XI	1		22/05/1940	Herts FA	Watford	W	3–1			
	War Reserve Police	3		29/10/1941	Met. Police	Imber Court	W	2–1	1		
	Met. Police	1		18/02/1942	Combined Services	Ipswich	W	3–2	2		
	Met. Police	2		02/01/1943	Army	Aldershot	D	5–5			

Name	Country	Caps	Level	Date	Against	Venue	W/D/L	Score	Goals	Sub	Capt
	Met. Police	3		20/01/1943	Stan Cullis XI	Chichester	L	1–5			
	Police & Civil Defence	1		06/03/1943	RAF	Preston	L	2–4			
	National Police	1		05/05/1943	RAF	Wembley	L	3–4			
	Civil Defence	1		05/02/1944	Army	Derby	L	3–4			
	Police & Civil Defence	2		10/05/1944	Combined Services	Wembley	L	2–5			
	National Civil Defence	1		13/05/1944	Royal Navy	Selhurst	D	4–4	1		
Richard MARCH	FA XI	1		01/01/1940	Chelmsford	Chelmsford	W	5–0			
Rodney MARSH	England	1	U23	07/02/1968	Scotland	Glasgow	W	2–1	1		
	England	2	U23	01/05/1968	Hungary	Everton	W	4–0	1		
	England	1	Full	10/11/1971	Switzerland	Wembley	D	1–1		Sub	
William MASON	Police Pros	1		03/04/1941	FA XI	New Cross	D	0–0			
Don MASSON	Scotland	1	Full	06/05/1976	Wales	Glasgow	W	3–1			
	Scotland	2	Full	08/05/1976	Northern Ireland	Glasgow	W	3–0	1		
	Scotland	3	Full	15/05/1976	England	Glasgow	W	2–1	1		
	Scotland	4	Full	08/09/1976	Finland	Glasgow	W	6–0	1		
	Scotland	5	Full	13/10/1976	Czechoslavakia	Prague	L	0–2			
	Scotland	6	Full	28/05/1977	Wales	Wrexham	D	0–0			
	Scotland	7	Full	01/06/1977	Northern Ireland	Glasgow	W	3–0			
	Scotland	8	Full	04/06/1977	England	Wembley	W	2–1			
	Scotland	9	Full	15/06/1977	Chile	Santiago	W	4–2			
	Scotland	10	Full	19/06/1977	Argentina	Buenos Aires	D	1–1	1		
	Scotland	11	Full	23/06/1977	Brazil	Sao Paulo	L	0–2			
	Scotland	12	Full	07/09/1977	East Germany	Berlin	L	0–1			
	Scotland	13	Full	21/09/1977	Czechoslavakia	Glasgow	W	3–1			
	Scotland	14	Full	12/10/1977	Wales	Liverpool	W	2–0	1		Capt
Michael MEAKER	Wales	1	U21	07/09/1993	RCS	Ebbw Vale	L	0–4		Sub	
	Wales	2	U21	16/11/1993	Romania	Ebbw Vale	L	1–2		Sub	
	Wales	1	B	02/02/1994	Scotland	Wrexham	W	2–1			
Don MILLS	FA	1		25/10/1950	RAF	Fulham	W	6–1			
	FA	2		01/11/1950	Diables Rouges						
	Southern League	1		11/10/1913	Irish League	Dublin	W	4–1			
	Southern League	2		13/10/1913	Scottish League	Glasgow	L	0–5			
	Southern League	3		09/02/1914	Football League	Millwall	L	1–3			
	Southern League	4		13/10/1914	Scottish League	Millwall	D	1–1			
	Southern League	5		26/10/1914	Football League	Highbury	L	1–2			
	Southern League	6		31/10/1914	Irish League	Swansea	D	1–1			
	FA XI	1		18/11/1920	Cambridge University	Cambridge	L	0–1			
Ian MORGAN	FA XI	1		21/05/1969	Tahiti	Papette	W	4–1			
	FA XI	2		02/06/1969	New Zealand	Wellington	W	7–1			
	FA XI	3		07/06/1969	New Zealand	Hamilton	W	5–0			
	FA XI	4		11/06/1969	New Zealand	Auckland	W	5–0			
	FA XI	5		14/06/1969	Singapore	Singapore	W	9–0			
	FA XI	6		16/06/1969	Hong Kong	Hong Kong	W	6–0	2		
Roger MORGAN	England	1	Youth	15/04/1964	Belgium	Ludwigshafen	W	3–0	2		
	England	2	Youth	17/04/1964	Spain	Heilbronn	D	0–0			
	England	3	Youth	21/04/1964	Hungary	Wuppertal	W	5–0	1		
	England	4	Youth	23/04/1964	Italy	Marl-Huels	W	3–1			
	England	5	Youth	25/04/1964	East Germany	Essen	L	2–3			
Steve MORROW	Northern Ireland	1	Full	02/04/1997	Ukraine	Kiev	L	1–2			
	Northern Ireland	2	Full	30/04/1997	Armenia	Yerevan	D	0–0			Capt
	Northern Ireland	3	Full	20/08/1997	Germany	Belfast	L	1–3			Capt
	Northern Ireland	4	Full	11/10/1997	Portugal	Lisbon	L	0–1			Capt
	Northern Ireland	5	Full	25/03/1998	Slovakia	Belfast	W	1–0			Capt
	Northern Ireland	6	Full	22/04/1998	Switzerland	Belfast	W	1–0			Capt
	Northern Ireland	7	Full	03/06/1998	Spain	Santander	L	1–4			Capt

Michael Meaker

Name	Country	Caps	Level	Date	Against	Venue	W/D/L	Score	Goals	Sub	Capt
	Northern Ireland	8	Full	05/09/1998	Turkey	Istanbul	L	0–3			
	Northern Ireland	9	Full	10/10/1998	Finland	Belfast	W	1–0			
	Northern Ireland	10	Full	18/11/1998	Moldova	Belfast	D	2–2			
	Northern Ireland	11	Full	27/03/1999	Germany	Belfast	L	0–3			
	Northern Ireland	12	Full	31/03/1999	Moldova	Chisinau	D	0–0			
	Northern Ireland	13	Full	08/09/1999	Germany	Dortmund	L	0–4			
	Northern Ireland	14	Full	09/10/1999	Finland	Helsinki	L	1–4			
Ian MUIR	England	1	Youth	17/10/1981	Romania	Adelaide	L	0–1			
Danny MURPHY	Eire	1	U17	1999	France		W	2–0			
	Eire	1	U18	20/09/2000	Switzerland	Dublin					
	Eire	2	U18	/04/2001	Portugal	Portugal	L				
	Eire	3	U18	/04/2001	Finland	Portugal	L				
	Eire	4	U18	/04/2001	Slovakia	Portugal	L				
Neil MURPHY	Ireland	1	Full	25/02/1905	England	Middlebrough	D	1–1			
	Ireland	2	Full	18/03/1905	Scotland	Glasgow	L	0–4			
	Ireland	3	Full	08/04/1905	Wales	Cliftonville	D	2–2	1		
Paul MURRAY	England	1	U21	12/02/1997	Italy	Bristol	W	1–0			
	England	2	U21	30/05/1997	Poland	Katowice	D	1–1			
	England	3	U21	10/10/1997	Italy	Rieti	W	1–0			
	England	4	U21	17/12/1997	Greece	Norwich	W	4–2			
	England	1	B	10/02/1998	Chile	West Bromwich	L	1–2		Sub	
Danny NARDIELLO	Wales	1	Full	22/08/2007	Bulgaria	Bourgas	W	1–0		Sub	
	Wales	2	Full	26/03/2008	Luxembourg	Luxembourg	W	2–0		Sub	
Brian NICHOLLS	London	1		04/06/1955	Basle	Basle	W	3–0		Sub	
Mick O'BRIEN	Ireland	1	Full	26/02/1921	Scotland	Belfast	L	0–2			
	Football League	1		10/11/1921	The Army	Leyton	W	4–1	1		
	Ireland	2	Full	04/03/1922	Scotland	Glasgow	L	1–2			
Karl OWEN	England	1	U16	09/03/1996	Spain	(Away)	L	0–2			
	England	2	U16	/02/1996	Eire	Lilleshall					
	England	3	U16	/02/1996	Denmark						
Paul PARKER	England	1	B	14/10/1987	Malta	Ta'Qali	W	2–0		Sub	
	England	1	Full	26/04/1989	Albania	Wembley	D	1–1		Sub	
	England	2	B	19/05/1989	Iceland	Reykjavik	W	2–0			
	England	2	Full	23/05/1989	Chile	Wembley	W	5–0			
	England	3	Full	07/06/1989	Denmark	Copenhagen	D	0–0			
	England	3	B	14/11/1989	Italy	Brighton	D	1–1			
	England	4	Full	13/12/1989	Yugoslavia	Wembley	W	2–1			
	England	5	Full	22/05/1990	Uruguay	Wembley	L	1–2			
	England	6	Full	16/06/1990	Holland	Cagliari	D	0–0			
	England	7	Full	21/06/1990	Egypt	Cagliari	W	1–0			
	England	8	Full	26/06/1990	Belgium	Bologna	W	1–0			
	England	9	Full	01/07/1990	Cameroon	Naples	W	3–2			
	England	10	Full	04/07/1990	West Germany	Turin	D	1–1			
	England	11	Full	07/07/1990	Italy	Bari	L	1–2			
	England	12	Full	12/09/1990	Hungary	Wembley	W	1–0			
	England	13	Full	17/10/1990	Poland	Wembley	W	2–0			
	England	14	Full	21/05/1991	USSR	Wembley	W	3–1			
	England	15	Full	01/06/1991	Australia	Sydney	W	1–0			
	England	16	Full	03/06/1991	New Zealand	Auckland	W	1–0			
Phil PARKES	England	1	U23	05/01/1972	Wales	Swindon	W	2–0			
	England	2	U23	16/02/1972	Scotland	Derby	D	2–2			
	England	3	U23	22/03/1972	East Germany	Bristol	L	0–1			
	England	4	U23	24/05/1973	Denmark	Naestved	D	1–1			
	England	5	U23	01/06/1973	Czechoslavakia	Bratislava	L	0–3			
	England	1	Full	03/04/1974	Portugal	Lisbon	D	0–0			

Name	Country	Caps	Level	Date	Against	Venue	W/D/L	Score	Goals	Sub	Capt
	England	6	U23	28/10/1975	Czechoslavakia	Trnava	D	1–1			
	England	1	U21	19/09/1978	Denmark	Hvidovre	W	2–1			
Dean PARRETT	England	1	U16	20/10/2006	Wales	Carmarthen	D	1–1			
	England	2	U16	09/11/2006	Northern Ireland	Ballymena	W	3–0			
	England	3	U16	08/12/2006	Scotland	Scuntorpe	W	2–1			
Gavin PEACOCK	England	1	Youth	03/04/1985	USSR	Cannes	L	1–3		Sub	
	England	2	Youth	08/04/1985	Scotland	Cannes	W	2–1			
	England	3	Youth	11/09/1985	Iceland	Reykjavik	W	5–0		Sub	
	England	4	Youth	02/06/1987	Brazil	Niteroi	L	0–2		Sub	
	England	5	Youth	10/06/1987	Uruguay	Montevideo	D	2–2	1	Sub	
Mark PERRY	England	1	Schools	12/03/1994	Switzerland	Wembley	W	3–0			
	England	2	Schools	1994	Wales	Coventry	W	2–0			
	England	3	Schools	1994	Holland		W	1–0			
	England	4	Schools	/06/1994	France	Wembley	W	2–1			
	England	1	U16	03/08/1994	Denmark	Vejle	L	0–1			
	England	2	U16	04/08/1994	Iceland	Vildbjerg	W	4–3			
	England	3	U16	06/08/1994	Norway	Aby	L	0–3			
	England	4	U16	07/08/1994	Austria	Vejle	L	0–3			
	England	5	U16	17/09/1994	Holland	Amsterdam	D	1–1			
	England	6	U16	16/11/1994	Turkey	Sakarya	W	3–2			
	England	1	U18	11/10/1996	Finland	York	W	1–0	1		
	England	2	U18	13/10/1996	Northern Ireland	York	W	4–0			
	England	3	U18	29/04/1997	Portugal	Bury	W	2–1			
	England	4	U18	13/05/1997	Portugal	Azores	L	0–3			
Mike PINNER	RAF	1		05/10/1960	FA	Old Trafford	D	2–2			
Chris PLUMMER	England	1	U16	26/04/1993	Belgium		D	1–1			
	England	2	U16	28/04/1993	Eire		W	1–0			
	England	3	U16	06/09/1994	France	Reading	L	2–3			
	England	1	U21	23/04/1996	Croatia	Sunderland	L	0–1		Sub	
	England	2	U21	24/05/1996	Belgium	Toulon	W	1–0			
	England	3	U21	28/05/1996	Angola	Cuers	L	0–2			
	England	4	U21	30/05/1996	Portugal	Arles	L	1–3		Sub	
	England	5	U21	01/06/1996	Brazil	Toulon	l	1–2			
Ivor POWELL	Wales	1		06/06/1942	Western Command	Wrexham	W	2–0			
	Wales	2		26/09/1942	RAF	Swansea	L	1–3			
	Wales	3		24/10/1942	England	Molineux	W	2–1			
	Wales	4		27/02/1943	England	Wembley	L	3–5			
	Wales	5		08/05/1943	England	Cardiff	D	1–1			
	Wales	6		25/09/1943	England	Wembley	L	3–8			
	Wales	1	Full	13/11/1946	England	Manchester	L	0–3			
	Wales	2	Full	18/10/1947	England	Cardiff	L	0–3			
	Wales	3	Full	12/11/1947	Scotland	Glasgow	W	2–1			
	Wales	4	Full	10/03/1948	Northern Ireland	Wrexham	W	2–0			
	Wales	5	Full	23/05/1949	Belgium	Liege	L	1–3			
Grahame POWER	England	1	Schools	1993	Italy	Wembley	D	1–1			
	England	1	U18	24/07/1994	Norway	Larvik	D	3–3			
	England	2	U18	26/07/1994	Norway	Vikersund	W	3–2			
	England	3	U18	06/09/1994	France	Reading	L	2–3		Sub	
Wayne PURSER	England	1	U16	09/03/1996	Spain	(Away)	L	0–2			
	England	2	U16	/02/1996	Eire	Lilleshall					
Nigel QUASHIE	England	1	U16	30/10/1993	Eire	Lilleshall	W	2–0			
	England	2	U16	24/11/1993	Holland	(Away)	D	1–1		Sub	
	England	3	U16	02/02/1994	Italy	Walsall	D	0–0		Sub	
	England	4	U16	08/03/1994	Holland	Hereford	W	1–0		Sub	
	England	5	U16	26/03/1994	Portugal	(Away)	W	1–0		Sub	

Paul Parker

Name	Country	Caps	Level	Date	Against	Venue	W/D/L	Score	Goals	Sub	Capt
	England	6	U16	28/04/1994	Eire	Dublin	D	1–1			
	England	7	U16	29/04/1994	RCS	Dublin	W	2–0		Sub	
	England	8	U16	02/05/1994	Ukraine	Dublin	D	2–2		Sub	
	England	1	U18	16/11/1995	Latvia	Rushden	W	2–0			
	England	1	U21	30/05/1997	Poland	Katowice	D	1–1			
	England	2	U21	09/09/1997	Moldova	Wycombe	W	1–0			
	England	3	U21	13/11/1997	Greece	Heraklion	L	0–2			
	England	1	B	10/02/1998	Chile	West Bromwich	L	1–2			
	England	4	U21	24/03/1998	Switzerland	Brugglifeld	L	0–2			
Karl READY	Wales	1	B	18/03/1992	Canada	Wrexham	L	1–1			
	Wales	1	U21	19/05/1992	Romania	Bucharest	W	3–2			
	Wales	2	U21	17/11/1992	Belgium	Kortrijk	L	1–3			
	Wales	3	U21	30/03/1993	Belgium	Cardiff	D	0–0			
	Wales	4	U21	27/04/1993	RCS	Frydek Mistek	D	1–1			
	Wales	5	U21	07/09/1993	RCS	Ebbw Vale	L	0–4			
	Wales	6	U21	13/10/1993	Cyprus	Cwmbran	W	6–2	1		
	Wales	2	B	02/02/1994	Scotland	Wrexham	W	2–1			
	Wales	1	Full	11/02/1997	Eire	Cardiff	D	0–0			
	Wales	2	Full	10/10/1997	Belgium	Brussels	L	2–3			
	Wales	3	Full	12/11/1997	Brazil	Brasilia	L	0–3			
	Wales	4	Full	03/06/1998	Malta	Valletta	W	3–0			
	Wales	5	Full	06/06/1998	Tunisia	Tunis	L	0–4			
Ted REAY	FA XI	1		22/05/1940	Herts FA	Watford	W	3–1			
Zesh REHMAN	Pakistan	1	Full	22/10/2007	Iraq	Lahore	L	0–7			
Alf RIDYARD	Met. Police	1		18/02/1942	Combined Services	Ipswich	W	3–2			
	Met. Police	2		08/04/1942	FA XI	New Cross	W	2–1			
	Met. Police	3		06/05/1942	RAF	Wembley	L	3–6			
	Met. Police	4		20/05/1942	Royal Navy	Ipswich	W	7–5			
	Civil Defence	1		05/09/1942	FA XI	Brentford	L	1–4			
	Met. Police	5		02/01/1943	Army	Aldershot	D	5–5			
	Met. Police	6		20/01/1943	Stan Cullis XI	Chichester	L	1–5			
	Football League	1		13/02/1943	Eastern Command	Ipswich	D	2–2			
	Police & Civil Defence	1		09/05/1945	Combined Services	Wembley	L	1–3			
RILEY	Eastern Command	1		30/10/1943	A.A. Command		L	1–4			
Tony ROBERTS	Wales	1	U21	15/12/1990	England	Tranmere	D	0–0			
	Wales	2	U21	30/05/1991	Poland	(Away)	W	2–1			
	Wales	1	B	18/03/1992	Canada	Wrexham	D	1–1			
	Wales	1	Full	17/02/1993	Eire	Dublin	L	1–2		Sub	
	Wales	2	Full	13/10/1993	Cyprus	Cardiff	W	2–0			
	Wales	2	B	02/02/1994	Scotland	Wrexham	W	2–1			
	Wales	3	Full	31/08/1996	San Marino	Cardiff	W	6–0		Sub	
Michael ROBINSON	Eire	1	Full	01/05/1985	Norway	Dublin	D	0–0			
	Eire	2	Full	26/05/1985	Spain	Cork	D	0–0			
	Eire	3	Full	02/06/1985	Switzerland	Dublin	W	3–0			
	Eire	4	Full	13/11/1985	Denmark	Dublin	L	1–4		Sub	
	Eire	5	Full	26/03/1986	Wales	Dublin	L	0–1			
	Eire	6	Full	27/05/1986	Czechoslavakia	Reykjavik	W	1–0			
Glenn ROEDER	England	1	B	15/10/1979	New Zealand	Leyton	W	4–1			
Keith ROWLAND	Northern Ireland	1	B	11/03/1998	Eire	Dublin	W	1–0			
	Northern Ireland	1	Full	05/09/1998	Turkey	Istanbul	L	0–3			
	Northern Ireland	2	Full	10/10/1998	Finland	Belfast	W	1–0	1		
	Northern Ireland	3	Full	18/11/1998	Moldova	Belfast	D	2–2			
	Northern Ireland	4	Full	27/03/1999	Germany	Belfast	L	0–3			
	Northern Ireland	5	Full	27/04/1999	Canada	Belfast	D	1–1			
	Northern Ireland	6	Full	29/05/1999	Republic of Ireland	Dublin	W	1–0			

Keith Rowland

Andy Sinton

Name	Country	Caps	Level	Date	Against	Venue	W/D/L	Score	Goals	Sub	Capt
Matin ROWLANDS	Eire	1	Full	27/05/2004	Romania	Dublin	W	1–0		Sub	
	Eire	2	Full	29/05/2004	Nigeria	Charlton	L	0–3		Sub	
	Eire	3	Full	02/06/2004	Jamaica	Charlton	W	1–0		Sub	
Reg SAPHIN	Met. Police	1		26/03/1942	Welsh Guards	Staines					
Steve SCOTT	England	1	Youth	24/08/1985	Paraguay	Baku	D	2–2		Sub	
	England	2	Youth	29/08/1985	Mexico	Baku	L	0–1			
Sam SCULLY	Wales	1	U19	07/08/2001	Faroe Islands	Swansea	W				
	Wales	2	U19	09/08/2001	Faroe Islands	Haverfordwest	W	8–2	1		
Tony SCULLY	Eire	1	B	16/02/1999	Irish League	Dublin	W	4–3		Sub	
David SEAMAN	England	1	B	14/10/1987	Malta	Ta'Qali	W	2–0			
	England	1	Full	16/11/1988	Saudi Arabia	Riyadh	D	1–1			
	England	2	Full	07/06/1989	Denmark	Copenhagen	D	1–1		Sub	
	England	2	B	27/03/1990	Eire	Cork	L	1–4		Sub	
	England	3	B	24/04/1990	Czechoslavakia	Sunderland	W	2–0			
	England	3	Full	25/04/1990	Czechoslavakia	Wembley	W	4–2		Sub	
Charlie SHAW	Southern League	1		09/10/1911	Football League	Stoke	L	1–2			
	Southern League	2		30/09/1912	Football League	Manchester	L	1–2			
	Southern League	3		14/10/1912	Scottish League	Millwall	W	1–0			
	Southern League	4		15/03/1913	Irish League	Millwall	D	1–1			
Ernest SHEPHERD	FA	1		01/11/1950	Diables Rouges						
	London	1		21/11/1951	Berlin	Berlin	D	1–1			
Dan SHITTU	Nigeria	1	Full	26/03/2002	Paraguay	Loftus Road	D	1–1		Sub	
Frank SIBLEY	England	1	Youth	21/05/1966	Czechoslavakia	Rijeka	L	2–3			
	England	2	Youth	23/05/1966	France	Rijeka	L	1–2			
	England	3	Youth	25/05/1966	Italy	Rijeka	D	1–1			
	England	4	Youth	30/06/1966	Spain	Swindon	W	3–0			
Trevor SINCLAIR	England	1	U21	12/10/1993	Holland	Utrecht	D	1–1			
	England	2	U21	17/11/1993	San Marino	Bologna	W	4–0			
	England	3	U21	08/03/1994	Denmark	Brentford	W	1–0	1		
	England	4	U21	30/05/1994	Russia	Bandol	W	2–0	1		
	England	5	U21	31/05/1994	France	Aubagne	L	0–3			
	England	6	U21	02/06/1994	USA	Arles	W	3–0			
	England	7	U21	05/06/1994	Belgium	Barres	W	2–1			
	England	8	U21	07/06/1994	Portugal	Toulon	W	2–0	1		
	England	9	U21	06/09/1994	Portugal	Leicester	D	0–0			
	England	10	U21	15/11/1994	Eire	Newcastle	W	1–0			
	England	11	U21	27/03/1995	Eire	Dublin	W	2–0	1		
	England	12	U21	25/04/1995	Latvia	Riga	W	1–0	1		
	England	13	U21	02/09/1995	Portugal	Oporto	L	0–2			
Andy SINTON	England	1	B	27/03/1990	Eire	Cork	L	1–4			
	England	1	Full	13/11/1991	Poland	Poznan	D	1–1			
	England	2	B	18/02/1992	France	QPR	W	3–0			
	England	3	B	24/03/1992	Czechoslavakia	Budejovice	W	1–0			
	England	2	Full	29/04/1992	CIS	Moscow	D	2–2			
	England	3	Full	12/05/1992	Hungary	Budapest	W	1–0		Sub	
	England	4	Full	17/05/1992	Brazil	Wembley	D	1–1			
	England	5	Full	14/06/1992	France	Malmo	D	0–0			
	England	6	Full	17/06/1992	Sweden	Stockholm	L	1–2			
	England	7	Full	09/09/1992	Spain	Santander	L	0–1			
	England	8	Full	31/03/1993	Turkey	Izmir	W	2–0			
	England	9	Full	16/06/1993	Brazil	Washington	D	1–1			
	England	10	Full	19/06/1993	Germany	Detroit	L	1–2			
Juergen SOMMER	USA	1	Full	08/10/1995	Saudi Arabia	Washington	W	4–3		Sub	
	USA	2	Full	26/05/1996	Scotland	Conneticut	W	2–1			
	USA	3	Full	/11/1997	El Salvador	(H)	W	4–2			

Name	Country	Caps	Level	Date	Against	Venue	W/D/L	Score	Goals	Sub	Capt
John SPENCER	Scotland	1	Full	27/05/1997	Wales	Kilmarnock	L	0–1		Sub	
Peter SPRINGETT	England	1	Youth	27/02/1964	Spain	Murcia	W	2–1			
	England	2	Youth	26/03/1964	Poland	Breda	D	1–1			
	England	3	Youth	30/03/1964	Eire	Middleburg	W	6–0			
	England	4	Youth	01/04/1964	Austria	Rotterdam	W	2–1			
	England	5	Youth	03/04/1964	Portugal	The Hague	W	4–0			
	England	6	Youth	05/04/1964	Spain	Amsterdam	W	4–0			
William STEER	England	1	Amateur	26/03/1910	Belgium	Brussels	D	2–2	1		
	England	2	Amateur	09/04/1910	Switzerland	Park Royal	W	6–1	2		
	Southern League	1		11/04/1910	Football League	Chelsea	D	2–2			
	England	3	Amateur	16/04/1910	France	Brighton	W	10–1	4		
	England	4	Amateur	05/05/1910	Denmark	Copenhagen	L	1–2	1		
	London	1		03/10/1910	Birmingham	Birmingham	W	3–0			
	England	5	Amateur	23/03/1911	France	Paris	W	3–0			
	England	6	Amateur	14/04/1911	Germany	Berlin	D	2–2			
Jan STEJSKAL	Czechoslavakia	1	Full	19/08/1992	Austria	Bratislava	D	2–2			
	Czechoslavakia	2	Full	02/09/1992	Belgium	Prague	L	1–2			
	Czechoslavakia	3	Full	23/09/1992	Faroe Islands	Kosice	W	4–0			
Damion STEWART	Jamaica	1	Full	03/06/2006	England	Manchester	L	0–6			
	Jamaica	2	Full	04/09/2006	Canada	Montreal	L	0–1			
	Jamaica	3	Full	08/10/2006	Canada	Kingston	W	2–1			
	Jamaica	4	Full	05/06/2007	Chile	Kingston	L	0–1		Sub	
	Jamaica	5	Full	18/11/2007	El Salvador	Kingston	W	3–0			
	Jamaica	6	Full	06/02/2008	Costa Rica	Kingston	D	1–1			
	Jamaica	7	Full	26/03/2008	Trinidad & Tobago	Kingston	D	2–2			
	Jamaica	8	Full	11/10/2008	Mexico	Kingston	W	1–0			
	Jamaica	9	Full	15/10/2008	Honduras	Kingston	W	1–0			
	Jamaica	10	Full	19/11/2008	Canada	Kingston	W	3–0			
	Jamaica	11	Full	11/02/2009	Nigeria	Millwall	D	0–0			
	Jamaica	12	Full	23/05/2009	Haiti	Fort Lauderdale	D	2–2	1		
	Jamaica	13	Full	30/05/2009	El Salvador	Washington	D	0–0			
	Jamaica	14	Full	07/06/2009	Panama	Kingston	W	3–2			
Ian STEWART	Northern Ireland	1	Full	24/03/1982	France	Paris	L	0–4		Sub	
	Northern Ireland	2	Full	04/07/1982	France	Madrid	L	1–4			
	Northern Ireland	3	Full	17/11/1982	West Germany	Belfast	W	1–0	1		
	Northern Ireland	4	Full	15/12/1982	Albania	Tirane	D	0–0			
	Northern Ireland	5	Full	30/03/1983	Turkey	Belfast	W	2–1			
	Northern Ireland	6	Full	27/04/1983	Albania	Belfast	W	1–0	1		
	Northern Ireland	7	Full	24/05/1983	Scotland	Glasgow	D	0–0			
	Northern Ireland	8	Full	28/05/1983	England	Belfast	D	0–0			
	Northern Ireland	9	Full	31/05/1983	Wales	Belfast	L	0–1			
	Northern Ireland	10	Full	21/09/1983	Austria	Belfast	W	3–1			
	Northern Ireland	11	Full	12/10/1983	Turkey	Ankara	L	0–1			
	Northern Ireland	12	Full	16/11/1983	West Germany	Hamburg	W	1–0			
	Northern Ireland	13	Full	13/12/1983	Scotland	Glasgow	W	2–0			
	Northern Ireland	14	Full	04/04/1984	England	Wembley	L	0–1			
	Northern Ireland	15	Full	22/05/1984	Wales	Swansea	D	1–1			
	Northern Ireland	16	Full	27/05/1984	Finland	Pori	L	0–1			
	Northern Ireland	17	Full	12/09/1984	Romania	Belfast	W	3–2			
	Northern Ireland	18	Full	16/10/1984	israel	Belfast	W	3–0			
	Northern Ireland	19	Full	14/11/1984	Finland	Belfast	W	2–1			
	Northern Ireland	20	Full	27/02/1985	England	Belfast	L	0–1			
	Northern Ireland	21	Full	27/03/1985	Spain	Palma	D	0–0			
	Northern Ireland	22	Full	01/05/1985	Turkey	Belfast	W	2–0			
Dave THOMAS	England	1	U23	13/11/1973	Denmark	Portsmouth	D	1–1		Sub	

Ian Stewart

Name	Country	Caps	Level	Date	Against	Venue	W/D/L	Score	Goals	Sub	Capt
	England	2	U23	11/05/1974	Turkey	Ankara	D	0–0			
	England	3	U23	19/05/1974	France	Valence	D	2–2			
	England	1	Full	30/10/1974	Czechoslavakia	Wembley	W	3–0		Sub	
	England	2	Full	02/11/1974	Portugal	Wembley	D	0–0			
	England	3	Full	16/04/1975	Cyprus	Wembley	W	5–0		Sub	
	England	4	Full	11/05/1975	Cyprus	Limassol	W	1–0			
	England	5	Full	21/05/1975	Wales	Wembley	D	2–2			
	England	6	Full	24/05/1975	Scotland	Wembley	W	5–1		Sub	
	England	7	Full	30/10/1975	Czechoslavakia	Bratislava	L	1–2		Sub	
	England	8	Full	19/11/1975	Portugal	Lisbon	D	1–1		Sub	
William THOMPSON	Southern League	1		26/10/1914	Football League	Highbury	L	1–2			
TOZER	FA XI	1		22/05/1940	Herts FA	Watford	W	3–1			
Gary WADDOCK	Eire	1	Full	30/04/1980	Switzerland	Dublin	W	2–0			
	Eire	2	Full	06/05/1980	Argentina	Dublin	L	0–1			
	Eire	3	Full	24/02/1981	Wales	Dublin	L	1–3			
	Eire	4	Full	23/05/1981	Poland	Bydgoszcz	L	0–3		Sub	
	Eire	5	Full	28/04/1982	Algeria	Algiers	L	0–2			
	Eire	6	Full	22/09/1982	Holland	Rotterdam	L	1–2		Sub	
	Eire	7	Full	13/10/1982	Iceland	Dublin	W	2–0			
	Eire	8	Full	30/03/1983	Malta	Valletta	W	1–0			
	Eire	9	Full	27/04/1983	Spain	Zaragoza	L	0–2			
	Eire	10	Full	21/09/1983	Iceland	Reykjavik	W	3–0	1		
	Eire	11	Full	12/10/1983	Holland	Dublin	L	2–3	1		
	Eire	12	Full	04/04/1984	Israel	Tel Aviv	L	0–3			
	Eire	13	Full	05/02/1985	Italy	Dublin	L	1–2	1		
	Eire	14	Full	26/03/1985	England	Wembley	L	1–2			
	Eire	15	Full	01/05/1985	Norway	Dublin	D	0–0			
	Eire	16	Full	26/05/1985	Spain	Cork	D	0–0			
	Eire	17	Full	27/05/1985	Israel	Tel Aviv	D	0–0			
	Eire	18	Full	16/10/1985	USSR	Moscow	L	0–2			
William WAKE	London	1		25/10/1909	Birmingham	Fulham	L	1–3			
	London	2		02/10/1911	Birmingham	Tottenham	L	2–3			
	Southern League	1		14/10/1912	Scottish League	Millwall	W	1–0			
Mick WALSH	Eire	1	Full	02/05/1979	Denmark	Dublin	W	2–0		Sub	
	Eire	2	Full	19/05/1979	Bulgaria	Sofia	L	0–1			
	Eire	3	Full	22/05/1979	West Germany	Dublin	L	1–3		Sub	
	Eire	4	Full	29/05/1979	Argentina	Dublin	D	0–0			
Nick WARD	Australia	1	U21	06/06/2007	Jordan	Amman	W	4–0	1	Sub	
	Australia	1	U23	17/11/2007	Iraq	Brisbane	W	2–0		Sub	
	Australia	2	U23	21/11/2007	North Korea	Pyongyang	D	1–1		Sub	
Gary WESTLEY	England	1	Youth	08/04/1985	Scotland	Cannes	W	1–0		Sub	
	England	2	Youth	11/09/1985	Iceland	Reykjavik	W	5–0		Sub	
David WHITTLE	Eire	1	U18		France	Opporto	D	1–1			
	Eire	2	U18		Russia	Opporto	D	1–1			
	Eire	3	U18		Portugal	Opporto	L	0–2			
Steve WICKS	England	1	U21	19/04/1982	Scotland	Glasgow	W	1–0			
Chris WOODS	England	1	U21	20/11/1979	Bulgaria	Leicester	W	5–0			
	England	2	U21	23/04/1980	East Germany	Jena	L	0–1			
	England	3	U21	18/11/1980	Switzerland	Ipswich	W	5–0			
Paul WRIGHT	Scotland	1	U21	05/09/1989	Yugoslavia	Slavonski Brod	L	1–4		Sub	
Karl YELLAND	Wales	1	U19	31/07/2006	USA	N.Ireland	L	0–3			
	Wales	2	U19	02/08/2006	Paraguay	N.Ireland	L	2–3			
	Wales	3	U19	04/08/2006	Turkey	N.Ireland	L	1–3			
	Wales	4	U19	07/09/2006	Germany	Chiemese	L	1–4			

PLAYER RECORDS

Surname	Christian	Born	Date	Debut	No	App	Sub	Goal	Signed From	Date	Signed Fee	Transferred To	Date	Transfer Fee
ABBOTT	HARRY	BLACKBURN	1883	3/9/1902	9	28		4	BLACKBURN ROVERS	1902		BOLTON WANDERERS	1904	
ABBOTT	RON	LAMBETH	2/8/1953	10/9/1973	7	38	16	4	Apprentice	7/1971		DROGHEDA		
ABBOTT	SHIRLEY	ALFRETON	10/2/1889	6/10/1923	5	12			PORTSMOUTH	1923		CHESTERFIELD	1924	
ABEL	SAM	NESTON	30/12/1908	15/9/1934	8	221		11	FULHAM	1934	400	Retired	1945	
ADAM	CHARLIE	GLASGOW	22/3/1919	1940		9		2	LEICESTER CITY			Guest		
ADAMS	ERNIE	WILLESDEN	3/4/1922	24/4/1948	7	5			PRESTON NORTH END	9/1947				
ADDINALL	ALBERT	PADDINGTON	30/1/1921	17/3/1945	9	172		73	RAF	1944		BRIGHTON & HOVE ALBION	1/1953	
ADLAM	LESLIE	GUILDFORD	24/6/1897	14/11/1931	4	64			OLDHAM ATHLETIC	11/1931	1500+Goodier	CARDIFF CITY	12/1933	
AGOGO	JUNIOR	ACCRA, GHANA	1/8/1979	6/4/2002	A		2		SAN JOSE EARTHQUAKES	3/2002	Non-Contract	BARNET	7/2002	Free
AGYEMANG	PATRICK	WALTHAMSTOW	29/9/1980	5/1/2008	A	29	12	11	PRESTON NORTH END	1/2008	350,000			
AINSWORTH	GARETH	BLACKBURN	10/5/1973	9/8/2003	6	109	41	21	CARDIFF CITY	7/2003	Free			
AINSWORTH	JACK			25/1/1908	11	2		2						
ALBERTI	MATTEO	BRESCIA, ITALY	4/8/1988	9/8/2008	B	7	6	2	AC CHIEVO VERONA	7/2008				
ALEXANDER	FRED			10/4/1944	5	4				10/1944				
ALLAN	JAMES	AMBLE	1913	14/9/1935	4	47		2	HUDDESFIELD TOWN	1935		CLAPTON ORIENT	7/1937	Free
ALLEN	BRADLEY	ROMFORD	13/9/1971	14/1/1989	14	65	29	32	Juniors	9/1988		CHARLTON ATHLETIC	3/1996	400,000
ALLEN	CLIVE	STEPNEY	20/5/1961	4/11/1978	12	147	10	83	Apprentice	9/ 1978	Free	ARSENAL	6/1980	1,200,000
									CRYSTAL PALACE	6/1981	450,000	TOTTENHAM HOTSPUR	8/1984	750,000
ALLEN	IAN	PAISLEY	27/1/1932	7/4/1954	7	1			BEITH JUNIORS	9/1952		BOURNEMOUTH	7/1954	
ALLEN	JOE	BLISTHORPE	30/12/1909	30/9/1933	8	58		7	TOTTENHAM HOTSPUR	1933		MANSFIELD TOWN		
ALLEN	LES	DAGENHAM	4/9/1937	21/8/1965	8	146	5	62	TOTTENHAM HOTSPUR	7/1965	20,000	WOODFORD TOWN		
ALLEN	MARTIN	READING	14/8/1965	2/10/1984	16	154	12	19	Apprentice	5/1983		WEST HAM UNITED	9/1989	550,000
ALLEN	REG	MARYLEBONE	3/5/1919	26/11/1938	1	255			CORONA	1938		MANCHESTER UNITED	6/1950	12,000
ALLUM	ALBERT	NOTTING HILL	15/10/1930	2/9/1957	7	1			BRENTFORD	6/1957		DOVER		
ANDERSON	EDWARD	SCOTLAND	1881	1/9/1906	9	19		3	SHEFFIELD UNITED	1906				
ANDERSON	GEORGE	SUNDERLAND	1881	7/9/1912	8	3		1	PRESTON NORTH END	1912				
ANDERSON	TOMMY	EDINBURGH	24/9/1934	29/11/1958	7	10		3	BOURNEMOUTH	11/1958		TORQUAY UNITED	7/1959	
ANDERTON	SYLVAN	READING	23/11/1934	20/1/1962	6	4			CHELSEA	1/1962		DOVER		
ANDREWS	CECIL	ALTON	1/11/1930	18/8/1956	6	65		1	CRYSTAL PALACE	6/1956		SITTINGBOURNE	7/1958	
ANDREWS	JIMMY	INVERGORDON	1/2/1927	22/8/1959	11	88		17	LEYTON ORIENT	6/1959		QPR Coaching Staff	6/1963	
ANGELL	BRETT	MARLBOROUGH	20/8/1968	23/11/2002	10	8	5		PORT VALE	11/2002	Free	Retired from football	5/2003	
ANGELL	PETER	CHALVEY	11/1/1932	12/9/1953	11	457		40	SLOUGH TOWN	7/1953		Charlton Athletic Coach	7/1965	
ARCHER	ARTHUR	ASHBY-DE-LA-ZOUCH	4/1877	5/9/1903	2	53			WINGFIELD HOUSE	1903		NORWICH CITY	1905	
ARCHIBALD	JIMMY			13/4/1918	10	4		2						
ARDILES	OSSIE	CORDOBA, ARGENTINA	3/8/1952	27/8/1988	6	7	5		TOTTENHAM HOTSPUR	8/1988	Free	SWINDON TOWN	7/1989	Free
ARMITAGE	STAN	WOOLWICH	5/6/1919	14/9/1946	10	2						GRAVESEND & NORTHFLEET	1947	Free
ARMSTRONG	JIMMY	LYMINGTON		10/11/1928	4	133		5	CLAPTON ORIENT	7/1928		WATFORD	1934	
ARMSTRONG	RICHARD	NEWBURN	31/8/1909	14/4/1941	6	13		3						
ASHFORD	HERBERT	SOUTHALL		12/2/1921	6	10			BRENTFORD	1920		AYR UNITED		
ASHMAN	DONALD	STAINDROP	9/10/1902	27/8/1932	2	87			MIDDLESBROUGH	7/1932		DARLINGTON	1935	
ASTON	CHARLES	BILSTON	1875	7/9/1901	3	28		1	ASTON VILLA	1901		BURTON UNITED	1902	
ATTWELL	REGINALD	SHIFNAL	23/2/1920	28/10/1944	10	12		1	WEST HAM UNITED			Guest		
BACON	SID			1940		3								
BAIDOO	SHABAZZ	HACKNEY	13/4/1988	5/4/2005	B	12	21	4	Youth Academy			DAGENHAM & REDBRIDGE	1/2008	Free
BAILEY	DENNIS	LAMBETH	13/11/1965	17/8/1991	7	39	8	13	BIRMINGHAM CITY	7/1991	175,000	GILLINGHAM	8/1995	50,000
BAILEY	SIDNEY	LONDON		22/4/1922	3	1								
BAILEY	STEFAN	BRENT	10/11/1987	9/4/2005	A	18	4		Youth Academy			GRAYS ATHLETIC	6/2008	free
BAIN	KEN	SCOTLAND	26/5/	12/11/1921	3	98			MID-RHONDA					

Surname	Christian	Born	Date	Debut	No	App	Sub	Goal	Signed From	Date	Signed Fee	Transferred To	Date	Transfer Fee
BAIN	WILLIAM			23/9/1944	8	5		1	ABERDEEN			Guest		
BAKER	PETER	WALTHAMSTOW	24/8/1934	4/3/1961	2	28			SHEFFIELD WEDNESDAY	3/1961		ROMFORD		
BAKHOLT	KURT	ODENSE	12/8/1963	8/2/1986	12		1		VEJIE					
BALANTA	ANGELO	COLUMBIA	1/7/1990	4/12/2007	B	9	16	3	Youth Academy					
BALDOCK	JOHN	SHADWELL	1893	6/12/1913	8	143		13						
BALLENTYNE	JOHNNY	GLASGOW	27/10/1899	16/11/1935	10	27		3	PARTICK THISTLE	1935		Not Re-registered	7/1937	
BALOGUN	TESI	NIGERIA	27/3/1931	13/10/1956	9	16		7	SKEGNESS	9/1956		HOLBEACH UNITED	7/1957	
BANKOLE	ADEMOLE	LAGOS, NIGERIA	9/9/1969	9/10/1999	A		1		CREWE ALEXANDRA	7/1998	Free	CREWE ALEXANDRA	7/2001	Free
BANKS	REG			31/8/1935	11	12		3	WEST BROMWICH ALBION	1935		TUNBRIDGE WELLS RANGERS	7/1937	Free
BANNER	WILLIAM			28/12/1903	5	4			CHESTERFIELD	1903		CHESTERFIELD	1904	
BANNISTER	GARY	WARRINGTON	22/7/1960	25/8/1984	9	172		72	SHEFFIELD WEDNESDAY	8/1981	150,000	COVENTRY CITY	3/1988	300,000
BARACLOUGH	IAN	LEICESTER	4/12/1970	21/3/1998	7	133	5	1	NOTTS COUNTY	3/1998	50,000	NOTTS COUNTY	7/2001	Free
BARBER	MICHAEL	KENSINGTON	24/8/1941	5/9/1960	7	70		13	ARSENAL	12/1959		NOTTS COUNTY	7/1963	10,000
BARDSLEY	DAVID	MANCHESTER	11/9/1964	16/9/1989	7	294	1	6	OXFORD UNITED	9/1989	375,000	BLACKPOOL	7/1998	Free
BARKAS	SAMUEL	WARLEY COLLIERY	29/12/1909	21/11/1942	2	1			MANCHESTER CITY			Guest		
BARKER	CHRIS	SHEFFIELD	2/3/1980	1/9/2007	5	26			CARDIFF CITY	7/2007	Free	PLYMOUTH ARGYLE	7/2008	
BARKER	SIMON	FARNWORTH	4/11/1964	27/8/1988	11	349	27	41	BLACKBURN ROVERS	7/1988	400,000	PORT VALE	7/1998	Free
BARLEY	DEREK	HIGHBURY	20/3/1932	29/8/1953	9	4			ARSENAL	5/1953		ALDERSHOT	7/1954	
BARLOW				24/3/1917	8	3		1				Guest		
BARNES	PHIL	SHEFFIELD	2/3/1979	4/2/2006	1	1			SHEFFIELD UNITED	2/2006	Emergency loan	SHEFFIELD UNITED	2/2006	Returned
BARNES	WILLIAM	WEST HAM	20/5/1879	2/9/1907	11	234		37	LUTON TOWN	1907		SOUTHEND UNITED		1913
BARR	HAMID	LEWISHAM	29/9/1976	16/10/2001	C		1		FISHER ATHLETIC	7/2001	Free	ST ALBANS CITY	8/2002	Free
BARR	JOHN	BRIDGE OF WEIR	9/9/1917	1940		12			THIRD LANARK	1939				
BARR	WILLIAM			5/9/1925	8	2								
BARRIE	WALTER	KIRKCALDY	9/8/1909	24/9/1932	2	174		1	WEST HAM UNITED	1932		CARLISLE UNITED	1938	
BARRINGTON				23/9/1916	4	1						Guest		
BARRON	PAUL	WOOLWICH	16/9/1953	24/9/1985	1	42			WEST BROMWICH ALBION		40,000	READING		
BARTLETT	FREDERICK	READING	5/3/1913	3/11/1934	5	51			READING DISTRICT	1933		CLAPTON ORIENT	7/1937	Free
BARTON	WARREN	ISLINGTON	19/3/1969	4/10/2003	A	4	1		DERBY COUNTY	9/2003	Free	WIMBLEDON	3/2004	Free
BEADELL	R.			29/8/1942		1		1						
BEALE	A.		25/11/1916		9	1						Guest		
BEAN	MARCUS	HAMMERSMITH	2/11/1984	26/8/2002	A	51	25	2	Youth Academy			BLACKPOOL	1/2006	Free
BEATS	EDDIE	BRISTOL		10/3/1928	9	1		1	ASTON VILLA					
BECK	JOHN	EDMONTON	25/5/1954	26/12/1972	12	38	8	1	Apprentice	5/1972		COVENTRY CITY	6/1976	70,000
BECK	MIKKEL	AARHUS, DENMARK	4/5/1973	12/2/2000	A	10	1	4	DERBY COUNTY	2/2000	Loan	DERBY COUNTY	4/2000	Returned
BECKERLEY				9/12/1916	3	1						Guest		
BEDFORD	BRIAN	FERNDALE	24/12/1933	22/8/1959	10	284		180	BOURNEMOUTH	7/1959		SCUNTHORPE UNITED	9/1965	
BEDINGFIELD	FRANK	SUNDERLAND	1877	9/9/1899	9	32		21	ASTON VILLA	8/1899		PORTSMOUTH	1900	
BEECHAM	ERNEST	HERTFORD	23/7/1896	27/8/1932	1	95			FULHAM	1932		BRIGHTON & HOVE ALBION	9/1935	
BELLAMY	JAMES	BARKING	10/1881	25/12/1915	2	1			FULHAM			Guest		
BELLINGHAM	JAMES	SCOTLAND	1878	8/9/1900	2	17			FALKIRK	1900		GRIMSBY TOWN	1901	
BEN ASKAR	AZIZ	CHATEAU GONTIER	30/3/1976	11/8/2001	3	20			STADE LAVALLOIS	8/2001	Loan	Returned to France	5/2002	
BENNETT	EDWARD	KILBURN	22/8/1925	19/3/1949	1	2			SOUTHALL	1948		SOUTHALL		
BENSON	GEORGE	BURNLEY	25/6/1893	25/8/1923	11	17			STALYBRIDGE CELTIC			PORT VALE		
BENSTEAD	GRAHAM	ALDERSHOT	20/8/1963	8/1/1982	1	1			Apprentice	7/1981		NORWICH CITY	3/1985	
BENTLEY	ROY	BRISTOL	17/5/1924	19/8/1961	5	52			FULHAM	6/1961		Reading (Manager)		
BERRY	FREDERICK		1891	14/2/1920	1	4								
BEST	LEON	NOTTINGHAM	19/9/1986	18/12/2004	A	2	3		SOUTHAMPTON	12/2004	Loan	SOUTHAMPTON	1/2005	Returned
BEST	TOM	MILFORD HAVEN	23/12/1920	10/12/1949	8	14		3	CARDIFF CITY	12/1949		HERTFORD TOWN	1950	
BEVAN	FRED	HACKNEY	1880	3/9/1904	9	59		30	READING	1904		BURY	7/1906	340
BIGNOT	MARCUS	BIRMINGHAM	28/8/1974	17/3/2001	A	182	11	2	BRISTOL ROVERS/	3/2001	Free	RUSHDEN & DIAMONDS	8/2002	Free
									RUSHDEN & DIAMONDS	3/2004	Free	MILLWALL	1/ 2008	Free

Surname	Christian	Born	Date	Debut	No	App	Sub	Goal	Signed From	Date	Signed Fee	Transferred To	Date	Transfer Fee
BIRCH	JIMMY	BLACKWELL	1888	5/9/1912	9	363		144	ASTON VILLA	8/1912		BRENTFORD	1926	
BIRCHAM	MARC	WEMBLEY	11/5/1978	10/8/2002	7	151	16	7	MILLWALL	7/2002	Free	Released	5/2007	
BIRKETT				25/11/1916	7	1						Guest		
BLACK	SAM	MOTHERWELL	18/11/1905	31/12/1938	11	5			PLYMOUTH ARGYLE	11/1938			1939	Free
BLACKMAN	FRED	KENNINGTON	8/2/1884	30/8/1919	2	62			LEEDS CITY	1919		Retired	1922	
BLACKMAN	JACK	BERMONDSEY	1/1911	9/1/1932	9	120		71	WESTON UNITED	1932		CRYSTAL PALACE	10/1935	
BLACKSTOCK	DEXTER	OXFORD	20/5/1986	12/8/2006	11	96	21	32	SOUTHAMPTON	8/2006	500,000			
BLACKWOOD	JOHN	GLASGOW	1877	29/11/1902	8	46		33	READING	11/1902		WEST HAM UNITED	1904	
BLAKE	ALBERT	FULHAM	1900	26/8/1933	6	89		10	WATFORD	1933		TUNBRIDGE WELLS	1936	
BLAKE	F.			2/10/1915	9	1						Guest		
BLAKE	F.J.C.			26/3/1914	9	2								
BLAKE	SID	WHITLEY BAY		1/9/1906	11	14			NEWCASTLE UNITED	1906		WHITLEY BAY	1908	
BLIZZARD	LES	ACTON	13/3/1923	8/11/1941	6	28			Local Club			BOURNEMOUTH	5/1947	Free
BOLAM	ROBERT	BIRTLEY	1896	6/12/1924	11	2			SOUTH SHIELDS					
BOLDER	ADAM	HULL	25/10/1980	30/1/2007	6	37	5	2	DERBY COUNTY	1/2007	Free	MILLWALL	9/2008	Loan
BONASS	ALBERT	YORK	1/1/1912	26/8/1939	11	61		7	CHESTERFIELD	1939		Died during WW2		
BONNOT	ALEX	POISSY	31/7/1973	11/8/2001	8	20	5		WATFORD	7/2001	Free	Released	2/2002	
BORROWDALE	GARY	SUTTON	16/7/1985	1985								COVENTRY CITY	1/2009	500,000
BOTT	WILFRED	FEATHERSTONE	25/4/1907	29/8/1936	11	110		45	NEWCASTLE UNITED	8/1936		COLCHESTER UNITED	1938	
BOTTOMS	MICHAEL	HARROW	11/1/1939	15/10/1960	10	3			HARROW TOWN	7/1960		OXFORD UNITED	7/1962	Free
BOWERS	ALFRED	CANNING TOWN	5/1899	2/10/1926	4	1			BRISTOL ROVERS					
BOWLES	STAN	MANCHESTER	24/12/1948	16/9/1972	10	315		96	CARLISLE UNITED	9/1972	112,000	NOTTINGHAM FOREST	12/1979	250,000
BOWMAN	JOHN	MIDDLESBROUGH	23/4/1879	7/9/1901	5	110		2	STOKE CITY	1901		NORWICH CITY	1905	
BOXSHALL	DANNY	BRADFORD	2/4/1920	1/1/1946	7	40		18	SALEM ATHLETIC			BRISTOL CITY	8/1948	
BRADSHAW	JOE	BURNLEY	1880	3/9/1910	8	2		2	CHELSEA			SOUTHEND UNITED		
BRADSHAW	JOHN	BURNLEY	1892	24/9/1921	7	5			ABERDARE ATHLETIC			BURNLEY		
BRADY	PAT	DUBLIN	11/3/1936	4/9/1963	3	70			MILLWALL	7/1963		GRAVESEND & NORTHFLEET		
BRADY	RAY	DUBLIN	3/6/1937	24/8/1963	5	97		1	MILLWALL	7/1963		HASTINGS UNITED		
BRANCO	SERGE	DOUALA, CONGO	11/10/1980	22/9/2004	8	5	4		LEEDS UNITED	9/2004	Free	Released	1/2005	
BRAZIER	MATTHEW	WHIPPS CROSS	2/7/1976	3/10/1995	A	42	15	3	Juniors			FULHAM	3/1998	65,000
BRAZIL	ALAN	GLASGOW	15/6/1959	23/8/1986	12	2	4	1	COVENTRY CITY	7/1986	130,000	WITHAM TOWN		
BREACKER	TIM	BICESTER	2/7/1965	3/10/1998	4	46	3	2	WEST HAM UNITED	2/1999	Free	Retired from football	4/2001	
BREVETT	RUFUS	DERBY	24/9/1969	23/3/1991	3	158	12	1	DONCASTER ROVERS	2/1991	250,000	FULHAM	1/1998	375,000
BREWIS	ROBERT		1885	7/10/1905	9	7		2				LINCOLN CITY	1907	
BRIDGES	BARRY	NORWICH	29/4/1941	24/8/1968	9	82		35	BIRMINGHAM CITY	8/1968	50,000	MILLWALL	9/1970	40,000
BRINDLEY	HORACE	KNUTTON	1/1/1885	3/9/1910	7	18			CREWE ALEXANDRA	1910		SUTTON TOWN	1913	
BRITTON				13/4/1918	7	1		1				Guest		
BROCK	KEVIN	BICESTER	9/9/1962	15/8/1987	11	50	2	3	OXFORD UNITED	8/1987	100,000	NEWCASTLE UNITED	12/1988	300,000
BROOK	HAROLD	SHEFFIELD	15/12/1921	23/9/1944	10	1			SHEFFIELD UNITED			Guest		
BROOMES	MARLON	MERIDEN	28/11/1977	25/10/2000	5	5			BLACKBURN ROVERS	10/2000	Loan	BLACKBURN ROVERS	11/2000	Returned
BROSTER	JOHN	EARLSTOWN		26/12/1912	6	74		4	CHORLEY			ROCHDALE	1920	
BROWN	AARON	BRISTOL	14/3/1980	23/4/2005	B	2	2		BRISTOL CITY	3/2005	Free	SWINDON TOWN	1/2006	Free
BROWN	ARTHUR	TAMWORTH	1879	25/10/1902	9	31		12	SOUTHAMPTON	1902		PRESTON NORTH END	1905	
BROWN	BERTIE			6/4/1942	7	1								
BROWN	CHARLES	STAKESFORD	14/1/1898	30/8/1924	7	73		3	SOUTHAMPTON	1924		POOLE TOWN	1926	
BROWN	DICK	PEGSWOOD	14/2/1911	27/8/1932	11	70		23	BLYTH SPARTANS	7/1932		NORTHAMPTON TOWN		
BROWN	HAROLD	SHILDON	1897	30/8/1924	9	13		3	SHILDON UNITED					
BROWN	HARRY	KINGSBURY	9/4/1924	15/11/1941	1	286						NOTTS COUNTY		
									DERBY COUNTY	8/1951		PLYMOUTH ARGYLE	8/1956	
BROWN	J.			2/12/1916	7	29		7						
BROWN	WAYNE	BARKING	20/8/1977	24/3/2001	3	2			IPSWICH TOWN	3/2001	Loan	IPSWICH TOWN	5/2001	Returned
BROWN	WILLIAM	SOUTH INCH		4/3/1911	8	6		2	KETTERING	1910		CHELSEA	1912	
BROWNING	ROBERT			8/10/1910	10	54		20				SOUTHAMPTON	1913	

Surname	Christian	Born	Date	Debut	No	App	Sub	Goal	Signed From	Date	Signed Fee	Transferred To	Date	Transfer Fee
BRUCE	PAUL	LONDON	18/2/1978	13/1/1998	14	35	10	3	Trainee	5/1996		DAGENHAM & REDBRIDGE	7/2002	Free
BUBB	ALVIN	PADDINGTON	11/10/1980	6/5/2001	C		1		Youth Academy			BRISTOL ROVERS	7/2001	Free
BULL	ALBERT	DERBY	1875	19/9/1903	6	15			READING	1903		NEW BROMPTON	1905	
BURGESS	DANIEL	GOLDENHILL	23/10	29/8/1925	10	50		9	ABERDARE ATHLETIC			SITTINGBOURNE		
BURGESS	OLIVER	ASCOT	12/10/1981	7/4/2001	A	9	5	1	Youth Academy			NORTHAMPTON TOWN	7/2003	Free
BURKE	STEVE	NOTTINGHAM	29/9/1960	8/9/1979	11	47	30	5	NOTTINGHAM FOREST	9/1979	150,000	DONCASTER ROVERS	9/1986	Free
BURLEY	BEN			5/9/1942	11	77		20	DARLINGTON					
BURNHAM	JOHN	SUNDERLAND	1896	26/11/1921	6	33			BRIGHTON	1921		DURHAM CITY	1923	
BURNS	JACK	FULHAM	27/11/1906	14/1/1928	8	125		36	CRYPTO			BRENTFORD	1931	
BURRIDGE	JOHN	WORKINGTON	3/12/1951	26/12/1980	1	45			CRYSTAL PALACE	12/1980	150,000	WOLVERHAMPTON WANDERERS	8/1982	75,000
BUSBY	MARTYN	SLOUGH	24/5/1953	18/4/1970	4	145	22	20	Apprentice	7/ 1970	Free	NOTTS COUNTY	10/1976	35,000
									NOTTS COUNTY	9/1977	35,000	Retired (Injury)	6/1981	
BUSBY	WALTER	WELLINGBOROUGH	1882	3/9/1902	10	15		3	WELLINGBOROUGH	1902		WOOLWICH ARSENAL		1903
BUTLER	ERNEST	STILLINGTON	17/6/1896	7/10/1922	7	35			EBBW VALE	1922		HARTLEPOOLS UNITED		
BUTLER	J.			26/12/1916	7	7							Killed in WW1	
BUTTERWORTH	HERBERT	UNSWORTH	1/1/1885	26/11/1910	6	41			OLDHAM ATHLETIC	1910		MILLWALL ATHLETIC	1912	
BUZSAKY	AKOS	HUNGARY	7/5/1982	3/11/2007	8	32	9	11	PLYMOUTH ARGYLE	11/2007	500,000			
BYRNE	JOHN	MANCHESTER	1/2/1961	27/10/1984	12	128	21	36	YORK CITY	10/1984	100,000	LE HARVE	5/1988	175,000
BYROM	WILLIAM	BLACKBURN	30/3/1915	1915/39/1940		1			BURNLEY	1939		ROCHDALE		
CABLE	TOMMY	BARKING	27/11/1900	25/12/1925	5	18		2	LEYTON			TOTTENHAM HOTSPUR		1928
CAESER	GUS	HARRINGEY	5/3/1966	1/12/1990	5	5			ARSENAL	11/1990	Loan	ARSENAL	12/1990	Returned
CAIN	THOMAS	EALING		22/3/1920	5	6						BRENTFORD	1924	
CAMERON	JAMES	INVERNESS		25/8/1923	6	25			HEART OF MIDLOTHIAN			INDIANA FLOORING		
CAMERON	KEN	HAMILTON	1905	29/8/1936	10	8		1	HULL CITY			ROTHERHAM UNITED	7/1937	Free
CAMERON	ROBERT	GREENOCK	23/11/1932	13/1/1951	8	278		62	PORT GLASGOW	6/1950		LEEDS UNITED	7/1959	
CAMP	LEE	DERBY	22/8/1984	13/3/2004	1	76			DERBY COUNTY	3/2004	Loan	DERBY COUNTY	5/2004	Returned
									DERBY COUNTY	2/2007	Loan	DERBY COUNTY	4/2007	Returned
									DERBY COUNTY	7/2007	300,000	NOTTINGHAM FOREST	10/2008	Loan
CAMPBELL	CHARLES	BLACKBURN		29/8/1925	9	4		1	PEMBROKE DOCK				READING	
CAMPBELL	DOUGOLD	KIRKINTILLOCH	14/12/1922	15/1/1949	7	1				3/1948		CREWE ALEXANDRA	7/1949	
CAMPBELL	ROBERT	GLASGOW	28/6/1922	31/5/1941		1			LUTON TOWN			Guest		
CAMPBELL	SANDY			24/11/1917	9	2		1				Guest		
CAMPBELL				11/10/1941	4	5								
CANNON	FRANK	HAMMERSMITH	8/11/1885	29/2/1908	8	29		10	HITCHIN TOWN	1906		WEST HAM UNITED	1910	
CAPE	JACK	CARLISLE	16/11/1910	28/8/1937	7	65		13	MANCHESTER UNITED	1937		CARLISLE UNITED	1939	
CAREY	PETER	BARKING	14/4/1933	20/5/1960	2	17		1	LEYTON ORIENT	7/1960		COLCHESTER UNITED	11/1960	
CARLISLE	CLARKE	PRESTON	14/10/1979	12/8/2000	3	109	3	6	BLACKPOOL	5/2000	250,000	LEEDS UNITED	5/2004	Free
CARR	WILLIAM	CAMBOIS	6/11/1901	31/8/1935	2	28			DERBY COUNTY	7/1935		BARROW	7/1937	Free
CERNY	RADEK	CZECH REPUBLIC	18/2/1974	9/8/2008	1	47			SLAVIA PRAGUE	7/2008				
CHALKLEY	ALFRED	PLAISTOW		30/12/1944	2	1			WEST HAM UNITED			Guest		
CHALLIS	TREVOR	PADDINGTON	23/10/1975	19/11/1995	A	14	1		Juniors			BRISTOL ROVERS	8/1998	Free
CHANDLER	ARTHUR	PADDINGTON	27/11/1895	1/1/1921	10	86		18	HAMPSTEAD TOWN	1920		LEICESTER CITY	1923	3,000
CHANNING	JUSTIN	READING	19/11/1968	1/11/1986	11	53	14	5	Apprentice	8/1986		BRISTOL ROVERS	1/1993	275,000
CHAPMAN	REG	SHEPHERDS BUSH	7/9/1921	12/1/1946	5	108		4						
CHARLES	JEREMY	SWANSEA	26/5/1959	10/12/1983	12	12	4	6	SWANSEA CITY	11/1983	80,000	OXFORD UNITED	2/1985	80,000
CHARLES	LEE	HILLINGDON	20/8/1971	25/11/1995	A	6	11	1	CHERTSEY TOWN	8/1995	65,000	HAYES	8/1998	Free
CHARLESWORTH	GEORGE	BRISTOL	29/11/1901	4/9/1926	7	23		3	BRISTOL ROVERS			CRYSTAL PALACE	1929	
CHARLTON	WILLIAM	SOUTH STONEHAM	4/6/1912	19/11/1936	8	21		10	WIMBLEDON			BARNET	1938	
CHEETHAM	TOMMY	BYKER	11/10/1910	12/9/1935	9	135		93	ROYAL ARTILLERY	1935		BRENTFORD	3/1939	5,000
CHESTER	ALBERT	HEXHAM		15/11/1919	7	1			CROYDON COMMON			BRENTFORD		
CHIVERS	GARY	STOCKWELL	15/5/1960	7/11/1984	2	67	2		SWANSEA CITY	2/1984	Free	WATFORD	9/1987	Free
CHRISTIE	DAVID	SCOTLAND	1873	1/9/1900	9	10		1	RYDE (I.O.W.)					
CINI	JOE	MALTA		22/8/1959	7	7		1	FLORIANA			Returned to Malta	3/1960	

Surname	Christian	Born	Date	Debut	No	App	Sub	Goal	Signed From	Date	Signed Fee	Transferred To	Date	Transfer Fee
CLARK	CLIVE	ROUNDHAY	19/12/1940	6/9/1958	11	73	1	8	LEEDS UNITED	8/1958		WEST BROMWICH ALBION	1/1961	
									WEST BROMWICH ALBION	6/1969	30,000	PRESTON NORTH END	1/1970	25,000
CLARK	WILLIE	LARKHILL	25/2/1932	6/2/1954	9	97		32	PETERSHILL	2/1954		BERWICK RANGERS	1956	
CLARKE	CHARLIE	FLEET		25/4/1936	8	6						LUTON TOWN	1938	
CLARKE	COLIN	NEWRY	30/10/1962	11/3/1989	9	49	7	14	SOUTHAMPTON	3/1989	750,000	PORTSMOUTH	8/1990	350,000
CLARKE	FRANK	WILLENHALL	15/7/1942	17/2/1968	9	74	2	24	SHREWSBURY TOWN	2/1968	35,000	IPSWICH TOWN	3/1970	38,000
CLARKE	GEORGE	BOLSOVER	24/7/1900	26/8/1933	11	16		6	CRYSTAL PALACE	7/1933		FOLKESTONE	1934	
CLARKE	LEON	BIRMINGHAM	10/2/1985	4/2/2006	10	1			WOLVERHAMPTON WANDERERS	1/2006	Loan	WOLVERHAMPTON WANDERERS	2/2006	Returned
CLAYTON	HORACE	HACKNEY	4/7/1898	17/3/1921	8	6		1						
CLAYTON	LEWIS	ROYSTON	7/6/1924	9/9/1950	4	92		5	BARNSLEY	8/1950		BOURNEMOUTH	5/1955	
CLEMENT	DAVE	BATTERSEA	2/2/1948	8/4/1967	5	472	4	28	Juniors	7/1965		BOLTON WANDERERS	6/1979	170,000
CLIPSHAM				1/11/1902	5	3			WANDSWORTH	1902				
CLUTTERBUCK	HENRY	WHEATENHURST	6/1873	9/9/1899	1	70			SMALL HEATH	8/1899		GRIMSBY TOWN	1901	
COCHRANE	JUSTIN	HACKNEY	26/1/1982	28/4/2001	C		1		Youth Academy			HAYES	8/2002	Free
COCKBURN	WILLIAM	WILLINGTON QUAY	1899	25/8/1928	5	62			LIVERPOOL	1928		SWINDON TOWN	1930	
COCKELL	DAVID	ASHFORD	1/2/1939	17/10/1960	6	11			HOUNSLOW TOWN	8/1960		CRAWLEY TOWN	7/1962	
COGGINS	WILLIAM	BRISTOL	16/9/1901	28/12/1935	1	6			EVERTON			BATH CITY	1936	
COLE	JACK	WALES		1/9/1900	2	1								
COLE	JAKE	HAMMERSMITH	11/9/1985	26/12/2005	1	6	2		Youth Academy			Released	5/2009	
COLEMAN	JOHN	KETTERING	26/10/1881	11/9/1915	8	7		2	NOTTINGHAM FOREST			TUNBRIDGE WELLS		
COLGAN	WALTER	CASTLEFORD	3/4/1937	28/12/1957	2	3			ASHLEY ROAD FC	7/1954			7/1960	
COLLIER	JOHN	DYSART	1/2/1897	28/8/1926	4	37		1	HULL CITY			YORK CITY	1928	
COLLINS	HARRY	WYNLATON	1876	7/9/1901	1	121			BURNLEY	1900		EVERTON	1905	
COLLINS	JAMES	BERMONDSEY	30/1/1911	7/11/1931	8	22		4	TOOTING & MITCHAM			TUNBRIDGE WELLS	1933	
COLLINS	JOHN	CHISWICK	10/8/1942	30/4/1960	8	193		56	Juniors	8/1959		OLDHAM ATHLETIC	10/1966	10,000
COLVIN	ROBERT	DUMFRIES	5/12/1876	3/9/1902	7	11		1	LUTON TOWN	1901		SWINDON TOWN	1903	
COMPTON	LESLIE	WOODFORD	12/9/1912	1940		2		2	ARSENAL			Guest		
CONEY	DEAN	DAGENHAM	18/9/1963	15/8/1987	8	47	15	9	FULHAM	6/1987	50,000	NORWICH CITY	3/1989	
CONGREVE				14/9/1918	6	12		4						
CONNOLLY	KARL	PRESCOT	9/2/1970	20/8/2000	A	61	21	12	WREXHAM	5/2000	Free	SWANSEA CITY	7/2003	Free
CONNOLLY	MATTHEW	BARNET	24/9/1987	5/1/2008	2	54	6		ARSENAL	1/2008	1,000,000			
CONNOR	ROBERT	NEWCASTLE	1913	26/1/1935	11	6						YEOVIL & PETTERS		
COOK	LEE	HAMMERSMITH	3/8/1982	21/12/2002	9	161	17	12	WATFORD	12/2002	Loan	WATFORD	3/2003	Returned
									WATFORD	7/2004	150,000	FULHAM	7/2007	2,500,000
									FULHAM	8/2008	800,000			
COOPER	GARY	EDGWARE	20/11/1965	2/10/1984	14	2	2		Apprentice			FISHER ATHLETIC		
COPE	WILLIAM	STOKE ON TRENT	25/11/1884	21/9/1918	7	3			WEST HAM UNITED					
CORBETT	WALTER	WELLINGTON	26/11/1880	7/9/1907	2	1			SOHO VILLA	1904	Loan	ASTON VILLA		
									BIRMINGHAM	1907	Loan	BIRMINGHAM		
COTTAM				25/12/1941	7	1								
COUSINS	HARRY			17/11/1917	8	3								
COWAN	DAVE			16/12/1905	11	1		1						
COWARD	WILLIAM	WINDSOR		31/3/1928	7	138		28	WINDSOR & ETON	1/1928		WALSALL		
COWIE	ANDREW	LOCHEE	1879	9/9/1899	11	16		2	MANCHESTER CITY	8/1899		WOOLWICH ARSENAL	1900	
CRACK	FREDERICK	LINCOLN	12/1/1919	25/8/1945	11	3		3	GRIMSBY TOWN			Guest		
CRANIE	MARTIN	YEOVIL	23/9/1986	8/10/2007	4	6			PORTSMOUTH	10/2007	Loan	PORTSMOUTH	11/2007	Returned
CRAWFORD	GAVIN	GALSTON	1867	9/9/1899	4	33		1	MILLWALL ATHLETIC	8/1899				
CRAWFORD	JACKIE	JARROW	26/9/1896	25/8/1934	11	59		18	CHELSEA	1934		Retired	1937	
CRIBB	STANLEY	GOSPORT	11/5/1905	29/8/1931	11	32		18	WEST HAM UNITED	1931		CARDIFF CITY		
CRICKSON	GEORGE	DOVER	21/9/1934	6/4/1953	4	6			Juniors	9/1951		DOVER		
CROMPTON	NORMAN	FARNWORTH	1905	3/5/1928	5	1			OLDHAM ATHLETIC	1928		HORWICH RMI		
CROSS	JOHN		1879	3/9/1904	6	24			THIRD LANARK	1904				
CROSS	WILLIAM			5/9/1903	7	33		4	THIRD LANARK	1903		BRENTFORD	1905	
CROSSLAND				29/12/1917	10	1						Guest		

Surname	Christian	Born	Date	Debut	No	App	Sub	Goal	Signed From	Date	Signed Fee	Transferred To	Date	Transfer Fee
CROSSLEY	CHARLIE	HEDNESFORD	1892	6/4/1917	11	3			SUNDERLAND			Guest		
CROUCH	PETER	MACCLESFIELD	30/1/1981	12/8/2000	10	42	5	12	TOTTENHAM HOTSPUR	7/2000	60,000	PORTSMOUTH	7/2001	1,250,000
CRUIKSHANK	J			20/1/1945	1	1						Guest		
CULKIN	NICK	YORK	6/7/1978	10/8/2002	1	25			MANCHESTER UNITED	7/2002	Free	Retired from football	5/2005	
CULLIP	DANNY	BRACKNELL	17/9/1976	3/2/2007	3	19	1		NOTTINGHAM FOREST	1/2007	Free	Released	11/2007	
CUNNINGHAM	JOEL	LOCHIE	1905	30/10/1926	1	174			NEWPORT COUNTY	1926		WALSALL		1932
CUNNINGHAM	TOMMY	BETHNAL GREEN	7/12/1955	2/10/1976	8	31	4	2	CHELSEA	5/1975	0	WIMBLEDON	3/1979	50,000
CURETON	JAMIE	BRISTOL	28/8/1975	7/2/2004	B	23	23	7	BUSCAN ICONS	2/2004	100,000	SWINDON TOWN	7/2005	Free
CURRIE	TONY	EDGWARE	1/1/1950	5/9/1979	10	96	2	6	LEEDS UNITED	8/1979	400,000	VANCOUVER WHITECAPS	5/1983	40,000
CURTIS	JOHN	NUNEATON	3/9/1978	11/8/2007	5	3	2		NOTTINGHAM FOREST	7/2007	Free	Released	12/2007	
CZERKAS	ADAM	SOKOLOW, POLAND	13/7/1984	5/8/2006	11	3	1		ODRA WODZISLAW, POLAND	7/2006	Loan	ODRA WODZISLAW, POLAND	1/2007	Returned
DALE	A.			25/12/1941	3	1						Guest		
DALE	GEORGE	NOTTINGHAM	2/5/1883	30/10/1915	8	110		40	NOTTS COUNTY			CHELSEA		
DALY	WES	HAMMERSMITH	7/3/1984	16/3/2002	8	5	6		Youth Academy			GRAYS ATHLETIC	3/2005	Free
DAND	ROBERT	ILFORD		25/12/1924	4	1			READING			MARGATE		
DANIELS	ARTHUR	MANCHESTER	9/5/	30/8/1930	11	14		3	WATFORD	1930				
DANIELS	HARRY	KENSINGTON	25/6/1920	1940		101		13	Local Club	10/1944		BRIGHTON & HOVE ALBION	8/1948	
DARLINGTON	JERMAINE	HACKNEY	11/4/1974	10/4/1999	4	78	1	2	AYLESBURY UNITED	3/1999	25,000	WIMBLEDON	7/2001	200,000
DARRAGON	W.			9/12/1944	7	12		2		1944				
DAVIDSON	PETER	NEWCASTLE	31/10/1956	25/8/1979	12		1		BERWICK RANGERS	7/1979	40,000	BERWICK RANGERS	12/1979	35,000
DAVIE	JOHN	DUMFERMLINE	19/2/1913	26/4/1941		9		7	BRIGHTON			Guest		
DAVIES	ANDREW	STOCKTON-ON-TEES	17/12/1984	14/1/2005	4	9			MIDDLESBROUGH	1/2005	Loan	MIDDLESBROUGH	4/2005	Returned
DAVIES	EDMUND	OSWESTRY	5/6/1927	27/1/1951	9	1		1	ARSENAL	4/1950		CREWE ALEXANDRA	7/1951	
DAVIS	ARTHUR	BIRMINGHAM	1900	28/8/1922	10	67		22	ASTON VILLA	1922		NOTTS COUNTY	1924	
DAWES	FREDERICK	FRIMLEY GREEN	2/5/1911	23/9/1944	3	11			CRYSTAL PALACE			Guest		
DAWES	IAN	CROYDON	22/2/1963	27/2/1982	3	270		4	Apprentice	12/1980		MILLWALL	8/1988	150,000
DAWSON	ALEC	GLASGOW	21/10/1933	13/4/1957	7	67		7	GOUROCK JUNIORS	2/1957		SITTINGBOURNE	7/1959	
DAWSON	GEORGE	GLASGOW	13/9/1930	10/3/1956	6	1			MOTHERWELL	5/1955				
DAY	CHRIS	WHIPPS CROSS	28/7/1975	11/8/2001	1	100			WATFORD	7/2001	Free	OLDHAM ATHLETIC	5/2005	
DAY				8/3/1913	9	4								
DE BUSSER	EMUIEL			28/8/1943	8	3		1	BELGIAN ARMY	8/1943				
DE LISLE				1/4/1944	7	1		1	SOUTHAMPTON	4/1944	Loan			
DE ORNELAS	FERNANDO	CARACAS, VENEZUELA	29/7/1976	27/10/2001	C	1	1		DEPORTIVO ITAL CHACAO	10/2001	Trial	(Not Taken on)	10/2001	
DEAN	JOBEY	CHESTERFIELD	25/11/1934	30/8/1955	9	17			THORESBY COLLIERY	11/1952		SUTTON TOWN	12/1957	
DEAN	W.			11/3/1944	7	2		2				Guest		
DELANEY	DAMIEN	CORK, IRELAND	20/7/1981	19/1/2008	5	57	2	3	HULL CITY	1/2008	600,000			
DELANEY	LOUIS	BOTHWELL	28/2/1921	6/4/1942	2	1			ARSENAL					
DELVE	JOHN	ISLEWORTH	27/9/1953	9/12/1972	9	10	7		Apprentice	7/1971		PLYMOUTH ARGYLE	7/1974	25,000
DENNIS	MARK	STREATHAM	2/5/1961	15/8/1987	3	33	3		SOUTHAMPTON	5/1987	50,000	CRYSTAL PALACE	8/1989	50,000
DENOON	JOCK	INVERNESS	10/4/1890	13/1/1917	1	89								
DEVINE	JOE	MOTHERWELL	8/9/1905	26/8/1933	10	65		10	SUNDERLAND	1933		BIRMINGHAM CITY	1/1935	
DEVINE	JOHN	ABERDEEN		27/8/1938	8	10		3	ABERDEEN	1938				
DI CARMINE	SAMUEL	FLORENCE, ITALY	20/9/1988	12/8/2008	A	18	14	3	FIORENTINA	7/2008	Loan	FIORENTINA	5/2009	Returned
DICHIO	DANIELE	HAMMERSMITH	19/10/1974	25/10/1994	24	66	22	23	Juniors			SAMPDORIA	6/1997	Free
DIGBY	FRAZER	SHEFFIELD	23/4/1967	3/11/2001	1	24	2		HUDDERSFIELD TOWN	11/2001	Loan	Released	1/2003	
DINES	JOSEPH	KINGS LYNN	12/4/1886	16/4/1910	4	1			KINGS LYNN			ILFORD		
DOBINSON	HAROLD	DARLINGTON	2/3/1898	20/10/1923	9	2			BURNLEY	7/1923				
DODD	GEORGE	WHITCHURCH	7/2/1885	14/9/1918	8	1			WEST HAM UNITED					
DOHERTY	TOMMY	BRISTOL	17/3/1979	6/8/2005	8	14	1		BRISTOL CITY	7/2005	Free	WYCOMBE WANDERERS	8/2006	Loan
												WYCOMBE WANDERERS	1/2007	Free
DOLDING	DESMOND	INDIA	13/12/1922	11/9/1943	10	1			CHELSEA					
DONALD	DAVID	COATBRIDGE	29/12/1878	12/9/1914	11	119		12	WATFORD	1914		HAMILTON	5/1921	
DONNELLY	SCOTT	HAMMERSMITH	25/12/1987	19/10/2004	A	3	11		Youth Academy			Released from contract	1/2007	
DOWIE	IAIN	HATFIELD	9/1/1965	31/1/1998	9	16	18	2	WEST HAM UNITED	1/1998	Sinclair (part)	Resigned	3/2001	

Surname	Christian	Born	Date	Debut	No	App	Sub	Goal	Signed From	Date	Signed Fee	Transferred To	Date	Transfer Fee
DOWNING	SAMUEL	WILLESDEN	19/1/1883	7/11/1903	6	170		13	WEST HAMPSTEAD	4/1903		CHELSEA	1909	
DOWNING	T.			1/9/1900	8	20		10						
DOWNING				2/3/1918	5	16		1						
DOYLE	MAURICE	ELLESMERE PORT	17/10/1969	9/2/1993	4	6			CREWE ALEXANDRA	4/1989	40,000	MILLWALL	5/1995	25,000
DRABBLE	FRANK	SOUTHPORT	8/7/1888	1/3/1924	1	2			SOUTHPORT				Retired	
DRAKE	ALONZO	ROTHERHAM	16/4/1884	1/9/1908	10	20		5	BIRMINGHAM	1908		HUDDERSFIELD TOWN	1910	
DRAPER	WILLIAM			4/9/1915	3	101								
DREW	WILLIAM			18/9/1926	7	1			BARNET					
DRINKWATER	RAY	JARROW	18/5/1931	15/3/1958	1	216			PORTSMOUTH	2/1958		BATH CITY	6/1963	
DRYSDALE				2/9/1916	10	1						Guest		
DUDLEY	REG	HEMEL HEMPSTEAD	3/2/1915	7/12/1946	2	62			MILLWALL	12/1946		WATFORD	7/1950	
DUFF	HARRY			7/9/1908	4	22			MANCHESTER CITY					
DUFFIELD	MARTIN	PARK ROYAL	28/2/1964	14/5/1983	12		1		Apprentice	1/1982		ENFIELD		
DUFFIELD				9/2/1918	1	4								
DUGDALE	JIMMY	LIVERPOOL	15/1/1932	22/10/1962	5	13			ASTON VILLA	10/1962	6,000	Retired		
DUGGAN	TED	WEST HAM	27/7/1922	5/2/1949	8	48		5	LUTON TOWN	2/1949		WORCESTER CITY		
DUKE	GEORGE	CHICHESTER	6/9/1920	16/9/1944	1	2			LUTON TOWN			Guest		
DUKES	HAROLD	PORTSMOUTH	31/3/1912	11/12/1943	1	2			NORWICH CITY			Guest		
DUMSDAY	JOHN			1940		1								
DURRANT	FRED	DOVER	19/6/1921	28/9/1946	9	53		26	BRENTFORD	9/1946	5,000	EXETER CITY	2/1949	4,000
DURSTON	JACK	CLOPHILL	11/7/1893	2/9/1916	1	13								
DUTHIE	JOHN	FRASERBURGH	7/1/1903	22/10/1927	10	11			NORWICH CITY			YORK CITY	1928	
DUTTON	TOM	SOUTHPORT	11/11/1906	25/8/1934	6	26		6	LEICESTER CITY	1934		DONCASTER ROVERS	6/1935	
DYER	LLOYD	ASTON	13/9/1982	27/9/2005	5	15			WEST BROMWICH ALBION	9/2005	Loan	WEST BROMWICH	12/2005	Returned
DYKSTRA	SIEB	KERKRADE, NETHERLANDS	20/10/1966	22/10/1994	13	12			MOTHERWELL	7/1994	250,000	DUNDEE UNITED	12/1996	50,000
EASTHAM	GEORGE	BLACKPOOL	13/8/1914	6/9/1941	8	9		2	BLACKPOOL			Guest		
EASTOE	PETER	TAMWORTH	2/8/1953	16/10/1976	12	80	5	20	SWINDON TOWN	3/1976	90,000	EVERTON	3/1979	WALSH
EATON	FRANK	STOCKPORT	12/11/1902	26/8/1933	8	19		2	READING	7/1933				
EDGHILL	RICHARD	OLDHAM	23/9/1974	30/8/2003	B	33	13		SHEFFIELD UNITED	8/2003	Free	BRADFORD CITY	7/2005	Free
EDGLEY	HAROLD	CREWE	1/1892	27/8/1921	7	75		6	ASTON VILLA	1921		STOCKPORT COUNTY	6/1923	
EDWARDS	ALBERT			29/11/1902	6	17		1	SWINDON TOWN	1902			1906	
EDWARDS	E.			1940		6								
EDWARDS	JOHN		1875	7/9/1901	6	29		2	GRAYS UNITED	1901				
EDWARDS	JOSEPH			2/4/1926	7	3								
EDWARDS	R.			11/4/1942	3	1								
EDWARDS				17/11/1917	10	1						Guest		
EGGLETON	JIMMY	HESTON	29/8/1897	27/12/1926	5	43			WATFORD	10/1926		Became Club Trainer		
ELLIOTT				16/10/1915	7	1						Guest		
ELSEY	KARL	SWANSEA	20/11/1958	24/3/1979	11	6	1		PEMBROKE BOROUGH	1/1979		NEWPORT COUNTY	7/1980	
EMBLETON	SID	POPLAR	1906	7/3/1931	7	2			WALTHAMSTOW AVENUE	1930				
EMMERSON	GEORGE	BISHOP AUCKLAND	15/5/1906	26/8/1933	7	60		16	CARDIFF CITY	7/1933	Marcroft	ROCHDALE	1935	
EPHRAIM	HOGAN	ISLINGTON	31/3/1988	11/8/2007	A	37	22	3	WEST HAM UNITED	7/2007	Loan	WEST HAM UNITED	11/2007	Returned
									WEST HAM UNITED	1/2008	800,000			
EVANS	BERNARD	CHESTER	4/1/1937	19/11/1960	9	84		39	WREXHAM	11/1960		OXFORD UNITED	12/1962	
EVANS	CHARLES	LUTON		1/2/1930	8	1				1/1929				
EVANS	F.			27/11/1943	2	1						Guest		
EVANS	IAN	EGHAM	30/1/1952	6/4/1971	5	42		2	Apprentice	1/1970		CRYSTAL PALACE	9/1974	30,000
EVANS	J. LLOYD			25/2/1905	7	1						BRENTFORD	1907	
EVANS	RHYS	SWINDON	27/1/1982	26/2/2002	1	11			CHELSEA	11/2001	Loan	CHELSEA	5/2002	Returned
EVANS	ROGER	BANGOR	17/11/1879	15/3/1902	9	1			ILFORD	1901		CLAPTON		1902
EVANS	WILLIAM	LLANGLOS		20/9/1924	2	17			SOUTHEND UNITED					
EVANS	WILLIAM	LLANSANTFFRAID		7/10/1899	11	13		6	LONDON WELSH	1899		LINCOLN CITY		
EVATT	IAN	COVENTRY	19/11/1981	23/8/2005	3	22	6		CHESTERFIELD	7/2005	100,000	BLACKPOOL	8/2006	Loan
												BLACKPOOL	1/2007	Free

Surname	Christian	Born	Date	Debut	No	App	Sub	Goal	Signed From	Date	Signed Fee	Transferred To	Date	Transfer Fee
FALCO	MARK	HACKNEY	22/10/1960	5/12/1987	8	81	25	33	GLASGOW RANGERS	12/1987	400,000	MILLWALL	8/1991	175,000
FALLON	PETER	DUBLIN	19/10/1922	19/9/1953	6	1			EXETER CITY	8/1953		Retired - injury	7/1954	
FARMER	ALEC	LOCHGELLY	9/10/1908	3/2/1934	5	178		11	NOTTINGHAM FOREST			QPR Assistant Trainer		
FARROW	DESMOND	PETERBOROUGH	11/2/1926	25/11/1944	6	158		7	LEICESTER CITY	1944		STOKE CITY	10/1952	
FAULKNER	ROBERT	GLASGOW		28/8/1920	7	52		1	BLACKBURN ROVERS			SOUTH SHIELDS	1923	
FENWICK	HARRISON	ASHINGTON		4/10/1924	4	19			SHILDON UNITED					
FENWICK	TERRY	SEAHAM	17/11/1959	19/12/1980	4	307	1	45	CRYSTAL PALACE	12/1980	100,000	TOTTENHAM HOTSPUR	12/1987	550,000
FERDINAND	LES	PADDINGTON	18/12/1966	20/4/1987	12	169	14	90	HAYES	4/1987	15,000	NEWCASTLE UNITED	6/1995	6,000,000
FEREDAY	WAYNE	WARLEY	16/6/1963	19/8/1980	7	206	36	25	Apprentice	9/1980		NEWCASTLE UNITED	7/1989	300,000
FERGUSON	CHRIS	KIRKCONNEL		13/9/1930	8	15		1	CHELSEA	1930		WREXHAM	1931	
FERGUSON	JAMES			19/2/1910	7	2								
FERGUSON	MIKE	BURNLEY	9/3/1943	22/11/1969	8	76	1	3	ASTON VILLA	11/1969	20,000	CAMBRIDGE UNITED	7/1973	Free
FERRIER	HAROLD	RATHO	20/5/1920	30/12/1944	4	1			BARNSLEY			Guest		
FIDLER	JOSEPH	SHEFFIELD	1885	29/9/1906	3	192			FULHAM	1906		WOOLWICH ARSENAL	1913	
FIDLER	TOM	HOUNSLOW	4/9/1933	24/8/1954	9	14		4	HOUNSLOW	5/1954		DOVER		
FIELD	WILLIAM	OXFORD		19/1/1924	1	29			OXFORD CITY					
FILLERY	MIKE	MITCHAM	17/9/1960	27/8/1983	12	114	3	10	CHELSEA	8/1983	175,000	PORTSMOUTH	7/1987	Free
FINCH	BOBBY	CAMBERWELL	24/8/1948	16/4/1968	2	6	1		Apprentice	8/1966		DURBAN CITY, SOUTH AFRICA		
FINNEY	WILLIAM	STOKE-ON-TRENT	5/9/1931	24/8/1957	9	10		1	BIRMINGHAM CITY	5/1957		CREWE ALEXANDRA	7/1958	
FITZGERALD	ALFRED	CONISBOROUGH	25/1/1911	7/11/1936	10	124		57	READING	1936		ALDERSHOT		
FITZGERALD	BRIAN	PERIVALE	23/10/1983	12/1/2002	B		1		Youth Academy			NORTHWOOD	7/2003	Free
FLANAGAN	MIKE	ILFORD	9/11/1952	19/12/1980	7	86	7	22	CRYSTAL PALACE	12/1980	150,000	CHARLTON ATHLETIC	1/1984	50,000
FLEMING	JIM			10/3/1917	9	1						Guest		
FLEMING	MARK	HAMMERSMITH	11/8/1969	27/2/1988	12	1	4		Trainee	1/1988		BRENTFORD	7/1989	Free
FLETCHER	JACK			23/12/1905	8	41		13	WEST HAM UNITED	1905				
FLETCHER	JACK	TYNE DOCK	1910	4/9/1935	8	20			BOURNEMOUTH	1935		CLAPTON ORIENT		
FOLEY	DOMINIC	CORK, IRELAND	7/7/1976	27/10/2001	11	3	2	1	WATFORD	10/2001	Loan	WATFORD	10/2001	Returned
									WATFORD	3/2002	Loan	WATFORD	5/2002	Returned
FORBES	TERREL	SOUTHWARK	17/8/1981	11/8/2001	2	128	2		WEST HAM UNITED	7/2001	Free	GRIMSBY TOWN	9/2004	
FORD	EWART	BEDWORTH		30/8/1924	11	64		4	HINKLEY UNITED			MERTHYR TOWN		
FORSTYH	JIM			6/1/1945	4	3						Guest		
FORTUNE	JAMES	DUBLIN	1890	11/10/1913	11	13			BARROW	1912		BRISTOL ROVERS		
FOSTER	CYRIL	AYLESBURY	1910	20/10/1928	8	5			WATFORD	1928				
FOWLER	ALAN	ROTHWELL	20/11/1911	31/5/1941		3			SWINDON TOWN			Guest		
FOX	GEORGE			4/9/1915		128		15						
FOX	T.S.			14/4/1906	3	1								
FOXALL	ABRAHAM	SHEFFIELD	1874	1/9/1900	11	31		4	LIVERPOOL	1900		WOOLWICH ARSENAL	1903	
FRANCIS	E.			1940		1								
FRANCIS	GEORGE	ACTON	4/2/1934	13/9/1961	9	3		3	BRENTFORD	5/1961	8,000 (inc Towers)	BRENTFORD	11/1961	
FRANCIS	GERRY	CHISWICK	6/12/1951	29/3/1969	12	347	5	65	Apprentice	6/1969	Free	CRYSTAL PALACE	7/1979	450,000
									CRYSTAL PALACE	2/1980	150,000	COVENTRY CITY	2/1982	150,000
FRANCIS	TREVOR	PLYMOUTH	19/4/1954	26/3/1988	12	40	2	15	GLASGOW RANGERS	3/1988	Free	SHEFFIELD WEDNESDAY	1/1990	Free
FREEMAN	BEN	BIRMINGHAM	10/1878	7/9/1901	4	53		1	GRAYS UNITED	1901				
FRY	BOB	PONTYPRIDD	29/6/1935	14/12/1957	1	2			BATH CITY	8/1957		BEXLEY HEATH		
FURLONG	PAUL	LONDON	1/10/1968	20/8/2000	10	149	34	58	BIRMINGHAM CITY	8/2000	Loan	BIRMINGHAM CITY	8/2000	Returned
									BIRMINGHAM CITY	8/2002	Free	Released	5/2007	
GADSDEN	RON			25/12/1942	8	10			Juniors					
GALLEN	KEVIN	CHISWICK	21/9/1975	20/8/1994	20	338	65	97	Juniors			HUDDERSFIELD TOWN	7/2000	Free
									BARNSLEY	10/2001		Released	5/2007	
GARDNER	ANDREW	LEITH	26/9/1877	2/9/1905	11	5			BRIGHTON	1905		Retired	1906	
GARDNER	WILLIAM	LANGLEY PARK	7/6/1893	7/4/1923	10	2			SPENNYMOOR	1922		ASHINGTON	1923	
GAUL	WILLIAM			21/12/1912	9	16		9						
GAYLARD	HUGH			30/9/1899	2	7				1899				
GERMAN	ANTONIO	LONDON	26/12/1991	14/3/2009	A	0	3		Youth Academy					

Surname	Christian	Born	Date	Debut	No	App	Sub	Goal	Signed From	Date	Signed Fee	Transferred To	Date	Transfer Fee
GIBBONS	JOHN	CHARLTON	8/4/1925	23/10/1948	9	9		2	DARTFORD	12/1947		IPSWICH TOWN	5/1949	
GIBBS	DEREK	FULHAM	22/12/1934	24/8/1963	6	29			LEYTON ORIENT	8/1963	5,000	ROMFORD		
GIBBS-KENNETT	R.			6/4/1942	9	1								
GILBERG	HARRY	TOTTENHAM	27/6/1923	18/8/1951	6	70		12	TOTTENHAM HOTSPUR	8/1951		BRIGHTON & HOVE ALBION	12/1952	
GILFILLAN	JOHN	TOWNHILL	29/9/1898	16/10/1937	1	24			PORTSMOUTH	1937				
GILHOOLEY	MICHAEL	GLENCRAIG	26/11/1896	27/8/1927	5	9			BRADFORD CITY				1928	
GILLARD	IAN	HAMMERSMITH	9/10/1950	23/11/1968	3	479	5	11	Apprentice	10/1968		ALDERSHOT	7/1982	
GILLESPIE	J.		1886	5/12/1908	2	1			THIRD LANARK					
GILLIES	MATTHEW	LOGANLEA	12/8/1921	11/3/1944	5	31		2	BOLTON WANDERERS			Guest		
GILMORE	HENRY	WEST HARTLEPOOL	1913	24/12/1938	6	10			BOURNEMOUTH	1937		HULL CITY	1939	Free
GITTENS	ALFRED	MANCHESTER	7/1886	2/9/1907	10	46		17	LUTON TOWN	1907		CROYDON COMMON	1908	
												ASTON VILLA	1909	
GIVENS	DON	LIMERICK	9/8/1949	12/8/1972	11	293	1	101	LUTON TOWN	7/1972	40,000	BIRMINGHAM CITY	8/1978	150,000
GLOVER	ALAN	LALEHAM	21/10/1950	4/1/1969	10	6	1		Apprentice	3/1968		WEST BROMWICH ALBION	6/1969	70,000
GNOHERE	ARTHUR	YAMOUSSOUKRO	20/11/1978	6/9/2003	4	22	1	1	BURNLEY	9/2003	Loan	BURNLEY	10/2003	Returned
									BURNLEY	2/2004		Contract Terminated	3/2005	
GODDARD	GEORGE	GOMSHALL	20/12/1903	11/9/1926	9	260		186	REDHILL	6/1926		BRENTFORD	12/1933	
GODDARD	PAUL	HARLINGTON	12/10/1959	11/4/1978	12	67	8	23	Apprentice	7/1977		WEST HAM UNITED	8/1980	1,000,000
GODDARD	THOMAS			2/12/1916	11	13		1						
GOFTON	GEORGE	HARTLEPOOL	28/2/1912	22/10/1932	9	11		8	NEWCASTLE UNITED	1932				
GOLDIE	WILLIAM	SCOTLAND		8/9/1900	9	9		3						
GOLDING	JIMMY	SOUTHWARK	23/1/1937	14/9/1959	7	32		6	TONBRIDGE	8/1959		KETTERING TOWN		
GOODIER	TED	FARNWORTH	15/10/1902	14/11/1931	6	155		2	OLDHAM ATHLETIC	11/1931	1500+Adlam	WATFORD	1935	LOWE
GOODMAN	WILLIAM	ISLINGTON	1894	18/4/1924	11	1								
GOODRIDGE	GREGORY	BARBADOS	10/7/1971	3/10/1995	B		9	1	TORQUAY UNITED	7/1995	300,000	BRISTOL CITY	7/1996	50,000
GORKSS	KASPARS	LATVIA	16/11/1981	9/8/2008	4	33	2		BLACKPOOL	7/2008				
GOUGH	CLAUDE	SOUTH CERNEY	17/10/1901	28/8/1926	6	19			CLAPTON ORIENT			TORQUAY UNITED		
GOULD	HARRY	LONDON		26/3/1921	1	2			X DIV MET POLICE	1920				
GRAHAM	MALCOLM	WAKEFIELD	26/1/1934	24/8/1963	10	23		8	LEYTON ORIENT	7/1963	5,000	BARNSLEY	7/1964	
GRAHAM	MARK	NEWRY	24/10/1974	18/9/1996	7	20	3		Trainee			CAMBRIDGE UNITED	7/1999	Free
GRAHAM	RICHARD	NEWRY	24/10/1974	29/9/1998	13		2		Trainee	5/1996		CHESHAM UNITED	9/2001	Free
GRANT	GEORGE	PLUMSTEAD	1891	28/8/1920	5	72		1	MILLWALL ATHLETIC	1920		NORTHFLEET	1922	
GRAY	ANDY	LAMBETH	22/2/1964	4/2/1989	8	11		2	ASTON VILLA	2/1989	450,000	CRYSTAL PALACE	8/1989	500,000
GRAY	TOM	GRIMSBY	1876	1/9/1900	7	32		10	NEW BROMPTON			BURY	1901	
GREEN	H.			2/9/1916	7	7								
GREEN	TOM	ROCK FERRY	25/11/1883	1/9/1906	7	39		8	MIDDLESBROUGH	1906		STOCKPORT COUNTY	1907	
GREENWOOD	RON	BURNLEY	11/11/1921	4/3/1944	5	1			CHELSEA			Guest		
GREER	WALTER			25/12/1908	9	34		7						
GREGORY	CLARENCE	BIRMINGHAM		26/8/1922	11	24		1	SUNDERLAND	1922		YEOVIL & PETTERS		
GREGORY	ERNEST	STRATFORD	10/11/1921	23/9/1944	1	20			WEST HAM UNITED			Guest		
GREGORY	JOHN	SCUNTHORPE	11/5/1954	29/8/1981	2	188	2	43	BRIGHTON	6/1981	275,000	DERBY COUNTY	12/1985	100,000
GREGORY	JOHN	BIRMINGHAM		7/12/1912	9	241		59	WILLENHALL SWIFTS	1912		YEOVIL TOWN (player / manager)	1923	
GRENDON	FRANK	FARNHAM	5/9/1891	9/12/1916	6	88		1				NORTHAMPTON TOWN		
GRETTON	THOMAS	WALSALL		7/12/1929	1	4			WOLVERHAMPTON UNITED	1929		WALSALL	1930	
GRIFFEN				13/10/1917	8	3								
GRIFFITHS	JAMES	STAIRFOOT	23/2/1914	30/10/1943	7	3		1	PORTSMOUTH			ALDERSHOT		
GRIFFITHS	LEROY	LONDON	30/12/1976	11/8/2001	A	27	10	3	HAMPTON & RICHMOND	6/2001	40,000	FARNBOROUGH TOWN	7/2003	Free
GRIFFITHS	ROBERT	CHAPELTOWN		9/11/1940		1			CHELSEA			Guest		
GRIMSDELL	ERNEST	WATFORD	1/1/1892	4/9/1920	3	23			WATFORD	1920		GUILDFORD UNITED		
									GUILDFORD UNITED			DARTFORD	1923	
GULLAN	STANLEY	EDINBURGH	26/1/1926	6/9/1950	1	48			CLYDE	7/1949		TUNBRIDGE WELLS		
GUNNER	R.			21/3/1942	4	14								
HAGGAN	JOHN			26/4/1920	5	1								
HALES				9/2/1918	7	1						Guest		

Surname	Christian	Born	Date	Debut	No	App	Sub	Goal	Signed From	Date	Signed Fee	Transferred To	Date	Transfer Fee
HALEY	WILLIAM	BEXLEYHEATH	16/2/1904	31/8/1931	8	17		5	FULHAM	1931		DARTFORD	1932	
HALFORD	DAVID	CROXLEY GREEN	19/10/1915	31/5/1941		12		3	OLDHAM ATHLETIC			Guest		
HALL	ERNEST	BARNDALE		5/9/1931	3	71			BEDWORTH TOWN	1930		CHESTER		
HALL	FITZ	LEYTONSTONE	20/12/1980	5/1/2008	3	36	6	2	WIGAN ATHLETIC	1/2008	700,000			
HAMILTON	BILLY	BELFAST	9/5/1957	2/12/1978	12	10	3	2	LINFIELD	4/1978	25,000	BURNLEY	11/1979	60,000
HAMILTON	DAVID	CARLISLE	8/2/1919	29/12/1945	7	3			SOUTHEND UNITED			Guest		
HAMILTON	JOHN	NOTTINGHAM		28/8/1926	7	10			BLACKPOOL	7/1926		SUTTON TOWN		
HAMILTON	JOHN	GLASGOW	1880	3/9/1902	8	50		3	MILLWALL ATHLETIC					
HAMILTON	LEWIS	DERBY	21/11/1984	19/4/2005	A		1		DERBY COUNTY	8/2005	Free	ALDERSHOT TOWN	7/2005	Free
HAMMOND	JOSEPH	WEST HAM	1909	14/4/1934	7	21		7	LONDON PAPER MILL	1/1934				
HANDFORTH	ERNEST			14/9/1901	11	3								
HANFORD				9/2/1918	9	1						Guest		
HANNAH	JAMES	GLASGOW		25/11/1899	8	20		2	SUNDERLAND	1899				
HARDY	EDGAR			10/4/1944	11	1						Guest		
HARKOUK	RACHID	CHELSEA	19/5/1956	26/8/1978	12	18	6	3	CRYSTAL PALACE	6/1978	100,000	NOTTS COUNTY	6/1980	50,000
HARPER	LEE	CHELSEA	30/10/1971	9/8/1997	1	129	2		ARSENAL	7/1997	250,000	WALSALL	7/2001	Free
HARRIS	ALLAN	HACKNEY	28/12/1942	19/8/1967	3	94	4		CHELSEA	7/1967	30,000	PLYMOUTH ARGYLE	3/1971	9,500
HARRIS	BERNARD	SHEFFIELD	14/3/1901	31/8/1929	3	67			LUTON TOWN	1929		SWINDON TOWN	7/1933	
HARRIS	GEORGE	HIGH WYCOMBE	1898	10/9/1924	6	43			NOTTS COUNTY			FULHAM	1926	
HARRIS	NEIL	GLASGOW	9/2/1920	25/12/1941	9	3		3	SWANSEA TOWN	9/1946			1947	Free
HARRISON	JAMES	HAMMERSMITH	31/7/1928	3/1/1953	6	6		1		2/1952				
HART	ERNEST	HUDDERSFIELD		4/11/1922	10	5		2	FOLKESTONE			GUILDFORD UNITED		
HART	GEORGE	GOSFORTH		27/10/1923	4	6		1	BEDLINGTON COLLIERY	7/1923		DURHAM CITY		
HARTBURN	JOHN	DURHAM	20/12/1920	23/8/1947	7	63		13	YEOVIL TOWN	3/1947		WATFORD	9/1949	
HARTWELL	AMBROSE	EXETER	28/6/1883	1/9/1909	5	64		4	BRADFORD (PA)	1909		KIDDERMINSTER	1911	
HASSAN	VICTOR			2/12/1916	8	25		10						
HASTY	PADDY	BELFAST	17/3/1932	26/12/1959	11	1			LEYTON ORIENT	10/1959		TOOTING & MITCHAM		
HATELEY	MARK	LIVERPOOL	7/11/1961	29/11/1995	A	21	12	5	GLASGOW RANGERS	10/1995	1,250,000	GLASGOW RANGERS	3/1997	400,000
HATTON	CYRIL	GRANTHAM	14/9/1918	14/2/1942	10	206		93	NOTTS COUNTY		Brown	CHESTERFIELD	6/1953	
HAWKINS	BERT	BRISTOL	29/9/1923	19/8/1953	9	8		3	WEST HAM UNITED	6/1953		CHELTENHAM	7/1954	
HAWKINS				9/2/1918	2	1						Guest		
HAWLEY	FRED	DERBY	28/7/1890	28/8/1926	5	29		1	BRIGHTON			LOUGHBOROUGH CORINTHIANS	1928	
HAYWOOD	ADAM	HORNINGLOW	23/3/1875	9/9/1899	8	27		9	WOOLWICH ARSENAL	8/1899		NEW BROMPTON	1900	
HAZELL	BOB	KINGSTON, JAMAICA	14/6/1959	5/9/1979	5	117	7	9	WOLVERHAMPTON	9/1979	240,000	LEICESTER CITY	9/1983	100,000
HAZELL	TONY	HIGH WYCOMBE	19/9/1947	3/10/1964	4	407	8	5	Juniors	10/1964		MILLWALL	12/1974	40,000
HEATH	BILL	STEPNEY	26/6/1920	7/3/1942	9	124		14				DOVER	7/1953	
HEATHCOTE	WILLIAM	HEMSWORTH	29/6/1911	13/2/1943	9	102		89				MILLWALL	12/1946	
HEBDEN	GEORGE	WEST HAM	2/6/1900	29/8/1925	1	64			LEICESTER CITY			GILLINGHAM	1927	
HEINOLA	ANTTI	HELSINKI, FINLAND	20/3/1973	21/1/1998	13	27	12		SC HERCULES	1/1998	150,000	Retired from football	3/2001	
HELGUSON	HEIDAR	AKUREYRI, ICELAND	22/8/1977	29/11/2008	A	15	6	5	BOLTON WANDERERS	11/2008	750,000			
HELLAWELL	MICHAEL	KEIGHLEY	30/6/1938	25/2/1956	11	50		8	SALTS	8/1955		BIRMINGHAM CITY	5/1957	
HENLEY	LESLIE	LAMBETH	26/9/1922	3/10/1942	4	3			ARSENAL			Guest		
HERRERA	ROBERT	TORQUAY	12/6/1970	14/1/1989	12	6	5		Trainee	2/1988		FULHAM	3/1994	60,000
HIBBS	R.			1/1/1946	8	1								
HICKS	A.			23/10/1915	7	21		3						
HIGGINS	ALEX	SHEFFIELD	17/11/1979	6/5/2001	B		1		SHEFFIELD WEDNESDAY	3/2001	Free	CHESTER	11/2001	
HIGGINS	DENNIS			21/3/1913	2	30								
HIGGINS	RONALD	SILVERTOWN	14/2/1923	28/2/1953	9	3		1	BRIGHTON & HOVE ALBION	1/1953		SITTINGBOURNE		
HILL	CHARLES	CARDIFF	6/9/1918	27/11/1948	9	20		1	TORQUAY UNITED	3/1949		SWINDON TOWN	9/1950	
HILL	GORDON	SUNBURY	1/4/1954	1/12/1979	11	12	4	1	DERBY COUNTY	11/1979	175,000	MONTREAL MANIC		
HILL	JOSEPH	SHEFFIELD	1906	1/9/1932	8	16		1	BARNSLEY	1932		STOCKPORT COUNTY		
HILL	LEONARD	ISLINGTON	15/2/1899	4/9/1920	1	176			SOUTHEND UNITED	8/1920		SOUTHAMPTON	1925	
HILL	WILLIAM	UXBRIDGE	9/6/1930	1/12/1951	8	11		1	UXBRIDGE TOWN	4/1951		RAMSGATE		
HILLARD	JOHN		3/9/1916	8/2/1941	7	1			TORQUAY UNITED			Guest		

Surname	Christian	Born	Date	Debut	No	App	Sub	Goal	Signed From	Date	Signed Fee	Transferred To	Date	Transfer Fee
HIRST	HENRY	HORBURY	24/10/1899	5/9/1925	4	30		1	PRESTON NORTH END	5/1925		CHARLTON ATHLETIC	6/1926	
HISLOP	MATTHEW	WOLVERHAMPTON	31/1/1987	24/9/2005	5	1			ARSENAL	3/2005	Free	Released from contract	1/2007	
HITCH	ALFRED	WALSALL	1878	7/10/1899	5	183		20	GRAYS	1899		NOTTINGHAM FOREST	7/1901	
									NOTTINGHAM FOREST	1902		WATFORD		
HITCHCOCK	ERNEST			2/9/1907	9	2		2	MANCHESTER CITY					
HODGE	STEVE	NOTTINGHAM	25/10/1962	29/10/1994	25	16			LEEDS UNITED	10/1994	300,000	WATFORD	12/1995	Free
HOLD	OSCAR	BARNSLEY	19/10/1918	8/3/1952	8	4		1	EVERTON	2/1952		MARCH TOWN (player/manager)	7/1953	
HOLLINS	JOHN	GUILDFORD	16/7/1946	16/8/1975	4	177	6	7	CHELSEA	6/1975	80,000	ARSENAL	7/1979	75,000
HOLLOWAY	IAN	KINGSWOOD	12/3/1963	17/8/1991	14	150	20	5	BRISTOL ROVERS	8/1991	225,000	BRISTOL ROVERS	6/1996	Free
HOOPER	H.			12/2/1916	3	13								
HOOPER	HAROLD	BRIERLEY HILL	1900	28/8/1926	2	16			LEICESTER CITY					
HORSFIELD	ALEC	SELBY	4/8/1921	5/9/1942	6	6			ARSENAL			Guest		
HOTEN	RALPH	PINXTON	27/12/1896	30/8/1930	10	9		4	NORTHAMPTON TOWN	1930				
HOWE	ERNIE	CHISWICK	15/2/1953	17/12/1977	5	106		6	FULHAM	12/1977	50,000	PORTSMOUTH	8/1982	50,000
HOWE	HAROLD	HEMEL HEMPSTEAD	9/4/1906	19/10/1929	11	75		14	WATFORD			CRYSTAL PALACE	1933	
HOWELL	ANDREW	GREAT YARMOUTH	18/3/1989	22/8/2006	5	1			Youth Academy				5/2008	Released
HOWES	ARTHUR	LEICESTER	1876	12/11/1904	1	53			BRIGHTON	1904				
HOWIE	DAVID			9/12/1916	8	2								
HUCKER	PETER	HAMPSTEAD	28/10/1959	2/5/1981	1	188			Apprentice	7/1977		OXFORD UNITED	2/1987	100,000
HUDSON	STAN	FULHAM	10/2/1923	9/10/1948	11	24		8		9/1948		Died 21/06/1951		
HUGHES	WILLIAM	COLWYN BAY	2/2/1919	22/1/1944	1	1			TOTTENHAM HOTSPUR			Guest		
HUGHES				11/3/1916	10	2								
HUMPHRIES	HOWARD			4/9/1915	9	22		9						
HUMPHRIES	PERCY	CAMBRIDGE	3/12/1880	8/9/1900	10	31		12	CAMBRIDGE ST MARYS	1900		NOTTS COUNTY	1901	
HUNT	RON	PADDINGTON	19/12/1945	28/12/1964	5	249	6	1	Apprentice	3/1963		Retired - injury	7/1973	
HUNTER				9/10/1915	7	1						Guest		
HURREL	WILLIE	DUNDEE	28/1/1920	16/9/1953	8	9		3	MILLWALL	7/1953		TUNBRIDGE WELLS		
HURST	WILLIAM	NEWCASTLE		2/2/1924	8	10		4	DERBY COUNTY	7/1923				
HUTCHINSON	R.			27/11/1943	7	1						Guest		
IDIAKEZ	INIGO	SAN SEBASTIAN, SPAIN	8/11/1973	10/3/2007	7	4	1	1	SOUTHAMPTON	3/2007	Loan	SOUTHAMPTON	4/2007	Returned
IMPEY	ANDREW	HAMMERSMITH	13/9/1971	9/10/1991	14	199	16	18	YEADING	8/1990	Free	WEST HAM UNITED	6/1997	1,200,000
INGHAM	TONY	HARROGATE	18/2/1925	25/11/1950	2	555		3	LEEDS UNITED	6/1950		Retired		
IORFA	DOMINIC	LAGOS, NIGERIA	1/10/1968	5/5/1990	12	2	7		STANDARD LIEGE	3/1990	175,000	GALATASARAY	12/1991	100,000
IVES	BEN	HACKNEY	1889	19/4/1913	7	37		3	EXETER CITY	1912		CLAPTON ORIENT	1919	
IVES	GEORGE	LINCOLNSHIRE		28/2/1938	7	1			BRENTFORD	7/1937				
JACKMAN	V.			21/3/1913	11	3								
JACKMAN				12/2/1916	8	1						Guest		
JACKS	GEORGE	STEPNEY	14/3/1946	23/4/1965	10	1			Apprentice	1/1964		MILLWALL	7/1965	
JACKSON	JAMES			1940		1			BOLTON WANDERERS			Guest		
JACKSON	MATT	LEEDS	19/10/1971	23/8/1996	2	7			EVERTON	8/1996	Loan	EVERTON	9/1996	Returned
JAMES	LEIGHTON	LOUGHOR	16/2/1953	29/10/1977	8	32	1	6	DERBY COUNTY	10/1977	MASSON	BURNLEY	9/1978	165,000
JAMES	NORMAN	BOOTLE	25/3/1908	31/10/1936	5	76		1	BRADFORD CITY	10/1936			1939	
JAMES	ROBBIE	SWANSEA	23/3/1957	17/11/1984	12	92	9	6	STOKE CITY	10/1984	100,000	LEICESTER CITY	6/1987	70,000
JAMES				14/4/1917	11	1						Guest		
JARRETT	JASON	BURY	14/9/1979	3/10/2007	8	1	1		PRESTON NORTH END	10/2007	Loan	PRESTON NORTH END	11/2007	Returned
JEANNE	LEON	CARDIFF	17/11/1980	20/2/1999	13	8	4		Trainee	11/1997		Contract terminated	3/2000	
JEFFERIES	H.	BRISTOL		27/9/1913	1	21			ABERDARE					
JEFFERSON	ARTHUR	GOLDTHORPE	14/12/1916	31/8/1936	3	368		1	PETERBOROUGH UNITED			ALDERSHOT	3/1950	
JEFFERSON	ROBERT			8/12/1917	7	38		5	SWINDON TOWN					
JENKINS				16/11/1918	2	1								
JOBSON	JOHN	HEBBURN	8/8/1903	27/8/1932	5	4			STOCKPORT COUNTY	1932		GATESHEAD		
JOHN	REG	ABERDARE	22/7/1899	6/11/1920	4	145		1	ABERDARE ATHLETIC	1920		CHARLTON ATHLETIC	1926	
JOHNS	NICKY	BRISTOL	8/6/1957	21/12/1987	1	16			CHARLTON ATHLETIC	12/1987	40,000	MAIDSTONE UNITED		
JOHNSON	HENRY	BIRMINGHAM	1897	16/2/1924	10	74		23	SOUTHAMPTON			CRADLEY HEATH		

Surname	Christian	Born	Date	Debut	No	App	Sub	Goal	Signed From	Date	Signed Fee	Transferred To	Date	Transfer Fee
JOHNSON	RICHARD	KURRI KURRI	27/4/1974	20/2/2004	C	17	1		WATFORD	2/2004	Free	Contract Cancelled	12/2004	
JOHNSTONE	JOE			1/1/1946	11	1			MOTHERWELL			Guest		
JONES	CHARLIE	SWANSEA	1911	10/9/1932	10	16		1	NORTHEND	1932				
JONES	ERIC	SWANSEA	12/11/1920	18/3/1944	7	14		8	WEST BROMWICH ALBION			Guest		
JONES	GEORGE			17/4/1946	9	1								
JONES	J.			9/2/1918	5	2		2				Guest		
JONES	PAUL	CHIRK	18/4/1967	11/2/2006	1	26			Unattached	2/2006	Free	Released from contract	5/2007	
JONES	RAY	NEWHAM	28/8/1988	24/4/2006	B	18	19	6	Youth Academy			(Died in car crash, 8/2007)	8/2007	
JONES	VINNIE	WATFORD	5/1/1965	28/3/1998	4	8	1	1	WIMBLEDON	3/1998	500,000	Retired from football	3/1999	
JORDAN	FRANK			14/9/1901	7	2								
JORDAN	HARRY			7/10/1899	7	2				1899				
KANYUKA	PATRICK	KINSHASHA, CONGO	19/7/1987	19/4/2005	3	10	5		Youth Academy			SWINDON TOWN	1/2008	Free
KEECH	WILLIAM	IRTHLINGBURGH	6/1876	9/9/1899	6	69		6	LOUGHBOROUGH TOWN	8/1899		BRENTFORD	1902	
KEEN	JAMES	WALKER	25/11/1897	25/8/1923	7	32			NEWCASTLE UNITED			HULL CITY	1924	
KEEN	MIKE	WYCOMBE	19/3/1940	7/9/1959	6	440		45	Juniors	6/1958		LUTON TOWN	1/1961	18,500
KEETCH	BOBBY	TOTTENHAM	25/10/1941	11/3/1967	3	53	3		FULHAM	11/1966	Free	DURBAN CITY	5/1969	5,000
KELLAR				9/2/1918	8	1						Guest		
KELLARD	THOMAS	OLDHAM	1905	3/5/1928	10	5		1	OLDHAM ATHLETIC	1928		BURTON TOWN	1929	
KELLY	BRIAN	ISLEWORTH	25/9/1937	13/12/1958	9	6			DOVER	11/1958		BEXLEYHEATH		
KELLY	EDDIE	GLASGOW	7/2/1951	11/9/1976	8	33		1	ARSENAL	9/1976	60,000	LEICESTER CITY	7/1977	50,000
KELLY	JAMES			1940		7			CAMBUSLANG RANGERS	1939				
KELLY	MIKE	NORTHAMPTON	18/10/1942	26/11/1966	1	64			WIMBLEDON	3/1966	1000 + Wicks	BIRMINGHAM CITY	8/1970	16,000
KELLY	STEPHEN	DUBLIN	6/9/1983	29/3/2003	2	9			TOTTENHAM HOTSPUR	3/2003	Loan	TOTTENHAM HOTSPUR	5/2003	Returned
KENNEDY	MARK	DUBLIN	15/5/1976	31/1/1998	11	8		2	LIVERPOOL	1/1998	Loan	LIVERPOOL	3/1998	Returned
KERR	ANDREW	FALKIRK		27/3/1926	9	2			READING					
KERRINS	PAT	FULHAM	13/9/1936	13/2/1954	11	158		31	Juniors	12/1953		CRYSTAL PALACE	6/1960	
KERSLAKE	DAVID	STEPNEY	19/6/1966	13/4/1985	12	48	26	10	Apprentice	6/1983		SWINDON TOWN	12/1989	110,000
KING	ANDY	LUTON	14/8/1956	20/9/1980	8	31	2	9	EVERTON	8/1980	425,000	WEST BROMWICH ALBION	9/1981	400,000
KING	ARTHUR			18/1/1912	9	4								
KING	ARTHUR			7/9/1901	7	22		2	GAINSBOROUGH TRINITY					
KING	P.			14/4/1945	7	2								
KING	R.			21/11/1908	8	3								
KINGSLEY	MATTHEW	TURTON	1876	2/9/1905	1	20			WEST HAM UNITED	1905		ROCHDALE	1907	
KINLIN				2/12/1916	10	1						Guest		
KIRK	T.			2/12/1916	2	1						Guest		
KIRKHAM	JOHN	ELLESMERE PORT	16/6/1918	11/10/1941	9	13		3	BOURNEMOUTH			Guest		
KIWOMYA	CHRIS	HUDDERSFIELD	2/12/1969	29/8/1998	14	81	15	30	ARSENAL	8/1998	Free	AAB	7/2001	Free
KNIGHT	ARNOLD	GAINSBOROUGH	30/5/1919	3/3/1945	10	1			LEEDS UNITED			Guest		
KNIGHT	FREDERICK			12/11/1921	9	2		1						
KNIGHT	LEON	HACKNEY	16/9/1982	10/3/2001	11	10	1		CHELSEA	3/2001	Loan	CHELSEA	5/2001	Returned
KNOWLES	FRANK	HYDE	1891	23/2/1924	5	40			NEWPORT COUNTY			ASHTON NATIONAL		
KNOWLES	JOE	MONKWEARMOUTH	1872	9/9/1899	2	29			SOUTH SHIELDS	8/1899				
KOEJOE	SAMUEL	PARAMARIBO, SURINAM	17/8/1974	4/12/1999	B	17	25	3	SALZBURG	11/1999	250,000	Released from contract	9/2001	
KULSCAR	GEORGE	BUDAPEST, HUNGARY	12/8/1967	21/12/1997	4	44	16	1	BRADFORD CITY	12/1997	250,000	Released	5/2001	
KUS	MARCIN	WARSAW, POLAND	2/9/1981	4/2/2006	2	3			POLINIA WARSAW	1/2006	Loan	Released	5/2006	
LAIDMAN	FREDERICK	DURHAM	20/6/1913	20/1/1945	2	1			STOCKTON			Guest		
LANE	HARRY	STONEY STRATTON	23/10/1894	4/11/1922	6	5			CHARLTON ATHLETIC	1922				
LANGFORD	THOMAS			24/3/1917	4	3						Guest		
LANGFORD	WALTER	WOLVERHAMPTON	24/3/1905	9/9/1933	10	13			LEICESTER CITY	1933		WELLINGTON TOWN		
LANGLEY	JIM	KILBURN	7/2/1929	21/8/1965	3	104	1	11	FULHAM	7/1965	5,000	HILLINGDON (player/manager)	11/1967	
LANGLEY	RICHARD	LONDON	27/12/1979	31/10/1998	13	161	21	24	Trainee	5/1996		CARDIFF CITY	8/2003	250,000
									CARDIFF CITY	8/2005	Free	Released	5/2006	
LANGLEY	TOMMY	LAMBETH	8/2/1958	23/8/1980	9	27	1	9	CHELSEA	8/1980	475,000	CRYSTAL PALACE	3/1981	200,000
LARGE	FRANK	LEEDS	26/1/1940	18/8/1962	10	22		7	HALIFAX TOWN	6/1962	8,000	NORTHAMPTON TOWN	3/1963	10,000

Surname	Christian	Born	Date	Debut	No	App	Sub	Goal	Signed From	Date	Signed Fee	Transferred To	Date	Transfer Fee
LAW	BRIAN	MERTHYR TYDFIL	1/1/1970	23/4/1988	12	25	2		Apprentice	8/1987		WOLVERHAMPTON WANDERERS	12/1994	100,000
LAW	R.			29/4/1911	7	1								
LAW	WILLIAM	PLECK	3/1882	16/9/1908	11	5		1	WATFORD	1908		GLOSSOP	1910	
LAWRENCE	WALTER			28/10/1916	10	20		10						
LAY	PETER	STRATFORD	4/12/1931	26/12/1956	5	1			NOTTINGHAM FOREST	7/1956		KINGS LYNN	1958	
LAZARUS	MARK	STEPNEY	5/12/1938	17/9/1960	7	233	2	84	LEYTON ORIENT	9/1960		WOLVERHAMPTON	9/1961	
									WOLVERHAMPTON WANDERERS	2/1962		BRENTFORD	4/1964	8,000
									BRENTFORD	11/1965	10,000	CRYSTAL PALACE	11/1967	10,000
LEABURN	CARL	LEWISHAM	30/3/1969	5/1/2002	C		1		CHARLTON ATHLETIC	12/2001	Loan	CHARLTON ATHLETIC	1/2002	Returned
LEACH	JAMES	SPENNYMOOR	7/1890	26/8/1922	6	1			ASTON VILLA					
LEACH	MICK	CLAPTON	16/1/1947	26/2/1965	8	337	24	70	Apprentice	2/1964		DETROIT EXPRESS	3/1978	30,000
LEARY	STUART	CAPE TOWN, SOUTH AFRICA	30/4/1933	15/12/1962	9	104		32	CHARLTON ATHLETIC	12/1962	17,000	Retired		
LEATHER	JACK		1875	26/3/1904	1	2			WOOLWICH ARSENAL					
LEDESMA	EMMANUEL	QUILMES, ARGENTINA	24/5/1988	9/8/2008	8	15	8	4	GENOA	7/2008	Loan	GENOA	5/2009	Returned
LEE	KIERAN	TAMESIDE	22/6/1988	5/1/2008	C	2	6		MANCHESTER UNITED	1/2008	Loan	MANCHESTER UNITED	5/2008	Returned
LEE	SAMMY	LIVERPOOL	7/2/1959	30/8/1986	7	33	2	1	LIVERPOOL	8/1986	175,000	OSASUNA	7/1987	200,000
LEE	THOMAS	BURY	1887	19/11/1910	2	4			FULHAM	1910				
LEGGE	ALBERT	HEDNESFORD	19/6/1901	30/8/1930	8	9			CHARLTON ATHLETIC	1930				
LEIGERTWOOD	MIKELE	ENFIELD	12/11/1982	1/9/2007	7	72	14	7	SHEFFIELD UNITED	8/2007	900,000			
LENNON	ALEC	GLASGOW	23/1/1925	25/12/1945	11	3			ROTHERHAM UNITED	1/1947		MANSFIELD TOWN	2/1949	
LENNOX	STUART			29/12/1900	4	11								
LEWIS	JIM	HAMMERSMITH		2/5/1931	8	12		5	WALTHAMSTOW AVENUE	1930		WALTHAMSTOW AVENUE		
LEWIS	L.			9/9/1916	10	21								
LIBBY	J.			11/4/1942	5	1								
LIEVSLEY	LESLIE	STAVELEY	7/9/1911	1940		1			CRYSTAL PALACE			Guest		
LILLIE	JOHN	NEWCASTLE		30/8/1924	3	3			LIVERPOOL			CLAPTON ORIENT	1925	
LING	L.			1940		7		4						
LINIGHAN	ANDY	HARTLEPOOL	18/6/1962	5/4/1999	14	4	3		CRYSTAL PALACE	3/1999	Loan	CRYSTAL PALACE	5/1999	Returned
LINKSON	OSCAR	BARNET	1888	11/9/1915	3	17			MANCHESTER UNITED				Died during WW1	
LINTOTT	EVELYN	GODALMING	2/11/1883	7/9/1907	6	35		1	PLYMOUTH ARGYLE	1907		BRADFORD	11/1908	1,000
LISBIE	KEVIN	HACKNEY	17/10/1978	2/12/2000	B	1	1		CHARLTON ATHLETIC	12/2000	Loan	CHARLTON ATHLETIC	12/2000	Returned
LITTLE	C.			8/1/1944	7	4		1				Guest		
LOCK	HERBERT	SOUTHAMPTON	21/1/1887	12/11/1921	1	6			GLASGOW RANGERS	1921		SOUTHAMPTON	1922	
LOCKE	LESLIE	PERTH	24/1/1934	27/8/1956	10	82		29	BROMLEY	5/1958		GUILDFORD CITY	7/1960	
LOFTHOUSE	JAMES	ST HELENS	24/3/1896	28/8/1926	11	81		27	BRISTOL ROVERS			ALDERSHOT		
LOGAN	W.	GOVANHILL	1887	1/9/1909	2	7			VALE OF LEVEN					
LOMAS	STEVE	HANOVER, GERMANY	18/1/1974	10/9/2005	B	46	11	2	WEST HAM UNITED	8/2005	Free	GILLINGHAM	8/2007	Free
LONEY	BASIL			24/4/1915	2	65								
LONGBOTTOM	ARTHUR	LEEDS	30/1/1933	12/3/1955	8	218		68	METHLEY UNITED	3/1954		PORT VALE	5/1961	
LOPEZ	JORDI	BARCELONA, SPAIN	28/2/1981	28/2/2009	B	7	3	1	MALLORCA	2/2009	Free			
LOWE	HARRY	KINGSKETTLE	24/2/1907	31/8/1935	8	250		51	WATFORD	6/1935	Goodier	GUILDFORD CITY	1939	
LOWE	KEITH	WOLVERHAMPTON	13/9/1985	4/2/2006	4	1			WOLVERHAMPTON WANDERERS	1/2006	Loan	WOLVERHAMPTON WANDERERS	2/2006	Returned
LOWE	OLIVER			25/4/1908	3	2								
LOWE	W.			8/11/1919	10	1								
LOWES	ARNOLD	SUNDERLAND	27/2/1919	25/12/1943	8	11		6	SHEFFIELD WEDNESDAY			Guest		
LUDFORD	GEORGE	BARNET	22/3/1915	2/12/1944	11	1			TOTTENHAM HOTSPUR			Guest		
LUMSDEN	FRANK	SUNDERLAND		21/9/1935	7	40		8	HUDDERSFIELD TOWN	1935		BURNLEY	7/1937	Free
LYON	FRANK	CREWE	23/9/1879	24/10/1903	2	60			WATFORD	1903		CHELSEA	4/1906	
M'BOMBO	EBEIL	ZAIRE	11/9/1980	21/8/2001	10	25	26	3	AS MONACO	8/2001	Free	Released	5/2003	
McADAMS	BILLY	BELFAST	20/1/1934	25/9/1964	9	38		12	BRENTFORD	9/1964	5,000	BARROW	7/1966	
McALLISTER	WILLIAM	GLASGOW		23/10/1926	8	26		1	MIDDLESBROUGH			RAITH ROVERS		
McCAIRNS	THOMAS	DINSDALE	22/12/1873	24/10/1903	8	3			WELLINGBOROUGH	1903		BRIGHTON & HOVE ALBION	1903	
McCARTHY	ALAN	WANDSWORTH	11/1/1972	14/2/1989	4	10	4		Juniors			LEYTON ORIENT	8/1995	25,000
McCARTHY	LEN	CAERAN		30/10/1937	10	68		23	PORTSMOUTH	1937				

Surname	Christian	Born	Date	Debut	No	App	Sub	Goal	Signed From	Date	Signed Fee	Transferred To	Date	Transfer Fee
McCLELLAND	JOHN	BRADFORD	5/3/1935	23/9/1961	7	79		24	LINCOLN CITY	9/1961	15,000	PORTSMOUTH	5/1963	
McCOLGAN	JOHN	LANARKSHIRE	20/6/1916	1940		2			PLYMOUTH ARGYLE	1939		IPSWICH TOWN		
McCONNELL	ALEX	GLENBUCK	1875	9/9/1899	3	64			WOOLWICH ARSENAL	8/1899		GRIMSBY TOWN	1901	
McCREEY	DAVID	BELFAST	16/9/1957	18/8/1979	4	65	2	5	MANCHESTER UNITED	8/1979	200,000	TULSA ROUGHNECKS	6/1981	225,000
McCULLOCH	ANDY	NORTHAMPTON	3/1/1950	17/10/1970	9	33	14	11	WALTON & HERSHAM	10/1970		CARDIFF CITY	10/1972	45,000
McDERMOTT	ANDREW	SYDNEY, AUSTRALIA	20/3/1977	14/12/1996	2	6		2	AUSTRALIAN I.O.S.	7/1995		WEST BROMWICH ALBION	3/1997	400,000
McDONALD	ALAN	BELFAST	12/10/1963	24/9/1983	5	476	7	18	Apprentice	8/1981		SWINDON TOWN	6/1997	Free
McDONALD	JOHN	AYR	1882	14/9/1907	2	198			GRIMSBY TOWN	1907		Retired	1913	
MacDONALD	JOHN			1/9/1908	7	20			LINCOLN CITY	1908				
McEWAN	BILLY	GLASGOW	29/8/1914	4/3/1939	7	173		51	PETERSHILL	1938		LEYTON ORIENT	2/1950	
McEWAN	DAVID	WESTMINSTER	2/11/1977	21/8/2001	A	2	4		TOTTENHAM HOTSPUR	7/2001	Free	Released	1/2002	
McEWAN	ROBERT		1881	26/12/1908	3	1			GLOSSOP	1908				
McFLYNN	TERRY	MAGHERAFELT	27/3/1981	28/4/2001	A	1	1		Youth Academy			WOKING	7/2001	Free
McGARGILL	H.			14/4/1906	6	4			GATESHEAD					
McGEE	PAUL	DUBLIN	19/6/1954	19/11/1977	7	35	9	8	SLIGO ROVERS	11/1977	15,000	PRESTON NORTH END	10/1979	100,000
McGOVERN	BRIAN	DUBLIN	28/4/1980	28/12/1999	A	3	2		ARSENAL	12/1999	Loan	ARSENAL	1/2000	Returned
McGOVERN	MICK	HAYES	15/2/1951	26/12/1967	9	11	2		Apprentice	11/1968		SWINDON TOWN	2/1973	10,000
McGOVERN	THOMAS	GLASGOW		28/8/1920	4	2			BRENTFORD					
McGOWAN	FRANK			19/9/1903	10	9		3						
McINNES	JAMES	AYR	1911	12/12/1942	6	1			LIVERPOOL			Guest		
McKAY	JOHNNY	PORT GLASGOW	27/6/1927	19/11/1949	11	16		1	IRVINE	3/1949		YEOVIL TOWN		
McKAY	WILLIAM	ROTHESAY	10/3/1927	30/8/1955	7	6			DEAL TOWN	7/1955		DOVER		
McKENZIE	TOMMY	INVERNESS		1/9/1908	9	9		1	GLOSSOP			BRENTFORD		
McKIE	DAN			12/9/1910	8	70		30	CHORLEY					
McKINLEY				26/10/1901	10	4								
McKINNEY	EDWARD			27/2/1915	7	2			BROOM ATHLETIC					
McLARNEY	PATRICK			2/9/1905	2	8								
McLEAN	JOHN	PORT GLASGOW	22/5/1872	1/9/1906	5	78			MILLWALL ATHLETIC	1906		Retired	1908	
McLEOD	GEORGE	INVERNESS	30/11/1932	11/1/1964	11	42		4	BRENTFORD	1/1964		SOUTH AFRICA		
McLEOD	KEVIN	LIVERPOOL	12/9/1980	22/3/2003	9	47	30	8	EVERTON	3/2003	Loan	EVERTON	5/2003	Returned
									EVERTON	8/2003	190,000	SWANSEA CITY	3/2005	100,000
McLEOD	ROBERT			1/9/1914	1	41			NEWPORT COUNTY					
McLINTOCK	FRANK	GLASGOW	28/12/1939	22/9/1973	6	162	1	6	ARSENAL	6/1973	30,000	Leicester City (manager)		
MacLINTON				2/3/1918	8	17		6						
McLUKIE	JAMES	STONEHOUSE	2/4/1908	22/4/1944	10	2			IPSWICH TOWN			Guest		
McMAHON	HUGH	GRANGETOWN	24/9/1909	12/9/1936	7	45		5	READING	1936		SUNDERLAND	11/1937	
McNAB	JOHN	CLELAND	17/4/1895	25/8/1928	4	59		2	LIVERPOOL	1928		Retired	1930	
McNAUGHT	JOHN	DUMBARTON	8/6/1870	29/8/1908	7	63		6	HOUNSLOW	1908				
McNICKLE				13/12/1941	3	1								
McQUADE	TERRY	HACKNEY	24/2/1941	4/9/1963	11	25		2	MILLWALL	7/1963		LEYTON ORIENT		
McQUEEN	HUGH	HART HILL	1/10/1867	7/9/1901	10	29		9	DERBY COUNTY	1901		GAINSBOROUGH TRINITY	1902	
McRAE				18/3/1916	10	1						Guest		
MADDIX	DANNY	ASHFORD	11/10/1967	28/11/1987	12	307	40	18	TOTTENHAM HOTSPUR	7/1987	Free	SHEFFIELD WEDNESDAY	7/2001	Free
MAGUIRE	GAVIN	HAMMERSMITH	28/12/1967	28/12/1986	11	39	10		Apprentice	10/1985		PORTSMOUTH	12/1988	175,000
MAHON	GAVIN	BIRMINGHAM	2/1/1977	1/1/2008	A	46	11	3	WATFORD	1/2008	200,000			
MAHON	JACK			1940		16		4				Guest		
MAHONEY-JOHNSON	MICHAEL	PADDINGTON	6/11/1976	2/10/1996	12		3		Trainee			Out of Contract	6/2000	
MALCOLM	ANDY	WEST HAM	4/5/1933	22/10/1962	4	94		6	CHELSEA	10/1962	12,000	PORT ELIZABETH		
MALCOLM	BOB	GLASGOW	12/11/1980	24/11/2007	4	10	1		DERBY COUNTY	11/2007	Loan	DERBY COUNTY	1/2008	Returned
MALLETT	JOE	GATESHEAD	8/1/1916	23/10/1937	8	297		60	CHARLTON ATHLETIC	1937	800	CHARLTON ATHLETIC	7/1938	
									CHARLTON ATHLETIC	2/1939		SOUTHAMPTON	2/1947	5,000
MANCIENNE	MICHAEL	ISLEWORTH	8/1/1988	21/10/2006	A	55	6		CHELSEA	10/2006	Loan	CHELSEA	5/2008	Returned
MANCINI	TERRY	CAMDEN TOWN	4/10/1942	16/10/1971	6	111		5	ORIENT	10/1971	25,000	ARSENAL	10/1974	25,000
MANGNALL	DAVE	WIGAN	21/9/1908	26/8/1939	9	138		97	MILLWALL	5/1939				

Surname	Christian	Born	Date	Debut	No	App	Sub	Goal	Signed From	Date	Signed Fee	Transferred To	Date	Transfer Fee
MANNING	JOHN	BOSTON	1886	23/10/1920	10	24		5	ROTHERHAM COUNTY			BOSTON TOWN		
MARCH	RICHARD	WASHINGTON	9/10/1908	24/12/1932	4	311		6	CRAWCROOK ALBION			Retired (QPR Catering Manager)		
MARCROFT	EDWARD	ROCHDALE	4/1910	27/8/1932	7	33		9	MIDDLESBROUGH	1932		CARDIFF CITY	7/1933	EMMERSON
MARNEY	DEAN	BARKING	31/1/1984	17/1/2004	B	2	1		TOTTENHAM HOTSPUR	1/2004	Loan	TOTTENHAM HOTSPUR	2/2004	Returned
MARSDEN	BEN	HANLEY		27/12/1920	2	132		6	PORT VALE	1920		READING		1925
MARSH	RODNEY	HATFIELD	11/10/1944	19/2/1966	10	242		134	FULHAM	3/1966	15,000	MANCHESTER CITY	3/1972	200,000
MARSHALL	ALF			27/1/1917	9	1						Guest		
MARTIN	J.			4/3/1944	6	1			ST MIRREN			Guest		
MASON	BILL	EARLSFIELD	31/10/1908	18/1/1934	1	269			FULHAM	7/1933		Retired during WW2		
MASSON	DON	BANCHORY	26/8/1946	14/12/1974	4	144		24	NOTTS COUNTY	12/1974	100,000	DERBY COUNTY	10/1977	JAMES
MATTHEWS	A.			27/11/1915	7	6		1						
MATTHEWS	F.W.			23/4/1914	1	7			HAMPSTEAD TOWN					
MAYES	TOM			6/12/1902	8	4			GRAYS UNITED					
MEAKER	MICHAEL	GREENFORD	18/8/1971	20/11/1990	14	26	14	3	Trainee			READING	7/1995	500,000
MERRICK	JOSEPH	GREAT BARR	1900	30/8/1919	1	39			ASTON VILLA			BIRMINGHAM CITY		
METCHICK	DAVE	BAKEWELL	14/8/1943	5/10/1968	12	1	3	1	PETERBOROUGH UNITED	3/1968	5,000	ARSENAL	9/1970	
MICKLEWHITE	GARY	SOUTHWARK	21/3/1961	5/11/1980	12	115	12	17	MANCHESTER UNITED	7/1979		DERBY COUNTY	2/1985	75,000
MIDDLEMISS	HERBERT	NEWCASTLE	19/12/1888	28/8/1920	11	16		1	TOTTENHAM HOTSPUR	1920		Retired	1921	
MIDDLETON	JACK	SUNDERLAND	19/4/1898	29/8/1925	8	54		9	LEICESTER CITY	1925		ALDERSHOT	1928	
MIKLOSKO	LUDEK	PROTESOV, CZECH	9/12/1961	3/10/1998	1	63	2		WEST HAM UNITED	12/1998	50,000	WEST HAM UNITED	7/2001	Free
MILANESE	MAURO	TRIESTE, ITALY	17/9/1971	20/8/2005	A	40	4		PERUGIA	7/2005	Free	SALERNITANA CALCIO	7/2007	Free
MILLAR	HARRY	PAISLEY	1874	7/9/1901	9	27		12	SHEFFIELD WEDNESDAY	1901				
MILLBANK	JOE	EDMONTON	30/9/1919	11/9/1948	4	1			CRYSTAL PALACE	7/1948		BEDFORD TOWN	1950	
MILLER	ADAM	HEMEL HEMPSTEAD	19/2/1982	4/12/2004	8	11	5		ALDERSHOT TOWN	11/2004	50,000	STEVENAGE BOROUGH	1/2006	Free
MILLER	JIMMY	GLASGOW		1/9/1913	9	71		31	VALE OF LEVEN			HARTLEPOOL	1921	
MILLER	LIAM	CORK	13/2/1981	27/1/2009	9	11	2		SUNDERLAND	1/2009	Free	Released	5/2009	
MILLINGTON	TOM	MANCHESTER		1/9/1914	2	34			BURY					
MILLS	DON	ROTHERHAM	17/8/1926	25/9/1946	10	78		12		8/1946		TORQUAY UNITED	3/1949	
									TORQUAY UNITED	1/1950		WEST HAM UNITED	2/1951	
MILLS	GEORGE	DEPTFORD	29/12/1908	1940		2		1	CHELSEA			Guest		
MILWARD	GEORGE			5/9/1903	8	46		14	CHESTERFIELD	1903				
MITCHELL	ARCHIE	SMETHWICK	15/12/1885	2/9/1907	4	467		25	ASTON VILLA	1907		BRENTFORD	1921	
MOBLEY	VIC	OXFORD	11/10/1943	4/10/1969	5	30	1		SHEFFIELD WEDNESDAY	10/1969	55,000	Retired - injury	7/1971	
MOFFATT	HUGH	CAMERTON	1900	31/8/1929	7	15		3	WALSALL	1929				
MOGER	HENRY	SOUTHAMPTON	9/1879	21/4/1906	1	3								
MOLLOY	PETER	HASLINGDEN	20/4/1909	14/9/1935	6	3			CARDIFF CITY	1935		STOCKPORT COUNTY		
MOORE	JAMES	FELLING-ON-TYNE	1/9/1891	30/8/1924	8	26		5	HALIFAX			CREWE ALEXANDRA	1925	
MOORE	JOHN			27/12/1941	9	1		1						
MOORE	STEFAN	BIRMINGHAM	28/9/1983	6/8/2005	C	21	21	3	ASTON VILLA	7/2005	Free	PORT VALE	8/2006	Loan
									PORT VALE	11/2006	Returned	Released	1/2008	
MORALEE	WILLIAM	CROOK	3/5/1906	21/1/1937	6	23			BOURNEMOUTH	1936				
MORGAN	IAN	WALTHAMSTOW	14/11/1946	25/9/1964	7	175	15	28	Apprentice	9/1964		WATFORD	10/1973	10,000
MORGAN	ROGER	WALTAHMSTOW	14/11/1946	3/10/1964	11	206		44	Apprentice	9/1964		TOTTENHAM HOTSPUR	2/1969	110,000
MORRIS	SAMUEL	HANDSWOTH	1888	25/4/1908	5	42		2	ASTON VILLA	1907		BRISTOL ROVERS	1911	
MORROW	STEVE	BELFAST	2/7/1970	5/4/1997	6	93	7	2	ARSENAL	3/1997	500,000	Released	5/2001	
MORTIMER	JOHNNY			25/1/1941	3	1			NEW BRIGHTON			Guest		
MORTIMORE	JOHN	FARNBOROUGH	23/9/1934	11/9/1965	5	10			CHELSEA	9/1965	8,000	SUNDERLAND	3/1966	
MOUGHTON	COLIN	HARROW	30/12/1947	21/5/1966	6	6			Apprentice	12/1965		COLCHESTER UNITED	7/1968	Free
MOUNTFORD	GEORGE	STOKE-ON-TRENT	30/3/1921	25/10/1952	7	38		2	STOKE CITY	10/1952		HEREFORD UNITED	10/1953	
MUIR	IAN	COVENTRY	5/5/1963	25/4/1981	11	2		2	Apprentice	9/1980		BIRMINGHAM CITY	8/1983	
MUIR	WILLIAM	AYR	27/8/1925	13/9/1948	3	17		4	IRVINE MEADOW	2/1948		TORQUAY UNITED	10/1952	
MULHOLLAND	SCOTT	BEXLEY	7/9/1986	19/4/2005	C		1		Youth Academy			Released	5/2005	
MUNSON				1/4/1918	8	1						Guest		
MURDIN	STEVE			25/2/1926	9	1								

Surname	Christian	Born	Date	Debut	No	App	Sub	Goal	Signed From	Date	Signed Fee	Transferred To	Date	Transfer Fee
MURPHY	DANNY	LONDON	4/12/1982	15/12/2001	6	14	10		Youth Academy			SWINDON TOWN	7/2003	Free
MURPHY	NEIL			26/9/1903	11	53		12	SHEFFIELD UNITED	1903		LUTON TOWN	1907	
MURRAY	PAUL	CARLISLE	31/8/1976	5/5/1996	30	132	25	8	CARLISLE UNITED	5/1996	300,000	SOUTHAMPTON	8/2001	Free
MUSSLEWHITE	JOHN			14/4/1900	5	2			WEST HAMPSTEAD	1899				
MUSTARD	JOHN	BOLDON-ON-TYNE	1905	11/12/1926	7	38		4	CRAWCROOK ALBION			SOUTH SHIELDS	1929	
MYERS	COLIN	CHAPEL TOWN	1894	25/10/1924	10	22		10	NORTHAMPTON TOWN			EXETER CITY	1925	
NARDIELLO	DANIEL	COVENTRY	22/10/1982	11/8/2007	10	4	4		BARNSLEY	7/2007	Free	BLACKPOOL	7/2008	Released
NASH	BOBBY	HAMMERSMITH	8/2/1946	25/9/1964	3	18			Juniors	2/1964		EXETER CITY	6/1966	
NEAL	DEAN	EDMONTON	5/1/1961	18/8/1979	7	22	2	9	Apprentice	8/1979		TULSA ROUGHNECKS	6/1981	
NEARY	FRANK	ALDERSHOT	6/3/1921	25/8/1945	7	58		34	FINCHLEY	8/1946	6,000	WEST HAM UNITED	1/1947	4,000
									LEYTON ORIENT	8/1949		MILLWALL	8/1950	
NEEDHAM	DAVE	LEICESTER	21/5/1949	20/8/1977	5	20		3	NOTTS COUNTY	6/1977	90,000	NOTTINGHAM FOREST	12/1977	140,000
NEEDHAM				9/12/1916	9	2						Guest		
NEIL	ANDY	KILMARNOCK	24/4/1895	27/8/1927	8	112		1	BRIGHTON			Retired	1930	
NEILL	WARREN	ACTON	21/11/1962	30/8/1980	12	209	6	7	Apprentice	9/1980		PORTSMOUTH	7/1988	110,000
NELSON	DAVE	DOUGLAS WATER	3/2/1918	18/2/1950	4	31			BRENTFORD	2/1950		CRYSTAL PALACE	3/1952	
NELSON	WILLIAM	SILVERTOWN	20/9/1929	24/9/1955	2	9			WEST HAM UNITED	7/1955		RAMSGATE ATHLETIC		
NEVINS	LAURENCE	GATESHEAD	2/7/1920	3/2/1945	11	2			NEWCASTLE UNITED			Guest		
NEWBIGGING	WILLIAM	SCOTLAND	27/12/1879	20/10/1900	9	7		1	LANARK UNITED	1900		NOTTINGHAM FOREST		
NEWLANDS	GEORGE	GLASGOW	1882	29/9/1900	3	186		1	PARKHEAD JUNIORS	1900		NORWICH CITY	1907	
NGONGE	MICHEL	HUY, BELGIUM	10/1/1967	16/12/2000	11	7	8	3	WATFORD	12/2000	60,000	KILMARNOCK	7/2001	Free
NICHOLAS	BRIAN	ABERDARE	20/4/1933	7/5/1949	4	122		2	Juniors	5/1950		CHELSEA	7/1955	
NICHOLLS	ARTHUR			20/1/1912	1	42								
NICHOLSON				16/10/1915	8	1						Guest		
NISBET	D.			4/9/1915	7	17		3						
NIXON	TOM	NEWCASTLE		9/3/1929	5	56		1	CRAWCROOK ALBION			CRYSTAL PALACE	10/1933	
NIXON	WILFRED			25/9/1915	1	11			FULHAM					
NUTT	PHIL	LONDON	18/5/1958	29/11/1975	12		4	1	Apprentice	7/1975		HOUNSLOW		
NYGAARD	MARC	DENMARK	1/9/1976	9/8/2005	B	46	26	14	BRESCIA	7/2005	Free	RANDERS, DENMARK	1/2008	Free
O'BRIEN	MICK	KILCOCK	10/8/1893	28/8/1920	6	70		4	SOUTH SHIELDS	1920		LEICESTER CITY	1922	
O'CONNOR	MARK	ROCHFORD	10/3/1963	26/12/1981	2	2	1		Apprentice	6/1980		BRISTOL ROVERS	8/1984	30,000
O'DONNELL	DENNIS	WILLINGTON QUAY	1880	1/9/1906	8	27		7	SUNDERLAND	1906		NOTTS COUNTY	1907	
O'NEILL	JOHN	DERRY	11/3/1958	31/10/1987	5	2			LEICESTER CITY	7/1987	90,000	NORWICH CITY	12/1987	100,000
O'ROURKE	JOHN	NORTHAMPTON	11/2/1945	19/10/1971	9	36	1	12	COVENTRY CITY	10/1971	60,000	BOURNEMOUTH	1/1974	40,000
OGLEY	WILLIAM	ROTHERHAM	1896	30/8/1924	6	41		2	NEWPORT COUNTY			CASTLEFORD TOWN	1925	
OLI	DENNIS	NEWHAM	28/1/1984	26/2/2002	B	11	19		Youth Academy			SWANSEA CITY	7/2004	Free
OLISEH	EGUTU	LAGOS, NIGERIA	18/11/1980	22/8/2006	A	2	1		LA LOUVIERE, BELGIUM			Released from contract	1/2007	
OLSEN	C.			3/4/1920	5	1								
ORR	DOUGLAS	GLASGOW	8/11/1937	16/9/1957	11	5			HENDON	7/1957		HENDON	5/1958	
OSBORN	SIMON	NEW ADDINGTON	19/1/1972	19/8/1995	A	7	3	1	READING	8/1995	1,000,000	WOLVERHAMPTON WANDERERS	12/1995	1,000,000
OVENS	GILBERT	BRISTOL		30/9/1911	3	112		4	BRISTOL ROVERS	1911			1915	
OVENSTONE	DAVID	ST MONANCE	17/6/1913	9/11/1935	11	16		3	BRISTOL ROVERS	1935		CARDIFF CITY	1936	
OVER				15/9/1917	8	2						Guest		
OXLEY	RICHARD	BARROW	10/4/1893	8/9/1923	10	18			SOUTHPORT			NORTHAMPTON TOWN	1925	
PACQUETTE	RICHARD	PADDINGTON	28/1/1983	21/4/2001	B	18	23	7	Youth Academy			MK DONS	7/2004	Free
PADULA	GINO	BUENOS AIRES	11/7/1976	17/8/2002	A	91	12	5	WIGAN ATHLETIC	7/2002	Free	NOTTINGHAM FOREST	7/2005	Free
PAGE				25/12/1918	9	1								
PAINTER	EDWARD	SWINDON	23/6/1921	27/9/1941	6	3			SWINDON TOWN					
PALMER	STEVE	BRIGHTON	31/3/1968	11/8/2001	4	130	13	10	WATFORD	7/2001	Free	MILTON KEYNES DONS	6/2004	Free
PAPE	ANDY	HAMMERSMITH	22/3/1962	19/4/1980	1	1			Juniors	7/1980		IKAST, DENMARK		
PAREJO	DANIEL	SPAIN	16/4/1989	9/8/2008	A	14	4		REAL MADRID	7/2008	Loan	REAL MADRID	12/2008	Returned
PARKER	PAUL	WEST HAM	4/4/1964	15/8/1987	4	156	4	1	FULHAM	6/1987	200,000	MANCHESTER UNITED	8/1981	2,000,000
PARKER	RICHARD	STOCKTON-ON-TEES	14/9/1894	26/8/1922	9	66		34	SOUTH SHIELDS	1922		MILLWALL ATHLETIC		
PARKES	PHIL	SEDGELEY	8/8/1950	22/8/1970	1	406			WALSALL	6/1970	15,000	WEST HAM UNITED	2/1979	565,000

Surname	Christian	Born	Date	Debut	No	App	Sub	Goal	Signed From	Date	Signed Fee	Transferred To	Date	Transfer Fee
PARKINSON	ALBERT	CAMDEN TOWN	30/4/1922	2/1/1943	10	88		9	Local Club				Retired	
PARRY	WILLIAM			22/4/1944	4	1			CHELMSFORD CITY			Guest		
PARSONS	DEREK	HAMMERSMITH	24/1/1929	8/11/1952	6	3		1		2/1950		ASHFORD TOWN		
PATERSON	JOCK	FIFE	1904	16/1/1926	8	36		6	MID-RHONDA UNITED	1/1926		WELLESLEY JUNIORS	1927	
PATON	TOMMY	SALTCOATS	22/12/1918	20/9/1941	9	3			BOURNEMOUTH			Guest		
PATTISON	JOHNNY	GLASGOW	19/12/1918	12/3/1938	11	168		50	MOTHERWELL		1937	LEYTON ORIENT	2/1950	
PEACOCK	DARREN	BRISTOL	3/2/1968	23/12/1990	5	140	3	7	HEREFORD UNITED	12/1990	350,000	NEWCASTLE UNITED	3/1994	2,750,000
PEACOCK	GAVIN	ELTHAM	18/11/1967	29/11/1986	11	206	19	42	Apprentice	11/1984		GILLINGHAM	12/1987	40,000
									CHELSEA	12/1996	800,000	Released from Contract	7/2002	
PEACOCK	TERENCE	HULL	18/4/1935	15/12/1956	9	17		4	HULL CITY	8/1956		SITTINGBOURNE	7/1958	
PEARSON	HARRY	BIRKENHEAD	1911	8/10/1938	7	15		1	COVENTRY CITY	1938		BARROW	1939	
PEARSON	JOHN	ISLEWORTH	23/4/1935	1/9/1958	11	21		9	BRENTFORD	6/1958		KETTERING TOWN		
PEARSON	STANLEY	SALFORD	11/1/1919	13/11/1943	10	4		1	MANCHESTER UNITED			Guest		
PENNIFER	JOHN			13/12/1913	9	9		1					Killed in WW1	
PENRICE	GARY	BRISTOL	23/3/1964	2/11/1991	14	63	31	23	ASTON VILLA	10/1991	650,000	WATFORD	11/1995	300,000
PENTLAND	FRED	WOLVERHAMPTON	18/9/1883	2/9/1907	7	40		14	BRENTFORD	1907		MIDDLESBROUGH	7/1908	350
PEPPITT	STANLEY	STOKE	18/9/1919	1/1/1946	10	1			STOKE CITY			Guest		
PERKINS	STEVE	STEPNEY	3/10/1954	1/4/1978	6	2			CHELSEA	6/1977		WIMBLEDON	10/1978	
PERRY	MARK	LONDON	19/10/1978	14/9/1996	8	63	12	1	Trainee	10/1995		Released	5/2002	
PESCHILSOLIDO	PAUL	CANADA	25/5/1971	4/11/2000	11	5		1	FULHAM	11/2000	Loan	FULHAM	12/2000	Returned
PETCHEY	GEORGE	WHITECHAPEL	24/6/1931	19/8/1953	10	278		24	WEST HAM UNITED	7/1953		CRYSTAL PALACE	6/1960	
PHILLIPS	W.			13/1/1945	6	1						Guest		
PICKETT	THOMAS	MERTHYR TYDFIL	5/2/1909	16/11/1929	1	52			KENTISH TOWN			BRISTOL CITY	1932	
PIDGEON	HENRY	TOTTENHAM		5/4/1920	7	6						SOUTHEND UNITED		
PIERCE	WILLIAM	ASHINGTON	29/10/1907	6/10/1923	3	193		3	BEDLINGTON COLLIERY	7/1923		CARLISLE UNITED	1931	
PIGG	WILLIAM	HIGH SPEN	1897	7/3/1925	6	25			ASHINGTON			CARLISLE UNITED	1926	
PINNER	MIKE	BOSTON	16/2/1934	22/8/1959	1	22			SHEFFIELD WEDNESDAY	1959		MANCHESTER UNITED	2/1961	
PIZANTI	DAVID	ISRAEL	27/5/1962	17/10/1987	14	26	6	1	FC KOLN	9/1987	150,000			
PLUMMER	CHRIS	ISLEWORTH	12/10/1976	5/5/1996	A	63	8	2	Juniors	7/1994		BARNET	7/2003	
PLUNKETT	ADAM	BLANTYRE	16/3/1903	29/8/1925	3	15			BURY	7/1925		GUILDFORD CITY		
POINTING	WILLIAM	ANDOVER	1872	22/9/1900	3	1			SOUTHAMPTON	1900				
POINTON	WILLIAM	HANLEY	25/11/1920	22/1/1949	9	26		6	PORT VALE	1/1949		BRENTFORD	2/1950	
POLLARD	ROBERT	WIGAN	25/8/1899	14/9/1929	2	73			EXETER CITY			CARDIFF CITY	1932	
POPPITT	JOHN	WEST SLEEKBURN	20/1/1923	23/9/1950	2	111			DERBY COUNTY	9/1950		CHELMSFORD CITY	7/1954	
POULTON	JERRY			4/12/1915	8	1			WEST BROMWICH ALBION			Guest		
POUNDER	ALBERT	CHARLTON	27/7/1931	13/2/1954	7	55		6	CHARLTON ATHLETIC	2/1954		SITTINGBOURNE	7/1957	
POWELL	GEORGE	FULHAM	11/10/1924	8/11/1947	2	155			FULHAM	12/1946		SNOWDON COLLIERY	6/1955	
POWELL	IVOR	BARGOED	5/7/1916	28/1/1939	4	159		2	BARGOED	1938		ASTON VILLA	12/1948	17,500
POWELL	MICHAEL	SLOUGH	18/4/1933	6/9/1952	5	109			Juniors	1/1951		YIEWSLEY	7/1959	
PRICE	EDWARD	WALSALL		28/8/1920	1	7			BRENTFORD					
PRICE	LLEWELLYN	CAERSWS	12/8/1896	25/8/1928	11	3			NOTTS COUNTY	1928		GRANTHAM		
PRIOR	STANLEY	SWINDON	20/12/1910	15/9/1937	9	6		3	CHARLTON ATHLETIC	1937		CHELTENHAM TOWN	1938	
PRITCHETT	KEITH	GLASGOW	8/11/1953	31/3/1975	3	4			DONCASTER ROVERS	1/1975		BRENTFORD	7/1976	
PRYCE	JOHN	RENTON	25/1/1874	7/9/1901	8	22		2	SHEFFIELD WEDNESDAY	1901		BRIGHTON & HOVE ALBION	1903	
PULLEN	HENRY	WELLINGBOROUGH	1888	29/4/1911	2	202		1	KETTERING	1910		NEWPORT COUNTY	1920	
QUASHIE	NIGEL	NUNHEAD	20/7/1978	30/12/1995	19	54	8	5	Juniors			NOTTINGHAM FOREST	8/1998	2,500,000
QUIGLEY	THOMAS	MID CALDER	26/3/1932	18/8/1956	9	17		7	PORTSMOUTH	6/1956		WORCESTER CITY	8/1957	
QUINN	GORDON	HAMMERSMITH	11/5/1932	18/10/1952	10	22		1	EASTCOTE B.C.	8/1952		PLYMOUTH ARGYLE	9/1956	
RADNAGE	JOSEPH			11/9/1909	5	3			READING					
RAMAGE	PETER	ASHINGTON	22/11/1983	9/8/2008	2	33	1		NEWCASTLE UNITED	7/2008	Free			
RAMSCAR	FRED	SALFORD	24/1/1919	4/12/1943	8	61		7	WOLVERHAMPTON	10/1947		PRESTON NORTH END	11/1949	
RAMSEY	ALEX	GATESHEAD		27/8/1921	11	6			NEWCASTLE UNITED	1921		ABERAMAN ATHLETIC		
RAMSEY	C.B.			6/12/1919	7	12		1						
RANCE	CHARLES	BOW	28/2/1899	30/9/1922	5	13			TOTTENHAM HOTSPUR	1922		GUILDFORD UNITED		

Surname	Christian	Born	Date	Debut	No	App	Sub	Goal	Signed From	Date	Signed Fee	Transferred To	Date	Transfer Fee
READ	A.			1/4/1918	4	1						Guest		
READ	ARTHUR	EALING	1899	27/8/1921	5	21			TUFNELL PARK	1921		READING	1922	
READY	KARL	NEATH	14/8/1972	9/10/1991	12	224	22	11	Trainee			MOTHERWELL	7/2001	Free
REAY	TED	TYNEMOUTH	5/8/1914	2/4/1938	3	88		1	SHEFFIELD UNITED	11/1937		QPR Assistant Trainer		
REED	GORDON	SPENNYMOOR	6/5/1913	25/8/1934	9	9		4	NEWPORT COUNTY	1934		DARLINGTON	1937	
REHMAN	ZESH	BIRMINGHAM	14/10/1983	12/8/2006	4	43	6		FULHAM	8/2006	250,000	BRADFORD CITY	7/2009	Free
REID	JOHNNY			1940		2			WISHAW JUNIORS	1/1938				
REID	PETER	HUYTON	20/6/1956	11/2/1989	11	31	1	1	EVERTON	2/1989	Free	MANCHESTER CITY	12/1989	Free
REVILL	EDWARD			2/9/1911	8	67		23	CHESTERFIELD	7/1911				
RHODES	ALBERT	DINNINGTON	29/4/1936	14/4/1956	2	5			WORKSOP TOWN	12/1954		TONBRIDGE		
RICHARDS	GEORGE			18/11/1916	4	1						Guest		
RICHARDSON	ANTHONY	SOUTHWARK	7/1/1932	19/1/1952	2	2			SLOUGH S.C.	4/1951				
RICHARDSON	DEREK	HACKNEY	13/7/1956	8/3/1977	1	32			CHELSEA	4/1976	Free	SHEFFIELD UNITED	12/1979	50,000
RICHARDSON	STUART	LEEDS	12/6/1938	3/1/1959	6	1			METHLEY UNITED	11/1956		OLDHAM ATHLETIC	7/1959	
RICHMOND	HUGH	KILMARNOCK		29/8/1925	5	10			COVENTRY CITY	5/1925		BLYTH SPARTANS	1926	
RICKETTS	ROHAN	CLAPHAM	22/12/1982	31/3/2007	C		2		WOLVERHAMPTON WANDERERS	3/2007	Loan	WOLVERHAMPTON WANDERERS	5/2007	Returned
RIDLEY	JOHN	BURDON MILL	19/1/1903	8/12/1934	2	21			READING	1934		NORTH SHIELDS	1935	
RIDYARD	ALFRED	CUDWORTH	5/5/1908	9/4/1938	5	243		9	WEST BROMWICH ALBION	3/1938		Retired – QPR Trainer	1948	
RIVERS	WALTER	THROCKLEY	8/1/1909	26/8/1933	4	4			CRYSTAL PALACE	7/1933		GATESHEAD		
ROBERTS	JOESPH	BIRKENHEAD	2/10/1900	5/11/1927	11	4			WATFORD			YORK CITY		
ROBERTS	TONY	BANGOR	4/8/1969	18/12/1987	1	145	1		Trainee	7/1987		MILLWALL	8/1998	Free
ROBERTS	WILLIAM			21/10/1905	11	22		1						
ROBINSON	JOHN	GRANGETOWN		27/10/1923	10	5		1	GUILDFORD	6/1923			1924	
ROBINSON	MICHAEL	LEICESTER	12/7/1958	29/12/1984	12	49	9	6	LIVERPOOL	12/1984	100,000	OSASUNA	1/1987	150,000
ROBINSON	PETER			16/9/1944	8	2			MANCHESTER UNITED			Guest		
ROEDER	GLENN	WOODFORD	13/12/1955	26/8/1978	2	181		18	ORIENT	8/1978	250,000	NEWCASTLE UNITED	12/1983	150,000
ROGERS	ALBERT			2/9/1907	8	34		10				BRISTOL ROVERS	1910	
ROGERS	ALBERT	MANCHESTER		15/12/1928	10	12		4	SOUTHALL	10/1928				
ROGERS	DON	PAULTON	25/10/1945	24/9/1974	12	13	6	5	CRYSTAL PALACE	9/1974	Venables	SWINDON TOWN	3/1976	33,000
ROGERS	MARTYN	NOTTINGHAM	26/1/1960	26/4/1980	2	2			MANCHESTER UNITED	7/1979		(Australia)		
RONALDSON	DUNCAN	BLYTHSWOOD	21/4/1879	1/12/1900	9	40		14	RUTHERGLEN			BURY	1900	
									GRIMSBY TOWN			NORWICH CITY		
ROSE	JACK	SHEFFIELD	26/10/1921	16/1/1943	2	138			PETERBOROUGH UNITED	3/1945		Retired	12/1949	
ROSE	MATTHEW	DARTFORD	24/9/1975	9/8/1997	2	236	24	8	ARSENAL	5/1997	500,000	Released	5/2007	
ROSE	RAMONE	READING	19/1/1990	4/5/2008	B	0	4		Youth Academy					
ROSENIOR	LEROY	CLAPTON	24/3/1964	3/9/1985	12	29	18	10	FULHAM	8/1982	100,000	FULHAM	6/1987	100,000
ROSSI	GENEROSO	NAPOLI, ITALY	3/1/1979	23/4/2005	1	3			LECCE	1/2005	Free	TRIESTINA	7/2005	Free
ROUNCE	GEORGE	GRAYS	1905	25/2/1928	8	188		71	UXBRIDGE TOWN	2/1928		FULHAM	3/1933	450
									GRIMSBY TOWN					
ROUTLEDGE	WAYNE	SIDCUP	7/1/1985	10/1/2009	7	18	1	1	ASTON VILLA	1/2009	600,000			
ROWE	ALFRED	POPLAR		5/4/1926	11	4		1	PLYMOUTH ARGYLE					
ROWE	JONTY	PACKMOOR		31/8/1935	3	57			READING	7/1935		PORT VALE	7/1937	Free
ROWLAND	KEITH	PORTADOWN	1/9/1971	31/1/1998	3	34	26	3	WEST HAM UNITED	1/1998	Sinclair (part)	CHESTERFIELD	7/2001	Free
ROWLANDS	MARTIN	HAMMERSMITH	8/2/1979	9/8/2003	B	191	14	37	BRENTFORD	7/2003	Free			
ROXBURGH	ALEXANDER	MANCHESTER	19/9/1910	4/3/1944	1	5			BLACKPOOL			Guest		
ROYCE	SIMON	NEWHAM	9/9/1971	24/8/2002	1	84			LEICESTER CITY	8/2002	Loan	LEICESTER CITY	11/2002	Returned
									CHARLTON ATHLETIC	2/2005	Loan	CHARLTON ATHLETIC	4/2005	Returned
									CHARLTON ATHLETIC	5/2005	Free	Released from Contract	5/2007	
RUDDOCK	NEIL	WANDSWORTH	9/5/1968	28/3/1998	6	7			LIVERPOOL	3/1998	Loan	LIVERPOOL	5/1998	Returned
RUSSELL	SIDNEY	STAINES	10/1911	4/2/1933	3	45			TUNBRIDGE WELLS	1933		NORTHAMPTON TOWN		
RUTHERFORD	MICHAEL	SIDCUP	6/6/1972	21/10/1989	12	1	2		Trainee					
RUTTER	KEITH	LEEDS	10/9/1931	24/8/1954	3	369		2	METHLEY UNITED	7/1954		COLCHESTER UNITED	2/1963	
RYDER	FRED			1/10/1904	10	73		21				BOLTON WANDERERS	1907	
SABIN	ERIC	SARCELLES	22/1/1975	9/8/2003	A	6	10	1	SWINDON TOWN	7/2003	Free	NORTHAMPTON TOWN	3/2004	Free

Surname	Christian	Born	Date	Debut	No	App	Sub	Goal	Signed From	Date	Signed Fee	Transferred To	Date	Transfer Fee
SAHAR	BEN	HOLON	10/9/1989	1/9/2007	10	6	3		CHELSEA	7/2007	Loan	CHESLEA	12/2007	Returned
SALES	ARTHUR	LEWES	4/3/1900	11/10/1930	4	38			CHELSEA	1930		BOURNEMOUTH	1933	
SALMON	LEONARD	WEST KIRBY	24/6/1912	12/9/1945	11	4		1	BURNLEY			Guest		
SALMON				7/10/1916	8	3		2				Guest		
SALT	HAROLD	SHEFFIELD		2/10/1926	5	5			PETERBOROUGH UNITED			GRAYS UNITED	1928	
SALVAGE	BARRY	BRISTOL	21/12/1947	27/3/1971	11	17	6	1	MILLWALL	3/1971	0	BRENTFORD	2/1973	9,000
SAME	FRANKIE	ST LOUIS, USA	13/10/1984	19/10/2004	3	5			ARSENAL	10/2004	Loan	ARSENAL	11/2004	Returned
SAMUEL	DAVID	SWANSEA	1911	31/8/1935	10	9		3	READING	6/1935		BARROW		
SANDERS	ARTHUR			23/2/1918	8	1						Guest		
SANDERSON	KEITH	HULL	9/10/1940	21/8/1965	10	118	6	12	PLYMOUTH ARGYLE	6/1965	4,000	GOOLE TOWN	3/1970	
SANGSTER	J.			21/9/1912	7	4			SOUTHALL					
SANSOM	KENNY	CAMBERWELL	26/9/1958	19/8/1989	3	82		2	NEWCASTLE UNITED	7/1989	300,000	COVENTRY CITY	3/1991	150,000
SANTOS	GEORGES	MARSEILLE	15/8/1970	7/8/2004	A	66	11	6	IPSWICH TOWN	7/2004	Free	Released	5/2006	
SAPHIN	REG	KILBURN	8/8/1916	4/12/1946	1	32			WALTHAMSTOW AVENUE	6/1946		WATFORD	7/1951	
SAUL	FRANK	CANVEY ISLAND	23/8/1943	15/8/1970	9	47	3	6	SOUTHAMPTON	5/1970	40,000	MILLWALL	3/1972	20,000
SAXON	VICTOR			16/9/1916	9	1						Guest		
SCOTT	LAURENCE	SHEFFIELD	23/4/1917	1940		1			ARSENAL			Guest		
SCULLY	TONY	DUBLIN	12/6/1976	21/3/1998	11	24	22	2	MANCHESTER CITY	3/1998	160,000	CAMBRIDGE UNITED	7/2001	Free
SEALY	TONY	HACKNEY	7/5/1959	21/3/1981	9	61	7	18	CRYSTAL PALACE	3/1981	80,000	FULHAM	1/1985	80,000
SEAMAN	DAVID	ROTHERHAM	19/9/1963	23/8/1986	1	175			BIRMINGHAM CITY	8/1986	225,000	ARSENAL	7/1990	1,300,000
SEARY	RAY	SLOUGH	18/9/1952	4/9/1971	12		1		Apprentice	9/1970		CAMBRIDGE UNITED	3/1974	3,000
SEELEY	GEORGE	SOUTHAMPTON	1879	7/9/1901	11	22		2	SOUTHAMPTON NEW BRIGHTON	1901		NEW BRIGHTON		
SHANKS	DON	HAMMERSMITH	2/10/1952	7/12/1974	4	201	5	11	LUTON TOWN	11/1974	35,000	BRIGHTON & HOVE ALBION	8/1981	Free
SHAW	ARTHUR	LIMEHOUSE	9/4/1924	10/4/1944	6	12		5						
SHAW	CHARLIE	TWECHAR	21/9/1885	2/9/1907	1	251			PORT GLASGOW	1907		GLASGOW CELTIC	1913	
SHEEN	JOHN	AIRDRIE	30/8/1920	5/2/1944	4	8		4	SHEFFIELD UNITED			Guest		
SHEPHERD	ERNEST	WOMBWELL	14/8/1919	19/8/1950	11	233		54	HULL CITY	8/1950		HASTINGS UNITED		
SHEPPARD	WILLIAM	FERRYHILL	1907	23/10/1930	10	13		4	WATFORD	6/1930		COVENTRY CITY	7/1931	
SHERON	MIKE	LIVERPOOL	11/1/1972	2/9/1997	10	61	8	20	STOKE CITY	7/1997	2,350,000	BARNSLEY	1/1999	1,500,000
SHIMMIN	DOMINIC	BERMONDSEY	13/10/1987	20/8/2005	4	3	1		ARSENAL	3/2005	Free	CRAWLEY TOWN	1/2008	Free
SHITTU	DANNY	LAGOS, NIGERIA	2/9/1980	23/10/2001	3	179	5	28	CHARLTON ATHLETIC	12/2001	250,000	WATFORD	8/2006	1,600,000
SHUFFLEBOTTOM	THOMAS		1881	18/3/1905	6	1			CHESTERFIELD	1904				
SHULT				2/12/1916	3	1						Guest		
SIBLEY	ALBERT	SOUTHEND	6/10/1919	21/2/1942	7	56		11	SOUTHEND UNITED			Guest		
SIBLEY	FRANK	UXBRIDGE	4/12/1947	4/9/1963	7	165	3	5	Apprentice	2/1965		QPR Coaching Staff		
SILKMAN	BARRY	LONDON	29/6/1952	1/11/1980	11	24	1	2	BRENTFORD	10/1980	20,000	ORIENT	9/1981	15,000
SILVER	ALAN			29/11/1954	1	1						TUNBRIDGE WELLS	7/1957	
SIMONS	TOMMY	CLAPTON	1887	14/11/1914	9	40		13	FULHAM	1914		NORWICH CITY		
SINCLAIR	SCOTT	BATH	26/3/1989	6/11/2007	9	8	1	1	CHELSEA	11/2007	Loan	CHELSEA	12/2007	Returned
SINCLAIR	TREVOR	DULWICH	2/3/1973	18/8/1993	11	185	5	21	BLACKPOOL	8/1993	750,000	WEST HAM UNITED	1/1998	2,000,000 + Dowie + Rowland
SINGLETON	HARRY	PRESCOTT	1877	3/9/1904	11	19			NEW BROMPTON	1904		LEEDS CITY	1905	
SINTON	ANDY	NEWCASTLE	19/3/1966	25/3/1989	7	190		25	BRENTFORD	3/1989	300,000	SHEFFIELD WEDNESDAY	8/1993	2,700,000
SKILTON	PERCY			30/4/1904	9	64		22	HARROW					
SKINNER	HARRY	MIDDLESEX	1875	16/9/1899	3	56		1	UXBRIDGE TOWN GRIMSBY TOWN	8/1899 1902		GRIMSBY TOWN	7/1901	
SLACK	RODNEY	FARCET	11/4/1940	14/10/1961	1	1			LEICESTER CITY	3/1961		CAMBRIDGE UNITED	7/1962	
SLADE	STEVE	ROMFORD	6/10/1975	28/8/1996	10	31	46	7	TOTTENHAM HOTSPUR	7/1996	350,000	CAMBRIDGE UNITED	7/2000	Free
SMALE	DOUGLAS	VICTORIA	27/2/1916	2/5/1942	6	2			CHELSEA			Guest		
SMITH	A.			4/9/1915	4	4								
SMITH	ALBERT	STOKE-ON-TRENT	27/8/1918	10/1/1942	7	144		3	BIRMINGHAM CITY	1939		Retired - knee injury		
SMITH	ARTHUR	STOURBRIDGE	1887	2/9/1911	7	37		8	BRIERLEY ATHLETIC	1911		BIRMINGHAM CITY	1912	
SMITH	B.			4/9/1915	8	1						Guest		

Surname	Christian	Born	Date	Debut	No	App	Sub	Goal	Signed From	Date	Signed Fee	Transferred To	Date	Transfer Fee
SMITH	CONWAY	HUDDERSFIELD	13/7/1926	17/3/1951	8	181		83	HUDDERSFIELD TOWN	3/1951		HALIFAX TOWN	6/1956	
SMITH	EDDIE			28/10/1944	8	3		1						
SMITH	EDWARD	LONDON	23/3/1929	24/8/1957	10	21		2	COLCHESTER UNITED	7/1957		CHELMSFORD	7/1958	
SMITH	FRANK	COLCHESTER	30/4/1936	24/9/1962	1	70			TOTTENHAM HOTSPUR	5/1962	Free	WIMBLEDON	11/1965	
SMITH	GEORGE	BROMLEY-BY-BOW	23/4/1915	23/8/1947	5	83		1	BRENTFORD	6/1947		IPSWICH TOWN	9/1949	
SMITH	J.			1940		1						Guest		
SMITH	JACK	DERBY		1/9/1917		159		66	THIRD LANARK	4/1919		SWANSEA TOWN	1922	
SMITH	JIMMY	NEWHAM	7/1/1987	30/9/2006	C	24	7	6	CHELSEA	9/2006	Loan	CHELSEA	5/2007	Returned
SMITH	LESLIE	EALING	13/3/1918	19/9/1945	7	1			BRENTFORD			Guest		
SMITH	NORMAN	NEWBURN	15/1/2/1897	30/8/1930	4	27			SHEFFIELD WEDNESDAY	8/1930		Retired	1932	
SMITH	NORMAN			28/8/1937	2	71		2	CHARLTON ATHLETIC	1937		CHELSEA	1939	Free
SMITH	STEPHEN C.	HEDNESFORD	27/3/1896	6/9/1928	11	25		1	CLAPTON ORIENT	5/1928		MANSFIELD TOWN	1929	
SMITH	STEPHEN R.			24/4/1926	1	2			GUILDFORD UNITED			GUILDFORD UNITED		
SMITH	TOM	ASHTON / MARKERFIELD	1876	9/9/1899	7	21		4	SOUTHAMPTON	8/1899		PRESTON NORTH END		
SNELGROVE	ERNIE		1886	18/4/1908	8	11		1	SITTINGBOURNE	1907			1909	
SOFFE	PERCY			2/12/1916	9	1						Guest		
SOMERFIELD	ALFRED	SOUTH KIRBY	22/3/1918	26/2/1944	8	19		7	WOLVERHAMPTON WANDERERS			Guest		
SOMERVILLE	J.			12/2/1916	6	8								
SOMMER	JUERGEN	NEW YORK, USA	22/2/1964	16/9/1995	25	71			LUTON TOWN	9/1995	600,000	COLUMBUS CREW	1/1998	175,000
SPACKMAN	NIGEL	ROMSEY	2/12/1960	4/2/1989	6	31	2	2	LIVERPOOL	2/1989	500,000	GLASGOW RANGERS	12/1989	500,000
SPENCE	WILLIAM	HARTLEPOOL	10/1/1926	25/12/1951	5	60			PORTSMOUTH	12/1951		Retired - injury	7/1955	
SPENCER	JOHN	GLASGOW	11/9/1970	23/11/1996	7	54		24	CHELSEA	11/1996	2,350,000	EVERTON	5/1998	1,500,000
SPOTISWOOD	JOE	CARLISLE		29/8/1925	11	22		2	SWANSEA TOWN					
SPRATLEY	ALAN	MAIDENHEAD	5/6/1949	4/1/1969	1	32			Apprentice	9/1968		SWINDON TOWN	7/1973	10,000
SPRINGETT	PETER	FULHAM	8/5/1946	18/5/1963	1	161			Apprentice	5/1963		SHEFFIELD WEDNESDAY	5/1967	35,000
SPRINGETT	RON	FULHAM	22/7/1935	5/11/1955	1	147			VICTORIA UNITED	2/1953		SHEFFIELD WEDNESDAY	3/1958	
									SHEFFIELD WEDNESDAY	6/1967		Retired		
ST AIMIE	KIERON	BRENT	4/5/1989	14/8/2007	A		1		Youth Academy			BARNET	1/2008	Free
STAINROD	SIMON	SHEFFIELD	1/2/1959	22/11/1980	10	175	2	62	OLDHAM ATHLETIC	11/1980	270,000	SHEFFIELD WEDNESDAY	2/1985	250,000
STANDLEY	THOMAS	POPLAR	23/12/1932	21/12/1957	9	14		2	BASILDON	5/1957		BOURNEMOUTH	11/1958	
STEER	J.H.			16/2/1918	2	25						BRISTOL CITY		
STEER	WILLIAM	KINGSTON ON THAMES	1888	1/9/1909	8	76		37	KINGSTON TOWN	1909		CHELSEA	1912	
STEIN	MARK	CAPE TOWN, SOUTH AFRICA	28/1/1966	27/8/1988	14	29	15	7	LUTON TOWN	8/1988	300,000	OXFORD UNITED	9/1989	200,000
STEINER	ROB	FINSPRONG, SWEDEN	20/6/1973	7/11/1998	14	32	7	9	BRADFORD CITY	11/1998	Loan	BRADFORD CITY	3/1999	Returned
									BRADFORD CITY	7/1999	300,000	Retired from football	12/2000	
STEJSKAL	JAN	CZECHOSLAVAKIA	15/1/1962	20/10/1990	1	122	1		SPARTA PRAGUE	10/1990	600,000	SLAVIA PRAGUE	7/1994	
STEPHENSON	HERBERT	LONDON		15/11/1930	8	2								
STEPHENSON	JAMES	NEW DELAVAL	2/1895	27/8/1927	7	18			WATFORD			NORWICH CITY		
STEVENS	RONALD	LUTON	26/11/1914	4/5/1939	11	1			LUTON TOWN	4/1939				
STEWART	DAMION	JAMAICA	18/8/1980	5/8/2006	3	128	5	11	BRADFORD CITY	7/2006	120,000			
STEWART	GEORGE	CHIRNSIDE	18/10/1920	13/4/1948	8	40		5	BRENTFORD	3/1948	4,000	SHREWSBURY TOWN	1/1953	
STEWART	IAN	BELFAST	10/9/1961	4/10/1980	12	65	17	4	Juniors	5/1980		NEWCASTLE UNITED	8/1985	100,000
STEWART	JOHN			5/10/1901	7	40		6	HIBERNIAN				7/1902	
STOCK	ALEC	PEASEDOWN	30/3/1917	26/2/1938	9	47		16	CHARLTON ATHLETIC	2/1938		YEOVIL TOWN (player/manager)		
STRICKLAND				3/2/1917	11	1						Guest		
STRUGNELL	HERBERT			25/10/1913	8	11			ASTON VILLA					
STURRIDGE	DEAN	BIRMINGHAM	27/7/1973	19/3/2005	B	6	5		WOLVERHAMPTON	3/2005	Free	KIDDERMINSTER HARRIERS	7/2006	
SUGDEN	SIDNEY	BATTERSEA	1880	2/9/1905	8	69		21	NOTTINGHAM FOREST	1905		BRENTFORD	1909	
SUTCH	W.H.			3/1/1920	10	1		2						
SWAN	JACK	EASINGTON	10/7/1893	12/2/1927	10	28		5	WATFORD				1928	
SWANN	HUBERT	LYTHAM	28/3/1882	9/10/1909	8	4		1	CRYSTAL PALACE	1909				
SWEETMAN	SIDNEY	LONDON		7/2/1925	5	102			HAMPSTEAD TOWN	2/1925		MILLWALL	1929	
SWINFEN	REG	BATTERSEA	4/5/1915	19/9/1936	8	124		42	CIVIL SERVICE			YEOVIL TOWN		
SYMES	ERNEST	FULHAM	22/8/1892	8/11/1924	3	30			ABERDARE ATHLETIC					

Surname	Christian	Born	Date	Debut	No	App	Sub	Goal	Signed From	Date	Signed Fee	Transferred To	Date	Transfer Fee
TAARABT	ADEL	Morroco	24/5/1989	14/3/2009	B	5	2	1	TOTTENHAM HOTSPUR	3/2009	Loan	TOTTENHAM HOTSPUR	5/2009	Returned
TAGG	TONY	EPSOM	10/4/1957	23/8/1975	6	4			Apprentice	3/1975		MILLWALL	7/1977	Free
TAYLOR	ANDY	BLACKBURN	14/3/1986	14/1/2006	A	1	2		BLACKBURN ROVERS	1/2006	Loan	BLACKBURN ROVERS	2/2006	Returned
TAYLOR	BRIAN	HAMMERSMITH	2/7/1944	23/3/1963	2	52			Juniors	3/1962		ROMFORD		
TAYLOR	GARETH	WESTON-SUPER-MARE	25/2/1973	18/3/2000	C	2	4	1	MANCHESTER CITY	3/2000	Loan	MANCHESTER CITY	4/2000	Returned
TAYLOR	GEOFF	HENSTEAD	22/1/1923	25/12/1953	7	2			BRISTOL ROVERS	11/1953		GUILDFORD	1954	
TAYLOR	GEORGE	WIGAN	21/3/1920	17/3/1945	1	3			WEST HAM UNITED			Guest		
TAYLOR	JIM	HILLINGDON	5/11/1917	19/8/1953	5	44			FULHAM	4/1953		TUNBRIDGE WELLS (p / m)	7/1954	
TAYLOR	ROBERT	NORWICH	30/4/1971	30/8/2001	11	3	1		WOLVERHAMPTON WANDERERS	8/2001	Loan	WOLVERHAMPTON WANDERERS	9/2001	Returned
TAYLOR				26/1/1907	4	2								
TEABAY				7/10/1916	9	2						Guest		
TEALE	RICHARD	MILLOM	27/2/1952	7/9/1974	1	2			WALTON & HERSHAM	7/1973		FULHAM	8/1976	
TEMBY	WILLIAM	DOVER	16/9/1934	5/11/1955	4	6		3	RHYL	12/1955		DOVER		
TENNANT	ALBERT	ILKESTON	29/10/1917	17/2/1945	8	1			CHELSEA			Guest		
TENNANT	WILLIAM	COATBRIDGE	1875	9/9/1899	5	15		5	ARTHURLIE	8/1899				
THOMAS	DAVE	KIRKBY	5/10/1950	21/10/1972	7	219	1	34	BURNLEY	10/1972	165,000	EVERTON	8/1977	200,000
THOMAS	JEROME	WEMBLEY	23/3/1983	30/3/2002	9	9	1	3	ARSENAL	3/2002	Loan	ARSENAL	5/2002	Returned
									ARSENAL	8/2002	Loan	ARSENAL	10/2002	Returned
THOMPSON	ANDY			28/10/1905	7	24		7						
THOMPSON	CHARLES	WREKENTON		29/10/1921	2	1			NEWCASTLE UNITED					
THOMPSON	GARRY	BIRMINGHAM	7/10/1959	21/8/1991	14	14	11	4	CRYSTAL PALACE	8/1991	100,000	CARDIFF CITY	8/1993	Free
THOMPSON	JOHN	WILLESDEN		27/12/1924	4	26			YEOVIL & PETTERS					
THOMPSON	OLIVER	WHEATLEY	11/5/1900	1/9/1928	6	18			CHESTERFIELD	1928		YORK CITY	1930	
THOMPSON	WILLIAM	MORPETH	8/1886	5/9/1912	7	139		8	PLYMOUTH ARGYLE	1912		SOUTH SHIELDS	1914	
									SOUTH SHIELDS			NEWPORT COUNTY	1920	
THOMSON	ANDY	MOTHERWELL	1/4/1971	24/3/2001	A	49	25	30	GILLINGHAM	3/2001	Free	PARTICK THISTLE	7/2003	Free
THORNTON	HENRY			9/9/1911	10	37		10		9/1911		Died in WW1		
THORPE	TONY	LEICESTER	10/4/1974	23/8/2003	10	28	18	11	LUTON TOWN	8/2003	50,000	SWINDON TOWN	7/2005	Free
THURMAN				22/9/1917	10	13		3						
THWAITES	A.			20/1/1917	5	2						Guest		
TILSON	ANDY	HUNTINGDON	30/6/1966	23/12/1990	4	30	2	2	GRIMSBY TOWN	12/1990	400,000	BRISTOL ROVERS	11/1992	375,000
TIMOSKA	SAMPSA	FINLAND	12/2/1979	13/1/2007	A	14	7		MyPa, FINLAND	1/2007	Free	MyPa	2/2008	Free
TOMKYS	MICHAEL	KENSINGTON	14/12/1932	24/11/1951	7	97		18	FULHAM	11/1951		YIEWSLEY	9/1959	
TOMMASI	DOMIANO	ITALY	17/5/1974	28/10/2008	8	5	2		LEVANTE	9/2008	Free	Contract Cancelled	1/2009	
TOMS	T.			25/11/1916	3	2						Guest		
TOSSWILL	JOHN	EASTBOURNE	1890	5/4/1912	8	3		1	MAIDSTONE UNITED	1911		LIVERPOOL	1912	
TOWERS	JIM	SHEPHERDS BUSH	15/4/1933	19/8/1961	10	32		16	BRENTFORD	5/1961	8,000 (inc. Francis)	MILLWALL	8/1962	
TOWNSEND	LUKE	GUILDFORD	28/9/1986	19/4/2005	B		2		Youth Academy			Released	5/2006	
TRAVERS	JAMES	BIRMINGHAM	4/11/1888	1/9/1909	9	41		8	ASTON VILLA	1909		LEICESTER FOSSE	1910	
TRINDALE				23/2/1918	7	1						Guest		
TRODD	WILLIAM			13/4/1935	4	7			LEYTON	1930				
TURNBULL	PETER	LANQUHAR	1875	9/9/1899	10	28		13	MILLWALL ATHLETIC	8/1899		BRENTFORD	1901	
TURNER	WILLIAM	SOUTH MOOR	22/12/1894	27/8/1927	6	39			BURY					
TURPIE	BOBBY	HAMPSTEAD	13/11/1949	13/9/1969	12	1	1		Apprentice	11/1967		PETERBOROUGH UNITED	7/1970	
TUTT	WALTER			14/1/1931	11	7		3	CANTERBURY WAVERLEY					
UKAH	UGO	NIGERIA	18/1/1984	20/8/2005	B	1	1			7/2005	Free	NOURESE CALICO, ITALY	7/2006	
UNDERWOOD	DAVE	ST PANCRAS	15/3/1928	26/1/1952	1	2			EDGWARE TOWN	12/1949		WATFORD	2/1952	
VAFIADIS	SETH	HAMMERSMITH	8/9/1945	28/9/1963	7	15		4	CHELSEA	11/1962		MILLWALL	9/1964	
VALLENCE	HUGH	WOLVERHAMPTON	14/6/1905	16/2/1929	8	1			ASTON VILLA	1928		BRIGHTON & HOVE ALBION	1929	
VANGO	ALFRED	WALTHAMSTOW	23/12/1900	14/1/1931	5	12			WALTHAMSTOW AVENUE			CLAPTON ORIENT		
VARCO	PERCY	FOWEY	17/4/1904	28/8/1926	8	16		4	ASTON VILLA			NORWICH CITY	1927	
VENABLES	TERRY	BETHNAL GREEN	6/1/1943	9/8/1969	4	205	1	22	TOTTENHAM HOTSPUR	6/1969	70,000	CRYSTAL PALACE	9/1974	Rogers
VIGRASS	JOHN	LEEK	4/1/	22/4/1922	6	71		1	LEEK ALEXANDRA			MACCLESFIELD TOWN		
VINCENT	ERNIE	SPENNYMOOR	28/10/1907	31/8/1935	5	31			MANCHESTER UNITED	1935		DONCASTER ROVERS	7/1937	Free

Surname	Christian	Born	Date	Debut	No	App	Sub	Goal	Signed From	Date	Signed Fee	Transferred To	Date	Transfer Fee
VINE	ROWAN	BASINGSTOKE	21/9/1982	3/10/2007	11	34	4	8	BIRMINGHAM CITY	10/2007	1,000,000			
VIRTUE				9/12/1916	2	2						Guest		
WADDOCK	GARY	KINGSBURY	17/3/1962	28/8/1979	12	227	13	10	Apprentice	7/1979		CHARLEROI		
									MILLWALL	2/1992		LUTON TOWN	11/1992	100,000
WAGSTAFF				4/3/1916	10	1		1				Guest		
WAKE	WILLIAM	BANBURY CASTLE	1887	1/9/1909	6	240		1	EXETER CITY	1909				
WALKER	ARTHUR	RIPLEY	8/1888	14/9/1907	9	30		16	NOTTINGHAM FOREST	1907		NOTTS COUNTY	1909	
WALKER	CLIVE	OXFORD	26/5/1957	17/12/1985	7	22	5	2	SUNDERLAND	12/1985	70,000	FULHAM	10/1987	Free
WALLACE	BARRY	PLAISTOW	17/4/1959	26/10/1977	11	20	8		Juniors	8/1977		TULSA ROUGHNECKS		
WALLER	WILLIAM	BOLTON		1/3/1924	10	2			CHORLEY					
WALSH	MICKEY	CHORLEY	13/8/1954	31/3/1979	9	15	5	3	EVERTON	3/1979	EASTOE	FC OPORTO	8/1980	175,000
WALSH	PAUL	PLUMSTEAD	1/10/1962	17/9/1991	9	2			TOTTENHAM HOTSPUR	9/1991	Loan	TOTTENHAM HOTSPUR	9/1991	Returned
WALSH				12/2/1916	10	1						Guest		
WALSHE	BEN	HARLESDEN	24/5/1983	28/4/2001	B	1	1		Youth Academy			ST ALBANS CITY	7/2004	Free
WALTERS				15/9/1917	11	29		11						
WALTON	SIMON	SHERBURN-IN-ELMET	13/9/1987	11/12/2007	B	1	4		CHARLTON ATHLETIC	8/2007	200,000	PLYMOUTH ARGYLE	7/2008	750,000
WARBURTON	ARTHUR	BURY	10/9/1908	10/9/1938	10	21			FULHAM	1938		Retired		
WARD	DARREN	HARROW	13/9/1978	18/12/1999	3	15			WATFORD	12/1999	Loan	WATFORD	3/2000	Returned
WARD	NICK	PERTH, AUSTRALIA	24/3/1985	5/8/2006	10	14	9	1	PERTH GLORY, AUSTRALIA	7/2006	120,000	MELBOURNE VICTORY	12/2007	Free
WARDLE	GEORGE	KIMBLESWORTH	24/9/1919	29/1/1949	7	55		4	CARDIFF CITY	1/1949		DARLINGTON	8/1951	
WARDLEY	STUART	CAMBRIDGE	10/9/1974	7/9/1999	A	78	17	17	SAFFRON WALDEN TOWN	7/1999	15,000	RUSHDEN & DIAMONDS	3/2002	Free
WARREN	CHRISTER	POOLE	10/10/1974	26/8/2000	A	26	12		BOURNEMOUTH	6/2000	Free	BRISTOL ROVERS	8/2002	Free
WASH	J.			25/11/1916	8	2						Guest		
WASSEL	HAROLD	STOURBRIDGE	21/9/1879	18/11/1905	3	3			BRISTOL ROVERS	1905				
WATERALL	ALBERT	NOTTINGHAM	1/3/1887	18/9/1926	5	2			STOCKPORT COUNTY			CLAPTON ORIENT		
WATSON	EDWARD	SHOTTON	1899	11/9/1922	2	8			SUNDERLAND			ROCHDALE		
WATSON	GEORGE	SHOTTON COLLIERY	1914	6/10/1934	7	8		1	DURHAM CITY	2/1934				
WATSON	GUY			28/4/1906	1	1								
WATSON	IAN	HAMMERSMITH	7/1/1944	21/8/1965	2	226	6	2	CHELSEA	7/1965	5,000	Retired		
WATTS	FRED	LONDON		30/4/1920	3	5						YEOVIL & PETTERS		
WAUGH	LYLE	NEWCASTLE	1899	12/9/1923	5	5			BEDLINGTON COLLIERY			CRAMLINGTON WE		
WAUGH	WILLIAM	EDINBURGH	27/11/1921	19/8/1950	7	78		6	LUTON TOWN	7/1950		BOURNEMOUTH	7/1953	
WEARE	ROSS	PERIVALE	19/3/1977	20/11/1999	B		5		EAST HAM UNITED	3/1999	10,000	BRISTOL ROVERS	7/2001	Free
WEBB	DAVID	EAST HAM	9/4/1946	16/8/1974	6	146	1	11	CHELSEA	7/1974	120,000	LEICESTER CITY	9/1977	50,000
WEBB	ISAAC	WORCESTER	10/10/1874	11/3/1907	1	10			SUNDERLAND	1906		WEST BROMWICH ALBION		
									WEST BROMWICH ALBION			Retired	1910	
WEBB	J.			1940		20		1						
WEBB	RON	BRENTFORD	13/3/1925	11/9/1943	8	6				1944		CRYSTAL PALACE	9/1946	
WEBLIN	FRANCES			14/12/1912	2	11			WEST NORWOOD					
WEGERLE	ROY	JOHANESBURG, S. AFRICA	19/3/1964	16/12/1989	14	88	4	31	LUTON TOWN	12/1989	1,000,000	BLACKBURN ROVERS	3/1992	1,000,000
WELTON	PAT	ELTHAM	3/5/1928	7/2/1959	1	3			LEYTON ORIENT	3/1958		ST ALBANS (manager)		
WENTWORTH	F.			1/9/1909	4	7			SALISBURY CITY					
WESTWOOD	DANNY	DAGENHAM	25/7/1953	8/10/1974	9	1	1	1	BILLERICAY TOWN	7/1974		GILLINGHAM	11/1975	5,000
WHATMORE	ERNEST	KIDDERMINSTER	25/4/1900	25/8/1928	10	82		3	BRISTOL ROVERS	1928		SHEPHERD'S BUSH		
WHELDON	GEORGE	BIRMINGHAM	1/11/1871	16/11/1901	10	14		6	WEST BROMWICH ALBION	1901		PORTSMOUTH	1902	
WHITAKER	COLIN	LEEDS	14/6/1932	18/2/1961	11	8			SHREWSBURY TOWN	2/1961		ROCHDALE	5/1961	
WHITE	DEVON	NOTTINGHAM	2/3/1964	27/1/1993	14	18	11	9	CAMBRIDGE UNITED	1/1993	100,000	NOTTS COUNTY	12/1994	100,000
WHITE	J.			6/4/1917	2	25								
WHITE	JABEZ	DROYLESDON	1879	28/9/1901	5	140		1	GRAYS UNITED	1901		LEEDS CITY	1908	
WHITE	WILLIAM			11/11/1899	9	25		8	NEW BROMPTON	1899		LIVERPOOL	1901	
WHITEHEAD	WILLIAM	SAFFRON WALDEN		17/10/1925	9	28		5	SWANSEA TOWN			PRESTON NORTH END		
WHITEHEAD	WILLIAM	MALTBY	6/2/1920	22/9/1945	11	10		1	MALTBY M.C.W.			ALDERSHOT	8/1947	Free
WHITELAW	GEORGE	PAISLEY	1/1/1937	16/3/1959	9	27		10	SUNDERLAND	3/1959		HALIFAX TOWN	11/1959	
WHITFIELD	KEN	BISHOPS AUCKLAND	24/3/1930	26/9/1959	10	23		3	BRIGHTON	7/1959		BIDEFORD (player/manager)	4/1961	

Surname	Christian	Born	Date	Debut	No	App	Sub	Goal	Signed From	Date	Signed Fee	Transferred To	Date	Transfer Fee
WHITFIELD	WILF	CHESTERFIELD	17/11/1916	31/5/1941		4			BRISTOL ROVERS			Guest		
WHITING	J.			3/2/1917	9	8		1						
WHITTAKER	DICK	DUBLIN	10/10/1934	24/8/1963	2	18			PETERBOROUGH UNITED	7/1963		KINGS LYNN	7/1964	
WHYMAN	ALFRED		1887	1/9/1909	10	206		25	NEW BROMPTON	1909			1920	
WICKS	JIM	READING		8/11/1924	1	5			READING					
WICKS	STEVE	READING	3/10/1956	25/9/1979	12	220	1	6	DERBY COUNTY	9/1979	275,000	CRYSTAL PALACE	6/1981	250,000+Allen
									CRYSTAL PALACE	3/1982	325,000	CHELSEA	8/1986	400,000
WILCOX	JONAH	COLEFORD	9/1/1894	28/8/1926	9	9		2	BRISTOL ROVERS			GILLINGHAM	1927	
WILDE	J.			29/4/1914	5	13			SHEFFIELD UNITED					
WILES	GEORGE	EAST HAM	5/1905	5/9/1929	3	18			SITTINGBOURNE	1929		WALSALL	7/1933	
WILES	HARRY	EAST HAM		31/8/1929	8	43		25	SITTINGBOURNE	1929		WALSALL	7/1933	
WILKINS	DEAN	HILLINGDON	12/7/1962	1/11/1980	12	2	5		Apprentice	5/1980		BRIGHTON & HOVE ALBION	8/1983	Free
WILKINS	RAY	HILLINGDON	14/9/1956	2/12/1989	7	200	7	10	GLASGOW RANGERS	12/1989	Free	CRYSTAL PALACE	5/1994	Free
									CRYSTAL PALACE	11/1994	Free	WYCOMBE WANDERERS	9/1996	Free
WILKS	ALAN	SLOUGH	5/10/1946	27/12/1966	9	47	7	19	CHELSEA	5/1965	Free	GILLINGHAM	7/1971	5,000
WILLIAMS	BILL	ESHER	23/8/1942	16/9/1961	3	48			PORTSMOUTH	7/1961		WEST BROMWICH ALBION	6/1963	
WILLIAMS	BRIAN	SALFORD	5/11/1955	20/8/1977	12	10	13		BURY	7/1977	70,000	SWINDON TOWN	6/1978	50,000
WILLIAMS	TOMMY	CARSHALTON	8/7/1980	10/8/2002	C	31	7	1	BIRMINGHAM CITY	8/2002	Loan	BIRMINGHAM CITY	5/2003	Returned
									BIRMINGHAM CITY	8/2003	Loan	BIRMINGHAM CITY	9/2003	Returned
WILLOCK	CALUM	LONDON	29/10/1981	9/11/2002	10	3			FULHAM	11/2002	Loan	FULHAM	12/2002	Returned
WILSON	ANDY	NEWMAINS	14/2/1896	10/10/1931	10	23		3	CHELSEA	10/1931		NIMES		1932
WILSON	CLIVE	MANCHESTER	13/11/1961	25/8/1990	8	196	3	14	CHELSEA	8/1990	450,000	TOTTENHAM HOTSPUR	6/95	Free
WILSON	K.			1940		1								
WILSON	TOM	PRESTON	20/10/1877	3/9/1902	11	62		3	LONDON CALEDONIA	1902		BOLTON WANDERERS	1904	
WILSON	TOM	PRESTON	20/10/1877	25/12/1909	10	6		1	MANCHESTER UNITED	1909		Retired	1911	
WINGROVE	JOSEPH	SOUTHALL		23/4/1913	2	88			UXBRIDGE TOWN					
WINYARD	WILLIAM			14/10/1916	1	8			MILLWALL					
WISE	E.			2/12/1916	4	1						Guest		
WITTER	TONY	LONDON	12/8/1965	14/8/1993	6	1			CRYSTAL PALACE	8/1991	25,000	MILLWALL	12/94	100,000
WODEHOUSE	GEORGE			3/4/1920	4	1								
WOOD	ARTHUR	SOUTHAMPTON	8/5/1890	15/12/1923	10	20			NEWPORT COUNTY			Retired - Injury	1927	
WOOD				16/10/1915	2	9								
WOODS	CHRIS	SWINESHEAD	14/11/1959	18/8/1979	1	72			NOTTINGHAM FOREST	7/1979	250,000	NORWICH CITY	3/1981	250,000
WOODS	PAT	ISLINGTON	29/4/1933	3/1/1953	2	333		16	Juniors	6/1950		HELLENIC, AUSTRALIA	5/1961	
WOODWARD	HORACE	ISLINGTON	16/1/1924	20/8/1949	5	58			TOTTENHAM HOTSPUR	6/1949		WALSALL	7/1953	
WOODWARD	JOSEPH	CATFORD	2/1904	3/3/1928	1	11			CLAPTON ORIENT			MERTHYR TOWN	1929	
WREN	A.			18/11/1916	1	1					Guest			
WRIGGLESWORTH	WILLIAM	SOUTH ELMSALL	12/11/1912	19/9/1945	11	1			MANCHESTER UNITED		Guest			
WRIGHT	ARTHUR			4/11/1916	6	52								
WRIGHT	ERNIE	MIDDLETON	1912	26/1/1935	10	1			SEDGLEY PARK			CREWE ALEXANDRA	1935	
WRIGHT	PAUL	EAST KILBRIDE	17/8/1967	19/8/1989	10	11	8	6	ABERDEEN	7/1989	275,000	HIBERNIAN	1/1990	300,000
WYATT	A.			12/3/1910	7	10								
WYPER	THOMAS	CALTON	8/10/1900	29/8/1931	7	11			CHARLTON ATHLETIC	1931		CHESTER	1932	
									CHESTER			BRISTOL ROVERS	19333	
YATES	JOHN	MANCHESTER	26/9/1903	9/9/1929	6	10			ASTON VILLA	1929		STOURBRIDGE		
YATES	STEVE	BRISTOL	29/1/1970	18/8/1993	6	137	12	2	BRISTOL ROVERS	8/1993	750,000	TRANMERE ROVERS	8/1999	Free
YENSON	WILLIAM	KINGSTON BAGPUIZE	1880	2/9/1905	6	94		4	BOLTON WANDERERS	1905		WEST HAM UNITED	1908	
									WEST HAM UNITED			CROYDON COMMON	1909	
YIELLEYOYE	H.			4/12/1943	11	1			BELGIAN ARMY	12/1943				
YOUNG	HERBERT	LIVERPOOL	4/9/1899	31/8/1929	11	15		1	NEWPORT COUNTY	1929		BRISTOL ROVERS	1930	
YOUNG	JOHN	WHITBURN	1895	28/8/1926	3	91		12	WEST HAM UNITED			ACCRINGTON STANLEY		
YOUNG	WILLIAM	FERRYBRIDGE	1898	21/3/1925	8	8		2	TYNESIDE DISTRICT	2/1925		KETTERING TOWN	1927	
YOUSSOUF	SAMMY	COPENHAGEN, DENMARK	7/9/1976	4/2/2006	B	2	4		MARITIMO, PORTUGAL	1/2006	Free	Released	5/2006	
ZELIC	NED	SYDNEY, AUSTRALIA	4/7/1971	23/8/1995	A	3	1		BORUSSIA DORTMUND	8/1995	1,200,000	EINTRACHT FRANKFURT	3/1996	750,000

Roll of Honour

Don Heather
Raymond J. F. Brown
David R. Brown
Jeffrey N. Brown
Graham R. Brown
Mark Scott
David Coulson
Mark (HoopsOfEssex) Dunbar
Raymond Cutler
Ron Hill
Paul Varcoe
James Luck
Chris Hewitt
John Kenna - Republic of Ireland
Patrick John O'Dwyer
Michael Patrick Malachy O'Dwyer
Brian Robertson
John Plumridge
Francis Atkinson
David Robinson
Keith Smith
Steve Quashie
Andy Evans
Katie Ashby
Gavin Taylor
Boyd Brinkman
Malcolm Oakley
Mark Breagan
Barry Anthony William Strong
Terry Springett
Sarah Holt
Dave Dore
John Macdonald
Julie Newman
Ian Taylor
Paul Morrissey
Joe Kyle
Nigel Blackman
Jeffrey Seward
Mr. William A. Powell
Neil A. Austin
Keith James Hetherington
Henry P. Holder
Oliver P. Holder
Keith Porter
Damian Boys
David Jackson
Stephen Jenkins
Paul, Ben and Luke Mason
Mark Mosselson
John-Paul Yuill
Joe McCarthy
James P. Doherty
Stuart Leslie Ian Mason
Peter Howard
William Joseph (AKA Joe) English
J. L. Gurr
Scott Row
Richard Sawyer
Anders Nygard
Max Smith
Mark James Winmill
Michael Webster
Mark Matthews
Mark Bewsey
Geoff Langridge
Andy Barrett
Steve Lewington
Steve Betts
Michael O'Halloran
David Bowman
Anders Hove
Mike Hawdon
Allan Barnard
Pete Key
Ray Marno

Tony Raffermati
Mike Pelizzoni
Brian Dallamore
Roy Dallamore
Fred Hartman
Joseph Hartman
Alan Green
Roy Morris
Martin Simmonds
John Davidson
Simon J. Godley
John McNeill
Les Carder
Colin Speller
Nik Speller
Harry H. Hayward
Phillip Tureck
John Harris
Anne Dickerson
Nikk Gunns
Ian Ellis
Colin Mark Dawes
Steve Roome
John Leyson
Katie Everton
Hugh Phillipps
Trish Phillips
Steve Parkin
John Barrett
Lee Barrett
Craig Barrett
Terry Smith
Dave Burt
Robin Lomas
Stephen Charles Smith
Neil Truckle
Tony Brind
Jason Attridge
Mike Ray
Marcus Ray

Roger Stokes
Paul Stokes (Stokesy)
David Ohl
Michael Beevor
Jamie Stuart
Trevor Douglas Parsons
Chris Dolan
Brian Green
David Green
Richard Haynes (Bedford_R)
Tim Kelleher
Brian Walden
Wendy Haynes
Raymond Haynes
Susan Haynes
Anthony Ryan (Stodge)
Richard Fraser
Nich Carter
Steve Clarke
Stanley Murphy
Paul Bargery
Iain Martin Procter
Andrew K. W. Harvey
Andrew Beckett
Scott Bailey
Martin Percival
Eamon P. Farrell
Oliver Saragoussi
Mungo Penfold
Joseph Daniel Morris
Stanley Hadley
Jim Watts
Norman M. Davies
Noel McKeown
Alf Henrik Hansen
Niall Reilly
Adam Witkover
Alan Power
Charles Diggons
Gary Buchan

Roar Eskild Jacobsen
Emil Harkness
Nathan, Toby and Abby Burchall
Martyn Royle
Tom Barrow
Patrick Connolly
Jason Mark Robertson
Adrian Powers
Ian Harris
Andrew O'Loughlin
Adam George Maher
Paul Stych
Brendan P. Byrne
Michael Reid
Michael Cartin
Jim Simms
Geoffrey Quick
David Quick
Michael Coles
Adrian Cummings
John Summers
Tony Mackenzie
Steve Colwell
George Simissen
Eric Stuart
Juan Pedro Adrados
Richard, Stuart & Oliver Franks
Richard Powell
Louis Moir
Simon Kingham
Steve Overall
Denis O'Sullivan
Isabella and Joe Robertson
Clive Collins
Daniel John Weston
Ricky Don Weston
Perry John Weston
James Privett
Geoff Privett
Mark Levander

Terry Brown
Rodney Brazier
Peter Pike
Andrew Holland
Roy William Hendy
Terry Dodd
Steven Grover
Declan Finnegan
John Williams
David Jones
Benjamin J. Reisman
Desmond Reynolds
Adrian David Cooke
David Hancy
David Cowdrey
Darren Hetherington
Simon Mahoney
Jeff Budd
Daniel Gristwood
Denis George Gristwood
Graham Black
Jonathan Silvester
Joshua Silvester
Kelly Speller
Mark Smedley
Rob Anderson
Larry and Tom Barker
John Hopkins
Christopher Smithers
David Jones
Robert Stuart Hill
Gary McIlfatrick
Andy Hamilton
Raymond David Adams
Nigel Biggs
Darren Billing
Les Walsh
Gareth Ebenezer
Henry Besant
Robert Grey

Kevin Roy Powell
Iain Pithers
Paul McGinnes
John F. Sharp
Phil and Jack Boswell
Chris Martin
Roy Newstead
Matt Kilshaw
David L. Osborn
Graham Smith
Stuart Ratcliffe
Harry Meades
Ronald William Whyley
Jamie David John Carbery
Adrian Bland
Mr Graham Charlton
Vesa Pirnes
Susanna Pirnes
Martin Masterson-Andrews (55y)
Simon Ingall
John Blakemore
Barry Hodson
Terry Tew
Richard Ellis
Kenneth Westerberg
Bernard Lambert
Paul Willis
Andrew John Jones
Clive and James Thompson
Scott Richard Weaver
Ian Jones
William Hodges
Jim Johnson
Brian Loader
Seagry Teagle
Robin Jeeps
Nigel Pickering
Robert Overington
Robin Neary
Dave Crouch

Antony Simmons
Gareth Brennan
David Dresch
Zack Speller
Stuart Hearn
Stephen Harris
Andrew Melham
Tony Duffy
Graham Whitehead
Daniel Dylan Stoddart
Stephen J. Brown
Duncan Gamble
Nick (slaphead) Granger
Bob Pitcher
Kirsty Pitcher
Philip Beach
Alan Penson
Michael Penson
Ron and Sophie Risbridger
Glen Robert Dauwalder
Joe Slane
Brian A. Humphreys
John Wood
Frode Rekve
James Halsey
Alan Kerr
Jamie Allen
Alex Baxter
Alexander Cocks
Chris Stormer
Jamie Duncan Macfarlane
Andrea Price
Ian Bannister
Gregg Chapman
Jari Sulonen
Kjetil Huseboe
John Fisher
Jan Merling
Naomi Jones
James Humphreys

George Harper
Robert Alan Davis
Russell Peter Davis
Peter William Davis
Graham Fidler
John Francis Hanafin
Paul John Hanafin
Raymond Thomas
Dave Morrison
Philip Johnston-Smith
Sam Heptinstall
Terry Johns
Gary Hatton
Michael Treby
Euen Weeks
Tony Kavanagh
Anders Bergenholtz
Luke Durrant
Graham Weekes
Ben Handley - Pritchard
Field Handley - Pritchard
Paul Handley
Daniel Callan
Gary Salter
Angus The Batman Senior
David Fairclough
Lawrence A. Meek
Simon Cheshire
Michelle Cheshire
Stuart Wilson
Michael White
Rickie Jones
Robert Blakey
Jeff Maslin
Jim Heels
Gordon A. & B. Roberts
Shamit Biswas
Dag HÃ¥kon Hellevik
Pete Sadler
The Maddox Family (Blackpool)
Darren Davey
William John Soden
Kenneth Johansen
Barry Thorn
Steve Webb
Gary Munson
Chris Brooks
Andrew David Newham
Nigel Tilson
Georgia, Amicia & Laurel Nelson
Bob Alderton
Ernest Albert Underwood
Steven Wayne
Roger J. Stokes
Andrew Foley
Bill Freer
Moreno Ferrari
Luke & James Duffy
Robert Dawe
Ken Green
Conrad Svard
Karl Svard
Joshua Fisk
Edward Grayson
Richard S. Grayson
Gillian Maureen Collings
John Joseph Taylor
W. E. Keywood (Jersey)
David Vyvyan
Joseph Higgins
Paul Kerrin
Jacob Cashman
David and Ben Adams
Stephen John Smith
Paul Robert Hull
Dave Clayton 1965
Adam Richard Daryl Smith
Keith McRobert
Gary Richards
Justin Burden

Julian Dromgoole
Sidney Giles
Martin Davis
Andy Shorter
Mano Singh Ladhar
Tony Warrick
Bill Fleming
Lauren & Emma Cass
Steve Rhodes
Alan Lawson
Bill Gristwood
Andy Barnard
Louis Bremner
John O'Driscoll
Kevin David Gamblin
Jamie Peters
Jon Cerasale
Roger Payne
Mr Len Hillier
James Chatterley
Gary Morgan
Antony Eastmond
John Quigley
James Farrell
Teddy Twohig
Paul Blue and White Blood Heaphy
Steve Russell
Roland Stallings
Ian Miles
Yngve Ness
Leslie R. J. Bentley
David Smith
Jeremy Bartholomew
Daniel Hodgkins
Alan McEwan
John Southgate
Robin Churchill
Ross Churchill
Robert Armstrong
Harry Armstrong

Joseph Christopher Aherne
Richard Drake
Ricky Brooks
Geoff Merrett
Luke Emberton
Mason Emberton
Charles Hambi
Simon Oxborrow
Tony Binks
John Fowler
Roy Curtis
Stella Cheesman
Oliver Drumm
Nick McMaster
Ray Gartland
Mike Gartland
Mark Capell
Joe Palazzo
James Daly
Sandra and Liam Duggan
Christopher King
Richard Brown
Sean Sadler
Terry Carter
Burt Shane Madhoo
Harold Havelock
Chris Tisdall
David Barton
Alan Barton
Mark 'Bod' Alder
Stephen John Alder
Paul Ashman
Paul J. Ahearn
The Hume Family
Paul Snape Stoke
Niall Shute
Danilo 'Dan' Ronzani (Bologna - Italia)
Karen Macey
Andrew Macey
Neil Macey

ND - #0171 - 090625 - C0 - 240/170/37 - PB - 9781780914091 - Gloss Lamination